THEORY AND PRACTICE OF THE EUROPEAN CONVENTION ON HUMAN RIGHTS

Fourth Edition

Editors:
PIETER VAN DIJK
FRIED VAN HOOF
ARJEN VAN RIJN
LEO ZWAAK

Authors:

YUTAKA ARAI
EDWIN BLEICHRODT
CEES FLINTERMAN
AALT WILLEM HERINGA
JEROEN SCHOKKENBROEK
PIETER VAN DIJK

FRIED VAN HOOF
ARJEN VAN RIJN
BEN VERMEULEN
MARC VIERING
LEO ZWAAK

intersentia

Antwerpen – Oxford

Distribution for the UK:
Hart Publishing
Salter's Boat Yard
Folly Bridge
Abingdon Road
Oxford OX1 4LB
UK
Tel: + 44 1865 24 55 33
Fax: + 44 1865 79 48 82

*Distribution for Switzerland and
Germany:*
Schulthess Verlag
Zwingliplatz 2
CH-8022 Zürich
Switzerland
Tel: + 41 1 251 93 36
Fax: + 41 1 261 63 94

Distribution for North America:
Gaunt Inc.
Gaunt Building
3011 Gulf Drive
Holmes Beach
Florida 34217-2199
USA
Tel: + 1 941 778 5211
Fax: + 1 941 778 5252

Distribution for other countries:
Intersentia Publishers
Groenstraat 31
2640 Mortsel
Belgium
Tel: + 32 3 680 15 50
Fax: + 32 3 658 71 21

Theory and Practice of the European Convention on Human Rights
Fourth Edition
Pieter van Dijk, Fried van Hoof, Arjen van Rijn and Leo Zwaak (eds.)

© 2006 Intersentia
Antwerpen – Oxford
http://www.intersentia.be

ISBN-10: 90-5095-546-0 (hardback)
ISBN-10: 90-5095-616-5 (paperback)
ISBN-13: 978-90-5095-546-1 (hardback)
ISBN-13: 978-90-5095-616-1 (paperback)
D/2006/7849/42
NUR 828

PREFACE TO THE FOURTH EDITION

The publication of this fourth edition of *Theory and Practice of the European Convention on Human Rights* is a cause of great satisfaction and gratitude for the editors. The preparation of the previous edition of the book was completed before Protocol No. 11 to the Convention, with its fundamental procedural reforms, had entered into force. Consequently, the "new" Court, which as a full-time court would produce a very extensive case law, had not yet been established. Therefore, at that moment it was already evident that the preparations for a next edition were imminent and would lead to drastic revision and considerable extension of the book.

This demanding task could only be accomplished through the willingness of those who contributed to the third edition as well as three additional experts who joined the group of authors in relation to this edition, to put so much effort and time into researching the case law of the "new" Court and to revise their respective chapters while taking developments in that case law into account. Notwithstanding their efforts however, this fourth edition would not have been completed without the support of the law firm of Pels Rijcken & Droogleever Fortuijn, which enabled one of its partners, Arjen van Rijn, to use time and facilities of the firm in order to coordinate the work of the editors and authors, and liaise with the publisher.

As pointed out, the entry into force of Protocol No. 11 and the extensive case law of the "new" Court made a drastic revision of most of the chapters necessary, even including complete rewriting of large parts of the text. It is therefore only fair that the name of the "reviser" is expressly mentioned at the beginning of each chapter. In order to keep the resulting extension of the book within reasonable limits, the "case law" of the former Commission has been deleted insofar as inclusion of such case law was deemed no longer necessary to shed light on the development of the jurisprudence concerning the Convention or that the Commission's case law has been incorporated or replaced by case law of the Court. As part of the same effort to keep the size of the volume manageable, references to the case law have been simplified, assuming that most readers will not turn to the official reports but rather to the site of the Court for further reference. Therefore, the references only provide the information necessary to identify the case and to enable the reader to find access to the full text of the judgment, decision or report concerned. The register of cases annexed to the book contains the full name of the parties to each case referred to. As in the previous editions of this book references to literature are almost completely absent; these references are easily available to the reader through other sources and would have overburdened the footnotes.

It almost seems a whim of fate that, whilst the previous edition had to anticipate the entry into force of Protocol No. 11, the date of which was uncertain at the moment of writing, the present edition has to anticipate the entry into force of Protocol No. 14, which was also unpredictable at the moment the editing had to be concluded. In each of the relevant chapters the future effects of Protocol No. 14 have been indicated, which however would appear to be less far-reaching than those of Protocol No. 11.

The editors gratefully acknowledge the assistance that they, as well as the authors, received from others in relation to research, documentation and secretarial support. This assistance has been of vital importance to an operation that has acquired mammoth proportions. In particular they wish to mention with appreciation the most valuable assistance of Ms. Fleur van der Meer of the law firm of Pels Rijcken & Droogleever Fortuijn, Ms. Ingrid Neumann of the Netherlands Council of State and Ms. Desislava Stoitchkova of the Netherlands Institute of Human Rights (SIM). In addition the editors also gratefully mention the excellent cooperation with the new publisher of the book, Intersentia. Mr. Kris Moeremans and his staff have shown an invaluable and unfailing capacity for indulgence, inventiveness and perseverance, as well as a genuine appreciation of pure quality. It was a real pleasure to embark on this project with them and to be able to disembark at the destination that we all had in mind.

July 2006

Pieter van Dijk
Fried van Hoof
Arjen van Rijn
Leo Zwaak

TABLE OF CONTENTS*

---

* You will find a detailed table of contents at the beginning of each Chapter.

ABOUT THE AUTHORS

Yutaka Arai (1969), PhD, senior lecturer in International Law and International Human Rights Law at University of Kent and at the Brussels School of International Studies. His thesis (1998) dealt with the margin of appreciation doctrine and the principle of proportionality in the jurisprudence of the European Court of Human Rights. He has published extensively in the fields of European human rights law (ECHR and EU law) and international humanitarian law.

Edwin Bleichrodt (1968), PhD, lawyer and partner at the law firm Pels Rijcken & Droogleever Fortuijn in The Hague, professor of Penitentiary Law at Groningen University and deputy-justice at the Arnhem Court of Appeal. His thesis (1996) dealt with the conditional sentences and other conditional modalities in Dutch criminal law. He has published extensively on issues in the field of criminal law and penal sanctions.

Cees Flinterman (1944), PhD, professor of Human Rights at Utrecht University, director of the Netherlands Institute of Human Rights and academic director of the Netherlands School of Human Rights Research. He is a member of the Advisory Council on International Affairs to the Netherlands Government and member of the United Nations Committee on the Elimination of Discrimination Against Women. His thesis (1981) dealt with the Act of State doctrine in a comparative perspective. He has published extensively in the fields of international human rights law and comparative public law.

Aalt Willem Heringa (1955), PhD, professor of Comparative Constitutional and Administrative Law at Maastricht University, dean of the Faculty of Law, deputy-judge at the Maastricht and Roermond District Courts and member of the Dutch Equal Treatment Commission. His thesis (1989) dealt with Social Rights. He has published extensively in the fields of (comparative) constitutional law and human rights law.

Jeroen Schokkenbroek (1960), PhD, head of the Human Rights Intergovernmental Programmes Department of the Directorate General of Human Rights of the Council of Europe. Previously he worked as a lecturer of Constitutional and Administrative Law at Leiden University. His thesis (1996) dealt with judicial control of restrictions on European Convention rights (Strasbourg and Dutch case-law). He has published extensively on issues relating to the European Convention on Human Rights such as the margin of appreciation and the reform of the control system of the Convention (Protocol No. 14).

Pieter van Dijk (1943), PhD, member of the Council of State of the Netherlands, member of the Venice Commission of the Council of Europe and member of the Royal Netherlands Academy of Arts and Sciences. Previously he has been professor of the Law of International Organizations at Utrecht University. He is a former judge at the European Court of Human Rights and former vice-president of the Administrative Tribunal of the Council of Europe. He is co-founder of the Netherlands Institute of Human Rights. His thesis (1976) dealt with judicial review of governmental action (comparative and international law). He has published extensively in the fields of the law of international organizations and human rights law.

Fried van Hoof (1949), PhD, professor of International Law and Human Rights at the Netherlands Institute of Human Rights of Utrecht University, member of the Advisory Commission for Foreigners' Affairs to the Netherlands Government and lawyer at the law firm Kaiser Van As. Previously he has been a member of the United Nations Sub-Commission on the Promotion and Protection of Human Rights. His thesis (1983) dealt with the sources of international law. He has published extensively in the fields of the theory of international law and international human rights law.

Arjen van Rijn (1956), PhD, lawyer and partner at the law firm Pels Rijcken & Droogleever Fortuijn in The Hague, with specialization in constitutional and administrative law. Previously he worked as a journalist in Germany and as a deputy-professor at the University of the Netherlands Antilles in Curaçao. His thesis (1985) dealt with the freedom of opinion in the Federal Republic of Germany and (former) East-Germany. He has published extensively in the fields of the Netherlands Antilles and the Kingdom of the Netherlands constitutional law and human rights law.

Ben Vermeulen (1957), PhD, professor of Constitutional and Administrative Law at the Free University Amsterdam and professor of Education Law at the Free University Amsterdam and the Radboud University Nijmegen, member of the Education Council and of the Advisory Board for Immigration Policy to the Netherlands Government. His thesis (1989) dealt with the freedom of conscience. He has published extensively on human rights issues such as asylum, the right to education, the freedom of conscience and religion and the separation of church and state.

Marc Viering (1960), PhD, criminal court judge in the 's-Hertogenbosch District Court. Previously he worked as a lawyer and as a university lecturer at the Radboud University Nijmegen and Utrecht University. His thesis (1994) dealt with the applicability of Article 6 of the European Convention on Human Rights. He has published extensively in the fields of constitutional law and human rights law.

Leo Zwaak (1947), LL.M (1975), senior lecturer in the field of International Protection of Human Rights at Utrecht University, senior researcher at the Netherlands Institute of Human Rights, visiting professor at the Washington College of Law, American University, and visiting professor at the University of Malta. He has published extensively on issues such as the application and interpretation of the European Convention on Human Rights and the effectiveness of the supervisory mechanism.

LIST OF ABBREVIATIONS

A.	Publications of the European Court of Human Rights; Judgments and Decisions, Series A
AJIL	American Journal of International Law
Appl(s)	Application(s) lodged with the Commission under Article 24 of the Convention
B.	Publications of the European Court of Human Rights; Pleadings, Oral Arguments and Documents, Series B
Coll.	Collection of Decisions of the European Commission of Human Rights
Cons. Ass.	Consultative Assembly of the Council of Europe
D&R	Decisions and Reports of the European Commission of Human Rights
HRLJ	Human Rights Law Journal
ICJ Reports	International Court of Justice, Reports of Judgments, Advisory Opinions and Orders
ILM	International Legal Materials
ILO	International Labour Organization
Para(s)	Paragraph(s)
Parl. Ass.	Parliamentary Assembly of the Council of Europe
RCADI	Recueil des Cours de l'Académie de Droit International de la Haye
Reports	Reports of Judgments and Decisions. Publication of the case-law of the Commission and the Court (as from 1996)
Res.	Resolution
UN	United Nations
UN Doc.	United Nations Documents
UNHCR	United Nations High Commissioner for Refugees
UNTS	United Nations Treaty Series
Yearbook	Yearbook of the European Convention on Human Rights

CHAPTER 1
GENERAL SURVEY OF THE EUROPEAN CONVENTION

REVISED BY LEO ZWAAK

CONTENTS

1.1 GENESIS OF THE CONVENTION

The European Convention for the Protection of Human Rights and Fundamental Freedoms is a product of the period shortly after the Second World War, when the issue of international protection of human rights attracted a great deal of attention. These rights had been crushed by the atrocities of National Socialism, and the guarantee of their protection at the national level had proved completely inadequate.

As early as 1941 Churchill and Roosevelt, in the Atlantic Charter, launched their four freedoms: freedom of life, freedom of religion, freedom from want and freedom from fear. After the Second World War the promotion of respect for human rights and fundamental freedoms became one of the purposes of the United Nations. Within that framework the Universal Declaration of Human Rights, adopted by the General Assembly of the United Nations on 10 December 1948, became a significant milestone.

Meanwhile, preliminary steps were also taken at the European level. In May 1948 the International Committee of the Movements for European Unity organised a 'Congress of Europe' at The Hague. This initiative gave the decisive impetus to the foundation of the Council of Europe in 1949. At the Congress a resolution was adopted, the introductory part of which reads as follows:

> The Congress
> *Considers* that the resultant union or federation should be open to all European nations democratically governed and which undertake to respect a Charter of Human Rights;
> *Resolves* that a Commission should be set up to undertake immediately the double task of drafting such a Charter and of laying down standards to which a State must conform if it is to deserve the name of democracy.

After the Council of Europe had been founded, the matter was discussed during the first session of the Consultative Assembly (at present called the Parliamentary Assembly) of the Council of Europe in August 1949. The Assembly charged its Committee on Legal and Administrative Questions to consider in more detail the matter of a collective guarantee of human rights.

From that moment onwards the Convention was drafted in a comparatively short period of time. In September of the same year the Consultative Assembly adopted the Committee's report, in which ten rights were included that were to be the subject of a collective guarantee, with a view to which the establishment of a European Commission of Human Rights and a European Court of Justice was proposed. In November of that year the Committee of Ministers of the Council of Europe decided to appoint a Committee of Government Experts, which was entrusted with the task of preparing a draft text on the basis of this report.

This Committee completed its work in the spring of 1950. It had made considerable headway, but had failed to find a solution to a number of political problems. The subsequently appointed Committee of Senior Officials also had to leave the ultimate decision on a number of matters to the Committee of Ministers, even though it reached agreement on the greater part of the text of the Committee of Experts.

On 7 August 1950 the Committee of Ministers approved a revised draft text, which was less far-reaching than the original proposals on a number of points. For example, the system of individual applications and the jurisdiction of the Court were made optional. This draft text was not substantially altered afterwards.

On 4 November 1950 the Convention, which according to its preamble was framed "to take the first steps for collective enforcement of certain rights stated in the Universal Declaration", was signed in Rome.[1] It entered into force on 3 September 1953 and to date (October 2005) has been ratified by the 46 Member States of the Council of Europe: Albania, Armenia, Andorra, Austria, Azerbaijan, Belgium, Bosnia Herzegovina, Bulgaria, Croatia, Cyprus, the Czech Republic, Denmark, Estonia, Finland, France, Georgia, Germany, Greece,[2] Hungary, Iceland, Ireland, Italy, Latvia, Liechtenstein, Lithuania, Luxembourg, Macedonia ('FYROM'), Malta, Moldova, Monaco, the Netherlands, Norway, Poland, Portugal, Romania, Russia, San Marino, Serbia and Montenegro, Slovakia, Slovenia, Spain, Sweden, Switzerland, Turkey, Ukraine and the United Kingdom. Belarus has also shown its desire to become a member of the Council of Europe and as a consequence thereof to become a party to the Convention. To date, 14 Protocols have been added to the Convention,[3] but not all of them have been ratified by all the Contracting States.[4] As a result of the entry into force of Protocol No. 11, Protocols Nos 8, 9 and 10 were repealed. Protocol No. 2, conferring the competence upon the Court to give advisory opinions, has been included almost in its entirety in Protocol No. 11 and has thus become part of the Convention.[5]

1.2 SCOPE OF THE CONVENTION AS TO THE GUARANTEED RIGHTS AND FREEDOMS

As stated in the preamble to the Convention, the aim which the Contracting States wished to achieve was "to take the first steps for the collective enforcement of certain of the Rights stated in the Universal Declaration". The purpose of the Convention was therefore, within the framework of the Council of Europe, to lay down certain human rights, proclaimed in 1948 by the United Nations in the Universal Declaration of Human Rights, in a binding agreement, and at the same time to provide for supervision of the observance of those human rights provisions.

---

[1]   213 UNTS, No. 2889, p. 221; Council of Europe, *European Treaty Series*, No. 5, 4 November 1950; See: http://conventions.coe.int.

[2]   Greece withdrew from the Council of Europe in 1969, but became a member again in 1974 and re-ratified the Convention.

[3]   See Appendix I.

[4]   See Appendix I.

[5]   Article 47 of the Convention.

Only certain rights were included in these 'first steps'. A comparison with the Universal Declaration discloses that not all the rights mentioned there have been laid down in the Convention. It covers mainly those rights which would be referred to, in the later elaboration of the Universal Declaration in the two Covenants, as `civil and political rights', and not even all of those. The principle of equality before the law, the right to freedom of movement and residence, the right to seek and to enjoy asylum in other countries from persecution, the right to a nationality, the right to own property and the right to take part in the Government, which are included in the Universal Declaration,[6] are not to be found in the Convention.

However, in that respect subsequent steps have been taken within the framework of the Council of Europe, both in the form of additional Protocols to the Convention[7] and in the form of other conventions, including in particular the European Social Charter of 1961.

The reason for the limited scope of the Convention was explained as follows by Teitgen, the rapporteur of the Legal Committee of the Consultative Assembly of the Council of Europe, which prepared the first draft of the Convention: "It [i.e. the Committee] considered that, for the moment, it is preferable to limit the collective guarantee to those rights and essential freedoms which are practised, after long usage and experience, in all the democratic countries. While they are the first triumph of democratic regimes, they are also the necessary condition under which they operate. Certainly, professional freedoms and social rights, which have themselves an intrinsic value, must also, in the future, be defined and protected. Everyone will, however, understand that it is necessary to begin at the beginning and to guarantee political democracy in the European Union and then to co-ordinate our economies, before undertaking the generalization of social democracy."[8] The drafters, therefore, concentrated on those rights which were considered essential elements of the foundation of European democracies and with regard to which one might expect that an agreement could easily be reached about their formulation and about the international supervision of their implementation, since they could be deemed to have been recognised in the Member States of the Council of Europe. On the other hand, both the detailed formulation of these rights, with the possibilities of limitations and the creation of a supervisory mechanism in a binding treaty, were novel and revolutionary.[9]

It was precisely these two points – the formulation of the rights and freedoms and the supervisory mechanism – which were used as arguments for separate regulation

---

[6]   Articles 7, 13, 14, 15, 17 and 21 respectively of the Universal Declaration.
[7]   For ratifications, see Appendix I.
[8]   Council of Europe, Cons. Ass., First Session, *Reports* (1949), p. 1144.
[9]   In view of the emphasis placed by the drafters on democracy it may be a matter of surprise that no provision was included on the right of participation in government and on free elections. Evidently the matter was considered too complex and would have delayed the signing of the Convention. The issue of free elections was covered by the First Additional Protocol soon thereafter (Article 3).

of, on the one hand, civil and political rights, and, on the other hand, economic, social, and cultural rights; a solution which was ultimately also chosen within the framework of the UN. The first category of rights was considered to concern the sphere of freedom of the individual vis-à-vis the Government. These rights and liberties and their limitations would lend themselves to detailed regulation, while the implementation of the resulting duty on the part of the Government to abstain from interference could be reviewed by national and/or international bodies. The second category, on the other hand, was considered to consist not of legal rights but of programmatic rights, the formulation of which necessarily is much vaguer and for the realisation of which the States must pursue a given policy, an obligation which does not lend itself to incidental review of government action for its lawfulness.[10]

It is undeniable that there are differences, roughly speaking, between the two categories of rights with respect to their legal character and their implementation. However, such differences also present themselves *within* those categories. Thus, the right to a fair trial and the right to periodic elections by secret ballot call not only for abstention but also for affirmative action on the part of the Governments. And in the other category the right to strike has less the character of a programmatic right than has the right to work. In the modern welfare state which is typical for most of the Member States of the Council of Europe, the civil rights and liberties are being 'socialised' increasingly, while the social, economic and cultural rights are becoming more concrete as to their content. Therefore, a stringent distinction between the two categories becomes less justified, while too strict a distinction entails the risk of the necessary connection between the two categories of rights being misunderstood. This connection was emphasised in the Proclamation of Teheran of 1968[11] and reaffirmed in the Vienna Declaration and Programme of Action, where it has been set forth that "All human rights are universal, indivisible and interdependent and interrelated. The international community must treat human rights globally in a fair and equal manner, on the same footing, and with the same emphasis. While the significance of national and regional particularities and various historical, cultural and religious backgrounds must be borne in mind, it is the duty of States, regardless of their political, economic and cultural systems, to promote and protect all human rights and fundamental freedoms."[12]

---

[10] See 'Annotations on the text of the draft International Covenant on Human Rights, prepared by the Secretary-General', Document A/2929, pp. 7-8. See also the statement of Henri Rolin, member of the Consultative Assembly, before the Belgian Senate, quoted in H. Golsong, *'Implementation of International Protection of Human Rights'*, RCADI 110, 1963-III, p. 58.

[11] Text of the Proclamation in Res. 2442(XLII) of the General Assembly of the United Nations, 19 December 1968.

[12] UN Doc. A/Cont.157/23, para. 5.

This connection, and the recognition of the relative value of the distinction between the two categories of rights, also led the Council of Europe to investigate whether certain economic and social rights should be added to the Convention, and, if so, which ones. The investigation led to Protocol No. 7. The original aim of this Protocol, as recommended by the Parliamentary Assembly in 1972, was "to insert as many as possible of the substantive provisions of the Covenant on Civil and Political Rights in the Convention".[13] However, the Committee of Experts which prepared the draft of the Protocol, followed a more restrictive approach, keeping in mind "the need to include in the Convention only such rights as could be stated in sufficiently specific terms to be guaranteed within the framework of the system of control instituted by the Convention".[14] Although the idea of such an extension was born in the early seventies, it was not until 22 November 1984 that the Protocol was opened for signature. And it was only in 1988 that sufficient States had ratified the Protocol for it to enter into force.[15]

Enthusiasm for Protocol No. 7 appears not to be very great. This has to do with the fact that the original aim of the Protocol can hardly be said to have been achieved. In a comparative report[16] a series of rights had been enumerated which were included in the UN Covenant on Civil and Political Rights but not in the Convention. Only some of these rights are now included in this Protocol. A clarification of the reasons for it, other than the above-mentioned general viewpoint of the Committee of Experts, is not to be found in the Explanatory Report. Although it is true that some of the other rights do not fulfill the requirement of 'sufficiently specific terms to be guaranteed', it is by no means clear why, for example, the right of the accused to be informed of his right to have legal assistance or the right of equality before the law, have not been included in the Protocol. Furthermore, the rights that have been incorporated are, on the whole, formulated rather narrowly. Most of the rights are framed in more restricted terms than their counterparts in the UN Covenant on Civil and Political Rights. It may be concluded, therefore, that the outcome of this lengthy exercise is rather disappointing.

In Part II the rights and freedoms laid down in the Convention and in its Protocols Nos 1, 4, 5, 6, 7, 12, 13 and 14 are discussed by reference to the Decisions and Reports of the former Commission and the case-law of the Court. As indicated above, although a number of provisions of the International Covenant on Civil and Political Rights may entail for those Contracting States which have also ratified that Covenant[17] more

---

[13]   Explanatory Report on Protocol No. 7 to the Convention for the Protection of Human Rights and Fundamental Freedoms, Council of Europe, Strasbourg, 1985, p. 5.

[14]   *Ibidem*, p. 6.

[15]   Protocol No. 7 entered into force on 1 November 1988. For the state of ratifications, see Appendix I.

[16]   Problems arising from the co-existence of the United Nations Covenants on Human Rights and the European Convention on Human Rights, Doc. H(70)7, Strasbourg 1970, pp. 4-5.

[17]   These are all Contracting States except Andorra.

far-reaching obligations than rest on them under the Convention;[18] such obligations are left intact by virtue of Article 53 of the Convention.[19]

1.3 STRUCTURE OF THE CONVENTION

1.3.1 RIGHTS AND FREEDOMS LAID DOWN IN THE CONVENTION

After Article 1, which deals with the scope of the Convention and will be discussed in para. 3, the Convention lists the rights and freedoms that it guarantees.

Section I of the Convention contains the following rights and freedoms:

Article 2:   right to life;
Article 3:   freedom from torture and inhuman or degrading treatment or punishment;
Article 4:   freedom from slavery and forced or compulsory labour;
Article 5:   right to liberty and security of the person;
Article 6:   right to a fair and public trial within a reasonable time;
Article 7:   freedom from retrospective effect of penal legislation;
Article 8:   right to respect for private and family life, home and correspondence;
Article 9:   freedom of thought, conscience and religion;
Article 10:   freedom of expression;
Article 11:   freedom of assembly and association;
Article 12:   right to marry and found a family.

Protocol No. 1 has added the following rights:

Article 1:   right to peaceful enjoyment of possessions;
Article 2:   right to education and free choice of education;
Article 3:   right to free elections by secret ballot.

Protocol No. 4 has added the following rights and freedoms:

Article 1:   prohibition of deprivation of liberty on the ground of inability to fulfil a contractual obligation;
Article 2:   freedom to move within and choose residence in a country;

---

[18]   See the report of the Committee of Experts on Human Rights to the Committee of Ministers, *Problems arising from the Co-Existence of the United Nations Covenants on Human Rights and the European Convention on Human Rights*, Doc. H(70)7, Strasbourg, 1970. In Protocol No. 7 the differences between the obligations resulting from the Covenant and those resulting from the Convention have been partly removed. This Protocol entered into force on 1 November 1988.
[19]   On this, see *infra* 1.3.4.

Article 3:   prohibition of expulsion of nationals and right of nationals to enter the
              territory of the State of which they are nationals;
Article 4:   prohibition of collective expulsion of aliens.

Protocol No. 6 has added the prohibition of the condemnation to and execution of
the death penalty (Article 1).

Protocol No. 7 has added the following rights and freedoms:
Article 1:   procedural safeguards in case of expulsion of aliens lawfully resident in
              the territory of a State;
Article 2:   right of review by a higher tribunal in criminal cases;
Article 3:   right to compensation of a person convicted of a criminal offence, on
              the ground that a new or newly discovered fact shows that there has
              been a miscarriage of justice;
Article 4:   prohibition of a second trial or punishment for offences for which one
              has already been finally acquitted or convicted (*ne bis in idem*);
Article 5:   equality of rights and responsibilities between spouses.

Protocol No. 12 enlarges the scope of the prohibition of discrimination of Article 14
to the effect that the prohibition is no longer limited to the rights and freedoms
enshrined in the Convention, but is extended to "any right set forth by law".[20]

Protocol No. 13 prescribes the abolition of the death penalty in all circumstances.

1.3.2   GENERAL PROVISIONS CONCERNING THE ENJOYMENT, THE PROTECTION AND THE LIMITATION OF THE RIGHTS AND FREEDOMS

Article 13 stipulates that everyone whose rights and freedoms set forth in the Convention are violated shall have an effective remedy before a national authority, notwithstanding that the violation has been committed by persons acting in an official
capacity. Article 14 obliges the Contracting States to secure the rights and freedoms
set forth in the Convention without discrimination on any ground. Article 15 allows
States to derogate from a number of provisions of the Convention in time of war or
other public emergency threatening the life of the nation. Under Article 16 States are
allowed to impose restrictions on the political activity of aliens notwithstanding
Articles 10, 11 and 14 of the Convention. Article 17 provides that nothing in the Convention may be interpreted as implying for any State, group or person any right to

---

[20]   Protocol No. 12 entered into force on 1 April 2005.

engage in any activity or perform any act aimed at the destruction of any of the rights and freedoms set forth in the Convention or at their limitation to a greater extent than is provided for in the Convention. Finally, Article 18 implies a prohibition of misuse of power (*détournement de pouvoir*) as to the right of Contracting States to impose restrictions on the rights and freedoms guaranteed by the Convention.

1.3.3 PROVISIONS TO ENSURE THE OBSERVANCE BY THE CONTRACTING PARTIES OF THEIR OBLIGATIONS

Besides the above-mentioned substantive provisions, the European Convention also contains a number of provisions to ensure the observance by the Contracting States of their obligations under the Convention. The responsibility for the implementation of the Convention rests primarily with the national authorities, in particular the national courts (at least in States where the courts are allowed to directly apply the Convention).[21] This is implied in Article 13 where, in connection with violations of the rights and freedoms set forth in the Convention, reference is made to an 'effective remedy before a national authority'. For those cases where a national procedure is not available or does not provide for an adequate remedy, or in the last resort has not produced a satisfactory result in the opinion of the injured party or of any of the other Contracting States, the Convention itself provides for a supervisory mechanism on the basis of individual and State complaints. In addition, the Secretary General of the Council of Europe may take part in the supervision of the observance of the Convention (Article 52).

1.3.4 FINAL PROVISIONS

Section III contains miscellaneous provisions (Articles 52 to 59). Article 52, relating to inquiries by the Secretary-General, will be discussed separately.[22] The same holds good for Article 56, concerning territorial scope, and Article 58, which deals with denunciation of the Convention.[23] Article 57, concerning reservations, will be dealt with separately in Chapter 38.

    Article 53 embodies what has become a general rule of international human rights law, *viz.* that a legal obligation implying a more far-reaching protection takes priority over any less far-reaching obligation. The article provides that nothing in the Con-

---

[21] On this, see *infra* 1.6 and 2.2.9.
[22] *Infra*, Chapter 4.
[23] *Infra*, 1.4, and 1.5.3, respectively.

vention may be construed as limiting or derogating from any of the human rights and fundamental freedoms which may be ensured under the laws of any Contracting State or under any other agreement to which the latter is a party.

Article 54 stipulates that the Convention shall not prejudice the powers conferred on the Committee of Ministers by the Statute of the Council of Europe.

Article 55 is aimed at leaving the supervision of the observance of the Convention at the international level exclusively in the hands of the organs designated by the Convention. The article provides that the Contracting States, except by special agreement, will not avail themselves of treaties, conventions or declarations in force between them for the purpose of submitting, by way of petition, a dispute arising out of the interpretation and application of this Convention to a means of settlement other than those provided for in this Convention. Article 55 applies in those instances where the Convention is expressly invoked. With respect to disputes where this is not the case, but where nevertheless a right is at issue that is also protected by the Convention, the rationale for such an exclusive competence is much less self-evident. It is submitted that the text of Article 55 does not dictate the exclusivity of the procedure provided for in the Convention as far as those latter cases are concerned. There is, however, still some difference of opinion as to the exact scope of the obligation of the Contracting States under Article 55.

In the Case of *Cyprus v. Turkey* the respondent Government alleged that a special agreement was in force between the States concerned to settle the dispute by means of other international procedures. In that respect they invoked Article 62 (the present Article 55). They claimed that, in fact, all the matters raised by the application were directly or indirectly handled within the United Nations, by the Secretary General acting under the direction of the Security Council. The Commission considered that, having regard to the wording of Article 62 (55) itself and the aim and purpose of the Convention as a whole, the possibility for a High Contracting Party of withdrawing a case from the jurisdiction of the Convention organs on the ground that it has entered into a special agreement with another High Contracting Party concerned, is given only in exceptional circumstances. The principle stipulated in Article 62 (55) starts from a monopoly of the Convention institutions for deciding disputes arising out of the interpretation and application of the Convention. The High Contracting Parties agree not to avail themselves of other treaties, conventions and declarations in force between them for the purpose of submitting such disputes to other means of settlement. Only exceptionally is a departure from this principle permitted, subject to the existence of a 'special agreement' between the High Contracting Parties concerned, permitting the submission of a dispute concerning 'the interpretation or application of the Convention' to an alternative means of settlement 'by way of petition'. The Commission considered that the conditions for invoking such a special agreement were not fulfilled in the present case. A primary condition, namely the consent of both High Contracting

Parties concerned to withdraw the particular dispute from the jurisdiction of the Convention organs, was lacking, the applicant Government clearly opposing such a way of proceeding.[24]

In a resolution of 1970 the Committee of Ministers declared "that, as long as the problem of interpretation of Article 62 [the present Article 55] of the European Convention is not resolved, States Parties to the Convention which ratify or accede to the UN Covenant on Civil and Political Rights and make a declaration under Article 41 of the Covenant should normally utilize only the procedure established by the European Convention in respect of complaints against another Contracting Party of the European Convention relating to an alleged violation of a right which in substance is covered both (by) the European Convention (or its Protocols) and by the UN Covenant on Civil and Political Rights, it being understood that the UN procedure may be invoked in relation to rights not guaranteed in the European Convention (or its Protocols) or in relation to States which are not Parties to the European Convention."[25]

In practice no problems have yet arisen in this respect. Since the entry into force of the UN Covenant on Civil and Political Rights in 1976, only three inter-State complaints have been dealt with in the context of the European Convention: two cases of *Cyprus v. Turkey*[26] and the joint cases of *France, Norway, Denmark, Sweden and the Netherlands v. Turkey*.[27] Since Turkey had not ratified the UN Covenant on Civil and Political Rights,[28] and Cyprus and France had not recognised the competence of the Human Rights Committee to receive inter-State complaints, there was no other possibility than to submit the case to the European Commission. In the inter-State complaint of *Cyprus v. Turkey* the Court referred to the preliminary objection of the Turkish Government which had alleged the existence of a special agreement between the respective Governments to settle the dispute by means of other international procedures and noted that the Commission in its admissibility decision of 28 June 1996 had rejected the respondent Government's objections.[29]

Finally, Article 59 contains a number of provisions about the ratification and the entry into force of the Convention.

---

[24]   Decision of 28 June 1996.
[25]   Res. (70)17 of 15 May 1970, Council of Europe, *Collected Texts*, Strasbourg, 1994, pp. 331-332.
[26]   Appl. 8007/77, Yearbook XX (1977), p. 98; D&R 13 (1979), p. 85; Appl. 25781/94, D&R 86 A (1995), p. 104 (134).
[27]   Appls 9940-9944/82, D&R 35 (1984), p. 143.
[28]   Turkey ratified the Covenant on 23 September 2003.
[29]   Judgment of 10 May 2001, para 57.

1.4   PERSONAL AND TERRITORIAL SCOPE OF THE CONVENTION

1.4.1   EVERYONE WITHIN THEIR JURISDICTION, IRRESPECTIVE OF RESIDENCE

Under Article 1 of the Convention the Contracting States are bound to secure to everyone within their jurisdiction the rights and freedoms set forth in Section I of the Convention. To the extent that a State has ratified any of the Protocols Nos 1, 4, 6, 7, 12 and 13, this obligation also applies to the rights and freedoms laid down in these Protocols, since the latter are considered to contain additional provisions of the Convention, to which all the provisions of the Convention apply accordingly.[30]

Under Article 1 of the Convention, the State is required to 'secure' the Convention rights to everyone within its jurisdiction. In certain cases it may therefore be necessary for the State to take positive action with a view to effectively securing these rights.[31] The Court has held that where an individual raises an arguable claim that there has been a breach of Article 2 or 3 that those provisions, read in conjunction with the State's general duty under Article 1 of the Convention to 'secure to everyone within their jurisdiction the rights and freedoms defined in … [the] Convention', requires by implication that there should be an effective official investigation.[32] If this were not the case, the right to life and the prohibition of torture and inhuman and degrading treatment and punishment, despite their fundamental importance, would be ineffective in practice and it would be possible in some cases for agents of the State to abuse the rights of those within their control with virtual impunity.[33]

The Contracting States must secure these rights and freedoms to 'everyone within their jurisdiction'. These words do not imply any limitation as to nationality. Even those alleged victims who are neither nationals of the State concerned nor of any of the other Contracting States are entitled to protection when they are in some respect subject to the jurisdiction of the State from which they claim that guarantee.[34] Further

---

[30]   See Article 5 of Protocol No. 1, Article 6(1) of Protocol No. 4, Article 6 of Protocol No. 6, Article 7(1) of Protocol No. 7, Article 3 of Protocol No. 12 and Article 5 of Protocol No. 13.

[31]   Judgment of 13 June 1979, *Marckx*, para. 31; judgment of 26 May 1985, *X and Y v. the Netherlands*, para. 23; judgment of 9 June 1998, *L.C.B. v. the United Kingdom*, para. 36; judgment of 28 October 1998, *Osman*, para. 115; judgment of 10 October 2000, *Akkoç*, para. 77.

[32]   Judgment of 28 October 1998, *Assenov*, para. 102; judgment of 27 September 1995, *McCann*, para. 161; judgment of 19 February 1998, *Kaya*, para. 86; judgment 22 September 1998, *Yasa*, para. 98; judgment of 27 June 2000, *Salman*, para. 104; judgment of 10 May 2001, *Cyprus v. Turkey*, para. 425; judgment of 23 May 2001, *Denizci*, para. 378; judgment of 10 July 2001, *Avşar*, para. 393.

[33]   Judgment of 28 May 1998, *McShane*, para. 94.

[34]   See, *e.g.*, Appl. 788/60, *Austria v. Italy*, Yearbook IV (1961), p. 116 (138 and 140): "Whereas, therefore, in becoming a Party to the Convention, a State undertakes, *vis-à-vis* the other High Contracting Parties, to secure the rights and freedoms defined in Section I to every person within

more, it is irrelevant whether they have their residence inside or outside the territory of that State.[35] Moreover, in several cases the Commission and the Court held that although Article 1 sets limits on the scope of the Convention, the concept of 'jurisdiction' under this provision does not imply that the responsibility of the Contracting Parties is restricted to acts committed on their territory.

In the same vein the Court held that the extradition or expulsion of a person by a Contracting Party to a country where there is a serious risk of torture or inhuman or degrading treatment or punishment, may give rise to an issue under Article 3, and hence engage responsibility of that State under the Convention.[36] In cases where provisions other than Article 3 are at stake, the extraditing State may equally be held responsible for acts which take place thereafter in another country.[37]

In the *Assanidze* Case the Government, in their preliminary objections, accepted that the Ajarian Autonomous Republic was an integral part of Georgia and that the matters complained of were within the jurisdiction of the Georgian State. However, consideration should be given to the difficulties encountered by the central State authorities in exercising their jurisdiction in the Ajarian Autonomous Republic. As a general rule, the notion of 'jurisdiction' within the meaning of Article 1 of the Convention must be considered as reflecting the position under public international law. That notion is 'primarily' or 'essentially' territorial.[38] The Court held that the Ajarian Autonomous Republic is indisputably an integral part of the territory of Georgia and subject to its competence and control. In other words, there is a presumption of competence. In that connection, the Court noted, firstly, that Georgia had ratified the Convention for the whole of its territory. Furthermore, it was common ground that the Ajarian

---

its jurisdiction, regardless of their nationality or status; whereas, in short, it undertakes to secure these rights and freedoms not only to its own nationals and those of other High Contracting Parties, but also to nationals of States not parties to the Convention and to stateless persons."

[35] The Consultative Assembly had proposed in the draft of the Convention the words 'all persons residing within the territories of the signatory States', but these were changed by the Committee of Experts in the sense mentioned. See report of the Committee of Experts to the Committee of Ministers, Council of Europe, *Collected Edition of the 'Travaux Préparatoires' of the European Convention on Human Rights*, Vol. IV, The Hague, 1977, p. 20: "It was felt that there were good grounds for extending the benefits of the Convention to all persons in the territories of the signatory States, even those who could not be considered as residing there in the legal sense of the word." See also Appl. 1611/62, *X v. Federal Republic of Germany*, Yearbook VIII (1965), p. 158 (168), where the Commission held: "in certain respects the nationals of a Contracting State are within its jurisdiction even when domiciled or resident abroad." See also *infra* 1.4.3.

[36] Judgment of 7 July 1989, *Soering*, para. 90; judgment of 20 March 1991, *Cruz Varas and Others*, para. 69; judgment of 30 October 1991, *Vilvarajah*, para. 103; judgment of 23 March 1995, *Loizidou* (preliminary objections), para. 62. See also *infra* 7.6.

[37] Appl. 10427/83, *X v. the United Kingdom*, D&R 47 (1986), p. 85 (95-96), where the applicant, a suspected deserter from the Indian army, had been extradited to India and claimed that he had been deprived of a fair trial within a reasonable time.

[38] Decision of 12 December 2001, *Bankovic*, paras 59-61.

Autonomous Republic had no separatist aspirations and that no other State exercised effective overall control there. On ratifying the Convention, Georgia did not make any specific reservation under Article 57 of the Convention with regard to the Ajarian Autonomous Republic or to difficulties in exercising its jurisdiction over that territory.[39]

The Court went on by stating that: "Unlike the American Convention on Human Rights of 22 November 1969 (Article 28), the European Convention does not contain a 'federal clause' limiting the obligations of the federal State for events occurring on the territory of the states forming part of the federation. Moreover, since Georgia is not a federal State, the Ajarian Autonomous Republic is not part of a federation. It forms an entity which – like others (the Autonomous Republic of Abkhazia and, before 1991, the Autonomous District of South Ossetia) – must have an autonomous status, which is a different matter. Besides, even if an implied federal clause similar in content to that of Article 28 of the American Convention were found to exist in the European Convention (which is impossible in practice), it could not be construed as releasing the federal State from all responsibility, since Article 28 of the American Convention requires the federal State to "immediately take suitable measures, in accordance with its constitution ..., to the end that the [states forming part of the federation] may adopt appropriate provisions for the fulfillment of [the] Convention." The Court, therefore, found that the actual facts out of which the allegations of violations arose were within the 'jurisdiction' of the Georgian State within the meaning of Article 1 of the Convention.[40]

In the *Ilascu* Case the Court considered that the Moldovan Government, the only legitimate government of the Republic of Moldova under international law, did not exercise authority over part of its territory, namely that part which was under the effective control of the 'MRT'. However, even in the absence of effective control over the Transdniestrian region, Moldova still had a positive obligation under Article 1 of the Convention to take the measures in its power and in accordance with international law to secure the rights guaranteed by the Convention. Consequently, the applicants were within the jurisdiction of the Republic of Moldova for the purposes of Article 1, but its responsibility for the acts complained of was to be assessed in the light of its positive obligations under the Convention. These related both to the measures needed to re-establish its control over Transdniestrian territory, as an expression of its jurisdiction, and to measures to ensure respect for the applicants' rights, including attempts to secure their release. As regards the applicants' situation, the Court noted

---

[39]   Such a reservation would in any event have been ineffective, as the case-law precludes territorial exclusions other than in the instance referred to in Article 56(1) of the Convention (dependent territories); see the judgment of 18 February 1999, *Matthews*, para. 29.

[40]   Judgment of 8 April 2004, paras 139-143.

that before ratification of the Convention in 1997 and even after that date the Moldovan authorities had taken a number of measures to secure the applicants' rights. On the other hand, it did not have any evidence that since Mr. Ilaşcu's release in May 2001 effective measures had been taken to put an end to the continuing infringements of their Convention rights complained of by the other applicants. In their bilateral relations with the Russian Federation the Moldovan authorities had not been any more attentive to the applicants' fate; the Court had not been informed of any approach by the Moldovan authorities to the Russian authorities after May 2001 aimed at obtaining the remaining applicants' release. Even after Mr. Ilaşcu's release in May 2001, it had been within the power of the Moldovan Government to take measures to secure to the other applicants their rights under the Convention. The Court accordingly concluded that Moldova's responsibility was capable of being engaged on account of its failure to discharge its positive obligations with regard to the acts complained of which had occurred after May 2001.

With respect to the Russian Federation, the Court observed that during the Moldovan conflict in 1991-92 forces of the former Fourteenth Army (which owed allegiance to the USSR, the CIS and the Russian Federation in turn, and later became the ROG) stationed in Transdniestria, an integral part of the territory of the Republic of Moldova, fought with and on behalf of the Transdniestrian separatist forces. Moreover, large quantities of weapons from the stores of the Fourteenth Army were voluntarily transferred to the separatists, who were also able to seize possession of other weapons unopposed by Russian soldiers. The Court noted that from December 1991 onwards the Moldovan authorities systematically complained, to international bodies among others, of what they called 'the acts of aggression' of the former Fourteenth Army against the Republic of Moldova and accused the Russian Federation of supporting the Transdniestrian separatists. Throughout the clashes between the Moldovan authorities and the Transdniestrian separatists the leaders of the Russian Federation supported the separatist authorities through political declarations. The Russian Federation drafted the main lines of the ceasefire agreement of 21 July 1992, and moreover signed it as a party.

In the light of all these circumstances the Court considered that the Russian Federation's responsibility was engaged in respect of the unlawful acts committed by the Transdniestrian separatists, regard being had to the military and political support it gave them to help them set up the separatist regime and the participation of its military personnel in the fighting. In acting thus the authorities of the Russian Federation contributed both militarily and politically to the creation of a separatist regime in the region of Transdniestria, which was part of the territory of the Republic of Moldova. The applicants were arrested in June 1992 with the participation of soldiers of the Fourteenth Army. The first three applicants were then detained on Fourteenth Army premises and guarded by Fourteenth Army troops. During their detention these three applicants were interrogated and subjected to treatment which could be considered contrary to Article 3 of the Convention. They were then handed over to the Transdniestrian police. The Court considered that on account of these events the applicants came within the jurisdiction of the Russian Federation within the meaning of Article 1 of the Convention, although at the time when these events occurred the Convention was not in force with regard to the Russian Federation. The events which gave rise to the responsibility of the Russian Federation must be considered to include not only the acts in which the agents of that State participated, like the applicants' arrest and detention, but also their transfer into the hands of the Transdniestrian police and regime, and the subsequent ill-treatment inflicted on them by the police, since in acting in that way the agents of the Russian Federation were fully aware that they were handing them over to an illegal and unconstitutional regime. The Court considered that there was a continuous and uninterrupted link of responsibility on the part of the Russian Federation for the applicants' fate, as the Russian Federation's policy of support for the regime and collaboration with it continued beyond 5 May 1998,[41] and after that date the Russian Federation made no attempt to put an end to the applicants' situation brought about by its agents, and did not act to prevent the violations allegedly committed after 5 May 1998. In conclusion, the applicants came within the "jurisdiction" of the Russian Federation for the purposes of Article 1 of the Convention and its responsibility was engaged with regard to the acts complained of.[42]

A Contracting State is responsible for acts or omissions on its territory only to the extent that those are the responsibility of its own organs. Thus it was decided that the alleged violations of the Convention by the Supreme Restitution Court could not be held against the Federal Republic of Germany, even though this tribunal had its sessions on West German territory. It was to be considered as an international tribunal, in respect of which Germany had neither legislative nor supervisory powers.[43]

1.4.2   TERRITORIES FOR WHOSE INTERNATIONAL RELATIONS A STATE IS RESPONSIBLE

Article 56 contains a *lex specialis* in respect of the principle of Article 1 according to which the Convention is applicable to everyone within the jurisdiction of the Contracting States. According to general international law a treaty is applicable to the

---

[41]   On that date the Convention entered into force with respect to Russia.
[42]   Judgment of 8 July 2004, paras 380-385.
[43]   Appl. 2095/63, *X v. Sweden, Federal Republic of Germany and other States*, Yearbook VIII (1965), p. 272 (282). See also Appl. 235/56, *X v. Federal Republic of Germany*, Yearbook II (1958-1959), p. 256 (304), where the Commission reached the same conclusion with respect to the American Court of Restitution Appeals in Germany.

whole territory of a Contracting State, including those territories for whose international relations the State in question is responsible.[44] This is different only when a reservation has been made for one or more of those territories in the treaty itself, or at the time of its ratification. Under Article 56(1), however, the European Convention applies to the latter territories only when the Contracting State concerned has agreed to this *via* a declaration to that effect addressed to the Secretary General of the Council of Europe. Such declarations were made in due course by Denmark with respect to Greenland,[45] by the Netherlands with respect to Suriname[46] and the Netherlands Antilles[47] and by the United Kingdom with respect to most of the non-self-governing territories belonging to the Commonwealth.[48]

The question of what has to be understood by the words 'territory for whose international relations a State is responsible' was raised in a case concerning the former Belgian Congo. The applicants submitted that their complaint related to a time when this area formed part of the national territory of Belgium, and that accordingly the Convention, including the Belgian declaration under Article 25 [the present Article 34], was applicable to the Belgian Congo even though Belgium had not made any declaration as referred to in Article 56 with reference thereto. The Commission, however, held that the Belgian Congo had to be regarded as a territory for whose international relations Belgium was responsible in the sense of Article 56. It reached the conclusion that the complaint was not admissible *ratione loci*, since Belgium had not made any declaration under Article 56 with reference to this territory.[49]

According to paragraph 3, the provisions of the Convention are applied to the territories referred to in Article 56 [former Article 63] with due regard to local requirements. In the *Tyrer* Case the British Government submitted in this context that corporal punishment on the Isle of Man was justified as a preventive measure based on public opinion on the island. The Court, however, held that "for the application of Article 63(3), more would be needed: there would have to be positive and conclusive proof of a requirement, and the Court could not regard beliefs and local 'public' opinion on their own as constituting such proof."[50]

---

[44]   See Article 29 of the 1969 Vienna Convention on the Law of Treaties, ILM 8, (1969), p. 679.

[45]   Since 1953 Greenland has been an integral part of Denmark.

[46]   Suriname became independent in 1975.

[47]   The reservation made with respect to the Netherlands Antilles with reference to Article 6(3)(c) has since been withdrawn.

[48]   See Council of Europe, *Collected Texts*, Strasbourg, 1994, p. 88.

[49]   Appl. 1065/61, *X v. Belgium*, Yearbook IV (1961), p. 260 (266-268).

[50]   Judgment of 25 April 1978, paras 36-40, from which it likewise appears that, even apart from the correctness of public opinion, the Court does not wish to regard corporal punishment itself, intended as a preventive measure, as a local requirement in the sense of Article 63(3), which would have to be taken into account in the application of Article 3. See also Appl. 7456/76, *Wiggins v. the United Kingdom*, D&R 13 (1979), p. 40 (48).

In the *Piermont* Case a German member of the European Parliament had been expelled from French Polynesia and had been prohibited from returning, while a decision was taken prohibiting her from entering New Caledonia, because of certain statements which she had made at a demonstration in Tahiti. The applicant complained that these orders infringed, amongst others, her right to freedom of expression. The French Government submitted that the 'local requirements' of French Polynesia made the interference legitimate. According to the Government the 'local requirements' were the indisputable special features of protecting public order in the Pacific territories, namely their island status and distance from metropolitan France and also the especially tense political atmosphere. The Court noted that the arguments put forward by the Government related essentially to the tense local political atmosphere taken together with an election campaign and, therefore, emphasised circumstances and conditions rather than requirements. A political situation, which admittedly was a sensitive one but also one which could occur in the mother country, did not suffice to interpret the phrase 'local requirements' as justifying an interference with the right secured in Article 10.[51]

When territories become independent, a declaration under Article 56 automatically ceases to apply because the Contracting State which made it is no longer responsible for the international relations of the new State.[52] This new State does not automatically become a Party to the Convention. In the majority of cases[53] it will not even be able to become a Party, since Article 59(1) makes signature possible only for member States of the Council of Europe and membership of the latter organisation is open only to European States.[54]

1.4.3   STATE RESPONSIBILITY FOR ACTS OF ITS ORGANS THAT HAVE BEEN COMMITTED OUTSIDE ITS TERRITORY

The fact that the Convention is applicable only to the territory of the Contracting States, with the qualification of Article 56, does not imply that a Contracting State cannot be responsible under the Convention for acts of its organs that have been committed outside its territory. Thus the Commission decided that in principle the acts of functionaries of the German embassy in Morocco might involve the responsibility

---

[51]   Judgment of 27 April 1995, para. 59.
[52]   See, *e.g.*, Appl. 7230/75, *X v. the Netherlands*, D&R 7 (1977), p. 109 (110-111).
[53]   This was different in the cases of Cyprus and Malta only, which after their independence became members of the Council of Europe and Parties to the Convention.
[54]   Article 4 of the Statute of the Council of Europe.

of the Federal Republic of Germany.[55] Switzerland was deemed responsible for acts committed under a treaty of 1923 concerning the incorporation of Liechtenstein into the Swiss customs area. The Commission held that acts of Swiss authorities having effect in Liechtenstein place all those to whom these acts are applicable under Swiss jurisdiction in the sense of Article 1 of the Convention.[56]

In the *Loizidou* Case the Court held Turkey responsible for alleged violations of Article 8 of the Convention and Article 1 of Protocol No. 1, which took place in the northern part of Cyprus, because that part was under control of Turkish forces in Cyprus which exercised overall control in that area. The Court held that the responsibility of a Contracting Party might also arise when as a consequence of military action, 'whether lawful or unlawful', it exercises effective control of an area outside its national territory. The obligation to secure, in such an area, the rights and freedoms set out in the Convention, derives from the fact of such control whether it is exercised directly, through its armed forces, or through a subordinate local administration.[57]

In *Cyprus v. Turkey* the Court held more generally that "It is of course true that the Court in the *Loizidou* Case was addressing an individual's complaint concerning the continuing refusal of the authorities to allow her access to her property. However, it is to be observed that the Court's reasoning is framed in terms of a broad statement of principle as regards Turkey's general responsibility under the Convention for the policies and actions of the 'TRNC' authorities. Having effective overall control over northern Cyprus, its responsibility cannot be confined to the acts of its own soldiers or officials in northern Cyprus but must also be engaged by virtue of the acts of the local administration which survives by virtue of Turkish military and other support. It follows that, in terms of Article 1 of the Convention, Turkey's 'jurisdiction' must be considered to extend to securing the entire range of substantive rights set out in the Convention and those additional Protocols which she has ratified, and that violations of those rights are imputable to Turkey."[58]

The responsibility of Contracting Parties can also be incurred by acts or omissions of their authorities, whether performed within or outside national boundaries, which

---

[55]   Appl. 1611/62, *X v. Federal Republic of Germany*, Yearbook VIII (1965), p. 158 (163).

[56]   Appls 7289/75 and 7349/76, *X and Y v. Switzerland*, D&R 9 (1978), p. 57 (73). In this context see, however, Appl. 6231/73, *Ilse Hess v. Federal Republic of Germany*, Yearbook XVIII (1975), p. 146 (174-176), where the British Government was not held responsible in terms of the Convention for alleged violations in Spandau Prison, because the Commission concluded that the responsibility for the prison was exercised on a Four-Power basis and that the United Kingdom acted only as a partner in the joint responsibility. Since decisions could only be taken unanimously, the prison was not under the jurisdiction of the United Kingdom in the sense of Art. 1.

[57]   Judgment of 23 March 1995 (preliminary objections), para. 62. See in this respect also the judgment of 8 July 2004, *Ilascu and Others*, paras 386-394.

[58]   Judgment of 10 May 2001, para. 77.

produce effects outside their own territory.[59] The Court noted, however, in the *Al-Adsani* Case that liability is incurred in such cases by an action of the respondent State *vis à vis* a person who is at the relevant moment on its territory and clearly within its jurisdiction, and that such cases do not concern the actual exercise of a State's competence or jurisdiction abroad.[60]

In the *Drozd and Janousek* Case the applicants complained that they had not had a fair trial before the *Tribunal de Corts* of the Principality of Andorra. They held France and Spain responsible at the international level for the conduct of the Andorran authorities. As regards the objection of lack of jurisdiction *ratione loci*, the Court agreed in substance with the Governments' arguments and the Commission's opinion that the Convention was not applicable to the territory of Andorra, notwithstanding its ratification by France and Spain. It took into consideration various circumstances: the Principality was not a member of the Council of Europe, which prevented it from being a Party to the Convention in its own right, and appeared never to have taken any steps to seek admission as an 'associate member' of the organisation. The territory of Andorra was not an area common to France and Spain or a Franco-Spanish condominium. Next the Court examined whether the applicants came under the jurisdiction of one of the Contracting States separately. The Principality's relations with France and Spain did not follow the normal pattern of relations between sovereign States and did not take the form of international agreements, even though the development of the Andorran institutions might, according to the French Co-Prince, allow Andorra to 'join the international community'. The objection of lack of jurisdiction *ratione loci* was considered well-founded. The Court also noted that judges from France and Spain sat as members of the Andorran courts, and but did not do so in their capacity as French or Spanish judges. Those courts, in particular the *Tribunal de Corts*, exercised their functions in an autonomous manner, while their judgments were not subject to supervision by the authorities of France or Spain. There was nothing in the case-file to suggest that those authorities had attempted to interfere with the applicants' trial.[61]

In sum, the case law of the Court demonstrates that its recognition of the exercise of extra-territorial jurisdiction by a Contracting State is exceptional: it has done so when the respondent State, through the effective control of the relevant territory and its inhabitants as a consequence of military occupation, or through the consent, invitation or acquiescence of the authorities of that territory, exercises all or some of the public powers normally exercised by the latter. In addition, the Court held in the *Banković* Case that other recognised instances of the extraterritorial exercise of jurisdiction by a State include cases involving the activities of its diplomatic or consular agents abroad

---

59   Judgment of 26 June 1992, *Drozd and Janousek*, para. 91.
60   Judgment of 21 November 2001, para. 39.
61   Judgment of 26 June 1992, paras 84-98.

and on board aircraft and vessels registered in, or flying the flag of, that State. In these specific situations, customary international law and treaty provisions have recognised the extraterritorial exercise of jurisdiction by the relevant State.[62] In contrast, the Court fairly recently found that the participation of a State in the defence of proceedings against it in another State does not, without more, amount to an exercise of extra-territorial jurisdiction. The Court considered that, in the particular circumstances of the case, the fact that the United Kingdom Government raised the defence of sovereign immunity before the Irish courts, where the applicant had decided to sue, does not suffice to bring them within the jurisdiction of the United Kingdom within the meaning of Article 1 of the Convention.[63]

In the Öcelan Case, the applicant maintained that there was prima facie evidence that he had been abducted by the Turkish authorities operating overseas, beyond their jurisdiction, and that it was for the Government to prove that the arrest was not unlawful. The fact that arrest warrants had been issued by the Turkish authorities and a red notice had been circulated by Interpol, did not give officials of the Turkish State jurisdiction to operate overseas. The applicant pointed out that no proceedings had been brought for his extradition from Kenya, whose authorities had denied all responsibility for his transfer to Turkey. Mere collusion between Kenyan officials operating without authority and the Turkish Government could not constitute inter-State co-operation. The Kenyan Minister of Foreign Affairs had stated that the Kenyan authorities had played no role in the applicant's departure and that there had been no Turkish troops on Kenyan territory. The applicant further alleged that the Kenyan officials implicated in his arrest had been bribed. The Turkish Government on their part maintained that the applicant had been arrested and detained in accordance with a procedure prescribed by law, following co-operation between two States, Turkey and Kenya. They said that the applicant had entered Kenya not as an asylum-seeker, but by using false identity papers. Since Kenya was a sovereign State, Turkey had no means of exercising its authority there. The Government also pointed to the fact that there was no extradition treaty between Kenya and Turkey. The Court held that the applicant was arrested by members of the Turkish security forces inside an aircraft in the international zone of Nairobi Airport. Directly after he had been handed over by the Kenyan officials to the Turkish officials the applicant was effectively under Turkish authority and was, therefore, brought within the 'jurisdiction' of that State for the purposes of Article 1 of the Convention, even though in this instance Turkey exercised its authority outside its territory. The Court considered that the circum-stances of this case were distinguishable from those in the Bankovic Case, notably in

---

[62]   Decision of 12 December 2001, para. 73
[63]   Judgment of 21 November 2001, McElhinney, para. 39.

that the applicant was physically forced to return to Turkey by Turkish officials and was subject to their authority and control following his arrest and return to Turkey.[64]

1.5   TEMPORAL SCOPE OF THE CONVENTION

1.5.1   GENERAL OBSERVATIONS

By virtue of a generally accepted principle of international law a treaty is not applicable to acts or facts that have occurred, or to situations that have ceased to exist, before the treaty entered into force and was ratified by the State in question.[65] This also applies to the European Convention.[66] In the *Pfunders* Case the Commission inferred from the nature of the obligations under the Convention that the fact that the respondent State (in this case Italy) was a party to the Convention at the time of the alleged violation was decisive, without it being necessary for the applicant State (in this case Austria) to have ratified the Convention at that time.[67]

1.5.2   CONTINUING VIOLATIONS

Of particular note is the case law developed by the Commission concerning complaints which relate to a continuing situation, i.e. to violations of the Convention which are caused by an act committed at a given moment, but which continue owing to the consequences of the original act. Such a case occurred with respect to a Belgian national who lodged a complaint concerning a conviction by a Belgian court for treason during the Second World War. The verdict had been pronounced before Belgium had ratified the Convention, but the situation complained about, *viz.* the punishment in the form of, *inter alia*, a limitation of the right of free expression, continued after the Convention had become binding upon Belgium. According to the Commission the latter fact was decisive and the complaint accordingly was declared admissible.[68]

---

[64]   Judgment of 12 March 2003, paras 93-94; see also the judgment of 30 March 2005, *Issea*, para. 38.

[65]   See Art. 28 of the Vienna Convention on the Law of Treaties, ILM 8 (1969), p. 679.

[66]   Judgment of 16 December 1997, *Proszak*, para. 31; judgment of 8 July 2004, *Ilascu and Others*, para. 400; judgment of 23 September 2004, *Dimitrov*, para. 54.

[67]   Appl. 788/60, *Austria v. Italy*, Yearbook IV (1961), p. 116 (142).

[68]   Appl. 214/56, *De Becker*, Yearbook II (1958-1959), p. 214 (244). See also Appl. 7031/75, *X v. Switzerland*, D&R 6 (1977), p. 124; Appl. 7202/75, *X v. the United Kingdom*, D&R 7 (1977), p. 102; and Appl. 8701/79, *X v. Belgium*, D&R 18 (1980), p. 250 (251) concerning disfranchise. See, however, the decision of the Commission on the joined Appls 8560/79 and 8613/79, *X and Y v. Portugal*, D&R 16 (1979), p. 209 (211-212), in which two servicemen complained that their transfer had taken place in contravention of Art. 6.

Similarly the Court held in the *Papamichalopoulos* Case that the expropriation of land amounted to a continuing violation of Article 1 of Protocol No. 1. The alleged violations had begun in 1967. At that time Greece had already ratified the Convention and Protocol No. 1, and their denunciation by Greece from 13 June 1970 until 28 November 1974 during the military regime had not released it from its obligations under them "in respect of any act which, being capable of constituting a violation of such obligations, [might] have been performed by it" earlier, as stated in Article 58(2) of the Convention. Greece had, however, not recognised the Commission's competence to receive individual petitions until 20 November 1985 and then only in relation to acts, decisions, facts and events subsequent to that date. However, the Government had not raised any preliminary objection in that regard and the Court held that the question did not call for consideration by the Court on its own motion. The Court merely noted that the applicants' claim related to a continuing situation.[69]

In the *Stamoulakatos* Case the applicant had been convicted, *in absentia*, by the Greek criminal courts on several occasions. The Government's preliminary objection was that the applicant's complaints did not come within the Court's jurisdiction *ratione temporis* because they related to events which had taken place before 20 November 1985, when Greece's acceptance of the right of individual complaint took effect. The breach which the applicant complained of originated from three convictions dating from 1979 and 1980. The fact that he had subsequently lodged appeals could not affect the period that the Court had to consider in order to rule on the objection. The Court found that the events which gave rise to the proceedings against the applicant, together with the three judgments, were covered by the time-limit in Greece's declaration in respect of [the old] Article 25 of the Convention. As to his appeals and applications against those judgments, the applicant only complained that they were ineffective in that they did not enable him to obtain from a court which had heard him, as he was entitled to under the Convention, "a fresh determination of the merits of the charges on which he had been tried *in absentia*". Thus, although those appeals and applications were lodged after the 'critical' date of 19 November 1985, according to the Court they were closely bound up with the proceedings that had led to his conviction. The Court was of the opinion that divorcing these appeals and applications from the events which gave rise to them would, in the instant case, be tantamount to rendering Greece's aforementioned declaration nugatory. It was reasonable to infer from that declaration that Greece could not be held to have violated its obligation for not affording any possibility of a retrial to those who had been convicted *in absentia*

---

[69]   Judgment of 24 June 1993, para. 40; Judgment of 22 May 1998, *Vasilescu*, para. 49; judgment of 10 May 2001, *Cyprus v. Turkey*, para. 189; Judgment of 31 July 2003, *Eugenia Michaelidou Developments Ltd. and Michael Tymvios*, para. 31.

before 20 November 1985. The objection was well-founded and the Court found it could not deal with the merits of the case.[70]

In the cases of *Yağci and Saragin,* and *Mansur* the Court rejected the preliminary objection of the Turkish Government that the Court's jurisdiction was excluded in respect of events subsequent to the date of the acceptance by Turkey of the Court's compulsory jurisdiction but which by their nature were merely "extensions of ones occurring before that date". According to the Court, having regard to the wording of the declaration Turkey made under [the old] Article 46 of the Convention, it could not entertain complaints about events which occurred before the acceptance of the Court's compulsory jurisdiction. However, when examining the complaints relating to Articles 5(3) and 6(1) of the Convention – the articles in question – the Court took account of the state of proceedings at the time when the declaration was deposited. It, therefore, could not accept the Government's argument that even facts subsequent to the date of the Turkey's declaration were excluded from its jurisdiction if they were extensions of an already existing situation. 'From the critical date onwards all the State's acts and omissions not only must conform to the Convention but are also undoubtedly subject to review by the Convention institutions.'[71]

In the *Ilascu* Case the Court held that, insofar the complaint concerned Article 6(1), it did not have jurisdiction *ratione temporis*, since the proceedings ended with the judgment of 9 December 1993. However, the applicants also submitted that their detention was not lawful, since the judgment pursuant to which they had been detained, and in three cases still were detained, had not been given by a competent court. Furthermore, they alleged that while in prison they had not been able to correspond freely or receive visits from their families. They also complained about their conditions of detention. The Court noted that those alleged violations concerned events which began with the applicants' incarceration in 1992 and were still going on. The Court, therefore, had jurisdiction *ratione temporis* to examine the complaints made insofar as they concerned events subsequent to 12 September 1997 as regards the Republic of Moldova and 5 May 1998 as regards the Russian Federation, the dates on which the Convention entered into force with respect to those States.[72]

1.5.3   DENUNCIATION OF THE CONVENTION

Even after a State has denounced the Convention in accordance with Article 58(1), the Convention remains fully applicable to that State for another six months (Article 58(2)). A complaint submitted between the date of denunciation of the Convention

---

[70]   Judgment of 26 October 1993, paras 13-14. See also decision of 9 July 2002, *Kresović*.
[71]   Judgments of 8 June 1995, para. 40 and para. 44. See also the decision of 7 March 2002, *Trajkovski*.
[72]   Judgment of 8 July 2004, paras 401-403.

and that on which that denunciation becomes effective thus falls within the scope of the Convention *ratione temporis*. This occurred in the case of the second complaint, of April 1970, by Denmark, Norway and Sweden against Greece. On 12 December 1969 Greece had denounced the Convention. This denunciation was, therefore, to become effective on 13 June 1970. The Commission decided that in virtue of Article 65(2) [the present Article 58(2)] Greece was still bound, at the time of the complaint, to comply with the obligations ensuing from the Convention, and that consequently the Commission could examine the complaint.[73]

1.6 EFFECT OF THE CONVENTION WITHIN THE NATIONAL LEGAL SYSTEMS

It is primarily the task of the national authorities of the Contracting States to secure the rights and freedoms set forth in the Convention. To what extent the national courts can play a part in this, by reviewing the acts and omissions of those national authorities, depends mainly on the question of whether the provisions of the Convention are directly applicable in proceedings before those national courts. The answer to this question depends in turn on the effect of the Convention within the national legal system concerned. The Convention does not impose upon the Contracting States the obligation to make the Convention part of domestic law or otherwise to guarantee its domestic applicability and supremacy over national law.

In the context of the relationship between international law and municipal law there are two contrasting views. According to the so-called *dualistic* view the international and the national legal system form two separate legal spheres and international law has effect within the national legal system only after it has been 'transformed' into national law via the required procedure. The legal subjects depend on this transformation for the protection of the rights laid down in international law; their rights and duties exist only under national law. This is the case, for instance, in the United Kingdom; only recently has the Convention been incorporated, under the Human Rights Act. It is only through this Act that the rights and freedoms in the Convention can be invoked. However, under this Human Rights Act, the British courts are not allowed to disapply an (other) Act of Parliament, which they consider to conflict with the Convention / Human Rights Act. They can only go so far as to give a declaratory judgment, leaving it to the legislature to remedy the situation of conflict

---

[73] Appl. 4448/70, *Denmark, Norway and Sweden v. Greece*, Yearbook XIII (1970), p. 108 (120). After the admissibility declaration the Commission desisted from further examination. However, on 18 November 1974 Greece became a Party again to the Convention, and the Commission then resumed its examination of the complaint. Finally, on 4 October 1976, after both the applicant States and the defendant State had intimated that they were no longer interested in proceeding with the case, the Commission struck the case off the list; D&R 6 (1977), p. 6 (8).

between the two Acts of Parliament. In another dualistic system, that of the Federal Republic of Germany, the Convention has been transformed by a federal law (*Zustimmungsgesetz*) according to Article 59(2) of the Constitution, thereby becoming part of the domestic law of the Federal Republic.

In a dualistic system, after the Convention has been approved and transformed into domestic law, the question remains as to what status it has within the national legal system. The answer to this question is to be found in national constitutional law and practice. Under German constitutional law, for instance, the Convention has no priority over the Federal Constitution nor is it of equal rank. It has, however, the rank of a federal statute. The consequences of this have been mitigated by interpreting German statutes in line with the Convention; the German *Bundesverfassungsgericht* has even decided that priority should be given to the provisions of the Convention over subsequent legislation unless a contrary intention of the legislature could be clearly established. Even provisions of the Federal Constitution have to be interpreted in light of the Convention. As pointed out above, the British courts cannot disapply Acts of Parliament considered not to be in conformity with the Human Rights Act. However, it can be safely assumed that many discrepancies can and will be resolved by interpreting the conflicting Act of Parliament in conformity with the Human Rights Act, meaning conformity with the Convention and the accompanying case law of the Court.

According to the so-called *monistic* view, on the other hand, the various domestic legal systems are viewed as elements of the all-embracing international legal system, within which the national authorities are bound by international law in their relations with individuals as well, regardless of whether or not the rules of international law have been transformed into national law. In this view the individual derives rights and duties directly from international law, so that in national proceedings he may directly invoke rules of international law, which must be applied by the national courts and to which the latter must give priority over any national law conflicting with it.

However, even among the monistic systems many differences exist. Although as a general rule they accept the domestic legal effect of (approved) international treaties, the scope of this acceptance varies considerably. In the Netherlands self-executing provisions of treaties and of decisions of international organisations (i.e. written international law) may be invoked before domestic courts and may set aside conflicting (*anterior* and *posterior*) statutory law, including provisions in the Constitution. In fact, the Dutch courts have actively made use of the Convention in setting aside or interpreting Acts of Parliament. In France the *Cour de Cassation*, relying upon Article 55 of the French Constitution, has accepted the prevalence of treaties (including EC-law) over national *lois* since 1975. The *Conseil d'Etat* has been much more hesitant, but finally, in 1989, accepted the supremacy of treaties over domestic legislation.

The prevailing opinion is that the system resulting from the monistic view is not prescribed by international law at its present stage of development. International law leaves the States full discretion to decide for themselves in what way they will fulfil their international obligations and implement the pertinent international rules within their national legal system; they are internationally responsible only for the ultimate result of this implementation. This holds good for the European Convention as well,[74] although the Court indicated that the system according to which the Convention has internal effect is a particularly faithful reflection of the intention of the drafters.[75] The consequence is that there is no legal obligation to assign internal effect to the Convention nor to afford it prevalence over national law. However, the great majority of Contracting States have provided for internal effect; many also accept that the Convention prevails over national legislation.

In States in which the Convention has internal effect one must ascertain for each provision separately whether it is directly applicable (i.e. is self-executing), so that individuals may directly invoke such a provision before the national courts. The self-executing character of a Convention provision may generally be presumed when the content of such a provision can be applied in a concrete case without there being a need for supplementary measures on the part of the national legislative or executive authorities.

1.7 DRITTWIRKUNG

Drittwirkung is a complicated phenomenon about which there are widely divergent views. Here only those general aspects which are directly connected with the Convention will be dealt with. Hereafter, in the discussion of the separate rights and freedoms, certain aspects of *Drittwirkung* will be discussed insofar as the case law of the Commission and the Court calls for it. For a detailed treatment of *Drittwirkung*, in particular also as to its recognition and effect under national law, reference may be made to the literature.[76]

---

[74] See the judgment of 6 February 1976, *Swedish Engine Drivers' Union*, para. 50, in which the Court held that "neither Article 13 nor the Convention in general lays down for the Contracting States any given manner for ensuring within their internal law the effective implementation of any of the provisions of the Convention." Similary, see the judgment of 23 July 1968, *Belgian Linguistic* Case, section 2, para. 11 and the judgment of 27 October 1975, *National Union of Belgian Police*, para. 38. See also the dissenting opinion of the Commission members Sperduti and Opsahl in the report of the Commission in *Ireland v. the United Kingdom*, B.23-I (1980), pp. 503-505.

[75] Judgment of 18 January 1978, *Ireland v. the United Kingdom*, para. 239.

[76] See, *e.g.*, E.A. Alkema, "The third-party applicability or "Drittwirkung" of the ECHR", in: *Protecting Human Rights; The European Dimension,* Köln, 1988, pp. 33-45; A. Clapham, 'The "Drittwirkung" of the Convention', in: R.St.J. McDonald, F. Matscher, H. Petzold (eds.), *The European System for the Protection of Human Rights,* Dordrecht/Boston/London, 1993, pp. 163-206; A. Drzemczewski, 'The domestic status of the European Convention on Human Rights; new dimensions', *Legal Issues*

What does the term *Drittwirkung* mean? Two views in particular must be distinguished. According to the first view, *Drittwirkung* of provisions concerning human rights means that these provisions also *apply* to legal relations between private parties and not only to legal relations between an individual and the public authorities. According to the second view, *Drittwirkung* of human rights provisions is defined as the possibility for an individual to *enforce* these rights against another individual. Advocates of the latter view consider that *Drittwirkung* of human rights is present only if an individual in his legal relations with other individuals is able to enforce the observance of the law concerning human rights via some procedure or other.

As to the latter view it may at once be pointed out that no *Drittwirkung* of the rights and freedoms set forth in the Convention can be directly effectuated via the procedure set up by the Convention. In fact in Strasbourg it is possible to lodge complaints only about violations of the Convention by one of the Contracting States; a complaint directed against an individual is inadmissible for reason of incompatibility with the Convention *ratione personae*. This follows from Articles 19, 32, 33 and 34 of the Convention and has also been confirmed by the Strasbourg case law.[77] As a consequence, an individual can bring up an alleged violation of his fundamental rights and freedoms by other individuals in Strasbourg only indirectly, *viz.* when a Contracting State can be held responsible for the violation in one way or another.[78] In that case the supervision in the Strasbourg procedure concerns the responsibility of the State and not that of the private actor. It is, therefore, no surprise that the Strasbourg case law provides little clarity as far as *Drittwirkung* is concerned. Any urgency for a more straightforward approach is not felt. In the *Verein gegen Tierfabriken* Case the Court even explicitly stated that it does not consider it desirable, let alone necessary, to elaborate a general theory concerning the extent to which the Convention guarantees should be extended to relations between private individuals *inter se*.[79] At best a kind of 'indirect *Drittwirkung*'[80] is recognised in cases where from a provision of the Convention – notably Articles 3, 10 and 11 – rights are inferred for individuals which, on the basis of a positive obligation on the part of Contracting States to take measures

---

of European Integration, No. 1, 1977, pp. 1-85; M.A. Eissen, 'La convention et les devoirs des individus', in: *La protection des droits de l'homme dans le cadre européen*, Paris, 1961, pp. 167-194; H. Guradze, 'Die Schutzrichtung der Grundrechtsnormen in der Europäischen Menschenrechtskonvention', *Festschrift Nipperdy*, Vol. II, 1965, pp. 759-769; M.M. Hahne, *Das Drittwirkungsproblem in der Europäischen Konvention zum Schutz der Menschenrechte und Grundfreiheiten*, Heidelberg, 1973; D.J. Harris, M. O'Boyle, C. Warbrick, *Law of the European Convention of Human Rights*, London/Dublin/Edinburgh 1995, pp. 19-22; D.H.M. Meuwissen, *De Europese Conventie en het Nederlandse Recht* [The European Convention and Dutch Law], Leyden, 1968, pp. 201-211.

[77]   See *infra* 2.2.11.8.2.

[78]   As a rule a State is not internationally responsible for the acts and omissions of its nationals or of individuals within its jurisdiction; on this, see *infra* 2.2.11.8.2.

[79]   Judgment of 28 June 2001, para. 40.

[80]   See Alkema, *supra* note 76, p. 33.

in order to make their exercise possible, must also be enforced vis-à-vis private third parties.[81]

The fact that in Strasbourg no complaints can be lodged against individuals need not, however, bar the recognition of *Drittwirkung* of the Convention, not even in the second sense referred to above. The possibility of enforcement, which in this view is required, does not necessarily have to be enforcement under international law, but may also arise from national law.[82] In that context two situations must be distinguished. In the first place there are States where those rights and freedoms included in the Convention, which are self-executing, can be directly applied by the national courts.[83] In those States the relevant provisions of the Convention can be directly invoked by individuals against other individuals insofar as their *Drittwirkung* is recognised by the national courts. Judgments of these national courts which conflict with the Convention, for which indeed the Contracting State concerned is responsible under the Convention, may then be submitted to the Strasbourg Court via the procedure under Article 34 or via the procedure under Article 33. In addition, there are those States in whose national legal systems the provisions of the Convention are not directly applicable. Those States are also obliged under the general guarantee clause of Article 1 of the Convention to secure the rights and freedoms set forth in the Convention. If one starts from the principle of *Drittwirkung*, such States also have to secure for individuals protection against violations of their fundamental rights by other individuals in their national legal system. If the competent national authorities default in this respect or if the applicable provisions of national law are not enforced, responsibility arises for the State concerned, a responsibility which may be invoked via the procedure under Article 34 or Article 33 of the Convention.[84]

At the same time the existence of a supervisory system as described above does not in itself imply *Drittwirkung*. It does not necessarily imply that the Convention is applicable to legal relations between private parties if, in a given State, individuals may directly invoke the Convention before the courts. And the nature of the obligation arising from Article 1 of the Convention for those States in whose legal system the Convention is not directly applicable, is also in itself not decisive for the question concerning that type of *Drittwirkung*. In fact one cannot deduce from Article 1 whether the Contracting States are obliged to secure the rights and freedoms only in relation to the public authorities or also in relation to other individuals. For a possible *Drittwirkung*, therefore, other arguments have to be put forward.

---

[81] For an elaborate survey of such cases of 'indirect *Drittwirkung*' and other comparable cases of 'private abuse of human rights', see Clapham, *supra* note 76.

[82] See Hahne, *supra* note 76, pp. 81-94.

[83] That this so-called 'internal effect' of the Convention does not necessarily follow from international law according to its present state, has been explained *supra* 1.6.

[84] For the above, see Hahne, *supra* note 76, pp. 89-90.

What arguments for *Drittwirkung* can be inferred from the Convention itself? It is beyond doubt that the issue of *Drittwirkung* was not taken into account when the Convention was drafted, if it played any part at all in the discussions. One can infer from the formulation of various provisions that they were not written with a view to relations between private parties. On the other hand, the subject-matter regulated by the Convention – fundamental rights and freedoms – lends itself eminently to *Drittwirkung*. It is precisely on account of the fundamental character of these rights that it is difficult to appreciate why they should deserve protection in relation to public authorities, but not in relation to private parties.

It is submitted that it is not very relevant whether the drafters of the Convention had *Drittwirkung* in mind. Of greater importance is what conclusions may be drawn for the present situation from the principles set forth in the Convention, and specifically in its Preamble. In the Preamble the drafters of the Convention gave evidence of the great value they attached to general respect for the fundamental rights and freedoms.[85] From this emphasis on general respect an argument pro rather than contra *Drittwirkung* can be inferred. But, as has been observed above, the drafters dit not make any pronouncement on this.

Neither do the separate provisions of the Convention provide any clear arguments for or against *Drittwirkung*. Article 1 has already been discussed above. Article 13 is also mentioned in this context. From the last words of this article, *viz.* 'notwithstanding that the violation has been committed by persons in their official capacity', it is inferred by some that the Convention evidently also intends to provide a remedy against violations by individuals,[86] whereas others assert that those words merely indicate that the State is responsible for violations committed by its officials,[87] or that Article 13 does not afford an independent argument for *Drittwirkung*.[88] In addition, it is sometimes inferred from Article 17 that the Convention has *Drittwirkung*. It is, however, doubtful whether such a general conclusion may be drawn from Article 17.[89] That provision forbids not only public authorities, but also individuals from invoking the Convention for the justification of an act aimed at the destruction of fundamental rights of other persons. Such a prohibition of abuse of the Convention is quite another matter than a general obligation for individuals to respect the fundamental rights of other persons in their private legal relationships.

---

[85]   It states, among other things, that the Universal Declaration, of which the Convention is an elaboration, "aims at securing universal and effective recognition and observance of the rights therein declared", while the Contracting States affirm "their profound belief in those Fundamental Freedoms which are the foundation of justice and peace in the world."

[86]   See Eissen, *supra* note 76, pp. 177 *et seq.*

[87]   See Guradze, *supra* note 76, p. 764.

[88]   See Meuwissen, *supra* note 76, p. 210.

[89]   *Ibidem.*

In summary, one may conclude that *Drittwirkung* does not imperatively ensue from the Convention. On the other hand, nothing in the Convention prevents the States from conferring *Drittwirkung* upon the rights and freedoms laid down in the Convention within their national legal systems insofar as they lend themselves to it. In some States *Drittwirkung* of the rights and freedoms guaranteed by the Convention is already recognised, whilst in other States this *Drittwirkung* at least is not excluded in principle.[90] Some have adopted the view that it may be inferred from the changing social circumstances and legal opinions that the purport of the Convention is *going to be* to secure a certain minimum guarantee for the individual as well as in his relations with other persons.[91] It would seem that with regard to the spirit of the Convention a good deal may be said for this view, although in the case of such a subsequent interpretation one must ask oneself whether one does not thus assign to the Convention an effect which may be unacceptable to (a number of) the Contracting States, and consequently is insufficiently supported by their implied mutual consent.

At the same time, whether *Drittwirkung* can be assigned to the Convention at all also depends in particular on the nature and formulation of each separate right embodied in the Convention. In this context Alkema warns us that the nature of the legal relations between private parties may be widely divergent and that consequently *Drittwirkung* is a multiform phenomenon about which general statements are hardly possible.[92]

1.8 THE SUPERVISORY MECHANISM UNTIL 1998

1.8.1 THE SYSTEM BEFORE PROTOCOL NO. 11

In order to ensure the rights and freedoms laid down in the Convention, two bodies were originally established: the European Commission of Human Rights and the European Court of Human Rights. Furthermore, the Committee of Ministers of the Council of Europe and the Secretary General of the Council of Europe played a part in the supervisory mechanism. The European Commission of Human Rights and the European Court of Human Rights were set up specifically to ensure the observance of the engagements undertaken by the Contracting States under the Convention (Article 19 old). The other two organs were established by the Statute of the Council of Europe and not by the Convention.

---

[90] See Drzemczewski, *supra* note 76, p. 63 et seq.
[91] See Meuwissen, *supra* note 76, p. 211; and Clapham, *supra* note 76, in particular pp. 200-206.
[92] See Alkema, *supra* note 76, pp. 254-255.

1.8.2   THE EUROPEAN COMMISSION ON HUMAN RIGHTS

The individual complaints procedure covered the following two phases:

1   *The decisions on admissibility.* After the Secretariat of the Commission had decided to register an application, the Commission examined the admissibility of the complaint. If the application was ruled inadmissible, the procedure ended.

2.   *The examination of the merits.* If the application was declared admissible, the Commission examined the merits of the case. The procedure could, at this point, end in a friendly settlement or some other arrangement. If no settlement was reached, the Commission stated its opinion in a report. The case could subsequently be submitted to the Court,[93] which then gave the final decision on the merits. If a case was not submitted to the Court, the Committee of Ministers gave the final decision on the merits.

The Commission did not sit permanently. After the entry into force of Protocol No. 8 in 1990, Chambers were set up which exercised all the powers of the plenary Commission relating to individual complaints which could be dealt with on the basis of established case law or which raised no serious questions affecting the interpretation or application of the Convention. Each Chamber was composed of at least seven members. The Protocol, in addition, opened up the possibility of setting up Committees, each composed of at least three members, with the power to unanimously declare inadmissible or strike off its list of cases applications submitted under (the old) Article 25 when such a decision could be taken without further examination.

The most important decisions of the Commission on admissibility as well as the great majority of its reports have been published.[94]

---

[93]   According to article 48 (old) of the Convention "The following may bring a case before the Court, provided that the High Contracting Party concerned, if there is only one, or the High Contracting Parties concerned, if there is more than one, are subject to the compulsory jurisdiction of the Court, failing that, with the consent of the High Contracting Parties concerned, if there is only one, or of the High Contracting Parties concerned if there is more than one:
(a)   the Commission;
(b)   a High Contracting Party whose national is alleged to be a victim;
(c)   a High Contracting Party which referred the case to the Commission;
(d)   a High Contracting Party against which the complaint has been lodged."

[94]   The publication system of the Commission was rather complicated and therefore requires some elucidation. Not all decisions of the Commission were published, especially not those taken after summary proceedings. A number of the decisions concerning admissibility are to be found in the *Yearbook of the European Convention on Human Rights* and in the *Collection of Decisions*, continued after 1975 as *Decisions and Reports*. The reports of the Commission were published separately; in addition they were sometimes included in the *Yearbooks* and in the *Decisions and Reports*. Sometimes a decision was included in the *Yearbooks* but not in the *Collection of Decisions/Decisions and Reports* and vice versa. In the *Digest of Strasbourg case-law relating to the European Convention on Human Rights*, published by Carl Heymans Verlag, the case law of the Commission and the Court has been incorporated. For those cases that were referred to the Court, the main parts of the reports of the Commission were since 1985 also published as an Annex to the judgment of the Court (Series A),

1.8.3 THE EUROPEAN COURT OF HUMAN RIGHTS

As with the Commission, the European Court of Human Rights was specifically set up to supervise the observance by the Contracting States of their engagements arising from the Convention (under the old Article 19). Unlike the Commission, the number of members of the Court was not related to the number of the Contracting States, but to the number of Member States of the Council of Europe which originally was not the same number, as the Member States were not obliged to accede to the Convention.

For the consideration of each case a Chamber composed of nine judges was constituted from the Court (under the old Article 43). Persons sitting as *ex officio* members of the Chambers were those judges who were elected in respect of the States Parties to the case. If such a judge was not available, the place was taken by a judge *ad hoc*; a person chosen by the State in question. In addition, either the President or the Vice-President sat as an *ex officio* member of the Chamber. The other members of the Chamber were chosen by lot. For that purpose the judges were divided into three regional groups. The Chamber thus constituted was able, or was obliged, under certain conditions, to relinquish jurisdiction in favour of, originally, the plenary Court, and later a Grand Chamber of 17 judges.[95] To prevent inconsistencies in the case law, the Court, in its Rules, had assigned to the Chambers the right to relinquish jurisdiction in favour of the plenary Court/Grand Chamber when a case pending before a Chamber raised serious questions affecting the interpretation of the Convention. A Chamber was obliged to do so where the resolution of such questions might have a result inconsistent with a judgment previously delivered by a Chamber or by the plenary Court/Grand Chamber. According to Rule 51(5) of the old Rules of Court the Grand Chamber could exceptionally, when the issues raised were particularly serious or involved a significant change of existing case law, relinquish jurisdiction in favour of the plenary Court.

No case could be brought before the Court unless it had been declared admissible by the Commission, and the Commission had stated its opinion on the merits in a report.

All the judgments of the Court were published, as were the documents relating to the proceedings, including the report of the Commission, but excluding any document which the President considered unnecessary to publish.[96]

---

while before 1985 they were included in the materials published in Series B. As from 1996 the case law of the Commission was and that of the Court still is published in *Reports of Judgments and Decisions*.

[95] On 27 October 1993 the Court decided to establish a Grand Chamber to exercise the jurisdiction of the plenary Court in most cases.

[96] The judgments and decisions of the Court were published in the *Publications of the European Court of Human Rights, Series A*. The documents of the case, including the report of the Commission, were published in the *Publications of the European Court of Human Rights, Series B*. Since 1985, the main parts of reports of the Commission were also published as an annex to the Court judgments in Series

1.8.4 THE COMMITTEE OF MINISTERS OF THE COUNCIL OF EUROPE

Unlike the Commission and the Court, the Committee of Ministers was not set up by the Convention. Here a supervisory function had been entrusted to an already existing body of the Council of Europe. Accordingly, the composition, organisation, and general functions and powers of the Committee of Ministers are not regulated in the Convention, but by the Statute of the Council of Europe.[97]

The function assigned to the Committee of Ministers in the Convention was the result of a compromise. On the one hand, during the drafting of the Convention there was a body of opinion which wished to institute, in addition to the Commission, a Court with compulsory jurisdiction. Others, however, held that it was preferable to entrust supervision, apart from the Commission, only to the Committee of Ministers. Ultimately the two alternatives were combined by making the jurisdiction of the Court optional and granting the Committee the power, in those cases that were not, or could not be, submitted to the Court, to decide on the question of whether there had been a violation of the Convention.

1.9 THE SUPERVISORY MECHANISM SINCE 1998

1.9.1 THE REVISED SYSTEM UNDER PROTOCOL NO. 11

Since 1982 several proposals had been forwarded concerning the possibility of 'merging' the Commission and the Court into a single body. Apart from the idea of 'merging' there was a Dutch-Swedish initiative in 1990 which proposed making the opinions of the Commission under (the old) Article 31 – in so far as individual applications were concerned – legally binding decisions. Thus, there would be a two-tier judicial system, where the Commission would operate as a court of first instance from which individual applicants and States might be granted a right of appeal to the Court. In both proposals no role was left for the Committee of Ministers under (the old) Article 32 in respect of individual applications. As no consensus could be reached on either proposal, they were referred to the Committee of Ministers in order to obtain a clear mandate for further work on the reform. At the Vienna Summit of October 1993, the Council of Europe's Heads of State and Government adopted the 'Vienna

---

A. In addition, a summary was published in the *Yearbook of the European Convention on Human Rights*. In 1996 the Series A ceased to exist. Subsequently the judgments of the Court were published in *Reports of Judgments and Decisions*.

[97]   See Articles 13-21 of the Statute of the Council of Europe.

Declaration' of 9 October 1993, which finally resulted in the reform enshrined in Protocol No. 11.

One of the most important reasons that prompted the revision of the supervisory system was the increasing workload of the existing institutions. For example, the yearly number of individual applications registered had grown from 1,013 in 1988 to 4,721 in 1997, and the number of judgments – including decisions rejecting applications submitted under Protocol No. 9 – delivered by the Court had risen from 19 in 1988 to 150 in 1997. Another important reason was the increasing length of time needed to deal with applications.

The entry into force of Protocol No. 11 on 1 November 1998 meant a considerable alteration of the supervisory mechanism under the Convention. A new, permanent Court took the place of the European Commission of Human Rights and the European Court of Human Rights. In addition, the role of the Committee of Ministers of the Council of Europe in the individual complaint procedure was dropped. Under Article 42, para 2, the Committee of Ministers has, however, retained its supervisory role with respect to the execution of the Court's judgments. The European Commission of Human Rights continued to function until 1 November 1999, in order to handle the cases that were still in progress. The new Court handled the cases of the old Court that were still pending on 1 November 1998. The secretariat of the Commission was combined with the registry to form the registry of the new Court. Another important change was that the individual right of complaint was no longer dependent on the optional recognition by the State. Henceforth ratification of the Convention automatically entailed recognition of the individual right of complaint.[98] Acceptance of the Court's jurisdiction by the State was also no longer required. The new system provides for the Court's jurisdiction as the only and compulsory jurisdiction. The State's right of complaint continues to exist in addition to that of the individual.[99]

1.9.2 THE FUTURE SYSTEM UNDER PROTOCOL NO. 14

The reform under Protocol No. 11 has, however, proven to be insufficient to cope with the prevailing situation. Since 1998 the number of applications increased from 18,164 to 34,546 in 2002, while at the end of 2003 approximately 65,000 applications were pending before the Court. The problem of the excessive case-load is characterized by two phenomena in particular: i. The number of inadmissible applications, and ii. the number of repetitive cases following a so-called 'pilot judgment'. In 2003 some 17,270 applications were declared inadmissible (or struck off the list of cases) and 753 cases were declared admissible. With respect to the remaining cases, the Court delivered

---

[98]   Article 34 of the Convention.
[99]   Article 33 of the Convention.

703 judgments in 2003, of which some 60% concerned repetitive cases.[100] As a result of the massive increase of individual applications, the effectiveness of the system and thus the credibility and authority of the Court are seriously endangered.

In order to cope with this problem, Protocol No. 14 was drafted to amend the control system of the Convention. It was opened for signature on 13 May 2004, but has not entered into force yet. Unlike Protocol No.11, Protocol 14 makes no radical changes to the control system. The changes it does make relate more to the functioning of the system rather than to its structure. Its main purpose is to improve the system, giving the Court the procedural means and flexibility it needs to process all applications in a timely fashion, while allowing it to concentrate on the most important cases which require in-depth examination.

The amendments concern the following aspects: (a) reinforcement of the Court's filtering capacity in respect of the flux of unmeritorious applications; (b) a new admissibility criterion concerning cases in which the applicant has not suffered a significant disadvantage; (c) measures for dealing with repetitive cases. Together these elements of the reform seek to reduce the time spent by the Court on clearly inadmissible, repetitive and less important applications, in order to enable the Court to concentrate on those cases that raise important human rights issues.[101]

1.9.3   THE EUROPEAN COURT OF HUMAN RIGHTS

The European Court of Human Rights, set up under the Convention as amended by Protocol No. 11, is composed of a number of judges equal to that of the Contracting States.[102] The Court functions on a permanent basis. Judges sit on the Court in their individual capacity and do not represent any State. They cannot engage in any activity which is incompatible with their independence or impartiality or with the demands of full-time office.

The purpose of Protocol No. 11 was to streamline procedures rather than to change substantive matters. Thus the Court now also exercises the filter function that in the past was performed by the Commission. The Court consists of Committees, Chambers and the Grand Chamber. Subject to powers specifically attributed to the Committees and the Grand Chamber, Chambers have inherent competence to examine the admissibility and the merits of all individual and interstate applications. The Committees only play a role at the admissibility stage of the proceedings, and only in respect of cases brought by individuals. In accordance with Article 28, a Committee may, by unanimous vote, declare an application inadmissible or strike a case off its list of cases

---

[100]   Explanatory Report to Protocol No.14, para. 7.
[101]   See *infra* 1.9.6.
[102]   Article 20 of the Convention.

where such a decision can be taken without further examination. The decision is final. According to Article 29(2) a Chamber is to decide on the admissibility (and the merits) of inter-state complaints.

When Protocol No. 14 will enter into force, paragraphs 1 and 2 of Article 28 will be amended. On the basis of the new paragraph 1.b of Article 28, the Committee may also, in a joint decision, declare individual applications admissible and decide on their merits, when the questions they raise concerning the interpretation or application of the Convention are covered by well-established case law of the Court. The Committees may rule on all aspects of the case (admissibility, merits, just satisfaction) in a single judgment or decision. Unanimity is required on each aspect. Failure to reach a unanimous decision counts as no decision, in which event the Chamber procedure applies (Article 29). It will then fall to the Chamber to decide whether all aspects of the case should be covered in a single judgment. Even when the Committee initially intends to apply the procedure provided for in Article 28(1)(b), it may declare an application inadmissible under Article 28(1)(a). This may happen, for example, if the respondent Party has persuaded the Committee that domestic remedies have not been exhausted.

When a three-judge Committee gives a judgment on the merits, the judge elected in respect of the High Contracting Party concerned will not be an *ex officio* member of the decision-making body, in contrast with the situation under the Convention as it stands. According to the *Explanatory Report to Protocol No. 14* the presence of this judge would not appear necessary, since Committees will deal with cases on which well-established case law exist. However, paragraph 3 of Article 28 provides that a Committee may invite the judge elected in respect of the High Contracting Party concerned to replace one of its members. In certain circumstances it may, in particular, be useful to do so if questions relating to the domestic legal system concerned need to be clarified. Article 28(3) explicitly mentions as one of the factors which a Committee may take into account in deciding whether to invite the judge elected in respect of the Respondent Party to join it, the situation where the Party has contested the applicability of paragraph 28(1)(b). The *Explanatory Report to Protocol No. 14* mentions in this respect that it was considered important to have at least some reference in the Convention itself to giving respondent Parties the opportunity to contest the application of the simplified procedure.[103]

After the entry into force of Protocol No. 14, a new Article 27 containing provisions defining the competence of the new single-judge formation will be inserted into the Convention. Paragraph 1 specifies that the competence of the single judge is limited to taking decisions of inadmissibility or decisions to strike cases off the list "where such a decision can be taken without further examination". This means that the judge will take such decisions only in clear-cut cases, where the inadmissibility of the application is manifest from the outset. The single-judge formations will be assisted by rapporteurs

---

[103] Explanatory Report to Protocol No.14, para. 71.

from the Registry with knowledge of the language and the legal system of the respondent Party concerned (Article 24(2) (new)). The decision itself remains the sole responsibility of the judge. In case of doubt the judge will refer the application to a Committee or a Chamber.[104]

Under Protocol No. 14, Article 29 needed to be amended to take into account the new provisions in Articles 27 and 28. Paragraph 1 of the amended Article 29(1) reads as follows:

> *If no decision is taken under Article 27 or 28, or no judgment rendered under Article 28, a Chamber shall decide on the admissibility and merits of individual applications submitted under Article 34. The decision on admissibility may be taken separately.*

The text of the old Article 29(3) will be included in the new paragraph 2 of Article 29 which will read as follows:

> *A Chamber shall decide on the admissibility and merits of inter-State applications submitted under Article 33. The decision on admissibility shall be taken separately unless the Court, in exceptional cases, decides otherwise.*

1.9.4 ELECTION OF THE MEMBERS OF THE COURT

For the election of the judges every member of the Council of Europe nominates three candidates of whom two at least must be its nationals. The third candidate may be a national of another Contracting State, any other State, or stateless. There is no longer a provision that no two judges may be of the same nationality. From the list thus produced the Parliamentary Assembly elects the members of the Court by a majority of the votes cast (Article 22(1)).

Article 22(2) provides that the same procedure must be followed when new members are admitted to the Council of Europe and in filling interim vacancies. In the former case the new Member State puts forward the three candidates and in the latter case this is done by the State which had nominated the candidate to whose resignation or death the vacancy is due. After the entry into force of Protocol No. 14, Article 22(2) shall be deleted since it will no longer serve any useful purpose in view of the changes made to Article 23.

According to the present Article 23(1) judges will be elected for a period of six years, and may be re-elected. However, the terms of office of half of the judges elected at the first election expired at the end of three years. The judges whose term of office expired at the end of the initial period of three years were chosen by lot by the Secretary General of the Council of Europe immediately after their election. Judges may be re-

---

[104]   *Ibidem*, para. 67.

elected. Article 23(6) (the new Article 23(2) provides that the term of office of the judges shall expire when they reach the age of 70. The members of the Court hold office until replaced. After having been replaced they continue to deal with such cases as they already had under consideration (Article 23(7) (the new Article 23(3)). The end of the terms of office is staggered in the sense that, as far as possible, every three years half of the terms of office expire (Article 23(1) and (3)).

After the entry into force of Protocol 14 the term of office will be nine years and the judges may not be re-elected. (Article 23(1) (new). The system whereby large groups of judges were renewed at three-year intervals will be abolished. This will be brought about by the new wording of paragraph 1 and the deletion of paragraphs 2 to 4 of Article 23. In addition, paragraph 5 of the old Article 23 will be deleted so that, in the event of an interim vacancy, a judge will no longer be elected to hold office for the remainder of his or her predecessor's term. Judges will hold office until replaced, while they will continue to deal with such cases as they already have under consideration. Paragraph 4 will read that no judge may be dismissed from office unless the other judges decide by a majority of two-thirds that that judge has ceased to fulfil the required conditions.

The Court functions on a permanent basis.[105] The judges have a full-time office (Article 21, paragraph 3), and have their home basis in Strasbourg.

The Plenary Court elects its President, two Vice-Presidents and three Presidents of Section for a period of three years (Article 26).

1.9.5 REQUIREMENTS FOR MEMBERSHIP OF THE COURT

The Convention lays down certain requirements for members of the Court. Candidates must be of high moral character and must either possess the qualifications required for appointment to high judicial office or be jurisconsults of recognised competence (Article 21(1)). The judges shall sit on the Court in their individual capacity (Article 21(2)). During their term of office the judges shall not engage in any activity which is incompatible with their independence, impartiality, or with the demands of a full-time office (Article 21(3)). According to Rule 3 of the Rules of Court,[106] before taking up their duties, the judges must take an oath or make a declaration to the effect that they will exercise their function independently and impartially. Similarly, a judge may not exercise his function when he is a member of a government or holds a post or exercises a profession which is incompatible with his independence and impartiality (Rule 4 of the Rules of Court).

---

[105] Article 19.
[106] http://www.echr.coe.int/Eng/EDocs/RulesOfCourt.html.

Article 51 provides that the members of the Court, during the exercise of their functions, are entitled to the privileges and immunities provided for in Article 40 of the Statute of the Council of Europe and in the agreements made thereunder,[107] which furthers the independent exercise of their function.

1.9.6   SESSIONS OF THE COURT

The seat of the Court is in Strasbourg, but if it considers it expedient, the Court may exercise its functions elsewhere in the territories of the Member States of the Council of Europe (Rule 19 of the Rules of Court). Rule 20 of the Rules of Court provides that the President convenes the Court whenever the performance of its functions under the Convention and under these Rules so requires in a plenary session and also at the request of at least one-third of the members. The quorum for the sessions of the plenary Court is two-thirds of the judges (Rule 20(2) of the Rules of Court).

In order to consider cases brought before it, the Court shall sit in Committees, Chambers and the Grand Chamber.[108] In plenary the Court will only deal with administrative matters, such as the election of the President, the Vice-Presidents and the Presidents of the Chambers, and the adoption of the Rules of Procedure (Article 26) (new Article 25). After the entry into force of Protocol No. 14 a new paragraph will be added in order to reflect the new function attributed to the plenary Court. Under new Article 26(2) the Committee of Ministers may, by a unanimous decision and for a fixed period, at the request of the plenary Court, reduce the number of judges of the Chambers to five.

The Chambers, consisting of seven judges, as provided for in Article 26(b) of the Convention, shall be set up by the plenary Court. In fact the Court divides its membership into Sections. There shall be at least four Sections. Each judge shall be a member of a Section. The composition of the Sections shall be geographically and gender balanced and shall reflect the different legal systems of the Contracting Parties. Where a judge ceases to be a member of the Court before the expiry of the period for which the Section has been constituted, the judge's place in the Section shall be taken by his or her successor as a member of the Court. The President of the Court may exceptionally make modifications to the composition of the Sections if circumstances so require. On the basis of a proposal by the President the plenary Court may constitute an additional Section (Rule 25). Meanwhile, a fifth Section has been constituted.

The Committees, as provided for in Article 27(1) of the Convention, are composed of three judges belonging to the same Section. The Committees are constituted for a period of twelve months by rotation among the members of each Section, excepting

---

[107]   See Sixth Protocol to the General Agreement on Privileges and Immunities of the Council of Europe, Strasbourg, 5 March 1996, ETS, No. 162.
[108]   Article 27(1) of the Convention.

the President of the Section. The judges of the Section who are not members of a Committee may be called upon to take the place of members who are unable to sit. Each Committee shall be chaired by the member having precedence in the Section.[109]

The Grand Chamber, consisting of seventeen judges, includes the President of the Court, the Vice-Presidents, the Presidents of the Chambers and other judges chosen in accordance with the Rules of Court. There shall sit as an *ex officio* member of the Chamber and the Grand Chamber the judge elected in respect of the State Party concerned or, if there is none or if he or she is unable to sit, a person of that State's choice. To make sure that the Grand Chamber looks into the matter afresh when it examines a case referred to it under Article 43, judges from the Chamber which rendered the judgment are excluded, with the exception of the President of the Chamber and the judge who sat in respect of the State concerned (Article 27).

For the consideration of a case a Chamber is constituted from the Section (Article 27(1) and Rule 26(1)). Persons sitting as *ex officio* members of the Chambers are the President of the Section and those judges who are elected in respect of any State Party to the case. If such a judge is unable to sit or withdraws, the President of the Chamber shall invite that Party to indicate within thirty days whether it wishes to appoint to sit as judge either another elected judge or, as an *ad hoc* judge, any other person possessing the qualifications required by Article 21(1) of the Convention and, if so, to state at the same time the name of the person to be appointed. The Contracting Party concerned shall be presumed to have waived its right of appointment if it does not reply within thirty days (Rule 29). The other members of the Chamber are chosen by lot (Rule 21 of the Rules of Court).

In order to prevent inconsistencies in the Court's case law, according to the Rules, the Chambers have the right to relinquish jurisdiction in favour of the Grand Chamber. Rule 72(1) provides in that respect that in accordance with Article 30 of the Convention, where a case pending before a Chamber raises a serious question affecting the interpretation of the Convention or the Protocols thereto or where the resolution of a question before it might have a result inconsistent with a judgment previously delivered by the Court, the Chamber may, at any time before it has rendered its judgment, relinquish jurisdiction in favour of the Grand Chamber, unless one of the parties to the case has objected in accordance with paragraph 2 of this Rule. Reasons need not be given for the decision to relinquish. The Registrar shall notify the parties of the Chamber's intention to relinquish jurisdiction. The parties shall have one month from the date of that notification within which to file at the Registry a duly reasoned objection. An objection which does not fulfil these conditions shall be considered invalid by the Chamber.[110]

---

[109]   Rule 27 of the Rules of Court.
[110]   See for an overview of judgments, in which Rule 72 of the Rules has been applied: Appendix IV.

Judges may not take part in the consideration of any case in which they have a personal interest or with respect to which they have previously acted as agent, advocate, or adviser of a party or of a person having an interest in the case, or as a member of a tribunal or commission of enquiry, or in any other capacity. If a judge considers that he or she should not take part in the consideration of a particular case, he or she informs the President, who shall exempt the judge concerned from sitting. The initiative may also be taken by the President, when the latter considers that such a withdrawal is desirable. In case of disagreement the Court decides (Rule 28(2), (3) and (4) of the Rules of Court).

The hearings of the Court are public, unless the Court decides otherwise in exceptional circumstances (Rule 33 of the Rules of Court). This publicity is a logical implication of the judicial character of the procedure. The deliberations of the Court, on the other hand, are in private (Rule 22 of the Rules of Court).

The Court takes its decisions by a majority of votes of the judges present. If the voting is equal, the President of the (Grand) Chamber has a casting vote (Rule 23 of the Rules of Court).

In accordance with Article 44(3) of the Convention final judgments of the Court shall be published, under the responsibility of the Registrar, in an appropriate form. The Registrar shall in addition be responsible for the publication of official reports of selected judgments and decisions and of any document which the President of the Court considers useful to publish.[111]

After the entry into force of Protocol No.14 the following changes will be brought about. The present Article 25 will become Article 24 and will be amended in two respects. First of all, the second sentence of Article 25 will be deleted since the legal secretaries, created by Protocol 11, have in practice never had an existence of their own, independent from the registry. Secondly, a new paragraph 2 will be added so as to introduce the function of rapporteur as a means of assisting the new single judge formation as provided for in the new Article 27.

Article 27 will become Article 26 and its text will be amended in several respects. In paragraph 1 a single judge formation will be introduced in the list of judicial formations of the Court and a new rule will be inserted in a new paragraph 3 to the effect that a single judge shall not sit in cases concerning a High Contracting Party in respect of which he or she has been elected. A new paragraph 2 will be introduced as regards a possible reduction of the size of the Court's Chambers. Application of this paragraph by the Committee of Ministers at the request of the Court will reduce to five the number of judges of the Chambers. It will not allow, however, for setting up a system of Chambers of different sizes which would operate simultaneously for different types

---

[111]   Rule 78 of the Rules of Court.

of cases.[112] Finally, paragraph 2 of Article 27 will be amended to make provision for a new system of *ad hoc* judges. Under the new rule, contained in paragraph 4 of the new Article 26, each High Contracting Party is required to draw up a reserve list of *ad hoc* judges from which the President of the Court shall choose someone when the need arises to appoint an *ad hoc* judge.

Under Protocol No. 14 an amendment of Article 31 concerning the powers of the Grand Chamber will be needed. A new paragraph will be added to this Article in order to reflect the new function attributed to the Grand Chamber by this Protocol, namely to decide on issues referred to the Court by the Committee of Ministers under the new paragraph 4 of Article 46 of the Convention. This concerns the question whether a High Contracting Party has failed to fulfill its obligations to comply with a judgment. Finally, in Article 32 of the Convention concerning the jurisdiction of the Court a reference will be inserted to the new procedure provided for in the amended Article 46. According to the amended Article 46 the Committee of Ministers may, if it considers that the supervision of the execution of a final judgment is hindered by a problem of interpretation of the judgment, refer the matter to the Court for a ruling on the question of interpretation.

1.10 THE COMMITTEE OF MINISTERS

1.10.1 GENERAL OBSERVATIONS

Unlike the Court, the Committee of Ministers was not set up by the Convention. Here a function was entrusted to an already existing body of the Council of Europe. Accordingly, the composition, organisation, general functions and powers, and procedure of the Committee of Ministers are not regulated by the Convention, but by the Statute of the Council of Europe.[113] After the entry into force of Protocol No. 11, under Article 46 (2) the Committee of Ministers retained its function of supervising the execution of judgments of the Court, while its power under former Article 32 in respect of individual applications was abolished.

Under Protocol No. 14, Article 46 will be amended. Article 46(3) will empower the Committee of Ministers to ask the Court to interpret a final judgment, for the purpose of facilitating the supervision of its execution. The Court's reply will settle any argument concerning a judgment's exact meaning. According to Article 46(3) a referral decision shall require a majority vote of two thirds of the representatives entitled to sit on the Committee. According to the Explanatory Report to this Protocol the aim of the new paragraph 3 is to enable the Court to give an interpretation of a

---

[112] Explanatory Report to Protocol No. 14, 194, para. 63.
[113] See Articles 13-21 of the Statute of the Council of Europe.

judgment, not to pronounce on the measures taken by the High Contracting Parties to comply with that judgment. No time-limit will be set for making requests for interpretation, since a question of interpretation may arise at any time during the Committee of Ministers' examination of the execution of a judgment.[114]

Paragraphs 4 and 5 of Article 46 will empower the Committee of Ministers to bring infringement proceedings before the Court.[115] On the basis of paragraph 4 the Committee of Ministers may – if it considers that a High Contracting Party has refused to abide by a final judgment in a case to which it is a party, after serving formal notice on that Party and by decision adopted by a majority vote of two thirds of the representatives entitled to sit on the Committee – refer to the Court the question of whether that Party has failed to fulfil its obligation under paragraph 1. If the Court finds a violation of paragraph 1, it shall refer the case to the Committee of Ministers for consideration of the measures to be taken. If the Court finds no violation of paragraph 1, it shall return the case to the Committee of Ministers, which shall close its examination of the case.[116] The new Article 46 thus introduces a wider range of measures of bringing pressure to secure execution of judgments. Currently the ultimate measure available to the Committee of Ministers is recourse to Article 8 of the Statute of the Council of Europe (suspension of voting rights in the Committee of Ministers or even expulsion from the Council of Europe), which in most cases would be an overkill.

1.10.2   COMPOSITION OF THE COMMITTEE OF MINISTERS

The Committee of Ministers consists of one representative from each Member State of the Council of Europe – as a rule the Minister for Foreign Affairs. In case of the latter's inability to be present, or if other circumstances make it desirable, an alternate may be nominated, who shall, whenever possible, be a member of government (Article 14 of the Statute). In practice the Committee has sessions only twice annually (see Article 21(c) of the Statute). In the intervening periods its duties are discharged by the so-called 'Committee of the Ministers' Deputies', consisting of high officials who are generally the permanent representatives of their governments to the Council of Europe. Every representative on the Committee of Ministers appoints an alternate (Rule 14 of the Rules of the Committee of Ministers).

---

[114]   Explanatory Report to Protocol No. 14, para. 97.
[115]   According to Article 35(b) (new), the Court sit as a Grand Chamber, having first served the State concerned with notice to comply.
[116]   Article 46(5) of the Convention.

1.10.3 SESSIONS OF THE COMMITTEE OF MINISTERS

The sessions of the Committee of Ministers are not public, unless the Committee decides otherwise (Article 21(a) of the Statute). In principle the rules of procedure that apply to the Committee as executive organ of the Council of Europe are equally applicable to its functions within the context of the Convention.

1.11 THE SECRETARY GENERAL OF THE COUNCIL OF EUROPE

The Secretary General of the Council of Europe also plays a part within the framework of the Convention. The Secretary General is the highest official of the Council of Europe and is elected for a period of five years by the Parliamentary Assembly from a list of candidates which is drawn up by the Committee of Ministers (Article 36 of the Statute of the Council of Europe).

The Secretary General is involved in the Convention system in various ways, on the one hand by reason of his administrative functions as they result from the Statute of the Council of Europe, and on the other hand in connection with a specific supervisory task created by the Convention.

Ratifications of the Convention must be deposited with the Secretary General (Article 59(1)), who has to notify the Members of the Council of Europe of the entry into force of the Convention and keep them informed of the names of the States which have become parties to the Convention (Article 59(4)).[117] A denunciation of the Convention must also be notified to the Secretary General, who informs the other Contracting States (Article 58). Deposition with the Secretary General is also required for the notification by which a State declares that the Convention extends to a territory for whose international relations that State is responsible (Article 56(1)).

Moreover, the Secretary General fulfils an important administrative function under Article 15(3) of the Convention. Any State availing itself under Article 15 of the right to derogate from one or more provisions of the Convention in time of war or another emergency threatening the life of the nation, must keep the Secretary General fully informed of the measures taken in that context and the reasons therefore. It must also inform him when such measures have ceased to operate.

The most important function assigned to the Secretary General in the Convention, however, is of quite a different nature. Under Article 52 he has the task of supervising the effective implementation by the Contracting States of the provisions of the Convention. This supervisory task of the Secretary General will be dealt with in chapter 4.

---

[117]   The same applies for Protocols to the Convention.

1.12   THE RIGHT OF COMPLAINT OF STATES

1.12.1   INTRODUCTION

What is called here the 'right of complaint' under the Convention is the right to take the initiative for the supervisory procedure provided for in the Convention on the ground that the Convention has allegedly been violated by a Contracting State. The Convention differentiates between the right of complaint for States on the one hand (Article 33) and that for individuals on the other hand (Artice 34).

When the Convention enters into force for a State, that State acquires the right to lodge, through the Secretary General, an application with the Court on the ground of an alleged violation of one or more provisions of the Convention by another Contracting State.

1.12.2   OBJECTIVE CHARACTER

This right of complaint for States constitutes an important divergence from the traditional principles of international law concerning inter-State action. According to these principles a State can bring an international action against another State only when a right of the former is at stake, or when that State takes up the case of one of its nationals whom it considers to have been treated by the other State in a way contrary to the rules of international law – so-called 'diplomatic protection'.

Under the Convention a State may also lodge a complaint about violations committed against persons who are not its nationals or against persons who are not nationals of any of the Contracting States or are stateless, and even about violations against nationals of the respondent State. States may equally lodge a complaint about the incompatibility with the Convention of legislation or an administrative practice of another State without having to allege a violation of a right of any specified person – the so-called 'abstract applications'. Thus the right of complaint for States assumes the character of an *actio popularis*: any Contracting State has the right to lodge a complaint about any alleged violation of the Convention, regardless of whether there is a special relationship between the rights and interests of the applicant State and the alleged violation.

In the *Pfunders* Case between Austria and Italy, the Commission stressed that a State which brings an application under Article 33, "is not to be regarded as exercising a right of action for the purpose of enforcing its own rights, but rather as bringing before the Commission an alleged violation of the public order of Europe."[118] The Court similarly held that, unlike international treaties of the classic kind, "the Convention comprises more than mere reciprocal engagements between Contracting States. It creates, over and above a network of mutual, bilateral undertakings, objective obligations which, in the words of the Preamble, benefit from a 'collective enforcement'."[119] The supervisory procedure provided for in the Convention, therefore, has an objective character; its aim is to protect the fundamental rights of individuals against violations by the Contracting States, rather than to implement mutual rights and obligations between those States. This objective character of the procedure is also reflected in other respects, which will be mentioned later.[120]

Clear examples of inter-State applications within the framework of the 'collective enforcement' mentioned by the Court are the applications of Denmark, Norway, Sweden and the Netherlands of September 1967 and the joint application of the three Scandinavian countries of April 1970 against Greece,[121] and the application of the Scandinavian countries, France and the Netherlands of July 1982 against Turkey.[122] The complaints against Greece were in fact lodged at the instance of the Parliamentary Assembly, which considered it the duty of the Contracting States to lodge an application under Article 33 in the case of an alleged serious violation.[123]

1.12.3 CASES IN WHICH A SPECIAL INTEREST OF THE CONTRACTING STATE IS INVOLVED

The Convention, of course, at the same time protects the particular interests of the Contracting States when they claim that the rights set forth in the Convention must be secured to their nationals coming under the jurisdiction of another Contracting State. And even though States have the right to initiate a procedure in which they have no special interest, in practice they will more readily be inclined to bring an application

---

[118] Appl. 788/60, *Austria v. Italy*, Yearbook VI (1961), p. 116 (140). See also Appls 9940/82-9944/82, *France, Norway, Denmark, Sweden and the Netherlands v. Turkey*, D&R 35 (1984), p. 143 (169); joined Appls 15299/89, 15300/89 and 15318/89, *Chrysostomos, Papachrysostomou* and *Loizidou*, D&R 68 (1991), p. 216 (242).

[119] Judgment of 18 January 1978, *Ireland v. the United Kingdom*, para. 239; report of 4 October 1983, *Cyprus v. Turkey*, D&R 72 (1992), p. 5 (19), where the Commission further noted that a Government cannot avoid this collective enforcement by not recognising the Government of the applicant State.

[120] See *infra* 1.13.3.1.

[121] Appls 3321-3323 and 3344/67, *Denmark, Norway, Sweden and the Netherlands v. Greece*, Yearbook XI (1968), p. 690, and Appl. 4448/70, *Denmark, Norway and Sweden v. Greece*, Yearbook XIII (1970), p. 108.

[122] Appls 9940-9944/82, *France, Norway, Denmark, Sweden and the Netherlands v. Turkey*, D&R 35 (1984), p. 143.

[123] Res. 346 (1967), 'On the situation in Greece', Council of Europe, Cons. Ass., Nineteenth Ordinary Session, Second Part, 25-28 September 1967, *Texts Adopted*.

when there has been a violation against persons who are their nationals or with whom they have some other special link.

A case in which the applicant State's own nationals were involved occurred for the first time when Cyprus brought applications against Turkey concerning the treatment of nationals of Cyprus during the Turkish invasion and the subsequent occupation of that island.[124] In total three applications emanated from this dispute.[125] In November 1994 Cyprus lodged another complaint against Turkey. The Court found that several Articles of the Convention had been violated.[126]

Examples of applications concerning persons with whom the applicant State had a special relationship other than the link of nationality are the applications of Greece against the United Kingdom, which concerned the treatment of Cypriots of Greek origin.[127] Further, Austria lodged a complaint in the so-called *Pfunders* Case in connection with the prosecution of six young men by Italy for the murder of an Italian customs officer in the boundary region of Alto Adige (South Tyrol) disputed by both States.[128] Finally, the applications of Ireland against the United Kingdom concerned the treatment of, and the legislation concerning Roman Catholics in Northern Ireland, who aspire for union with the Irish Republic.[129]

1.12.4   REQUIREMENTS OF ADMISSIBILITY

In order for State complaints to be admissible hardly any *prima facie* evidence is required. The Commission deduced from the English text (alleged breach) and from the French wording (*qu'elle croira pouvoir être imputé*) that the mere allegation of such a breach was, in principle, sufficient under this provision (Article 24; the present Article 33).[130] The Commission based this point of view on the fact that the provisions of Article 27(2) [the present Article 34(3)] "empowering it to declare inadmissible any petition submitted under Article 25 [the present Article 34], which it considers either incompatible with the provisions of the Convention or "manifestly ill-founded" apply, according to their express terms, to individual applications under Article 25 [the present Article 34] only, and that, consequently, any examination of the merits of State applications must in such cases be entirely reserved for the post-admissibility stage".[131]

---

[124]   Appls 6780/74 and 6950/75, *Cyprus v. Turkey*, Yearbook XVIII (1975), p. 82.
[125]   See also: Appl. 8007/77, *Cyprus v. Turkey*, Yearbook XX (1977), p. 98.
[126]   Judgment of 10 May 2001, *Cyprus v. Turkey*.
[127]   Appls 176/56 and 299/57, *Greece v. the United Kingdom*, Yearbook II (1958-1959), pp. 182 and 186, respectively.
[128]   Appl. 788/60, *Austria v. Italy*, Yearbook IV (1961), p. 116.
[129]   Appls 5310/71 and 5451/72, *Ireland v. the United Kingdom*, Yearbook XV (1972), p. 76.
[130]   Appls 9940/82-9944/82, *France, Norway, Denmark, Sweden and the Netherlands v. Turkey*, D&R 35 (1984), p. 143 (161).
[131]   *Ibidem.*

On the other hand, the Commission was of the opinion that Article 27 [the present Article 35] did not exclude the application of the general rule according to which an application under Article 24 [the present Article 33] may be declared inadmissible if it is clear from the outset that it is wholly unsubstantiated or otherwise lacking the requirements of a genuine allegation in the sense of Article 24 [the present Article 33] of the Convention.[132]

The Commission held, on the other hand, that the rule requiring the exhaustion of domestic remedies applied not only to individual applications lodged under Article 34 but also to cases brought by States under Article 33 of the Convention.[133]

1.12.5 THE PRACTICE OF INTER-STATE COMPLAINTS

Up to January 2006 a total of 19 applications had been lodged by States. Even this very low number provides a distorted picture. In fact only six situations in different States have been put forward in Strasbourg by means of an inter-State application. In the 1950s Greece complained twice about the conduct of the United Kingdom in Cyprus; Austria filed a complaint in 1960 about the course of events during proceedings against South Tyrolean activists in Italy; the five applications of the Scandinavian countries and the Netherlands concerned the situation in Greece during the military regime; Ireland lodged two applications against the United Kingdom about the activities of the military and the police in Ulster; and all four applications of Cyprus were connected with the Turkish invasion of that island, while the five applications in 1982 all related to the situation in Turkey under the military regime.

Given the number of violations that have occurred during the more than 50 years that the Convention has been in force, it is evident that the right of complaint of States has not proved to be a very effective supervisory tool. The idea contained in the Preamble – as it was also formulated by the Commission in the *Pfunders* Case and by the Court in *Ireland v. the United Kingdom, viz.* that the Contracting States were to guarantee the protection of the rights and freedoms collectively – has hardly materialised. Save for two instances,[134] the Contracting States have not been willing to lodge complaints about situations in other States where no special interest of their own was involved. Such a step is generally considered to run counter to their interest in that charging another State with violating the Convention is bound to be considered an unfriendly act by the other party, with all the political repercussions that may be

---

[132]   *Ibidem*, p. 162.
[133]   Appl. 25781/94, *Cyprus v. Turkey*, D&R 86-B (1996), p. 104 (139).
[134]   The applications of the Scandinavian countries and the Netherlands against Greece in 1967 and 1970 and the applications of France, the Netherlands and the Scandinavian countries against Turkey in 1982.

involved. Moreover, an application by a State that does have a special interest of its own may create negative effects in that it may stir up the underlying conflict.

In comparison with inter-State applications individual complaints have the advantage that in general political considerations will not play as important a part.[135] For this reason as well it is of the utmost importance that individual complaints may now be lodged against all Contracting States. At the time when some Contracting States had not recognised the individual right of complaint, the inter-State procedure – apart from the remedy of Article 52, which so far has not functioned very adequately – was the only mechanism for supervising the observance by all Contracting States of their obligations under the Convention. That situation was far from satisfactory.

1.13 THE RIGHT OF COMPLAINT OF INDIVIDUALS

1.13.1 INTRODUCTION

Article 34 undoubtedly constitutes the most progressive provision of the Convention. It has removed the principal limitation by which the position of the individual in international law was traditionally characterised. One improvement as compared to the traditional practice of diplomatic protection, mentioned above, was brought about by the elimination of the condition of the link of nationality in the case of an action by a State. However, the individual right of complaint, despite its limitations, constituted an even greater improvement over the classic system. It is precisely because States are generally reluctant to submit an application against another State that the individual right of complaint constitutes a necessary expedient for achieving the aim of the Convention, to secure the rights and freedoms of individuals against the States.

The importance of the individual right of complaint for the functioning of the supervisory system under the European Convention becomes clear from the large number of individual applications that have been submitted. On 31 December 2005 a total of 201,072 applications had been registered, on 145,706 of which a decision had been taken with respect to admissibility. However, to put these figures within the right context, it should be pointed out that a great many cases were immediately declared inadmissible. Of the remaining cases, the majority were declared inadmissible after having been transmitted to the government concerned for its observations. In the course of the examination of the merits an additional number of cases were subsequently rejected. Only a total of 10,676 cases were ultimately declared admissible. It is significant that the annual number of provisional applications grew from 4,044

---

[135]   Here, too, political motives may sometimes constitute the real incentive for an application, while even if that is not the case, the application may have some political implications.

in 1988 to 41,516 in 2005, i.e. by some 1.026% over the full period. The annual number of registered applications grew from 1,013 in 1988 to 35,402 in 2003. Since the new Court commenced its activities in November 1998, its 'productivity' has significantly increased. In 1999 the Court rendered 4,251 decisions, while in 2005 this number increased to 28,648. The number of judgments in the same period increased from 177 to 1,105.[136]

1.13.2 WHO MAY LODGE A COMPLAINT?

Anyone who in a relevant respect is subject to the jurisdiction of a State Party and is allegedly a victim of a violation of the Convention by that State may lodge an application. The nationality of the applicant is irrelevant. This means that the right of complaint is conferred not only on the nationals of the State concerned, but also on those of other Contracting States, on the nationals of States which are not Parties to the Convention, and on stateless persons, provided that they satisfy the condition referred to in Article 1, *viz.* that they were subject to the jurisdiction of the respondent State at the moment the violation allegedly took place. Lack of legal capacity does not affect the natural person's right of complaint. In several cases the Court held thats minors have the right, of their own accord and without being represented by their guardians, to lodge a complaint.[137] In the *Scozzari and Giunta* Case the Court held that "In particular, minors can apply to the Court even, or indeed especially, if they are represented by a mother who is in conflict with the authorities and criticizes their decisions and conduct as not being consistent with the rights guaranteed by the Convention. Like the Commission, the Court considers that in the event of a conflict over a minor's interests between a natural parent and the person appointed by the authorities to act as the child's guardian, there is a danger that some of those interests will never be brought to the Court's attention and that the minor will be deprived of effective protection of his rights under the Convention. Consequently, as the Commission observed, even though the mother has been deprived of parental rights – indeed that is one of the causes of the dispute which she has referred to the Court – her standing as the natural mother suffices to afford her the necessary power to apply to the Court on the children's behalf, too, in order to protect their interests."[138] The same

---

[136] See Council of Europe, *Survey of Activities and Statistics*, 2005.
[137] See, *e.g.*, the judgment of 28 November 1988, *Nielsen*, para. 58.
[138] Judgment of 13 July 2000, *Scozzari and Giuntay*, para. 138; judgment of 24 January 2002, *Covezzi and Morseli*, paras 103-105.

applies to persons who have lost their legal capacity after being committed to a psychiatric hospital.[139]

Besides individuals, non-governmental organisations and groups of persons may also file an application. With respect to the last-mentioned category the Commission decided during its first session that these must be groups which have been established in a regular way according to the law of one of the Contracting States. If that is not the case, the application must have been signed by all the persons belonging to the group.[140] As to the category of non-governmental organisations the Commission decided that they must be *private* organisations, and that municipalities, for instance, cannot be considered as such.[141] In the *Danderyds Kommun* Case the Court held in this respect that it is not only the central organs of the State that are clearly governmental organisations, as opposed to non-governmental organisations, but also decentralised authorities that exercise public functions, notwithstanding the extent of their autonomy vis-à-vis the central organs. This is the case even if the municipality is claiming that in this particular situation it is acting as a private organ.[142]

A wide range of organisations, such as newspapers,[143] churches and other religious institutions,[144] associations,[145] political parties[146] and companies[147] have submitted applications. Although the rights and freedoms laid down in the Convention apply to individuals as well as to non-governmental organisations, some of the rights and freedoms are by their nature not susceptible of being exercised by a legal person. Insofar as Article 9 is concerned, the Commission made a distinction between the freedom of conscience and the freedom of religion. In contrast to freedom of

---

[139]   Judgment of 24 October 1979, *Winterwerp*, para. 10; judgment of 21 February 1990, *Van der Leer*, para. 6; judgment of 24 September 1992, *Herczegfalvy*, para. 13; Decision of 15 June 1999, *Croke*; Decision of 16 March 2000, *Valle*.

[140]   See the report of the session: DH(54)3, p. 8.

[141]   Joined Appls 5767/72, 5922/72, 5929-5931/72, 5953-5957/72, 5984-5988/73 and 6011/73, *Austrian municipalities*, Yearbook XVII (1974), p. 338 (352); Appl. 15090/89, *Ayuntamiento M. v. Spain*, D&R 68 (1991), p. 209 (214); Appls 26114/95 and 26455/95, *Consejo General de Colegios Oficiales de Economistas de Espaòa*, D&R 82 (1995), p. 150.

[142]   Decision of 7 June 2001.

[143]   Judgment of 17 July 2001, *Association Ekin*, para. 38; Judgment of 11 July 2002, *Alithia Publishing Company*, para.1.

[144]   Appl. 28626, *Christian Association Jehovah's Witnesses*; Judgment of 9 December 1994, *Holy Monasteries*, paras 48-49; judgment of 13 December 2001, *Metropolotan Church of Bessarabia*, para. 101.

[145]   Judgment of 2 July 2002, *Wilson, National Union of Journalists and Others*, para. 41.

[146]   Judgment of 8 December 1999, *Freedom and Democracy Party (Özdep)*; judgment of 31 July 2001, *Refah Partisi (Prosperity Party)*.

[147]   Judgment of 24 October 1986, *AGOSI*, para. 25; judgment of 7 July 1989, *Tre Traktörer AB*, para. 35.

religion,[148] freedom of conscience cannot be exercised by a legal person.[149] The right not to be subjected to degrading treatment and punishment can also not be exercised by a legal person[150] and the same holds good for respect to the right to education.[151] The Court and the Commission have also examined complaints brought by a trade union concerning collective aspects of trade union freedom[152] including strike action.[153]

In other cases, too, it was stressed that some of the rights and freedoms included in the Convention apply only to natural persons. In the Case of *X Union v. France* the Commission stated: "In the present case, the applicant union as a legal person does not itself claim to be the victim of an infringement of the right to free choice of residence guaranteed by Article 2 of Protocol No. 4, since the legislative restrictions in question are only applicable to natural persons. (...) It might however be considered that the application really emanates from the members of the union, which is empowered (...) to initiate proceedings on behalf of its members. (...) However, it is noted in this context that the petition does not mention any specific case of one or more teachers alleged to be subjected to a measure constituting an infringement."[154]

In the Case of *Asselbourg and 78 Others and Greenpeace Association* the Court held with regard to the association Greenpeace-Luxembourg, that a non-governmental organisation cannot claim to be the victim of an infringement of the right to respect for its "home", within the meaning of Article 8 of the Convention, merely because it has its registered office close to the steelworks that it is criticising, where the infringement of the right to respect for the home results, as alleged in this case, from nuisances or problems which can be encountered only by natural persons. In so far as Greenpeace-Luxembourg sought to rely on the difficulties suffered by its members or employees working or spending time at its registered office, the Court considered that the association may only act as a representative of its members or employees, in the same way as, for example, a lawyer represents his client, but cannot itself claim to be the victim of a violation of Article 8.[155]

Obviously, other rights or freedoms are clearly applicable to legal persons. In the Case of *A Association and H v. Austria*, lodged by a political party and its chairman/legal representative alleging violation of Article 11 because of the prohibition

---

148 Judgment of 13 December 2001, *Metropolitan Church of Bessarabia,* para 101; Appl. 27417/95, *Cha'are Shalom Ve Tsedek,* para 72.
149 Appl. 11921/86, *Verein Kontakt Information Therapie and Hagen,* D&R 57 (1988), p. 81 (88).
150 *Idem.*
151 Appl. 11533/85, *Ingrid Jordebo Foundation of Christian Schools and Ingrid Jordebo,* D&R 51 (1987), p. 125 (128).
152 Judgment of 27 October 1975, *National Union of Belgian Police,* paras 38-42; judgment of 6 February 1976, *Swedish Engine Drivers' Union,* paras 35-43; Decision of 27 June 2002, *Federation of Offshore Workers' Trade Union.*
153 Appl. 53574/99, *UNISON v. the United Kingdom.*
154 Appl. 9900/82, *X Union v. France,* D&R 32 (1983), p. 261 (264).
155 Decision of 29 June 1999, 29121/95, *Asselbourg and 78 Others and Greenpeace Association.*

of a meeting, the Commission held that, as the right invoked could be exercised by both the organiser of a meeting, even if it is a legal person as in the present case, and by individual participants, both applicants could claim to be victims of a violation of their rights under Article 11.[156]

1.13.3   THE VICTIM REQUIREMENT

1.13.3.1 General

Whereas States may complain about 'any alleged breach of the provisions of the Convention and the Protocols thereto by another High Contracting Party' (Article 33), and consequently also about national legislation or administrative practices *in abstracto*, individuals must claim 'to be the victim of a violation by one of the High Contracting Parties of the rights set forth in this Convention and the Protocols thereto' (Article 34). The special relationship required is that the individual applicant himself is the victim of the alleged violation.[157] He may not bring an *actio popularis*, nor may he submit abstract complaints.[158] The Commission held that the mere fact that trade unions considered themselves as guardians of the collective interests of their members, did not suffice to make them victims within the meaning of Article 34, of measures affecting those members.[159]

The Commission has, however, declared admissible individual applications which had a *partly* abstract character. Thus, a number of Northern Irishmen complained, on the one hand, about torture to which they had allegedly been subjected by the British during their detention, while they claimed, on the other hand, that this treatment formed part of "a systematic administrative pattern which permits and encourages brutality." They requested the Commission, *inter alia*, to conduct "a full investigation of the allegations made in the present application as well as of the system of interrogation currently employed by security forces under the control of the United Kingdom in Northern Ireland, for the purpose of determining whether or not such specific acts and administrative practices are incompatible with the European Convention for the Protection of Human Rights and Fundamental Freedoms."[160] The British Government submitted that the second part of the application was not

---

[156]   Appl. 9905/82, *A Association and H v. Austria*, D&R 36 (1984), p. 187 (191-192).

[157]   This question remains relevant throughout the examination of the application: Appl. 9320/81, *D. v. Federal Republic of Germany*, D&R 36 (1984), p. 24 (30-31).

[158]   Judgment of 6 September 1978, *Klass*, para. 33; judgment of 13 June 1979, *Marckx*, para. 27; Appl. 31924/96, *Di Lazzaro*, D&R 90, p. 134; judgment of 27 June 2000, *İlhan*, para 52; decision of 6 November 2001, *Christian Federation of Jehova's Witnesses*.

[159]   Appl. 15404/89, *Purcell*, D&R 70 (1991), p. 262 (273); Appl. 24581/94, *Greek Federation of Custom Officers, Gialouris and Others*, D&R 81, p. 123.

[160]   Appls 5577-5583/72, *Donnelly*, Yearbook XVI (1973), p. 212 (216).

admissible and referred to the case law of the Commission with respect to abstract complaints. The Commission held, however, that "neither Article 25[the present Article 34], nor any other provisions in the Convention, *inter alia* Article 27(1)(b)[the present Article 35(2)(b)], prevent an individual applicant from raising before the Commission a complaint in respect of an alleged administrative practice in breach of the Convention provided that he brings *prima facie* evidence of such a practice and of his being a victim of it."[161]

An individual application may, therefore, be concerned not only with the personal interest of the applicant, but also with the public interest. Consequently, the procedure that originates from an individual complaint may in some respects also assume an objective character. Thus the Commission adopted the view that, on the ground of the general function assigned to it in Article 19 [old] 'to ensure the observance of the engagements undertaken by the High Contracting Parties in the present Convention', it was competent to examine *ex officio*, also in case of an application by an individual, whether there had been a violation. It did not need to confine itself to an examination of the violations expressly alleged by the applicant.[162]

Another implication of this objective character was manifested in the Commission's view that, when an applicant withdraws his application or no longer shows any interest in the case, the procedure does not necessarily come to an end, but might be pursued in the public interest. Thus, in its decision in the *Gericke* Case, the Commission expressly held "that the interests served by the protection of human rights and fundamental freedoms guaranteed by the Convention extend beyond the individual interests of the persons concerned; (...) whereas, consequently, the withdrawal of an application and the respondent Government's agreement thereto cannot deprive the Commission of the competence to pursue its examination of the case."[163]

For his application to be admissible the applicant is not required to *prove* that he is the victim of the alleged violation. Article 34 only provides that the applicant must be a person 'claiming to be the victim' (*qui se prétend victime*).[164] However, this does not mean that the mere submission of the applicant that he is a victim, is in itself sufficient. The test is whether, assuming that the alleged violation has taken place, it is

---

161   *Ibidem*, p. 260. In the second instance, via application of Art. 29 [the present Article 35(4)], the said complaints were declared inadmissible, because of non-exhaustion of domestic remedies: Yearbook XIX (1976), p. 82 (252-254).

162   See, *e.g.*, Appl. 202/56, *X v. Belgium*, Yearbook I (1955-1957), p. 190 (192) and the joined Appls 7604/76, 7719/76 and 7781/77, *Foti, Lentini* and *Cenerini v. Italy*, D&R 14 (1979), p. 133 (143).

163   Appl. 2294/64, Yearbook VIII (1965), p. 314 (320). See also Appl. 2686/65, *Heinz Kornmann v. Federal Republic of Germany*, Yearbook IX (1966), p. 494 (506-508).

164   An amendment to replace these words by 'which has been the victim', tabled at the Consultative Assembly, was withdrawn after discussion, because it was recognised that this was a 'right to complain from the point of view of procedure' and not a 'substantial right of action': Council of Europe, Cons. Ass., First Session, Fourth Part, *Reports*, 1949, pp. 1272-1274.

to be deemed plausible that the applicant is a victim, on the basis of the facts submitted by the applicant and the facts, if any, advanced against them by the defendant State. If this is not the case, the application is declared 'incompatible with the provisions of the present Convention' and, on the ground of Article 27(2) [the present Article 35(2)], pronounced inadmissible.[165] On the other hand, even if the applicant does not expressly submit that he is the victim of the challenged act or omission, the application may still be declared admissible if there appears to be sufficient ground for this.[166]

In the *Gayduk* Case the applicants alleged a violation of Article 1 of Protocol I. However, the Court held that it did not appear from the material in the case file that any of them had sought to exercise a property right. On the contrary, some of the applicants had stated that they had no need of the initial deposits and had emphasised that the main purpose of their applications was to recover the indexed amounts. In these circumstances, and in so far as the applications concerned repayment of the deposits themselves, the Court found that the applicants could not claim to have standing as "victims" within the meaning of Article 34 of the Convention.[167]

In the *Lacko* Case the applicants complained that by publicly and formally referring to certain persons as *Roma*, i.e. their ethnic identity, by singling out such persons for special treatment, by prohibiting them from entering and settling in the respective municipalities and by publicly threatening to enforce such exclusion orders through physical expulsion the Slovakian authorities discriminated against them on the grounds of their race and ethnicity in a manner which constituted degrading treatment. The Court noted that the third applicant had not alleged that he lived or intended to live in the settlements and it did not appear from the documents submitted that he needed to visit those municipalities and was prevented from doing so. In these circumstances, the Court considered that the third applicant could not claim to be a victim of a violation of his rights under Article 2 of Protocol No. 4, taken alone or in conjunction with Article 14 of the Convention. As regards the first and the second applicant the Court recalled that a decision or measure favourable to the applicant is not in principle sufficient to deprive the applicant of his or her status as a 'victim' unless the national authorities have acknowledged, either expressly or in substance, and then afforded

---

[165]   See, *e.g.*, Appl. 1983/63, *X v. the Netherlands*, Yearbook IX (1966), p. 286 (304). In a few cases the Commission declared the application 'manifestly ill-founded' because in its view the applicant could not be regarded as a victim: see, *e.g.*, Appl. 2291/64, *X v. Austria*, Coll. 24 (1967), p. 20 (33 and 35); and Appl. 4653/70, *X v. Federal Republic of Germany*, Yearbook XVII (1974), p. 148 (178). This also leads to a declaration of inadmissibility, but the ground was indicated wrongly here, since the question of whether the application is well-founded depends on whether there has been a violation of the Convention, not on the question of the effect of such a violation, if any, for the applicant. See also the decision of 25 November 1999, *Oćić*, where the Court observed that there was no sufficiently direct connection between the applicant as such and the injury he maintained he suffered as a result of the alleged breach of the Convention.

[166]   See, *e.g.*, Appl. 99/55, *X v. Federal Republic of Germany*, Yearbook I (1955-1957), p. 160 (161).

[167]   Decision of 2 July 2002.

redress for, the breach of the Convention. In the present case the resolutions in question were quashed by unanimous vote of the municipal councils concerned. In the Court's view these actions, considered as a whole, could be qualified as acknowledgement by the Slovakian authorities, at least in substance, of a violation of the rights of the *Romani* families affected by the municipal resolutions in question including the first and the second applicant. Having regard to the particular circumstances of the case, the Court was satisfied that in doing so the domestic authorities provided the first and the second applicant with adequate redress for the breach of their rights under Article 2 of Protocol No. 4 and under Article 14 of the Convention which they alleged before the Court. In this respect they could, therefore, no longer claim to be victims within the meaning of Article 34 of the Convention.[168]

1.13.3.2 Personally affected

The requirement of "victim" implies that the violation of the Convention must have *affected* the applicant in some way. According to the Court's well-established case law "the word 'victim' in Article 34 refers to the person directly affected by the act or omission at issue."[169] To this the Court usually adds, however, a phrase of the sort that "the existence of a violation being conceivable even in the absence of prejudice; prejudice is relevant only in the context of Article 41."[170] In the *Gayduk* Case the Court held that the issue of whether of an applicant may claim to be a 'victim' within the meaning of Article 34 of the Convention does not turn on the substance or content of the right in issue, but solely on the question of whether it is linked to the person who relies on it.[171]

The requirement that the applicant be *personally* affected by the alleged violation was stressed by the Commission right from the beginning. Thus, an application in which it was submitted that the Norwegian legislation concerning *abortus provocatus* conflicted with Article 2(1) of the Convention, was declared inadmissible because of the fact that the applicant had not alleged that he himself was the victim of this legislation, but had lodged his application on behalf of parents who without their own consent or knowledge (...) have or will have their offspring taken away by *abortus provocatus*, and on behalf of those taken away by such operations "all unfit or unable to plead on their own behalf."[172]

---

[168]   Decision of 2 July 2002.
[169]   Judgment of 15 June 1992, *Lüdi*, para. 34. See also the judgment of 28 March 1990, *Groppera Radio AG*, para. 47; judgment of 25 September 1996, *Buckley*, paras 56-59; judgment of 23 March 1999, *Valmont;* Decision of 6 April 2004, *Skubenko.*
[170]   Judgment of 27 June 2000, *İlhan*, para. 52.
[171]   Decision of 2 July 2002.
[172]   Appl. 867/60, *X v. Norway*, Yearbook IV (1961), p. 270 (276).

In an almost identical case an Austrian applicant submitted that the abortion legislation of his country conflicted with Articles 2 and 8 of the Convention. His application was also not admitted, because the Commission held that it was "not competent to examine *in abstracto* its [the disputed legislation's] compatibility with the Convention." According to the Commission the applicant had meant to bring an *actio popularis*. He had submitted that the legislation in question actually concerned every Austrian citizen "because of its effects for the future of the nation and for the moral and legal standard of the nation", and had declared himself willing "to be nominated curator to act on behalf of the unborn in general".[173]

A somewhat divergent view was taken by the Commission in some other decisions concerning cases in which abortion legislation was involved. A German Act of 1974, which removed penalties for abortion, had been declared by the *Bundesverfassungsgericht* to conflict with the German Constitution. A regulation concerning abortion was subsequently enacted which met the requirement laid down in this judicial decision and was incorporated into a new Act of 1976. With respect to the judgment of the *Bundesverfassungsgericht* and its consequences, an application was lodged on the ground of alleged violation of Article 8 of the Convention by an organisation, a man and two women. The application of the organisation was declared inadmissible by the Commission, which was fully in line with its decision in the above-mentioned Norwegian case, because it did not concern a physical, but a legal person; the abortion legislation could not be applicable to the organisation, and the latter could not, therefore, itself be considered the victim. The same also applied to the application of the man; the law had not been applied to him and according to the Commission he had not proved at all that the mere existence of the law had injured him to such an extent that he could claim to be the victim of a violation of the Convention.[174] However, the Commission here seemed to leave open the possibility that the bare existence of abortion legislation would injure a man to such an extent that he must be considered its victim.

This impression is corroborated by the decision of the Commission with respect to the two women. According to their submissions they themselves were not pregnant nor had an interruption of pregnancy been refused to them, and they had not been prosecuted for illegal abortion either. However, they were of the opinion that the Convention had been violated with regard to themselves because in consequence of the legislation in question they were obliged to either abstain from sexual relations or use contraceptives of which they disapproved for several reasons, including health,

---

[173]   Appl. 7045/75, *X v. Austria*, D&R 7 (1977), p. 87 (88). See also Appl. 7806/77, *Webster v. the United Kingdom*, D&R 12 (1978), p. 168 (174).
[174]   Report of 12 July 1977, *Brüggemann and Scheuten v. Federal Republic of Germany*, D&R 10 (1978), p. 100 (117-118).

or become pregnant against their will. The Commission recognised that both women were victims in the sense of Article 25 [the present Article 34] on the following ground: "The Commission considers that pregnancy and the interruption of pregnancy are part of private life and also in certain circumstances of family life. It further considers that respect for private life comprises also, to a certain degree, the right to establish and develop relationships with other human beings, especially in the emotional field, for the development and fulfilment of one's own personality (...) and that therefore sexual life is also part of private life; and in particular that legal regulation of abortion is an intervention in private life which may or may not be justified under Article 8(2)."[175]

The Commission thus took the position that a legal regulation of abortion constituted an interference with private life and under certain circumstances with family life as well, which might or might not be justified on the ground of Article 8(2). Women may allege to be the victims of that regulation even if it has not actually been enforced against them. The consideration quoted above is formulated in very general terms and leaves scope for the interpretation that in certain cases men may also be considered victims because of the mere existence of abortion legislation. As said before, the application of the man was not admitted, because the victim-requirement was not satisfied as he had lodged his application in his capacity as chairman of the above-mentioned organisation. The decision, therefore, does not exclude that a man's application be declared admissible if he complains about abortion legislation in his capacity as a husband or partner. In a case in 1980 the Commission confirmed this interpretation. There the applicant challenged the English legislation under which his wife had undergone *abortus provocatus*. According to the Commission the requirement of Article 25 [the present Article 34] had been satisfied on the simple consideration that "the applicant, as potential father, was so closely affected by the termination of his wife's pregnancy that he may claim to be a victim."[176]

In a case where a journalist and two newspapers alleged violation of their right to receive and impart information as a result of a ruling by the House of Lords that a lawyer had acted in contempt of court because she had allowed inspection of confidential documents by the journalist after these had been read out in the course of a public hearing, the Commission took a more restrictive position. It declared the application inadmissible because it did "not consider that the concept of 'victim' in Article 25(1)[the present Article 34] may be interpreted so broadly, in the present case, as to encompass every newspaper or journalist in the United Kingdom who might

---

[175]   Appl. 6959/75, *Brüggemann and Scheuten*, D&R 5 (1976), p. 103 (115).
[176]   Appl. 8416/78, *X v. the United Kingdom*, D&R 19 (1980), p. 244 (248). See also Appl. 17004/90, *Hercz*, D&R 73 (1992), p. 155 (166).

conceivably be affected by the decision of the House of Lords. The form of detriment required must be of a less indirect and remote nature."[177]

This decision would seem to deviate from the Commission's above-mentioned case law, as the ruling by the House of Lords clearly implied a restraint for the applicants. Furthermore, the reasoning upon which it was based is not very convincing. The argument that the applicants remained free to publish articles on the disputed subject overlooked that not only the right to impart but also the right to receive information was invoked. Similarly, the fact that the decision of the House of Lords was, according to the Commission, "one which affected every interested journalist in the United Kingdom", does not justify the conclusion that, therefore, the applicants cannot be considered victims within the meaning of Article 34. In fact, a year later, in a case where the applicants, an editor of a newspaper and a journalist, complained that the law of contempt of court prevented the preparation of a newspaper article on a case which was *sub judice*, the Commission considered that in view of the applicants' professional activities, the applicants might be directly affected by the Contempt of Court Act 1981 and, therefore, might claim to be victims in respect of this legislation.[178]

1.13.3.3 Potential victim

The Commission and the Court have accepted as victims in the sense of Article 34 a category of persons of whom it could not be ascertained with certainty that they had suffered an injury. The reason for this acceptance was due to the fact that the applicants could not know whether the challenged legislation had or had not been applied to them. This matter came up in the *Klass* Case.[179] Three lawyers, a judge and a public prosecutor alleged violation of the secrecy of their mail and telecommunications by the authorities. The measures concerned were secret insofar that the persons in question were not informed of them in all cases, and if they were informed, then only afterwards. The Commission settled the matter of the victim-requirement in a brief consideration, stressing the secret character of the measures and concluding as follows: "In view of this particularity of the case the applicants have to be considered as victims for purposes of Article 25."[180]

The Court dealt with the matter much more in detail. It stated at the outset that according to Article 25 [the present Article 34] individuals in principle may neither

---

[177]   Appl. 10039/82, *Leigh and Others*, D&R 38 (1984), p. 74 (78).
[178]   Appl. 10243/83, *Times Newspapers Ltd, Giles, Knightly and Potter v. the United Kingdom*, D&R 41 (1985), p. 123 (130).
[179]   For the examination of the merits, see *infra* 10.4.6.6.
[180]   Appl. 5029/71, *Klass v. Federal Republic of Germany*, Yearbook XVII (1974), p. 178 (208).

bring an *actio popularis* nor complain about legislation *in abstracto*.[181] The principle of effectiveness (*l'effet utile*), however, according to the Court, calls for exceptions to this rule. This principle implies that the procedural provisions of the Convention are to be applied in such a way as to contribute to the effectiveness of the system of individual applications. All this induced the Court to conclude that "an individual may, *under certain conditions*, claim to be the victim of a violation occasioned by the mere existence of secret measures or of legislation permitting secret measures, without having to allege that such measures were in fact applied to him. "[182] Such conditions were satisfied in the case under consideration since "the contested legislation institutes a system of surveillance under which all persons in the Federal Republic of Germany can potentially have their mail, post and telecommunications monitored, without their even knowing this unless there has been either some indiscretion or subsequent notification."[183]

This may be summarised to imply that in case of the existence of secret measures (whether based on legislation or not) the victim-requirement under Article 34 may already be satisfied when the applicant is a *potential* victim. A comparable line of reasoning was followed by the Commission in the *Malone* Case, in which it found that the "applicant is directly affected by the law and practice in England and Wales (...) under which the secret surveillance of postal and telephone communications on behalf of the police is permitted and takes place. His communication has at all relevant times been liable to such surveillance without his being able to obtain knowledge of it. Accordingly (...) he is entitled to claim (...) to be a victim (...) irrespective of whether or to what extent he is able to show that it has actually been applied to him."[184]

The reasoning of the Court in the *Klass* Case was relied upon by two mothers who submitted, on behalf of their children, violation of Article 3 of the Convention on the ground of the existence of a system of corporal punishment at the schools in Scotland attended by their children. According to the Commission there was no direct analogy with the *Klass* Case, but it did refer to the criterion of effectiveness relied upon by the Court in that case and held as follows: "that in order to be accepted as victims under Article 25 [the present Article 34] of the Convention, individuals must satisfy the Commission that they run the risk of being directly affected by the particular matter

---

181   Judgment of 6 September 1978, para. 33. On this see also the judgment of 4 May 2000, *Rotaru*, para 35; Decision of 23 May 2002, *Segi and Others*; decision of 6 November 2001, *Christian Federation of Jehova's Witnesses*.
182   Judgment of 6 September 1978, para. 34.
183   *Ibidem*, para. 37
184   Report of 17 December 1982, para. 114. See also the report of 9 May 1989, *Hewitt and Harman v. the United Kingdom*, D&R 67 (1991), p. 89 (98); Appl. 10799/84, *Radio X, S, W & A v. Switzerland*, D&R 37 (1984), p. 236 (239).

which they wish to bring before it."[185] Thus, here again, the mere fact of running a risk was deemed sufficient to be considered as 'victims'. According to the Commission it would be too restrictive an interpretation of Article 25 [the present Article 34] to require that the children had in actual fact been subjected to corporal punishment. It, therefore, considered the children as victims because they "may be affected by the existence of physical violence around them and by the threat of a potential use on themselves of corporal punishment."[186]

Shortly afterwards, in the *Marckx* Case, the Court adopted the same approach by express reference to the *Klass* Case. In the *Marckx* Case it had been advanced that the Belgian legislation concerning illegitimate children conflicted with the Convention. The Belgian Government submitted that this was in reality an abstract complaint, since the challenged legislation had not been applied to the applicant. The Court held that: "Article 25 [the present Article 34] of the Convention entitles individuals to contend that a law violates their rights by itself, in the absence of an individual measure of implementation, if they run the risk of being directly affected by it."[187] This was considered to be the case here. According to the Court the question of whether the applicant has actually been placed in an unfavourable position is not a criterion of the victim-requirement: "the question of prejudice is not a matter for Article 25 [the present Article 34] which, in its use of the word 'victim', denotes 'the person directly affected by the act or omission which is in issue'."[188]

In the *Dudgeon* Case, and later in the *Norris* Case and the *Modinos* Case, the applicants complained about the existence of laws which had the effect of making certain homosexual acts, between consenting adult males, criminal offences. The Court held that "in the personal circumstances of the applicant, the very existence of this legislation continuously and directly affects his private life."[189]

In the *Rekvéni* Case a police officer complained about a constitutional prohibition preventing members of the police force from joining political parties or engaging in

---

[185]   Report of 16 May 1980, *Campbell and Cosans*, B.42 (1985), p. 36. However, in a case where a mother and her son complained about the existence of corporal punishment for breach of school discipline the Commission held that having failed to inquire about the disciplinary methods when she put her child in a private school, a mother cannot claim to be a victim, direct or indirect, of a violation of the rights guaranteed in the Convention in respect of corporal punishment inflicted on the child for a breach of school discipline; Appl. 13134/87, *Costello-Roberts v. the United Kingdom*, D&R 67 (1991), p. 216 (224).

[186]   *Ibidem*, pp. 36-37. The Court in its judgment of 25 February 1982 did not deal with this question, as it had concluded that Art. 3 of the Convention had not been violated, (para. 31). See also the judgment of 29 October 1992, *Open Door and Dublin Well Woman*, para. 44; decision of 18 January 2000, *Association Ekin*; Decision of 19 February 2002, *Rosca Stanescu and Ardeleanu*.

[187]   Judgment of 13 June 1979, para. 27.

[188]   *Ibidem*.

[189]   Judgment of 22 October 1981, para. 41; judgment of 26 October 1988, paras 31-34; judgment of 22 April 1993, para. 24. See also the judgment of 19 February 1998, *Bowman*, para. 29; decision of 22 November 2001, *S.L. v. Austria*; decision of 19 February 2002, *Bland*.

political activities. The Government submitted that the applicant had failed to specify the political activities which he felt he was prevented from pursuing. In their view the applicant had thus failed to substantiate his complaint for the purposes of admissibility. In these circumstances the Government raised the question of whether the applicant could claim to be a victim of any breach of his Convention rights, within the meaning of Article 25 [the present Article 34] of the Convention. The Commission held that it was true that, notwithstanding the impugned provision of the Constitution, in the relevant period the applicant was not completely prevented from engaging in political activities. There was no indication that he could not nominate a third person as a candidate for the elections by submitting his nomination coupon. Moreover, he was free to accept a nomination as a candidate for the elections on condition that, if elected, he would resign from any position incompatible with his mandate. Furthermore, neither the impugned constitutional prohibition nor the other relevant laws entailed any formal sanction for illegitimate political activities potentially assumed by the applicant. However, the Commission, having regard to the limited nature of these possibilities to articulate political preferences and, in particular, to the circular letters issued by the Head of the National Police, considered that the applicant could be reasonably concerned by the consequences of his expression of political views. In these circumstances the Commission found that the applicant could claim to be a victim within the meaning of Article 34 of the Convention.[190]

In the *Segi* Case the applicant organisations complained that they had been described by the fifteen member States of the European Union as terrorist organisations. The applications concerned the ways in which the applicants were affected, allegedly in a manner incompatible with certain rights guaranteed by the Convention, by Common Position 2001/930/CFSP on combating terrorism and Common Position 2001/931/CFSP on the application of specific measures to combat terrorism, both adopted by the Council of the European Union on 27 December 2001. The applicants claimed to be both direct and potential victims of the texts concerned. The Court noted that the two common positions were adopted in the context of implementation of the CFSP by the member States of the European Union and consequently came within the field of intergovernmental cooperation. With regard, firstly, to Common Position 2001/930/CFSP, the Court observed that this contains measures of principle to be taken by the European Union and its member States to combat terrorism. To that end Article 14 recommended that member States became parties as soon as possible to the international conventions and protocols relating to terrorism listed in an annex. The Court noted that this common position was not directly applicable in the member States and could not form the direct basis for any criminal or administrative proceedings against individuals, especially as it did not mention any particular organisa-

---

[190]   Appl. 25390/94, *Rekvényi v. Hungary*, D&R 89 (1997), p. 47 (51-52).

tion or person. As such, therefore, it does not give rise to legally binding obligations for the applicants. The mere fact that the names of two of the applicants (*Segi* and *Gestoras Pro-Amnistía*) appeared in the list referred to in that provision as "groups or entities involved in terrorist acts" might be embarrassing, but the link was much too tenuous to justify application of the Convention. Consequently, the Court considered that the situation complained of did not give the applicant associations, and *a fortiori* their spokespersons, the status of victims of a violation of the Convention within the meaning of Article 34 of the Convention.[191]

In the Case of *The Christian Federation of Jehova's Witnesses* the Court pointed out that the applicant association complained of a series of hostile reactions to Jehovah's Witnesses (a press campaign, the establishment of civic action groups, the holding of public debates on sects, etc.) and measures such as judicial or administrative decisions allegedly affecting certain Jehovah's Witnesses individually or associations of Jehovah's Witnesses. The Court held that, even supposing that the applicant association could claim to be directly affected by the measures in question, as the federal body of all Jehovah's Witnesses with responsibility for protecting their interests, some of the measures were not based on the report complained of and, where reference was made to the report, it was merely a passing mention which could not in any way be regarded as the reason for taking the measures. The Court noted, moreover, that a parliamentary report had no legal effect and could not serve as the basis for any criminal or administrative proceedings. As to the Law of 12 June 2001, the Court noted that its aim, as its title indicated, is to strengthen preventive and punitive action against sectarian movements infringing human rights and fundamental freedoms. The Court held, furthermore, that the impugned law provided for the possibility of dissolving sects, a term which it did not define, but that such a measure could be ordered only by the courts when certain conditions were satisfied, in particular where there had been final convictions of the sect concerned or of those in control of it for one or more of an exhaustively listed set of offences – a situation in which the applicant association should not normally have any reason to fear finding itself. Impugning Parliament's motives for passing this legislation, when it was concerned to settle a burning social issue, did not amount to proof that the applicant association was likely to run any risk. Moreover, it would be inconsistent for the latter to rely on the fact that it was not a movement that infringed freedoms and at the same time to claim that it is, at least potentially, a victim of the application that might be made of the law concerned. It followed that the applicant association could not claim to be a victim within the meaning of Article 34 of the Convention.[192]

---

[191]   Decision of 23 May 2002, *Segi and Others.*
[192]   Decision of 6 November 2001.

1.13.3.4 Future victim

The question of whether applicants having a *future* interest may also be considered victims in the sense of Article 34 was avoided by the Commission in a case concerning Article 2 of Protocol No. 1. In this case forty mothers claimed that, in consequence of an Act on pre-school education promulgated in Sweden on 21 December 1973, they had been deprived of the right to send their children to the school of their choice. As to the admissibility of their application, the Commission divided the mothers into three groups. The mothers from the first group could not be regarded as victims, because their children had passed the pre-school age at the moment of the Act's effective date. The second group consisted of mothers whose children had not yet reached pre-school age at that moment. With respect to this group the Commission held as follows: "The Commission understands that these applicants consider themselves to be victims of a violation of the Convention in that the Act on Pre-School Activities may affect them in the future. The Commission notes that the children of these applicants in some cases might have reached pre-school age in the course of proceedings before the Commission. However, having regard to the fact that the applicants in Group 3 [the mothers of children that had pre-school age at the moment referred to] can be considered to be victims within the meaning of Article 25 [the present Article 34] of the Convention for the purpose of the present application, the Commission can abstain from examining as to whether the applicants in Group 2 also can be so considered."[193]

From an earlier decision of the Commission in a similar case, however, one may infer that the Commission was indeed prepared to recognise a future interest in certain cases. In that case two parents complained about legal and administrative measures concerning sexual instruction at primary schools. The measures were not yet applicable to their school-age daughter. Nevertheless, the Commission admitted their application. Curiously enough, however, it did not mention the victim-requirement at all.[194] The admissibility of the application may have been justified on the ground that in cases like this one, the alleged violation – in this case the application of the said measures to the child – would certainly take place in the near future. It is particularly in cases where the interests of the applicant would otherwise be irreparably prejudiced, that admissibility ensues imperatively from the purpose of the legal protection envisaged by the Convention and the requirement of effectiveness.[195]

In the *Kirkwood* Case such a situation was at stake. The case concerned a man who complained that his envisaged extradition from the United Kingdom to California would amount to inhuman and degrading treatment contrary to Article 3 of the

---

[193]   Appl. 6853/74, *40 Mothers v. Sweden*, Yearbook XX (1977), p. 214 (236).
[194]   Appl. 5095/71, *V. and A. Kjeldsen v. Denmark*, Yearbook XV (1972), pp. 482-502.
[195]   Decision of 23 May 2002, *Segi and Others*.

Convention since, if extradited, he would be tried for two accusations of murder and one of attempt to murder, and would very probably be sentenced to death. He argued that the circumstances surrounding the implementation of such a death penalty would constitute inhuman and degrading treatment. He referred in particular to the 'death row' phenomenon of excessive delay due to a prolonged appeal procedure which might last several years, during which he would be gripped with uncertainty as to the outcome of his appeal and, therefore, as to his fate. The Commission held as follows with respect to the victim-requirement: "In these circumstances, faced with an imminent act of the executive, the consequences of which for the applicant will allegedly expose him to Article 3 treatment, the Commission finds that the applicant is able to claim to be a victim of an alleged violation of Article 3."[196]

In several cases where a decision had been taken to expel a person to a country where he claimed he risked being treated contrary to Article 3, the Commission has held that a person who is about to be subjected to a violation of the Convention may claim to be a victim.[197] If, however, the order to leave the territory of the State concerned is not enforceable, the person concerned may not yet claim to be a victim. Only the notification of an expulsion order to him, with reference to the country of destination, can confer on him the status of victim, provided that domestic remedies have been exhausted. Thus, in the *Vijayanthan and Pusparajah* Case the Court made a distinction between, on the one hand, the *Soering* Case, where the Home Secretary had signed the warrant for the applicant's extradition, and that of *Vilvarajah,* where the deportation of the applicants to Sri Lanka had taken place during the proceedings before the Commission and, on the other hand, that of *Vijayanthand and Pusparajah.* In respect of the latter case, the Court found that, despite the direction to leave French territory, not enforceable in itself, and the rejection of their application for exceptional leave to remain, no expulsion order had been made with respect to the applicants. If the Commissioner of Police were to decide that they should be removed, the appeal provided for in French law would be open to the applicants, with all its attendant safeguards, but at the moment here at issue such an appeal would probably have been declared inadmissible as premature or devoid of purpose by the competent court. The applicants could not, as matters stood, claim 'to be the victim(s) of a violation' within the meaning of Article 25(1) [the present Article 34].[198]

In a case where the applicants complained about the decision of the French President to resume nuclear testing on Mururoa and Fangataufa atolls in French Polynesia, which allegedly violated their rights under Articles 2, 3 and 8 of the Convention and Article 1 of Protocol No. 1, the Commission found the consequences, if any, of the

---

[196]   Appl. 10479/83, D&R 37 (1984), p. 158 (182).
[197]   Appl. 17262/90, *A. v. France,* D&R 68 (1991), p. 319 (334); Appls 17550/90 and 17825/91, *V. and P. v. France,* D&R 70 (1991), p. 298 (314); Appl. 19373/92, *Voulfovitch and Oulianova,* D&R 74 (1993), p. 199 (207).
[198]   Judgment of 27 August 1992, para. 46.

resumption of the tests at issue too remote to affect the applicants' personal situation directly. Therefore, they could not claim to be a victim under Article 25 [the present Article 34].[199] In a case where the complaint concerned restrictions on the exercise of the right of ownership the Commission held that the only subject of the proceedings was whether or not a particular prefectoral order was lawful. The Commission recalled that is was only in highly exceptional circumstances that an applicant may claim to be a victim of a violation of the Convention owing to the risk of a future violation. An example of this would be a piece of legislation which, while not having been applied to the applicant personally, subjects him to the risk of being directly affected in specific circumstances of his life. In the instant case the Commission noted that the applicants, taken individually, had not submitted any evidence in support of their allegations, such as their title-deeds to property or documents relating to the consequences or losses they had allegedly suffered as a result of the implementation of the prefectoral order.[200]

In the Case of *Asselbourg and 78 Others and Greenpeace Association* the Court considered that the mere mention of the pollution risks inherent in the production of steel from scrap iron was not enough to justify the applicants' assertion that they were the victims of a violation of the Convention. They should be able to assert, arguably and in a detailed manner, that for lack of adequate precautions taken by the authorities the degree of probability of the occurrence of damage was such that it could be considered to constitute a violation, on condition that the consequences of the act complained of were not too remote. In the Court's opinion it was not evident from the file that the conditions of operation imposed by the Luxembourg authorities and in particular the norms dealing with the discharge of air-polluting wastes were so inadequate as to constitute a serious infringement of the principle of precaution.[201]

1.13.3.5 Indirect victim

It is conceivable that an individual may experience a personal injury owing to a violation of the Convention against another person. Under certain circumstances, therefore, an individual may lodge an application on his own account concerning a violation of the Convention against another person, without the applicant himself having directly suffered a violation of one of his rights or freedoms. In such a case the applicant must have so close a link with the direct victim of the violation that he himself is also to be considered a victim. On that basis the Commission developed in its case law the concept of 'indirect victim', meaning that a near relative of the victim or certain other third parties can refer the matter to the Commission on their own

---

[199] Appl. 28204/95, *Tauira and 18 Others v. the United Kingdom*, D&R 83 (1995), p. 112 (131-133). See also decision of 6 November 2001, *Christian Federation of Jehova's Witnesses*.

[200] Appl. 38912/97, *Association des Amis de Saint Raphaël et de Fréjus and Others*, D&R 94 (1998), p. 124 (132).

[201] Decision of 29 June 1999.

initiative insofar as the violation concerned is (also) prejudicial to them or insofar as they have a personal interest in the termination of that violation.[202] Thus, a spouse was considered a victim in view of the fact that she had suffered financial and moral injury in consequence of a violation of the Convention committed against her husband.[203] Another applicant was regarded as an indirect victim because he had submitted that his twin brother had wrongfully been detained in a State institution, in which he had later died.[204] That a purely non-material interest is sufficient for the admissibility of the action of an applicant as the indirect victim becomes evident, for example, from the decision by the Commission that a complaint of a mother about the treatment of her detained son was admissible.[205] And in the Case of *X, Cabales and Balkandali* the Commission held: "When the alleged violation concerns a refusal of a leave to remain or an entry clearance, the spouse of the individual concerned can claim to be a victim, even if the individual concerned is in fact staying with her, but unlawfully and under constant threat of deportation."[206]

The father of a hostage-taker killed by special police was considered as an indirect victim of an alleged violation of Article 2. The same applied to the deceased's sister, notwithstanding the fact that under national law the deceased's children, who where not among the applicants, were his heirs.[207] On the other hand, an applicant was not admitted who submitted that his sisters had wrongfully failed to receive compensation for their sufferings during the Nazi regime and who now claimed this as yet in his own name. This compensation related only to the sufferings of the sisters, not to those of the applicant, so that the latter could not be considered as a victim himself.[208] In the Case of *Becker v. Denmark* a German journalist, who was director of a body called Project Children's Protection & Security International, challenged the repatriation of 199 Vietnamese children, proposed by the Danish Government, as contrary to Art. 3 of the Convention. It was held that he was not a direct victim but considered to be an indirect victim because the children depended on him and he had been entrusted with at least the care of the children by the Vietnamese authorities on behalf of their parents.[209] And in the Case of *D v. Federal Republic of Germany* the Commission held: "The answer to this question (whether an applicant could claim to be a victim) depended largely on the legal interest which the applicant has in a determina-

---

[202]   Appl. 100/55, *X v. Federal Republic of Germany*, Yearbook I (1955-1957), p. 162 (162-163); decision of 26 January 1999, *Hibbert;* decision of 22 June 1999, *Çelikbilek.*
[203]   Appl. 1478/62, *Y v. Belgium*, Yearbook VI (1963), p. 590 (620).
[204]   Appl. 7467/76, *X v. Belgium*, D&R 8 (1978), p. 220 (221).
[205]   Appl. 898/60, *Y v. Austria*, Coll. 8 (1962), p. 136.
[206]   Appls 9214/80, 9473/81 and 9474/81, *X, Cabales and Balkandali v. the United Kingdom*, D&R 29 (1982), p. 176 (182).
[207]   Appl. 25952/94, *Andronicou Constantinou v. Cyprus*, D&R 85-A (1996), p. 102.
[208]   Appl. 113/55, *X v. Federal Republic of Germany*, Yearbook I (1955-1957), p. 161 (162). See also Appl. 9639/82, *B., R. and J. v. Federal Republic of Germany*, D&R 36 (1984), p. 139.
[209]   Appl. 7011/75, *Becker v. Denmark*, Yearbook XIX (1976), p. 416 (450).

tion of his allegations of Convention breaches. In assessing this interest, any material or immaterial damage suffered (...) as a result of the alleged violation must be taken into account."[210]

In the Case of *A. V. v. Bulgaria* the Government contended that the applicant had no standing to bring an application, as she was never married to Mr T. The only legal heirs of Mr T., who had twice been married and divorced, were his seven children. The Court first noted that the Bulgarian Supreme Court had recognised the right of an unmarried partner to damages in tort in respect of the wrongful killing of the other partner on the basis of the understanding, notably, that such a partner 'sustains moral damages' and that awarding compensation is 'just'. Moreover, none of the domestic authorities which were involved in the applicant's complaints in respect of Mr T.'s death questioned her *locus standi*. The prosecution authorities examined and ruled on her appeal against the suspension of the criminal proceedings. The Court recalled that a couple who have lived together for many years constitutes a 'family' for the purposes of Article 8 of the Convention and is entitled to its protection notwithstanding the fact that their relationship exists outside marriage. In the present case the applicant raised complaints in respect of the death of Mr T., with whom she had lived for more than 12 years. They had three children together. In these circumstances the Court had no doubt that the applicant could claim to be personally affected by, and, therefore, be a victim of, the alleged violations of the Convention in respect of the death of Mr T. and the subsequent investigation into this event. There was no valid reason for the purposes of *locus standi* to distinguish the applicant's situation from that of a spouse. The Court found, therefore, that the applicant had standing to bring an application under Article 34 of the Convention in respect of the death of Mr T. and the ensuing investigation.[211]

In the Case of *Open Door Counselling Ltd. and Dublin Well Women Centre Ltd.* the Court extended the group of persons who may claim to be indirect victims. The applications concerned restrictions imposed on the two applicant companies as a result of a court injunction prohibiting them from providing information to pregnant women as to the location or identity of, or method of communication with, abortion clinics in Great Britain. The applicant companies were engaged at the time in non-directive counselling of pregnant women. The other applicants were two of the counsellors employed by one of the companies and two women of child-bearing age. The Government argued that the complaint submitted by the two women of child-bearing

---

[210]   Appl. 9320/81, *D. v. Federal Republic of Germany*, D&R 36 (1984), p. 24 (31). See also Appl. 9348/81, *W v. the United Kingdom*, D&R 32 (1983), p. 190 (198-200) and Appl. 9360/81, *W v. Ireland*, D&R 32 (1983), p. 211 (212-216); Appl. 20948/92, *Işiltan*, D&R 81(1995) p. 35 where the father of a minor who died following an operation could claim to be an indirect victim of an alleged violation of Article 2.

[211]   Decision of 18 May 1999.

age amounted to an *actio popularis*, since they could not claim to be victims of an infringement of their Convention rights. The Court held: "Although it has not been asserted that Mrs X and Mrs Geragthy are pregnant, it is not disputed that they belong to a class of women of child-bearing age which may be adversely affected by the restrictions imposed by the injunction. They are not seeking to challenge *in abstracto* the compatibility of Irish law with the Convention since they run a risk of being directly prejudiced by the measures complained of. They can thus claim to be 'victims' within the meaning of Article 25(1) [the present Article 34]."[212]

Although the Court's reasoning seems to relate rather to the concept of 'potential victim', in fact the concept of 'indirect victim' is also at issue here, and has been considerably extended. A measure may be challenged not only by the persons to whom it is directed, but also by those who may be affected by it in another way.

This extension was foreshadowed by the judgment in the *Groppera Radio AG* Case. A company which owned a radio station, its sole shareholder and two of its employees complained about an Ordinance adopted by the Federal Council prohibiting Swiss cable companies which had a community-antenna licence, from re-broadcasting programmes from transmitters which did not satisfy the requirement of the international agreements on radio and telecommunications. Groppera Radio did not satisfy these requirements. The applicants alleged a violation of Article 10. The Court dismissed the Government's preliminary objection that the applicants were not 'victims' within the meaning of Article 34 of the Convention since the Ordinance was not directed against them.[213]

Finally, it should be mentioned that in certain cases the Commission considered shareholders as victims of alleged violations of rights and freedoms of the company. It appears from its case law that the Commission did not regard shareholders in such cases as indirect but as direct victims.[214] In the cases concerned the applicant held a majority share in the company. On the other hand, in the *Yarrow* Case, the Commission held that a minority shareholder of Company A could not claim to be a victim of an interference with property rights of Company B, all the securities in which were owned by Company A, because the nationalisation measure complained of did not involve him personally. In the view of the Commission it was only open to Company A to lodge a complaint under the Convention.[215]

In the Case of *Wasa Liv Ömsesidigt* the Commission found that a group of persons who were policyholders in an insurance company, could not be considered as victims,

---

[212]   Judgment of 29 October 1992, para. 44.
[213]   Judgment of 28 March 1990, paras 48-51.
[214]   Appl. 1706/62, *X v. Austria*, Yearbook IX (1966), p. 112 (130) and the report of 17 July 1980, *Kaplan v. the United Kingdom*, D&R 21 (1981), p. 5 (23-24); Appl. 14807/89, *Agrotexim Hellas S.A. v. Greece*, D&R 72 (1992), p. 148 (155).
[215]   Appl. 9266/81, D&R 30 (1983), p. 155 (184-185).

since the policyholders did not have any legal claim to direct ownership of the company's assets as such.[216]

In the *Agrotexim Hellas* Case the Commission found that the question of whether a shareholder could claim to be a victim of measures against a company, could not be determined on the basis of the sole criterion of whether the shareholders held the majority of the company shares. The Commission took into account, in addition to the fact that the applicants as a group held the majority of the shares in the company, that they had a direct interest in the subject matter of the application. Moreover, the company was in liquidation and was under a special regime of effective State control. Consequently, the company could not reasonably be expected to lodge an application with the Commission against the State. In these specific circumstances, the Commission found that the applicant shareholders were entitled, by lifting the veil of the company's legal personality, to claim that they were victims of the measures affecting the company's property, within the meaning of Article 25 [new Article 34].[217]

The Court did not share the view of the Commission. In the first place, when the applicant companies lodged their application with the Commission in 1988, Fix Brewery, although in the process of liquidation, had not ceased to exist as a legal person. It was at that time represented by its two liquidators, who had legal capacity to defend its rights and, therefore, to apply to the Convention institutions, if they considered it appropriate. There was no evidence to suggest that at the material time it would have been impossible as a matter of fact or of law for the liquidators to do so. The Court concluded that it had not been clearly established that at the time when the application was lodged with the Commission it was not possible for Fix Brewery to apply through its liquidators to the Convention institutions in respect of the alleged violation of Article 1 of Protocol No. 1 which was the basis of the applicant companies' complaint. It followed that the latter companies could not be regarded as being entitled to apply to the Convention institutions.[218]

In the *Ankarcrona* Case the applicant submitted that he and his business were in practice the same and that he had, therefore, to be regarded as a victim within the meaning of Article 34 of the Convention. The Court recalled that the applicant was the sole owner of Skyddsvakt Herbert Ankarcrona AB. Consequently, there was no risk of differences of opinion among shareholders or between shareholders and a board of directors as to the reality of infringements of the rights protected under the Convention and its Protocols, or concerning the most appropriate way of reacting to such infringements. Having regard to the absence of competing interests which could create difficulties, for example, in determining who was entitled to apply to the Court, and in the light of the circumstances of the case as a whole, the applicant could, in the

---

216 Appl. 13013/87, D&R 58 (1988), p. 163(183-185).
217 Appl. 14807/89, D&R 72 (1992), p. 148 (156).
218 Judgment of 24 October 1995, paras 68-70.

Court's opinion, reasonably claim to be a victim within the meaning of Article 34 of the Convention, in so far as the impugned measures taken with regard to his company were concerned.[219]

In the Case of *CDI Holding Aktiengeschellschaft and Others* the Court held that it had found earlier that disregarding an applicant company's legal personality in similar cases could be justified only in exceptional circumstances, in particular where it was clearly established that it was impossible for the company to apply to the Convention institutions through the organs set up under its articles of incorporation or – in the event of liquidation – through its liquidators, as in the *Agrotexim Hellas* Case. However, no such exceptional circumstances had been established in the present case. The Court further found that the applicants could not claim to be victims of a violation of Article 10 of the Convention as a result of the termination of the applicant company's broadcasts as any rights susceptible of attracting the protection of Article 10 in the present case were linked to the applicant company as such and not to its shareholders or official representatives.[220] In the *Lebedev* Case the Court reiterated that the piercing of the 'corporate veil' or the disregarding of a company's legal personality would be justified only in exceptional circumstances, in particular where it was clearly established that it was impossible for the company to apply to the Court through the organs set up under its articles of incorporation.[221]

From the above it may be concluded that the doctrine of 'indirect victim' has not yet been established with full clarity in the case law as far as holders of financial interests in a company are concerned.

1.13.3.6 The alleged violation must still exist

Cases may occur in which the violation complained of has meanwhile been terminated or at least no longer exists at the moment the Court examines the case. The applicant will then not be admitted, because he can no longer allege to be a victim.[222] If, for instance, in the meantime the violation of the Convention complained of has been recognised by the authorities and the applicant has received sufficient redress, he can no longer claim to be a victim of that violation.[223] In the *Amuur* Case the Court consi-

---

[219]   Decision of 27 June 2000.

[220]   Decision of 18 October 2001.

[221]   Decision of 25 November 2004.

[222]   See, *e.g.*, the report of 15 October 1980, *Foti*, B.48 (1986), p. 30; report of 6 July 1983, *Dores and Silveira*, D&R 41 (1985), p. 60 (19-20); Appl. 10103/82, *Faragut*, D&R 39 (1984), p. 186 (207); judgment of 25 September 2001, *Gulsen and Haul Yasin Ketenoglou*, paras 36-37.

[223]   Appl. 8865/80, *Verband Deutscher Flugleiter and Others v. Federal Republic of Germany*, D&R 25 (1982), p. 252 (254-255); Appl. 10092/82, *Baraona v. Portugal*, D&R 40 (1985), p. 118 (137); Appl. 10259/83, *Anca and Others v. the United Kingdom*, D&R 40 (1985), p. 170 (177-178); Appl. 13156/87, *Byrn v. the United Kingdom*, D&R 73 (1993), p. 5 (9), and as regards 'reasonable time': Appl. 8858/80, *G. v. Federal Republic of Germany*, D&R 33 (1983), p. 5 (6-7).

dered that the notion of 'victim' within the meaning of Article 34 of the Convention denotes the person directly affected by the act or omission in issue, the existence of a violation of the Convention being conceivable even in the absence of prejudice; prejudice is relevant only in the context of Article 41 of the Convention. Consequently, a decision or measure favourable to the applicant is not in principle sufficient to deprive him of his status as 'victim', unless the national authorities have acknowledged, either expressly or in substance and have afforded redress for, the breach of the Convention.[224]

In the Case of *Aydin and 10 Others* the first applicant submitted that the *ex gratia* financial aid he had received had no connection with the disappearance of his father and, therefore, could not form a basis of a finding that he could no longer claim to be a victim within the meaning of Article 34 of the Convention. The Court held that since it did not appear that the financial aid, which had in fact been paid to the first applicant, was based on an acknowledgement, either expressly or in substance, and since the first applicant's rights under the Convention had been disrespected by the authorities, the financial aid at issue could not be regarded as sufficient for a deprivation of the first applicant's status as a 'victim' in respect of his material losses. The Court, therefore, accepted that the first applicant could claim to be a victim.[225]

In the *Burdov* Case the Court held that a decision or measure favourable to the applicant was in principle not sufficient to deprive him of his status as a 'victim' unless the national authorities have acknowledged, either expressly or in substance, and then afforded redress for, the breach of the Convention.[226] In the *Doubtfire* Case the Court noted that the applicant's conviction was quashed on the grounds that the proceedings had been unfair because of the lack of full disclosure by the prosecution. It was open to the applicant to apply for compensation in respect of his conviction and imprisonment. In these circumstances, the applicant could no longer claim to be a victim of the alleged violation of Article 6 of the Convention.[227]

As to the question of whether the applicant may continue to claim to be a victim of a violation of Article 6(1) of the Convention on the grounds of the length of the criminal proceedings against him, the Court has held that the mitigation of a sentence on the ground of the excessive length of proceedings does not in principle deprive the individual concerned of his status as a victim within the meaning of Article 34 of the Convention. However, according to the Court, this general rule is subject to an exception when the national authorities have acknowledged in a sufficiently clear way the

---

[224]   Judgment of 25 June 1996, para. 36.
[225]   Decision of 1 February 2000.
[226]   Judgment of 7 May 2002, para. 31. See also decision of 6 April 2004, *Skubenko*.
[227]   Decisions of 23 April 2002.

failure to observe the reasonable time requirement and have afforded redress by reducing the sentence in an express and measurable manner.[228]

In the *Wejrup* Case the Court noted that the High Court expressly stated that it concurred entirely with the comments stated by the City Court concerning the penal merits of the counts adjudicated and the other circumstances emphasised in the sentencing (which did not entail considerations about the length of the proceedings). Moreover, the Court noted that in finding a violation of the Convention in respect of the three accountants, the High Court mitigated the sentences as such with regard to two accountants and upheld the sentence with regard to one, despite the fact that this accountant was convicted of a longer sentence than before the City Court, in addition to exempting them from paying costs. When reducing the applicant's and the co-accuseds' share of costs, the High Court had partly taken into account the proportion between the charge and the outcome of the judgment and, in the light of the quite extraordinary level of legal costs in the case, all the accused's circumstances together with the fact that the consolidation of the cases against the applicant and the two top executives and the cases against the accountants should not be detrimental to them. However, the High Court had also partly and particularly taken into account its statement as to the length of the proceeding. As regards the applicant it was unclear how much of the reduction of the costs were attributable to the length of the proceedings alone. Having regard to the above, the Court was not convinced that the national authorities, in view of their initial finding that the Convention could not be considered violated, nevertheless in a sufficiently clear way acknowledged a failure to comply with the 'reasonable time' requirement within the meaning of Article 6(1) of the Convention. Neither was the Court convinced that the national authorities afforded the applicant redress therefore by reducing the sentence in an express and measurable manner or exempted the applicant from paying such an amount of costs that it constitutes a redress in relation to the alleged violation of the Convention thereby precluding the examination of the application. Accordingly, the Court found that the applicant might claim to be a victim of a violation of his right to trial within a reasonable time as guaranteed by Article 6(1) of the Convention.[229]

In a case where applicants submitted that the authorities' recording of their telephone conversations with counsels was contrary to the Convention, the records in question had since been destroyed. In view of this the German Government advanced that the alleged violation had become a moot point. The Commission, however, decided that since the destruction had not taken place in response to a request from the applicants and the latter had not received reparation otherwise, "the applicants still have to be considered as victims although the records in question no

---

[228]   Judgment of 26 June 2001, *Beck*, para. 27; decision of 20 September 2001, *Jansen*; decision of 7 March 2002, *Wejrup*.
[229]   Decision of 7 March 2002.

longer exist."[230] In a case where a settlement between the parties had been reached which disposed of previous applications to the Commission and the Court concerning criminal proceedings against the applicant, the Commission found that the declaration made by the applicant in the context of those applications were unequivocal in that it was intended to prevent him from bringing further applications before the Convention organs.[231]

In the *Caraher* Case the Court held that the possibility of obtaining compensation for the death of a person will generally, and in normal circumstances, constitute an adequate and sufficient remedy for a substantive complaint of an unjustified use of lethal force by a State agent in violation of Article 2 of the Convention. Separate procedural obligations may also arise under Article 2 concerning the provision of effective investigations into the use of lethal force. Where a relative accepts a sum of compensation in settlement of civil claims and renounces further use of local remedies, he or she will generally no longer be able to claim to be a victim in respect of those matters.[232] However, in the Case of *Z.W. v. the United Kingdom* the Court observed that the compensation accepted by the applicant was not in settlement of her civil claims and not part of the process of exhaustion of domestic remedies. Her claims in the civil court were struck out and the award of GBP 50,000 was made as compensation for criminal injuries. This statutory scheme was not concerned with any alleged failings by the local authority in their duty to protect the applicant, which was being the essence of the complaint raised by her under Article 3 of the Convention, but rather with the injuries attributable to her as a victim of a criminal offence committed by her foster parents. The Court, therefore, found that the applicant might still claim to be a victim of a violation of Article 3 of the Convention in respect of her complaints against the local authority.[233]

In the cases of *Van den Brink* and *Zuiderveld and Klappe* the respondent Government contended before the Court that the applicants could not claim to be victims of a breach of Article 5(3) as the time each one spent in custody on remand was deducted in its entirety from the sentence ultimately imposed on them. According to the Court the relevant deduction did not *per se* deprive the individual concerned of his status as an alleged victim within the meaning of Article 34 of a breach of Article 5(3). The Court added that "the position might be otherwise if the deduction from sentence had been based upon an acknowledgement by the national courts of a violation of the Convention."[234]

---

[230] Appl. 8290/78, *A, B, C and D v. Federal Republic of Germany*, D&R 18 (1980), p. 176 (180).
[231] Appl. 22634/93, *Mlynek v. Austria*, D&R 79 (1994), p. 103 (107).
[232] Decision of 11 January 2000, *Caraher*.
[233] Decision of 27 November 2001.
[234] Judgments of 22 May 1984, para. 41 and para. 37 respectively.

Similarly, in the *Inze* Case the fact that a judicial settlement had been reached between the parties that might have mitigated the disadvantage suffered by the applicant, was considered insufficient reason to deprive the applicant of his status as victim. Here again the Court added: "The position might have been otherwise if, for instance, the national authorities had acknowledged either expressly or in substance, and then afforded redress for, the alleged breach of the Convention."[235]

Indeed, in cases where the applicant's sentence had been reduced in an express and measurable manner after a judicial finding concerning the undue length of the proceedings, the Commission took the position that he could no longer be considered to be a victim of a violation of Article 6(1).[236]

In the *East African Asians* Cases the Commission held that where Article 3 is violated by a State's exclusion from its territory of a person on the ground of race, the violation is substantially terminated, but not redressed, by that person's admission. Such a person can claim to be a victim of a violation notwithstanding admission.[237]

In the *Moustaquim* Case the applicant, a Moroccan national living in Belgium, had been deported by the Belgian authorities in 1984. The deportation order was suspended in 1989 for a trial period of two years during which the applicant was authorised to reside in Belgium. The applicant alleged that his deportation had violated, *inter alia*, Article 8. The Belgian Government submitted that the application had become devoid of purpose in that the deportation order had been suspended for a trial period of two years and the applicant was thus authorised to reside in Belgium. Since the new order had only suspended the deportation order and had not made reparation for the consequences which the applicant had suffered for more than five years, the Court did not consider that the case had become devoid of purpose. According to the Court there had been an interference with the right to respect for his family life.[238]

In the *Hamaïdi* Case the applicant submitted that the decision of 5 March 1998 dismissing his application for the exclusion order to be lifted, infringed his right to respect for his private and family life. The Court noted that the applicant was deported to Tunisia in 1995 and that the exclusion order did not expire until 18 July 1998, which was eight months after the application had been lodged and four months after the decision of 5 March 1998 dismissing his application to the Court of Appeal for the order to be lifted. Consequently, the Court concluded that the applicant did not lose his 'victim' status on account of the exclusion order expiring on 18 July 1998.[239]

---

235   Judgment of 28 October 1987, para. 32.
236   Appl. 17669/91, *Van Laak v. the Netherlands*, D&R 74 (1993), p. 156 (158); report of 16 February 1993, *Byrn v. the United Kingdom*, D&R 74 (1993), p. 5 (9).
237   Report of 14 December 1973, D&R 78-A (1994), p. 5 (63).
238   Judgment of 18 February 1991, para. 33.
239   Decision of 6 March 2001.

In the *Ilaşcu* Case the Moldovan Government asked the Court to dismiss Mr. Ilaşcu's application on the ground that he had ceased to be a victim in view of his release on 5 May 2001. The Court noted, firstly, that the applicant's conviction was still in existence and that there was accordingly a risk that the sentence would be executed. Furthermore, the Court had not been informed of any pardon or amnesty to which the applicant's release might have been due. It noted, secondly, that the applicant complained not only of his death sentence but also of the unlawfulness of his detention, the unfairness of the proceedings which led to his conviction, the conditions in which he was held from 1992 to 5 May 2001, and the confiscation of his possessions. In conclusion, the Court considered that Mr. Ilaşcu could still claim to be a 'victim' within the meaning of Article 34 of the Convention.[240]

1.13.4 REPRESENTATION OF AN APPLICANT; SUBSTITUTION FOR A DECEASED VICTIM

The requirement that the violation of the Convention must have caused the applicant a personal injury does not, of course, prevent an application from being lodged by his representative.[241] Furthermore, if the victim himself is not able, or is not adequately able, to undertake an action – for example a detained person, a patient in a mental clinic, a very young person – a close relative, a guardian, a curator, or another person may act on his behalf. In that case the name of the victim must be made known and, if possible, he must have given his consent to lodging the application.[242]

In case of the death of the victim his heir may lodge an application or uphold a previously lodged application only if the allegedly violated right forms part of the estate or if on other grounds he himself is to be considered the (direct or indirect) victim.[243] In the *Kofler* Case the Commission stated that "the heirs of a deceased applicant cannot claim a general right that the examination of the application introduced by the *de cujus* be continued by the Commission". The nature of the complaint (which concerned

---

[240] Decision of 4 July 2001.

[241] Appl. 282/57, *X v. Federal Republic of Germany*, Yearbook I (1955-1957), p. 164 (166).

[242] See, *e.g.*, Appl. 5076/71, *X v. the United Kingdom*, Coll. 40 (1972), p. 64 (66); decision of 26 June 2001, *Saniewski*.

[243] See, on the one hand, Appl. 282/57, *X v. Federal Republic of Germany*, Yearbook I (1955-1957), p. 164 (166), and on the other hand Appl. 1706/62, *X v. Austria*, Yearbook IX (1966), p. 112 (124). See also Appls 7572/76, 7586/76 and 7587/76, *Ensslin, Baader and Raspe v. Federal Republic of Germany*, Yearbook XXI (1978), p. 418 (452). See, however, Appl. 6166/73, *Baader, Meins, Meinhof, Grundmann*, Yearbook XVIII (1975), p. 132 (142); Appl. 12526/86, *Björkgren and Ed v. Norway*, D&R 68 (1991), p. 104 (105), where the Commission recognised the right of action of a widow and sole heir with regard to an action relating to property; Appl. 16744/90, *Dujardin v. France*, D&R 72 (1992), p. 236 (243).

the duration of the proceedings that resulted in the applicant's conviction and sentence) did not allow that complaint to be considered as transferable because the complaint was closely linked with the late applicant personally and his heirs "cannot now claim (...) to have themselves a sufficient legal interest to justify the further examination of the application on their behalf". Interestingly, from the viewpoint of the issue of 'abstract complaints', the Commission considered next whether any question of general interest would justify a further examination of the application. It stated: "Such a situation can arise in particular where an application in fact concerns (...) the legislation or a legal system or practice of the defendant State". The Commission concluded that in this case such a general interest did not exist.[244]

Accordingly, the issue is whether the widow(er) or heir can claim that the applicant's original interest in having the alleged violation of the Convention established might be considered as an interest vested in them. Such an interest was found to exist in a case where the deceased applicant had complained about his criminal conviction. In particular he had claimed that he had not had a 'fair hearing' nor had he benefited from the 'presumption of innocence'. The Commission emphasised that, by their very nature, complaints relating to Article 6 were closely linked to the person of the deceased applicant. However, the Commission continued by saying that "this link is not exclusive and it cannot be claimed that they have no bearing at all on the person of the widow." The widow could claim to be a victim, since she suffered the effects of the decisions concerning the seizure of property and a daily fine and civil imprisonment, both of which were enforceable against her.[245] In X v. France the Court took an even more liberal position. In this case the applicant, who was given a number of blood transfusions, was found to have been infected with HIV. The applicant died shortly after the referral of his case to the Court, but his parents expressed the wish to continue the proceedings. The Court accepted that they were entitled to take Mr X's place in the proceedings before it.[246] Also, in other cases concerning the length of proceedings the Court without restrictions showed itself to be willing to continue the proceedings at the wish of the heirs of the deceased applicant.[247]

If the death of the direct victim is the result of the alleged violation, e.g. in the case of torture, his relatives will as a rule qualify as indirect victims.[248] This was, however, different in the Scherer Case where the applicant's executor had not expressed any intention whatsoever of seeking, on Mr Scherer's behalf, to have the criminal procee-

---

[244]   Report of 9 October 1982, D&R 30 (1983), p. 5 (9-10). See also the report of 7 March 1984, Altun, D&R 36 (1984), p. 236 (259-260) and the judgment of 25 August 1987, Nölkenbockhoff, para. 33.
[245]   Appl. 10828/84, Funke, D&R 57 (1988), p. 5 (25-26).
[246]   Judgment of 31 March 1992, para. 26.
[247]   Judgment of 24 May 1991, Vocaturo, para. 2 and judgment of 27 February 1992, G v. Italy, paras. 2-3. See also Appl. 14660/89, Prisca and De Santis, D&R 72 (1992), p. 141 (147).
[248]   Judgment of 24 May 1991, Vocaturo, para. 2; judgment of 27 February 1992, G. v. Italy, para. 2; Judgment of 22 February 1994 Raimondo, para. 2; judgment of 2 September 1998, Yaşa, para. 66; judgment of 23 September 1998, Aytekin; Decision of 4 September 2001, Kakoulli.

dings reopened in Switzerland or to claim compensation for non-pecuniary damage in Strasbourg. Under these circumstances Mr Scherer's death could be held to constitute a "fact of a kind to provide a solution of the matter".[249]

In the *Scozzari and Giunta* Case the Italian Government contested the first applicant's standing to also act on behalf of her children, because, as her parental rights had been suspended, there was a conflict of interest between her and the children, and criminal proceedings were pending against her for offences against her children. The Court pointed out that in principle a person who is not entitled under domestic law to represent another may nevertheless, in certain circumstances, act before the Court in the name of the other person. In particular, minors can apply to the Court even, or indeed especially, if they are represented by a mother who is in conflict with the authorities and criticises their decisions and conduct as not being consistent with the rights guaranteed by the Convention. The Court considered that in the event of a conflict over a minor's interests between a natural parent and the person appointed by the authorities to act as the child's guardian, there is a danger that some of those interests will never be brought to the Court's attention and that the minor will be deprived of effective protection of his rights under the Convention. Consequently, even though the mother had been deprived of parental rights – indeed that was one of the causes of the dispute which she had referred to the Court – her standing as the natural mother sufficed to afford her the necessary power to apply to the Court on the children's behalf as well, in order to protect their interests. Moreover, the conditions governing individual applications are not necessarily the same as national criteria relating to *locus standi*. National rules in this respect may serve different purposes from those contemplated by Article 34 of the Convention and, whilst those purposes may sometimes be analogous, they need not always be so.[250]

In the Case of *P., C. and S. v. the United Kingdom* the applicants P. and C. complained on behalf of their daughter S. concerning the failure to make post-adoption provision for any form of direct contact with her and the reduction in indirect contact. The Government disputed that the applicants – the natural parents – could claim to bring an application on behalf of S. as they retained no residual parental authority over her and had no standing domestically to represent S. The Court reiterated the principle that the object and purpose of the Convention as an instrument for the protection of individual human beings requires that its provisions, both procedural and substantive, be interpreted and applied so as to render its safeguards both practical and effective. The Court held that a restrictive or technical approach in this area is to be avoided. The Court found that the key consideration in such a case is that any serious issues concerning respect for a child's rights should be examined.

---

[249] Judgment of 25 March 1993, paras 31-32.
[250] Judgment of 13 July 2000, paras 135-139.

It was claimed on behalf of S. that since the freeing for adoption proceedings she had been deprived of the opportunity to maintain a meaningful relationship with her birth parents. It could not be disputed that this was a right which S. should enjoy without unjustified interference. The necessity and proportionality of the interference had been put in issue in this application. The adoptive parents had, according the Government, objected to direct contact between P. and C. and S., and it was their decision to restrict indirect contact to one letter per year. In the circumstances it could not be expected that they introduce an application on behalf of S. raising the point. Therefore, given the issues raised in this application and the standing of P. and C. as S.'s natural parents, P. and C. might apply to the Court on her behalf in order to protect her interests.[251]

In the *Petersen* Case the applicant raised several complaints about German court decisions concerning his parental rights in his own name, but also on behalf of his child. The Court held that the case related to disputes between the mother, who had custody over the child, and the applicant, its natural father. Such conflicts concerning parental rights other than custody do not oppose parents and the State on the question of deprivation of custody where the State as holder of custodial rights cannot be deemed to ensure the children's Convention rights. In cases arising out of disputes between parents it is the parent entitled to custody who is entrusted with safeguarding the child's interests. In these situations the position as natural parent cannot be regarded as a sufficient basis to also bring an application on behalf of a child. Consequently, the applicant had no standing to act on the child's behalf.[252]

1.13.5   CONTRACTING PARTIES MAY NOT HINDER THE RIGHT OF INDIVIDUAL COMPLAINT

According to the last sentence of Article 34 the Contracting States undertake not to interfere in any way with the exercise of the individual right of complaint. In this respect the Court held in the *Cruz Varas* Case that Article 25 [the present Article 34] imposes an obligation not to interfere with the right of the individual to effectively present and pursue his complaint with the Commission. Although such a right is of a procedural nature distinguishable from the substantive rights contained in the Convention, it must be open to individuals to complain of alleged infringements of it in Convention proceedings. In this respect also the Convention must be interpreted as guaranteeing rights which are practical and effective as opposed to theoretical and illusory.[253]

---

[251]   Decision of 11 December 2001; decision of 26 September 2002, *Sylveste*.
[252]   Decision of 6 December 2001.
[253]   Judgment of 20 March 1991, para. 99. See also the Commission in Appl. 14807, *Agrotexim Hellas v. Greece*, D&R 72 (1992), p. 148 (156).

In the *Cruz Varas* Case the question arose of whether the failure on the part of the respondent State to comply with the Commission's indication of provisional measures under Rule 36 of the Rules of Procedure of the Commission[254] amounted to a violation of the obligation not to hinder the effective exercise of the right of individual petition. The Court took the position that the Convention did not contain any provision empowering the Convention organs to order interim measures. In the absence of a specific provision for such a power a Rule 36 indication could not give rise to a binding obligation.[255] In the subsequent Cases of *Öcalan*[256] and *Mamatkulov and Abdurasulovic*[257] the Court changed its position and held that its interim measures under Rule 39 of the Rules of Court are legally binding. That position was confirmed by the Grand Chamber after a referral (by virtue of Article 43 of the Convention).[258]

In the *Akdivar* Case concerning the alleged burning of houses by security forces in south-east Turkey, the question arose whether the Turkish authorities had hindered the effective exercise of the right of individual petition. Some of the applicants, or persons thought to be applicants, had been directly interrogated by the Turkish authorities about their applications to the Commission and had been asked to sign statements declaring that no such applications had been made. Furthermore, in the case of two of the applicants the interview had been filmed. The Court found a violation of Article 25(1) [the present Article 34] in this respect. It held that the applicants must be able to communicate freely with the Commission without being subjected to any form of pressure from the authorities to withdraw or modify their complaints. Given their vulnerable position and the reality that in south-east Turkey complaints against the authorities might well give rise to a legitimate fear of reprisals, the matters complained of amounted to a form of illicit and unacceptable pressure on the applicants to withdraw their applications. Moreover, it could not be excluded that the filming of the two persons, who were subsequently declared not to be applicants, could have contributed to this pressure. The Court also held that the fact that the applicants actually pursued their application to the Commission did not prevent such behaviour on the part of the authorities from amounting to a hindrance in respect of the applicants in breach of this provision.[259]

In the *Kurt* Case the Court held that the threat of criminal proceedings against an applicant's lawyer concerning the contents of a statement drawn up by him must be

---

[254] See 2.2.8.2.
[255] See judgment of 20 March 1991, para. 98.
[256] Decision of 14 December 2000.
[257] Judgment of 6 February 2003, paras 94-96.
[258] See 2.2.8.2.
[259] Judgment of 16 September 1996, para. 105; judgment of 25 May 1998, *Kurt*, para. 165; judgment of 18 June 2002, *Orhan*, para. 406; judgment of 30 January 2001, *Dulaş*, para. 79.

considered as interfering with the exercise of the applicant's right of petition.[260] The same was the case as regards the institution of criminal proceedings against a lawyer involved in the preparation of an application to the Commission.[261] In the *McShane* Case the Court considered that the threat of disciplinary proceedings may also infringe this guarantee of free and unhindered access to the Convention system.[262]

In the *Tanrıkulu* Case the Court observed that it was of the utmost importance for the effective operation of the system of individual petition instituted under Article 34, not only that applicants or potential applicants should be able to communicate freely with the Convention organs without being subject to any form of pressure from the authorities, but also that States should furnish all necessary facilities to make possible a proper and effective examination of applications. According to the Court it is inherent in proceedings relating to cases of this nature, where an individual applicant accuses State agents of violating rights under the Convention – his own or someone else's – that in certain instances solely the respondent Government have access to information capable of corroborating or refuting these allegations. A failure on a Government's part to submit such information which is in their hands without a satisfactory explanation may not only give rise to the drawing of inferences as to the well-foundedness of the applicant's allegations, but may also reflect negatively on the level of compliance by a respondent State with its obligations under Article 38(1)(a) of the Convention.[263] The same applies to delays by the State in submitting information which prejudices the establishment of facts in a case.[264]

In the *Tepe* Case the Court concluded that the Government had failed to provide any convincing explanation for its delays and omissions in response to the Court's requests for relevant documents, information and witnesses. The Court considered, therefore, that it could draw inferences from the Government's conduct in the instant case. Bearing in mind the difficulties arising from a fact-finding exercise of this nature and in view of the importance of a respondent Government's co-operation in Convention proceedings, the Court found that the Government had failed to furnish all necessary facilities to the Court in its task of establishing the facts within the meaning of Article 38(1) (a) of the Convention. Accordingly, it did not consider it necessary to also examine these matters under Article 34 of the Convention.[265]

In the *Salman* Case the Court found that the document recording the first interview showed that the applicant was questioned, not only about her declaration of means, but also about how she introduced her application to the Commission and with whose

---

[260]   Judgment of 25 May 1998, paras 164-165.
[261]   Judgment of 22 May 2001, Şarlı, paras 85-86; judgment of 13 November 2003, *Elci*, para. 711.
[262]   Judgment of 28 May 2002, para. 149.
[263]   Judgment of 8 July 1999, paras 66 and 70.
[264]   Judgment of 18 June 2002, *Orhan*, para. 266; judgment of 24 April 2003, *Aktas*, para. 341.
[265]   Judgment of 9 May 2003, para. 135; See also the judgment of 8 April 2004, *Tahsin Acar,* para. 254.

assistance. Furthermore, the Government had not denied that the applicant was blindfolded while at the Adana anti-terrorism branch headquarters. The Court found that blindfolding had increased the applicant's vulnerability, causing her anxiety and distress, and disclosed, in the circumstances of this case, oppressive treatment. Furthermore, there was no plausible explanation as to why the applicant was questioned twice about her legal aid application and in particular why the questioning was conducted on the first occasion by police officers of the anti-terrorism branch, whom the applicant had claimed were responsible for the death of her husband. The applicant must have felt intimidated by these contacts with the authorities. This constituted undue interference with her petition to the Convention organs.[266]

In the *Dulaş* Case the Court recalled that the Government had not provided any information to the Commission about the authorities' contacts with the applicant and that the Commission reached its finding of undue interference on the basis of the oral testimony of the applicant and her son. The statement provided to the Court indicated that the applicant was shown the statement made by her to the Human Rights Association (HRA) and the letter of authority concerning her legal representation before the Commission. It also appeared that she was asked to verify her thumbprint and to verify the contents of the statement as accurate. The text of the statement also implied that the applicant was questioned as to whether she wanted to maintain an application to the Commission in Europe and whether she wished to pursue a complaint against the HRA lawyer. Though the applicant maintained that her statement to the HRA was accurate and repeated the substance of her allegation against the security forces, it did not appear that the public prosecutor pursued any questions with a view to adding to the factual details of the applicant's complaints. In these circumstances the Court was not satisfied that the interview related solely to the public prosecutor's duty to collect information about the applicant's complaints for the purpose of his own investigation. It also trespassed into verifying the authenticity of the applicant's application and whether she wanted to continue it. The applicant not unreasonably must have felt intimidated by this interview and felt under pressure to withdraw complaints considered as being against the State. This constituted undue interference with her petition to the Convention organs.[267]

In the *Orhan* Case the Government submitted that the purpose of the applicant's summons was to question him about his recollection of his apprehension and to verify the authenticity of the power of attorney he had signed in favour of English lawyers. The Court emphasised that 'pressure' included not only direct coercion and flagrant acts of intimidation but also other improper indirect acts or contacts designed to dissuade or discourage applicants from pursuing a Convention remedy. The fact that the individual actually managed to pursue his application did not prevent an issue

---

[266]   Judgment of 27 June 2000, paras 131-132.
[267]   Judgment of 30 January 2001, paras 80-81.

arising under Article 34: should the Government's action make it more difficult for the individual to exercise the right of petition, this amounted to 'hindering' his rights under Article 34.[268] The Court further emphasised that it was inappropriate for the authorities of a respondent State to enter into direct contact with an applicant even on the pretext of verifying whether an applicant had, in fact, signed a form of authority in favour of legal representatives before the former Commission or the Court. Even if a Government had reason to believe that in a particular case the right of individual petition was being abused, the appropriate course for that Government was to alert the Court and inform it of their misgivings. To proceed as the Government had done in the present case was reasonably interpreted by the applicant as an attempt to intimidate him. In addition, the Court held that an attempt was made by the authorities to cast doubt on the validity of the application and thereby on the credibility of the applicant. These actions could only be interpreted as a bid to try to frustrate the applicant's successful pursuance of his claims, which also constituted a negation of the very essence of the right of individual petition.[269]

In the *Ilascu* Case the applicants submitted in the first place that they had not been permitted to apply to the Court from prison so that their wives had had to do that on their behalf. They also alleged that they had been persecuted in prison because they had tried to apply to the Court. They further submitted that the statement by the President of Moldova, that the applicant's refusal to withdraw his application had been the cause of the remaining applicants' continued detention, had been a flagrant interference with their right of individual petition. Lastly, they submitted that the note from the Russian Ministry of Foreign Affairs had been a serious interference with their right of individual petition. The Court reiterated that the expression 'any form of pressure' must be taken to cover not only direct coercion and flagrant acts of intimidation but also improper indirect acts or contacts designed to dissuade or discourage applicants from pursuing a Convention remedy. Moreover, the question whether contacts between the authorities and an applicant constitute unacceptable practices from the standpoint of Article 34 must be determined in the light of the particular circumstances of the case. In that connection the Court must assess the vulnerability of the complainant and the risk of his being influenced by the authorities.

The Court had also regard to the threats made against the applicants by the Transdniestrian prison authorities and the deterioration in their conditions of detention after their application was lodged. It took the view that such acts constituted an improper and unacceptable form of pressure which hindered their exercise of the right of individual petition. In addition the Court noted with concern the content of the diplomatic note of 19 April 2001 sent by the Russian Federation to the Moldovan authorities. It appeared from that note that the Russian authorities requested the

---

[268]   Judgment of 18 June 2002, para. 406.
[269]   *Ibidem*, paras 409-410.

Republic of Moldova to withdraw the observations they had submitted to the Court in so far as these implied responsibility for the alleged violations on the part of the Russian Federation on account of the fact that its troops were stationed in Moldovan territory in Transdniestria. Subsequently, at the hearing, the Moldovan Government did indeed declare that it wished to withdraw the part of its observations concerning the Russian Federation. The Court considered that such conduct on the part of the Government of the Russian Federation represented a negation of the common heritage of political traditions, ideals, freedom and the rule of law mentioned in the Preamble to the Convention and were capable of seriously hindering its examination of an application lodged in exercise of the right of individual petition and thereby interfering with the right guaranteed by Article 34 of the Convention itself. There had, therefore, been a breach by the Russian Federation of Article 34 of the Convention. The Court further noted that after the applicant's release he spoke to the Moldovan authorities about the possibility of obtaining the release of the other applicants, and that in that context the President of Moldova publicly accused the applicant of being the cause of his comrades' continued detention, through his refusal to withdraw his application against Moldova and the Russian Federation. In the Court's opinion, such remarks by the highest authority of a Contracting State, that improvement in the applicants' situation depended on withdrawal of the application lodged against that State or another Contracting State, represented direct pressure intended to hinder the exercise of the right of individual petition. That conclusion held good whatever real or theoretical influence that authority might have on the applicants' situation. Consequently, the remarks amounted to an interference by the Republic of Moldova with the applicants' exercise of their right of individual petition, in breach of Article 34.[270]

In practice, difficulties arise particularly with respect to persons who have been deprived of their liberty in one way or another. The Court does not regard every form of monitoring of the mail of detained persons addressed to it as unlawful, although it considers it more in conformity with the spirit of the Convention that the letters are forwarded unopened. According to the Court there is a conflict with Article 34 only when an applicant cannot freely submit his grievances in a complete and detailed way.[271] In the *Manoussos* Case the applicant complained that he was not allowed to send telegrams or make telephone calls to the Court's Registry, and that letters sent to him by the latter were opened on several occasions. The Court considered that such complaints fell to be examined under Article 8 of the Convention rather than under Article 34. In particular, the voluminous correspondence which the applicant had sent to the Court confirmed that he was able to submit all his complaints to the Court by ordinary mail, and there was no indication that the correspondence between the Court

---

[270]   Judgment of 8 July 2004, paras 476-482.
[271]   Judgment of 8 February 2000, *Cooke,* para. 48: decision of 30 April 2002, *Salapa.*

and the applicant was unduly delayed or tampered with. Finally, the Court noted that the applicant was granted free legal aid under the legal aid scheme funded by the Council of Europe, and that the Czech Bar Association recommended a lawyer who was willing to represent the applicant in the proceedings before the Court following his failure to appoint a lawyer. However, the applicant declined the lawyer's assistance for reasons which the Court considered groundless. Accordingly, he bore full responsibility for any alleged inadequacies in the presentation of his case to the Court. In view of the above facts and considerations the Court found that the alleged violation of Article 34 of the Convention had not been established.[272]

In this context the European Agreement relating to persons participating in proceedings before the European Court of Human Rights is also of interest.[273] In Article 3(2) of this Agreement States undertake to guarantee also to detained persons the right to free correspondence with the Court. This means that, if their correspondence is at all examined by the competent authorities, this may not entail undue delay or alteration of the correspondence. Nor may detained persons be subjected to disciplinary measures on account of any correspondence with the Court. Finally, they have a right to speak, out of hearing of other persons, with their lawyer concerning their application to the Court, provided that the lawyer is qualified to appear as a barrister before the courts of the State concerned. With respect to these provisions the authorities may impose limitations only insofar as they are in accordance with the law and are necessary in a democratic society in the interests of national security, for the detection and prosecution of a crime, or for the protection of health. Despite the fact that individuals cannot rely directly on this Agreement in the form of separate application, it is of importance for the promotion of an undisturbed exercise of the individual right of complaint, because the Court can take its provisions into account in connection with Article 34. The scope of the State's obligation under Article 34, however, is not necessarily confined to the provisions of this Agreement.

In the *Klyakhin* Case the issue concerned the alleged refusal of the prison authorities to forward the applicant's letters to the Court, delays in posting the letters and an alleged failure of the authorities to give the incoming letters from the Court to the applicant. While there was no allegation of undue pressure, interception of letters by prison authorities can hinder applicants in bringing their cases to the Court. As to exhaustion of domestic remedies in this respect, the Court observed that Article 34 of the Convention imposes an obligation on the Contracting States not to interfere with the right of the individual effectively to present and pursue his application before the Court. Such an obligation confers upon the applicant a right distinguishable from

---

[272]   Decision of 9 July 2002.

[273]   This agreement entered into force on 1 January 1999. This agreement replaces the 1969 Agreement. For the text see: Council of Europe, *European Treaty Series*, No. 161. For ratifications, see Appendix I.

the rights set out in Section I of the Convention or its Protocols. In view of the nature of this right the requirement to exhaust domestic remedies does not apply to it. Given the importance attached to the right of individual petition it would be unreasonable to require the applicant to make recourse to a normal judicial procedure within the domestic jurisdiction in every event where the prison authorities interfere in his correspondence with the Court. In these circumstances, the Court considered that the applicant's complaint under Article 34 could not be rejected for failure to exhaust domestic remedies. It found that this part of the application raised complex questions of fact and law, the determination of which should depend on an examination of the merits.[274]

Finally, it deserves attention that neither the Convention nor the above-mentioned European Agreement impose an obligation on the Contracting States to inform private parties of the possibility of filing an application with the Court after they have exhausted the domestic remedies. At any rate, according to the Commission, such an obligation could not be inferred from the words 'not to hinder in any way the effective exercise of this right' of Article 25 [present Article 34].[275] Considering the text of Article 34 this interpretation is not incomprehensible. Still, it would be in keeping with the spirit of the Convention if, in appropriate cases, after the domestic remedies have been exhausted, the attention of individuals were drawn to the possibility of lodging a complaint with the Court. After all, a State, which by becoming a party to the Convention recognises the right of complaint under Article 34, may be expected to assure the effective exercise of this right by giving adequate publicity to the existence of the right of complaint.

Correspondence with the Court in which the applicants complain about interference with the exercise of the right of complaint is not considered as a separate 'application' or '*requête*' to which the rules of admissibility are applicable. As a rule the case will be settled between the Court and the Contracting State concerned on an administrative basis, the applicant being permitted to react to any observations which a State may make. However, if along with another complaint such a complaint is also lodged, the Court appears to be prepared to examine the latter together with the first complaint.[276]

---

[274]   Decision of 14 October 2003.
[275]   See, *e.g.*, Appl. 1877/63, *X v. Austria*, 22 July 1963 (not published).
[276]   Judgment of 24 July 2001, *Valasinas*, para. 134; judgment of 20 January 2004, *D.P. v. Poland*, para. 92.

1.13.6   CO-EXISTENCE OF THE EUROPEAN CONVENTION AND THE UN COVENANT ON CIVIL AND POLITICAL RIGHTS

The co-existence of the possibilities of an individual right of complaint under the UN Covenant on Civil and Political Rights and the Convention raises two questions in particular. Is an individual, when he considers that one or more of his rights and freedoms, laid down in both treaties, has been violated, allowed to choose which action to institute? And may he also bring both actions for the same matter, either simultaneously or successively?

The first question may at once be answered in the affirmative. An individual who regards himself as the victim of a violation of one of the rights and freedoms guaranteed in the Convention as well as in the UN Covenant on Civil and Political Rights, must be considered free to use the procedure which he regards as the most favourable for his case, since neither of the two treaties prohibits this choice.[277] This freedom of choice does not apply with respect to inter-State complaints, since Article 55 of the Convention provides that the Contracting Parties agree that, except by special agreement, they will not avail themselves of treaties, conventions or declarations in force between them for the purpose of submitting, by way of petition, a dispute arising out of the interpretation or application of the Convention to a means of settlement other than those provided for in the Convention.

With respect to the second question, three situations may arise: (1) identical applications are lodged at the same time under both instruments; (2) the applicant first tries the procedure of the UN Covenant on Civil and Political Rights and then, if he is not satisfied with the outcome, that of the Convention; and (3) the applicant applies first to the European Court and subsequently, if he is not satisfied with the outcome, to the Human Rights Committee.

In the first case the applicant incurs the risk of being received by neither the Court nor the Committee. According to Article 35(2)(b) the Court cannot consider an application which is substantially the same as a matter which has already been submitted to another procedure of international investigation or settlement and if it contains no relevant new information.[278] On its part, Article 5(2) of the Optional Protocol of the UN Covenant on Civil and Political Rights provides that the Committee shall not consider any communication from an individual unless it has

---

[277]   See *Secretariat Memorandum prepared by the Directorate of Human Rights on the effects of the various international human rights instruments providing a mechanism for individual communications on the machinery of protection established by the European Convention on Human Rights*, H(85)3, No. 23, p. 9.

[278]   On this, see 2.2.12.4.

ascertained that the same matter is not being examined under another procedure of international investigation or settlement. From these provisions it appears that there is a real possibility that the application may be rejected by both organs. Such a highly unsatisfactory situation may be avoided if the Commission and the Committee pursue a flexible policy on this point. They might postpone consideration so as to enable the applicant to withdraw one of the two complaints. However, the situation where two applications are lodged at the same moment is likely to occur only rarely.

It is more likely that applications in Geneva and Strasbourg are lodged successively. If, as in the case mentioned above sub (2), the second application is lodged in Strasbourg, this leads to its being declared inadmissible under Article 35(2)(b), unless relevant new information is put forward. In the opposite case, that of sub. (3), such a conclusion does not follow imperatively from the text of Article 5(2)(a) of the Protocol. This provision provides for inadmissibility of a matter which is 'being examined under another procedure'. It is thus only the fact that the matter *is being* examined elsewhere which bars its admissibility, not the fact that the matter *has been* examined elsewhere. The Human Rights Committee, therefore, has actually taken the view that no complaint submitted to it is inadmissible merely on account of the fact that this case has already been examined in another procedure.[279]

It is questionable whether it is desirable that cases dealt with in Strasbourg may afterwards be brought up before the Committee again. An argument against this is that such a form of 'appeal' against decisions of the Strasbourg organs is contrary to the intention of the drafters of the Convention that the outcome of the procedure provided there is final. This intention may be inferred from Articles 35 and 42 of the Convention. Moreover, reasons of procedural economy may be advanced against renewed consideration of the same case by the Human Rights Committee. In general it takes a number of years for a case to pass through the Strasbourg procedure and the preceding national procedures. One may well wonder whether after such a long procedure the case should be reopened again.

In any event the Committee of Ministers of the Council of Europe has answered that question in the negative. In 1970 it urged those Contracting States, which were to ratify the Optional Protocol to the UN Covenant on Civil and Political Rights, to attach to their ratification a declaration denying the competence of the Human Rights Committee to receive communications from individuals concerning matters which have already been or are being examined in a procedure under the Convention, unless rights or freedoms not set forth in the Convention are invoked in such communications.[280] Several of the Contracting States which are also parties to the Protocol, have followed up this suggestion by making a declaration or a reservation. The Netherlands,

---

[279] See *Report of the Human Rights Committee of 1978*, General Assembly Official Records (A/33/40), p. 100.
[280] See Yearbook XIII (1970), pp. 74-76.

however, has refrained from making such a declaration or reservation. In the opinion of the Dutch Government there are indeed some practical objections to possible double procedures concerning the same matter, but they constitute an insufficient argument for preventing individuals from applying to the Human Rights Committee after having done so to the European Commission. Moreover, the Dutch Government submits that the Committee and the Commission/Court have different powers in a number of respects. Finally, the making of declarations as suggested by the Committee of Ministers might be imitated in other regional arrangements, which might be detrimental to the worldwide system for the protection of human rights.[281] For individuals subject to the jurisdiction of the Netherlands, therefore, it is possible to initiate, after the Strasbourg procedure, the procedure provided for in the Optional Protocol to the UN Covenant on Civil and Political Rights.

As regards the relevant practice of the two bodies concerned, the following may be observed. Only a few cases have been rejected by the European Commission under Article 35(2)(b) of the European Convention. The Secretariat usually prevents this by advising an applicant, who lodges a complaint already brought before the Committee, about the content of Article 35(2)(b). In a case where two members of the *Grapo* (an anti-fascist revolutionary group) had brought a complaint before the Commission, the Commission noted that it appeared from their letters to the Commissions that, before bringing his complaint in Strasbourg, the first applicant had brought a communication to the Human Rights Committee. The second applicant had joined this individual communication after having brought his complaint before the Commission. The Commission noted that in the relevant part of their application form the applicants omitted to mention the existence of the communication in question, then pending before the Human Rights Committee. Therefore, the Commission took the view that a situation of this type was incompatible with the spirit and letter of the Convention, which seeks to avoid a plurality of international proceedings relating to the same cases. According to the Commission the application was substantially the same as the petition submitted by the applicants to the Human Rights Committee, which was still pending before that Committee and was, therefore, inadmissible under Article 27(1)(b) [new Article 35(2)(b)].[282] The Commission also noted that a request for suspension of the proceedings before an international body (the applicants had requested the Human Rights Committee to grant such a suspension) did not have the same effect as a complete withdrawal of the application, which was the only step allowing the Commission to examine an application also brought before it.[283]

---

[281]   Second Chamber, Session 1975-1976, 13 932 (R 1037), Nos 1-6, p. 42.
[282]   Appl. 17512/90, *Calcerrada Fornielles and Cabeza Mato*, D&R 73 (1992), p. 214 (223-224).
[283]   *Ibidem*, p. 224.

An interesting issue came up in the case of *A.N. v. Denmark*. Denmark had made a reservation, with reference to Article 5(2)(a) of the Optional Protocol, in respect of the competence of the Committee to consider a communication from an individual if the matter has already been considered under other procedures of international investigation. The author of the communication had already filed an application concerning the same matter with the Commission, which was declared inadmissible as manifestly ill-founded. On the basis of these facts but without any further argument the Committee concluded that it was not competent to consider the communication. It thus implicitly dismissed the position taken by one of its members in his individual opinion, who argued that an application that had been declared inadmissible had not, in the meaning of the Danish reservation, been 'considered' in such a way that the Human Rights Committee was precluded from it. According to this point of view, the reservation aims at preventing a review of cases but does not seek to limit the competence of the Human Rights Committee merely on the ground that the rights of the UN Covenant on Civil and Political Rights allegedly violated may also be covered by the European Convention and its procedural requirements since it concerns a separate and independent international instrument.[284]

In the Case of *Pauger* the Committee decided that, irrespective of whether the State party has invoked its reservation to article 5, paragraph 2 (a), of the Optional Protocol or not, the European Court has based the decision of inadmissibility solely on procedural grounds, rather than on reasons that include a certain consideration of the merits of the case. This meant that the same matter had not been 'examined' within the meaning of the Austrian reservation to article 5, paragraph 2 (a), of the Optional Protocol.[285] In the Case of *Franz and Maria Deisl* the Committee noted that the European Court declared the authors' application inadmissible for failure to comply with the six-month rule, and that no such procedural requirement existed under the Optional Protocol. In the absence of an 'examination' of the same matter by the European Court, the Committee concluded that it was not precluded from considering the authors' communication by virtue of the Austrian reservation to article 5, paragraph 2 (a), of the Optional Protocol.[286]

In the Case of *Rupert Althammer* the Committee recalled that it on earlier occasions had already decided that the independent right to equality and non-discrimination embedded in article 26 of the Covenant provides a greater protection than the

---

[284] *Report of the Human Rights Committee of 1982*, General Assembly Official Records (A/37/40), p. 213, and the individual opinion of the East German expert, Mr Graefrath, appended to this decision, p. 214. See also Communication No. 168/1984, *Report of the Human Rights Committee of 1985*, General Assembly Official Records (A/40/40), p. 235; see also Communication No. 744/1997, *Linderholm*, decision on admissibility adopted on 23 July 1999, UN Doc. CCPR/C/66/D/744/1997, at para. 4.2. where the Committee decided in the same way.

[285] Communication No. 716/1996, *Pauger*, Views adopted on 25 March 1999, at para. 6.4.

[286] Communication No. 1069/202, Views adopted on 27 July 2004 at para. 10.2.

accessory right to non-discrimination contained in article 14 of the European Convention. The Committee had taken note of the decision taken by the European Court on 12 January 2001 rejecting the authors' application as inadmissible as well as of the letter from the Secretariat of the European Court explaining the possible grounds of inadmissibility. It noted that the authors' application was rejected because it did not disclose any appearance of a violation of the rights and freedoms set out in the Convention or its Protocols as it did not raise issues under the right to property protected by article 1 of Protocol No. 1. As a consequence, in the absence of an independent claim under the Convention or its Protocols, the Court could not have examined whether the authors' accessory rights under article 14 of the Convention had been breached. In the circumstances of the case, therefore, the Committee concluded that the question of whether or not the authors' rights to equality before the law and non-discrimination had been violated under article 26 of the Covenant was not the same matter that was before the European Court. The Committee, therefore, decided that the communication was admissible.[287] The outcome will now be different in respect of those States which have ratified Protocol No. 12.

---

[287] Communication No. 998/2001, Views adopted on 8 August 2003 at para 7.1.

CHAPTER 2
THE PROCEDURE BEFORE THE EUROPEAN COURT OF HUMAN RIGHTS

REVISED BY LEO ZWAAK

CONTENTS

2.1 INTRODUCTION

As stated above, a year after Protocol No. 11 to the Convention entered into force the Commission ceased to exist. Its functions have been merged with those of the Court in the newly established Court. In its sifting task the Court has until now followed the previous practice of the Commission. The Registry of the Court establishes all necessary contacts with the applicants and, if necessary, requests further information. Next, the application is registered and assigned to one of the Sections of the Court. A judge-rapporteur is designated by the President of the Section, who may refer the application to a three-judge committee, which may include the judge-rapporteur. The committee may, by unanimous decision, declare the application inadmissible. Such a decision is final. When the judge-rapporteur considers the application to be not inadmissible or when the committee does not unanimously reject the complaint, the application will be examined by a Chamber.

2.2 THE EXAMINATION OF ADMISSIBILITY

2.2.1 REGISTRATION OF AN APPLICATION

A complaint usually reaches the Registry of the Court by way of a letter. As a rule such letters have the character of a first contact and not of a formal application. They do not (yet) lend themselves to official registration. Applicants may approach the Registry by sending a letter by facsimile ('fax'). However, they must send the signed original by post within 5 days following the dispatch by fax. The Registry makes a provisional file for each case in order to obtain at the earliest possible stage as complete a picture as possible of any complaint. It is in the interest of the applicant to be diligent in conducting the correspondence with the Registry. Any delay in replying or failure to reply is likely to be regarded as a sign that the applicant is not or is no longer interested in having his case dealt with. Thus, if he does not answer a letter sent to him by the Registry within one year of its dispatch to him, his file will be destroyed.

The applicant receives a form for him to fill out which should be returned to the Registry within six weeks at the latest. He may also submit documents in addition to this form. The application, which must bear his signature, must contain: the name, age, occupation and address of the applicant; the name, occupation and address of his representative, if any; the name of the Contracting State against which the application is lodged; as specific as possible, the object of the application and the provision(s) of the Convention allegedly violated; a statement of the facts and arguments on which the application is based; and finally any relevant documents, and in particular any judgments or other act relating to the object of the application.[1] Moreover, in his application the applicant must provide information showing that the conditions laid down in Article 35(1) concerning the exhaustion of domestic remedies and the six-month time-limit for filing the application have been complied with. In general, procedural rules are not treated in Strasbourg with the same rigidity as they are by national courts.[2] However, a communication containing only an allegation that a particular act violates one or more provisions of the Convention was considered by the Commission insufficient to constitute a full application, unless this communication sets out summarily the object of the application.[3]

If the above-mentioned requirements are satisfied and the complaint, *prima facie*, discloses a violation of the Convention, it will in general be entered in the official register of the Court. Registration has no other meaning than that the complaint is pending before the Court; no indications as to its admissibility may be inferred from it.

Until 1 January 2002 registration of a complaint – save in the event of failure to supply certain documents or information – was not refused if the party submitting it insisted on registration. Nevertheless, only a small part of all complaints received were actually registered.[4] The other cases were withdrawn during the phase of the first correspondence with the Registry of the Court. The Registry had been instructed to draw the attention of potential applicants to the possibility of rejection of the complaint in cases where the existing case law pointed in that direction. The Registry did so by means of standard letters. At present, however, in the interest of efficiency, the Court has decided to dispense with the warning letter. In accordance with Rule 49 of

---

[1]   Rule 47(1) of the Rules of Court of the European Court of Human Rights, Strasbourg, November 2003 (hereafter: the Rules of Court). See: http://www.echr.coe.int/Eng/EDocs/RULES%20OF%20COURTNOV2003.htm.

[2]   For the Commission, see Appl. 332/57, *Lawless v. Ireland*, Yearbook II (1958-1959), p. 308 (326).

[3]   Appl. 18660/91, *Bengtsston v. Sweden*, D&R 79-A (1994), p. 11 (19).

[4]   In 2005, the Registry of the Court received 41,510 communications, 35,402 of which were registered; *Survey of Activities and Statistics*, 2005.

the Rules of Court once the case is ready, the President of the Section to which the case is assigned shall designate a judge as rapporteur, who will examine the application and decide whether it should be considered by a Committee or a Chamber.[5]

2.2.2 LANGUAGES

The official languages for the Court are English and French, but the President of the Chamber may permit the parties to use another language. In connection with individual complaints, and for as long as no Contracting Party has been given notice of such an application, all communications with and oral and written submissions by applicants or their representatives, if not in one of the Court's official languages, will be in one of the official languages of the Contracting Parties. If a Contracting Party is informed or given notice of an application, the application and any accompanying documents will be communicated to that State in the language in which they were lodged with the Registry by the applicant. In practice this means that the parties may also use any of the other languages of the Contracting States, and that the correspondence may also be conducted in those languages.

All communications with and pleadings by such applicants or their representatives in respect of a hearing, or after a case has been declared admissible, will be in one of the Court's official languages, unless the President of the Chamber authorises the continued use of the official language of a Contracting Party. If such leave is granted, the Registrar will make the necessary arrangements for the interpretation and translation into English or French of the applicant's oral and written submissions, respectively, in full or in part, where the President of the Chamber considers it to be in the interests of the proper conduct of the proceedings. Exceptionally the President of the Chamber may make the grant of leave subject to the condition that the applicant bears all or part of the costs of making such arrangements. Unless the President of the Chamber decides otherwise, any decision made in this respect will remain valid in all subsequent proceedings in the case, including those in respect of requests for referral of the case to the Grand Chamber and requests for interpretation or revision of a judgment.

All communications with and oral and written submissions by a Contracting Party which is a party to the case will be in one of the Court's official languages. The President of the Chamber may grant the Contracting Party concerned leave to use one of its official languages for its oral and written submissions. If such leave is granted, it is the responsibility of the requesting Party to file a translation of its written submissions into one of the official languages of the Court within a time-limit fixed

---

[5]   See in this respect: Reflection Group on the Reinforcement of the Human Rights Protection Mechanism, CDDH-GDR (2001) 010, 15 June 2001, p. 9.

by the President of the Chamber. Should that Party not file the translation within that time-limit, the Registrar may make the necessary arrangements for such translation, the expenses to be charged to the requesting Party. The Contracting Party will bear the expenses of interpreting its oral submissions into English or French. The Registrar is responsible for making the necessary arrangements for such interpretation.

The President of the Chamber may direct that a Contracting Party which is a party to the case will, within a specified time, provide a translation into, or a summary in, English or French of all or certain annexes to its written submissions or of any other relevant document, or of extracts therefrom. The President of the Chamber may invite the respondent Contracting Party to provide a translation of its written submissions in the or an official language of that Party in order to facilitate the applicant's understanding of those submissions. Any witness, expert or other person appearing before the Court may use his or her own language if he or she does not have sufficient knowledge of either of the two official languages. In that event the Registrar shall make the necessary arrangements for interpreting or translation.[6]

2.2.3   REPRESENTATION

States are represented before the Court by their Agents, who may be assisted by advocates or advisers.[7] Individuals, non-governmental organisations, or groups of individuals may present and conduct applications before the Court on their own behalf, but may also be represented or assisted by an advocate authorised to practice in any of the Contracting Parties and residing in the territory of one of them, or any other person approved by the President of the Chamber. The President of the Chamber may, where representation would otherwise be obligatory, grant leave to the applicant to present his or her own case, subject, if necessary, to being assisted by an advocate or other approved representative. In exceptional circumstances and at any stage of the procedure, the President of the Chamber may, where he or she considers that the circumstances or the conduct of the advocate or other person appointed so warrant, direct that the latter may no longer represent or assist the applicant and that the applicant should seek alternative representation.[8] The advocate or other approved representative, or the applicant in person who seeks leave to present his or her own case, must even if leave is granted to use one of the (other) languages of the Contracting States, have an adequate understanding of one of the Court's official languages. In case he or she does not have sufficient proficiency to express himself or herself in the

---

6   Rule 34 of the Rules of Court.
7   Rule 35 of the Rules of Court.
8   Rule 36(4)(b) of the Rules of Court.

Court's official languages, leave may be given to use one of the official languages of the Contracting States.[9]

2.2.4 COSTS OF THE PROCEEDINGS

The procedure before the Court is free of charge for the parties; the expenses are accounted for by the Council of Europe.[10] Where a witness, expert or other person is summoned at the request or on behalf of a Contracting Party, the costs of their appearance shall be borne by that Party unless the Chamber decides otherwise. The costs of the appearance of any such person who is in detention in the Contracting Party on whose territory on-site proceedings before a delegation takes place, shall be borne by that Party unless the Chamber decides otherwise. In all other cases, the Chamber shall decide whether such costs are to be borne by the Council of Europe or awarded against the applicant or third party at whose request or on whose behalf the person appears. In all cases, such costs will be taxed by the President of the Chamber.[11] Finally, at every stage of the procedure, after the written observations of the respondent government concerning the admissibility have been received or the time-limit for this has expired, the President of the Chamber may grant the applicant free legal aid if he deems this necessary for the proper conduct of the case before the Chamber and the applicant does not have sufficient means.[12]

The President of the Chamber will conclude that free legal aid is necessary when it is evident that the applicant has had no legal training, or when it appears from the written documents submitted by him that he is unable to defend his case adequately before the Court. In order to establish that he does not have sufficient means, the applicant must submit a declaration to that effect, certified by the appropriate domestic authorities.[13]

Free legal aid may comprise not only lawyer's fees but also the travelling and subsistence expenses and any other necessary expenses incurred by the applicant and his lawyer.[14]

---

[9]   Rule 36(5) of the Rules of Court.
[10]   Art. 50 of the Convention.
[11]   Rule A5(6) of the Annex to the Rules of Court.
[12]   Rules 91-96 of the Rules of Court.
[13]   Rule 93 of the Rules of Court.
[14]   Rule 94 of the Rules of Court.

2.2.5   HANDLING OF THE CASE AFTER THE APPLICATION HAS BEEN RECEIVED

Any individual application will be assigned to a Section of a Chamber by the President of the Court. If the application is brought by a State, the President gives notice of the application to the State against which the claim is made and assigns the application to one of the Sections. The President of the Section constitutes the Chamber and invites the respondent State to submit written observations on admissibility.[15]

In the case of a (registered) individual complaint the President of the Section to which the case has been assigned by the President of the Court nominates a member of the Section to act as judge-rapporteur, who examines the application. The latter will thereafter work in close co-operation with the case-processing lawyer to whom the case has been allocated. The rapporteur may request relevant further information on the complaint as well as documents and other material from the applicant and/or the State concerned.[16] He communicates any information obtained from the State to the applicant for comments. The same holds good with respect to the information obtained from the applicant, which will be communicated to the State for comment. The tasks of the judge-rapporteur cover examination and preparation of the case, channelling it towards a Committee of three judges or a Chamber of seven judges and making proposals as to its processing. The judge-rapporteur will seize one of the Committees (at present twelve have been constituted) of the case if it is not complex and appears to be inadmissible *de plano*.[17] This procedure is known as the 'summary procedure', by which the Committee of three, by unanimous vote ('global formula'), may declare an application inadmissible or strike it off the list, when such a decision can be taken without further examination.[18] In 1999, 79% of all inadmissibility decisions were taken by Committees; that percentage had increased to 92% in 2000.[19] Since January 2002 the applicant no longer receives a copy of the decision. He or she will receive a letter from the Registry stating that the application has been declared inadmissible and a brief outline of the grounds. The letter states that the Registry is not able to give any further information or reasons in connection with the decision. This decision is final.[20]

If the application is not declared inadmissible by unanimous vote of the Committee of three, the case will be examined by a Chamber. It is for the judge-rapporteur to prepare a report summarising the facts of the case, indicating the issues which it raises

---

[15]   Rule 51 of the Rules of Court.
[16]   Rule 49(2)(a) of the Rules of Court.
[17]   Rule 49(2) of the Rules of Court.
[18]   Rule 53(2) of the Rules of Court.
[19]   Reflection Group on the Reinforcement of the Human Rights Protection Mechanism, CDDH-GDR (2001) 010, 15 June 2001, p. 11.
[20]   Art. 28 of the Convention.

and making a proposal as to the procedure to be followed. The Chamber may request additional relevant information from the applicant or the State concerned and/or give notice of the application to the State and invite the State to present written observations on the admissibility of the application.[21] The information and/or observations of the State are communicated to the applicant, so that the latter may comment on it. The same holds true with respect to the information and/or observations obtained from the applicant, which will be communicated to the respondent State. After receipt of the observations of the State against which the application is brought, the application is examined by the judge-rapporteur. Before deciding upon the latter's report on admissibility, the Chamber may invite the parties to submit further observations in writing or orally.[22] If the Chamber decides to hold a hearing in this phase, the parties are also invited to plead on the merits. Such a combined procedure is intended to save time.[23]

The above-mentioned difference in treatment between individual applications and applications by States as far as referring the application to the defendant State is concerned, would seem to be justified. A State may be assumed not to lodge an application lightly, on account of the political complications which such a step may involve. In the case of individual applications the chances for this to happen are greater. It would, therefore, not be right to also communicate for comments to the governments concerned those numerous applications which, *prima facie*, fail to satisfy the admissibility conditions. Nor does it appear to be objectionable that among individual applications a first selection is made via a simplified procedure, provided that the legal position of the applicant is not negatively affected by such a procedure. It is, therefore, of the greatest importance that the rapporteur be obliged to transmit any information he obtains from a Government to the applicant, upon which the latter may comment. Thus, the equality of the parties is secured. It would seem less satisfactory that the outcome of the simplified procedure is not communicated to the applicant in the form of a decision, signed by the President of the Committee concerned, with a specification of the ground(s) of inadmissibility. The letter, signed by a member of the Registry, and which is not in the applicant's own language, is far from a public and reasoned decision and is often experienced as a denial of justice.

In the event that the application is handled by a Chamber, the latter decides on the admissibility and the merits.[24] At this stage of the proceedings an oral hearing will be held if necessary. The Chamber may declare the case inadmissible at any stage of the proceedings, even if the case was initially declared admissible.[25] The decision on

---

[21]   Rule 54(2) of the Rules of Court.
[22]   Rule 54(2)(c) of the Rules of Court.
[23]   Rules 54(3) and 54 A of the Rules of Court.
[24]   Article 29(1) of the Convention.
[25]   Article 35(4) of the Convention.

admissibility must be reasoned and as a rule is taken separately.[26] According to the Explanatory Report to Protocol 11, in its decision declaring the application admissible the Chamber may give the parties an indication of its opinion on the merits. A separate decision on admissibility is important to the parties if they are considering starting negotiations to reach a friendly settlement. There may, however, be situations in which the Court does not take a separate admissibility decision. This could occur, for example, where a State does not object to a case being declared admissible.[27] In fact, joint decisions on admissibility and merits have become more and more common.

The entry into force of Protocol No. 14 will change the procedure considerably. The main aim of this Protocol is to reduce the time spent by the Court on clearly inadmissible applications and repetitive applications. The filtering capacity will be increased by making a single judge competent to declare inadmissible or to strike out an individual application. This new mechanism maintains the judicial character of decision-making on admissibility. The single judges will be assisted by non-judicial rapporteurs, who will be staff members of the Registry. Former Article 25 will be renumbered as Article 24 and will be amended in two respects. The legal secretaries as created by Protocol No.11 will cease to exist, since they never had an existence of their own. A new paragraph 2 will be added so as to introduce the function of rapporteur to assist the new single-judge formation provided for in the new Article 27. The work of rapporteurs will be carried out by persons other than judges in order to achieve a significant potential increase in the filtering capacity which the institution of single-judge formations aims at. It will be for the Court to implement the new paragraph 2 by deciding in particular on the number of rapporteurs needed and the manner and duration of appointment. The *Explanatory Report* to the Protocol points out that it would be advisable to diversify the recruitment channels for Registry lawyers and rapporteurs. Without prejudice to the possibility of entrusting existing Registry lawyers with rapporteur functions, it is deemed desirable to reinforce the Registry, for fixed periods, with lawyers who have an appropriate practical experience in the functioning of their respective domestic legal systems. Moreover, it is understood that the new function of rapporteur should be conferred on persons with solid legal experience, expertise in the Convention and its case law and a very good knowledge of at least one of the two official languages of the Council of Europe, and who meet the requirements of independence and impartiality.[28] According to Article 26(3)(new) the single judge shall not sit in cases concerning the High Contracting Party in respect of which he or she has been elected.

---

[26]   Article 45(1) of the Convention.
[27]   Protocol No. 11 to the European Convention on Human Rights and Explanatory Report, para 77 and 78, Council of Europe, Strasbourg May 1994, H(94)5, (hereinafter: Explanatory Report).
[28]   *Explanatory Report to Protocol No. 14*, para. 59.

The establishment of this system will lead to a significant increase in the Court's filtering capacity, on the one hand, on account of the reduction, compared to the old Committee practice, of the number of actors involved in the preparation and adoption of decisions (one judge instead of three; the new rapporteurs may combine the function of case-lawyer and rapporteur), and on the other hand because judges will be relieved of the rapporteur role when sitting in a single-judge formation. As a result, there will be a multiplication of filtering formations operating simultaneously.

Article 26(1)(new) sets out the competence of the single-judge formations. Their competence will be limited to taking decisions of inadmissibility and decisions to strike a case off the list "where such a decision can be taken without further examination". The purpose of this amendment is to provide the Court with an additional tool which should assist it in its filtering work and allow it to devote more time to cases which warrant examination on the merits, whether seen from the perspective of the legal interest of the individual applicant or considered from the broader perspective of the law of the Convention and the European public order to which it contributes. The latter point is important with regard to the new admissibility criterion introduced in Article 35, and which relates to the interest of the applicant and the interest of respect for human rights, but in respect of which the Court's Chambers and Grand Chamber will have to develop case-law at first.[29] In case of doubt as to admissibility, the judge will refer the application to a Committee or Chamber.

Finally, paragraph 2 of Article 27 will be amended to make a provision for a new system of appointment of *ad hoc* judges. This new system is a response to criticism of the old system, which allowed the High Contracting Party to choose an *ad hoc* judge after the beginning of proceedings.[30] Under the new rule contained in Article 26(4)(new), each High Contracting Party will be required to draw up a reserve list of *ad hoc* judges from which the President of the Court shall choose someone when the need arises to appoint an *ad hoc* judge. It is understood that the list of potential *ad hoc* judges may include names of judges elected in respect of other High Contracting Parties. More detailed rules on the implementation of this new system may be included in the Rules of Court.

Paragraphs 1 and 2 of the amended Article 28 will extend the powers of three-judge Committees. Under the present system these committees may unanimously declare applications inadmissible. Under paragraph 28(1)(b)(new), they may also, in a joint decision, declare individual applications admissible and decide on the merits, when the questions raised concerning the interpretation and application of the Convention are covered by well-established case law of the Court. 'Well-established case-law' normally means case law which has been consistently applied by a Chamber. Excep-

---

[29]   See *infra*, 2.2.9.
[30]   *Ibidem*, para. 64.

tionally, however, it is conceivable that a single judgment on a question of principle may constitute 'well-established case law', particularly when rendered by the Grand Chamber. This new competence will apply, in particular, to repetitive cases, which account for a significant proportion of the Court's judgments (in 2003, approximately 60%). Parties may, of course, contest the 'well-established' character of the case law before the Committee.[31]

The new procedure concerning admissible repetitive cases will be both simplified and accelerated, although it preserves the adversarial character of proceedings and the principle of judicial and collegiate decision-making on the merits. It will be simplified in that the Court will bring the case (or possibly a group of similar cases) to the attention of the respondent Party, pointing out that it concerns an issue which is already the subject of well-established case law holding a violation. Should the respondent Party agree with the Court's position, the latter will be able to give its judgment very rapidly. The respondent Party may contest the application, for example, if it considers that domestic remedies have not been exhausted or that the case at issue differs from applications which have resulted in well-established case law. However, it may not veto the use of this procedure which lies within the Committee's sole competence. The Committee will rule on all aspects of the case (admissibility, merits and just satisfaction) in a single judgment or decision. The procedure still requires unanimity on each aspect. Failure to reach a unanimous decision counts as no decision, in which event the Chamber procedure will apply.[32] It will then fall to the Chamber to decide whether all aspects of the case should be covered in a single judgment. Even when the Committee initially intends to apply the procedure provided for in Article 28(1)(b), it may still declare an application inadmissible under Article 28(1)(a). This may happen, for example, if the respondent Party has persuaded the Committee that domestic remedies have not been exhausted. The implementation of the new procedure will substantially increase the Court's decision-making capacity and effectiveness, since many cases can be decided by three judges, instead of the seven currently required for admissible applications.

Even when, in the new procedure, a three-judge Committee gives a judgment on the merits, the judge elected in respect of the High Contracting Party concerned will not be an *ex officio* member of the Committee, in contrast with the situation with regard to judgments on the merits under the Convention as it stands. The presence of this judge would not appear necessary, since the Committee will deal with cases on which well-established case law exists. However, a Committee may invite the judge elected in respect of the High Contracting Party concerned to replace one of its members, if it deems the presence of this judge to be useful. For example, it may be felt that this judge, who is familiar with the legal system of the respondent Party,

---

[31]   *Ibidem,* para. 68.
[32]   Article 29 (1) of the Convention.

should be involved in taking the decision, particularly when such questions as the exhaustion of domestic remedies need to be clarified. One of the factors which a Committee may consider relevant in this respect is whether the respondent Party has contested the applicability of Article 28(1)(b).[33] According to the *Explanatory Report* the reason why this factor has been explicitly mentioned in Article 28(3) is that it was considered important to have at least some reference in the Convention itself to the possibility for respondent Parties to contest the application of the simplified procedure.[34] A respondent Party may contest the new procedure, for example, on the basis that the case in question differs in some material respect from the established case law cited. It is likely that the expertise that the national judge has in domestic law and practice will be relevant to this issue and, therefore, helpful to the Committee. Should this judge be absent or unable to sit, the procedure provided for in Article 26(4)(new) *in fine* will apply.[35]

While separate decisions on admissibility were the rule before the entry into force of Protocol No. 11, joint decisions on the admissibility and merits of individual applications has become more and more common, which allows the registry and judges to process faster while respecting fully the principle of adversarial proceedings. This practice will be formalised in the amended Article 29.[36] However, the Court may always decide that it prefers to take a separate decision on the admissibility of a particular application. According to the second paragraph of Article 29 (new) separate decisions are the rule in the case of inter-State applications.

2.2.6 RELINQUISHMENT OF JURISDICTION IN FAVOUR OF THE GRAND CHAMBER

Where cases pending before a Chamber raise serious questions affecting the interpretation of the Convention or its Protocols, or where the resolution of a question before the Chamber might have a result inconsistent with a judgment previously delivered by the Court, the Chamber may, at any time before it has rendered its judgment, relinquish jurisdiction in favour of the Grand Chamber, unless one of the parties to

---

[33] Article 28(3) (new) of the Convention.
[34] *Explanatory Report to Protocol No. 14*, CETS 194, para. 71.
[35] "If there is none or if the judge is unable to sit, a person chosen by the President of the Court from a list submitted in advance by that Party shall sit in the capacity of judge".
[36] This Article reads as follows:
    1 If no decision is taken under Article 27 or 28, or no judgment rendered under Article 28, a Chamber shall decide on the admissibility and merits of individual applications submitted under Article 34. The decision on admissibility may be taken separately.
    2 A Chamber shall decide on the admissibility and merits of inter-State applications submitted under Article 33. The decision on admissibility shall be taken separately unless the Court, in exceptional cases, decides otherwise.

the case objects.[37] The Chamber may take this decision of its own motion and does not have to give reasons for it. The Registrar notifies the parties of the Chamber's intention to relinquish jurisdiction. The parties will have one month from the date of that notification within which to file at the Registry a duly reasoned objection. An objection which does not fulfil these conditions will be considered invalid by the Chamber.[38]

2.2.7   PUBLIC CHARACTER OF THE HEARING

In accordance with Rule 63 of the Rules of Court the hearings are public unless, in accordance with paragraph 2 of that Rule, the Chamber in exceptional circumstances decides otherwise, either of its own motion or at the request of a party or another person concerned. Paragraph 2 provides that the press and the public may be excluded from all or part of a hearing in the interests of morals, public order or national security in a democratic society, where the interests of juveniles or the private life of the parties so require, or to the extent strictly necessary in the opinion of the Chamber in special circumstances where publicity would prejudice the interests of justice. In accordance with paragraph 3, any request for a hearing to be held in camera must include reasons and specify whether it concerns all or only part of the hearing.

Rule 33 provides that all documents deposited with the Registry in connection with an application, with the exception of those deposited within the framework of friendly-settlements negotiations, must be accessible to the public unless the President of the Chamber decides otherwise, either of his own motion or at the request of a party or another person concerned. According to its paragraph 2, public access to a document or to any part of it may be restricted in the interests of morals, public order or national security in a democratic society, where the interests of juveniles or the protection of the private life of the parties so require, or to the extent strictly necessary in the opinion of the President in special circumstances where publicity would prejudice the interests of justice.

Decisions and judgments given by a Chamber are accessible to the public. The Court periodically makes accessible to the public general information about decisions taken by the Committees.[39] According to Rule 77(2) the judgment may be read out at a public hearing.

---

[37]   Article 30 of the Convention.
[38]   Rule 72(2) of the Rules of Court.
[39]   Rule 33(4) of the Rules of Court.

2.2.8 MEASURES IN URGENT CASES

2.2.8.1 Interim measures

The Convention does not provide for applications for measures in urgent cases. This is regulated under Rules 39, 40 and 41 of the Rules of Court. The Chamber or, where appropriate, its President may, at the request of a party or of any other person concerned, or of his own motion, indicate to the parties any interim measure which it considers should be adopted in the interests of the parties or of the proper conduct of the proceedings before it. Notice of these measures is given to the Committee of Ministers.[40] In any case of urgency the Registrar, with the authorisation of the President of the Chamber, may, without prejudice to the taking of any other procedural steps and by any available means, inform a Contracting Party concerned in an application of the introduction of the application and of a summary of its objects.[41] Finally, in urgent cases the Chamber or its President may decide to give priority to a particular application, thus derogating from its normal procedure, according to which applications are dealt with in the order in which they become ready for examination.[42]

2.2.8.2 Legal character of interim measures

In the *Cruz Varas* Case the Court had to decide on the argument that the failure to comply with the Commission's indication of an interim measure amounted to a violation of Sweden's obligation under Article 25 [the present Article 34] not to hinder the effective exercise of the right of individual petition. The Court took the position that the Convention did not contain any provision empowering the Convention organs to order interim measures.[43] The Court further noted that the practice of States revealed almost total compliance with the indications of interim measures. Subsequent practice could indeed be taken as establishing the agreement of States regarding the interpretation of a Convention provision, but not to create new rights and obligations which were not included in the Convention at the outset. The practice of complying with Rule 36 [the present Rule 39] was rather based on good faith co-operation with the Commission. Furthermore, no assistance could be derived from general principles of international law since no uniform legal rule existed on the matter. Accordingly, the Court found that the power to order binding interim measures could not be inferred from Article 25 [the present Article 34] or from other sources. According to the Court it was within the province of the Contracting Parties to decide whether it

---

[40]   Rule 39 of the Rules of Court.
[41]   Rule 40 of the Rules of Court.
[42]   Rule 41 of the Rules of Court.
[43]   Judgment of 20 March 1991, para. 102.

was expedient to remedy this situation. However, the Court observed that where a State decides not to comply with a Rule 36 [the present Rule 39] indication, it knowingly assumes the risk of being found in breach of Article 3 by the Convention organs.[44] This interpretation by the Court of Article 25 [the present Article 34], which deviated from that of the majority of the Commission, was adopted by ten to nine votes. The Court confirmed this interpretation in the Case of *Conka*. The applicants, who were of Slovak origin, were victims of a number of assaults by skinheads in Slovakia and were unable to obtain police protection. In November 1998 they arrived in Belgium, where they sought political asylum. On 18 June 1999 the General Commissioner for Refugees and Stateless Persons refused asylum and ordered them to leave the territory within five days of being put on notice. On 5 October 1999 the applicants and 74 other gypsy refugees who had been refused asylum, were put on board a plane bound for Slovakia notwithstanding the Court's interim measure under Rule 39 of the Rules of Court.[45]

In subsequent cases, i.e. in the *Mamatkulov and Abdurasulovic* Case and in the *Öcalan* Case, however, the Court changed its position and held that its interim measures under Rule 39 of the Rules of Court are legally binding. In the *Mamatkulov and Abdurasulovic* Case the Court held for the first time that a State Party to the Convention to which interim measures have been indicated in order to avoid irreparable harm being caused to the victim of an alleged violation must comply with those measures and refrain from any act or omission that will undermine the authority and effectiveness of the final judgment.[46] If a State does not comply with an interim measure, this can lead to a violation of the right of individual application (under Article 34 ECHR), at least if the contested act – *in casu* an extradition – has affected the core of the right of individual application.[47] In this case the applicants, two Uzbek nationals who were members of an opposition party, were arrested at Istanbul airport with an international arrest warrant on suspicion of involvement in terrorist activities in their home country. The Uzbek authorities asked for their extradition. The applicants claimed, *inter alia*, that, if extradited to Uzbekistan, their lives would be at risk and they would be in danger of being subjected to torture. They asked the Court under Rule 39 of the Rules of Court to indicate an interim measure to Turkey not to extradite them to Uzbekistan. The President of the Chamber indicated to the Turkish Government that it was desirable in the interest of the parties and the proper conduct of the proceedings before the Court not to extradite the applicants to Uzbekistan until the Court had had an opportunity to examine the applications further at the forthcoming sessions of the Chamber on 23 and 30 March 1999. On 19 March 1999, the Turkish Cabinet issued a decree for the applicants' extradition and handed

---

44   *Ibidem*, para. 103.
45   Decision of 13 March 2001.
46   Judgment of 6 February 2003, 110.
47   *Ibidem*, para. 96.

information to the Court regarding guarantees obtained from the Uzbek Government. Notwithstanding the decision of the Chamber of 23 March to extend the interim measures until further notice, the applicants were extradited on 27 March.[48] The Court recalled that the object and purpose of the Convention as an instrument for the protection of individual human beings require that its provisions be interpreted and applied so as to make its safeguards practical and effective, as part of the system of individual applications. It also reiterated that the Convention is a living instrument which must be interpreted in the light of the present-day conditions. Next, it stressed that it is of utmost importance for the effective operation of the system of individual applications instituted under Article 34, that applicants or potential applicants should be able to communicate freely with the Court without being subjected to any form of pressure from the authorities to withdraw or modify their complaints. It noticed in that connection that the applicants, once extradited, were unable to remain in contact with their representatives, while it is implicit in the notion of the effective exercise of the right of individual application that for the duration of the proceedings in Strasbourg the principle of equality of arms should be observed and an applicant's right to sufficient time and necessary facilities in which to prepare his or her case respected. With reference to its previous case law the Court observed that it is not formally bound by it, although in the interests of legal certainty and foreseeability it should not depart, without good reasons, from its own precedents. Re-examining the problem, and also taking account of the jurisprudence of other international courts on the matter, the Court reached the conclusion that since the applicants' extradition, in disregard of the indications given under Rule 39, had rendered nugatory their right to individual application, it amounted to a breach by Turkey of its obligations under Article 34 of the Convention by failing to comply with the interim measures.[49]

If a State decides not to comply with an interim measure, this will not amount automatically to a violation of Article 34. The Court will decide on a case-by-case basis as to what the effect of the refusal has been on the exercise of the right of individual application. This is demonstrated by the *Öcalan* Case. In this case the Court asked Turkey, *inter alia*, to take all necessary measures to protect the rights under Article 6 of the Convention of PKK leader Öcalan, who had been arrested in Kenya and brought before a court where he faced the death penalty. This request was set aside by the Turkish Government. In its judgment the Court, without prejudice to its view on the binding nature of interim measures, did not find a violation of the right of individual petition. For this the Court gave the following reasons. The Government had later on furnished the information requested by the Court, as part of their observations on the admissibility of the application. Furthermore, the Government's refusal to supply that information earlier had not prevented the applicant from making

---

out his case on the complaints concerning the criminal proceedings that had been brought against him.[50]

Both cases were referred to the Grand Chamber of the Court for a 're-hearing' by virtue of Article 43 of the Convention. In the *Mamatkulov and Abdurasulovic* Case, the Grand Chamber agreed with the line of reasoning of the Chamber and also found that Turkey had failed to comply with its obligations under Article 34.[51]

2.2.8.3 Practice

In the majority of cases the interim measures are taken seriously by the national authorities. In fact it is only in cases of extreme urgency that interim measures are indicated: the facts must *prima facie* point to a violation of the Convention, and the omission to take the proposed measures must result or threaten to result in irreparable injury to certain vital interests of the parties or to the progress of the examination. Such would be the case, for instance, if an expulsion threatens to constitute a violation of Article 3 of the Convention, in view of a serious risk that the person concerned will be exposed to torture or inhuman treatment or punishment. In that case a stay of expulsion may be requested until the Court has had the opportunity to investigate the case. However, it will do so only if there is a high degree of probability that a violation of Article 3 is likely to occur.[52] This requires that the applicant state his case in a convincing manner and possibly also presents some evidence showing the danger to life or limb to which he may be exposed if expelled or extradited to a particular country. It is not sufficient for the applicant to provide information about the danger or uncertain situation in the country of destination and/or his being an opponent of the ruling Government.

Interim measures cannot only be indicated to the respondent State but also to the applicant. The *Altun* Case concerned a pending extradition from Germany to Turkey. The Commission gave an indication to the German Government to suspend the applicant's extradition until it had had the opportunity to examine the case. The Government complied but urged the Commission to decide quickly as it was no longer possible under German law to keep the applicant in detention pending extradition. The Government maintained that, if released, the applicant would abscond. In these circumstances the Commission gave an indication to the applicant, that if he was released, he should remain at the disposal of the German authorities pending the decision which the Commission was to take at its next session. During the domestic

---

[50]   Judgment of 12 March 2003, para. 241.
[51]   Judgment of 4 February 2005, para. 132.
[52]   Appl. 29966/96, *Venezia v. Italy*, D&R 87, p. 140 (150).

proceedings in this case the applicant committed suicide. The Commission decided that no general interest existed for further examination of the case.[53]

In the *Urrutikoetxea* Case the Commission decided to indicate an interim measure to uphold the expulsion of the applicant until it had had the opportunity to make a more thorough examination of the application. A letter from the applicant's lawyer informed the Commission that the expulsion order had been enforced. The Commission referred to its earlier case law in this respect and held that when a Contracting Party expels an alien from its territory, its responsibility is engaged under Article 3. It declared the application, however, inadmissible noting that the French Government, having taken note of the recommendations made by the European Commission for the Prevention of Torture, Inhuman or Degrading Treatment or Punishment (CPT), considered that there were no substantial grounds for believing that the applicant would be subjected to treatment in Spain contrary to Article 3. Furthermore, the applicant had not suffered any inhuman or degrading treatment since his arrival in Spain.[54]

In the *Soering* Case the applicant argued that, notwithstanding the assurance given to the United Kingdom Government, there was a serious likelihood that he would be sentenced to death if extradited to the United States of America. He maintained that in the circumstances and, in particular, having regard to the 'death row phenomenon', he would thereby be subjected to inhuman and degrading treatment and punishment contrary to Article 3 of the Convention. He also submitted that his extradition to the United States would constitute a violation of Article 6(3)(c), because of the absence of legal aid in the State of Virginia to pursue various appeals. Finally he claimed that, in breach of Article 13, he had no effective remedy under United Kingdom law in respect of his complaint under Article 3. The President of the Commission indicated to the United Kingdom Government, in accordance with Rule 36 [the present Rule 39], that it was desirable, in the interests of the parties and the proper conduct of the proceedings, not to extradite the applicant to the United States until the Commission had had an opportunity to examine the application. This indication was subsequently prolonged by the Commission on several occasions until the case was referred to the Court, which in turn indicated an interim measure.[55]

In the *Nivette* Case the Court even went one step further by applying Rule 36 [the present Rule 39] in a case where an American national ran the risk of being extradited and, according to the applicant, was in danger of having to serve a full life sentence.[56]

---

[53] Report of 7 March 1984, D&R 36 (1984), p. 236 (259-260).
[54] Appl. 31113/96, D&R 87 (1996), p. 151(158). See also Appl. 22742/93, *Aylor-Davis v. France*, D&R 76 (1994), p. 164 (172).
[55] Judgment of 7 July 1989, paras 4 and 77.
[56] Decisions of 14 December 2000 and 3 July 2001, *Nivette*. See also Information Note No. 25, 8-9.

In the *Einhorn* Case, having received information that the applicant had tried to commit suicide, the acting President of the Chamber decided to indicate interim measures, under Rule 39 of the Rules of Court, "in the interests of the proper conduct of the proceedings before the Court". Specifically, the acting President asked the French Government to provide information about the applicant's state of health and not to extradite him prior to 19 July 2001, when a further decision was to be taken. A medical report dated 12 July was sent to the Court by the French Government on 17 July 2001, indicating that the applicant was fit to travel to the US by plane under medical and police supervision. In his application before the Court the applicant complained, among other things, that his extradition was granted despite the risk of his facing the death penalty and being exposed to inhuman and degrading conditions on "death row". However, it appeared from the documents submitted to the Court, in particular from the decision of the *Conseil d'Etat*, that satisfactory assurances had been provided by various US authorities that the applicant would not face the death penalty in any circumstances. Thereupon the Court lifted the interim measure. The applicant was extradited to the United States on the same day. In its decision on admissibility the Court noted that the circumstances of the case and the assurances obtained by the Government were such as to remove the danger of the applicant's being sentenced to death in Pennsylvania. Since, in addition, the decree of 24 July 2000 granting the applicant's extradition expressly provided that "the death penalty may not be sought, imposed or carried out in respect of Ira Samuel Einhorn", the Court considered that the applicant was not exposed to a serious risk of treatment or punishment prohibited under Article 3 of the Convention on account of his extradition to the United States.[57]

In the *Azzouza Rachid* Case the applicant, who was a member of the Islamic Liberation Front (FIS), which was outlawed in Algeria after having won the general elections, alleged that he ran the danger of being maltreated or killed in Algeria upon his deportation. Thereupon, the President of the Commission asked the Belgian State (one day prior to the expulsion) to suspend the implementation of the decision in view of the fact that the person concerned risked losing his life if he were sent back to Algeria. The request was honoured.[58]

In the *Poku* Case the applicant alleged that her deportation posed an immediate threat to her health and the life of her unborn child. The Commission indicated to the United Kingdom that it was desirable in the interests of the parties and the proper conduct of the proceedings before the Commission not to deport the applicant.[59] In the cases of *Ammouche* and *Lenga* an interim measure was given not because the applicants, if extradited, ran the risk of being tortured or losing their lives, but because

---

[57]   Decision of 16 October 2001.
[58]   Appl. 27276/95, D&R 82 A (1995), pp. 156-157.
[59]   Appl. 26985/95.

they were suffering from AIDS and ran the risk of being exposed to a lack of adequate medical treatment and living conditions.[60] In the *Bodika* Case the applicant, an Angolan national, stated that following a failed coup d'Etat led by a Government Minister, who he claimed was his uncle, there had been severe reprisals in his village, in which his mother and sisters were killed. He said that he then joined an Angolan liberation group but was taken prisoner by Government forces, convicted, imprisoned and brutally treated. He succeeded in escaping and entered France in 1983. He was granted political asylum. After various criminal convictions in France his refugee status had been withdrawn in the light of the seriousness of his offences. His application to have the exclusion orders lifted was dismissed. The applicant maintained that if he was sent back to his country of origin, he would be at risk of treatment contrary to Article 3, and requested a Rule 39 indication. The Chamber considered that it was necessary, on the facts, to apply Rule 39.[61]

In the *Jabari* Case the applicant alleged that her expulsion to Iran would constitute a breach of Article 3 of the Convention. She maintained that she risked ill-treatment and death by stoning on account of her adultery. The Commission decided that it was desirable in the interests of the parties and the proper conduct of the proceedings not to return the applicant to Iran until the Commission had had an opportunity to examine the application. It further decided to bring the applicant's complaints under Article 3 of the Convention to the notice of the respondent Government and to invite them to submit written observations on their admissibility and merits.[62] The Court, when dealing with the case, confirmed the application of Rule 39 until further notice.[63]

In the Cases of *Venkadajalasarma* and *Thampibillai* a provisional measure was indicated in response to complaints under Articles 2 and 3 of the Convention that the expulsion of the applicants, Sri Lankan Tamils, to Sri Lanka would expose them to a real risk of death and torture in the hands of the authorities, due to hostilities between the Tamil Tigers and Sri Lankan Government forces. The cases were declared admissible under Article 3 and are still pending.[64]

Recently, in a number of cases an interim measure was indicated against the Netherlands concerning the envisaged expulsion of asylum seekers to Somalia. In one case concerning the expulsion of the applicant via Abu Dhabi, the President asked the Government to submit information on the following issues: 1 the actual situation in Somalia, including UNHCR's most recent view on forced repatriation to that county; and 2 the likelihood of the applicant being sent to Somalia by the Abu Dhabi authorities.[65] In a subsequent case the President had regard to the current situation

---

[60]   Appl. 29481/95, 12 September 1996; App. 30011/96, 25 October 1996.
[61]   Decision of 18 May 1999; See also Decision of 28 June 2001, *Amrollahi*, Information Note 18.
[62]   Decision of 28 October 1999.
[63]   Judgment of 11 July 2000, para. 6.
[64]   Decisions of 9 July 2002.
[65]   Note Verbale of 21 January 2004, 2683/04.

in Northern Somalia and in particular to the absence of an effective public authority capable of providing protection to the applicant, who submitted that he belonged to a minority and had no family or clan ties in Northern Somalia. The President further noted that there was no guarantee that the applicant would be admitted to Northern Somalia.[66] At present, these cases are still pending and the Dutch Government has adhered to the interim measures.

If the expulsion allegedly violates Article 8 of the Convention (respect for family life), an interim measure will not readily be indicated because the damage can easily be reversed by allowing the expelled person's re-entry into the State concerned.

So far there have been only a few situations in which an indication was given in circumstances other than expulsion or extradition. In one case it was deemed necessary by the Commission in order to secure evidence. After the death of three members of the RAF, who had brought claims before the Commission concerning their treatment in prison, the President of the Commission decided that a delegation of the Commission should visit the prison concerned. This visit was intended to examine, on the spot, the conditions in which the applicants had been detained.[67] The other situation arose in the case of *Patane v. Italy*, where the Commission was faced with an application of a person serving a five-year prison sentence. This person was suffering from a severe state of depression and her health was, according to medical certificates, continuously deteriorating to the point where an acute threat to her life existed. In this case the Commission gave an indication to the Italian Government that it was desirable to take at once all necessary measures to preserve the applicant's health, either by transferring her to an institution better suited for her or by granting her provisional release. The Government informed the Commission that the applicant had been released from detention by order of an Italian court. As the applicant subsequently disappeared, the Commission decided to strike the case off its list.[68]

In the *Ilijkov* Case the applicant complained that he was subjected to torture and inhuman and degrading treatment contrary to Article 3. He claimed that the forced feeding during his hunger strike was administered by unqualified personnel through a dirty rubber hose, in a manner which caused violent pain and a sense of helplessness, and represented a serious risk for his life. In particular, according to independent medical advice obtained from the London Medical Foundation for the Care of Victims of Torture, forced feeding administered without qualified medical supervision on persons on hunger strike might result in cardiac arrest and death. The Commission also decided to indicate to the Government of Bulgaria that it was desirable in the

---

[66]   Note Verbale of 3 May 2004, 15243/04.
[67]   Appls 7572/76, 7586/76, 7587/76, *Ensslin, Baader and Raspe v. Federal Republic of Germany*, Yearbook XVIII (1975), p. 132.
[68]   Appl. 11488/85.

interest of the parties and the proper conduct of the proceedings before the Commission that all necessary steps be taken by the Government to preserve the applicant's health. The Commission decided to invite the applicant to stop his hunger strike.[69]

In the *Öcalan* Case the Chamber, which had initially held that it was unnecessary to apply Rule 39, had nonetheless decided, under Rule 54(3)(a), to request the Turkish authorities to clarify a number of points concerning the conditions of the applicant's arrest and detention and had indicated that it considered respect of the applicant's rights to put forward his case both in the criminal proceedings and in the proceedings concerning his application to the Court to be of particular importance. It accordingly sought information about whether the applicant would be permitted to receive assistance by counsel in both sets of proceedings. The Government provided certain information concerning the applicant's detention and the circumstances in which he received a visit from two lawyers. On 4 March 1999 the Court asked the respondent Government to take interim measures within the meaning of Rule 39, with particular regard to compliance with the requirements of Article 6 in the proceedings brought against the applicant in the National Security Court and the effective use by the applicant of his right to lodge an individual petition with the Court through lawyers of his choice. On 23 March 1999 the Court requested the Government to supply further information on particular points concerning the measures taken in application of Rule 39 of the Rules of Court. On 9 April 1999 the legal adviser to the Turkish Permanent Delegation indicated that the Government were not prepared to answer the Court's questions on the ground that these went well beyond the scope of interim measures within the meaning of Rule 39. On 2 July 1999 one of the applicant's representatives asked the Court to request the Government "to suspend execution of the death sentence imposed on 29 June 1999 until the Court [had] decided on the merits of his complaints". On 6 July 1999 the Court decided that the request for application of Rule 39 could be allowed if the applicant's sentence were to be upheld by the Court of Cassation. By a judgment of 25 November 1999 the Court of Cassation dismissed the applicant's appeal on points of law and upheld the judgment of 29 June 1999. On the same day one of the applicant's representatives asked the Court to apply Rule 39 and to request the Government to stay execution of the death sentence imposed on the applicant until the end of the proceedings concerning his application to the Court. On 30 November 1999 the Court decided to indicate to the Government the following interim measure: "The Court requests the respondent Government to take all necessary steps to ensure that the death penalty is not carried out so as to enable the Court to proceed effectively with the examination of the admissibility and merits of the applicant's complaints under the Convention." On 12 January 2000 the Turkish Prime Minister announced that the applicant's file was to be transmitted to the Turkish Grand National Assembly (which is empowered to approve or disapprove

---

[69] Appl. 33977/96.

enforcement of the death penalty) when the proceedings before the Court were over. The application was declared admissible with respect to the complaints under Articles 2, 3, 6 and 34.[70] In its subsequent judgment the Court stated that, in the special circumstances of the case, the Government's refusal to provide the Court with the requested information did not amount to a violation for the following reasons: firstly, the Government had furnished the information later as part of their observations on the admissibility of the application, and secondly and above all, the refusal to supply that information earlier had not prevented the applicant from making out his case on the complaints concerning the criminal proceedings that had been brought against him. Indeed, these complaints, which mainly concerned Article 6, were examined by the Court, which subsequently found a violation. The Court also reiterated in that connection that the information requested from the Government concerned the fairness of the proceedings that could have led to the death penalty imposed on the applicant being carried out. That risk had now effectively disappeared following the abolition of the death penalty in peacetime in Turkey.[71]

An indication under Rule 39 will not be given if it is still possible to apply for domestic remedies with suspensive effect. The Commission has also never given an indication under Rule 36 [the present Rule 39] if in the case of an expulsion or extradition the receiving State was a Member State of the Council of Europe and had recognised the right of individual complaint. Apparently, the Commission was of the opinion that in such a case there was a sufficient guarantee that the Convention – in particular Articles 2, 3, 5 and 6 – would be respected by the receiving State, if necessary through a new application under Article 25 [the present Article 34], this time directed against the latter State.

As regards the manner in which requests under Rule 39 are to be presented, the following points are the most important to be mentioned. Firstly, the request should be submitted as soon as the final domestic decision has been taken, and sufficiently in advance of the execution of the decision, for instance an expulsion order, so that an intervention by the Court is still possible. A certain time is required for the Registry to prepare the case and, when necessary, to communicate with the President of the Chamber. The Chamber or its President should also have sufficient time to obtain information on the matter, for instance by contacting the Agent of the Government to inquire about the Government's intentions. For these reasons, making a preliminary request under Rule 39 pending the decision of the domestic authorities or courts might be advisable.

---

[70]   Decision of 14 December 2000, *Öcalan*.
[71]   Judgment of 12 March 2003, *Öcalan*, paras 241-242.

Secondly, the request must be in writing and should contain the required information. A telephone conversation might serve as an announcement of the request, but it cannot as such set in motion the procedure under Rule 39. On the other hand, communication by e-mail or fax is sufficient provided it contains adequate information. In this connection it is also very important to provide the Chamber with copies of relevant national judgments and decisions showing the arguments which have been put before the domestic authorities and courts and the reasons for the refusal to grant the claim.[72]

2.2.8.4 Urgent notification

According to Rule 40, in case of urgency the Registrar, with the authorisation of the President of the Chamber, may inform the respondent State of the introduction of the application and of a summary of its objects. The purpose of this provision is to prevent surprise on the part of the Contracting State concerned if afterwards any interim measures prove desirable.

2.2.8.5 Case priority

According to Rule 41 of the Rules of Court the Chamber shall deal with applications in the order in which they become ready for examination. It may, however, decide to give priority to a particular application. In the Case of *X v. France* the applicant was a haemophiliac who had undergone several blood transfusions and was discovered to be HIV positive. He started proceedings for indemnity. He lodged his application with the Commission on 19 February 1991, alleging that his case had not been heard within a reasonable time as required under Article 6(1) of the Convention. The Commission found a violation of Article 6(1) on 17 October 1991. The Court was prepared to give priority to the case and delivered its judgment on 31 March 1992, finding a violation of Article 6(1).[73] However, in February 1992 the applicant had died.

In the Case of *D. v. the United Kingdom* the applicant, who suffered from AIDS, maintained that his removal from the United Kingdom to St Kitts would expose him to inhuman and degrading treatment. His case was dealt with by the Court with priority.[74] In a case where the application had been brought by the pretender to the Italian throne, who had been excluded from Italy for fifty-three years, the Court

---

[72] See C.A. Nørgaard and H. Krüger, "Interim and Conservatory Measures under the European System of Protection of Human Rights", in: Manfred Nowak, Dorothea Steurer and Hannes Tretter (eds.), *Progress in the Spirit of Human Rights*, Festschrift für Felix Ermacora, Kehl am Rhein, 1998, pp. 114-115. On this more recently: Yves Haeck and Clara Burbano Herrera, *Interim Measures in the Case Law of the European Court of Human Rights*, NQHR, Vol. 21/4, 2003, pp. 625-675.

[73] Judgment of 31 March 1992.

[74] Judgment of 2 May 1997.

decided that, although the application was unquestionably important, there was no reason to give it priority or, *a fortiori*, to communicate it as a matter of urgency.[75] With respect to the disappearance of two members of a Kurdish political party the Court applied Rule 41.[76] In a case against Moldova and the Russian Federation concerning the responsibility for violations of the Convention in Transdniestria, a region which was separated from Moldova and was under the control of the Russian Federation, the Court decided to give priority to the examination.[77]

The *Pretty* Case concerned an applicant who was dying of motor neurone disease, a degenerative disease affecting the muscles, for which there is no cure. The disease was at an advanced stage and the applicant's life expectancy was very poor. Given that the final stages of the disease were distressing and undignified, she wished to be able to control how and when she would die and be spared suffering and indignity. Although it is not a crime to commit suicide in English law, the applicant was prevented by her disease from taking such a step without assistance. It is, however, a crime to assist another to commit suicide under Section 2 para. 1 of the Suicide Act 1961. Ms Pretty wished to be assisted by her husband, but the Director of Public Prosecutions had refused her request to guarantee her husband freedom from prosecution if he did so. Her appeals against that decision were unsuccessful. The applicant complained of a violation amongst others of Articles 2 and 3 of the Convention. The application was registered on 18 January 2002. On 22 January 2002 the Court decided to apply Rule 41 and to give the case priority, and to apply Rule 40 concerning an urgent notification to the application to the Respondent Government. On 29 April 2002 the Court gave its judgment in the case and found no violation of the Convention.[78] Ms Pretty died afterwards in a natural way.

2.2.9   THE ADMISSIBILITY CONDITIONS

Two of the admissibility conditions set forth in the Convention apply to applications submitted by States as well as to those submitted by individuals. These are the condition that all remedies within the legal system of the respondent State must have been exhausted before the case is submitted to the Court, and the condition that the application must have been submitted within a period of six months from the date on which the final national decision was taken (Article 35(1)). For the admissibility of an individual application additional requirements are that the application is not anonymous; that the application is not substantially the same as a matter that has

---

[75]   Appl. 53360/99, *VittorioEmanuele Di Savoia v. Italy*, Information Note 16.
[76]   Appl. 65899/01, *Tanis and Deniz v. Turkey*, Information Note 27.
[77]   Decision of 4 July 2001, *Ilaşcu, Leşco, Ivanşoc and Petrov-Popa*.
[78]   Judgment of 29 April 2002 , para. 42.

already been examined by the Court or has already been submitted to another procedure of international investigation or settlement and contains no relevant new information; that the application is not incompatible with the provisions of the Convention or the Protocols thereto; that the application is not manifestly ill-founded; and that the application does not constitute an abuse of the right to lodge an application (Article 35(2) and (3)).

Paragraph 4 of Article 35 provides that the Court may reject an application which it considers inadmissible under this Article at any stage of the proceedings. Thus, it may do so also after having declared the case admissible at an earlier stage. This competence of the Court resembles the competence of the former Commission under Article 29 (old) to reject a case if in the course of the examination of a petition it found that the existence of one of the grounds for non-acceptance had been established.

Strictly speaking, one ought to differentiate between applications which are inadmissible and applications falling outside the competence of the Court, even though the Convention does not provide a clear basis for such a distinction. Applications by States may only be rejected on the grounds mentioned in Article 35(1), and not on the ground of incompatibility with the Convention mentioned in Article 35(2), a ground on which the Commission sometimes rejected individual applications with respect to which it had no jurisdiction.[79] All the same, it is evident that applications by States may also fall outside the jurisdiction of the Court, for instance when the application relates to a period in which the Convention was not yet binding upon the respondent State. The Court will have to reject such an application, but in this case, properly speaking, on account of lack of jurisdiction, not on account of inadmissibility, the grounds for which are enumerated exhaustively in the Convention. The practice concerning individual applications, however, shows that the Court usually rejects applications outside its competence *ratione personae*, *ratione materiae*, *ratione loci*, or *ratione temporis* on account of inadmissibility. That is why issues relating to the jurisdiction of the Court will here be discussed under the heading of admissibility conditions.

In practice the Court applies a particular sequence in the admissibility conditions by reference to which an application is examined. This sequence is based partly on logical and partly on practical grounds. But on the ground of practical considerations the case law of the Court diverges from this sequence on numerous occasions. The use of the so-called 'global formula' is especially striking.[80] The Court uses this formula for rejecting an application, which contains various separate complaints, as a whole on account of its manifestly ill-founded character, although the separate complaints

---

[79]   See, *e.g.*, Appl. 473/59, *I. v. Austria*, Yearbook II (1958-1959), p. 400 (406) and Appl. 1452/62, *X v. Austria*, Yearbook VI (1963), p. 268 (276).

[80]   This is often formulated as follows: 'An examination by the Court of this complaint as it has been submitted does not disclose any appearance of a violation of the rights and freedoms set out in the Convention.'

might be inadmissible on different grounds. The Court bases this approach on the fact that it does not consider it necessary in such a case to make a detailed examination of the separate elements of the application. Although according to Article 45, paragraph 1, reasons must be given for judgments in which an application is declared admissible or inadmissible, the Explanatory Report points out that such reasons can be given in summary form.[81]

Protocol No. 14, once it has entered into force, might change the procedure considerably. This Protocol will introduce a new admissibility criterion to the criteria laid down in Article 35. Paragraph 3 of Article 35 will be amended and read as follows:

> The Court shall declare inadmissible any individual application submitted under Article 34 if it considers that:
> a   the application is incompatible with the provisions of the Convention or the Protocols thereto, manifestly ill-founded, or an abuse of the right of individual application; or
> b   the applicant has not suffered a significant disadvantage, unless respect for human rights as defined in the Convention and the Protocols thereto requires an examination of the application on the merits and provided that no case may be rejected on this ground which has not been duly considered by a domestic tribunal.

This new admissibility requirement provides the Court with an additional tool which should assist it in concentrating on cases which warrant an examination on the merits, by empowering it to declare inadmissible applications where the applicant has not suffered any significant disadvantage, and which in terms of respect for human rights do not otherwise require an examination on the merits by the Court. Furthermore, the new admissibility criterion contains an explicit exception to ensure that it does not lead to the rejection of cases which have not been duly considered by a domestic tribunal. In the *Explanatory Report to Protocol No. 14* it is stressed that the new criterion does not restrict the right of individuals to apply to the Court or alter the principle that all individual applications are examined on their admissibility. While the Court alone is competent to interpret the new admissibility requirement and decide on its application, its terms should ensure that rejection of cases requiring an examination on the merits is avoided. The latter will notably include cases which, notwithstanding their trivial nature, raise serious questions affecting the application or interpretation of the Convention or important questions concerning national law.[82]

The new criterion is meant as a tool for the Court in its filtering capacity. It was introduced in Protocol No. 14 to allow the Court to devote more time to cases which warrant examination on the merits. Its introduction was considered necessary in view of the ever increasing caseload of the Court. According to the *Explanatory Report to*

---

[81]   *Explanatory Report to Protocol No. 11*, para 105.
[82]   *Explanatory Report to Protocol No. 14*, CETS 194, para. 39.

Protocol No. 14 it was necessary to give the Court some degree of flexibility in addition to that already provided for by the existing admissibility criteria. The interpretation of these criteria has been established in the case law that has been developed over several decades and is, therefore, difficult to change. It further pointed out that it is very likely that the numbers of individual applications to the Court will continue to increase, up to a point where other measures set out in this Protocol may well prove insufficient to prevent the Convention system from becoming totally paralysed and unable to fulfil its central mission of providing legal protection of human rights at the European level, thus rendering the right of individual application illusory in practice.[83]

In our opinion the new criterion may have a filtering effect only after the Court has developed clear-cut jurisprudential criteria of an objective character capable of straightforward application. The terms 'has not suffered a significant disadvantage' are open to interpretation. Like many other terms used in the Convention, they are legal terms capable of, and indeed requiring, interpretation establishing objective criteria through gradual development of the case law of the Court. Moreover, even in a case where the applicant has not suffered any significant disadvantage, the application will not be declared inadmissible if respect for human rights as defined in the Convention or the Protocols thereto requires an examination on the merits.[84] This exception also requires clear and objective criteria. Furthermore, it will never be possible for the Court to reject an application on account of its trivial nature if the case has not been duly considered by a domestic tribunal.[85] It might be questioned if this element of subsidiarity could ever be applied in a consistent and well-balanced way, given the considerable differences between the domestic legal systems and judicial practices of the High Contracting Parties. In any case it is to be expected that examination of whether this exception clause does apply, will require a thorough examination of the part of the file concerning domestic proceedings, and consequently reduce the gain of time that the application of the new admissibility criteria is meant to produce. On the other hand, the psychological costs on the part of the applicant of seeing his or her application being declared inadmissible for lack of significant disadvantage should not be underestimated.

It may be expected that it will take quite some time before the Court's Chambers and Grand Chamber will have developed case law in so-called 'pilot cases'. From the wording of articles 27 and 28 it may be clear that single-judge formations and Committees will not be able to apply the new criterion in absence of such guidance. The drafters of Protocol No. 14 were rather optimistic about the time needed to examine sufficient "pilot cases", since in Article 20(2), second sentence, single-judge

---

[83]   *Ibidem*, para. 78.
[84]   Compare with Article 37(1) of the Convention.
[85]   *Explanatory Report to Protocol No. 14*, CETS 194, paras 81-82.

formations and Committees will be prevented from applying the new criterion for a period of two years following the entry into force of Protocol No. 14. According to the transitional rule set out in Article 20(2), first sentence, the new admissibility criterion may not be applied to applications declared admissible before the entry into force of Protocol No. 14.

Protocol No. 14 will also amend Article 38 of the Convention, which according to its wording was intended to apply after a case had been declared admissible. In its new wording the text will read as follows:

> The Court shall examine the case together with the representatives of the parties and, if need be, undertake an investigation, for the effective conduct of which the High Contracting Parties concerned shall furnish all necessary facilities.

The changes are intended to allow the Court to examine cases together with the Parties' representatives, and to undertake an investigation, not only when the decision on admissibility has been taken, but at any stage of the proceedings. Since this provision even applies before the decision on admissibility has been taken, High Contracting Parties are required to provide the Court with all necessary facilities prior to that decision. Any problem which the Court might encounter in this respect can be brought to the attention of the Committee of Ministers so that the latter can take any step it deems necessary.[86]

The separate admissibility conditions are discussed here in the sequence referred to above.

2.2.10 THE OBLIGATION TO EXHAUST DOMESTIC REMEDIES

2.2.10.1 General

Article 35(1) provides:

> The Court may only deal with the matter after all domestic remedies have been exhausted, according to the generally recognised rules of international law, and within a period of six months from the date on which the final decision was taken.

This is the so-called rule of the 'exhaustion of local remedies' (épuisement des voies de recours internes) (hereafter: the local remedies rule), which is to be regarded as a general rule of international procedural law.

---

[86] Ibidem, para 90.

It should be mentioned at the outset that the local remedies rule does not apply to procedures for affording satisfaction under Article 41 of the Convention.[87] In fact such procedures do not ensue from a new application, but constitute a continuation of the original application after a violation has been found by the Court. Questions of admissibility are not involved here at all.[88] Article 35(1) refers expressly to the general rules of international law in the matter, and in its case law the Commission was indeed frequently guided by international judicial and arbitral decisions with respect to this rule. It, for instance, referred expressly to the judgment of the International Court of Justice in the *Interhandel* Case concerning the rationale of the local remedies rule.[89] In the *Nielsen* Case the Commission formulated this rationale as follows: "The Respondent State must first have an opportunity to redress by its own means within the framework of its own domestic legal system the wrong alleged to have been done to the individual."[90]

In the *Akdivar* Case the Court recalled that the rule of exhaustion of domestic remedies obliges those seeking to bring their case against the State before an international judicial or arbitral organ to use first the remedies provided by the national legal system. Consequently, States are dispensed from answering before an international body for their acts before they have had an opportunity to put matters right through their own legal systems. The rule is based on the assumption, reflected in Article 13 of the Convention – with which it has close affinity – that there is an effective remedy available in respect of the alleged breach in the domestic system whether or not the provisions of the Convention are incorporated in national law. In this way it is an important aspect of the principle that the machinery of protection established by the Convention is subsidiary to the national systems safeguarding human rights.[91]

The local remedies rule applies in principle to applications by States as well as to individual applications. This ensues from the wording of Article 35(2) and (3) as compared to that of Article 35(1). The second and third paragraphs of Article 35 expressly declare the admissibility conditions mentioned therein to be applicable only to applications lodged under Article 34, while the first paragraph of Article 35, where the local remedies rule is laid down, is formulated in a general way and is, therefore, also applicable to applications by States. The same conclusion flows from the fact that the local remedies rule is a general rule of international procedural law.

---

[87] On this, see *infra* 2.6.2.

[88] Judgment of 10 March 1972, *De Wilde, Ooms and Versyp* (*'Vagrancy'* Cases), para 16.

[89] *ICJ Reports*, 1959, p. 6 (27).

[90] Appl. 343/57, *Schouw Nielsen v. Denmark*, Yearbook II (1958-1959), p. 412 (438). See also Appl. 5964/72, *X v. Federal Republic of Germany*, D&R 3 (1976), p. 57 (60); Appl. 12945/87, *Hatjianastasiou v. Greece*, D&R 65 (1990), p. 173 (177); judgment of 20 September 1993, *Saïdi*, para 38.

[91] Judgment of 16 September 1996, para. 65; judgment of 18 December 1996, *Aksoy*, para.51; judgment of 27 June 2000, *Ilhan*, para. 61; judgment of 14 May 2002, *Şenmse Öner*, para. 77; judgment of 26 July 2002, *Horvath*, para. 37.

While in the case of an individual application the local remedies must have been exhausted by the applicant himself, with respect to applications by States the rule implies that the local remedies must have been exhausted by those individuals in respect to whom, according to the allegation of the applicant State, the Convention has been violated.[92]

In the *Pfunders* Case Austria submitted that, since the right of complaint of States is based on the principle of the collective guarantee and the public interest, and since an applicant State need not prove that an injury has been sustained, the local remedies rule does not hold for States.[93] The Commission, however, rejected this line of reasoning by referring to the terms of Articles 26 and 27 [the present Article 35 (1), (2) and (3)], and held that the principle on which the local remedies rule is based should be applied *a fortiori* in an international system which affords protection not only to the applicant State's own nationals, but to everyone who is in one way or another subject to the jurisdiction of the respondent State.[94] By this statement the Commission confirmed its earlier point of view in the second *Cyprus* Case.[95] The Court followed this approach.[96]

The local remedies rule is not an admissibility condition of an *absolute* character. In the *Aksoy* Case the Court held that the rule of exhaustion is neither absolute nor capable of being applied automatically.[97] On the basis of the reference in Article 35(1) to the 'generally recognised rules of international law', this rule is applied with flexibility.[98] One point of departure is that each concrete case should be judged 'in the light of its particular facts'.[99] According to the Court this means, amongst other things, that it must take realistic account not only of the existence of formal remedies in the legal system of the Contracting Party concerned but also of the general legal and political context in which they operate, as well as the personal circumstances of the applicants.[100] In this respect the Court noted in the *Akdivar* Case that "the situation

---

[92]   The condition applies in international law only when the action of a State is concerned with the treatment of individuals. If a State puts forward its own legal position, the condition is not applied, since as a rule a State cannot be subjected against its will to the jurisdiction of another State.

[93]   Appl. 788/60, Yearbook IV (1961), p. 116 (146-148); judgment of 2 September 1998, *Yasa v. Turkey*, para. 64; judgment of 27 June 2000, *Ilhan* , para 51.

[94]   Ibidem, pp. 148-152. See also Appls 6780/74 and 6950/75, *Cyprus v. Turkey*, Yearbook XVIII (1975), p. 82 (100).

[95]   Appl. 299/57, Yearbook II (1958-1959), p. 186 (190-196).

[96]   See the judgment of 10 May 2001, *Cyprus v. Turkey*, para 102.

[97]   Judgment of 18 December 1996, para. 53; judgment of 28 July 1999, *Selmouni*, para. 77.

[98]   The Court has frequently stated that Article 35 must be applied with some degree of flexibility and without excessive formalism. See *e.g.* judgment of 19 March 1991, *Cardot*, para. 36; judgment of 16 September 1996, *Akdivar*, para. 69; judgment of 29 August 1997, *Worm*, para 33; judgment of 27 June 2000, *Ilhan*, para. 51.

[99]   Appl. 343/57, *Schouw Nielsen v. Denmark*, Yearbook II (1958-1959), p. 412 (442-444).

[100]   Judgment of 16 September 1996, *Akdivar*, para. 69.

existing in South-East Turkey at the time of the applicants' complaints was – and continued to be – characterised by significant civil strife due to the campaign of terrorist violence waged by the PKK and the counter-insurgency measures taken by the Government in response to it. In such a situation it must be recognised that there may be obstacles to the proper functioning of the system of the administration of justice. In particular, the difficulties in securing probative evidence for the purposes of domestic legal proceedings, inherent in such a troubled situation, may make the pursuit of judicial remedies futile and the administrative inquiries on which such remedies depend may be prevented from taking place."[101]

2.2.10.2 Measures and practices to which the local remedies rule does not apply

2.2.10.2.1 Inter-State complaints

The rule does not apply when a State brings up the legislation or administrative practice of another State without the complaint being related to one or more concrete persons as victims of this legislation or administrative practice (the so-called 'abstract' complaints). In such a case individuals are not required to have exhausted the local remedies, while the applicant State itself cannot be expected to institute proceedings before the national authorities of the respondent State. An example is the first *Cyprus* Case where Greece submitted that a number of emergency acts which were in force in Cyprus at that time conflicted with the provisions of the Convention. In this case the Commission decided that "the provision of Article 26 [the present Article 35(1)] concerning the exhaustion of domestic remedies (...) does not apply to the present application, the scope of which is to determine the compatibility with the Convention of legislative measures and administrative practices in Cyprus."[102]

Later case law concerning inter-State applications has confirmed this position.[103] According to the case law an administrative practice comprises two elements: repetition of acts and official tolerance. The first element is defined as: "an accumulation of identical or analogous breaches which are sufficiently numerous and interconnected to amount not merely to isolated incidents or exceptions but to a pattern or system."[104] By official tolerance it is meant that "though acts of torture or ill-treatment are plainly

---

[101]   *Ibidem*, para. 70; See also judgment of 28 November 1997, *Mentes and Others*, para. 58; judgment of 30 January 2001, *Dulas*, para. 45; judgment of 8 January 2004, *Ayder*, para. 89.

[102]   Appl. 176/56, *Greece v. the United Kingdom*, Yearbook II (1958-1959), p. 182 (184).

[103]   See, *e.g.*, Appl. 5310/71, *Ireland v. the United Kingdom*, Yearbook XV (1972), p. 76 (242); Appl. 4448/70, *Second Greek* Case, Yearbook XIII (1970), p. 108 (134-136); and Appls 9940-9944/82, *France, Norway, Denmark, Sweden and the Netherlands v. Turkey*, D&R 35 (1984), p. 143 (162-163); Appl. 25781/94 *Cyprus v. Turkey*, D&R 86A p. 104(138). See also the judgment of 16 September 1996, *Akdivar*, para. 67.

[104]   Judgment of 18 January 1978, *Ireland v. the United Kingdom*, para 159; judgment of 16 September 1996, *Akdivar*, para. 67.

illegal, they are tolerated in the sense that the superiors of those immediately responsible, though cognisant of such acts, take no action to punish them or to prevent
their repetition; or that a higher authority, in face of numerous allegations, manifests
indifference by refusing any adequate investigation of their truth or falsity, or that in
judicial proceedings a fair hearing of such complaints is denied."[105] In the Case of
France, Norway, Denmark, Sweden and the Netherlands v. Turkey the Commission
added that for it to reach the conclusion that there was no official tolerance, "any
action taken by the higher authority must be on a scale which is sufficient to put an
end to the repetition of acts or to interrupt the pattern or system."[106]

A condition is always that the applicant State should give 'substantial evidence'
of the existence of the national legislation or administrative practice concerned. This
requirement of 'substantial evidence' may take on a different meaning depending on
whether the admissibility stage or the examination of the merits is concerned. According to the Commission: "The question whether the existence of an administrative
practice is established or not can only be determined after an examination of the
merits. At the stage of admissibility *prima facie* evidence, while required, must also
be considered as sufficient. (...) There is *prima facie* evidence of an alleged administrative practice where the allegations concerning individual cases are sufficiently substantiated, considered as a whole and in the light of the submissions of the applicant
and the respondent Party. It is in this sense that the term 'substantial evidence' is to
be understood."[107] If the applicant State does not succeed in doing so, the local remedies rule applies.

2.2.10.2.2   Individual complaints

In the case of individual applicants there can be no question of a completely abstract
complaint about an administrative practice. The applicant must submit that he is the
victim of the alleged violation, which means that he is at the same time the person who
must have exhausted all available local remedies.

When an applicant submitted that no local remedy had been available to him,
because his complaint concerned the compatibility of Belgian divorce legislation with
the Convention, the Commission decided that nothing had prevented him from
submitting this question to the Belgian Court of Cassation.[108] And in the case of an
application against the Netherlands concerning the discriminatory character of fiscal
legislation with respect to married women, the Commission pointed out that the
applicant could have submitted the question of the compatibility of the challenged

---

105   Report of 5 November 1969, *Greek* Case, Yearbook XII (1969), p. 196.
106   Appl. 9940-9944/82, D&R 35 (1984), p. 143 (164).
107   *Ibidem*, pp. 164-165.
108   Appl. 1488/62, *X v. Belgium*, Coll. 13 (1964), p. 93 (96).

provisions with the Convention, under (the then) Article 66 of the Dutch Constitution, to the Dutch courts.[109] Both applications were declared inadmissible under Article 26 [the present Article 35(1)].[110] It may be assumed that the Court will take a similar position when, in the case of an application by a State, certain legislation or an administrative practice is submitted for review, but the complaint at the same time concerns concrete persons to whom an effective and adequate local remedy is available. The latter must than have exhausted these remedies.

As has been mentioned above, however, a legislative measure or administrative practice may indeed be challenged by an individual applicant, provided that he proves satisfactorily that he himself is the victim of it. A legislative measure or administrative practice may be of such a nature as to justify the presumption that the remedies of the State in question offer no prospects of effective redress. This is clearly the case if the situation complained of specifically involves the absence of an effective judicial remedy required by one of the provisions of the Convention. Thus, in *G. v. Belgium* the Commission concluded that "as far as Article 5(4) is concerned, the question of exhaustion of domestic remedies does not arise." The reason, according to the Commission, was "that Belgian law does not provide for a judicial remedy which would make it possible to take a speedy decision as to the lawfulness of the detention of a person placed at the Government's disposal." The procedures referred to by the Belgian Government did not fulfil the requirement of effectiveness.[111]

Ineffectiveness of remedies may particularly occur in the case of practices of torture and inhuman treatment. On that ground, in the *Donnelly* Case the Commission took the view that in such a situation the local remedies rule is not applicable, provided that the applicant gives *prima facie* evidence that such a practice has occurred and that he was the victim of it.[112] Unlike in the above-mentioned inter-State applications here the rule is not inapplicable because the application is assumed to have an abstract character, but as a result of the principle, also recognised in general international law, that remedies which in advance are certain not to be effective or adequate need not be exhausted.[113] This became quite clear when in the next stage of the same *Donnelly*

---

[109] Appl. 2780/66, *X v. the Netherlands* (not published).

[110] The two applications mentioned were rejected on the ground of Article 35(1), but might also have been declared inadmissible on the ground of Article 35(3). In both cases the applicants had not submitted that they were victims of the alleged violation, so that these cases in reality concerned completely abstract complaints, which the Commission usually rejected on account of incompatibility with the provisions of the Convention.

[111] Appl. 9107/80, D&R 33 (1983), p. 76 (79).

[112] Appls 5577-5583/72, Yearbook XVI (1973), p. 212 (262). See also the report of the Commission of 5 November 1969 in the *Greek* Case, Yearbook XII (1969), p. 194. Cf. Appls 9911/82 and 9945/82, *R, S, A and C v. Portugal*, D&R 36 (1984), p. 200 (207), in which the Commission stated that the applicant must provide detailed allegations, if the remedy is to be considered ineffective.

[113] For this principle, see with respect to inter-State applications Appl. 299/57, *Greece v. the United Kingdom*, Yearbook II (1958-1959), p. 186 (192-194), and with respect to individual applications Appl. 5493/72, *Handyside v. the United Kingdom*, Yearbook XVII (1974), p. 228 (288-290).

Case the Commission, quite unexpectedly, on the basis of its examination of the facts concluded that effective possibilities of redress were indeed present, and on that ground, by applying former Article 29, declared the application inadmissible because the local remedies rule had not been complied with.[114] A given administrative practice may, therefore, give rise to the presumption that the local remedies are not effective, but whether that is indeed the case is a question subject to investigation by the Strasbourg organs.[115]

Several cases have been submitted by Kurdish citizens alleging that an administrative practice existed on the part of the Turkish authorities of tolerating abuses of human rights in relation to persons in police custody.[116] In one case an applicant had been killed following the submission of his application to the Commission and there were indications that to pursue the available remedies might have entailed serious risks for other applicants. The Commission held that in these circumstances it was not necessary to resolve the question if an administrative practice existed, because the applicants had done all that could be expected in the circumstances in relation to the local remedies. In the *Aksoy* Case the Commission noted the applicant's declaration that he had told the public prosecutor that he had been tortured. Moreover, when asked to sign a statement, he had answered that he could not sign because he could not move his hands. Although it was found that it was not possible to establish in detail what had happened during the applicant's meeting with the public prosecutor, the Commission found no reason to doubt that during their conversation there were elements which should have made the public prosecutor initiate an investigation or, at the very least, try to obtain further information from the applicant about his state of health or about the treatment to which he had been subjected. The Commission further noted that, after his detention, the applicant was in a vulnerable position, if he had, as he stated, been subjected to torture during his detention. The threats to which the applicant claimed to have been exposed after he had complained to the Commission, as well as his tragic death in circumstances which had not been fully clarified, were further elements which could at least support the view that the pursuance of remedies was not devoid of serious risks. The applicant could be said to have complied with the domestic remedies rule.[117] The Court accepted the facts as they had been established by the Commission and, on that basis, held that these constituted special circumstances

---

[114] Appls 5577-5583/72, Yearbook XIX (1976), p. 84 (248-254).

[115] Cf. also Appl. 9471/81, *X and Y v. the United Kingdom*, D&R 36 (1984), p. 49 (61). Here the Commission simply concluded that, since there was no dispute between the parties as far as compliance with Article 26 was concerned, it was not necessary to go into the question of whether Article 26 was inapplicable in the present case because of the existence of a State practice.

[116] Appl. 21987/93, *Aksoy v. Turkey*, D&R 79-A (1994), p. 60 (70-71); Appl. 21893/93, *Akdivar v. Turkey*; Appl. 21895/93, *Çagirga*.

[117] Appl. 21987/93, *Aksoy v. Turkey*, D&R 79-A (1994), p. 60 (70-71).

which absolved Mr Aksoy from the obligation to exhaust the local remedies. Having reached that conclusion the Court did not find it necessary to pronounce on whether an administrative practice existed obstructing applications being made.[118]

On an earlier occasion three applicants who had been placed in police custody, suspected of an offence coming within the jurisdiction of the State Security Council, alleged violations of Article 3 in that they were subjected to torture while held incommunicado in police custody. The Commission held that the Government had not mentioned any domestic remedy available to the applicants with regard to their detention incommunicado by the police as such. Apparently this particular form of detention was an administrative practice.[119] In the *Akdivar* Case the applicants maintained their allegations before the Court, which they had already made before the Commission, that the destruction of their homes was part of a State-inspired policy. That policy, in their submissions, was tolerated, condoned and possibly ordered by the highest authorities in the State aimed at massive population displacement in the emergency region of South-East Turkey. There was thus an administrative practice which rendered any remedies illusory, inadequate and ineffective. The Court concluded that there were special circumstances absolving the applicants from the obligation to exhaust their domestic remedies. The Court also emphasised that its ruling was confined to the particular circumstances of that case. It was not to be interpreted as a general statement that remedies were ineffective in that area of Turkey.[120]

2.2.10.3 Available remedies; procedural requirements

In connection with the local remedies rule it is first of all important to know what remedies are available. That question is to be answered on the basis of national law. It is for the respondent State to introduce any objection that the applicant has not exhausted domestic remedies[121] and to meet the burden of proving the existence of available and sufficient domestic remedies.[122] The respondent State also has the burden of proving that the existing remedies are effective, albeit only in cases where there is 'serious doubt'.[123]

---

[118] Judgment of 18 December 1996, paras 55-57.
[119] Appls 16311/90 and 16313/90, *Hazar and Acik v. Turkey*, D&R 72 (1992), p. 200 (208).
[120] Judgment of 16 September 1996, para. 77.
[121] Appl. 9120/80, *Unterpertinger v. Austria*, D&R 33 (1983), p. 80 (83); Appl. 25006/94, *I.S. v. Slovak Republic*, D&R 88-A, p. 34 (39); judgment of 28 July 1999, *Selmouni*, para. 76.
[122] Appl. 9013/80, *Farrel v. the United Kingdom*, D&R 30 (1983), p. 96 (101-102); Judgment of 9 December 1994, *Stran Greek Refineries and Stratis Andreadis*, para. 35; judgment of 16 September 1996, *Akdivar*, para. 68; judgment of 20 February 2003, *Djavit*, para. 29.
[123] Appls 8805/79 and 8806/79, *De Jong and Baljet v. the Netherlands*, D&R 24 (1981), p. 144 (150); Judgment of 16 September 1996, *Akdtvar*, para. 68; judgment of 29 June 2004, *Dogan and Others*, para. 102.

No definition of the term 'remedy' is to be found in the case law. In various places there are, however, indications as to its meaning. The concept of 'remedy' in any event does not cover those procedures in which one does not claim a right, but attempts to obtain a favour. Examples are the action for rehabilitation in Belgium,[124] the so-called 'petition to the Queen' in England,[125] the right of petition under Article 5 of the Dutch Constitution,[126] application to the Principal State Counsel at the Court of Cassation in Turkey,[127] and request for supervisory review.[128]

It is not only the *judicial* remedies which must be sought, but every remedy available under national law which may lead to a decision that is binding on the authorities,[129] including the possibility of appeal to administrative bodies, provided that the remedy concerned is adequate and effective. In a case concerning the nationalisation of *Yarrow Shipbuilders* under the British Aircraft and Shipbuilding Industries Act 1977, the Commission had to face the question of whether the reference of a dispute on compensation to an arbitration tribunal provided for in the 1977 Act constituted an effective remedy to be exhausted. According to the Commission the tribunal had jurisdiction to determine the amount of compensation under the statutory formula, but did not sit as a tribunal of appeal pronouncing on the adequacy of the offers made in the negotiations by the Secretary of State. It thus represented an alternative means of assessing the compensation due under the statutory formula, if agreement as to the appropriate amount could not be reached. As the substance of the applicant company's complaint was not that it received less than the Act entitled it to, but that the very nature of the statutory compensation formula was such that it inevitably failed to reflect the company's proper value, the Commission held that resort to arbitration would not have constituted an effective and sufficient remedy.[130]

The question of whether extraordinary remedies must also have been sought cannot be answered in a general way.[131] In the *Nielsen* Case the Commission required such exhaustion, insofar as this could be expected to produce an effective and adequate result. It must be decided for each individual case whether the remedy is effective and adequate. The Commission considered an application to the Special Court of Revision as a remedy that should be exhausted.[132] In subsequent case law, however, applications for reopening of the proceedings were not regarded as 'domestic remedies' in the sense

---

[124]   Appl. 214/56, *De Becker v. Belgium*, Yearbook II (1958-1959), p. 214 (236-238).

[125]   Appl. 299/57, *Greece v. the United Kingdom*, Yearbook II (1958-1959), p. 186 (192).

[126]   See the report of the Budget Committee for Foreign Affairs of the Dutch Parliament, Yearbook II (1958-1959), p. 566.

[127]   Judgment of 28 October 1998, *Çiraklar*, paras 29-32.

[128]   Decision of 8 February 2001, *Pitkevich*.

[129]   Appl. 332/57, *Lawless v. Ireland*, Yearbook II (1958-1959), p. 308 (322-324); judgment of 29 July 1999, *Selmouni*, para. 75.

[130]   Appl. 9266/81, *Yarrow P.L.C. and Others v. the United Kingdom*, D&R 30 (1983), p. 155 (188-190).

[131]   Appl. 20471/92, *Kustannus Oy Vapaa Ajattelija and Others v. Finland*, D&R 85 A (1996), p. 29(39).

[132]   Appl. 343/57, Yearbook II (1958-1959), p. 412 (438-442).

of Article 26 [the present Article 35(1)] of the Convention,[133] unless it was established under domestic law that such a request in fact constituted an effective remedy.[134] An application for retrial or similar extraordinary remedies cannot, as a general rule, be taken into account for the purpose of applying Article 35 of the Convention.[135]

When the applicant has sought an apparently effective remedy in vain, he cannot be required to try others which may be available but are probably ineffective.[136] Moreover, for a remedy to be considered effective it must be capable of directly remedying the situation complained of.[137]

With respect to the way in which and the time-limits within which proceedings must be instituted, national law is decisive. If in his appeal to a national court an applicant has failed to observe the procedural requirements or the time-limits, and his case accordingly has been rejected, the local remedies rule has not been complied with and his application is declared inadmissible.[138] However, non-exhaustion of domestic remedies cannot be held against the applicant if in spite of the latter's failure to observe the forms prescribed by law, the competent authority nevertheless examined the appeal.[139] It may be necessary for the applicant to call in the assistance of counsel to correctly exhaust the local remedies, if national law requires this.[140]

In some legal systems, such as that of Italy, individuals have no direct access to the constitutional court; they are dependent on a decision of the ordinary court to refer the issue of constitutionality of a specific law to the constitutional court. In such a case, according to the Commission, the individual applicant is required to have raised the question of that constitutionality in the proceedings before the ordinary court. If he has not done so, he cannot claim that he had no access to the constitutional court.[141]

The interpretation and application of the relevant provisions of national law in principle belong to the competence of the national authorities concerned. The Court, on the other hand, is competent to judge whether, as a result of such an interpretation

---

[133] See, *e.g.*, Appl. 2385/64, *X v. Norway*, Coll. 22 (1967), p. 85 (88). In a case which was practically identical to the *Nielsen* Case, with regard to the future the Commission expressly left open the question of whether a petition to the Danish Special Court of Revision constitutes an effective remedy: Appl. 4311/69, *X v. Denmark*, Yearbook XIV (1971), p. 280 (316-320); Appl. 23949/94 *Pufler v. France* D&R 77 B, (1994) p. 140 (142).
[134] Appl. 19117/91, *K. S. and K. S. AG v. Switzerland*, D&R 78-A (1994), p. 70 (74).
[135] Decision of 22 June 1999, *Tumilovich;* decision of 29 January 2004, *Berdzehnishvili.*
[136] Appl. 9248/81, *Leander v. Sweden*, D&R 34 (1983), p. 78 (33); Appl. 14838/89, *A. v. France*, D&R 69 (1991), p. 286 (302); decision of 25 April 2002, *Günaydin;* decision of 29 April 2004, *Moreira Barbosa.*
[137] Appl. 11660/85, *X v. Portugal*, D&R 59 (1983), p. 85 (92); judgment of 16 September 1996, *Akdivar*, para. 66; judgment of 28 July 1999, *Selmouni*, para. 66.
[138] See, *e.g.*, Appl. 2854/66, *X and Y v. Austria*, Coll. 26 (1968), p. 46 (53-54).
[139] Appl. 12784/87, *Huber v. Switzerland*, D&R 57 (1988), p. 251 (259).
[140] Appl. 6878/75, *Le Compte v. Belgium*, Yearbook XX (1977), p. 254 (274).
[141] See Appl. 6452/74, *Sacchi v. Italy*, D&R 5 (1976), p. 43 (51).

or application, the applicant has become the victim of a denial of justice. In the *Akdivar* Case the Court held that this means, amongst other things, that it must take realistic account not only of the existence of formal remedies in the legal system of the Contracting Party concerned, but also of the general legal and political context in which they operate, as well as the personal circumstances of the applicants.[142]

A question which for a long time had been left undecided in the case law is what an applicant should do when different remedies are open to him. Must he pursue them all, or may he confine himself to bringing the action which in his view is most likely to be successful? The text of Article 35(1) appears to suggest the former, because it refers to 'all domestic remedies'. The Commission, in a 1974 decision, seemed to take a less stringent approach. It held that, where there is a single remedy it should be pursued up to the highest level. The position is not so certain where the domestic law provides a number of different remedies. In such cases the Commission tends to admit that Article 26 [the present Article 35(1)] has been complied with if the applicant exhausts only the remedy or remedies which are reasonably likely to prove effective.[143] In a later case the Commission added: "Where (...) there is a choice of remedies open to the applicant to redress an alleged violation of the Convention, Article 26 [the present Article 35(1)] of the Convention must be applied to reflect the practical realities of the applicant's position in order to ensure the effective protection of the rights and freedoms guaranteed by the Convention."[144]

In the *Airey* Case the Court held that it was primarily for the applicant to select which legal remedy to pursue.[145] It is up to the applicant in those cases to indicate which remedy he has chosen and for what reasons. These grounds have to be objective and reasonable.[146]

2.2.10.4 Dispensation for remedies which are not effective and adequate

2.2.10.4.1 Introduction

Another important question in connection with Article 35(1) is whether all the available legal remedies must have been pursued. Here, too, a good deal depends on the relevant national law, and the answer to this question can only be given on a case-

---

[142] Judgment of 16 September 1996, para. 69; See also: judgment of 28 July 1999, *Selmouni*, para. 77.
[143] Appl. 5874/72, *Monika Berberich v. Federal Republic of Germany*, Yearbook XVII (1974), p. 386 (418).
[144] Appl. 9118/80, *Allgemeine Gold- und Silberscheideanstalt A.G. v. the United Kingdom*, D&R 32 (1983), p. 159 (165).
[145] Judgment of 9 October 1979, para. 23.
[146] *Idem.*

by-case basis.[147] From the very voluminous and rather casuistic case law, the following trends may be inferred.

In the *Nielsen* Case the Commission stated quite generally that "the rules governing the exhaustion of the local remedies, as they are generally recognised today, in principle require that recourse should be had to all legal remedies available under the local law which are in principle capable of providing an effective and sufficient means of redressing the wrongs for which, on the international plane, the Respondent State is alleged to be responsible."[148]

2.2.10.4.2 Effective and adequate remedies

An individual is dispensed from the obligation to exhaust certain local remedies, if in the circumstances of his case these remedies are ineffective or inadequate.[149] In the same vein the answer to the question of whether non-judicial procedures belong to the local remedies that have to be exhausted depends on whether those procedures are provided with sufficient guarantees to ensure an effective legal protection against the authorities.[150] Recourse to an organ which supervises the administration but cannot take binding decisions, such as an ombudsman, does not constitute an adequate and effective remedy in the sense of Article 35(1).[151]

For a given local remedy to be considered adequate and effective it is, of course, not required that the claim in question would actually have been recognised by the

---

[147] See Appl. 343/57, *Schouw Nielsen v. Denmark*, Yearbook II (1958-1959), p. 412 (442-444): "the competence which the Commission has in every case to appreciate in the light of its particular facts whether any given remedy at any given date appeared to offer the applicant the possibility of an effective and sufficient remedy."

[148] Appl. 343/57, Yearbook II (1958-1959), p. 412 (440). See also Appl. 10092/82, *Baraona v. Portugal*, D&R 40 (1985), p. 118 (136), where the Commission held that "the crucial point is (...) whether an appeal might have secured redress in the form of direct, rather than indirect, protection of the rights laid down in (...) the Convention." See also see the judgment of 18 September 1996, *Aksoy*, paras 51-52, and the judgment of 16 September 1996, *Akdivar*, paras 65-67.

[149] See, *e.g.*, Appl. 7011/75, *Becker v. Denmark*, D&R 4 (1976), p. 215 (232-233); Appl. 7465/76, *X v. Denmark*, D&R 7 (1977), p. 153 (154). A special case is Appl. 7397/76, *Peyer v. Switzerland*, D&R 11 (1978), p. 58 (75-76), in which in the opinion of the Commission the applicant did not need to appeal, since he could not rely on the Convention before the national court, as it had not yet entered into force with respect to Switzerland, while in addition there was no legal ground on which such an appeal could be based. See also joint Appls 8805/79 and 8806/79, *De Jong and Baljet v. the Netherlands*, D&R 24 (1981), p. 144 (150), in which the action for damages of Art. 1401 of the Netherlands Civil Code was not considered effective to question a detention which was in conformity with domestic law. Similarly, in the case of *Z v. the Netherlands,* the appeal to the Judicial Division of the Council of State against the Deputy Minister of Justice was considered not effective because such proceedings did not suspend the execution of the decision to deport the applicant; See also judgment of 9 October 1997, *Andronicou and Constantinou*, para 159.

[150] See, *e.g.*, Appl. 155/56, *X v. Federal Republic of Germany*, Yearbook I (1955-1957), p. 163 (164).

[151] Appl. 11192/84, *Montion v. France*, D&R 52 (1987), p. 227 (235) ; judgment of 23 May 2001, *Denizci*, para. 362.

national court. In this stage of the examination by the Court the question of whether the application is well-founded is not at issue, but only the question of whether, assuming that the complaint is well-founded, this particular remedy would have provided the applicant the possibility of redress.[152] In this context it must be noted that the applicant's personal view of the effectiveness or ineffectiveness of a given remedy is in itself not decisive.[153]

Where the national authorities remain passive in the face of serious allegations of misconduct or infliction of harm by State agents, this is a relevant criterion in absolving the applicant from the obligation to exhaust domestic remedies. The speed with which a remedy can be exercised may also be a relevant factor in assessing its effectiveness.[154]

In the *Tsomtsos* Case the Court reiterated that the only remedies Article 35 of the Convention requires to be exhausted are those that are available and sufficient and relate to the breaches alleged.[155] In the *Iatridis* Case the Court observed that the applicant made a special application – provided for in section 2(3) of Law no. 263/1968 – to the Athens Court of First Instance, specifically seeking to have the administrative eviction order quashed. The court found in his favour, holding that the conditions for issuing such an order had not been satisfied. The Minister of Finance, however, refused to give approval for the cinema to be returned to him. In light of the Minister's stance, an action under Articles 987 and 989 of the Civil Code – assuming it had succeeded – would in all probability not have led to a different outcome from that of the application to have the eviction order quashed. The applicant could not, therefore, be criticised for not having made use of a legal remedy which would have been directed to essentially the same end and which moreover would not have had a better prospect of success. As regards the second limb of the objection, the Court considered that an action for damages might sometimes be deemed a sufficient remedy, in particular where compensation is the only means of redressing the wrong suffered. In the instant case, however, compensation would not have been an alternative to the measures which the Greek legal system should have afforded the applicant to overcome the fact that he was unable to regain possession of the cinema despite a court decision quashing the eviction order. Furthermore, the various proceedings pending in the Athens Court of First Instance were decisive only in respect of an award of just satisfaction under Article 41 of the Convention. As to the third limb of the objection, the Court reiterated that Article 35 only requires the exhaustion of remedies that relate to the breaches

---

[152] Appl. 1474/62, *Belgian Linguistic* Case, Coll. 12 (1964), p. 18 (27).
[153] Appl. 289/57, *X v. Federal Republic of Germany*, Yearbook I (1955-1957), p. 148 (149). See also Appl. 6271/73, *X v. Federal Republic of Germany*, D&R 6 (1976), p. 62 (64); Appl. 7317/75, *Lynas v. Switzerland*, Yearbook XX (1977), p. 412 (442); and Appl. 10148/82, *Garcia v. Switzerland*, D&R 42 (1985), p. 98 (122).
[154] App. 25803/94, *Selmouni v. France*, D&R 88 B (1997), p. 55 (62-63).
[155] Judgment of 15 November 1996, para. 32.

alleged: sueing a private individual cannot be regarded as such a remedy in respect of an act on the part of the State, in this instance the refusal to implement a judicial decision and return the cinema to the applicant.[156]

The Commission and the Court have built up a voluminous case law concerning what may be regarded as an effective and adequate remedy. From this case law the following elements emerge as the most important.

In the first place the applicant must have used the remedies provided for up to the highest level, only if and insofar as the appeal to a higher tribunal can still substantially affect the decision on the merits.[157] In addition any procedural means which might have prevented a breach of the Convention should have been used.[158] An applicant may of course refrain from an appeal if the tribunal in question is not competent in the matter of his claim.[159] In some legal systems a higher or the highest court has jurisdiction only with respect to legal issues and cannot pronounce on the facts. If the application submitted to the Commission specifically concerns facts, the applicant need not have previously applied to such a court.[160] The same holds good with respect to the possibility of appeal to a constitutional court from a decision of another court. Such an appeal belongs to the remedies that must have been exhausted if and insofar as the decision of the constitutional court may have any impact on the situation about which a complaint is lodged with the Commission.[161] In Slovakia a petition to the Constitutional Court is not an effective remedy, in so far as the formal institution of the proceedings depends on a decision of that court and the court cannot interfere with or quash decisions of the ordinary courts.[162] In Ireland the granting of leave for appeal to the Supreme Court lies at the discretion of the Attorney-General and in Denmark it is the Minister of Justice who has wide discretion in granting leave for appeal. In both legal systems, moreover, such a leave is granted only exceptionally. With respect to both cases the Commission has decided that the appeal to the Supreme

---

[156]   Judgment of 25 March 1999, para. 47.

[157]   Appl. 788/60, *Austria v. Italy*, Yearbook IV (1961), p. 116 (172) and Appl. 2690/65, *Televizier v. the Netherlands*, Yearbook IX (1966), p. 512 (548). See also Appl. 6289/73, *Airey v. Ireland*, Yearbook XX (1977), p. 180 (200); Appl. 6870/75, *Y v. the United Kingdom*, D&R 10 (1978), p. 37 (67); Appls 9362/81, 9363/81 and 9387/81, *Van der Sluijs, Zuiderveld and Klappe v. the Netherlands*, D&R 28 (1982), p. 212 (219); Appl. 16839/90, *Remli v. France*, D&R 77-A (1994), p. 22 (29); judgment of 19 March 1991, *Cardot,*, para. 39.

[158]   Judgment of 6 December 1988, *Barberà, Messegué and Jarbardo*, para 59; judgment of 19 March 1991, *Cardot*, para. 36.

[159]   See, *e.g.*, Appl. 7598/76, *Kaplan v. the United Kingdom*, D&R 15 (1979), p. 120 (122). Thus also the Court: judgment of 6 November 1980, *Guzzardi*, para 69.

[160]   See, *e.g.*, Appl. 1437/62, *X v. Belgium* (not published) and Appl. 10741/84, *S v. the United Kingdom*, D&R 41 (1985), p. 226 (231).

[161]   See, *e.g.*, Appl. 1086/61, *X v. Federal Republic of Germany*, Yearbook V (1962), p. 149 (154); Appls 5573 and 5670/72, *Adler v. Federal Republic of Germany*, Yearbook XX (1977), p. 102 (132).

[162]   Appl. 26384/95, *Šamková v. Slovak Republic*, D&R 86 A (1997) p. 143 (151-152).

Court does not constitute an effective remedy in the sense of Article 26.[163] In the *Brozicek* Case the Court observed that in the Italian legal system an individual was not entitled to apply directly to the Constitutional Court for review of a law's constitutionality. Only a court trying the merits of a case has the right to make a reference to the Constitutional Court, either of its own motion or at the request of a party. Accordingly, such an application cannot be a remedy whose exhaustion is required under Article 35 of the Convention.[164]

In the *Boyle and Rice* Case the Court held that recourse to the administrative bodies could be considered an effective remedy in respect of complaints concerning the application or implementation of prison regulations.[165] In the *Cenbauer* Case the Court considered that it had not been demonstrated that an appeal to the administrative bodies or to a judge responsible for supervising the execution of sentences offered the applicant the possibility of securing redress for his complaints. In particular, the Court noted that section 15 para. 1 of the amended Act on Enforcement of Prison Terms refers to a complaint concerning the "acts or decisions of a prison employee" and accordingly did not provide a remedy in respect of complaints relating to the general conditions in prison.[166] In the *Tumilovich* Case the Court held that an application for retrial or similar extraordinary remedies could not, as a general rule, be taken into account for the purpose of applying Article 35 of the Convention.[167] With regard to the right to have a court decide speedily on the lawfulness of detention, an action for damages against the State is not a remedy which has to be exhausted, because the purpose of an action for damages on the ground of the defective operation of the machinery of justice is to secure compensation for the prejudice caused by deprivation of liberty, not to assert the right to have the lawfulness of that deprivation of liberty decided speedily by that court.[168]

With regard to the length of detention in Turkey in the case of a complaint about violation of Article 5 of the Convention the Commission noted that on a number of occasions the martial law court had considered whether to continue the applicants'

---

[163]   Appl. 9136/80, *X v. Ireland*, D&R 26 (1982), p. 242 (244); and Appl. 8395/78, *X v. Denmark*, D&R 27 (1982), p. 50 (52). Cf. also Appl. 8950/80, *H v. Belgium*, D&R 37 (1984), p. 5 (13); Appls 14116/88 and 14117/88, *Sargin and Yağci v. Turkey*, D&R 61 (1989), p. 250; Appl. 12604/86, *G. v. Belgium*, D&R 70 (1991), p. 125 (136); Appl. 20471/92, *Kustannus Oy Vapaa Ajattelija and others v. Finland*, D&R 85 (1996), p. 29 (39).

[164]   Judgment of 19 December 1989, para. 34; decision of 6 March 2003, *De Jorio*.

[165]   Judgment of 27 April 1988, para. 65.

[166]   Decision of 5 February 2004.

[167]   Decision of 22 June 1999; decision of 29 January 2004, *Berdzenishvili*; decision of 4 May 2004, *Denisov*.

[168]   Appl. 10868/84, *Woukam Moudefo v. France*, D&R 51 (1987), p. 62 (81); Appl. 11256/84, *Egue v. France*, D&R 57 (1988), p. 47 (67); Appl. 13190/87, *Navarra v. France*, D&R 69 (1991), p. 165 (171); Appls 16419/90 and 16426/90, *Yağci and Sargin v. Turkey*, D&R 71 (1991), p. 253 (268); judgment of 27 August 1992, *Tomasi*, para. 81; judgment of 23 November 1993, *Navarra*, para. 24.

detention on remand and refused their conditional release. It followed that the judicial authorities had the opportunity to put an end to the applicants' allegedly excessive detention. The Commission further noted that no appeal was possible against decisions by a martial law court which refused to grant conditional release. In connection with this it pointed out that in Turkish law there is a distinction between an order remanding the accused in custody and an order to continue detention on remand, the latter being issued at final instance by the court dealing with the case. With regard to the length of the criminal proceedings, for the purposes of Article 6(1) of the Convention, the Commission referred to previous decisions in which it had held that, having regard to the relatively protracted duration of proceedings, it was not bound to reject a complaint for failure to exhaust domestic remedies because appeals were still pending at the time when an application was introduced. The Commission further observed that the respondent Government had not established that the applicants had an effective remedy in Turkish law to expedite the proceedings whose length they complained of. The judgment to be given by the Military Court of Cassation, to which the Government alluded, was not as such a remedy capable of affording the applicants redress for the situation they complained of. Therefore, there was no effective remedy available.[169]

In a case where the applicant complained about the conditions of detention, the Government in question observed that she had not exhausted the domestic remedies, since she had not requested a transfer to another prison. The Commission, however, opined that even if this might have led to an improvement in the conditions of her detention, it would by no means have enabled her to assert her rights under the Convention, and in particular to raise her complaint under Article 3. Consequently, the Commission considered that these steps could not be taken into account for the purpose of deciding whether domestic remedies had been exhausted as required.[170]

The Commission held in respect of alleged ill-treatment contrary to Article 3, that raising criminal charges against the officials concerned, or filing a civil action for compensation, are effective remedies to be examined pursuant to Article 35(1).[171] However, in a case against Turkey the Commission observed that, under Turkish law, the applicants were entitled to complain at the trial if their statements to the police had been made under torture and that ill-treatment of prisoners by police officers was to be prosecuted *ex officio*. The Commission was, therefore, satisfied that the applicants had availed themselves of a proper remedy under Turkish law in that they had raised

---

[169] Appls 15530/89 and 15531/89, *Mitap and Müftüoglu v. Turkey*, D&R 72 (1992), p. 169 (189). See also Appls 16419/90 and 16426/90, *Yağci and Sargin v. Turkey*, D&R 71 (1991) p. 253 (267).

[170] Appl. 14986/89, *Kuijk v. Greece*, D&R 70 (1991), p. 240 (250).

[171] Appl. 10078/82, *M v. France*, D&R 41 (1985), p. 103 (119); Appl. 11208/84, *McQuiston v. the United Kingdom*, D&R 46 (1986), p. 182 (187); Appl. 17544/90, *Ribitsch v. Austria*, D&R 74 (1993), p. 129 (133).

their complaint of ill-treatment at their trial, first with the Public Prosecutor and subsequently before the State Security Court and the Court of Cassation. It concluded from the Government's submissions that the Public Prosecutor did not refer the complaint to the competent local Public Prosecutor, because he did not consider the allegations to be credible, and that, for the same reason, the court did not discard the evidence obtained during the applicant's detention incommunicado. The Commission subsequently examined whether the applicants were nevertheless required to avail themselves of the further remedy indicated by the Government by addressing a complaint of criminal behaviour to the competent Public Prosecutor. The Commission here observed that the complaint concerned primarily a question of evidence and that the reason why the applicants were unsuccessful in raising it at their trial was that the State Security Court and the Public Prosecutor did not find that there was sufficient evidence to support their detailed allegations. The Commission, therefore, assumed that the applicants, if they had availed themselves of the remedy indicated by the Government, would have been faced with the same problem of proving that they had in fact been ill-treated. For this reason the applicants were not obliged to exhaust the said remedy in order to comply with Article 35(1) of the Convention.[172]

In another case against Turkey the Commission observed in this respect, however, that the legal authorities to which the complaint of criminal behaviour was referred had held the decisions on detention to be in conformity with law and procedure. According to the case law quoted by the Government, Turkish courts only grant compensation in cases where those responsible for criminal acts of the kind in question have previously been found guilty in a criminal prosecution. In these circumstances the Commission was of the opinion that the applicants were not bound to attempt the means of redress indicated by the Government, given that the legal authorities to which the question of the lawfulness of their detention was referred had already taken a position and rejected the claim that the applicants' deprivation of freedom was illegal. In the circumstances it would have served no purpose had the applicants undertaken proceedings for compensation.[173]

In the *Akdivar* Case the applicants alleged that there was no effective remedy available for obtaining compensation before the administrative courts in respect of injuries or damage to property arising out of criminal acts of members of the security forces. In order to demonstrate that the available remedies were not ineffective, the Turkish Government referred to a number of judgments of the administrative courts. Some of these decisions concerned cases in which the State Council had awarded compensation to individuals for damage inflicted by public officials or by terrorists, or suffered

---

[172]   Appls 16311/90 and 16313/90, *Hazar and Acik v. Turkey*, D&R 72 (1992), p. 200 (207-208); Appls 14116/88 and 14117/88, *Sargin and Yağci v. Turkey*, D&R 61 (1989), p. 250 (280).

[173]   Appls 14116/88 and 14117/88, *Sargin and Yağci v. Turkey*, D&R 61 (1989), p. 250 (278).

in the course of confrontations between the Government, the public and the *PKK*. According to the Government, claims for compensation could also have been lodged in the ordinary civil courts. The Court considered it significant that the Government, despite the extent of the problem of village destruction, had not been able to point to examples of compensation being awarded in respect of allegations that property had been purposely destroyed by members of the security forces or to prosecutions having been brought against them in respect of such allegations. In this connection the Court noted the evidence referred to by the Delegate of the Commission as regards the general reluctance of the authorities to admit that this type of illicit behaviour by members of the security forces had occurred. It further noted the lack of any impartial investigation, any offer to co-operate with a view to obtaining evidence or any *ex gratia* payments made by the authorities to the applicants. Moreover, the Court did not consider that a remedy before the administrative courts could be regarded as adequate and sufficient in respect of the applicants' complaints, since it was not satisfied that a determination could be made in the course of such proceedings concerning the claim that their property was destroyed by members of the gendarmerie.[174] As regards the civil remedy invoked by the respondent Government, the Court attached particular significance to the absence of any meaningful investigation by the authorities into the applicants' allegations and of any official expression of concern or assistance notwithstanding the fact that statements by the applicants had been given to various State officials. It appeared to have taken two years before statements were taken from the applicants by the authorities about the events complained of, which was probably done in response to the communication of the complaint by the Commission to the Government.[175]

In the *Egmez* Case the applicant made a complaint to the Ombudsman which resulted in a report naming some of the officers responsible for the alleged ill-treatment of the applicant. Having regard to the Attorney-General's refusal to take any action the Court decided that the applicant's complaint to the Ombudsman had not discharged the authorities of the Republic of Cyprus of the duty to "undertake an investigation capable of leading to the punishment (as opposed to the mere identification) of those responsible".[176] The same was true in the *Denizci Case*, where the Attorney-General refrained from taking any action despite the power he had to conduct an *ex officio* enquiry and where, under Cypriot law, the Ombudsman would have had no power to order any measures or impose any sanctions. In those circumstances the Court considered that the applicants were justified in considering that no other legal remedy on the national level would be effective in respect of their

---

174 Judgment of 16 September 1996, paras 71-72.
175 *Ibidem*, para. 73.
176 Judgment 21 December 2000, para 67.

complaints.[177] In the *Yasa* Case the Court held that with respect to an action in administrative law under Article 125 of the Turkish Constitution based on the authorities' strict liability, that a Contracting State's obligation under Articles 2 and 13 of the Convention to conduct an investigation capable of leading to the identification and punishment of those responsible in cases of fatal assault might be rendered illusory if in respect of complaints under those Articles an applicant were to be required to exhaust an administrative-law action leading only to an award of damages. Consequently, the applicant was not required to bring the administrative proceedings in question.[178]

In the *Dogan* Case the Court stated that, when an individual formulates an arguable claim in respect of forced eviction and destruction of property involving the responsibility of the State, the notion of an 'effective remedy' in the sense of Article 13 of the Convention, entails, in addition to the payment of compensation where appropriate, a thorough and effective investigation capable of leading to the identification and punishment of those responsible and including effective access by the complainant to the investigative procedure. Otherwise, if an action based on the State's strict liability were to be considered a legal action that had to be exhausted in respect of complaints under Article 8 of the Convention or Article 1 of Protocol No. 1, the State's obligation to pursue those guilty of such serious breaches might thereby disappear. As regards a civil action for redress for damage sustained through illegal acts or patently unlawful conduct on the part of State agents, the Court recalled that a plaintiff must, in addition to establishing a causal link between the tort and the damage he had sustained, identify the person believed to have committed the tort. In the instant case, however, the identity of those responsible for the forced eviction of the applicants from their village were still not known. Accordingly, the Court did not consider that a remedy before the administrative or civil courts could be regarded as adequate and effective in respect of the applicants' complaints, since it was not satisfied that a determination could be made in the course of such proceedings concerning the allegations that villages were forcibly evacuated by members of the security forces.[179]

In the *Hobbs* Case the Court held that a declaration of incompatibility issued by a British court to the effect that a particular legislative provision infringed the Convention cannot be regarded as an effective remedy within the meaning of Article 35(1). It stated: "In particular, a declaration is not binding on the parties to the proceedings in which it is made. Furthermore, by virtue of section 10(2) of the 1998 Act, a declaration of incompatibility provides the appropriate minister with a power, not a duty, to amend the offending legislation by order so as to make it compatible with the

---

[177]   Judgment of 21 May 2001, paras 362-363.
[178]   Judgment of 2 September 1998, para. 74.
[179]   Judgment of 18 November 2004, paras 106-108.

Convention. The minister concerned can only exercise that power if he considers that there are 'compelling reasons' for doing so."[180] Thus a remedy which is not enforceable or binding, or which is dependent on the discretion of the executive, falls outside the concept of effectiveness as established in the Convention case law, notwithstanding that it may furnish adequate redress in cases in which it has a successful outcome.[181]

In a case against Ireland the Court held that in a legal system which provides constitutional protection for fundamental rights, it is incumbent on the aggrieved individual to test the extent of that protection and, in a common law system, to allow the domestic courts to develop those rights by way of interpretation. In this respect it was recalled that a declaratory action before the High Court, with a possibility of an appeal to the Supreme Court, constitutes the most appropriate method under Irish law of seeking to assert and vindicate constitutional rights.[182]

The possibility of obtaining compensation may in some circumstances constitute an adequate remedy, in particular where it is likely to be the only possible or practical means whereby redress can be given to the individual for the wrong he has suffered.[183] Applying this case law, the Commission declared an application concerning the dismissal of police officers inadmissible under the local remedies rule since the police officers' action for compensation was pending before the Greek courts and the compensation capable of being awarded was potentially substantial enough to remedy the alleged violations.[184] However, the Commission has also held that compensation machinery could only be seen as an adequate remedy in a situation where the authorities had taken reasonable steps to comply with their obligations under the Convention.[185]

The personal appearance of the applicant before the court taking the decision may constitute so substantial an element of the procedure that the rejection of a request to that effect renders the procedure ineffective.[186]

In the *Tomé Mota* Case the Court supported the Government's view that an application against the administration's failure to decide constituted an effective remedy. In particular, the Government had pointed out that administrative authorities are under an obligation to decide on any request made by a party within six months. In proceedings under the Tax Offences Act where no other remedy, such as a request for a transfer of jurisdiction, lies against the failure to decide within the general six-month

---

[180] Decision of 18 June 2002; decision of 16 March 2004, *Walker*; decision of 27 April 2004, *Pearson*.
[181] Decision of 29 June 2004, *B. and L. v. the United Kingdom*.
[182] Decision of 19 June 2003, *Independent News and Media plc and Independent Newspapers (Ireland) Limited*.
[183] Appl. 12719/87, *Frederiksen and Others v. Denmark*, D&R 56 (1988), p. 237 (244).
[184] Appl. 18598/91, *Sygounis, Kotsis and 'Union of Police Officers' v. Greece*, D&R 78-B (1994), p. 71 (80).
[185] Appl. 12719/87, *Frederiksen and Others v. Denmark*, D&R 56 (1988), p. 237 (244).
[186] Appl. 434/58, *X v. Sweden*, Yearbook II (1958-1959), p. 354 (374-376).

time-limit, the party is entitled to lodge an application directly with the Administrative Court against the administration's failure to decide under Article 132 of the Federal Constitution.[187] The Court relied in essence on the Commission's case law according to which measures available to an individual which might speed up the proceedings are matters which fall to be considered in the context of the merits of an application relating to the length of proceedings rather than in the context of the exhaustion of domestic remedies.[188] In the *Basic* Case the Court referred to its decision in the *Tomé Mota* Case, where it had found that a request under Articles 108 and 109 of the Portuguese Code of Criminal Procedure to speed up the proceedings was an effective remedy. As there were a number of similarities between this remedy and the remedy at issue in the present case, the Court found that it was required to review the question whether the application against the administration's failure to decide under Article 132 of the Federal Constitution constituted an effective remedy. The Court noted that Portuguese law provided time-limits within which each stage of the criminal proceedings had to be completed. If they were not complied with, the person concerned might file a request to speed up the proceedings which, if successful, might, *inter alia*, result in a decision fixing a time-limit within which the competent court or public prosecutor had to take a particular procedural measure, such as closing the investigations or setting a date for a hearing. Given the strict time-limits within which the authorities had to decide upon a request to speed up the proceedings, the use of this remedy did not itself contribute to the length of the proceedings. Similarly, Austrian law provided in the field of administrative proceedings that the competent authority had, unless provided otherwise, to decide within six months upon any request by a party. If this time-limit was not complied with, the party might – in a case like the present one where the possibility to request a transfer of jurisdiction to the higher authority was excluded – lodge an application under Article 132 of the Federal Constitution with the Administrative Court. If deemed admissible, it resulted in an order addressed to the authority to give the decision within three months, a time-limit which could be extended only once. The Court further noted the information given by the Government and not contested by the applicant, namely, that in the vast majority of cases the use of the application under Article 132 of the Federal Constitution did not cause a further delay in the proceedings, as the Administrative Court usually takes no more than a month to issue its order. The Court found that there were no fundamental differences which would distinguish the application under Article 132 of the Austrian Federal Constitution under review in the present case from the remedy which was at issue in *Tomé Mota*. The Court concluded that this application

---

[187] Decision of 16 March 1999, judgment of 26 July 2001, *Horvat*, para. 48.
[188] Appl. 11296/84, *Moreira de Azevedo v. Portugal*, D&R 56 (1988), p. 126.

constituted an effective remedy as regards a complaint about the length of proceedings.[189]

In the *Horvat* Case the Court noted that proceedings pursuant to section 59(4) of the Constitutional Court Act of Croatia are considered as being instituted only if the Constitutional Court, after a preliminary examination of the complaint, decides to admit it. Thus, although the person concerned can lodge a complaint directly with the Constitutional Court, the formal institution of proceedings depends on the latter's discretion. Furthermore, for a party to be able to lodge a constitutional complaint pursuant to that provision, two cumulative conditions must be satisfied. Firstly, the applicant's constitutional rights have to be grossly violated by the fact that no decision has been issued within a reasonable time and, secondly, there should be a risk of serious and irreparable consequences for the applicant. The Court noted that terms such as 'grossly violated' and 'serious and irreparable consequences' are susceptible to various and wide interpretation. It remained open to what extent the applicant risked irreparable consequences in so far as the case involved her civil claims for repayment. The Government produced before the Court only one case in which the Constitutional Court had ruled under section 59(4) of the Constitutional Court Act to support their argument concerning the sufficiency and effectiveness of the remedy. The absence of further case law did, however, indicate the uncertainty of this remedy in practical terms. In the Court's view the single case cited by the Government did not suffice to show the existence of settled national case law that would prove the effectiveness of the remedy. In light of this the Court considered that a complaint pursuant to section 59(4) of the Constitutional Court Act could not be regarded with a sufficient degree of certainty as an effective remedy in the applicant's case.[190]

Finally, in cases of expulsion, the Commission has constantly held that a remedy which does not suspend execution of a decision to expel an alien to a specified country is not effective for the purposes of Article 26 [new Article 35(1)] and there is no obligation to have recourse to such a remedy.[191] In the *Said* Case the Government argued that the applicant had failed to exhaust domestic remedies in view of the fact that he had independently and voluntarily withdrawn his application for a provisional measure in the proceedings before the Administrative Jurisdiction Division of the Council of State. The Court noted that according to the case law of the President of the Administrative Jurisdiction Division a request for a provisional measure will be declared

---

[189]   Judgment of 30 January 2001, paras. 34-39; Judgment of 30 January 2001, *Pallanich*, para. 32.
[190]   Judgment of 26 July 2001, paras. 42-48.
[191]   Appl. 10400/83, *Z v. the Netherlands*, D&R 38 (1984), p. 145 (150); Appl. 10760/84, *X v. the Netherlands*, D&R 38 (1984), p. 224 (225); Appl. 10564/83, *X v. Federal Republic of Germany*, D&R 40 (1985), p. 262 (265); joined Appls 17550/90 and 17825/91, *V. and P. v. France*, D&R 70 (1991), p. 298 (315).

inadmissible if the date for the expulsion has not yet been made known. No reproach could, therefore, be made of the applicant for withdrawing his request.[192]

2.2.10.4.3   Remedy and real chance of success

A remedy is ineffective and does not, therefore, have to be sought if, considering well-established case law, it does not offer any real chance of success.[193] In that case, however, the applicant must give some evidence of the existence of such case law.[194] That the Commission was not inclined to accept an argument to that effect easily, if the case law proved not to be as well-established as was alleged, appeared from its decision in the *Retimag* Case. Retimag was a Swiss company, but it was actually controlled by the German Communist Party. The latter was declared unconstitutional by the German courts and consequently the property of Retimag was confiscated. The company invoked before the Commission the right to the peaceful enjoyment of possessions. Article 19 of the German Constitution declares the provisions on fundamental rights to be applicable to *internal* legal persons. As a result Retimag argued that it had not been able to appeal to the *Bundesverfassungsgericht* because it was a Swiss company, and accordingly not an internal legal person. However, after Retimag had lodged its application with the Commission, the *Bundesverfassungsgericht* decided that Article 19 was not to be interpreted *a contrario* and did not exclude an appeal by external legal persons. On this basis the Commission decided that Retimag had not exhausted the local remedies and it declared the application inadmissible under Article 35(1).[195]

A comparable situation presented itself in the *De Varga-Hirsch* Case, which concerned, *inter alia*, the requirement of 'reasonable time' of Article 5(3). The applicant had been held in detention on remand for almost five years. Although he had repeatedly applied to the courts for release on bail, he had not appealed to the Court of Cassation, except in two cases. In these two cases, however, he did not rely on the Convention or on comparable provisions of domestic law. The applicant contended that, because of its limited jurisdiction, the Court of Cassation could not be considered as an effective remedy. The Commission rejected this argument by referring to case law of the Court of Cassation with regard to detention on remand, dating from after

---

[192]   Decision of 5 October 2004.

[193]   Appl. 27/55, *X v. Federal Republic of Germany*, Yearbook I (1955-1957), p. 138 (139). See also Appl. 8378/78, *Kamal v. the United Kingdom*, D&R 20 (1980), p. 168 (170); Appls 9362/81, 9363/81 and 9387/81, *Van der Sluijs, Zuiderveld and Klappe v. the Netherlands*, D&R 28 (1982), p. 212 (219); Appl. 9697/82, *J and others v. Ireland*, D&R 34 (1983) p. 131; Appl. 10103/82, *Farragut v. France*, D&R 39 (1984), p. 186 (205); Appl. 13134/87, *Costello-Roberts v. the United Kingdom*, D&R 67 (1991), p. 216 (224); Appl. 20948/92, *Işiltan v. Turkey*, D&R 81 B (1997), p. 35 (38); judgment of 20 February 1991, *Vernillo*, para. 66; judgment of 19 February 1998, *Dalia*, para. 38; decision of 11 March 2004, *Merger and Cros*.

[194]   See, *e.g.*, Appl. 788/60, *Austria v. Italy*, Yearbook IV (1961), p. 116 (168); Appl. 15404/89, *Purcell v. Ireland*, D&R 70 (1991), p. 262 (274).

[195]   Appl. 712/60, Yearbook IV (1961), p. 384 (404-406).

the applicant's detention on remand had ended. It held that the appeal to the Court of Cassation was neither a new remedy nor an appeal likely to be dismissed as inadmissible. The Commission added that, "if there is any doubt as to whether a given remedy is or is not intrinsically able to offer a real chance of success, that is a point which must be submitted to the domestic courts themselves, before any appeal can be made to the international court."[196]

Particularly in a common law system where the courts extend and develop principles through case law, it is generally incumbent on an aggrieved individual to allow the domestic courts the opportunity to develop existing rights by way of interpretation.[197]

It thus appears to be hazardous for an applicant to rely on a particular interpretation if the latter is not supported by clear and constant national case law.[198] Moreover, an applicant cannot rely on case law if the legal provisions on which that case law is based, have meanwhile been altered. Indeed, in such a case there is no certainty that the decision in his case would have been identical with previous decisions, so that the relevant remedy cannot in advance be qualified as ineffective and inadequate.[199]

For a situation where reliance on standing case, law was honoured, reference may be made to the decision of the Commission in the so-called 'Vagrancy' Cases, where three Belgians claimed that they had been unlawfully detained for vagrancy.[200] Prior to these applications being lodged, it had been established case law of the Belgian Council of State that the latter had no jurisdiction with respect to an appeal against such detention. After the applications had been declared admissible, the Council of State reversed its approach. According to the Commission this was no reason for declaring the applications as yet inadmissible because of non-exhaustion of an effective local remedy.[201]

---

[196] Appl. 23548/94, *E.F. v. Czech Republic*, D&R 78-B (1994), p. 146 (151); Appl. 57039/00, *Epözdemir v. Turkey* and Appl. 20357/92, *Epözdemir v. Turkey;* Appl. 20357/92, *Whiteside v. the United Kingdom*. D&R. 76-A (1994), p. 80 (87); decision of 19 January 1999, *Allaoui;* decision of 26 October 2004, *Storck.*

[197] Appl. 20357/92, *Whiteside v. the United Kingdom*, D&R 76-A (1994), p. 80 (88); decision 27 March 2003, *Martin.*

[198] See also Appl. 10789/84, *K., F. and P. v. the United Kingdom*, D&R 40 (1985), p. 298 (299).

[199] See Appl. 8408/78, *X v. Federal Republic of Germany* (not published), where the Commission also attached importance to the fact that the case law had been formed before the Commission itself had shown in a decision that it took a different view. In other words, the Commission assumes that the relevant national court will take the Commission' view by taking a new case into consideration, and consequently will take a different decision.

[200] Appls 2832, 2835 and 2899/66, *De Wilde, Ooms and Versyp v. Belgium*, Yearbook X (1967), p. 420.

[201] Report of 19 July 1969, *De Wilde, Ooms and Versyp* ('Vagrancy' Cases), B.10 (1971), p. 94. See also Appl. 8544/79, *Öztürk v. Federal Republic of Germany*, D&R 26 (1982), p. 55 (69).

2.2.10.4.4   The length of proceedings

Effectiveness is also considered to be lacking when the procedure is exceptionally protracted.[202] However, that is only the case if a given procedure is structurally protracted, i.e. in all cases;[203] the fact that a given procedure is very lengthy in a concrete case does not in itself set aside the condition of the Convention that a remedy in such a procedure must be sought. In fact, in that case the applicant will first of all have to seek redress against that long duration within the national legal system concerned. It was perhaps mainly for this reason that the Commission rejected an application filed by a Belgian as the Court of Appeal had yet to pronounce a verdict, although the applicant had filed his appeal more than six years before. Curiously enough the Commission held: "It is true that the Commission finds that the length of the procedure before Belgian jurisdiction cannot be held against either the applicant or his lawyer. However, the Commission considers that it should put an end to a procedure pending before it for five years."[204]

More sense can be made of the Commission's decision with respect to a complaint concerning the length of criminal proceedings. The question arose whether the accused should have instituted a procedure designed to accelerate proceedings but which could not have led to any other effect. In the Commission's opinion, such a procedure could not be considered an effective and sufficient remedy as required by Article 26 [the present Article 35(1)].[205] The Commission also held that, in case of relatively protracted criminal proceedings, it was not bound to reject a complaint for failure to have exhausted domestic remedies even though appeals were still pending at the moment an application was introduced.[206] In a case against Cyprus, where the Attorney General had refused, in the light of findings by a Commission of Inquiry, to institute criminal proceedings in connection with the killing of two persons by special police, the relatives of the deceased could be considered to have exhausted the domestic remedies, given the fact that the scope of an inquest would not be broader than that of the inquiry and

---

[202]   See, e.g., Appl. 222/56, *X v. Federal Republic of Germany*, Yearbook II (1958-1959), p. 344 (350-351); Appl. 7161/75, *X v. the United Kingdom*, D&R 7 (1977), p. 100 (101); Appl. 13156/87, *Byrn v. Denmark*, D&R 73 (1992), p. 5 (12);. Appl. 26757/95, *Wójcik v. Poland*, D&R 90 (1997), p. 24.

[203]   See, e.g., Appl. 14556/89, *Papamichalopoulos v. Greece*, D&R 68 (1991), p. 261 (270); judgment of 29 April 2004, *Plaksin*, para. 35.

[204]   Appl. 5024/71, *X v. Belgium*, D&R 7 (1977), p. 5 (7). See, however, Appl. 6699/74, *X v. Federal Republic of Germany*, D&R 11 (1978), p. 16 (23-24), where the Commission found differently, even despite the fact that the applicant had consented to postponement of the national procedure. In this case the Commission evidently reached an 'equity' standpoint in view of the emergency in which the applicant found herself.

[205]   Appl. 8435/78, *X v. the United Kingdom*, D&R 26 (1982), p. 18 (20); Appl. 24559/94, *Gibas v. Poland*, D&R 82 A (1995), p. 76(81).

[206]   See, *inter alia*, Appl. 12850/87, *Tomasi v. France*, D&R 64 (1990), p. 128 (131); Appls 15530/89 and 15531/89, *Mitap and Müftüoglu v. Turkey*, D&R 72 (1992), p. 169 (189).

that it was undisputed that civil proceedings normally lasted eight years in all instances.[207]

In the *Plaskin* Case the Court noted that, according to the Convention organs' constant case law, complaints concerning length of procedure could be brought before it before the final termination of the proceedings in question.[208]

2.2.10.4.5 Independence of court

The prior exhaustion of local remedies is not required if the competent court is not fully independent, i.e. the necessary guarantees for a fair trial are not present. In the First *Greek* Case where Denmark, Norway, Sweden and the Netherlands complained about the torture of political prisoners in Greece, the applicant States alleged the existence of an administrative practice to which the local remedies rule was not applicable. In the Commission's opinion, however, the applicant States had not given 'substantial evidence' for the existence of such a practice. Nevertheless, the applications were not rejected under Article 26 [the present Article 35(1)]. The Greek Government had discharged several judges for political reasons. Under those circumstances the Commission found that there was insufficient independence of the judiciary. It concluded that the judicial procedures provided for under Greek law no longer constituted effective remedies which should have been exhausted.[209]

A comparable situation arose as a result of the Turkish military action in Cyprus. According to the Commission, the action had "deeply and seriously affected the life of the population in Cyprus and, in particular, that of the Greek Cypriots."[210] The circumstances were such that the existing remedies available in domestic courts in Turkey or before Turkish military courts in Cyprus could be considered as effective remedies which had to be exhausted according to Article 35(1) with respect to complaints of inhabitants from Cyprus, only "if it were shown that such remedies are both practicable and normally functioning in such cases."[211] The Commission found that this had not been proved by the Turkish Government.

In the *Yöyler* Case the Court considered that a complaint to the chief public prosecutor's office could in principle provide redress for the kind of violations alleged by the applicants. However, any prosecutor who receives a complaint alleging a criminal act by a member of the security forces must decline jurisdiction and transfer the file to the Administrative Council. On account of this, the Court reiterated that it had already found in a number of cases that the investigation carried out by the latter

---

[207] Appl. 25052/94, *Andronicou and Constanttinou v. Cyprus*, D&R 82 A (1995), p. 102 (115).

[208] Judgment of 29 April 2004, para. 35.

[209] Appls 3321-3323 and 3344/67, *Denmark, Norway, Sweden and the Netherlands v. Greece*, Yearbook XI (1968), p. 730 (774).

[210] Appls 6780/74 and 6950/75, *Cyprus v. Turkey*, D&R 2 (1975), p. 125 (137).

[211] *Ibidem*, pp. 137-138.

body could not be regarded as independent since it was composed of civil servants, who were hierarchically dependent on the governor, while an executive officer was linked to the security forces under investigation.[212] In the *Dogan* Case the Court noted in this connection that the applicants had filed petitions with various administrative authorities complaining about the forced evacuation of their village by the security forces. These proceedings did not result in the opening of a criminal investigation or any inquiry into the applicants' allegations. The Court was, therefore, of the opinion that the applicants were not required to make a further explicit request to this effect by filing a criminal complaint with the chief public prosecutor's office, as this would not have led to different result.[213]

2.2.10.5   Submission in substance of the alleged violations to the competent national authorities

The local remedies rule is considered to be complied with only if the points on which an application is lodged in Strasbourg have also been put forward in the relevant national procedure.[214] That the Commission took a stringent attitude in this respect became clear from the case where a complaint was lodged against Norway on account of the refusal of a Norwegian judicial organ to publish the reasons for its judgment. Since this point had not been put forward before the highest court in Norway, in the opinion of the Commission the local remedies rule had not been complied with, although a number of other objections against the judgment in question had indeed been raised in those proceedings.[215] This decision of the Commission showed at the same time that the injured person cannot rely on an alleged obligation on the part of the national court to supplement the legal grounds *ex officio*.[216] This was expressly confirmed by the Court: "The fact that the Belgian courts might have been able, or even obliged, to examine the case of their own motion under the Convention cannot be regarded as having dispensed the applicant from pleading before them the Convention or arguments to the same or like effect."[217]

In the *Kröcher and Möller* Case the applicants alleged violation of Article 3 because of the conditions imposed on them both during the period of their detention on remand, and during their preventive detention and while serving their sentences. As

---

[212]   Judgment of 24 July 2003, para. 93; judgment of 17 February 1994, *Ipek*, para. 207.

[213]   Judgment of 18 November 2004, para. 109.

[214]   Appl. 26629/95, *Litwa v. Poland*, D&R 90 A (1997), p. 13(21); judgment of 15 November 1996, *Ahmed Sadik*, para. 30; judgment of 28 July 1999, *Selmouni*, para. 74; decision of 11 December 2003, *Debelic*.

[215]   Appl. 2002/63, *X v. Norway*, Yearbook VII (1964), p. 262 (266). See also Appl. 11244/84, *Pirotte v. Belgium*, D&R 55 (1988), p. 98 (104).

[216]   See Appl. 2322/64, *X v. Belgium*, Coll. 24 (1967), p. 36 (42); Appl. 15123/89, *Braithwaite v. the United Kingdom*, D&R 70 (1991), p. 252 (256).

[217]   Judgment of 6 November 1980, *Van Oosterwijck*, para. 39.

far as the first-mentioned period was concerned, it was not disputed that the applicants had properly exhausted the domestic remedies available. The final national decision, however, referred solely to the conditions of detention on remand. With respect to the last-mentioned period the Commission investigated whether the facts or conditions complained of constituted a mere extension of those complained of at the outset. It concluded that this was not the case and declared the applicants' complaint inadmissible for not having properly exhausted the domestic remedies, since the last-mentioned period had not been expressly at issue in the national proceedings.[218]

The formula used in the case law requires that the point concerned must have been submitted 'in substance' to the national authorities.[219] The precise implications of this requirement will depend on the concrete circumstances of the case. In general the applicant will not be required to have explicitly referred to the relevant articles of the Convention in the national procedure.[220] Thus, in a case where an applicant alleged a violation of Article 3, the Commission concluded that the applicant had in substance raised the argument of degrading treatment in the domestic procedure by alleging that compliance with a court order complained of would bring him into disgrace.[221]

In the Case of *Gasus Dosier- und Fördertechnik GmbH* the Court observed that it was true that Article 1 of Protocol No. 1 was referred to for the first time by the Tax Collector and that the applicant company consistently denied its applicability, and argued it before the Supreme Court only in an alternative submission. Nevertheless, both the Court of Appeal and the Dutch Supreme Court were able to deal with the allegation of a violation of that provision and in fact did so. Accordingly, the applicant company did provide the Dutch courts, and more particularly the Supreme Court, with the opportunity of preventing or putting right the alleged violation of Article 1 of Protocol No. 1.[222]

In the *Cajella* Case the applicant had lodged a constitutional application, in accordance with the relevant domestic rules, in which he alleged a violation of Article 5(3) and Article 6(1) of the Convention on account of the length of his detention on

---

[218]   Appl. 8463/78, D&R 26 (1982), p. 24 (48-52).

[219]   See, *e.g.*, Appl. 9186/80, *De Cubber v. Belgium*, D&R 28 (1982), p. 172 (175); Appl. 16810/90, *Reyntjes v. Belgium*, D&R 73 (1992), p. 136 (154); Appl. 14524/89, *Yanasik v. Turkey*, D&R 74 (1993), p. 14 (25); and judgment of 28 August 1986, *Glasenapp*, para. 44; judgment of 16 September 1996, *Akdivar*, paras 65-67; judgment of 18 December 1996, *Aksoy*, paras 51-52.

[220]   Thus the Court in the *Van Oosterwijck* judgment of 6 November 1980, para. 39. See also the Commission in Appl. 1661/62, *X and Y v. Belgium*, Yearbook VI (1963), p. 360 (366): "whereas an application against a State where the Convention is an integral part of municipal law (...) may thus prove to be inadmissible if the victim of the alleged violation has not given his judges an opportunity to remedy that violation because the Convention was not invoked or no other arguments to the same effect were raised." See also Appl. 9228/80, *X v. Federal Republic of Germany*, D&R 30 (1983), pp. 132 (141-142); Appl. 17128/90, *Erdagöz v. Turkey*, D&R 71 (1991), p. 275 (282).

[221]   Appl. 11921/86, *Verein Kontakt Information Therapie and Hagen v. Austria*, D&R 57 (1988), p. 81 (89).

[222]   Judgment of 23 February 1995, para. 49.

remand and of the criminal proceedings concerning the charge of complicity in attempted murder. The application was examined both by the First Hall of the Civil Court and by the Constitutional Court. In the Court's view, by raising the 'reasonable time' issue before the competent domestic courts, the applicant had invited them to examine the length of his trial and of his deprivation of liberty in light of the Court's case law and to determine whether, during the relevant periods, there had been excessive delays for which the authorities might be held responsible. By doing so, he had complied with his obligation to make normal use of the available domestic remedies. Against this background it was considered of little relevance that the applicant might not have explicitly drawn the attention of the Civil Court and of the Constitutional Court to the shortcomings which, according to him, had occurred during a specific stage of the proceedings.[223]

Express reference to provisions of the Convention may, however, be necessary in certain cases: "In certain circumstances it may nonetheless happen that express reliance on the Convention before the national authorities constitutes the sole appropriate manner of raising before those authorities first, as is required by Article 26 [the present Article 35], an issue intended, if need be, to be brought subsequently before the European review bodies."[224] In other words, express reference to the provisions of the Convention is necessary if there is no other possibility of submitting the issue 'in substance' in the appropriate way to the national organs.[225]

The above exposé holds true for those Contracting States where the Convention has internal effect. Things are different, of course, in Contracting States where the Convention has no domestic status and has not been incorporated. Indeed, in such a case, directly invoking the Convention before the national authorities will be of no avail in most cases. Consequently, the Commission decided in a case against the United Kingdom: "Before lodging this application the applicant lodged an appeal against her conviction and sentence. Although in the appeal proceedings she did not invoke the rights guaranteed in Articles 5, 9 and 10, she has to be considered to have exhausted domestic remedies because the Convention which guarantees the said rights is not binding law for the British courts and it is doubtful whether the rights and liberties in question constitute general principles which could successfully be invoked by the

---

[223]   Decision of 18 March 2004.
[224]   Judgment of 6 November 1980, *Van Oosterwijck*, para. 37.
[225]   See the Court's judgment of the same date, *Guzzardi*, para. 72, where it was held: 'However, a more specific reference was not essential in the circumstances since it did not constitute the sole means of achieving the aim pursued (...). He [the applicant] (...) derived from the Italian legislation pleas equivalent, in the Court's view, to an allegation of a breach of the right guaranteed by Article 5 of the Convention.' See also Appl. 8130/78, *Hans and Marianne Eckle v. Federal Republic of Germany*, D&R 16 (1979), p. 120 (127-128); App. 20948/92, *Işiltan v. Turkey*, D&R 81 B (1996), p. 35(39).

defence in criminal proceedings before the British courts."[226] Here again, however, the applicant may be required to have invoked legal rules or principles of domestic law which are 'in substance' the same as the relevant provisions of the Convention.[227]

2.2.10.6 The burden of proof

In general the Court is well informed – especially through its member elected with respect to the State concerned – about the remedies available under the different national systems of law and, in dubious cases, may ascertain their existence via its Registry. If the Court has established which remedies exist under national law, it is for the applicant to prove that these remedies have been exhausted or that they are not effective or adequate.

The main source of information in that respect is the respondent State. However, the Court investigates *ex officio* whether the local remedies rule has been complied with. In many cases of individual applications which were declared inadmissible under this rule, that conclusion was reached on the basis of such an *ex officio* investigation, without the application first having been transmitted to the State against which it was directed. If the application is transmitted to the State concerned – and with inter-State applications this is always the case (Rule 51 of the Rules of Court) – the burden of proof with respect to the local remedies rule is divided as follows: the respondent State which relies on the rule must prove that certain effective and adequate remedies exist under its system of law which should have been sought.[228] In the *Bozano* Case the Court held that the Government had to indicate in a sufficiently clear way the remedies that were open to the applicant: "it is not for the Convention bodies to cure of their own motion any want of precision or shortcomings in respondent States' arguments."[229] If the State succeeds in proving its plea, subsequently it is for the applicant to prove that those remedies have been exhausted or that they are not effective or adequate.[230] In the *Akdivar* Case the Court elaborated this rule of the burden of proof by indicating that there may be special circumstances absolving the applicant from the requirement of exhaustion of domestic remedies. According to the Court one such reason may be constituted by the national authorities remaining totally passive in the face of serious

---

[226] Appl. 7050/75, *Arrowsmith v. the United Kingdom*, Yearbook XX (1977), p. 316 (334-336). See Appl. 6871/75, *Caprino v. the United Kingdom*, Yearbook XXI (1978), p. 284 (286-288).

[227] Judgment of 16 December 1992, *Geouffre de la Pradelle*, para. 26.

[228] Judgment of 18 June 1971, *De Wilde, Ooms and Versyp* ('*Vagrancy*' Cases), para. 16; judgment of 27 February 1980, *De Weer*, para. 29; judgment of 16 September 1996, *Akdivar*, para. 68; judgment of 28 November 1997, *Mentes and Others*, para. 57; judgment of 29 April 2003, *Dankevich*, para. 107; judgment of 29 June 2004, *Dogan and Others*, para. 102.

[229] Judgment of 18 December 1986, para. 46. See also Appl. 14461/88, *Chave née Julien v. France*, D&R 71 (1991), p. 141 (153).

[230] See, *e.g.*, Appl. 788/60, *Austria v. Italy*, Yearbook IV (1961), p. 116 (168) and Appl. 4649/70, *X v. Federal Republic of Germany*, Coll. 46 (1974), p. 1 (17).

allegations of misconduct or infliction of harm by State agents, for example where they failed to undertake investigations or offer assistance. In such circumstances it can be said that the burden of proof shifts once again, so that it becomes incumbent on the respondent Government to justify its response in relation to the scale and seriousness of the matters complained of.[231]

2.2.10.7 The moment the preliminary objection must be raised; ex officio inquiry

The Court takes cognisance of preliminary objections concerning the exhaustion of local remedies only insofar as the respondent State has raised them at the stage of the initial examination of admissibility, if their character and the circumstances permitted the State to do so at that moment.[232] The latter qualification was at issue in the *Campbell and Fell* Case. Here the Government raised the plea of non-exhaustion in its observations on the merits after the case had been declared admissible, because new developments had taken place in the relevant English case law only a few days before the Government had submitted its observations on admissibility. According to the Court, the Government could not reasonably have been expected to raise the plea of non-exhaustion at an earlier stage. There was, therefore, no estoppel on its part to do so at this stage of the proceedings. On the other hand, the Court held that it would now be unjust to find these complaints inadmissible for failure to exhaust domestic remedies, because after the Government had raised the issue the Commission had decided on the basis of former Article 29 not to reject the application on this ground. Consequently, the applicant was justified in relying on the Commission's decision by pursuing his case under the Convention instead of applying to the domestic courts.[233]

The question may be raised as to whether the Court should institute *ex officio* an inquiry into the compliance with the local remedies rule after the case has been transmitted to the State, in case the respondent Government has not raised an exception as to the admissibility under Article 35(1). The Commission did not institute an inquiry into the admissibility of the complaint under Article 26 [the present Article 35(1)] if the respondent State expressly waived or had waived its right to rely on the local remedies rule.[234] If the State had not waived this right, the Commission appeared

---

[231]   Judgment of 16 September 1996, para. 68; judgment of 18 December 1996, *Aksoy*, paras. 56-57; judgment of 9 December 1994, *Stran Greek Refineries and Stratis Andreadis*, para. 35; decision of 5 February 2004, *Cenbauer*.

[232]   See, *inter alia*, judgment of 18 June 1971, *De Wilde, Ooms and Versyp* ('*Vagrancy*' Cases), para. 60; judgment of 13 May 1980, *Artico*, para 27; judgment of 6 November 1980, *Guzzardi*, para. 63; and judgment of 10 December 1982, *Foti*, para. 44.

[233]   Judgment of 28 June 1984, para. 58-63.

[234]   See, *e.g.*, Appl. 1727/62, *Boeckmans v. Belgium*, Yearbook VI (1963), p. 370 (396); Appl. 1994/63, *Fifty-seven inhabitants of Leuven and environs v. Belgium*, Yearbook VII (1964), p. 252 (258-260); and Appl. 8919/80, *Van der Mussele v. Belgium*, D&R 23 (1981), p. 244 (257). This is different with regard to the six-month rule. There the Commission holds that "in view of the importance of this

prepared to declare an application inadmissible on the ground of non-exhaustion without the respondent State having raised an exception to that effect.[235] Despite the general wording of Article 35(1), one might wonder whether the Commission – and the Court – ought not to take a somewhat more passive attitude in this matter. The local remedies rule is intended primarily to protect the interest of the respondent State. The fact that the latter has failed to rely on that protection may indicate that it does not consider it to be in its interest to raise the exception. After all, the rejection of an application after a thorough investigation may be more convincing and, consequently, more satisfactory for the respondent State than a declaration of inadmissibility on formal grounds.[236] And, indeed, usually in cases which have been communicated to the respondent Government, the Commission has not declared the application inadmissible for failure to exhaust domestic remedies unless this matter had been raised by the Government in their observations. The Commission took the same attitude if the respondent Government had not submitted any observations at all,[237] or if the Government, following extensions of the time-limit, had neither submitted observations nor requested further extension but had raised the question of non-exhaustion in 'preliminary observations' long after the expiry of the time-limits fixed by the Commission.[238] In the *Kurt* Case the Court noted that the Government's objection was not raised in their memorial but only at the hearing and, therefore, outside the time-limit prescribed in Rule 48(1) of Rules of the Court [cf. the present Rule 55], which stipulated: "A Party wishing to raise a preliminary objection must file a statement setting out the objection and the grounds therefore not later than the time when that Party informs the President of its intention not to submit a memorial or, alternatively, not later than the expiry of the time-limit laid down in Rule 37 para. 1 for the filing of its first memorial." The objection was therefore dismissed.[239]

In the *Malama* Case the Court pointed out that according to Rule 55 of the Rules of Court, "[a]ny plea of inadmissibility must, in so far as its character and the circumstances permit, be raised by the respondent Contracting Party in its written or oral observations on the admissibility of the application". It was clear from the case file that that condition had not been satisfied in this instance. The Government were

---

rule; the Convention system, the Contracting States cannot on their own authority waive compliance with it": Appl. 9587/81, *X v. France*, D&R 29 (1982), p. 228 (240) and Appl. 10416/83, *K v. Ireland*, D&R 38 (1984), p. 158 (160).

[235] See Appl. 2547/65, *X v. Austria*, Coll. 20 (1966), p. 79 (83) and Appl. 5207/71, *X v. Federal Republic of Germany*, Yearbook XIV (1971), p. 698 (708-710).

[236] The decision on Appl. 9120/80, *Unterpertinger v. Austria*, D&R 33 (1983), p. 80 (83), seems to go in this direction.

[237] Appl. 23178/94, *Aydin v. Turkey*, D&R 79-A (1994), p. 116 (119); Appl. 23182/94, *Dündar v. Turkey*; Appl. 23185/94, *Asker v. Turkey*; joined Appls 22947/93 and 22948/93, *Akkoç v. Turkey*, D&R 79-A (1994), p. 108 (115).

[238] Appl. 22493/93, *Berktay v. Turkey*, D&R 79-A (1994), p. 97 (102).

[239] Judgment of 25 May 1998, para. 81.

consequently estopped from raising this objection. Nor could the Court accept that the applicant had altered the subject matter of her application, since her complaints had manifestly always concerned the absence of fair compensation for the expropriation of her land. The subsequent payment of an amount of compensation contested by the applicant was, admittedly, a new fact, but one which was linked to her original complaints.[240]

2.2.10.8 Moment at which the local remedies must have been exhausted

The Commission has taken a flexible attitude with respect to the moment at which the local remedies must have been exhausted. It considered it sufficient if the decision of the highest national court had been given at the moment when the Commission decided on the admissibility of the application.[241] Thus the Commission held that it was not obliged to reject a complaint for failure to exhaust domestic remedies on account of the fact that appeals were still pending at the time when the application was lodged.[242] And in a case concerning the length of proceedings the Commission held that for the purposes of Article 6(1), having regard to the protracted duration of proceedings, it was not bound to reject a complaint for failure to exhaust domestic remedies because appeals were still pending at the time when the application was introduced.[243]

The Commission's flexible attitude in this respect could, on the other hand, also cause problems for the applicant. The Commission has, for instance, decided that a remedy which was not open to the applicant at the time of the lodging of his application, but became available only afterwards as a result of a change in the case law of the national court concerned, had nevertheless to be exhausted in order to satisfy the requirements flowing from the local remedies rule.[244]

In the *Baumann* Case the Court held that the assessment of whether domestic remedies have been exhausted is normally carried out with reference to the date on which the application was lodged with it.[245] Nevertheless, this rule is subject to exceptions, which may be justified by the particular circumstances of a case. Thus, after the Italian Parliament passed a special act designed to provide a domestic remedy for

---

[240]   Judgment of 1 March 2001, para. 40.
[241]   Appl. 2614/65, *Ringeisen v. Austria*, Yearbook XI (1968), p. 268 (306); Appl. 13370/87, *Deschamps v. Belgium*, D&R 70 (1991), p. 177 (187). See also the judgment of 16 July 1971, *Ringeisen*, para. 91; Appl. 16278/90, *Karaduman v. Turkey*, D&R 74 (1993), p. 93 (106).
[242]   Appl. 9019/80, *Luberti v. Italy*, D&R 27 (1982), p. 181 (193); Appls 15530/89 and 15531/89, *Mitap and Müftüoglu v. Turkey*, D&R 72 (1992), p. 169 (189); Appl. 16278/90, *Karaduman v. Turkey*, D&R 74 (1993), p. 93 (106).
[243]   Appl. 12850/87, *Tomasi v. France*, D&R 64 (1990), p. 128; Appls 15530/89 and 15531/89, *Mitap and Müftüoglu v. Turkey*, D&R 72 (1992), p. 169 (189).
[244]   Appl. 7878/77, *Fell v. the United Kingdom*, D&R 23 (1981), p. 102 (112).
[245]   Decision of 22 May 2001.

alleged violations of the 'reasonable-time' requirement ('the Pinto Act'), the Court found a departure from that general principle justified because the growing number of identical applications threatened to "affect the operation, at both national and international level, of the system of human-rights protection set up by the Convention".[246]

2.2.10.9 The effect of the declaration of inadmissibility

The effect of a declaration of inadmissibility on account of non-exhaustion of the local remedies is generally of a *dilatory* character. The applicant may submit his case again to the Court after having obtained a decision from the national court concerned. In fact such a decision is considered as relevant new information by the Court, so that the application will not be rejected as being substantially the same as a matter already examined by the Court in the sense of Article 35(2)(b). The question of whether the local remedies rule must also be applied if meanwhile the national time-limits for appeal have expired, so that in fact local remedies are no longer available, will have to be decided on a case-by-case basis. Application of the rule in such a case has *peremptory* effect, since both the national and the international procedure are then barred. Such a consequence appears justified only when the individual in question is to be blamed for having allowed the time-limit to expire. A clear-cut answer to this, as well as several other questions concerning the application of the local remedies rule, cannot be given *in abstracto*. For guidance, use may be made of the general starting-point that that which can be demanded of the individual is not "what is impossible or ineffective, but only what is required by common sense, namely 'the diligence of a bonus pater familias'".[247]

2.2.10.10 Special circumstances absolving from the obligation of prior exhaustion

The Commission and the Court have accepted the possibility that according to the generally recognised rules of international law there may be special circumstances in which even effective and adequate remedies may be left unutilised.[248] The following special circumstances have been invoked by applicants: doubt on the part of the applicant as to the effectiveness of the relevant remedy;[249] lack of knowledge on his part as

---

[246]   Decision of 8 November 2001, *Giacometti*.

[247]   Judge Tanaka in his separate opinion in the *Barcelona Traction* Case, *ICJ Reports*, 1970, p. 148.

[248]   Appl. 2257/64, *Soltikow v. Federal Republic of Germany*, Yearbook XI (1968), p. 180 (224). See also Appl. 6861/75, *X v. the United Kingdom*, D&R 3 (1976), p. 147 (152).

[249]   Appl. 3651/68, *X v. the United Kingdom*, Yearbook XIII (1970), p. 476 (510-514); Appl. 19819/92, *Størksen v. Norway*, D&R 78-A (1994), p. 88 (93).

to (the existence of) a particular remedy;[250] non-admittance of an appeal because of a procedural mistake by the applicant;[251] poor health of the applicant;[252] advanced age of the applicant;[253] poor financial position of the applicant or the high costs of the procedure;[254] lack of free legal aid;[255] fear of repercussions;[256] errors or wrong advice by counsel or by the authorities;[257] the fact that two applicants had filed the same complaint, while only one applicant has exhausted the domestic remedies.[258] So far, special circumstances justifying the non-exhaustion have been recognised only exceptionally in the case law.

In the *Akdivar* Case the Court took account of the fact that the events complained of took place in an area of Turkey subject to martial law and characterised by severe civil strife. In such a situation the Court was of the opinion that it must bear in mind the insecurity and vulnerability of the applicants' position following the destruction of their homes and the fact that they must have become dependent on the authorities in respect of their basic needs. Against such a background the prospects of success of civil proceedings based on allegations against the security forces had to be considered negligible in the absence of any official inquiry into their allegations, even assuming that they would have been able to secure the services of lawyers willing to press their claims before the courts. In this context the Court found particularly striking the Commission's observation that the statements made by villagers following the events complained of gave the impression of having been prepared by the police. Nor could the Court exclude from its considerations the risk of reprisals against the applicants or their lawyers if they had sought to introduce legal proceedings alleging that the security forces were responsible for burning down their houses as part of a deliberate State policy of village clearance. Therefore, the Court considered that, in the absence of convincing explanations from the Government in rebuttal, the applicants had demonstrated the existence of special circumstances which dispensed them at the time of the events complained of from the obligation to exhaust the domestic remedies.[259] In the

---

[250]   Appl. 5006/71, *X v. the United Kingdom*, Coll. 39 (1972), p. 91 (95) Appl.15488/89, *Dello Preite v. Italy*, D&R 80 (1995), p. 14.

[251]   Appl. 23256/94, *Hava v. Czech Republic*, D&R 78-B (1994), p. 139 (144); 25046/94, *Grof v. Austria*, D&R 93 (1998), p. 29.

[252]   Appl. 3788/68, *X v. Sweden*, Yearbook XIII (1970), p. 548 (580-582).

[253]   Appl. 568/59, *X v. Federal Republic of Germany*, Coll. 2 (1960), p. 1 (3).

[254]   Appl. 181/56, *X v. Federal Republic of Germany*, Yearbook I (1955-1957), p. 139 (140-141).

[255]   Appl. 1295/61, *X v. Federal Republic of Germany* (not published).

[256]   Appl. 2257/64, *Soltikow v. Federal Republic of Germany*, Yearbook XI (1968), p. 180 (228).

[257]   Appl. 41250/98, *Steglich-Petersen v. Denmark*, D&R 94 (1998), p 163; See, however, the Court's judgment of 13 May 1980, *Artico*, para. 27. In Appl. 10000/82, *H v. the United Kingdom*, D&R 33 (1983), p. 247 (253), the Commission accepted that all domestic remedies were exhausted, since the applicant had received counsel's advice that a domestic remedy would have no prospect of success.

[258]   Appl. 9905/82, *A. Association and H v. Austria*, D&R 36 (1984), p. 187 (192) where the Commission also considered the second applicant's case to be admissible.

[259]   Judgment of 16 September 1996, paras 73-75; judgment of 24 April 1998, *Selçuk and Asker*, para. 65; judgment of 8 January 2004, *Ayder*, para. 91.

Selmouni Case the Commission had previously held that a situation where national authorities had remained passive in the face of serious allegations of misconduct or infliction of harm by State agents, was a relevant criterion in absolving the applicant from the obligation to exhaust domestic remedies.[260]

In the *Bahaddar* Case the Government maintained that the applicant had not exhausted the domestic remedies available to him. The Deputy Minister of Justice had rejected the application for revision of his refusal to recognise the applicant's refugee status or, in the alternative, to grant him a residence permit on humanitarian grounds. The applicant's lawyer had appealed against this decision to the Judicial Division of the Council of State, stating that the grounds for the appeal would be submitted as soon as possible. The lawyer was reminded by the Judicial Division three months later that no such grounds had yet been received and was invited to submit them within a month. She failed to do so, submitting her grounds of appeal only three months later; she had not asked for an extension of the time-limit, as she might have done. The Court held that even in cases of expulsion to a country where there is an alleged risk of ill-treatment contrary to Article 3, the formal requirements and time-limits laid down in domestic law should normally be complied with, such rules being designed to enable the national jurisdictions to discharge their caseload in an orderly manner. Whether there are special circumstances which absolve an applicant from the obligation to comply with such rules will depend on the facts of each case. It should be borne in mind in this regard that in the case of applications for recognition of refugee status it may be difficult, if not impossible, for the person concerned to supply evidence within a short time, especially if – as in the present case – such evidence must be obtained from the country from which he or she claims to have fled. Accordingly, time-limits should not be so short, or applied so inflexibly, as to deny an applicant for recognition of refugee status a realistic opportunity to prove his or her claim. In the case under examination, however, it would have been possible for the applicant to request an extension of the time-limit.[261]

In the Case of *R.M.D. v. Switzerland* the applicant complained about the fact that he had been detained for two months in seven different cantons, which had deprived him of any possibility of having the lawfulness of his detention reviewed by a court as required by Article 5(4) of the Convention. Regarding the question of whether the applicant had fulfilled the requirement of exhaustion of domestic remedies, the Court noted that it must take realistic account not only of the *existence of formal remedies* in the legal system of the Contracting Parties concerned, but also of the *context* in which they operate and the *personal circumstances* of the applicant. In this case the applicant was transferred to different counties of Switzerland in a short period of time. The applicant filed a complaint about his detention at the court in the first county,

---

[260]   Appl. 25803/94, D&R 88 B (1997), p. 55 (62-63).
[261]   Judgment of 19 February 1998, paras 45-46.

but when he was transferred, that court declared itself unable to decide on the matter. The applicant did not file another complaint at any of the other counties. According to the Court, the applicant could not be blamed for failing to avail himself of the remedies available in the other counties, since he was in a position of great legal uncertainty, because he could be transferred to another county soon. Furthermore, he had many practical difficulties in arranging effective representation, as many detained persons have. The problem in this case was not that remedies were unavailable in each of the cantons, but that they were ineffective in the applicant's particular situation. Because of the constant transfers he was unable to obtain a decision from a court regarding his detention as he was entitled to under Article 5(4).[262]

In the *Ayder* Case, where an unqualified undertaking was given by a senior public official that all property owners would be compensated for damage sustained and damage assessment reports were subsequently prepared with respect to each property, the Court found that, in the absence of a clear indication to the contrary, property owners could legitimately expect that compensation would be paid without the necessity of their commencing proceedings in the administrative courts. The Court did not consider that it had been shown that the need for each property owner to bring separate judicial proceedings was made sufficiently clear. In the light of the foregoing, the Court concluded that special circumstances existed which dispensed the applicants from the obligation to exhaust domestic remedies.[263]

2.2.10.11 Final observations

In certain cases the issue of the exhaustion of the local remedies may coincide with the question of whether or not the Convention has been violated. In *X v. the United Kingdom*, for example, the Commission decided that: "Having regard to the fact that the applicant has included in his application a complaint under Article 13 of the Convention concerning the absence of an effective remedy, (...) the Commission considers that it cannot reject all or part of the application as being inadmissible for failure to comply with the requirements as to the exhaustion of domestic remedies."[264]

Finally, it deserves mentioning that an applicant deprives himself of the ability to exhaust local remedies when he consents to the settlement of his claim with the national authorities. If that is the case, his application is declared inadmissible in Strasbourg on account of non-exhaustion.[265]

---

[262]   Judgment of 26 September 1997, paras 43-45
[263]   Judgment of 8 January 2004, paras 101-102.
[264]   Appl. 7990/77, *X v. the United Kingdom*, D&R 24 (1981), p. 57 (60).
[265]   See, *e.g.*, Appl. 7704/76, *X v. Federal Republic of Germany* (not published).

2.2.11 THE OBLIGATION TO SUBMIT THE APPLICATION WITHIN SIX MONTHS AFTER THE FINAL NATIONAL DECISION

2.2.11.1 General

The six-month time-limit set forth in Article 35(1) serves to prevent the compatibility of a national decision, action or omission with the Convention being questioned after a considerable lapse of time by the submission of an application to the Court. Its purpose is to maintain reasonable legal certainty and to ensure that cases raising issues under the Convention are examined within a reasonable time. It ought also to prevent the authorities and other persons concerned from being kept in a state of uncertainty for a long period of time. Lastly, the rule is designed to facilitate establishment of the facts of the case, which otherwise, with the passage of time, would become more and more difficult, thus making a fair examination of the issue raised under the Convention problematic.[266] On the other hand, the period of six months is considered to leave the person concerned with sufficient time to evaluate the desirability of submitting an application to the Court and to decide on the content thereof.[267]

The introduction of the application, and not its registration by the Registry to the Court, has to take place within a period of six months from the final decision.[268] In the *Cajella* Case the Court considered that the date of introduction of the application was, at the latest, 17 July 2001, which was less than six months after 23 January 2001, the date on which the Constitutional Court gave its judgment on the issue.[269]

The six-month rule is an admissibility condition which applies to applications by States as well as by individuals.

2.2.11.2 Final decision

There is a close relationship between the admissibility condition of the six-month period and the one concerning the exhaustion of local remedies.[270] Not only are they combined in the same Article, but they are also expressed in a single sentence whose grammatical construction implies such correlation. From the grammatical construction of Article 26 [the present Article 35(1)], in which the two conditions were set forth, the Commission inferred that "the term 'final decision', therefore, in Article 26 refers exclusively to the final decision concerned in the exhaustion of all local

---

[266]   Appl. 15213/89, *M v. Belgium*, D&R 71 (1991), p. 230 (234).
[267]   Appl. 22714/93, *Worm v. Austria*, D&R 83 (1995), p. 17; Appl. 32026/96, *Lacour v. France*, D&R 90 (1997), p. 141.
[268]   Appl. 24909/94, *Bonomo v. Italy*, D&R 92 (1998), p. 5; decision of 6 February 2003, *Belchev*.
[269]   Decision of 18 March 2004.
[270]   Decision of 29 January 2004, *Berdzenishvili*.

remedies according to the generally recognised rules of international law, so that the six-month period is operative only in this context."[271] From this the Commission concluded at a later instance that, if no local remedy is available, the challenged act or decision itself must be considered as the 'final decision'.[272]

In the case of *Christians against Racism and Fascism* the applicant association complained about a police order prohibiting all public processions other than those of a religious, educational, festive or ceremonial character, for a period running from 24 February to 23 April 1978. No remedy was available to challenge the ensuing measures or their application to the association's planned procession on 22 April 1978. With respect to the six-month period the Commission decided: "This period must normally be calculated from the final domestic decision, but where, as in the present case, no domestic decision is required for the application of a general measure to the particular case, the relevant date is the time when the applicant was actually affected by that measure. In the present case, this was the date of the procession planned by the applicant association, i.e. 22 April 1978."[273]

The Commission took a similar line in the case of an applicant who complained that he had not been entitled to have the lawfulness of his detention determined by a court contrary to Article 5(4). As the right guaranteed in Article 5(4) is applicable only to persons deprived of their liberty, the Commission decided that a person alleging a breach of that provision must, in the absence of a particular constitutional remedy or other similar remedies which could redress an alleged breach of Article 5(4), submit such a complaint to the Commission within six months from the date of his release.[274] And in the case of an application concerning the level of compensation after nationalisation of an industry, the Commission took the position that the six-month period did not run from the date of the nationalisation Act but from the date on which the amount of compensation for shareholders was fixed. In the Commission's opinion Article 26 [the present Article 35(1)] could not be interpreted so as to require an applicant to seize the Commission at any time before his position in connection with the matter complained of had been finally determined or settled at the domestic level.[275]

---

[271] Appl. 214/56, *De Becker v. Belgium*, Yearbook II (1958-1959), p. 214 (242).

[272] See, *e.g.*, Appl. 7379/76, *X v. the United Kingdom*, D&R 8 (1977), p. 211 (212-213); decision of 10 January 2002, *Hazar*; Decision of 6 May 2004, *Miconi*.

[273] Appl. 8440/78, D&R 21 (1981), p. 138 (147).

[274] Appl. 10230/82, *X v. Sweden*, D&R 32 (1983), p. 303 (304-305).

[275] Appl. 9266/81, *Yarrow P.L.C. and Others v. the United Kingdom*, D&R 30 (1983), p. 155 (187). Similarly, in Appls 8588/79 and 8589/79, *Bramelid and Malmström v. Sweden*, D&R 29 (1982), p. 64 (84), the Commission decided that in proceedings concerning the right to purchase company shares leading to two subsequent decisions, one on the right to purchase and the other on the price, the six-month time-limit runs from the second decision to the extent that the individuals concerned complain in particular about the price.

The above-mentioned link between the two admissibility conditions laid down in Article 35(1) has as a further consequence, that the criteria used by the Court in answering the question of whether a given local remedy must or must not be sought, are also relevant for determing the question of whether the time-limit has been observed;[276] the time-limit starts at the moment of the last national decision in the chain of local remedies that had to be exhausted. This means that remedies which the applicant did not have to pursue, for instance because they are not effective and adequate, are not taken into account as the starting-point of the time-limit. An applicant cannot, therefore, defer the time-limit, for instance by lodging a request for pardon, applying to an incompetent organ, or asking for reopening of his case. Decisions on such requests are not regarded as final national decisions in the sense of Article 35(1).[277]

A curious decision of the Commission in this connection is the one in the *Nielsen Case*. Although Nielsen's application had been lodged more than six months after the decision of the highest Danish court, the Commission did not declare it inadmissible on that account. Nielsen had in the meantime addressed a request to the Special Court of Revision and the Commission took the date of the decision of that court as the starting-point of the time-limit for appeal.[278]

The close relation between the two admissibility conditions of Article 35(1) may place the applicant in a difficult situation if he is not sure whether a particular remedy must or must not be pursued. If he first brings a certain action and waits for the outcome, he incurs the risk of subsequently not being received by the Court on account of exceeding the time-limit of six months, if the remedy in question did not have to be sought in the Court's opinion. If, on the other hand, he does not seek that remedy, he incurs the risk of not being received on the ground of non-exhaustion. In such a case an applicant is well-advised to lodge an application with the Court and at the same time to seek the remedy concerned. If later on the Court concludes that exhaustion of the remedy concerned was not required, at least the time-limit will have been complied with. And if the Court decides otherwise, the final national decision will as a rule still be in time, since the local remedies have to be exhausted only at the moment at which the Court decides on admissibility. If the national decision is not in time, the applicant may again lodge an application with the Court, the final national decision constituting a new fact. In matters like these the Commission used to take a flexible attitude. An Italian applicant contacted the Commission for the first time on 21 July

---

[276]   See, *e.g.*, Appl. 5759/72, *X v. Austria*, D&R 6 (1977), p. 15 (16); Appl. 7805/77, *Pastor X and Church of Scientology v. Sweden*, D&R 16 (1979), p. 68 (71); Appl. 15213/89, *M. v. Belgium*, D&R 71 (1991), p. 230 (235).

[277]   See, for example, with regard to a request to reopen the case Appl. 10431/83, *G. v. Federal Republic of Germany*, D&R 35 (1984), p. 241 (243) and Appl. 10308/83, *Altun v. Federal Republic of Germany*, D&R 36 (1984), p. 209 (231).

[278]   Appl. 343/57, Yearbook II (1958-1959), p. 412 (434-444).

1978, setting out in his letter the substance of his complaint. Subsequently he sought reopening of proceedings in Italy, possibly as a result of the information provided by the Commission's Secretariat. The applicant did not contact the Commission again until 17 February 1981, at the end of the reopening procedure. The Commission nevertheless considered his application to have been introduced on 21 July 1978, and, therefore, in time.[279]

In the *Miconi* Case the Court observed that in Italy there is no time-limit on the filing of an application for review of a law's constitutionality after the entry into force of the law. As this application for review can be made several times at any stage of proceedings, the Court noted that this could have unreasonable consequences as far as the six-months rule is concerned if the Constitutional Court's judgment was to be considered the final decision within the meaning of Article 35 of the Convention. Therefore, in the circumstances of the case, the Court found that the decision of the Constitutional Court given on 20 July 2000 was not the final decision within the meaning of Article 35(1) of the Convention. As a result, the six-month period ran from the entry into force of the law complained of. In this respect the Court considered that where the law complained of is a provisional act, such as the legislative decree in the present case, the 'final decision' within the meaning of the Convention is the definitive law which embodies that act. As Legislative Decree no. 166/1996 was never converted into a law, the Court found that Law no. 448/1998 was the final decision, as it maintained the effects of the said legislative decree. Consequently, the six-month period started to run from the date of entry into force of that law, i.e. on 1 January 1999.[280]

2.2.11.3 Starting-point of the time-limit

Although the six-month time-limit formally starts running from the moment at which the final national decision is taken, the Commission accepted the date on which that decision was notified to the applicant as the relevant moment, provided that the applicant was previously ignorant of the decision.[281] If a judgment is not delivered at a public hearing, the six-month period starts at the moment it was served on the applicant.[282] In the *Worm* Case the Court noted that, under domestic law and practice, the applicant was entitled to be served *ex officio* with a written copy of the Court of Appeal's judgment, and that the long delay for this service was exclusively the responsibility of the judicial authorities. The said judgment, which in its final version ran to over nine pages, contained detailed legal reasoning. In these circumstances the Court

---

[279]   Appls 9024/80 and 9317/81, *Colozza and Rubinat v. Italy*, D&R 28 (1982), p. 138 (158).
[280]   Decision of 6 May 2004.
[281]   Appl. 899/60, *X v. Federal Republic of Germany*, Yearbook V (1962), p. 136 (144-146). *Cf.* Appl. 9991/82, *Bozano v. Italy*, D&R 39 (1984), p. 147 (155).
[282]   Decision of 9 July 2002, *Venkadajalasarma*.

shared the Commission's view that the object and purpose of Article 26 [the present Article 35(1)] were best served by counting the six-month period as running from the date of service of the written judgment. Moreover, this was the solution adopted by Austrian law in respect of time-limits for lodging domestic appeals.[283] The position adopted by the Commission that the period started at the moment the applicant's lawyer became aware of the decision completing the exhaustion of domestic remedies, notwithstanding the fact that the applicant only became aware of the decision later, would seem to be disputable. After all it is the applicant's own decision whether or not to file an application in Strasbourg.[284]

Depending on the nature of the case concerned, notification of the operative part of the judgment might be insufficient. For the six-month period to start running, the subsequent notification of the full text giving the reasons for the judgment may be decisive.[285] In this respect, the Commission emphasised that the need to provide the person concerned with sufficient time to evaluate the desirability of submitting an application to the Commission and to decide on the content thereof, can only be satisfied from the moment when the applicant has been able to acquaint himself not only with the decision rendered by the national judicial authorities but also with the factual and legal grounds for that decision.[286] However, if the applicant knew that the decision was taken, but has made no further efforts to become acquainted with its contents, the date of the decision is considered the starting-point of the time-limit.[287]

Unlike in the case of the local remedies rule, where the moment at which the Court decides on admissibility is decisive, for the time-limit of the six-month period it is the date of receipt of the application that counts. In the case of the local remedies rule, the Commission evidently relied on the English version of Article 26 [the present Article 35(1)], which includes the words 'may only deal with the matter', while for its position concerning the time-limit for bringing the application it found support in the French text, which reads: *'ne peut être saisie que'*. In the *Iversen* Case the Norwegian Government submitted that the date of registration of the application with the Secretariat was to be considered as the decisive date. The Commission, however, decided that for the question of whether an applicant had or had not lodged the complaint in due time, the relevant date was "at the latest the date of its acknowledged arrival at the Secretariat-General."[288] In practice, the Commission took the date of the applicant's first letter as the decisive moment, in which he stated that he wished to

---

[283] Judgment of 27 August 1997, para. 33.
[284] Appl. 14056/88, *Aarts v. the Netherlands*, D&R 70 (1991), p. 208 (212); Decision of 7 September 1999, *Keskin*; Decision of 19 December 2002, *Pejic*.
[285] Appl. 9299/81, *P v. Switzerland*, D&R 36 (1984), p. 20 (22).
[286] Appl. 10889/84, *C. v. Italy*, D&R 56 (1988), p. 40 (57).
[287] Appl. 458/59, *X v. Belgium*, Yearbook III (1960), p. 222 (234); Decision of 23 September 2004, *Çelik*.
[288] Appl. 1468/62, *Iversen v. Norway*, Yearbook VI (1963), p. 278 (322).

lodge an application and gave some indication of the nature of the complaint.[289] The mere submission of certain documents was considered insufficient.[290]

Since the scope of an application in respect of the date of introduction is circumscribed by the terms of the applicant's first communication, the Court must also examine whether the further details of the application should be considered as legal submissions in respect of the applicant's main complaint to which the six-month rule would not be opposable,[291] or whether they should be considered as separate complaints introduced at a later stage.[292] The Commission concluded in a case where the applicant initially complained under Article 6(1) of lack of access to court, that his subsequent submissions alleging the lack of an oral hearing amounted to a fresh complaint. The Commission found that the complaint of a lack of an oral hearing contained a distinct, precise fact in respect of the right to a fair hearing. In these circumstances, for the purposes of the six-month rule, the complaints had to be considered separately.[293]

In the case of *19 Chilean nationals and the S. Association* the Commission was faced with the question of how to treat the declaration of 18 Chileans that they adhered to an application already lodged with the Commission by another Chilean. The Commission took the date of application for the 18 persons as their declaration and not the date of the filing of the original application.[294]

In a case where a period of almost seven years had elapsed between the initial letter to the Commission and the final completion of the application, the Commission first examined the question of the date of introduction of the application. The applicant wrote to the Commission for the first time on 12 December 1982 in a letter briefly setting out all her complaints. On 8 February 1983 the Secretariat sent her a letter drawing her attention to the need to exhaust domestic remedies. The letter also informed her that the application would be registered as soon as she returned the application form she had been given during a visit to the Secretariat. No more was heard from the applicant until 28 April 1989, on which date she sent the Commission a letter setting out in detail the complaints raised in December 1982 and including the relevant documents. On 30 June 1989 she sent the Commission a duly completed and signed application form. The Commission recalled that, according to its established practice, it considered the date of introduction of an application to be the date of the applicant's first letter indicating his intention to lodge an application and giving

---

[289]   Appl. 4429/70, *X v. Federal Republic of Germany*, Coll. 37 (1971), p. 109 (110). See also Appl. 8299/78, *X and Y v. Ireland*, D&R 22 (1981), p. 51 (72); Appl. 10293/83, *X v. the United Kingdom*, D&R 45 (1986), p. 41 (48).

[290]   Appl. 9314/81, *N v. Federal Republic of Germany*, D&R 31 (1983), p. 200 (201).

[291]   Appl. 12015/86, *Hilton v. the United Kingdom*, D&R 57 (1988), p. 108 (113).

[292]   Appl. 10857/84, *Bricmont v. Belgium*, D&R 48 (1986), p. 106 (153).

[293]   Appl. 18660/91, *Bengtsson v. Sweden*, D&R 79-A (1994), p. 11 (19-20).

[294]   Appls 9959/82 and 10357/83, *19 Chilean nationals and the S. Association v. Sweden*, D&R 37 (1984), p. 87 (89).

some indication of the nature of the complaints he wishes to raise. However, where a substantial interval followed before the applicant submitted further information, the particular circumstances of the case had to be examined in order to decide which date should be regarded as the date of introduction of the application.[295] Although the express obligation laid down in Article 26 [the present Article 35(1)] of the Convention concerned only the introduction of an application, and the Commission had hitherto shown generosity in this respect by accepting that the date of introduction should be held to be the date on which the first letter setting out the complaint was submitted, without imposing any other restrictions, the Commission held that it would be contrary to the spirit and purpose of the six-month rule laid down in Article 35(1) of the Convention to accept that by means of an initial letter an applicant could set in motion the procedure provided for in Article 34 of the Convention only to remain inactive thereafter for an unlimited and unexplained period of time.[296] The Commission pointed to the fact that it had always rejected applications submitted more than six months after the date of the final decision, if the running of time had not been interrupted by any special circumstance. It considered that it would be inconsistent with the object and purpose of the six-month rule to deviate from this practice when the application had actually been introduced within six months of the final decision but has not been pursued thereafter.[297]

In the *Papageorgiou* Case the Court held that an application is lodged on the date of the applicant's first letter, provided the applicant has sufficiently indicated the purpose of the application. Registration – which is effected when the Secretary to the Commission [at present: the Registrar of the Court] receives the full case file relating to the application – has only one practical consequence: it determines the order in which applications will be dealt with. As to the applicant's alleged negligence, the Court considered that parties to proceedings could not be required to enquire day after day whether a judgment that has not been served on them has been delivered.[298]

In the *Monory* Case the Court recalled that it had previously stated that when the reasons for a decision are necessary for the introduction of an application, the six-month period ordinarily runs not from the date of notification of the operative part of the decision but from the date on which the full reasons for the decision were given. It noted that on 7 April 2000, when the letter enquiring about the outcome of the proceedings before the Romanian courts was sent by the Hungarian Ministry to their Romanian counterpart, the applicant was already acquainted with the outcome of his appeal on points of law but not with the reasons given by the court. The date on which

---

[295] Appl. 15213/89, *M v. Belgium*, D&R 71 (1991), p. 230 (234).
[296] *Ibidem.*
[297] See Appl 10626/83, *Kelly v. the United Kingdom*, D&R 42 (1985), p. 205 (206).
[298] Judgment 22 October 1997, para 32.

he found out about the reasons for the decision was, at the earliest, 24 May 2001 when the Romanian Ministry communicated the text of the final decision to the applicant.[299] The Court noted that the Romanian Ministry represented the applicant in all the proceedings before the Romanian courts. All documents in the case, including previous court decisions, were sent by the Romanian Ministry to their Hungarian counterpart, which then forwarded them to the applicant. Furthermore, the letter addressed by the Romanian Ministry to their Hungarian counterpart on 5 March 2001 indicated that the Romanian Ministry alone played an active role in the proceedings before the Romanian courts. At no time did the courts communicate directly with the applicant. All documents, including subpoenas, were sent to the Romanian Ministry in their capacity of representative of the applicant. Furthermore, the Court acknowledged that the final decision was not subject to *ex officio* service on the parties. It recalled that according to its case law, if the applicant or his representative fails to make reasonable efforts to obtain a copy of the final decision, the delay in the lodging of the application with the Court is deemed to be due to their own negligence.[300] Accordingly, in the present case, the obligation to make all reasonable efforts to obtain a copy of the decision fell equally on the applicant and on his representative, the Romanian Ministry. As for the applicant, the Court noted that he had made reasonable efforts in order to obtain the decision. When he found out, unofficially, that the Oradea Appellate Court had adopted the decision, he used the customary channel of communication and asked for a copy of this decision. Hence, on 7 April 2000, the Hungarian Ministry asked their Romanian counterpart for a copy of the decision to be transmitted to them. As a consequence of his action, the applicant received the final decision of 2 February 2000 on 29 May 2000 by letter of 24 May 2000. Given the Romanian Ministry's role as representative of the applicant, its obligation to make all reasonable efforts in order to obtain the copy of the final decision was implied. Given that the Romanian Ministry was part of the Romanian Government, the Court noted that the Government enjoyed a dual capacity in the instant case: that of the representative of the applicant in the Hague Convention proceedings and that of the respondent Government of the High Contracting Party. In these circumstances it considered that the Romanian Ministry's failure to obtain a copy of the decision in their capacity as representative of the applicant could not be likened to the negligence of a private representative. The Romanian Ministry constituted part of the respondent Government and that Government could not invoke in their defence their own failures or negligence. The fact could not be overlooked that the applicant was a foreign national living outside the territory of Romania and could not be expected to know the language of the Romanian courts, i.e. Romanian. Accordingly, for any such contacts, the applicant would have needed the services of a representative. Under the Hague Convention, this

---

[299]   Decision of 17 February 2004.
[300]   See the decision of 9 April 2002, *Züleyha Yilmaz*.

role was played by the Romanian Ministry. The Court acknowledged that the Hague Convention does not impose on the Government the obligation to serve final decisions on the applicant. Notwithstanding this, it noted that the Hague Convention does impose on the Government an obligation to represent the applicant and, in this capacity, to make all reasonable efforts to secure to the applicant the enjoyment of his parental rights. Therefore, the Court considered that the applicant made all reasonable efforts to obtain a copy of the final decision of 2 February 2000. It thus considered that the starting date for the calculation of the six-month period was, at the earliest, 24 May 2000. It followed that the application, lodged with the Court on 23 November 2000, was within the six-month time limit.[301]

2.2.11.4 Continuing situation

A special starting date for the time-limit applies to cases involving a so-called 'continuing situation', where the violation is not (only) constituted by an act performed or a decision taken at a given moment, but (also) by its consequences, which continue and thus repeat the violation day by day. As long as that continuing situation exists, the six-month period does not commence, since it serves to make acts and decisions *from the past* unassailable after a given period.[302]

A well-known example is the *De Becker* Case. De Becker had been sentenced to death in 1946 for treason during the Second World War. Later this sentence was converted into imprisonment and in 1961 he was released under certain conditions. Under Belgian criminal law such a sentence resulted in the limitation of certain rights – including the right to freedom of expression – which limitation continued to apply after the release. The Commission held that this was a continuing situation and considered the complaint admissible *ratione temporis*. It considered that the six-month rule was not applicable here, because the issue was whether, by the application to De Becker of the Belgian legislation in question, the Convention was still being violated.[303]

The Commission disagreed, however, with an applicant who alleged the existence of a continuing violation of Article 13 insofar as no domestic remedy was available to him in respect of a deprivation of possession. According to the Commission: "Where domestic law gives no remedy against such a measure, it is inevitable that unless the law changes that situation will continue indefinitely. However the person affected suffers no additional prejudice beyond that which arose directly and immediately

---

[301] Decision of 17 February 2004.
[302] See in this respect Appl. 14807/89, *Agrotexim Hellas S.A. v. Greece*, D&R 72 (1992), p. 148 (158); Appl. 17864/91, *Çinar v. Turkey*, D&R 79-A (1994), p. 5 (7); judgment of 25 March 1999, *Iatridis*, para. 50; judgment of 1 March 2001, *Malama*, para. 35.
[303] Appl. 214/56, *De Becker v. Belgium*, Yearbook II (1958-1959), p. 214 (230-234). See also Appl. 4859/71, *X v. Belgium*, Coll. 44 (1973), p. 1 (18).

from the initial measure. His position is not therefore to be compared to that of a person subject to a continuing restriction on his substantive Convention rights."[304]

In another case the Commission held that the failure of the State to pay certain sums which were due to the applicant, created an ongoing situation in which the six-month rule did not apply.[305] The same was held to be the case when the administration failed to comply with the judgment of the Council of State which annulled the administrative decision refusing the applicants' application for a licence to establish a foreign language school.[306]

In the above-mentioned *De Becker* Case the continuing situation ensued from a legal provision. In those cases where the continuing situation was due to a judicial decision or a decision of the executive, the Commission applied the time-limit in the usual way.[307] The Commission adopted the view with respect to the latter that they were pronounced at a clearly defined moment and that the resulting consequences could be of a temporary nature and might be terminated. However, it is difficult to understand why a continuing situation could not thus be called into existence as well. Legislative measures are of course also taken at a clearly defined moment and, in the case of De Becker, the legal provision concerned became effective with respect to him at a specific moment. Moreover, the legal consequences of legislative measures may also be of a temporary nature and may be terminated by the legislator. The distinction made by the Commission would, therefore, seem to require more convincing reasoning. In the case of *McDaid and Others* the Commission held that a 'continuing situation' referred to a state of affairs which operated by continuous activities by or on the part of the State to render the applicants victim. Where complaints relate to specific events which occurred on identifiable dates, the fact that the events continue to have serious repercussions on the applicants' lives does not constitute a continuing situation.[308]

In the *Malama* Case the Court noted that, following the judgment of 12 September 1997 in which the Athens Court of First Instance had declared that the applicant was entitled to the amount of compensation determined in 1993, the applicant repeatedly requested payment of the compensation, but to no avail. She subsequently applied to the Commission complaining that she had been unable to obtain fair compensation for the expropriation of her land. Those circumstances indicated the existence of a continuing situation in relation to her complaints concerning the fairness of the pro-

---

[304] Appl. 8206/78, *X v. the United Kingdom*, D&R 25 (1982), p. 147 (151).
[305] Appl. 11698/85, *X v. Belgium* (not published); Appl. 11966/86, *X v. Belgium* (not published).
[306] Appl. 18357/91, *D. and A. H. v. Greece*, HRLJ, Vol. 16, No. 1-3, 1995, p. 50 (52). See also Appls 7572/76, 7586/76 and 7587/76, *Ensslin, Baader and Raspe v. Federal Republic of Germany*, D&R 14 (1979), p. 66 (113).
[307] See, *e.g.*, Appl. 1038/61, *X v. Belgium*, Yearbook IV (1961), p. 324 (334) and Appls 8560/79 and 8613/79, *X and Y v. Portugal*, D&R 16 (1979), p. 209.
[308] Appl. 25681/94, D&R 85(1996), p. 134: Decision of 30 March 2004, *Koval*.

ceedings and her right to peaceful enjoyment of her possessions; accordingly, the six-month rule could not be relied on against her. Although the compensation payable for the expropriation was indeed assessed by the Court of Appeal in 1993, it was quite clear that the applicant could not at that time have ascertained the precise value of 10 (old) paper drachmas per square metre, since that sum was not converted into new drachmas until 21 December 1998. Not until that date did she know how much she had been awarded. The six-month rule was, therefore, not applicable.[309]

2.2.11.5 Special circumstances absolving from the requirement of the six-month rule

With respect to the six-month rule, the Commission has also admitted that special circumstances might occur in which the applicant need not satisfy this requirement. The case law on this point is almost identical to that regarding special circumstances in connection with the local remedies rule.[310] In the *Toth* Case the Court adopted the liberal approach taken by the Commission and held that it was hardly realistic to expect a detainee without legal training to fully understand the complexity of the case concerned particulary with regard to the difference between the two types of procedure involved. The applicant was, therefore, excused for not strictly complying with the six-month rule.[311]

Special considerations could apply in exceptional cases where an applicant first avails himself of a domestic remedy and only at a later stage becomes aware, or should have become aware, of the circumstances which make that remedy ineffective. In such a situation, the six-month period might be calculated from the time when the applicant becomes aware, or should have become aware, of these circumstances.[312]

2.2.11.6 Anonymous applications

Article 35(2)(a) provides that the application must not be anonymous. This condition makes it possible to bar applications which have been lodged for purely political or propaganda reasons, although cases are also conceivable in which an applicant wishes to remain anonymous for fear of repercussions. However, after having lodged his complaint, the applicant is asked if he objects to his identity being disclosed. If he objects, his identity will not be disclosed during the procedure before the Court nor in the judgment or decision.[313] For obvious reasons the condition does not apply to inter-State applications.

---

[309] Judgment of 1 March 2001, para. 35.
[310] See *supra* 2.2.10.10.
[311] Judgment of 12 December 1991, para. 82.
[312] Judgment of 29 June 2004, *Dogan and Others*, para.113.
[313] Rule 47(3) of the Rules of Court.

In practice this admissibility condition does not present many problems. The overwhelming majority of applications contain the name of the applicant and the other information which has to be supplied according to the Rules of Court. Moreover, the Commission has developed a flexible attitude as regards the identity of the applicant. Thus, although it declared inadmissible an application that was signed 'lover of tranquillity', it did so only because the documents filed did not contain a single clue as to the identity of the applicant.[314] The Commission's flexible attitude was also evident in a case in which a number of applications had been submitted by an association. The Commission considered both the association and its individual members as applicants. With respect to the individual members the Commission held that their identity had been insufficiently established and that accordingly their application, properly speaking, was inadmissible under Article 27(1)(a) [the present Article 35(2)(a)]. Nevertheless, the Commission pursued the examination of the case on the presumption that this procedural defect would subsequently be redressed. Eventually, however, the application was declared inadmissible on other grounds.[315] In a case where two organisations of doctors and nurses complained of unjustified and discriminatory interference with the right of their member doctors and nurses to respect for their private lives, the Commission noted that they did not claim to be victims of a violation of the Convention themselves. Once they had stated that they were representing various individuals, who had thus become applicants, it became essential for the associations to identify these individuals and to show that they had received specific instructions from each of them. Since this had not been done, the rest of the application had to be rejected as anonymous within the meaning of Article 35(2)(a).[316]

2.2.12   SUBSTANTIALLY THE SAME APPLICATIONS

2.2.12.1 Introduction

Article 35(2)(b) provides that the application must not be substantially the same as a matter which has already been examined by the Commission or has already been submitted to another procedure of international investigation or settlement unless it contains relevant new information. This ground of inadmissibility does not apply with respect to inter-State complaints.[317] However, this does not prelude the Court

---

[314]   Appl. 361/58, *X v. Ireland, Case-Law Topics, No. 3, Bringing an application before the European Commission of Human Rights*, Strasbourg, 1972, p. 10.

[315]   Appl. 3798/68, *Church of X v. the United Kingdom*, Yearbook XII (1969), p. 306 (318).

[316]   Appl. 10983/84, *Confédération des Syndicats Médicaux Français and Fédération Nationale des Infirmiers v. France*, D&R 47 (1986), p. 224 (229).

[317]   Report of 4 October 1983, *Cyprus v. Turkey*, D&R 72 (1992), p. 5 (23); Appl. 25781/94, *Cyprus v. Turkey*, D&R, 86 A (1996), p. 104 (133-134).

from considering at the merits stage whether and, if so, to what extent an inter-State application is substantially the same as a previous one. As the Commission observed in its Report on the Case of *Cyprus v. Turkey*,[318] Article 27(1)(b) [the present Article 35(2)(b)] reflects a basic legal principle of procedure which in inter-State cases arises during the examination of the merits. The Commission held that it could not be its task to investigate complaints already examined in a previous case, and a State could not, therefore, except in specific circumstances, claim an interest to have new findings made where the Commission has already adopted a Report under former Article 31 of the Convention concerning the same matter.[319] The same holds good for Court judgments.

In practice, declarations of inadmissibility on the ground of the identical character of two or more applications do not occur frequently.[320] In the *Times Newspapers Ltd.* Case[321] the applicants referred to their earlier application[322] and alleged the failure of the United Kingdom Government to implement the judgment of the Court in that case.[323] With respect to this part of the application the Commission first pointed out that the supervision of judgments of the Court under Article 54 [the present Article 46] is entrusted to the Committee of Ministers and subsequently decided that it "cannot now examine these new developments in relation to the facts of the former case (...), as it is barred from doing so by Article 27 paragraph 1(b) [the present Article 35(2)(b)] of the Convention".[324] In the case of *Cyprus v. Turkey* (the fourth inter-state case) the Commission recalled that in its Report of 10 July 1976 concerning applications Nos. 6780/74 and 6950/75, *Cyprus v. Turkey* (the first and second inter-State cases), it had considered that the evidence before it did not allow a definitive finding with regard to the fate of Greek Cypriots declared to be missing. Although in its Report of 4 October 1983 concerning application No. 8007/77, *Cyprus v. Turkey* (the third inter-State case), the Commission had considered that it had found sufficient indications, in an indefinite number of cases, that Greek Cypriots who were still missing at the time had been unlawfully deprived of their liberty, it could not be

---

318   Report of the Commission of 4 October 1983, D&R 72 (1992), p. 5(22).
319   Appl. 25781/94, *Cyprus v. Turkey*, D&R 86 A (1996), p. 104(132-133).
320   Some of the rare published cases in which this aspect came up for discussion are Appls 5145/71, 5246/71, 5333/72, 5586/72, 5587/72 and 5332/72, *Michael and Margarethe Ringeisen v. Austria*, Coll. 43 (1973), p. 152 (153); Appls 5070/71, 5171/71 and 5186/71, *X v. Federal Republic of Germany*, Yearbook XV (1972), p. 474 (482); and Appls 7572/76, 7586/72 and 7587/76, *Ensslin, Baader and Raspe v. Federal Republic of Germany*, Yearbook XXI (1978), p. 418 (452). In Appl. 3479/68, *X v. Austria and the Federal Republic of Germany*, Coll. 28 (1969), p. 132 (138), the Commission took into account a previously lodged complaint, "even if it cannot strictly be said to be substantially the same".
321   Appl. 10243/83, D&R 41 (1985), p. 123.
322   Appl. 6538/74, *Times Newspapers Ltd, Sunday Times and Harold Evens v. the United Kingdom*, D&R 2 (1975), p. 90.
323   Judgment of 26 April 1979, para. 21.
324   Appl. 10243/83, *Times Newspapers Ltd. and Others v. the United Kingdom*, D&R 41 (1985), p. 123 (129).

established with any certainty that this finding also concerned the cases in the present applications. Finally, the Commission recalled that an examination of the merits of application No. 25781/94, *Cyprus v. Turkey* (the fourth inter-State case) still remained to be carried out. In these circumstances the Commission reserved the question of whether the present applications did concern a "matter" which had "already been examined" by the Commission in the context of one of the inter-State cases. For the same reason the Commission postponed to the merits stage the Government's arguments about the *res judicata* effect of the Committee of Ministers' resolution in the third inter-State case.[325]

In the *Oberschlick* Case the applicant complained under Article 10 of the Convention that his right to freedom of expression had been violated because the Supreme Court had dismissed the plea of nullity for the preservation of the law as regards his conviction for defamation, which the European Court of Human Rights had found to be in violation of Article 10 of the Convention. The Commission found that the applicant was not complaining about his previous conviction, but about the Supreme Court's decision of 17 September 1992, which was taken after the European Court of Human Rights had given its *Oberschlick* judgment on 23 May 1991.[326] Consequently, the application was not considered identical.

2.2.12.2 An application which is substantially the same

Although in the case of *Cyprus v. Turkey*, mentioned above, the Commission decided that Article 35(2)(b) did not apply with respect to inter-state complaints, it did not exclude that it would have to consider at the merits stage whether and, if so, to what extent the present inter-State application was substantially the same as a previous one.[327] The Commission, therefore, reserved the question whether and, if so, to what extent the applicant Government could have a valid legal interest in the determination of the alleged continuing violations of the Convention insofar as they had already been dealt with in previous Reports of the Commission. The Commission noted in this context that at least some of the complaints raised did not seem to be covered by definitive findings in earlier Reports, while some others seemed to concern entirely new facts.

For an answer to the question of whether a concrete case concerns a matter which is substantially the same as a matter which has already been examined by the Court, it is decisive whether new facts have been put forward in the application. These facts must be of such a nature that they cause a change in the legal and/or factual data on which the Court based its earlier decision. The mere submission of one or more new

---

[325] Appl. 25781/94, *Cyprus v. Turkey*, D&R 86 A (1996) p. 104 (133-134).
[326] Appl. 19255/92 and 21655/93, D&R 81 A (1995), p. 5(10).
[327] Appl. 25781/94, *Cyprus v. Turkey*, D&R 86 A (1996), p. 104 (134).

legal arguments is, therefore, insufficient, if the facts on which the application is based are the same.[328] The Commission did not consider as new facts those which were already known to the applicant at the time of the introduction of his application and could, therefore, have been presented by him on that occasion.[329]

A new fact is indeed involved when an applicant, whose earlier application has been declared inadmissible on account of non-exhaustion of local remedies, has afterwards obtained a decision in the last resort in the national legal system. The Commission's flexibility in this respect became evident in the following example. An applicant had submitted in a previous application that the final decision in his case had been taken by the Court of Appeal at Liège. On that basis his application was declared inadmissible because he was considered not to have exhausted the local remedies. In a new application he proved that he had made a mistake, since the decision in question had in reality been taken by the Court of Cassation, from whose decisions there is no appeal. The Commission considered this as relevant new information in the sense of Article 35(2)(b).[330] Obviously, a subsequent appeal in the last resort does not avail an applicant if his earlier application has been declared inadmissible on another ground as well.

A new fact is also involved when new obligations arise from the Convention for the Contracting State in question. An example is the case where a detained person complained about the refusal of the German authorities to permit him to leave Germany and live in Poland. His application was declared inadmissible on account of incompatibility with the provisions of the Convention, because the right to leave the country was not guaranteed in the Convention. In his new application he invoked Protocol No. 4, which had meanwhile become binding on Germany and whose Article 2(2) confers on everyone the right to leave a country, including that of which he is a national. As a result, the application was admissible under Article 35(2)(b). However, it was then rejected as being manifestly ill-founded, because paragraph 3 of Article 2 of Protocol No. 4 was held to permit an exception with respect to detained persons.[331]

Those cases in which the requirement of 'a fair and public hearing within a reasonable time' of Article 6 is at issue may present a somewhat special feature, as is shown by the following decision of the Commission. In his first complaint the applicant alleged a violation of the Convention, because a bankruptcy procedure had been pending against him for the past three years. This application was declared manifestly ill-founded. At the time when the Commission had to give its opinion on his second,

---

[328] See Appl. 202/56, *X v. Belgium*, Yearbook I (1955-1957), p. 190 (191) and Appl. 8206/78, *X v. the United Kingdom*, D&R 25 (1982), p. 147 (150).

[329] Appl. 13365/86, *Ajinaja v. the United Kingdom*, D&R 55 (1988), p. 294 (296).

[330] Appl. 3780/68, *X v. Belgium*, Coll. 37 (1971), p. 6 (8). See also Appl. 21962/93, *A.D. v. the Netherlands*, D&R 76-A (1994), p. 157 (161). See also, on the one hand, Appl. 4517/70, *Huber v. Austria*, Yearbook XIV (1971), p. 548, on the other hand, Appl. 6821/74, *Huber v. Austria*, D&R 6 (1977), p. 65.

[331] Appl. 4256/69, *X v. Federal Republic of Germany*, Coll. 37 (1971), p. 67 (68-69).

'identical' complaint, the period had meanwhile increased to four years and eight months. This time the applicant was not dismissed by the Commission on the ground that "the time aspect constitutes in itself the relevant new information in the sense of Article 27(1)(b)."[332]

In *I.J.L v. the United Kingdom* the applicant complained about a report prepared by Inspectors appointed by the Department of Trade and Industry under sections 432(2) and 442 of the Companies Act 1985 to investigate allegations of an unlawful share support operation at the time of the take-over by Guinness PLC of the Distillers Company PLC. The applicant maintained that the Report referred quite extensively to him and was pejorative, containing criticisms of his honesty both in relation to the events which were the principal subject matter of the Report and his responses to the Inspectors. The content of the Report was seriously detrimental to his reputation, all the more so in view of the intense media interest generated by it. The Court noted that the applicant complained in a separate application (no. 29522/95), *inter alia*, that the Inspectors' investigation, his trial and conviction and the resultant publicity had blighted his reputation and led to the annulment of his knighthood. As a result he invoked Article 8 of the Convention. In its partial inadmissibility decision on this complaint the Commission found that, insofar as these matters could be considered an unjustified interference with the applicant's right under Article 8, that interference would in any event be justified under Article 8(2) of the Convention because it fulfilled the 'in accordance with the law' requirement. The Commission had found, as a result, that the applicant's complaint was inadmissible as being manifestly ill-founded. For the Court the publication of the Report could not be said to have caused the applicant any further prejudice to his private life including reputation over and above that attendant on his conviction following a lengthy jury trial. It further considered that in the circumstances the applicant's new application had the same factual basis as that of his previously rejected complaint under Article 8 notwithstanding that he had sought to support it with a new legal argument. Since the application was substantially the same as a matter that had previously been examined by the Convention institutions, it was inadmissible within the meaning of Article 35(2)(b) and (4) of the Convention.[333]

2.2.12.3 The same applicant

From the formulation of Article 35(2)(b) it could be inferred that the words 'substantially the same matter' also cover an application that is otherwise identical but

---

is lodged by another applicant. The provision is, however, to be interpreted in the sense that it is only directed against identical applications by the same applicant. It would not be in conformity with the purpose of the Convention to provide individual legal protection, if an application from X, who considers himself to be the victim of a violation of the Convention, would not be admitted on the ground of the fact that an identical violation in relation to Y is already being examined or has already been examined. In fact, the Commission did not object to identical applications from different applicants, although it then joined such cases, if possible.[334]

Article 35(2)(b) may, however, bar applications from different applicants which concern the same violation against the same person, for instance if, in connection with the same violation both the direct and the indirect victim lodge an application. In its earlier case law the Commission considered a new examination of the case justified only if in each individual case a new fact was involved.[335] In a later case, however, the Commission was less strict. This case concerned the execution of an expulsion order from the Federal Republic of Germany to Yugoslavia. At first instance the fiancee of the person to be expelled lodged a complaint with the Commission, which was followed several years later by a complaint by the person himself. With respect to the latter application the Commission decided that it could not be rejected under Article 35(2)(b) as being substantially the same as the first application, because "this applicant has a specific personal interest in bringing an application before the Commission".[336] Here the criterion was not the identity of the case, but the identity of the interests of the applicants involved. In the *Peltonen* Case the applicant complained about a refusal to issue a passport. The Government drew the Commission's attention to the fact that the applicant's brother had submitted a communication with similar contents to the Human Rights Committee under the Optional Protocol to the Covenant on Civil and Political Rights. The Commission held that it was true that the freedom guaranteed by Article 2(2) of Protocol No. 4 resembled that protected by Article 12 of the International Covenant on Civil and Political Rights. The Commission recalled, however, that if the complainants before the Commission and, for instance, the United Nations Human Rights Committee were not identical, the complaint to the Commission could not be considered as being substantially the same as the communication to the Committee.[337]

---

[334] See, *e.g.*, the successive Appls 6878/75, *Le Compte v. Belgium*, D&R 6 (1977), p. 79 and 7238/75, *Van Leuven and De Meyere v. Belgium*, D&R 8 (1977), p. 140. In its decision in the last-mentioned case the Commission held (p. 160): "In view of all the similarities between the two applications it is desirable that they should be examined together". The same conclusion can also be drawn from the opinion of the Commission on the Appls 5577/72-5583/72, *Donnelly and Others v. the United Kingdom*, Yearbook XVI (1973), p. 212 (266) that "apart from the fact that the applicants are different in each case (...) this complaint could still not be rejected under Article 27(1)(b) of the Convention."

[335] Appl. 499/59, *X v. Federal Republic of Germany*, Yearbook II (1958-1959), p. 397 (399).

[336] Appl. 9028/80, *X v. Federal Republic of Germany*, D&R 22 (1981), p. 236 (237).

[337] Appl. 19583/92, D&R 80 A (1995), p. 38(43).

The question of identical complaints may also arise in connection with the lodging of a complaint by a State as well as by an individual. Thus, in the applications of a number of Northern Irishmen matters were denounced which had already formed the subject of the application of the Irish Government against the United Kingdom. The latter application had meanwhile been declared admissible, but the examination of the merits was still pending. The Commission did not decide on the question of whether the individual applications were now to be rejected on account of their having the same character as the application by a State, because "the relevant part of the inter-State case has (...) not yet been examined within the meaning of Article 27(1)(b) of the Convention."[338] This result in itself may be welcomed, but the reasoning on which it is based is less satisfactory. Indeed, the argument set forth by the Commission leaves wide open the possibility that in similar cases, where the examination has already been completed, the Commission may decide differently. On the ground of the emphasis which the Convention puts on individual legal protection this would be regrettable since it might discourage individual applicants. The application of a State and that of an individual are distinctly different, both in character and as to the interests involved. The latter specicically concerns the personal interests of the individual applicant, while the former is aimed much more at denouncing a general situation concerning 'European public order'. It is, therefore, questionable whether in the case of a succession of two applications of so different a character it is still possible to speak of 'a matter which is substantially the same'.

2.2.12.4 A matter which has already been submitted to another procedure of international investigation or settlement

So far very few decisions have been published in which an application was declared inadmissible on the ground that a matter had already been submitted to another international body for investigation or settlement. In view of the small number of international organs charged with the supervision of the implementation of human rights obligations this is not surprising. It is, however, somewhat surprising in connection with the UN Covenant on Civil and Political Rights and the Optional Protocol accompanying it.[339] This Protocol confers on individuals the right to submit an application ('communication') to the Human Rights Committee,[340] so that a case referred to in Article 35(2)(b) is quite conceivable.[341] The Commission held that it would be against the letter and spirit of the Convention if the same matter was simultaneously submitted to two international institutions. Article 35(2)(b) of the Convention aims at avoiding

---

[338]   Appls 5577-5583/72, *Donnelly and Others v. the United Kingdom*, Yearbook XVI (1973), p. 212 (266).
[339]   The UN Covenant on Civil and Political Rights and the Optional Protocol belonging thereto entered into force on 26 March 1976.
[340]   See Art. 1 of the Protocol.
[341]   See *supra* 1.13.6.

the plurality of international procedures concerning the same case.[342] In considering this issue the Commission needed, and the Court now needs to verify whether the applications to the different institutions concern substantially the same person, facts and complaints.[343] An application introduced with the Commission alleging a violation of Article 6(1) in the proceedings concerning a pension claim, where simultaneously an application had been submitted to the Human Rights Committee alleging discrimination contrary to Article 26 of the Covenant, could in the opinion of the Commission not be considered as being substantially the same notwithstanding that they emanated from the same facts.[344]

In order not to run the risk of being declared inadmissible by the Court under Article 35(2)(b), the applicant has to withdraw his application lodged with the other body. It is not sufficient to request a suspension of the proceedings pending before that body, because this does not have the same effect as a complete withdrawal of the application, which is the only step that allows the Court to examine an application also brought before it.[345]

New events subsequent to the introduction of an application but directly related to the facts adverted to therein will be taken into account by the Court at the time of the examination of the application. Therefore, an application introduced before the Commission by two applicants, which had the same object as the application submitted to the Human Rights Committee by one of the applicants and joined by the second after the introduction of the application before the Commission, was considered to be substantially the same as the one submitted to the Human Rights Committee.[346]

In a case where the application had been submitted by the Council of Civil Service Unions and six individuals the Commission held that these applicants were not identical to complaints before the ILO organs concerned. The complaints before the ILO were brought by the Trade Union Congress, through its General Secretary, on its own behalf. The six individual applicants before the Commission would not have been able to bring such complaints since the Committee on Freedom of Association only examines complaints from organisations of workers and employees. Accordingly, the application could not be regarded as being substantially the same as the complaints before the ILO.[347] However, in a subsequent case the Commission decided the opposite. The applicants in this case were 23 former employees of a company. They had been dismissed because of the attitude they had taken as members of the works

---

[342]   Appl. 17512/90, *Calcerrada Fornielles and Cabeza Mato v. Spain*, D&R 73 (1992), p. 214 (223).
[343]   Appl. 11603/85, *Council of Civil Service Unions v. the United Kingdom*, D&R 50 (1987), p. 228 (251); App. 24872/94, *Pauger v. Austria*, D&R 80 A (1995), p. 170(174).
[344]   Appl. 16717/90, *Pauger v. Austria*, D&R 80 A (1995), p. 24(32).
[345]   *Ibidem.*
[346]   *Ibidem.*
[347]   Appl. 11603/85, *Council of Civil Service Unions and Others v. the United Kingdom*, D&R 50 (1987), p. 228 (237).

council. The Government submitted that the World Federation of Industry Workers (WFIW) had submitted a complaint to the Freedom of Association Committee of the ILO. Therefore, the complaint should be rejected as being substantially the same. The Commission noted that in the present case, although the main complainant was the WFIW, the four trade unions representing the workers at the company on the works council joined the proceedings, which specifically concerned the dismissal of the 23 applicants – the very persons who petitioned the Commission. Although formally the 23 individual applicants before the Commission were not the complainants who appeared before the ILO organs, the Commission adopted the view that the complaint was, in substance, submitted by the same applicants. On that basis the Commission concluded that the parties were substantially the same.[348] It seems that the Commission considered it conclusive that the original applicants were members of the trade union branches which participated in the proceedings before the ILO organs, although the Commission admitted that individual applicants could not complain before the Freedom of Association Committee of the ILO.[349]

In the *Lukanov* Case the applicant complained about conditions of detention. In the same case the Human Rights Committee of the Inter-Parliamentary Union examined in particular the conditions of the applicant's detention. On 12 September 1992, at the 88th Conference of the Inter-Parliamentary Council, the Committee issued a Report on the applicant's case. The matter was still under consideration by the Union. The Commission observed that the Inter-Parliamentary Union was an association of parliamentarians from all over the world, set up *inter alia* to unite parliamentarians in common action and to advance international peace and cooperation. The Union is a non-governmental organisation. The organs of the Union may adopt resolutions which are communicated by the parliamentarians concerned to the national parliaments and to international organisations. The Commission considered that the term 'another procedure' referred to judicial or quasi-judicial proceedings similar to those set up by the Convention. Moreover, the term 'international investigation or settlement' refers to institutions and procedures set up by States, thus excluding non-governmental bodies. The Commission considered that the Inter-Parliamentary Union constituted a non-governmental organisation, whereas Article 35(2)(b) referred to inter-governmental institutions and procedures. It followed that the procedures of the Inter-Parliamentary Union did not constitute 'another procedure of international investigation or settlement' within the meaning of Article 35(2)(b) of the Convention.[350]

---

[348]   Appl. 16358/90, *Cereceda Martin and Others v. Spain*, D&R 73 (1992), p. 120 (134).
[349]   Appl. 11603/85, *Council of Civil Service Unions and Others v. the United Kingdom*, D&R 50 (1987), p. 228 (237); Appl. 16358/90, *Cereceda Martin and Others v. Spain*, D&R 73 (1992), p. 120 (134).
[350]   Appl. 21915/93, D&R 80 A (1995), p. 108(123-124).

In the *Hill* Case the Court noted that it appeared from the file that the applicant and his brother had introduced an application with the UN Human Rights Committee set up under the International Covenant on Civil and Political Rights complaining that their right to a fair trial had been breached by the Spanish courts, namely the Provincial High Court of Valencia. The Court observed that on 2 April 1997 the Human Rights Committee had given its view on the case, finding Spain to be in breach of several provisions of the Covenant. In an effort to execute this finding, the applicant had instituted two separate sets of proceedings before the Spanish authorities which had still not ended. The Court noted that the application did not concern the breach of the applicant's right to a fair trial guaranteed by Article 6 of the Convention in the framework of the criminal proceedings against him in the Provincial High Court of Valencia. The complaints submitted to the Court concerned the execution of the decision of the UN Human Rights Committee finding a violation of several rights guaranteed by the International Covenant. However, the Court did not need to decide whether the application could be rejected as being substantially the same as those submitted to the Human Rights Committee, as it was in any case inadmissible *ratione materiae*.[351]

In the *Smirnova and Smirnova* Case the Court ascertained to what extent the proceedings before it overlapped with those before the United Nations Human Rights Committee. The Court noted, first, that the communication pending before the Human Rights Committee was lodged by and concerned only the first applicant and its effects could not for this reason be extended to the second applicant. Next, the first applicant's complaints in that case were directed against her arrest on 26 August 1995 and raised, in particular, the question whether this arrest was justified, the impossibility of challenging it in the courts, and the conditions of detention. The scope of the factual basis for the first applicant's application to the Court, although going back to the arrest of 26 August 1995, was significantly wider. It extended to the whole of the proceedings which terminated in 2002 and included the first applicant's arrest on three more occasions since 26 August 1995. It followed that the first applicant's application was not substantially the same as the petition pending before the Human Rights Committee, and that being so, it fell outside the scope of Article 35(2)(b) of the Convention and could not be rejected pursuant to that provision.[352] In the Case of *Kovacic, Mrkonjic and Golubovic* the Court acknowledged that the Convention institutions have interpreted the concept of 'substantially the same application' very restrictively. They have found themselves prevented from dealing with an application if the applicant in the other international procedure was the same as the applicant who lodged the

---

[351] Decision of 4 December 2001.
[352] Decision of 3 October 2002.

application with the Commission or with the Court.[353] The Court continued that, even assuming that arbitration proceedings before the International Monetary Fund and mediation proceedings under the auspices of the Bank for International Settlement in the framework of succession negotiations were pending and that their subject matter were the same as that in the present cases, that the parties to the IMF and BIS procedures were not the same as those to the proceedings before the Court. It followed that it had not been shown that an application identical to, or substantially the same as, those before the Court in the present cases had already been submitted to another procedure of international investigation or settlement.[354]

The Court of Justice of the European Communities also has jurisdiction to deal with human rights issues within the Community context.[355] The applicable human rights issues may be identical to issues covered by the Convention. This will be even more so after the EU Charter of Fundamental Human Rights has become binding. This raises the question of whether the examination of those issues by the Court of Justice has to be considered 'another procedure of international investigation or settlement' in the sense of Article 35(2)(b) of the Convention. Leaving apart the fact that in the most of the procedures the issues raised before the two Courts will not be 'substantially the same',[356] since all the member States of the EU are also parties to the Convention and the European Court of Human Rights considers itself competent to also deal with complaints against member States of the EU that have a community context,[357] it may be expected that the Court will consider the procedure before the Court of Justice as a '"omestic remedy'. This will certainly be the case after the EU has acceded to the Convention.

---

[353]   Appl. 11603/85, *Council of Civil Service Unions and others v. the United Kingdom*, D&R 50 (1987), p. 228 (236-237)

[354]   Decision of 9 October 2003.

[355]   Standing case law since Case 11/70, *Internationale Handelsgesellschaft*, ECR, 1970, p. 1134.

[356]   Judgment of 18 February 1999, *Matthews*, paras 33-35.

[357]   An example of this is Appl. 6452/74, *Sacchi v. Italy*, D&R 5 (1976), p. 43, the core of which was also discussed by the Court of Justice in Luxembourg, of which the court of Biella had requested a preliminary ruling in Case 155/73, *Sacchi*, ECR, 1974, p. 409. Mr Sacchi, operator of a cable television firm (Telebiella) without a licence, refused to pay the contribution for the TV receiving sets, which was punishable under Italian law. Upon this, he was convicted. A request for a licence for transmission via a cable system was refused. A presidential decree of 29 March 1973 equated cable TV equipment with radio and TV equipment, thus making it subject to the RAI/TV monopoly. Sacchi lodged a complaint with the Commission in Strasbourg about violation of Art. 10(1) of the Convention. Questions were submitted to the Court in Luxembourg, *inter alia,* about free movement of goods and services, competition and national monopolies of a commercial nature.

2.2.13 APPLICATIONS INCOMPATIBLE WITH THE PROVISIONS OF THE CONVENTION

2.2.13.1 Introduction

Incompatibility with the Convention was concluded in the case law of the Commission: (1) if the application fell outside the scope of the Convention *ratione personae, ratione materiae, ratione loci,* or *ratione temporis*; (2) if the individual applicant did not satisfy the condition of Article 34; and (3) if the applicant, contrary to Article 17, aimed at the destruction of one of the rights and freedoms guaranteed in the Convention.

In relation to the categories referred to (1) it has been observed above that the Commission did not differentiate clearly between its competence and the admissibility of the application.[358] Of these categories the territorial and the temporal scope of the Convention have already been discussed above.[359] In the Case of *Cyprus v. Turkey* the Commission held that an inter-state complaint could not be rejected as being incompatible with the provisions of the Convention.[360]

2.2.13.2 Jurisdiction ratione personae

Whether an application falls within the scope of the Convention *ratione personae* is determined by the answer to the question of who may submit an application to the Court (active legitimation) and against whom such an application may be lodged (passive legitimation). This question has been answered *passim* above. An application may be lodged by any of the Contracting States as well as by those natural and legal persons, non-governmental organisations and groups of individuals who are within the jurisdiction of the State against which the complaint is directed. With respect to applications by States it should also be noted that they must be lodged by a national authority competent to act on behalf of the State in international relations. In that respect, regard must be had not only to the text of the Constitution but also to how it is applied in practice.[361]

The Court cannot receive applications directed against a State which is not a party to the Convention[362] or, as the case may be, to the Protocols relied upon in the applica-

---

[358] See *supra* 2.2.9.
[359] See *supra* 1.5.2.
[360] App. 25781/94, D&R 86 A (1996), p. 104(135)
[361] Appls 6780/74 and 6950/75, *Cyprus v. Turkey*, Yearbook XVIII (1975), p. 82 (116).
[362] For some of the numerous examples, see Appl. 262/57, *X v. Czechoslovakia*, Yearbook I (1955-1957), p. 170; Appl. 8030/77, *Confédération Française Démocratique du Travail v. European Communities*, Yearbook XXI (1978), p. 530 (536-538); Appl. 21090/92, *Heinz v. Contracting States also Parties to the European Patent Convention*, D&R 76-A (1994), p. 125 (127).

tion.[363] Furthermore, an application will be declared inadmissible *ratione personae* if the alleged violation does not come under the responsibility of the respondent State. In general, a State is internationally responsible for the acts of its legislative, executive and judicial branches of government. The question may arise as to whether a particular organ or person can be considered as belonging to these government organs for the purpose of the Convention. The case has already been mentioned of a foreign or international organ which is active in the territory of a Contracting State, but does not fall under its responsibility.[364] Thus, an application brought in substance against the European Patent Office falls outside the scope of the Court's jurisdiction *ratione personae*.[365] In the *Calabro* Case the Court held that, in so far as the applicants' complaint concerned the Greek authorities' apparent reluctance to co-operate with their Hungarian counterparts, it was competent to assure the respect of the European Convention on Human Rights and not that of any other international agreement.[366]

Furthermore, the situation may arise where a State is responsible for the international relations of a given territory without it being possible for an application to be lodged against it on account of the acts of the authorities in those territories. Indeed, the Convention is only applicable to those territories if the State in question has made a declaration as referred to in Article 56(1).[367]

Applications may be directed only against States and consequently not against individuals or groups of individuals. Applications against individuals are, therefore, declared inadmissible *ratione personae*.[368] In practice, a number of complaints are directed against the most varied categories of individuals and organisations, such as judges and lawyers in their personal capacity, employers, private radio and TV stations and banks. For the rejection of such complaints the Commission generally invoked former Article 19, under which the Commission and the Court had to ensure the observance of the engagements which the Contracting States have undertaken, and former Article 25, which permitted it to receive applications if the applicant claimed to be the victim of a violation of the Convention by a Contracting State.[369] It appears from its case law, however, that the Commission did investigate whether a violation

---

[363]   See, *e.g.*, the Appls 5351/72 and 6579/74, *X v. Belgium*, Coll. 46 (1974), p. 71 (80-81); Appl. 22564/93, *Grice v. the United Kingdom*, D&R 77-A (1994), p. 90 (97).

[364]   For the special position of the British Judicial Committee of the Privy Council, see Appl. 3813/68, *X v. the United Kingdom*, Yearbook XIII (1970), p. 586 (598-600).

[365]   Appl. 21090/92, *Heinz v. Contracting States also Parties to the European Patent Convention*, D&R 76 A (1992), p. 125 (127); Appl. 38817/97, *Lenzing AG v. the United Kingdom*, D&R 94 A (1998), p. 136 (146).

[366]   Decision of 21 March 2002. See also the judgment of 6 April 2004, *Karalyos and Huber*, para. 40, where the question concerned the European Convention on Information on Foreign Law.

[367]   On this, see *supra* 1.4.2.

[368]   See Appl. 6956/75, *X v. the United Kingdom*, D&R 8 (1978), p. 103 (104); Appl. 19217/91, *Durini v. Italy*, D&R 76-A (1994), p. 76 (79), where the complaints concerning the contents of a will were directed against the testator and did not engage the responsibility of the State.

[369]   See, *e.g.*, Appl. 2413/65, *X v. Federal Republic of Germany*, Coll. 23 (1967), p. 1 (7).

of the Convention by an individual may involve the responsibility of a State. Under international law a State is responsible for acts of individuals to the extent that the State has urged the individuals to commit the acts in question, has given its consent to them, or in violation of its international obligations has neglected to prevent those acts, to punish the perpetrators, or to impose an obligation to redress the injury caused.[370] These principles also apply within the framework of the European Convention,[371] because Article 1 creates that responsibility with respect to the treatment of 'everyone within their jurisdiction', and not only of foreigners. The Court has also held that a State cannot absolve itself from this responsibility by delegating its obligations to private bodies or individuals.[372]

The starting-point for State responsibility under the Convention is that it applies to all organs of the State, even those which under national law are independent of the Government, such as the judiciary.[373] However, it is not crystal clear in all cases whether a particular institution must be considered, with respect to the Convention, as an organ of the State concerned for which the latter is responsible. It is not possible to provide general answers to this question; a good deal depends, in each concrete case, on the precise position of the said institution under national law[374] and the involvement of public authorities. Thus, in the *Campbell and Cosans* Case the Court held the Government of the United Kingdom responsible for acts occurring at state schools, since the State had assumed responsibility for formulating general school policy.[375] In a subsequent case, where an applicant and his mother complained about corporal punishment at a private school, the punishment of the applicant was administered by the headmaster of the private school for whose disciplinary regime the Government had declined responsibility under the Convention. The Commission held, however, that the United Kingdom was responsible under the Convention, Articles 1, 3 and 8 of which having imposed a positive obligation on High Contracting Parties to ensure a legal system which provides adequate protection for children's physical and emotional integrity: "The Commission considers that Contracting States do have an obligation under Article 1 of the Convention to secure that children within their jurisdiction are not subjected to torture, inhuman or degrading treatment or punishment, contrary to Article 3 of the Convention. This duty is recognised in English law which provides certain criminal and civil law safeguards against assault or unreasonable punishment. Moreover, children subjected to, or at risk of being subjected to ill-treat-

---

[370] See I. Brownlie, *Principles of Public International Law*, Oxford, 1990, pp. 444-476.
[371] See Appl. 852/60, *X v. Federal Republic of Germany*, Yearbook IV (1961), p. 346 (350-352).
[372] Judgment of 23 November 1983, *Van der Mussele*, para 29.
[373] See, *e.g.*, Appl. 7743/76, *J.Y. Cosans v. the United Kingdom*, D&R 12 (1978), p. 140 (149).
[374] See, *e.g.*, Appl. 1706/62, *X v. Austria*, Yearbook IX (1966), p. 112 (162-164).
[375] Judgment of 25 February 1982, para. 26.

ment by their parents, including excessive corporal punishment, may be removed from their parents' custody and placed in local authority care."[376]

The Commission also noted that the State obliges parents to educate their children or have them educated in schools, and that the State has the function of supervising educational standards and the suitability of teaching staff, even in independent schools. Furthermore, the effect of compulsory education is that parents are normally obliged to put their children in the charge of teachers. If parents choose a private school, the teachers assume the parental role in matters of discipline under the national law while the children are in their care by virtue of the *in loco parentis* doctrine. In these circumstances the Commission considered that the United Kingdom had a duty under the Convention to secure that all pupils, including pupils at private schools, were not exposed to treatment contrary to Article 3 of the Convention. The Commission considered that the United Kingdom's liability also extended to Article 8 of the Convention, under which provision it had to protect the right to respect for private life of pupils in private schools to the extent that corporal punishment in such schools might involve an unjustified interference with children's physical and emotional integrity.[377] The case ended in a friendly settlement, after it had been referred to the Court. In the *Costello-Roberts* Case, however, the Court has occasion to point out that the State has an obligation to secure to children their right to education under Article 2 of Protocol No. 1. Functions relating to the internal administration of a school, such as discipline, cannot be said to be ancillary to the educational process. In this respect the Court noted that a school's disciplinary system fell within the ambit of the right to education which has also been recognised in Article 28 of the UN Convention on the Rights of the Child. Secondly, it held that in the United Kingdom independent schools co-existed with a system of public education. The fundamental right of everyone to education is a right guaranteed equally to pupils in State schools and independent schools, with no distinction being made between the two. Finally, the Court referred to the *Van der Mussele* judgment where it held that a State could not absolve itself from responsibility by delegating its obligations to private bodies or individuals.[378]

With respect to so-called public industries and enterprises the case law of the Commission has been rather casuistic. In a number of cases it did not reach a decision on responsibility.[379] In one case the Commission described public transport companies as *entreprises para-étatiques*, for which the Government was not responsible.[380] Two

---

[376] Appl. 14229/88, *Y v. the United Kingdom* (not published). See also the report of the Commission in this case of 8 October 1991, A.247-A, pp. 11-12.

[377] *Ibidem.*

[378] Judgment of 25 March 1993, para. 30.

[379] Appl. 3059/67, *X v. the United Kingdom*, Coll. 28 (1969), p. 89 (93) and Appl. 4515/70, *X and the Association of Z v. the United Kingdom*, Yearbook XIV (1971), p. 538 (544).

[380] Appl. 3789/68, *X v. Belgium*, Coll. 33 (1970), p. 1 (3-4).

later decisions, however, pointed in the other direction. In both cases the applicants had been discharged by British Rail, because they had refused to join a trade union (the so-called 'closed-shop system'). The Commission reached the conclusion that, as a public industry, British Rail came under the responsibility of the United Kingdom and that accordingly the applications were admissible *ratione personae*.[381]

Does the responsibility of the Contracting States under the Convention extend still further in the sense that it also covers cases where there is no question of direct responsibility for the acts or omissions of governmental organs or of negligence with respect to the acts of individuals? One decision of the Commission seemed to point in that direction. At issue was whether the Irish Government was responsible for certain acts of an institution which had been called into existence by law, but which otherwise was largely independent of the State. The Commission came to the conclusion that the acts concerned in this case (alleged violation of Article 11) did not fall under the direct responsibility of the Irish Government. However, the Commission subsequently accepted the submission that, despite this, the Irish Government would have violated the Convention if it were to be established that national law did not protect the right or freedom guaranteed by the Convention, the violation of which was alleged before the Commission, or at least did not provide a remedy for enforcing such protection.[382] However, rather than being a matter of State responsibility for acts of individuals, this is a case of the possible violation by the State of a specific obligation resulting from the Convention, *viz.* from Article 13.

In the *Nielsen* Case the Government argued that the placement of a minor in a psychiatric hospital was the sole responsibility of the mother. The majority of the Commission found, however, that the final decision on the question of hospitalisation of the applicant was not taken by the holder of parental rights but by the Chief Physician of the Child Psychiatric Ward of the State Hospital, thus engaging the responsibility of the State under Article 5(1).[383] The Court disagreed with the Commission and held that the decision on the hospitalisation was in fact taken by the mother in her capacity as holder of parental rights.[384]

In the *Ciobanu* Case the Court noted that the applicants' representatives failed to submit to the Court all information of relevance to the case under the Convention by introducing a complaint in the name of a deceased person, by signing the power of attorney on behalf of the deceased applicant and by omitting to inform the Court of the applicant's death. The Court further noted that the applicant died on 31 December 1996, i.e. before the submission of his complaint to the Court. Therefore, the applicant had not expressed any intention to lodge such a complaint, nor claimed

---

[381]   Appl. 7601/76, *Young and James v. the United Kingdom*, Yearbook XX (1977), p. 520 (560-562) and
        Appl. 7806/77, *Webster v. the United Kingdom*, D&R 12 (1978), p. 168 (173-175).
[382]   Appl. 4125/69, *X v. Ireland*, Yearbook XIV (1971), p. 198 (218-224).
[383]   Report of 12 March 1987, A.144, p. 38.
[384]   Judgment of 28 November 1988, para. 73.

to be a victim, as required by Article 34 of the Convention, on the date of the application. Accordingly, it found that the case was not legally brought before it as regards the applicant who, as a consequence, lacked *locus standi*. Moreover, it recalled that the representatives did not lodge any complaint with the Court in their own name, nor did they manifest their intention to continue the case of the deceased in their own capacity. It followed from this that the representatives also lacked *locus standi* for the purpose of the proceedings before the Court. Accordingly, the application was incompatible *ratione personae*.[385]

In the *Mykhaylenky* Case the issue arose whether the State was liable for the debts of a State-owned company which was a separate legal entity and could be held responsible for the ultimate failure to pay the applicants the amounts awarded to them in the judgments against that company. The Court considered that the Government had not demonstrated that the company enjoyed sufficient institutional and operational independence from the State in order to absolve the State from responsibility under the Convention for its acts and omissions. The Court noted that it was not suggested by the Government or by the materials in the case-file that the State's debts to the company had ever been paid in full or in part, which implied the State's liability as regards the ensuing debts of the company. The debtor company had operated in the highly regulated sphere of nuclear energy and conducted its construction activities in the Chernobyl zone of compulsory evacuation, which was placed under strict Governmental control due to environmental and public health considerations. This control even extended to the applicants' terms of employment by the company, including their salaries. The State had prohibited the attachment of the company's property due to possible contamination. Moreover, the management of the company was transferred to the Ministry of Energy as of May 1998. In the Court's opinion these elements confirmed the public nature of the debtor enterprise, regardless of its formal classification under domestic law. Accordingly, the Court concluded that there were sufficient grounds to deem the State liable for the debts of the company to the applicants in the special circumstances of the case, despite the fact that the company was a separate legal entity. The Court found, therefore, that the applicants' complaint was compatible *ratione personae* with the provisions of the Convention.[386]

2.2.13.3 Jurisdiction ratione materiae

In order to answer the question of whether an application falls within the scope of the Convention *ratione materiae* it is necessary to differentiate between State applications and individual applications.[387]

---

[385]   Decision of 16 December 2003.
[386]   Judgment of 30 November 2004, paras 44-46; judgment of 21 December 2004, *Derkach and Palek*, para. 32.
[387]   Strictly speaking, inter-State applications cannot be rejected on this ground.

Article 33, which permits the Contracting States to lodge applications on 'any alleged breach of the provisions of the Convention by another High Contracting Party', leaves open the possibility for States to submit applications which relate to provisions of the Convention other than the articles of Section I. Articles that might be considered as such, for instance, are Article 1 concerning the obligation for a Contracting State to secure to everyone within its jurisdiction the rights and freedoms of Section I of the Convention, and Article 34 in case of interference with the exercise of the individual right of complaint. The same applies to Article 46 in case of refusal to give effect to a judgment of the Court, and Article 52 in case of refusal to furnish the requested information to the Secretary General of the Council of Europe concerning the implementation of the provisions of the Convention. So far the Contracting States have not availed themselves of this wider right of action, except as far as Article 1 is concerned.

The right of complaint of individuals has a somewhat more limited character. It appears from Article 34 that individuals may lodge complaints only about 'the rights set forth in this Convention', which implies that their complaints may relate only to the articles of Section I and the articles of the Protocols containing additional rights.[388] The question arises whether an exception must be made for Article 34; in other words, whether the right of complaint itself, the exercise of which the Contracting States have undertaken not to hinder, may be considered a 'right'. As a rule the Commission dealt with such a complaint in a way different from that of a complaint concerning the violation of one of the rights or freedoms of Section I, in that it consulted directly with the Government concerned.

It might be argued that, apart from the right of individual complaint under Article 34, if an individual who has been successful before the Court feels that the judgment has not been complied with, he or she may properly claim to be a victim of a violation of Article 46, which contains the obligation to abide by the judgment of the Court. In the case of *Olsson I* the main issue was whether the decision of the Swedish authorities to take the children of the applicants into care had given rise to a violation of Article 8 of the Convention. The Court found a violation of that provision and awarded the applicants just satisfaction under Article 41 of the Convention.[389] In the case of *Olsson II* the applicants complained that despite the Court's *Olsson I* judgment the Swedish authorities had continued to hinder their reunion with their children. The applicants had still not been allowed to meet the children under circumstances which would have enabled them to re-establish parent-child relationships. In their view Sweden had continued to act in breach of Article 8 and had thereby failed to comply with its obligations under Article 46(1) of the Convention. The Court referred to Resolution DH (88)18, adopted on 26 October 1988, concerning the execution of the *Olsson I* judgment, where the Committee of Ministers, "having satisfied itself that

---

[388] For the meaning and scope of Article 1, see *supra* 1.4.1.
[389] Judgment of 24 March 1988, para. 84.

the Government of Sweden has paid to the applicants the sums provided for in the judgment", declared that the Committee had "exercised its functions under Article 46(2) of the Convention." The Court held that in the circumstances of the case no separate issue arose under Article 46, since the present complaint raised a new issue which had not been determined by the *Olsson I* judgment.[390] The Court thus left open the possibility that there might be circumstances under which a complaint under Article 46 of the Convention could be examined by it. The late Judge Martens questioned the position that the Committee of Ministers' competence under Article 46(2) of the Convention is an exclusive one. He gave two reasons for taking the view that complaints under Article 46(1) should not be decided by the Committee of Ministers but by the Court. In the first place, the interpretation of its judgments is, in the nature of things, better left to the Court than to a gathering of professional diplomats who are not necessarily trained lawyers possessing the qualifications laid down in the Convention. Secondly, the members of the Committee of Ministers are under the direct authority of their national administrations and cannot be considered as a 'tribunal' in the sense of the Convention.[391] Under Protocol No. 14 the Committee of Ministers will has the option to refer to the Court the question of whether a Contracting Party has failed to fulfil its obligations under Article 46 (the new paragraph 4 of Article 46).

The Court cannot deal with complaints about rights or freedoms not set forth in the Convention. Complaints concerning such rights and freedoms are declared inadmissible by the Court as being incompatible with the Convention. In practice, a great many complaints concern a variety of 'rights and freedoms'. From the colourful case law of the Commission the following examples of incompatibility *ratione materiae* may be cited: right to a university degree, right to asylum, right to start a business, right to diplomatic protection, right to a divorce, right to a driving licence, a general right to free legal aid, right to free medical aid, right to adequate housing, right to a nationality, right to a passport, right to a pension, right to a promotion and the right to be recognised as a scholar. In this context it should, however, be borne in mind that a right which is not set forth in the Convention, may find protection indirectly via one of the provisions of the Convention. Thus, it is conceivable that, although the right to admission to a country of which one is not a national, has not been included in the Convention, under certain circumstances a person cannot be denied admission to a country if his right to respect for his family life (Article 8) would be violated. Similarly, although the Convention does not recognise a right to a pension, violation of an

---

[390]   Judgment of 27 November 1992, para.75.
[391]   S.K. Martens, 'Individual Complaints under Article 53 of the European Convention on Human Rights', in: Rick Lawson and Matthijs de Blois (eds.), *The Dynamics of the Protection of Human Rights in Europe. Essays in Honour of Henry G. Schermers*, Vol. III, Dordrecht, 1994, pp. 253-286 (284-286).

existing right to a pension may be contrary to Article 1 of Protocol No. 1, in which the right to the enjoyment of one's possessions is protected.

Complaints to be equated with those concerning rights not protected in the Convention are complaints concerning rights which are indeed incorporated in the Convention, but with respect to which the respondent State has made a reservation.[392] Complaints relating to such rights are also declared inadmissible on account of incompatibility with the Convention.[393]

The applicant is not required to indicate accurately in his application the rights set forth in the Convention which in his opinion have been violated. The Commission showed prepared to investigate *ex officio*, by reference to the submissions of the applicant, whether there has been a violation of one or more of the provisions of Section I. This approach is in conformity with the above-mentioned objective character of the European Convention.[394] Nevertheless, it remains advisable for an applicant or counsel to raise all important points of fact and law during the examination of admissibility. The possible consequences if this is not done are apparent from the *Winterwerp* Case. The Court held that there was an evident connection between the issue of Article 6 raised before it and the initial complaints. This, in combination with the fact that the Dutch Government had not raised a preliminary objection on the point, induced the Court to take the alleged violation of Article 6 into consideration,[395] but its observations indicate that the Court would not be prepared to adopt such a lenient attitude in all circumstances.

2.2.13.4 The requirement of victim

The second of the above-mentioned categories of cases in which the application is not compatible with the provisions of the Convention – those cases where the applicant does not satisfy the condition of Article 34 – concerns the condition which has already been discussed at length, *viz.* that an individual applicant must be able to furnish *prima facie* evidence that he is personally the victim of the violation of the Convention alleged by him, or at least has well-founded reasons for considering himself to be the victim. If he merely puts forward a violation *in abstracto* or a violation which has done a wrong

---

[392] See *infra* 38.2.

[393] See, *e.g.*, Appl. 1452/62, *X v. Austria*, Yearbook VI (1963), p. 268 (276).

[394] The approach was confirmed expressly by the Court in its judgment of 6 November 1980, *Guzzardi*, para. 106. In that case the Commission had – wrongly, according to the Italian Government – also considered the complaint in light of Art. 5, whereas the applicant had not expressly referred to it. On the basis of a detailed motivation the Court held as follows: "The Commission and the Court have to examine in the light of the Convention as a whole the situation impugned by an applicant. In the performance of this task, they are, notably, free to give to the facts of the case, as found to be established by the material before them (...), a characterisation in law different from that given to them by the applicant" (para. 58).

[395] Judgment of 24 October 1979, para. 72.

only to other persons, his application is incompatible with the provisions of the Convention.[396]

2.2.13.5 Destruction or limitation of a right or freedom

The most obvious case of incompatibility with the provisions of the Convention is the third of the above-mentioned categories. This concerns applications which are directed at the destruction or limitation of one of the rights or freedoms guaranteed in the Convention, and as such conflict with Article 17, which will hereafter be discussed in greater detail.[397] Even if Article 17 had not been written, such applications of course would still be inadmissible, *viz.* on account of abuse of the right of complaint in the sense of Article 35(3), which will now be discussed.

2.2.14   APPLICATIONS WHICH CONSTITUTE AN ABUSE OF THE RIGHT OF COMPLAINT

Article 35(3) provides that the application must not constitute an abuse of the right of complaint. On this ground, too, in practice very few applications are declared inadmissible. This may probably be accounted for by the fact that it is very difficult to establish such an abuse, since the applicant's motives cannot easily be ascertained – certainly not in so early a stage of the examination.

The prudence of the Commission in this respect appeared from its interpretation of the term 'abuse'. Thus, the fact that the applicant is inspired by motives of publicity and political propaganda does not necessarily have to imply that the application constitutes an abuse of the right of complaint.[398] In such a case it is only justified to speak of an abuse if an applicant unduly stresses the political aspects of the case.[399] Similarly, with respect to a complaint by a teacher of Turkish ethnic origin about disciplinary proceedings brought against him for using the term 'Turkish' to describe the Muslim minority in Western Thrace, the Commission noted that an application is not an abuse merely by virtue of the fact that it is motivated by the desire for publicity or propaganda.[400]

---

[396]   See *supra* 1.13.3.2.

[397]   See *infra* chapter 36.

[398]   Appl. 332/57, *Lawless v. Ireland*, Yearbook II (1958-1959), p. 308 (338). See also Appl. 8317/78, *McFeeley v. the United Kingdom*, D&R 20 (1980), p. 44 (70-71).

[399]   Appl. 1468/62, *Iversen v. Norway*, Yearbook VI (1963), p. 278 (326).

[400]   Appl. 21782/93, *Raif v. Greece*, D&R 82 A (1995), p. 5(9)

The Commission also left open the question of whether an abuse is involved on the mere ground that no practical effects are envisaged regarding the application.[401] It took a quite lenient attitude in this respect and held that an application that was said to be devoid of any sound juridical basis and to have been lodged for propaganda purposes, may not be rejected as constituting an abuse of the right of petition unless it is clearly based on untrue statements of fact.[402]

An abuse may consist primarily in the object one wishes to attain with the application. Such an abuse of the right of complaint was found to exist in the case of *Ilse Koch*. This wife of the former commander of the Buchenwald concentration camp had been convicted for violation of the most elementary human rights. She submitted that she was innocent and requested that she be released, without invoking a specific provision of the Convention. In her application she voiced a number of accusations and complaints which were not supported in any way by the Convention. The Commission declared her application inadmissible, because her sole aim was evidently to escape the consequences of her conviction, so that her application constituted a 'clear and manifest abuse'.[403]

The condition that an application must not constitute an abuse is also an expedient tool for holding querulous applicants at bay. A German had in the course of time lodged a great many applications which had been rejected without exception, either because they were manifestly ill-founded or because of non-exhaustion of the local remedies. When – together with his wife – he once again lodged several applications, which were moreover substantially the same as previous applications submitted by him, the Commission declared them inadmissible on account of abuse, and gave the applicant to understand: "It cannot be the task of the Commission, a body which was set up under the Convention 'to ensure the observance of the engagements undertaken by the High Contracting Parties in the present Convention', to deal with a succession of ill-founded and querulous complaints, creating unnecessary work which is incompatible with its real functions, and which hinders it in carrying them out."[404]

Not only the aim pursued in lodging an application, but also the applicant's conduct during the procedure may lead to a declaration of inadmissibility on account of abuse.

---

[401]   Appls 7289/75 and 7349/76, *X and Y v. Switzerland*, Yearbook XX (1977), p. 372 (406): "even assuming that the concept of abuse within the meaning of Art. 27(2) in fine may be understood as including the case of an application serving no practical purpose."

[402]   Appl. 21987/93, *Aksoy v. Turkey*, D&R 79-A (1994), p. 60 (71); Appl. 22497/93, *Aslan v. Turkey*, D&R 80 A (1995), p. 138(146); Decision of 5 October 2000, *Verbanov*.

[403]   Appl. 1270/61, *Ilse Koch v. Federal Republic of Germany*, Yearbook V (1962), p. 126 (134-136). See also Appl. 5207/71, *Raupp v. Federal Republic of Germany*, Coll. 42 (1973), p. 85 (90).

[404]   Appls 5070/71, 5171/71, 5186/71, *X v. Federal Republic of Germany*, Yearbook XV (1972), p. 474 (482). See also Appls 5145/71, 5246/71, 5333/72, 5586/72, 5587/72 and 5332/72, *Michael and Margarethe Ringeisen v. Austria*, Coll. 43 (1973), p. 152 (153); Appl. 13284/87, *M v. the United Kingdom*, D&R 54 (1987), p. 214 (218).

Thus, applications were rejected because the applicant had deliberately made false declarations in an attempt to mislead the Commission,[405] or because the applicant failed to furnish the necessary information even after repeated requests,[406] or because the applicant had broken bail and had fled,[407] or because he had used threatening or insulting language vis-à-vis the Commission or the respondent Government.[408]

The Court has repeatedly held that, although the use of offensive language in proceedings before the Court is undoubtedly inappropriate, except in extraordinary cases, an application may only be rejected as abusive if it is knowingly based on untrue facts.[409]

In the *Al-Nashif* Case the Court, while considering that an application deliberately grounded on a description of facts omitting events of central importance may in principle constitute an abuse of the right of petition, did not find it established that such a situation obtained in the present case, regard being had to the stage of the proceedings, to the fact that the information allegedly withheld only concerned new developments after the deportation complained of, and to the explanation by the applicants' lawyer.[410] In the *Klyakhin* Case the Court considered that, although some of the applicant's statements were inappropriate, they did not give rise to such extraordinary circumstances justifying a decision to declare the application inadmissible as an abuse of the right of petition.[411]

In the *Manoussos* Case the Court noted, on the one hand, that in some of the applicant's submissions he used insulting expressions about Czech people in general and about certain Czech authorities, and found nothing to warrant the use of such language. On the other hand, the Court took into consideration that such expressions were of rare occurrence in the applicant's voluminous submissions and that they had not recurred since the Section Registrar's letter in which the applicant was advised of the possible consequences of his continued use of insulting language. Considering all circumstances of the case, the Court did not find it appropriate to declare the application inadmissible as being abusive within the meaning of Article 35(3) of the Convention.[412]

---

[405]   Appls 2364/64, 2584/65, 2662/65 and 2748/66, *X v. Federal Republic of Germany*, Coll. 22 (1967), p. 103 (109) and Appl. 6029/73, *X v. Austria*, Coll. 44 (1973), p. 134.

[406]   Appl. 244/57, *X v. Federal Republic of Germany*, Yearbook I (1955-1957), p. 196 (197) and Appl. 1297/61, *X v. Federal Republic of Germany*, Coll. 10 (1963), p. 47 (48).

[407]   Appl. 9742/82, *X v. Ireland*, D&R 32 (1983), p. 251 (253).

[408]   Appl. 2625/65, *X v. Federal Republic of Germany*, Coll. 28 (1969), p. 26 (41-42) and Appl. 5267/71, *X v. Federal Republic of Germany*, Coll. 43 (1973), p. 154.; Appls 29221/95 and 29225/95, *Stankov and United Macedonian Organisation "Ilinden" v. Bulgaria*, D&R 94 A (1998), p. 68(76).

[409]   Judgment of 16 September 1996, *Akdivar*, paras 53-54; judgment of 5 October 2000, *Varbanov*, para. 36; Decision of 6 April 2000, *I.S. v. Bulgaria*; Decision of 10 April 2003, *S.H.K. v. Bulgaria*.

[410]   Judgment of 20 June 2002, para. 89.

[411]   Decision of 14 October 2003.

[412]   Decision of 9 July 2002.

In the *Duringer* Case the Court held that the applicant had sent numerous communications by letter and electronic mail, making serious accusations touching the integrity of certain judges of the Court and members of its Registry. In particular, the applicant, who had systematically tried to cast aspersions on judges of the Court, members of its Registry and politicians of the respondent State, accused certain judges of extremely serious crimes. Moreover, in seeking to ensure the widest possible circulation of his accusations and insults the applicant had evinced his determination to harm and tarnish the image of the institution and its members. The Court noted in addition that the application lodged, by a person who claimed to be called Forest Grunge, contained the same expressions as those the applicant used. It noted, furthermore, that in most passages the texts of these communications were similar, if not identical, such as with regard to their presentation and the long lists of their addressees. Even supposing that the name 'Forest Grunge' was not an alias used by the applicant, the Court considered that the applicant had repeatedly made, remarks without any foundation which were totally offensive and preposterous, and could not fall within the scope of the provisions of Article 34 of the Convention. In the Court's opinion the intolerable conduct of the applicant and Mr Forest Grunge – always supposing that the latter actually existed – was contrary to the purpose of the right of individual petition, as provided for in Articles 34 and 35 of the Convention. There was no doubt whatsoever that it constituted an abuse of the right of application within the meaning of Article 35(3) of the Convention.[413]

The fact that an applicant had omitted to inform the Commission that after the introduction of his application he had instituted proceedings before domestic courts concerning the same facts, was not considered an abuse of the right of petition.[414] The fact that an applicant publishes certain details of the examination of his case, may cause the application to be declared inadmissible on account of abuse. However, the Commission held that the appearance of an article disclosing confidential information relating to the proceedings before the Commission did not constitute an abuse of the right of petition, since the applicant's representative had merely answered questions put to him by the press, who had secured their information from other sources. The Commission considered that there was no conclusive evidence that the applicant's representative was responsible for the disclosure of this information.[415] The Commission made a similar decision in a case where the applicants had told the press of their intention to apply to the Convention organs. The confidentiality of the Commission proceedings was respected, since the applicants did not make public any information once their application had been introduced.[416]

---

[413]   Decision of 4 February 2003.
[414]   Appl. 13524/88, *F v. Spain*, D&R 69 (1991), p. 185 (194).
[415]   *Ibidem.*
[416]   Appl. 24645/94, *Buscarini, Balda and Manzaroli v. San Marino*, D&R 89 B (1997) p. 35(42).

As was pointed out above, the present admissibility condition does not apply to applications by States. Nevertheless, the case law of the Commission shows that the Commission did not exclude the possibility that an application by a State might likewise be rejected on account of abuse. This would not be done on the ground of the admissibility condition mentioned in Article 35(2), but on the ground of the general legal principle that the right to bring an action before an international organ must not be abused. Referring to its decision in the first *Greek* Case[417] the Commission stated in the case of *Cyprus v. Turkey* that "even assuming that it is empowered on general principle to make such a finding, [the Commission] considers that the applicant Government have, at this stage of the proceedings, provided sufficient particularised information of alleged breaches of the Convention for the purpose of Article 24."[418]

In its preliminary objection in the Case of *Cyprus v. Turkey* before the Court the Turkish Government pleaded that the applicant Government had no legal interest in bringing the application. They argued that Resolutions DH (79) 1 and DH (92) 12, adopted by the Committee of Ministers on the previous inter-State applications, constituted *res judicata* in respect of the complaints raised in the instant application which, they maintained, were essentially the same as those which were settled by the aforementioned decisions of the Committee of Ministers. The Court did not agree and added that this was the first occasion on which it had been seized of the complaints invoked by the applicant Government in the context of an inter-State application, it being observed that, as regards the previous applications, it was not open to the parties or to the Commission to refer them to the Court under former Article 45 of the Convention read in conjunction with former Article 48. The Court continued that, without prejudice to the question of whether and in what circumstances the Court had jurisdiction to examine a case which was the subject of a decision taken by the Committee of Ministers pursuant to former Article 32 of the Convention, it should be noted that, in respect of the previous inter-State applications, neither Resolution DH (79) 1 nor Resolution DH (92) 12 resulted in a 'decision' within the meaning of Article 32(1). This was clear from the terms of these texts. Indeed, it was to be further observed that the respondent Government accepted in their pleadings on their preliminary objections in the *Loizidou* Case that the Committee of Ministers did not endorse the Commission's findings in the previous inter-State cases. The Court accordingly concluded that the applicant Government had a legitimate interest in having the merits of the instant application examined by the Court.[419]

---

[417]   Appls 3321-3323/67 and 3344/67, *Denmark, Norway, Sweden and the Netherlands v. Greece*, Yearbook XI (1968), p. 690 (764).

[418]   Appls 6780/74 and 6950/75, *Cyprus v. Turkey*, Yearbook XVIII (1975), p. 82 (124); Appl. 25781/94, *Cyprus v. Turkey*, D&R 86 A (1995), p. 104 (134).

[419]   Judgment of 10 May 2001, paras. 65-68.

2.2.15 THE CONDITION OF NOT MANIFESTLY ILL-FOUNDEDNESS

2.2.15.1 General

Article 35(3) provides that the application must not be manifestly ill-founded. This admissibility condition, again, applies only to individual applications. Inter-State applications, which may be assumed to be filed only after extensive deliberation and to have been prepared by expert legal advisers of the Government, may in general be expected not to be manifestly ill-founded. Nevertheless, while reiterating that the wording of Article 35(2) and (3) makes reference only to Article 34, the Commission "does not exclude the application of a general rule providing for the possibility of declaring an application under Article 24 [the present Article 33] inadmissible, if it is clear from the outset that it is wholly unsubstantiated or otherwise lacking the requirements of a genuine allegation in the sense of Article 24 of the Convention."[420] Until now this has not occurred in practice. On the other hand a great many individual applications have been declared inadmissible on the ground of being manifestly ill-founded.

In practice, applications are declared manifestly ill-founded in particular if the facts about which a complaint is lodged evidently do not indicate a violation of the Convention, or if those facts cannot been proven or are manifestly incorrect. As to the latter, the applicant is required to give *prima facie* evidence of the facts put forward by him.[421] As regards the former ground, it is not always possible to distinguish clearly between manifest ill-foundedness and incompatibility with the Convention. There is incompatibility *ratione materiae* if an application concerns the violation of a right not protected by the Convention.[422] In that case the application falls entirely outside the scope of the Convention and no examination of the merits is possible. An application is manifestly ill-founded if it does indeed relate to a right protected by the Convention, but a *prima facie* examination discloses that the facts put forward cannot by any means justify the claim of violation, so that an examination of the merits is superfluous.

The case law in this matter has not always been consistent. An obvious example is the case law with respect to Article 14. According to this article the enjoyment of the rights and freedoms set forth in the Convention must be guaranteed without discrimination on any ground. Applications containing complaints about discrimina-

---

[420]   Appls 9940-9944/82, *France, Norway, Denmark, Sweden and the Netherlands v. Turkey*, D&R 35 (1984), p. 143 (161-162).
[421]   See, *e.g.*, Appl. 556/59, *X v. Austria*, Yearbook III (1960), p. 288. Similary, see the Court judgment of 9 October 1979, *Airey*, para. 18.
[422]   See *supra* 2.2.11.8.3.

tion with respect to rights or freedoms which the Convention does not protect, have sometimes been declared manifestly ill-founded and sometimes incompatible with the Convention.[423]

It has been stated above that the power to declare an application inadmissible on the ground that it is manifestly ill-founded fits into the screening function which the drafters of the Convention intended the admissibility examination to perform. For a proper discharge of that function no more is needed than the power to reject those applications the ill-founded character of which is actually *manifest*. In several cases, however, the Commission has used this competence in a way which clearly went beyond this.

A clear example is the *Iversen* Case in which the applicant complained about the possibility that existed in Norway that dentists who had recently completed their studies could be obliged to work for some time in the public service. The complaint was declared "manifestly ill-founded" by the Commission, while it raised complicated questions concerning Article 4, which moreover divided the members of the Commission.[424] Therefore, a more detailed examination of the merits would decidedly have been justified. Similarly, an application on account of violation of the freedom of expression was declared manifestly ill-founded by the Commission on the basis of the finding that a prohibition that prevented a Buddhist prisoner from sending a manuscript to the publisher of a Buddhist journal constituted a reasonable application of the prison rule concerned and that this rule itself "is necessary in a democratic society for the prevention of disorder or crime within the meaning of Article 10(2)."[425] There again, to put it mildly, it was doubtful whether this was so obvious an interpretation of the said provision of the Convention that no difference of opinion was possible among reasonable persons. It is submitted that an application should be declared to be manifestly ill-founded only if its ill-founded character is actually evident at first sight or if the decision is based on standing case law.

Therefore, it is difficult to accept as a correct interpretation and application of this 'admissibility' requirement the position of the Commission, contained in its report in the *Powell and Rayner* Case, that the term 'manifestly ill-founded' under Article 27(2) [the present Article 34(3)] of the Convention extends further than the literal meaning of the word 'manifestly' would suggest at first reading. However, this would also appear to be the Court's position. In certain cases where the Court considers at an early stage in the proceedings that a *prima facie* issue arises, it seeks the observations of the parties on admissibility and merits. The Court may then proceed to a full

---

[423]   For a declaration of manifest ill-foundedness, see, *e.g.*, Appl. 1452/62, *X v. Austria*, Yearbook VI (1963), p. 268 (278), and for a declaration of incompatibility, see, *e.g.*, Appl. 2333/64, *Inhabitants of Leeuw-St. Pierre v. Belgium*, Yearbook VIII (1965), p. 338 (360-362).

[424]   Appl. 1468/62, *Iversen v. Norway*, Yearbook VI (1963), p. 278 (326-332).

[425]   Appl. 5442/72, *X v. the United Kingdom*, D&R 1 (1975), p. 41 (42).

examination of the facts and legal issues of a case, but nevertheless may finally reject the applicant's substantive claims as manifestly ill-founded notwithstanding their 'arguable' character. In such cases the rejection of a claim under this head of inadmissibility amounts to the following finding: after full information has been provided by both parties, without the need of further formal investigation, it has now become manifest that the claim of a breach of the Convention is unfounded.[426]

2.2.15.2 Rejection of the application under Article 35(4)

Under the old system the Commission could, in the course of its examination of the merits of an individual application which it had accepted as admissible, decide to reject the application as inadmissible if, on the basis of these examinations, it reached the conclusion that not all the conditions of admissibility had been complied with (Article 29). Such a decision of the Commission required a two-third majority of its members and had to state the reasons on which it was based. Former Article 29 thus enabled the Commission to stop the procedure even at this phase on the ground of inadmissibility, thus preventing the Court or the Committee of Ministers from having to deal with the case.[427] Although the wording of Article 35(4) is not exactly the same as the former Article 29 of the Convention, the Explanatory Report to Protocol No. 11 indicates no significant differences. According to the Explanatory Report, paragraph 4 of Article 35 does not signify that a State is able to raise an admissibility question at any stage of the proceedings, if it could have been raised earlier. However, the Court will be able to reject an application at any stage of the proceedings – even without an oral hearing – if it finds the existence of one of the grounds of non-acceptance provided in Article 35. Copies of all decisions declaring applications inadmissible should be transmitted to the States concerned for information.[428] From the text of Article 35(4) it cannot be inferred that this provision may be applied only if *new* facts have become known to the Court. The principle of legal security and that of honouring justified expectations might be said to plead for such a restriction of the rule.[429]

---

[426] Report of 19 January 1989, A.172, p. 27. See also Appl. 15404/89, *Purcell v. Ireland*, D&R 70 (1991), p. 262, where it could hardly be said that the applicant did not have an 'arguable claim'. See also Judgment of 21 February 1990, *Powell and Rayner*, para. 29.

[427] See Committee of Experts, *Explanatory Report on the Second to Fifth Protocols to the European Convention for the Protection of Human Rights and Fundamental Freedoms*, H(71)11, Strasbourg, 1971, p. 27.

[428] Council of Europe, Explanatory Report to Protocol No. 11 to the European Convention of Human Rights and Fundamental Freedoms restructuring the control machinery established thereby, ETS, No. 155.

[429] A new fact was concerned, for example, when the Commission found during the examination of the merits that the applicant had used the procedure before the Commission to evade her obligations of payments vis-à-vis her creditor and thus had abused her right of complaint in the sense of Art. 27(2) of the Convention; Appl. 5207/71, *Raupp v. Federal Republic of Germany*, Coll. 42 (1973), p. 85 (89-90).

However, the case law shows that the Commission took the view that former Article 29 might also be applied on the basis of facts which were already known or might have been known to the Commission during the admissibility examination.[430]

From the *Schiesser* Case one might conclude that the Court was prepared to apply Article 29 even by analogy.[431] In that case the applicant had adduced a violation of Article 5(4), after his complaint concerning Article 5(3) had already been declared admissible by the Commission. In its report the Commission stated that, as regards Article 5(4), the requirement of previous exhaustion of local remedies had not been complied with. When the Swiss Government subsequently requested the Court to declare the application incompatible with the requirements of former Article 26, the latter took the position that it had no jurisdiction to deal with the issue, holding among other things: "The Court takes the view that, on the point now being considered, the Commission's report amounts, in substance, to an implicit decision of inadmissibility, although it does not expressly refer to Article 29(1) or even to Article 27(3)."[432] However, there could not possibly be a question of an implicit decision on the basis of Article 29, since the decision of the Commission had been taken with eleven votes in favour, one against and two abstentions. Since Article 29 (old) explicitly required unanimity, reference by the Court to Article 29(1) would seem to be out of place.

The Court reaffirmed its position in the *Artico* Case where it held with reference to its *Schiesser* judgment that "despite the apparent generality of the wording of Article 29, the respondent State is entitled by analogy to the benefit of the provisions governing the initial stage of the proceedings, in other words to obtain from the Commission, in a supplementary decision, *a ruling by majority vote* (Article 34) on the questions of jurisdiction or admissibility submitted to the Commission by the State immediately it has been led to do so by the change in the legal situation."[433]

In the Case of *K. and T. v. Finland* the Grand Chamber noted that neither the Convention nor the Rules of Court empowered it to review a decision by the panel to accept a request for a rehearing. What is more, the terms of Article 43(3) of the Convention (which provides: "If the panel accepts the request, the Grand Chamber shall decide the case by means of a judgment") make clear that once the panel has

---

[430]   See Appls 5577-5583/72, *Donnelly v. the United Kingdom*, Yearbook XIX (1976), p. 85 (252-254). See also the decision of the Commission on the Appls 5100/71, 5354/72 and 5370/72, *Engel, Dona and Schul v. the Netherlands*, B.20 (1974-76), pp. 134-140; and the decision of 29 May 1973 on Appl. 4771/71, *Kamma v. the Netherlands* (not published). Application of Art. 29 (old) in those cases did not lead to rejection of the applications, because the Commission held that all the conditions of admissibility had been satisfied. However, it may be inferred from the above-mentioned decisions that the Commission would have rejected them if the said conditions had not been satisfied, even if this could have been known during the admissibility examination.

[431]   Judgment of 4 December 1979.

[432]   *Ibidem*, para. 41.

[433]   Judgment of 13 May 1980, para. 27 (emphasis added).

accepted a request for a rehearing, the Grand Chamber has no option but to examine the case. Consequently, once the panel has noted that the case raises, or might raise, a serious question or issue within the meaning of Article 43(2), it is the entire "case", in so far as it has been declared admissible, that is automatically referred to the Grand Chamber, which in principle decides the case by means of a new judgment. However, that does not mean that the Grand Chamber may not be called upon to examine, where appropriate, issues relating to the admissibility of the application in the same manner as is possible in normal Chamber proceedings, for example by virtue of Article 35(4) *in fine* of the Convention (which empowers the Court to 'reject any application which it considers inadmissible ... at any stage of the proceedings'), or where such issues have been joined to the merits, or where they are otherwise relevant at the merits stage.[434]

The Grand Chamber may likewise be required to apply other provisions of the Convention that enable it to terminate the proceedings by a means other than a judgment on the merits, for example by approving a friendly settlement (Article 39 of the Convention) or striking the application out of the list of cases (Article 37). The principle governing proceedings before the Grand Chamber, as before the other Chambers of the Court, is that it must assess the facts as they appear at the time of its decision by applying the appropriate legal solution. Once a case is referred to it, the Grand Chamber may accordingly employ the full range of judicial powers conferred on the Court.[435]

In the *Pisano* Case the Government made a preliminary objection in which they asked the Court to declare the application inadmissible. The Court held that Article 35(4) allows the Court, even at the merits stage, subject to Rule 55 of the Rules of Court, to reconsider a decision to declare an application admissible where it concludes that it should have been declared inadmissible for one of the reasons given in the first three paragraphs of Article 35, including that of incompatibility with the provisions of the Convention (Article 35(3) taken together with Article 34). According to the Court's settled case law incompatibility *ratione personae* is present if the applicant cannot or can no longer claim to be a victim of the alleged violation. The Court held, however, that in the instant case both at the time when the applicant lodged his application and at the time when the Chamber declared it admissible, the applicant was perfectly entitled to complain of the criminal proceedings in which he had been sentenced to life imprisonment without evidence being heard from a defence witness whom he regarded as crucial. His conviction had become final, as he had exhausted all the remedies available in domestic law for the submission of arguments concerning the failure to call the witness. His complaints to the Court on that account under Article 6(1) and (3)(d) of the Convention were not manifestly ill-founded, as the

---

[434]   Judgment of 12 July 2001, paras 140-141.
[435]   Judgment of 24 October 2002, *Pisano*, para. 28.

Chamber held in its decision on the admissibility of the application, and the panel of the Grand Chamber subsequently agreed, that those complaints raised serious questions affecting the interpretation or application of the Convention. It was true that the applicant failed to inform the Court in good time of his application for a retrial, but, contrary to the Government's assertion, such an application was not a remedy of which he was required to avail himself for the purposes of Article 35(1) of the Convention. It remained to be determined whether the application should be rejected as being incompatible *ratione personae* with the provisions of the Convention on the ground that, as a result of his acquittal with final effect after a retrial at which the witness concerned gave evidence, the applicant could no longer claim to be the 'victim' within the meaning of Article 34 of a violation of the Convention. In connection with this the Court noted that, although the situation of which the applicant complained had been remedied, the Italian courts dealing with the case had not found a violation of the relevant provisions of the Convention as regards the failure to examine the witness concerned during the initial trial. In the absence of such an acknowledgement by the national authorities the Court considered that it could not, in the light of events which occurred after the initial declaration of admissibility, subsequently declare the application inadmissible and reject it pursuant to Article 35(4) *in fine* of the Convention on the ground that the applicant could no longer claim to be the 'victim' of the alleged violation.[436]

In the *Assanidze* Case the Chamber to which the case was originally assigned, declared the whole of the applicant's complaint under Article 5(1) of the Convention admissible in its decision on 12 November 2002. At the hearing on 19 November 2003 the applicant complained for the first time about his prosecution in December 1999 and his ensuing detention in the second set of criminal proceedings. The Court held that, by virtue of Article 35(4) of the Convention, it might declare a complaint inadmissible "at any stage of the proceedings" and that the six-month rule is a mandatory one which the Court has jurisdiction to apply of its own motion. In light of the Government's observations and the special circumstances of the case, the Court considered that it was necessary to take this rule into account when examining the various periods for which the applicant was detained. With regard to the first period of detention it held that the complaint under Article 5(1) was made outside the six-month time-limit, since the applicant lodged his application with the Court on 2 July 2001. It followed that this part of the application had to be declared inadmissible as being out of time. As to the complaint concerning the applicant's prosecution on 11 December 1999 in the second set of criminal proceedings and his detention between that date and his acquittal, the Court noted that the first occasion this was raised before it was on 23 September and 19 November 2003. Consequently, it had not been dealt with in the admissibility decision of 12 November 2002, which defined the scope of

---

[436]   *Ibidem,* paras 34-38; judgment of 13 January 2003, *Odievre,* para. 22.

the Court's examination. It followed that this complaint fell outside the scope of the case referred to the Grand Chamber for examination.[437]

2.3 THE PROCEDURE AFTER AN APPLICATION HAS BEEN DECLARED ADMISSIBLE

2.3.1 GENERAL

The decision declaring an application admissible is communicated by the Registrar to the applicant, to the Contracting Party or Parties concerned and to any third party where these have previously been informed of the application.[438] According to Article 37 the Court may at any stage of the proceedings decide to strike an application out of the list of cases where the circumstances lead to the conclusion that one of the situations mentioned there presents itself.

After the Court has declared an application admissible, it subjects the complaint contained therein to an examination of the merits (Article 38(1)(a)). The Court also places itself at the disposal of the parties 'with a view to securing a friendly settlement of the matter on the basis of respect for human rights as defined in the Convention and the Protocols thereto' (Article 38(1)(b)). If no settlement can be reached in the case of an individual application, the President of the Chamber will set deadlines for the submission of further written observations and the Chamber may decide, either at the request of a party or of its own motion, to hold a hearing on the merits.[439] In the case of an inter-State complaint the President of the Chamber will, after consulting the Contracting Parties concerned, lay down the time-limits for the filing of written observations on the merits and for the production of any further evidence. A hearing on the merits shall be held if one or more of the Contracting Parties concerned so requests, or if the Chamber so decides on its own motion.[440]

2.3.2 THIRD PARTY INTERVENTION

A Contracting Party, one of whose nationals is an applicant, has the right to submit written comments and to take part in hearings.[441] When notice of an application is given to the respondent Party, a copy of the application will at the same time be

---

[437] Judgment of 8 April 2004, paras 160-162.
[438] Rule 56(2) of the Rules of Court.
[439] Rule 59 of the Rules of Court.
[440] Rule 58 of the Rules of Court.
[441] Article 36(1) of the Convention.

transmitted to any other Contracting Party one of whose nationals is an applicant in the case. If a Contracting Party wishes to exercise its right to submit written comments or to take part in a hearing, it must so advise the Registrar in writing not later than twelve weeks after the transmission or notification.[442] Another time limit may be fixed by the President of the Chamber for exceptional reasons.[443] In accordance with Article 36(2) of the Convention, the President of the Chamber or the Grand Chamber[444] may, in the interests of the proper administration of justice, invite any Contracting Party which is not a party to the proceedings, or any person concerned who is not the applicant, to submit written comments or take part in hearings. The President of a Chamber or the Grand Chamber is left a certain margin of discretion in this respect.

Third party intervention is only possible before a Chamber or the Grand Chamber and not before a Committee of three judges.[445] The drafters of Protocol 11 have provided States whose nationals have lodged applications against other States Parties to the Convention, with the opportunity to submit written comments and take part in hearings, only in relation to applications that have been declared admissible.[446] Nevertheless, the Court has admitted third party intervention in cases where it had not yet decided on admissibility. In the Case of *T.I. v. the United Kingdom* the Court took note of the comments of the German Government and of the United Nations High Commissioner for Refugees, while the German Government also took part in the oral hearing.[447] The interventions were made at the request of the Court and related to the admissibility of the case. In fact the case finally was declared manifestly ill-founded.

Individuals, non-governmental organisations or groups of individuals must have a perceptible interest in the outcome of the case, if they want to intervene.[448] In the Cases of *T. v. the United Kingdom* concerning the trial and sentencing of two minors who had murdered a child, the President granted leave to the non-governmental organisation Justice and to the parents of the child who had been murdered, to submit written comments in connection with the case. The President, furthermore, granted leave to the victim's parents to attend the hearing and to make oral submissions to the Court.[449] In the *Soering* Case, which concerned the extradition to the United States, and the ristk of the applicant being put on 'deathrow' for a long period of time,

---

[442]   See the judgment of 7 July 1989, *Soering*: Germany intervened because the applicant was a German national.

[443]   Rule 44(1)(2) of the Rules of Court.

[444]   From Rule 44(2)(a) it appears that this power of the President is exercised by the President of the (Grand) Chamber.

[445]   Article 36(1) of the Convention only mentions the Chamber and Grand Chamber.

[446]   Explanatory Report to Protocol No. 11, para 48.

[447]   Decision of 7 March 2000.

[448]   The Explanatory Report to Protocol No. 11 states in this respect in para 48: "establishing an interest in the result of any case".

[449]   Judgments of 16 December 1999, para. 4.

Amnesty International was granted leave to intervene as '*amicus curiae*'.[450] Other examples of non-governmental organisations which have been granted leave to intervene are Human Rights Watch, Interights, Article 19, Liberty, and Aire.[451] On the other hand, in the *Modinos* Case concerning the prohibition of homosexual activities in Cyprus, the intervention of the International Lesbian and Gay Association was refused. Given the Court's previous judgments in the case of Northern Ireland and the United Kingdom, the Court did not see any need for third party intervention.[452]

Requests for leave for this purpose must be duly reasoned and submitted in one of the official languages, within a reasonable time after the fixing of the written procedure. Any invitation or grant of leave referred to in paragraph 2 of Rule 41 of the Rules of the Court may be subject to any conditions, including time-limits, set by the President. Where such conditions are not complied with, the President may decide not to include the comments in the case file. Written comments have to be submitted in one of the official languages, save where leave to use another language has been granted. They are forwarded by the Registrar to the parties to the case, who are entitled, subject to any conditions, including time-limits, set by the President, to file written observations in reply or, where appropriate, to reply at the hearing.[453]

Protocol No.14, will amend Article 36, by adding a third paragraph which reads as follows:

> In all cases before a Chamber or the Grand Chamber, the Council of Europe Commissioner for Human Rights may submit written comments and take part in hearings.

This provision originates from an express request by the Council of Europe's Commissioner, supported by the Parliamentary Assembly.[454] At present it is already possible for the President of the Court to invite the Commissioner on Human Rights to intervene in pending cases. However, with a view to protecting the general interest more effectively, the Commissioner will be explicitly given the right to intervene as third party, even if not invited by the Court to do so.

---

[450] Judgment of 7 July 1989, para 8.
[451] Judgment of 23 September 1994, *Jersild* , para. 5 (Human Rights Watch); judgment of 27 September 1995, *McCann*, para. 5 (Amnesty International, Liberty, the Committee on the Administration of Justice, Inquest, British Irish Rights Watch); judgment of 16 September 1996, *Akdivar*, para. 7 (Amnesty International); judgment of 17 December 1996, *Saunders,* para 5 (Liberty); judgment of 15 November 1996, *Chahal*, para. 6 (Amnesty) International, Justice, Liberty, Aire Centre, Joint Council for the Welfare of Immigrants); judgment of 20 July 2001, *Pellegrini*, para. 10 (Aire).
[452] Judgment of 22 April 1993, para. 4.
[453] Rule 44(5) of the Rules of the Court.
[454] Recommendation 1640(2004), adopted on 26 January 2004.

2.3.3   STRIKING THE APPLICATION OFF THE LIST OF CASES UNDER ARTICLE 37

Article 37 provides that the Court may at any stage of the proceedings – i.e. including during its examinations of the merits – decide to strike an application off its list of cases where the circumstances lead to the conclusion that the applicant does not intend to pursue his petition, or that the matter has been resolved, or that for any other reason established by the Court, it is no longer justified to continue the examination of the application.

In the case of an inter-State application the Chamber may only strike a case off the list if the applicant Contracting Party notifies the Registrar of its intention not to proceed with the case and the other Contracting Party or Parties concerned in the case agree to such discontinuance.[455] The Chamber will not make such a decision if it holds that any reason of a general character affecting the observance of the Convention and the Protocols thereto justifies further examination of the application.[456]

The decision to strike out an application which has been declared admissible, is given in the form of a judgment. The President of the Chamber forwards that judgment, once it has become final, to the Committee of Ministers in order to allow the latter to supervise, in accordance with Article 46(2) of the Convention, the execution of any undertakings which may have been attached to the discontinuance, friendly settlement or solution of the matter.[457] When an application has been struck out, the costs are at the discretion of the Court. If an award of costs is made in a decision striking out an application which has not been declared admissible, the President of the Chamber also forwards that decision to the Committee of Ministers.[458]

The Court may also decide to strike a case off its list of cases if the applicant shows a lack of interest by not responding to the request to provide further information. Thus in a number of cases concerning the length of civil proceedings, a lack of interest was manifested by the applicants in the proceedings pending before the Court, which the Court considered to be an implied withdrawal constituting a "fact of a kind to provide a solution of the matter". In the opinion of the Court there were no reasons of *ordre public* for continuing the proceedings. The Court, therefore, ordered these cases to be struck off the list, subject to the possibility of their being restored thereto in the event of a new situation justifying such a course.[459]

---

[455]   Rule 43(2) of the Rules of Court.
[456]   Appl. 24276/94, *Kurt v. Turkey*, D&R 81 (1995), p. 112. In this case, account was taken of the serious nature of the complaint (the disappearance of a detainee) and grave allegations of intimidation.
[457]   Rule 43(3) of the Rules of Court.
[458]   Rule 43(4) of the Rules of Court.
[459]   Judgments of 3 December 1991, *Gilberti, Nonnis, Trotto, Cattivera, Seri, Gori, Casadio, Testa, Covitti, Zonetti, Simonetti, Dal Sasso*; decision of 21 March 2002, *Zhukov*; decision of 23 April 2002, *Shepelev*.

According to Article 37(2) the Court may decide to restore an application to its list of cases if it considers that the circumstances justify such a course. In a case which had been struck off the list because the applicant's lawyer did not reply to letters from the Secretariat, the Commission decided to restore the case to its list of cases, since the applicant could prove that the letters had been received at the office of his lawyer after the latter's death, but had not been forwarded to him.[460] It is evident that the same possibility of re-acceptance does not exist with respect to cases which have been declared inadmissible.[461]

In the *Drozd* Case confidential information about the proceedings before the Commission was made public, for which the applicant was responsible. This responsibility was established by the fact that the applicant was on the editorial boards of the newspapers concerned. Given the serious and unjustified breach of the confidentiality of the Commission's proceedings it was considered no longer justified to continue the examination of the application.[462]

In the *Bunkate* Case the Dutch Government, which had referred the case to the Court after the Commission has adopted its report, notified the Court that they did not wish to proceed with the case, since the Court had already found a violation in the similar *Abdoella* Case.[463] The applicant did not comment on this proposal of the Dutch Government. The Commission, however, disagreed with the Government, because in this way there would be no formal decision and the applicant would not be able to receive any just satisfaction to which, in the Commission's opinion, he was entitled. The Court agreed with the Commission that the applicant's entitlement to a formal and binding decision on the merits and to just satisfaction overrode any interest the Government may have had in discontinuance of the case.[464]

In the *Skoogström* Case a friendly settlement between the applicant and the Swedish Government was reached during the proceedings before the Court. The Swedish Commission for Revision of Certain Parts of the Code of Judicial Procedure had been asked to propose and elaborate the details for an amendment of the Code in order to put it beyond any doubt that it was in conformity with Article 5(3) of the Convention. In connection with this settlement the applicant was paid a sum of SEK 5,000 for his legal costs. In light of the settlement reached, the Swedish Government requested the Court to strike the case off its list. The Delegate of the Commission proposed that the Court should not strike the case off its list but should adjourn examination of the case "in order to ascertain what progress has been made in the work to amend the legislation, or alternatively to ascertain the timetable for the work which will lead to

---

[460] Appl. 13549/88, *M v. Italy*, D&R 69 (1991), p. 195 (197).
[461] Appl. 16542/90, *J v. France*, D&R 72 (1992), p. 226 (227).
[462] Appl. 25403/94, D&R 84 (1995), p. 114; Appl. 26135/95, *Malige v. France*, D&R 84 (1995), p. 156.
[463] Judgment of 25 November 1992.
[464] Judgment of 26 May 1993, para 25.

those amendments".[465] The Court, however, stated that it had no cause to believe that the settlement did not reflect the free will of the applicant. As far as the general interest was concerned, the Court did not feel able to defer judgment, nor did it see any reason of public policy sufficiently compelling to warrant continuation of its proceeding on the merits of the case. The Court, therefore, concluded that it would be appropriate to strike the case off the list.[466]

In the *Baggetta* Case the Italian Government contended that the applicant could no longer claim to be a victim of a violation of the Convention owing to two events that had occurred after the case was referred to the Court, namely the judgment of the Italian Court of Cassation holding that the applicant's prosecution was time-barred and the decision to recruit the applicant for a post on the railways, subject to a medical examination. The Court noted, however, that there had been neither a friendly settlement nor an arrangement. It considered that the two new facts brought to its notice were not of a kind to provide a solution to the matter and that a decision had accordingly to be taken on the merits.[467]

In the Case of *B.B v. France* the Government invited the Court to strike the case out of the list. They relied on two factors of which the Commission had been unaware, since the relevant information had been communicated to it on the day its report had been adopted: the Versailles Administrative Court had quashed the decision to enforce the order excluding the applicant from French territory and a compulsory residence order had been made against the applicant. Those measures meant that the applicant no longer risked being deported to the Democratic Republic of Congo and was no longer a 'victim'. The Court noted that there had been no friendly settlement or arrangement in the instant case. The compulsory residence order made was unilateral in character and issued by the French authorities after the Commission had adopted its report. It considered, however, that the order constituted an 'other fact of a kind to provide a solution of the matter'. In his initial application to the Convention institutions the applicant's main argument was that if he was deported to what was formerly Zaïre, there would be a considerable risk of his being exposed to treatment which was contrary to Article 3 of the Convention, as he would not be able to receive the treatment his serious medical condition required in his country of origin. It appeared that as regards Article 3 the measure reflected, through its continuity and duration, the French authorities' intention to allow Mr B.B. to receive the treatment his present condition required and to guarantee him, for the time being, the right to remain in France. The Court saw this as tantamount to an undertaking by the French Government not to expel the applicant to his country of origin, the risk of a potential violation therefore having ceased, at least until such time as any new factors emerged justifying

---

[465]   Judgment of 2 October 1984, para. 24.
[466]   *Ibidem*, para 25.
[467]   Judgment of 25 June 1987, para. 18.

a fresh examination of the case. The Court saw no reason of public policy to proceed with the case. In that connection it pointed out that it had had occasion to rule on the risk that a person suffering from Aids would run if expelled to his country of origin in which he would be unable to receive the medical care that was absolutely necessary for his condition.[468] Accordingly, it was appropriate to strike the case out of the list.[469]

Although on a number of occasions the Court has accepted that the parents, spouses or children of a deceased applicant are entitled to take his place in the proceedings,[470] in the *Scherer* Case the Court held that the applicant's executor had not expressed any intention whatsoever of seeking, on the applicant's behalf, to have the proceedings reopened in Switzerland or to claim compensation for non-pecuniary damage in Strasbourg. Under these circumstances the applicant's death could be held to constitute a 'fact of a kind to provide a solution of the matter'.[471] Two other cases were struck off the list since the applicant's death, together with the silence of the heirs who showed no interest in the proceedings pending before the Court, constituted a 'fact of a kind to provide a solution of the matter', while there was no reason of *ordre public* for continuing the proceedings.[472]

In the Cases of *Aydin*[473] and *Akman*[474] the applicants did not agree with the terms of a proposed friendly settlement of the case. They stressed, *inter alia*, that the proposed declaration omitted any reference to the unlawful nature of the killing of the son and failed to highlight that he was unarmed at the material time. In the applicants' submission the terms of the declaration did not determine any of the fundamental human rights questions raised by the application. They urged the Court to proceed with its decision to take evidence in the case with a view to establishing the facts. The Court observed at the outset that the parties were unable to agree on the terms of a friendly settlement of the case. It recalled that, according to Article 38(2) of the Convention, friendly-settlement negotiations are confidential. Rule 62(2) of the Rules of Court stipulates in this connection that no written or oral communication and no offer or concession made in the framework of the attempt to secure a friendly settlement may be referred to or relied on in the contentious proceedings. The Court, therefore, proceeded on the basis of the declaration made outside the framework of the friendly-

---

[468] See in this respect: judgment of 2 May 1997, *D v. the United Kingdom*, para. 53, where the Court held that in view of these exceptional circumstances and bearing in mind the critical stage now reached in the applicant's fatal illness, the implementation of the decision to remove him would amount to inhuman treatment by the respondent State in violation of Article 3.

[469] Judgment of 7 September 1998. paras 37-40.

[470] See, *e.g.*, the judgment of 24 May 1991, *Vocaturo*, para. 9; judgment of 31 March 1992, *X v. France*, para 1; and judgment of 22 February 1994, *Raimondo*, para. 2.

[471] Judgment of 25 March 1994, para. 32.

[472] Judgments of 3 December 1991, *Macaluso and Manunza*, para. 12.

[473] Judgment of 10 July 2001, para. 32.

[474] Judgment of 26 June 2001, para. 25

settlement negotiations by the respondent Government. Having examined carefully the terms of the respondent Government's declaration and having regard to the nature of the admissions contained in the declaration, as well as the scope and extent of the various undertakings referred to therein, together with the amount of compensation proposed, the Court considered that it was no longer justified to continue the examination of the application. Moreover, the Court was satisfied that respect for human rights as defined in the Convention and the Protocols thereto did not require it to continue the examination of the application. The Court noted in this regard that it had specified the nature and extent of the obligations which arose for the respondent Government in cases of alleged unlawful killings by members of the security forces under Articles 2 and 13 of the Convention. In two more recent judgments, the Cases of *Togcu* and *T.A. v. Turkey*, both concerning disappearances of the applicants' relatives, the Court based its decision to strike out these cases on a formal statement from the Turkish Government, notwithstanding the rejection of a friendly settlement by the applicants.[475]

In a dissenting opinion, Judge Loucaides opposed this 'striking out' process of the applications in a way which was very similar to the arguments of the applicants. He argued that there was no acceptance by the Government of responsibility for the violations complained of and that there was no undertaking to carry out any investigation of the disappearances. He further argued: "Instead, the Government undertake in the declaration generally 'to issue appropriate instructions and adopt all necessary measures with a view to ensuring that all deprivations of liberty are fully and accurately recorded by the authorities and that effective investigations into alleged disappearances are carried out in accordance with their obligations under the Convention'. However such an 'undertaking' does not add anything to the already existing obligation of the respondent Government under the Convention." He also disagreed with the Turkish Government's statement: "The Government consider that the supervision by the Committee of Ministers of the execution of Court judgments concerning Turkey in this and similar cases is an appropriate mechanism for ensuring that improvements will be made in this context." In his opinion that seemed to imply that the Government considered the Committee of Ministers as a more appropriate mechanism for ensuring improvements in cases like the one in respect of which the declaration was made than an examination of 'this and similar' cases by the Court. He feared that "the solution adopted may encourage a practice by States – especially those facing serious or numerous applications – of 'buying off' complaints for violations of human rights through the payment of *ex gratia* compensation, without admitting any responsibility and without any adverse publicity, such payments being simply accompanied by a general undertaking to adopt measures for preventing situations like those complained of, from arising in the future on the basis of unilateral declarations which are approved

---

[475]   Judgments of 9 April 2002, para. 32.

by the Court even though they are unacceptable to the complainants. This practice will inevitably undermine the effectiveness of the judicial system of condemning publicly violations of human rights through legally binding judgments and, as a consequence, it will reduce substantially the required pressure on those Governments that are violating human rights."[476] The Cases of *Akman* and *Aydin* could, in his opinion, be distinguished from the precious decisions in the *Togcu* Case and in *T.A. v. Turkey*, because the *Akman* Case concerned an alleged instantaneous violation, i.e. murder, and the *Aydin* Case concerned the disappearance of a person in respect of which an investigation was still being pursued at the time of the decision of the Court to strike the case out of the list, while the Cases of *Togcu* and *T.A. v. Turkey* concerned an alleged continuing violation, i.e. the disappearance of a person. As Judge Loucaides pointed out: "Departure from both decisions is justified for cogent reasons, namely to ensure more effective implementation of the obligations of the High Contracting Parties to the Convention through ceasing to strike cases out as a result of approving the method of compensation proposed by the respondent States on the basis of unilateral declarations unacceptable to the latter, like the one in the present case."[477]

The President of the Chamber, Judge Costa, stated in his concurring opinion that he came close to the views of Judge Loucaides and stressed that striking out should not be abused and should only be used in narrowly defined cases.[478] He continued by saying that "in the circumstances of the present cases, and without calling into question the good faith and sincerity of the respondent State, I am very concerned by the unilateral nature of its undertakings".[479]

The *Tahsin Acar* Case concerning the disappearance of the applicant's brother was referred to the Grand Chamber. The Turkish Government had sent the Court a text of a unilateral declaration expressing regret for the actions that had led to the application and offering to make an *ex gratia* payment of 70,000 pounds sterling to the applicant for any pecuniary and non-pecuniary damage and for costs. The Government requested the Court to strike the case out of the list under Article 37 of the Convention. The Grand Chamber considered that, under certain circumstances, it might be appropriate to strike out an application under Article 37(1)(c) of the Convention on the basis of a unilateral declaration by the respondent Government, even if the applicant wished the examination of the case to be continued. Depending on the particular circum-

---

[476]   Dissenting opinion of Judge Loucaides.

[477]   *Ibidem.*

[478]   Such as where the applicant dies and the proceedings are not continued by his heirs: judgment of 14 May 2000, *Gladkowski,* or where proceedings are taken over by a legal entity which does not, in that particular case, have a legitimate interest allowing it to pursue the proceedings: judgment of 18 September 2001, *S.G. v. France.*

[479]   Judgments of 9 April 2002, concurring opinion of the President of the Chamber Judge Costa. On 9 September 2002 the Case of *T.A. v. Turkey* was referred to the Grand Chamber.

stances of each case various considerations could come into play in the assessment of a unilateral declaration. It might be appropriate to examine whether the facts are in dispute between the parties, and, if so, to what extent. Other factors that might be taken into account are the nature of the complaints made, whether the Court has ruled on similar issues in previous cases, the nature and scope of any measures taken to enforce judgments delivered in such cases, and the impact of those measures on the case before the Court. The Court should also ascertain, among other things, whether in their declaration the Government made any admissions concerning the alleged violations of the Convention and, if so, should determine the scope of such admissions and the manner in which the Government intended to provide redress to the applicant. The Grand Chamber held that the unilateral declaration made in the present case did not adequately address the applicant's grievances. In the Chamber's view, where a person had disappeared or had been killed by unknown persons and there was *prima facie* evidence that supported allegations that the domestic investigation had fallen short of what was necessary under the Convention, a unilateral declaration should at the very least contain an admission to that effect, combined with an undertaking by the respondent Government to conduct, under the supervision of the Committee of Ministers, an investigation that fully complies with the requirements of the Convention as defined by the Court in previous cases of a similar nature. As the Government's unilateral declaration in the present case did not contain any such admission or undertaking, it did not offer a sufficient basis for the Court to hold that it was no longer justified to continue the examination of the application. The Grand Chamber accordingly rejected the Government's request to strike the application out under Article 37(1)(c) of the Convention and decided to pursue its examination of the merits of the case.[480]

2.3.4   THE EXAMINATION OF THE MERITS

2.3.4.1 General

Article 29 states that, except for cases declared inadmissible by a Committee, the Chamber has to examine the admissibility and the merits of the case. There may, however, be situations in which the Court will not take a separate admissibility decision. This could occur, for example, where a State does not object to a case being declared admissible.

According to Rule 58(1) of the Rules of Court, once the Chamber has decided to admit an inter-State application, the President of the Chamber will, after consulting the Contracting Parties concerned, lay down the time-limits for the filing of written

---

[480]   Judgment of 6 May 2003, paras. 74-82.

observations on the merits and for the production of any further evidence. The President may however, with the agreement of the Contracting Parties concerned, direct that a written procedure is to be dispensed with. According to Rule 59(1), in the case of an individual application the Chamber or its President may invite the parties to submit further evidence and written observations.

An application is initially examined by one or more judges as Judge Rapporteurs whom the Chamber appoints from among its members[481] and who submit such reports, drafts and other documents as may assist the Chamber in carrying out its functions. The merits of an application will be examined by a Chamber and, exceptionally, by the Grand Chamber. The parties will present their submissions by means of a written procedure. The oral procedure will consist of a hearing at which the applicant, or a State Party in an inter-State case, and the respondent State may present their arguments orally. The President of the Chamber fixes the written and oral procedure.[482]

Article 40 of the Convention indicates that oral proceedings are, in principle, to be conducted in public. It also specifies that documents submitted in the written proceedings (memorials and formal written information) are also, in principle, accessible to the public. Thus, documents deposited with the Registrar and not published will be accessible to the public unless otherwise decided by the President, either on his own initiative or at the request of a party or of any other person concerned.

2.3.4.2 The written procedure

According to Rule 38(1) of the Rules of Court, no written observations or other documents may be filed after the time-limit set by the President of the Chamber or the Judge Rapporteur. For the purposes of observing this time-limit the material date is the certified date of dispatch of the document or, if there is none, the actual date of receipt at the Registry.[483]

According to Rules 17-19 of Practice Direction 3, a time-limit set under Rule 38 may be extended on request from a party. A party must make such a request as soon as it has become aware of the circumstances justifying such an extension and, in any event, before the expiry of the time-limit. It should state the reason for the delay. If an extension is granted, it applies to all parties for which the relevant time-limit is running, including those which have not asked for it. According to Rules 3 and 7 of Practice Direction 3, all pleadings as well as documents should be sent in triplicate by

---

[481] Rule 48(2) with respect to inter-State applications and Rule 49(1) with respect to individual applications.

[482] Rule 59(4) of the Rules of Court. See in this respect Practice Direction 3 to the Rules of Court.

[483] Rule 38(2) of the Rules of Court.

post with one copy sent, if possible, by fax. In case of the use of fax, the name of the person signing a pleading must also be printed on it so that he or she can be identified.

Concerning form and contents, Practice Direction 3 in Rule 8 prescribes that a pleading should include: (a) the application number and the name of the case; (b) a title indicating the nature and content (*e.g.* observations on admissibility [and the merits]; reply to the Government's/the applicant's observations on admissibility [and the merits]; observations on the merits; additional observations on admissibility [and the merits]; memorial etc.). In addition, Rule 9 prescribes that a pleading should normally: (a) be on A4 paper having a margin of not less than 3.5 cm wide; (b) be wholly legible and, preferably, typed; (c) have all numbers expressed as figures; (d) have pages numbered consecutively; (e) be divided into numbered paragraphs; (f) be divided into chapters and/or headings corresponding to the form and style of the Court's decisions and judgments; (g) place any answer to a question by the Court or to the other party's arguments under a separate heading; and (h) give a reference for every document or piece of evidence. According to Rule 10, if a pleading exceeds 30 pages, a short summary should also be filed with it. Finally, according to Rule 11, where a party produces documents or other exhibits together with a pleading, every piece of evidence should be listed in a separate annex. Concerning the contents, Rule 13 prescribes that the pleadings should include: (i) a short statement confirming a party's position on the facts of the case as established in the decision on admissibility; (ii) legal arguments relating to the merits of the case; and (iii) a reply to any specific questions on a factual or legal point put by the Court. An applicant submitting claims for just satisfaction should do so in the written observations on the merits. Itemised particulars of all claims made, together with the relevant supporting documents or vouchers, should be submitted. If the applicant fails to do so, the Chamber may reject the claim in whole or in part.[484]

2.3.4.3 The oral hearing

The examination of the merits usually takes a good deal of time; apart from exceptional cases, approximately two years. In some cases this is inevitable, *viz.* if it is difficult to ascertain the facts, or if the attempts to reach a friendly settlement take a long time. On the whole, however, the desirability of shortening the procedure is evident, especially if it is borne in mind that the time which elapses between the moment at which an application is submitted and the date of the decision on admissibility is also rather long in many cases. In this respect it has to be noted that the Rules of Court have been amended and that the rule which provided that in general an oral hearing would be held, has been deleted. Instead, Rule 59(3) of the Rules of Court provides

---

[484]   Rule 60 of the Rules of Court. The Practice Direction with respect to claims under Article 41 has not yet been issued.

that the Chamber may decide, either at the request of a party or of its own motion, to hold a hearing on the merits if it considers that the discharge of its functions under the Convention so requires. It is now current practice for oral hearings to be held only in a limited number of cases.

The applicant must be represented at any hearing decided on by the Chamber, unless the President of the Chamber exceptionally grants leave to the applicant to present his or her own case, subject, if necessary, to being assisted by an advocate or other approved representative.[485] According to Rule 64 of the Rules of Court, the President of the Chamber organises and directs hearings and prescribes the order in which those appearing before the Chamber will be called upon to speak. Where a party or any other person due to appear fails or declines to do so, the Chamber may, provided that it is satisfied that such a course is consistent with the proper administration of justice, nonetheless proceed with the hearing.[486] In the *Diennet* Case the hearing took place even though at a preparatory meeting the Court was informed that the applicant's lawyer was stranded in Paris as a result of an airline strike. It decided to hold the hearing at the fixed time and to fax a provisional record of it to applicant's lawyer so that she could submit any observations in writing before the deliberations.[487]

All communications with and pleadings by individual applicants or their representatives, witnesses or experts in respect of a hearing, or after a case has been declared admissible, shall be in one of the Court's official languages, unless the President of the Chamber authorises the continued use of the official language of a Contracting Party.[488]

2.3.4.4 Investigative measures and inquiry on the spot

The Chamber may, at the request of a party or of its own motion, adopt any investigative measures which it considers capable of clarifying the facts of the case. The Chamber may, *inter alia*, invite the parties to produce documentary evidence and decide to hear as a witness or expert or in any other capacity any person whose evidence or statements seem likely to assist it in carrying out its tasks.[489] The Chamber may also ask any person or institution of its choice to express an opinion or make a written report on any matter considered by it to be relevant to the case. According to Rule A1(3) of the Annex to the Rules of Court, after a case has been declared admissible or, exceptionally, before the decision on admissibility, the Chamber may appoint one or more of its members or of the other judges of the Court, as its delegate or delegates, to conduct an inquiry, carry out an on-site investigation or take evidence in

---

[485]   Rule 36(3) of the Rules of Court.
[486]   Rule 65 of the Rules of Court.
[487]   Judgment of 26 September 1995, para 5.
[488]   Rule 34 of the Rules of Court.
[489]   Rule A1(1) and (2) of the Annex to the Rules of Court.

some other manner. The Chamber may also appoint any person or institution of its choice to assist the delegation in such manner as it sees fit. Under the Convention, the Contracting States are obliged to furnish the facilities required (Article 38(1)(a)). In accordance with Rule A1(5) of the Annex to the Rules of Court, proceedings forming part of any investigation by a Chamber or its delegation will be held in camera, save in so far as the President of the Chamber or the head of the delegation decides otherwise.

The parties must assist the Chamber, or its delegation, in implementing any measure for taking evidence. The Contracting Party on whose territory on-site proceedings before a delegation take place must extend to the delegation the facilities and co-operation necessary for the proper conduct of the proceedings. These include, to the full extent necessary, freedom of movement within the territory and all adequate security arrangements for the delegation, for the applicant and for all witnesses, experts and others who may be heard by the delegation. It is the responsibility of the Contracting Party concerned to take steps to ensure that no adverse consequences are suffered by any person or organisation on account of any evidence given, or of any assistance provided, to the delegation.[490] The Court does not have any means for compelling a witness, expert or other person to appear before it. Rule A3 of the Annex to the Rules of Court provides that, where a party or any other person due to appear fails or declines to do so, the delegation [and the Chamber, as the case may be] may, provided that it is satisfied that such a course is consistent with the proper administration of justice, nonetheless continue with the proceedings. Even without an express provision in the Rules of Procedure it would seem possible for the Court to communicate such failure to the Contracting State concerned. This State will then have to take any appropriate measures necessary to ensure that the persons in question will co-operate. In fact the Contracting States are obliged to give the Court the necessary assistance in the performance of its duties. This would seem to also ensue by analogy from Article 38(1)(a) of the Convention, which provides that, if the Court decides to carry out an inquiry on the spot, 'the States concerned shall furnish all necessary facilities.'

The head of the delegation may request the attendance of witnesses, experts and other persons during on-site proceedings before a delegation. The Contracting Party on whose territory such proceedings are held must, if so requested, take all reasonable steps to facilitate that attendance. In accordance with Rule 37(2), the Contracting Party in whose territory the witness resides is responsible for servicing any summons sent to it by the Chamber for service. In the event of such service not being possible, the Contracting Party must give reasons in writing. The Contracting Party shall further

---

[490]   Rule A2 of the Annex to the Rules of Court.

take all reasonable steps to ensure the attendance of persons summoned who are under its authority or control.[491]

The President of the Chamber may, as he or she considers appropriate, invite, or grant leave to, any third party to participate in an investigative measure. The President lays down the conditions of any such participation and may limit that participation if those conditions are not complied with.[492]

The former Commission availed itself of the power to conduct an inquiry on the spot for the first time in connection with the first complaint by Greece against the United Kingdom.[493] On that occasion an inquiry was made in Cyprus into the existence of certain practices of torture and into whether the threat to public order was such that the measures taken by the British authorities were justified. In September 1975 the Commission again went to Cyprus, this time, *inter alia*, to visit two refugee camps in connection with complaints by Cyprus against Turkey.[494] In the *Northern Ireland* Case the Court expressed its disapproval of the fact that, as the Commission had hinted in its report, the British Government had not always afforded the desirable assistance. In its judgment the Court emphasised the importance of the obligation of Contracting States set forth in Article 28(a) (the present Article 28(1)(a)).[495] In connection with the five applications which were lodged against Turkey the Commission decided to send a delegation to that country in order to continue its efforts to reach a friendly settlement. The delegation had discussions with, *inter alia*, the Minister of Justice, members of the Grand National Assembly and members of the Military Court of Cassation. The delegation also met with journalists, academics and trade unionists, and visited Military Detention Centres, where it was able to talk in private with prisoners.[496]

Within the framework of a number of individual complaints against Turkey, the Commission and the Court organised fact-finding missions to Turkey.[497] This concerned allegations of gross violations, such as disappearances, killing and torture in south east Turkey. In most of these cases the domestic authorities had neither made an effective inquiry into the alleged violations nor started any serious investigation against the perpetrators of the cruelties.[498] Recently a delegation of three Judges of the Court took evidence from witnesses in Ankara in the *Abdürrezzak Ipek* Case. The applicant complained about the disappearance of his two sons, who were allegedly

---

[491] Rule A 5(4) of the Annex to the Rules of Court.
[492] Rule A 1(6) of the Annex to the Rules of Court.
[493] Appl. 176/56, *Greece v. the United Kingdom*, Yearbook II (1958-1959), p. 182.
[494] Appls 6780/74 and 6950/74, *Cyprus v. Turkey*, Yearbook XVIII (1975), p. 82.
[495] Judgment of 18 January 1978, *Ireland v. the United Kingdom*, para. 93.
[496] Report of 7 December 1985, *France, Norway, Denmark, Sweden and the Netherlands v. Turkey*, D&R 44 (1985), p. 31 (36-37).
[497] Judgment of 18 December 1996, *Aksoy*, para 23; judgment 25 May 1998, *Kurt*, para 13; judgment of 8 July 1999, *Cakici*, para 13.
[498] Report of the Commission of 10 September 1999, *Akdeniz*, para 384.

last seen by three people taken into detention with them. He also alleged that his family home and property had been destroyed by security forces in the course of an operation conducted in his village. The Turkish Government submitted that the investigation carried out by the authorities proved that no operation was conducted in the area by security forces. They further maintained that the applicant's sons were never detained.[499]

On 11 September 2002 the Grand Chamber decided that a delegation of judges should carry out an on-the-spot investigation in Moldova in the *Ilaşcu* Case. The Court also decided to ask the parties to provide further clarification in writing about the case. The applicants had been convicted in 1993 for various crimes by a court of the 'Moldovan Republic of Transdniestria' (MRT), a region of Moldova which declared its independence in 1991 but is not recognised by the international community. The first applicant had been sentenced to capital punishment and the other three applicants to prison sentences between 12 and 15 years. The judgment was subsequently declared unconstitutional by the Supreme Court of Moldova. Three of the applicants were detained in Transdniestria, while the first applicant was released on 5 May 2001 and moved to Romania. The applicants complained about the proceedings which led to their conviction in 1993 and claimed that their detention since then had been unlawful. They also complained of the conditions of their detention and, in substance, of a violation of their right not to be hindered in the effective exercise of the right of individual application. The applicants considered that the Moldovan authorities were responsible under the Convention for the alleged violations of their Convention rights since they had not taken adequate measures to stop them. They further contended that the Russian Federation shared that responsibility as the territory of Transdniestria was and continues to be *de facto* under Russia's control owing to the stationing of its troops and military equipment and its alleged support of the separatist regime.[500]

Article 38(1)(a) of the Convention provides for measures to enforce the duty of co-operation on the part of a Contracting State. In cases in which, in the Court's opinion, an inquiry on the spot is absolutely necessary while the Contracting Party refuses to co-operate, it would appear most appropriate for the Court to appeal to the Committee of Ministers. Through a resolution the latter organ may bring pressure to bear on the recalcitrant State to comply with its obligations and to co-operate by making an investigation on its territory possible. In addition, although in practice this is not very likely to occur, another Contracting State might lodge an application against the recalcitrant State for alleged violation of Article 38. As was stated above, Article 33 permits the Contracting States to complain about 'any alleged breach of the provisions of the Convention by another High Contracting Party', so that they need not confine

---

[499]   Press release issued by the Registrar, 20 November 2002.
[500]   Press release issued by the Registrar, 11 October 2002.

themselves to the rights and freedoms of Section I of the Convention and of the Protocols, but may also refer to an article such as Article 38. In the *Timurtas* Case the Court held that "It is inherent in proceedings relating to cases of this nature, where an individual applicant accuses State agents of violating his rights under the Convention, that in certain instances solely the respondent State has access to information capable of corroborating or refuting these allegations. A failure on a Government's part to submit such information as is in their hands without a satisfactory explanation may not only reflect negatively on the level of compliance by a respondent State with its obligations under Article 38 para. 1 (a) of the Convention, but may also give rise to the drawing of inferences as to the well-foundedness of the allegations. In this respect, the Court reiterates that the conduct of the parties may be taken into account when evidence is being obtained."[501]

Where a witness, expert or other person is summoned at the request or on behalf of a Contracting Party, the costs of their appearance will be borne by that Party unless the Chamber decides otherwise. The costs of the appearance of any such person who is in detention in the Contracting Party on whose territory on-site proceedings before a delegation take place, will be borne by that Party unless the Chamber decides otherwise. In all other cases the Chamber decides whether such costs are to be borne by the Council of Europe or awarded against the applicant or third party at whose request or on whose behalf the person appears. In all cases such costs are taxed by the President of the Chamber.[502]

Rule A 6 lays down the oath or solemn declaration by witnesses and experts heard by a delegation.

Any delegate may put questions to the Agents, advocates or advisers of the parties, to the applicant, witnesses and experts, and to any other persons appearing before the delegation. Witnesses, experts and other persons appearing before the delegation may, subject to the control of the head of the delegation, be examined by the Agents and advocates or advisers of the parties. In the event of an objection to a question put, the head of the delegation decides. Save in exceptional circumstances and with the consent of the head of the delegation, witnesses, experts and other persons to be heard by a delegation will not be admitted to the hearing room before they give evidence. The head of the delegation may make special arrangements for witnesses, experts or other persons to be heard in the absence of the parties where that is required for the proper administration of justice. The head of the delegation decides in the event of any dispute

---

[501] Judgment of 13 June 2000, para 66. See also judgment of 24 April 2003, *Aktas*, paras. 272-277; judgment of 9 May 2003, *Tepe*, paras. 128-135 and judgment of 15 January 2004, *Tekdag*, paras. 57-61.
[502] Rule A5(6) of the Annex to the Rules of Court.

arising from an objection to a witness or expert. The delegation may hear for information purposes a person who is not qualified to be heard as a witness or expert.[503]

A verbatim record is prepared by the Registrar of any proceedings concerning an investigative measure. If all or part of the verbatim record is in a non-official language, the Registrar arranges for its translation into one of the official languages. The representatives of the parties receive a copy of the verbatim record in order that they may, subject to the control of the Registrar or the head of the delegation, make corrections, but in no case may such corrections affect the sense and bearing of what was said. The Registrar sets, in accordance with the instructions of the head of the delegation, the time-limits granted for this purpose. The verbatim record, once so corrected, is signed by the head of the delegation and the Registrar and then constitutes certified matters of record.[504]

2.3.4.5 Hearing of witnesses or experts by the Chamber

Since the amendment of the Rules of Court the provisions concerning the hearing of witnesses and experts are to be found in the Annex to the Rules of Court concerning investigative measures. The provisions concerning investigative measures by a delegation apply, *mutatis mutandis*, to any such proceedings conducted by the Chamber itself.[505] According to Rule A 1(1) of the Annex to the Rules of Court, the Chamber may, at the request of a party or of its own motion, adopt any investigative measure which it considers capable of clarifying the facts of the case.

Witnesses, experts and other persons to be heard by a Chamber are summoned by the Registrar. The summons has to indicate (a) the case in connection with which it has been issued; (b) the object of the inquiry, expert opinion or other investigative measure ordered by the Chamber or the President of the Chamber; and (c) any provisions for the payment of sums due to the person summoned.[506]

The Chamber may, *inter alia*, invite the parties to produce documentary evidence and decide to hear as a witness or expert or in any other capacity any person whose evidence or statements seem likely to assist it in carrying out its tasks.[507] For example in the case of *Brozicek* the Court decided to hear five witnesses on a specific point and to order an opinion by a handwriting expert.[508] The Chamber may also ask any person or institution of its choice to express an opinion or make a written report on any matter considered by it to be relevant to the case.[509]

---

[503]   Rule A7 of the Annex to the Rules of Court.
[504]   Rule A8 of the Annex to the Rules of Court.
[505]   Rule A3(3) of the Annex to the Rules of Court.
[506]   Rule A5(2) in conjunction with Rule A1(4) of the Annex to the Rules of Court.
[507]   Rule A1 of the Annex to the Rules of Court.
[508]   Judgment of 19 December 1989, para. 5.
[509]   Rule A1(2) of the Annex to the Rules of Court.

2.3.5 FRIENDLY SETTLEMENT

2.3.5.1 General

From the terms of Article 38 it is clear that the drafters of the Convention intended the attempts to reach a friendly settlement to take place simultaneously with the examination of the merits. This makes sense. In fact, on the one hand, a complete examination of the merits is superfluous if a friendly settlement is reached. On the other hand, the Chamber cannot mediate in an effective way with a view to reaching such a settlement until it has gained some insight into the question of whether or not the application is well-founded. Moreover, the provisional views within the Chamber on the latter question may put pressure on (one of) the parties to co-operate with reaching a settlement.

The friendly settlement is a form of *conciliation*, one of the traditional methods of peaceful settlement of international disputes. The term 'conciliation', which refers particularly to inter-State disputes, has been replaced in the European Convention by 'friendly settlement' because disputes between States and individuals may be – and for the most greater part are – concerned.[510] A non-legal element has been introduced into the friendly settlement procedure. Indeed, this method is not necessarily based on exclusively legal considerations; other factors may also play a part in it. Experience demonstrates the great utility of the conciliation element in Convention proceedings. Thus, for instance, 20 percent of the cases declared admissible in 2001 have resulted in a friendly settlement, often providing for pecuniary compensation for the victim and sometimes referring to a change in the law of the State concerned.[511]

Friendly settlement negotiations could be 'guided', or even encouraged, by a judge (with the help of the registry of the Court). Also, during friendly settlement negotiations, parties may call upon the services of the Court's registry to help them in these negotiations. A member of a Chamber might at any stage assist the parties in settling their case.

As far as Protocol No. 14 is concerned, the provisions of Article 39 (new) are taken partly from the present Article 38(1)(b) and 2 and also from the present Article 39. However, since under the present Article 38(1)(b) it is only after an application has been declared admissible that the Court places itself at the disposal of the parties with a view to securing a friendly settlement, this procedure will be more flexible. The Court will be free to place itself at the parties' disposal at any stage of the proceedings.

---

[510] See *Collected Edition of the 'Travaux Préparatoires' of the European Convention on Human Rights*, Vol. III, The Hague, 1977, pp. 271-272.

[511] See: Council of Europe, Report of the Evaluation Group to the Committee of Minister on the European Court of Human Rights, EG(2001)1 27 September 2001, p. 21.

Friendly settlements will thus be encouraged and may prove particularly useful in repetitive cases as well as in other cases where questions of principle or changes in domestic law are not involved. It goes without saying that these friendly settlements, will also have to be based on respect for human rights, pursuant to Article 39(1)(new).[512]

The new Article 39 will provide for supervision of the execution of friendly settlements by the Committee of Ministers. This new provision was inserted to reflect a practice which the Court has already developed. Within the framework of the text of Article 46(2) the Court uses to endorse friendly settlements through *judgments* and not – as provided for in the present Article 39 of the Convention – through *decisions*, since the execution of the latter is not subject to supervision by the Committee of Ministers. It was recognised that adopting a judgment instead of a decision, might have negative connotations for respondent Parties and make it harder to secure a friendly settlement. The new procedure will make this easier and thus reduce the Court's work-load.[513]

2.3.5.2 The way in which the Court secures a friendly settlement

The Court has wide discretion as to how it may try to secure a friendly settlement. The Convention does not impose any limitations on the Court in this matter, with the exception of the requirement to be discussed below that the settlement reached must be based on respect for human rights as defined in the Convention.[514]

This flexible and informal character of the procedure enables the Court to create an atmosphere which makes it easier for the parties to reach a compromise. In this context, the fact that the procedure is confidential plays an important part. Further-more, the fact that it may be attractive for the respondent State to avoid continuation of the procedure, which would lead to a thorough examination of the facts and might result in public condemnation, helps to create a situation in which States may be willing to accept a compromise. The individual applicant may also benefit from the compromise by having certainty about the outcome of the dispute and reparation, if any, of the damages incurred, at the earliest possible moment. He or she may, therefore, generally also wish to avoid lengthy proceedings before the Court, involving the risk of an unfavourable judgment. The Chamber may provide the parties with an indication of its provisional opinion on the merits. The separate decision on admissibility is important for the parties when considering whether they should start friendly settlement negotiations.[515]

---

[512] Explanatory Report to Protocol No. 14, CETS 194, para 93.
[513] *Ibidem*, para 94.
[514] Article 38(1)(b) of the Convention.
[515] Explanatory Report to Protocol No. 11, para 78.

On the other hand, the friendly settlement procedure entails the drawbacks of a non-public procedure. Owing to the fact that it is a compromise, the friendly settlement, without further qualifications, would involve the risk that ultimately an agreement may be reached which does not meet the standards with respect to human rights set by the Convention. However, the concluding words of Article 38(1)(b) require the settlement to be reached 'on the basis of respect for Human Rights as defined in this Convention.' It is the duty of the Court to see to this. Besides the parties concerned, the Court must agree to the content of the settlement. It is possible that the victim of a violation is ready to accept a given sum of money with which the Government concerned might wish to buy off the violation, while the cause of the violation, for instance in the form of a legal provision or an administrative practice conflicting with the Convention, would continue to exist. In such a case the Court will have to demand that the Contracting State concerned, in addition to giving compensation to the victim, takes measures to alter the law or administrative practice in question. In its attempts to secure a friendly settlement, the Court also has a duty with respect to the public interest, which constitutes a further indication of the 'objective' character of the procedure provided for in the Convention.

Besides the public interest in the maintenance of the legal order created by the Convention, the issue of the *Rechtsfrieden* (peace through justice) also plays a part here. Indeed, if the Court did not see to it that the existing violation be ended, there would be considerable risk that repeated applications might be submitted about the same situation conflicting with the Convention in a given Contracting State.

The former Commission has never refused a proposed settlement for the reason that it had not been reached 'on the basis of respect for Human Rights as defined in this Convention'.[516] And as far as information is available, up to present the same holds good with respect to the Court.

About the actual course of the attempts to reach a friendly settlement and the role of the Court, only a few general remarks can be made, precisely because the procedure is confidential and data about it are, therefore, scanty.

Article 38 states that the Court places itself at the disposal of the parties. Immediately after a complaint has been declared admissible, the Registrar, acting on instructions from the Chamber or its President, invites the parties to state whether they wish to make proposals for a possible settlement. A friendly settlement will even be possible after the case has been referred to the Grand Chamber.[517]

---

[516]   See H. Krüger and C.A. Nørgaard, 'Reflections concerning friendly settlement under the European Convention on Human Rights', in: F. Matscher and H. Petzold (eds.), *Protecting Human Rights: The European Dimension*, Cologne, 1988, pp. 329-334 (332).

[517]   See in this respect judgment of 24 October 2002, *Pisano*, para 28.

Sometimes the Court will first examine the possibilities for a friendly settlement in discussions with one or both of the parties separately. In other cases it will immediately bring the parties into contact with each other because it considers it possible for a settlement to be reached. The Court may provide the parties with an indication of its provisional opinion on the merits. This separate decision on admissibility is important for the parties when considering whether they should start friendly settlement negotiations. The Court only makes use of these methods in cases where a friendly settlement is justified and not in those cases where a decision on the merits of the case is important for the further development of the case law.[518]

The degree to which the Court has to be proactive depends on whether it is dealing with an inter-State application or an individual application. In the first case the parties are more or less on equal terms, so that the Court may confine itself to a more passive role. Whilst it may also be true in the case of an individual application that the parties are formally on equal terms, the respondent State is generally better equipped to conduct negotiations within the framework of a friendly settlement than an individual applicant. Therefore, the latter, in taking a decision on whether or not to agree to a given settlement, may be guided by the Court. The Court, owing to its expertise and experience, will often be better able to evaluate the content of the settlement and may, by playing a guiding role, neutralise factual inequality between the parties to the negotiations to some extent. However, the role of the Court should not dominate to such an extent that it is actually the Court which determines the terms of the settlement and imposes it more or less upon the individual applicant. Up to the present, however, there have been no indications of such a situation.

The Court is responsible for the establishment of the facts and may conduct an investigation on the understanding that the parties furnish the Court with all the relevant information. Parties to friendly settlement proceedings are not at liberty to disclose the nature and content of any communication made with a view to and in connection with a friendly settlement. Material relating to the friendly settlement negotiations must remain confidential.[519] In the *Familiapress Zeitung* Case the applicant had used confidential information of a provisional measure in a procedure before the domestic court. The Commission considered that to be "a serious breach of confidentiality" and decided to strike the case of the list.[520]

If a friendly settlement in the sense of Article 38 is reached, the Court strikes the case out of its list by means of a decision which is confined to a brief statement of the facts and of the solutions reached.[521] As stated above, the Court now endorses friendly

---

[518]   See in this respect: N. Bratza en M. O'Boyle, "The Legacy of the Commission to the New Court under the Protocol No. 11", in *The Birth of European Human Rights Law. Liber Amicorum Carl Aage Norgaard*, M. de Salvia en M.E. Villiger (eds.), Baden-baden, Nomos, 1998, p. 387.

[519]   Rule 62(2) of the Rules of Court.

[520]   Report of 3 March 1995, D&R 80 (1996), pp. 76-77.

[521]   Article 39 of the Convention.

settlements through *judgments* and not – as provided for in Article 39 – through *decisions*, of which execution is not subject to supervision by the Committee of Ministers. If the Court is informed that an agreement has been reached between the applicant and the respondent State, it verifies the equitable nature of the agreement and, where it finds the agreement to be equitable, strikes the case out of its list in accordance with Rule 43(3).[522]

2.3.5.3 Friendly settlements reached

The number of cases in which a friendly settlement has been reached has increased dramatically since the entry into force of Protocol No. 11. From 1999 up to the end of 2003, according to the available information, 695 friendly settlements have been reached.[523]

The first friendly settlement concerned a special case. In the *Boeckmans* Case the applicant complained about remarks made by a judge during his trial, which were alleged to be incompatible with the right to a fair trial under Article 6 of the Convention. The Belgian Government, while upholding the validity of the judgment in question, agreed to pay Boeckmans compensation of 65,000 Belgian francs, because the remarks were such "as to disturb the serenity of the atmosphere during the proceedings in a manner contrary to the Convention and may have caused the applicant a moral injury."[524]

In a great number of cases the substance of the settlement has consisted merely of the Government concerned paying compensation and/or redressing the consequences of the violation for the victim as much as possible.[525] A number of settlements have in fact been based on judgments of the Court in cases which raised identical issues. In a case against the United Kingdom, for instance, six applicants complained about their dismissal from employment after refusal to join a trade union. After the Court's judgment in the *Young, James and Webster* Case the Government settled the case by offering the applicants compensation in respect of loss of earnings, pension rights and other employment benefits.[526] Similarly, in the *Geniets* Case the admissible part of the application was similar to the *Van Droogenbroeck* Case where the Court found a breach of Article 5(4) because of the absence of an effective and accessible judicial remedy which satisfied the requirements of that provision. As a result, the

---

[522] Rule 75(4) of the Rules of Court.

[523] See *European Court of Human Rights: Survey of Activities and Statistics*, Council of Europe, Strasbourg, 2001, 2002 and 2003.

[524] Report of 17 February 1965, Yearbook VIII (1965), p. 410 (422).

[525] See, *e.g.*, judgment of 20 March 2001, *Köksal*, para 14; judgment of 21 May 2001, *Değerli*, para. 14; judgment of 12 February 2002, *Gawracz*, para. 9; judgment of 18 June 2002, *Samy*, para. 14; judgment of 6 May 2003, *Sêdek*, para 14; judgment of 21 October 2004, *Binbay*, para. 19.

[526] Report of 10 December 1984, *Eaton and Others v. the United Kingdom*, D&R 39 (1984), p. 11 (15).

Belgian Government showed itself prepared to pay compensation to Geniets.[527] With respect to three complaints regarding corporal punishment of children at school, the way to a settlement was paved by the Court's judgment in the *Campbell and Cosans* Case as a result of which Government of the United Kingdom changed the relevant legislation and in addition made *ex gratia* payments to the applicants concerned.[528]

In the *Tsavachidis* Case a Jehova Witness complained that the Greek intelligence services kept him under surveillance on account of his religious beliefs. The Court pointed out that in a number of earlier cases it had had to consider systems of secret surveillance in States other than Greece and to ascertain, under Article 8 of the Convention, that there were adequate and effective safeguards against abuses of such systems. Furthermore, in the cases of *Kokkinakis* and *Manoussakis* – in which the facts had, however, been different from those of the *Tsavachidis* Case – the Court had had to rule under Article 9 of the Convention on the application of the relevant Greek legislation to the Jehovah's Witnesses. In so doing it had clarified the nature and extent of the Contracting States' obligations in that regard, including payment of compensation. It followed that the case was ripe for a settlement and should be struck out of the list.[529]

In a case where the applicant complained under Articles 8, 13 and 14 of the Convention about the investigation and inquiries into his sexual orientation and about his discharge from the RAF by reason of his homosexuality, the Court noted that it considered the issues raised in its judgment in, *inter alia, Smith and Grady*, in which violations of Articles 8 and 13 of the Convention were found. The Court further observed that following that judgment, the policy of the Ministry of Defence was abandoned and homosexuals had been allowed to serve in the United Kingdom is armed forces as from 12 January 2000. Furthermore, the respondent State paid a certain amount in compensation.[530]

In several cases the Court was notified of a friendly settlement reached between the Government and the applicant in respect of the latter's claim under Article 41. When delivering the principal judgment, the Court took formal note of the settlement and concluded that it was appropriate to strike the case out of its list.[531]

Many applications received in Strasbourg allege that the length of domestic criminal, civil or administrative court proceedings has exceeded the 'reasonable time' stipulated

---

[527]   Report of 15 March 1985, *Geniets v. Belgium*, D&R 41 (1985), p. 5 (12).

[528]   Report of 23 January 1987, *Townend v. the United Kingdom*, D&R 50 (1987), p. 36; report of 16 July 1987, *Durairaj and Baker v. the United Kingdom*, D&R 52 (1987), p. 13; report of 16 July 1987, *Family A v. the United Kingdom*, D&R 52 (1987), p. 150.

[529]   Judgment of 21 January 1999.

[530]   Judgment of 29 July 2003, *Brown*, para 13.

[531]   See *e.g.* judgment of 29 September 1987, *Erkner and Hofauer*; judgment of 29 March 1990, *Kostovski*; judgment of 2 September 1996, *Vogt*; judgment of 31 March 1998, *Tsomtsos*.

in Article 6(1) of the Convention (more than 3,129 of a total of 5,307 applications declared admissible between 1955 and 1999). A particularly high number of such applications concerned Italy. Of the applications registered in the period from 1 November 1998 to 31 January 2001, 2,211 were directed against Italy. Of these, 1,516 related to the length of proceedings. Again, of the 1,085 applications declared admissible in 2000, 486 concerned Italy, of which 428 cases related to this issue. In addition, as of July 2001, there were about 10,000 further provisional applications in total against Italy which fell into this category, of which 3,177 files were ready for registration but could not be processed for lack of human resources at the Registry. In the period from 1 January 1999 to 31 December 2003, 177 of these cases against Italy ended in a friendly settlement in which the Italian Government was prepared to pay a certain amount for just satisfaction.[532]

In a very high number of applications against Turkey the applicants complained in relation to the payment of compensation following the expropriation of their property. They alleged that the compensation they received did not reflect the real increase in inflation during the period between the date the amount was fixed and the date of payment. The great majority of these cases ended by reaching a friendly settlement in which the Turkish Government agreed to pay a certain amount of compensation.

There are also examples of more substantive settlements. In this respect mention could be made of the settlement in the case of *France, Norway, Denmark, Sweden and the Netherlands v. Turkey*, which was accepted by the Commission in 1985. The substantive parts of the settlement included the assurance by the Turkish Government that they would strictly observe their obligations under Article 3 of the Convention, a vague promise concerning the granting of amnesty and – as regards the derogations under Article 15 of the Convention – a reference to an even more vague declaration by the Turkish Prime Minister of 4 April 1985, stating that "I hope that we will be able to lift martial law from the remaining provinces within 18 months."[533] In particular the acceptance by the applicant States of the latter part of the settlement was striking in view of the fact that, when lodging their complaint, the applicant States upheld that a public emergency threatening the life of the nation did not exist in Turkey in 1982. Although the application, as declared admissible, also included alleged violations of the Articles 5, 6, 9, 10, 11 and 17 of the Convention, those provisions were not explicitly mentioned in the settlement.

Due to their rather lenient attitude, the applicant Governments had manoeuvred the Commission into a very difficult position. It may even be argued that the Commission was left with no choice but to accept the settlement. Indeed, in the alternative

---

[532] See *Survey of Activities of the European Court of Human Rights*, http://www.echr.coe.int/Eng/InfoNotes AndSurveys.htm.
[533] Report of 7 December 1985, D&R 44 (1985), p. 31 (39).

the case would have been decided by the Committee of Ministers – Turkey had not recognised the jurisdiction of the Court at that time – in which case the applicant States and Turkey would obviously have played a prominent if not decisive role. Be this as it may, it does not turn the settlement into one which was reached 'on the basis of respect for Human Rights as defined in this Convention.' It is, therefore, questionable whether the Commission sufficiently upheld this requirement of former Article 28(1)(b). It is submitted that the Commission should at least have insisted on a stricter type of supervision over the observance by Turkey regarding its commitments under the settlement. With respect to Article 15, as well as to the granting of amnesty, there was in fact no supervision at all: the Turkish Government only undertook to keep the Commission informed of further developments. As far as Article 3 was concerned, supervision was confined to a commitment by Turkey to submit three reports under former Article 57 during 1986, to enter into a dialogue with the Commission on each of those reports, and to prepare a short final report on the implementation of the settlement no later than 1 February 1987. All this, moreover, was to be conducted in a confidential manner.[534] As was to be expected, these supervisory arrangements turned out to be inadequate. Although martial law was lifted in Turkey in the course of 1987, allegations of serious violations of human rights continued.[535]

After Turkey had accepted the right of individual petition and the compulsory jurisdiction of the Court in 1989, many applications were brought against Turkey alleging violations of Article 2 and 3 of the Convention. Several cases ended in a friendly settlement. In some of those the Court accepted the friendly settlement. The Court stated that, in view of its responsibilities under Article 19 of the Convention, it would nevertheless be open to the Court to proceed with its consideration of the case if a reason of public policy (*ordre public*) appeared to necessitate such a course, but that it discerned no such reason.[536] In other cases the Turkish Government accepted that the use of excessive or disproportionate force resulting in death constitutes a violation of Article 2 of the Convention and undertook to issue appropriate instructions and adopt all necessary measures to ensure that the right to life – including the obligation to carry out effective investigations – would be respected in the future. In fact, new legal and administrative measures were adopted which resulted in a reduction in the occurrence of deaths in circumstances similar to those of the application referred to here, as well as more effective investigations.[537] In the case of *Denmark v. Turkey* the Court observed that the friendly settlement, *inter alia*,

---

[534]   *Ibidem.*

[535]   See Amnesty International, *Turkey, Brutal and Systematic Abuse of Human Rights*, London, 1989.

[536]   Judgment of 3 October 1997, *Sur*, para 31; judgment of 25 September 2001, *Ercan*, para. 29; judgment of 31 October 2001, *Saki*, para. 14; judgment of 9 April 2002, *Toğcu*, para. 37; judgment of 19 June 2003, *Ulku Dogan and Others*, para. 21.

[537]   Judgment of 26 June 2001, *Akman*, para 31; judgment of 26 November 2002, *Yakar*, para. 32; judgment of 15 July 2004, *Örnek and Eren*, para 24; judgment of 27 July 2004, *Çelik*, para.16.

made provision for the payment of a sum of money to the applicant Government and included a statement of regret by the respondent Government concerning the occurrence of occasional and individual cases of torture and ill-treatment in Turkey, which emphasised, with reference to Turkey's continued participation in the Council of Europe's police-training project, the importance of the training of Turkish police officers, and provided for the establishment of a new bilateral project in this area. Furthermore, it had been decided to establish a continuous Danish-Turkish political dialogue that would also focus on human rights issues and within which individual cases might be raised. The Court also took note of the changes to the legal and administrative framework which had been introduced in Turkey in response to instances of torture and ill-treatment as well as the respondent Government's undertaking to make further improvements in the field of human rights – especially concerning the occurrence of incidents of torture and ill-treatment – and to continue their co-operation with international human rights bodies, in particular the Committee for the Prevention of Torture. Against that background the Court was satisfied that the settlement was based on respect for human rights as defined in the Convention or its Protocols.[538]

In cases of deportation or extradition, a friendly settlement may sometimes lead to an immediate solution. The threatened deportation of a South African who had gone into exile, allegedly for political reasons, raised questions in connection with the prohibition of degrading and inhuman treatment set forth in Article 3 of the Convention. This case was eventually resolved because the Belgian authorities provided the applicant with the documents required for emigration to Senegal as desired by him and paid his travelling expenses.[539] In another case a Jordanian citizen had been expelled to Jordan after the Commission had decided, in accordance with Rule 36 of the Commission's Rules of Procedure, to indicate to the Swedish Government that it was desirable in the interest of the parties and the proper conduct of the proceedings before the Commission not to deport the applicant to Jordan until the Commission had had an opportunity to examine the application at its forthcoming session. In the settlement reached the applicant was granted permission to return to Sweden and to reside in Sweden permanently.[540] Complaints concerning inhuman treatment and a breach of the right to respect for family life were raised in a similar case against Sweden by a 12-year-old Lebanese boy whose deportation was at issue. The application also was originally filed on behalf of his two elder brothers who had already been deported from Sweden. Under the terms of the friendly settlement that was eventually arrived at, the Swedish Government agreed to grant permission to the applicant's brothers to reside and work in Sweden, their travel expenses being paid by the Government,

---

[538] Judgment of 5 April 2000, paras 24-25.
[539] Report of 17 July 1980, *Giama v. Belgium*, D&R 21 (1982), p. 73.
[540] Report of 7 December 1989, *Mansi v. Sweden*, D&R 64 (1990), p. 253(258).

to make an *ex gratia* payment as well as a payment for legal expenses, and to revise the relevant regulations concerning expulsion.[541] In the case of *Yang Chun Jin Alias Yang Xiaolin v. Hungary* the applicant alleged that, if extradited to China, he risked having an unfair trial, being detained under harsh conditions, being subjected to torture, or being sentenced to death. Noting that the Hungarian Minister of Justice had decided to refuse the applicant's extradition to China and that he had left Hungary for Sierra Leone, the Court found that the applicant was no longer threatened with extradition to China from Hungary and that the matter was resolved.[542]

Friendly settlements can also be found in which there is, apart from financial compensation, the willingness on the part of the respondent State to amend the legislation which gave rise to the complaint. In a case concerning the refusal to grant legal aid for appeal against a sentence the Government of the United Kingdom issued a practice note to all appeal court chairmen and clerks opening the possibility of review in cases where legal aid had been refused and the court concerned considered that, *prima facie*, an appellant might have substantial grounds for lodging the appeal.[543] In the *Gussenbauer* Case against Austria the settlement resulted in radical changes to the Austrian system of counsel assigned to prisoners.[544] In the *Zimmermann* Case the Austrian Government was willing to propose to the Federal President to quash, by an act of grace, the conditional prison sentence of seven months imposed on Zimmermann by the Vienna Regional Court. In this case financial compensation was also offered.[545] In the *Selim* Case the applicant wished to contract a civil marriage with a Romanian citizen. The Municipality of Nicosia informed the applicant that Section 34 of the Marriage Act did not allow a Turkish Cypriot professing the Muslim faith to contract a civil marriage. The applicant was thus forced to marry in Romania without any of his family or friends being able to attend. The case ended in a friendly settlement. The Court took note of the agreement reached between the Government and the applicant. It noted, in addition, that new legislation had been enacted, which provided for the application of the Marriage Act Cap. 279 to members of the Turkish Community, thus conferring on them the right to marry. It further noted that a new law (The Civil Marriage Act 2002), which would apply to all Cypriots without distinction of origin, was also to be tabled in Parliament for enactment.[546]

---

[541]   Report of 8 December 1984, *Bulus v. Sweden*, D&R 39 (1984), p. 75 (78-79). See also the report of 7 October 1986, *Min, Min and Min Paik v. the United Kingdom*, D&R 48 (1986), p. 58, and the report of 4 July 1991, *Fadelle v. the United Kingdom*, D&R 70 (1991), p. 159 (162).

[542]   Judgment of 8 March 2001; see also judgment of 21 December 2001, *K.K.C. v. the Netherlands*.

[543]   Report of 13 February 1992, *Higgins v. the United Kingdom*, D&R 73 (1992), p. 95 (97-98).

[544]   Report of 8 October 1974, *Gussenbauer v. Austria*, Yearbook XV (1972), p. 558.

[545]   Report of 6 July 1982, *Zimmermann v. Austria*, D&R 30 (1983), p. 15 (20).

[546]   Judgment of 16 July 2002, para. 16

In some cases considerations of public interest also play a part, especially in relation to the prospect that the challenged law will be amended. In the *Alam* Case in which a complaint was lodged, *inter alia*, about Article 6(1), the Commission included in its considerations the fact that the British Government had introduced Bills in which aliens were granted the right to appeal against decisions of immigration officers.[547] Again, in a case against Austria concerning Article 6(1) the principal element of the settlement reached was the fact that the Government had proposed an amendment of the law as a result of which detained persons henceforth could also be present at hearings where an appeal lodged to their detriment was dealt with.[548] In two other cases the friendly settlement included the readiness on the part of the Governement of the United Kingdom to amend prison administrative practices in order to inform a prisoner's relatives in due time of his imminent transfer to another prison,[549] and to better safeguard the prisoners' right to respect for their correspondence.[550]

In a complaint against the United Kingdom the applicant, in addition to alleging violation of his right to respect for his family life and home as a result of noise and vibration nuisance, complained that this also affected his property located a quarter of a mile from Heathrow Airport. The matter was settled by an *ex gratia* payment by the Government.[551]

In a number of cases, matters of family law were at issue. In two of these cases, both against Sweden, the applicants complained about the taking into public care of their respective children. Due to the fact that in both cases the children had in the meantime been returned to their mothers, they could be settled on the basis of compensation paid by the Government.[552]

2.3.5.4 Other forms of similar arrangements

Apart from the friendly settlement referred to in Article 37(1)(b) the parties sometimes reach a settlement of the dispute themselves. In those cases the applicant withdraws his complaint after having come to some kind of arrangement with the Government concerned.[553]

A well-known example is the *Televizier* Case. In that case the applicant, who was the owner of a radio and T.V magazine, complained about violation of the freedom of expression (Article 10) and about discriminatory treatment (Article 14) in con-

---

[547] Report of 17 December 1968, *Mohammed Alam v. the United Kingdom*, Yearbook X (1967), p. 478.
[548] Report of 13 October 1981, *Peschke v. Austria*, D&R 25 (1982), p. 182.
[549] Report of 15 May 1986, *Seale v. the United Kingdom*, D&R 50 (1987), p. 70.
[550] Report of 15 May 1986, *McComb v. the United Kingdom*, D&R 50 (1987), p. 81.
[551] Report of 8 July 1987, *Baggs v. the United Kingdom*, D&R 52 (1987), p. 29.
[552] Report of 10 October 1986, *Aminoff v. Sweden*, D&R 48 (1986), p. 82; and report of 10 October 1986, *Widén v. Sweden, Ibidem*, p. 93.
[553] Rule 43(1) of the Rules of Court.

nection with a judgment of the Dutch Supreme Court, which was based on the Copyright Act. The case concerned information provided and comments given on radio and television programmes, for which use had been made of summaries of programmes of the Central Broadcasting Bureau in the Netherlands. Some years after the application had been submitted the parties informed the Commission that they had arrived at an arrangement and that the applicant wished to withdraw the application. Televizier had meanwhile concluded an agreement with one of the broadcasting organisations about the publication of the latter's radio and TV guide.[554] In the Case of *Denmark, Norway and Sweden v. Greece* the Commission took note of the Parties' concordant requests that the proceedings should be closed. It found that the texts of the relevant provisions of Greek law were sufficient to show that remedies were open in Greece to persons claiming to have been victim of political prosecution under the former regime and that these remedies also provided compensation. It decided to close the proceedings in this case and to strike it off its list.[555]

In cases like these the Commission was (and the Court is) willing to accept the withdrawal of the application and to strike the case off the list only if considerations of public interest do not oppose to its doing so. Thus, in the *Gericke* Case the Commission at first refused to agree to the withdrawal of the application on the ground that "the present application raises problems of individual freedom involved in the application of Article 5, paragraph 3, of the Convention, which may extend beyond the interests of the particular applicants."[556] After the adoption of its report in the *Wemhoff* Case[557] in May 1966, the Commission discontinued the procedure in the case of *Gericke*, who had been condemned as an accomplice of Wemhoff, because it held that reasons of public interest no longer made it necessary to examine the case any further.[558] A number of other cases were terminated because the issue(s) at stake had in the meantime been decided by the Court in comparable cases.[559] In some cases the main element of the informal settlement consisted of an amendment of the legislation which was the cause of the alleged violation.[560]

There is also a possibility that the Court may decide to strike a case off the list of cases if a solution is reached by way of a unilateral measure. In accordance with Article

---

[554]   Report of 3 October 1968, *N.V. Televizier v. the Netherlands*, Yearbook XI (1968), p. 783.

[555]   Report of 4 October 1976, D&R 6 (1977), p. 5 (8).

[556]   Report of 22 July 1966, *Gericke v. Federal Republic of Germany*, Yearbook VIII (1965), p. 314 (320).

[557]   Report of 1 April 1966, B.5 (1969).

[558]   See Council of Europe, *Stock-Taking on the European Convention on Human Rights* (1954-1984), Strasbourg, 1984, p. 145.

[559]   Report of 9 May 1987, *Bozano v. Switzerland*, D&R 52 (1987), p. 5 (11); the case was terminated after the Court's *Sanchez-Reisse* judgment, while the Case of *Scotts' of Greenock Ltd and Lithgow Ltd v. the United Kingdom*, report of 5 March 1987, D&R 51 (1987), p. 34 (37), was withdrawn on the basis of the *Lithgow* judgment.

[560]   Appl. 10664/83, *Bowen v. Norway*, D&R 45 (1986), p. 158 (161); see also the report of 7 May 1986, *Prasser v. Austria*, D&R 46 (1986), p. 81.

37(1)(c) the Court may at any stage of the proceedings decide to strike an application off its list of cases where the circumstances lead to the conclusion that it is no longer justified to continue the examination of the application. The Court may, however, decide to restore the case to the list again if new circumstance justify this. Thus, in one case the applicant complained that, if he was deported to what was formerly Zaire it would amount to treatment contrary to Article 3 of the Convention, as it would reduce his life expectancy because he would not receive the medical treatment his condition demanded. The Government invited the Court to strike the case off the list. They relied on two factors of which the Commission had been unaware, since the relevant information had been communicated to it on the day its report had been adopted: the Versailles Administrative Court had quashed the decision to enforce the order excluding the applicant from French territory, while a compulsory residence order had been made. Those measures meant that the applicant no longer risked being deported to the Democratic Republic of Congo and was no longer a 'victim'. The Court noted that there had been no friendly settlement or arrangement in the instant case. The compulsory residence order made was unilateral in character and issued by the French authorities after the Commission had adopted its report. It considered, however, that the order constituted an 'other fact of a kind to provide a solution of the matter'. Accordingly, it was appropriate to strike the case out of the list. The Court, however, reserved the power to restore it to the list if new circumstances were to arise justifying such a measure.[561]

As described above,[562] in the cases of *Aydin,*[563] *Akman*[564] and *Tahsin Acar*[565] the applicants did not agree to a friendly settlement of the case. The Court held that having examined the terms of the respondent Government's declaration carefully and having regard to the nature of the admissions contained in the declaration as well as the scope and extent of the various undertakings referred to therein, together with the amount of compensation proposed, it considered that it was no longer justified to continue the examination of the applications. In the case of *Tahsin Acar* the Grand Chamber held that, under certain circumstances, it might be appropriate to strike out an application under Article 37(1)(c) of the Convention on the basis of a unilateral declaration by the respondent Government even if the applicant wished the examination of the case to be continued. It will, however, depend on the particular circumstances whether the unilateral declaration offers a sufficient basis for finding that

---

[561]   Judgment of 7 September 1998, *B.B. v. France*, para 37.
[562]   See *supra* 2.3.3.
[563]   Judgment of 10 July 2001, para. 15.
[564]   Judgment of 26 June 2001, para 30.
[565]   Judgment of 29 April 2002, para. 65.

respect for human rights as defined in the Convention does not require the Court to continue its examination of the case.[566]

As a non-exhaustive list the Court indicated that relevant factors for deciding whether a unilateral declaration is sufficient to decide to strike a case off the list of cases include the nature of the complaints made, the question of whether the issues raised are comparable to issues already determined by the Court in previous cases, the nature and scope of any measures taken by the respondent Government in the context of the execution of judgments delivered by the Court in any such previous cases, and the impact of these measures on the case at issue. It may also be material whether the facts are in dispute between the parties, and if so to what extent, and what *prima facie* evidentiary value is to be attributed to the parties' submissions on the facts. In that connection it will be of significance whether the Court itself has already taken evidence in the case for the purposes of establishing disputed facts. Other relevant factors may include the question of whether in their unilateral declaration the respondent Government has made any admission(s) in relation to the alleged violations of the Convention, and if so, the scope of such admissions and the manner in which they intend to provide redress to the applicant. As to the last-mentioned point, in cases in which it is possible to eliminate the effects of an alleged violation (as, for example, in some property cases) and the respondent Government declares its readiness to do so, the intended redress is more likely to be regarded as appropriate for the purposes of striking out the application, although the Court, as always, retains its power to restore the application to its list as provided in Article 37(2) of the Convention and Rule 43(5) of the Rules of Court.[567]

A full admission of liability in respect of an applicant's allegations under the Convention cannot be regarded as a condition *sine qua non* for the Court to be prepared to strike an application out on the basis of a unilateral declaration by a respondent Government. However, in cases concerning persons who have disappeared or have been killed by unknown perpetrators and where there is *prima facie* evidence in the case-file supporting allegations that the domestic investigation fell short of what is necessary under the Convention, a unilateral declaration should at the very least contain an admission to that effect, combined with an undertaking by the respondent Government to conduct, under the supervision of the Committee of Ministers in the context of the latter's duties under Article 46(2) of the Convention, an investigation that is in full compliance with the requirements of the Convention.[568]

In the *Kalantari* Case the applicant complained that his expulsion to Iran would expose him to a risk of inhuman and degrading treatment contrary to Article 3 of the Convention. The Government took the position that, since the Federal Office for

---

[566]   Judgment of 6 May 2003, para. 75.
[567]   *Ibidem*, para 76.
[568]   *Ibidem*, para 84.

Refugees had set aside its decision of 31 August 1998 and ruled that there were bars to the applicant's expulsion under section 53(4) of the Aliens Act, the applicant was now fully protected against an expulsion to Iran in breach of Article 3 of the Convention. The new decision could only be set aside by the Federal Office for Refugees itself and, in such event, an appeal would be available to the administrative courts. Furthermore, the federal government as such could not give assurances concerning the grant of a residence permit, as the issue of such permits was the responsibility of the relevant *Länder* authorities. The Court held that the decision of the Federal Office for Refugees was binding on the Aliens Office and might only be set aside by the Federal Office for Refugees itself; an appeal would lie to the administrative courts against any new decision. In light of the Federal Office for Refugees' decision, the continued examination of the application was no longer justified.[569]

2.3.5.5 Non-compliance with the terms of a friendly settlement

There is no express provision in the Convention concerning non-compliance. It would seem to be possible for one of the Contracting States to submit a complaint concerning non-compliance with a friendly settlement to the Committee of Ministers. In fact, as members of the Council of Europe the Contracting States may take the initiative for the much more far-reaching procedure of expulsion of a Member State from the organisation under Article 8 of the Statute of the Council of Europe, when the latter has seriously violated its engagements concerning human rights and fundamental freedoms. Therefore, they must certainly also be considered as being authorised to put non-compliance with a friendly settlement before the Committee of Ministers in order to try, through that organ, to induce the State in question to comply with its obligations under the settlement. In view thereof it would be advisable for the Committee of Ministers, when stating that no further steps in the respective case are necessary in view of the settlement reached, to reserve to itself the right to take appropriate measures at a later date should one of the parties not comply with its obligations. Since the entry into force of Protocol No.11 a practice has been developed by which the Court endorses friendly settlements through *judgments* and not – as provided for in Article 39 of the Convention – through *decisions*, whose execution are not subject to supervision by the Committee of Ministers.

Under Protocol No. 14 the new Article 39 will expressly provide for supervision of the execution of friendly settlements by the Committee of Ministers. According to the *Explanatory Report to Protocol No. 14* this amendment is in no way intended to reduce the Committee's present supervisory powers, particularly concerning the strike-out decisions covered by Article 37. It would be advisable for the Committee of Ministers to distinguish more clearly, in its practice, between its supervision function

---

[569]   Judgment of 11 October 2001, paras 52-57.

by virtue of the new Article 39, paragraph 4 (friendly settlements), on the one hand, and that under Article 46, paragraph 2 (execution of judgments), on the other.[570]

A non-official settlement may also be reached when the Court's examination of the merits is quite complete, or almost so. It must, therefore, be determined for each individual case what is the best solution if such a settlement is not complied with by the Contracting State in question: supervision by the Committee of Ministers, or restoration of the application to the list. When a thorough examination of the merits has not yet taken place, it would seem to be most appropriate for the Court to place the case on the list of cases again when 'the circumstances of the case as a whole justify such restoration.' The consequence of this is that the original application as a whole is resuscitated, so that no additional difficulties may arise in connection with the admissibility conditions. Here again, however, the Court will first have to ascertain whether the settlement has really not been complied with, and it will, therefore, have to give the State concerned an opportunity to prove the contrary.

2.4   PROCEEDINGS BEFORE THE GRAND CHAMBER

2.4.1.   GENERAL

The Grand Chamber has competence both with regard to inter-State applications referred to it under Article 30 or Article 43 of the Convention as well as to individual applications when they are referred to it under Article 30 or Article 43. The Grand Chamber is also competent to consider requests for advisory opinions, a function which the plenary Court carried out under the former system.[571] In cases with specified serious implications a Chamber will be able to relinquish jurisdiction *proprio motu* in favour of the Grand Chamber at any time, as long as it has not yet rendered judgment, unless one of the parties to the case objects.[572] Such relinquishment should also speed up proceedings. Once a judgment has been rendered by a Chamber, any of the parties may request that the case be referred to the Grand Chamber for a re-hearing.[573]

---

[570]   *Explanatory Report to Protocol No. 14*, para 94.
[571]   Rule 88 of the Rules of Court.
[572]   Rule 72 of the Rules of Court.
[573]   Rule 73 of the Rules of Court.

2.4.2 RELINQUISHMENT OF JURISDICTION IN FAVOUR OF THE GRAND CHAMBER

In accordance with Article 30 of the Convention, where a case pending before a Chamber raises a serious question affecting the interpretation of the Convention or the Protocols thereto or where the resolution of a question before it might have a result inconsistent with a judgment previously delivered by the Court, the Chamber may, at any time before it has rendered its judgment, relinquish jurisdiction in favour of the Grand Chamber, unless one of the parties to the case has objected in accordance with paragraph 2 of this Rule. Reasons need not be given for the decision to relinquish.[574] Conferring a veto right on the parties keeps open the possibility for their case to receive a handling in two instances. However, the objection against relinquishment of jurisdiction has to be duly reasoned; otherwise it will be considered invalid.[575]

2.4.3 REFERRAL TO THE GRAND CHAMBER

In accordance with Article 43(1) of the Convention within a period of three months from the date of the judgment of the Chamber, any party to the case may, in exceptional cases, request that the case be referred to the Grand Chamber. A re-hearing of the case, as envisaged in Article 43, will take place only exceptionally, when a case raises a serious question affecting the interpretation or application of the Convention or a serious issue of general importance.[576] The purpose is to ensure the quality and consistency of the Court's case law by allowing for a re-examination of the most important cases. The intention is that these conditions will be applied in a strict sense.[577]

The party must specify in its request the serious question affecting the interpretation or application of the Convention or the Protocols thereto, or the serious issue of general importance, which in its view warrants consideration by the Grand Chamber.[578]

According to the *Explanatory Report to Protocol No. 11* serious questions affecting the interpretation of the Convention are involved when a question of importance not yet decided by the Court is at stake, or when the decision is of importance for future cases and for the development of the Court's case law. Moreover, a serious question may be particularly evident when the judgment concerned is not consistent with a previous judgment of the Court. A serious question concerning the application of the

---

[574]   Rule 72(1) of the Rules of Court.
[575]   Rule 72(2) of the Rules of Court.
[576]   Article 43(2) of the Convention and Rule 73(2) of the Rules of Court.
[577]   *Explanatory Report to Protocol No. 11*, para. 99. See in this respect Article 43(1) of the Convention and Rule 73(1) of the Rules of Court, where the term 'exceptionally' has been used.
[578]   Rule 73(1) of the Rules of Court.

Convention may be at stake when a judgment necessitates a substantial change of national law or administrative practice but does not itself raise a serious question of interpretation of the Convention. A serious issue of general importance could involve a substantial political issue or an important issue of policy.[579]

A request for a re-hearing may concern the admissibility as well as the merits of a case. A request may also be made if a party to the case has a disagreement with respect to a judgment concerning the award of just satisfaction under Article 41 of the Convention.[580]

In order to ensure that the parties are in a position to observe the time limit of three months from the date of delivery of the judgment, they will be informed about the date on which the judgment is delivered. A panel of five judges of the Grand Chamber decides on the acceptance of the request. If the request is accepted, the Grand Chamber has to make the final determination as to whether the Convention has been violated after written and, if the Court so decides, oral proceedings. If the conditions for a request of referral are not met, the panel rejects the request and the Chamber's judgment becomes final. It will accept the request only if it considers that the case does raise a serious question as defined in Article 43(2). Reasons need not be given for a refusal of the request.[581] In practice it seems to be rather difficult to have a case be referred to the Grand Chamber. In the period from 1 January 2000 to 31 December 2003 only 26 requests were accepted.[582]

In the *Pisano* Case the Italian Government asked the Grand Chamber to review the decision of the panel of five judges to accept the request for referral. They argued that the request did not satisfy the conditions laid down in Article 43 of the Convention. In the Government's submission the case did not raise any serious questions affecting the interpretation or application of the Convention, or indeed any serious issues of general importance. They emphasised that the applicant had not produced any evidence to suggest that it did but had merely referred to the dissenting opinion appended to the Chamber judgment. The latter opinion, however, was not sufficient to justify a rehearing of the case as it did not in any way call into question the manner in which Article 6 of the Convention had been construed. Lastly, the Government argued that the Grand Chamber, seeing that it had the final say about its own jurisdiction and whether it had been validly seized, was not bound by the opinion of the five judges. The Grand Chamber noted that neither the Convention nor the Rules of Court empowered it to review a decision by the panel to accept a request for a rehearing. What is more, the terms of Article 43(3) of the Convention provide as follows: 'If the panel accepts the request, the Grand Chamber shall decide the case by means

---

[579]   *Explanatory Report to Protocol No. 11*, paras 100-102.
[580]   Judgment of 28 May 2002, *Kingsley*, para. 7
[581]   Rule 73(2) of the Rules of Court.
[582]   See Grand Chamber, Annual Activity Reports 2000-2003.

of a judgment' and thus make it clear that, once the panel has accepted a request for a rehearing, the Grand Chamber has no option but to examine the case.[583]

2.4.4 THE PROCEDURE BEFORE THE GRAND CHAMBER

According to Rule 71(1) of the Rules of Court, any provisions governing proceedings before the Chambers shall apply, *mutatis mutandis*, to proceedings before the Grand Chamber.

Where a case has been submitted to the Grand Chamber either under Article 30 or under Article 43 of the Convention, the President of the Grand Chamber designates as Judge Rapporteur(s) one or, in the case of an inter-State application, one or more of its members.[584] The Judge Rapporteur of the Grand Chamber is always a judge other than the judge elected in respect of the respondent Party. The proceedings of the Grand Chamber are normally written proceedings but, if the Court so decides, oral proceedings may be held. The powers conferred on a Chamber in relation to the holding of a hearing may, in proceedings before the Grand Chamber, also be exercised by the President of the Grand Chamber.[585] From the text of Article 31(a) of the Convention it may be deduced that, if the decision to relinquish jurisdiction in favour of the Grand Chamber is taken before a decision as to admissibility has been taken, the Grand Chamber will also decide on admissibility. After all, in accordance with Article 35(4) of the Convention, the Court rejects any application which it considers inadmissible. It may do so at any stage of the proceedings. At this stage third party intervention is also possible.[586]

As holds good for the Chambers of the Court, the Grand Chamber must assess the facts as they appear at the time of its decision by applying the appropriate legal solution. Once a case is referred to it, the Grand Chamber deals with the case afresh and may employ the full range of judicial powers conferred on the Court.[587] In this respect the Court held: "The Court would first note that all three paragraphs of Article 43 use the term 'the case' ('*l'affaire*') for describing the matter which is being brought before the Grand Chamber. In particular, paragraph 3 of Article 43 provides that the Grand Chamber is to 'decide *the case*' – that is the whole case and not simply the 'serious question' or 'serious issue' mentioned in paragraph 2 – 'by means of a judgment'. The wording of Article 43 makes it clear that, whilst the existence of 'a serious question affecting the interpretation or application of the Convention or the Protocols thereto, or a serious issue of general importance' (paragraph 2) is a

---

[583]   Judgment of 24 October 2002, para. 26.
[584]   Rule 50 of the Rules of Court.
[585]   Rule 71(2) of the Rules of Court.
[586]   Rule 44 (3) of the Rules of Court.
[587]   Judgment of 24 October 2002, *Pisano*, para. 28.

prerequisite for acceptance of a party's request, the consequence of acceptance is that the whole 'case' is referred to the Grand Chamber to be decided afresh by means of a new judgment (paragraph 3). The same term 'the case' (*l'affaire*) is also used in Article 44 para. 2 which defines the conditions under which the judgments of a Chamber become final. If a request by a party for referral under Article 43 has been accepted, Article 44 can only be understood as meaning that the entire judgment of the Chamber will be set aside in order to be replaced by the new judgment of the Grand Chamber envisaged by Article 43 para. 3. This being so, the 'case' referred to the Grand Chamber necessarily embraces all aspects of the application previously examined by the Chamber in its judgment, and not only the serious 'question' or 'issue' at the basis of the referral. In sum, there is no basis for a merely partial referral of the case to the Grand Chamber."[588]

The Grand Chamber may also re-examine, where appropriate, issues relating to the admissibility of the application in the same manner as this is possible in normal Chamber proceedings, for example by virtue of Article 35(4) *in fine* of the Convention.[589]

The Grand Chamber may likewise be required to apply other provisions of the Convention that enable it to terminate the proceedings by a means other than a judgment on the merits, for example by approving a friendly settlement (Article 39 of the Convention) or striking the application off the list of cases (Article 37).

2.5   JUDGMENT OF THE COURT

Where the Chamber finds that there has been a violation of the Convention or the Protocols thereto, it gives in the same judgment a ruling on the application of Article 41 of the Convention if that question, after being raised in accordance with Rule 60 of the Rules of Court, is ready for decision. If the question is not ready for decision, the Chamber reserves it in whole or in part and fixes the further procedure.[590]

According to Article 42 in conjunction with Article 44(2) of the Convention, judgments of Chambers become final (a) when the parties declare that they will not request that the case be referred to the Grand Chamber; or (b) three months after the date of the judgment, if reference of the case to the Grand Chamber has not been requested; or (c) when the panel of the Grand Chamber rejects the request to refer the case to the Grand Chamber. According to Article 44(1) of the Convention, the judgment of the Grand Chamber is final. Judgments have to be reasoned (Article 45,

---

[588]   Judgment of 12 July 2001, *K. and T. v. Finland*, para. 140; judgment of 11 July 2002, *Göc*, para. 36; judgment of 24 October 2002, *Pisano*, para. 28; judgment of 6 May 2003, *Perna*, para.23; judgment of 6 May 2003, *Tahsin Acar*, para.63; judgment of 28 April 2004, *Azinas*, para. 32.

[589]   Judgment of 28 April 2004, *Azinas*, para. 32.

[590]   Rule 75(1) of the Rules of Court.

paragraph 1). This article does not concern decisions taken by the panel of five judges of the Grand Chamber in accordance with Article 43, nor Committee decisions on admissibility under Article 28.

The judgment will be transmitted to the parties but will not be published until it has become final (Article 44, paragraph 3). Unless the Court decides that a judgment will be given in both official languages, all judgments will be given either in English or in French.[591] According to Rule 77 of the Rules of Court the judgment may be read out at a public hearing by the President of the Chamber or by another judge delegated by him or her. The Agents and representatives of the parties are informed in due time of the date of the hearing. Final judgments of the Court are published under the responsibility of the Registrar in an appropriate form. In addition, the Registrar is responsible for the publication of official reports of selected judgments and decisions and of any document which the President of the Court considers it useful to publish.[592]

According to Article 46, the High Contracting Parties undertake to abide by the final judgment of the Court in any case to which they are parties. The final judgment is transmitted to the Committee of Ministers, which will supervise its execution.

With respect to the binding force and execution of judgments, Protocol No. 14 will amend Article 46 of the Convention. Three new paragraphs will be added to Article 46. The new Article 46, in its paragraph 3, will empower the Committee of Ministers to ask the Court to interpret a final judgment for the purpose of facilitating the supervision of its execution. The Committee of Ministers' experience of supervising the execution of judgments shows that difficulties are sometimes encountered due to disagreement as to the interpretation of judgments. The Court's reply settles any argument concerning a judgment's exact meaning. The qualified majority vote required on the part of the Committee of Ministers by the last sentence of paragraph 3 shows that the Committee of Ministers should use this possibility sparingly in order to avoid over-burdening the Court. The aim of the new paragraph 3 is to enable the Court to give an interpretation of a judgment, not to pronounce on the measures taken by a High Contracting Party to comply with that judgment. No time-limit has been set for making requests for interpretation, since a question of interpretation may arise at any time during the Committee of Ministers' examination of the execution of a judgment.

The Court is free to decide on the manner and form in which it wishes to reply to the request. Normally, it would be for the formation of the Court which delivered the original judgment to rule on the question of interpretation. More detailed rules governing this new procedure may be included in the Rules of Court.[593]

---

[591] Rule 76 of the Rules of Court.
[592] Rule 78 of the Rules of Court.
[593] *Explanatory Report to Protocol No. 14*, paras 96-97.

Paragraphs 4 and 5 of Article 46 will empower the Committee of Ministers to bring infringement proceedings before the Court. The Court will sit as a Grand Chamber,[594] having first served the State concerned with notice to comply. The Committee of Ministers' decision to do so requires a qualified majority of two thirds of the representatives entitled to sit on the Committee. This infringement procedure does not aim to reopen the question of violation, already decided in the Court's first judgment. Nor does it provide for payment of a financial penalty by a High Contracting Party found in violation of Article 46, paragraph 1. It is felt that the political pressure exerted by proceedings for non-compliance in the Grand Chamber and by the latter's judgment should suffice to secure execution of the Court's initial judgment by the state concerned.[595]

In fulfilling its supervisory task the Committee of Ministers has invited the Court to identify, as far as possible, in its judgments in which a violation of the Convention is found, what it considers to be an underlying systemic problem and the source of this problem, particularly when it is likely to give rise to numerous applications, so as to assist States in finding the appropriate solution and the Committee of Ministers in supervising the execution of judgments.[596]

In this respect the Court held in the *Broniowski* Case that above all the measures adopted must be such as to remedy the systemic defect underlying the Court's finding of a violation so as not to overburden the Convention system with large numbers of applications deriving from the same cause. Such measures should, therefore, include a scheme which offers redress to those affected for the Convention violation identified in the instant judgment in relation to the present applicant. In this context the Court's concern is to facilitate the most speedy and effective resolution of a dysfunction established in national human rights protection. Once such a defect has been identified, it falls to the national authorities, under the supervision of the Committee of Ministers, to take, retroactively if appropriate, the necessary remedial measures in accordance with the subsidiary character of the Convention, so that the Court does not have to repeat its finding in a lengthy series of comparable cases. The Court held that, with a view to assisting the respondent State in fulfilling its obligations under Article 46, the Court has sought to indicate the type of measure that might be taken by the Polish State in order to put an end to the systemic situation identified in the present case. The Court was not in a position to assess whether the December 2003 Act can be treated as an adequate measure in this connection since no practice of its implementation has been established as yet. In any event, this Act does not cover persons who – like Mr Broniowski – had already received partial compensation, irre-

---

[594]   New Article 31(b).
[595]   *Explanatory Report to Protocol No. 14*, para 98.
[596]   Resolution Res. (2004) 3 van 12 May 2004 on judgments revealing an underlying systemic problem.

spective of the amount of such compensation. Thus, it was clear that for this group of Bug River claimants the Act could not be regarded as a measure capable of putting an end to the systemic situation identified in the present judgment as adversely affecting them. Nevertheless, as regards general measures to be taken, the Court considered that the respondent State must, primarily, either remove any hindrance to the implementation of the right of the numerous persons affected by the situation found, in respect of the applicant, to have been in breach of the Convention, or provide equivalent redress in lieu. As to the former option, the respondent State should, therefore, through appropriate legal and administrative measures secure the effective and expeditious realisation of the entitlement in question in respect of the remaining Bug River claimants, in accordance with the principles for the protection of property rights laid down in Article 1 of Protocol No. 1, having particular regard to the principles relating to compensation.[597] Since the applicant belonged to a fairly large group of victims of similar violations, on 4 July 2004 the Court used the 'leading case' procedure for the first time, whereby examination of the many similar cases is being suspended until the required measures have been taken. This procedure is one of the means chosen to reduce the Court's workload.[598]

In the *Sejdovic* Case the Court held that the infringement of the applicant's right to a fair trial had originated in a problem resulting from Italian legislation on the question of trial *in absentia* and had been caused by the wording of the provisions of the CCP relating to the conditions for lodging an application for the lifting of a procedural bar. There was a shortcoming in the Italian legal system which meant that every person convicted *in absentia* who had not been effectively informed of the proceedings against him could be deprived of a retrial. The Court considered that the shortcomings of domestic law and practice revealed in the present case could lead to a large number of well-founded applications in the future. Italy had a duty to remove every legal obstacle that might prevent either the reopening of the time allowed for an appeal or a retrial in the case of every person convicted by default who, not having been effectively informed of the proceedings against him, had not unequivocally waived the right to appear at his own trial. Such persons would thus be guaranteed the right to obtain a new ruling on the charges brought against them from a court which had heard them in accordance with the requirements of Article 6 of the Convention. Consequently, Italy should take appropriate measures to make provision for and regulate further proceedings capable of effectively securing the right to the reopening of proceedings, in accordance with the principles of the protection of the rights enshrined in Article 6 of the Convention.[599]

---

[597]   Judgment of 22 June 2004, paras 193-194.
[598]   Human Rights Information Bulletin, H Inf (2005) 1, p. 23.
[599]   Judgment of 10 November 2004, paras 46-47.

According to the *Explanatory Report to Protocol No. 14* the Committee of Ministers should bring infringement proceedings only in exceptional circumstances. Nevertheless, it appeared necessary to give the Committee of Ministers, as the competent organ for supervising execution of the Court's judgments, a wider range of means of pressure to secure execution of judgments. Currently, the ultimate measure available to the Committee of Ministers is recourse to Article 8 of the Council of Europe's Statute (suspension of voting rights in the Committee of Ministers or even expulsion from the Organisation). This is an extreme measure, which would prove counterproductive in most cases; indeed, the High Contracting Party which finds itself in the situation foreseen in paragraph 4 of Article 46 continues to need the discipline of the Council of Europe. The new Article 46, therefore, adds further possibilities of bringing pressure to bear to the existing ones. The procedure's mere existence, and the threat of using it, should act as an effective new incentive to execute the Court's judgments. It is foreseen that the outcome of infringement proceedings will be expressed in a judgment of the Court.

2.6   THE AWARD OF COMPENSATION UNDER ARTICLE 41

2.6.1   GENERAL

When the Court finds that a violation of the Convention by a Contracting State has taken place, under Article 41 it may afford just satisfaction to the injured party provided that the consequences of the violation cannot be fully repaired according to the internal law of the State concerned. The initiative for having the claim for just satisfaction determined lies with the original applicant as the injured person.[600] According to Rule 75(1) of the Rules of the Court, where the Chamber finds that there has been a violation of the Convention or the Protocols thereto, it gives in the same judgment a ruling on the application of Article 41 of the Convention if that question, after being raised in accordance with Rule 60 of the Rules of Court, is ready for decision; if the question is not ready for decision, the Chamber reserves it in whole or in part and fixes the further procedure. In that case, and also in cases where the claim by the applicant is finalized after the judgment on the merits, the Chamber which rules on the application of Article 41 will, as far as possible, be composed of those judges who sat to consider the merits of the case. Where it is not possible to constitute the original Chamber, the President of the Court completes or composes the Chamber by drawing lots (Rule 75(2) of the Rules of Court). This would seem appropriate from

---

[600]   See Rule 60 of the Rules of Court.

the viewpoint of procedural economy. The judges who examined the merits are best informed of the different aspects of the case and for that reason most competent to determine the amount of compensation to be awarded, if any. Any claim which the applicant Contracting Party or the applicant may wish to make for just satisfaction under Article 41 of the Convention must, unless the President of the Chamber directs otherwise, be set out in the written observations on the merits or, if no such written observations are filed, in a special document filed no later than two months after the decision declaring the application admissible. Thus, in the *Nasri* Case, despite several reminders, counsel for the applicant did not file any claims for just satisfaction. The Court, for its part, saw no ground for examining this question of its own motion.[601]

In the *Haase* Case the applicants were separated from their children in December 2001 and never saw them again. In this respect they claimed non-pecuniary damage on behalf of the children. However, in accordance with Rule 38(1) of the Rules of Court no written observations filed outside the time-limit set by the President of the Chamber will be included in the case file unless the President of the Chamber decides otherwise. The applicants' request to present the application on behalf of their children as well was submitted on 19 December 2002, which was after the close of the written procedure on the admissibility of the application. The Court, therefore, considered that it could not take the damage claimed on behalf of the children into account.[602]

The Court specifies in its judgment the period, which is usually three months, within which the specified sum must be paid to the individual.[603] And in accordance with Rule 75(3) of the Rules of Court, the Chamber may, when affording just satisfaction under Article 41 of the Convention, direct that if settlement is not made within a specified time, interest is to be payable on any sums awarded. It is subsequently up to the Committee of Ministers under Article 54 to determine if the specified sum has been paid within the time-limit set by the Court.

The Court will award financial compensation under Article 41 only where it is satisfied that the loss or damage complained of was actually caused by the violation it has found, since the State cannot be required to pay damages in respect of losses for which it is not responsible.[604]

---

[601] Judgment of 13 July 1995, para. 49; judgment of 13 February 2001, *Schöps*, para. 57

[602] Judgment of 8 April 2004, para. 121.

[603] See, *e.g.*, the judgment of 28 August 1991, *Moreira De Azevedo*; judgment of 21 September 1993, *Kremzow*; judgment of 27 October 1993, *Dombo Beheer B.V*; judgment of 11 January 2001, *Platakou*; judgment of 23 July 2002, *Västberga Taxi Aktiebolag and Vulic*.

[604] Judgment of 28 May 2002, *Kingsley*, para. 40.

2.6.2   NO INDEPENDENT PROCEDURE

From the Court's case law it becomes clear that an application for compensation on the basis of Article 41 is not considered as an independent procedure, but is dealt with as an element of a larger whole, of which the examination of the merits forms the first part. In the '*Vagrancy*' Cases the Court stated that the application for compensation is closely linked to the proceedings concerning the merits before the Court and cannot, therefore, be regarded as a new complaint, to which former Articles 25, 26 and 27 [the present Articles 34 and 35] of the Convention apply. For that reason the original applicant did not need to exhaust the local remedies once more with respect to his application for compensation.[605] In the *Barberà, Messegué and Jarbardo* Case the Court noted that under Spanish law a remedy existed making it possible to obtain compensation in the event of the malfunctioning of the system of justice. However, referring to the aforementioned '*Vagrancy*' Cases it did not consider itself bound to stay the proceedings relating to the applicants' claims. In this respect, the Court held: "If, after having exhausted domestic remedies without success before complaining in Strasbourg of a violation of their rights, then doing so a second time, successfully, to secure the setting aside of the convictions, and finally going through a new trial, the applicants were required to exhaust domestic remedies a third time in order to be able to obtain just satisfaction from the Court, the total duration of the proceedings would be hardly consistent with the effective protection of human rights and would lead to a situation incompatible with the aim and object of the Convention."[606] Furthermore, in the *Ogur* Case the Court took into account the fact that the events complained of took place more than eight years before.[607]

In the *Neumeister* Case the Austrian Government argued that the Commission had committed an error by transmitting Neumeister's application for compensation directly to the Court, whereas it ought to have considered and examined it as a new complaint under Article 25 [the present Article 34]. This complaint was assumed to concern the alleged violation of Article 5(5) of the Convention, in which it is provided that 'Everyone who has been the victim of arrest or detention in contravention of the provisions of this Article shall have an enforceable right to compensation'. The principal argument of the Court against this line of reasoning was as follows: "the proceedings in the present case no longer fall within Section III of the Convention but are the final phase of proceedings brought before the Court under Section IV on the con-

---

[605]   Judgment of 10 March 1972, para. 20. See also the judgment of 6 November 1980, *Guzzardi*, para. 113; judgment of 18 December 1986, *Bozano*, para. 9; judgment of 13 June 1994, *Barberà, Messegué and Jabardo*, para. 17; judgment of 4 May 2000, *Rotaru*, para. 83; judgment of 26 July 2001, *Ilijkov*, para. 123; judgment of 13 June 2002, *Anguelova*, para. 172.

[606]   Judgment of 13 June 1994, para. 17; judgment of 20 May 1999, *Ogur*, para. 98.

[607]   Judgment of 20 May 1999, para. 98.

clusion of those to which the original petition of Neumeister gave rise in 1963 before the Commission."[608]

In the *Anguelova* Case the Bulgarian Government argued that, since Article 362 para. 1 (4) of the Bulgarian Code of Criminal Procedure provided for the possibility of reopening criminal proceedings in cases where the European Court of Human Rights had found a violation of the Convention, the applicant should, if the Court found a violation in the present case, submit a civil claim for damages once the criminal proceedings were reopened. The Court noted that the provision of the Code of Criminal Procedure referred to by the Government concerned the reopening of criminal proceedings which were ended by a judicial decision, whereas the investigation in the applicant's case was terminated by a decision of the prosecuting authorities. It was, therefore, unclear whether the Code of Criminal Procedure required the reopening of the investigation after the Court's findings in the present case. Furthermore, the Court held that Article 41 of the Convention does not require applicants to exhaust domestic remedies a second time in order to obtain just satisfaction if they have already done so in vain in respect of their substantive complaints. In this connection the Court considered that the hypothetical possibility that the investigation might be resumed many years after the death of the applicant's son in police custody and after the first ineffective investigation, and that the applicant might then have the opportunity to bring a civil claim, which would only be successful if the fresh investigation produced results, could not reasonably be interpreted as *restitutio in integrum* under domestic law.[609]

2.6.3 QUESTIONS REGARDING ARTICLE 41 WHICH ARE NOT READY FOR DECISION

Article 41 appears to imply that the decision on an award of compensation must be given together with the judgment on the merits. Rule 75 of the Rules of Court, however, leaves the moment of the decision on an award of compensation entirely open. If the Chamber of the Court which deals with the case finds that there is a violation of the Convention, the Chamber gives a decision on the application of Article 41 in the same judgment if the question, after being raised under Rule 75, is ready for decision. As an example, reference could be made to the judgment in the *Golder* Case, in which the Court, after having found that there had been a violation of Article 6(1) and Article 8, decided that in the circumstances of the case it was not necessary to afford to the applicant any just satisfaction other than that resulting from the finding

---

[608]   Judgment of 7 May 1974, para. 30.
[609]   Judgment of 13 June 2002, para. 172.

of a violation of his rights.[610] The majority of the decisions concerning Article 41 are made simultaneously with the judgment on the merits.

If the question of compensation has been raised, but is not yet ready for decision, the Chamber reserves it in whole or in part and fixes the ensuing procedure. If the question of compensation has not been raised, the Chamber lays down a time-limit within which this may be done by the original applicant.[611] Thus the possibilities for raising the question of compensation have been left as wide as possible. At the same time the interests of the respondent States are served in this way because, as the Court formulated it: "they may be reluctant to argue the consequences of a violation the existence of which they dispute and they may wish, in the event of a finding of a violation, to maintain the possibility of settling the issue of reparation directly with the injured party without the Court being further concerned."[612]

In a number of cases applicants complained that as a consequence of the length of domestic proceedings they were deprived of the enjoyment of their property, thereby relying on Article 1 of Protocol No. 1. Since the Court already found a violation of Article 6(1), it did not find it necessary to examine the complaint based on Article 1 of Protocol No. 1. Nevertheless, in the *Brigandi* Case, where the applicant had sought compensation for loss of enjoyment of property, the Court found that the measures already taken by the national courts – which included compensation for loss of enjoyment – had not made full reparation for the consequences of the breach found. The Court, therefore, awarded the applicant a specified sum on an equitable basis.[613]

In the *Zanghì* Case the applicant had only claimed compensation in respect of damage resulting from the alleged violation on Article 1 of Protocol No. 1. In its judgment of the same day as that of the *Brigandi* Case, concerning the same respondent State, in connection with the same type of violation, the Court observed that it was still possible that the national courts before which the applicant's action remained pending, might make reparation for the final consequences of the failure to try the case within a reasonable time. Therefore, as a matters stood, it dismissed the applicant's claim for compensation of damage.[614] After having obtained a final domestic decision, Mr Zanghì again requested compensation for the financial consequences of the failure to try the case within a reasonable time. The Court decided to re-enter the case on its list. This means that the dismissal of the claim for just satisfaction 'as the matter stood' in the Court's earlier judgment was only provisional. It also means, by implication, that the applicant was not estopped, because he relied

---

[610]   Judgment of 21 February 1975, para. 46; judgment of 26 February 2002, *Morris*, para. 98; judgment of 27 February 2003, *Niederböster*, para. 49.

[611]   See, for example, the judgment of 28 June 1978, *König*, para. 140.

[612]   Judgment of 22 June 1972, *Ringeisen*, para. 18.

[613]   Judgment of 19 February 1991, para. 33.

[614]   Judgment of 19 February 1991, para. 9.

the first time, in support of his claim, on Article 1 of Protocol No. 1 and not on Article 6 of the Convention. The Court found, however, that, as it held it unnecessary to rule on the complaint based on Article 1 of Protocol No. 1, the financial consequences of an infringement of the applicant's right to the peaceful enjoyment of his possessions could not be taken into consideration. As to the consequences of the breach of Article 6(1) of the Convention, which was found by the Court on 19 February 1991, it noted at the time, even though no claim for just satisfaction had been made under that head, that it was still possible that the national courts might make reparation for them. The final domestic decision, in the opinion of the Court, was not of such a nature as to call for a reconsideration of the decision delivered on 19 February 1991.[615] Thus for the second time, and this time finally, the applicant's claim for compensation was dismissed. In its final judgment the Court did not make clear in which way and to what extent the final domestic decision compensated the applicant in respect of the alleged violation of Article 6, nor did it indicate how its final judgment in the *Zanghi* Case was to be reconciled with that in the *Birgandi* Case.

In the *Windisch* Case the Government referred to the possibility of the applicant's case being reopened if the Attorney General decided – as had in fact since happened – to lodge a plea of nullity for the preservation of the law. The applicant's counsel mentioned, as an example, the *Unterpertinger* Case (judgment of 24 November 1986) where the criminal proceedings involved had been reopened as a result of the Court's judgment. The Court considered that the compensation sought in respect of the length of the national proceedings was not recoverable because the violation found in the principal judgment did not concern this point.[616]

In the *Vogt* Case the Court was of the opinion that the question of reparation was not ready for decision. It was accordingly necessary to reserve it and to fix the further procedure, account being taken of the possibility of an agreement between the respondent State and the applicant.[617] In the *Papamichalopoulos* Case the Court invited the Government and the applicants to submit, within two months, the names and positions of experts chosen by agreement for the purpose of valuing the disputed land and to inform it, within eight months from the expiry of that period, of any friendly settlement that they might reach before the valuation.[618]

---

[615] Judgment of 10 February 1993, para. 8.
[616] Judgment of 28 June 1993, para. 15.
[617] Judgment of 26 September 1995, para. 74. See also the judgment of 30 May 2000, *Carbonara and Ventura*, para. 79.
[618] Judgment of 31 October 1995, para. 3.

2.6.4   SUPERVISION BY THE COURT OF AN AGREEMENT ON COMPENSATION

Even if an agreement is reached between the injured party and the State found to be liable of a violation, the Court is still involved in the matter. In fact, according to Rule 75(4) of its Rules of Court, the Court will have to verify the equitable nature of such agreement and, when it finds the agreement to be equitable, will strike the case off the list by means of a judgment. Such supervision of the equitable nature of the agreement on compensation was exercised by the Court in, *e.g.*, the *Luedicke, Belkacem and Koç* Case,[619] the *Airey* Case,[620] the *Malone* Case,[621] the *Kostovski* Case[622] and the *Katikaridis* Case.[623]

In the *Winterwerp* Case the judgment under Article 41 consisted of the unanimous decision by the Court to strike the case off the list. The reason for this was that the Government of the Netherlands and Winterwerp had come to an agreement, which was judged on its equitable nature by the Court. This arrangement, in part, even went beyond that originally suggested by Winterwerp's counsel. The principal elements of the arrangement were as follows: "(1) The State shall promote that Mr. Winterwerp be placed as soon as possible in a hostel. The State Psychiatric Establishment at Eindhoven is and will remain prepared to give Mr. Winterwerp medical treatment whenever this might be necessary; (2) The State shall transfer a lump sum of 10,000 (ten thousand guilders) to Mr. Winterwerp's new guardian to be used for the resocialisation of Mr. Winterwerp."[624]

Sometimes the agreement concerns only a part of the claim of the applicant and the Court has to decide about the rest of the claim. Thus in the *Barthold* Case the settlement only concerned the claims for fees and expenses and for loss of earnings.[625] The Court took note of this agreement and considered it appropriate to strike the case off the list as far as those claims were concerned.

---

[619]   Judgment of 10 March 1980, para. 13.
[620]   Judgment of 6 February 1981, para. 10.
[621]   Judgment of 26 April 1985, para. 9. See also the judgments of 29 September 1987, *Erkner and Hofauer*, para. 8; and the judgment of 27 June 1988, *Bouamar*, para. 8.
[622]   Judgment of 29 March 1990, para. 7.
[623]   Judgment of 31 March 1998, para. 11.
[624]   Judgment of 27 November 1981.
[625]   Judgment of 31 January 1986, para. 9. See also the judgments of 9 June 1988, *O., H., W. and R. v. the United Kingdom*.

2.6.5 THE QUESTION OF RESTITUTIO IN INTEGRUM

As to the merits of the procedure for compensation under Article 41, it is especially the passage which states that, 'if the internal law of the said Party allows only partial reparation to be made for the consequences of this decision or measure' which has caused problems.

In the 'Vagrancy' Cases the Belgian Government submitted that the application for compensation was ill-founded, because under Belgian law compensation could be obtained from the State for damage caused by an unlawful situation for which the State was responsible under national or international law. Those who claimed compensation before the Court, therefore, ought to have applied first to the national court.[626] The Court held that the treaties from which the text of Article 41 has been derived, undoubtedly related in particular to cases where the nature of the injury would make it possible to wipe out entirely the consequences of a violation but where the internal law of the State involved precludes this being done. However, according to the Court, this did not alter the fact that Article 41 is also applicable to cases in which such a *restitutio in integrum* is not possible precisely on account of the nature of the injury concerned.[627] The Court added the following: "indeed, common sense suggests that this must be so *a fortiori*".[628] The Court distinguished here between those cases in which, considering the nature of the injury, *restitutio in integrum* is possible and those in which it is not, and considered it has jurisdiction in both cases; in the first case, however, only when such *restitutio in integrum* is precluded under national law. Thus, in the 'Vagrancy' Cases which according to the Court belonged to the second category, the Court declared that it had jurisdiction to award compensation. It held, however, that the applicants' claims for damages were not well-founded. Although in this case the decision not to grant compensation was taken unanimously, there were considerable differences of opinion within the Court on the argument described above.

In their joint separate opinion the judges Holmback, Ross and Wold asserted that the argument followed by the Court was "unsound" and "completely alien to the text of Article 50" [the present Article 41] for those cases in which *restitutio in integrum* was impossible.[629] In the first place they submitted with regard to the Court's argument: "It presupposes that there is an absolute obligation on the State to restore to the applicants the liberty of which they have been deprived. But this cannot be so because of the maxim *impossibilium nulla est obligatio*."[630] Furthermore, they opined that in the two cases distinguished by the Court the jurisdiction of the Court should

---

[626] Judgment of 10 March 1972, para. 15.
[627] *Ibidem,* para. 20. See in this respect also the judgment of 31 October 1995, *Papamichalopoulos,* para. 34; judgment of 23 January 2001, *Brumărescu,* para. 20.
[628] *Ibidem.*
[629] See the opinion annexed to the judgment.
[630] *Ibidem.*

depend on the fact that "the internal law does not allow full reparation".[631] On the ground of Articles 5(5), 13, 53 and 54 [the present Article 46] they were of the opinion that the general rule underlying the Convention is that "a party claiming to be injured must seek redress before national courts and not before the European Court of Human Rights". The only exception to this is the jurisdiction conferred on the Court by Article 41 to award compensation in case the internal law in question does not make full reparation possible.[632] In their view the Court's conception led "to the Court in fact assuming jurisdiction in respect to claims for reparation in all cases where *restitutio* is impossible, regardless of the state of internal law."[633]

In its judgment in the '*Vagrancy*' Cases as well as in the subsequent *Ringeisen* Case the Court did take into account the fact that the Belgian and the Austrian Government, respectively, had refused the applicant compensation.[634] But in the '*Vagrancy*' Cases it immediately added: "The mere fact that the applicants could have brought and could still bring their claims for damages before a Belgian Court does not therefore require the Court to dismiss their claims as being ill-founded any more than it raises an obstacle to their admissibility."[635]

In the *Ringeisen* Case the Court was even more explicit. The necessity to apply Article 41 exists "once a respondent government refuses the applicant reparation to which he considers he is entitled."[636]

A considerable difference between the view of the three above-mentioned judges and that of the Court remains. According to the three judges, the Court may award compensation only in one exceptional case, *viz.* when under internal law there is no possibility of obtaining full compensation. In the Court's view it is sufficient for the application of Article 41 that a Government has refused the compensation claimed by the applicant. The view of the three judges resembles most closely the principle of general international law that a State must previously have been enabled as much as possible to redress the consequences of any violation of its international obligations itself within the context of its own national legal system.[637] On the other hand, the Court has argued that, if for the consideration of an application under Article 41 it should be required that the local remedies have first been exhausted, the total length of the procedure provided for in the Convention could hardly be considered compatible with the idea of effective protection of human rights.[638] Moreover, it might be

---

[631]   *Ibidem.*
[632]   *Ibidem.*
[633]   *Ibidem.*
[634]   Judgment of 10 March 1972, para. 16. and judgment of 22 June 1972, para. 14 respectively.
[635]   Judgment of 10 March 1972, para. 20.
[636]   Judgment of 22 June 1972, para. 20.
[637]   Compare the corresponding principle of general international law underlying the local remedies rule, *supra* 2.2.10.1.
[638]   Judgment of 10 March 1972, *De Wilde, Ooms and Versyp* ('*Vagrancy*' Cases), para. 20.

argued in support of the Court's view that the consideration of applications under Article 41 and the examination of the merits should be regarded as one and indivisible,[639] so that the decision that the local remedies have been exhausted, in combination with the finding that a friendly settlement has not been reached and that the State has not been found willing to pay damages, must be considered a sufficient basis for the application of Article 41. The consequence of the latter approach is that, with respect to the decision on an application for compensation under Article 41 of the Convention, the internal law of the State concerned becomes irrelevant.

In the final analysis, the middle course suggested by judge Verdross in his separate opinion would appear the most attractive. From the text of Article 41 he infers that the Court, when dealing with an application for compensation, should first of all ascertain whether the injured individual is able to obtain adequate compensation under internal law. If that is the case, the respondent State should be enabled to award compensation according to its own procedures, but with the Court remaining competent to assure itself that just satisfaction has indeed duly been given and to fix a time within which this should take place.[640] In this construction the State concerned is given the opportunity to settle the matter within the context of its own legal system, while the Court can judge afterwards whether the compensation is equitable and at the same time keep the total duration of the procedure within reasonable limits.

The viewpoint of the Court set forth above appears to have become constant case law, however, since it has been confirmed explicitly or implicitly in a series of judgments.[641] Thus, in the *De Cubber* Case the Court noted that Article 50 [the present Article 41] was applicable, because the conditions were fulfilled: "the proceedings in Belgium after 26 October 1984 (...) have not redressed the violation found in its judgment of that date; they have not brought about a result as close to *restitutio in integrum* as was possible in the nature of things."[642]

In the *Barberà, Messegué and Jarbardo* Case the Spanish Government submitted that the Court's principal judgment[643] had been executed in Spain in the fullest possible manner. The Constitutional Court's judgment quashing the convictions and ordering that the proceedings in the *Audiencia Nacional* be reopened, represented an innovation for the Spanish legal system under which previously the finding of a violation by the European Court of Human Rights could not constitute a ground for reopening

---

[639]   See *supra* 2.6.2.

[640]   Separate opinion of Judge Verdross in the '*Vagrancy*' Cases, judgment of 10 March 1972.

[641]   Judgment of 10 March 1980, *König*, para. 15; judgment of 13 May 1980, *Artico*, paras. 44-45; judgment of 6 November 1980, *The Sunday Times*, para. 16; and the judgment of 6 November 1980, *Guzzardi*, para. 113.

[642]   Judgment of 14 September 1987, para. 21.

[643]   Judgment of 6 December 1988, para. 2, where the Court found a violation of Art. 6(1) based above all on "the fact that very important pieces of evidence were not adequately adduced and discussed at the trial in the applicants' presence and under the watchful eye of the public".

proceedings. In the subsequent proceedings all the guarantees laid down in Article 6 had been scrupulously complied with and they, therefore, afforded the most complete *restitutio in integrum* that could be obtained from the point of view of Article 41. However, the Court observed that it could not speculate as to what the outcome of the proceedings would have been had the violation of the Convention not occurred. Nevertheless, the applicants were kept in prison as a direct consequence of the trial found by the Court to be in violation of the Convention. There was thus, in the opinion of the Court, a clear causal connection between the damage claimed by the applicants and the violation of the Convention. In the nature of things, the subsequent release and acquittal of the applicants could not in themselves afford *restitutio in integrum* or complete reparation for damage derived from their detention.[644] Accordingly, the Court considered that the question to be decided was the level of just satisfaction in respect of those damages, to be determined by the Court at its discretion having regard to what was equitable.[645]

In the *Papamichalopoulos* Case the Court found a violation on the basis of an irregular *de facto* expropriation (occupation of land by the Greek Navy since 1967) which had lasted for more than twenty-five years by the date of the principal judgment of 24 June 1993. In its judgment on just satisfaction the Court held: "the unlawfulness of such a dispossession inevitably affects the criteria to be used for determining the reparation owed by the respondent State, since the pecuniary consequences of a lawful expropriation cannot be assimilated to those of an unlawful dispossession."[646] Consequently, the Court ordered the Greek State to pay the applicants "for damage and loss of enjoyment since the authorities took the possession of the land in 1967, the current value of the land, increased by the appreciation brought about by the existence" of certain buildings which had been erected on the land since the occupation, as well as the construction costs of those buildings.[647]

In the *Iatridis* Case the applicant owned a cinema but did not own the land on which the cinema that he ran was situated. The ownership of the cinema site had been a matter of dispute between the lessors of the cinema and the State since 1953 and this dispute had still not been resolved by the date of adoption of the judgment. In its principle judgment in the case the Court held: "on 23 October 1989 the Athens Court of First Instance heard the case under summary procedure and quashed the eviction order on the grounds that the conditions for issuing it had not been satisfied. No appeal lay against that decision. From that moment on, the applicant's eviction thus ceased to have any legal basis and Ilioupolis Town Council became an unlawful occupier and should have returned the cinema to the applicant, as was indeed recom-

---

[644]   Judgment of 13 June 1994, para. 16.
[645]   *Ibidem*, paras 18-20. In the same sense judgment of 25 July 2000, *Smith and Grady*, paras 18-19.
[646]   Judgment of 31 October 1995, para. 36.
[647]   *Ibidem*, para. 39. See also the judgment of 10 June 2003, *Serghides*, para. 23.

mended by all the bodies from whom the Minister of Finance sought an opinion, namely the Ministry of Finance, the State Legal Council and the State Lands Authority."[648] Consequently, the Court considered that the manifest unlawfulness under Greek law of the interference complained of would justify awarding the applicant full compensation. Nothing short of returning the use of the cinema to the applicant would put him, as far as possible, in a situation equivalent to the one in which he would have found himself had there not been a breach of Article 1 of Protocol No. 1. The Court pointed out that the applicant did not own the land on which the cinema that he ran was situated. He rented that land from a third party under a lease valid until 30 November 2002. The issue of the ownership of the land was at the material time the subject of proceedings in the national courts. In all these circumstances the Court considered that the applicant should be awarded only compensation that would cover loss of the earnings that he could have derived from running the cinema until the end of the current lease (30 November 2002).[649]

In the principal judgment in the Case of the *Former King of Greece* the Court held that the interference in question satisfied the requirement of lawfulness and was not arbitrary. The act of the Greek Government which the Court held to be contrary to the Convention was an expropriation that would have been legitimate but for the failure to pay any compensation. The lawfulness of such a dispossession inevitably affects the criteria to be used for determining the reparation owed by the respondent State, since the pecuniary consequences of a lawful taking cannot be assimilated to those of an unlawful dispossession. In this context the Court noted that international case law of courts and arbitration tribunals, gave the Court valuable guidance; although that case law concerned more particularly the expropriation of industrial and commercial undertakings, the principles identified in that field are valid for situations such as the one in the instant case. In the *Amoco International Finance Corporation* Case the Iran-United States Claims Tribunal stated, referring to the judgment of the Permanent Court of International Justice in the *Case Concerning the Factory at Chorzów*, that: "a clear distinction must be made between lawful and unlawful expropriations, since the rules applicable to the compensation to be paid by the expropriating State differ according to the legal characterisation of the taking." (Amoco International Finance Corporation v. Iran, Interlocutory Award of 14 July 1987, Iran-U.S. Claims Tribunal Reports (1987-II), para. 192)."[650] In view of the above, the Court was of the opinion that in the present case the nature of the breach found in the principal judgment did not allow the Court to proceed on the basis of the principle of *restitutio in integrum*. That said, the Government were of course free to decide on their own initiative to return all or part of the properties to the applicants. In conclusion, the

---

[648]   Judgment of 25 March 1999, para. 61.
[649]   Judgment of 19 October 2000, para. 37.
[650]   Judgment of 28 November 2002, paras. 74-75.

Court held that, unless the Government would decide on their own initiative to return the properties to the applicants, it deemed it appropriate to fix a lump sum based, as far as possible, on an amount "reasonably related" to the value of the property taken, i.e. an amount which the Court would have found acceptable under Article 1 of Protocol No. 1, had the Greek State compensated the applicants. In determining this amount the Court took into account the claims of each applicant, the question of the movable property, the valuations submitted by the parties and the possible options for calculating the pecuniary damage, as well as the lapse of time between the dispossession and the present judgment. The Court considered that in the unique circumstances of the present case resort to equitable considerations was particularly called for.[651]

2.6.6   MEASURES OF REDRESS

In several cases the Court noted that it is well established that the principle underlying the provision of just satisfaction for a breach of the Convention is that the applicant should as far as possible be put in the position he would have enjoyed had the procee-dings complied with the Convention's requirements.[652]

The Court has indicated that, in the context of the execution of judgments in accor-dance with Article 46 of the Convention, a judgment in which it finds that a breach has occurred, imposes on the respondent State a legal obligation under that provision to put an end to the breach and make reparation for its consequences in such a way as to restore as far as possible the situation existing before the breach. If, on the other hand, national law does not allow – or allows only partially – reparation to be made for the consequences of the breach, Article 41 empowers the Court to afford the injured party such satisfaction as appears to it to be appropriate. It follows, *inter alia*, that a judgment in which the Court finds a violation of the Convention or its Protocols imposes on the respondent State a legal obligation not just to pay those concerned the sums awarded by way of just satisfaction, but also to choose, subject to supervision by the Committee of Ministers, the general and/or, if appropriate, individual measures to be adopted in its domestic legal order to put an end to the violation found by the Court and to redress so far as possible the effects.[653] Furthermore, it follows from the Convention and from Article 1 in particular that in ratifying the Convention the Contracting States undertake to ensure that their domestic legislation is compatible with it. Consequently, it is for the respondent State to remove any obstacles in its

---

[651]   *Ibidem*, para. 79.
[652]   See *e.g.* judgment of 26 October 1984, *Piersack*, para 12; judgment of 28 May 2002, *Kingsley*, para. 40.
[653]   Judgment of 13 July 2000, *Scozzari and Giunta*, para. 249; judgment of 24 October 2002, *Pisano*, para. 43; judgment of 8 April 2004, *Haase*, para. 115.

domestic legal system that might prevent the applicant's situation from being adequately redressed.[654]

2.6.7 THE INJURED PARTY

The term 'injured party' is fairly clear in the Court's view. 'Injured party' is a synonym for 'victim' in Article 34, and as such may be considered "the person directly affected by the failure to observe the Convention".[655] This also includes legal persons.[656] From this it follows, for instance, that counsel for the applicant cannot bring his fee directly under the claim for reparation pursuant to Article 41, although it may after all form part of the reparation awarded to the applicant. In the *Belkacem* Case the applicant had received free legal aid with respect to the Strasbourg proceedings and had not stated that he owed his counsel any additional amount. When the latter nevertheless claimed a supplementary fee, the Court decided that a lawyer "cannot rely on Article 50 to seek just satisfaction on his own account".[657]

In the *Pakelli* Case counsel had not claimed an immediate payment of his fee because of the financial situation of his client. Reparation of costs for legal assistance was nevertheless awarded, because counsel had not waived his right to reparation of his costs (as the Government suggested). The Court noted that "in a human rights case a lawyer will be acting in the general interest if he agrees to represent or assist a litigant even if the latter is not in a position to pay him immediately"[658] and included the payment in the the reparation awarded.

In *X v. France* the applicant had died during the proceedings before the Court. His parents, however, had expressed their wish to continue the proceedings. The Court decided that the parents were entitled to take his place. The applicant had claimed 150,000 francs for non-pecuniary damage. The case concerned the length of compensation proceedings brought by a haemophiliac inflicted with the AIDS virus following a blood transfusion. The applicant had claimed that the length of proceedings had prevented him from obtaining the compensation which he had hoped for, and thus

---

[654] Judgment of 17 February 2004, *Meastri*, para. 47.
[655] Judgment of 6 November 1980, *The Sunday Times*, para. 13. See also the judgment of 14 September 1987, *Gillow*, para. 23: "Since this case relates to events and their consequences which were experienced by Mr and Mrs Gillow together, the Court considers it equitable that all sums awarded in this judgment should be paid to the survivor of them, Mrs Gillow."
[656] Judgment of 7 July 1989, *Unión Alimentaria Sanders S.A.*, para. 45; judgment of 6 April 2000, *S.A. v. Portugal*, paras 15-20; judgment of 19 March 2002, *Société industrielle d'Entretien et de Service (SIES)*, paras. 18-24.
[657] Judgment of 10 March 1980, para. 15. See also the judgment of 13 May 1980, *Artico*, para. 40; judgment of 19 December 1990, *Delta*, para. 47; judgment 28 May 2002, *Beyeler*, para. 27; Judgment of 28 November 2002, *The former King of Greece and Others*, para. 105.
[658] Judgment of 25 April 1983, para. 47.

from being able to live independently and in better psychological conditions for the remaining period of his life. Without further observation the Court found that the applicant had sustained non-pecuniary damage and held that France was to pay the applicant's parents the entire sum sought.[659] In case the Court has awarded just satisfaction to the next of kin and the respondent State requests a revision of that judgment because the next of kin cannot be traced, the Court may revise its judgment in such a way that the earlier compensation does not have to be paid.[660]

The Court has frequently been requested to award damages to the relatives of a person who was unlawfully killed by agents of the State or had disappeared and for whose disappearance the respondent State was held responsible.[661] In the *Kurt* Case the applicant maintained that both she and her son had been victims of specific violations of the Convention as well as of a practice of such violations. She requested the Court to award a total amount of 70,000 pounds sterling (GBP) which she justified as follows: GBP 30,000 for her son in respect of his disappearance and the absence of safeguards and effective investigative mechanisms in that regard; GBP 10,000 for herself to compensate for the suffering to which she had been subjected on account of her son's disappearance and the denial of an effective remedy with respect to his disappearance; and GBP 30,000 to compensate both of them on account of the fact that they were victims of a practice of 'disappearances' in south-east Turkey. The Court recalled that it had found the respondent State in breach of Article 5 in respect of the applicant's son. It considered that an award of compensation should be made in his favour having regard to the gravity of the breach in question. It awarded the sum of GBP 15,000, which amount was to be paid to the applicant and held by her for her son and his heirs. Moreover, given that the authorities had not assisted the applicant in her search for the truth about the whereabouts of her son, which had led it to find a breach of Articles 3 and 13 in her respect, the Court considered that an award of compensation was also justified in her favour. It accordingly awarded the applicant the sum of GBP 10,000.[662]

If the Court decides that there has been a violation of the Convention, this does not mean that the next of kin will be automatically awarded compensation. First of all there should be a causal link between the violation found and the damage alleged. Secondly, the alleged damage should be substantiated. In the *Ogur* Case the Court noted that, as regards pecuniary damage, the file contained no information on the applicant's son's income from his work as a night-watchman, the amount of financial

---

[659]   Judgment of 31 March 1992, para. 54.
[660]   Judgment of 3 May 2001, *E.P. v. Italy*, paras 7-9.
[661]   Judgment of 27 September 1995, *McCann, Farrell and Savage*, para. 142; judgment of 9 October 1997, *Andronicou and Constantinou*, para 153; judgment of 19 February 1998, *Kaya*, para. 1; judgment of 25 May 1998, *Kurt*, para. 73; judgment of 8 July 1999, *Cakici*, para. 8.
[662]   Judgmant of 25 May 1998, para. 321; see also judgment of 28 July 1998, *Ergi*, para. 330.

assistance he gave the applicant, the composition of her family or any other relevant circumstances. That being so, the Court could not allow the compensation claim submitted under this head in accordance with Rule 60(2) of the Rules of Court.[663] In most of such cases only non-pecuniary damage is taken into consideration.[664] In the Case of *McCann, Farrell and Savage* the Court held that, having regard to the fact that the three terrorist suspects who were killed had been intending to plant a bomb in Gibraltar, the Court did not consider it appropriate to make an award under this head. It, therefore, dismissed the applicants' claim for damages.[665]

In the *Haase* Case the applicants claimed non-pecuniary damage on behalf of their children. The Court pointed out that in principle a person who is not entitled under domestic law to represent another may nevertheless, in certain circumstances, act before the Court in the name of the other person.[666] The Court referred in this respect to the *Aksoy* Case where the pecuniary claims made by the applicant prior to his death for loss of earnings and medical expenses arising out of detention and torture were taken into account by the Court in making an award to the applicant's father who had continued the application.[667]

In the *Caciki* Case the Court found that it might be taken as established that the applicant died following his apprehension by the security forces and that the State's responsibility was engaged under Article 2 of the Convention. In these circumstances there was a direct causal link between the violation of Article 2 and the loss by his widow and children of the financial support which he provided for them. The Court noted that the Government had not queried the amount claimed by the applicant. Having regard to the detailed submissions by the applicant concerning the actuarial basis of calculation of the appropriate capital sum to reflect the loss of income due to applicant's death, the Court awarded compensation to be held by the applicant on behalf of his brother's surviving spouse and children.[668]

In the *Ciliç* Case the claims for pecuniary damage related to alleged losses accruing subsequent to the death of the applicant's brother. They did not represent losses actually incurred either by the applicant's brother before his death or by the applicant after his brother's death. The Court refused compensation. It noted that the applicant's brother was unmarried and had no children. It was not claimed that the applicant was in any way dependent on him. More in general, however, the Court held that an award in respect of pecuniary damage was not excluded regarding an applicant who has

---

[663] Judgment of 20 May 1999, para, 98; judgment of 8 July 1999, *Cakici*, para.127.
[664] Judgment of 19 February 1998, *Kaya*, para. 122; judgment of 20 May 1999, *Ogur*, para. 98.
[665] Judgment of 27 September 1995, para. 218.
[666] See judgment of 8 April 2004, paras. 113-120.
[667] Judgment of 18 December 1996, para. 113.
[668] Judgment of 8 July 1999, para. 127. See also judgment of 31 May 2001, *Akdeniz*, para. 127.

established that a close member of the family has suffered a violation of the Convention.[669]

In the event of a conflict over a minor's interests between a natural parent and the person appointed by the authorities to act as the child's guardian there is a danger that some of those interests will never be brought to the Court's attention and that the minor will be deprived of effective protection of his rights under the Convention. Consequently, even though the parents have been deprived of parental rights – indeed that is one of the causes of the dispute which they have referred to the Court – their standing suffices to afford them the necessary power to apply to the Court on the children's behalf, as well as in order to protect their interests.[670]

2.6.8 JUST SATISFACTION

2.6.8.1 General

As to the term 'just satisfaction', the formulation of Article 41 makes it plain in the first place that the Court has a certain discretion in determining it: "as is borne out by the adjective 'just' and the phrase 'if necessary', the Court enjoys a certain discretion in the exercise of the power conferred by Article 41".[671] Taking this as a point of departure the Court strictly upholds that the only element qualifying for satisfaction is the injury due to the previously found violation of the Convention. Injury which is connected therewith, but which in fact is due to other causes, does not qualify for satisfaction.[672] The Court, therefore, requires a causal link between the injury and the violation.[673] In the *Quaranta* Case the applicant had claimed compensation in respect of the main complaint concerning the right to liberty under Article 5, whereas the Court had only found a violation in relation to one of the subsidiary complaints. The Court rejected the compensation claim for lack of causal link.[674] In cases where the Court finds a violation of the reasonable time requirement of Article 6, it usually does not find that a causal link exists between the violation and the alleged damage.[675]

In the *Albert and Le Compte* Case the first claim concerned a request to the Court to direct the State to annul the disciplinary sanctions imposed on the applicants. The

---

[669]   Judgment of 28 March 2000, para 102.
[670]   Judgment of 8 April 2004, *Haase*, para. 120.
[671]   Judgment of 6 November 1980, *Guzzardi*, para. 114.
[672]   Judgment of 10 March 1980, *König*, para. 18; judgment of 6 February 1981, *Airey*, para. 12.
[673]   Judgment of 23 October 1985, *Benthem*, para. 46; judgment of 2 June 1986, *Bönisch*, para. 11; judgment of 22 June 2000, *Cöeme*, para. 155; judgment of 27 February 2001, *Lucà*, para. 48; judgment of 17 February 2004, *Maestri*, para.46.
[674]   Judgment of 24 May 1991, para. 43.
[675]   Judgment of 1 March 2002, *K*utic, para 39; judgment of 6 June 2002, *Marques Francisco*, para. 27; judgment of 13 June 2002, *Mereu and S. Maria Navarrese S.R.L.*, para. 19.

Court decided that, even when leaving aside the fact that the Court is not empowered to do this, "the disciplinary sanctions, which were the outcome of proceedings found by the Court not to have complied with one of the rules of Article 6 § 1 of the Convention, cannot on that account alone be regarded as the consequences of that breach. As for the criminal sentence, there is no connection whatsoever between them and the violation (...) As for the applicant's second series of claims (...), the Court considers it proper to distinguish here, as in the Case of *Le Compte, Van Leuven and De Meyere* (...), between damage caused by a violation of the Convention and the costs incurred by the applicant."[676]

In the *Canea Catholic Church* Case the Court opined that in holding that the applicant church had no capacity to take legal proceedings, the Court of Cassation did not only penalise the failure to comply with a simple formality necessary for the protection of public order, as the Government maintained. It also imposed a real restriction on the applicant church preventing it on this particular occasion and for the future from having any dispute relating to its property rights determined by the courts. Such a limitation impaired the very substance of the applicant church's 'right to a court' and, therefore, constituted a breach of Article 6(1) of the Convention. Making its assessment on an equitable basis, the Court awarded the applicant church the whole of the sum sought for the pecuniary damage it sustained on account of its inability to take legal proceedings.[677] In the *Ajdenize* Case the Court held that a precise calculation of the sums necessary to make complete reparation in respect of the pecuniary losses suffered by an applicant may be prevented by the inherently uncertain character of the damage flowing from the violation. An award may still be made notwithstanding the large number of imponderables involved in the assessment of future losses, though the greater the lapse of time involved the more uncertain the link between the breach and the damage becomes. The question to be decided in such cases is the level of just satisfaction in respect of either past and future pecuniary loss, which it is necessary to award to an applicant, the matter to be determined by the Court at its discretion having regard to what is equitable.[678]

2.6.8.2 Factors determining whether just satisfaction will be awarded

The reparation under Article 41 is intended to place the applicant as far as possible in the position he would have been, had the violation of the Convention not taken

---

[676] Judgment of 24 October 1983, para. 9. See on the said distinction also, *e.g.*, judgment of 6 November 1980, *The Sunday Times*, para. 16; judgment of 18 October 1982, *Le Compte, Van Leuven and De Meyere*, para. 13; judgment of 25 April 1983, *Van Droogen-broeck*, para. 13.

[677] Judgment of 16 December 1997, para.55.

[678] Judgment of 31 May 2001, paras. 128 and 130.

place.[679] Whether and to what extent satisfaction will be awarded by the Court depends on the circumstances of the case.

In the *Neumeister* Case there had been a violation of Article 5(3) and the Court awarded the applicant compensation amounting to 30,000 Austrian Schillings. An important factor in the determination of the amount was the degree to which the detention under remand had exceeded reasonable limits. In this case, however, there were a number of circumstances which induced the Court to decide that compensation for material injury was not necessary. In particular, the duration of the detention under remand counted towards the ultimately imposed imprisonment. For the remainder, the applicant had been granted a pardon. These factors also amply counterbalanced, in the Court's opinion, the moral injury which Neumeister had sustained. Even though this did not, according to the Court, constitute a genuine *restitutio in integrum*, it approached this very closely. The sum of money was, therefore, awarded to him as compensation for the damage he had incurred in the form of costs in the matter of legal assistance in his attempts to prevent the violation of the Convention, subsequently to request the Commission and the Court to establish this violation, and finally to obtain compensation.[680]

In the *Engel* Case only a symbolic amount of compensation of Dfl. 100 was awarded to Engel. Compensation was refused to De Wit, Dona and Schul, because the violation of the Convention in regard to them only consisted in the fact that the Supreme Military Court had dealt with their cases *in camera*. In its judgment on the merits the Court had already found that they did not seem to have suffered as a result. They had not since then advanced any new arguments for their claims for damages. In awarding Dfl. 100 to Engel the Court took into account the very short duration of the detention and the fact that the injury caused by the violation of Article 5(1) had been largely compensated by the circumstance that Engel had not actually had to undergo his punishment.[681]

On the other hand, in the *Guincho* Case the Court found a violation of the reasonable-time requirement of Article 6(1), which stemmed from two periods of almost total inactivity on the part of the State. The resultant lapse of time, totaling more than two years, did not only "reduce the effectiveness of the action brought, but it also placed the applicant in a state of uncertainty which still persists and in such a position that even a final decision in his favour will not be able to provide compensation for the lost interest". Accordingly, the Court awarded the applicant compensation of 150,000 Escudos.[682]

---

[679]   Judgment of 23 October 1984, *Piersack*, para. 12.
[680]   Judgment of 7 May 1974, paras. 30-31.
[681]   Judgment of 23 November 1976, para. 10.
[682]   Judgment of 10 July 1984, paras. 29-30. See also, *inter alia*, the judgment of 22 March 1983, *Campbell and Cosans*, paras. 12-14 and the judgment of 14 September 1987, *Gillow*, para. 11.

Other factors may also play a part in the awarding of reparation of costs and expenses. In the *Airey* Case, for instance, it seems to have been an important factor that the British Government had already declared itself prepared before the proceedings started to award a given amount.[683] On the other hand, no compensation is awarded if the fees are borne by an insurance company, since in that case "there is no prejudice capable of being the subject of a claim for restitution".[684] The same argument applies, if the applicant has received free legal aid.[685] In the *Wassink* Case the applicant also sought a specified amount for the expenses and fees of the lawyer who represented him before the Commission and the Court. The Dutch Government argued that the applicant, who had received legal aid in Strasbourg, had not shown that he had to pay his lawyer additional fees whose reimbursement he was entitled to request. In the Court's view, the mere fact that the applicant was granted legal aid did not mean that he was not under an obligation to pay the fee note drawn up by his counsel and attached to the claim submitted under Article 41. In the absence of proof to the contrary, the Court must accept that the applicant was required to pay his lawyer the amount set out in the fee note, from which the sums received from the Council of Europe are to be deducted.[686] And in the *Pakelli* Case, although the applicant did not have to pay the bill of his lawyer immediately, because of his financial situation, he could ask for the amount he needed to pay that bill.[687]

The fact that an applicant has accepted an out-of-court settlement does not exclude the award of compensation. In the *Silva Pontes* Case where the applicant had concluded an agreement with the private party defendant, the Court held that the agreement concerned the consequences of a road accident and not those, for which the State could be held responsible, flowing from the failure to comply with the reasonable time requirement. The Court, therefore, awarded the applicant a specified sum for pecuniary and non-pecuniary damage.[688]

The Court also takes into consideration whether the finding of a violation has effects beyond the confines of a particular case. The respondent State is then under the obligation to take the necessary measures in its domestic legal system to ensure the performance of its obligations under Article 46 of the Convention. Thus in the *Norris* Case the Court took into account that Ireland had to take the necessary steps to ensure its obligations under Article 46. In this respect the Court referred to the change in the law which had been effected with regard to Northern Ireland in compliance with the

---

[683]   Judgment of 6 February 1981, para. 10.
[684]   Judgment of 23 October 1984, *Öztürk*, para. 9.
[685]   Judgment of 18 December 1986, *Johnston*, para. 86; judgment of 25 June 1987, *Baggetta*, para. 28; judgment of 27 July 1987, *Feldbrugge*, para. 18.
[686]   Judgment of 27 September 1990, para. 42. Similarly, see the judgment of 25 October 1990, *Koendjbiharie*, para. 35.
[687]   Judgment of 25 April 1983, para. 47.
[688]   Judgment of 23 March 1994, para. 46.

Court's finding of a violation in the *Dudgeon* Case. This lead the Court to the decision that its finding of a violation constituted adequate just satisfaction for the purposes of Article 41.[689] However, the Court held in the *Dudgeon* Case that changes in the contested legislation or practice after the finding of a violation cannot constitute *per se* just satisfaction in respect of facts which occurred previously, although they may be taken into account for the award of non-pecuniary damage.[690] Moreover, it may take several years before the respondent State has made the necessary changes. In fact in Ireland it took almost four years before the Criminal Law (Sexual Offences) Act 1993 modified Irish Law to decriminalise consensual homosexual acts between adult males. In *S. L. v. Austria* the Court noted that the judgments concerned had been given ten to twento years previously. The Court considered it now appropriate to award just satisfaction for non-pecuniary damage in a case like the present one, even though the Criminal Code concerned had recently been repealed and the applicant had, in part therefore, achieved the objective of his application. In fact the Court attached weight to the fact that the applicant had been prevented from entering into relations corresponding to his disposition until he reached the age of eighteen.[691]

A trend appears to have developed in the case law of the Court to the effect that injury pursuant to Article 41 can be made good, as far as it was "incurred by the applicants in order to try to prevent the violation found by the Court or to obtain redress therefore" and only if, in particular, three criteria are fulfilled: costs and expenses susceptible of satisfaction must have been (1) 'actually incurred', (2) 'necessarily incurred' and (3) 'reasonable as to quantum'.[692] These criteria apply to costs described as material damage as well as to costs referable to proceedings.[693]

2.6.8.3 The costs of the proceedings

Legal costs are only recoverable insofar as they relate to the violation found.[694] In the *Eckle* Case the Court went into the matter of restitution of costs of proceedings extensively. The Court held that an applicant is entitled to an award of costs and expenses

---

[689]   Judgment of 26 October 1988, para. 50.
[690]   Judgment of 24 February 1983, para.14.
[691]   Judgment of 9 January 2003, para. 52. See also 10 February 2004, *B.B. v. the United Kingdom*, para. 34.
[692]   Judgment of 18 October 1982, *Le Compte, Van Leuven and De Meyere*, para. 14; judgment of 24 February 1983, *Dudgeon*, para. 14; judgment of 27 August 1991, *Philis*, para. 76; judgment of 12 May 1992, *Megyeri*, para. 34; judgment of 28 March 2000, *Baranowski,*para. 82; judgment of 29 June 2000, *Sabeur Ben Ali*, para.49; judgment of 26 July 2001, *Ilijkov*, para. 124.
[693]   See, *e.g.*, judgment of 6 November 1980, *The Sunday Times*, paras 23-42; judgment of 24 February 1983, *Dudgeon*, paras 19-22; 43; judgment of 25 April 2000, *Punzelt*, para. 106; judgment of 22 June 2000, *Coëme*, para. 155.
[694]   Judgment of 25 September 1992, *Pham Hoang*, para. 45; judgment of 19 April 1994, *Van der Hurk*, para. 66; judgment of 28 May 2002, *Beyeler*, para. 27; judgment of 28 November 2002, *The former King of Greece and Others*, para. 105; judgment of 10 June 2003, *Serghides*, para. 38.

---

under Article 41 when these costs are incurred in order to seek, through the domestic legal order, prevention or redress of a violation, to have the same established by the Commission and later by the Court, or to obtain reparation therefore, and when they "were actually incurred, were necessarily incurred and were also reasonable as to quantum". Considering, however, the proceedings in which the costs were incurred in this case, the claim for restitution of costs and expenses incurred in the proceedings before the Koblenz Court of Appeal was rejected because: "it should not be overlooked that the complaint in question was not aimed at securing a more expeditious conduct of the proceeding: the complaint was directed against the unreasonable length of the detention on remand and had as its sole object Mr. Eckle's release from custody. It could have been of relevance in relation to Article 5, para. 3 – if (...) the Commission had not declared the application inadmissible on that score – but not in relation to Article 6, para. 1."[695] In relation to the claims for restitution of costs incurred in the 'review' procedure before the Regional Court of Trier, the Court considered that "in view of his not having raised the issue of 'reasonable time' himself the applicant cannot recover in full Mr von Stackelberg's fees and disbursements".[696] Concerning the recovery of costs in relation to the procedure in Strasbourg, the Government expressed the view "that a deduction should be made in view of the applications having been unsuccessful in relation to three complaints declared inadmissible by the Commission". The Court did not agree with this, because "in contrast to what occurred in the case of *Le Compte, Van Leuven and De Meyere*, to which the Government referred (...), the complaints in question failed at the admissibility stage. Furthermore, the Commission did not reject them as being manifestly ill-founded, and hence after a preliminary inquiry into the merits, but for being out of time and for non-exhaustion of domestic remedies. (...) As is apparent from the decision on admissibility, the examination of these two questions of admissibility (...) was not of such complexity that its outcome could warrant the deduction called for by the Government."[697]

On the other hand, in the *Campbell and Fell* Case[698] the restitution of costs and expenses was made conditional on the degree to which the complaints were successful.

The costs made with respect to the Strasbourg proceedings must have been made with a view to establishing the violation of the Convention by the Court. Just satisfaction may be afforded for costs incurred at all stages of the proceedings. The reimbursement may cover the costs and fees of the lawyer as well as travel and subsistence expenses. The Court will also take other costs, such as services of experts, photocopying and postal costs, and translation fees, into consideration, as long as these costs are neces-

---

[695] Judgment of 21 June 1983, para. 30.
[696] *Ibidem*, para. 28.
[697] *Ibidem*, para. 51.
[698] Judgment of 28 June 1984, para. 146. See also the judgment of 18 December 1986, *Johnston*, para. 86.

sarily incurred. However, the applicant must seek the reimbursement of these costs himself, because according to the Court, this is not a matter which it has to examine of its own motion.[699] In the *Brogan* Case the applicants did not submit any claim for reimbursement of costs and expenses and the Court held that the question of the application of Article 41 was not ready for decision in relation to the claim for compensation for prejudice suffered.[700] When the Court had to deal with the question of compensation under Article 41, the applicants sought not only compensation for prejudice sustained but also for reimbursement of costs and expenses incurred before the Convention organs. However, the Court stated that it had held that in its principal judgment there was no call to examine the application of Article 50 [the present Article 41] in relation to reimbursement of any costs or expenses incurred. The Court referred to Article 52 [the present Article 42] according to which the earlier decision was final. Therefore, the Court could not entertain the applicants' subsequent claim in this respect.[701]

In the Case of *L. and v. v Austria* the applicants asserted that following the Court's judgment further costs had to be incurred in order to remove the consequences flowing from the violation of the Convention. They argued in particular that – in case of a finding of a violation by the Court – they would be entitled, pursuant to Article 363a of the Code of Criminal Procedure, to have the criminal proceedings reopened in order to have their convictions set aside and to have them removed from their criminal records. The applicants, therefore, requested the Court to rule that the respondent State was obliged to pay any future costs necessary for removing the consequences of the violation at issue and to reserve the fixing of the exact amount to a separate decision. The Court considered that such a claim was speculative. The Court noted in particular that both applicants were sentenced to a prison term suspended on probation in 1997 and that the three-year probationary period had already expired. What remained was the entry of their convictions in their criminal records. In this situation it was open to doubt whether there would be any need for the applicants to have the criminal proceedings against them reopened, as the respondent State might well choose other means to have their convictions expunged. The respondent State might, for instance, decide to grant the applicants a pardon and have their convictions removed from their criminal records. Having regard to these circumstances the Court dismissed the applicants' claim for future costs.[702]

In the *Akdivar* Case the applicants complained that notwithstanding the order in the principal judgment for costs to be paid in pounds sterling, the respondent Government

---

[699]   Judgment of 24 April 1990, *Huvig*, para. 38; judgment of 19 February 1991, *Colacioppo*, para. 16.
[700]   Judgment of 29 November 1988, para. 71.
[701]   Judgment of 30 May 1989, *Brogan and Others*, para. 7.
[702]   Judgment of 9 January 2003, para. 68.

had paid only part of the costs owed, in equal divisions, into bank accounts opened by the authorities on behalf of each of the applicants. The sums had been paid in Turkish liras some four months after the delivery of the principal judgment on 13 January 1997. As a result, the applicants stated that there was a shortfall of GBP 5,681.89 as of 13 January 1997, a sum which had accumulated 8% interest since then. The Court pointed out that by Article 53 [the present Article 46] of the Convention the High Contracting Parties undertake to abide by the decision of the Court in any case to which they are parties. Furthermore, it considered that the issue of a shortfall in the payment of costs ordered in the principal judgment is a matter which concerns the proper execution of a judgment of the Court by the respondent State. Accordingly, it is a question which falls to be decided by the Committee of Ministers of the Council of Europe.[703]

2.6.8.4 Other damages that might be compensated

hat other kind of damage may be compensated in addition to direct costs of proceedings? In the *König* Case, according to the Court, the extent to which the 'reasonable time' had been exceeded had left the applicant in prolonged uncertainty regarding his career, which in the Court's opinion ought to be compensated in the form of DM 30,000 of damages.[704] In the *Goddi* Case the applicant maintained that, if he had had an opportunity to have his defence adequately presented, he would certainly have received a lighter sentence. The Court did not accept so categorical an allegation. However, it held that the outcome might possibly have been different if the applicant had had the benefit of a practical and effective defence and that, therefore, such a loss of real opportunities warranted the award of just satisfaction.[705] A similar reasoning was followed by the Court in the *Colozza* Case, where it had found a violation of Article 6(1) of the Convention, since the applicant was never heard in his presence by a 'tribunal' which was competent to determine all the aspects of the matter. The Court noted that an award of just satisfaction could only be based on the fact that the applicant had not had the benefit of the guarantees of Article 6 and awarded just satisfaction to the applicant's widow for loss of real opportunities.[706] Reparation for loss of earnings is also possible,[707] as well as the repayment of fines and costs unjustly awarded against

---

[703]   Judgment of 1 April 1998, para. 59

[704]   Judgment of 10 March 1980, para. 19.

[705]   Judgment of 9 April 1984, para. 35.

[706]   Judgment of 12 February 1985, para. 38. See also the judgment of 2 June 1986, *Bönisch*, para. 13; judgment of 8 July 1986, *Lingens*, para. 50; judgment of 28 October 1987, *Inze*, para. 47.

[707]   Judgment of 24 November 1986, *Unterpertinger*, para. 35; judgment of 21 June 1988, *Berrehab*, para. 34, where, however, no reparation of loss of earnings was awarded because of the lack of a causal link.

the applicant,[708] and reimbursement of the travel and subsistence expenses met by the applicant in attending the hearings before the Commission and the Court.[709] Reparation of immaterial damage can be awarded for suffered uncertainty,[710] feeling of unequal treatment,[711] unjust imprisonment[712] and feeling of frustration.[713]

Several factors can play a part in the determination of the amount of such kinds of compensation. In the *Ringeisen* Case the Court had found that there had been a violation of Article 5(3). The Court awarded the applicant compensation of DM 20,000, and in fixing the amount of this sum, took into account the following factors. Firstly, the fact that the detention under remand had exceeded reasonable limits by 22 months. Although the period of imprisonment to which he had ultimately been condemned was reduced by the duration of the detention under remand, he had always maintained that he was innocent and on that account had undoubtedly felt so long a detention under remand as unjust. Secondly, the fact that his detention had been hard on him, since it had been impossible for him to undertake anything to avoid bankruptcy.[714]

In the *Artico* Case the Court took three elements into consideration, *viz.* the imprisonment actually served, the additional imprisonment which the applicant had possibly incurred in consequence of the lack of effective legal aid and the isolated position in which he had been placed as a result of this. The Court held that "none of the above elements of damage lends itself to a process of calculation. Taking them together on an equitable basis, as is required by Article 50, the Court considers that Mr. Artico should be afforded satisfaction assessed at three million (3,000,000) Lire."[715]

In the *Sporrong and Lönnroth* Case the Court had found a violation of Article 1 of Protocol No. 1 of the Convention. In order to decide whether or not the applicants had been prejudiced, the Court had to determine during which periods the continuation of the measures complained of had been in violation of Protocol No. 1, and in addition which constituent elements of damage warranted examination. The Court found it reasonable that a municipality should, after obtaining an expropriation permit, require some time to undertake and complete the planning needed to prepare

---

[708]   Judgment of 27 February 1980, *De Weer*, para. 60; judgment of 8 July 1986, *Lingens*, para. 53; judgment of 28 August 1992, *Schwabe*, para. 40.

[709]   Judgment of 10 December 1982, *Corigliano*, para. 53.

[710]   Judgment of 10 July 1984, *Guincho*, para. 44.

[711]   Judgment of 2 June 1986, *Bönisch*, para. 11; judgment of 23 April 1987, *Lechner and Hess*, para. 65; judgment of 8 July 1987, *Baraona*, para. 61.

[712]   Judgment of 24 November 1986, *Unterpertinger*, para. 35.

[713]   Judgment of 26 May 1994, *Keegan*, para. 68; judgment of 31 October 1995, *Papamichalopoulos*, para. 36.

[714]   Judgment of 22 June 1972, paras. 25-26. The Court did not exclude that a third factor – the deteriorated health due to the detention – could also have played a role, but Ringeisen had not advanced any evidence for that fact while from medical reports the contrary could be inferred.

[715]   Judgment of 13 May 1980, para. 48. See further the judgment of 21 June 1983, *Eckle*, para. 14; and particularly the judgment of 18 December 1984, *Sporrong and Lönnroth*, paras. 19-21.

the final decision on the expropriation contemplated. Whilst a comparison between the beginning and the end of the periods of damage did not show that the applicants were prejudiced in financial terms, the Court nevertheless did not conclude that there was no loss within that period. There were, in fact, other factors which also warranted attention. Firstly, there were limitations on the utilization of the properties. In addition, during the periods of damage the value of the properties in question fell. Furthermore, there were difficulties in obtaining loans, secured by way of mortgage. Above all, the applicants were left in prolonged uncertainty as they did not know what the fate of their properties would be. To these factors had to be added the non-pecuniary damage occasioned by the violation of Article 6(1) of the Convention: the applicants' case could not be heard by a tribunal competent to determine all the aspects of the matter. The applicants thus suffered damage for which reparation was not provided by the withdrawal of the expropriation permits.[716] As regards claims for loss of earnings, the Court's case law establishes that there must be a clear causal connection between the damage claimed by the applicant and the violation of the Convention and that this may, in the appropriate case, include compensation in respect of loss of earnings.[717]

In the *Bozano* Case the applicant claimed just satisfaction for the violation of Article 5(1) of the Convention. The Court concluded that the applicant's detention in France involved a serious breach of the Convention, which inevitably caused him substantial non-pecuniary damage. With regard to his subsequent detention in Switzerland and Italy the Court found that it had no jurisdiction to review the compatibility of that detention with the Convention, since the Commission had either declared the applicant's complaints against those two States inadmissible or struck them off its list. Nonetheless, there was a need to have regard to the applicant's detention as it took place prior to the enforcement of the deportation order. In the Court's view the real damage was that sustained as a consequence of the process of enforcing the deportation order and of the unlawful and arbitrary deprivation of liberty.[718]

If the damage or the costs do not lend themselves to a process of calculation, or the calculation presented to the Court is unreasonable, the Court fixes them on an equitable basis.[719] In the *Young, James and Webster* Case there was no dispute that all three applicants had incurred pecuniary and non-pecuniary losses and also liability for legal costs and expenses referable to the Strasbourg proceedings, but certain claims exceeded with regards to their quantum, the sums offered by the British Government during

---

[716]   Judgment of 18 December 1984, para. 26.
[717]   Judgment of 13 June 1994, *Barberà, Messegué and Jabardo*, paras. 16-20; judgment of 8 July 1999, *Cakici*, para. 127; judgment of 10 April 2001, *Tanli*, para. 181.
[718]   Judgment of 2 December 1987, para. 9.
[719]   Judgment of 13 May 1980, *Artico*, para. 48; judgment of 18 October 1982, *Young, James and Webster*, para. 11; judgment of 2 June 1986, *Bönisch*, para. 11.

unsuccessful friendly settlement negotiations. The Court observed that "high costs of litigation may themselves constitute a serious impediment to the effective protection of human rights. It would be wrong for the Court to give encouragement to such a situation in its decisions awarding costs under Article 50. It is important that applicants should not encounter undue financial difficulties in bringing complaints under the Convention and the Court considers that it may expect that lawyers in Contracting States will cooperate to this end in the fixing of their fees."[720] During the settlement negotiations the British Government offered to have the costs in question independently assessed or 'taxed' by a Taxing Master. In the opinion of the Court this would have been a reasonable method of assessment. However, the applicants did not take up this offer. In these circumstances the Court accepted the figure of 65,000 offered by the Government in respect of all legal costs and expenses.[721]

A claim for compensation will be rejected when there is nothing to suggest with reasonable certainty that without the violation the result would have been different.[722] Other possible reasons for rejection of reparation claims are: the Court's finding that, by holding that the violation has occurred, its judgment has already furnished sufficient satisfaction for the purposes of Article 50;[723] the conclusion that the applicants did not suffer any damage;[724] the fact that the domestic court has imposed a sentence identical to that given before the judgment of the Court, but now after a trial attended by all the guarantees laid down by the Convention;[725] the circumstance that the applicant has adduced insufficient evidence or information in support of his claim;[726] or the Court's holding that the "claims stem from matters in respect of which it has found no violation".[727]

In the Case of *Abdulaziz, Cabales and Balkandali*, the applicants sought 'substantial', but unquantified, compensation for non-pecuniary damage in the form of distress, humiliation and anxiety. They argued that the interference complained of concerned a vital element in society, namely family life; that sexual discrimination was universally condemned; and that the existence of a practice in breach of the Convention was an aggravating factor. The Court held that by reason of its very nature, non-pecuniary damage of the kind alleged could not always be the object of concrete proof.

---

[720]   Judgment of 18 October 1982, para. 11.
[721]   Judgment of 18 October 1982, para. 12.
[722]   Judgment of 10 March 1972, *De Wilde, Ooms and Versyp* ('*Vagrancy*' Cases), para. 20; judgment of 23 February 1984, *Luberti*, para. 40.
[723]   Judgment of 18 October 1982, *Le Compte, Van Leuven and De Meyere*, para. 12; judgment of 18 December 1987, *F. v. Switzerland*, para. 45; judgment of 22 April 1993, *Modinos*, para. 30.
[724]   Judgment of 23 November 1976, *Engel*, para. 10.
[725]   Judgment of 26 October 1984, *Piersack*, para. 15; judgment of 28 June 1993, *Windisch*, para. 11.
[726]   Judgment of 21 November 1983, *Foti*, para. 18; judgment of 29 May 1986, *Deumeland*, para. 98; judgment of 14 September 1987, *Gillow*, para. 14; judgment of 20 June 1988, *Schönenberger and Durmaz*, para. 38.
[727]   Judgment of 18 December 1986, *Johnston*, para. 85.

However, it is reasonable to assume that persons who, like the applicants, find themselves faced with problems relating to the continuation or inception of their married life may suffer distress and anxiety. The Court, however, considered that in the circumstances of these cases its findings of violation of themselves constituted sufficient just satisfaction. The applicants' claim for monetary compensation could not therefore be accepted.[728]

In the Case of *A.D.T. v. the United Kingdom* concerning a conviction for homosexual acts with a number of consenting adults, the Court awarded 10,000 pounds sterling in respect of non-pecuniary damage.[729] In the *Smith and Davies* Case the applicants submitted that both the investigation of their sexual orientation and their consequent discharge from the armed forces on the sole ground of their homosexuality were profoundly degrading and humiliating events. Moreover, and as a result, they could not now pursue a career in a profession which they enjoyed and in which they excelled.[730] In its principal judgment the Court recalled that it had found that both the investigations and consequent discharges constituted 'especially grave' interferences with the applicants' private lives for three reasons. In the first place, the Court considered that the investigation process was of an 'exceptionally intrusive character', noting that certain lines of questioning were 'particularly intrusive and offensive'. Secondly, the Court considered that the discharge of the applicants had a 'profound effect on their careers and prospects' and, thirdly, it found the absolute and general character of the policy striking, leading as it did to the discharge of the applicants on the ground of an innate personal characteristic irrespective of their conduct or service records. The principal judgment had also noted that the High Court, in its judgment delivered on 7 June 1995 in the domestic judicial review proceedings, had described the applicants' service records as 'exemplary' and had found that they had been 'devastated' by their discharge. Although not found to give rise to a violation of Article 3, these events were described in that context as having been 'undoubtedly distressing and humiliating for each of the applicants'. The Court considered it clear that the investigations and discharges described in the principal judgment were profoundly destabilising events in the applicants' lives which had and, it cannot be excluded, continue to have a significant emotional and psychological impact on each of them. The Court, therefore, awarded, on an equitable basis, GBP 19,000 to each applicant in compensation for non-pecuniary damage.[731] With respect to the pecuniary damages, the Court referred to the *Vogt* Case and recalled that one of the reasons why it considered Mrs Vogt's dismissal from her post as a schoolteacher to be a 'very severe measure', was

---

[728] Judgment of 28 May 1985, para. 96.
[729] Judgment of 31 July 2000, paras 43-45.
[730] Judgment of 25 July 2000, para. 10.
[731] *Ibidem*, paras 12-13.

the finding that schoolteachers in her situation would 'almost certainly be deprived of the opportunity to exercise the sole profession for which they have a calling, for which they have been trained and in which they have acquired skills and experience'.[732] In the *Smith and Davies* Case the Court was of the opinion that the significant differences between military service and civilian life and qualifications, together with the emotional and psychological impact of the investigations and of the consequent discharges, rendered it difficult for the applicants to find civilian careers which were, and would continue to be, equivalent to their service careers. Both applicants had access to certain armed forces' resettlement services. However, the first applicant submitted that she was too psychologically affected by the events surrounding her discharge to take immediate and full advantage of those services. The second applicant did participate in a resettlement programme and received a resettlement grant of GBP 5,583.[733] Moreover, the Court considered significant the loss to the applicants of the non-contributory service pension scheme. The lump sum and service pension which the first applicant would receive on retirement were substantially less than the amounts she would have received had she not been discharged, even if she had not achieved her predicted promotions before retirement. The same held true, but to a lesser extent, for the second applicant. In such circumstances, and making its assessment on an equitable basis, the Court awarded compensation (inclusive of interest claimed) to the applicants for past loss of earnings, for future loss of earnings and for the loss of the benefit of the non-contributory service pension scheme.[734]

In the *Davies* Case the Government contended that the applicant was not entitled to any compensation because he had not shown that he had suffered any stress or distress as a result of the violation. The Court observed that some forms of non-pecuniary damage, including emotional distress, by their very nature cannot always be the object of concrete proof. This did not prevent the Court from making an award if it considered that it was reasonable to assume that an applicant had suffered injury requiring financial compensation. It was reasonable to assume that the applicant suffered distress, anxiety and frustration exacerbated by the unreasonable length of the proceedings. The Court awarded the applicant 4,500 euros.[735]

In the *Stran Greek Refineries and Stratis Andreadis* Case the Court held that the adequacy of compensation might be diminished if it is paid without reference to various circumstances likely to reduce its value, such as the lapse of a considerable

---

[732]   Judgment of 26 September 1995, para. 60
[733]   Judgment of 25 July 2000, para. 20.
[734]   *Ibidem,* paras. 20-25.
[735]   Judgment of 16 July 2002, para. 38. Similarly, see judgment of 10 October 2002, *D.P. and J.C. v. the United Kingdom*, para. 142, and judgment of 28 January 2003, *Peck*, para.119.

period of time.[736] In the *Guillemin* Case the Court took note of the excessive and continuing duration of the proceedings the applicant had brought to secure compensation for an expropriation which the Court of Cassation had held to be unlawful. The Court observed that since the principal judgment was given, the proceedings in the national courts, which were still pending, had deprived the applicant of the compensation to which she was entitled and would doubtless continue to deprive her of it, at least until the Court of Cassation gave judgment. The Court considered it appropriate, without prejudice to the amount that would finally be paid to the applicant at the end of the proceedings in the Court of Cassation, to award her compensation for the loss of availability of the sum already awarded in the judgment of the Evry *Tribunal de Grande Instance* on 26 May 1997 that has been caused by the town council's refusal to comply with that judgment.[737]

In the *Selim Sadak* Case the applicants alleged that they had sustained pecuniary damage corresponding to what they would have earned as members of parliament had they not been forced to vacate their seats and the loss of earnings they endured as a result of the restrictions to their civic rights. The Court considered that, irrespective of the dissolution of the DEP, because of the forfeiture of their parliamentary seats the applicants undoubtedly sustained pecuniary damage, which, however, could not be assessed with precision. To that must be added non-pecuniary damage, which the finding of a violation in this judgment was not sufficient to make good.[738]

In the *Teixeira de Castro* Case the applicant claimed, firstly, compensation for loss of earnings during the three years of the six-year sentence he spent in prison on the ground that without the two police officers' intervention he would not have been convicted. He also requested compensation for loss of earnings because, when he came out of prison, he had been dismissed and was unable to find another job as he was labelled a drug trafficker. Owing to the fact that he had been in prison and consequently had no earnings, his wife and son had gone hungry and had known periods of intense anxiety. Since his conviction their life had been a series of humiliations; he had lost friends and become estranged from members of his family. The Court held that the documents in the case file suggested that the term of imprisonment complained of would not have been imposed if the two police officers had not intervened. The loss by the applicant both of his earnings while he was deprived of his liberty and of opportunities when he came out of prison were actual and entitled him to an award of just satisfaction.[739] However, in cases of deprivation of liberty, compensation for pecuniary damages will not be given if a causal link between the violation found and the claimed damages does not exist.[740]

---

[736] Judgment of 19 December 1994, para. 82.
[737] Judgment of 2 September 1998, paras 24-25.
[738] Judgment of 11 June 2002, para. 56.
[739] Judgment of 9 June 1998, para. 49.
[740] Judgment of 4 June 2002, *Yagmurdereli*, para. 69

2.6.8.5 No Jurisdiction to direct a State to take certain measures

Repeatedly the Court has declared that it lacked jurisdiction to direct the States to take certain measures, such as to abolish the violation found by the Court and to repair the costs, etc. The Court notes regularly that it is left to the State concerned to choose the means within its domestic legal system to give effect to its obligations under Article 53.[741]

In the *Corigliano* Case the Court declared the claim inadmissible to order the State to make certain articles of the Penal Code inapplicable to 'political and social trials'. This "falls outside the scope of the case brought before the Court".[742] Also, the request to publish a summary of the Court's judgment in local newspapers or the removal of any reference to the applicant's conviction in the central criminal record fall outside the scope of the jurisdiction of the Court.[743]

In the *Bozano* Case the applicant had requested the Court to recommend that the French Government to approach the Italian authorities through diplomatic channels with a view to securing either a 'presidential pardon' – leading to his 'rapid release' – or a reopening of the criminal proceedings taken against him in Italy from 1971 to 1976. The Government argued that the Court did not have the power to take such a course of action. Furthermore, they maintained that it would in any case be unconnected with the subject-matter of the dispute, since it would amount to recommending France to intervene in the enforcement of final decisions of the Italian courts. The Court did not go into these arguments. It merely pointed out that Mr Bozano's complaints against Italy were not in issue before it, as the Commission had declared them inadmissible.[744] One cannot escape the impression that the Court did not want to enter into the issue of whether or not it had the power to make a recommendation as requested by the applicant. It might be argued that in cases where *restitutio in integrum* is impossible, as in the present case, the Court has no other option but to award just satisfaction. However, what Mr Bozano in addition requested from the Court was only a *recommendation* and such a recommendation should, in general, not be deemed inappropriate, comparable as it would seem to be with the recommendation of provisional measures, for which there is also no express basis in the Convention.

In the *Akdivar* Case the applicants claimed, *inter alia*, compensation under this provision for the losses incurred as a result of the destruction of their houses by the security forces which forced them to abandon their village. They further submitted that the Court should confirm, as a necessary implication of an award of just satis-

---

[741]   Judgment of 20 September 1993, *Saïdi*, para. 47; judgment of 13 July 1995, *Tolstoy Miloslavsky*, paras 69-72; judgment of 30 October 1995, *Papamichalopoulos*, para. 34; judgment of 1 April 1998, *Akdiva*, para. 62.

[742]   Judgment of 10 December 1982, para. 51.

[743]   Judgment of 27 February 1992, *Manifattura FL*, para. 26; judgment of 23 April 1992, *Castells*, para. 54.

[744]   Judgment of 18 December 1986, para. 65.

faction, that the Government should (1) bear the costs of necessary repairs in their village to enable the applicants to continue their way of life there; and (2) remove any obstacle preventing the applicants from returning to their village. The Court held that, if *restitutio in integrum* is in practice impossible, the respondent States are free to choose the means whereby they will comply with a judgment in which the Court has found a breach, and the Court will not make consequential orders or declaratory statements in this regard. It falls to the Committee of Ministers acting under Article 54 of the Convention to supervise compliance in this respect.[745]

In the *Papamichalopoulos* Case the Court held that "the loss of all ability to dispose of the land in issue, taken together with the failure of the attempts made [up to then] to remedy the situation complained of, [had] entailed sufficiently serious consequences for the applicants de facto to have been expropriated in a manner incompatible with their right to the peaceful enjoyment of their possessions". The act of the Greek Government which the Court held to be contrary to the Convention, was not an expropriation that would have been legitimate but the failure to pay fair compensation; it was a taking by the State of land belonging to private individuals, which had lasted twenty-eight years, the authorities having ignored the decisions of national courts and their own promises to the applicants to redress the injustice committed in 1967 by the dictatorial regime.[746] Consequently, the Court considered that the return of the land in issue – as defined in 1983 by the Athens second Expropriation Board – would put the applicants as far as possible in a situation equivalent to the one in which they would have been if there had not been a breach of Article 1 of Protocol No. 1; the award of the existing buildings would then fully compensate them for the consequences of the alleged loss of enjoyment. The Court held that if the respondent State did not make such restitution within six months from the delivery of this judgment, it was to pay the applicants for damage and loss of enjoyment since the authorities took possession of the land in 1967, the current value of the land increased by the appreciation brought about by the existence of the buildings and the construction costs of the latter.[747]

In the *Scozzari and Giunta* Case the Court held that a judgment in which the Court finds a breach of the Convention imposes on the respondent state a legal obligation not just to pay those concerned the sums awarded by way of just satisfaction, but also to choose, subject to supervision by the Committee of Ministers, the general and/or, if appropriate, individual measures to be adopted in their domestic legal order to put an end to the violation found by the Court and to redress so far as possible the effects.[748]

---

[745] Judgment of 1 April 1998, para. 62; judgment of 24 April 1998, *Selçuk and Asker*, para. 154; judgment of 24 July 1998, *Mentes and Others*, para. 423.

[746] Judgment of 24 June 1993, para. 45.

[747] Judgment of 31 October 1995, paras 38-40.

[748] Judgment of 13 July 2000, para. 249.

In the *Velikova* Case the applicant claimed 100,000 French francs in compensation for the pain and suffering resulting from the violations of the Convention. She asked for an order of the Court that this amount be paid directly to her in full, free of taxes or of any claim or attachment by the government or by third persons. The applicant also requested the Court to order that there should be no negative consequences for her, such as reduction in social benefits due to her as a result of the receipt of the above amount. The Court considered that the compensation fixed pursuant to Article 41 and due by virtue of a judgment of the Court should be exempted from attachment. It held that it would be incongruous to award the applicant an amount in compensation for, *inter alia*, deprivation of life constituting a violation of Article 2, if the State itself were then allowed to attach this amount. The purpose of compensation for non-pecuniary damage would inevitably be frustrated and the Article 41 system perverted, if such a situation were to be deemed satisfactory. However, the Court held that it had no jurisdiction to make an order exempting compensation from attachment. It, therefore, left this point to the discretion of the Bulgarian authorities.[749]

Where the choice of measures is theoretical in the sense that it is constrained by the nature of the violation, the Court can itself directly require certain steps to be taken. To date it has made use of this possibility only on two occasions. In the *Assanidze* Case the Court ordered the release of the applicant who was being arbitrarily detained in breach of Article 5 of the Convention. It held that as regards the measures which the Georgian State had to take, subject to supervision by the Committee of Ministers, in order to put an end to the violation that had been found, its judgments are essentially declaratory in nature and that, in general, it is primarily for the State concerned to choose the means to be used in its domestic legal order in order to discharge its legal obligation under Article 46 of the Convention, provided that such means are compatible with the conclusions set out in the Court's judgment. This discretion as to the manner of execution of a judgment reflects the freedom of choice attaching to the primary obligation of the Contracting States under the Convention to secure the rights and freedoms guaranteed. However, by its very nature the violation found in the instant case did not leave any real choice as to the measures required to remedy it. In these conditions, having regard to the particular circumstances of the case and the urgent need to put an end to the violation of Article 5(1) and Article 6(1) of the Convention, the Court considered that the respondent State had to secure the applicant's release at the earliest possible date.[750] In the *Ilaşcu* Case the Court considered that any continuation of the unlawful and arbitrary detention of the three applicants would necessarily entail a serious prolongation of the violation of Article 5 found by the Court and a breach of the respondent States' obligation under Article

---

[749]   Judgment of 18 May 2000, para. 99.
[750]   Judgment of 8 April 2004, paras 202-203.

46(1) of the Convention to abide by the Court's judgment. Regard being had to the grounds on which the respondent States had been found by the Court to be in violation of the Convention, they had to take every measure to put an end to the arbitrary detention of the applicants still detained and to secure their immediate release.[751]

In this respect it should be noted that the Committee of Ministers in a fairly recent Resolution considered that the execution of judgments would be facilitated if the existence of a systemic problem is already identified in the judgment of the Court. Therefore, it invited the Court: "I. as far as possible, to identify, in its judgments finding a violation of the Convention, what it considers to be an underlying systemic problem and the source of this problem, in particular when it is likely to give rise to numerous applications, so as to assist states in finding the appropriate solution and the Committee of Ministers in supervising the execution of judgments; II. to specially notify any judgment containing indications of the existence of a systemic problem and of the source of this problem not only to the state concerned and to the Committee of Ministers, but also to the Parliamentary Assembly, to the Secretary General of the Council of Europe and to the Council of Europe Commissioner for Human Rights, and to highlight such judgments in an appropriate manner in the database of the Court."[752]

In the Explanatory Report to Protocol No. 14 it is indicated that it would be useful if the Court and, as regards the supervision of the execution of judgments the Committee of Ministers, adopt a special procedure so as to give priority treatment to judgments that identify a structural problem capable of generating a significant number of repetitive applications with a view to securing speedy execution of the judgment.[753]

In virtue of Protocol No. 14, paragraphs 4 and 5 of Article 46 of the Convention accordingly will empower the Committee of Ministers to bring infringement proceedings before the Court (which will sit as a Grand Chamber), having first served the State concerned with notice to comply. The Committee of Ministers' decision to do so requires a qualified majority of two thirds of the representatives entitled to sit on the Committee. This infringement procedure does not aim to reopen the question of violation already decided in the Court's first judgment. Nor does it provide for payment of a financial penalty by a High Contracting Party found in violation of Article 46, paragraph 1. It is felt that the political pressure exerted by proceedings for non-compliance in the Grand Chamber and by the latter's judgment should suffice to secure execution of the Court's initial judgment by the state concerned.[754]

---

[751] Judgment of 8 July 2004, para. 490.
[752] Resolution (2004)3 of 12 May 2004.
[753] *Explanatory Report to Protocol No.14*, para. 16.
[754] *Ibidem*, para. 98.

2.7   REQUEST FOR INTERPRETATION OF A JUDGMENT OF THE COURT

Rule 79 of the Rules of Court deals with the possibility of requesting the Court to interpret a judgment. A party may request such an interpretation within one year following the delivery of the judgment. The request must state precisely the point or points in the operative provisions of the judgment of which interpretation is required. The original Chamber may decide of its own motion to refuse the request on the ground that there is no reason to warrant considering it. Where it is not possible to constitute the original Chamber the President of the Court will complete or compose the Chamber by drawing lots. If the Chamber does not refuse the request, the Registrar will communicate it to the other party or parties and will invite them to submit any written comments within a time-limit laid down by the President of the Chamber. The President of the Chamber will also fix the date of the hearing should the Chamber decide to hold one. The Chamber will decide by means of a judgment. A request for interpretation will be dealt with, according to Rule 102 of the Rules of Court, in proceedings largely resembling the normal proceedings before the Court.

Until 2005 the Court only decided on a request for interpretation on three occasions. On 21 December 1972, on the basis of a letter from the original individual applicant, the Commission submitted to the Court a request for interpretation of the Court's second judgment in the *Ringeisen* Case of 22 June 1972. In this judgment Ringeisen had been awarded compensation of DM 20,000. The question whether this amount would have to be paid directly to Ringeisen or whether it might be claimed by the trustee in the bankruptcy of Ringeisen had been left by the Court to the discretion of the Austrian Government. In this connection, however, the Court had referred to the Austrian legislation concerning compensation on account of detention under remand, which implied that no attachment or seizure may be made against such compensation. The money was, however, sent by the Austrian authorities on consignment to a judicial tribunal. The latter decided that upon request of the persons entitled to it or after a final judicial decision the money was to be paid. The Commission asked the Court what was meant by the order to pay compensation, in particular with respect to the currency and the place of the payment, and whether the term 'compensation' was to be understood as an amount that was exempt from any judicial claims under Austrian law or, on the contrary, was subject to such claims. The Court replied that the compensation was to be paid in German marks and was to be made payable in the Federal Republic of Germany. Furthermore the Court ruled that the money was to be paid to Ringeisen and was personally exempt from any claim or title to it. This ruling, therefore, implied disapproval of the position taken by the Austrian authorities. Austria had called into question the competence of the Court in the matter, stating that "the competence of the (...) Court (...) for interpretation of its judgments

(...) is based solely on the Rules of the Court. Therefore, in the light of Article 52 of the (...) Convention, the well-founded question may even be raised whether this legal institution is compatible at all with the Convention." The Court pointed out that the sole purpose of Article 52 [the present Article 42] is to exclude appeal to another authority from decisions of the Court.[755] It submitted that there is no question of appeal when the Court deals with a request for interpretation. In such a case the Court exercises inherent jurisdiction, because such a request concerns only elucidation of the purport and scope of a preceding judgment. Furthermore, the Court pointed out that Rule 56 (the present Rule 57) had been submitted to the Contracting States at the time of its adoption and that no objections had been raised against it by those States.[756]

In its judgment of 10 February 1995 in the *Allenet de Ribemont* Case the Court awarded the applicant under Article 50 an overall sum of FRF 2,000,000 for pecuniary and non-pecuniary damage, together with FRF 100,000 for costs and expenses. In response to the applicant's request for a ruling that France should guarantee him against any application for enforcement of a judgment delivered by the Paris *Tribunal de Grande Instance* on 14 March 1979, the Court said that "under Article 41 it does not have jurisdiction to issue such an order to a Contracting State".[757] In July-August 1995 the applicant was informed that an attachment of the sums awarded to him by the Court had been effected at the request of the parties in whose favour the judgment of the Paris *Tribunal de Grande Instance* had been given. Following a request from Mr Allenet de Ribemont the Commission submitted to the Court a request for interpretation of the judgment of 10 February 1995. The request was worded as follows: "*Firstly*: Is it to be understood that Article 50 of the Convention, which provides for an award of just satisfaction to the injured party if the domestic law of the High Contracting Party allows only partial reparation to be made for the consequences of the decision or measure held to be in conflict with the obligations arising from the Convention, means that any sum awarded under this head must be paid to the injured party personally and be exempt from attachment? *Secondly*: In respect of sums subject to legal claims under French law, should a distinction be made between the part of the sum awarded under the head of pecuniary damage and the part awarded under the head of non-pecuniary damage? and *Thirdly*: If so, what were the sums which the Court intended to grant the applicant in respect of pecuniary damage and non-pecuniary damage respectively?"

The Court observed, firstly, that when considering a request for interpretation it is exercising inherent jurisdiction: it goes no further than to clarify the meaning and

---

[755] See *supra* 2.5.
[756] Judgment of 23 June 1973, paras 12-15.
[757] Judgment of 10 February 1995, para. 23.

scope which it intended to give to a previous decision which issued from its own deliberations, specifying if need be what it thereby decided with binding force. The Court understood the first question put by the Commission as an invitation to interpret Article 50 in a general, abstract way. That, however, went outside not only the bounds laid down by Rule 57 of Rules of Court, but also those of the Court's contentious jurisdiction under the Convention. In any event, the Court had not in the instant case ruled that any sum awarded to Mr Allenet de Ribemont was to be free from attachment. The applicant had asked the Court to hold that the State should guarantee him against any application for enforcement of the judgment delivered by the Paris *Tribunal de Grande Instance* on 14 March 1979. In response the Court had said that "under Article 50 it does not have jurisdiction to issue such an order to a Contracting State". Accordingly, the question had been left to the national authorities acting under the relevant domestic law. In short, the Court had no jurisdiction to answer the first question put by the Commission. As to the Commission's second and third questions the Court said that in its judgment of 10 February 1995 it had awarded the applicant FRF 2,000,000 'for damage' without distinguishing between pecuniary and non-pecuniary damage. In relation to the sum awarded the Court had considered that it did not have to identify the proportions corresponding to pecuniary and non-pecuniary damage respectively. It was not bound to do so when affording 'just satisfaction' under Article 50 of the Convention. In point of fact it was often difficult, if not impossible, to make any such distinction. The Court held that the judgment it had delivered on 10 February 1995 was clear on the points in the operative provisions on which interpretation had been requested. To hold otherwise would not be to clarify 'the meaning and scope' of that judgment but rather to modify it in respect of an issue which the Court had decided with binding force. Accordingly, it was unnecessary to answer the Commission's second and third questions.[758]

In the *Hentrich* Case the Court had ruled in its judgment of 3 July 1995 on just satisfaction that the French Government should pay a specified amount of money. In her request for interpretation the applicant complained of the delay in paying the just satisfaction – payment being made on 1 December 1995 – and she claimed default interest on the sums awarded. This was not considered a matter for interpretation.[759]

Protocol No. 14 will amend Article 46(3) to empower the Committee of Ministers to ask the Court to interpret a final judgment for the purpose of facilitating the supervision of its execution. The Committee of Ministers' experience of supervising the execution of judgments shows that difficulties are sometimes encountered due to disagreement as to the interpretation of judgments. The Court's reply is designed to settle any argument concerning a judgment's exact meaning. The qualified majority vote

---

[758]   Judgment of 7 August 1996, para. 23.
[759]   Judgment of 3 July 1997, paras 14-16.

required by the last sentence of paragraph 3 shows that the Committee of Ministers should use this possibility sparingly, in order to avoid over-burdening the Court.

No time-limit has been set for making requests for interpretation since a question of interpretation may arise at any time during the Committee of Ministers' examination of the execution of a judgment. The Court is free to decide on the manner and form in which it wishes to reply to the request. Normally it would be for the formation of the Court which delivered the original judgment to rule on the question of interpretation. More detailed rules governing this new procedure may be included in the Rules of Court.[760]

2.8 REQUEST FOR REVISION OF A JUDGMENT

The competence of the Court to deal with requests for revision of its judgments is likewise not regulated by the Convention. Like the competence to give an interpretation of a judgment at the request of a party, the competence to revise a judgment may also be considered as inherent in the jurisdiction of the Court. The procedure to be followed in connection with a request for revision is also to be found in the Rules of Court, *viz.* in Rule 80.

A party may, in the event of the discovery of a fact which might by its nature have a decisive influence and which, when a judgment was delivered, was unknown to the Court and could not reasonably have been known to that party, request the Court, within a period of six months after that party acquired knowledge of the fact, to revise that judgment. The original Chamber may decide of its own motion to refuse the request on the ground that there is no reason to warrant considering it. Where it is not possible to constitute the original Chamber, the President of the Court will complete or compose the Chamber by drawing lots. If the Chamber does not refuse the request, the Registrar will communicate it to the other party or parties and invite them to submit any written comments within a time-limit laid down by the President of the Chamber. The President of the Chamber will also fix the date of the hearing should the Chamber decide to hold one. The Chamber decides by means of a judgment. A request for revision will be dealt with, according to Rule 102 of the Rules of Court, in proceedings largely resembling the normal proceedings before the Court.

---

[760]   *Explanatory Report to Protocol No. 14*, paras 96-97.

Up to the present (February 2005) eight requests for revision had been honoured by the Court,[761] while four requests had been dismissed.[762] This rather low figure is not surprising. In general, cases in which an originally unknown fact of decisive importance is discovered after the final judgment are very rare. It is even less likely that such a situation will occur after lengthy local proceedings and the elaborate proceedings before the Court.

In the *Pardo* Case the applicant complained, *inter alia*, of a breach of his right to a fair trial. He claimed that as a party in commercial litigation in the Aix-en-Provence Court of Appeal he had not had the opportunity to present oral arguments on the merits despite the fact that the President had announced that there would be a further hearing at a later date. In its judgment the Court held that there had been no violation of Article 6(1).[763] At Mr Pardo's request the Commission submitted to the Court a request for the revision of that judgment. The Commission noted that the Court, prior to its hearing on 22 March 1993, had asked the participants in the proceedings to produce some documents. For the reasons given at the hearing these requests were not complied with. Since then the applicant had been able to obtain certain of these documents and in particular the letter from Mr de Chessé to Mr Davin (both lawyers) of 25 March 1985 and the list of documents contained in the appeal file. The Commission took the view that, as the Court had asked for these documents to be produced, they might by their nature have had a decisive influence on its judgment. The Court took the view that the two documents submitted in support of the Commission's request (the letter from Mr de Chessé to Mr Davin of 25 March 1985 and the list of documents in the appeal file), documents to which Mr Pardo did not have access until after the delivery of the judgment of 20 September 1993, could be regarded as facts for the purposes of Rule 58(1) [the present Rule 80(1)]. The Court noted that, under the terms of the second sentence of Rule 58(4) [the present Rule 80(4)], the Chamber constituted to consider the request for revision could only determine the admissibility of that request. It had, accordingly, to confine itself to examining whether, *prima facie*, the facts submitted were such as 'might by [their] nature have a decisive influence'. The task of considering whether they actually had a 'decisive influence' lay in principle with the Chamber which gave the original judgment. A decision on the admissibility of the request, therefore, in no way prejudged the merits of the request. However, in carrying out its examination the Court had to bear in mind that, by virtue of Article 52 [the present Article 42] of the Convention, its judgments were final. Inasmuch as it called

---

761   Judgment of 3 May 2001, *E.P. v. Italy*; judgment of 23 October 2001, *Tripodi*; judgment of 7 November 2002, *Viola*; judgment of 26 November 2002, *Frattini*; judgment of 8 April 2003, *Perhirin and 29 Others*; judgment of 29 April 2003, *Grasso*; judgment of 8 July 2004, *Karagiannis*; judgment of 21 September 2004, *Stoiescu*.

762   Judgment of 10 July 1996, *Pardo*; judgment of 30 July 1998, *Gustafsson*; judgment of 28 January 2000, *McGingley and Egan*; judgment of 2 October 2003, *Corsi*.

763   Judgment of 20 September 1993, para. 29.

into question the final character of judgments, the possibility of revision, which was not provided for in the Convention but had been introduced by the Rules of Court, was an exceptional procedure. That was why the admissibility of any request for revision of a judgment of the Court under this procedure was subject to strict scrutiny. In order to establish whether the facts on which a request for revision were based 'might by [their] nature have a decisive influence', they had to be considered in relation to the decision of the Court the revision of which was sought. The Court observed in this connection that a request to those appearing before the Court for documents to be produced was not in itself sufficient to warrant the conclusion that the documents in question 'might by [their] nature have a decisive influence'. On the other hand, the Court could not exclude the possibility that the documents in question 'might by [their] nature have a decisive influence'. It fell to the Chamber which gave the original judgment to determine whether those documents actually cast doubt on the conclusions it reached in 1993. The Court accordingly declared the request for revision admissible and referred it to the Chamber which gave the original judgment.[764] In its judgment of 29 April 1997 the Court decided that the documents in question did not provide any information on the proceedings concerned whose course had been in dispute before the Court. The documents would not have had a decisive influence on the original judgment and did not constitute any grounds for revision. Therefore, the request was dismissed.[765]

In the *Gustafsson* Case the applicant complained that the lack of State protection against industrial action conducted by the Hotel and Restaurant Workers' Union (HRF) against his restaurant, gave rise to a violation of his right to freedom of association as guaranteed by Article 11 of the Convention. The Court concluded that Article 11 of the Convention was applicable in the applicant's case but that there had been no violation of this Article.[766] In requesting the Court to revise its judgment of 25 April 1996 the applicant adduced evidence in relation to two allegations advanced by the Government for the first time in their memorial to the Court during the main proceedings. This concerned firstly their assertion that in 1986 one of his employees, who was also a member of HRF, had contacted the HRF to complain about the terms of employment. Secondly, it concerned the Government's allegation that the applicant could not substantiate his own assertion that the employment terms which he offered were, as regards salaries, equal to or better than those required under a collective agreement with the HRF. The Court held that, although the judgment referred to the additional information in question, this only disposed of a point of procedure in reply to the applicant's contention that the Government were estopped from changing the

---

[764] Judgment of 10 July 1996, paras 24-25.
[765] Judgment of 29 April 1997, paras 20-22; see also in this respect the judgment of 28 January 2000, *McGinley and Egan*, paras 35-36.
[766] Judgment of 25 April 1996, paras 51-55.

stance they had adopted before the Commission and from adducing the evidence before the Court. The Court's answer that it was not prevented from taking the information into account if it considered it relevant could not of its own be taken to mean that the Court actually did have regard to the information. The reasons stated in the ensuing part of the original judgment were sufficient to support, and were decisive for, the Court's conclusion that there had been no violation of Article 11 of the Convention. It contained no mention of the additional evidence and arguments submitted by the Government. Nor was there anything to indicate that the evidence had been relied on here. Nor did other parts of the Court's reasoning and conclusions mention the first set of facts in dispute, namely the Government's allegation that the trade union action had its background in a complaint in 1986 by an HRF member employed by the applicant. Only the second set of disputed facts concerning the terms and conditions of employment was alluded to. However, the reasons contained in the relevant part of the judgment were merely accessory to those mentioned above. Furthermore, the Court did not state anything suggesting an acceptance on its part of the arguments and evidence advanced by the Government in rebuttal. It did not regard the additional facts submitted by them as established facts. Rather than determining the disagreement between the applicant and the Government as to the terms and conditions of employment, the Court had regard to the general interest sought to be achieved through the union action, in particular the special role and importance of collective agreements in the regulation of labour relations in Sweden. It followed that the evidence adduced by the applicant would not have had a decisive influence on the Court's judgment of 25 April 1996 as far as the applicant's complaint under Article 11 of the Convention was concerned. Nor would it have had any such bearing on its conclusions with respect to his complaints under Article 1 of Protocol No. 1 or Article 6 or 13 of the Convention. Accordingly, the evidence did not offer any ground for revision.[767]

Most of the requests for revision concerned the issue of just satisfaction under Article 41 of the Convention. In a number of cases the applicant had died before the Court had taken a decision in his case, finding a violation of the Convention and awarding the applicant compensation under Article 41. Subsequently, the respondent State requested for revision of the principal judgment concerning Article 41 of the Convention. The Court found that it had not been informed to whom it could legitimately award the just satisfaction due, and decided to revise its principal judgment so that no amount be awarded for non-pecuniary damage.[768] In the Case of E.P. v. Italy the Court decided to revise its principal judgment and not to award costs and expenses,

---

[767]   Judgment of 30 July 1998, paras 27-32.
[768]   Judgment of 3 May 2001, *E.P. v. Italy*, para. 6; judgment of 23 October 2001, *Tripodi*, para. 5. See also the judgment of 26 November 2002, *Frattini*, para. 3, and the judgment of 8 April 2003, *Perhirin and 29 Others*, para. 5, where the Court revised the judgment concerning Article 41 with respect to the moral damage awarded to the deceased applicants and their heirs.

because the applicant's lawyer had not provided the information requested.[769] In the *Grasso* Case the Court revised its principal judgment concerning Article 41 in the sense that the payment for moral damage should be paid to the legitimate heirs of the deceased applicant.[770] In the *Viola* Case the applicant's lawyer informed the Court that he had received news of the applicant's death. He, therefore, requested the Court to take the necessary steps in order to pay the just satisfaction to the applicant's widow. The Court agreed and revised its principal judgment in that sense.[771] In the *Corsi* Case the applicant requested revision of the judgment previously delivered by the Court concerning his application, in which the Court found a violation of Article 6(1) on account of the length of the proceedings but made no financial award in respect of damage. Noting that no sum had been awarded to the applicant because no claim had reached the Registry within the time allowed, and that no new information warranting revision of the earlier judgment had been received, the Court decided to dismiss the application for revision.[772]

In the *Stoiescu* Case the Court had held that there had been a violation of Article 6(1) on account of the lack of a fair hearing and the denial of access to court as well as a violation of Article 1 of Protocol No. 1. The Court had ordered the Romanian State to return the property in question to the applicant or, failing that, to pay him EUR 270,000 for pecuniary damage. It also awarded him EUR 6,000 for non-pecuniary damage.[773] The Romanian Government requested revision of the Court's judgment on account of the discovery of a new fact, namely that the applicant had lost his status as heir when his certificate of inheritance was declared null and void following an application by a third-party who inherited under the terms of a will. The Court noted that following proceedings in the Romanian courts between 1995 and 1999 the applicant's certificate of inheritance, which formed the basis of his claim for the return of the property, had been declared null and void. That decision could have decisively affected the admissibility decision and the judgment that had been handed down by the Court in the case in 2000 and 2003. The Court considered that, due to the lack of a computerised database of pending cases in Romania at the material time, the Romanian Government could not reasonably have been aware of events. However, the applicant had been involved in the proceedings concerning the validity of his certificate of inheritance for over seven years and could have informed the Court of the position before it gave its judgment, but had knowingly declined to do so. Since 20 May 1999, when the Bucharest Court of Appeal declared his certificate of inheritance null and void, the applicant had lost his status as his aunt's heir and his right to the return of the property. In those circumstances he could no longer claim to be a victim, within

---

[769] Judgment of 3 May 2001, para. 7.
[770] Judgment of 29 April 2003, para. 7.
[771] Judgment of 7 November 2002, paras 5-10.
[772] Judgment of 2 October 2003, para. 10.
[773] Judgment of 4 March 2003.

the meaning of the Convention, of a violation of his rights. Accordingly, the Court unanimously declared the Government's application for revision admissible. Consequently, it declared Mr Stoicescu's application inadmissible and revised the judgment of 4 March 2003 in full.[774]

2.9   ADVISORY JURISDICTION OF THE COURT

Since the entry into force of Protocol No. 2 on 21 September 1970, the Court has jurisdiction to give advisory opinions on legal questions concerning the interpretation of the Convention and the Protocols thereto (Article 1(1) of Protocol No. 2).

The advisory jurisdiction of a court may be of great importance for a uniform interpretation and the further development of the law. With regard to international law this is quite evident from the practice of the International Court of Justice and the Court of Justice of the European Communities. Via its advisory opinions the International Court of Justice has made an important contribution to the interpretation and the progressive development of the law of the United Nations in particular. The advisory jurisdiction of the International Court of Justice is formulated very broadly, without any conditions being made as to the scope of such advisory opinions. According to Article 96 of the Charter of the United Nations in conjunction with Article 65 of the Court's Statute, the Court may give advisory opinions 'on any legal question', so that the most varied issues of international law may be submitted to the Court. The jurisdiction of the Court of Justice of the European Communities is very limited as to its scope, but still comprises the field of the conclusion of treaties, which is of great importance for the Communities.

The practical importance of the advisory jurisdiction of the European Court of Human Rights, on the other hand, has been reduced to a minimum from the outset because of the restrictions which are put on it in the said Protocol. In fact, Article 1(2) provides that advisory opinions of the European Court:

> shall not deal with any question relating to the content or scope of the rights or freedoms defined in Section I of the Convention and in the Protocols thereto, or with any other question which the Commission, the Court, or the Committee of Ministers might have to consider in consequence of any such proceedings as could be instituted in accordance with the Convention.

A request for an advisory opinion must indicate in precise terms the question on which the opinion of the Court is sought, and in addition the date on which the Committee of Ministers decided to request an advisory opinion, as well as the names and addresses of the person or persons appointed by the Committee to give the Court any explana-

---

[774]   Judgment of 21 September 2004, para. 33.

tions which it may require (Rule 83 of the Rules of Court). A copy of the request is transmitted to the members of the Court (Rule 84 of the Rules of Court). The President lays down the time-limits for the filing of written comments or other documents (Rule 85 of the Rules of Court). The President also decides whether after the closure of the written procedure an oral hearing is to be held (Rule 86 of the Rules of Court).

Advisory opinions are given by majority vote of the plenary Court. They mention the number of judges constituting the majority, while any judge may attach to the opinion of the Court either a separate opinion, concurring with or dissenting from the advisory opinion, or a bare statement of dissent (Rule 88 of the Rules of Court).

The advisory opinion is read out by the President or his delegate at a public hearing, and certified copies are sent to the Committee of Ministers, the Contracting States and the Secretary General of the Council of Europe (Rules 89 and 90 of the Rules of Court).

If the Court considers that the request for an advisory opinion is not within its consultative competence, it so declares in a reasoned decision (Rule 87 of the Rules of Court).

It is obvious that a high degree of inventiveness is required for the formulation of a question of any importance which could stand the test of Article 1(2) of Protocol No. 2 and could, therefore, be submitted to the Court.

So far, at any rate, in June 2004 the Court delivered its first decision on its competence to give an advisory opinion. The request concerned the Commonwealth of Independent States (CIS) which was established in 1991 by a number of former Soviet Republics and at present comprises 12 States. It provides for the establishment of a Human Rights Commission of the Commonwealth of Independent States (the CIS Commission) to monitor the fulfilment of the human rights obligations entered into by States. The CIS Convention entered into force on 11 August 1998. In May 2001 the Parliamentary Assembly of the Council of Europe adopted a Recommendation that the Committee of Ministers request the Court to give an advisory opinion on the question of whether the CIS Commission should be regarded as 'another procedure of international investigation or settlement' within the meaning of Article 35(2)(b) of the Convention. The Parliamentary Assembly referred to 'the weakness of the CIS Commission as an institution for the protection of human rights' and expressed the view that it should not be regarded as a procedure falling within the scope of Article 35(2)(b).[775] The Committee of Ministers followed the recommendation and requested the Court to give an advisory opinion on "the co-existence of the Convention on Human Rights and Fundamental Freedoms of the Commonwealth of Independent States and the European Convention on Human Rights". The Court considered that the request for an advisory opinion related essentially to the specific question whether the CIS Com-

---

[775] Recommendation 1519(2001).

mission could be regarded as 'another procedure of international investigation or settlement' within the meaning of Article 35(2)(b) of the Convention and was satisfied that the request related to a legal question concerning the interpretation of the Convention, as required by Article 47(1). It was, however, necessary to examine whether the Court's competence was excluded by Article 47(2), on the ground that the request raised a 'question which the Court or the Committee of Ministers might have to consider in consequence of any such proceedings as could be instituted in accordance with the Convention'. The Court considered that 'proceedings' in this context referred to proceedings relating to applications lodged with it by States or individuals under Articles 33 and 34 of the Convention respectively and that the term 'question' extended to issues concerning the admissibility of applications under Article 35 of the Convention. It observed that the question whether an individual application should be declared inadmissible on the ground that the matter had already been submitted to 'another procedure of international investigation or settlement' had been addressed in a number of concrete cases in the past, in particular by the former European Commission of Human Rights.

In that connection the Court endorsed the Commission's approach, which showed that the examination of this question was not limited to a formal verification of whether the matter had been submitted to another procedure but extended, where appropriate, to an assessment of the nature of the supervisory body concerned, its procedure and the effect of its decisions. The question whether a particular procedure fell within the scope of Article 35(2)(b) was, therefore, one which the Court might have to consider in connection with proceedings instituted under the Convention, so that its competence to give an advisory opinion was in principle excluded. As far as the CIS Convention procedure was concerned the Court noted that several States Parties to the European Convention on Human Rights were members of the CIS and that three had signed and one had ratified the CIS Convention. Moreover, the rights set out in the CIS Convention were broadly similar to those in the European Convention on Human Rights. It could not, therefore, be excluded that the Court might have to consider, in the context of a future individual application, whether the CIS procedure was 'another procedure of international investigation or settlement'. The Court concluded that the request for an advisory opinion did not come within its advisory competence.[776]

It is submitted that it is regrettable that the advisory jurisdiction of the Court does not have a wider scope. Widening of the scope of the Court's advisory jurisdiction would, however, require amendment of Protocol No. 2. It would seem desirable that the subject-matter to which requests for an advisory opinion may relate be extended to any legal question concerning the Convention and the Protocols, though on condition

---

[776]   Decision of 2 June 2004.

that the giving of an advisory opinion by the Court must not amount to a decision of the Court under Section IV of the Convention and that the request must not directly relate to a dispute which is pending before the Court, while wide discretion ought to be given to the Court to comply with the request or not, on the basis of the character and/or the importance of the question submitted to it and in view of its case load.

Secondly, more entities should be entitled to submit a request for an advisory opinion. In the present situation only the Committee of Ministers may address a request for an advisory opinion to the Court (Article 1(1) of Protocol No. 2). In addition, the Parliamentary Assembly of the Council of Europe, and perhaps each of the individual Contracting States, might be considered for entitlement to make a request.

However, such changes depend on the consent of the Contracting States and the recent negotiations concerning Protocol No. 14 provide little evidence of willingness on their part to widen the scope of the advisory jurisdiction of the Court.

CHAPTER 3

THE SUPERVISORY TASK OF THE COMMITTEE OF MINISTERS

REVISED BY LEO ZWAAK

INDEX

3.1 INTRODUCTION

Unlike the Court, the Committee of Ministers was not set up in connection with the adoption of the European Convention. It is the policy-making and executive organ of the Council of Europe.[1]

One of the tasks of the Committee of Ministers concerning human rights results directly from the Statute of the Council of Europe, *viz.* from Article 8. By virtue of this article the Committee supervises the observance of the obligation contained in Article 3 of the Statute, according to which every member of the Council of Europe 'must

---

[1]   On the Committee, see also *supra* 1.10.

accept the principles of the rule of law and of the enjoyment by all persons within its jurisdiction of human rights and fundamental freedoms'. The more specific tasks of the Committee of Ministers with regard to human rights, however, have been laid down in the Convention.

3.2 THE DECISION-MAKING COMPETENCE UNTIL 1998

Apart from its function of supervising the judgments of the Court under the former Article 54 (the present Article 46(2)), before the entry into force of Protocol No. 11 the most important function of the Committee of Ministers was that which ensued from the former Article 32. In those instances where, after a complaint had been declared admissible by the Commission and a report on the merits had been sent to the Committee of Ministers, the case was not referred to the Court within a period of three months, the Committee of Ministers decided whether there had been a violation of the Convention. With respect to those cases the Committee of Ministers had a task comparable to that of the Court, although the procedure followed by the two organs differed quite substantially. The decisions of both organs were binding: the Contracting States had also undertaken to regard as binding the decisions taken by the Committee of Ministers under former Article 32(4). However, the State which was declared in default by the Committee of Ministers, had to take 'satisfactory' measures within a prescribed period (former Article 32(3)), while a decision of the Court had to be complied with directly (former Article 53).

Under former Article 32(2), when the Committee of Ministers had found that there had been a violation of the Convention, the Contracting State concerned was obliged to take the measures required by that decision within a period to be prescribed by the Committee of Ministers. The Committee of Ministers exercised this recommendatory power for the first time in the *Greek* Case.[2] During the examination in the *Houart* Case concerning a violation of Article 6 on the ground of the non-public character of disciplinary proceedings, the Committee of Ministers was informed by the Belgian Government that it accepted the opinion of the Commission and that, following two judgments of the Court,[3] it had changed its legislation to the effect that certain disciplinary proceedings would henceforth be held in public. The Committee of Ministers took note of this information and recommended that the Government

---

[2] Yearbook XII (1969), pp. 513-514.
[3] Judgment of 23 June 1981, *Le Compte, Van Leuven and De Meyere*, and judgment of 10 February 1983, *Albert and Le Compte*.

should pay the applicant a certain amount for the costs of the proceedings and for the defence.[4]

Since 1987 it had become standing practice for the Committee of Ministers to also recommend that a certain amount of money be paid to the original applicant for expenses incurred in the proceedings before the Commission or as just satisfaction for other damages suffered.[5]

In the first case of *Greece v. the United Kingdom* the Committee of Ministers decided that no further steps were needed after Greece and the United Kingdom had reached a settlement.[6] The Committee of Ministers was also inclined to stop the proceedings if no settlement between the parties had been reached but certain measures had improved the situation complained of. In the *Bramelid and Malmström* Case the applicants complained that they had been compelled to surrender their shares for a price below their real value and alleged, *inter alia*, that the arbitrators to whom their dispute was referred did not constitute a 'tribunal' within the meaning of Article 6(1) of the Convention. In its report the Commission had expressed the opinion that there had been a violation of Article 6(1) of the Convention.[7] During the examination of the case, the Government of Sweden informed the Committee of Ministers that the Swedish Parliament had adopted an amendment to the legislation according to which a party not satisfied with an arbitral decision could start a procedure before an ordinary court. The Committee of Ministers decided that, having regard to the information supplied by the Government of Sweden, no further action was called for.[8]

A situation which had not been provided for in former Article 32 of the Convention was the one which arose when the required two-thirds majority in the Committee of Ministers could not be found, either for the view that there had been an violation, or for the view that no violation had occurred. In such a case no decision as required by the former Article 32 was taken, while there was no question of some kind of settlement between the parties, nor was there any guarantee that the situation held by the Commission to conflict with the Convention, would be corrected or made good with respect to the victim by the respondent State. An example of the above situation was the *Huber* Case. In its report the Commission had expressed the opinion that Austria had violated Article 6(1) of the Convention with respect to the applicant.[9] The most important passage from the resolution of the Committee of Ministers in this case reads as follows: "Voting in accordance with the provisions of Article 32(1) of the

---

4   Res. DH(87)10 of 25 September 1987.
5   Res. DH(89)1 of 18 January 1989, *Sallustio*; Res. DH(89)6 of 2 March 1989, *Veit*.
6   Res. DH(59)12 of 20 April 1959, Council of Europe, *Collection of Resolutions adopted by the Committee of Ministers in application of Article 32 of the European Convention for the Protection of Human Rights and Fundamental Freedoms 1959-1981*, Strasbourg, 1981.
7   Report of 12 December 1983, D&R 38 (1984), p. 18 (38-41).
8   Res. DH(84)4 of 25 October 1984, *ibidem*, p. 43.
9   Report of 8 February 1973, D&R 2 (1975), p. 11 (29).

Convention, but without attaining the majority of two thirds of the members entitled to sit... [D]ecides therefore that no further action is called for in this case."[10] The power of the Committee of Ministers under former Article 32 was designed to guarantee that the supervisory procedure should ultimately result in a binding decision on whether or not there had been a violation. However, a consequence of the two-thirds requirement was that such a guarantee did not exist in practice, as was evident from the *Huber* Case and also from the *East Africans* Case,[11] the *Dores and Silveira* Case,[12] the *Dobbertin* Case[13] and the *Warwick* Case.[14]

When the Committee of Ministers found a violation of the Convention, it was obliged, under former Article 32(2), to prescribe a period within which the State in question was to take the measures required in the light of the Committee's decision. However, no cases have been reported in which such a period has been prescribed for measures other than remunerations. This might be accounted for partly by the fact that only in a few cases has the Committee of Ministers found a violation of the Convention which in its opinion called for further action other than the payment of satisfaction and costs.

The first case in which the Committee of Ministers would have had the opportunity to prescribe a compliance period for measures other than remuneration was the *Greek* Case, in which the Commission had concluded that a great many articles of the Convention had been violated.[15] However, before the Committee of Ministers had found in its resolution that there had been a violation of the Convention, Greece had already withdrawn from the Council of Europe and denounced the Convention.[16] Under these circumstances the Committee of Ministers observed that it was "called upon to deal with the case in conditions which are not precisely those envisaged in the Convention" and concluded "that in the present case there is no basis for further action under paragraph 2 of (former) Article 32 of the Convention".[17]

The only other occasion known to us, in which the Committee of Ministers considered imposing a compliance period for measures other than remuneration, was offered by the first two cases of *Cyprus v. Turkey*. On 21 October 1977 the Committee of Ministers decided in those cases that "events which occurred in Cyprus constitute violations of the Convention". In addition, the Committee of Ministers requested Turkey to take measures "in order to put an end to such violations as might continue to occur and so that such events are not repeated", and urged the parties "to resume

---

10   Res. DH(75)2 of 15 April 1975, Yearbook XVIII (1975), p. 325 (326).
11   Res. DH(77)2 of 21 October 1977, Yearbook XX (1977), p. 642 (644).
12   Res. DH(85)7 of 11 April 1985.
13   Res. DH(88)12 of 28 September 1988.
14   Res. DH(89)5 of 2 March 1989.
15   Yearbook XII (1969), p. 512.
16   *Ibidem.*
17   *Ibidem*, p. 513.

intercommunal talks".[18] By a resolution of 20 January 1979 the Committee of Ministers dealt with the matter again. It regretted to find that its request that the negotiations between the Turkish and the Greek-Cypriotic community be resumed, had not been complied with by the parties and subsequently decided "strongly to urge the parties to resume intercommunal talks under the auspices of the Secretary General of the United Nations in order to agree upon solutions on all aspects of the dispute", after which it stated that it considered this decision "as completing its consideration of the case Cyprus versus Turkey".[19] Cyprus and Turkey, contrary to former Article 32(4), had not given effect to the original decision of the Committee of Ministers. When the second resolution was adopted, there were no indications that they would as yet take the measures prescribed in the original decision. In fact, therefore, the Committee of Ministers backed out of the case and shirked its responsibilities under the Convention by shifting the matter to the Secretary General of the United Nations.

3.3   THE SUPERVISORY TASK SINCE 1998

3.3.1   GENERAL

Since the entry into force of Protocol No. 11 the Committee of Ministers performs only a supervisory task under the European Convention in connection with judgments of the Court. As pointed out above, Article 46(1) of the Convention provides that the Contracting Parties "undertake to abide by the final judgment of the Court in any case to which they are parties". This undertaking entails precise obligations for respondent States which are found to be in violation of the Convention. On the one hand they must take measures in favour of applicants to put an end to these violations and, as far as possible, erase their consequences (*restitutio in integrum*), while, on the other hand, they must take the measures needed to prevent new, similar violations. A primary obligation is the payment of just satisfaction (normally a sum of money), which the Court may award the applicant under Article 41 of the Convention and which covers, as the case may be, pecuniary and/or non-pecuniary damage and/or costs and expenses. The payment of such compensation is a strict obligation which is clearly defined in each judgment.[20]

According to Article 46(2) of the Convention, once the Court's final judgment has been transmitted to the Committee of Ministers, the latter invites the respondent State to inform it of the steps taken to pay the amounts awarded by the Court in respect of just satisfaction and, where appropriate, of the individual and general measures taken

---

[18]   Res. DH(79)1 of 20 January 1979, Yearbook XXII (1979), p. 440.
[19]   *Ibidem.*
[20]   See *supra* 2.6.1.

to abide by the judgment.[21] Once it has received this information, the Committee examines it closely. According to Rule 1(c) of the Rules of the Committee of Ministers for the application of Article 46(2) of the Convention, in case the chairmanship of the Committee of Ministers is held by the representative of a State which is a party to a case referred to the Committee of Ministers under Article 46(2), that representative shall relinquish the chairmanship during any discussion of that case.

The Directorate General of Human Rights helps the Committee of Ministers to carry out this responsibility under the Convention. In close co-operation with the authorities of the State concerned it considers what measures need to be taken in order to comply with the Court's judgment. At the Committee of Ministers' request it supplies opinions and advice based on the experience and practice of the Convention bodies.

In accordance with Rule 3(b) the Committee of Ministers shall examine whether any just satisfaction awarded by the Court has been paid, including, as the case may be, default interest. To the extent required the Committee shall also take into account the discretion of the State concerned to choose the means necessary to comply with the judgment. In all cases it will strive to ascertain whether individual measures have been taken to ensure that the violation has ceased and that the injured party is put, as far as possible, in the same situation as that party enjoyed prior to the violation of the Convention, and/or, whether general measures have been adopted, preventing new violations similar to that or those found or putting an end to continuing violations. It is the Committee of Ministers' well-established practice to keep cases on its agenda until the States concerned have taken satisfactory measures and to continue to require explanations or action.[22] When there is a delay in the execution of a judgment, the Committee of Ministers may adopt an interim resolution assessing the progress towards execution. As a rule this type of interim resolution contains information about any interim measures taken and indicates a timetable for the reforms designed to resolve the problem or problems raised by the judgment once and for all. If there are obstacles to execution, the Committee will adopt a more strongly worded interim resolution urging the authorities of the respondent State to take the necessary steps in order to ensure that the judgment is complied with.

According to Rule 4(b), if the State concerned informs the Committee of Ministers that it is not yet in a position to inform the Committee that the general measures

---

[21] See the Rules of the Committee of Ministers for the application of Article 46(2) of the Convention; http://www.coe.int/T/E/Human_rights/execution/. Unless indicated otherwise, in this chapter the Rules refer to this set of Rules.

[22] Rule 4(a) provides that, until the State concerned has provided information on the payment of the just satisfaction awarded by the Court or concerning possible individual measures, the case will be placed on the agenda of each human rights meeting of the Committee of Ministers, unless the Committee decides otherwise.

necessary to ensure compliance with the judgment have been taken, the case will be placed again on the agenda of a meeting of the Committee of Ministers taking place no more than six months later, unless the Committee decides otherwise; the same rule applies when this period expires and for each subsequent period. The Committee may bring its full weight to bear in order to induce the State concerned to comply with the Court's judgment. In practice the Committee of Ministers rarely resorts to political and diplomatic pressure but tends, instead, to function as a forum for constructive dialogue enabling States to work out satisfactory solutions with regard to the execution of judgments. On a number of occasions, however, interim resolutions have been drafted and adopted in order to pressurise States that had refused to afford applicants just satisfaction or to take specific measures in compliance with judgments. Under the Statute of the Council Europe tougher political sanctions could be considered such as suspension or termination of membership of the Council of Europe under Article 8 of the Statute, but obviously these are *ultima remedia* that will be considered in very exceptional circumstances only.

The Committee of Ministers is entitled to consider any communication from the injured party with regard to the payment of the just satisfaction or the taking of individual measures.[23]

With respect to access to information, Rule 5 provides as follows: "Without prejudice to the confidential nature of Committee of Ministers' deliberations, in accordance with Article 21 of the Statute of the Council of Europe, information provided by the State to the Committee of Ministers in accordance with Article 46 of the Convention and the documents relating thereto shall be accessible to the public, unless the Committee decides otherwise in order to protect legitimate public or private interests. In deciding such matters, the Committee of Ministers shall take into account reasoned requests by the State or States concerned, as well as the interest of an injured party or a third party not to disclose their identity."

In accordance with Rule 7 the Committee of Ministers may in the course of its supervision of the execution of a judgment adopt interim resolutions in order to provide information on the state of progress of the execution or, where appropriate, to express concern and/or to make relevant suggestions with respect to the execution. There may be situations in which the adverse consequences of the violation suffered by an injured party are not always adequately remedied by the payment of just satisfaction. Depending on the circumstances the execution of the judgment may also require the respondent State to take individual measures in favour of the applicant, such as the reopening of unfair proceedings if domestic law allows for such reopening, the destruction of information gathered in breach of the right to privacy or the revocation of a deportation order issued despite of the risk of inhumane treatment in the

---

[23]   Rule 6(a).

country of destination. It may also require general measures – such as an adaptation of legislation, rules and regulations, or of a judicial practice – to prevent new, similar violations.

After having established that the State concerned has taken all the necessary measures to abide by the judgment, the Committee adopts a resolution concluding that its functions under Article 46(2) of the Convention have been exercised.

Finally, Article 17 of the Statute of the Council of Europe provides for still another tool for the Committee in fulfilling its supervisory powers. According to that article, the Committee of Ministers may set up advisory or technical committees or commissions if it deems this desirable. The Committee of Ministers might proceed to do so for the purpose of taking evidence and other tasks within the context of its functions under the Convention.

3.3.2 SCOPE OF THE OBLIGATION TO COMPLY WITH A JUDGMENT

A judgment of the Court does not expressly order the respondent State to take specific measures to rectify the applicant's situation and prevent further violations. Under the Convention States are free to choose the means whereby they implement individual or general measures.

This is not to say, however, that the payment of just satisfaction is the only obligation that may derive from a judgment of the Court. To execute a judgment finding one or more violations of the Convention the respondent State may, depending on the circumstances, also be required to take certain measures. This may be, firstly, individual measures for the applicant's benefit, so as to end an unlawful situation, if that situation still continues, and to redress its consequence (*restitutio in integrum*),[24] and secondly, general measures to prevent further violations of a similar nature.[25]

This has been stressed by the Court in the *Papamichalopoulos* Case. There the Court pointed out that from the obligation under Article 46 of the Convention it follows, *inter alia*, that a judgment, in which the Court finds a breach, imposes on the respondent State a legal obligation not only to pay those concerned the sums awarded by way of just satisfaction, but also to choose, subject to supervision by the Committee

---

[24] For instance, the striking out of an unjustified criminal conviction from the criminal records, the granting of a residence permit or the reopening of impugned domestic proceedings: Recommendation No. R (2000) 2 of the Committee of Ministers to the member States on the re-examination or reopening of certain cases at domestic level following judgments of the European Court of Human Rights, of 19 January 2000.

[25] For instance, legislative or regulatory amendments, changes of case law or administrative practice or publication of the Court's judgment in the language of the respondent State and its dissemination to the authorities concerned.

of Ministers, the general and/or, if appropriate, individual measures to be taken in their domestic legal order to put an end to the violation found by the Court and to redress so far as possible its effects.[26]

3.3.3 JUST SATISFACTION

If the Court has decided that the respondent State has to pay just satisfaction under Article 41 of the Convention within three months of the delivery of its judgment, the Committee of Ministers will examine the case at its meeting following the delivery of that judgment.[27] In a number of cases against Italy concerning violations of the requirement of a reasonable length of proceedings, the Committee had recommended that the Government pay, within a time-limit of three months, just satisfaction to the applicants. The Italian Government disagreed with the proposals of the Committee of Ministers and refused to pay the applicants. The Committee subsequently noted at its next meeting that, although the time-limit had been extended, the Government still had not paid the sums it had agreed to pay following the Committee's recommendation. It decided to strongly urge the Government to proceed without delay to pay the specified amount to the applicants. It further decided, if need be, to resume consideration of these cases at each of its forthcoming meetings.[28] In its subsequent session the Committee of Ministers again adopted resolutions in the Italian cases and then firmly stated that, in accordance with (former) Article 32(2) of the Convention, the Government of Italy was to pay the applicants before a fixed date a certain amount in respect of just satisfaction. The Committee of Ministers invited the Government to inform it of the measures taken in consequence of its decision, having regard to the Government's obligations under (former) Article 32(4) of the Convention to abide by it.[29] Finally, on 17 September 1992 the Committee of Ministers ended the consideration of these cases by declaring, after having taken note of the measures taken by the Italian Government, that it had exercised its functions under (former) Article 32 of the Convention.[30]

---

[26]   Judgment of 31 October 1995, para. 34; see also the judgment of 13 July 2000, *Scozzari and Giunta v. Italy*, para. 249.

[27]   The three month time-limit has become standing practice since the judgment of 28 August 1991, *Moreira de Azevedo*, para. 1 of the operative part of the judgment.

[28]   Res. DH(91)12 of 6 June 1991, *Azzi*; Res. DH(91)13 of 6 June 1991, *Lo Giacco*; Res. DH(91)21 of 27 September 1991, *Savoldi*; Res. DH(91)22 of 27 September 1991, *Van Eesbeeck*; Res. DH(91)23 of 27 September 1991, *Sallustio*; Res. DH 91(24) of 27 September 1991, *Minniti*.

[29]   Res. DH(92)3 of 20 February 1992, *Lo Giacco*; Res. DH92(4) of 20 February 1992, *Savoldi*; Res. DH(92)5 of 20 February 1992, *Van Eesbeeck*; Res. DH(92)6 of 20 February 1992, *Sallustio*; Res. DH(92)7 of 20 February 1992, *Minniti*.

[30]   Res. DH(92)45 of 17 September 1992, *Azzi*; Res. DH(92)46 of 17 September 1992, *Lo Giacco*, Res. DH(92)47 of 17 September 1992, *Savoldi*; Res. DH(92)48 of 17 September 1992, *Van Eesbeeck*; Res. DH(92)49 of 17 September 1992, *Sallustio*; Res. DH(92)50 of 17 September 1992, *Minniti*.

In case the respondent State is unable to show proof of payment, the case will stay on the agenda of the Committee of Ministers and will be dealt with at every subsequent meeting of the Committee until it is satisfied that the payment has been made in full.

It has become practice that, from the expiry of the initial three-month period set for the payment until the final settlement, interest should be payable on the amount at a rate equal to the marginal lending rate of the European Central Bank during the default period.[31]

On the whole the respondent States are willing to pay the compensation awarded by the Court to the applicant. However, apart from the above-mentioned reasonable-time cases concerning Italy, in a few instances, such as in the *Stran Greek Refineries and Stratis Andreas* Case and the *Loizidiou* Case, the Committee of Ministers had to deal with the unwillingness of the respondent State to pay compensation.

After delivery of the judgment of the Court in the *Stran Greek Refineries and Stratis Andreas* Case[32] the Greek Government informed the Committee of Ministers that, considering the size of the just satisfaction awarded to the applicants and the economic problems in Greece, it was not able to make immediate full payment. The Committee of Ministers strongly urged the Greek Government to pay the amount corresponding to the value of just satisfaction as of March 1995 and decided, if need be, to resume consideration of the case at each of its forthcoming meetings.[33] Subsequently, in September 1996, the Chairman of the Committee of Ministers wrote to the Minister of Foreign Affairs of Greece underlining the fact that the credibility and effectiveness of the mechanism for the collective enforcement of human rights established under the Convention is based on the respect of the obligations freely entered into by the Contracting Parties and in particular on respect for the decisions of the supervisory bodies. According to its Final Resolution of 20 March 1997 the Committee of Ministers was informed that the Greek Government had transferred 30,863,828.50 US dollars to the applicants, which sum the applicants were entitled to enjoy without any interference whatsoever. The Committee, having satisfied itself that the amount paid, increased in order to provide compensation for the loss of value caused by the delay in payment, corresponded to the just satisfaction awarded by the Court, declared that it had exercised its supervisory function under the Convention.[34]

In its Interim Resolution concerning the judgment in the *Loizidou* Case, the Committee of Ministers noted that the Government of Turkey had indicated that the sums awarded by the Court could only be paid to the applicant in the context of a

---

[31]   Judgment of 18 June 2002, *Önyerildiz*, para. 168; judgment of 30 November 2004, *Gumusten*, para. 34; judgment of 30 November 2004, *Klyakhin*, para. 134; judgment of 2 December 2004, *Yaroslavtsev*, para. 42.

[32]   Judgment of 9 December 1994.

[33]   Interim Resolution of 15 May 1996, DH (96) 251.

[34]   Final Resolution of 20 March 1997, DH (97) 184.

global settlement of all property cases in Cyprus. It concluded that the conditions of payment envisaged by the Government of Turkey could not be considered to be in conformity with the obligations flowing from the Court's judgment. It strongly urged Turkey to review its position and to pay the just satisfaction awarded in this case in accordance with the conditions set out by the Court so as to ensure that Turkey, as a High Contracting Party, met its obligations under the Convention.[35]

In its second Interim Resolution the Committee once more stressed that Turkey had had ample time to fulfil in good faith its obligations in the case concerned. It emphasised that the failure on the part of a High Contracting Party to comply with a judgment of the Court was unprecedented. It declared that the refusal of Turkey to execute the judgment of the Court demonstrated a manifest disregard for its international obligations, both as a High Contracting Party to the Convention and as a Member State of the Council of Europe. In view of the gravity of the matter it strongly insisted that Turkey comply fully and without any further delay with the Court's judgment of 28 July 1998.[36] At its subsequent meeting on 26 June 2001 the Committee declared that it very deeply deplored the fact that Turkey still had not complied with its obligations under the judgment of the Court.[37]

At its meeting on 12 November 2003 the Committee urged the Turkish Government to reconsider its position and to pay without any conditions whatsoever the just satisfaction awarded to the applicant by the Court, within one week at the latest. It declared the Committee's resolve to take all adequate measures against Turkey, if the Turkish Government failed once more to pay the just satisfaction to the applicant.[38] On 12 December 2003 the Chairman of the Committee of Ministers announced that the Turkish Government had executed the judgment of 28 July 1998 in the *Loizidou* Case by paying to the applicant the sum which had been awarded to her by the Court in respect of just satisfaction.[39]

3.3.4   INDIVIDUAL MEASURES

The need to take individual measures at the domestic level, in addition to the payment of pecuniary compensation if determined by the Court, is considered by the Committee of Ministers where the established breach continues to have negative consequences for the applicant, which cannot be redressed through pecuniary compensation.

---

[35]   Interim Resolution of 6 October 1999, DH (99) 680.
[36]   Interim Resolution of 24 July 2000, DH (2000) 105.
[37]   Interim Resolution of 26 June 2002, DH (2001) 80.
[38]   Interim Resolution of 12 November 2003, DH (2003) 174.
[39]   Press Release Council of Europe: http://press.coe.int/cp/2003/620a(2003).htm.

The reopening of proceedings at the domestic level may constitute an important means of redressing the effects of a violation of the Convention, where there were serious shortcomings in the procedure before the national courts. In fact, the reopening of domestic proceedings was also within the powers of the Committee of Ministers to suggest during the period before the entry into force of Protocol No. 11, in cases which had not been referred to the Court and where the Committee of Ministers acted under the former Article 32 as the final arbiter.

In the joint cases of *Pataki* and *Durnshirn* the applicants had alleged violation of the right to a fair trial, because they were not represented in a particular phase of the criminal proceedings against them, whereas the Public Prosecutor was present.[40] The Commission considered that the Austrian Penal Code conflicted with the Convention on this point. In the last phase of the proceedings before the Commission Austria amended its legislation to eliminate this conflict. At the same time a temporary arrangement was made which enabled the applicants to have their case re-examined by the Austrian judicial authorities. At the suggestion of the Commission, the Committee of Ministers then expressed its satisfaction with the amendment of the law and decided that no further steps were necessary.[41]

In the *Unterpertinger* Case the applicant claimed that he had been convicted on the basis of testimony, namely statements made to the police by his former wife and stepdaughter, in respect of which his defence rights had been appreciably restricted. The Court found a violation of Article 6.[42] The Austrian Government informed the Committee of Ministers that the Austrian Supreme Court, on the ground of unlawful refusal to admit supplementary evidence, had quashed the judgment of the Court of Appeal by which the latter had dismissed the applicant's appeal against his conviction by the Innsbruck Regional Court. As a result, the case was referred back to the Innsbruck Court of Appeal for re-examination and decision. That court quashed the applicant's conviction and acquitted him on the ground of lack of evidence. The Committee of Ministers decided, on the basis of the information supplied by the Austrian Government, that it had exercised its supervisory function.[43]

In the *Barbarà Messegué and Jarbardo* Case the Court found a violation on the ground that the applicants had not received a fair trial.[44] The Spanish Government informed the Committee of Ministers that the Constitutional Court had ordered the reopening of the proceedings before the *Audiencia Nacional* in the applicants' case. That court acquitted the applicants as there was not sufficient evidence against them. The problems of a general nature raised by the Court in its judgment had been resolved

40   Yearbook VI (1963), p. 714 (738).
41   *Ibidem*, p. 730. See also Res. DH(64)1 of 5 June 1964 concerning the *Glaser* Case.
42   Judgment of 6 December 1988, para. 33.
43   Resolution of 18 January 1989, DH (89) 002.
44   Judgment of 6 December 1988 on the merits, para. 89; judgment of 13 June 1994 on the question of just satisfaction, para. 16.

by legislative changes and by the development of the case law of the Constitutional Court and the Supreme Court. The Committee of Ministers agreed and decided that Spain had fulfilled its obligations.[45]

In the *Open Door and Dublin Well Women* Case the Court found a violation of Article 10 in that the High Court's injunction had prohibited the dissemination of information to pregnant women about abortion services in the United Kingdom.[46] The High Court lifted the injunction with regard tot the Dublin Well Women Centre. Having taken note of the information supplied by the Irish Government, the Committee of Ministers decided that it had exercised its supervisory function.[47]

In the *Daktaras* Case the Court held that there were insufficient guarantees to exclude all reasonable doubt as to the impartiality of the Supreme Court which had examined the applicant's cassation petition.[48] The Government informed the Committee of Ministers that the domestic proceedings had been reopened on 29 January 2002 by a decision of the Criminal Chamber of the Supreme Court. This reopening was made possible by the application of the new section of the Code of Criminal Procedure called "Reopening of criminal cases following a judgment of the European Court of Human Rights", which entered into force on 15 October 2001. Following the reopening of the national proceedings, on 2 April 2002 a plenary session of the Criminal Chamber of the Supreme Court annulled the previous cassation judgment. According to the new judgment, the cassation petition submitted by the President of the Criminal Chamber of the Supreme Court was not taken into account. The cassation petition submitted by Mr Daktaras, as well as that of his legal representative, were rejected.[49]

Sometimes reopening of the domestic proceedings is the only form of *restitutio in integrum* regarding a violation of Article 6 by previous proceedings. In view of the problem raised in certain cases of the lack of appropriate national legislation, the Committee of Ministers has adopted a recommendation to Member States on the re-examination or reopening of certain cases at the domestic level following judgments of the Court.[50] In the recommendation the Committee of Ministers invites the Contracting Parties to ensure that adequate possibilities exist at the national level to achieve, as far as possible, *restitutio in integrum*. It further encourages them "to examine their national legal systems with a view to ensuring that there exist adequate

---

45   Resolution of 16 November 1994, DH (94) 84.
46   Judgment of 29 October 1992, para. 80.
47   Resolution of 25 June 1996, DH (96) 368.
48   Judgment of 10 October 2000, para. 38.
49   Resolution of 6 July 2004, DH(2004)43.
50   Recommendation of 19 January 2000, on the re-examination or reopening of certain cases at domestic level following judgments of the European Court of Human Rights, R (2000) 2.

possibilities of re-examination of the case, including reopening of proceedings, in instances where the Court has found a violation of the Convention, especially where:

(i)   the injured party continues to suffer very serious negative consequences because of the outcome of the domestic decision at issue, which are not adequately remedied by the just satisfaction and cannot be rectified except by re-examination or reopening, and

(ii)   the judgment of the Court leads to the conclusion that

   (a)   the impugned domestic decision is on the merits contrary to the Convention, or

   (b)   the violation found is based on procedural errors or shortcomings of such gravity that a serious doubt is cast on the outcome of the domestic proceedings complained of."

In the explanatory memorandum to this recommendation it is indicated that, as regards the terms, the recommendation uses "re-examination" as the generic term. The term "reopening of proceedings" denotes the reopening of court proceedings as a specific means of re-examination. Violations of the Convention may be remedied by different measures ranging from administrative re-examination of a case (*e.g.* granting a residence permit previously refused) to the full reopening of judicial proceedings (*e.g.* in cases of criminal convictions). The recommendation applies primarily to judicial proceedings where existing law may pose the greatest obstacles to reopening. The recommendation is, however, also applicable to administrative or other measures or proceedings, although legal obstacles will usually be less serious in these areas.

Sub-paragraph (i) of the recommendation is intended to cover the situation in which the injured party continues to suffer very serious negative consequences, not capable of being remedied by just satisfaction, because of the outcome of domestic proceedings. It applies in particular to persons who have been sentenced to lengthy prison sentences and who are still in prison when the Court examines the 'case'. It also applies, however, in other areas, such as when a person is unjustifiably denied certain civil or political rights (in particular in case of loss of, or non-recognition of legal capacity or personality, bankruptcy declarations, or prohibitions of political activity), if a person is expelled in violation of his or her right to family life, or if a child has been unjustifiably forbidden contact with his or her parents. It is understood that a direct causal link must exist between the violation found and the continuing suffering of the injured party.

Sub-paragraph (ii) is intended to indicate, in cases where the above-mentioned conditions are met, the kind of violations in which re-examination of the case or reopening of the proceedings will be of particular importance. Examples of situations mentioned under item (a) are criminal convictions violating Article 10, because the statements characterized as criminal by the national authorities constitute a legitimate exercise of the injured party's freedom of expression, or violating Article 9 because the behaviour characterised as criminal is a legitimate exercise of freedom of religion. Examples of situations mentioned under item (b) are those where the injured party did not have the time and facilities to prepare his or her defence in criminal proceedings, where the conviction was based on statements extracted under torture or on material which the injured party had no possibility of verifying, or where in civil proceedings the parties were not treated with due respect for the principle of equality of arms.

As appears from the text of the recommendation, any such shortcomings must be of such gravity that serious doubt is cast on the outcome of the domestic proceedings. The recommendation does not deal with the problem of who ought to be empowered to ask for reopening or re-examination. Considering that the basic aim of the recommendation is to ensure adequate redress for the victims of certain grave violations of the Convention found by the Court, the logic of the system implies that the individuals concerned should have the right to submit the necessary requests to the competent court or other domestic organ. Considering the different traditions of the Contracting Parties, no provision to this effect has, however, been included in the recommendation. The recommendation also does not address the special problem of 'mass cases', i.e. cases in which a certain structural deficiency leads to a great number of violations of the Convention. It was considered preferable to leave it to the State concerned to decide it in such cases reopening or re-examination is a realistic solution, or whether other measures are more appropriate.

Another example of an individual measure that may be called for following a judgment is cancellation of a person's criminal record in respect of a conviction that led to a violation of the Convention. Such a measure may be taken, for instance, where the applicant has already served a sentence and the reference to his conviction in his judicial record is the only remaining consequence of the violation. In the *Marijnissen* Case the Commission had found a violation of the reasonable time requirement under Article 6.[51] The case was not referred to the Court, so the Committee of Ministers had to act under (former) Article 32 as the final supervisory body. It agreed with the Commission. The Government of the Netherlands informed the Committee of Ministers that it accepted its decision; the sentence served against the applicant would not be executed and no mention of this sentence would appear in the applicant's judicial record. The Committee of Ministers decided that no further action was called for in this case.[52]

In the *Van Mechelen* Case the Court had found a violation of Article 6(3)(d) on the ground that the applicants' conviction was based to a decisive extent on statements given by unidentified witnesses who were members of the police and whose reliability

---

[51]   Report of 12 March 1984, D&R 40 (1985), p. 83.
[52]   Resolution of 25 February 1985, DH (85) 004

could not be tested by the defence.[53] During the examination of the case by the Committee of Ministers the Government of the Netherlands gave the Committee information about the measures taken with a view to remedying the applicants' situation and preventing new violations. The applicants were provisionally released on 25 April 1997 on the orders of the Minister of Justice and were subsequently, by letter of 22 July 1997, informed that they would not be required to serve the remainder of their sentences. Furthermore, the reasons why the sentences were not executed in their entirety were mentioned in their criminal records.[54]

In the *Ben Yaacoub* Case a friendly settlement was reached as the Belgian Government had decided to lift, as of 30 August 1992, the effects of an expulsion order made against the applicant.[55] The Belgian Government notified the Committee of Ministers of the date on which the effects of the expulsion order against the applicant were lifted. Prior to that date, it undertook to examine any request for safe-conduct enabling the applicant to enter Belgium, provided that it was based on valid reasons and was supported by appropriate evidence. The Committee of Ministers decided to resume consideration of this case at its first meeting after 30 August 1992, or earlier if appropriate.[56]

In the Case of *D. v. the United Kingdom* the Court had held that the applicant's proposed removal from the United Kingdom to St. Kitts would place him at risk of reduced life expectancy, of inhuman and degrading treatment and of invasion of his physical integrity.[57] The Government of the United Kingdom gave the Committee information about the measures taken to avoid the impending violation as found in the judgment. The applicant was granted an indefinite leave which would permit him to remain in the country, where he would continue to receive adequate medical treatment and palliative care.[58]

In the Case of *A.P and T.P. v. Switzerland* the Court had found a violation of Article 6(2) since, irrespective of any personal guilt, the applicants had been convicted, as heirs, of an offence allegedly committed by a deceased person.[59] The Swiss Government informed the Committee of Ministers that by a judgment of the Federal Court the case of the applicants had been revised. Following this revision the cantonal tax authorities were obliged to reimburse the fine imposed on the applicants, with interest accruing on the sum. The Committee of Ministers decided to resume consideration of the case as far as general measures were concerned when the legislative reforms had been carried out, or at the latest at its first meeting in 2001.[60]

---

[53] Judgment of 23 April 1997, para. 66.
[54] Resolution 19 February 1999, DH (99) 124.
[55] Judgment of 27 November 1987, para. 14.
[56] Resolution of 29 September 1988, DH (88) 13.
[57] Judgment of 2 May 1997, para. 54.
[58] Resolution of 18 February 1998, DH (98) 10.
[59] Judgment of 29 August 1997, para. 48.
[60] Interim Resolution of 18 January 1999, DH (99) 110.

In the *Vasilescu* Case, which related to, firstly, the unlawful seizure and the continued retention of valuables with respect to which the domestic courts had accepted the applicant's property rights and, secondly, the lack of access to an independent tribunal that could order their return, the Court had found a violation of Article 6(1) and Article 1 of Protocol No. 1.[61] The Romanian Government informed the Committee of Ministers that the Constitutional Court of Romania had rendered a decision declaring that, in order to comply with the Constitution, Article 278 of the Code of Criminal Procedure – concerning the right to appeal decisions of the public prosecutor – would be interpreted to the effect that a person who had an interest could challenge before a court any measure decided by the prosecutor. This decision became final and binding under Romanian law with its publication in the Official Journal of Romania and accordingly enforceable *erga omnes*. The Government considered that similar cases – where the valuables in question had been confiscated without any order from a competent judicial authority – were not likely to recur. The Committee of Ministers decided to resume consideration of the case until legislative reforms had been carried out, or at the latest at one of its meetings at the beginning of 2001.[62]

In the Case of the *Socialist Party v. Turkey*, relating to the dissolution of this party on account of certain statements made in 1991 by one of the applicants, the Party's chairman, Mr Perinçek, the Court had found a violation of Article 11.[63] The Committee of Ministers noted that it had been informed that in a judgment of 8 July 1998 – i.e. after the judgment of the Court – the Court of Cassation of Turkey had confirmed a criminal conviction imposed on Mr. Perinçek by the First State Security Court of Ankara on 15 October 1996, according to which the sanction of dissolution of the party also carried with it personal criminal responsibility. It noted, furthermore, that by virtue of this conviction, Mr Perinçek had been sentenced to a 14-month prison sentence, which he started to serve on 29 September 1998. He had furthermore been banned from further political activities. The Committee of Ministers insisted on Turkey's obligation under Article 53 (the present Article 46) of the Convention to erase, without delay, through action by the competent Turkish authorities, all the consequences resulting from the applicant's criminal conviction on 8 July 1998 and decided, if need be, to resume consideration of the case at each forthcoming meeting.[64] During its next session the Committee of Ministers noted with regret that action had still not been taken by the Turkish authorities to give full effect to the judgment of the Court and to the Committee's interim resolution. It urged Turkey, without further delay, to take all necessary action to remedy the situation of the former Chairman of the Socialist Party, Mr Perinçek.[65]

---

[61] Judgment of 22 May 1998, paras. 41 and 54.
[62] Interim Resolution of 8 October 1999, DH (99) 676.
[63] Judgment of 25 May 1998, para. 54.
[64] Interim Resolution of 4 March 1999, DH (99) 245.
[65] Interim Resolution of 28 July 1999, DH (99) 529.

In the area of the execution of the Court's judgments positive developments were taken note of in the *Sadak, Zana, Dicle* and *Dogan* Cases against Turkey. After the decision by the Ankara Court of Cassation suspending the prison sentences of the four Turkish former members of Parliament, this court decided, on 14 July 2004, to quash the Ankara State Security Court's verdict in the retrial of four former Kurdish MPs, and to order a fresh hearing in an ordinary court. The Committee of Ministers noted that the Court of Cassation had found that shortcomings identified by the European Court of Human Rights in the 1994 trial had not been properly addressed in the retrial proceedings. It considered this to be a convincing example of the positive impact of recent constitutional amendments, which were aimed at ensuring the direct application of the European Convention of Human Rights to the Turkish legal system.[66]

With respect to the fourth inter-State case of *Cyprus against Turkey* the Committee of Ministers had noted that after a period of some years during which progress seemed rare, at recent meetings concrete information had been presented making it possible to register progress towards the execution of this complex and controversial judgment. In particular, the Committee of Ministers had been informed that a school had opened for Greek Cypriot pupils in the north of the island and that the Committee on Missing Persons had taken steps to bring its terms of reference further into line with the requirements of the Court judgment. That said, there were obviously still serious issues to be resolved.[67]

3.3.5 GENERAL MEASURES

In certain cases it is clear from the circumstances that the violation resulted from particular domestic legislation or from the absence of legislation. In such cases, in order to comply with the Court's judgments, the State concerned must either amend existing laws or introduce appropriate new ones. In many cases, however, the structural problem that led to a violation, lies not in an obvious conflict between domestic law and the Convention but rather in case law of the national courts. In that situation a change of case law of the national courts may preclude possible future violations. When courts adjust their legal stance and their interpretation of national law to meet the demands of the Convention, as reflected in the Court's judgments, they implement these judgments by virtue of their domestic law. In this way further similar violations may be effectively prevented. However, it is precondition that the judgment concerned is published and circulated among the national authorities, including the courts, and accompanied, where appropriate, by an explanatory circular.

---

[66] Documents of the Committee of Ministers, CM/AS (2004)9 of 4 October 2004.
[67] *Ibidem.*

Following the judgment of the Court in the *Jersild* Case, the Danish Supreme Court acquitted, in a judgment of 28 October 1994, a journalist who had been charged with invasion of privacy by entering an area without permission which was not accessible to the public. In the City Court of Copenhagen and in the Eastern Division of the High Court the journalist had been found guilty as charged. However, the Supreme Court acquitted the journalist as it found that this result was most in keeping with the jurisprudence of the European Court of Human Rights concerning Article 10. In this connection the Supreme Court made a special reference to the *Jersild* judgment as the latest authority. Moreover, following the *Jersild* judgment of the Court, the Special Court of Revision decided on 24 January 1995 to allow the case against, *inter alia*, Mr Jersild to be reopened.[68]

In the *Vogt* Case the Court had held that the exclusion from public service in the Land of Lower-Saxony, on account of the applicants' political activities as a member of the German Communist Party, constituted a violation of her right to freedom of expression and of her freedom of association and also discrimination in the enjoyment of these rights.[69] The German Government informed the Committee of Ministers that the German Federal Ministry of the Interior had transmitted the judgment of the Court with a letter to the Länder indicating that the authorities would have to examine all future cases of this kind in detail, in the light of the Court's judgment, in order to prevent the repetition of violations similar to those found in the present case. The ministry was, however, of the opinion that it would not be possible to reopen old dismissal procedures on the basis of judgments of the Court. The Government noted further that the Convention is directly applicable in German law and considered that the German courts will not fail, in case they were to be seized with new cases of the same kind, to interpret the law in accordance with the judgments of the European Court.[70]

In the *Gaygusuz* Case a Turkish national complained about violation of Articles 6(1), 8 and 14 of the Convention and of Article 1 of Protocol No. 1 by the Austrian authorities' refusal to grant emergency assistance to the applicant, an unemployed man who had exhausted entitlement to unemployment benefit, on the ground that he did not have Austrian nationality. The Court found a violation of Article 14 in conjunction of Article 1 of Protocol No. 1.[71] The Austrian Government informed the Committee of Ministers that the Austrian Constitutional Court, which was seized with several complaints regarding the constitutionality of the discrimination against foreigners provided for in Articles 33 and 34 of the Unemployment Insurance Act, had changed its earlier jurisprudence according to which benefits such as emergency assistance did

---

[68]   Resolution of 11 September 1995, DH(95)212.
[69]   Judgment of 26 September 1995, paras. 61 and 68.
[70]   Resolution of 28 January 1997, DH(97)12.
[71]   Judgment of 16 September 1996, para. 52.

not fall under Article 1 of Protocol No 1, and had aligned it with that of the Court in the *Gaygasuz* Case. In consequence, the Austrian Constitutional Court had annulled with immediate effect the two provisions in question insofar as they reserved the right to emergency assistance to Austrian nationals. It had found it appropriate in the circumstances to deviate from its usual practice of postponing the full effects of its judgment to a future date. Immediately after this judgment the Austrian Parliament had adopted a new law providing that the amendments to the Unemployment Insurance Act entered into force on 1 April 1998 and not on 1 January 2000.[72]

In the *Kalashnikov* Case concerning the poor conditions in which the applicant was held in detention before trial between 1995 and 2000, due in particular to severe prison overcrowding and to an insanitary environment, and concerning the excessive length of both this detention and the criminal proceedings, the Court had found a violation of Articles 3, 5(1) and 6(1).[73] The Russian Government, in its information to the Committee of Ministers, referred in particular to two major reforms which had already resulted in significant improvement of the conditions of pre-trial detention and their progressive alignment with the Convention's requirements. The Committee of Ministers decided to examine at one of its meetings, no later than 2004, whether any further progress had been achieved in the adoption of the general measures necessary to effectively prevent these kind of violations of the Convention.[74]

With respect to the length of proceedings in Italy the Court has been faced with continuous problems. In the *Bottazzi* Case the Court drew attention to the fact that since 25 June 1987, the date of the *Capuano* Case, it had delivered 65 judgments in which it had found violations of Article 6(1) in proceedings exceeding a 'reasonable time' in the civil courts of the various regions of Italy. Similarly, under former Articles 31 and 32 of the Convention, more than 1,400 reports of the Commission resulted in resolutions by the Committee of Ministers finding Italy in breach of Article 6 for the same reason. The frequency with which violations were found showed that there was an accumulation of identical breaches which were sufficiently numerous to amount not merely to isolated incidents. Such breaches reflected a continuing situation that had not yet been remedied and in respect of which litigants had no domestic remedy. This accumulation of breaches accordingly constituted a practice that was incompatible with the Convention.[75]

In its Interim Resolution the Committee of Ministers recalled that excessive delays in the administration of justice constitute an important danger, in particular to respect for the rule of law. The Committee further noted that the question of Italy's adoption

---

[72]   Resolution of 12 November 1998, DH(98)372.
[73]   Judgment of 15 July 2002, paras. 103, 121 and 135.
[74]   Interim Resolution of 4 June 2003, DH (2003) 123.
[75]   Judgment of 28 July 1999, para. 22; see also judgment of 28 July 1999, *Di Mauro*, para. 23.

of general measures to prevent new violations of the Convention of this kind had been before the Committee of Ministers since the judgments of the Court in the 1990s and, therefore, highlighted the existence of serious structural problems in the functioning of the Italian judicial system.[76] At its session in October 2000 the Committee of Ministers noted with satisfaction that recently the highest Italian authorities had manifested – both at the national level and before the organs of the Council of Europe – their solemn commitment to eventually finding an effective solution to the situation.

The Committee also expressed appreciation regarding the progress made in the implementation of major reform to the Italian judicial system, undertaken in order to find long-term remedies, to ensure special expediency in the treatment of the oldest and most deserving cases and to alleviate the burden of the Court. It noted that the reforms, undertaken by the Italian authorities, had included three different lines of action: 1. deep structural modernisation of the judicial system for better long-term efficiency (notably through the introduction of Article 6 of the Convention into the Italian Constitution, the streamlining of the jurisdictions of the civil and administrative courts, the increased reliance on the single judge, the creation of the office of justices of the peace and also the subsequent extension of their competence to minor criminal offences, new simplified dispute settlement mechanisms, and the modernisation of a number of procedural rules); 2. special actions dealing with the oldest cases pending before the national civil courts or aiming at improvements which, while being of a structural nature, could already produce positive effects in the near future (in particular the creation of provisional court chambers composed of honorary judges, entrusted with the solution of civil cases pending since May 1995, an important increase in the number of judges and administrative personnel and two important resolutions by the Supreme Council of the Magistrature laying down a number of monitoring mechanisms and guidelines for judges in order to prevent further unreasonably long proceedings and also in order to speed up those which have already been incriminated by the European Court of Human Rights); and 3. reduction of the flow of applications to the Court and the speeding up of compensation procedures by means of the creation of a domestic remedy in cases of excessive length of procedures.

The Committee acknowledged that the measures in the first group, aiming at a structural reform of the entire Italian judicial system, could not be expected to produce major effects before a reasonable time had elapsed, although it was already possible to see the first signs of a positive trend in the statistics recently provided to the Committee of Ministers by the Italian authorities. The Committee concluded that Italy, while making undeniable efforts to solve the problem and having adopted measures of various kinds which allowed concrete hope for an improvement within a reasonable

---

[76]   See in this respect Resolution of 11 July 1997, DH(97)336; Interim Resolutions of 15 July 1999, DH (99) 436 and DH (99) 437.

time, had not, so far, thoroughly complied with its obligations to abide by the Court's judgments and the Committee of Ministers' decisions finding violations of Article 6 of the Convention on account of the excessive length of judicial proceedings. It called upon the Italian authorities, in view of the gravity and persistence of the problem, to maintain the high priority now given to the reform of the Italian judicial system and to continue to make rapid and visible progress in the implementation of the reforms; to continue their examination of further measures that could help effectively prevent new violations of the Convention on account of the excessive length of judicial proceedings; and to inform the Committee of Ministers with the greatest diligence of all steps undertaken to this effect. It decided to continue the attentive examination of this problem until the reforms of the Italian judicial system had become thoroughly effective and a reversal of the trend at the domestic level had be fully confirmed.

Meanwhile, the Committee of Ministers resumed its consideration of the progress made, at least at yearly intervals, on the basis of a comprehensive report to be presented each year by the Italian authorities.[77] In concluding its examination of the third annual report presented by the Italian authorities, on 29 September 2004, the Committee of Ministers noted with concern that an important number of reforms announced since 2000 were still pending for adoption and/or for effective implementation, and reminded the Italian authorities of the importance of respecting their undertaking to maintain the high priority initially given to the reforms of the judicial system and to continue to make rapid and visible progress in the implementation of these reforms. As regards the effectiveness of the measures adopted so far, the Committee of Ministers deplored the fact that no stable improvement could yet be seen: subject to a few exceptions, the situation generally worsened between 2002 and 2003[78] with an increase in both the average length of proceedings and the backlog of pending cases. The Committee of Ministers accordingly confirmed its willingness to pursue the monitoring until a reversal of the trend at the national level had been fully confirmed by reliable and consistent data. In light of this situation the Committee of Ministers took note of the information provided by Italy concerning a follow-up plan aimed at ensuring the respect of the expected execution objectives. It invited Italy to rapidly submit the complementary information requested, as well as to complete the above-mentioned follow-up plan by implementing an action plan. It also decided to examine the 4th report by April 2005 at the latest.[79]

In the Cases of *Akdivar, Aksoy, Çetin, Aydin, Mentes, Kaya, Yilmaz, Selçuk and Asker, Kurt, Tekin, Güleç, Ergi,* and *Yasa,* the Court had found various violations of the Convention by Turkey, which all resulted from the actions of its security forces in the

---

[77]   Interim Resolution DH(2000)135 of 25 October 2000.
[78]   See CM/Inf(2004)23 rev.
[79]   Documents of the Committee of Ministers, CM/AS (2004)9 of 4 October 2004.

south-east of the country, a region subject to a state of emergency for the purposes of the fight against terrorism. The Turkish Government informed the Committee of Ministers that it had engaged in an important process, including notably the drafting of measures in respect of regulations and training, in order to implement fully and in all circumstances the constitutional and legal prohibition of the use of torture and ill-treatment. The Committee of Ministers noted that the actions of the security forces challenged in these cases took place in a particular context, i.e. the rise of terrorism during the years 1991-1993. However, it also noted that the principal problems, which gave rise to the violations found, had subsequently remained unaddressed, and that, in particular, investigations relating to these violations, when they took place, had not produced concrete and satisfactory results.

The Committee of Ministers noted, in respect of the efficiency of criminal proceedings directed against agents of the security forces, that still, more than two years after the first judgments of the Court denouncing the serious violations of the human rights at issue in the case at hand, the information provided to the Committee of Ministers did not indicate any significant improvement of the situation with regard to offences falling within the jurisdiction of the state Security Courts and/or committed in the regions subject to a state of emergency. The Committee of Ministers called upon the Turkish authorities to rapidly complete the announced reform of the existing system of criminal proceedings against members of the security forces, in particular by abolishing the special powers of the local administrative councils in engaging criminal proceedings, and to reform the prosecutor's office in order to ensure that prosecutors in the future had the independence and necessary means to ensure the identification and punishment of agents of the security forces who abuse their powers so as to violate human rights. The Committee of Ministers decided to continue, in accordance with its responsibilities under the Convention, the examination of the above cases until measures had been adopted which would effectively prevent new violations of the Convention.[80]

In its follow-up Resolution the Committee of Ministers noted with satisfaction that Turkey had pursued and enhanced its reform process with a view to ensuring that its security forces and other law enforcement authorities respect the Convention in all circumstances and thus prevent new violations. In particular, the Committee expressed appreciation for the Government's efforts to effectively implement the existing laws and regulations concerning police custody through administrative instructions and circulars issued to all personnel of the Police and *Gendarmerie*, which, *inter alia*, provided for stricter supervision of their activities. It also took note of the recent constitutional and legislative amendments, particularly those which limited to 4 days the maximum periods of detention before persons accused of collective offences are presented to a judge, and those which introduced the right of access to

---

[80]   Interim Resolution of 9 June 1999, DH (99) 434.

a lawyer after a maximum period of 48 hours in police custody in cases of collective offences committed in the state of emergency regions and falling within the jurisdiction of the State Security Courts. The Committee of Ministers expressed, however, concern about the continuing existence of new complaints of alleged torture and ill-treatment as evidenced notably through the new applications lodged with the Court. It noted with concern that, three years after the adoption of Interim Resolution DH(99)434, Turkey's undertaking to engage in a global reform of basic, in-service and management training of the Police and *Gendarmerie* remained to be fulfilled and stressed that concrete and visible progress in the implementation of the Council of Europe's Police Training Project was very urgent. The Committee of Ministers urged Turkey to accelerate without delay the reform of its system of criminal prosecution for abuses by members of the security forces, in particular by abolishing all restrictions on prosecutors' competence to conduct criminal investigations against State officials, by reforming the prosecutor's office and by establishing sufficiently deterring minimum prison sentences for persons found guilty of grave abuses such as torture and ill-treatment. It called upon the Turkish Government to continue to improve the protection of persons deprived of their liberty in the light of the recommendations of the Committee for the Prevention of Torture (CPT) and decided to pursue the supervision of the execution of the judgments concerned until all necessary measures had been adopted and their effectiveness in preventing new similar violations had been established.[81]

In 27 judgments against Turkey the Court had found that the criminal convictions of the applicants, on account of statements contained in articles, books, leaflets or messages addressed to, or prepared for, a public audience, had violated their freedom of expression guaranteed by Article 10 of the Convention. In its Interim Resolution on violations of the freedom of expression in Turkey, the Committee of Ministers encouraged the Turkish authorities to bring to a successful conclusion the comprehensive reforms planned to bring Turkish law into conformity with the requirements of Article 10 of the Convention.[82] At its subsequent meeting, having examined the significant progress achieved in a series of reforms undertaken with a view to aligning Turkish law and practice with the requirements of the Convention in the field of freedom of expression, the Committee of Ministers welcomed the changes made to the Turkish Constitution, in particular to its Preamble, to the effect that only anti-constitutional activities instead of thoughts or opinions could be restricted, as well as to Articles 13 and 26, which introduced the principle of proportionality and indicated grounds for restrictions of the exercise of freedom of expression, similar to those contained in paragraph 2 of Article 10 of the Convention. It noted also the recent, important legislative measures adopted as a result of these reforms, in particular the

---

[81]   Interim Resolution of 10 July 2002, DH (2002) 98.
[82]   Interim Resolution of 23 July 2001, DH(2001) 106.

repeal of Article 8 of the Anti-terrorism Law and the modification of Articles 159 and 312 of the Turkish Criminal Code. The Committee of Ministers welcomed in this context also the 'train the trainers' programme currently being carried out in the framework of the Council of Europe/European Commission Joint Initiative with Turkey: to enhance the ability of the Turkish authorities to implement the National Programme for the adoption of the Community acquis (NPAA) in the accession partnership priority area of democratization and human rights, noting that this programme aims, among other things, at devising a long-term strategy for integrating Convention training into the initial and in-service training of judges and prosecutors. The Committee of Ministers expressed appreciation in this context of the recent establishment of the Judicial Academy, as well as many Convention awareness-raising and training activities for judges and prosecutors initiated by the Turkish authorities. Furthermore, it welcomed the amendment of Article 90 of the Constitution, which had recently been adopted by the Turkish Parliament to facilitate the direct application of the Convention and Strasbourg case law in the interpretation of Turkish law. It encouraged the Turkish authorities to consolidate their efforts to bring Turkish law fully into conformity with the requirements of Article 10 of the Convention. The Committee of Ministers decided to resume consideration of the general measures in these cases within nine months, and outstanding individual measures concerning the respective applicants at its 897th meeting (September 2004), it being understood that the Committee's examination of those cases involving applicants convicted on the basis of former Article 8 of the Anti-terrorism Law would be closed upon confirmation that the necessary individual measures had been taken.[83]

In the *Scozzari and Giunta* Case the Court found two violations of Article 8 of the Convention by Italy on account, on the one hand, of the delays in organising contact visits and the limited number of such visits between the first applicant and her children, after they had been taken into public care and, on the other hand, of the placement of the children in a community among whose managers were persons convicted for ill-treatment and sexual abuse of handicapped persons placed in the community.[84] The Committee of Ministers noted that, following Ms Scozzari's taking up residence in Belgium, the Belgian Government had approached the Italian authorities in order to examine the possibilities of organising, by judicial means, the placement of the children in Belgium, near the mother's place of residence, under the guardianship of the competent youth court. It found that such a proposal could provide the basis for a solution respecting the Court's judgment. Considering the urgency of the

---

[83]   Interim Resolution of 2 June 2004, DH(2004) 38.
[84]   Judgment of 13 July 2000, paras. 183 and 216.

situation the Committee of Ministers encouraged the Belgian and Italian authorities to implement the proposal without delay so as to put an end to the violations found.[85]

At its next session the Committee of Ministers expressed regret that, more than one year after the Court's judgment, the latter had still not been fully executed; in fact, several problems that lay at the basis of the Court's finding of a violation in respect of the placement in the *Forteto* community had not been remedied. It invited the Italian authorities to rapidly take concrete and effective measures in order to prevent the children from being irreversibly separated from their mother and to ensure that their placement respects the superior interests of the children and the mother's rights, as defined by the Court in its judgment.[86] The Committee of Ministers noted that certain general measures remained to be taken and that further information and clarifications were outstanding with regard to a number of other measures, including, where appropriate, information on the impact of these measures in practice. It recalled that the obligation to take all such measures is all the more pressing in cases where procedural safeguards surrounding investigations into cases raising issues under Article 2 of the Convention are concerned. The Committee of Ministers decided to pursue the supervision of the execution of the judgments concerned until all necessary general measures had been adopted and their effectiveness in preventing new, similar violations had been established and the Committee of Ministers had satisfied itself that all necessary individual measures had been taken to erase the consequences of the violations found with respect to the applicants. It resumed consideration of these cases, as far as individual measures were concerned, at each of its DH meetings, and with regard to outstanding general measures it decided to review their adoption within nine months from the date of its interim resolution at the latest.[87]

Following the idea submitted in the context of the Committee of Ministers' supervision of the implementation of the *Ryabykh* judgment, a high-level seminar was held with the participation of the highest Russian judiciary, *prokuratura*, executive authorities and the Bar to discuss the prospects for further reforms of the supervisory review procedure, one of the topics at the heart of Russian judicial reform. The violation of the Convention found in the *Ryabykh* Case was due to the quashing, by the Presidium of the Belgorod Regional Court in March 1999, of a final judicial decision in the applicant's favour, following an application for supervisory review lodged by the President of the same court under Articles 319 and 320 of the Code of Civil Procedure as they were then in force. The latter gave the President discretionary powers to challenge at any moment final court decisions. The Court found that this supervisory review by the Presidium infringed the principle of legal certainty and thus the ap-

---

[85]   Interim Resolution of 29 May 2001, DH (2001) 65.
[86]   Interim Resolution of 3 October 2001, DH (2001) 151.
[87]   Interim Resolution of 23 February 2005, DH(2005) 20.

plicant's right to a court.[88] Subsequently, the Russian Federation adopted some general measures with a view to remedying the systemic problem at the basis of the violation. According to the new Code of Civil Procedure, the time period for lodging an application for supervisory review was limited to one year (Article 376) and the list of state officials empowered to lodge such an application was significantly narrowed (Article 377).

While these measures were welcomed by the Committee of Ministers, doubts were expressed as to whether the measures taken were sufficient to prevent new, similar violations of the principle of legal certainty. The Russian authorities were thus invited to continue the reform of the supervisory review procedure, bringing it in line with the Convention's requirements, as highlighted, *inter alia*, by the *Riabykh* judgment. Given the complexity of the issue and the ongoing reflection on the matter in Russian legal circles, it was suggested, at the Committee of Ministers' meeting (8-9 December 2004), that a high-level seminar be held with a view to taking stock of the current *nadzor* practice and to discussing prospects for further reform of this procedure in conformity with the Convention's requirements.[89]

As a result, the Directorate General of Human Rights organized a seminar in Strasbourg, from 21–22 February 2005, in close co-operation with the Russian authorities. The participants at the Conference welcomed the reforms of the supervisory review procedure adopted by the Russian Federation through the new Codes of Criminal, Commercial (Arbitration) and Civil Procedure (in force respectively since 1 July 2002, 1 January 2003 and 1 February 2003). Notably it was suggested by many participants that the supervisory review in its amended form more closely respected the legal certainty principle enshrined in the Convention, especially in criminal and commercial matters. More reservations were, however, expressed, from the Convention viewpoint, as to the existing supervisory review procedure in civil matters. The conclusions of the seminar will be reported to competent Russian authorities with a view to contributing to their reflection on possible further reforms of the *nadzor* procedure. The Committee of Ministers will also be informed regarding the seminar in the context of its supervision of the execution of the Court's judgment in the *Riabykh* case. Given the time needed for the enactment of the new legislative measures, the Committee of Ministers decided to postpone its examination of the case until the legislative reforms have been carried out, or at the latest, until its first meeting in 2006.[90]

---

[88] Judgment of 24 July 2003, paras. 57–58.
[89] Interim Resolution of 8 February 2006, DH(2006)1.
[90] http://www.coe.int/T/E/Human_rights/execution/.

3.4 MONITORING FUNCTIONS PERFORMED BY THE COMMITTEE OF MINISTERS

3.4.1 GENERAL

During the Council of Europe Summit in Vienna in October 1993 one of the points discussed was the implications of the geographical enlargement of the Council of Europe as a result of the political changes which had taken place in Central and Eastern Europe as from 1989. On that occasion the Heads of State and Government of the Member States of the Council of Europe stated that "the Council is the pre-eminent European political institution capable of welcoming, on an equal footing and in permanent structures, the democracies of Europe freed from communist oppression. For that reason the accession of those countries to the Council of Europe is a central factor in the process of European construction based on our Organisation's values. Such accession presupposes that the applicant country has brought its institutions and legal system into line with the basic principles of democracy, the rule of law and respect of human rights."[91]

In that context the Committee of Ministers has repeatedly expressed the view that the opening up of Central and Eastern European countries cannot take place at the cost of lowering the norms and standards of human rights protection established by the Council of Europe. In connection with the requests for accession of new Member States, the question arose of how to determine whether the State concerned fulfilled the requirements for membership. Apart from the procedure of Article 52 of the Convention,[92] the Council of Europe lacks a mechanism under which the Member States can be kept under constant surveillance regaring their compliance with the commitments accepted within the framework of the Council of Europe.

Against this background and inspired by the Vienna Summit, where the Heads of State and Government resolved to ensure full compliance with the commitments accepted by all Member States within the Council of Europe, the Committee of Ministers adopted a declaration on compliance with these commitments.[93] The declaration envisages a political mechanism under which the Members States of the Council of Europe, its Secretary General or its Parliamentary Assembly may refer questions of implementation of commitments concerning the situations of democracy, human rights and the rule of law to the Committee of Ministers. On 20 April 1995, the Committee of Ministers adopted the procedure for implementing the above-men-

---

[91]   Council of Europe Summit, Vienna, 9 October 1993; see NQHR, Vol. 11, No. 4, 1993, p. 513.
[92]   See *infra*, Chapter 4.
[93]   Declaration of the Committee of Ministers of the Council of Europe of 10 November 1994 on the Compliance with Commitments accepted by Member States of the Council of Europe, Yearbook XXXVII (1994), pp. 461-462.

tioned declaration. When considering issues referred to it, the Committee of Ministers will take account of all relevant information available from different sources such as the Parliamentary Assembly and the Organisation for Security and Co-operation in Europe (OSCE). The mechanism will not affect the existing procedures arising from statutory or conventional control mechanisms. At least three meetings of the Ministers' Deputies at A level, fixed in advance, will be devoted to this question every year. At the first meeting and subsequently every second year, unless decided otherwise, the Secretary General will present a factual overview of compliance with the commitments. The discussions will be confidential and held in camera "with a view to ensuring compliance with commitments, in the framework of a constructive dialogue". The Committee of Ministers will then consider, in a constructive manner, matters brought to its attention, encouraging member States, through dialogue and co-operation, to take all appropriate steps to conform with the principles of the Statute in the cases under discussion. Finally, in cases requiring specific action, the Committee of Ministers may decide to request the Secretary General to make contacts, collect information or furnish advice; to issue an opinion or recommendation; to forward a communication to the Parliamentary Assembly or; to take any other decision within its statutory powers.

3.4.2   MONITORING IN PRACTICE

By virtue of paragraph 1 of the 1994 Declaration on Compliance with Commitments, "questions of implementation of commitments concerning the situation of democracy, human rights and the rule of law in any member State" may be brought before the Committee of Ministers by member States, by the Secretary General, or on the basis of a recommendation from the Parliamentary Assembly. To date, the Committee of Ministers has been seized twice on the basis of this paragraph. On both occasions this concerned the specific situation in the Chechen Republic of the Russian Federation. This was done for the first time by the Secretary General in June 2000 and a second time by the Parliamentary Assembly in April 2003 in its Recommendation 1600 (2003).

Likewise, by virtue of paragraphs 5 and 6 of the 1995 Procedure for implementing the 1994 Declaration, any Delegation within the Committee of Ministers or the Secretary General may ask to put the situation in any member State on the agenda of a special (*in camera*) monitoring meeting, on the basis of its own concerns or with reference to a discussion in the Parliamentary Assembly. The request should be accompanied by specific questions. These paragraphs were used once by the Secretary General in early 2002 concerning the situation in Moldova.[94]

---

[94]   See Monitor/Inf (2005)1, 19 January 2005, p. 2.

3.4.2.1 Thematic Monitoring

Thematic monitoring was set up in 1996 and covers all member States. In the years 1996-2004 ten themes were dealt with by the Committee of Ministers, namely: Freedom of expression and information; Functioning and protection of democratic institutions; Functioning of the judicial system; Local democracy; Capital punishment; Police and security forces; Effectiveness of judicial remedies; Non-discrimination, with emphasis on the fight against intolerance and racism; Freedom of conscience and religion and Equality between women and men. Work on these themes has now been terminated.[95]

Further to discussions on the theme relating to the functioning of democratic institutions, the Committee of Ministers, by virtue of paragraph 4, second indent, of the 1994 Declaration, forwarded a communication to the Parliamentary Assembly in January 2000 on the basis of its thematic monitoring on the functioning of democratic institutions.[96]

In June 2000 and 2001, following the examination of the theme 'Freedom of expression and information', the Secretary General was instructed, by virtue of paragraph 4, first indent, of the 1994 Declaration, to make contacts and collect information on this theme.[97] The Secretary General carried out the request through, notably, *in loco* visits to 4 Member States in 2000 and 2001 (Albania, the Russian Federation, Turkey and Ukraine) and to nine Member States in 2002 and 2003 (the four States previously mentioned as well as Azerbaijan, Georgia, Moldova, Romania and the former Yugoslav Republic of Macedonia).[98]

3.4.2.2 Specific Post Accession Monitoring

Since Armenia and Azerbaijan joined the Council of Europe in 2001, an ad hoc Ministers' Deputies Monitoring Group (GT-SUIVI.AGO) has reviewed democratic developments in both countries through dialogue and *in loco* visits. Progress reports are discussed by the Committee of Ministers on a regular basis. Independent experts, appointed by the Secretary General and assisted by the Monitoring Department, have examined cases of alleged political prisoners in both countries.

---

[95] Monitor/Inf (2005)1, 19 January 2005, p. 3.

[96] See document CM/Monitor(2000)2 (also issued as AS/Inf(2000)01). See also Resolution 1308 (2002) on *restrictions concerning political parties in the member States of the Council of Europe* adopted by the Assembly in November 2002, as well as, for instance, Assembly Resolutions 1280 (2002), 1358 (2004) and 1363 (2004) on the functioning of democratic institutions in Azerbaijan, Moldova and Georgia.

[97] See Monitor/Inf (2005)1.

[98] See CM/Monitor(2003)8 final 2.

Regular monitoring procedures have been instituted with respect to the obligations and commitments of Bosnia and Herzegovina, Georgia, and Serbia and Montenegro. The reports, which are submitted on a quarterly basis with respect to Bosnia and Herzegovina, and Serbia and Montenegro, and on a six-monthly basis with respect to Georgia, are examined by the Ministers' Deputies' Rapporteur Group on Democratic Stability.

3.4.3. CONCLUDING OBSERVATIONS

Although the monitoring mechanism has been in existence for more then ten years, it is still difficult to make an evaluation of its functioning. It in fact does not provide the Committee of Ministers with more powers than it already had. It also may result in even less willingness on the part of the member States to make use of the inter-State complaint mechanism under Article 33 of the Convention. The new mechanism has, however, the advantage that it may create a platform for the Committee of Ministers and the Member States to discuss and examine on a structural basis the human rights situation in all Member States of the Council of Europe. It also provides a more convenient tool for the Member States to employ a kind of 'early warning system' when there are indications that one of the Member States does not fulfil its obligations. If the Member States are fully aware of their responsibilities concerning the collective enforcement of human rights, the new mechanism may add a new dimension to the protection of human rights in Europe. In the more than 50 years of the Council of Europe's existence, there have been situations in which silent diplomacy might have had a better result than the existing complaint procedures.

Since the adoption of its 1994 Declaration on compliance with commitments, the Committee of Ministers has developed three distinct and sometimes interrelated, monitoring procedures: monitoring the application of the 1994 Declaration, thematic monitoring and specific post-accession monitoring. The 1994 Declaration may be perceived as a special mechanism that enables the Committee of Ministers to examine any situation or subject related to the implementation of commitments in the fields of democracy, human rights and the rule of law and to take specific action, when required. Thematic monitoring is a Committee of Ministers' tool which permits it to verify the implementation of commitments accepted by member States from the angle of specific topics. This procedure can lead to the re-adjustment of co-operation and assistance programmes and intergovernmental work, where appropriate. Specific action, in application of the 1994 Declaration, may also be taken to this effect. The Committee of Ministers has also set up country specific post-accession monitoring procedures in order to closely follow progress achieved and difficulties encountered by new Member States with respect to their specific obligations and commitments.

CHAPTER 4
THE SUPERVISORY FUNCTION OF THE SECRETARY GENERAL OF THE COUNCIL OF EUROPE

REVISED BY JEROEN SCHOKKENBROEK

INDEX

4.1   INTRODUCTION

In addition to the complaint procedure, the Convention provides for yet another procedure for supervising the observance by the Contracting States of their obligations under the Convention. This form of supervision is based on Article 52 (formerly Article 57) of the Convention and is entrusted to the Secretary General of the Council of Europe. Article 52 reads as follows:

> On receipt of a request from the Secretary General of the Council of Europe any High Contracting Party shall furnish an explanation of the manner in which its internal law ensures the effective implementation of any of the provisions of this Convention.

This provision originates from the work of the United Nations. In 1947, within the context of the *travaux préparatoires* of what later developed into the Universal Declaration and the two Covenants on Human Rights, a text was drawn up which related to civil and political rights. This text contained a provision according to which the Secretary General of the United Nations would have the right to request States, after they had become Parties to the treaty then under preparation, to report on the manner in which the effective implementation of the provisions of the treaty was ensured in their internal law. During the preparation of the European Convention this idea was adopted in a British proposal to the Committee of Experts and accepted by that Committee.

Under international law there are several examples of procedures in which States have to submit reports to make possible the assessment of the observance of their obligations. This system of supervision, which in general is referred to as the reporting procedure, may also constitute an effective instrument of control in the field of the protection of human rights.

Treaties for the protection of human rights are not concerned primarily with the interests of the State, but with the interests of the individual. If such a treaty provides for an inter-State complaint procedure, the Contracting States' decisions on whether to file an application will also depend on political considerations. And precisely because the interests of a State are affected to a lesser extent by a violation, States are likely to lodge an application against another State only in very exceptional cases. In this respect, the practice with regard to Article 33 (formerly 24) of the European Convention is self-explanatory.[1] As a result of the lack of initiative on the part of States to start a complaint procedure, a gap in the supervision of the treaty concerned may readily arise. A reporting procedure, such as is provided for in Article 52, may fill this gap, because the initiative for the reporting procedure may be taken by an international organ and is not dependent on a decision of one of the Contracting States.

In the case of treaties providing for an individual right of complaint, the States' lack of initiative to start the complaint procedure has less serious consequences, because the initiative may also be taken by those individuals who have a personal and direct interest at stake. It should, however, be borne in mind that the individual right of complaint is optional under most human rights treaties that provide for such a right, which implies that it can only be exercised if the State concerned has accepted that possibility. In this respect the Convention constitutes an exception. Since the entry into force of Protocol No. 11 on 1 November 1998 the right of individual application has been set out in Article 34 without any condition or requirement as to acceptance of this right by Contracting States. However, situations which allegedly conflict with the Convention but have not yet created any victims in the sense of Article 34, can be submitted for review by the Court only by Contracting States.[2] In such cases the supervision of the observance of the obligations under the Convention, therefore, is again dependent on the lodging of a complaint by a State, with all the disadvantages and restrictions involved. Here again a reporting procedure may have an important supplementary value. Moreover, there may be situations where there *are* victims, who, however, for one reason or another, do not take the initiative to lodge a complaint.

---

[1]   See *supra*, 1.12.5.
[2]   See *supra*, 1.12.2 and 1.13.3.1.

Even apart from the question of whether the complaint procedure provided for in a human rights treaty functions effectively or not and whether or not the initiative has been laid also in the hands of the individual concerned, the existence of a reporting procedure side by side with a complaint procedure may be of great value. A reporting procedure may, precisely because its character differs from that of a complaint procedure, enhance the effectiveness of the international supervision in a number of respects. Thus, via a reporting procedure all the Contracting States can be supervised at the same time, while in a complaint procedure usually the acts or omissions of only one State are examined. The first advantage of this is that the resistance to the supervision may be less if all the States are equally subjected to examination. Further, because of the possibility of comparison, a more balanced picture may be obtained of the state of affairs with respect to the implementation of the treaty in question within the whole group of Contracting States, which may facilitate the taking of measures for the improvement of the situation. In addition, the reporting procedure makes it possible to complete the picture of implementation, because this form of supervision may comprise all the provisions of the treaty in question simultaneously, while in a complaint procedure only one, or at best a few of the provisions at a time will be examined. Furthermore, a reporting procedure has the advantage that the international organ concerned may assure a certain continuity in the supervision, because it can itself decide which aspects are to be examined and when, while in the case of a complaint procedure one must wait until a complaint is submitted, in which case the supervision has more of an *ad hoc* character. The continuity of the reporting procedure allows a comparison with the situation in the past and may thus greatly enhance the effectiveness of the supervision. Finally, the reporting system will in general assume a form that is more flexible than the much more formal complaint procedure.

In view of the above-mentioned advantages it is not surprising that many international instruments for the protection of human rights, both those concerning civil and political rights and those concerning economic, social and cultural rights, provide for a reporting procedure.[3]

---

[3]   See, *e.g.*, Articles 22 and 23 of the Constitution of the International Labour Organisation; Article 9 of the Convention on the Elimination of All Forms of Racial Discrimination; Articles 40 *et seq.* of the International Covenant on Civil and Political Rights; Articles 16 *et seq.* of the International Covenant on Economic, Social and Cultural Rights; Article 19 of the Torture Convention; Article 18 of the Convention on the Elimination of all forms of Discrimination against Women, Article 44 of the Convention on the Rights of the Child. At the European level, see, *e.g.*, Article 21 of the European Social Charter and Articles 24-26 of the Framework Convention for the Protection of National Minorities.

4.2 THE REPORTING PROCEDURE UNDER ARTICLE 52 OF THE CONVENTION

In comparison with most other human-rights treaties that contain reporting obligations for the Contracting States the provision of Article 52 of the European Convention is very concise and leaves a great number of questions unanswered. Most of this lack of clarity, however, has been removed by practice. At any rate it is clear from the text of the article that the Secretary General has the power to request the Contracting States to furnish an explanation of the manner in which in their internal law the effective implementation of the provisions of the Convention is ensured, and that the Contracting States have the duty to provide him with this information. For the remainder, little can be inferred with certainty from the article itself and it is thus important to look at the practice which has developed under this provision.

To date, the Secretary General has used the power under Article 52 on seven occasions. On the first five occasions, all Contracting States were invited to submit reports on the application of the rights laid down in the Convention.[4] An important development of the practice was initiated in December 1999, when for the first time the Secretary General addressed a request to a single Contracting Party, namely the Russian Federation, asking it "to furnish, in the light of the case-law of the European Court of Human Rights, explanations concerning the manner in which the Convention is currently being implemented in Chechnya, and the risks of violation which may result therefrom." And the next recourse to the Article 52 procedure (in February 2002) also concerned a single State: Moldova was requested to provide explanations about the implementation of the Convention in the light of certain recent developments in that country.

As regards the subject-matter of the request for explanations under Article 52, the Secretary General has, on some occasions, referred to all or to a few of the provisions of the Convention, and in others to only one of them. In 1964 the Contracting States were requested to furnish information on the question of "how their laws, their case-law and their administration practice give effect to the fundamental rights and freedoms guaranteed by the Convention and its first Protocol". In that case, therefore, they had to report on all the rights set forth in the Convention and the Protocol. In 1970, on the other hand, the request of the Secretary General concerned only Article 5(5), while in 1975 information was required on the application of Articles 8, 9, 10

---

[4]   In October 1964, July 1970, April 1975, March 1983 and July 1988, respectively. In a very recent development, which therefore cannot be examined further in this edition, the Secretary General used Article 52 for the eighth time on 21 November 2005, requesting all Contracting Parties to provide certain explanations in the context of media and NGO reports about operations conducted by foreign agencies on the territory of Contracting Parties involving unacknowledged deprivation of liberty and transport of individuals suspected of terrorist activities: Council of Europe Document SG/Inf (2006) 5.

and 11. Moreover, on the latter occasion the Secretary General reserved for himself the right to ask for a further explanation of certain points in connection with the reports submitted by the States. In 1983 the Secretary General carried out an enquiry into the implementation of the Convention "in respect of children and young persons placed in care or in institutions following a decision of the administrative or judicial authorities", while in 1988 the request concerned Article 6(1).[5] The 1999 enquiry concerning the Russian Federation referred to recent developments in Chechnya (notably the armed intervention by Russian forces in the autumn of 1999) which raised serious questions concerning the effective implementation of the Convention. The request was not limited to one or more specific provisions of the Convention.[6] The use of the Article 52 procedure in relation to Moldova was prompted by the decision of the Moldovan authorities to suspend for one month the activities of a political opposition party and to lift the administrative parliamentary immunity of three leaders of that party. The request concerned all provisions of the Convention and additional Protocols, but fixed a shorter deadline for the explanations to be given concerning Articles 9-11, 13 and 14 of the Convention.[7]

This practice shows that, compared to traditional reporting procedures provided for under human rights treaties, the Article 52 procedure is unique in that the Secretary General's power is of a discretionary nature.

As early as 1964, before the first use was made of this procedure, then under Article 57 of the Convention, the Secretary General expressed this view in a statement made before the Legal Committee of the Parliamentary Assembly: "The Secretary General in making a request under Article 57 is acting under his own responsibility and at his own discretion, in virtue of powers conferred upon him by the Convention independently of any powers he may have in virtue of the Statute of the Council of Europe. His power under Article 57 is not subject to control or instruction."[8] To date not a single Contracting State has officially objected to this interpretation by the Secretary General of his supervisory powers. It may, therefore, be assumed that the above-mentioned statement constitutes a generally accepted interpretation of Article 52. This is not to say, however, that the Secretary General's actions in this field are always welcomed by the Contracting States. Three States have refused to furnish a reply to his fourth

---

[5]   Council of Europe, *Information Sheet*, No. 21, Strasbourg, 1988, p. 95.

[6]   *Request for explanations concerning the manner in which the Convention is implemented in Chechnya and the risks of violation which may result therefrom, Report by the Secretary General on the use of his powers under Article 52 of the European Convention on Human Rights in respect of the Russian Federation*, Council of Europe document SG/Inf (2000) 21 and Addendum of 10 May 2000.

[7]   *Report by the Secretary General on the use of his powers under Article 52 of the European Convention on Human Rights in respect of Moldova*, Council of Europe document SG/Inf (2002) 20 of 6 May 2002.

[8]   *Statement by the Secretary General on Art. 57 of the European Convention on Human Rights made before the Legal Committee of the Consultative Assembly in Oslo on 29 August 1964*, Council of Europe, *Collected Texts*, Strasbourg, 1994, pp. 235-236.

request: the Federal Republic of Germany, Iceland and Malta, while his fifth request has met with broad opposition so far. The sixth request has not been met by adequate explanations from the Russian authorities.[9] It should be noted, however, that the more recent practice of using Article 52 powers in respect of a single State has not been contested by any Contracting Party, including the two States concerned.

It follows from the discretionary nature of this power that the Secretary General has discretion notably in deciding whether and when to issue the request, in choosing the State or States to which it will be addressed, in determining the subject-matter of the request, and in fixing time-limits for the submission of the explanations. This also appears from the above-mentioned practice under Article 52.

An interesting development occurred in the context of the 1999 request to the Russian Federation about Chechnya. The Secretary General considered that the lengthy initial reply from the Russian authorities only referred to the Convention in a general and summary way and that it did not contain the explanations requested. He sent a second letter to clarify his request, referring *inter alia* to the requirement of strict proportionality of the use of force set out in Article 2 of the Convention and asking for precise details of precautions taken by the authorities in the choice of means and methods of the operation of the federal forces in Chechnya so as to respect the obligations under Article 2. The second reply was still not considered satisfactory and a subsequent reply to a third and last letter of the Secretary General did not add much either. In a report transmitted to the Committee of Ministers and the Parliamentary Assembly,[10] the Secretary General, therefore, concluded that the "affirmations of a general nature" contained in the replies "cannot be considered as satisfactory 'explanations' for the purposes of Article 52 of the Convention". He requested a team of recognised experts in international human rights law to analyse the correspondence in greater depth "in the light of the obligations incumbent on a High Contracting Party which is the recipient of a request under Art 52".[11]

The report submitted by the three experts opens with a general analysis of the legal framework of the Secretary General's request set out in Article 52.[12] They affirmed the discretionary nature of the power (which includes the possibility of requesting information from one specific Contracting Party in a specific context), but added that

---

[9]   The recent request about detention and transport of suspects of terrorism has not met with any refusal, but some of the reactions led to a second round.

[10] Copies were sent, for information, to the European Court of Human Rights, the Council of Europe Commissioner for Human Rights and the United Nations High Commissioner for Human Rights.

[11] See *supra* note 6.

[12] *Consolidated report containing an analysis of the correspondence between the Secretary General of the Council of Europe and the Russian Federation under Article 52 of the European Convention on Human Rights*, prepared by Tamas Ban, Frédéric Sudre and Pieter van Dijk, Council of Europe document SG/Inf (2000) 24 of 26 June 2000. The three individual reports which formed the basis for this consolidated report are contained in document SG/Inf (2000) 24 Addendum of the same date.

this does not mean that there are no guiding principles at all for the exercise of this discretionary power.[13] The experts' report listed six principles derived from the effectiveness principle, which is the principle according to which the provisions of the Convention shall be interpreted and applied in such a manner as will make them effective. These principles are:

- the Secretary General's choice of the State and of the occasion must be obvious or based on sound arguments;
- the request for explanations must be as specific as possible;
- the Article 52 procedure must be exercised in an objective manner;
- the answer(s) must be adequate and sufficiently detailed; if necessary, additional information must be requested and provided;
- channels for dialogue must be open;
- the Secretary General must draw conclusions from the outcome of the procedure and submit these to the political and legal bodies within the framework of the Council of Europe.[14]

As regards the obligations of a recipient State, the experts stressed that such a State has the obligation to provide truthful explanations about the effective implementation of the Convention in its internal law. This is an obligation of result: the State cannot limit itself to giving explanations of a formal nature. Bearing in mind also the obligation to execute treaty obligations in good faith (Article 26 of the 1969 Vienna Convention on the Law of Treaties), the State must provide precise and adequate explanations which make it possible to verify whether the Convention is actually implemented in its internal law. According to the experts, this necessarily implies that sufficiently detailed information must be provided about national law and practice, particularly about judicial authorities, and about their conformity with Convention and the case law of its supervisory organs.[15]

After having analysed the correspondence under Article 52 in light of these requirements, the experts concluded that the replies were not adequate and that the Russian Federation had failed in its legal obligations as a Contracting State under Article 52 of the Convention.[16]

---

[13]   *Ibidem*, paras 4 and 5.
[14]   *Ibidem*, para. 7.
[15]   *Ibidem*, para. 6.
[16]   *Ibidem*, para. 32.

4.3 THE FOLLOW-UP TO EXPLANATIONS RECEIVED UNDER ARTICLE 52

Practice under Article 52 has also produced some clarity concerning the question about what is to be done with the reports submitted by the Contracting States and what consequences, if any, may be attached to a violation of the Convention discovered in this way. The Secretary General compiles the answers of the Contracting States to his requests in a document which is subsequently brought to the notice of all the Contracting States and of the Parliamentary Assembly of the Council of Europe.[17]

Therefore, the answers of the Contracting States are made public. This in itself may already constitute an element of sanction for those cases in which, according to those answers, there has been a violation of the Convention. For that purpose some kind of (comparative) analysis with the assistance of independent experts might be desirable, as was done with the results of the third inquiry by the Secretary General.

In this way the defaulting State is exposed to criticism of the other States, the Parliamentary Assembly and public opinion. However, it is doubtful whether, when serious violations have been found, this sanction will be sufficiently effective to put an end to the violation. The Secretary General has not been empowered to refer a case via a complaint procedure to the Court. Such a possibility might enhance the effectiveness of the supervision under Article 52, although one may wonder whether this power would not place the Secretary General too far outside his proper function. It would seem more appropriate to place such a right of application in the public interest with a separate institution. During the drafting of Protocol No. 14 to the Convention (opened for signature on 13 May 2004) the Council of Europe Commissioner for Human Rights suggested that he be given such a right of application. The drafting body, the Steering Committee for Human Rights, considered that such an 'accusatory' role could easily interfere with the Commissioner's main tasks defined in Committee of Ministers Resolution (99) 50, which are based on a co-operative relationship between the Commissioner and the Member States. However, the Steering Committee did agree that it would be useful to give the Commissioner a right (as opposed to merely the option of asking to be invited, which already existed) to intervene as third party in proceedings before a Chamber or Grand Chamber of the Court, as a way of strengthening the general interest factor in Convention proceedings.[18] This resulted in Article 13 of Protocol No. 14, which introduces a new third paragraph in Article 36 of the Convention, granting the Commissioner such a right of intervention.

Under the present circumstances, in many cases a violation found via the reporting procedure can be subjected to a further examination resulting in a binding decision

---

[17]   The more recent reports were also transmitted, for information purposes, to other bodies, including the Court.

[18]   Explanatory Report to Protocol No. 14, paras 86-88.

only if one of the other States is prepared – perhaps also on the basis of the information obtained by means of Article 52 – to make use of its right under Article 33, provided that the admissibility conditions of Article 35(1) are fulfilled. It should be noted, however, that, as concerns the compliance with the Convention by Russia in the context of its actions in Chechnya, no inter-State application was brought during or following the conclusion of the Article 52 procedure, despite clear appeals from the Parliamentary Assembly.[19]

The Secretary General himself can do little else but bring the issue, if there has been a very serious violation, to the notice of the Committee of Ministers. Under a political monitoring procedure created by the Committee of Ministers' Declaration on compliance with commitments accepted by Member States of the Council of Europe (10 November 1994), Member States, the Secretary General or the Parliamentary Assembly may refer matters to the Committee of Ministers regarding 'questions of implementation of commitments concerning the situation of democracy, human rights and the rule of law in any member State.' This is in fact what the Secretary General did in June 2000, after having received the expert analysis of his correspondence with the Russian Federation under Article 52. In October 2000 the Committee of Ministers decided to deal with this matter as part of the regular discussions on the Council of Europe's contribution to re-establishing the rule of law, respect for human rights and democracy in Chechnya.[20] No measures were taken on the ground of Article 8 of the Statute of the Council of Europe.

By contrast, there was specific follow-up to the next Article 52 enquiry. The replies received from the Moldovan authorities not only indicated that the decision to suspend the activities of the opposition party in question had been revoked but also that they recognised that there were numerous elements of Moldovan law which raised serious questions as to their conformity with the Convention. In his report the Secretary General also noted some essential additional problems of compatibility and stated that he expected the Moldovan authorities to conduct a thorough review of domestic law and practice and to take steps rapidly to rectify the shortcomings already found. Furthermore, he expected the authorities to provide him with further information resulting from these actions. This indicates that the Article 52 procedure in respect of Moldova was left open, pending receipt of information about such domestic follow-up measures.[21] The Committee of Ministers subsequently adopted a targeted co-operation programme which was partly designed to assist the Moldovan authorities in conducting the necessary reviews of domestic law and practice in areas identified

---

[19]   Parliamentary Assembly Resolution 1221 (2000) on the conflict in the Chechen Republic, para. 22.
[20]   See *Council of Europe monitoring procedures: an overview*, Council of Europe document Monitor/Inf (2004) 2 of 5 April 2004, para. 12.
[21]   See *supra* note 7, paras 35-36.

in the Article 52 procedure. The Council of Europe has on many occasions provided comments by Convention experts on existing and draft legislation. This process has not yet been completed.

The comparison with the follow-up given to the Article 52 procedure in respect of the Russian Federation concerning Chechnya indicates that, especially in cases of allegations of massive and serious human rights violations, recourse to Article 52 will not bring any practical results if the State concerned is not willing to fulfil its obligations under Article 52 and if the procedure's outcome is not backed up by political support, notably from the Committee of Ministers. On the other hand, where the State co-operates in the procedure, and if the Committee of Ministers is willing to act, the procedure has the potential to lead to concrete steps to improve compliance with the Convention.

CHAPTER 5

THE SYSTEM OF RESTRICTIONS

REVISED BY YUTAKA ARAI

CONTENTS

5.1 INTRODUCTION

This Chapter deals with the nature and scope of restrictions that are contemplated in the Convention. The analysis of the case law reveals four types of restrictions: first, the general type of restrictions applicable to all the substantive rights under Articles 2-14 of the Convention and under the Protocols; second, the limitation clauses attached to Articles 8-11 of the Convention, Article 2 of Protocol No. 4, and Article 1 of Protocol No. 7; third, the possibility of restrictions allowed to demarcate or delimit the scope of protection of certain Convention rights; and fourth, the question of inherent or implied limitations. The first type of restrictions on the Convention rights include qualifications on the rights of individuals as contemplated under Articles 15,

17-18, which are discussed in connection with these articles.[1] This section focuses only on the other three types of restrictions. The assessment starts with restrictions under the limitation clauses and thereafter turns to 'limitations by delimitation' and the theory of inherent limitations.

5.2 LIMITATION CLAUSES AND THE CRITERIA FOR APPRAISAL

5.2.1 GENERAL REMARKS

The structure of the second paragraphs of Articles 8-11 of the Convention and the third paragraph of Article 2 of Protocol No. 4 is almost identical, with these paragraphs designed to qualify the exercise of the rights guaranteed under the first paragraph of those provisions.[2] The limitations based on similar textual formula are also seen under the second sentence of Article 6(1) relating to the right to a public trial, and Article 1 of the Seventh Protocol which guarantees the right of an alien lawfully resident in the territory of a Member State not to be expelled.[3] Despite a variety of denominations used to describe possibilities of qualifying the exercise of Convention rights in these paragraphs, such as 'interference',[4] 'limitations',[5] 'restrictions',[6] 'formalities, conditions, restrictions or penalties',[7] 'depriv[ation]'[8] and 'control',[9] they can all be categorized as 'limitations'.

With respect to the limitation clauses under Articles 8-11 of the Convention and Article 2 of the Fourth Protocol, the same principles apply in assessing the compliance of interference with the requirements of the Convention provisions (*Conventionnalité*). When the Court identifies an interference with a right provided in these provisions, a further examination is required to determine whether such interference can be justified on the basis of the three standards laid down in the Convention and elaborated upon in the case law. The first standard demands that any interference with the Convention right must be 'in accordance with law' or 'prescribed by law'. Second,

---

[1] *Infra* Chapters 34, 36 and 37.

[2] In the case of Article 2(3) of the Fourth Protocol, this clause qualifies the rights under the first paragraph and the second paragraph.

[3] The case law on Article 1 of the Seventh Protocol is limited to admissibility decisions. See, for instance, decision of 8 July 2004, *Bolat* (admissible).

[4] Article 8(2) of the Convention.

[5] Article 9(2) of the Convention.

[6] First and second sentences of Article 11(2) of the Convention; and Article 2 (3) and (4) of the Fourth Protocol.

[7] Article 10(2) of the Convention.

[8] Second sentence of Article 1(1) of the First Protocol.

[9] Article 1(2) of the First Protocol.

such interference must pursue any of the legitimate aims that are exhaustively laid down in the second paragraphs of Articles 8-11. Third, an interfering measure must be considered as 'necessary in a democratic society'. The methodology established in the case law is to examine the three standards in sequence. Yet, it is clear that in case of any finding of a breach of the first or the second standard, this will obliterate the need for evaluations based on the third standard, save in very special circumstances where the nature of issues relating to these standards is such as to require examinations in conjunction.[10] A survey of the case law reveals the tendency of the Court to focus its rigorous scrutiny on the third standard.[11] As regards cases relating to the second paragraphs of Articles 8-11, the general policy of the Court has been to stress the fundamental importance of those rights in a democratic society and to intensify the standard of review, taking as a point of departure that "those paragraphs of Articles of the Convention which provide for an exception to a right guaranteed are to be narrowly interpreted"[12] and any restriction "must be convincingly established".[13]

As regards restrictions on the rights under Article 11, a caveat must be entered that the second sentence of Article 11(2) expressly recognises 'lawful restrictions' on the exercise of the Article 11 rights by members of the armed forces, the police or the administration of the State. Where such issues arise, the Strasbourg organs have evaluated the merits exclusively under the second sentence, finding it unnecessary to examine it under the first sentence. This methodology may be considered as a variation of the 'limitations by delimitation', which will be discussed below. It is submitted that rather than allowing the implicit operation of the margin of appreciation to justify this evasive technique,[14] the principle of proportionality should be deployed to examine such restrictions as well. The Court has stressed that the phrase 'lawful restrictions' must be interpreted in the same manner as the expressions 'in accordance with the law' and 'prescribed by law' in the second paragraphs of Articles 9-11 and entail the requirements of forseeability and of non-arbitrariness.[15] However, the case law has left open the question of whether the principle of proportionality can be deduced from that phrase.[16]

Furthermore, the first and second paragraphs of Article 1 of Protocol No. 1 contemplate certain restrictions based on deprivation of possession or on control of the use of property. The survey of the case law reveals elaborate criteria for assessing the lawfulness of such restrictions, including the legal basis test, which is similar

---

[10] See, for instance, judgment of 22 February 1994, *Raimondo*, paras. 39-40; and judgment of 23 May 2001, *Denizci and Others*, para. 406 (Article 2 of Protocol No. 4).

[11] See, for instance, judgment of 28 October 1999, *Wille*, paras 55-56.

[12] Judgment of 25 March 1983, *Silver and Others*, para. 97. See also judgment of 6 September 1978, *Klass and Others*, para. 42.

[13] See, for example, judgment of 25 February 1993, *Funke*, para. 55.

[14] Report of 9 July 1998, *Rekvényi*, paras. 62-64; and judgment of 20 May 1999, para. 61.

[15] Judgment of 20 May 1999, *Rekvényi*, para. 59.

[16] See, in particular, Appl. 11603/85, *Council of Civil Service Unions and Others*, 50 D&R (1987), p. 228.

to the 'in accordance with law' standard (or the requirement of lawfulness), legitimate aims, the public interest test, the fair balance test, and the principle of proportionality.[17] The development of the case law has also seen the recognition of the test of accessibility and precision/foreseeability as part of the requirement of lawfulness[18], and of the principle of legitimate expectation inherent to the notion of proportionality.[19] In that sense, restrictions as allowed under Article 1 of the First Protocol can be assimilated with the limitation clauses as seen under the second paragraph of Articles 8-11 and are discussed in detail in the context of the right to property.[20]

5.2.2 PRESCRIBED BY LAW/IN ACCORDANCE WITH THE LAW

The English text uses the different terms 'in accordance with the law'[21] 'prescribed by law',[22] as well as 'subject to the conditions provided for by law',[23] but it has been established in the case law that all of them must be interpreted in the light of the same general principles.[24] The French text, which is equally authentic, uses the same expression, *'prévue(s) par la loi'*, in the second paragraphs of Articles 8-11 of the Convention and Article 2(3) of the Fourth Protocol. The requirement does not merely mean literal conformity with national law. What matters most here is the 'quality of law'. The case law reveals three essential components of the notion of 'quality of law'.[25] First, the national legal provision that provides for an interfering measure must be accessible to the citizens, which means that "the citizen must be able to have an indication that is adequate, in the circumstances, of the legal rules applicable to a given case".[26] The test of accessibility does not require States to codify every law, allowing

---

[17]   See, for instance, the report of 8 October 1980, *Sporrong and Lönnroth*, B. 46, para. 42.
[18]   Judgment of 22 September 1994, *Hentrich*, paras 42 and 47; judgment of 27 September 2005. *'Amat-G' Ltd and Mebaghishvili*, paras 61-63.
[19]   Judgment of 6 October 2005 (Grand Chamber), *Maurice*, para. 88.
[20]   As will be discussed, Article 1 of the First Protocol is the only provision that is equipped with qualifying phrases akin to limitation clauses but is nonetheless subject to inherent limitations.
[21]   Article 8(2) of the Convention, Article 2(3) and (4) of the Fourth Protocol, and Article 1(1) of the Seventh Protocol.
[22]   Articles 9(2), 10(2), 11(2) of the Convention as well as Article 2(2) of the Seventh protocol.
[23]   Article 1 of the First Protocol.
[24]   Judgment of 25 March 1983, *Silver and Others*, para. 85; and judgment of 2 August 1984, *Malone*, para. 66. See also judgment of 26 April 1979, *Sunday Times* (No. 1), paras 47 and 49.
[25]   See, for instance, the judgment of 26 April 1979, *Sunday Times* (No. 1), para. 49; judgment of 25 March 1983, *Silver and Others*, paras 86-88; judgment of 24 March 1988, *Olsson (No. 1)*, para. 61; and judgment of 20 May 1999, *Rekvényi*, para. 34.
[26]   See, *inter alia*, the judgment of 26 April 1979, *Sunday Times* (No. 1), paras 47 and 49; judgment of 25 November 1999, *Hashman and Harrup*, para. 31(Article 10); judgment of 25 March 1983, *Silver and Others*, paras 86-88 (Article 8); judgment of 24 February 1998, *Larissis and Others*, p. 378, para.

room for common law.[27] It is sufficient that the law is at the reasonable disposal of the citizens with the advice of legal experts. The test of adequate accessibility has not given rise to serious problems for national authorities, and the Strasbourg organs' assessment based on this test has remained relatively curt.

Second, the law must be formulated in such a way as to enable citizens to foresee with precision the exact scope and meaning of the provision so as to enable them to regulate their conduct. The Court has noted that a citizen 'must be able – if need be with appropriate advice – to foresee, to a degree that is reasonable in the circumstances, the consequences which a given action may entail'[28] This foreseeability or precision test has been deployed as a crucial interpretive device to heighten the standard of review. It furnishes a crucial safeguard for the citizen, requiring the law at issue to be 'sufficiently clear' and precise, with 'adequate indication' as to the conditions under which any intrusive measures, such as secret surveillance and interception, are to be employed.[29]

Third, as enunciated in the *Olsson (No. 1)* Case,[30] the notion of 'quality of the law' requires that, as a corollary of the foreseeability test, adequate safeguards against abuses must be proffered in a manner that would clearly demarcate the extent of the authorities' discretion and define the circumstances in which it is to be exercised.[31] The Court has continuously stressed the importance of such safeguards, linking the notion of 'in accordance with law' with the overarching principle of the rule of law. According to the Court, a law that confers discretion is not in itself contrary to the requirement of foreseeability. However, such law must satisfy the condition that "the scope of the discretion and the manner of its exercise are indicated with sufficient clarity, having regard to the legitimate aim of the measure in question, to give the individual adequate protection against arbitrary interference".[32] The need for legal safeguard against arbitrary intrusions is all the more important where the executive exercises a power in

---

40 (Article 9); judgment of 17 February 2004 (Grand Chamber), *Maestri*, para. 30 (Article 11); and judgment of 4 June 2002, *Landvreugd*, para. 54 (Article 2 of Protocol No. 4).

[27] For instance, in judgment of 26 April 1979, *Sunday Times* (No. 1), paras 46-53, the issue was the common law notion of contempt of court.

[28] See, *inter alia*, judgment of 26 April 1979, *Sunday Times* (No. 1), paras 47 and 49 (Article 10); judgment of 25 March 1983, *Silver and Others*, paras 86-88 (Article 8); judgment of 24 February 1998, *Larissis and Others*, p. 378, para. 40 (Article 9); judgment of 17 February 2004 (Grand Chamber), *Maestri*, para. 30 (Article 11); and judgment of 4 June 2002, *Landvreugd*, para. 54 (Article 2 of Protocol No. 4).

[29] See, for instance, judgment of 25 June 1997, *Halford*, para. 49; and judgment of 25 March 1998, *Kopp*, paras 64 & 72. See also judgment of 24 April 1990, *Kruslin*, para. 33; and judgment of 24 April 1990, *Huvig*, para. 32.

[30] Judgment of 24 March 1988, para. 61.

[31] See, *inter alia*, judgment of 2 August 1984, *Malone*, para. 67; judgment of 24 March 1988, *Olsson* (No. 1), para. 61; and report of 11 April 1997, *Valenzuela Contreras*, para. 52; and judgment of 30 July 1998, paras 59-60.

[32] See, for instance, judgment of 24 November 1986, *Gillow*, p. 21, para. 51; and judgment of 24 March 1988, *Olsson (No. 1)*, para. 61.

secret.[33] The Court has, however, recognized the relative nature of the level of precision required, which depends on three factors: the content of the legislative instrument, the field it is designed to cover, and the number and status of addressees.[34] On this matter, the Court has consistently recognised that "many laws are inevitably couched in terms which, to a greater or lesser extent, are vague and whose interpretation and application are questions of practice", referring to the impossibility of attaining absolute certainty in framing laws and the risk that the search for certainty may entail excessive rigidity.[35]

The 'in accordance with law' standard has served as a crucial interpretive device to condemn national measures under Article 8. With respect to surveillance of communication and a prisoner's right to correspondence, the foreseeability test has been invoked to curb the Member State's discretionary power.[36] In relation to the rights of inmates or detainees to correspondence[37] as well as the protection of private life against surveillance measures,[38] the Court has engaged in thorough and solid appraisal of impugned national measures on the basis of the foreseeability or precision test.[39] In contrast, the same standard has not provided much of an elaborate analysis by the Strasbourg organs under Articles 9,[40] 10 and 11 of the Convention and Article 2 of Protocol No. 4, except for a small number of cases.[41] Yet, when ascertaining measures

---

[33] See, *inter alia*, judgment of 24 April 1990, *Kruslin*, para. 25; and Commission's report of 27 February 1996, *Kalaç*, para. 42.

[34] Judgment of 25 August 1993, *Chorherr*, para. 25; and report of 27 February 1996, *Kalaç*, para. 42. See also judgment of 25 March 1983, *Silver and Others*, p. 33, para. 88; judgment of 28 March 1990, *Groppera Radio AG and Others*, para. 68; and judgment of 24 September 1992, *Herczegfalvy*, p. 27, para. 89.

[35] See, among others, judgment of 26 April 1979, *Sunday Times*, p. 31, para. 49; judgment of 20 May 1999, *Rekvényi*, para. 34; judgment of 21 December 2004, *Busuioc*, para. 52. See also the judgment of 4 June 2002, *Landvreugd*, para. 61 (Article 2 of the Fourth Protocol).

[36] Very exceptionally, a State has been condemned for the violation of Article 8 by reason of the absence of any formal law authorising interference. See, *inter alia*, judgment of 25 June 1997, *Halford*; and judgment of 25 March 1998, *Kopp*.

[37] See, among others, judgment of 25 March 1983, *Silver and Others*; judgment of 24 September 1992, *Herczegfalvy*; and judgment of 13 September 2005, *Ostrovar*, paras 100-102 and 107-108.

[38] See, *inter alia*, judgment of 2 August 1984, *Malone*; and judgment of 24 April 1990, *Kruslin*.

[39] See the Commission's meticulous assessment of the foreseeability test in: report of 27 February 1996, *Kalaç*, paras 41 *et seq.*

[40] Here again, this standard has been construed as meaning that "the law in question must be both adequately accessible to the individual and formulated with sufficient precision to enable him to regulate his conduct". This suggests the requirements of accessibility and foreseeability. See for instance, judgment of 24 February 1998, *Larissis and Others*, para. 44.

[41] For findings of violation of Article 9 based on the stringent evaluation of the foreseeability test, see, for instance, judgment of 26 October 2000, *Hasan and Chaush*, para. 86. In the context of Article 10, see, for instance, judgment of 25 November 1999, *Hashman and Harrup*; and Commission's Report of 9 July 1998, *Rekvényi* (the Court, in contrast, found the requirement of sufficient precision to be met: judgment of 20 May 1999). With respect to a decisive role played by the foreseeability test under Article 11, see, for instance, judgment of 17 February 2004 (Grand Chamber), *Maestri*, paras.

touching on the inner core of freedom of religion and conscience under Article 9, the Court has at least called for enhanced vigilance in applying the precision test. For instance, where the relevant law allows public authorities discretion to impose sanctions on military officers for breach of the constitutional principle of secularism, the respondent State must define the scope of such discretion and the manner of its exercise with sufficient clarity and provide them with an "adequate protection against arbitrary interference".[42]

Apart from the limitation clauses under Articles 8-11, the test of foreseeability or precision can be inferred from the expressions 'lawful' and 'in accordance with a procedure prescribed by law' in Article 5(1).[43] This test also serves as a crucial safeguard in the evaluation of the notion of 'very essence' as regards the right of access to a court under Article 6.[44] Further, the development of the tests of accessibility and foreseeability has been instrumental in ascertaining the principle of *nullum crimen, nulla poena sine lege* embodied in Article 7,[45] and its derivative principle that criminal law must not be extensively construed to the detriment of the accused, for instance, by analogy.[46]

5.2.3 LEGITIMATE AIM(S)

States may invoke legitimate aims or purposes laid down in the limitation clauses under Articles 8-11 of the Convention and Article 2 of Protocol No.4. The catalogue of such aims includes interests of national security, territorial integrity or public safety, the prevention of disorder or crime, the protection of health or morals, the interest

---

[32-42]. Reference should also be made to judgment of 5 October 2004, *Presidential Party of Mordovia*, para. 32 (clear absence of legal basis for the interference in question). As to the detailed evaluation based on the foreseeability requirement under Article 2 of Protocol No. 4, see, for instance, judgment of 4 June 2002, *Landvreugd*, paras 59-66 (no breach of the foreseeability test in a close vote of four to three); and the joint dissenting opinion of Judges Gaukur Jörundsson, Türmen and Maruste (breach of the foreseeability test); judgment of 4 June 2002, *Olivieira*, paras 52-59 (no breach of the foreseeability test in a close vote of four to three); and the joint dissenting opinion of Judges Gaukur Jörundsson, Türmen and Maruste (breach of the foreseeability test). Note should also be taken of judgment of 23 May 2001, *Denizci and Others*, paras 405-406 (sheer absence of legal basis for the interference in question, and the lack of necessity).

[42] Report of 27 February 1996, *Kalaç*, paras 44-5. While the Commission found the precision test to be breached, the Court, apparently relying on the theory of inherent limitations, did not consider that there existed any interference: judgment of 1 July 1997.

[43] Judgment of 23 September 1998, *Steel and Others*, para. 54.

[44] See, for instance, judgment of 23 October 1996, *Levage Prestations Services*, para. 42; and judgment of 28 October 1998, *Pérez de Rada Cavanilles*, para. 47.

[45] The Court has recognized that the requirements of certainty and foreseeability are inherent in Article 7: judgment of 25 May 1993, *Kokkinakis*, p. 22, para. 52; and judgment of 24 February 1998, *Larissis and Others*, para. 34.

[46] Judgment of 22 November 1995, *SW*, para. 35; and judgment of 22 November 1995, *CR*, para. 33.

of well-being of the country, the protection of public order, the maintenance of *ordre public*, the protection of the reputation, the protection of rights and freedoms of others, the prevention of the disclosure of information received in confidence, and the maintenance of the authority and impartiality of the judiciary. The list of legitimate purposes enumerated under the second paragraphs of Articles 8-11 and the third paragraph of Article 2 of Protocol No. 4 is exhaustive. The Strasbourg organs have very rarely found a violation of Convention rights by reference to the legitimate aim standard.[47] This can be explained partly by the strong commitment to democratic governance and the protection of human rights, which is a precondition for membership of the Council of Europe. A more substantial reason is that the assessment of this standard is normally carried out in conjunction with the third standard, 'necessary in a democratic society', and in particular, with the application of proportionality.

5.2.4 NECESSARY IN A DEMOCRATIC SOCIETY

The Strasbourg organs' detailed assessment of the merits is concerned mostly with the third standard, 'necessary in a democratic society', which is commonly found in the limitation clauses (the second paragraph of Articles 8-11 and third paragraph of Article 2 of Protocol No. 4). It is the concept of democratic necessity that has spawned the most significant principles of interpretation, including the margin of appreciation doctrine, the principle of proportionality, the evolutive interpretation, the less restrictive alternative doctrine[48] and the chilling effect doctrine. The Court has consistently held that the adjective 'necessary' is not synonymous with 'indispensable'; neither has it the flexibility of such expressions as 'admissible', 'ordinary', 'useful', 'reasonable' or 'desirable',[49] but it suggests that the interference must, *inter alia*, correspond to a 'pressing social need' and be 'proportionate to the legitimate aim pursued'.[50] The

---

[47] See, for example, judgment of 23 October 1990, *Darby*, in which the Court found that the refusal to exempt a non-registered foreign worker, as opposed to a registered foreign worker from a church tax, did not pursue the legitimate aim.

[48] For the application of this doctrine under Article 9, see judgment of 16 December 2004, *Supreme Holy Council of the Muslim Community*, para. 97. For its application under Article 10, see, for instance, judgment of 9 June 1998, *Incal*, para. 54; judgment of 8 July 1999, *Ceylan*, para. 34; Commission's report of 4 April 1995, *Ahmet Sadik*, para. 51; judgment of 8 July 1999, *Arslan*, paras. 46-50; judgment of 8 July 1999, *Baskaya and Okçuoglu*, paras 62-67. In the context of Article 11, see, for instance, judgment of 25 May 1998, *The Socialist Party and Others*, para. 51.

[49] Judgment of 25 March 1983, *Silver and Others*, para. 97.

[50] See, *inter alia*, judgment of 25 March 1983, *Silver and Others*, para. 97 (Article 8); judgment of 14 December 1999, *Serif*, paras 49 and 54; judgment of 13 December 2001, *Metropolitan Church of Bessarabia and Others*, paras 119 and 121 (Article 9); judgment of 7 December 1976, *Handyside*, paras 48-49; and judgment of 25 November 1996, *Wingrove*, para. 53 (Article 10); judgment, of 25 May 1998, *The Socialist Party and Others*, para. 49 (Article 11); judgment of 22 May 2001, *Baumann*, para.

Contracting States enjoy a 'certain but not unlimited margin of appreciation' in evaluating such 'pressing social need',[51] including the necessity and extent of the interfering measure. Yet, the Court has consistently emphasized that it is for the Court to give the final ruling on whether the limitations as applied are compatible with the Convention.[52]

The Strasbourg organs have held that the principle of proportionality employed under the second paragraph of Articles 8-11 entails a subsidiary requirement that the reasons adduced by a respondent State for justifying interference must be both 'relevant and sufficient'.[53] The 'relevant reasons' test, which is related to the legitimate aim standard, can readily be met. In contrast, the 'sufficient reasons' test requires a more careful analysis of factors including the nature, severity and effects of obstructing measures in tandem with any expected harm caused to the rights of a citizen.[54] It is closely intertwined with the proportionality assessment, with the failure to meet the sufficient reasons test resulting in the proportionate balance being upset.[55] Assessment of the sufficiency of reasons can be facilitated by the method of evolutive interpretation,[56] which allows a departure from precedent through a progressive decision-making

---

67; judgment of 4 June 2002, *Landvreugd*, para. 74; judgment of 17 July 2003, *Luordo*, paras 96-97 (Article 2 of Protocol No. 4).

[51] See, for instance, judgment of 7 December 1976, *Handyside*, paras 48-49; judgment of 17 February 2004 (Grand Chamber), *Gorzelik and Others*, para. 96.

[52] See, *inter alia*, judgment of 25 March 1983, *Silver and Others*, para. 97 (Article 8); judgment of 25 May 1993, *Kokkinakis*, para. 47; judgment of 26 September 1996, *Manoussakis and Others*, para. 44 (Article 9); judgment of 21 January 1999, *Janowski*, para. 30; and judgment of 16 November 2004, *Karhuvaara and Iltalehti*, para. 38 (Article 10).

[53] For cases recognizing the 'relevant and sufficient reasons' test under Article 8, see, *inter alia*, judgment of 22 October 1981, *Dudgeon*, para. 54; judgment of 24 March 1988, *Olsson* (No. 1), para. 68; and judgment of 27 November 1992, *Olsson* (No. 2), para. 87. For cases involving Article 10, see, *inter alia*, judgment of 7 December 1976, *Handyside*, para. 50; judgment of 26 April 1979, *The Sunday Times (No. 1)*, p. 38, para. 62; judgment of 8 July 1986, *Lingens*, para. 40; judgment of 22 February 1989, *Barfod*, para. 28; judgment of 11 January 2000, *News Verlags GmbH & CoKG*, para. 52; judgment of 29 June 2004, *Chauvy and Others*, para. 70; judgment of 17 December 2004, *Pedersen and Baadsgaard*, para. 70 (Article 10). For cases relating to Article 11, see, for instance, judgment of 30 January 1998, *The United Communist Party of Turkey and Others*, paras 46-47; judgment of 13 February 2003, *Refah Partisi (The Welfare Party) and Others*, para. 100; and judgment of 17 February 2004 (Grand Chamber), *Gorzelik and Others*, para. 96. In contrast, with respect to Article 9 of the Convention and to Article 2 of Protocol No. 4, the Strasbourg organs, presumably due to the meager body of the relevant case law, have yet to enunciate the 'relevant and sufficient reasons' test.

[54] See, for instance, the judgment of 8 July 1999, *Ceylan*, para. 37; judgment of 6 February 2001, *Tammer*, para. 69; judgment of 11 March 2003, *Lešník*, para. 63; judgment of 16 November 2004, *Selistö*, paras 63-70; and judgment of 21 December 2004, *Busuioc*, para. 95.

[55] See, for instance, the judgment of 16 November 2004, *Karhuvaara and Iltalehti*, para. 54; and judgment of 11 January 2005, *Halis*, para. 38.

[56] The first clear recourse to this interpretative method was seen in the *Tyrer* case, which involved birching inflicted on a teenager as a form of judicial corporal punishment. When finding the exercise of whipping to constitute 'degrading treatment' as proscribed by Article 3, the Court held that "the Convention is a living instrument which . . . must be interpreted in the light of present-day conditions. In the case now before it the Court cannot but be influenced by the developments and

policy. Further, the chilling effect doctrine comes into operation in this context, with the Court emphasizing the importance that obstructing measures must not have any deterrent effect on the exercise of the rights by the general public. However, reliance on this doctrine in the case law is limited to cases concerning freedom of expression and freedom of association. Applied under Article 10, this doctrine means that journalists, press or the public in general should not be discouraged from criticizing public authorities by the threat of criminal or civil proceedings for defamation. In view of the 'dominant position' that it occupies, a Government must display restraint in sanctions against freedom of expression and show prudence in choosing the measure of a less restrictive kind.[57]

5.3 LIMITATIONS ARISING FROM DELIMITATION

Restrictions on the Convention rights may ensue from the way in which a right has been formulated, with a clause or phrase delimiting the scope of protection of certain rights and explicitly excluding specific areas or persons from their scope of protection, or 'delegating' to State authorities the responsibility of regulating the exercise of certain rights. First, such 'limitations by delimitation' can be seen in the case where provisions expressly refer to certain areas or subject-matters as not encompassed by their scope of application *ratione materiae*. Article 2(2) expressly rules out three circumstances as not constituting a violation of Article 2, subject to the condition that the use of force that results in deprivation of life is no more than absolutely necessary. Similarly, Article 4(3) excludes from the notion of 'forced or compulsory labour' within the meaning of the second paragraph the four types of service or work, whereas Article 5 (1) envisages six exhaustive cases of lawful arrest or detention as exceptions to the right to liberty and security as provided in the first sentence.

Second, 'limitations by delimitation' may be conceived in circumstances where a provision expressly states that national authorities should take certain positive steps, such as regulatory measures, to govern their scope of guarantees. In other words, national authorities are given a margin of appreciation in demarcating the scope of application of certain rights, with the result that certain areas are excluded from the reach of those rights. The phrase under Article 12 'according to the national law governing the exercise of this right' suggests that national authorities are entrusted to the task of delineating the ambit of protection of the right to marriage based on their law,

---

commonly accepted standards in the penal policy of the member States of the Council of Europe in this field"; judgment of 25 April 1978, *Tyrer*, para. 31.

[57] See, for instance, judgment of 23 April 1992, *Castells*, para. 46; judgment of 27 March 1996, *Goodwin*, para. 39; judgment of 28 October 1999, *Wille*, para. 50; judgment of 21 March 2002, *Nikula*, para. 54; judgment of 13 November 2003, *Elci and Others*, para. 714; judgment of 16 November 2004, *Selistö*, para. 53; and judgment of 17 December 2004, *Cumpănă and Mazăre*, para. 114.

and providing both 'institutional guarantees' and conditions for the exercise of the rights under this provision. The national authorities are 'assigned' to govern the scope of application of certain rights also in relation to the four rights guaranteed under Protocol No. 7. The present chapter does not examine issues relating to those provisions, as the 'restrictions' of this nature are discussed in connection with the respective rights and freedoms.

5.4   THE DOCTRINE OF INHERENT LIMITATIONS

5.4.1   INTRODUCTION

For a long time the Commission took a view that, apart from expressly provided restrictions, the scope of the Convention rights may be subordinated to implied limitations.[58] Unlike 'limitations' flowing from delimitation as described above, the legal basis of inherent limitations cannot be found in the express textual formulation. According to the theory of 'inherent limitations', restrictions on certain Convention rights are considered as not amounting to 'interference' on the ground that they are 'ingrained' in the scope of guarantee of these rights. When invoked in relation to the Convention rights that are subject to limitation clauses, denying that a specific restricting measure amounts to interference would exonerate national authorities and the Strasbourg Court from scrutinizing whether or not such a measure can be justified under the limitation clauses based on the established criteria. It must, however, be noted that four non-derogable rights are logically impervious to implied limitations under any circumstances, even with respect to 'special categories of persons'.

An analysis of the case law demonstrates that the Court's recognition of 'implied limitations' is confined to specific contexts (rather than in a general manner). This may be seen in relation to the right of access to court, which, as an implied right derived from Article 6(1), has been held to be susceptible to inherent limitations.[59] Further, the theory of 'implied limitations' has been invoked by the Court to broaden the width of the margin of appreciation in relation to the right to vote and to stand for election under Article 3 of the First Protocol.[60]

---

[58]   See, for instance, Appl. 2749/66, *Kenneth Hugh de Courcy, Yearbook* X (1967), p. 388.

[59]   See, *inter alia*, the judgment of 21 February 1975, *Golder*, paras 21, 37-41; judgment of 29 July 1998, *Omar*, para. 34; and judgment of 28 October 1998, *Osman*, para. 147. See also the dissenting opinion of Judge Loucaides in the judgment of 21 November 2001, *McElhinney*, para. 6 (as regards the doctrine of sovereign immunity which had an effect of denying the applicant the right to a judicial determination of his compensation claim, Judge Loucaides recognized that Article 6 may be subject to 'inherent limitations', albeit he stressed that these limitations should not affect the 'core' of the right).

[60]   See, for instance, the judgment of 2 March 1987, *Mathieu- Mohin and Clerfayt*, para. 52; judgment of 1 July 1997, *Gitonas*, para. 39; and judgment of 18 February 1999, *Matthews*, para. 63.

The application of implied limitations can also be seen with respect to limitations on the right to property under Article 1 of Protocol I. According to the Court's case law, restrictions on the right to property as guaranteed under this provision must first be analysed under the second sentence of the first paragraph. It must be ascertained whether a contested measure amounts to a deprivation or expropriation of the property concerned. Then it must be examined whether such interference constitutes the control of use of properties within the meaning of the second paragraph. Even after these two possibilities of limitations are found to be incapable of justifying the interference in question, this may fall within the 'inherent' limitations under the first sentence of the first paragraph. The Court has repeatedly observed that the "fact that the permits fell within the ambit neither of the second sentence of the first paragraph nor of the second paragraph does not mean that the interference with the said right violated the rule contained in the first sentence of the first paragraph".[61] The Court justified the recognition of implied limitations under the first sentence of the first paragraph on the basis of the need to strike a fair balance between the general interest of the community as a whole and the individual's right to property.[62]

The most controversial application of the theory of inherent limitations is the one in relation to the rights accompanied by express limitation clauses, such as the second paragraphs of Articles 8-11. In its earlier decisions the Commission flirted with this theory concerning prisoners' rights under Articles 8 and 10.[63] For instance, in the *K.H.C.* Case the Commission took the view that with respect to the control and stopping of a prisoner's letters in general 'the limitation of the right of a detained person to conduct correspondence is a necessary part of his deprivation of liberty which is *inherent* in the punishment of imprisonment… not disclos[ing] any violation of Article 8, paragraph (1)'.[64] However, such methodology was expressly rejected by

---

[61] This principle has been established since the judgment of 23 September 1982, *Sporrong and Lönnroth*, para. 69. See also the judgment of 23 October 1997, *The National & Provincial Building Society, The Leeds Permanent Building Society and The Yorkshire Building Society*, para. 78.

[62] According to the Court, the search for such a balance is inherent in the whole of the Convention and reflected in the structure of Article 1: judgment of 23 September 1982, *Sporrong and Lönnroth*, para. 69; and judgment of 27 October 1994, *Katte Klitsche de la Grange*, para. 42.

[63] See, for instance, Appl. No. 1860/63, *X v. Federal Republic of Germany*, which concerned the refusal by the prison authorities to make available to a prisoner a copy of the provisional regulations on the execution of penalties. The Commission observed that 'the limitations imposed on the right referred to in Article 10 are the consequence of a prisoner's special situation': Decision of 15 December 1965, Yearbook VIII (1965), p. 204 (216). See also Appl. No. 5270/72, *X v. the United Kingdom*, decision of 8 July 1974, Coll. 46 (1972), para. 7 ('THE LAW') (a prisoner's complaint of the stopping of periodicals outside the quota under Articles 8 and 10).

[64] Appl. No. 2749/66, *Kenneth Hugh de Courcy*, decision of 11 July 1967, Yearbook X (1967), p. 388 (emphasis added).

the Court's subsequent decisions in the *Vagrancy*[65] *and Golder* Cases[66] on the ground that the possibility of lawful restrictions on the Convention rights are enumerated in an exhaustive manner, with no room for 'inherent limitations'. Similarly, in the context of the right to public pronouncement of judgments under Article 6(1) the Court has rejected any room for the notion of implied limitations.[67] However, in the *Klamecki (No. 2)* Case the Court recognized that a detention regime is susceptible to 'inherent limitations' on the exercise of certain Convention rights, such as the right to private and family life.[68] Similarly, a methodology akin to the theory of implied limitations, which would justify the non-recognition of interference itself, resurfaced in the Court's approach in the *Kalaç* Case. There, the Court, contrary to the Commission, did not find any interference with the right under the first paragraph of Article 9 in relation to the forced retirement of a judge advocate from the air force due to his alleged sympathy with Islamic fundamentalism.[69] These cases must be treated as deviations in the case law. There is an encouraging sign that, except for *Kalaç*, whenever such fundamental rights as freedom of religion or free speech are involved, the Court has engaged in critical evaluation of the merits under the second paragraphs of Articles 9 and 10.[70]

5.4.2 THE THEORY OF SPECIAL STATUS REGIME AND INHERENT LIMITATIONS

Akin to national constitutional theories,[71] the Commission developed the doctrine of inherent limitations specifically to justify greater restrictions on certain Convention rights exercised by persons of a special legal status or regime, such as detained persons, psychiatric patients, soldiers and civil servants. For instance, the Commission held

---

[65] Judgment of 18 June 1971, De Wilde, Ooms and Versyp (Vagrancy Case), para. 93 (the supervision of detained persons' correspondence).

[66] The Commission expressly rejected the submission of the respondent State based on this doctrine, whereas the Court simply refused to follow the methodology of implied limitations and examined the complaint under the second paragraph of Article 8: judgment of 21 February 1975, *Golder*, paras 44-45.

[67] See, for instance, judgment of 28 June 1984, *Campbell and Fell*, para. 90; and judgment of 24 April 2001, *B. and P. v. the United Kingdom*, para. 44; concurring opinion of Judge Bratza, para. 1; dissenting opinion of Judge Loucaides, joined by Judge Tulken, para. 2.

[68] Judgment of 3 April 2003, *Klamecki (No. 2)*, paras. 144 and 152.

[69] Judgment of 1 July 1997, paras 27 *et seq.*

[70] See, for instance, *Vereinigung Demokratischer Soldaten Österreichs and Gubi*, para. 36; judgment of 25 November 1997, *Grigoriades*.

[71] See, for instance, A. Bleckmann, *Staatsrecht II – Die Grundrechte*, 4th ed., (1997) section 3, para. 24; and section 12, paras 94 *et seq.*

that the right to respect for family life[72] and correspondence[73] under Article 8 was susceptible to broader restrictions with respect to a detained person. Textual interpretation of the Convention may support possible exceptions for particular categories of individuals such as members of the military and civil services under Articles 4(3) and under the second sentence of 11(2).[74] According to these theories and practices, the rights of those belonging to such a special regime, such as members of the army, can be subject to inherently greater limitations than a civilian on the basis of hierarchical and disciplinary features of the military. Such categories of persons are subject to the application of inherent limitations, with the consequence that restrictions on their rights do not amount to 'interference', and hence that in case of the affected provisions containing limitation clauses there is no need of assessment under these clauses, such as under the second paragraphs of Articles 8-11. It must be questioned whether the Convention ever allows room for inherent restrictions on the rights of individuals pertaining to 'special regime'. The implications flowing from this controversial approach would be that the State or local government could restrict rights and freedoms of those belonging to this special power relationship without *specific* legal basis, and that they could be denied the right of judicial review.

5.4.3 CRITICISMS OF THE DOCTRINE OF INHERENT LIMITATIONS

Three arguments can be put forward to support the exclusion of inherent limitations applied in the context of rights susceptible to limitation clauses.[75] First, both the second paragraphs of Articles 8-11 and the requirement for public pronouncements of judgments under Article 6(1) are formulated in such a way as to leave no room for the concept of implied limitations. This textual formulation needs to be interpreted in light of the fact that the ECHR is a law-making treaty designed to create and give effect to rights of individuals, as can be supported by Article 1 of the Convention and

---

[72] Appl. No. 2676/65, *X v. Austria*, Coll. 23 (1967), p. 31.
[73] Appl. No. 2375/64, *X v. Federal Republic of Germany*, Coll. 22 (1967), p. 45; and No. 2749/66, *Kenneth Hugh de Courcy*, Yearbook X (1967) p. 388.
[74] The Strasbourg organs consider that once the two requirements of foreseeability and non-arbitrariness are met under the second sentence of Article 11(2), there is no separate need for examinations based on the three common standards in the first sentence: judgment of 20 May 1999, *Rekvényi*, para. 61. In the context of Article 10(2), the Strasbourg organs have interpreted the phrase 'duties and responsibilities' as providing a justification for 'a certain margin of appreciation': *ibidem*, para. 43; and judgment of 28 October 1999, *Wille*, para. 64.
[75] The one exception of inherent limitations that the Court has allowed with respect to provisions accompanied by limitation clauses relates to the issues of positive obligations under Article 8. It has so far examined these issues solely under the first paragraph to the exclusion of having them examined under the second paragraph.

the effective protection principle.[76] The limitation clauses include phrases such as '[t]here shall be no interference (...) except such as',[77] 'shall be subject only to such limitations as'[78] or '[n]o restrictions shall be placed on the exercise of these rights other than such as'.[79] The absence of a comparable, qualifying adverbial expression and the use of 'may' under Article 10(2)[80] suggests that the enumerated list of public objectives may be exemplary and not exhaustive. However, in line with the effective protection principle that requires any possible restrictions on the rights to be construed 'narrowly', it is more consistent to argue that all the limitation clauses must be interpreted in the same fashion for the benefit of applicants. Once the exhaustive nature of the legitimate aims enumerated in the second paragraph of Articles 8-11, which can be adduced to justify restrictions on the rights under the first paragraph of those provisions, is ascertained, the better view should be that possibilities of limitations are provided equally in an exhaustive manner and only in express form.[81] If the drafters had wished to allow special restrictions on the rights of particular categories of persons, they could have expressly stated this in each individual provision. Second, the principle of non-discrimination as recognized under Article 14 militates against 'inherently' greater restrictions on the rights of certain categories of individuals. As the Commission clarified in the Kalaç Case,[82] any exclusion of the Convention's application and the Strasbourg organs' judicial review will run counter to Articles 1 and 14. It held that 'everyone within [the] jurisdiction' of the Contracting States shall enjoy the Convention rights and 'without discrimination on any ground'. Third, Article 18 ensures that the restrictions allowed under the Convention may not be applied for any purpose other than those for which they have been prescribed.

---

[76] The Court has expressly recognized the law-making, rather than, contracting, character of the ECHR. See, for instance, *Wemhoff*, in which the Court emphasized that "[g]iven that it [the Convention] is a law-making treaty, it is also necessary to seek the interpretation that is most appropriate in order to release the aim and achieve the object of the treaty, and not that which would restrict to the greatest possible degree the obligations undertaken by the parties": judgment of 27 June 1968, para. 8. See also judgment of 21 February 1975, *Golder*, para. 36. A similar tenor can be found in *Austria v. Italy*, in which the Commission observed that "the purpose of the High Contracting Parties in concluding the Convention was not to concede to each other reciprocal rights and obligations in pursuance of their individual national interest but (...) to establish a common public order of the free democracies of Europe with the object of safeguarding their common heritage of political traditions, ideals, freedom and the rule of law": Appl. No. 788/60, *Yearbook* IV (1961), p. 116 (138).

[77] Article 8(2) of the Convention.

[78] Article 9(2) of the Convention.

[79] Article 11(2) of the Convention. See also Article 2(3) of the fourth Protocol.

[80] See also the second sentence of Article 6(1) of the Convention, and Article 1(2) of the Seventh Protocol.

[81] Note also the Commission's Report of 19 July 1974 in *Engel and Others*, in which the Commission observed that "[f]rom this analysis of the Convention, and the method adopted therein, it is clear that the Convention is not conceived in terms of whose rights shall be protected but in terms of what rights shall be guaranteed and to what extent": B.20 (1978), p. 58.

[82] Commission's Report of 27 February 1996, para. 35.

It is submitted that the theory of implied limitations in the sense of excluding review of interfering measures cannot be applied in the Convention without much overhaul. Its application must be confined to cases where certain Convention provisions, which are susceptible to derogation, lack express reference to limitations, whether by limitation clauses or by 'limitations by delimitation'. In particular, in case of restrictions on the rights subject to limitations clauses, they must be assessed under these clauses based on established criteria. A caveat must be entered that even in such circumstances the application of an amorphous doctrine of the margin of appreciation in evaluating the rights of persons belonging to 'special categories' such as prisoners and members of armed forces might result in as wide a scope of restrictions as can be contemplated by the inherent limitations doctrine.[83] Yet, this methodology of the Court should be capable of providing greater transparency, as all the limitations are at least subordinated to the judicial scrutiny under the limitations clauses of Articles 8-11 and to the general restriction clauses such as Article 18.[84]

Whenever the theory of implied limitations is invoked in relation to provisions accompanied neither by limitation clauses nor by qualifying phrases purported to delimit their scope of protection, the Court must scrutinise the lawfulness of such limitations based on transparent and consistent criteria. For instance, in relation to the 'implied right' of access to a court under Article 6(1) the Court has emulated the methodology of assessing the limitation clauses of Articles 8-11, enunciating the principle of proportionality. It is submitted that the articulation of this principle should serve to ascertain whether a contested measure applied to specific categories of persons are 'ordinary and reasonable', as envisaged within the framework of special regimes such as prisons and military hierarchy.[85] The proportionality appraisal should include critical evaluations of the necessity and severity of restrictions as well as the nature of the rights affected.

5.4.4 VARIATIONS OF IMPLIED LIMITATIONS: POSITIVE OBLIGATIONS

The variation of inherent limitations can be seen in the Strasbourg organs' approach in assessing the scope of positive obligations under Article 8 of the Convention. The

---

[83] See, for instance, judgment of 21 February 1975, *Golder*.
[84] See the observations made by the Commission in its report of 11 October 1980, *Silver and Others*, B. 51 (1987), p. 72.
[85] Judgment of 21 February 1975, *Golder*, para. 45. See also *Engel*, where the Court speaks of 'specific demands' of military service and 'normal restrictions' under Article 5: judgment of 8 June 1976, para. 59. In relation to detained persons, common European standards as to modern penitentiary requirements must be taken into account. See, for instance, *Hamer*, report of 13 December 1979, DR 24, (1981), p. 5, where the Commission considered that a two-year delay in a detained persons' possibility of marrying would be an encroachment on this right to marry.

methodology of the Court has been to treat a failure to comply with a certain positive duty as not amounting to 'interference' within the meaning of the first paragraph of Article 8, excluding the possibility that contested omissions relating to the right to private and family life can be examined pursuant to the tripartite criteria under the second paragraph. In *Abdulaziz* Judge Bernhardt criticized that the Court's reasoning that there is no 'lack of respect' for family life under Article 8(1) would result in recognition of 'inherent limitations' not susceptible to justifications by reference to the second paragraph of Article 8.[86]

On this matter the reasoning of the Court suggests that the applicable principles are the same both in relation to negative obligations and to positive duties under Article 8, with the notion of fair balance serving as a criterion.[87] However, the very notion of fair balance is obscure and amenable to a varying margin of appreciation, with the Court broadening the scope of margin in respect of issues of positive obligations. In that way issues of positive obligations have not attracted rigorous scrutiny, which in turn suggests that though not explicitly mentioned, they may be subject to 'inherent limitations'. In the *Stjerna* Case Judge Wildhaber proposed a 'unified' approach to issues of both positive and negative obligations, arguing that the word, 'interference' under the first paragraph should be interpreted as covering both action and omissions,[88] but his proposal has not been followed in the case law. However, the perusal of the case law demonstrates two innovative features of the Court's assessment of a 'fair balance' with respect to the bounds of positive duties. First, the Court has come to embrace elements of legitimate aims under the second paragraph of Article 8 as factors relevant for assessing a fair balance under the first paragraph of this provision.[89] Second, it has incorporated the principle of effective protection (the requirement that the Convention rights must be 'practical and effective', and 'not theoretical or illusory') into this assessment and reinforced the rigour of review.[90] However, the Court has yet to integrate the principle of proportionality into the appraisal of implied limitations relating to positive duties.

---

[86] Judgment of 28 May 1985, *Abdulaziz, Cabales and Balkandali,* concurrent opinion of Judge Bernhardt, para. 1.

[87] See, *inter alia*, the judgment of 26 May 1994, *Keegan*, para. 49; and judgment of 24 February 1998, *Botta*, para. 33.

[88] Judgment of 25 November 1994, concurring opinion of Judge Wildhaber.

[89] See, for instance, the judgment of 7 August 2003, *Hatton and Others*, para. 98; and judgment of 16 November 2004, *Moreno Gómez*, para. 55.

[90] See, for instance, the judgment of 16 November 2004, *Moreno Gómez*, paras 56, 61-62; and judgment of 10 November 2004, *Taşkin and Others*, para. 117. Note that in cases involving environmental pollution raised under Article 8, the Court also emphasized the procedural safeguards, such as appropriate investigations and studies into effects of certain economic activities on environment, and access to conclusions of such studies by the public: judgment of 19 February 1998, *Guerra and Others*, para. 60; judgment of 9 June 1998, *McGinley and Egan*, para. 97; and judgment of 10 November 2004, *Taşkin and Others*, para. 119.

Limitations can also be deemed as 'inherent' in respect of other rights that require a greater degree of positive obligations on the part of State authorities, such as the right to effective (domestic) remedies under Article 13 of the Convention and the right to education and to periodic free elections under Articles 2 and 3, respectively, of Protocol No. 1. The fact that these provisions do not contain limitation clauses makes it easier for the notion of implied limitations to be slipped into the appraisal of their scope of protection.

CHAPTER 6
RIGHT TO LIFE (Article 2)

REVISED BY LEO ZWAAK

CONTENTS

6.1 TEXT OF ARTICLE 2

1. *Everyone's right to life shall be protected by law. No one shall be deprived of his life intentionally save in the execution of a sentence of a court following his conviction of a crime for which this penalty is provided by law.*
2. *Deprivation of life shall not be regarded as inflicted in contravention of this Article when it results from the use of force which is no more than absolutely necessary:*

(a)   in defence of any person from unlawful violence;
*(b)   in order to effect a lawful arrest or to prevent the escape of a person
        lawfully detained;*
(c)   in action lawfully taken for the purpose of quelling a riot or insurrection.

6.2   INTRODUCTION

Article 2 is formulated in a somewhat strange way. Unlike the corresponding Article 6 of the Covenant, it does not expressly recognise the existence of the right to life, but imposes upon the national authorities an obligation to protect everyone's right to life, followed by a prohibition of intentional deprivation of life.

As to that prohibition, the question may be raised whether this is addressed only to the national authorities or also to private persons. In any case, Article 2 can be invoked in Strasbourg only when its violation is (also) due to a lack of protection on the part of the national authorities, because complaints can only be directed against acts and omissions for which the State bears responsibility.[1] The prohibition of intentional deprivation of life implies the duty to abstain from acts which needlessly endanger life.[2]

The duty to protect the right to life seems to have been imposed by Article 2 in particular on the legislator: 'shall be protected by law'. What does this obligation imply? Is a State in default under this provision if, for instance, drivers are not subjected to certain speed limits, although such a measure might reduce the number of road victims? The right to life does not afford a guarantee against all threats to life, but against intentional deprivation and careless endangering of life. The latter must be prohibited and made punishable by law except for those cases in which Article 2 permits such deprivation of life. The protection provided by the law, however, is a reality only if that law is implemented. Omission on the part of the authorities to trace

---

[1]   The Contracting State's obligation to guarantee protection against the acts and omissions of individuals may be deemed implied in the first sentence of Article 2 in conjunction with the provision of Article 1. The content and the scope of this obligation, however, are difficult to indicate *in abstracto*. For the issue of *Drittwirkung* in general, see *supra* 1.7.

[2]   See, *e.g.*, Appl. 5207/71, *X v. Federal Republic of Germany*, Yearbook XIV (1971), p. 698 (710), where a complaint based on Article 2 on account of an order of the national court to evict a person in poor health from her house was not considered manifestly ill-founded by the Commission; Appl. 4340/69, *Simon-Herold v. Austria*, Yearbook XIV (1971), p. 352 (394-398), where the complaint based on Artcile 2 concerned the medical care in a prison; Appl. 7154/75, *Association X v. the United Kingdom*, D&R 14 (1979), p. 31 (32-33), where the Commission decided that in the case of a vaccination programme to which certain risks to life were attached, it could not be said that the Government envisaged such possible consequences; and Appl. 7317/75, *X v. Switzerland*, Yearbook XX (1977), p. 412 (436-438), where extradition to the United States was concerned and the person in question feared reprisals on the part of the CIA, but the Commission held that this fear had been made insufficiently concrete.

and prosecute the offender in case of an unlawful deprivation of life is, therefore, in principle subjected to review by the Court.[3] Consequently, the first sentence of the first paragraph is not addressed exclusively to the legislator, but refers to a general obligation of the authorities to take appropriate measures for the protection of life.[4]

In its decision in *X v. Austria* the Commission held that Article 2 "does (...) primarily provide protection against deprivation of life only". At the same time it did not wish to entirely rule out the possibility that protection of physical integrity also comes under this provision, but if so, then exclusively protection against such injuries as involve a threat to life.[5] Other injuries to the physical – and mental – integrity may in many cases be brought under Article 3.

6.3   POSITIVE OBLIGATIONS

6.3.1   INTRODUCTION

To what extent are the authorities obliged to prevent deprivation of life by individuals? They can hardly be required to put a bodyguard at the disposal of each citizen.[6] Their task of guarding public security does involve, however, the duty to observe a certain vigilance with respect to the lives of the individual citizens, but in this duty they cannot go so far that their obligations towards other citizens are jeopardised. They will have

---

[3]   See the report of the Committee of Experts on Human Rights to the Committee of Ministers, *Problems arising from the Co-Existence of the United Nations Covenants on Human Right and the European Convention on Human Rights*, Doc. H(70)7, Strasbourg, 1970, where it speaks of "an obligation of States to take the necessary deterrent measures with a view to preventing by law (i.e. by adequate legislation and its enforcement) intentional interference with life whether by a State or by individuals". Of course, certain discretion will have to be allowed to the national authorities as regards the prosecution policy, but the fundamental character of the right to life stringently restricts that scope. As in the case of an individual complaint the applicant must be able to prove that he himself is the victim of the omission of the authorities, a complaint concerning deprivation of life will be possible only in the case of a so-called 'indirect' victim; see *supra*, 1.13.3.5.

[4]   Whereas in Appl. 6839/74, *X v. Ireland*, D&R 7 (1977), p. 78, the Commission still left open the question of whether Article 2 may also entail an obligation to take measures, it held in Appl. 7154/75, *Association X v. the United Kingdom*, D&R 14 (1979), p. 31 (32), that the State has a duty to take appropriate steps to safeguard life. See also Appl. 9348/81, *W v. the United Kingdom*, D&R 32 (1983), p. 190 (199-200) and Appl. 16734/90, *Dujardin v. France*, D&R 72 (1992), p. 236 (243), where the Commission stated that Article 2 "may indeed give rise to positive obligations on the part of the State".

[5]   Appl. 8278/78, D&R 18 (1980), p. 154 (156).

[6]   In Appl. 9348/81, *W v. the United Kingdom*, D&R 32 (1983), p. 190 (200) and Appl. 9829/82, *X v. the United Kingdom and Ireland* (not published), the Commission added, that from Article 2 one cannot deduce a positive obligation to exclude any possible violence.

to weigh these obligations against each other and the way they do this may be reviewed in Strasbourg for its reasonableness.[7]

Thus, in the *Dujardin* Case weighing the protection of the individual's right to life against the State's legitimate interests, the Commission decided that the fact that the French amnesty law adopted in the context of a settlement between various communities in New Caledonia, resulting in a discontinuation of the prosecution of the suspected murderers of the applicants' close relatives, did not infringe the right protected by Article 2.[8] In the *Taylor, Crampton, Gibson and King families* Case the applicants submitted that the State, in view of its positive obligation to protect the right to life where an unlawful killing or life-threatening attack has taken place in an environment for which it is responsible, must show that it has sought out the perpetrator and brought him/her to justice. The Commission held that the obligation to protect life includes a procedural aspect, involving the minimum requirements of a mechanism whereby the circumstances of a deprivation of life by agents of a State receive public and independent scrutiny. In this case the death and serious injuries of the children of the applicants in a public hospital had been caused by a nurse suffering from mental illness. According to the Commission the procedural requirements of Article 2 were satisfied because there had been criminal proceedings against the nurse, which led to her conviction and imprisonment.[9] In *Cyprus v. Turkey* the balance of interests weighed in favour of the applicant State. Cyprus accused the Turkish invasion forces of having murdered citizens, including women and aged people, in cold blood. These cases were declared admissible by the Commission,[10] and the Committee of Ministers decided on the basis of the Commission's report "that events which occurred in Cyprus constitute violations of the Convention".[11]

In the *Ergi* Case the Court held that under Article 2 of the Convention, read in conjunction with Article 1, the State may be required to take certain measures in order to 'secure' an effective enjoyment of the right to life.[12]

---

[7]   However, in Appl. 9348/81, *W v. the United Kingdom*, D&R 32 (1983), p. 190 (200), where the applicant complained about her husband's and her brother's death in Northern Ireland, the Commission came to the conclusion that it was not its task, when examining a complaint under Article 2, to consider in detail the appropriateness and efficiency of the measures taken by the United Kingdom to combat terrorism in Northern Ireland.

[8]   Appl. 16734/90, D&R 72 (1992), p. 236 (243-244).

[9]   Appl. 23412/94, D&R 79-A (1993), p. 127 (136).

[10]   Appls 6780/74 and 6950/75, *Yearbook* XVIII (1975), p. 82 (124).

[11]   Resolution of the Committee of Ministers, DH(79)1 of 20 January 1979, Yearbook XXII (1979), p. 440. See the report of 10 July 1976, *Cyprus v. Turkey*, in particular paras 352-354, pp. 118-119.

[12]   Judgment of 28 July 1998, para. 79.

6.3.2   OBLIGATION TO PROTECT LIFE

It has been firmly established in the Court's case law that where an individual is taken into police custody in good health but is later found dead, it is incumbent on the State to provide a plausible explanation of the events leading to his death, failing which the authorities will be held responsible under Article 2 of the Convention.[13] Thus, in the *Salman* Case the Court ruled that where the events in issue lie wholly, or in large part, within the exclusive knowledge of the authorities, as in the case of persons within their control in detention, strong presumptions of fact will arise in respect of injuries and death occurring during that detention. Indeed, the burden of proof may be regarded as resting on the authorities to provide a satisfactory and convincing explanation.[14] The general principle applied by the Court in such instances is the 'beyond reasonable doubt' standard of proof. Such proof may follow from the co-existence of sufficiently strong, clear and concordant inferences or of similar unrebutted presumptions of facts. As persons in custody are in a vulnerable position, the authorities are under a duty to protect them and to provide a plausible explanation of how injuries in custody have been caused.[15]

The obligation on the part of the authorities to account for the treatment of an individual in custody is particularly stringent where that individual dies. Deprivations of life in such context are generally subjected to the most careful scrutiny by the Court, which takes into consideration not only the actions of State agents but also all the surrounding circumstances.[16] Thus in the *Velikova* Case, in which the applicant complained about the death of a relative in police custody following intentional infliction of injuries and subsequent failure of the authorities to provide him with adequate medical help, the Court noted the implausibility of the explanation by the Government that Mr. Tsonchev had fallen, and thus injured himself, in light of the autopsy reports detailing severe injuries inflicted through beating. Considering further the failure of the authorities to provide any evidence that Mr. Tsonchev had been examined by a medical professional while in custody with care warranted by the severity of his condition, the Court concluded that there had been a violation of Article 2.[17] In the *Anguelova* Case the Court observed that the fact that police officers were not medical professionals, did not relieve them from the responsibility for failing to detect a medical emergency, particularly in the light of strong evidence that death had occurred

---

[13]   Judgment of 18 May 2000, *Velikova*, para. 70; judgment of 27 June 2000, *Salman*, para. 99; judgment of 10 July 2001, *Avşar*, para. 391; judgment of 18 June 2002, *Orhan*, para. 326

[14]   Judgment of 27 June 2000, para. 100. See also the judgment of 8 July 1999, *Çakici*, para. 85; judgment of 9 May 2000, *Ertak*, para. 32; judgment of 13 June 2000, *Timurtaş*, para. 82; judgment of 18 June 2002, *Orhan*, para. 327. See also the judgment of 14 February 2004, *Ipek*, para. 164.

[15]   Judgment of 27 August 1992, *Tomasi*, para. 108; judgment of 28 July 1999, *Selmouni*, para. 87

[16]   Judgment of 27 June 2000, *Salman*, para. 99. See also the judgment of 13 June 2000, *Timurtaş*, para. 327; judgment of 18 June 2002, *Orhan*, para. 327; judgment of 14 February 2004, *Ipek*, para. 165.

[17]   Judgment of 18 May 2000, para. 97.

in their custody and also in light of their failure to provide a credible explanation as to the skull fracture and serious bodily injuries of the applicant's relative. The Court held that there had been a violation of Article 2.[18]

In the *Tanli* Case the Court noted that, where an individual was taken into police custody in good health and died, it was incumbent on the State to provide a plausible explanation. The Court recalled that Mahmut Tanli, a 22-year-old man, was in good health when taken into custody, with no medical history of illness. He had completed his military service one year before without any medical problems. However, some twenty four to thirty six hours after being taken into custody, he died during interrogation at the Uluyol police station. The Court considered that the post mortem procedure was defective in fundamental aspects. The Istanbul Forensic Medicine Institute, which carried out a second examination of the body on 12 June 1995, found there had been no dissection of the heart. It concluded that in these circumstances the findings in the first report were without scientific value. The expert report provided by the applicant also considered that the alleged basis for the cause of death was insufficiently recorded or detailed to be relied on. Nor did the examination of the body rebut the allegations made by the applicant that his son was tortured to death. No tests apt to establish the presence of subtle signs of torture were carried out. The domestic post mortem procedures accordingly failed to provide an explanation for Mahmut Tanli's death. It certainly could not be considered as established, as submitted by the Government, that he had died from natural causes. The Court, therefore, found that the Government had not accounted for the death of Mahmut Tanli during his detention at the Uluyol police station and that their responsibility for his death was engaged.[19]

The Court has also dealt, in a number of cases, with allegations that the State has not fulfilled its positive obligation to protect the right to life of prisoners under its jurisdiction, who either committed suicide or were killed by other prisoners while detained. In such circumstances the Court applies a two-pronged analysis in the determination of whether a State has failed in its positive obligation under Article 2. Firstly, it is ascertained whether the authorities knew or ought to have known that the individual concerned was in any real and immediate risk, and secondly, it considers whether the authorities took all necessary operational measures that could reasonably be expected from them to prevent that risk from materialising. In the *Keenan* Case the applicant complained that the prison authorities, through their treatment of her son prior to his suicide, had failed to protect his right to life contrary to Article 2. She alleged in particular that by not assessing properly his fitness for segregation and by inflicting disciplinary punishment on him, the prison authorities had increased the stresses on

---

[18]   Judgment of 13 June 2002, paras 126-131.
[19]   Judgment of 10 April 2001, paras 143-146.

her son's schizophrenic mind and had, therefore, induced his suicide. In its judgment the Court noted that there was no formal evidence pointing to the fact that the applicant's son was suffering from schizophrenia and concluded that the applicant's allegations were to some extent speculative as the reason for Mark Keenan's suicide had not been established. Despite the lack of evidence pointing to Mark Keenan suffering from schizophrenia, the prison authorities, being put on notice upon his detention that he exhibited suicidal tendencies, considered that his unstable mental condition required that he be monitored carefully for symptoms of deterioration. Therefore, in all the various instances in which Mark Keenan evinced suicidal tendencies, he was placed in hospital care and subjected to regular consultations with psychiatrists. In these circumstances the Court was of the opinion that the authorities had taken all steps that could reasonably be expected from them to protect the life of the applicant's son. Accordingly, the Court concluded that there had been no violation of Article 2.[20]

A breach of Article 2 was found, however, in the *Paul and Audrey Edwards* Case, in which the applicants complained of the authorities' failure to protect their son's life while in detention. Christopher Edwards was killed while detained on remand by a dangerous, mentally ill prisoner, Richard Linford, who was placed in his cell. Noting the failure of the different agencies involved in the case – medical profession, police, prosecution and court – to pass information about the condition of Richard Linford (of which condition they were all aware as it was considered to permanently commit Linford to mental care) on to the prison authorities, and also taking notice of the inadequate nature of the screening process on Richard Linford's arrival in prison (during which process it was observed that his behaviour was disturbing), the Court held that the State had failed in its positive obligation to protect the life of Christopher Edwards in violation of Article 2.[21]

In the Case of *L.C.B. v. the United Kingdom*, where the applicant, who suffered from leukaemia, was the daughter of a soldier who had been on Christmas Island during the United Kingdom's nuclear tests, the Court noted that it was not suggested that the State had intentionally sought to deprive her of her life but examined under Article 2 whether the State had done all that could have been required of it to prevent the applicant's life from being avoidably put at risk. It found that the State had not failed in this regard.[22]

---

[20]   Judgment of 3 April 2001, paras 97-104.
[21]   Judgment of 14 March 2002, para. 64.
[22]   Judgment of 9 June 1998, paras 36-41.

6.3.3 OBLIGATION TO PROTECT THE LIFE OF INDIVIDUALS AGAINST THE ACTS OF THIRD PARTIES

The Court has firmly established in its case law that the first sentence of Article 2(1) enjoins the State not only to refrain from the intentional and unlawful taking of life, but also to take appropriate steps to safeguard the lives of those within its jurisdiction.

The *Osman* Case concerned the alleged failure of the authorities to protect the right to life of the first applicant's husband and of the second applicant, her wounded son, from the threat posed by an individual, and the lawfulness of restrictions on the applicants' right to access to a court to sue the authorities for damage caused by the said failure. The Court noted that it was not disputed that Article 2 may in well-defined circumstances imply a positive obligation on the authorities to take preventive operational measures to protect an individual whose life is at risk from the criminal acts of another individual. As to the scope of that obligation the Court considered that, bearing in mind the difficulties involved in policing modern societies, the unpredictability of human conduct and the operational choices which must be made in terms of priorities and resources, any such obligation must be interpreted in a way which does not impose an impossible or disproportionate burden on the authorities. Accordingly, not every claimed risk to life can entail for the authorities a Convention requirement to take operational measures to prevent that risk from materialising. For a positive obligation to arise it must be established that the authorities knew or ought to have known at the time of the existence of a real and immediate risk to the life of an identified individual or individuals from the criminal acts of a third party and that they failed to take measures within the scope of their powers which, judged reasonably, might have been expected to avoid that risk.

According to the Court it is common ground that the State's obligation in this respect extends beyond its primary duty to secure the right to life by putting in place effective criminal law provisions to deter the commission of offences against the person backed up by law-enforcement machinery for the prevention, suppression and sanctioning of breaches of such provisions. Another relevant consideration is the need to ensure that the police exercise their powers to control and prevent crime in a manner which fully respects the due process and other guarantees which legitimately place restraints on the scope of their action to investigate crime and bring offenders to justice. In the particular case the Court did not accept the Government's view that the failure to perceive the risk to life in the circumstances known at the time or to take preventive measures to avoid that risk must be tantamount to gross negligence or willful disregard of the duty to protect life. Such a rigid standard must be considered to be incompatible with the requirements of Article 1 of the Convention and the obligations of Contracting States under that Article to secure the practical and effective protection of the rights and freedoms laid down therein, including Article 2. Having regard to the nature of the right protected by Article 2, a right fundamental in the scheme of the Convention, it is sufficient for an applicant to show that the authorities did not do all that could be reasonably expected of them to avoid a real and immediate risk to life of which they have or ought to have knowledge. This is a question which can only be answered in the light of all the circumstances of any particular case. In the case under consideration the Court noted that the applicants had failed to point to any decisive stage in the sequence of the events leading up to the tragic shooting when it could be said that the police knew or ought to have known that the lives of the victims were at real and immediate risk from the shooter. Therefore, the Court found no violation of Article 2 in this case.[23]

In the *Denizci* Case the Court held that there was nothing to suggest that, even supposing that the applicant's son feared that his life was at real and immediate risk, he had ever reported these fears to the Cypriot police. Nor was there anything to indicate that the Cypriot authorities ought to have known that the applicant's son was at risk of attack from criminal acts of a third party and failed to take steps to protect him. For these reasons the Court concluded that there had been no violation of Article 2 of the Convention on this account.[24]

The *Mastromatteo* Case concerned the murder of the applicant's son by three criminals who were making their getaway after robbing a bank. It was subsequently proved that two of the three had been serving prison sentences pursuant to final criminal convictions for repeated violent offences. At the material time one of these two, who had fired the fatal shot, had been released on prison leave; the other was subject to a semi-custodial regime. The judges responsible for the execution of their sentences had granted prison leave and the semi-custodial measure on the ground that, according to the prison authorities' reports on their conduct in prison, they were not a danger to society. The three criminals were later sentenced to lengthy terms of imprisonment. The applicant applied for compensation under a law which made provision for aid to be paid to the victims of terrorism and organised crime, but his claim was refused, first by the Minister of the Interior and then by the President of Italy. Relying on Article 2 of the Convention, the applicant alleged that the decisions of the judges responsible for the execution of sentences who had granted his son's killers prison leave, had led to his death.

In this regard the Court recalled the situations it had earlier examined in the *Osman* and *Paul and Audrey Edwards* Cases concerning the requirement of personal protection of one or more individuals identifiable in advance as the potential target of a lethal act. It held, however, that the *Mastromatteo* Case differed from those cases in that it

---

[23]   Judgment of 28 October 1998, *Osman*, paras 115-116. See also the judgment of 28 March 2000, *Kiliç*, para. 62; judgment of 23 May 2001, *Denizci*, para. 375; judgment of 17 January 2002, *Calvelli and Ciglio*, para. 55; judgment of 18 June 2002, *Öneryildiz*, para. 63; judgment of 20 December 2004, *Makaratzis*, para. 57.

[24]   Judgment of 23 May 2001, paras 376-377.

was not a question here of determining whether the responsibility of the authorities was engaged for failing to provide personal protection to Mastromatteo. What was at issue was the obligation to afford general protection to society against the potential acts of one or of several persons serving a prison sentence for a violent crime and the determination of the scope of that protection. On the question of whether the system of alternative measures to imprisonment engaged the responsibility of the State under Article 2 of the Convention, the Court observed that one of the essential functions of a prison sentence was to protect society, but it recognised the legitimate aim of a policy of social reintegration. The Court noted that Italian legislation laid down restrictions on alternative measures where crimes committed by members of criminal organisations were concerned. It considered that the system introduced in Italy provided sufficient protective measures for society, as evidenced by the statistics supplied by the respondent State, which showed that few crimes were committed by prisoners subject to a semi-custodial regime or by prisoners who had absconded while on prison leave. Accordingly, there was nothing to suggest that the system of reintegration measures applicable in Italy at the material time should be called into question under Article 2.

As to whether the adoption and implementation of the alternative measures disclosed a breach of the duty of care required in this area by Article 2 of the Convention, the Court pointed out that the relevant risk in the present case was a risk to life for members of the public at large rather than for one or more identified individuals. In granting the alternative measures the judges responsible for the execution of sentences had based their decisions on reports from the prison authorities which gave positive accounts of the conduct of the two prisoners. The Court considered that there was nothing to make the national authorities fear that the release of these two men might pose a real and immediate threat to life. Nor was there anything to alert the authorities to the need to take additional measures against them once they had been released. Admittedly, one of them had been granted prison leave after an accomplice had taken advantage of his own prison leave to abscond, but that did not, in the Court's view, establish a special need for caution, since there was no way of knowing that they would commit an offence which would result in the loss of life.

Consequently, the Court considered that it had not been established that the prison leave granted to the prisoners gave rise to any failure on the part of the judicial authorities to protect the right to life of the applicant's son. It concluded that there had been no violation of Article 2 as regards the complaint relating to the authorities lack of diligence.[25] As the killers had been prisoners in the State's charge at the material time, the Court indicated that a procedural obligation arose to determine the circumstances of the applicant's son's death. As a result of the investigation the criminals had been found guilty of murder, sentenced to lengthy terms of imprisonment and ordered

---

[25]   Judgment of 24 October 2002, paras 69-76.

to compensate the applicant. Consequently, the Court was of the opinion that the State had satisfied the obligation under Article 2 of the Convention to guarantee a criminal investigation. As to whether the procedural obligations under Article 2 required a remedy by which a claim could be lodged against the State, the Court noted that the applicant's compensation claim had been dismissed on the ground that the statute relied on was not applicable to the case. However, he could have sued the State for negligence, for which purpose there had been two remedies available to him, namely an action against the State under Article 2043 of the Civil Code and an action against the judges responsible for the execution of sentences under the Judges' Liability Act. In that connection the Court observed that Article 2 of the Convention did not impose on States an obligation to provide compensation on the basis of strict liability. Consequently, the Court held that the procedural requirements under Article 2 of the Convention had been satisfied.[26]

In the Case of *L.C.B v. the United Kingdom* the applicant claimed that both the State's failure to warn her parents of the possible risk to her health caused by her father's participation in the nuclear tests and its earlier failure to monitor her father's radiation dose levels, gave rise to violations of Article 2 of the Convention. The Court held that the first sentence of article 2(1) enjoins the State not only to refrain from the intentional and unlawful taking of life, but also to take appropriate steps to safeguard the lives of those within its jurisdiction. The Court's task is to determine whether the State did all that could have been required of it in order to prevent the applicant's life from being avoidably put at risk.[27] Having examined the evidence submitted to it, the Court was not satisfied that it had been established that there was a causal link between the exposure of the father to radiation and the leukemia found in a child that was subsequently conceived. Therefore, the Court could not reasonably hold that at the time of the nuclear testings the United Kingdom could or should have taken action in respect of the applicant. In addition, the Court found it clearly uncertain whether monitoring of the applicant's health from birth would have lead to earlier diagnosis and medical intervention such as to diminish the severity of her disease.[28]

In the *Calvelli and Ciglio* Case the Court held that the same principles applied in the public-health sphere as well. The positive obligations implied in Article 2 require States to make regulations compelling hospitals, whether public or private, to adopt appropriate measures for the protection of patients' lives. They also require an effective independent judicial system to be set up so that the cause of death of patients in the care of the medical profession, whether in the public or the private sector, can be

---

[26]   *Ibidem*, paras 92-97.
[27]   Judgment of 9 June 1998, para. 36. See also the judgment of 28 March 2000, *Kaya*, para. 85; judgment of 17 January 2002, *Calvelli and Ciglio*, para. 48; judgment of 18 June 2002, *Öneryildiz*, para. 62.
[28]   *Ibidem*, paras 38-41.

determined and those responsible made accountable. However, if the infringement of the right to life or to personal integrity was not caused intentionally, the positive obligation imposed by Article 2 to set up an effective judicial system does not necessarily require the provision of a criminal law remedy in every case. In the specific sphere of medical negligence the obligation may, for instance, also be satisfied if the legal system affords victims a remedy in the civil courts, either alone or in conjunction with a remedy in the criminal courts, enabling any liability of the doctors concerned to be established and any appropriate civil redress, such as an order for damages and for the publication of the decision, to be obtained. Disciplinary measures may also be envisaged.[29]

In the particular case the applicants complained of a violation of Article 2 of the Convention on the ground that, due to procedural delays, a time-bar had arisen making it impossible to prosecute the doctor responsible for the delivery of their child that had died shortly after birth. The applicants' complaint was essentially that no criminal penalty was imposed on the doctor found liable for the death of their child in the criminal proceedings at first instance because of the operation of the time bar. The Court noted that, in cases of death through medical negligence, the Italian legal system affords injured parties both mandatory criminal proceedings and the possibility of bringing an action in the relevant civil court. The Government had affirmed, and the applicants did not deny, that disciplinary proceedings could be brought if the doctor was held liable in the civil courts. Consequently, the Italian system offers litigants remedies which, in theory, meet the requirements of Article 2. However, that provision will not be satisfied if the protection afforded by domestic law exists only in theory: above all, it must also operate effectively in practice within a time-span such that the courts can complete their examination of the merits of each individual case. The Court noted that the criminal proceedings instituted against the doctor concerned became time-barred because of procedural shortcomings that led to delays, particularly during the police inquiry and judicial investigation. However, the applicants were also entitled to institute proceedings in the civil courts and that is what they did. It was true that no finding of liability was ever made against the doctor by a civil court. However, the case file showed that in the civil proceedings in the Cosenza Court of First Instance, the applicants entered into a settlement agreement with the doctor's and the clinic's insurers and voluntarily waived their right to pursue the civil proceedings, which could have led to an order against the doctor for the payment of damages and possibly to the publication of the judgment in the press.

The Court accordingly considered that the applicants had denied themselves access to the best means – and one that, in the special circumstances of the instant case, would have satisfied the positive obligations arising under Article 2 – of elucidating the extent of the doctor's responsibility for the death of their child. Consequently, the Court

---

[29]   Judgment of 17 January 2002, para. 53.

concluded that, where a relative of a deceased person accepts compensation in settlement of a civil claim based on medical negligence, he or she is in principle no longer able to claim to be a victim. That conclusion made it unnecessary for the Court to examine, in the special circumstances of the instant case, whether the fact that a time-bar prevented the doctor being prosecuted for the alleged offence was compatible with Article 2.[30]

The *Öneryildiz* Case concerned the death of nine members of the family of the applicant who lived in a shanty town that comprised a collection of slums haphazardly built on land surrounding a rubbish tip which had been used jointly by four district councils since the 1970s and was under the authority and responsibility of the main City Council of Istanbul. An expert report drawn up on 7 May 1991 at the request of the Üsküdar District Court, to which the case had been referred by the Ümraniye District Council, drew the authorities' attention to, among other things, the fact that no measure had been taken with regard to the tip in question to prevent a possible explosion of the methane gas being given off by the decomposing refuse. The report gave rise to a series of disputes between the mayors concerned. Before the proceedings instituted by either of them had been concluded a methane-gas explosion occurred on 28 April 1993 on the waste-collection site and the refuse erupting from the pile of waste buried eleven houses situated below it, including the one belonging to the applicant, who lost nine members of his family. The Turkish Government submitted that the operation of an installation for the storage of household waste, which involved only a very slight risk, should not be regarded as the exercise of a potentially dangerous activity or situation, comparable to those pertaining to the spheres of public health and nuclear or industrial installations.

Referring to the principle set out in the *Osman* Case, the Grand Chamber held that, if it is established that the authorities knew or ought to have known at the time of the existence of a real and immediate risk to the life of an individual or individuals, they had a positive obligation under Article 2 of the Convention to take such preventive measures as were necessary and sufficient to protect those individuals, especially as the authorities themselves had set up the rubbish site and authorised its operation, which gave rise to the risk in question.[31] Among these preventive measures particular emphasis should be placed on the public's right to information, as established in the case law of the Convention institutions. This obligation indisputably applies in the particular context of dangerous activities, where, in addition, special emphasis must be placed on regulations geared to the special features of the activity in question, particularly with regard to the level of the potential risk to human lives. They must govern the licensing, setting up, operation, security and supervision of the activity and must

---

[30]   *Ibidem,* paras 58-61.
[31]   Judgment of 30 November 2004, *Öneryildiz,* para. 101.

make it compulsory for all those concerned to take practical measures to ensure the effective protection of citizens whose lives might be endangered by the inherent risks. The Grand Chamber held that this right, which had already been recognised under Article 8,[32] may also, in principle, be relied on for the protection of the right to life, particularly as this interpretation is supported by current developments in European standards. In any event, the relevant regulations must also provide for appropriate procedures, taking into account the technical aspects of the activity in question, for identifying shortcomings in the processes concerned and any errors committed by those responsible at different levels.[33]

The Court continued by considering that the obligations deriving from Article 2 do not end there. Where lives have been lost in circumstances potentially engaging the responsibility of the State, that provision entails a duty for the State to ensure, by all means at its disposal, an adequate response – judicial or otherwise – so that the legislative and administrative framework set up to protect the right to life is properly implemented and any breaches of that right are repressed and punished.[34] If the infringement of the right to life or to physical integrity is not caused intentionally, the positive obligation to set up an 'effective judicial system' does not necessarily require criminal proceedings to be brought in every case and may be satisfied if civil, administrative or even disciplinary remedies were available to the victims.[35]

According to the Court, however, in areas such as that in issue in the *Öneryildiz* Case, the applicable principles are rather to be found in those which the Court has already had occasion to develop in relation notably to the use of lethal force, principles which lend themselves to application in other categories of cases. In this connection it should be pointed out that in cases of homicide the interpretation of Article 2 as entailing an obligation to conduct an official investigation is justified not only because any allegations of such an offence normally give rise to criminal liability[36], but also because often, in practice, the true circumstances of the death are, or may be, largely confined within the knowledge of State officials or authorities.[37] Where it is established that the negligence attributable to State officials or bodies on that account goes beyond an error of judgment or carelessness, in that the authorities in question, fully realising the likely consequences and disregarding the powers vested in them, failed to take measures that were necessary and sufficient to avert the risks inherent in a dangerous activity, the fact that those responsible for endangering life have not been charged with

---

[32]   Judgment of 19 February 1998, *Guerra and Others*; para. 228.
[33]   Judgment of 30 November 2004, *Öneryildiz*, paras 89-90.
[34]   See also judgment of 28 October 1998, *Osman*, paras 115-116.
[35]   Judgment of 30 November 2004, *Öneryildiz*, paras 91-92. See also the judgment of 17 January 2002, *Calvelli and Ciglio*, para. 51; judgment of 24 October 2002, *Mastromatteo*, para. 90; Judgment of 8 July 2004, *Vo*, para. 90.
[36]   Decision of 11 January 2000, *Caraher*.
[37]   Judgment of 27 September 1995, *McCann*, paras 157-164.

a criminal offence or prosecuted may amount to a violation of Article 2, irrespective of any other types of remedy which individuals may exercise on their own initiative; this is amply evidenced by developments in the relevant European standards.[38]

The Court summed up its position as follows: "the judicial system required by Article 2 must make provision for an independent and impartial official investigation procedure that satisfies certain minimum standards as to effectiveness and is capable of ensuring that criminal penalties are applied where lives are lost as a result of a dangerous activity if and to the extent that this is justified by the findings of the investigation. In such cases, the competent authorities must act with exemplary diligence and promptness and must of their own motion initiate investigations capable of, firstly, ascertaining the circumstances in which the incident took place and any shortcomings in the operation of the regulatory system and, secondly, identifying the State officials or authorities involved in whatever capacity in the chain of events in issue. That said, the requirements of Article 2 go beyond the stage of the official investigation, where this has led to the institution of proceedings in the national courts; the proceedings as a whole, including the trial stage, must satisfy the requirements of the positive obligation to protect lives through the law. It should in no way be inferred from the foregoing that Article 2 may entail the right for an applicant to have third parties prosecuted or sentenced for a criminal offence or an absolute obligation for all prosecutions to result in conviction, or indeed in a particular sentence. On the other hand, the national courts should not under any circumstances be prepared to allow life-endangering offences to go unpunished. This is essential for maintaining public confidence and ensuring adherence to the rule of law and for preventing any appearance of tolerance of or collusion in unlawful acts. The Court's task therefore consists in reviewing whether and to what extent the courts, in reaching their conclusion, may be deemed to have submitted the case to the careful scrutiny required by Article 2 of the Convention, so that the deterrent effect of the judicial system in place and the significance of the role it is required to play in preventing violations of the right to life are not undermined."[39]

With respect to the responsibility borne by the State for the deaths in the *Öneryildiz* Case, the Court noted at the outset that there were safety regulations in force in Turkey in both of the fields of activity central to the present case – the operation of household-refuse tips and the rehabilitation of slum areas. The expert report submitted on 7 May 1991 had specifically referred to the danger of an explosion due to methanogenesis, as the tip had had "no means of preventing an explosion of methane occurring as a result of the decomposition" of household waste. The Court considered that neither the reality nor the immediacy of the danger in question was in dispute, seeing that the risk of an explosion had clearly come into being long before it was highlighted in the

---

[38]   Judgment of 30 November 2004, *Öneryildiz*, para. 93.
[39]   Judgment of 30 November 2004, *Öneryildiz*, paras 94-96.

report of 7 May 1991 and that, given the site's continued operation in the same conditions, that risk could only have increased over time. It was impossible for the administrative and municipal departments responsible for supervising and managing the tip not to have known of the risks inherent in methanogenesis or of the necessary preventive measures, particularly as there were specific regulations on the matter.

The Court likewise regarded it as established that various authorities had also been aware of those risks, at least by 27 May 1991, when they had been notified of the report of 7 May 1991. Since the Turkish authorities had known or ought to have known that there was a real or immediate risk to persons living near the rubbish tip, they had had an obligation under Article 2 of the Convention to take such preventive operational measures as were necessary and sufficient to protect those individuals, especially as they themselves had set up the site and authorised its operation, which had given rise to the risk in question. However, Istanbul City Council had not only failed to take the necessary urgent measures but had also opposed the recommendation by the Prime Minister's Environment Office to bring the tip into line with the applicable standards. It had also opposed the attempt, in August 1992, by the mayor of Ümraniye to obtain a court order for the temporary closure of the waste-collection site. As to the Government's argument that the applicant had acted illegally in settling by the rubbish tip, the Court observed that in spite of the statutory prohibitions in the field of town planning, the Turkish State's consistent policy on slum areas had encouraged the integration of such areas into the urban environment and had thus acknowledged their existence and the way of life of the citizens who had gradually caused them to build up since 1960, either of their own free will or simply as a result of that policy. From 1988 until the accident of 28 April 1993 the applicant and his close relatives had lived entirely undisturbed in their house, in the social and family environment they had created. It also appeared that the authorities had levied council tax on the applicant and other inhabitants of the Ümraniye slums and had provided them with public services, for which they were charged. Accordingly, the Government could not maintain that they were absolved of responsibility on account of the victims' negligence or lack of foresight.

As to the policy required for dealing with the social, economic and urban problems in that part of Istanbul, the Court acknowledged that it was not its task to substitute its own views for those of the local authorities. However, the timely installation of a gas-extraction system at the Ümraniye tip before the situation became fatal could have been an effective measure which would have complied with Turkish legislation and general practice in such matters without placing an impossible or excessive burden on the authorities. Such a measure would also have been a better reflection of the humanitarian considerations which the Government had relied on before the Court to justify the fact that they had not taken any steps entailing the immediate and wholesale destruction of the slum areas. The Court further noted that the Government had not shown that any measures had been taken to provide the slum inhabitants with information about the risks they were running. In any event, even if the Turkish authorities had respected the right to information, they would not have been absolved of responsibility in the absence of more practical measures to avoid the risks to the slum inhabitants' lives. In conclusion the Court held that the regulatory framework applicable in the present case had proved defective in that the tip had been allowed to operate and there had been no coherent supervisory system. That situation had been exacerbated by a general policy which had proved powerless in dealing with general town-planning issues and had undoubtedly played a part in the sequence of events leading to the accident. The Court accordingly held that there had been a violation of Article 2.[40]

6.3.4   OBLIGATION TO CONDUCT AN EFFECTIVE INVESTIGATION

In the *McCann* Case the parents of the victims who were shot dead in Gibraltar by members of the Special Air Service (SAS), which is a regiment of the British Army, alleged a violation of Article 2. The Court held that the obligation to protect the right to life required some form of effective official investigation when individuals have been killed as a result of the use of force by agents of the State. However, the Court did not deem it necessary to decide what form such an investigation should take and under what conditions it should be conducted, since public inquest proceedings in which the applicants were legally represented and which involved the hearing of seventy-nine witnesses, had in fact taken place. Moreover, the lawyers acting on behalf of the applicants were able to examine and cross-examine key witnesses, including the military and police personnel involved in the planning and conduct of the anti-terrorist operation, and to make the submissions they wished to make in the course of the proceedings. Against this background the Court did not consider that the alleged shortcomings in the inquest proceedings substantially hampered the carrying out of a thorough, impartial and careful examination of the circumstances surrounding the killings. In this respect there had thus been no breach of Article 2(1).[41]

A different conclusion was reached in the *Jordan* Case, in which the applicant also submitted that there had been no effective investigation into the circumstances surrounding the death of his son, who had been shot and killed by a police officer. The Court considered that a number of factors distinguished this case from the *McCann* Case. Firstly, the investigation into the killing was headed and carried out by police officers who, albeit subject to the supervision of an independent police monitoring authority, were hierarchically linked to the officer subject to the investigation.

---

[40]   *Ibidem*, paras 97-110.
[41]   Judgment of 27 September 1995, para. 162.

Secondly, the investigation report did not contain any reasoned justification as to why the shooting was to be regarded as not disclosing a criminal offence or as not meriting a prosecution of the officer concerned. The lack of such reasoned opinion, in the Court's view, could not be considered compatible with Article 2 as it did not reassure a concerned public and the relatives affected that the rule of law had been respected. Thirdly, the inquest proceedings conducted into the killing of the applicant's son did not provide, according to the Court, the same procedural guarantees as those in the *McCann* Case. In Northern Ireland, unlike in England and Wales, not every person suspected of causing death could be compelled to give evidence. In the particular case under consideration, the failure of the authorities to require the officer investigated for the killing to provide them with his testimony, detracted, in the Court's view, from the inquest's capacity to establish the facts immediately relevant to the death, specifically the lawfulness of the use of force, and thereby to comply with the requirements of Article 2. Furthermore, the absence of legal aid for the representation of the victim's family in the proceedings and the non-disclosure of witness statements prior to their appearance (on the basis of public interest immunity, without a fair balance being struck between the interests of the two sides concerned) at the inquest, prejudiced, according to the Court, the ability of the applicant to participate in the inquest and contributed to the long adjournments of proceedings. Lastly, the Court considered that the inquest had not been pursued with reasonable expedition as at the date of the Court's judgment, more than eight years after the inquest's initiation, proceedings had still not been concluded. On the basis of the aforementioned considerations the Court concluded that the procedural shortcomings of the investigation into the applicant son's death had been such so as to substantially hamper an independent and thorough examination into the killing in question. Accordingly, Article 2 had been breached.[42]

A slightly different set of circumstances compelled the Court to also find a violation of Article 2 in the *McKerr* Case, in which the applicant alleged that his father had been unjustifiably killed by security forces and that there had been no effective investigation into his death. It was noted that the existence of an independent police authority supervising the officers carrying out the investigation could not be regarded as a sufficient safeguard where the investigation itself had been – for all practical purposes – conducted by police officers connected to those being investigated.[43] Moreover, although three police officers were put to criminal trial for the death of the applicant's father, the same shortcomings of the inquest procedure, as those detailed above with reference to the *Jordan* Case, did oblige the Court to find a breach of Article 2. Different from the *Jordan* Case, however, the afore-mentioned considerations were evaluated in a broader context, warranted by a violation of the procedural require-

---

[42]   Judgment of 4 May 2001, para. 145.
[43]   Judgment of 4 May 2001, para. 67.

ments of Article 2 on one additional account – particularly disturbing in the Court's view – namely, the decision of the authorities not to charge the three police officers, alleged as responsible for the killing of the applicant's father, with an attempt to pervert the course of justice. Although in the course of investigation it had been established that they were instructed to withhold information concerning their belonging to a special police branch unit and their acting on intelligence information, the inquest proceedings failed to properly examine the matter. The Court, in its turn, considered that the attempts at concealment of information and the investigators' failure to react adequately, raised serious and legitimate doubts as to the integrity of the investigative process, particularly in a case in which it had been established that a person had been killed in the course of security operations – a situation raising issues pertaining to the proportionate use of force in counter-terrorism procedures.[44]

A similar failure on the part of the national authorities to include in the inquest proceedings concerns about possible collusion by security force personnel in the targetting and killing of the applicant's son in the *Shanaghan* Case, led the Court to the conclusion that there had been a breach of the procedural requirements of Article 2. The Court noted that, although the investigating officers had been made aware of evidence pointing to the fact that Patrick Shanaghan had been subjected to harassment and threats by the police force, it had not been deemed necessary to extend the inquest to allegations concerning events having taken place before the particular incident under consideration. Considering this drawback of the investigation proceedings in the light of the failure of the authorities to identify the perpetrator of the applicant son's killing, the lack of independence of the investigating authorities and the general defects of the inquest procedure in Northern Ireland (as discussed above with reference to the *Jordan* Case and the *McKerr* Case), the Court concluded that there had been a breach of Article 2.[45]

The inadequacy of inquest procedures in Northern Ireland and the lack of independence of the authorities investigating allegations of police involvement in killings, as detailed in the cases of *Jordan*, *McKerr* and *Shanaghan* above, were once again confirmed by the Court in the *Kelly* Case[46] and in the more recent *Finucane*[47] Case, in which the procedural requirements of Article 2 were deemed violated, the Court's reasoning and conclusion being in conformity with its previous judgments. The Court re-affirmed the requirement, imposed on States by Article 2, to carry out effective official investigation when individuals had been killed as a result of the use of force, and particularly when there had been allegations of complicity of police or security

---

44   *Ibidem*, para. 76.
45   Judgment of 4 May 2001, paras 122-125.
46   Judgment of 4 May 2001, para. 139.
47   Judgment of 1 July 2003, para. 84.

forces in the killings.[48] It also stressed the need for the investigating authorities to be independent – hierarchically, institutionally and also practically – from those persons implicated in the events under investigation.[49] The Court further emphasised the obligation of States to ensure promptness of the investigation and a degree of public scrutiny, which may vary from case to case but must always allow for the involvement of the next-of-kin of victims in all investigative proceedings so as to safeguard their legitimate interests.[50]

In the *Denizci* Case the Court noted that with respect to the investigation that immediately after the killing was reported to the authorities, the police went to the scene, a plan of the incident site was drawn up and a list of the objects found was established. Relevant samples were taken and scientifically examined. A pathologist who arrived at the scene a few hours after the killing proceeded to the post mortem examination and, later on the same day, carried out an autopsy on the bodies. The Court also noted the numerous acts accomplished by the local police during the investigation opened into the killing of the applicant's son and his friend, which led, in less than a year, to a case-file of more than 600 pages. In the light of the above and having examined the investigation file submitted by the domestic authorities, the Court saw no element which would allow it to conclude that the investigation into the killing was inadequate. There had been accordingly no violation of Article 2 on this account.[51]

In the *Öneryildiz* Case, discussed *supra* in subsection 6.3.3, the positive obligation under Article 2 to conduct an independent and impartial investigation was also at issue. With respect to the responsibility borne by the State as regards the nature of the investigation the Court considered that the administrative remedy used by the applicant to claim compensation could not satisfy the requirement to conduct an effective investigation into the deaths of the applicant's close relatives. As to the criminal law remedies used, the Court considered that the investigating authorities could be regarded as having acted with exemplary promptness and as having shown diligence in seeking to establish the circumstances that had led both to the accident of 28 April 1993 and to the ensuing deaths. Those responsible for the events in question had been identified and prosecuted, eventually being sentenced to the minimum penalty applicable under the Criminal Code. However, the sole purpose of the criminal proceedings in the present case had been to establish whether the authorities could be held liable for 'negligence in the performance of their duties' under Article 230 of the Criminal Code, which provision did not in any way relate to life-endangering acts or

---

[48]   See, *mutatis mutandis*, the judgment of 27 September 1995, *McCann*, para. 161; and decision of 20 February 1995, *Kaya*, para. 86.

[49]   See, *mutatis mutandis*, the judgments of 4 May 2001, *Kelly and Others*, para. 95; *McKerr*, para. 112; and *Hugh Jordan*, para. 106; judgment of 27 July 1998, *Güleç*, paras 81-82; and judgment of 28 July 1998, *Ergi*, paras 83-84.

[50]   *Ibidem.*

[51]   Judgment of 23 May 2001, paras 378-379.

to the protection of the right to life within the meaning of Article 2. The judgment of 4 April 1996 had left in abeyance any question of the authorities' possible responsibility for the death of the applicant's close relatives. Accordingly, it could not be said that the Turkish criminal justice system had secured the full accountability of State officials or authorities for their role in the tragedy, or the effective implementation of provisions of domestic law guaranteeing respect for the right to life, in particular the deterrent function of criminal law. The Court, therefore, held that there had also been a violation of Article 2 concerning the inadequate investigation into the deaths of the applicant's close relatives.[52]

In the *Makaratzis* Case, even though an administrative investigation had been carried out following the incident, the Court observed that there had been striking omissions in its conduct. In particular, the Court attached significant weight to the fact that the domestic authorities had failed to identify all the policemen who had taken part in the chase. Some policemen had left the spot without identifying themselves and without handing over their weapons so that some of the firearms which were used had never been reported. It also appeared that nothing had been done to identify the policemen who had been on duty in the area when the incident had taken place. Moreover, it was remarkable that only three bullets had been collected and that, other than the bullet which had been removed from Mr Makaratzis's foot and the one which was still in his buttock, the police had never found or identified the other bullets which had injured the applicant. Those omissions had prevented the Greek court from making as full a finding of fact as it might otherwise have done and had resulted in the acquittal of the police officers on the ground that it had not been shown beyond reasonable doubt that it was they who had injured the applicant, since many other shots had been fired from unidentified weapons. In those circumstances the Court concluded that the authorities had failed to carry out an effective investigation into the incident. The incomplete and inadequate character of the investigation was highlighted by the fact that, even before the Court, the Government had been unable to identify all the officers who had been involved in the shooting and wounding of the applicant. The Court concluded that there had accordingly been a violation of Article 2 of the Convention in that respect. Having regard to that conclusion, it did not find it necessary to determine whether the failings identified in this case were part of a practice adopted by the authorities, as asserted by the applicant.[53]

---

[52]   Judgment of 30 November 2004, paras 111-118.
[53]   Judgment of 20 December 2004, paras 76-80.

6.3.5 MEASURES AND PROCEDURES IN TURKEY DURING THE EMERGENCY SITUATION OF THE 1990S

The Court has also examined a great number of complaints against Turkey concerning the emergency situation in the South-East region in the 1990s, which complaints have produced a series of findings of failures by the authorities to investigate allegations of wrongdoing by the security forces, both in the context of the procedural obligations under Article 2 of the Convention and the requirement for effective remedies imposed by Article 13 of the Convention.[54] A common feature of these cases is a finding that the public prosecutor had failed to pursue complaints by individuals claiming that the security forces were involved in an unlawful act, for example not interviewing or taking statements from members of the security forces implicated, accepting at face value the reports of incidents submitted by members of the security forces and attributing incidents to the PKK on the basis of minimal or no evidence.

In the *Ergi* Case the Court observed that the responsibility of the State was not confined to circumstances where there was significant evidence that misdirected fire from agents of the State has killed a civilian. It may also be engaged where they fail to take all feasible precautions in the choice of means and methods of a security operation mounted against an opposing group with a view to avoiding and, in any event, to minimising incidental loss of civilian life. Thus, even though it had not been established beyond reasonable doubt that the bullet which killed the victim had been fired by the security forces, the Court had to consider whether the security forces' operation had been planned and conducted in such a way as to avoid or minimise, to the greatest extent possible, any risk to the lives of the villagers, including from the firepower of the PKK members caught in the ambush. In this case the ambush operation took place in a village. Even though the security forces had been careful not to hit the civilians in their fire, the terrorists of the PKK could not be assumed to do the same. Therefore, the Court found that it could reasonably be inferred that insufficient precautions had been taken to protect the lives of the civilian population. As for the investigation of the situation by the State, the Court attached particular weight to the procedural requirement implicit in Article 2. It recalled that, according to its case law, the obligation to protect the right to life under Article 2, read in conjunction with the State's general duty under Article 1, requires by implication that there should be some form of effective official investigation when individuals have been killed as a result of the use of force by agents of the State. However, this obligation is not confined to

---

[54] Judgment of 19 February 1998, *Kaya*, paras 86-92; judgment of 28 July 1998, *Ergi*, paras 82-85; judgment of 2 September 1998, *Yaşa*, paras 98-108; judgment of 8 July 1999, *Çakici*, para. 87; judgment of 8 July 1999, *Tanrikulu*, paras 101-111; judgment of 9 May 2000, *Ertak*, paras 134-135; judgment of 13 June 2000, *Timurtaş*, paras 87-90; judgment of 14 November 2000, *Demiray*, para. 48.

cases where it has been established that the killing was caused by an agent of the State, nor is it decisive whether members of the deceased's family or others have lodged a formal complaint about the killing with the relevant investigatory authority. In the case under consideration the mere knowledge of the killing on the part of the authorities gave rise to an obligation under Article 2 to carry out an effective investigation into the circumstances surrounding the death.[55]

In the *Ertak* Case the Court noted one particular omission in that the investigating officer responsible for the preliminary investigation did not have in his possession the case file in which was to be found, among other documents, a deposition referring to other people who had been in custody, and had not in the course of his investigations taken a statement from the applicant or other persons named by the applicant in his complaint.[56]

In the *Akkoç* Case the Court found that it had not been established beyond reasonable doubt that any State agent or person acting on behalf of the State authorities was involved in the killing of Zübeyir Akkoç. It found that Zübeyir Akkoç, a teacher of Kurdish origin and engaged in trade union activities perceived by the authorities as unlawful and against the State interest, was at particular risk of falling victim to an unlawful attack. The authorities were aware of this risk, in particular as he and the applicant had informed the public prosecutor that they had received telephone calls during which threats to their lives were made. The authorities were also aware, or ought to have been aware, of the possibility that this risk derived from the activities of persons or groups acting with the knowledge or acquiescence of elements in the security forces. The Court, therefore, had to consider whether the authorities had done all that could be reasonably expected of them to avoid the risk to Zübeyir Akkoç. While there were large numbers of security force personnel in the south-east and a framework of law in place with the aim of protecting life, the implementation of criminal law in respect of unlawful acts allegedly carried out with the involvement of the security forces disclosed particular characteristics in the south-east region during this period. Firstly, where offences were committed by State officials in certain circumstances, the public prosecutor's competence to investigate was removed to administrative councils which took the decision whether or not to prosecute. The Court had already found in two previous cases that these councils, made up of civil servants under the orders of the Governor, did not provide an independent or effective procedure for investigating deaths implicating the security forces. Secondly, the attribution of responsibility for incidents to the PKK had particular significance as regards investigations and judicial procedures, since jurisdiction for terrorist crimes had been given to the State Security Courts, which had been found by the Court not to fulfil the requirement of independence imposed by

---

[55]   Judgment of 28 July 1998, paras 82-85.
[56]   Judgment of 9 May 2000, para. 135.

Article 6 of the Convention, due to the presence of a military judge whose participation gave rise to legitimate fears that the court may be unduly influenced by considerations extraneous to the case.

The Court found that these defects undermined the effectiveness of criminal law protection, permitting or fostering a lack of accountability of members of the security forces for their actions incompatible with the rule of law in a democratic society respecting the fundamental rights and freedoms guaranteed under the Convention. This removed from Zübeyir Akkoç the protection which he should have received by law. Furthermore, the Government had not provided any information concerning steps to investigate the existence of contra-guerrilla groups or the extent to which State officials were implicated in unlawful killings during this period. Nor had any steps been taken by the public prosecutor in response to the applicant's petitions concerning the threats to their lives. The Court concluded that in the circumstances of this case the authorities had failed to take reasonable measures available to them to prevent a real and immediate risk to the life of Zübeyir Akkoç and, accordingly, there had been a violation of Article 2.[57] The Court also noted that the investigation into the killing by the gendarmes had effectively ended by 25 January 1993. Only one statement was taken at the scene. Though Seyithan Araz, tried for separatist offences as a Hizbollah member, was alleged in an indictment before the Diyarbakir State Security Court to have killed Zübeyir Akkoç, there was no direct evidence linking him with that particular crime. There was no explanation either as to why he had not been charged with the killing of the teacher, shot with the same gun at the same time as Zübeyir Akkoç. Seyithan Araz was in any event acquitted of the offences. No steps had been taken to investigate the possible source of the threats to the applicant and her husband prior to the shooting. Having regard, therefore, to the limited scope and short duration of the investigation in this case, the Court found that the authorities failed to carry out an effective investigation into the circumstances surrounding the death of Zübeyir Akkoç. It concluded that there had been, in this respect too, a violation of Article 2.[58]

In the *Tanli* Case, concerning a 22-year old individual who was taken into police custody in good health but died during interrogation twenty-four to thirty-six hours later, the Court observed that the autopsy investigation was of critical importance in determining the facts surrounding Mahmut Tanli's death. This investigation, while launched promptly by the public prosecutor, had been shown to be defective in a number of fundamental respects. It also appeared that the doctors who had signed the post mortem report were not qualified forensic pathologists, notwithstanding the provision in the Code of Criminal Procedure which required the presence of a forensic doctor. In the light of the defective forensic investigation it was not surprising that the court proceedings resulted in the acquittal for lack of evidence of the three police

---

[57]   Judgment of 10 October 2000, paras 83-94.
[58]   *Ibidem*, paras 95-99.

officers who had been interrogating Mahmut Tanli before he died. The Court con-cluded that the authorities failed to carry out an effective investigation into the circum-stances surrounding Mahmut Tanli's death.[59]

In the *Avşar* Case the Court held that the mere fact that the authorities were informed of the abduction of Mehmet Şerif Avşar by village guards and others holding themselves out as security officers, following which he was found dead, gave rise of itself to an obligation under Article 2 to carry out an effective investigation into the circumstances surrounding this incident. The Court concluded that the investigation by the gendarmes and public prosecutor, and before the criminal court, did not provide a prompt or adequate investigation of the circumstances surrounding the killing of Mehmet Şerif Avşar and was, therefore, in breach of the State's procedural obligation to protect the right to life. This rendered recourse to civil remedies equally ineffective in the circumstances. The Court, therefore, held that there had been a violation of Article 2 in this respect. The Court was satisfied that Mehmet Şerif Avşar might be regarded as having died after having been taken into custody by agents of the State. It did not accept that the crime was committed by persons acting in their private capacity without the knowledge of the authorities and thereby beyond the scope of the State's responsibility. The Court recalled that there was a lack of accountability as regards the security forces in south-east Turkey in or about 1993 and further noted that this case additionally highlighted the risks attached to the use of civilian volunteers in a quasi-police function. It had been established in this case that guards were used regularly on a variety of official operations, including the apprehension of suspects. According to the regulations provided by the Government, village guards were hierarchically subordinate to the district gendarme commander. However, it was not apparent what supervision was, or could be exerted over guards who were engaged in duties outside the jurisdiction of the district gendarme commander. Nor, as the village guards were outside the normal structure of discipline and training applicable to gendarmes and police officers, was it apparent what safeguards there were against wilful or unintentional abuses of position carried out by the village guards either on their own initiative or under the instructions of security officers who themselves were acting outside the law. Although there had been a prosecution which had resulted in the conviction of the village guards and Mehmet Mehmetoğlu, there was a failure to investigate promptly or effectively the identity of the seventh person, the security official, and thereby to establish the extent of official knowledge of or connivance in the abduction and killing of Mehmet Şerif Avşar. As the investigation and court pro-ceedings had not provided sufficient redress for the applicant's complaints concerning the authorities' responsibility for his brother's death, he might still claim to be a victim, on behalf of his brother, of a violation of Article 2. No justification for the killing of Mehmet Şerif Avşar being provided, the Court concluded that the Turkish Govern-

---

[59]   Judgment of 10 April 2001, paras 147-151.

ment was liable for his death. There had accordingly been a breach of Article 2 in this respect.[60]

With regard to the investigative measures taken following a complaint, the Court noted in the *Demiray* Case, firstly, that the Lice public prosecutor's office did not appear to have arranged a visit to the site of the incident in order to carry out any investigations or, at the very least, to confirm the accuracy of the sketch map drawn up by the gendarmes. Furthermore, none of the gendarmes present at the scene of Ahmet Demiray's death appeared to have been questioned. Lastly, the autopsy was performed by a general practitioner and contained little forensic evidence. The authority's conclusion that a classic autopsy by a forensic medical examiner was not necessary, was, in the Court's view, inadequate given that a death occurred in the circumstances described in the present case. The Lice public prosecutor's office appeared to have confined itself to giving a decision on 29 May 1996 that it had no jurisdiction *ratione materiae*. In that decision it established that Ahmet Demiray had been killed by a booby-trapped grenade planted by the PKK. The Lice public prosecutor's office based that conclusion solely on two documents which had been sent to it by the provincial gendarmerie command which constituted "all the information in the case file". The Court considered, in the light of its observations on the lack of investigative measures, that such a conclusion could be regarded as hasty given the scant amount of information available at the time to the Lice public prosecutor's office. The subsequent investigation carried out by the administrative bodies hardly remedied the shortcomings referred to above. The Government asserted that this investigation was still pending, but had not provided any concrete information on the progress of the investigation despite the fact that four years had elapsed since the case file was transferred to the Kocaköy District Commissioner's Office. The Court felt it important to point out, as it had done in earlier cases, that serious doubts arose as to the ability of the administrative authorities concerned to carry out an independent investigation, as required by Article 2 of the Convention, having regard to their nature and composition. Lastly, the investigation referred to by the Government, which they maintained was initiated in order to identify and arrest those suspected of having murdered the applicant's husband, was apparently also pending, but the Government had not produced any evidence concerning such an investigation. The Court considered that the authorities had failed to carry out an effective investigation into the circumstances of Ahmet Demiray's death. It found that the authorities concerned had disregarded their essential responsibilities in this respect. The Court was prepared to take into account, as indicated in the *Yaşa* Case and *Tanrikulu* Case, the fact that loss of life was a tragic and frequent occurrence in the context of the security situation in south-east Turkey, which might have hampered the search for conclusive evidence. Nonetheless, such

---

[60]   Judgment of 10 July 2001, paras 399-416.

circumstances could not have the effect of relieving the authorities of the obligation imposed by Article 2 to carry out an effective investigation.[61]

In the *Gül* Case the Court found that, while an investigation into the incident had been carried out by the public prosecutor, there were a number of significant omissions. Furthermore, although the actions of the officers involved required careful and prompt scrutiny by the responsible authorities, the public prosecutor did not take any statements from them. Nor were the officers required to account for the use of their weapons and ammunition. As regards the investigation by the administrative council, the Court noted its previous findings that the investigations undertaken by administrative councils into killings by security forces failed to satisfy the requirements of an independent investigation, in particular since the council and the officers under investigation were both hierarchically subordinate to the governor. The Court considered whether the criminal proceedings cured the defects in the investigation into the events up to that date. The criminal court heard evidence from the three officers charged, who gave brief statements. It called no other witnesses. The applicant and members of his family were not informed that the proceedings were taking place and were not afforded the opportunity of submitting to the court their very different version of events. The court requested two expert opinions (from a gendarme lieutenant and from police experts) which contained an evaluation of events based on the assumption that the police officers' account was the correct one. They both reached conclusions as to the lack of fault of the officers which were based on that general evaluation rather than on any findings of technical expertise. The court's decision to acquit the three officers was based entirely on the opinion that there was no fault. There was no reasoning as to why the police officers' account was preferred to that of the family. In basing itself without any additional explanation on the experts' legal classification of the officers' actions, the court in this case effectively deprived itself of its jurisdiction to decide the factual and legal issues of the case.[62]

In the *Şemse Önen* Case the Court held that rather than carrying out a serious and effective investigation in the preliminary phase, the competent authorities appeared to have proceeded on the assumption that it was the PKK, not State security forces or gendarmes, who were responsible for the killings. Similar criticism could also be made about the subsequent investigation before the State Security Court. The Court noted that, since the conclusion of those proceedings, nothing had come to light which suggested that the authorities had taken further investigative measures that could be regarded as effective for the purposes of Article 2. The Court, therefore, found that the authorities had failed to carry out an adequate and effective investigation into

---

[61]   Judgment of 14 November 2000, paras 51-53.
[62]   Judgment of 14 December 2000, paras 88-93.

the circumstances surrounding the killings and that there had been a violation of Article 2 in that respect.[63]

6.3.6 MISSING PERSONS

In the Case of *Cyprus v. Turkey* the applicant Government upheld that the number of missing Greek-Cypriots was 1,485 and that the evidence clearly pointed to the fact that the missing Greek-Cypriots were either detained by, or were in the custody or under the actual authority and responsibility of the Turkish army or its militia, and were last seen in areas which were under the effective control of the respondent State. They maintained, in addition, that the Court should proceed on the assumption that the missing persons were still alive, unless there was evidence to the contrary. The Court noted at the outset that the applicant Government had not contested the facts as found by the Commission. Like the Commission the Court did not consider it appropriate to estimate the number of persons that fell into the category of "missing persons". It limited itself to observing that figures were communicated by the applicant Government to the United Nations Committee on Missing Persons ("CMP") and revised in accordance with the most recent information which became available. Furthermore, the Court shared the Commission's concern to limit its inquiry to ascertaining the extent, if any, to which the authorities of the respondent State had clarified the fate or whereabouts of the missing persons. It was not its task to make findings on the evidence on whether any of these persons were alive or dead or had been killed in circumstances which engaged the liability of the respondent State.

The Court observed that the applicant Government contended first and foremost that the missing persons must be presumed to be still alive unless there was clear evidence to the contrary. Although the evidence adduced before the Commission confirmed a very high incidence of military and civilian deaths during the military operations of July and August 1974, the Court reiterated that it could not speculate as to whether any of the missing persons had in fact been killed by either the Turkish forces or Turkish-Cypriot paramilitaries into whose hands they might have fallen. It was true that the head of the "TRNC", Mr Denktaş, broadcasted a statement on 1 March 1996 admitting that the Turkish army had handed over Greek-Cypriot prisoners to Turkish-Cypriot fighters under Turkish command and that these prisoners had then been killed. It was equally the case that, in February 1998, Professor Yalçin Küçük, who was a serving Turkish officer in 1974, asserted that the Turkish army had engaged in widespread killings of civilians. Although all of these statements had given rise to undoubted concern, especially in the minds of the relatives of the missing persons, the Court considered that they were insufficient to establish the respondent State's liability

---

[63]   Judgment of 14 May 2002, paras 88-92.

for the deaths of any of the missing persons. It was mere speculation that any of these persons were killed in the circumstances described in these accounts. The Court noted that the evidence given of killings carried out directly by Turkish soldiers or with their connivance, related to a period which was outside the scope of the present application. Indeed, it was to be noted that the Commission had been unable to establish on the facts whether any of the missing persons were killed in circumstances for which the respondent State could be held responsible under the substantive limb of Article 2 of the Convention. The Court concluded, therefore, that it could not accept the applicant Government's allegations that the facts disclosed a substantive violation of Article 2 of the Convention in respect of any of the missing persons.

The Court recalled that there was no proof that any of the missing persons had been unlawfully killed. However, in its opinion, and of relevance to the instant case, the above-mentioned procedural obligation also arose upon proof of an arguable claim that an individual, who was last seen in the custody of agents of the State, subsequently disappeared in a context which might be considered life-threatening. Against this background the Court observed that the evidence bore out the applicant Government's claim that many persons now missing were detained either by Turkish or Turkish-Cypriot forces. Their detention occurred at a time when the conduct of military operations was accompanied by arrests and killings on a large scale. The Commission correctly described the situation as life-threatening. That the missing persons disappeared against this background could not be denied. The Court could not but note that the authorities of the respondent State had never undertaken any investigation into the claims made by the relatives of the missing persons that the latter had disappeared after being detained in circumstances in which there was real cause to fear for their welfare. It must be noted in this connection that there was no official follow-up to Mr Denktaş's alarming statement. No attempt was made to identify the names of the persons who were reportedly released from Turkish custody into the hands of Turkish-Cypriot paramilitaries or to inquire into the whereabouts of the places where the bodies were disposed of. It did not appear either that any official inquiry was made into the claim that Greek-Cypriot prisoners were transferred to Turkey. The Court noted that, although the CMP's procedures were undoubtedly useful for the humanitarian purpose for which they were established, they were not of themselves sufficient to meet the standard of an effective investigation required by Article 2 of the Convention, especially in view of the narrow scope of that body's investigations. The Court concluded that there had been a continuing violation of Article 2 on account of the failure of the authorities of the respondent State to conduct an effective investigation aimed at clarifying the whereabouts and fate of Greek-Cypriot missing persons who had disappeared in life-threatening circumstances.[64]

---

[64]   Judgment of 10 May 2001, paras 125-136.

6.3.7 FORCED DISAPPEARANCES

It was not until 1998 that the Court had to deal with the question of forced disappearances. In the *Kurt* Case the applicant requested the Court to find on the basis of the facts established by the Commission that the disappearance of her son engaged the responsibility of the respondent State under Articles 2, 3 and 5 of the Convention, and that each of those Articles had been violated. The Court recalled at the outset that it had accepted the Commission's findings of fact in respect of the detention of the applicant's son by soldiers and village guards. Subsequent to this detention almost four and a half years had passed without information as to his whereabouts or fate. According to the applicant, in such circumstances there were compelling grounds for drawing the conclusion that her son had in fact been killed in unacknowledged custody at the hands of his captors. However, the Court held that it would have to carefully scrutinise whether there in fact existed concrete evidence, which would lead it to conclude that the applicant's son was, beyond reasonable doubt, killed by the authorities either while in detention or at some subsequent stage. It noted that in those cases where it had found that a Contracting State had a positive obligation under Article 2 to conduct an effective investigation into the circumstances surrounding an alleged unlawful killing by the agents of that State, there had existed concrete evidence of a fatal shooting, which had brought that obligation into play.[65]

Turning to the particular case before it, the Court then observed that the applicant's claims rested entirely on presumptions deduced from the circumstances of her son's initial detention, bolstered by more general analyses of an alleged officially tolerated practice of disappearances and associated ill-treatment and extra-judicial killings of detainees in the respondent State. The Court considered that these arguments were not in themselves sufficient to compensate for the absence of more persuasive indications that the applicant's son had in fact met his death in custody. As to the applicant's argument that there existed a practice of violations of, *inter alia*, Article 2 in the respondent State, the Court considered that the evidence which she had adduced, did not substantiate such a claim. In the light of these considerations the Court concluded that the applicant's assertions that the respondent State had failed in its obligation to protect her son's life in the circumstances described fell, instead, to be assessed from the standpoint of Article 5 of the Convention.[66]

In the *Çakici* Case the applicant put forward a similar claim alleging that his brother had been taken into unacknowledged detention and had since disappeared. According to the Court, however, this case had to be distinguished from the *Kurt* Case where, although the applicant's son had been taken into detention, no other elements of evidence existed regarding his treatment or fate subsequent to that. In the *Çakici* Case

---

[65]   Judgment of 27 September 1995, *McCann*; judgment of 19 February 1998, *Kaya*.
[66]   Judgment of 25 May 1998, paras 106-109.

the Court pointed out that very strong inferences could be drawn from the authorities' claim that the identity card of the applicant's brother was found on the body of a dead terrorist. The Court considered on that basis that there was sufficient circumstantial evidence, based on concrete elements, on which it could be concluded beyond reasonable doubt that the applicant's brother had died following his apprehension and detention by the security forces.[67] The Court furthermore held that, as Ahmet Çakici had to be presumed dead following an unacknowledged detention by the security forces, the responsibility of the respondent State for his death was, therefore, engaged. It observed that the authorities had not offered any explanation as to what had occurred following his apprehension, nor any ground of justification in respect of any use of lethal force by the Government's agents. Liability for Ahmet Çakici's death was, therefore, attributable to the respondent State and there had accordingly been a violation of Article 2 on that account. Furthermore, having regard to the lack of effective procedural safeguards, disclosed by the inadequate investigation carried out into the disappearance and the alleged finding of Ahmet Çakici's body, the Court found that the respondent State had failed in its obligation to carry out an effective investigation into Ahmet Çakici's death. Accordingly, there had been a violation of Article 2 of the Convention on this account also.[68]

Despite its initial reluctance, as evidenced by the *Kurt* Case, to accept that there existed in south-east Turkey in the early 1990s an officially tolerated practice of forced disappearances, ill-treatment and extra-judicial killings by security forces of detainees, suspected of PKK involvement, the Court subsequently re-examined its position. The landmark cases, which served as a central point of reference in later cases concerning forced disappearances and alleged killings, were the *Mahmut Kaya* Case and the *Kiliç* Case.[69] In both of these cases the Court considered that for lack of concrete evidence it could not be established beyond reasonable doubt that any State agents were involved in the alleged killings. However, the Court did acknowledge the so-called 'unknown perpetrator phenomenon' increasingly spreading in the south-east parts of Turkey.[70] It also deemed that the Turkish authorities were aware, or ought to have been aware, that this phenomenon was largely attributable to the activities of persons or groups acting with the knowledge or acquiescence of certain elements in the security forces. In reaching this conclusion the Court based itself on a report by a 1993 Parliamentary Investigation Commission, presented to the Turkish Prime Minister's Office. The report provided strong substantiations for allegations, current at the time

---

[67]   Judgment of 8 July 1999, para. 85. See also the judgment of 9 May 2000, *Ertak,* para. 131; judgment of 13 June 2000, *Timurtaş,* para. 85.
[68]   Judgment of 8 July 1999, para. 87.
[69]   Judgments of 28 March 2000.
[70]   See also judgment of 2 September 1998, *Yaşa,* para. 106.

and since, that certain 'counter-guerrilla' groups, involving terrorists and confessors, were targetting individuals perceived to be acting against the State interests and in support of the PKK, with the acquiescence and possible assistance of members of the security forces. Although the Turkish Government had refused to accede any judicial value to this report, it had relied on it in taking appropriate counter-measures. Therefore, the report was considered by the Court to be a significant document.[71]

Furthermore, the Court recalled previous judgments in which it had established that there existed substantial defects undermining the effectiveness of the protection afforded by criminal law in south-east Turkey during the emergency period in the 1990s against alleged unlawful acts on the part of the security forces, namely, unwillingness of the prosecution authorities to undertake investigations of alleged wrongdoings and also lack of independent and impartial procedure for investigating deaths involving security agents. In the light of the above considerations the Court concluded that any person, identified by the security forces as a PKK suspect and therefore apprehended and detained, could be considered as having been exposed to a real and immediate risk of being killed, especially if disappearance upon detention had remained unaccounted for by the authorities. The failure of the State to prevent such a risk from materialising, even in the absence of a body, and to carry out a prompt and adequate investigation into any instance of disappearance involving security forces, did, in the Court's opinion, suffice to engage the responsibility of the State under Article 2 of the Convention.[72]

In the *Timurtaş* Case the Court held as follows: "Article 5 imposes an obligation on the State to account for the whereabouts of any person taken into detention and who has thus been placed under the control of the authorities (...). Whether the failure on the part of the authorities to provide a plausible explanation as to a detainee's fate, in the absence of a body, might also raise issues under Article 2 of the Convention will depend on all the circumstances of the case, and in particular on the existence of sufficient circumstantial evidence, based on concrete elements, from which it may be concluded to the requisite standard of proof that the detainee must be presumed to have died in custody (...). In this respect the period of time which has elapsed since the person was placed in detention, although not decisive in itself, is a relevant factor to be taken into account. It must be accepted that the more time goes by without any news of the detained person, the greater the likelihood that he or she has died. The passage of time may therefore to some extent affect the weight to be attached to other elements of circumstantial evidence before it can be concluded that the person concerned is to be presumed dead. In this respect the Court considers that this situation gives rise to issues which go beyond a mere irregular detention in violation of Article 5. Such an interpretation is in keeping with the effective protection of the right to life

---

[71]   Judgment of 28 March 2000, *Kaya*, para. 91; judgment of 28 March 2000, *Kiliç*, para. 68.
[72]   Judgment of 28 March 2000, *Kaya*, paras 94-99; judgment of 28 March 2000 *Kiliç*, paras 71-75.

as afforded by Article 2, which ranks as one of the most fundamental provisions in the Convention (...).”[73]

The Court considered that there were a number of elements distinguishing this case from cases such as the *Kurt* Case. In the first place, six and a half years had elapsed since Abdulvahap Timurtaş was apprehended and detained – a period markedly longer than the four and a half years between the taking into detention of the applicant's son and the Court's judgment in the *Kurt* Case. Furthermore, whereas Üzeyir Kurt was last seen surrounded by soldiers in his village, it had been established in the present case that Abdulvahap Timurtaş was taken to a place of detention – first at Silopi, then at Şirnak – by authorities for whom the State is responsible. Finally, there were few elements in the *Kurt* Case file identifying Üzeyir Kurt as a person under suspicion by the authorities, whereas the facts of the present case left no doubt that Abdulvahap Timurtaş was wanted by the authorities for his alleged PKK activities. In the general context of the situation in south-east Turkey in 1993 it could by no means be excluded that an unacknowledged detention of such a person would be life-threatening. It was recalled that the Court had held in the *Kiliç* Case and the *Mahmut Kaya* Case that defects undermining the effectiveness of criminal law protection in the south-east region during the period relevant also to this case permitted or fostered a lack of accountability of members of the security forces for their actions. The Court was satisfied that Abdulvahap Timurtaş must be presumed dead following an unacknowledged detention by the security forces. Consequently, the responsibility of the respondent State for his death was engaged. Noting that the authorities had not provided any explanation as to what occurred after Abdulvahap Timurtaş's apprehension and that they did not rely on any ground of justification in respect of any use of lethal force by their agents, it followed that liability for his death was attributable to the respondent State.[74]

In the *Taş* Case the Court observed that, although the applicant's son was taken into custody on 14 October 1993, no entries were subsequently made in any custody records and that no reliable evidence has been forthcoming as to where he was held. Although he was injured in the knee by a bullet, there were no medical records showing that he had continued to receive treatment after being seen by Dr Can at Şirnak Military Hospital on the day of his apprehension. When, finally, more than a month later, the applicant received news of his son on or about 18 November 1993, he was told that his son had escaped from the security forces during an operation with them in the Gabar mountains on 9 November 1993. This assertion, based on a report by three officers who allegedly used code names and could not be identified by the

[73] Judgment of 13 June 2000, paras 82-83. See also the judgment of 27 February 2001, *Çiçek*, para. 145; judgment of 18 June 2002, *Orhan*, para. 329; judgment of 14 February 2004, *Ipek*, para. 166.
[74] Judgment of 13 June 2000, *Timurtaş*, para. 86; See also judgment of 14 November 2000, *Taş*, paras 66; judgment of 27 February 2001, *Çiçek*, para. 146; judgment of 18 June 2002, *Orhan*, para. 330.

Government, was lacking entirely in credibility and was not substantiated by any reliable evidence. The Court drew very strong inferences from the lack of any documentary evidence relating to where Muhsin Tas was detained and from the inability of the Government to provide a satisfactory and plausible explanation as to what happened to him. It also observed that in the general context of the situation in south-east Turkey in 1993, it could by no means be excluded that an unacknowledged detention of such a person would be life-threatening. For these reasons the Court found that Muhsin Taş must be presumed dead following his detention by the security forces. Consequently, the responsibility of the respondent State for his death was engaged. Noting that the authorities had not accounted for what happened during Muhsin Taş's detention and that they did not rely on any ground of justification in respect of any use of lethal force by their agents, it followed that liability for his death was attributable to the respondent Government. Accordingly, there had been a violation of Article 2 on that account.[75] The Court recalled that the public prosecutor at Cizre undertook no investigative steps in response to the petitions of the applicant, in which he expressed his fear that his son had been killed in detention. While the Government maintained that the public prosecutor was not required to investigate an unsubstantiated claim, the Court observed that it is incumbent on the competent authorities to ensure that persons in detention enjoy the safeguards accorded by law and judicial process. The lack of any reaction to a report that the security forces had 'lost' a person detained on suspicion of committing serious offences was incompatible with this obligation. Also in the light of its previous case-law the Court found that the investigation carried out into the disappearance of the applicant's son was neither prompt, adequate or effective and, therefore, disclosed a breach of the State's procedural obligations to protect the right to life.[76]

The Court further refined its reasoning in the Çiçek Case,[77] in which the applicant complained about the unacknowledged detention and disappearance of her two sons who had been taken into custody during a military operation in the south-east region of Turkey. Six and a half years had elapsed since their detention but the whereabouts of the applicant's sons and their fate had remained unknown. They had last been seen in the hands of soldiers. It was considered that a number of elements distinguished this case from the Kurt Case and, therefore, warranted a different conclusion. The applicant's sons were identified as persons under suspicion by the authorities; they were taken to a place of detention by state security forces and subsequently disappeared. The Government for their part had failed to adduce any information concerning the whereabouts of the applicant's sons, although the facts of the case had established that the two men had been taken to a detention centre by authorities for whom the respon-

---

[75]   Judgment of 14 November 2000, paras 65-67.
[76]   Ibidem, paras 68-71.
[77]   Judgment of 27 February 2001.

dent State was responsible. The Court also recalled that in the context of the situation in south-east Turkey in the period relevant to the case, it could by no means be excluded that the unacknowledged detention of a person, regarded as suspicious by the security forces, would be life-threatening.[78] For the above reasons the Court was satisfied that the applicant's sons could be presumed dead and held that the responsibility of the respondent State for their death was engaged. Accordingly, there had been a violation of Article 2 on that account. As the official investigation into Tahsin and Ali Çiçek's deaths had gone on for an unreasonably long time, the authorities failing to procure sufficient testimony from co-detainees of the Çiçek brothers and ignoring various relevant information, the Court also found that the investigation had been inadequate and, therefore, in breach of the State's procedural obligations to protect the right to life. There had accordingly been a violation of Article 2 on this account also.

In the *Akdeniz* Case the Court observed that, although the applicants' relatives were detained on or about 9 to 12 October 1993, no entries were subsequently made in any custody records. The evidence of the applicants and other villagers indicated that they were held at Kepir until about 17 to 19 October 1993, at which point some of them at least were seen being loaded onto a helicopter. There had been no news of the missing men since. The Court drew very strong inferences from the length of time which had elapsed, the lack of any documentary evidence relating to their detention, and the inability of the Government to provide a satisfactory and plausible explanation as to what had happened to them. It also observed that in the general context of the situation in south-east Turkey in 1993, it could by no means be excluded that an unacknowledged detention of such persons would be life-threatening. The Court also recalled that in two recent judgments it had held that defects undermining the effectiveness of criminal law protection in the south-east region during the period relevant also to this case permitted or fostered a lack of accountability of members of the security forces for their actions. For these reasons the Court concluded that the applicants' relatives might be presumed dead following their detention by the security forces. Consequently, the responsibility of the respondent State for their death was engaged. Noting that the authorities had not accounted for what happened during the period of alleged detention and that they had not relied on any ground of justification in respect of any use of lethal force by their agents, the Court found that the liability for the deaths of the applicants' relatives was attributable to the respondent Government. Accordingly, there had been a violation of Article 2 on that account.[79]

---

[78]   Judgment of 13 June 2000, *Timurtaş*, para. 85; judgment of 18 June 2002, *Orhan*, para. 330.
[79]   Judgment of 31 May 2001, paras 87-89.

The Court followed the same line of reasoning, and reached the same conclusion in the *Avşar* Case,[80] in the *Bilgin* Case,[81] and in the *Orhan* Case.[82]

In July 2002 the Committee of Ministers adopted an interim resolution on the above-mentioned judgments, where the Court had established a violation of Article 2 in respect of forced disappearances. The Committee of Ministers took regard to the forty-two judgments and decisions finding that Turkey was responsible for numerous breaches of the Convention relating notably to homicides, torture and destruction of property inflicted by its security forces and the lack of effective domestic remedies against the State officers who had committed these abuses. It also mentioned a number of other cases involving similar complaints which were struck off the list by the Court following friendly settlements or other solutions found, notably on the basis of the Government's undertaking to take rapid remedial measures. The Committee of Ministers noted that most of the violations in the cases here discussed took place against a background of the fight against terrorism in the first half of the 1990s and recalling that each member State, in combating terrorism, must act in full respect of its obligations under the Convention, as set out in the European Court's judgments. It recalled that since 1996-1997, when the Court adopted its first judgments relating to the violations of the Convention committed by the Turkish security forces, it had consistently emphasised that Turkey's compliance with them must *inter alia* entail the adoption of general measures so as to prevent new violations similar to those found in these cases.

The Committee of Ministers also referred to its earlier Interim Resolution, in which it noted with satisfaction some progress in the adoption of such measures, while at the same time calling on Turkey to rapidly adopt further comprehensive measures.[83] The Committee of Ministers finally urged Turkey to accelerate without delay the re-form of its system of criminal prosecution for abuses by members of the security forces, in particular by abolishing all restrictions on the prosecutor's competence to conduct criminal investigations against State officials, by reforming the prosecutor's office and by establishing sufficiently deterring minimum prison sentences for persons found guilty of grave abuses such as torture and ill-treatment, and decided to pursue the supervision of the execution of the judgments concerned until all necessary measures had been adopted and their effectiveness in preventing new similar violations had been established.[84]

---

[80]   Judgment of 10 July 2001, para. 416.
[81]   Judgment of 17 July 2001, para. 144.
[82]   Judgment of 18 June 2002, paras 330-331.
[83]   Interim Resolution DH(99)434 of 9 June 1999.
[84]   Interim Resolution ResDH(2002)98 of 10 July 2002.

6.4   BEGINNING AND END OF PHYSICAL LIFE

6.4.1   ABORTION

The most difficult interpretation problem that Article 2 raises concerns the question of the beginning and the end of the physical life of the human person.

The word 'everyone' does not exclude the possibility that unborn life falls under the protection of Article 2, no more than this is true of 'every human being' in Article 6 of the Covenant.[85] If one takes the view that such protection is indeed included, it implies that *abortus provocatus* must in principle be prohibited by the legislator and prosecuted by the authorities.

On this point, however, there is no consensus yet at the national and the international level.[86] The question was expressly left open by the Commission in its report in the *Brüggeman and Scheuten* Case.[87] In a later decision in *X v. the United Kingdom* the Commission held with respect to the word 'everyone' in Article 2 that both the use of this term in the Convention in general and the context in which the term has been used in Article 2 (for this, the Commission paid attention in particular to the exceptions mentioned in Article 2, which apply exclusively to individuals already born) indicate that the term is not meant to include the unborn child.[88] The Commission did not confine itself to this, but subsequently examined whether the term 'life' in Article 2 refers only to the life of an individual already born or also includes the unborn life. In this connection it stated, first of all, that the views as to the question at what moment there is life tend to diverge widely, and that the term 'life' may also have a different meaning according to the context in which it is used.[89] Next, the Commission distinguished the following three possibilities: (1) Article 2 is not applicable to the foetus at all; (2) Article 2 recognises the right to life of the foetus with specific implied restrictions; or (3) Article 2 recognises an unqualified right to life for the foetus.[90]

---

85   As to the latter article this point was expressly left open: UN Doc. A/3764, para. 112.

86   See Recommendation 874 (1979) of the Parliamentary Assembly concerning a "European Charter on the Rights of the Child", Parl. Ass., *Documents*, Doc. 4376, which contains the words "the right of every child to life from the moment of conception". See also Recommendation 1046 (1986) on the use of human embryos and foetuses for diagnostic, therapeutic, scientific, industrial and commercial purposes, where the Parliamentary Assembly stresses that a definition of the biological status of the embryo is necessary and expresses its awareness of the fact that scientific progress has made the legal position of the embryo and foetus particularly precarious, and that their legal status is at present not defined by law.

87   Report of 12 July 1977, D&R 10 (1978), p. 100 (116).

88   Appl. 8416/78, D&R 19 (1980), p. 244 (249-250). This argument would not seem very convincing, since, as the Commission itself mentioned, Article 4 of the American Convention, which uses the term 'every person', expressly protects the unborn life.

89   *Ibidem*, pp. 250-251.

90   *Ibidem*, p. 252.

The third possibility was excluded by the Commission, since from the mere fact that Article 2 also protects the life of the mother, certain restrictions ensue with respect to the life of the unborn child, as it cannot have been intended by the drafters that priority should be given to the latter life, particularly in view of the fact that, when the Convention was drafted, nearly all the States Parties allowed abortion for the protection of the mother's life.[91] The Commission subsequently noted that there was no need for it to take a position in a general sense on the two other possibilities, because the case under discussion concerned an interruption of pregnancy in the early stages of pregnancy and exclusively on medical opinion. Even if one were to assume that Article 2 is applicable to the first months of pregnancy, in any case an implied restriction was concerned here, *viz.* the protection of the life and the health of the mother.[92]

The line of reasoning of the Commission makes it all too evident that it felt confronted here with a complicated question, which it thought could hardly be answered in a general way.[93] The rejection of the third possibility was not very problematic. However, the Commission subsequently seemed to extend the exceptional case in which abortion is necessary to spare the life of the mother rather readily to the situation where it is not the life of the mother that is at stake, but the abortion is considered desirable for some other medical reason. There is, however, an essential difference between the protection of the life of the mother as a ground for restriction, which ensues directly from Article 2 itself and is narrowly defined, and the much wider ground 'medical opinion', which Article 2 is held to also imply. Even if one assumes that a woman's right to physical and mental integrity, which may be based on Article 3,[94] may be interpreted in so wide a manner that it provides protection against any conscious injury to physical and mental health, and if on the other hand one does not rule out that Article 2 protects the unborn life, it is by no means self-evident that the former right has priority, so that the protection of that right implicitly restricts the enjoyment of the latter right by the foetus. The only point that has been decided here by the Commission is, therefore, that, in the Commission's opinion, in the present case, even if one assumes that Article 2 protects the unborn life, the rights and interests involved had been weighed against each other in a reasonable way. As long as the question of whether Article 2 is applicable to the unborn life has not been answered in the negative, this reasonableness will have to be reviewed in each individual case. Since a generally accepted standard still seems to be lacking, such a review is likely to be a rather marginal one.

---

[91]   *Ibidem.*

[92]   *Ibidem*, pp. 252-253.

[93]   As in other difficult and highly controversial cases, here too it is astonishing that the Commission declared the complaint to be *manifestly* ill-founded; *ibidem*, p. 253.

[94]   Article 2 protects the physical integrity only insofar as an injury to it constitutes a threat to life. See *supra* 6.2. and Appl. 8278/78, *X v. Austria*, D&R 18 (1980), p. 154 (156).

In a later decision the Commission took a somewhat different approach, but with a rather far-reaching result. Here again it started by observing that it did not exclude that in certain circumstances the foetus may enjoy a certain protection under Article 2, notwithstanding the fact that the Contracting States show a considerable divergence of views on whether or to what extent Article 2 protects the unborn life. The Commission continued that it did not have to decide this question because it was clear that national laws on abortion differ considerably. In these circumstances, and assuming that the Convention may be considered to have a certain bearing in this field, the Commission found that in such a delicate area the Contracting States must have a certain discretion. The Norwegian legislation in this respect was rather liberal. It allowed self-determined abortion within the first 12 weeks of pregnancy. From the 12th week until the 18th week of pregnancy, a termination could be authorised by a board of doctors, if certain conditions had been fulfilled. After the 18th week, termination was not allowed, unless there were serious reasons for such a step. According to the Commission, this legislation did not exceed the discretion allowed to States in this matter.[95]

It follows from the aforementioned recapitulation of the position of the Commission that in the circumstances examined by it – i.e. regarding various national laws on abortion – it did not consider the unborn child as a 'person' directly protected by Article 2 of the Convention and that, in its opinion, even if the 'unborn child' were to be considered having a 'right to life', such a right is implicitly limited by the mother's rights and interests. It did not rule out, however, the possibility that in certain circumstances safeguards might be extended to the unborn child notwithstanding the fact that there is in the Contracting Parties a considerable divergence of views on whether or to what extent Article 2 protects unborn life, and accordingly notwithstanding the discretion afforded to member States in this area. This is what appears to have been contemplated by the Commission in the *Brüggeman and Scheuten* Case, where it held that "pregnancy cannot be said to pertain uniquely to the sphere of private life. Whenever a woman is pregnant, her private life becomes closely connected with the developing foetus".[96]

As far as the Court's case law is concerned, in the *Boso* Case, although holding that it was not required to determine "whether the foetus may qualify for protection under the first sentence of Article 2", the Court went on to also examine the claim in the particular case under the supposition that in certain circumstances the foetus's right to life might be protected by Article 2. Although this did not alter the Court's conclusion that Italian law had struck a fair balance between the woman's interests and the need to ensure the protection of the foetus, the Court did leave open the

---

95   Appl. 17004/90, *H v. Norway*, D&R 73 (1992), p. 155 (167).
96   *Brüggeman and Scheuten v. Federal Republic of Germany*, D&R 10 (1978), pp. 116-7.

possibility that Article 2 might apply to the unborn child, provided that certain conditions are in place. However, no indication was given as to what these conditions might be. Nor is the Court's hesitation on this point a guarantee that eventually, in the course of further case law development, the protection of Article 2 will be extended to the unborn child. In any case each particular complaint will have to be determined on its own merits by weighing the rights, freedoms and interests of parents in relation to one another or vis-à-vis an unborn child.[97]

The Court re-affirmed its position in the *Vo* Case, in which it was faced with a complaint by a woman who intended to carry her pregnancy to term and whose unborn child was expected to be viable, but whose pregnancy was terminated as a result of a negligent error of a doctor. She claimed that the refusal of the French authorities to classify the taking of her unborn child's life as unintentional homicide was in breach of Article 2 of the Convention. In its judgment the Court considered that it was neither possible, nor desirable, to answer in the abstract the question whether an unborn child is a person for the purpose of Article 2. The Court relied on the lack of consensus – scientific and legal – as to the nature and status of the embryo and/or foetus, the difficulty in seeking the harmonisation of national laws as well as the inappropriateness of imposing one exclusive moral code. It, therefore, reiterated that the issue of when the right to life begins comes within the margin of appreciation which States enjoy.

The Court furthermore affirmed, albeit indirectly, the position it had taken in its earlier case law, stipulating that the lack of a clear legal status, under either national or Convention law, did not necessarily deprive the unborn child's life of all protection. As Article 2 imposes on States a duty to refrain from intentional killing as well as an obligation to take appropriate steps to safeguard the lives of those within their jurisdictions, States are required to regulate their public health sector so as to protect patients' rights. This requirement extends also to the existence of an effective independent judicial system, set up so as to hold medical professionals accountable for any misconduct. When such misconduct, however, has resulted in a negligent infringement of the right to life, the positive obligation imposed on States by Article 2 does not necessarily require the provision of a criminal-law remedy in every case; an administrative procedure accompanied by all requisite safeguards, including the possibility for civil redress, should suffice. As such a procedure had been available to the applicant in the particular case under consideration the Court considered that there had been no procedural violation of Article 2 of the Convention. Thus the Court once again re-affirmed its unwillingness to rule on whether an unborn child enjoys the direct protection of Article 2 but left open the possibility that Article 2 might have some role

---

[97]   Decision of 5 September 2002.

to play in abortion cases, although always subject to certain restrictions derived from the parents' rights and interests.[98]

Who is entitled to complain in the case of abortion? Apart from the highly unlikely case of a complaint by a State, the parents will be entitled to vindicate the rights of their unborn child. However, they will proceed to do so only if abortion has been performed against their will or without their consent or the consent of one of them. If such a case concerns parents who are married or are living together in an extramarital relationship, it would seem more appropriate for them to invoke Article 8 (the right to respect for private and family life)[99] or Article 12 (the right to found a family).[100]

6.4.2   EUTHANASIA

The question not as to the beginning, but as to the end of the life protected in Article 2, arises in connection with euthanasia. Here again a uniform regulation in the laws of the Contracting States and an international standard are lacking. It would seem, however, that even in those situations where it must in reason be assumed that human life still exists, euthanasia does not *per se* conflict with the Convention. It might be argued that the value of the life to be protected should be weighed against other rights of the person in question, particularly his right, laid down in Article 3, to be protected from inhuman and degrading treatment. Whether the will of the person is decisive in such a case, depends on whether the right to life is or is not to be regarded as inalienable. In this respect, too, a certain trend may be discerned, but not yet a *communis opinio*.[101] There is as yet hardly any standard for a strict review by the

---

[98]   Judgment of 8 July 2004, paras 91-95.

[99]   See Appl. 6959/75, *Brüggemann and Scheuten v. Federal Republic of Germany*, D&R 10 (1978), p. 100; and Appl. 8416/78, *X v. the United Kingdom*, D&R 19 (1980), p. 244 (253). In its decision on Appl. 11045/84, *Knudsen v. Norway*, D&R 42 (1985), p. 247 (256), the Commission took the position that, since the applicant was not a potential father, but a minister of religion within a State church, he was not affected differently by the abortion legislation than other citizens and therefore could not claim to be a victim. That he lost his office was, according to the Commission, not due to the Abortion Act but to the fact that he, because of his views on the Act, refused to perform functions that were duties of his office.

[100]   This holds good also for cases of sterilisation and other forms of birth control against the will of the person concerned, or at least without the latter's consent. In fact, in these cases there is not yet any question of destruction of life. It is therefore curious that in connection with a man's complaint about the sterilisation of his wife without his consent the Commission held that "an operation of this nature might in certain circumstances involve a breach of the Convention, in particular of Articles 2 and 3"; In Appl. 1287/61, *X v. Denmark* (not published) it was postulated that the right to life and the right to produce life are not to be equated.

[101]   See the discussion of the so-called 'euthanasia declaration' in the Hubinek/Voogd report concerning the rights of the sick and the dying, which was submitted early in 1976 in the Parliamentary Assembly of the Council of Europe; Council of Europe, Parl. Ass., Twenty-Seventh Session, *Documents*, Doc. 3699.

Strasbourg organs, neither as to the weighing between the various rights of the person in question, nor as to the establishment of the dividing line between human and merely vegetative life.[102]

According to the Strasbourg case law as it stands at the moment, the choice as to whether to permit euthanasia and assisted suicide falls within the States' margin of appreciation. According to the Court Article 2 cannot be said to guarantee to anyone a right to die, and, therefore, it cannot be regarded as an avenue for challenging national legislation prohibiting euthanasia. The aforementioned was expressly established by the Court in the *Pretty* Case. There the Court recalled that in all the cases it had dealt with concerning Article 2, it had consistently placed the emphasis on States' positive obligation to protect life. The Court was also explicit in stating that Article 2 is unconcerned with issues having to do with the quality of living or what a person chooses to do with his or her own life. Such issues, as far as they require protection from State interference, might be reflected in other Articles of the Convention (*e.g.* Article 8) or other international human rights instruments. However, to claim that Article 2 creates a right to self-determination in the sense of conferring on the individual an entitlement to choose death rather than life, would in the Court's view constitute a gross distortion of interpretation. Therefore, the Court held that the applicant's claim that the national authorities' refusal to permit her to commit assisted suicide, despite her suffering and imminent death, and her having taken the decision on the basis of informed consent, violated Article 2, was ill-founded. As to the question of whether countries that do permit euthanasia, are to be considered in breach of Article 2, the Court noted that the extent to which a State permits, or seeks to regulate, the possibility for the infliction of harm on individuals at liberty, by their own or another's hand, may raise conflicting considerations of personal freedom and public interest that can only be resolved on examination of the concrete circumstances of each particular case.[103]

6.5 EXCEPTIONS

6.5.1 DEATH PENALTY

Article 2 mentions a number of cases to which the prohibition of deprivation of life does not apply.

---

[102] The Hubinek/Voogd report mentioned in the preceding note, also only indicates the framework for a more uniform regulation. It holds that "the prolongation of life should not in itself constitute the overriding aim of medical practice, which must be concerned equally with the relief of suffering". The report contains a recommendation to the Committee of Ministers to invite the Governments of the Member States to set up committees for the drafting of ethical rules; Doc. 3699, pp. 2-3.
[103] Judgment of 29 April 2002, para. 41.

In the first paragraph, in the very formulation of the prohibition, an exception is made for the case where a person is deprived of his life in the execution of a sentence of a court following his conviction of a crime for which the death penalty is provided by law. Consequently, execution of the death penalty or extradition to a country where the death penalty is still executed, does not in itself constitute a violation of Article 2.[104] In the meantime however, Protocol No. 6 concerning the abolition of the death penalty has entered into force.[105] And for those States which have not yet ratified this Protocol, it follows from other provisions of the Convention that not every death sentence pronounced by a court is permitted under the Convention: (1) the judicial decision in question must have been preceded by a fair and public hearing in the sense of Article 6; (2) the punishment must not be so disproportionate to the crime committed, and the choice of the place and manner of execution must not be such, that these amount to an inhuman and degrading treatment in the sense of Article 3; (3) under Article 7 the crime must have been punishable by death at the moment it was committed; (4) under Article 14 no discrimination is permitted in the imposition and execution of the death penalty, and in the granting of pardon.[106] Finally, Protocol No. 13 concerning the abolishment of the death penalty in all circumstances has entered into force.[107] Therefore, the issue of whether the death penalty is still allowed under the Convention has to be considered in the context of several Convention provisions.

As appears from the *Kirkwood* Case,[108] a difficult dilemma may present itself with regard to appeal proceedings, which will inevitably delay execution of the death sentence and during which the convicted person will be gripped with uncertainty as to the outcome of his appeal and, therefore, as to his fate. On the one hand, a prolonged appeal system generates acute anxiety over long periods owing to the uncertain, but possibly favourable outcome of each successive appeal. This anxiety could possibly constitute an inhuman or degrading treatment and punishment contrary to Article 3. On the other hand, a sound appeal system serves to ensure protection of the right to life as guaranteed by Article 2 and to prevent arbitrariness. The Commission declared the application inadmissible, because the applicant had not been tried or convicted, and it could therefore not be established whether the treatment to which the applicant would be exposed, and the risk of his exposure to it, was so serious as to constitute inhuman or degrading treatment or punishment contrary to Article 3. The British Government had taken the position that, since the second sentence of Article 2(1) of the Convention expressly provides for the imposition of the death sentence by a court,

---

[104]   Appl. 10227/82, *H v. Spain*, D&R 37 (1984), p. 93.
[105]   This Protocol entered into force on 1 March 1985. See *infra*, Chapter 24.
[106]   In the case of States which have abolished the death penalty in general, but have maintained it in respect of acts committed in time of war or imminent threat of war, the requirements under (1) and (4) apply only to the extent that derogation from them is not justified under Article 15.
[107]   This Protocol entered into force on 1 July 2002. See *infra*, Chapter 31.
[108]   Appl. 10479/83, D&R 37 (1984), p. 158 (181-190).

following conviction for a crime for which that penalty is provided by law, delays associated with the appeal procedure must be assumed to be compatible with Article 2 and Article 3 of the Convention read together.

The Commission rejected this argument. It acknowledged that the Convention must be read as a whole, but it stressed on the other hand that "its respective provisions must be given appropriate weight where there may be implicit overlap, and the Convention organs must be reluctant to draw interferences from one text which would restrict the express terms of another. As both the Court and the Commission have recognized, Article 3 is not subject to any qualification. Its terms are bald and absolute. This fundamental aspect of Article 3 reflects its key position in the structure of the rights of the Convention, and is further illustrated by the terms of Article 15(2), which permit no derogation from it even in time of war or other public emergency threatening the life of the nation. In these circumstances the Commission considers that notwithstanding the terms of Article 2(1), it cannot be excluded that the circumstances surrounding the protection of one of the other rights contained in the Convention might give rise to an issue under Article 3."[109]

The *Soering* Case concerned the imminent extradition of the applicant from the United Kingdom to the United States of America, where he feared being sentenced to death on a charge of capital murder and would be subjected to the 'death row phenomenon'. The Court held that extradition of a person to a country where he risks the death penalty could not, in itself, raise any issue under either Article 2 or Article 3 of the Convention. The Court considered that Article 3 could not "have been intended by the drafters of the Convention to include a general prohibition of the death penalty since that would nullify the clear wording of Article 2(1)". Also, the opening for signature in 1983 of Protocol No. 6 showed that "the intention of the Contracting Parties as recently as 1983 was to adopt the normal method of amendment of the text in order to introduce a new obligation to abolish capital punishment in time of peace and, what is more, to do so by an optional instrument allowing each state to choose the moment when to undertake such an engagement."[110] The Court continued, however, that the manner in which the death penalty is imposed or executed, the personal circumstances of the condemned person and a disproportionality to the gravity of the crime committed, as well as the condition of the detention must not be such that an inhuman treatment in the sense of Article 3 arises.[111]

---

[109] *Ibidem*, p. 184. For further details, see the discussion of Article 3, *infra* 7.6.2.
[110] Judgment of 7 July 1989, para. 103.
[111] *Ibidem*. See also the discussion in this respect in connection with Art. 3, *infra* 7.6.2.

6.5.2   MORE FORCE THAN ABSOLUTELY NECESSARY

In the second paragraph three cases of deprivation of life are mentioned which also do not fall under the prohibition of the first paragraph. These are cases where deprivation of life results from the use of force for a given purpose. This is, however, subject to the condition that the force used 'is no more than absolutely necessary'. There must, therefore, be proportionality between the measure of force used and the purpose pursued, which moreover must be among the purposes mentioned in the second paragraph. Thus, for instance, the use of force in the case of an arrest, where the arrested person neither uses force nor attempts to flee, but only refuses to furnish certain data, will not be proportional and consequently cannot constitute a justification for a resulting deprivation of life. Moreover, the words 'absolutely necessary' have to be interpreted in such a way that there must also be some proportionality between the force used and the interest pursued. Thus, the use of force resulting in death will not be justified in the case of the escape of a prisoner, or to effect an arrest, when no serious danger is reasonably to be feared from the person concerned.

When the widow of a man killed by the police during a riot complained of a breach of Article 2 by the Belgian State, the Commission declared her complaint to be 'manifestly ill-founded', arguing that it was a case of lawful self-defence of a policeman who felt himself threatened, while there was no reason to assume that the latter had intended to kill the man.[112] By the latter argument the Commission obviously referred to the fact that the prohibition of deprivation of life in the first paragraph of Article 2 speaks of 'intentionally'. Since there was no question of intent in the case under discussion, in the Commission's reasoning there was no need to examine whether the force used was absolutely necessary for one of the purposes mentioned in the second paragraph. However, in this way the Commission largely deprived the second paragraph of its meaning. In fact, in the cases mentioned in the second paragraph the killing will seldom be intentional, but on the contrary will be the unintended result of the force used for a different purpose. This is also evident from the words 'when it results from the use of force'. It has, therefore, to be presumed that the function of the second paragraph is not merely to impose a restriction on the prohibition in the second sentence of the first paragraph. If the latter was intended, it would have been more appropriate to add the cases, mentioned in the second paragraph, to the exception of capital punishment in the first paragraph, or to refer expressly to the second sentence of the first paragraph in the second paragraph. Instead, the second paragraph contains the words 'in contravention of this Article', which imply at the same time a reference to the first sentence of the first paragraph and the general protection of the right to life contained therein. The correct interpretation, therefore, seems to be that the second paragraph prohibits any use by the authorities of force in such a

---

[112]   Appl. 2758/66, *X v. Belgium*, Yearbook XII (1969), p. 174 (192).

measure or form that it results in death, with as the only exceptions the ones mentioned there and irrespective of the question whether the result was intended or not.

This interpretation was indeed adopted by the Commission in its decision in the *Stewart* Case. The case concerned the death of a boy as a consequence of an injury caused by a plastic baton, fired by a British soldier during a riot in Northern Ireland. The Commission had to examine whether the death of the boy was a consequence of the use of force contrary to Article 2. The British Government submitted that "Article 2 extends only to intentional acts and has no application to negligent or accidental acts". The Commission, however, adopted the broader view that the sphere of protection afforded by Article 2 goes beyond the intentional deprivation of life. In view of the object and purpose of the Convention the Commission was of the opinion that it could not accept another interpretation. The text of Article 2, read as a whole, indicates in the Commission's opinion that paragraph 2 does not primarily define situations where it is permitted intentionally to kill an individual, but situations where the use of violence is permitted, which may then, as an unintentional consequence, result in a deprivation of life. This use of force has to be absolutely necessary for one of the purposes in subparagraphs (a), (b) or (c). With regard to this last condition the Commission held, with reference, *inter alia*, to the *Sunday Times* Case, that (1) 'necessary' implies a 'pressing social need'; (2) the 'necessity test' includes an assessment as to whether the interference with the Convention right was proportionate to the legitimate aim pursued; and (3) the qualification of the word 'necessary' in Article 2(2) by the adverb 'absolutely' indicates that a stricter and more compelling test of necessity must be applied. This led the Commission to the conclusion that Article 2(2) permits the use of force for the purposes enumerated in (a), (b) and (c) under the condition that the employed force is strictly proportionate to the achievement of the permitted purpose. In assessing whether this condition is fulfilled regard must be had to "the nature of the aim pursued, the dangers to life and limb inherent in the situation and the degree of risk that the force employed might result in loss of life".[113]

The Commission followed the same line of reasoning in a case where a boy in Northern Ireland had been shot by soldiers as he attempted to drive round a vehicle checkpoint in a stolen car. In the circumstances of the case and having regard to the background of events in Northern Ireland, which was facing a situation in which killings had become a feature of life, the soldiers had reasons to believe that they were

---

[113]   Appl. 10044/82, D&R 39 (1985), p. 162 (169-171). See also Appl. 9013/80, *Farrell v. the United Kingdom*, Yearbook XXV (1982), p. 124 (143); Appl. 16734/90, *Dujardin v. France*, D&R 72 (1992), p. 236 (243).

dealing with terrorists. Therefore, the use of force was justified in the terms of the second paragraph of Article 2.[114]

In the *McCann* Case the Court also applied a very strict proportionality test. The Court held that Article 2, which safeguards the right to life and sets out the circumstances when deprivation of life may be justified, ranks as one of the most fundamental provisions in the Convention, from which no derogation is permitted. Together with Article 3 it also enshrines one of the basic values of the democratic societies making up the Council of Europe. The circumstances in which deprivation of life may be justified must, therefore, be strictly construed. The object and purpose of the Convention as an instrument for the protection of individual human beings also requires that Article 2 be interpreted and applied so as to make its safeguards practical and effective.[115] The text of Article 2, read as a whole, demonstrates that it covers not only intentional killing but also the situations where it is permitted to 'use force' which may result, as an unintended outcome, in the deprivation of life. The deliberate or intended use of lethal force is, however, only one factor to be taken into account in assessing its necessity. Any use of force must be no more than 'absolutely necessary' for the achievement of one or more of the purposes set out in sub-paragraphs (a) to (c). This term indicates that a stricter and more compelling test of necessity must be employed from that normally applicable when determining whether State action is 'necessary in a democratic society' under paragraphs 2 of Articles 8 to 11 of the Convention. Consequently, the force used must be strictly proportionate to the achievement of the permitted aims.[116] In the light of the importance of the protection afforded by Article 2, the Court must subject deprivations of life to the most careful scrutiny, taking into consideration not only the actions of State agents but also all the surrounding circumstances.

In the *McCann* Case the British, Spanish and Gibraltar authorities were aware that the Provisional IRA was planning a terrorist attack on Gibraltar. The intelligence assessment of the British and Gibraltar authorities was that an IRA unit (which had been identified) would carry out an attack by means of a car bomb which would probably be detonated by a remote control device. It was decided that the three suspects should be arrested. Soldiers of the SAS in plain clothes were standing by for that purpose. Allegedly thinking that the three suspects were trying to detonate remote control devices, the soldiers shot them at close range. No weapons or detonator devices

---

[114]   Appl. 17579/90, *Kelly v. the United Kingdom*, D&R 74 (1993), p. 139 (146-147).

[115]   Judgment of 27 September 1995, paras 146-147. See also the judgment of 9 October 1997, *Andronicou and Constantinou*, para. 171; judgment of 28 July 1998, *Ergi*, para. 79; judgment of 27 June 2001, *Salman*, paras 97-98; judgment of 10 July 2001, *Avşar*, para. 390; judgment of 18 June 2002, *Orhan*, para. 325; judgment of 17 February 2004, *Ipek*, para. 163.

[116]   Judgment of 27 September 1995, *McCann*, paras 148-149; judgment of 27 June 2000, *İlhan*, para. 74; judgment of 20 December 2004, *Makaratzis*, para. 56.

were found on the bodies of the three suspects. The car which had been parked by one of the suspects was revealed on inspection not to contain any explosive device or bomb. The Court accepted that the soldiers believed that it was necessary to shoot the suspects in order to prevent them from detonating a bomb and causing serious loss of life. The actions which they took, in obedience to superior orders, were thus perceived as absolutely necessary in order to safeguard innocent lives. The Court held that the use of force by agents of the State in pursuit of one of the aims delineated in paragraph 2 of Article 2 may be justified under this provision where it is based on an honest belief which is perceived, for good reasons, to be valid at the time, but which subsequently turns out to be mistaken. Having regard to the dilemma confronting the authorities in the circumstances of the case, the reactions of the soldiers did not, in themselves, give rise to a violation of Article 2.[117]

In connection with the control and organisation of the operation, the Court first observed that it had been the intention of the authorities to arrest the suspects at an appropriate stage and that evidence had been given at the inquest that arrest procedures had been practised by the soldiers and that efforts had been made to find a suitable place to detain the suspects after their arrest. The Court questioned, however, why the three suspects had not been arrested at the border immediately on their arrival in Gibraltar and why the decision was not taken to prevent them from entering Gibraltar if they were believed to be on a bombing mission. Having had advance warning of the terrorists' intentions, it would certainly have been possible for the authorities to have mounted an arrest operation. The security services and the Spanish authorities had photographs of the three suspects, knew their names, as well as their aliases, and would have known what passports to look for. The Court further noted that the authorities had made a number of key assessments, in particular, that the terrorists would not use a blocking car; that the bomb would be detonated by a radio-controlled device; that the detonation could be effected by the pressing of a button; that it was likely that the suspects would detonate the bomb if challenged; that they would be armed and would be likely to use their arms if confronted. In the event, all of these crucial assumptions, apart from the terrorists' intention to carry out an attack, turned out to be erroneous. In the Court's view insufficient allowances appeared to have been made for other assumptions. A series of working hypotheses were conveyed by the authorities to the soldiers as certainties, thereby making the use of force almost unavoidable. In the Court's view, the above failure to make provision for a margin of error had to be considered in combination with the training of the soldiers to continue shooting once they opened fire until the suspect was dead. As noted by the coroner in the inquest proceedings, all four soldiers shot to kill the suspects. Against this background the authorities were bound by their obligation to respect the right to life of the suspects to exercise the greatest of care in evaluating the information at

---

[117] Judgment of 27 September 1995, para. 200.

their disposal before transmitting it to soldiers whose use of firearms automatically involved shooting to kill. This failure by the authorities suggested a lack of appropriate care in the control and organisation of the arrest operation. In sum, the Court was not persuaded that the killing of the three terrorists constituted a use of force which was no more than absolutely necessary in defence of persons from unlawful violence within the meaning of Article 2(2)(a). There thus had been a breach of Article 2.[118]

In the *İlhan* Case the applicant alleged that his brother had been unlawfully subjected to a life-threatening attack by gendarmes and that the authorities had failed to carry out an adequate and effective investigation into the attack. He argued that there had been a breach of Article 2 of the Convention. The Court recalled that the force used against Abdüllatif İlhan was not in the event lethal. This does not exclude an examination of the applicant's complaints under Article 2. In three previous cases the Court had examined complaints under this provision where the alleged victim had not died as a result of the impugned conduct.[119] In the *Osman* Case the applicant had been shot and seriously injured when a man fired a shotgun at close range at him and his father. His father had died. The Court concluded on the facts of that case that the United Kingdom authorities had not failed in any positive obligation under Article 2 to provide protection of their right to life within the meaning of the first sentence of Article 2.[120]

In the *Yaşa* Case the applicant was shot in the street by an unknown gunman, receiving eight bullet wounds but surviving. The Court, finding that the authorities had not failed to protect the applicant's life, held nonetheless that they had failed to comply with the procedural obligation under Article 2 to conduct an effective investigation into the attack.[121]

In the *İlhan* Case the Court noted that Abdüllatif İlhan suffered brain damage following at least one blow to the head with a rifle butt inflicted by gendarmes who had been ordered to apprehend him during an operation and who kicked and beat him when they found him hiding in some bushes. Two contemporaneous medical reports identified the head injury as being of a life-threatening character. This had left him with a long-term loss of function. The seriousness of his injury was, therefore, not in doubt. However, the Court was not persuaded in the circumstances of this case that the use of force applied by the gendarmes when they apprehended Abdüllatif İlhan, was of such a nature or degree as to breach Article 2 of the Convention. Nor did any separate issue arise in this context concerning the alleged lack of prompt

---

[118] *Ibidem*, paras 206-213.
[119] Judgment of 27 June 2000, para. 75.
[120] Judgment of 28 October 1998, paras 115-122.
[121] Judgment 22 September 1998, paras 92-108.

medical treatment for his injuries. It followed that there had been no violation of Article 2 of the Convention.[122]

The *Andronicou and Constantinou* Case concerned the death of a couple after an armed intervention by a unit of the Special Police Forces ("MMAD"). Following a domestic dispute between Lefteris Andronicou and Elsie Constantinou, the police were called by neighbours to the flat which they shared. Mr Andronicou was said to be armed and was apparently holding Ms Constantinou against her will. There ensued a lengthy period of negotiations involving, among others, senior police officers, Andronicou's doctor and members of Ms Constantinou's family. Throughout the afternoon, efforts were made to persuade him to release Ms Constantinou. The Chief of Police decided to approve a MMAD rescue plan. Earlier he had telephoned the Minister of Justice, who had left the decision to the police authorities. The post-mortem examination found that death was caused by a shot fired from a submachine gun. As regards the planning and control the Court held that its sole concern should be to evaluate whether in the circumstances the planning and control of the rescue operation showed that the authorities had taken appropriate care to ensure that any risk to the lives of the couple had been minimised and that they were not negligent in their choice of action. Within the framework of this evaluation the Court had particular regard to the context in which the incident occurred as well as to the way in which the situation developed over the course of the day. As far as the context was concerned the Court stated that the fact that the kidnapper was armed, taken together with the fact that the woman was constantly shouting for help, gave the State's special armed forces every right to enter the apartment where the woman was being held and to use force in order to free her and to arrest the kidnapper. In addition, the armed forces where strictly instructed as to when and in what way to use their weapons. Moreover, the State never intended to use weapons; in fact the authorities were very anxious to avoid any harm to the couple. The officers that shot the kidnapper dead were justified in their belief that it was necessary to kill him in order to save the life of the woman and their own lives. Therefore, the use of force under Article 2(2) is justified where it is based on an honest belief which is perceived, for good reasons, to be valid at the time but subsequently turns out to be mistaken. To hold otherwise, according to the Court, would impose an unrealistic burden on the State and its law-enforcement personnel in the execution of their duty. In this case the officers were entitled to open fire for the purpose of saving lives and to take all measures which they honestly and reasonably believed were necessary to eliminate any risk. Furthermore, the accuracy of the officers' fire was impaired through the kidnapper's action in clinging on to the woman and thereby exposing her to risk. Therefore, there was no breach of Article 2 (2) (a) of the Convention.[123]

---

[122]   Judgment of 27 June 2000, *Ilhan*, paras 77-78.
[123]   Judgment of 9 October 1997, paras 183-186.

In the *Güleç* Case the Court held again that the use of force may be justified under para. (2)(c) of Article 2, provided that a balance is struck between the aim pursued and the means employed to achieve it. The gendarmes had used a very powerful weapon, since they did not have any lighter weapons available to them. The lack of such lighter equipment was all the more incomprehensible and unacceptable because the province in which the demonstration in question took place, was a region in which a state of emergency had been declared and where at that time disorder could have been expected. As to the question of whether there were armed terrorists among the demonstrators, the Court noted that the Government produced no evidence to support that assertion. In the first place, no gendarme sustained a bullet wound either in the place where the applicant's son died or in other places passed by the demonstration. Secondly, no weapons or spent cartridges supposed to have belonged to PKK members were found at the spot. Moreover, prosecutions brought in the Diyarbakir National Security Court against the owners of thirteen rifles confiscated after the incidents, from which spent cartridges had been collected by the security forces, ended in acquittals, because the defendants had not taken part in the events in issue. In conclusion, the Court considered that the force used to disperse the demonstrators, which caused the death of Ahmet Güleç, was not absolutely necessary within the meaning of Article 2.[124]

In the *Nachova* Case the applicants complained that their relatives had been deprived of their life in violation of Article 2(2) of the Convention, as they had died as a result of deficient law and practice, which permitted the use of lethal force without absolute necessity, and thus violated Article 2(1) per se. The applicants' relatives had been fatally shot by police officers in an operation to effect their lawful arrest. Considering the circumstances of the case the Court noted that the two men shot had escaped from detention, where they had been serving short sentences for being absent without leave from compulsory military service. They had escaped without using violence, simply by leaving their place of work, which was outside of the detention facility. Neither man was armed or represented a danger to the police officers or to third parties, as neither man had a previous record of violence. Against this background the Court considered that it was in no circumstances 'absolutely necessary' within the meaning of Article 2(2) to use firearms to arrest a person suspected of a non-violent offence who was known not to pose a threat to life or limb, even where the failure to do so might have resulted in the opportunity to arrest the fugitive being lost.

The Court further took notice of evidence suggesting that automatic rifles had been used in place of handguns, that the fugitives had been shot while attempting to surrender and that at no point had the police officers attempted to minimise the risk of loss of life. Observing in a broader context that relevant national regulations on the use of firearms by the police were not published, did not make the use of firearms

---

[124]   Judgment of 27 July 1998, paras 71-73.

dependant on an assessment of the surrounding circumstances, and most importantly, did not require an evaluation of the nature of the offence committed by the fugitive and of the threat that he or she posed, the Court concluded that there had been a violation of Article 2 of the Convention. The Court was furthermore careful to differentiate this case from earlier judgments in which the use of firearms was found to have been justified. All of these other cases concerned situations where State agents involved had acted in the belief that there was a threat of violence or in order to apprehend fugitives suspected of violent offences.[125]

In the *Makaratzis* Case the applicant complained that the police officers who pursued him used excessive firepower against him, putting his life at risk, and that the authorities failed to carry out an adequate and effective investigation into the incident. The applicant had been chased by a large number of police officers who had made repeated use of revolvers, pistols and submachine guns. According to the Court it was clear from the evidence adduced before it that the police had used their weapons in order to immobilise the applicant's car and effect his arrest, this being one of the instances contemplated by the second paragraph of Article 2. Having regard to the circumstances of the case and in particular to the degree and type of force used, the Court concluded that, irrespective of whether or not the police had actually intended to kill him, the applicant had been the victim of conduct which, by its very nature, had put his life at risk, even though, in the event, he had survived. Article 2 was thus applicable.[126] Although the Greek State had since passed a new law in 2003 regulating the use of firearms by the police, at the relevant time the applicable legislation dated from the Second World War when Greece had been occupied by German armed forces. Greek law did not contain any other provisions regulating the use of weapons during police actions or laying down guidelines on planning and control of police operations. Having regard to the criminal conduct of the applicant and to the climate at the time, marked by terrorist actions against foreign interests, the Court accepted that the use of force against him had been based on an honest belief which had been perceived, for good reasons, to be valid at the time. However, the Court was struck by the chaotic way in which the firearms had actually been used by the police and serious questions arose as to the conduct and the organisation of the operation. While accepting that the police officers who had been involved in the incident, had not had sufficient time to evaluate all the parameters of the situation and to carefully organise their operation, the Court considered that the degeneration of the situation had largely been due to the fact that at that time neither the individual police officers nor the chase, seen as a collective police operation, had had the benefit of the appropriate structure which should have been provided by domestic law and practice. At the time the use of

---

[125]   Judgment of 26 February 2004, para. 105; judgment of 6 July 2005 (Grand Chamber), paras 114-119.

[126]   Judgment of 20 December 2004, paras 50-55.

weapons by State officials had still been regulated by an obsolete and incomplete law for a modern democratic society. The system in place had not afforded to law-enforcement officials clear guidelines and criteria governing the use of force in peacetime. The police officers concerned had thus enjoyed a greater autonomy of action and had been able to take unconsidered initiatives, which would probably not have been the case had they had the benefit of proper training and instructions. Consequently, the Court found that the Greek authorities had failed to comply with the positive obligation to put in place an adequate legislative and administrative framework and had not done all that could be reasonably expected of them to afford to citizens the level of safeguards required by Article 2. Accordingly, the Court held that there had been a violation of Article 2 of the Convention.[127]

6.6 THE RIGHT TO LIFE IS NON-DEROGABLE

Article 2 has been included in the list of articles from which under Article 15(2) no derogation is permitted in any circumstances; it belongs to the so-called 'non-derogable' rights.[128] Consequently, as was correctly submitted by the Irish Government in the case of *Ireland v. the United Kingdom*, the British declarations addressed to the Secretary General, announcing that with respect to Northern Ireland measures derogating from the Convention had been taken, could not be invoked against accusations of violation of Article 2.[129]

In the *McCann* Case the Court held that Article 2 ranks as one of the most fundamental provisions in the Convention, from which no derogation is permitted. Together with Article 3 it also enshrines one of the basic values of the democratic societies making up the Council of Europe. The circumstances in which deprivation of life may be justified must, therefore, be strictly construed. The object and purpose of the Convention as an instrument for the protection of individual human beings also requires that Article 2 be interpreted and applied so as to make its safeguards practical and effective.[130]

---

[127]   *Ibidem*, paras 61-72.
[128]   Article 3 of Protocol No. 6 and Article 2 of Protocol No. 13 concerning the abolition of the death penalty also prohibits any derogation from Article 15 of the Convention.
[129]   Appl. 5310/71, Yearbook XV (1972), p. 76 (96).
[130]   Judgment of 27 September 1995, para. 146; See also the judgment of 27 June 2000, *Salman*, para. 97; judgment of 9 October 1997, *Andronicou and Constantinou*, para. 171; judgment of 13 June 2002, *Anguelova*, para. 110.

CHAPTER 7
FREEDOM FROM TORTURE AND OTHER INHUMAN OR DEGRADING TREATMENT OR PUNISHMENT
(Article 3)

REVISED BY BEN VERMEULEN

CONTENTS

7.1 TEXT OF ARTICLE 3

No one shall be subjected to torture or to inhuman or degrading treatment or punishment.

7.2   TORTURE; INHUMANT TREATMENT OR PUNISHMENT; DEGRADING TREATMENT OR PUNISHMENT

Article 3 undoubtedly is one of the core provisions of the Convention. It forbids submitting a person to torture, inhuman treatment or punishment, and degrading treatment or punishment. The distinction between the notion of torture and that of inhuman or degrading treatment or punishment "derives principally from a difference in the intensity of the suffering inflicted."[1] As the Commission stated in its report in the *Greek* Case: "It is plain that there may be treatment to which all these descriptions apply, for all torture must be inhuman and degrading treatment, and inhuman treatment also degrading." Starting from the concept of inhuman treatment, the Commission elaborated the following specifications: "The notion of inhuman treatment covers at least such treatment as deliberately causes severe suffering, mental or physical, which, in the particular situation, is unjustifiable. The word 'torture' is often used to describe inhuman treatment, which has a purpose, such as the obtaining of information or confession, or the infliction of punishment, and is generally an aggravated form of inhuman treatment.[2] Treatment or punishment of an individual may be said to be degrading if it grossly humiliates him before others or drives him to act against his will or conscience."[3] In the *Greek* Case the Commission came to the conclusion that it had been established that in several individual cases torture or ill-treatment had been inflicted, that there had been a practice of torture and ill-treatment by the Athens Security Police and that the conditions in the cells of the Security Police building were contrary to Article 3.[4]

In its report in *Ireland v. the United Kingdom* the Commission based itself again on this definition. In doing so, it held unanimously that the challenged English techniques of interrogation – obliging the interrogated persons to stand for a long period on their toes against the wall, covering their heads with black hoods, subjecting them to constant intense noise, depriving them of sleep and sufficient food and drink – constituted torture and inhuman treatment in the sense of Article 3.[5]

However, in the same case the Court reached the conclusion that these techniques of interrogation did involve inhuman treatment, but not torture. It mentioned as a distinctive element that by the term 'torture' a special stigma is attached to "deliberate

---

[1]   Judgment of 18 January 1978, *Ireland v. the United Kingdom*, para. 167.
[2]   Cf. Article 1 of the Declaration on the protection of all persons from being subjected to torture and other cruel, inhuman or degrading treatment or punishment, UNGA Res. 3452 (XXX) of 9 December 1975: "Torture constitutes an aggravated and deliberate form of cruel, inhuman and degrading treatment or punishment".
[3]   Report of 5 November 1969, *The Greek Case*, Yearbook XII (1969), p. 186.
[4]   *Ibidem*, pp. 503-505.
[5]   Report of 25 January 1976, B.23/I (1976-1978), p. 411.

inhuman treatment causing very serious and cruel suffering",[6] and held that the particular acts complained of "did not occasion suffering of the particular intensity and cruelty implied by the word torture as so understood".[7] In addition to the severity of the treatment there must, according to the Court, be a purposive element, as has been recognised in the United Nations Convention against Torture and Other Cruel, Inhuman or Degrading Treatment or Punishment, which defines torture in terms of the intentional infliction of severe pain or suffering.[8]

In the *Aksoy* Case the Court, referring to the qualification in the *Ireland v. the United Kingdom* judgment, for the first time found that treatment had to be described as torture. It concerned an applicant who was subjected to 'Palestinian hanging': he was stripped naked, with his arms tied together behind his back, and suspended by his arms. The Court argued that "this treatment could only have been deliberately inflicted; indeed, a certain amount of preparation and exertion would have been required to carry it out. It would appear to have been administered with the aim of obtaining admissions or information from the applicant. In addition to the severe pain which it must have caused at the time, the medical evidence shows that it led to a paralysis of both arms which lasted for some time [...]. The Court considers that this treatment was of such a serious and cruel nature that it can only be described as torture."[9]

In the *Aydin* Case the Court concluded that the accumulation of acts of physical and mental violence inflicted on the applicant and the especially cruel act of rape amounted to torture, considering that "rape of a detainee by an official of the State must be considered to be an especially grave and abhorrent form of ill-treatment given the ease with which the offender can exploit the vulnerability and weakened resistance of his victim. Furthermore, rape leaves deep psychological scars on the victim which do not respond to the passage of time as quickly as other forms of physical and mental violence. The applicant also experienced the acute physical pain of forced penetration, which must have left her feeling debased and violated both physically and emotionally."[10]

In the *Selmouni* Case the Court again concluded that the physical and mental violence inflicted on the applicant caused severe pain and suffering, and was so serious and cruel that it amounted to torture. The body of the applicant was covered with a large number of blows, he was dragged along by his hair, had to run along a corridor

---

[6]   Cf. also the judgment of 18 December 1996, *Aksoy*, para. 63.

[7]   Judgment of 18 January 1978, *Ireland v. the United Kingdom*, para. 167.

[8]   Judgment of 27 June 2000, *Salman*, para. 114.

[9]   Judgment of 18 December 1996, para. 64. The Court's interpretation of the notion of "torture" probably has been inspired by the definition of "torture" in Article 1 of the 1984 UN Convention against torture and other cruel, inhuman or degrading treatment or punishment. Cf. also the judgment of 27 June 2000, *Salman*, para. 114.

[10] Judgment of 25 September 1997, paras 83 and 86.

with police officers positioned at either side to trip him up, had to suck a police officer's penis, was urinated upon and was threatened with a blowlamp and a syringe.[11]

In the *Ilaşcu* Case the applicant had spent a very long period on death row in uncertainty and fear of execution, and while this sentence had no legal basis or legitimacy, he was detained in very strict isolation, his cell was unheated and had no natural light or ventilation, he was deprived of food as a punishment, could take showers only very rarely and did not receive appropriate health care. The Court concluded that the death sentence coupled with the harsh conditions he was living in were particularly serious and cruel so that they could be considered to amount to torture.[12]

Finally, in the *Krastanov* Case the Court found that the treatment was inhuman, but that it could not be qualified as torture, because it did not appear to be inflicted on the applicant intentionally for the purpose of, for instance, making him confess or breaking his physical and moral resistance, and because it lasted only for a short period of time.[13]

The difference between inhuman treatment or punishment and degrading treatment or punishment is likewise one of gradation in the suffering inflicted, though it should be kept in mind that the Court does not always draw a sharp distinction and often uses qualifications such as 'inhuman *and* degrading treatment'.[14] In the *Kudla* Case the Court held that it "has considered treatment to be 'inhuman' because, *inter alia*, it was premeditated, was applied for hours at a stretch and caused either actual bodily injury or intense physical or mental suffering. It has deemed treatment to be 'degrading' because it was such as to arouse in the victims feelings of fear, anguish and inferiority capable of humiliating and debasing them."[15]

Inhuman treatment can take many forms. For instance, in the *Selçuk and Asker* Case the Court held that the destruction of the applicant's homes, considering their personal circumstances, caused them suffering of sufficient severity to be categorised as inhuman treatment. The applicants were 54 and 60 years old at that time and had lived in the village all their lives. The destruction of their homes and most of their property forced them to leave their village. The destruction was premeditated and carried out without respect for the feelings of the applicants: they were taken unprepared, had to watch the burning of their homes, their safety was not adequately secured, their protests were ignored and no assistance was provided afterwards. The Court concluded

---

[11]   Judgment of 28 July 1999, paras 102-105.

[12]   Judgment of 8 July 2004, paras 435-440.

[13]   Judgment of 30 September 2004, para. 53.

[14]   Cf. the judgment of 27 August 1992, *Tomasi*, para. 115; judgment of 4 December 1995, *Ribitsch*, para. 36; report of 7 March 1996, *Mentes, Turhalli, Turhalli and Uvat*, para. 190 (burning of the applicants' homes by security forces amounts to "inhuman and degrading treatment within the meaning of Article 3 of the Convention").

[15]   Judgment of 26 October 2000, para. 92.

that, even if the destruction had the purpose of preventing their homes being used by terrorists or as a discouragement to others, this would not provide a justification for the ill-treatment.[16]

In the *Tyrer* Case the Court held "that the suffering occasioned must attain a particular level before a punishment can be classified as 'inhuman' within the meaning of Article 3". The complaint concerned the punishment of caning for certain offences, which was provided by law and actually applied in the Isle of Man to boys between ten and seventeen. The Court concluded, in conformity with the opinion of the Commission, that this did not constitute torture or inhuman punishment.[17] Then it examined whether the punishment was to be considered degrading. Assuming that every punishment involves an element of degradation, the Court indicated as a distinctive element of degrading punishment the degree of humiliation, which must then be judged according to the circumstances of each separate case, in particular "the nature and context of the punishment itself and the manner and method of its execution."[18] Present views were decisive, rather then the views at the moment the Convention was drawn up, since "the Convention is a living instrument which (...) must be interpreted in the light of present-day conditions".[19] Having regard to all the circumstances, the Court, according particular weight to the fact that physical force was used by a complete stranger in an institutionalized form, concluded that the punishment concerned was degrading.[20]

As may be gathered from the *Tyrer* Case, a serious degree of humiliation or debasement can be an important argument to qualify a certain treatment or punishment as degrading. Publicity can be a relevant factor to assess whether a punishment is degrading, but the absence of publicity will not necessarily mean that the punishment is not degrading, because the victim can be humiliated in his own eyes.[21] So, in a number of cases the Commission held that there is question of a degrading treatment or punishment of the person concerned "if it grossly humiliates him before others or drives him to act against his will or conscience".[22]

In the *Tyrer* Case the Court held that humiliation or debasement of a particular level may be regarded as 'degrading'.[23] In the *Albert and Le Compte* Case it ruled that

---

[16] Judgment of 24 April 1998, paras 77-79. See also the judgment of 8 January 2004, *Ayder*, paras 109-110.

[17] Judgment of 25 April 1978, para. 29.

[18] *Ibidem*, para. 30.

[19] *Ibidem*, para. 31.

[20] *Ibidem*, para. 33.

[21] *Ibidem*, para. 32.

[22] Report of 5 November 1969, *Greece v. the United Kingdom*, Yearbook XII (1969), p. 186; report of 25 January 1976, *Ireland v. the United Kingdom*, B.23-I (1976-1978), p. 388; report of 14 December 1976, *Tyrer*, B.24 (1977-1978), p. 23; and report of 7 December 1978, *Guzzardi*, B.35 (1979-1980), p. 33.

[23] Judgment of 25 April 1978, para. 30. Cf. also the judgment of 26 October 2000, *Kudla*, para. 92.

while the withdrawal from the register of the *Ordre des médicins* had as its object the imposition of a sanction for misconduct and not the debasement of his personality, it did not amount to a breach of Article 3;[24] and in the *Abdulaziz, Cabales and Balkandali* Case the Court observed that the difference of treatment as part of the United Kingdom immigration policy, while it did not denote any contempt or lack of respect for the personality of the applicants and was not designed to, and did not, humiliate or debase them, could not, therefore, be regarded as degrading.[25] In the *Peers* Case, however, the Court held that the mere absence of a purpose to humiliate or debase cannot conclusively rule out a finding of violation of Article 3.[26]

A family member of a 'disappeared person' can himself be a victim of treatment contrary to Article 3. Relevant elements which should be taken into account are "the proximity of the family tie – in that context, a certain weight will attach to the parent-child bond – the particular circumstances of the relationship, the extent to which the family member witnessed the events in question, the involvement of the family member in the attempts to obtain information about the disappeared person and the way in which the authorities responded to those enquiries".[27]

The Court often applies as standard of proof that the applicant must show that it is beyond reasonable doubt that a violation of Article 3 took place. This is a rather strict criterion. However, "such proof may follow from the coexistence of sufficiently strong, clear and concordant inferences or of similar unrebutted presumptions of fact. The conduct of the Parties when evidence is being obtained has to be taken into account."[28] Furthermore, this standard is not always applied; not, for instance in detention cases (see 7.5) and in asylum cases (see 7.6.3).

From Article 3 flow some important positive obligations, especially of a procedural nature. In the case that an individual raises an arguable claim that he has been seriously ill-treated by the police or other State agents – unlawfully and in breach of Article 3 – this provision requires that there should be an effective official investigation, which should be capable of leading to the identification and punishment of those responsible. Otherwise the protection of Article 3, "despite its fundamental importance, would be ineffective in practice and it would be possible in some cases for agents of the State

---

24   Judgment of 10 February 1983, para. 22.
25   Judgment of 28 May 1985, para. 91. Cf. also Judgment of 25 February 1982, *Campbell and Cosans*, paras 28-30.
26   Judgment of 19 April 2001, para. 74.
27   Judgment of 8 July 1999, *Çakici*, para. 98; judgment of 17 February 2004, *Ipek*, para. 181; judgment of 31 May 2005, *Akdeniz*, para. 121.
28   See for instance the judgment of 18 January 1978, *Ireland v. the United Kingdom*, para. 161; judgment of 25 September 1997, *Aydin*, para. 73; judgment of 28 July 1999, *Selmouni*, para. 88; judgment of 12 April 2005, *Chamaïev*, para. 338.

to abuse the rights of those within their control with virtual impunity".[29] The Court
further held that authorities who are confronted with clear information in official
documents concerning a possible violation of Article 3 and are not competent to take
any investigative steps themselves, should bring this information to the attention of
those authorities who are competent in the matter.[30]

This procedural obligation under Article 3 is more or less similar to the obligation
to carry out an effective investigation under Article 2.[31] Under Article 2 there are some
minimal conditions for the investigation to be effective: it should be independent from
those implicated in the events, all reasonable steps available should be taken to secure
the evidence concerning the incident, including eye witness testimony, forensic evidence or an autopsy, it should be a prompt response and a reasonable expedition and
there must be a sufficient element of public scrutiny.[32]

It is not clear why the Court sometimes discusses flaws in procedures and investigations under Article 3 and sometimes under Article 13.[33] In the *Jabari* Case it found
that the automatic and mechanical application of short time-limits for submitting an
asylum application violated Article 13 as well as Article 3.[34]

A relevant element in answering the question of whether a family member of a
'disappeared person' is a victim of treatment contrary to Article 3, is the way in which
the authorities respond to inquiries of the family. Here the violation does not lie in
the fact of the 'disappearance' but rather concerns the reactions of the authorities and
their attitudes to the situation when it is brought to their attention.[35]

It has to be noted that in asylum and extradition cases States also have an obligation
to abstain from removing aliens when the Court or its President by way of interim
measures based on Rule 39 of the Rules of Court has so requested. In general such requests concern cases where Article 3 plays a prominent role. In the *Mamatkulov* Case
the Court ruled that by virtue of Article 34 of the Convention States undertake to
refrain from any act or omission that may hinder the effective exercise of the right of
application, and that a failure of a State to comply with such interim measures must
be regarded as preventing the Court from effectively examining the complaint and

---

[29]   Judgment of 28 October 1998, *Assenov and Others,* para. 102; judgment of 6 April 2000, *Labita,*
      para. 131.
[30]   Judgment of 6 April 2004, *Ahmet Özkan,* para. 359.
[31]   Judgment of 28 October 1998, *Assenov,* para. 102 ("this investigation, as with that under Article 2");
      judgment of 27 July 2004, *Slimani,* para. 31 ("an investigation of that sort (under Article 2) must
      also be carried out where an individual makes a credible assertion that he has suffered treatment
      infringing Article 3").
[32]   Judgment of 4 May 2001, *Kelly,* paras 95-98; judgment of 27 July 2004, *Slimani,* para. 32.
[33]   Judgment of 27 June 2000, *İlhan,* paras 91-93; judgment of 31 May 2005, *Yasin Ateş,* para. 134.
[34]   Judgment of 11 July 2000, paras 39-40 and 49-50.
[35]   Judgment of 8 July 1999, *Çakici,* para. 98; judgment of 17 February 2004, *Ipek,* para. 181; judgment
      of 31 May 2005, *Akdeniz,* para. 121.

as hindering the effective exercise of his right to complain, and thus as a violation of Article 34.[36]

States are also required to take measures designed to ensure that individuals within their jurisdiction are not subjected to treatment by private individuals violating Article 3. "Children and other vulnerable individuals, in particular, are entitled to State protection, in the form of effective deterrence, against serious breaches of personal integrity."[37] In the Case of *A. v. the United Kingdom* a nine years old boy was hit by his stepfather with a garden cane applied with considerable force on more than one occasion. The stepfather was charged with assault, but the jury did not find him guilty, because the treatment was considered to amount to 'reasonable chastisement'. The Court held that the law did not provide adequate protection to the boy against this ill-treatment, which constituted a violation of Article 3.[38] In the Case of *Z. and Others v. the United Kingdom* the four applicant children suffered appalling neglect and physical and psychological injury and had been subjected in their home to horrific experiences. Although the Court acknowledged the difficult and sensitive decisions facing social services and the important countervailing principle of respecting and preserving family life, it concluded that the failure of the system to protect these children from serious, long-term neglect and abuse amounted to a violation of Article 3.[39] And although the treatment complained of in the *Costello-Roberts* Case was the act of a headmaster of an independent school, the State could be held responsible under the Convention if that treatment was incompatible with Article 3.[40]

7.3 MINIMUM LEVEL OF SEVERITY

"The borderline between harsh treatment on the one hand and a violation of Article 3 on the other is sometimes difficult to establish."[41] There is no abstract, absolute standard for the kinds of treatment and punishment prohibited by Article 3. The question whether treatment or punishment is inhuman or degrading must be judged by the circumstances of the case and the prevalent views of the time. Thus, in its report in the *Greek* Case, the Commission considered with respect to the treatment of detainees: "It appears from the testimony of a number of witnesses that a certain

---

[36]   Judgment of 6 February 2003, paras 109-111; judgment of 4 February 2005 (Grand Chamber), *Mamatkulov*, para. 128.

[37]   Judgment of 23 September 1998, *A. v. the United Kingdom,* para. 22; judgment of 10 May 2001, *Z. and Others v. United Kongdom,* para. 73.

[38]   Judgment of 23 September 1998, paras 23-24.

[39]   Judgment of 10 May 2001, para. 74.

[40]   Judgment of 25 March 1993, para. 28.

[41]   Report of 4 May 1989, *McCallum,* para. 77.

roughness of treatment of detainees by both police and military authorities is tolerated by most detainees and even taken for granted (...). This underlines the fact that the point up to which prisoners and the public may accept physical violence as being neither cruel nor excessive, varies between different societies and even between different sections of them."[42] And in its judgment in *Ireland v. the United Kingdom* the Court held: "Ill-treatment must attain a minimum level of severity if it is to fall within the scope of Article 3. The assessment of this minimum is, in the nature of things, relative; it depends on all the circumstances of the case, such as the duration of the treatment, its physical or mental effects and, in some cases, the sex, age and state of health of the victim."[43]

Thus, a certain qualification is introduced in a norm formulated in absolute terms, which is almost inevitable in the case of the application of an abstract norm, containing subjective concepts, to concrete cases. For instance, the question whether a penalty is inhuman or not may depend on the crime committed. "An exceptionally harsh punishment for a trivial offence might raise a question under Article 3",[44] while the same punishment could be acceptable in case of a more serious crime. Likewise a punishment for a certain crime may be so out of proportion because of the age or the mental or physical condition of the offender that there may be an issue under Article 3, while such a punishment is entirely justified for others having committed the same type of crime. And an unfair procedure resulting in a sentence may make it inhuman, although the sentence as such is not.[45]

It has to be stressed, however, that the national authorities are often allowed a wide margin of appreciation. The Commission has held that "the Convention does not provide as such any general right to call into question the length of a sentence imposed by a competent court."[46] Only under exceptional circumstances a particular sentence may raise an issue under Article 3. For instance, the mere fact "that an offence is punished more severely in one country than in another does not suffice to establish that the punishment is inhuman or degrading".[47] So, although the death penalty has *de facto* been abolished in Western Europe, having regard to Article 2 that expressly permits it, the Court has not yet been prepared to state explicitly that this penalty should now be considered as an inhuman and degrading punishment within the mea-

---

[42]   Report of 5 November 1969, Yearbook XII (1969), p. 501.
[43]   Judgment of 18 January 1978, para. 162. Cf. also the judgment of 25 April 1978, *Tyrer*, paras 29-30 and judgment of 7 July 1989, *Soering*, para. 100.
[44]   Appl. 5471/72, *X. v. the United Kingdom*, Coll. 43 (1973), p. 160 (160).
[45]   Judgment of 12 March 2003, *Öcalan*, paras 212-213 and judgment of 12 May 2005 (Grand Chamber), *Öcalan*, paras 174-175.
[46]   Appl. 5871/72, *X. v. the United Kingdom*, D&R 1 (1975), p. 54 (55); Appl. 7057/75, *X. v. Federal Republic of Germany*, D&R 6 (1977), p. 127 (127).
[47]   Appl. 11017/84, *C. v. Federal Republic of Germany*, D&R 46 (1986), p. 176 (181).

ning of Article 3.[48] However, the legal status of the death penalty has undergone a considerable evolution since the *Soering* Case. All Contracting States have signed Protocol No. 6 concerning abolition of the death penalty, and almost all States have ratified it. Moreover, Protocol No. 13 provides for the abolition of the death penalty in time of war. Consequently, the Court has adopted the position that "it cannot now be excluded, in the light of the developments that have taken place in this area, that the States have agreed through their practice to modify the second sentence in Article 2 para. 1 in so far as it permits capital punishment in peacetime. Against this background it can also be argued that the implementation of the death penalty can be regarded as inhuman and degrading treatment contrary to Article 3".[49] This suggests that the Court may qualify the death penalty as inhumant treatment in the future. However, in the *Öcalan* Case the Court found it not necessary to reach any firm conclusion on this point.[50]

In the *Weeks* Case the Court found a sentence of life imprisonment for a seventeen-year-old who had committed an armed robbery, to be not inhuman, albeit with certain reservations: "Having regard to Mr. Weeks' age at the time and to the particular facts of the offence he committed (...), if it had not been for the specific reasons advanced for the sentence imposed, one could have serious doubts as to its compatibility with Article 3 of the Convention, which prohibits, *inter alia*, inhuman punishment."[51]

In the *Bonnechaux* Case both the Commission and the Committee of Ministers agreed that there was no violation of Article 3 in the case of a 74 year old man suffering from diabetes and cardiovascular disease who had been detained on remand for 35 months.[52] More generally, the Commission seemed unwilling, in dealing with the conditions of detention, to attach much importance to developments in penitentiary views.[53]

---

[48] Judgment of 7 July 1989, *Soering*, para. 103.

[49] Judgment of 12 March 2003, paras 195-198; judgment of 12 May 2005 (Grand Chamber), *Öcalan*, paras 164-165.

[50] *Ibidem*. It is rather surprising that in the judgment of 12 April 2005, *Chamaïev*, para. 333, the Court reaffirmed the position it took in the *Soering* Case, that Article 3 can not be interpreted as generally prohibiting the death penalty because that would nullify the clear wording of Article 2(1).

[51] Judgment of 2 March 1987, para. 47.

[52] Appl. 8224/78, D&R 15 (1979), p. 211 (241) and Report of 5 December 1979, D&R 18 (1980), p. 100 (148); Resolution DH (80)1, D&R 18 (1980), p. 149.

[53] In this connection, see the "Minimum Rules for the Treatment of Prisoners", Resolution (73)5 of the Committee of Ministers, European Yearbook XXI (1973), pp. 322-350; and more recently the "European Prison Rules", laid down in Resolution (87)3, adopted by the Committee of Ministers on 12 February 1987. In its decision on Appl. 7341/76, *Eggs*, Yearbook XX (1977), p. 448 (460), the Commission took the position that "the conditions of detention which in certain aspects did not come up to the standard of the 'Minimum Rules' did not thereby alone amount to inhuman or degrading treatment". See also Appl. 7408/76, *X. v. Federal Republic of Germany*, D&R 10 (1978), p. 221 (222), where, on the one hand, the Commission found that the punishment imposed on the applicant was not in conformity with modern views of penitentiary policy, but, on the other hand, came to the conclusion that the treatment was not inhuman or degrading.

It is clear that the answer to the question whether Article 3 has been violated, although depending on all the circumstances of the case, including such factors as the mental effects on the person concerned, is not entirely dependent on his subjective appreciations and feelings. So, in the *East African Asians* Case the Commission did not accept the 'subjective' definition that the treatment of a person is degrading in the sense of Article 3 "if it lowers him in rank, position, reputation or character, whether in his own eyes or in the eyes of other people", and argued that – given the general purpose of this provision to prevent interferences with the dignity of man of a particularly serious nature – "an action which lowers a person in rank, position, reputation or character can only be regarded as 'degrading treatment' in the sense of Article 3 where it reaches a certain level of severity".[54] And in *B. v. France* the Commission found that the situation in which there is a discrepancy between the appearance of a transsexual and her identity papers, although creating embarrassment for her in respect of third persons to whom she is forced to reveal her particular situation, does not attain the requisite minimum degree of severity for an infringement of Article 3.[55]

The Court has followed the same approach. For instance, in the *Campbell and Cosans* Case, when it had to rule on the application of corporal punishment in British schools, the Court reached the conclusion that in that case it could not be said that a degrading treatment was involved, because the corporal punishment had not been actually applied to the children of the two applicants and the gravity of the punishment and its degrading effect on the person concerned could not therefore be measured. They might have experienced feelings of apprehension, disquiet or alienation, but "these effects fall into a different category from humiliation or debasement".[56] And in the *Marckx* Case the Court held that "while the legal rules at issue probably present aspects which the applicants may feel to be humiliating, they do not constitute degrading treatment coming within the ambit of Article 3."[57]

Thus, like the Commission, the Court is of the opinion that ill-treatment must reach a certain (objective) level of severity in order to fall within the ambit of Article 3.[58] In the *Costello-Roberts* Case the Court once again had to address the issue of corporal punishment in British schools. The applicant was a young boy punished in accordance with the disciplinary rules of his school. The Court distinguished the circumstances of this punishment from those in the *Tyrer* Case which was found to

---

[54]   Report of 14 December 1973, D&R 78-A (1994), p. 5 (55). Cf. also *ibidem*, p. 57: "The Commission finally recalls its own statement in the First Greek Case that treatment of an individual may be said to be 'degrading' in the sense of Article 3 'if it grossly humiliates him before others or drives him to act against his will or conscience'. This definition is similar to the indication reached (...) above; in particular, the word 'grossly' indicates that Article 3 is only concerned with 'degrading treatment' which reaches a certain level of severity."

[55]   Report of 6 September 1990, paras 84-87.

[56]   Judgment of 25 February 1982, paras 25-30.

[57]   Judgment of 13 June 1979, para. 66.

[58]   Judgment of 18 January 1978, *Ireland v. the United Kingdom*, para. 162.

be degrading within the meaning of Article 3. Tyrer was sentenced in a juvenile court to three strokes of the birch on the bare posterior; his punishment was administered three weeks later in a police station where he was held by two policemen whilst a third administered the punishment. Costello-Robert's punishment, on the other hand, amounted to being slippered three times on his buttocks through his shorts with a gym shoe by the headmaster in private. In his case the Court found that the minimum level of severity required to conclude that Article 3 was violated, was not attained.[59]

In several other cases the Court likewise ruled that the treatment, although unpleasant or even harsh, did not amount to inhuman or degrading treatment. The situation of Mr. *Guzzardi*, detained on an island, was "undoubtedly unpleasant or even irksome"; nevertheless, his treatment did not attain the level of severity above which it falls within the scope of Article 3.[60] The refusal to grant Mr. *Berrehab* a new residence permit after his divorce and his resulting deportation did not infringe Article 3; he did not undergo suffering of a degree corresponding to the concepts of "inhuman" or "degrading" treatment.[61] The conditions in which Mrs *López Ostra* and her family lived – near a plant for the treatment of liquid and solid waste, which despite a partial shutdown continued to emit fumes, repetitive noise and strong smells – did not amount to degrading treatment within the meaning of Article 3.[62] And the suffering that Mr. *Popov* might have experienced due to the non-execution of the judgment to give him back his parents' house was insufficient to amount to inhuman and degrading treatment.[63]

7.4 OTHER GENERAL ASPECTS

7.4.1 MENTAL SUFFERING

Both the Commission and the Court have left no doubt about the fact that Article 3 does not refer exclusively to the infliction of physical but also of mental suffering. The Commission defined the latter as covering "the infliction of mental suffering

---

[59] Judgment of 25 March 1993, paras. 31-32. The United Kingdom has responded to this judgment by passing legislation to prohibit corporal punishment in schools.
[60] Judgment of 6 November 1980, para. 107.
[61] Judgment of 21 June 1988, paras. 30-31.
[62] Judgment of 9 December 1994, para. 60.
[63] Judgment of 18 January 2005, paras 26-27.

by creating a state of anguish and stress by means other than bodily assault".[64] Even
torture does not necessarily require a "physical act or condition".[65]

Often there will be a combination of mental and physical suffering, as may be
clearly seen in *X and Y v. the Netherlands*, in which the Commission dealt with the
question of mental suffering as a result of the sexual abuse of the victim.[66] There the
Commission stated that "mental suffering leading to acute psychiatric disturbances
falls into the category of treatment prohibited by Article 3 of the Convention".[67] However, as was stressed in 7.3, not every measure taken by a public authority that has
emotional consequences of any kind for the individual falls within the scope of
inhuman treatment, but only such measures as "inflict severe mental or physical
suffering on an individual".[68]

7.4.2 INTENTION AND MOTIVE

Does the intention or motive of the acting person to cause physical or mental suffering,
in addition to the suffering inflicted or the humiliation experienced, constitute a
necessary element of the types of treatment prohibited in Article 3? It is obvious, for
example, that a medically necessary operation or treatment, however painful it may
be for the patient, is not to be considered as torture or inhuman or degrading treatment, provided that unnecessary suffering is avoided. So, in the *Herczegfalvy* Case
the Court held that mental patients are under the protection of Article 3, but that
the "established principles of medicine are (...) decisive in such cases; as a general rule,
a measure which is therapeutic cannot be regarded as inhuman or degrading."[69] But,
of course, the national courts and the Strasbourg Court must satisfy themselves as to
the medical necessity of a particular form of treatment. Thus, a medical experiment
may for lack of this necessity infringe Article 3, although the aim is not to inflict

---

[64] Report of 5 November 1969, *The Greek Case*, Yearbook XII (1969), p. 461. For the Court, see, *inter
alia*, the judgment of 7 July 1989, *Soering*, para. 100.

[65] Report in *The Greek Case*, ibidem; report of 14 December 1973, *East African Asians*, D&R 78-A
(1994), p. 5 (56). Cf. also the definition of "torture" in Article 1 of the UN Convention against
Torture and other Cruel, Inhuman or Degrading Treatment or Punishment: "the term 'torture'
means any act by which severe pain or suffering, whether physical or mental, is intentionally inflicted
on a person".

[66] Report of 5 July 1983, para. 93. In its judgment of 26 March 1985 in that case, para. 34, the Court,
having found a violation of Article 8, decided that it was not necessary to examine the case under
Article 3 as well.

[67] *Ibidem.*

[68] Appl. 9191/80, *X. v. Federal Republic of Germany* (not published). See also the judgment of 28 October
2004, *Zengin*, para. 55-57: that the governor has declared that Zengin's husband was a terrorist and
was legally killed did not fall within the scope of Article 3.

[69] Judgment of 24 September 1992, para. 82.

suffering, but to advance medical science.[70] In the *Herczegfalvy* Case the Commission had concluded by unanimous vote that there had been a violation of Article 3, because the treatment accorded to the applicant, who had been diagnosed as suffering from a mental illness, went beyond what was strictly necessary and extended beyond the period necessary to serve its purpose: he was forcibly administered food and neuroleptics, isolated, and attached with handcuffs to his security bed for several weeks.[71] Rather surprisingly, the Court, though expressing its worries concerning the length of time during which the handcuffs and security bed were used, considered the necessity test to be met.[72]

In the *Peers* Case the Court held that the absence of a purpose to humiliate or debase, cannot conclusively rule out a finding of degrading treatment under Article 3.[73] Similarly treatment of a detainee which in itself is inhuman does not lose this character through the mere fact that its only motive is the enhancement of security or the combat against crime. As the Court stated in the *Tomasi* Case, the requirements of the investigation and the undeniable difficulties inherent in the fight against terrorism cannot result in limits being placed on the protection by Article 3 to be afforded in respect of the physical integrity of individuals.[74]

It is, therefore, not the intention of the acting person, but the nature of the act and its effect on the person undergoing the treatment which are decisive. Therefore, the Court used too general a phrase when it observed in the *Albert and Le Compte* Case that the disciplinary measure of withdrawal of the right to practise, imposed upon a doctor, had as its object the imposition of a sanction and not the debasement of his personality; not this is decisive but the question raised next by the Court, *viz.* whether the consequences of the measure adversely affected the doctor's personality in a manner incompatible with Article 3.[75]

7.4.3 CONSENT

It cannot be said in general whether the absence of consent to the treatment on the part of the person in question constitutes a necessary element of the prohibition of

---

[70] See, for example, Appl. 9974/82, *X. v. Denmark*, D&R 32 (1983), p. 282 (283-284), concerning an experiment made with a slightly different instrument, but which did not change the procedure of the operation as such. According to the Commission, the operation "cannot be considered as such a medical experiment which, if carried out without consent, could constitute a violation of Article 3 of the Convention".

[71] Report of 1 March 1991, paras 245-254.

[72] Judgment of 24 September 1992, para. 83.

[73] Judgment of 19 April 2001, para. 74.

[74] Judgment of 27 August 1992, para. 115; cf. also the judgment of 4 December 1995, *Ribitsch*, para. 38.

[75] Judgment of 10 February 1983, para. 22.

Article 3, but evidently it is a relevant factor.[76] The consent of the person concerned may deprive an act, which would be felt by another to be inhuman or degrading, of that character. However, experiments and treatments are conceivable which are so inhuman or degrade the human person to such an extent that the person in question, in spite of his previous consent, may feel himself to be the victim of a violation of Article 3. And in any case the consent of a particular victim need not bar a complaint by an indirect victim[77] or an abstract complaint by a State concerning a general practice. On the other hand, the absence of consent does not in all cases give an inhuman character to treatment affecting human integrity. Thus the Commission decided that the enforced administration of medicine to a mentally deranged detainee did not have that character, since that treatment had been declared medically necessary and this had been confirmed by a court decision.[78] The Court endorsed a similar view in the *Herczegfalvy* Case.[79] However, the will of the person in question, in so far as he can be deemed capable of expressing it, must weigh heavily, since in principle he must be able himself to decide about his life and body as long as the life and the health of others are not at stake.

7.5 IMPRISONMENT, DETENTION AND ARREST

It is not surprising that in the Strasbourg case law Article 3 has frequently been an issue in connection with detained persons. Of course, as the Court held in the *Kudla* Case, "it cannot be said that the execution of detention on remand in itself raises an issue under Article 3 of the Convention. Nor can that Article be interpreted as laying down a general obligation to release a detainee on health grounds or to place him in a civil hospital to enable him to obtain a particular kind of medical treatment."[80] Neverthe-less, a balancing of interests is necessary. In the *Kröcher and Möller* Case the Commission opined that "the question that arises is whether the balance between the requirements of security and basic individual rights was not disrupted to the detriment of the latter."[81] In this case the prison conditions included, *inter alia*, isolation, constant artificial lighting, permanent surveillance by closed-circuit television, denial of access to newspapers and radio and the lack of physical exercise. Although the Commission expressed "serious concern with the need for such measures, their usefulness and their compatibility with Article 3 of the Convention", it concluded that the special conditions imposed on the applicants could not be construed as inhuman or degrading treat-

---

[76] Appl. 9974/82, *X. v. Denmark*, D&R 32 (1983), p. 282 (283-284).
[77] On this, see *supra*, 1.13.3.5.
[78] Appl. 8518/79, *X. v. Federal Republic of Germany*, D&R 20 (1980), p. 193 (194).
[79] Judgment of 24 September 1992, paras 82-83.
[80] Judgment of 26 October 2000, para. 93.
[81] Report of 16 December 1982, D&R 34 (1983), p. 52.

ment. This conclusion was reached after it had been sufficiently shown, in the opinion of the Commission, that these conditions were necessary to ensure security inside and outside the prison. Furthermore, the applicants were considered dangerous, they were alleged to be terrorists and there was a risk of escape and collusion.[82] Other factors that have been accepted by the Commission to justify stringent measures are the extremely dangerous behaviour of the prisoner, the ability to manipulate situations and encourage other prisoners to acts of indiscipline, the safety of the applicant, and the use of firearms at the time of arrest.[83]

In the *Kudla* Case the Court held that "a State must ensure that a person is detained in conditions which are compatible with respect for his human dignity, that the manner and method of the execution of the measure do not subject him to distress or hardship of an intensity exceeding the unavoidable level of suffering inherent in detention and that, given the practical demands of imprisonment, his health and well-being are adequately secured by, among other things, providing him with the requisite medical assistance".[84] The Court further observed that, when assessing conditions of detention, account has to be taken of the cumulative effects of these conditions, as well as the applicant's specific allegations.[85] Attention should be paid to "all the circumstances, such as the size of the cell and the degree of overcrowding, sanitary conditions, opportunities for recreation and exercise, medical treatment and supervision and the prisoner's state of health".[86] That the detention centre is not adequately funded is no justification: "lack of resources cannot in principle justify prison conditions which are so poor as to reach the threshold of treatment contrary to Article 3."[87]

As may be concluded from the *Weeks* Case,[88] life imprisonment is not in itself a breach of Article 3. Further, the Commission has held that Article 3 can not be read "as requiring that an individual serving a lawful sentence of life imprisonment must have that sentence reconsidered by a national authority, judicial or administrative, with a view to its remission or termination".[89]

It is as yet unclear whether a death penalty in peacetime in itself is contrary to Article 3 (*supra* 7.3). It is at least clear, however, that additional factors may cause this sentence to be contrary to this provision. Relevant factors are "the manner in which

---

[82]   *Ibidem*, pp. 52 and 57, respectively.

[83]   See, respectively, Appl. 9907/82, *M. v. the United Kingdom*, D&R 35 (1984), p. 13 (34); Appl. 8324/78, *X. v. the United Kingdom*, not published; Appl. 8241/78, *X. v. the United Kingdom*, not published; Appls. 7572/76, 7586/76, 7587/76, *Ensslin, Baader and Raspe*, Yearbook XXI (1978), p. 418 (454).

[84]   Judgment of 26 October 2000, para. 94; *cf.* the judgment of 24 July 2001, *Valašinas*, para. 102.

[85]   Judgment of 6 March 2001, *Dougoz*, para. 46.

[86]   Judgment of 28 October 1998, *Assenov and Others*, para. 135.

[87]   Judgment of 29 April 2003, *Poltoratskiy*, para. 148.

[88]   Judgment of 2 March 1987, para. 47.

[89]   Appl. 7994/77, *Kotälla*, D&R 14 (1979), p. 238 (240); Appl. 15776/89, *B., H. and L. v. Austria*, D&R 64 (1990), p. 264 (270).

the death sentence is imposed or executed, the personal circumstances of the con-demned person and a disproportionality to the gravity of the crime committed, as well as the conditions of detention awaiting execution".[90] Moreover, according to the Court, "to impose a death sentence on a person after an unfair trial is to subject that person wrongfully to the fear that he will be executed. Having regard to the rejection by the Contracting Parties of capital punishment, which is no longer seen as having any legitimate place in a democratic society, the imposition of a capital sentence after an unfair trial must be considered, in itself, to amount to a form of inhuman treatment."[91] The Court seems prepared to take into account a moratorium on executions, on the ground that feelings of fear and anxiety may diminish as time goes on and the morato-rium continues in force.[92] Nevertheless, in every single case regard must be had to the risk that the sentence in the long run will be implemented.[93]

In cases where the question was raised of whether solitary confinement of a detainee constituted an inhuman treatment, the Commission took the position that such confinement was in principle undesirable, particularly when the prisoner concerned was in detention on remand, and might only be justified for exceptional reasons. For the question of whether an inhuman or degrading treatment is concerned, regard must be had to the surrounding circumstances, including the particular conditions, the stringency of the measure, its duration, the objective pursued and its effects on the person concerned, and also the question of whether a given minimum of possibilities for human contact has been left to the person in question.[94] Absolute sensory isolation combined with complete social isolation can destroy the personality and constitutes an inhuman treatment for which no security requirements can form a justification in view of the absolute character of the right laid down in Article 3.[95] Moreover, the Commission has made a distinction between absolute sensory and social isolation on the one hand, and "removal from association with other prisoners for security, disciplinary and protective reasons" on the other, and has taken the view that the latter form of segregation from the prison community normally does not amount to

---

[90]   Judgment of 7 July 1989, *Soering*, para. 104.
[91]   Judgment of 12 March 2003, *Öcalan*, para. 207; judgment of 12 may 2005 (Grand Chamber), *Öcalan*, para. 169.
[92]   Judgment of 11 March 2004, *G.B. v. Bulgaria*, para. 80; judgment of 11 March 2004, *Iorgov*, para.79.
[93]   Judgment of 12 March 2003, *Öcalan*, paras 209-210; judgment of 12 May 2005 (Grand Chamber), *Öcalan*, paras 171-172.
[94]   Appl. 6038/73, *X. v. Federal Republic of Germany*, Coll. 44 (1973), p. 115 (119); Appl. 6166/73, *Baader, Meins, Meinhof and Grundmann*, Yearbook XVIII (1975), p. 132 (144-146); Appls 7572/76, 7586/76, and 7587/76, *Ensslin, Baader and Raspe*, Yearbook XXI (1978), p. 418 (454-460); report of 16 December 1982, *Kröcher and Möller*, D&R 34 (1983), p. 24 (51-55); judgment of 4 February 2003, *Van der Ven*, para. 51.
[95]   Appls 7572/76, 7586/76 and 7587/76, *Ensslin, Baader and Raspe*, Yearbook XXI (1978), p. 418 (456).

inhuman or degrading treatment or punishment.[96] In the latter case it is still possible to meet prison officers, medical officers, lawyers, relatives etc., and to have contact with the outside world through newspapers, radio and television. According to the Court in the *Sadak* Case and the *Yurttas* Case, the duration of the isolation should also be taken into account to decide whether this measure is in accordance with Article 3.[97] However, in the *Ramirez Sanchez* Case, in which the applicant was subjected to relative social isolation, because otherwise he could use communications inside or outside the prison to re-establish contact with members of his terrorist group, seek to proselytise other prisoners or prepare an escape, the Court held that "irrespective of its duration (eight years and two months), which in itself is regrettable, the applicant's continued solitary confinement has not, given his age and health, caused him suffering of the level of severity required to constitute a violation of Article 3".[98]

On the other hand, a detention cell may not be overcrowded and must have sufficient sanitary and sleeping facilities.[99] The European Committee for the Prevention of Torture and Inhuman and Degrading Treatment or Punishment (CPT) has set 7 square metres per prisoner as a desirable guideline. It is not surprising, then, that the Court concluded in the *Kalashnikov* Case that a detention cell where there is 0.9-1.9 square metres of space per inmate, is severely overcrowded, which in itself raises an issue under Article 3.[100] In the *Novoselov* Case the Court concluded that "the fact that the detainee was obliged to live, sleep and use the toilet in the same cell with so many other inmates and with less that 1 square metre of personal space was itself sufficient to cause distress or hardship of an intensity exceeding the unavoidable level of suffering inherent in detention".[101] In the *Peers* Case the applicant had to share a cell of approximately 7 square metres with another inmate. The Court concluded that there was a violation of Article 3 because the applicant had to use the toilet in the presence of the other inmate and had to spend almost the whole 24-hour period practically confined

---

[96] Report of 25 January 1976, *Ireland v. the United Kingdom*, B.23/I, p. 379; Appls 7572/76, 7586/76 and 7587/76, *Ensslin, Baader and Raspe*, Yearbook XXI (1978), p. 418 (456); Appl. 8317/78, *McFeeley*, D&R 20 (1980), p. 44 (82); report of 16 December 1982, *Kröcher and Möller*, D&R 34 (1983), p. 24 (53); Appl. 10263/83, *R. v. Denmark*, D&R 41 (1985), p. 149; Appl. 14610/89, *Treholt*, D&R 71 (1991), p. 168 (190-191). See for example the decision of 8 June 1999, *Messina*, where the Court concluded that the relative social isolation (prevention of meeting prisoners subject to different prison regimes, prevention of receiving visits from persons other than family members and making telephone calls, prohibition of recreational and sporting activities and handicraft work in his cell, limited access to outdoor exercise and withdrawal of the right to receive certain foods and objects from the outside) was in accordance with Article 3 because of the danger that the applicant might re-establish contact with criminal organizations and the risk of bringing dangerous tools into the prison's high-security wing.

[97] Judgment of 8 April 2004, para. 46; judgment of 27 May 2004, para. 48.

[98] Judgment of 27 January 2005, paras 113 and 120.

[99] Judgment of 6 March 2001, *Dougoz*, para. 45. The Court, concluding that Article 3 was violated, observed that "it was even impossible for him to read a book because his cell was so overcrowded"!

[100] Judgment of 15 July 2002, para. 97.

[101] Judgment of 2 June 2005, para. 43.

to his bed, in a cell where there was neither ventilation nor a window.[102] In contrast, in the *Valašinas* Case no violation of Article 3 was found, because the restricted space in the sleeping facilities was counterbalanced by the unlimited freedom of movement during the day.[103]

Article 3 imposes an obligation on the State to protect the physical well-being of persons deprived of their liberty. Health, age and severe physical disability are amongst the most relevant factors to be taken into account.[104] In the *Keenan* Case the Court held that the vulnerability and inability of mentally ill persons had to be taken into account. Treatment of a mentally ill person could be incompatible with Article 3, even though the person may not be able to complain coherently, or to point to any specific ill-effects.[105] In the *Price* Case the Court concluded that to detain a person who was four-limb deficient, in conditions which were inappropriate to her state of health, constituted degrading treatment.[106] The detention of elderly, sick persons for a prolonged period was discussed in the *Papon* Case, where the Court held that this situation could amount to a violation of Article 3.[107] In the *Mouisel* Case the Court concluded that the treatment of a detainee suffering from cancer amounted to inhuman and degrading treatment, because the prison was scarcely equipped to deal with his illness, while no special measures were taken and he was handcuffed and kept in chains while taken to a hospital.[108]

In a series of cases violation of Article 3 was alleged, because of the adverse effects of the mere fact of being detained on the health of the detainee. In such cases reports by medical experts appear to be of great importance.[109] The question to be answered is whether the (mental) health of the detainee is directly affected by his detention. Furthermore, the frequency of visits by medical staff and medical treatment are taken into account,[110] as well as the question of whether the detainee has sought medical opinion.[111] However, the latter does not take away the primary responsibility of the authorities for the medical care of the detainees.

In some cases it is not the negative consequences of detention as such on the health of the detainee, but the lack of proper medical care while being detained which is the

---

[102]   Judgment of 19 April 2001, para. 75.
[103]   Judgment of 24 July 2001, paras 103 and 107.
[104]   Judgment of 14 November 2002, *Mouisel,* paras 38-40.
[105]   Judgment of 3 April 2001, paras 111 and 113. See also the judgment of 30 July 1998, *Aerts,* para. 66.
[106]   Judgment of 10 July 2001, para. 30.
[107]   Decision of 7 June 2001.
[108]   Judgment of 14 November 2002, paras 46-48.
[109]   See, for example, Appl. 9554/81, *X. v. Ireland* (not published) and the report of 7 October 1981, *B. v. the United Kingdom,* D&R 32 (1983), p. 5 (35).
[110]   See for example the report of 8 December 1982, *Chartier,* D&R 33 (1983), p. 41 (57-58); Appl. 21915/93, *Lukanov,* D&R 80-A (1995), p. 108 (128-130); judgment of 29 April 2003, *McGlinchey,* para. 57.
[111]   Appl. 9813/82, *X. v. the United Kingdom,* not published.

main issue.[112] In the *Hurtado* Case the Commission found that it constituted a breach of Article 3 not to bring the applicant to a doctor for a medical examination until eight days after his arrest in the course of which he suffered a fracture of one of his ribs.[113] In the *Nevmerzhitsky* Case the applicant contracted various skin diseases while he was detained in an unsanitary environment with no respect for basic hygiene. The Court concluded that these conditions had a detrimental effect on his health and well-being and amounted to degrading treatment. Furthermore, the force-feeding of the applicant without any medical justification was considered to amount to torture.[114]

In two cases the Commission declared the applications admissible of persons detained in a mental hospital who complained of violation of Article 3 on account of the treatment and living conditions in the hospitals in question. It held that at first sight these complaints were sufficiently well-founded to justify further inquiry.[115] In a case which concerned the question of whether a detainee who was not mentally deranged, could be detained in a closed ward of a mental hospital, a friendly settlement was reached with the respondent Austrian Government; the Minister of Justice issued a general order that was to prevent such treatment in the future.[116] The placement of a mentally deranged person in a normal prison was considered acceptable by the Commission after it had found that the person in question received adequate care there.[117] Segregation of accused persons from convicted persons is not prescribed by the Convention, nor does it ensue *per se* from Article 3.[118]

In subsection 7.2 it was mentioned that the Court often applies a 'beyond reasonable doubt'-test as standard of proof, but that "such proof may follow from the coexistence of sufficiently strong, clear and concordant inferences or of similar unrebutted presumptions of fact. The conduct of the Parties when evidence is being

---

[112] See Appl. 7994/77, *Kotälla*, Yearbook XXI (1978), p. 522 (528), where the Commission followed the view of the Dutch court that the deterioration of the physical and mental condition of the applicant was not due to his detention. See also the report of 7 December 1978, *Guzzardi*, B.35 (1979-1980), pp. 34-35 and the report of 5 December 1979, *Bonnechaux*, D&R 18 (1980), p. 100 (148).

[113] Report of 8 July 1993, paras 75-80. Cf. also the judgment of 29 April 2003, *McGlinchey*, paras 53-58.

[114] Judgment of 5 April 2005, paras 87 and 98.

[115] Appl. 6840/74, *X. v. the United Kingdom*, Yearbook XXI (1978), p. 250 (282); Appl. 6870/75, *B. v. the United Kingdom*, D&R 10 (1978), p. 37 (67). In the first-mentioned case a friendly settlement was reached, by which the authorities promised a clearer regulation concerning solitary confinement of patients: D&R 20 (1980), p. 5 (8-11). In the latter case, the Commission concluded in its report of 7 October 1981 that, although the facilities in the hospital at that time were "extremely unsatisfactory", they did not amount to inhuman or degrading treatment contrary to Art. 3 of the Convention: D&R 32 (1983), p. 5 (30).

[116] Appl. 4340/69, *Simon-Herold*, Coll. 38 (1972), p. 18.

[117] Appl. 5229/71, *X. v. the United Kingdom*, Coll. 42 (1973), p. 140.

[118] Appl. 6337/73, *X. v. Belgium*, D&R 3 (1976), p. 83 (85). See, however, Article 10(2)(a) of the International Covenant on Civil and Political Rights. See also Article 11(3) 3 of the European Prison Rules, which stipulates that "in principle untried prisoners shall be detained separately from convicted persons unless they consent to being accommodated or involved together in organised activities beneficial to them".

obtained has to be taken into account."[119] It seems that this rather strict standard is
modified when detention conditions are concerned. This was not always manifest in
the case law of the Commission. As regards the effects on detainees, the Commission
required applicants to submit medical evidence to show that the prison conditions
had adverse effects on their mental or physical health.[120] This medical evidence should
not only show that there is a direct relationship between the prison conditions
complained of and the deteriorating health of the applicant,[121] but also that these
conditions were such that they could "destroy the personality and cause severe mental
and physical suffering" to the applicant.[122] From the Court's case law we may also
conclude that an important source of evidence concerning detention conditions are
the General Reports of the European Committee for the Prevention of Torture and
Inhuman or Degrading Treatment or Punishment (CPT).[123]

As is clear from the above discussion of the case law concerning solitary confinement, other major elements the Commission regularly has taken into account in
answering the question whether a violation of Article 3 has occurred, are the behaviour
of the detainee, his personality and the seriousness of his crimes. In particular, when
the measures complained of were a result of the unco-operative attitude of the detainee, the Commission has been very reticent in concluding that a violation had
occurred.[124] For this reason the Commission declared complaints of IRA prisoners
about the situation in the Maze prison and the treatment they received there inadmissible.[125] However its decision does contain the important finding that the fact of
the detainees carrying on a campaign against the authorities does not relieve the latter
from their obligations under Article 3.[126]

---

[119]   See, for instance, the judgment of 18 January 1978, *Ireland v. the United Kingdom*, para. 161.
[120]   See, for example, Appl. 8116/77, *X. v. the United Kingdom*, not published, and Appl. 8601/79, *X. v.
Switzerland*, not published.
[121]   In the applications of *Ensslin, Baader and Raspe*, medical reports were presented, but they did not
"make it possible to establish accurately the specific effect of this isolation in relation to their physical
and mental health, as compared with other factors", Yearbook XXI (1978), p. 418 (458).
[122]   Appl. 8158/78, *X. v. the United Kingdom*, D&R 21 (1981), p. 95 (99) and report of 16 December 1982,
Kröcher and Möller, D&R 34 (1983), p. 24 (56).
[123]   Judgment of 6 March 2001, *Dougoz*, paras. 46-47; judgment of 15 July 2002, *Kalashnikov*, para. 97;
judgment of 2 June 2005, *Novoselov*, para. 43.
[124]   See, *e.g.*, Appl. 8231/78, *X. v. the United Kingdom*, D&R 28 (1982), p. 5 (27-28), where the detainee
refused to wear prison clothes, and the report of 7 October 1981, *B. v. the United Kingdom*, D&R
32 (1983), p. 5 (34-35 and 38), where the applicant had constantly refused to accept medical
treatment and had refused to clean his cell himself. See also Appls. 9911/82 and 9945/82, *R., S., A.,
and C. v. Portugal*, D&R 36 (1984), p. 200 (208).
[125]   Appl. 8317/78, *McFeeley*, D&R 20 (1980), p. 44 (77-89). See also Appl. 8231/78, *X. v. the United
Kingdom*, D&R 28 (1982), p. 5 (27-33) concerning the obligation to wear prison clothes.
[126]   Appl. 8317/78, *McFeeley*, D&R 20 (1980), p. 44 (81). See also Appls. 7572/76, 7586/76 and 7587/76,
Ensslin, Baader and Raspe, Yearbook XXI (1978), p. 418 (458-460); and Appl. 9907/82, *M. v. the
United Kingdom*, D&R 35 (1984), p. 130 (133-136). In the latter case the measures taken with respect
to the detainee were the result of his extremely dangerous behaviour.

Not infrequently the complaint concerns physical force used against an arrested person or a detainee by policemen or prison officers. On the one hand, it is obvious that the use of a certain amount of force in case of resistance to arrest, an attempt to flee or an assault on a prison officer or fellow prisoner may be inevitable. On the other hand, the form as well as the intensity of the force used should be proportionate to the nature and the seriousness of the resistance or threat.

The Court has laid down some general principles, which to a certain extent also alleviate the applicant's burden of proof. In the *Ribitsch* Case the Court (obviously inspired by the concurring opinion of Judge De Meyer in the *Tomasi* judgment)[127] ruled that "in respect of a person deprived of his liberty, any recourse to physical force which has not been made strictly necessary by his own conduct diminishes human dignity and is in principle an infringement of the right set forth in Article 3".[128] Of course, it has to be established that the injuries actually occurred in the way alleged by the applicant, in that they resulted from physical force applied during arrest or detention.[129] In the *Aksoy* Case – making explicit the principle underlying *Tomasi* and *Ribitsch* – the Court considered that "where an individual is taken into police custody in good health but is found to be injured at the time of release, it is incumbent on the State to provide a plausible explanation as to the causing of the injury, particularly if those allegations were backed up by medical reports, failing which a clear issue arises under Article 3".[130] In the *Salman* Case the Court held that in a situation "where the events in issue lie wholly, or in large part, within the exclusive knowledge of the authorities, as in the case of persons within their control in custody, strong presumptions of fact will arise in respect of injuries and death occurring during such detention. Indeed, the burden of proof may be regarded as resting on the authorities to provide a satisfactory and convincing explanation."[131] A fact also taken into account by the Court is the time the applicant has been waiting before he seeks medical help. In the *Balogh* Case the applicant waited two days, but immediately sought medical assistance on his arrival in his home town. The Court stated to be "reluctant to attribute any decisive importance to this delay, which, in any event, cannot be considered so significant as to undermine his case under Article 3."[132] Finally, it is important to note that neither the acquittal of the police officers suspected of having inflicted ill-treatment,

---

[127]   Concurring opinion attached to the judgment of 27 August 1992.

[128]   Judgment of 4 December 1995, para. 38. See the judgment of 19 May 2004, *R.L. and M.-J.D. v. France*, paras. 69-72, where the Court concluded that the force used by the police was not strictly necessary, while on the one hand the police intervened because of a simple breach of the peace and had no reasons to assume that the applicants were violent, dangerous or armed, and on the other hand the applicants had many and significant marks of inflictions on their body, and after there release were temporarily unable to work.

[129]   Appl. 18764/91, *Hippin*, D&R 79-A (1994), p. 23 (29).

[130]   Judgment of 18 December 1996, para. 61. See also the judgment of 28 July 1999, *Selmouni*, para. 87.

[131]   Judgment of 27 June 2000, para. 100.

[132]   Judgment of 20 July 2004, para. 49.

nor a successful prosecution of State agents, nor the failure to find State agents guilty of a crime against detainees absolves the State of its responsibility under Article 3.[133]

It is not normally for the Court to substitute its own assessment of the facts for that of the domestic courts. This has been made particularly clear in the *Klaas* Case. Mrs Klaas was requested to provide a specimen of breath after allegedly committing a road offence. A struggle ensued, resulting in Mrs Klaas being handcuffed. She suffered bruising, was unconscious for a short period when she banged her head on a window-ledge and received a serious long-lasting injury to her shoulder. The Commission, basing itself on the *Tomasi* judgment, concluded that the Government had not produced any convincing explanation and the treatment of Mrs Klaas, therefore, had to be regarded as a disproportionate use of force that violated Article 3. The Court disagreed with the Commission. According to the Court the injuries were consistent with either the applicant's and the arresting officers' version of events. While the national courts found against the applicant and while there were no cogent reasons adduced to depart from their findings, the Court had to assume that the officers had not used excessive force and no violation of Article 3 had occurred.[134] The relevant factor distinguishing this case from the *Tomasi* and *Ribitsch* Cases seems to be that in the latter the Governments were not able to provide a plausible explanation of how the applicant's injuries were caused.

7.6 ADMISSION AND ASYLUM, EXPULSION AND EXTRADITION

7.6.1 GENERAL OBSERVATIONS

The Convention does not contain a general right of admission to a certain country and does not contain an explicit right to asylum. Article 3 of Protocol No. 4 prohibits the expulsion of nationals, and gives them the right to be admitted to their country; Article 4 of Protocol No. 4 prohibits only collective expulsion of aliens; and Article 1 of Protocol No. 7 only contains certain procedural guarantees against expulsion.[135] The refusal of admission to or the expulsion of an alien from a country may, however, constitute treatment that infringes Article 3. In the *East African Asians* Case the Com-

---

[133]   Judgment of 8 January 2004, *Çolak and Filizer*, para. 33; judgment of 20 July 2004, *Balogh*, para. 51; judgment of 5 April 2005, *Afanasyev*, para. 64.

[134]   Judgment of 22 September 1993, paras 29-30.

[135]   Judgment of 30 October 1991, *Vilvarajah and Others*, para. 102: "the Court observes that Contracting States have the right, as a matter of well-established international law and subject to their treaty obligations including Article 3, to control the entry, residence and expulsion of aliens (...). Moreover, it must be noted that the right to political asylum is not contained in either the Convention or its Protocols."

mission concluded that legislation imposing restrictions on admission to the United Kingdom of UK citizens and Commonwealth residents in East Africa discriminated against persons of Asian origin on the ground of race and thus constituted an interference with their human dignity which amounted to "degrading treatment" in the sense of Article 3.[136] A report of 1983 seems to imply that "sexual and other forms of discrimination" in immigration rules may also have such degrading aspects that Article 3 may be applicable.[137] However, because these aspects had already been dealt with in connection with Article 14, the Commission did not consider it necessary to pursue a further examination in the light of Article 3.[138] Furthermore, repeated expulsion of an individual whose identity is impossible to establish, to a country where his admission is not guaranteed, may raise an issue under Article 3.[139]

Expulsion and extradition may infringe Article 3 because of their direct physical or mental effects. The Strasbourg case law indicates the application of rather strict criteria. The Commission has held that extradition within a day after a second attempt to commit suicide did not violate Article 3.[140] In the *Cruz Varas* Case the Court did not consider that the applicant's expulsion to Chile exceeded the threshold set by Article 3, although he suffered from a post-traumatic stress disorder prior to his expulsion and his mental health deteriorated following his return to Chile.[141] And in the *Nsona* Case the return of a nine-year-old child to Zaïre that took seven days, part of which was unaccompanied, was not regarded as inhuman or degrading treatment.[142]

An issue under Article 3 may also arise in that expulsion might result in the person in question being separated from a person or group of persons with whom he has a close link, even apart from the protection of family life under Article 8.[143]

Finally, the violation of Article 3 may also consist in ill-treatment – torture, inhuman or degrading treatment or punishment – to which, on the basis of objective facts, the

---

[136]   Report of 14 December 1973, D&R 78-A (1994), p. 5 (62).
[137]   Report of 12 May 1983, *Abdulaziz, Cabales and Balkandali*, paras 121-122.
[138]   *Ibidem*. In its Judgment of 28 May 1985 in this case, para. 91, the Court did not find a violation of Article 3, because the difference of treatment did not denote any contempt or lack of respect for the personality of the applicants and the measures complained of were not designed to, and did not, humiliate or debase them.
[139]   Report of 17 July 1980, *Giama*, D&R 21 (1981), p. 73 (89).
[140]   Appl. 25342/94, *Raidl*, D&R 82-A (1995), p. 134 (146-147).
[141]   Judgment of 20 March 1991, para. 84. Cf. also the decision of 22 October 2002, *Ammari*.
[142]   Judgment of 28 November 1996, para. 99.
[143]   Judgment of 24 March 1988, *Olsson*, para. 86, where the applicants alleged a violation of Article 3 mainly in two different respects. First, they contended that the taking away of the children from them without sufficient reasons was a deprivation of the children's right to grow up in their family. Secondly, they put forward the frequent moving of one child from one home to another and the ill-treatment in his foster-family. In the Court's view, the allegations were not substantiated. See also Appl. 10730/84, *Berrehab and Koster*, D&R 41 (1985), p. 196 (209), where the Commission stated that where an expulsion raises issues under Article 8, a complaint under Article 3 on the same facts should not, for that reason alone, be declared inadmissible.

person in question may be expected to be subjected in the country to which he will
be deported. According to established case law of the Commission, "the deportation
of a foreigner might, in exceptional circumstances, raise an issue under Article 3 of
the Convention where there is serious reason to believe, that the deportee would be
liable, in the country of destination, to treatment prohibited by this provision."[144]

In the *Soering* Case, that concerned extradition, the Court had to deal for the first
time with the question whether deportation would engage the responsibility of the
deporting State. The Court, confirming the Commission's jurisprudence, gave an
affirmative answer. It held as follows: "That the abhorrence of torture has such implications is recognised in Article 3 of the United Nations Convention Against Torture
and Other Cruel, Inhuman or Degrading Treatment or Punishment, which provides
that 'no State Party shall (...) extradite a person where there are substantial grounds
for believing that he would be in danger of being subjected to torture'. The fact that
a specialised treaty should spell out in detail a specific obligation attaching to the
prohibition of torture does not mean that an essentially similar obligation is not
already inherent in the general terms of Article 3 of the European Convention. It would
hardly be compatible with the underlying values of the Convention, that 'common
heritage of political traditions, ideals, freedom and the rule of law' to which the
Preamble refers, were a Contracting State knowingly to surrender a fugitive to another
State where there were substantial grounds for believing that he would be in danger
of being subjected to torture, however heinous the crime allegedly committed. Extradition in such circumstances, while not explicitly referred to in the brief and general
wording of Article 3, would plainly be contrary to the spirit and intendment of the
Article, and in the Court's view this inherent obligation not to extradite also extends
to cases in which the fugitive would be faced in the receiving State by a real risk of exposure to inhuman or degrading treatment or punishment prescribed by that
Article."[145]

In other cases the Court has applied this principle also to expulsion.[146] The reasoning behind it is based on the idea that a State is violating Article 3 if its act of extradition or expulsion constitutes a crucial link in the chain of events leading to torture
or inhuman treatment or punishment in the State to which the person is returned.
Therefore, in such a case the State expelling or extraditing him must be held indirectly
responsible for the imminent treatment in that other State, regardless of whether that
treatment is to be expected from public authorities or from non-State actors,[147] regard-

---

[144]   See, *e.g.*, Appl. 11933/86, *A. v. Switzerland*, D&R 46 (1986), p. 257 (269).
[145]   Judgment of 7 July 1989, para. 88.
[146]   See, for instance, the judgment of 15 November 1996, *Chahal*, paras. 73-74; judgment of 17 December
1996, *Ahmed*, para. 39; judgment of 2 May 1997, *D. v. the United Kingdom*, paras. 47-49; judgment
of 11 July 2000, *Jabari*, para. 38; judgment of 6 March 2001, *Hilal*, para. 59.
[147]   Judgment of 17 December 1996, *Ahmed*, para. 46; judgment of 29 April 1997, *H.L.R. v. France*,
para. 40.

less of how great the – evidently not completely successful – efforts of the government have been to prevent such treatment[148] and regardless of whether the latter State is or is not a party to the Convention.[149] In exceptional circumstances the removal of a person to a country where his situation would be inhuman because of factors that cannot be attributed to human interference in that country – for instance a lack of adequate medical facilities – may equally engage the responsibility of the removing State:[150] the existence of the obligation under Article 3 is not dependent on the source of the risk. Finally, the expulsion by State A to State B that then removes the person to State C where he might run the risk of torture or inhuman or degrading treatment or punishment, may create a responsibility for State A for that risk, even when State B is (also) a party to the Convention.[151]

7.6.2 DEATH PENALTY AND LOSS OF LIFE

In the *Kirkwood* Case and in the *Soering* Case the Commission developed the view that, since Article 2 of the Convention expressly permits the imposition of the death penalty, extradition of a person to a country where he risks the death penalty cannot, in itself, raise an issue under either Article 2 or Article 3 of the Convention, but that this does not exclude the possibility of an issue arising under Article 3 in respect of the manner and circumstances in which the death penalty is implemented. The Commission gave as an example protracted delay in carrying out the death penalty. In the *Kirkwood* Case, which concerned a possible extradition to California, the Commission indicated as factors to be considered in assessing whether such a delay during the appeal procedure (the 'death row phenomenon') amounts to inhuman treatment, the relevance of the appeal system for the protection precisely of the right to life, the delays caused by the backlog of cases before the appeal courts and the control over them, and the possibility of a commutation of sentence by the very reason of the duration of the detention on the 'death row'. The Commission reached the following conclusion: "The essential purpose of the California appeal system is to ensure protection for the right to life and to prevent arbitrariness. Although the system is subject to severe delays, these delays themselves are subject to the controlling jurisdiction of the courts. In the present case the applicant has not been tried or convicted and his risk of exposure to death row

---

[148] Judgment of 7 July 1989, *Soering*, paras 97-98.

[149] See, *e.g.*, Appl. 1802/63, *X. v. Federal Republic of Germany*, Yearbook VI (1963), p. 462 (480). In Appl. 8088/77, *X. v. the Netherlands* and Appl. 9822/82, *X. v. Spain*, not published, the Commission did, however, take into account as a positive factor that the case concerned extradition to one of the State Parties to the European Convention which had accepted the right of individual petition. Cf. Appl. 10308/83, *Altun*, D&R 36 (1984), p. 209 (233-234), in which the fact that Turkey had not recognized the right of individual petition was taken into account as a negative factor.

[150] Judgment of 2 May 1997, *D. v. the United Kingdom*, para. 49.

[151] Decision of 7 March 2000, *T.I. v. the United Kingdom*.

is uncertain. In the light of these reasons (...) the Commission finds that it has not been established that the treatment to which the applicant will be exposed, and the risk of his exposure to it, is so serious as to constitute inhuman or degrading treatment or punishment contrary to Article 3 of the Convention."[152] The element which the Commission added here to its considerations, *viz.* that the applicant has not been tried or convicted and that his conviction to the death penalty is still uncertain, is a rather strange one, since that will often be the case when the complaint concerns extradition or expulsion; what matters in those cases is that there is a real risk of the applicant being sentenced to death.

In the *Soering* Case, which concerned a possible extradition to Virginia (USA), the British Government had contended that the applicant did not in reality risk the death penalty, pointing to the assurance that had been given by the Commonwealth Attorney that the trial judge would be informed of the wish of the British Government that the death penalty should not be imposed or carried out. The Commission observed that the sentencing judge was not obliged under Virginia law to accept the representation made to him on behalf of the British Government and that it could not be assumed that he would have regard to the diplomatic considerations relating to the continuing effectiveness of the extradition relationship between the two countries. Therefore, the risk that the applicant would be sentenced to death was considered a serious one.[153] The Commission repeated the view endorsed in *Kirkwood* that extradition of a person to a country where he risks the death penalty cannot, in itself, raise an issue either under Article 2 or Article 3 of the Convention. As to the question whether an issue arose under Article 3 in respect of the manner and circumstances in which the death penalty would be implemented, the Commission reached the conclusion – be it with only six votes against five – that there was no indication that the machinery of justice to which the applicant would be subjected, was an arbitrary or unreasonable one. Therefore, the treatment was not contrary to Article 3.[154]

The Court likewise held that the Convention has to be read as a whole and that Article 3 should therefore be construed in harmony with the provisions of Article 2: "On this basis Article 3 evidently cannot have been intended by the drafters of the Convention to include a general prohibition of the death penalty since that would nullify the clear wording of Article 2, paragraph 1."[155] Furthermore, the Court emphasized that Protocol No. 6, as a subsequent written agreement, showed the intention

---

[152]   Appl. 10479/83, D&R 37 (1984), p. 158 (190).
[153]   Report of 19 January 1989, paras 114-120. In the same sense the Court in its judgment of 7 July 1989 in this case, paras 97-99. In appl. 22742/93, *Aylor-Davis*, D&R 76-B (1994), p. 164 (172), the Commission considered that there was no issue under Article 3, while the undertaking under oath of the Dallas County prosecutor that he would not call for the death penalty excluded the risk that the applicant, after France had extradited her to the United States, would be sentenced to death and would be exposed to the 'death row phenomenon'.
[154]   Report of 19 January 1989, *Soering*, paras 151-152.
[155]   Judgment of 7 July 1989, *Soering*, para. 103.

of the contracting States to adopt the normal method of amendment of the text in order to introduce a new obligation to abolish capital punishment and to do so by an optional instrument allowing each State to choose the moment when to undertake such an engagement. In these conditions Article 3 could not be interpreted as generally prohibiting the death penalty.[156]

The Court added, however, that this did not mean that the circumstances relating to a death sentence could never give rise to an issue under Article 3. Whether the treatment or punishment was to be brought under Article 3 in this case depended on the particular circumstances of the case, the length of detention prior to execution, conditions on death row and the applicant's age and mental state. The Court agreed with the Commission that the machinery of justice to which the applicant would be subject in the United States, was in itself neither arbitrary nor unreasonable, but, rather, respected the rule of law and afforded considerable procedural safeguards to the defendant in a capital trial. Nevertheless, it concluded – unlike the Commission – that in this case the decision to extradite would amount to a violation of Article 3. It held as follows: "However, in the Court's view, having regard to the very long period of time spent on death row in such extreme conditions, with the ever present and mounting anguish of awaiting execution of the death penalty, and to the personal circumstances of the applicant, especially his age and mental state at the time of the offence, the applicant's extradition to the United States would expose him to a real risk of treatment going beyond the threshold set by Article 3. A further consideration of relevance is that in the particular instance the legitimate purpose of extradition could be achieved by another means which would not involve suffering of such exceptional intensity or duration. Accordingly, the Secretary of State's decision to extradite the applicant to the United States would, if implemented, give rise to a breach of Article 3."[157]

Although the Court held in the *Soering* Case that the death penalty as such is not incompatible with Article 3, there has since been a considerable evolution. All Contracting States have signed Protocol No. 6 and almost all States have ratified it. Moreover, Protocol No. 13 provides for the abolition of the death penalty in times of war. The Court observed in the *Öçalan* Case that "it cannot now be excluded, in the light of the developments that have taken place in this area, that the States have agreed through their practice to modify the second sentence in Article 2 para. 1 in so far as it permits capital punishment in peacetime. Against this background it can also be argued that the implementation of the death penalty can be regarded as inhuman

---

[156]   *Ibidem.*
[157]   *Ibidem*, para. 111.

and degrading treatment contrary to Article 3".[158] This suggests that at the present time expulsion or extradition to a country where the person involved runs the risk of a death penalty should be regarded as a breach of Article 3. Although in the *Öcalan* Case the Court found that it was not necessary to reach any firm conclusion on this point, it is rather surprising that the Court, in its judgment in the *Chamaïev* Case, reaffirmed the earlier position it took in the *Soering* Case, that Article 3 cannot be interpreted as generally prohibiting the death penalty because that would nullify the clear wording of Article 2(1).[159]

If there is a real risk that a person after deportation will lose his life, not as a consequence of the execution of a death sentence within the meaning of Article 2(1) but otherwise, it seems that deportation will amount to a violation of Article 2 and/or Article 3. The Commission considered that in such a case a real risk of loss of life "would not as such necessarily suffice to make expulsion 'an intentional deprivation of life' prohibited by Article 2, although it would amount to inhuman treatment within the meaning of Article 3."[160] The Court, however, has not yet decided whether deportation would then amount to an infringement of Article 2, or Article 3, or both provisions.[161]

7.6.3   ASYLUM

In recent years Article 3 has become a very important factor in asylum cases, although the right to political asylum as such is not contained in either the Convention or its Protocols.[162] While it is not the task of the Court to decide whether the expulsion of an asylum seeker violates the Refugee Convention,[163] expulsion of an asylum seeker/refugee to his country of origin in violation of the prohibition of *refoulement* (Article 33(1) of the Refugee Convention) may also infringe Article 3 when he is thus exposed to a real risk of being subjected to treatment going beyond the threshold set by Article 3. As the Court held in the *Vilvarajah* Case (and many other cases), "expulsion by a Contracting State of an asylum seeker may give rise to an issue under Article 3, and hence engage the responsibility of that State under the Convention, where substantial grounds have been shown for believing that the person concerned

---

[158]   Judgment of 12 March 2003, paras 195-198; judgment of 12 May 2005 (Grand Chamber), paras 164-165.

[159]   Judgment of 12 April 2005, para. 333.

[160]   Report of 13 September 1996, *Bahaddar*, para. 78.

[161]   See the decision of 29 June 1999, *Gonzalez*.

[162]   See, for instance, the judgment of 30 October 1991, *Vilvarajah*, para. 102 and the judgment of 17 December 1996, *Ahmed*, para. 38.

[163]   Appl. 4165/69, *X. v. the Federal Republic of Germany*, Yearbook XIII (1970), p. 806 (822).

faced a real risk of being subjected to torture or to inhuman or degrading treatment or punishment in the country to which he was returned."[164]

This raises the question what the relation is between Article 3 and the Refugee Convention. It is submitted that these norms are overlapping, in that if a person – in the sense of Article 1(A) of the Refugee Convention – has a well-founded fear of being persecuted in his country of origin, his forced return to this country would violate Article 3. It has to be admitted that for a long time the Strasbourg case law strictly differentiated between these norms. The Commission has held that the question whether or not a decision to deport is "covered by the Geneva Convention of 1951 on the Status of Refugees is not at issue as such",[165] and has ruled that "the risk of political persecution, as such, cannot be equated to torture, inhuman or degrading treatment".[166] The Commission has often stressed that the right to asylum as such does not figure among the Convention rights, and that the expulsion or extradition of an individual could prove to be a breach of Article 3 only in exceptional cases or circumstances.[167] This case law implies that *refoulement* only raises an issue under Article 3 if the ensuing persecution will reach a high level of severity.[168] Consequently, *refoulement* of refugees leading to persecution that does not reach that level of severity, has been held by the Commission to be compatible with Article 3.[169]

The protection to asylum-seekers provided by Article 3 has been further limited in that the Commission and the Court have adopted a rather restrictive approach with regard to the assessment of the risk of ill-treatment. According to their case law, the decision to expel an asylum-seeker only gives rise to an issue under Article 3 "where substantial grounds have been shown for believing that the person concerned (...) faces a real risk of being subjected to torture or to inhuman or degrading treatment or

---

[164] Judgment of 30 October 1991, para. 103. Constant case law, see for instance the judgment of 15 November 1996, *Chahal*, paras 73-74, and the judgment of 17 December 1996, *Ahmed*, para. 39.

[165] Appl. 4165/69, *X. v. the Federal Republic of Germany*, Yearbook XIII (1970), p. 806 (822).

[166] Appl. 10760/84, *C. v. the Netherlands*, D&R 38 (1984), p. 224 (226).

[167] Appl. 4162/69, *X. v. Federal Republic of Germany*, Yearbook XIII (1970), p. 806 (822); Appl. 4134/69, *X. v. Federal Republic of Germany*, Yearbook XIII (1970), p. 900 (902); Appl. 6315/73, *X. v. Federal Republic of Germany*, D&R 1 (1973), p. 73 (75); Appl. 7465/76, *X. v. Denmark*, D&R 7, p. 153 (154); Appl. 11017/84, *C. v. Federal Republic of Germany*, D&R 46 (1986), p. 176 (181); Appl. 12122/86, *Lukka*, D&R 50 (1987), p. 268 (273).

[168] Appl. 10633/83, *X. v. the Netherlands* (not published): "although the risk of political persecution, as such, cannot be equated to torture, inhuman or degrading treatment, the Commission does not exclude that expulsion or 'refoulement' may, in a particular case, raise an issue under Article 3 if it brings about a prejudice for the individual concerned which reaches such level of severity as to bring it within the scope of this provision"; cf. also Appl. 10760/84, *C. v. the Netherlands*, D&R 38 (1984), p. 224 (226).

[169] Appl. 4162/69, *X. v. Federal Republic of Germany*, Yearbook XIII (1970), p. 806 (822-284); Appl. 10032/82, *X. v. Sweden*, not published.

punishment" in the country to which he is to be returned.[170] It did not come as a
surprise that in the *Cruz Varas* Case the Court found that such substantial grounds
had not been shown: the (Chilean) asylum-seeker had remained silent about his alleged
clandestine activities and torture until more than 18 months after the first interrogation by the Swedish authorities; each time he was interviewed he changed his story;
and in the meantime democratic reform was taking place in Chile which had led to
improvements in the political situation.[171] However, in the *Vilvarajah* Case concerning
the removal of five Tamil asylum-seekers to Sri Lanka, where a civil war was going
on, the 'substantial grounds' test was applied by the Court in a rather restrictive way:
"The evidence before the Court concerning the background of the applicants, as well
as the general situation, does not establish that their personal situation was any worse
than the generality of other members of the Tamil community or other young male
Tamils who were returning to their country. Since the situation was still unsettled there
existed the possibility that they might be detained and ill-treated as appears to have
occurred previously in the cases of some of the applicants (...). A mere possibility of
ill-treatment, however, in such circumstances, is not in itself sufficient to give rise to
a breach of Article 3. It is claimed that the second, third and fourth applicants were
in fact subjected to ill-treatment following their return (...) Be this as it may, however,
there existed no special distinguishing features in their cases that could or ought to
have enabled the Secretary of State to foresee that they would be treated in this way."[172]

It is respectfully submitted that this approach is open to criticism. The crux of the
Court's reasoning seems to be that, because of the absence of special distinguishing
features in their cases, there was only a general risk – "a mere possibility" – that the
asylum-seekers upon return would be treated in a manner inconsistent with Article
3. This risk, that every young male Tamil returning to his country would run, was in
itself not sufficiently high to qualify as a 'real risk' to bring their removal within the
scope of Article 3. From the facts of the case, however, it appears that there were
sufficient special distinguishing features to conclude that there was a real risk that the
asylum-seekers would be exposed to inhuman treatment. Indeed, after the applicants
had been removed to Sri Lanka in February 1988, appeals were instituted on their
behalf. In March 1989 the Adjudicator concluded that the applicants had had a well-
founded fear of persecution, and that they were entitled to political asylum and should
be returned to the United Kingdom. In fact, they were allowed to return. The
Adjudicator largely believed the accounts given by the applicants of their personal
situations.[173] The Government did not contest these findings, nor did the Court. It
is, therefore, difficult to understand why the Court held that these facts were not

---

[170]   Judgment of 20 March 1991, *Cruz Varas and Others*, paras 69-70; judgment of 30 October 1991,
Vilvarajah, para. 103.
[171]   Judgment of 20 March 1991, paras 77-82.
[172]   Judgment of 30 October 1991, *Vilvarajah*, paras 111-112.
[173]   See *ibidem*, paras 9-66.

sufficient as special distinguishing features justifying the conclusion that there was indeed a real risk of treatment contrary to Article 3 after the deportation to Sri Lanka. The Court applied a standard of assessment that was even more restrictive than the already very strict test in refugee law that the asylum-seeker has to show that he is "singled out for persecution". Such a restrictive approach would seem to be incompatible with the Court's position that its examination of a risk of ill-treatment in breach of Article 3 must be a rigorous one in view of the absolute character of this provision.[174]

It seems, however, that in more recent cases a more liberal approach has been adopted, which amounts to the assumption that returning a person to his country of origin where he has a well-founded fear of being persecuted *ipso facto* violates Article 3. The Commission had already applied concepts that were related to the refugee definition in earlier case law. For instance, in a case concerning extradition the Commission found it necessary "to determine whether in this case there would be a certain risk of prosecution for political reasons which could lead to an unjustified or disproportionate sentence being passed on the applicant and as a result inhuman treatment".[175] This criterion is often applied in refugee cases.[176] A more explicit reference to the concept of refugee can be found in the Commission's report concerning a Somalian national, *Ahmed*, whose refugee status was forfeited by the Austrian authorities on the ground that he was convicted for particularly serious crimes within the meaning of Article 33(2) of the Refugee Convention. The Commission "attached particular weight to the fact that the applicant was granted asylum in May 1992. The Austrian Ministry for the Interior (...) found that he would risk persecution in Somalia. In the asylum proceedings, the Austrian authorities had to consider basically the same elements under Austrian law as the Commission must consider under Article 3." As the situation in Somalia had not changed fundamentally since the time when the applicant was granted asylum, the Commission concluded that he still would risk persecution, if returned to Somalia, and found that substantial grounds had been shown for believing that the applicant would then face a real risk of being subjected to treatment in breach of Article 3.[177] The Court followed the same reasoning, and reached a similar conclusion.[178] In the same way in the *Jabari* Case the Court, in concluding that expulsion would give rise to a violation of Article 3, attached great weight to the findings of UNHCR that the applicant qualified as a refugee.[179]

---

[174] *Ibidem*, para. 108.
[175] Appl. 10308/83, *Altun*, D&R 36 (1984), p. 209 (233); cf. also Appl. 11933/86, *A. v. Switzerland*, D&R 46 (1986), p. 257 (271).
[176] See UNHCR, *Handbook on Procedures and Criteria for Determining Refugee Status*, Geneva 1988, paras 57, 85 and 169.
[177] Report of 5 July 1995, paras 65, 66 and 70.
[178] Judgment of 17 December 1996, paras 42–47.
[179] Judgment of 11 July 2000, *Jabari*, paras 18 and 41–42.

Moreover, there seems to be a tendency in the Strasbourg case law to adopt a less strict 'real risk' criterion, which is not fundamentally different from a liberal "singling out" test. That the Commission adopted a less stringent standard of proof is evident from the *Bahaddar* Case, in which it concluded that expulsion of the applicant to Bangladesh would be in violation of Article 3, although he had not supplied much direct evidence: the Commission gave him the benefit of the doubt while it considered his account to be credible and on the whole consistent.[180]

Whether the Court also applies a more liberal criterion is less clear. The fact is that the Court has not expressly repeated that there should be 'special distinguishing features', in order to assume that there is a real risk. In several post-*Vilvarajah* judgments the Court has reached the conclusion that there was a violation of Article 3. In the *Chahal* Case the deportation to India of an alleged Sikh terrorist was regarded as infringing Article 3; particular weight was accorded to the general situation, especially the (non-)observance of human rights.[181] In the *Ahmed* Case the Court found that Article 3 would be violated by the deportation because the asylum-seeker earlier was recognized by the State as a refugee and the situation in his country of origin had not changed.[182] In the *Jabari* Case the Court concluded that no substantive examination had taken place, and regarded as a relevant factor that UNHCR had recognized the applicant as a refugee.[183] In the *Hilal* Case it was found that the 'internal flight option' on which the British Government had relied, was not really secure.[184] Finally, in the *Said* Case the Court held that in the light of credible statements of the asylum seeker in the context of general information concerning the situation in Eritrea, expulsion of the asylum seeker would amount to a violation of Article 3.[185]

Another indication of a more liberal approach is provided by the decision in the *T.I. v. the United Kingdom* Case. This case was about the removal of the applicant by the United Kingdom to Germany and the risk that Germany would subsequently deport the asylum seeker to his home country, Sri Lanka. The Court found it sufficient to observe that the facts gave "rise to concerns as to the risks faced by the applicant should he be returned to Sri Lanka", and only after a thorough investigation of the German asylum system did the Court come to the conclusion that removal to Germany would not create a risk of a violation of Article 3.[186]

Nevertheless, it is not clear whether and to what extent the Court has departed from the individualizing *Vilvarajah*-test. Chahal had a high profile as a leading figure

---

[180]   Report of 13 September 1996, paras 83-102. The Court did not decide on the merits of this case, because it found that the local remedies had not been exhausted: judgment of 19 February 1988, para. 49.
[181]   Judgment of 15 November 1996, paras 98-107.
[182]   Judgment of 17 December 1996, paras 42-47.
[183]   Judgment of 11 July 2000, paras 18 and 41-42.
[184]   Judgment of 6 March 2001, para. 67.
[185]   Judgment of 5 July 2005, paras 50-52.
[186]   Decision of 7 March 2000.

supporting the cause of Sikh separatism which in itself set him apart from Sikhs in general, and thus made it plausible that he was "singled out".[187] And Ahmed and Jabari were recognized as refugees by the Government and by UNHCR, respectively, which also implied that to a certain extent they were 'targeted'.

It is, therefore, plausible to assume that the Court still requires that the applicant's personal situation gives substantial grounds for believing that he would face a real risk of being subjected to treatment contrary to Article 3.[188] However, what level of individualization and what standard of proof is applied is yet uncertain. It would seem that the Court does not demand that there be 'special distinguishing features' any more. In the *Said* Case, a combination of consistent, more or less credible statements and information of a general nature supporting these statements were held to be sufficient to conclude that deportation to his home country would expose him to a real risk of being treated contrary to Article 3.[189] Furthermore, from the *Said* Case it may be concluded that the standard of proof that the Court has recently applied to extraditions – the criterion of a proof 'beyond reasaonable doubt'[190] – is not applicable in asylum cases.

A conceptual argument against the thesis that the deportation of an individual to a country where he has a well-founded fear of being persecuted in principle always amounts to a violation of Article 3 might be, that persecution in the sense of Article 1(A) of the Refugee Convention does not always attain the minimum level of severity required to fall within the scope of Article 3. Such a counter-argument misunderstands the said thesis, which does not equate "persecution" with "treatment prohibited by Article 3", but posits that the deportation of a person to a country where he has *a well-founded fear* of being persecuted will in general amount to *a real risk* of being exposed to ill-treatment in the sense of Article 3. It may be true that not every act of persecution can be qualified as torture or inhuman or degrading treatment or punishment, but it is plausible to assume that when a well-founded fear has been established that a person, if returned to his country, will suffer from such an act of persecution, there is a real risk that he will also be subjected to (additional) harsh treatment that falls within the scope of Article 3.

It, therefore, may be concluded that a person who has a well-founded fear of persecution within the meaning of Article 1(A) of the Refugee Convention and is

---

[187] Judgment of 15 November 1996, *Chahal*, para. 106.
[188] Decision of 22 October 2002, *Ammari*; judgment of 17 February 2004, *Venkadajalasarma*, paras 65-68; judgment of 17 February 2004, *Thampibillai*, paras 62-66; judgment of 26 July 2005, *N. v. Finland*, paras 162-165.
[189] Judgment of 5 July 2005, paras 50-56.
[190] Judgment of 12 April 2005, *Chamaïev*, para. 338. It is respectfully submitted that the application of such a strict standard in extradition cases is difficult to be reconciled with the *Soering* judgment of 7 July 1989.

protected by the prohibition of *refoulement* in Article 33(1) of the same Convention, can also claim that he may not be returned to his country of origin because that would expose him to a real risk of being subjected to treatment prohibited by Article 3. The reverse does not hold; Article 3 has a wider scope than Article 33(1) of the Refugee Convention. A person who fulfils the criteria of Article 1(A) of the Refugee Convention can be denied the protection of Article 33(1) when there are serious reasons for considering that he has committed crimes as mentioned in Article 1(F), as well as when he may reasonably be regarded as a danger to the security of the country of reception or if he, having been convicted of a particularly serious crime, constitutes a danger to the community of that country (Article 33(2) of the Refugee Convention). In all these cases he is still protected by Article 3. As the Court observed, "the activities of the individual in question, however undesirable or dangerous, cannot be a material consideration. The protection afforded by Article 3 is thus wider than that provided by Article 32 and 33 of the United Nations 1951 Convention on the Status of Refugees."[191]

The protection afforded by Article 3 is also wider than the prohibition of *refoulement* in that the concept of persecution in Article 1(A) of the Refugee Convention and thus the protection against *refoulement* (Article 33(1)) is often believed to presuppose the existence of State authority, and is linked to a limited number of grounds of persecution (race, religion, nationality, membership of a particular social group or political opinion), whereas the applicability of Article 3 solely depends on the character of the treatment, not on the source or the grounds of this treatment. Thus the Commission held that the "position of the Austrian authorities that there is no substantial risk for the applicant since the State authority had ceased to exist in Somalia cannot be accepted. It is sufficient that those who hold substantial power within the State, even though they are not the Government, threaten the life and security of the applicant."[192] And Soering was protected by Article 3 although the inhuman treatment that he feared was not related to one of the persecution grounds mentioned in the Refugee Convention.[193]

---

[191]   Judgment of 15 November 1996, *Chahal*, para. 80; judgment of 17 December 1996, *Ahmed*, para. 41. Cf. also the judgment of 7 July 1989, *Soering*, para. 88: "it would hardly be compatible with the underlying values of the Convention (...) were a Contracting State knowingly to surrender a fugitive to another State where there are substantial grounds for believing that he would be in danger of being subjected to torture, however heinous the crime allegedly committed."

[192]   Report of 5 July 1995, *Ahmed*, para. 68. Cf. also the judgment of 17 December 1996, *Ahmed*, para. 46: the conclusion the applicant's deportation to Somalia would amount to a violation of Article 3 is not invalidated by "the current lack of State authority in Somalia".

[193]   Judgment of 7 July 1989.

7.6.4 MEDICAL CASES

In exceptional circumstances the removal of a person to a country where his situation would be inhuman because of factors that cannot be attributed to human interference in that country, may engage the responsibility of the removing State: the existence of the obligation under Article 3 is not dependent on the source of the risk. Complaints mostly concern the lack of adequate medical facilities in the country where one is deported to. In *D. v. the United Kingdom* the Court concluded that the removal of a terminally ill person (in the final stage of AIDS) to a country where there was no adequate medical care, would expose him to a real risk of dying under most distressing circumstances and would thus amount to inhuman treatment.[194] However, as the Court stressed in this judgment, aliens cannot in principle claim any entitlement to remain on the territory of a State in order to benefit from medical, social or other forms of assistance.[195] The mere fact that the circumstances elsewhere would be less favourable than those in the country where one is currently staying, is not decisive from the point of view of Article 3.[196] And indeed, that *D. v. the United Kingdom* was an exceptional case becomes clear in the *Bensaid* Case concerning a schizophrenic patient. The Court did not deny the seriousness of the applicant's condition, nor that there would be difficulties in obtaining medication in the country where he would be deported to, nor that the suffering associated with a relapse could fall within the scope of Article 3. Nevertheless, it found that the risk that the applicant would suffer a deterioration in his condition if returned and that, if he did, he would not receive adequate support or care, was to a large extent speculative. The Court concluded that his removal would not violate Article 3.[197]

Recent decisions also arrive at the conclusion that although adequate medical and social care will be scarce, removal will not violate Article 3. As in the *Bensaid* Case the main factors are that it does not appear that the applicant's illness has attained an advanced or final stage, nor that he has no prospect of medical care or family support in his country of origin.[198]

7.7 DEROGATION

Article 3, which "enshrines one of the fundamental values of the democratic societies making up the Council of Europe",[199] is included in the list of rights which are declared

---

[194]   Judgment of 2 May 1997, para. 53.

[195]   *Ibidem*, para. 54.

[196]   Judgment of 6 February 2001, *Bensaid*, para. 38.

[197]   *Ibidem*, paras 36-41.

[198]   Decision of 23 June 2003, *Henao*; decision of 20 January 2004, *Meho*; decision of 22 June 2004, *Ndangoya*; decision of 29 June 2004, *Salkic*.

[199]   Judgment of 7 July 1989, *Soering*, para. 88.

non-derogable in Article 15(2). It guarantees an absolute right, not only in the sense
that the provision itself leaves no scope for limitations by law, as a number of other
provisions do, but also in the sense that no derogation is permitted, not even in the
event of a public emergency threatening the life of the nation.[200] The Commission
accordingly set forth in its report in *Ireland v. the United Kingdom*: "It follows that the
prohibition under Article 3 of the Convention is an absolute one and that there can
never be under the Convention, or under international law, a justification for acts in
breach of that provision."[201] This implies, for instance, that "it is never permissible
to have recourse to punishments which are contrary to Article 3, whatever their
deterrent effect may be."[202] Likewise, the requirements of the investigation of, and the
difficulties inherent in the fight against crime, cannot result in limits being placed on
the protection afforded by this provision.[203] "Even in the most difficult circumstances,
like the fight against terrorism and organised crime, the Convention prohibits in
absolute terms torture and inhuman or degrading treatment or punishment."[204]

The prohibition provided by Article 3 against ill-treatment is equally absolute in
expulsion and extradition cases. The States, even when protecting their communities
from terrorist violence, cannot invoke national interests to override the interests of
the individual where substantial grounds have been shown for believing that he would
be subjected to ill-treatment when expelled.[205] Nor can they invoke the interest of the
international community that suspected offenders who flee abroad should be brought
to justice. That the State might be allowed to do so was suggested by the Court in the
Soering judgment, where it remarked that the risk of undermining the foundations
of extradition was included among the factors to be taken into account in the
interpretation and application of Article 3.[206] However, in the *Chahal* Case the Court
made it clear that from these remarks it should *not* be inferred "that there is any room
for balancing the risk of ill-treatment against the reasons for expulsion in determining
whether a State's responsibility under Article 3 is engaged."[207]

---

[200]   Judgment of 18 January 1978, *Ireland v. the United Kingdom*, para. 163; judgment of 15 November
1996, *Chahal*, para. 79; judgment of 17 December 1996, *Ahmed*, para. 40.
[201]   Report of 25 January 1976, B.23-I (1976-1978), p. 390.
[202]   Judgment of 25 April 1978, *Tyrer*, para. 31.
[203]   Judgment of 27 August 1992, *Tomasi*, para. 115.
[204]   Judgment of 28 July 1999, *Selmouni*, para. 95; judgment of 6 April 2000, *Labita*, para. 119.
[205]   Judgment of 15 November 1996, *Chahal*, paras 78-80; cf. also the judgment of 17 December 1996,
Ahmed, paras 40-41.
[206]   Judgment of 7 July 1989, para. 89.
[207]   Judgment of 15 November 1996, para. 81.

CHAPTER 8
FREEDOM FROM SLAVERY, SERVITUDE AND FORCED OR COMPULSORY LABOUR (Article 4)

REVISED BY LEO ZWAAK

CONTENTS

8.1 TEXT OF ARTICLE 4

1. *No one shall be held in slavery or servitude.*
2. *No one shall be required to perform forced or compulsory labour.*
3. *For the purpose of this Article the term 'forced or compulsory labour' shall not include:*

    a) *any work required to be done in the ordinary course of detention imposed according to the provisions of Article 5 of this Convention or during conditional release from such detention;*
    b) *any service of a military character or, in case of conscientious objectors in countries where they are recognised, service exacted instead of compulsory military service;*
    c) *any service exacted in case of an emergency or calamity threatening the life or well-being of the community;*
    d) *any work or service which forms part of normal civic obligations.*

8.2   INTRODUCTION

In Article 4 slavery and servitude are dealt with separately from forced and compulsory labour. The first two terms refer to the entire status or situation of the person concerned. Slavery indicates that the person is wholly in the legal ownership of another person, while servitude concerns less far-reaching forms of restraint and refers, for instance, to the total of the labour conditions and/or of the obligations to work or to render services from which the person in question cannot escape and which he cannot change.[1] Forced labour and compulsory labour, on the other hand, do not refer to the entire situation of the person concerned, but exclusively to the involuntary character of the work and services to be performed by him, which may, and usually will, also have a temporary or incidental character.

Since the entry into force of Protocol No. 11, the Court has very rarely dealt with complaints concerning Article 4. For this reasons, the present analysis is based, primarily, on the decisions and reports of the former Commission.

8.3   SLAVERY AND SERVITUDE

The first paragraph of Article 4 has been invoked mainly in connection with complaints of detainees against the obligation to perform work in prison. In those cases the Commission took the position that the terms 'slavery' and 'servitude' are not applicable to such a situation, while from the third paragraph under (a) of Article 4 it is evident that the drafters of the Convention did not wish to prohibit the imposition of such an obligation.[2]

In the *Van Droogenbroeck* Case the applicant submitted that the fact that he had been placed at the disposal of the Government as a recidivist, had reduced him to a condition of servitude, since in fact he was subject to arbitrary supervision by the administrative authorities. The Commission took the view that there was no question of servitude, because the measure was one of limited duration only, was subject to judicial review and did not affect the legal status of the person in question.[3]

The first paragraph was also invoked before the Commission by four young men who, at the age of 15 and 16, had joined the Navy for a period of nine years and after some time had applied for discharge. In their complaint against the refusal of the authorities to discharge them they claimed, *inter alia*, that in view of their age their

---

[1]   See the report of 9 July 1980, *Van Droogenbroeck*, B.44 (1985), p. 30: "in addition to the obligation to provide another with certain services, the concept of servitude includes the obligation on the part of the 'serf' to live on another's property and the impossibility of changing his condition."

[2]   Appls 3134/67, 3172/67 and 3188-3206/67, *Twenty-one detainees v. Federal Republic of Germany*, Yearbook XI (1968), p. 528 (552). See also Appl. 7549/76, *X v. Ireland* (not published).

[3]   Report of 9 July 1980, B.44 (1985), p. 30.

service constituted a form of servitude in the sense of Article 4(1). After first having stated that military service did form an exception to the second, but not necessarily to the first paragraph, the Commission rejected the complaint as being manifestly ill-founded. This finding was based in particular on the circumstance that the relevant law prescribed for minors the consent of the parents and that in this case such consent had indeed been given.[4]

8.4   FORCED OR COMPULSORY LABOUR

The second paragraph of Article 4 has played a greater part in the case law. Hitherto the Commission and the Court have refrained from giving a definition of the term 'forced or compulsory labour'. However, in the *Schmidt* Case the Court reiterated that "paragraph 3 of Article 4 is not intended to 'limit' the exercise of the right guaranteed by paragraph 2, but to 'delimit' the very content of that right, for it forms a whole with paragraph 2 and indicates what the term 'forced or compulsory labour' shall not include (ce qui n'est pas considéré comme 'travail forcé ou obligatoire'). This being so, paragraph 3 serves as an aid to the interpretation of paragraph 2. The four subparagraphs of paragraph 3, notwithstanding their diversity, are grounded on the governing ideas of the general interest, social solidarity and what is normal in the ordinary course of affairs."[5]

Both the Commission and the Court have made reference to conventions of the International Labour Organisation, which contain far more detailed norms in this respect.[6] For the meaning of the term 'forced or compulsory labour', the Commission referred to the five categories enumerated in Convention No. 105 of the International Labour Organisation: "political coercion or education or as a punishment for holding or expressing political views or views ideologically opposed to the established political, social, or economic system; mobilising and using labour for purposes of economic development; labour discipline; punishment for having participated in strikes; and racial, social or religious discrimination."[7]

Elements of the concept 'forced or compulsory labour' mentioned by the Commission are "first, that the work or service is performed by the worker against his will

---

[4]   Appls 3435-3438/67, *W, X, Y and Z v. the United Kingdom*, Yearbook XI (1968), p. 562 (596-598).
[5]   Judgment of 18 July 1994, para. 22.
[6]   See, *e.g.*, the references to ILO Convention No. 29 by the Court in its judgment of 23 November 1983, *Van der Mussele*, para. 32.
[7]   Appl. 7641/76, *X and Y v. Federal Republic of Germany*, D&R 10 (1978), p. 224 (230).

and, secondly, that the requirement that the work or service be performed is unjust or oppressive or the work or service itself involves avoidable hardship."[8]

With respect to the first element – its involuntary nature – the Commission has adopted the view that consent, once given, deprives the work or service of its compulsory character. If the decision mentioned above concerning the boys who had joined the Navy, which related to the first paragraph, were followed analogously in connection with the second paragraph, the consent of the parents could presumably take the place of that of their children under age.

Such an interpretation of 'forced' and 'compulsory' would appear to be too restrictive. Even if a person has voluntarily entered into a labour contract or has agreed to perform certain services, the circumstances may change in such a way or the objections to the work in question, especially in engagements of long duration, may become so far-reaching that holding the person unqualifiedly to his consent may indeed bring in issue Article 4(2). It is submitted that this provision implies in such a case that alternative possibilities should be offered to the person in question, for instance different work if the objections are directed against the nature of the work, or termination of the contract coupled with the obligation to pay a reasonable compensation. And, indeed, in the *Van der Mussele* Case the Court did not hold the issue of consent to be decisive.[9]

Within the framework of the second criterion, *viz.* that the obligation to perform the work must have an unjustifiable or oppressive character, or that the work itself involves avoidable hardship for the person concerned, the Commission has introduced a number of elements which allow a considerable margin of discretion to the national authorities. If this second criterion were to be applied cumulatively to the first one, in fact a general ground of justification would be added to the specific grounds of the third paragraph to be discussed hereafter. Even work or a service which a person has to perform against his will and which is felt by him to be oppressive would not, in that view, constitute a violation of Article 4(2), provided that the national authorities can submit *prima facie* evidence that this oppressive character is not as bad as is alleged, or that the hardship was unavoidable. The text of Article 4 would thus be strained and, therefore, the second criterion should rather be handled *alternatively* in the sense suggested above, *viz.* that even work or a service to which the person concerned has previously consented may assume a compulsory character for him if the obligations resulting therefrom involve such unjustified or avoidable hardship that they can no longer be deemed to be covered by his consent. In its report in the *Van der Mussele*

---

[8]   Appl. 4653/70, *X v. Federal Republic of Germany*, Yearbook XVII (1974), p. 148 (172). Likewise Appl. 8410/78, *X v. Federal Republic of Germany*, D&R 18 (1980), p. 216 (219) and Appl. 9322/81, *X v. the Netherlands*, D&R 32 (1983), p. 180 (182-183); Appl. 27633/95, *Stadler v. Austria* (not published).

[9]   Judgment of 23 November 1983, para. 36.

Case the Commission indeed speaks of 'a subsidiary argument' in connection with the second criterion.[10]

There has been considerable dissension within the Commission about the elements of the concept of 'forced' labour. This is evident from the *Iversen* Case. In that case a piece of Norwegian legislation was brought into issue concerning the basis on which a dentist might be required to fill a vacancy for some time that had failed to be filled after having been duly advertised. The complaint was declared by the Commission to be manifestly ill-founded. Two of the members of the Commission belonging to the majority considered the Norwegian measure justified on the basis of the ground mentioned in the third paragraph under (c), *viz.* 'emergency or calamity threatening the life or well-being of the community'.[11] Four members of the majority of six, however, held that there was no question of forced or compulsory labour, because the service to be rendered was exacted for a limited time, was properly remunerated and was in keeping with the profession chosen by Iversen, while the law in question had not been applied against him in an arbitrary or discriminatory manner.[12] A minority of four members of the Commission, finally, were of the opinion that the above-mentioned circumstances did not exclude the applicability of the second paragraph, and that the possible application of the third paragraph called for a further examination.[13] In the light of this diversity of views within the Commission it is very curious indeed that the complaint was rejected as being manifestly ill-founded, which barred a thorough examination of the facts and a decision of the Court on this evidently controversial interpretation of the second paragraph.

In the case of a German lawyer who complained about having to act as unpaid or insufficiently paid defence counsel the Commission decided that the imposed obligation was not unreasonable and did not, therefore, fall under the prohibition of Article 4(2). The Commission did not review this form of compulsory service for its conformity with the third paragraph. In fact, the Commission based its decision partly on the consideration that anyone who voluntarily chooses the profession of a lawyer knows that under German law lawyers are obliged to defend clients who lack the means to pay counsel's fees, in those cases where they have been nominated to do so by a judicial body. In those circumstances it could not be said that such a service had to be rendered against the will of the person in question.[14] Here the Commission seems

---

[10]   Report of 3 March 1982, B.55 (1987), p. 33.
[11]   Appl. 1468/62, Yearbook VI (1963), p. 278 (328-330).
[12]   *Ibidem*, pp. 326-328.
[13]   *Ibidem*, pp. 330-332.
[14]   Appl. 4653/70, *X v. Federal Republic of Germany*, Yearbook XVII (1974), p. 148 (172). Previously, two complaints of an Austrian lawyer about free legal aid had been declared admissible by the Commission, on the ground that "these complaints raise issues of a complex nature" and could not therefore be declared manifestly ill-founded: Appls 4897/71 and 5219/71, *Gussenbauer v. Austria*, Coll. 42 (1973), p. 41 (48) and Yearbook XV (1972), p. 558 (562) respectively. These cases led to a

to follow the reasoning which already was hinted at by four of its members in the *Iversen* Case, *viz.* that when certain obligations are attached to a profession, the person choosing that profession accepts those obligations implicitly.

A similar decision was taken in the case of a notary public who complained about the system according to which in specific cases he was only allowed to charge reduced fees for his services. The Commission observed first of all that the applicant had not advanced that he had been forced in one way or another to give his services in specific cases, so that the question might be asked whether the first element had been satisfied. With respect to the second element the Commission found that the impugned system could not be qualified as 'unjust or oppressive', since it related to a normal part of the tasks of a notary public and ensued from his almost exclusive competence as regards the services concerned.[15] And also in the case of a Dutch football player who complained that he was, after renouncing the contract with his former football club, prevented from joining another football club in view of the prohibitive transfer sum requested by the former, the Commission took the view that the applicant freely chose to become a professional football player, knowing that by doing so he would be affected by the rules governing the relationships between his future employers. Moreover, the Commission was of the opinion that the system complained of, even if it could produce certain inconveniences for the applicant, could not be considered as being oppressive or constituting avoidable hardship, especially since it did not directly affect his contractual freedom.[16]

The above-mentioned argument applies only if the obligations form part of the normal exercise of a profession. The Commission, therefore, speaks of 'normal professional work'.[17] The obligation to lend free legal aid formed part of the normal obligations of a lawyer in the Federal Republic of Germany, as it does in most other member States of the Council of Europe, and the obligation to take for some time, if necessary, a position in the public dental service in the northern part of the country formed part of the normal obligations of a dentist in Norway after he has completed his studies.[18] This does not, however, alter the fact that it must still be ascertained for each individual case whether the concrete content of the obligation in question is not so oppressive for the person concerned that he can no longer be assumed to have consented to it by choosing his profession.

---

friendly settlement, so that the merits have not been dealt with; report of 8 October 1974, *Stock-Taking on the European Convention on Human Rights. A periodic Note on the Concrete Results Achieved Under the Convention. The First Thirty Years: 1954 Until 1984*, Strasbourg 1984, p. 123.

[15]   Appl. 8410/78, *X v. Federal Republic of Germany*, D&R 18 (1980), p. 216 (219).

[16]   Appl. 9322/81, *X v. the Netherlands*, D&R 32 (1983), p. 180 (182-183).

[17]   Appl. 4653/70, *X v. Federal Republic of Germany*, Yearbook XVII (1974), p. 148 (172).

[18]   See, however, the report of 3 March 1982, *Van der Mussele*, B.55 (1987), p. 34, where the Commission distinguishes the situation from that of the *Iversen* Case.

In another case where a lawyer invoked Article 4(2) on account of his obligation to act as a free legal aid counsel, the Commission followed a somewhat different line of reasoning. It referred to Article 6(3)(c) and submitted that, since in the Convention the right to free legal aid has been recognised, the obligation for a lawyer to give legal aid in a concrete case cannot constitute forced or compulsory labour in the sense of Article 4(2).[19] The connection established here by the Commission between the two provisions does not seem to be a very logical one. Indeed, the right to legal aid *per se* does not say anything about the way in which the authorities must effectuate this right and does not necessarily imply that this should be done via an obligation for lawyers to give such legal aid under conditions to be laid down by the authorities. In its report in the *Van der Mussele* Case the Commission impliedly indicated that this line of reasoning is rather unsatisfactory, by holding that the obligation of the State to provide free legal aid was not decisive in that case because legal aid was organised by the Bar Association. It, therefore, again emphasised that the obligation imposed on the applicant formed part of his normal professional work and left him so much freedom that one could not speak of forced or compulsory labour, though the Commission considered it unfortunate that pupil barristers such as the applicant were not paid at all when appointed to defend indigent persons.[20]

In the same *Van der Mussele* Case the Court took a somewhat different approach. It used as a starting point for the interpretation of 'compulsory labour' the definition given in Article 2 of ILO Convention No. 29:[21] "all work or service which is exacted from any person under the menace of any penalty and for which the said person has not offered himself voluntarily."[22] Although a refusal to act as a free legal aid counsel was not punishable by any sanction of a criminal law character, the Court concluded that there was a 'menace of any penalty', since with such a refusal the applicant would run the risk of his name being struck off the roll of pupils or of a rejection of his application for entry in the register of advocates.[23] As regards the voluntary character of the service exacted, the Court held that the argument used by the Commission that the applicant consented in advance "correctly reflects one aspect of the situation; nevertheless, the Court cannot attach decisive weight thereto".[24] The Court subsequently observed that the applicant had to accept the requirement concerned, whether he wanted to or not, in order to become an *avocat* and that his consent was determined by the normal conditions of exercise of the profession at the relevant time. Moreover, according to the Court, it should not be overlooked that the acceptance by the

---

[19]   Appl. 7641/76, *X and Y v. Federal Republic of Germany*, D&R 10 (1978), p. 224 (230).
[20]   Report of 3 March 1982, B.55 (1987), p. 34.
[21]   International Labour Office, *Conventions and Recommendations 1919-1966* (1966), p. 155.
[22]   Judgment of 23 November 1983, *Van der Mussele*, paras 32-33.
[23]   *Ibidem*, para. 35.
[24]   *Ibidem*, para. 36.

applicant was the acceptance of a legal regime of a general character.[25] In order to decide whether the service required fell within the prohibition of compulsory labour, the Court held that it should have regard to all the circumstances of the case in the light of the underlying objectives of Article 4.[26]

At first sight the approach of the Court seems different from that of the Commission, especially since the Court distances itself from the second criterion developed by the Commission, *viz.* that of the 'unjust' or 'oppressive' character of the service to be performed.[27] It is, however, striking to see that most of the circumstances of the case taken into consideration by the Court have also been dealt with by the Commission in its report. In fact, the main difference lies in the weight attached to the element of 'consent in advance'. Indeed, the view expressed by the Commission in this respect was too restrictive. The approach of the Court, therefore, is to be welcomed. However, the Court also fails to give clear guidelines with respect to the interpretation of 'forced or compulsory labour'. It restricts itself to an investigation of all the circumstances of the case, each of which, according to the Court, "provides a standard of evaluation".[28] These standards were in this case the following: the services did not fall outside the ambit of the normal activities of an *avocat*; a compensatory factor was to be found in the advantages attaching to the profession; the services contributed to the professional training of the applicant; the service is a means of securing the benefit, laid down in Article 6(3)(c), and can be seen as a 'normal civic obligation' as referred to in Article 4(3)(d); and, lastly, the burden imposed was not disproportionate, since it only took up about 18 hours of working time.[29]

Both the Commission and the Court concluded that, although the situation could be characterised as unsatisfactory because of the absence of any fee and the non-reimbursement of incurred expenditure, it did not constitute a violation of Article 4 of the Convention.[30]

8.5 EXCEPTIONS

With respect to the exceptions mentioned in the third paragraph the following observations may be made. The exception formulated under (a) for the work of detainees and conditionally released persons is put in quite general terms and – unlike Article 2(2)(c) of ILO Convention No. 29 – does not exclude work on behalf of private

---

[25] *Ibidem.*
[26] *Ibidem.*
[27] *Ibidem*, para. 37.
[28] *Ibidem*, para. 39.
[29] *Ibidem*, para. 39. Cf. the report of 3 March 1982, *Van der Mussele*, B.55 (1987), p. 34.
[30] *Ibidem*, para. 40. See also Appl. 20781/92, *Ackerl, Grötzback, Glawischnig, Schwalm, Klein, Sladeck and Limberger v. Austria*, D&R 78-A (1994), p. 116 (118).

enterprises and foundations. Complaints with respect to work of such a character have, therefore, been declared inadmissible by the Commission.[31]

The exception under (a) applies only to work 'in the ordinary course of detention'. In the '*Vagrancy*' Cases these words were interpreted by the Court to mean that it must be work directed at the rehabilitation of the prisoner.[32] Moreover, the Court's judgment would seem to imply that Article 4 is violated if the detention itself, in the course of which the work must be performed, conflicts with the first paragraph of Article 5.[33] However, the view of the Commission that also in case of a conflict with the fourth paragraph of Article 5 reliance on Article 4(3)(a) by the authorities is excluded,[34] was not adopted by the Court. This is curious, since the authorities may thus refer to a detention which is found to be in conformity with Article 5(1), but whose lawfulness – contrary to Article 5(4) – the applicant has not been able to have reviewed by the domestic court. Such a review could precisely result in the domestic court ordering his release, as a consequence of which the ground for the obligation to work would have ceased to exist.[35] It should finally be pointed out with respect to the exception under (a) that this exception does not relate exclusively to convicts – such as is the case in ILO Convention No. 29 – nor exclusively to persons whose detention is based on a judicial order – as Article 8 of the UN Covenant on Civil and Political Rights provides – but to all the situations of lawful deprivation of liberty mentioned in the first paragraph of Article 5.[36]

The formulation of the exception under (b) departs from that of Convention No. 29, where Article 2(2)(a) speaks of 'any work or service exacted in virtue of compulsory military service laws for work of a purely military character'. Due to the fact that in Article 4(3)(b) the confinement to 'compulsory military service' has not been adopted, the Commission concluded that "it was intended to cover also the obligation to continue a service entered into on a voluntary basis".[37] However, in view of the rationale of this exception, as it appears in particular from the reference to the service

---

[31]   Appls 3134/67, 3172/67 and 3188-3206/67, *Twenty-one detainees v. Federal Republic of Germany*, Yearbook XI (1968), p. 528 (552-558) and Appl. 9449/81, *X v. Austria* (not published). In some of the Contracting States, however, the courts will have to apply that restriction on the ground of the direct applicability of ILO Convention No. 29, ratified by those States.

[32]   Judgment of 18 June 1971, para. 90. See also Appl. 8500/79, *X v. Switzerland*, D&R 18 (1980), p. 238 (248-249), where in the case of the detention of a minor the Commission examined under Article 5(1)(d) whether the required work "was abnormally long or arduous in view of the applicant's age or was of no educational value".

[33]   Judgment of 18 June 1971, para. 89.

[34]   Report of 19 July 1969, *De Wilde, Ooms and Versyp* ('*Vagrancy*' Cases), B.10 (1971), pp. 96-97.

[35]   One could argue that the respondent State should be confronted here with the adage *nemo suam turpitudinem allegans audiendum est*. However, the Commission followed the Court in its report of 9 July 1980, *Van Droogenbroeck*, B.44 (1985), p. 31.

[36]   Appl. 8500/79, *X v. Switzerland*, D&R 18 (1980), p. 238 (248), which was a case under Article 5(1)(d).

[37]   Appls 3435-3438/67, *W, X, Y and Z v. the United Kingdom*, Yearbook XI (1968), p. 562 (594).

exacted instead of compulsory military service, such an application is justified only for those cases where this voluntary military service takes the place of compulsory military service. In fact, in other cases it is not self-evident that military service should be entitled to a special position as compared with other public services in the national interest, such as, for instance, service in public medical institutions or for utility companies.

The fact that Article 4(3)(b) also mentions (civil) service exacted instead of compulsory military service in case of conscientious objectors does not in itself mean that the Convention contains a right to such alternative service for conscientious objectors; the provision contains the limitation 'in countries where they are recognised'. If such a right for conscientious objectors is not recognised in a given country, this situation might have to be reviewed for its conformity with Article 9.[38]

The exception mentioned under (c) is self explanatory. Here the central issue is in what situation an 'emergency or calamity threatening the life or well-being of the community' is involved. As has been pointed out above, in the opinion of some members of the Commission even a shortage of dentists could constitute such a situation.[39] It would, however, appear to be more in keeping with the terminology used not to think here of structural inconveniences like those concerned in that case, but of an acute emergency with a temporary character. Thus, one should think of services such as aid in extinguishing a fire, urgent repairs of transport systems and dams, supply of water and food in case of a sudden shortage, transport of wounded persons or the evacuation of persons threatened by some danger, and similar incidental services which can be required of everyone in the public interest depending on everybody's capabilities and possibilities.

The exception mentioned under (d), on the contrary, refers to 'normal' civic obligations, which means that no urgent and unforeseen calamity is required. It is still restricted, however, to work and services in the general interest. The difference with the provision under (c) is mainly one of degree: the circumstances do not have to be as serious and urgent, but on the other hand the duties which are imposed may not be as burdensome for the person involved.[40] The formulation of the provision does not exclude special duties for particular professions in the public interest. In fact, the word 'normal' does not necessarily refer to what may be required equally of everyone,

---

[38]   Appl. 10640/83, *A v. Switzerland*, D&R 38 (1984), p. 219 (222-223).
[39]   See *supra* 8.4.
[40]   In the Strasbourg case law a clear distinction has not yet been made, as appears from the decision on Appl. 9686/82, *S v. Federal Republic of Germany*, D&R 39 (1985), p. 90 (91), where the obligation of a person enjoying shooting rights in a hunting district (*Jagdpächter*) to participate in the gassing of fox holes was considered to be justified either under (c) or under (d) in view of the public interest to control epidemics.

but may also relate to what in the given circumstances may be required of the person in question according to general usage.[41] The rationale of the provision implies that it does not refer to the normal obligations resulting from a profession, such as free legal aid given by lawyers, normal night duties for nurses and the like, since no compulsion in the real sense is involved, as the person concerned may resign from the job. The Commission would seem to have stretched the concept of 'normal civic obligations' beyond any specification in a decision in which it declared this term to be applicable to the obligation of the lessor to keep the rented premises in good repair.[42]

Finally, it is to be noted that a practice based on any of the above-mentioned exceptions loses its permissible character if it involves discrimination. By virtue of Article 14 it then resumes the character of compulsory labour contrary to the Convention. This question played a part, for instance, in the *Grandrath* Case, where a member of the Jehovah's Witnesses complained that alternative civil service had been required of him as a conscientious objector to military service, although within his religious group he held a function similar to that of ministers of other religions, who were excused from service.[43] In the *Schmidt* Case the applicant complained about the system which made it compulsory for men, but not women, to serve in the fire brigade or pay a financial contribution in lieu of such service. He claimed to be the victim of discrimination on the ground of sex in breach of Article 14 taken in conjunction with Article 4(3)(d). The Court considered that compulsory fire service constituted "normal civic obligations" envisaged in Article 4(3)(d). It observed further that the financial contribution which was payable – in lieu of service – was a "compensatory charge". The Court therefore concluded that, on account of its close links with the obligation to serve, the obligation to pay also fell within the scope of Article 4(3)(d). However, the Court found a violation of Article 14 taken in conjunction with Article 4(3)(d).[44]

8.6   DEROGATION

Under Article 15(2) no derogation from the first paragraph of Article 4 is permitted under any circumstances. Derogations from the second paragraph, apart from the cases mentioned in the third paragraph, are allowed only under the conditions and restrictions mentioned in Article 15.

---

[41]   Cf. judgment of 23 November 1983, *Van der Mussele*, para. 36.
[42]   Appl. 5593/72, *X v. Austria*, Coll. 45 (1974), p. 113.
[43]   Appl. 2299/64, *Grandrath v. Federal Republic of Germany*.
[44]   Judgment of 18 July 1994, paras 23-29.

CHAPTER 9

RIGHT TO LIBERTY AND SECURITY
OF PERSON (Article 5)

REVISED BY EDWIN BLEICHRODT

CONTENTS

9.1   TEXT OF ARTICLE 5

1. *Everyone has the right to liberty and security of person. No one shall be deprived of his liberty save in the following cases and in accordance with a procedure prescribed by law:*

   (a)   the lawful detention of a person after conviction by a competent court;

   (b)   the lawful arrest or detention of a person for non-compliance with the lawful order of a court or in order to secure the fulfilment of any obligation prescribed by law;

   (c)   the lawful arrest or detention of a person effected for the purpose of bringing him before the competent legal authority on reasonable suspicion of having committed an offence or when it is reasonably considered necessary to prevent his committing an offence or fleeing after having done so;

   (d)   the detention of a minor by lawful order for the purpose of educational supervision or his lawful detention for the purpose of bringing him before the competent legal authority;

   (e)   the lawful detention of persons for the prevention of the spreading of infectious diseases, of persons of unsound mind, alcoholics or drug addicts or vagrants;

   (f)   the lawful arrest or detention of a person to prevent his effecting an unauthorised entry into the country or of a person against whom action is being taken with a view to deportation or extradition.

2. *Everyone who is arrested shall be informed promptly, in a language which he understands, of the reasons for his arrest and of any charge against him.*

3. *Everyone arrested or detained in accordance with the provisions of paragraph 1(c) of this Article shall be brought promptly before a judge or other officer authorised by law to exercise judicial power and shall be entitled to trial within a reasonable time or to release pending trial. Release may be conditioned by guarantees to appear for trial.*

4. *Everyone who is deprived of his liberty by arrest or detention shall be entitled to take proceedings by which the lawfulness of his detention shall be decided speedily by a court and his release ordered if the detention is not lawful.*

5. *Everyone who has been the victim of arrest or detention in contravention of the provisions of this Article shall have an enforceable right to compensation.*

9.2   INTRODUCTION

In Article 5 the right to liberty of person and that to security of person are mentioned in the same breath, while in the following part of the article it is only the right to liberty of person that is elaborated. The right to security of person must be seen in the light of the right to liberty of person and the protection of the individual against arbitrariness. The right to security of person has played a role in cases where prisoners have disappeared. In the *Kurt* Case the Court observed that the authorities did not conduct any meaningful investigation into the applicant's insistence that the individual concerned was in detention and that she was concerned for his life. The unacknowledged detention in the absence of the safeguards of Article 5 was considered a particularly grave violation of the right to liberty and the right to security of person.[1]

In the *Bozano* Case the Court held as follows: "The Convention here (...) also requires that any measure depriving the individual of his liberty must be compatible with the purpose of Art. 5, namely to protect the individual from arbitrariness (...). What is at stake here is not only the 'right to liberty', but also the 'right to security of person'."[2] The question arises, however, whether the purpose of the inclusion of the right to security of person is thus done justice. After all, the obligation to give legal protection to the right to liberty of person and the prohibition of arbitrariness in the restriction of that right result from Article 5 and the system of the Convention even without the addition of 'and security',[3] while the term 'security' according to normal usage refers to more than mere protection against limitation of liberty. The Contracting States also have to give guarantees against other encroachments on the physical[4] security of persons and groups by the authorities as well as individuals, for instance, against unnecessary threats to the physical integrity of spectators during police action or against incitement to action against a particular group of persons.

---

[1]   Judgment of 25 May 1998, paras 124-129.
[2]   Judgment of 18 December 1986, para. 54.
[3]   See the judgment of 8 June 1976, *Engel*, para 58.
[4]   From its inclusion in Art. 5 it follows that, here, 'security' refers exclusively to physical security and not, *e.g.*, to mental, economic, or social security. *Cf.*, for 'liberty', *ibidem*.

9.3 DEPRIVATION OF LIBERTY

9.3.1 THE DIFFERENCE BETWEEN DEPRIVATION AND RESTRICTION OF LIBERTY

With respect to the right to liberty of person, in the Court's opinion Article 5 affords protection exclusively against *deprivation* of liberty, not against other restrictions of the physical liberty of a person. The Court infers this from the further elaboration of Article 5, where the terms 'deprived of his liberty', 'arrest' and 'detention' are used, and also from the fact that Article 2 of Protocol No. 4 contains a separate provision concerning the restriction of freedom of movement.[5] The right to liberty refers to the individual liberty in its classic sense, the physical liberty of the person.

In order to determine whether there has been *deprivation* of liberty the starting point is, in the opinion of the Court, the individual situation of the person concerned. Further, account must be taken of the special circumstances such as the type, duration, effects and manner of implementation of the measure in question. The degree of supervision and the effects on the possibilities of maintaining normal social contacts are also relevant.

Certain restrictions of the liberty of movement of soldiers – the obligation to be present in the barracks at particular times, also during leisure – which would constitute a deprivation of liberty for civilians, may be permitted if those restrictions are not "beyond the exigencies of normal military service".[6] In the *Engel* Case the Court made the following distinction: it held the so-called 'light arrest' and 'aggravated arrest' not to be in violation of Article 5, because the soldiers concerned were not confined, but were able to perform their normal service; this in contrast with 'strict arrest', which did imply confinement and, therefore, had to be reviewed for its justification, by reference to the exceptions of Article 5.[7] In the *Raimondo* Case the person concerned was placed under police supervision. He was also required to lodge a security of 2,000,000 lire as a guarantee to ensure that he complied with the constraints attaching to this measure, *e.g.* an obligation to return to his house by 9 p.m. and not to leave it before 7 a.m. unless he had valid reasons for doing so and had first informed the relevant authorities of his intention. This measure did not, according to the Court, exceed the boundaries of the mere *restriction* of liberty.[8] A different result was reached in the *Guzzardi* Case. In this case a measure of police supervision was combined with

---

[5]   *Ibidem*; judgment of 24 October 1979, *Winterwerp*, para. 37; judgment of 6 November 1980, *Guzzardi*, para. 92; judgment of 22 February 1994, *Raimondo*, para. 39. In its report in the *Bozano* Case the Commission came to the conclusion that Art. 5 amounts to a *lex specialis* in relation to the freedom of movement; report of 7 December 1984, A.111, p. 35.

[6]   Report of 19 July 1974, *Engel and Others*, B.20 (1978), para. 69.

[7]   Judgment of 8 June 1976, paras 61-63.

[8]   Judgment of 22 February 1994, paras 13 and 39.

enforced stay on an island, where freedom of movement was limited at night to a few buildings and in the daytime to a small area of the island, while the possibilities of social contact with other persons apart from the nearest relatives was very limited. The Court held that deprivation of liberty was involved.[9] In the *Lavents* Case a detainee got a heart attack and was sent to a hospital. The Court found that the stay in the hospital implied a deprivation of liberty. It took into consideration that the applicant could not leave the hospital and was under constant supervision, while the restrictions were comparable to those in prison.[10] In the *Amuur* Case asylum-seekers from Somalia were refused entry to France. They stayed in a transit zone of the airport. The Court held that the possibility to leave the transit zone of an airport is only theoretical if there is no other country that is prepared to grant entrance to the asylum-seeker and to offer him protection comparable to the protection that he expects to find in the country where he is seeking asylum.[11] The measures amounted to a deprivation of liberty. From the above case law it appears that the dividing line between deprivation of liberty and other restrictions of liberty is by no means clear-cut; the distinction is one of degree or intensity rather than one of nature or substance.

The mere fact that a person has assented to his detention does not imply that the detention cannot be an unlawful deprivation of liberty. In the 'Vagrancy' Cases the Court held that "the right to liberty is too important in a 'democratic society' within the meaning of the Convention for a person to lose the benefit of the protection of the Convention for the single reason that he gives himself up to be taken into detention."[12] In the Case of *H.M. v. Switzerland* the adult applicant complained that she had been placed in a nursing home against her will. The relevant statutory provisions under Swiss law expressly referred to the measure at issue as one of 'deprivation of liberty'. The Court came to an autonomous interpretation on the basis of the specific situation. Relevant factors were the degree of freedom of movement, the possibilities to maintain social contact with the outside world and the fact that she, after moving to the nursing home, agreed to stay there. The Court also took in account that the Swiss commission had ordered the placement in her own interest to provide her with the necessary medical care and satisfactory living conditions. Although it is not very clear in which manner this element may influence the assessment of whether the circumstances in the nursing home can be considered as a deprivation of liberty, all things considered the Court concluded that the applicant's placement in the nursing home did not amount to a deprivation of liberty within the meaning of Article 5(1).[13]

---

[9]   Judgment of 6 November 1980, para. 95.
[10]   Judgment of 28 November 2002, para. 63.
[11]   Judgment of 25 June 1996, para. 48. See also the judgment of 27 November 2003, *Shamsa*, paras 22-25.
[12]   Judgment of 18 June 1971, *De Wilde, Ooms and Versyp ('Vagrancy'* Cases), para. 65.
[13]   Judgment of 26 February 2002, paras 44-48.

In some cases the (delay in the) transition from a stricter form of detention to a more liberal one is at stake. In the *Ashingdane* Case there had been a nineteen-month-long failure to implement the applicant's transfer from a special psychiatric hospital to an ordinary psychiatric hospital with a more liberal regime. The Court noted that the place and conditions of detention had not ceased to be those capable of accompanying the lawful detention of a person of unsound mind. The delay thus was not a mischief against which Article 5(1) afforded protection. The Court is stricter when the transfer implies a change of the type of deprivation of liberty to which an applicant is subjected. In the *Mancini* Case the District Court had replaced the pre-trial detention of the applicants with the security measure of house arrest. However, owing to an organisational shortcoming that was attributable to the State, the applicants had not been able to leave the prison until six days later. Although the Court considered both imprisonment and house arrest deprivations of liberty, it concluded that the delay complained of fell within the scope of Article 5(1) under (c) and constituted a violation. Decisive was that the replacement of detention in prison with house arrest entails a change in the nature of the place of detention from a public institution to a private home.[14] Besides the gradual difference between deprivation of liberty and restriction of liberty, the Court introduced change of the type of deprivation of liberty as a possible criterion that may bring a delay of such change within the scope of Article 5. This makes the case law rather casuistic. The place of the detention may also be relevant in connection of Article 5 (1) under e.[15] In that context, its relevance for the applicability of Article 5 is more easily understandable, because the basis of the deprivation of liberty in those cases is often directly related with the place of the detention, often a clinic, and the possibilities of treatment.

9.3.2 DEPRIVATION OF LIBERTY BY PRIVATE PERSONS

Under which circumstances are the Contracting States responsible for a deprivation of liberty that is primarily carried out by private persons? In the *Nielsen* Case the question arose whether a deprivation of liberty was at stake. The case concerned the hospitalisation for approximately six months of a 12-year-old boy in a psychiatric ward at a State hospital against his will, but with the consent of his mother as the sole holder of parental rights. The Government's primary contention was that Article 5 did not apply, because the deprivation of liberty resulted from the decision of the mother. The Court, although accepting that the powers of the holder of parental authority cannot be unlimited, was of the opinion that the applicant was still of an age at which it would be normal for a decision to be made by the parent even against the wishes of the child.

---

[14] Judgment of 2 August 2001, paras 17-26.
[15] See, *e.g.*, the judgments of 11 May 2004, *Morsink* and *Brand*.

In the Court's opinion it must be possible for a child like the applicant to be admitted to hospital at the request of the holder of parental rights. Furthermore, the Court considered the restrictions to which the applicant was subjected in the ward to be normal requirements for the care of a child of 12 years of age receiving treatment in hospital. Therefore, the Court reached the opinion that Article 5 was not applicable in the case, since the hospitalisation was a responsible exercise of custodial rights by the mother.[16] The situation is different when the containment of the juvenile applicant is ordered by a court, as in *D.G. v. Ireland*. The Court held that the applicant was deprived of his liberty within the meaning of Article 5.[17]

In the *Riera Blume* Case the applicants were members of a sect, who were arrested and released. After the decision to release them was taken, the applicants were taken by members of the police in official vehicles to a hotel, where they were handed over to their families with a view to their recovering their psychological balance. Once at the hotel, the applicants were subjected to a process of 'deprogramming'. They were taken to individual rooms under the supervision of private persons and they were not allowed to leave their rooms for the first three days. After ten days they were allowed to leave the hotel. On the last two days of their stay in the hotel they were questioned by public authorities. The Court considered the transferral to the hotel and the stay in the hotel for ten days, on account of the restrictions placed on the applicants, as a deprivation of liberty. Since there was no legal basis for the deprivation of liberty, it was relevant to assess whether the detention fell under the responsibility of the State. The Court answered that question in the affirmative. The contribution of the authorities had been so decisive that without it the deprivation of liberty would not have occurred.[18] This criterion implies a causal connection between the part played by the authorities and the deprivation of liberty.

In the *Riera Blume* Case the police had played an active role. The question arises whether Article 5 may also be violated if the authorities merely play a passive role and acquiesce in the loss of liberty. Depending on the circumstances of the case, it is desirable that the guarantees of Article 5 are also applicable in situations in which the authorities are fully aware of the deprivation of liberty and in the position to put it to an end but fail to do so. In the *Storck* Case the Court stressed that Article 5(1) implies a positive obligation for the State to protect its citizens. The lack of any effective State control over the lawfulness of the detention in a psychiatric clinic was held not to be in conformity with this positive obligation.[19] Article 5 also requires the authorities

---

[16]   Judgment of 28 November 1988, paras 70-72. In the *Ashingdane* Case the Court held that the enforced stay in an ordinary psychiatric hospital amounted to a deprivation of liberty. See the Judgment of 28 May 1985, para. 42.

[17]   Judgment of 16 May 2002, paras 72-73. See also the admissibility decision of 12 October 2000, *Koniarska*.

[18]   Judgment of 14 October 1999, paras 29-30. See also the judgment of 16 June 2005, *Storck*, paras 90-91.

[19]   Judgment of 16 June 2005, paras 102-107.

to take effective measures to safeguard against the risk of disappearance.[20] Complaints about the investigation after a disappearance in a case where it was not beyond reasonable doubt that the authorities had taken away the persons were, however, examined under Article 13.[21]

In cases where individuals are under control of the authorities, the Court is rather strict. In the *Bilgin* Case, the Court held as follows: "Bearing in mind the responsibility of the authorities to account for individuals under their control, Article 5 requires them to take effective measures to safeguard against the risk of disappearance and to conduct a prompt and effective investigation into an arguable claim that a person has been taken into custody and has not been seen since."[22] In the *Kurt* Case, the Court considered an unacknowledged detention of an individual a complete negation of the guarantees in the Convention and a most grave violation of Article 5. Having assumed control over that individual it is incumbent on the authorities to account for his or her whereabouts. For this reason Article 5 must be seen as requiring the authorities to take effective measures to safeguard against the risk of disappearance and to conduct a prompt and effective investigation into an arguable claim that a person has been taken into custody and has not been seen since.[23]

9.3.3 EXTRATERRITORIALITY

The applicability of Article 5 is not limited to actions of a State within the borders of its own territory. In the *Öcalan* Case the Court accepted that an arrest made by the authorities of one State on the territory of another State, without the consent of the latter, affects the person's individual rights to security under Article 5 (1). The Convention does not prevent co-operation between States for the purpose of bringing fugitive offenders to justice, provided that it does not interfere with any of the specific rights recognised in the Convention. In those cases the rules established by an extra-dition treaty or, in the absence of any such treaty, the co-operation between the States concerned are also relevant factors to be taken into account for determining whether the arrest that has led to the subsequent complaint to the Court was lawful. The Court noted: "Independently of the question whether the arrest amounts to a violation of the law of the State in which the fugitive has taken refuge – a question which only falls to be examined by the Court if the host State is a party to the Convention – it must be established to the Court 'beyond all reasonable doubt' that the authorities of the State to which the applicant has been transferred have acted extra-territorially in a

---

[20] Judgment of 25 May 1998, *Kurt*, para. 124; judgment of 13 June 2000, *Timurtas*, para. 103.
[21] Judgment of 22 May 2001, *Sarli*, para. 69.
[22] Judgment of 17 July 2001, para. 149. See also judgment of 18 June 2002, *Orhan*, para. 369.
[23] Judgment of 25 May 1998, para. 124. In the same sense the judgment of 13 June 2000, *Timurtas*, para. 103.

manner that is inconsistent with the sovereignty of the host State and therefore contrary to international law".[24]

9.4 EXCEPTIONS TO THE PROHIBITION OF DEPRIVATION OF LIBERTY

9.4.1 GENERAL OBSERVATIONS

Article 5(1) contains an enumeration of the cases in which deprivation of liberty is permitted. This is an exhaustive enumeration,[25] that must be interpreted narrowly. Only such an approach is consistent with the aim and purpose of Article 5 to ensure that no one is arbitrarily deprived of his liberty.[26]

As appears from the inclusion in the second sentence of the words 'in accordance with a procedure prescribed by law', it is required for all the cases mentioned that the procedure by means of which the deprivation of liberty has been imposed, be regulated in the law of the country in question. That law does not have to be written law. In the *Drozd and Janousek* Case there was no French statutory provision or any international treaty which permitted the enforcement on French territory of criminal convictions pronounced in the Principality of Andorra. Nevertheless, the Court held that Franco-Andorron customary law, dating back several centuries, had "sufficient stability and legal force to serve as a basis" for the detention of the applicants.[27] The words 'prescribed by law' do not imply that in all cases a judicial procedure must have been followed, as is evident in particular from the cases under (c) and (f).

The question of whether a detention complies with the requirement 'a procedure prescribed by law' is closely related to the question of whether the detention was 'lawful'. These requirements, the latter of which is expressly mentioned in the individual exceptions under (a)-(f), and which are usually bracketed together by the Court, essentially refer back to national law. It means that the deprivation of liberty must be imposed in conformity with the substantive and procedural rules of the applicable national law. The Court is competent to review whether this requirement has been complied with, but is not called upon to give its own interpretation of national law.[28]

---

[24]   Judgment of 12 March 2003, paras 88-92. The judgment in this case was referred to the Grand Chamber, which came to the same conclusion in its judgment of 12 May 2005. See also the judgment of 12 October 1989, *Stocké*, paras 54 and 167. For transfer with a view to serving a sentence in another country, see the judgment of 15 March 2005, *Veermäe*.

[25]   Judgment of 18 January 1978, *Ireland v. the United Kingdom*, para. 194.

[26]   Judgment of 22 March 1995, *Quinn*, para. 24. See also the judgment of 24 October 1979, *Winterwerp*, para. 37.

[27]   Judgment of 26 June 1992, para. 107.

[28]   See, *e.g.,* the judgment of 24 October 1979, *Winterwerp*, para. 46; judgment of 18 December 1986, *Bozano*, para. 58; judgment of 10 June 1996, *Benham*, paras 39-47.

It is also not its role to assess the facts which have led a national court to adopt one position rather than another.[29] The interpretation and application of national law is primarily left to the domestic authorities,[30] but in cases where a failure to comply with domestic law entails a breach of the Convention, the Court exercises a certain power to examine whether national law has been observed.

A period of detention is, in principle, 'lawful' within the meaning of Article 5(1) if it is based on a court order. Even flaws in the detention order do not necessarily render the detention unlawful, since not every defect is of a nature that it deprives the detention of its legal basis under domestic law.[31] Relevant is whether the meaning of the court order may be considered to have been clear to the applicant and whether the domestic court acted in bad faith or failed to apply domestic law correctly.[32] A detention which extends over a period of several months and which has not been ordered by a court or by a judge or any other person 'authorised ... to exercise judicial power' cannot be considered 'lawful' in the sense of Article 5(1). In the Court's opinion, the protection afforded by Article 5(1) against arbitrary deprivations of liberty would be seriously undermined if a person could be detained by executive order alone following a mere appearance before the judicial authorities referred to in paragraph 3 of Article 5, as happened in the *Baranowski* Case.[33] A failure to comply with a procedural rule of national law,[34] but even the non-fulfilment of a procedural aspect may lead to a violation of Article 5(1). The latter occurred in the *Wassink* Case, where a judge failed to comply with national law inasmuch as he authorised the confinement of the applicant after a hearing held without a registrar.[35]

Moreover, the Court must ascertain whether domestic law is in conformity with the Convention. The answer to the questions of whether the court is competent (under a, c and d) and whether the arrest and detention are lawful, is determined essentially on the basis of national law. In that respect Article 5(1) lays down an obligation to comply with the substantive and procedural provisions of national law. But lawfulness also requires that any measure depriving the individual of his liberty must be compatible with the purpose of Article 5, namely, to protect the individual from arbitrariness.[36]

The words 'prescribed by law' are not merely a reference to domestic law. They refer also to the 'quality of the law' and require that the law is 'sufficiently accessible

---

[29] Judgment of 24 November 1994, *Kemmache (No. 3)*, para. 44.
[30] Judgment of 18 December 1986, *Bozano*, para. 58 and judgment of 20 March 1997, *Lukanov*, para. 41.
[31] Judgment of 4 August 1999, *Douiyeb*, paras 44-45 and judgment of 30 January 2003, *Nikolov*, para. 63.
[32] See, *e.g.*, the judgment of 31 July 2000, *Jecius*, para. 68.
[33] Judgment of 28 March 2000, para. 57.
[34] Judgment of 18 December 1986, *Bozano*, para. 54; judgment of 21 February 1990, *Van der Leer*, para. 22.
[35] Judgment of 27 September 1990, paras. 23-27.
[36] See, for example, the *Lukanov* judgment of 20 March 1997, para. 41; the *Giulia Manzoni* judgment of 1 July 1997, para. 21, and *K.-F. v. Germany*, judgment of 27 November 1997, para. 63.

and precise'.[37] In addition, as the Court held in the *Kemmache* Case, "The notion underlying the term in question ['in accordance with a procedure prescribed by law'] is one of fair and proper procedure, namely that any measure depriving a person of his liberty should issue from and be executed by an appropriate authority and should not be arbitrary."[38] The last mentioned requirement – the measure should not be taken arbitrarily – as inferred from the terms 'in accordance with a procedure prescribed by law' and 'lawful',[39] can be regarded as the guiding principle for the interpretation of Article 5. In view of that principle it must also be examined whether less severe measures than the deprivation of liberty could have sufficed. The detention of an individual is such a serious measure that it is only justified where other, less severe measures have been considered and found to be insufficient to safeguard the individual or public interest.[40]

The notion 'lawful', which figures in the individual exceptions, may also imply other requirements. These are discussed in the next section.

9.4.2 EXCEPTION UNDER (A)

The exception under (a) concerns the lawful detention of a person after conviction by a competent court. Three notions are to be discussed: 'competent court', 'lawful' and 'after conviction'.

The word 'court' implies that the conviction must be imposed by a judicial organ. A decision of the police or a public prosecutor is not sufficient,[41] no more than a decision of a military commander[42] or of an administrative organ.[43] For an organ to be a judicial organ it must be 'independent both of the executive and of the parties

---

[37]   Judgment of 25 June 1996, *Amuur*, para. 50; judgment of 23 September 1998, *Steel and Others*, paras 54-65; judgment of 28 March 2000, *Baranowski*, paras 51-52.

[38]   Judgment of 24 November 1994, para. 34. See also the judgment of 24 October 1979, *Winterwerp*, para. 45.

[39]   See, *e.g.,* the judgment of 29 February 1988, *Bouamar*, para. 47; judgment of 21 February 1990, *Wassink*, para. 24.

[40]   Judgment of 4 April 2000, *Witold Litwa*, para. 78.

[41]   With respect to the Belgian Advocate-Fiscal, see the report of 4 March 1978, *Eggs*, D&R 15 (1979), p. 35 (62).

[42]   Report of 19 July 1974, *Engel and Others*, B.20 (1978), par 84. A military commander can, however, order custody on remand, which is covered by paragraph 1(c): judgment of 22 May 1984, *De Jong, Baljet and Van den Brink*, paras 43-44.

[43]   For the Austrian reservation with respect to this, see Council of Europe, *Collected Texts*, Strasbourg, 1994, p. 88. If the decision of the administrative organ is based on a judicial decision, the requirement under (a) has been complied with, provided that there is a sufficiently direct link between the two: report of 1 March 1979, *Christinet*, D&R 17 (1980), p. 35 (54); report of 9 July 1980, *Van Droogenbroeck*, B.44 (1985), p. 24.

to the case'.[44] It is not required that the members be jurists,[45] nor that they have been nominated for an indefinite period.[46] The question of whether the court is competent, is to be answered on the basis of national law.

The requirement that the deprivation of liberty must be lawful means not only that this particular penalty must find a sufficient basis in the conviction by the court concerned, but also – this in connection with Article 7 – that the facts to which the sentence relates constituted under municipal law, at the time the offence was committed, a punishable act for which the imposition of imprisonment was possible. In addition, the sentence on which the deprivation of liberty is based, must satisfy the provisions of the Convention. It must, for instance, have been pronounced on the basis of a fair and public hearing in the sense of Article 6. In the *Drozd and Janousek* Case the applicants were serving a term of 14 years imprisonment in France, following their conviction by a court of the Principality of Andorra. They claimed a violation of Article 5(1) because the French courts had not carried out any review of the judgment of the foreign court, whose composition and procedure was, according to the applicants, not in conformity with the requirements of Article 6. Thus, the question arose whether the above-mentioned requirement also applies to sentences that have been passed in another country. The Court expressed as its view that the Contracting States are obliged to refuse their co-operation if it emerges that the conviction is the result of a flagrant denial of justice. However, there is no obligation to verify whether the proceedings which resulted in the conviction were compatible with *all* the requirements of Article 6.[47] The application of this standard, which lead to the conclusion, by 12 votes to 11(!), that Article 5(1) was not violated, is criticised by the minority of the Court because of the fact that the French representatives in Andorra had the power to ensure that the Convention was respected: they had legislative powers and the competence to appoint judges in Andorra.[48]

The mere fact that a judicial sentence is annulled on appeal does not deprive the imprisonment imposed in execution of that sentence of its lawful character.[49] However, the matter may be different if the ground for annulment is precisely a manifest error

---

[44]   Judgment of 27 June 1968, *Neumeister*, para. 24. See also the judgment of 18 June 1971, *De Wilde, Ooms and Versyp* ('Vagrancy' Cases), para. 77; judgment of 16 July 1971, *Ringeisen*, para. 95; and judgment of 8 June 1976, *Engel*, para. 68.

[45]   Appl. 5258/71, *X v. Sweden*, Coll. 43 (1973), p. 71 (79).

[46]   The Dutch Supreme Military Court was recognised as a judicial organ in the *Engel* Case, although the four military members could be discharged from their function by the King. In the opinion of the Commission and the Court the fact that these members had taken not only the judicial, but also the military oath also did not bar their independence: judgment of 8 June 1976, para.68; report of 19 July 1974, B.20 (1978), para. 99.

[47]   Judgment of 26 June 1992, paras 108-110. See also the judgment of 24 October 1995, *Iribarne Pérez*, paras 30-32.

[48]   *Ibidem*, pp. 40-43.

[49]   Appl. 3245/67, *X v. Austria*, Yearbook XII (1969), p. 206 (236); report of 9 March 1978, *Krzycki*, D&R 13 (1979), p. 57 (61).

with respect to municipal law or a violation of one of the provisions of the Convention, in particular of Articles 6 and 7.

The word 'conviction' has to be understood as signifying both a finding of guilt after it has been established in accordance with the law that an offence has been committed, and the imposition of a penalty or other measure involving deprivation of liberty.[50] If a person is not convicted or sentenced in view of his lack of criminal responsibility, his detention comes under Article 5(1) under (e) instead of (a).[51] A person detained on remand is to be considered, from the moment of his conviction by a court of first instance, as a detainee 'after conviction', so that from that moment and during appeal proceedings the lawfulness of that detention must be reviewed by reference to the provision under (a) and no longer by reference to that under (c).[52] This holds true even if under domestic law the person is still considered as a remand prisoner. The word 'after' in Article 5(1)(a) does not, according to the Court, simply mean that "the 'detention' must follow the 'conviction' in point of time", but also that "the detention must result from, follow, and depend or occur by virtue of, the conviction".[53]

In the *Van Droogenbroeck* Case the applicant was sentenced by a criminal court to two years of imprisonment and was ordered to be 'placed at the Government's disposal' for ten years. The Court had to decide whether there was sufficient connection, for the purpose of Article 5, between the sentence and the order, and the subsequent deprivation of liberty on two occasions as a result of the decisions by the Minister of Justice, following applicant's disappearances. According to the Court, the sentence to imprisonment and the order to be placed at the Government's disposal constituted "an inseparable whole". The execution of the order could take several forms, which was a matter of discretion of the Minister of Justice. In this case the way in which this discretion was exercised respected the requirements of the Convention.[54]

In the *Weeks* Case, again, the "sufficient causal connection between conviction and deprivation of liberty" was at issue. Here the applicant was sentenced to life imprisonment, but released on licence some ten years later. However, the licence was revoked after 15 months by the Home Secretary. The reason for the sentence to life imprisonment was to make the applicant "subject to a continuing security measure in the interests of public safety". Since there was no medical evidence justifying an order to send him to a mental institution, this "indeterminate sentence" would enable the Home Secretary to monitor his progress. The Court took the position that there were

---

[50]   Judgment of 24 June 1982, *Van Droogenbroeck*, para. 35. See also the judgment of 6 November 1980, *Guzzardi*, para. 100 and the judgment of 28 March 1990, *B. v. Austria*, para. 38.

[51]   Judgment of 24 September 1992, *Herczegfalvy*, paras 62-64.

[52]   Judgment of 27 June 1968, *Wemhoff*, para. 9; judgment of 6 April 2000, *Labita*, paras 145 and 147; judgment of 30 November 2004, *Klyakhin*, para. 57.

[53]   Judgment of 5 November 1981, *I. v. the United Kingdom*, para. 39 and judgment of 28 March 1990, *B. v. Austria*, para. 38.

[54]   Judgment of 24 June 1982, paras 39-40.

several similarities with an order to place someone at the disposal of the Government. However, the Court continued as follows: "Applying the principles stated in the *Van Droogenbroeck* judgment, the formal legal connection between Mr. Weeks' conviction in 1966 and his recall to prison some ten years later is not on its own sufficient to justify the contested detention under Article 5, para. 1(a). The causal link required by subparagraph (a) (...) might eventually be broken if a position were reached in which a decision not to release or to re-detain was based on grounds that were inconsistent with the objectives of the sentencing court. In those circumstances, a detention that was lawful at the outset would be transformed into a deprivation of liberty that was arbitrary and, hence, incompatible with Article 5."[55] The Court reached the conclusion that the sentencing judges must be taken to have known and intended that it was inherent in Mr Weeks' life sentence that his liberty was at the discretion of the executive for the rest of his life, and that it was not for the Court, within the context of Article 5, to review the appropriateness of the original sentence.[56] Thus, the Court accepted a rather loose link between the original sentence and the renewed detention. However, the Court next examined whether the grounds on which the re-detention was based, were sufficient. Although, here again, the Court took as a starting-point that a certain discretion has to be left to the national authorities in this matter, it conducted its own examination of the grounds in a rather detailed manner against the background of the original sentence.[57]

In the *Stafford* Case the Court noted that the finding in previous judgments that the mandatory life sentence according to English law constituted punishment for life and had to be distinguished from the discretionary life sentence, could no longer be regarded as reflecting the real position in the domestic criminal justice system of the mandatory life prisoner. That means that, once the punishment element of the sentence (as reflected in the tariff) has been satisfied, continued detention, as in discretionary life and juvenile murderer cases, depends on considerations of risk and dangerousness associated with the objectives of the original sentence. In the applicant's case the continued detention relied on the risk of non-violent offences, while the original sentence was based on murder. The Court found no sufficient causal connection.[58]

In the *Eriksen* Case, which seems to be rather exceptional, the authorisation to use security measures was expired. The applicant, who had become aggressive after suffering brain damage as a result of a traffic accident, stayed in detention on remand pending proceedings instituted in order to have the authorisation extended. The Court stated that the detention in issue was directly linked to the applicant's initial conviction and could thus be regarded as "lawful detention ... after conviction by a competent

---

[55] Judgment of 2 March 1987, para. 49.
[56] *Ibidem,* paras 50-51. See also the judgment of 16 December 1999, *Ireland v. the United Kingdom,* para. 118.
[57] *Ibidem*, paras 50-51. See also the judgment of 10 December 2002, *Waite,* para. 68.
[58] Judgment of 28 May 2002, paras 79-81.

court" for the purposes of Article 5(1) under (a). It considered that the prolonged detention, if granted, would have been based on the offences which had grounded the applicant's initial conviction. Furthermore, the detention was consistent with the objectives of that authorisation, in particular the serious danger that the person concerned would commit further criminal offences.[59]

9.4.3   EXCEPTION UNDER (B)

The first permissible form of deprivation of liberty mentioned under (b) – on account of non-compliance with a lawful order of a court – is clear. Here one may think, for instance, of non-compliance with orders of the courts to pay a fine[60], of a refusal to comply with a civil sentence[61] or to submit to a blood test,[62] or of a measure to enforce an injunction concerning a statutory declaration of assets which the applicant had refused to make.[63]

In the *Steel* Case the Court examined whether the binding-over orders to keep the peace and to be of good behaviour that had been applied to the applicants, were specific enough properly to be described as 'lawful order[s] of a court'. In this respect it noted that the orders were expressed in rather vague and general terms; the expression 'to be of good behaviour' was particularly imprecise and offered little guidance to the person bound over as to the type of conduct which would amount to a breach of the order. However, in each applicant's case the binding-over order was imposed after a finding that she had committed a breach of the peace. Having considered all the circumstances, the Court was satisfied that it was sufficiently clear that the applicants were being requested to agree to refrain from causing further, similar, breaches of the peace during the ensuing twelve months.[64]

The duration of the detention must be assessed in connection with the specific aim of the order. In the *Nowicka* Case the applicant's detention was carried out pursuant to a court order to secure the fulfilment of her obligation to submit to a psychiatric examination. The applicant was held in custody during several days before the (brief) examination was conducted and she remained in detention after the examination ended. Article 5(1) under (b) was violated.[65]

---

[59]   Judgment of 27 May 1997, paras 82-84.
[60]   Decision of 4 September 1996, *Tyrrell*.
[61]   In which case Article 1 of Protocol No. 4 must be observed by those countries which have ratified that Protocol.
[62]   Appl. 8278/78, *I. v. Austria*, D&R 18 (1980), p. 154 (156).
[63]   Appl. 9546/81, *X. v. Federal Republic of Germany* (not published).
[64]   Judgment of 23 September 1998, paras 75-76.
[65]   Judgment of 3 December 2002, para. 61.

The second exception mentioned under (b) – deprivation of liberty in order to secure fulfilment of an obligation prescribed by law – is less clear. In fact, this wide formulation would seem to pave the way for a great many forms of deprivation of liberty without any judicial intervention, simply by the invocation of a legal norm, with the additional possibility of even taking preventive action before a norm has been violated. It is true that in those cases the fourth paragraph allows appeal to a court, but this does not alter the fact that such a wide interpretation of the second limb of paragraph 1(b) would erode many of the guarantees contained in the other provisions of Article 5. In the *Benham* Case the applicant claimed that his detention ordered by a court because he had not paid the Poll Tax owed by him, did not fall under subparagraph (b) since he did not have any means to pay the debt and, therefore, the detention could not have been intended 'to secure the fulfilment' of his obligation. The Court rejected this argument by merely stating that subparagraph (b) did apply because the purpose of the detention was 'to secure the fulfilment' of the applicant's legal obligations.[66]

In the *Engel* Case the Court held that 'any obligation' must relate to a "specific and concrete obligation which the applicant has until then failed to satisfy". In this case the Supreme Military Court had invoked Article 5(1)(b) in order to justify an imposed 'strict arrest' as a provisional measure. The Court rejected this position, because it considered the general obligation to comply with military discipline not sufficiently specific.[67] In the above-mentioned *Steel* Case the applicants argued that Article 5 para. 1 (b) was violated since a requirement in general terms 'to keep the peace' was not sufficiently concrete and specific to amount to an 'obligation prescribed by law'. The Court did not agree. It observed that the elements of breach of the peace were adequately defined by English law. Furthermore, it was clear that where magistrates are satisfied, on the basis of admissible evidence, that an individual had committed a breach of the peace and that there was a real risk that he or she would do so again, the accused may be required to enter into recognizances to keep the peace or be of good behaviour. Finally, it was also clear that, if the accused refuses to comply with such an order, he or she may be committed to prison for up to six months.

A balance must be drawn between the importance in a democratic society of securing the immediate fulfilment of the obligation in question and the importance of the right to liberty. The duration of the detention is a relevant factor in drawing such a balance.[68] Other relevant factors are: the nature of the obligation arising from the relevant legislation, including its underlying object and purpose; the person being detained; and the particular circumstances leading to the detention.[69] In the *Vasileva* Case the applicant had been arrested because she refused to comply with the obligation

---

[66] Judgment of 10 June 1996, para. 39.
[67] Judgment of 8 June 1976, para. 69; report of 19 July 1974, B.20 (1978), p. 64. See also the judgment of 6 November 1980, *Guzzardi*, para. 101.
[68] Judgment of 3 December 2002, *Nowicka*, para. 61; judgment of 24 March 2005, *Epple*, paras 43-45.
[69] Judgment of 25 September 2003, *Vasileva*, para. 38.

to disclose her identity to the police. Although the decision to arrest her was in conformity with Article 5(b), the duration of the detention was, in the context of the specific circumstances of the case, not proportionate to the cause of her detention.[70]

9.4.4   EXCEPTION UNDER (C)

The provision under (c) in Article 5(1) permits arrest or detention if there is a reasonable suspicion that an offence has been committed, or if this measure is reasonably considered necessary to prevent an offence or to prevent flight after an offence has been committed. First of all, the relation between these three situations will be discussed. Next the terms 'competent legal authority', 'lawful'[71] and 'reasonable suspicion' will be dealt with. The third paragraph of Article 5 requires that everyone who is detained under subparagraph (c), shall be brought *promptly* before a judicial authority and is entitled to trial *within a reasonable time* or to release pending trial. These requirements will be discussed in connection with that provision.

Since the three grounds mentioned in paragraph 1 under (c) have been placed side by side and have not been made cumulative, the provision would appear to justify detention as a measure against persons on suspicion that they will commit crimes without their having as yet committed them. This interpretation is also corroborated by the *travaux préparatoires, viz.* in the report of the Senior Officials, in which it is stated as follows: "it may (...) be necessary in certain circumstances to arrest an individual in order to prevent his committing a crime, even if the facts which show his intention to commit the crime do not of themselves constitute a criminal offence."[72] The same line of reasoning is expressed by the Commission in the *De Jong, Baljet and Van den Brink* Case. It assigned an independent meaning to each of the three grounds mentioned under (c): "The wording 'or' separating these three categories of persons clearly indicates that this enumeration is not cumulative and that it is sufficient if the arrested person falls under one of the above categories".[73]

One may wonder why the fear that the accused may flee after having committed an offence has been included as a separate ground, if the suspicion that such an offence has been committed or will be committed is in itself already a sufficient ground for arrest. A rational interpretation is reached if it is assumed that in this provision the

---

[70]   *Ibidem.*

[71]   The French version of Article 5(1) under (c) makes no express reference to '*regularity*'. This is without importance because the notion 'lawful' is a general one which applies to the whole of Article 5(1); judgment of 6 November 1980, *Guzzardi*, para. 102.

[72]   Council of Europe, *Collected Edition of the 'Travaux Préparatoires' of the European Convention on Human Rights*, Vol. IV, Strasbourg, 1977, p. 260.

[73]   Report of 11 October 1982, p. 34. In its judgment of 22 May 1984, para. 44, the Court did not dissociate itself from this interpretation.

grounds for arrest and those for continued detention have been joined. This would then produce the following picture: arrest is permitted in case of a reasonable suspicion that the accused has committed an offence or if the arrest may reasonably be considered necessary to prevent his committing an offence that he is reasonably suspected of planning to commit. For continuation of the detention it is additionally required that it is likely that he will abscond or that there are reasonable grounds for assuming that after his release the arrested person will again commit an offence.[74] This poses, however, the problem that it will then also have to be assumed that these latter grounds of continuation do not constitute an exhaustive enumeration, since the Strasbourg organs have also recognised as such grounds the risk of suppression of evidence[75] and the danger of collusion.[76]

If a person is arrested on reasonable suspicion that he has committed an offence or in order to prevent his committing an offence or to prevent his fleeing after having done so, the conditions of the Convention are only met if the arrest or detention is really aimed at bringing the accused before a competent judicial authority. The Court took this position as early as 1961 in the *Lawless* Case.[77] The same position was taken in *Ireland v. the United Kingdom* and the *Jecius* Case.[78] In the *Brogan* Case the applicants alleged that their arrest and detention were not intended to bring them before the competent legal authority; in fact they were neither charged nor brought before a court. The Court held that the existence of such a purpose must be considered independently of its achievement. There was no reason to believe that the applicants' detention was not intended to further police investigation by way of confirming or dispelling concrete suspicions which grounded their arrest.[79] In this context the very vague term 'legal authority' must, in conformity with the third paragraph of Article 5, be deemed to mean: 'judge or other officer authorised by law to exercise judicial power'.[80] The provision under (c) does not require that the warrant of arrest itself must also originate from a judicial authority.[81]

---

[74] See Recommendation R(80)11 of the Committee of Ministers of 27 June 1980 on detention on remand, where the grounds are indeed formulated cumulatively in Article 3, while Article 4 provides that detention on remand without one of the grounds of the second category presenting itself "may nevertheless exceptionally be justified in certain cases of particularly serious offences".

[75] Judgment of 27 June 1968, *Wemhoff*, p. 25, paras 13-14.

[76] Judgment of 28 March 1990, *B. v. Austria*, paras 42-43.

[77] Judgment of 1 July 1961, para. 14.

[78] Judgment of 18 January 1978, para. 196 and judgment of 31 July 2000, para. 50.

[79] Judgment of 29 November 1988, paras 52-54. See also the judgment of 28 October 1994, *Murray*, paras 67-68, where the applicant was arrested for only three hours and released without being charged or being brought before the competent legal authority.

[80] Judgment of 18 January 1978, *Ireland v. the United Kingdom*, para. 199. In its judgment of 1 July 1961, *Lawless*, para. 14, the Court speaks of 'judicial authority' and of 'judge'. *Cf.* also the judgment of 4 December 1979, *Schiesser*, para. 30.

[81] Appl. 7755/77, *A. v. Austria*, D&R 9 (1978), p. 210 (211).

The mere fact that a person detained on remand is later released under a judicial decision does not render the arrest unlawful with retroactive effect.[82] Article 5(1)(c) requires only that there be a 'reasonable suspicion'. At the moment the arrest is made it need not yet be firmly established that an offence has actually been committed or what the precise nature of that offence is. The object of questioning during detention under subparagraph (c) is to further the investigation by way of confirming or dispelling the reason for arrest. Whether the mere continuation of suspicion suffices to warrant the prolongation of the detention on remand is covered not by the first but by the third paragraph of Article 5.

The term 'reasonable suspicion' presupposes the existence of facts or information which would satisfy an objective observer that the person concerned may have committed or is about to commit the offence. Thus, the reasonableness depends on all the circumstances of the case.[83] The Court must also assess whether the conduct of the detainee can reasonably imply an offence.[84] In the *Fox, Campbell and Hartley* Case the special circumstances in Northern Ireland were at issue. The applicants complained that their arrest under criminal legislation enacted to deal with acts of terrorism was not based on a reasonable suspicion. The Court, although acknowledging that terrorist crime falls under a special category, stressed that this cannot justify stretching the notion of 'reasonableness' beyond the point where the essence of the safeguard secured by subparagraph (c) is impaired. Scrutiny lead the Court to the conclusion that previous convictions for acts of terrorism cannot constitute the sole basis of a suspicion justifying the arrest some seven years later.[85] In the *Murray* Case the Government of the United Kingdom, without revealing its secret source that formed at least part of the reason of suspicion, succeeded in convincing the Court that there was a 'plausible and objective basis' for the suspicion that the applicant might have committed the offence of involvement in the collection of funds for the IRA.[86]

As discussed above, the detention under Article 5(1) under (c) comes to an end whenever the person on remand is convicted by a court of first instance. His further detention must then be reviewed under subparagraph (a). If no conviction or sentencing takes place because of lack of criminal responsibility on the part of the person concerned in view of his mental capacity, the eventually ordered prolonged detention comes under subparagraph (e).[87] In the *Quinn* Case the Paris Court of Appeal set aside a judicial order extending the detention on remand of the applicant. It directed that Mr Quinn should be "released forthwith if he [was] not detained on other grounds".

---

[82]   Appl. 8083/77, *X. v. the United Kingdom*, D&R 19 (1980), p. 223 (225).
[83]   Judgment of 30 August 1990, *Fox, Campbell and Hartley*, para. 32.
[84]   Judgment of 20 March 1997, *Lukanov*, paras 42-45.
[85]   Judgment of 30 August 1990, paras 16-18.
[86]   Judgment of 28 October 1994, paras 50-63.
[87]   Judgment of 24 September 1992, *Herczegfalvy*, paras 62-64.

This decision was not notified to the applicant nor was any step being taken to commence its execution. On the same day, eleven hours after the Court of Appeal delivered its judgment, the applicant, who was still detained in prison, was arrested with a view to extradition. The Strasbourg Court recognised that some delay in execution of a decision ordering release of a detainee is understandable. The continued detention for 11 hours was nevertheless clearly not covered by subparagraph (c) and did not fall under the other subparagraphs of Article 5(1).[88] In the *Giulia Manzoni* Case there was a period of 7 hours between the decision which implied release and the moment the applicant left prison. The Courts concluded that Article 5 (c) was not violated. It took into account that some delay in carrying out a decision to release a detainee is often inevitable, although it must be kept to a minimum.[89]

The Court is stricter in cases where the period of detention does not end by a court order, but is laid down by law. In *K.-F. v. Germany* the maximum period of twelve hours' detention for the purposes of checking identity was exceeded with 45 minutes. Since the maximum period, which was laid down by law and was absolute, was known in advance, the authorities responsible for the detention were under a duty to take all necessary precautions to ensure that the permitted duration was not exceeded. The Court concluded unanimously that Article 5 under (c) was violated.[90]

As a rule Article 5 under (c) does not provide a justification for the re-detention or continued detention of a person who has served a sentence after conviction of a specific offence where there is a suspicion that he may commit a further similar offence. However, in the Court's opinion the position is different when a person is detained with a view to determining whether he should be subjected, after expiry of the maximum period prescribed by a court, to a further period of security detention imposed following conviction for a criminal offence. In the *Eriksen* Case the authorities were entitled, having regard to the applicant's impaired mental state and aggressive history as well as to his established and foreseeable propensity for violence, to detain the applicant pending the determination by a court of the prosecutor's request for a prolongation of the authorisation to detain him. Relevant was that such a 'bridging' detention was of a short duration, was imposed in order to bring the applicant before a judicial authority and was made necessary by the need to obtain updated medical reports.[91] The Court emphasised the exceptional character of the case, so the implications of the Court's judgment should not be overrated.

Article 6(2) of the Convention provides that a person who is charged with an offence must be presumed innocent until proved guilty. This presumption of innocence should

---

[88]   Judgment of 22 March 1995, para. 42.
[89]   Judgment of 1 July 1997, para. 25.
[90]   Judgment of 27 November 1997, *K.-F. v. Germany,* para. 72.
[91]   Judgment of 27 May 1997, *Eriksen,* para. 86.

be respected not only during the hearing in court; out of court, too, the accused – and thus also the person detained on remand – should not be treated as if his guilt were already established. The justification of the limitations to be imposed on the person detained on remand should, therefore, be based on other criteria than the limitations which result from a sentence of imprisonment.[92] This may also imply that persons detained on remand should be segregated if possible from convicted persons, although, unlike in the UN Covenant on Civil and Political Rights, this is not explicitly provided for in the Convention.

9.4.5 EXCEPTION UNDER (D)

In the first case mentioned under (d) one has to think of an order – judicial or not – to place a minor under supervision, combined with a restriction of freedom, for instance enforced stay in a reformatory institution or in a clinic. Most legal systems permit such restrictions of freedom in the interest of the minor, even if the latter is not suspected of having committed any criminal offence. It is then required that it may reasonably be assumed that the development or the health of the minor is seriously endangered – for instance in the case of drug addiction and/or prostitution – or that he is being ill-treated. The text speaks only of 'lawful order', so that it does not appear to be required that the order emanates from a judicial organ. Under paragraph 4 of Article 5, however, these minors too – or if the law so provides, their legal representatives – are entitled to institute court proceedings in order that the lawfulness of the restriction of their freedom may be reviewed.[93]

The far-reaching powers emanating from Article 5(1)(d) have led the Court to require rather strict guarantees that the educational purpose is indeed served by the detention. In the *Bouamar* Case a minor was repeatedly confined in a remand prison 'for the purpose of educational supervision'. Although the confinements never exceeded the statutory limit of 15 days, the detentions (nine in total) amounted to a deprivation of liberty for 119 days in less than one year. The Court held that, in order to consider the deprivation of liberty lawful for educational supervision, the Belgian Government was under an obligation to put in place appropriate institutional facilities which met the demands of security and educational objectives; the mere detention of a juvenile "in conditions of virtual isolation and without the assistance of staff with educational training cannot be regarded as furthering any educational aim".[94] In *D.G.*

---

92   See Res. (65) 11 of the Committee of Ministers of the Council of Europe on detention on remand. In this Resolution it is emphasised that detention on remand should be an exceptional measure, which is applied only if 'strictly necessary'.

93   See, *e.g.*, the judgment of 29 February 1988, *Bouamar*, paras 54-64, where a breach of this provision was established.

94   Judgment of 29 February 1988, para. 56.

v. Ireland the institution where the minor was placed was considered by the Court as a penal institution. The educational and other recreational services were entirely voluntary, while the minor was unwilling to cooperate with the authorities. The detention could also not be considered as an interim measure for the purpose of an educational supervisory regime which was followed speedily by the application of such a regime.[95]

When the applicant has passed the school leaving age, but is still a minor, detention 'for the purpose of educational supervision' may still fall within the scope of Article 5 (1) under (d).

According to the *travaux préparatoires* the second case mentioned under (d) is concerned with the detention of minors for the purpose of bringing them before the court to secure their removal from harmful surroundings, so that they are not covered by Article 5(1)(c). This would, therefore, seem to be a measure by which the minor is protected against himself in order to prevent his sliding into criminality. It is not clear, however, what specific reason could bring the person concerned before a court, if no crime has been committed. The only case known to the authors relating to such a measure concerned an enforced stay of eight months in an observation centre, while the authorities examined whether theft and traffic offences had been committed.[96] In any case, the measure of bringing a minor before a judicial authority who decides on the prolongation of the detention, must be the purpose of the initial deprivation of liberty; consequently, there must be a sufficient ground for that measure. Which organ is competent to execute this deprivation of liberty is determined by national law ('lawful detention').

Since Article 5(1) under (d) confers such far-reaching powers on the national authorities with regard to minors, the age at which a person attains majority is of the greatest importance. This age is determined by domestic law. In Resolution (72)29 the Committee of Ministers of the Council of Europe has recommended to fix this age at eighteen.[97] Domestic law also determines whether and in what cases a minor has the legal capacity to institute proceedings himself, so that a minor who has this right in the Strasbourg proceedings may be dependent on his parents or guardian for the exhaustion of the local remedies.

---

[95]   Judgment of 16 February 2002, paras 81-85.
[96]   Appl. 8500/79, *X. v. Switzerland,* D&R 18 (1980), p. 238.
[97]   Res. (72)29 'Lowering of the age of full legal capacity' and Explanatory Memorandum, Council of Europe, Strasbourg, 1972.

9.4.6   EXCEPTION UNDER (E)

The provision under (e) deals with widely divergent categories of persons. There is a link between all those persons in that they may be deprived of their liberty either in order to be given medical treatment or because of considerations dictated by social policy, or on both medical and social grounds.[98] A predominant reason why the Convention allows the persons mentioned in paragraph 1(e) of Article 5 to be deprived of their liberty is not only that they may be dangerous for public safety but also that their own interests may necessitate their detention.[99]

The word 'lawful' constitutes the general criterion, while under the fourth paragraph of Article 5 the categories here referred to are also entitled to have the lawfulness of their detention reviewed by a court in accordance with the legal rules applying in the country concerned. The latter is important in particular for those cases where the detention can be ordered under municipal law by an administrative organ. If and insofar as, in performing this review, the court determines a civil right in the sense of Article 6, the rules for a fair trial set forth therein have to be observed.[100]

The scope of application of subparagraph (e) is essentially determined by the terms 'infectious diseases', 'persons of unsound mind', 'alcoholics', 'drug addicts' and 'vagrants'. The Convention does not contain a definition of these concepts. In deciding whether an individual should be detained for one of the reasons stated in subparagraph (e), the national authorities do have a certain discretion. However, in reviewing these national decisions the Court is prepared to carry out an independent examination of the question of whether the deprivation of liberty is in conformity with the Convention. In the case law the concepts 'infectious diseases', 'persons of unsound mind', 'alcoholics' and 'vagrants' have been clarified to some extent.

The essential criteria to assess the lawfulness of the detention of a person 'for the prevention of the spreading of infectious diseases' are whether this spreading is dangerous for public health or safety, and whether less severe measures than detention have been considered and found to be insufficient to safeguard the public interest.[101]

In the *Winterwerp* Case the Court emphasised that the term 'of unsound mind' implies that three minimum conditions have to be satisfied: (1) the person concerned must be "reliably shown" to be of unsound mind (which "calls for objective medical expertise"), (2) the nature or degree of the mental disorder must be such as to justify the deprivation of liberty, and (3) continued confinement is only valid as long as the disorder persists.[102] In the *Luberti* Case the question of whether the detention had

---

[98]   Judgment of 4 April 2000, *Witold Litwa*, para. 60.
[99]   Judgment of 6 November 1980, *Guzzardi*, para. 98. See also the judgment of 20 February 2003, *Hutchison Reid*, para. 51.
[100]   See the judgment of 24 October 1979, *Winterwerp*, para. 73.
[101]   Judgment of 25 January 2005, *Enhorn*, para. 44.
[102]   Judgment of 24 October 1979, para. 39.

continued beyond the period justified by applicant's mental disorder, was investigated by the Court in great detail.[103] In *R.L. and M.-J.D. v. France* there was no medical reason for the continued detention of the applicant, but the release was postponed because the physician in charge was not allowed to release the detainee. The Court judged that the applicant was held on administrative grounds that were incompatible with Article 5(1) under (e).[104]

No deprivation of liberty of a person considered to be of unsound mind may be deemed in conformity with Article 5(1) under (e) of the Convention if it has been ordered without seeking the opinion of a medical expert. In urgent cases or in cases where a person is arrested because of his violent behaviour, it may be acceptable that such an opinion be obtained immediately after the arrest. In all other cases a prior consultation is necessary. Where no other possibility exists, for instance due to a refusal of the person concerned to appear for an examination, at least an assessment by a medical expert, based on the actual state of mental health, on the basis of the file must be sought.[105] In the Court's view, it does not automatically follow from a finding by an expert authority that the mental disorder which justified a patient's compulsory confinement no longer persists, that the latter must be immediately and unconditionally released into the community. The authorities should be able to retain some measure of supervision over the progress of the person once he is released into the community and to that end make his discharge subject to conditions. Appropriate safeguards are necessary to ensure that any deferral of discharge is consonant with the purpose of Article 5(1) and with the aim of the restriction in sub-paragraph (e) and that discharge is not unreasonably delayed.[106]

In the *Witold Litwa* Case the Court interpreted the term 'alcoholics' (*d'un alcoolique*) on the basis of the *ratio legis*. The Court considered that the object and purpose of the exception under (e) cannot be interpreted as only allowing the detention of 'alcoholics' in the limited sense of persons in a clinical state of 'alcoholism'. Persons who are not medically diagnosed as 'alcoholics', but whose conduct and behaviour under the influence of alcohol pose a threat to public order or themselves, can be taken into custody under Article 5(1) under (e) for the protection of the public or their own interests, such as their health or personal safety.[107] The mere fact that someone is under influence of alcohol, however, is not a sufficient basis for a deprivation of liberty. The detention must be assessed in the light of the above-mentioned *ratio legis* of the exception under (e). Decisive is whether the person

---

[103] Judgment of 23 February 1984, para. 29. See also the report of 7 October 1981, *B. v. the United Kingdom,* D&R 32 (1983), p. 5 (37-38).

[104] Judgment of 19 May 2004, paras 124-128.

[105] Judgment of 5 October 2000, *Varbanov,* para. 47 and judgment of 19 May 2004, *R.L. and M.-J.D. v. France,* para. 117.

[106] Judgment of 24 October 1997, *Johnson,* paras 61-63.

[107] Judgment of 4 April 2000, *Witold Litwa,* paras 60-63.

behaves when drunk in such a way as to pose a threat to public order.[108] The purpose of the measure must be to avert that threat. The same will apply to 'drug addicts'.

In the *De Wilde, Ooms and Versyp ('Vagrancy')* Cases the question arose whether the applicants could be considered as 'vagrants'. The Belgian Criminal Code defined vagrants as "persons who have no fixed abode, no means of subsistence and no regular trade or profession". According to the Court this definition did not appear to be in any way irreconcilable with the usual meaning of the term 'vagrant'. A person falling within the definition of the Belgian Criminal Code in principle comes under the exception of Article 5(1) under (e). In addition the Court held that the national courts could deduce from the information available that the persons concerned met the criteria.[109] The Court, although confining itself to a marginal review of the national law and its application, took a rather active position when it comes to a review of the conformity of that application with the wording and meaning of Article 5(1) under (e). Thus a guarantee has been created against too wide a national interpretation and application of the categories mentioned under (e).[110] The necessity of a restrictive interpretation was equally emphasised by the Court in the *Guzzardi* Case, where it held that it may not be inferred from the exception permitted under Article 5(1) under (e) that the detention of persons who may constitute a greater danger than the categories mentioned in that article, is permitted equally and *a fortiori*.[111]

The involuntary commitment of an accused person in an observation clinic in most cases cannot be brought under paragraph 1 under (e), because as a rule it is not certain in advance that he is of unsound mind. This deprivation of liberty may perhaps find its justification in paragraph 1 under (b), in case the measure is provided for in a judicial decision which may be enforced if it is not complied with voluntarily.

Since paragraph 1(e) does not contain any limitation as to the duration of the detention, this in contrast with the other categories of detention regulated in the same paragraph, the question is of great importance whether paragraph 4 confers on the person concerned only the right to have the lawfulness of the deprivation of his liberty as such reviewed by a court, or also the right to have recourse to a court periodically if the detention is prolonged. This question will be discussed under Article 5(4).

In the *Winterwerp* Case it had been argued on behalf of the applicant that Article 5(1)(e) entails for the person detained on one of the grounds mentioned there the right to appropriate treatment in order to ensure that he is not detained longer

---

[108]   Judgment of 8 June 2004, *Hilda Hafsteinsdottir*, para. 42.
[109]   Judgment of 18 June 1971, para. 68.
[110]   See also the judgment of 23 February 1984, *Luberti*, para. 27, and the judgment of 28 May 1985, *Ashingdane*, para. 37.
[111]   Judgment of 6 November 1980, para. 98.

than absolutely necessary. This submission, however, was rejected by the Court.[112] In the *Ashingdane* and *Aerts* Cases the Court further elaborated on this. According to the Court, the lawfulness of a deprivation of liberty concerns not only the issuance of the order of the liberty-depriving measures, but also its execution. In other words, the measure must not only be in conformity with domestic law, but also with the purposes of the restrictions laid down in Article 5(1). This also follows from Article 18 of the Convention. Therefore, there must be "some relationship between the ground of permitted deprivation of liberty relied on and the place and conditions of detention". Except for this relationship, however, Article 5(1)(e) is not concerned with suitable treatment or conditions.[113]

In the *Morsink* and *Brand* Cases the relationship between the deprivation of liberty and the place of the detention was at stake. During the first period of the execution of the non-punitive measure, the applicants were held in pre-placement detention in an ordinary remand centre until they could be placed in a custodial clinic. The Court noted that, in principle, the 'detention' of a person as a mental health patient will only be 'lawful' for the purposes of paragraph (1) under (e) if effected in a hospital, clinic or other appropriate institution. In the circumstances of both cases the failure to admit the applicants to a custodial clinic did not result automatically in the conclusion that the detention was unlawful under Article 5 (1). The Court found it not to be contrary to this provision to commence the procedure for selecting the most appropriate custodial clinic after the order had taken effect. It would be unrealistic to expect that a place be immediately available. The Court found a certain friction between available and required capacity in custodial clinics inevitable and acceptable. However, a delay of six months in the admission of a person to a custodial clinic is not acceptable in the view of the Court.[114]

In the *Winterwerp* Case the Court considered the interval of two weeks between the expiry of the earlier order and the making of the succeeding renewal order not unreasonable or excessive.[115] In the *Erkalo* Case the applicant was placed by a court at the government's disposal. The request of the public prosecutor for the extension of the placement order was not received by the competent court until two months after the expiry of the statutory period, and, as a result, for eighty-two days the placement of the applicant was not based on any judicial decision. The Court noticed that there was a lack of adequate safeguards to ensure that the applicant's release from detention would not be unreasonably delayed. The 'bridging detention' was unlawful and constituted a breach of Article 5(1) of the Convention.[116]

---

[112] Judgment of 24 October 1979, para. 51.

[113] Judgment of 28 May 1985, para. 44; judgment of 30 July 1998, *Aerts*, para. 46.

[114] Judgment of 11 May 2004, *Morsink*, paras 63-69 and judgment of 11 May 2004, *Brand*, paras 60-66.

[115] Judgment of 24 October 1979, para. 49.

[116] Judgment of 2 September 1998, paras 57-60. See for a justified 'bridging detention': judgment of 24 July 2001, *Rutten*, paras 39-46.

9.4.7   EXCEPTION UNDER (F)

The importance of the provision under (f) consists in that, although the Convention does not grant to aliens a right of admission to or residence in any of the Contracting States, Article 5 nevertheless contains certain guarantees in case the authorities proceed to arrest or to detain an alien pending the decision on his admission, deportation or extradition. These consist first of all in the guarantee that such arrest or detention must be lawful and must, therefore, be in conformity with the applicable provisions of both domestic and international law and may not be imposed arbitrarily.[117] This right is coupled with the right of the person in question under paragraph 4 to have this lawfulness reviewed by a court. However, Article 5 does not merely refer back to domestic law but requires also that the applicable national law is 'sufficiently accessible and precise'. According to the Court this is especially required with regard to asylum-seekers.[118] In the *Amuur* Case French national law did not meet this requirement and moreover the Court held, *inter alia,* that the national courts lacked jurisdiction to review the conditions of detention.[119]

Article 5 paragraph 1 under (f) does not require that the detention of a person against whom action is being taken with a view to deportation or extradition must be reasonably considered necessary, for example to prevent his committing an offence or fleeing. In this respect Article 5 (1) under (f) provides a lower level of protection than Article 5 paragraph 1 under (c): all that is required under (f) is that action is being taken with a view to deportation or extradition. It is, therefore, immaterial whether the underlying decision can be justified under national or Convention law.[120] It is obvious, however, that in reviewing the lawfulness of the detention, the lawfulness of the deportation or extradition will often also be at issue. This is especially the case when, according to national law, the lawfulness of the detention is made dependent on that of the deportation.[121]

In the *Conka* Case the applicants had received orders to leave the territory of Belgium. They did not obey these orders. The Belgian authorities tried to gain the trust of the applicants with an invitation to come to the Ghent police station. The authorities declared that their attendance was required "to enable the files concerning their applications for asylum to be completed". In fact the applicants were on their arrival at the police station arrested in view of their deportation to Slovakia. The Court emphasised that acts whereby the authorities sought to gain the trust of asylum-seekers

---

117   Judgment of 18 December 1986, *Bozano*, para. 54.
118   Judgment of 25 June 1996, *Amuur*, para. 50.
119   *Ibidem*, para. 53.
120   Judgment of 15 November 1996, *Chahal*, para. 112 and judgment of 5 February 2002, *Conka*, para. 38.
121   Report of 11 October 1983, *Zamir*, D&R 40 (1985), p. 42 (55). The fact that a domestic court has found the deportation procedure to be illegal does not deprive the applicant of his claim to be a victim of a violation of the Convention by reason of his arrest: report of 7 December 1984, *Bozano*, p. 32.

with a view to arresting and subsequently deporting them may be found to contravene the general principles stated or implicit in the Convention. The narrow interpretation of the exceptions of Article 5(1) must also be reflected in the reliability of communications. Misleading the individuals concerned about the purpose of a notice so as to make it easier to deprive them of their liberty is not compatible with Article 5.[122]

Article 5(1) under (f) implies the guarantee that the detention must have no purpose other than that of preventing the admission of the alien in question to the country or of making it possible to decide on his deportation or extradition. Article 18 of the Convention, which prohibits restrictions of the rights and freedoms for any purpose other than that for which they have been prescribed, applies here as well. In the first place, this means that the deprivation of liberty is unlawful if the deportation order, and the way in which it is enforced, constitute a misuse of power.[123] In the second place, it follows that the detention must not be attended with more restrictions for the person concerned and must not last longer than is required for a normal conduct of the proceedings. In the *Quinn* Case the Court held: "It is clear from the wording of both the French and the English versions of Article 5 § 1(f) that deprivation of liberty under this sub-paragraph is justified only for as long as extradition proceedings are actually taking place. It follows that if such proceedings are not being conducted with due diligence, the detention ceases to be justified under Article 5 § 1(f))".[124] Thus, although the duration of detention is only mentioned in paragraph 3 of Article 5 and this provision refers only to detentions under paragraph 1(c), the Court stipulates that the period of detention may not exceed a reasonable time.[125] The reasonableness of the length of detention has to be assessed in each individual case. In this respect not only the length of the extradition or deportation proceedings is properly relevant, but also the length of connected procedures such as, for instance, summary proceedings which may result in a stay of execution of the extradition. If it has been decided to prolong the detention in the interest and at the request of the person concerned, *e.g.* in order to find a suitable country which is prepared to admit him, or in order to obtain certain guarantees from the extradition-requesting State with regard to his treatment,[126] he cannot claim afterwards that he is the victim of this prolonged detention. Thus, in the *Kolompar* Case the Court found the period spent in detention – it lasted for over two years – pending extradition to be unusually long. Nevertheless, it held that it did not amount to a violation of Article 5(1) under (f)

---

[122] Judgment of 5 February 2002, *Conka*, paras 41-42.
[123] Report of 7 December 1984, *Bozano*, para. 69.
[124] Judgment of 22 March 1995, para. 48. See also the judgment of 15 November 1996, *Chahal*, paras 112-113 and the judgment of 9 October 2003, *Slivenko*, para. 146.
[125] See also judgment of 25 June 1996, *Amuur*, para. 53.
[126] Appl. 9706/82, *X. v. Federal Republic of Germany* (not published).

because the Belgian State could not be held responsible for the delays to which the applicant's conduct gave rise.[127]

A clear example of a violation of paragraph 1 under (f) is offered by the *Bozano* Case. Here the Court had to decide whether the deportation of Bozano from France to Switzerland was 'lawful' and 'in accordance with a procedure prescribed by law'. 'Lawfulness', according to the Court, also implies the absence of any arbitrariness. The circumstances of the case, *inter alia* the fact that the authorities waited about a month before serving the deportation order and prevented Bozano from making any effective use of the theoretically existing judicial remedies, and the fact that the French authorities contacted only the Swiss authorities, although the Spanish border was much closer to the place where Bozano was arrested, led the Court to decide that the deprivation of liberty was neither lawful nor compatible with the right to security of person. Several French courts had reached the same conclusion. The way the deportation was executed clearly indicated what the French authorities had in mind to get round the prohibition of extradition to Italy ordered by the Limoges Court of Appeal. That was also the reason why Bozano had been delivered to the Swiss authorities: Switzerland had an extradition treaty with Italy. The Court concluded, therefore, that the way Bozano was deprived of his liberty amounted in fact to a disguised form of extradition.[128]

9.4.8   INTERPLAY OF THE DIFFERENT EXCEPTIONS

A person may be detained under different subparagraphs of Article 5(1) successively. If a person detained on remand is convicted by a court of first instance, his detention falls no longer under subparagraph (c) but under subparagraph (a). In the *Herczegfalvy* Case, the decision by which the applicant was ordered to be placed in an institution for mentally ill offenders, without convicting or sentencing him, was quashed on appeal. From that moment the deprivation of liberty once more came under paragraph 1(c).[129] It is also possible that the detention falls under more than one subparagraph at the same time. In the *Eriksen* Case the 'bridging detention' between the expiry of an authorisation and the decision on a request for prolongation fell under the provisions of Article 5 under (a) and (c) simultaneously.[130] In the *Kolompar* Case the detention of the applicant came successively under Article 5(1)(c) only, under (c) and (f) at the same time, under (f) only, under (f) and (a) at the same time, and finally once more merely under (f).[131]

---

[127]   Judgment of 24 September 1992, paras 40-42.
[128]   Judgment of 18 December 1986, paras 59-60.
[129]   Judgment of 24 September 1992, para. 22.
[130]   Judgment of 27 May 1997, para. 86.
[131]   Judgment of 24 September 1992, paras 35-36.

It appears sometimes to be difficult to determine whether the exception under (a) or under (e) is applicable. In *X v. the United Kingdom* the applicant was convicted, but this conviction contained solely the establishment that he committed the criminal conduct concerned. No punishment was imposed on him. However, his admission to and detention in a mental hospital for insane offenders was ordered. In assessing under which subparagraph the detention of the applicant had to be dealt with, the Court came to the conclusion that, although it recognised the differences between the subparagraphs 5(1)(a) and 5(1)(e), both subparagraphs could be and were applicable to the applicant's deprivation of liberty, at least initially. In the *Erkalo* Case the applicant was placed at the disposal of the government in a psychiatric institution. The Court considered that the applicant's detention fell within the ambit of Article 5(1)(a) and (e) of the Convention.[132]

9.5 · THE RIGHT TO BE INFORMED PROMPTLY OF THE REASONS FOR ARREST

9.5.1 GENERAL OBSERVATIONS

Article 5(2) grants to everyone who is arrested the right to be informed promptly, in a language which he understands, of the reasons for his arrest and of any charge against him. If the national authorities fail to do so, the arrest and detention are unlawful, even if they can be brought under one of the cases mentioned in paragraph 1. The rationale of this second paragraph necessarily ensues from the idea underlying Article 5: the liberty of person is the rule and is guaranteed, and an encroachment on this is allowed only in the cases expressly provided for and in conformity with the law as it stands. In order for the person arrested to be able to judge, from the moment of arrest, whether these two conditions have been met and to decide whether there are reasons for recourse to a court, adequate information must be available to him. Three notions are to be discussed successively: the applicability of Article 5(2), the information that should be given to the arrested person and, finally, the requirement of promptness.

A violation of paragraph 2 of Article 5 may also imply a violation of the fourth paragraph of this article. This question will be dealt with in the framework of the discussion of the fourth paragraph.

---

[132] Judgment of 2 September 1998, para. 51. See also the judgment of 11 May 2004, *Morsink*, para. 62 and the judgment of 11 May 2004, *Brand*, para. 59.

9.5.2   APPLICABILITY

The words 'arrest' and 'charge' used in paragraph 2 could create the impression that this provision is only relevant to cases arising under criminal law. However, the Court took a different view: the second paragraph applies not only to the detentions referred to in paragraph 1 under (c), but to any person arrested.[133] Therefore, paragraph 2 applies to all cases mentioned in the first paragraph of Article 5(1). The Court clarified its position by invoking the autonomous meaning of the terms of the Convention and the aim and purpose of Article 5. In addition, according to the Court, the use of the words 'any charge' ('toute accusation') showed that the intention of the drafters was not to lay down a condition for the applicability of Article 5(2), but to indicate an eventuality of which it takes account. Finally, the close link between the paragraphs 2 and 4 of Article 5 was considered to support this interpretation.[134]

9.5.3   RELEVANT INFORMATION

Paragraph 2 of Article 5 requires that any arrested person shall be informed of the reasons of his arrest and of any charge made against him. As the Court held in the *Fox, Campbell and Hartley* Case he must "be told, in simple, non-technical language that he can understand, the essential legal and factual grounds for his arrest, so as to be able, if he sees fit, to apply to a court to challenge its lawfulness in accordance with paragraph 4."[135] Thus, the Court took the position that the information required by Article 5(2) need not be worded in a particular form and need not even be given in writing. Consequently, as the Court held in the *Lamy* Case, there exists at this stage of the proceedings no obligation to make the file available to the defence of the accused person for inspection.[136] In assessing whether the applicant is adequately informed, the Court takes into consideration the special features of the case and the person of the detainee.[137] In the *Fox, Campbell and Hartley* Case and the *Murray* Case the persons concerned were questioned about their alleged activities for the IRA. The Court held that the bare indication of the legal basis for the arrest, taken on its own, was insufficient for the purposes of Article 5(2).[138] However, here the obligation of paragraph 2 had been complied with because the persons concerned had been able to infer the

---

[133]   Judgment of 30 August 1990, *Fox, Campbell and Hartley*, para. 40; judgment of 28 October 1994, *Murray*, para. 72.

[134]   Judgment of 21 February 1990, *Van der Leer*, paras 27-28.

[135]   Judgment of 30 August 1990, para. 40; reiterated in the judgment of 28 October 1994, *Murray*, para. 72. See also the judgment of 5 April 2001, *H.B. v. Switzerland*, paras 48-49.

[136]   Judgment of 30 March 1989, para. 31.

[137]   See, among others, the judgment of 30 August 1990, *Fox, Campbell and Hartley*, para. 40; judgment of 28 October 1994, *Murray*, para. 72 and judgment of 5 April 2001, *H.B. v. Switzerland*, para. 47.

[138]   *Ibidem*, para. 41 and para. 76, respectively.

reasons for the arrest clearly enough from the content of the interrogations that took place after the arrest.[139] In the *Dikme* Case the Court even took into account the intensity and frequency of the interrogations, from which the applicant could have gained some idea of what he was suspected of.[140] The rationale of paragraph 2 raises the question of whether the Court should not be a little stricter in these respects. The interests of the arrested person which paragraph 2 is designed to protect, are sufficiently guaranteed only if the prescribed information is communicated to him explicitly and unambiguously.

9.5.4 PROMPTLY

Article 5(2) prescribes that the information about the reasons of arrest and of any charge must be given 'promptly' *('dans le plus court delai')*. The Court has indicated that it need not be conveyed in its entirety by the arresting officer at the very moment of the arrest. In the *Fox, Campbell and Hartley* Case the applicants were informed sufficiently about the reasons for their arrest during the interrogations. These interviews took place four and a half, six and a half and three hours, respectively, after their arrest. These intervals could not be regarded in the context of those cases as falling outside the constraints of time imposed by the notion of promptness in Article 5(2).[141] In its decision in the *Durgov* Case the Court concluded that, in the context of the case, a delay of ten and a half hours did not fall outside the constraints of time imposed by the notion of promptness, while in the *Lowry* Case even an interval of 48 hours between the applicant's arrest and his questioning was considered compatible with Article 5(2).[142]

According to the Court, the arresting officer is not obliged to give the full information at the very moment of the arrest. This implies that at least some relevant information should be given at once.

---

[139] In the same sense: judgment of 11 July 2000, *Dikme*, para. 56.
[140] Judgment of 11 July 2000, paras 55-56.
[141] Judgment of 30 August 1990, para. 42. In the *Murray* Case, judgment of 28 October 1994, para 78, an interval of one hour and 20 minutes did not violate the provision of Article 5(2) either.
[142] Decision of 2 September 2004, *Durgov*, and decision of 6 July 1999, *Lowry*.

9.6   THE RIGHT TO BE BROUGHT PROMPTLY BEFORE A JUDGE OR OTHER OFFICER

9.6.1   GENERAL OBSERVATIONS

Article 5(3) relates exclusively to the category of detainees mentioned in the first paragraph under (c): those detained on remand.[143] The main purpose of this paragraph, in relation to Article 5(1)(c), is to afford to individuals deprived of their liberty a special guarantee: a procedure of a judicial nature designed to ensure that no one should be arbitrarily deprived of his liberty[144] and, furthermore, to ensure that any arrest or detention will be kept as short as possible.

The judicial review of the detention must be an automatic one.[145] It cannot be made to depend on a preceding application by the detained person. Such a requirement would change the nature of the safeguard provided for under Article 5(3), a safeguard distinct from that in Article 5(4).[146] It might even defeat the purpose of the safeguard under Article 5(3), which is to protect the individual from arbitrary detention by ensuring that the act of deprivation of liberty is subject to independent judicial scrutiny.[147] Prompt judicial review of detention is also an important safeguard against ill treatment of the individual taken into custody.[148]

9.6.2   PROMPTLY

Paragraph 3 comprises, first of all, in addition to the right to prompt information conferred in the second paragraph, the right to be brought 'promptly' before a judicial authority. It is obvious that a person cannot always be heard by a judge immediately after being arrested. Unlike in the case of the obligation to inform him of the reasons for his arrest, there is a third person involved in his first contact with a judge. The word 'promptly' – the French text speaks of '*aussitôt*' – therefore must not be interpreted so literally that the investigating judge must be virtually dragged out of bed to arraign the detainee or must interrupt urgent activities for this. However, adequate provisions will indeed have to be made in order that the prisoner can be heard as soon as may reasonably be required in view of his interests.

---

[143]   See, *e.g.*, the judgment of 28 March 1990, *B. v. Austria*, paras 33-36; judgment of 22 March 1995, *Quinn*, paras 51-53.

[144]   Judgment of 4 December 1979, *Schiesser*, para. 30.

[145]   Judgment of 22 May 1984, *De Jong, Baljet and Van den Brink*, para. 51.

[146]   *Ibidem*, para. 57.

[147]   Judgment of 25 May 1998, *Kurt*, para. 123.

[148]   See the judgment of 18 December 1996, *Aksoy*, para. 76.

The Court gave its opinion about the interpretation of the word 'promptly' in the *De Jong, Baljet and Van den Brink* Case. The Court had to answer the question of whether the referral to a judicial authority seven, eleven and six days, respectively, after the arrest was in conformity with the requirement of promptness of Article 5(3). Although this question was answered in the negative, the Court refrained from developing a minimum standard. It only noted that "the issue of promptness must be assessed in each case according to its special features".[149] In other cases decided by the Court on the same day it also refrained from indicating a minimum standard.[150]

In the *Brogan* Case the Court had to deal with the question of 'promptness' in the case of arrest and detention, by virtue of powers granted under special legislation, of persons suspected of involvement in terrorism in Northern Ireland. The requirements under ordinary law in Northern Ireland for bringing an accused before a court were expressly made inapplicable to such arrest and detention. None of the applicants was in fact brought before a judge or judicial officer during his time in custody ranging from four days and six hours to six days and sixteen and a half hours. The Court accepted that the investigation of terrorist offences presented the authorities with special problems and that, subject to the existence of adequate safeguards, the context of terrorism in Northern Ireland had the effect of prolonging the period during which the authorities may, without violating Article 5(3), keep a person suspected of serious terrorist offences in custody before bringing him before a judge or other judicial officer. However, it also stressed that the scope for flexibility in interpreting and applying the notion of 'promptness' is very limited.; even the shortest of the four periods of detention, namely the four days and six hours spent in police custody, fell outside the strict constraints as to time permitted by the first part of Article 5(3). The Court held as follows: "To attach such importance to the special features of this case as to justify so lengthy a period of detention without appearance before a judge or other judicial officer would be an unacceptably wide interpretation of the plain meaning of the word 'promptly'. An interpretation to this effect would import into Article 5 § 3 a serious weakening of a procedural guarantee to the detriment of the individual and would entail consequences impairing the very essence of the right protected by this provision."[151] In the *O'Hara* Case the Court stated that detention periods exceeding 4 days for terrorist suspects are not compatible with Article 5(3).[152]

In the *Koster* Case the applicant was not brought before the Military Court until five days after his arrest. According to the Court this period was too long. The fact that the lapse of time had occurred because of the weekend, which fell in the intervening period, and the two-yearly major manoeuvres, in which the members of the court had

---

[149] Judgment of 22 May 1984, para. 52. See also the judgment of 28 November 1991, *Koster*, para. 24.
[150] Judgments of 22 May 1984, *Van der Sluijs, Zuiderveld and Klappe*, para. 49, and *Duinhof and Duijf*, para. 41.
[151] Judgment of 29 November 1988, para. 62.
[152] Judgment of 16 October 2001, para. 46.

been participating, did not justify any delay in the proceedings. The demands of military life and justice could not alter this point of view.[153]

9.6.3   JUDGE OR OTHER OFFICER

Paragraph 3 provides that the accused should be brought before a 'judge' or 'other officer authorised by law to exercise judicial power'. In the *Schiesser* Case the Court laid down criteria for the determination of whether a person can be regarded as such an 'officer'. It expressed that 'officer' is not identical with 'judge', but "nevertheless must have some of the latter's attributes". The first condition is independence of the executive and of the parties. This does not mean that the 'officer' may not be to some extent subordinate to other judges or officers provided that they themselves enjoy similar independence. Secondly, there is a procedural requirement: the 'officer' is obliged to himself hear the individual brought before him. Thirdly, there is a sub-stantive requirement which places the 'officer' under the obligation to review "the circumstances militating for or against detention", and to decide "by reference to legal criteria, whether there are reasons to justify detention" and, if this is not the case, to order the release of the person.[154] In this case the complaint concerned the fact that the same authority who was charged in certain cases with the prosecution also had to decide on the lawfulness of the detention. The Court concluded that the provision of paragraph 3 had not been violated. It held in particular that in the case under consi-deration there had been no blending of functions, that the functionary had been able to proceed, and had proceeded, independently, and that the procedural and substantive guarantees had been observed.[155]

In three cases against the Netherlands elements of the Dutch Military Code were considered to be in violation of Article 5(3). The first question raised was whether the *auditeur-militair* could be considered as an 'officer authorised by law to exercise judicial power'. Referring to its judgment in the *Schiesser* Case, the Court answered this question in the negative, since the *auditeur-militair* was only competent to make recommendations about the applicant's detention, but he had no power to order his release. The Government had submitted that, in practice, these recommendations were always followed, pending a total revision of the Military Code in order to comply with the Convention. However, in the opinion of the Court this practice was an insufficient

---

[153]   Judgment of 28 November 1991, para. 25.
[154]   Judgment of 4 December 1979, para. 31. See also, *e.g.*, the judgment of 22 May 1984, *Van der Sluijs, Zuiderveld and Klappe*, para. 46; judgment of 22 May 1984, *Duinhof and Duijf*, para. 36; and judgment of 29 April 1999, *Aquilina*, paras 48-55.
[155]   Judgment of 4 December 1979, paras 32-38. The presence of counsel was not included by the Court among the relevant guarantees; *ibidem*, para. 36.

guarantee.[156] Furthermore, as the *auditeur-militair* could also be in charge of prosecuting functions in the same case, he likewise could not be considered to be independent from the parties.[157] The Court reached the same conclusion with regard to the *officier-commissaris,* especially on the ground of the lack of power to decide on the continued detention or release.[158] In the *Pauwels* Case the investigation and prosecution functions were also performed by one and the same *auditeur-militair.* The Court held that although the *auditeur-militair* is hierarchically subordinate to the *auditeur-generaal* and the Minister of Justice, he is completely independent in the performance of his twin duties as a member of the public prosecutor's office and as chairman of the Board of Inquiry. However, the fact that the legislation entitled the *auditeur-militair* to perform investigation and prosecution functions in the same case and in respect of the same defendant, led the Court to the conclusion that the *auditeur-militair's* impartiality could give rise to doubt.[159]

In two of the three cases against the Netherlands,[160] and to a lesser extent also in the *Pauwels* Case, the impartiality[161] of the *auditeur-militair* was found open to doubt because he could also be in charge of prosecuting functions in the same case. With this reasoning, the Court implicitly deviated from its judgment in the *Schiesser* Case, where it was held that only the effective concurrent exercise of such functions infringed Article 5(3). This development was clearly confirmed by the *Huber* Case and the *Brincat* Case. In the *Brincat* Case, the Court held as follows: "only the objective appearances at the time of the decision are material: if it then appears that the 'officer authorised by law to exercise judicial power' may later intervene, in the subsequent proceedings, as a representative of the prosecuting authority, there is a risk that his impartiality may arouse doubts which are to be held objectively justified".[162] In the *Assenov* Case the prisoner was brought before an investigator who questioned him, formally charged him, and took the decision to detain him on remand. Under Bulgarian law, investigators do not have the power to make legally binding decisions as to the detention or release of a suspect. Instead, any decision made by an investigator is capable of being overturned by the prosecutor. It followed that the investigator was

---

[156]   Judgments of 22 May 1984, *De Jong, Baljet and Van den Brink,* paras 46-50; *Van der Sluijs, Zuiderveld and Klappe,* paras 42-44; and *Duinhof and Duijf,* paras 42-45.

[157]   *Ibidem.*

[158]   Judgments of 22 May 1984, *Van der Sluijs, Zuiderveld and Klappe,* paras 47-48 and *Duinhof and Duijf,* paras 39-40, respectively. See also the judgment of 26 May 1988, *Pauwels,* paras 37-38.

[159]   Judgment of 26 May 1988, para. 38. In the same sense: judgment of 18 February 1999, *Hood,* para. 57 and judgment of 14 March 2000, *Jordan,* para. 28.

[160]   Judgments of 22 May 1984, *De Jong, Baljet and Van den Brink,* para. 49 and *Van der Sluijs, Zuiderveld and Klappe,* para. 44.

[161]   In the cases against the Netherlands the Court used the word 'independent' instead of 'impartial'.

[162]   Judgment of 26 November 1992, para. 21. See also the judgment of 23 October 1990, *Huber,* para. 43. This case law is closely related to the case law concerning Art. 6(1).

not sufficiently independent properly to be described as an 'officer authorised by law to exercise judicial power' within the meaning of Article 5 (3).[163]

9.6.4   TRIAL WITHIN A REASONABLE TIME

Furthermore, the third paragraph contains for the person detained on remand the right to be tried within a reasonable time or otherwise to be released pending trial, if necessary subject to certain guarantees for his appearance at the trial. The way this provision is formulated seems at first sight to leave a free choice to the judicial authorities: either to prolong the detention on remand, provided that it has been imposed in accordance with paragraph 1(c), up to the moment of the judgment, which must then be given within a reasonable time, or to provisionally release the detainee pending trial, which trial would then no longer be subject to a given time-limit. Such an interpretation has been resolutely rejected by the Court. In the *Neumeister* Case the Court held with regard to Article 5(3) "that this provision cannot be understood as giving the judicial authorities a choice between either bringing the accused person to trial within a reasonable time or granting him provisional release even subject to guarantees. The reasonableness of the time spent by an accused person in detention up to the beginning of the trial must be assessed in relation to the very fact of his detention. Until conviction he must be presumed innocent, and the purpose of the provision under consideration is essentially to require his provisional release once his continuing detention ceases to be reasonable."[164] And in the *Wemhoff* Case the Court held as follows: "It is inconceivable that they [the Contracting States] should have intended to permit their judicial authorities, at the price of release of the accused, to protract proceedings beyond a reasonable time. This would, moreover, be flatly contrary to the provision in Article 6(1)."[165] The reference to Article 6(1) is indispensable for the Court's interpretation of Article 5(3); the word 'moreover', therefore, might as well have been omitted by the Court. In fact, as soon as the accused has been released, Article 5(3) is no longer applicable.[166] The obligation that in these cases, too, the trial takes place within a reasonable time, can be based only on Article 6(1). But precisely because Article 6(1) applies to all criminal proceedings, it is evident that Article 5(3) does not contain a choice between either release or trial within a reasonable time, but the obligation to keep a prisoner no longer in detention on remand than is reasonable and to try him within a reasonable time.

---

[163]   Judgment of 28 October 1998, *Assenov and Others*, para. 148. See also the judgment of 25 March 1999, *Nikolova*, para. 51.
[164]   Judgment of 27 June 1968, para. 4.
[165]   Judgment of 27 June 1968, para. 5.
[166]   See, *e.g.*, the judgment of 13 July 1995, *Van der Tang*, para. 58.

According to the quotation from the *Neumeister* Case, the Court does not associate the word 'reasonable' with the processing of the prosecution and the trial, but with the length of the detention. The long delay of the trial may in itself be reasonable in view, for instance, of the complexity of the case or the number of witnesses to be summoned, but this does not mean that the continued detention is therefore also reasonable. The Court takes the view that Article 5(3) refers to the latter aspect. This implies at the same time that the criteria for 'reasonable' in Article 5(3) are different from those for the same term in Article 6(1) or, at least, have to be applied in a different way.[167] Some delays may in fact violate Article 5(3) and still be compatible with Article 6(1).[168] This is also corroborated by the view of the Court in the *Wemhoff* Case, that "an accused person in detention is entitled to have his case given priority and conducted with particular expedition".[169]

With respect to the period that has to be taken into consideration for the determination of whether the trial has taken place within a reasonable time, the Court has taken the position in the *Wemhoff* Case that this is the period between the moment of arrest and that of the judgment at first instance.[170] If that judgment implies acquittal or discharge from further prosecution, at all events it will have to be followed by release, while in the case of conviction henceforth it is a matter of 'detention of a person after conviction' in the sense of Article 5(1)(a), to which the provisions concerning detention on remand no longer apply.[171] Later on the Court reaffirmed its position adopted in the *Wemhoff* Case; it may now be taken as established case law that the period to be taken into consideration ends with the pronouncement of the first-instance judgment.[172] Two different periods of detention on remand for the same charge, interrupted by a release, may be taken into consideration together when determining the total period and its reasonable character,[173] but they may also be assessed separately.[174] If a detention on remand has been preceded by a detention of another character or in relation to another criminal charge, the latter detention is not taken into consideration when determining the period to be considered in relation to the former one. The continuation of the detention pending appeal falls within the scope of Article 5(1) under (a). This period may not be taken into consideration when assessing whether the period is reasonable within the meaning of Article 5(3). If the first judgment is quashed, the period between the moment when the judgment is

---

[167]   The relation between the two provisions is dealt with explicitly in the judgments of 10 November 1969 in the *Stögmüller* Case and in the *Matznetter* Case, para. 5 and para 12, respectively.

[168]   Judgment of 10 November 1969, *Matznetter*, para. 12.

[169]   Judgment of 27 June 1968, para. 17.

[170]   *Ibidem,* paras 6-8.

[171]   *Ibidem*, para 9.

[172]   See, *e.g.* judgment of 28 March 1990, *B. v. Austria*, paras 34-40; judgment of 6 April 2000, *Labita*, para. 147; judgment of 15 July 2002, *Kalashnikov*, para. 110.

[173]   See, *e.g.,* the judgment of 26 June 1991, *Letellier*, para. 34.

[174]   Judgment of 27 November 1991, *Kemmache*, paras 46-48.

quashed and the moment when the second judgment is delivered must be taken into account to assess whether the length of the detention was reasonable.[175]

9.6.5   CONTINUED DETENTION

The persistence of the 'reasonable suspicion', as mentioned in subparagraph 5(1) under (c), is a condition *sine qua non* for the lawfulness of the continued detention.[176] When the 'reasonable suspicion' ceases to exist, the continued detention becomes unlawful and accordingly the question as to its reasonableness does not arise at all.

When is continued detention on remand to be considered reasonable? This question cannot be answered *in abstracto*; the answer depends on the special features of the case. For each individual case and at each moment the interests of the accused person will have to be weighed against the public interest, with due regard to the principle of the presumption of innocence.[177] The national authorities have to establish those relevant facts. It is not possible to shift the burden of proof to the detained person. That would be contrary to the principle that detention is an exceptional departure from the right to liberty and one that is only permissible in exhaustively enumerated and strictly defined cases.[178]

In the first instance this weighing is in the hands of the national authorities. They must set out the relevant arguments in their decisions on the applications for release.[179] The Court has clearly shown that it considers itself competent, on the basis of the reasons given in these decisions and the statements of the applicant, to review for their compatibility with the Convention the grounds on which a request for release has been rejected by the national authorities.[180] The mere fact that the 'reasonable suspicion' continues to exist is not sufficient, in the Court's opinion, to justify, after a certain lapse of time, the prolongation of the detention. According to the Court's case law, the question whether the period spent in detention on remand is reasonable, consists of two separate questions. The first question to be answered is whether the (other) grounds given by the national judicial authorities are 'relevant and sufficient' to justify the continued detention. If so, the second question to be answered is whether the national authorities displayed 'special diligence' in the conduct of the proceedings.

---

[175]   See, among others, judgment of 6 June 2000, *Cesky*, para. 71.
[176]   See, *e.g.*, the judgment of 10 November 1969, *Stögmüller*, para. 4; judgment of 27 August 1992, *Tomasi*, para. 84; judgment of 26 January 1993, *W. v. Switzerland*, para. 30; judgment of 6 April 2000, *Labita*, para. 152 and judgment of 9 January 2003, *Shishkov*, para. 58.
[177]   Judgment of 26 January 1993, *W v. Switzerland*, para. 30; judgment of 6 April 2000, *Labita*, para. 152.
[178]   Judgment of 26 July 2001, *Ilijkov*, para. 85.
[179]   See, *e.g.*, the judgment of 26 June 1991, *Letellier*, para. 35; judgment of 27 November 1991, *Kemmache*, para. 45; judgment of 27 August 1992, *Tomasi*, para. 84; and judgment of 8 June 1995, *Mansur*, para. 52.
[180]   *Ibidem.*

If they did, the period spent in detention can be considered reasonable.[181] However, in case the first or second question is to be answered in the negative, the period of detention on remand did exceed a 'reasonable time'.

Various grounds have been adduced by the national authorities to justify the continued detention. Thus, for example, in the *Neumeister* Case, the *Stögmüller* Case and the *Matznetter* Case the Court held that the danger of flight, even if it had initially constituted a sufficient ground for the detention on remand, afterwards had ceased to exist as a ground, specifically because of the possibility of bail.[182] The danger of absconding cannot be gauged solely on the basis of the severity of the sentence risked; it must be assessed with reference to a number of other relevant factors, such as the character of the person involved, his morals, his assets and his contacts abroad.[183]

The risk of a further offence is the other ground mentioned in paragraph 1(c). In the *Clooth* Case the danger of repetition was founded on the psychological deficiencies of the applicant. Nine months after the beginning of the detention an expert report described the applicant as dangerous and mentioned the need for him to be taken into psychiatric care. In these circumstances the national courts should not extend the period of detention on remand without ordering an accompanying therapeutic measure. They did not order such a measure, consequently the risk of repetition was not sufficient to justify the continued detention.[184] The Court considered that the mere reference to a person's antecedents cannot suffice to justify refusing release.[185] When reviewing the lawfulness of the (prolongation of the) detention, the Court does not consider itself confined to the grounds for detention on remand expressly mentioned in paragraph 1(c), but has also accepted as such grounds the risk of suppression of evidence,[186] the seriousness of the offence in connection with the public order,[187] the safety of a person under investigation[188], (implicitly) the danger of subornation of wit-

---

[181] See, *e.g.*, the judgment of 10 November 1969, *Matznetter*, para 12; judgment of 26 June 1991, *Letellier*, para. 35; judgment of 26 January 1993, *W. v. Switzerland*, para. 30; judgment of 8 June 1995, *Mansur*, para. 52; judgment of 17 March 1997, *Muller*, para. 35; judgment of 6 April 2000, *Labita*, paras 152-153 and judgment of 9 January 2003, *Shishkov*, para. 58.

[182] Judgment of 27 June 1968, paras 7-14, and judgments of 10 November 1969, *Stögmüller*, para 15 and *Matznetter*, para 11, respectively. In the *Wemhoff Case*, the Court involved in its different finding the fact that on the part of the detainee there was no evident willingness to give bail; judgment of 27 June 1968, para. 15.

[183] See, *e.g.*, judgment of 26 June 1991, *Letellier*, para. 43; judgment 27 August 1992, *Tomasi*, para. 98; judgment of 26 January 1993, *W. v. Switzerland*, para. 33; judgment 17 March 1997, *Muller*, para. 43.

[184] Judgment of 12 December 1991, para. 40.

[185] See also the judgment of 17 March 1997, *Muller*, para. 44.

[186] Judgment of 27 June 1968, *Wemhoff*, para. 14.

[187] Judgment of 27 November 1991, *Kemmache*, para. 49; judgment of 27 August 1992, *Tomasi*, paras 86-91, judgment of 23 September 1998, *I.A. v. France*, para. 104; judgment of 13 February 2001, *Gombert and Gochgarian*, para. 46.

[188] Judgment of 23 September 1998, *I.A. v. France*, para. 108.

nesses,[189] the danger of collusion[190] and the risk of pressure being brought to a witness.[191]

In the *Letellier* Case the French Government relied among other arguments on the preservation of public order to justify the continued detention. The Court held that, at least for a time, grave offences may give rise to a 'social disturbance' capable of justifying pre-trial detention. However, it added that "this ground can be regarded as relevant and sufficient only provided that it is based on facts capable of showing that the accused's release would actually disturb public order. In addition detention will continue to be legitimate only if public order remains actually threatened."[192] This wording, that can be regarded as established case law,[193] places the national courts under the obligation to state their reasons carefully when deciding to prolong the detention on remand. The mere use of stereotype criteria referring to the requirements of public order will not suffice for the purpose of Article 5(3). This conclusion *mutatis mutandis* seems to hold good for the other grounds capable of justifying the continued detention on remand.[194] In the *Labita* Case the grounds of the continued detention were the risk of pressure being brought to bear on witnesses and of evidence being tampered with, the fact that the accused were dangerous, the complexity of the case and the requirements of the investigation. The Court considered the grounds very general, but reasonable, at least initially. The grounds were not considered sufficient, however, to justify the applicant's being kept in detention for two years and seven months. Some grounds, like the risk of tampering with evidence, can lose their strength after a certain lapse of time.[195] In the *Labita* Case the allegations against the applicant came from a single source, a *pentito*. The Court considered that a suspect may validly be detained at the beginning of proceedings on the basis of statements by *pentiti*. Such statements become, because of their ambiguous nature, necessarily less relevant with the passage of time, especially where no further evidence is uncovered during the course of the investigation. The same reservations must be made with respect to hearsay evidence.[196]

---

[189]   See the judgment of 16 July 1971, *Ringeisen*, paras 105-106.

[190]   Judgment of 28 March 1990, *B. v. Austria*, paras 42-43; judgment of 12 December 1991, *Clooth*, para. 43; judgment of 26 January 1993, *W. v. Switzerland*, para. 35.

[191]   Judgment of 26 June 1991, *Letellier*, para. 39; judgment of 27 November 1991, *Kemmache*, para. 53; judgment of 27 August 1992, *Tomasi*, para. 95; judgment of 6 April 2000, *Labita*, paras 156-161.

[192]   Judgment of 26 June 1991, para. 51.

[193]   See the judgment of 27 November 1991, *Kemmache*, para. 52; judgment of 27 August 1992, *Tomasi*, para. 91; judgment of 23 September 1998, *I.A. v. France*, para. 104; judgment of 13 February 2001, *Gombert and Gochgarian*, para. 46.

[194]   See, *e.g.*, the judgment of 11 December 2003, *Yankov*, para. 172.

[195]   See also the judgment of 26 June 1991, *Letellier*, para. 39; judgment of 12 December 1991, *Clooth*, para. 43; judgment of 27 August 1992, *Tomasi*, para. 95; judgment of 26 January 1993, *W. v. Switzerland*, para. 35; judgment of 16 November 2000, *Vaccaro*, para. 38.

[196]   Judgment of 6 April 2000, paras 156-161.

Generalizations and Article 5(3) appear not to fit very well together. A system that excludes any possibility of the release of a person against whom more than one investigation is pending, is incompatible with Article 5(3).[197] However, the Court accepted in the *Pantano* Case in the specific circumstances of the crimes of the mafia a legal presumption of dangerousness. It was relevant that this presumption was not absolute.[198]

As has been observed above, if the prolongation of the detention on remand is based on well-founded reasons, the question remains whether the authorities showed 'special diligence' in the conduct of the proceedings. Article 5(3) does not imply a maximum length of pre-trial detention; the reasonableness cannot be assessed in the abstract.[199] The case law shows that even a very long duration of the detention on remand – in *W v. Switzerland* this was slightly more than four years – may still be deemed acceptable. On the other hand, in the *Shishkov* Case a period of approximately seven months and three weeks was considered to exceed the reasonable time, while in the *Belchev* Case even a period of four months and fourteen days constituted a violation of Article 5(3). The Court motivated, against the background of the relatively short periods, that Article 5(3) does not authorise pre-trial detention that lasts no longer than a certain minimum period. Justification for any period of detention, no matter how short, must be convincingly demonstrated by the authorities.[200]

With regard to the criteria by which the reasonableness of the duration of the procedure is to be assessed, three factors seem to be of crucial importance: the complexity of the case, the conduct of the detainee and the conduct of the authorities. In case the length of a period spent in detention on remand does not appear to be essentially attributable either to the complexity of the case or to the applicant's conduct[201] and the authorities did not act with the necessary promptness, Article 5(3) is violated.[202] If a detention on remand has been preceded by a detention of another character or in relation to another criminal charge, the latter detention is not taken into consideration when determining *the period* to be considered in relation to the former one. However, that preceding detention must be taken into account in assessing the *reasonable character* of the period spent in detention on remand.[203] The Court examines

---

[197] See the judgment of 11 December 2003, *Yankov*, para. 173.

[198] Judgment of 6 November 2003, paras 69-70.

[199] Judgment of 27 June 1968, *Wemhoff*, para 10, and judgment of 26 January 1993, *W. v. Switzerland*, para. 30.

[200] Judgment of 9 January 2003, *Shishkov*, para. 66; judgment of 8 April 2004, *Belchev*, para. 82.

[201] The right of a prisoner on remand "to have his case examined with particular expedition must not unduly hinder the efforts of the judicial authorities". See, *e.g.*, the judgment of 12 December 1991, *Toth*, para. 77.

[202] See the judgment of 12 December 1991, *Toth*, para. 77 and the judgment of 27 August 1992, *Tomasi*, para. 102.

[203] Judgment of 8 June 1995, *Mansur*, para. 51.

whether there have been periods of inactivity without a justification. In the *Kalashnikov* Case there had been significant delays in the proceedings. The hearing had to be postponed on account of the absence of the applicant's lawyer. The Court found that the applicant did not substantially contribute to the length of the proceedings. The proceedings exceeded a reasonable time.[204]

Article 5(3) expressly allows for making the release of the person detained on remand dependent on guarantees to appear for trial. The rationale of this is obvious: if and as long as prolongation of the detention would be allowed, certain guarantees may be asked for release. The provision is important in particular because of the obligation and the limitations resulting from it for the national authorities.

Although Article 5(3) does not guarantee an absolute right to release on bail, the possibility of demanding bail laid down there entails for the judicial authorities the obligation to ascertain whether by means of such a guarantee the same purpose can be achieved as is aimed at by the detention on remand. In the *Jablonski* Case the domestic courts did not take into account any other guarantees that the applicant would appear for trial. The Court concluded that the prolonged detention could not be considered as necessary from the point of view of ensuring the due course of the proceedings.[205]

In the case law four basic acceptable reasons for refusing bail can be distinguished: the risk that the accused will fail to appear for trial and the risk that the accused, if released, would take action to prejudice the administration of justice, commit further offences, or cause public disorder. If there are sufficient indications and guarantees for a bail, but this possibility is not offered to the detainee, the detention loses its reasonable, and as a consequence also its lawful, character. This will be the case in particular if the only ground for the detention is the risk of flight.[206] If the detainee declines the offer without suggesting an acceptable alternative, he has only himself to blame for the continued detention.[207] On the other hand, the guarantee demanded for release must not impose heavier burdens on the person in question than are required for obtaining a reasonable degree of security. If, for instance, the detainee is required to give bail the amount of which he cannot possibly raise, while it may be assumed that a lower sum would also provide adequate security for his compliance with a summons to appear for trial, the prolongation of the detention is unreasonable.[208] This also means that the nature and the amount of the security demanded must be related to

---

[204]   Judgment of 15 July 2002, para. 120.

[205]   Judgment of 21 December 2000, para. 84.

[206]   Thus also the Court in the *Wemhoff Case,* judgment of 27 June 1968, para. 15. See further the judgment of 26 June 1991, *Letellier,* para. 64 and the report of 11 December 1980, *Schertenleib,* D&R 23 (1981), p. 137 (195).

[207]   In the Court's opinion that was the situation in the *Wemhoff Case,* judgment of 27 June 1968.

[208]   Judgment of 27 June 1968, *Neumeister,* paras 12-15.

the grounds on which the detention on remand is based; thus, in the determination of the amount the damage caused by the accused may not be taken into account. On the other hand, the financial situation of the person concerned and/or his relation to the person who stands bail for him must be taken into consideration. The amount of the bail must be assessed principally in relation to the person concerned.[209] The accused must provide the requisite information about this, but this does not relieve the authorities from the duty of making an inquiry into it themselves, in order to be able to decide on the possibility of releasing him on bail.[210] In the *Iwanczuk* Case the inquiry about the sum and form of the bail lasted four months and fourteen days after the competent judicial authority found prolonged detention on remand unnecessary. The applicant had promptly provided the relevant information as to its assets. In view of these facts, the Court concluded that Article 5(3) was violated.

9.7 HABEAS CORPUS

9.7.1 GENERAL OBSERVATIONS

Article 5(4) grants to everyone who is deprived of his liberty by arrest or detention the right to take proceedings by which the lawfulness of such deprivation of liberty will be reviewed speedily by a court and his release ordered if the latter decides that the detention is unlawful. This resembles the remedy of *habeas corpus*, originating from English law.

The fourth paragraph constitutes an independent provision: even if the Court has found that the first paragraph has not been violated and that the detention, accordingly, had a lawful character, an inquiry into the possible violation of the fourth paragraph may nevertheless be made.[211] This implies that even if the review by the Court leads to the conclusion that the detention was lawful, an assessment must be made of whether the detained person at the time had the possibility to have the lawfulness reviewed by a domestic court. The procedure of paragraph 4 must, therefore, also be considered as independent of the possibility of applying for release on bail.[212]

The fourth paragraph of Article 5, like the second paragraph, requires that the arrested person be informed of the reasons of his arrest in order to be in a position to take proceedings with a view to having the lawfulness of his detention determined.[213] In *X. v. the United Kingdom* the Court considered that the issue under Article 5(2) was

---

[209]   See, *e.g.*, the judgment of 15 November 2001, *Iwanczuk*, para. 66.
[210]   Report of 11 December 1980, *Schertenleib*, D&R 23 (1981), p. 137 (197).
[211]   See, *inter alia*, the judgment of 24 October 1979, *Winterwerp*, para. 53 and the judgment of 24 September 1992, *Kolompar*, para. 45.
[212]   Report of 11 October 1983, *Zamir*, D&R 40 (1985), p. 42 (59).
[213]   Judgment of 5 November 1981, *X. v. the United Kingdom*, para 66.

absorbed by the fact that a violation was found of Article 5(4).[214] In the *Van der Leer* Case it stated, on the other hand, that it was not necessary to examine the question of information under paragraph 4 because it dealt with it under the second paragraph.[215]

9.7.2 APPLICABILITY

The *habeas corpus* guarantees extend to all cases of deprivation of liberty provided for in the first paragraph of Article 5. The content of the obligation is not necessarily the same in all circumstances and as regards every category of deprivation of liberty.[216] Where a national court, after convicting a person of a criminal offence, imposes a fixed sentence of imprisonment for the purposes of punishment, the supervision required by Article 5(4) is incorporated in that court decision. This view is based on the assumption that in those cases the judicial review of the lawfulness of the detention, which is guaranteed by Article 5(4), has already taken place. This situation must be distinguished from situations in which an indeterminate sanction is imposed. In *X. v. the United Kingdom* the applicant was convicted of causing bodily harm and was committed to a mental hospital for an indefinite period. According to the Court this deprivation of liberty fell, initially at least, within the ambit of both Article 5(1)(a) and Article 5(1)(e). The Court held that "By virtue of Article 5 § 4, a person of unsound mind compulsorily confined in a psychiatric institution for an indefinite or lengthy period is thus in principle entitled, at any rate where there is no automatic periodic review of a judicial character, to take proceedings at reasonable intervals before a court to put in issue the 'lawfulness' (...) of his detention, whether that detention was ordered by a civil or criminal court or by some other authority."[217]

The *Van Droogenbroeck* Case concerned the placing of a recidivist at the Government's disposal for ten years by court order. This order was given together with a sentence to two years imprisonment. On the completion of his principal sentence Van Droogenbroeck was placed in semi-custodial care, but he disappeared and, after his arrest, was sent to prison by a decision of the Minister of Justice. Although the Court held that the resulting deprivation of liberty occurred 'after conviction' in accordance with Article 5(1)(a), it considered the fourth paragraph of Article 5 to be applicable,

---

214 *Ibidem.*
215 Judgment of 21 February 1990, para. 34.
216 Judgment of 5 November 1981, *X. v. the United Kingdom*, para. 52; judgment of 20 January 2004, *König*, para. 19.
217 Judgment of 5 November 1981, para. 52. The Court, moreover, emphasised that given the scheme of Article 5, read as a whole, the notion of 'lawfulness' implies that the same deprivation of liberty should have the same significance in paragraphs 1(e) and 4. See also the judgment of 28 May 1985, *Ashingdane*, paras 51-52.

which required in the instant case "an appropriate procedure allowing a court to determine 'speedily' (...) whether the Minister of Justice was entitled to hold that detention was still consistent with the object and purpose of the 1964 Act."[218]

The same line of reasoning was followed in the *Weeks* Case. The applicant, at the age of 17, was convicted of armed robbery and sentenced to life imprisonment. This sanction was not imposed because of the gravity of the offence. The sentencing judge took account of the age and dangerous and unstable personality of the convict and decided that he should impose the sentence of life imprisonment to enable the Secretary of State to release him whenever he had become responsible with the passing of years. After nearly ten years the applicant was released on licence, but subsequently this license was revoked. He complained that he had not been able, either on his recall to prison or at reasonable intervals throughout his detention, to take proceedings as required by Article 5(4). The Court stated that the decisions of the executive to release or to re-detain the applicant should be consistent with the objectives of the sentencing court. If not, the detention would no longer be lawful for the purposes of subparagraph (a). Because the grounds relied on by the sentencing judges for deciding that the length of deprivation should be subject to the discretion of the executive were "by their nature susceptible of change", the Court concluded that Mr Weeks was entitled to take proceedings as mentioned under paragraph 4.[219]

In the *Thynne, Wilson and Gunnel* Case each of the applicants had committed grave offences and had been sentenced to life imprisonment. The question of whether this sentence should be imposed was at the discretion of the trial judge. In addition to the need of punishment the applicants were considered to be suffering from a mental disturbance and to be dangerous and in need of treatment. The discretionary life sentence was imposed to enable the administration to assess their improvements and to act accordingly. The Court decided, in line of the *Weeks* Case, that the applicants were entitled to take proceedings, but it had to establish from what point in time this would be the case. To this end it distinguished between the punitive and the security element of the sentence[220] and concluded that the punitive period of the life imprisonment had expired.[221] According to the judgment in the *Stafford* Case, this distinction is also applicable to mandatory life sentences.[222] To sum up, in fact the Court distinguishes between 'the conviction by a competent court' in the sense of Article 5(1)(a) as "the decision depriving a person of his liberty", on the one hand, and the "ensuing period of detention in which new issues affecting the lawfulness of the detention might subsequently arise", on the other hand. The 'conviction' does not

---

[218]   Judgment of 24 June 1982, para. 49.
[219]   Judgment of 2 March 1987, para. 59.
[220]   This distinction was confirmed by English law, at least according to the Court. The Government took the opposite view.
[221]   Judgment of 25 October 1990, paras 71-78.
[222]   Judgment of 28 May 2002, paras 87-89.

purport to deal with the latter period. Thus, whenever the latter period starts, the lawfulness of the detention is no longer incorporated in the initial conviction.

In connection with the fourth paragraph, the Court takes account not only of the formal existence of remedies in the legal system of the Contracting Party concerned, but also of the context in which they operate and the personal circumstances of the applicant. The domestic remedies have to be sufficiently certain, otherwise the require-ments of accessibility and effectiveness are not fulfilled.[223] In *R.M.D. v. Switzerland* the applicant was in a position of great legal uncertainty. He had to expect to be transferred from one canton to another at any moment, in which situation eventuality the courts of the transferring canton no longer had jurisdiction to decide the lawfulness of his detention; that rendered any remedy ineffective, which led to a violation of Article 5(4).[224]

Does the fourth paragraph also apply to the detention on remand, now that the third paragraph already prescribes that an accused person, after his arrest, shall be brought promptly before a judge or other officer authorised by law to exercise judicial power? Even in the case that the person in question has thus been brought to trial it can hardly be said that he has been able to exercise the right 'to take proceedings', while moreover not in all cases there is a decision on the lawfulness of the detention by a 'court' in the strict sense. The position would, therefore, appear justifiable that in certain cases Article 5(4) grants to the person detained on remand a right of (periodic) recourse to a court after the (judicial) decision to detain him or to prolong the detention has been taken.[225] In the *De Jong, Baljet and Van den Brink* Case the Court reached the same conclusion by holding that the procedure, prescribed in Article 5(3), "may admit-tedly have a certain incidence on compliance with paragraph 4. For example, where that procedure culminates in a decision by a 'court' ordering or confirming deprivation of the person's liberty, the judicial control of lawfulness required by paragraph 4 is incorporated in this initial decision. (...) However, the guarantee assured by paragraph 4 is of a different order from, and additional to, that provided by paragraph 3."[226]

In the *Toth* Case the Court held that Article 5(4) did not cover proceedings instituted by an investigating judge for the extension of the pre-trial period. The national court that had to decide on the request of the judge, had to confine itself to

---

[223]   See, among others, judgment of 24 June 1982, *Van Droogenbroeck*, para. 54 and judgment of 26 November 1997, *Sakik*, para 53.

[224]   Judgment of 26 September 1997, *R.M.D. v. Switzerland*, para. 47.

[225]   See Recommendation R(80)11 of the Committee of Ministers of 27 June 1980 on detention on remand, Article 14 of which provides: "Custody pending trial shall be reviewed at reasonably short intervals which the law or the judicial authority shall fix. In such a review, account shall be taken of all the changes in circumstances which have occurred since the person concerned was placed in custody".

[226]   Judgment of 22 May 1984, para. 57. See also the judgment of 25 October 1989, *Bezicheri*, para. 20.

'setting out a framework' within which the investigating judge was free to take decisions. The national court itself did not review the 'lawfulness' of the detention, nor gave it a decision on the question of whether the applicant should be released.[227]

9.7.3 REVIEW OF LAWFULNESS AT REASONABLE INTERVALS

In the *Winterwerp* Case the Court took the view that a case of detention of a person of unsound mind "would appear to require a review of lawfulness to be available at reasonable intervals".[228] This requirement was initially solely connected with persons of unsound mind.[229] In the *Bezicheri* Case, however, the applicant was detained on remand. Subsequent to a first judicial review of the lawfulness of the detention, he was, according to the Court, entitled "after a reasonable interval, to take proceedings by which the lawfulness of his continued detention" was decided.[230]

According to established case law the right to take proceedings exists *at any rate* where there is no "automatic periodic review of a judicial character".[231] It is not yet clear if this right also exists in case the national legislation does provide for such a system. Anyway, the wording of paragraph 4 suggests an answer in the affirmative. On the other hand, one might presume that the national authorities must be left the possibility to reject an application for judicial review if no new facts are adduced and if shortly before an automatic periodic review of judicial character amounted to a negative decision for the applicant.[232] In the *Bezicheri* Case, the person concerned, detained under Article 5(3), submitted his application for release one month after the first judicial review. The Italian Government argued that this period was too short to be reasonable, but the Court held that "detention on remand calls for short intervals". Consequently, in this case a period of one month was not unreasonable. In the *De Jong, Baljet and Van den Brink* Case the applicants were in remand seven, eleven and six days respectively without any remedy against their deprivation of liberty. The Court held that this amounted to be a breach of Article 5(4).[233]

---

[227] Judgment of 12 December 1991, para. 57.
[228] Judgment of 24 October 1979, para 55. See also the judgment of 23 February 1984, *Luberti*, para. 31, and the judgment of 22 May 1984, *De Jong, Baljet and Van den Brink*, para. 57.
[229] See, *e.g.*, the judgment of 23 February 1984, *Luberti*, p. 31.
[230] Judgment of 25 October 1989, para. 20. The restriction to 'persons of unsound mind' was reiterated in the judgment of 12 May 1992, *Megyeri*, para. 22, but, on the other hand, was lacking in the judgment of 23 November 1993, *Navarra*, para. 26 (concerning a prisoner on remand).
[231] See, *e.g.*, the judgment of 5 November 1981, *X v. the United Kingdom*, para. 52; judgment of 12 May 1992, *Megyeri*, para. 22.
[232] Compare the report of the Commission of 15 December 1977, *Winterwerp*, B.31 (1983), para. 94 and para. 109.
[233] Judgment of 22 May 1984, paras 58-59.

In case of detention of persons of unsound mind, the intervals can be longer than in case of detention under Article 5(3). In the *Herczegfalvy* Case concerning the automatic periodic review of the detention of a person of unsound mind, intervals of fifteen months and two years, respectively, between two judicial decisions were not considered as 'reasonable intervals'. However, a period of nine months was not criticised by the Court and, therefore, seemed to meet the requirements of the fourth paragraph.[234]

Life sentences may be imposed on offenders due to considerations of mental instability and dangerousness. These circumstances may change over the passage of time. In the *Oldham* Case the applicant, who was sentenced to life imprisonment, complained that a two-year delay between his Parole Board Reviews was unreasonable. The Court shared this opinion. The Court was not satisfied that the period of two years was justified by considerations of rehabilitation and monitoring and took into consideration that the courses that the applicant underwent to address his problems were concluded within eight months of his recall.[235] The Court seems to require a certain flexibility in determining the period, which must reflect the fact that there are significant differences in the personal circumstances of the prisoners under review.

9.7.4   REVIEW BY A COURT

Paragraph 4 entitles the accused to a decision by a 'court'. In the *Neumeister* Case, the Court indicated as the decisive criterion that the competent authority "must be independent both of the executive and of the parties to the case".[236] Subsequently the Court added that the right to judicial review is not of such a scope as to empower the national courts to substitute their own discretion for that of the decision-making authority on questions of pure expediency.[237] To satisfy the requirements of the Convention the review of the national court should comply with both the substantial and procedural rules of the national legislation and be conducted in conformity with the aim of Article 5, the protection of the individual against arbitrariness.[238] What guarantees must be attached to the procedure under the fourth paragraph of Article 5 must be judged by the circumstances of each case, in which context in particular the consequences resulting for the person concerned from the decision to be taken in that

---

[234]   Judgment of 24 September 1992, para. 77.

[235]   Judgment of 26 September 2000, *Oldham*, paras 34-35.

[236]   Judgment of 27 June 1968, para. 24. In this case the procedure itself was not yet considered decisive by the Court. See also the judgment of 18 June 1971, *De Wilde, Ooms and Versyp ('Vagrancy'* Cases), para. 78; judgment of 25 October 1989, *Bezicheri*, para. 20.

[237]   See, e.g., the judgment of 24 June 1982, *Van Droogenbroeck*, para. 49; judgment of 29 August 1990, *E. v. Norway*, para. 50; judgment of 25 October 1990, *Thynne, Wilson and Gunnell*, para. 79.

[238]   Judgments of 25 October 1990, *Koendjbiharie*, para. 27, and *Keus*, para. 66.

procedure must be considered.[239] Consequently, the guarantees which the procedure of Article 5(4) must afford need not necessarily be the same as those prescribed in Article 6(1) for a 'fair trial'.[240] Nevertheless, because of the impact of deprivation of liberty on the fundamental rights of the person concerned, proceedings conducted under Article 5(4) should in principle also meet, to the largest extent possible under the circumstances of an ongoing investigation, the basic requirements of a fair trial.[241] The proceeding must have a judicial character and provide guarantees appropriate to the kind of deprivation of liberty in question. The practical realities and the specific circumstances of the detained person must be taken into consideration.[242]

The procedure must be adversarial and must always ensure 'equality of arms' between the parties.[243] Equality of arms is not ensured if counsel is denied access to those documents in the investigation file which are essential in order effectively to challenge the lawfulness of his client's detention.[244] The authorities should ensure that both parties have the opportunity to be aware that observations have been filed and have a real opportunity to comment thereon.[245] Whether or not a submission by the prosecution deserves a reaction is a matter for the defence to assess.[246] Article 5(4) does not impose an obligation on a court examining an appeal against detention to address every argument contained in the appellant's submissions. However, the court cannot treat as irrelevant, or disregard, concrete facts invoked by the detainee and capable of putting into doubt the existence of the conditions essential for the 'lawfulness', in the sense of the Convention, of the deprivation of liberty.[247] In the *Lamy* Case the applicant's counsel did not have the opportunity to effectively challenge the statements or views which the prosecution based on these documents, while it was essential to inspect the documents in question in order to challenge the lawfulness of the arrest warrant effectively. Article 5(4) was violated.[248]

The Court recognises that the use of confidential material may be unavoidable where national security is at stake. This does not mean, however, that the national authorities are released from effective control by the domestic courts whenever they choose to assert that national security and terrorism are involved. The Court takes into account that techniques may be employed which both accommodate legitimate security concerns about the nature and sources of intelligence information and yet

---

[239] Judgment of 18 June 1971, *De Wilde, Ooms and Versyp* ('*Vagrancy*' Cases), para. 42.
[240] Judgment of 24 October 1979, *Winterwerp*, para. 60; judgment of 12 May 1992, *Megyeri*, para. 24.
[241] Judgment of 13 February 2001, *Schöps*, para. 44; judgment of 31 January 2002, *Lanz*, para. 41.
[242] Judgment of 9 January 2003, *Shishkov*, para. 85.
[243] See, *e.g.*, judgment of 21 October 1986, *Sanchez-Reisse*, para. 51; judgment of 25 March 1999, *Nikolova*, paras 58-59; judgment of 31 January 2002, *Lanz*, para 44.
[244] Judgment of 13 February 2001, *Garcia Alva*, para. 39.
[245] Judgment of 13 February 2001, *Schöps*, para. 44.
[246] Judgment of 31 January 2002, *Lanz*, para. 44.
[247] Judgment of 25 March 1999, *Nikolova*, para. 61; judgment of 26 July 2001, *Ilijkov*, para. 94.
[248] Judgment of 30 March 1989, para. 29.

accord the individual a substantial measure of procedural justice.[249] It is for the authorities to prove that an individual satisfies the conditions for detention.[250]

In the case of a person whose detention falls within the ambit of Article 5(1) under (c), a hearing is required.[251] The detainee must have adequate time to prepare the hearing.[252] Article 5(4) does not as a general rule require such a hearing to be public.[253]

In the *Winterwerp* Case the detention of a person of 'unsound mind' under paragraph 1(e) was at stake. The Court considered it essential for the person concerned to have access to court and to be enabled to be heard in person or, if necessary, through a representative. According to the Court it is possible that the mental condition of the person makes specific restrictions or derogations necessary as to the exercise of this right, but this cannot in any case justify an encroachment on the right in its essence, but on the contrary calls for special procedural guarantees.[254] The Court concluded that in this case the initial decision of detention was not taken by a 'court' and that later the applicant did not have access to a 'judicial procedure'.[255] In the *Megyeri* Case the national court had to assess whether the continued detention of the applicant was necessary. The applicant was heard in person but that did not meet the requirements of Article 5(4). The Court considered it doubtful whether the applicant was capable of adequately presenting the relevant points. It concluded, also taking into consideration the fact that the applicant had spent more than four years in a psychiatric hospital, that a counsel should have been appointed to assist the applicant in the proceedings.[256] The same point of view was adopted by the Court in the *Bouamar* Case, taking into consideration, *inter alia,* that the proceedings concerned a juvenile,[257] and in the *Magalhaes Pereira* Case. In the last mentioned case the decision to continue the detention relied, *inter alia,* on a medical report that had been obtained a year and eight months beforehand that did not necessarily reflect the applicant's condition at the time of the decision. The Court considered that a delay of that length between the preparation of a medical report and the decision whether or not the detention must be continued, in itself can run counter to the principle of protecting individuals from arbitrariness.[258]

In the *Sanchez-Reisse* Case the applicant, against whom action had been taken with a view to extradition, complained about the fact that he had not been able to apply

---

[249]   Judgment of 15 November 1996, *Chahal,* para. 131; judgment of 20 June 2002, *Al-Nashif,* para. 95.
[250]   Judgment of 20 February 2003, *Hutchison Reid,* para. 70.
[251]   Judgment of 4 December 1979, *Schiesser,* paras 30-31; judgment of 21 October 1986, *Sanchez-Reisse,* para. 51; judgment of 25 March 1999, *Nikolova,* para. 58.
[252]   Judgment of 24 June 2004, *Frommelt,* para. 33.
[253]   Judgment of 15 November 2005, *Reinprecht,* paras 38-41.
[254]   Judgment of 24 October 1979, para. 60.
[255]   *Ibidem,* para 67. See also the judgment of 21 February 1990, *Van der Leer,* paras 32-36.
[256]   Judgment of 12 May 1992, para. 25.
[257]   Judgment of 29 February 1988, paras 59-60.
[258]   Judgment of 26 February 2002, para. 49.

directly to a court. However, the Strasbourg Court had no objections to the requirement of a previous administrative procedure, provided that this did not violate the 'speed'-requirement.[259] In the *Singh* Case and the *Hussain* Case the Court held that the lack of an oral and adversarial hearing in the proceedings before the Parole Board could not be compensated by the possibility of instituting proceedings for judicial review. It was crucial for the Court that the applicants risked a considerable term of imprisonment and that the decision which had to be taken by the Parole Board on the dangerousness of the applicants involved questions with regard to their "personality and level of maturity".[260] In the *Wassink* Case a failure to comply with national law (according to the Court the requirement concerned was not an essential one) did not lead to the conclusion that Article 5(4) was violated.[261]

Article 5(4) does not stipulate the requirement of the court's independence and impartiality and thus differs from Article 6(1). However, the Court has held that independence is one of the most important constitutive elements of the notion of a 'court' and that it would be inconceivable that Article 5(4) should not equally envisage the impartiality of that court. In *D.N. v.* Switzerland the Court assessed the impartiality of a judge in conformity with the jurisprudence concerning Article 6(1). One of the judges – the only psychiatrist of the court – had previously given an expert opinion on the state of health of the detainee. The Court concluded that the circumstances of the case served objectively to justify the applicant's apprehension that the judge lacked the necessary impartiality.[262]

Article 5(4) does not require the institution of a second level of proceedings.[263] The intervention of one organ satisfies Article 5(4), on condition that the procedure has a judicial character and gives to the detainee guarantees appropriate to the kind of deprivation of liberty in question. However, in principle, if the question of whether the detained person should be released will be heard on appeal, then the Contracting States must offer the persons concerned the same guarantees as at first instance.[264]

In the *Brannigan and McBride* Case the Court concluded that the right, laid down in Article 5(4), is a *lex specialis* in relation to the right to an effective remedy, laid down in Article 13.[265]

---

[259] Judgment of 21 October 1986, paras 17 and 54.
[260] Judgments of 21 February 1996, paras 68-69 and paras 60-61, respectively.
[261] Judgment of 27 September 1990, paras 33-34.
[262] Judgment of 29 March 2001, *D.N. v. Switzerland*, paras 44-56.
[263] Judgment of 31 July 2000, *Jecius*, para. 100; judgment of 31 January 2002, *Lanz*, para. 42.
[264] Judgment of 12 December 1991, *Toth*, para. 84, and judgment of 23 November 1993, *Navarra*, para. 28.
[265] Judgment of 26 May 1993, para. 76.

9.7.5   SPEEDY DECISION

Paragraph 4 explicitly requires that the judicial review shall take place 'speedily'. Compliance must be assessed in the light of the specific circumstances of the case.[266] The complexity of medical issues involved in a determination of whether a person can be released may be taken into account.[267] With regard to the period that has to be taken into consideration the Court has taken as a starting point the day the application for release has been made. The relevant period comes to an end on the day the court has given judgment.[268] If the proceedings have been conducted at two levels of jurisdiction an overall assessment must be made in order to determine whether the requirement of 'speedily' has been complied with.[269]

In assessing the speedy character required by paragraph 4 comparable factors may be taken into consideration as those which play a role with respect to the requirement of trial within a reasonable time under Article 5(3) and under Article 6(1), such as, for instance, the conduct of the applicant and the way the authorities have handled the case.[270] Neither an excessive workload,[271] nor a vacation period[272] can justify a period of inactivity on the part of the judicial authorities.

The notion of 'speedily' ('à bref délai') indicates a lesser urgency than that of 'promptly' ('aussitôt') in Article 5(3).[273] In the *Sanchez-Reisse* Case the time which elapsed between the lodging of two requests and the decisions thereon, 31 days and 46 days, respectively, did not satisfy the 'speed'-requirement of Article 5(4). In the *Rehbock* Case a period of 23 days on remand was not considered 'speedily'.[274] In the *Kadem* Case the same conclusion was reached with respect to extradition proceedings for a period of 17 days.[275] With respect to a period of nearly one year and five months in which six judicial decisions were given[276], the Court expressed certain doubts about the overall length of the period. Nevertheless, it took into consideration the fact that the applicant had retained the right to submit further applications for release, which

---

[266] See, *e.g.*, the judgment of 21 October 1986, *Sanchez-Reisse*, para. 55, and the judgment of 29 August 1990, *E. v. Norway*, para. 64.

[267] Judgment of 21 December 2000, *Jablonski*, para. 92.

[268] See, *e.g.*, the judgment of 21 October 1986, *Sanchez-Reiss*, para. 54, and the judgment of 29 August 1990, *E. v. Norway*, para. 64.

[269] See, *e.g.*, the judgment of 23 February 1984, *Luberti*, para. 33, and the judgment of 23 November 1993, *Navarra*, para. 28.

[270] See, *e.g.*, the judgment of 23 February 1984, *Luberti*, paras 30-37, and the judgment of 21 February 1990, *Van der Leer*, para. 36.

[271] See, *e.g.*, the judgment of 25 October 1990, *Bezicheri*, para. 25.

[272] Judgment of 29 August 1990, *E. v. Norway*, para. 66.

[273] *Ibidem*, para. 64.

[274] Judgment of 28 November 2000, paras 85-86.

[275] Judgment of 9 January 2003, paras 44-45.

[276] With respect to one application for release the applicant appealed three times to the Court of Cassation.

were all dealt with in short periods,[277] and reached the conclusion that paragraph 4 was not violated.[278] In the *Fox, Campbell and Hartley* Case two applicants instituted proceedings for *habeas corpus*. They were released 44 hours after their arrest, before judicial control on the lawfulness of their detention had taken place. The Court held that they were released speedily and did not find it necessary to examine their complaint under Article 5(4).[279]

9.8 RIGHT TO COMPENSATION

Article 5(5) grants a right to compensation if an arrest or detention is found to be in contravention of the preceding provisions of Article 5. At first sight this provision appears superfluous by the side of the general provision concerning just satisfaction in Article 41 of the Convention. The difference, however, is that Article 41 confers a competence on the Court, while Article 5(5) grants an independent right *vis-à-vis* the national authorities, the violation of which right may constitute the object of a separate complaint and may subsequently lead to the Court's application of Article 41. This difference may be illustrated by the following example. If an arrest has been declared unlawful by the national court and the prisoner has subsequently been released under Article 5(4), he can still complain about a violation of Article 5 if his claim for compensation has not been received or has been rejected. If, on the other hand, a given treatment of a detainee has been stopped after having been found by the national court to conflict with Article 3, but no damages are awarded to the injured person, there is no ground for a separate complaint, since Article 3 itself does not grant a right to compensation and Article 41 applies only after the Court has established violation of – in this case – Article 3.

In the *Brogan* Case the Government argued that the aim of paragraph 5 is to ensure that the victim of an 'unlawful' arrest or detention should have an enforceable right to compensation. In this regard the Government also contended that 'lawful' is to be construed as essentially referring back to domestic law and in addition as excluding any element of arbitrariness. The Government concluded that even in the event of a violation being found of any of the first four paragraphs, there had been no violation of paragraph 5 because the applicants' deprivation was lawful under Northern Ireland law and was not arbitrary. The Court held that such a restrictive interpretation was incompatible with the terms of paragraph 5, which refers to arrest or detention 'in contravention of the provisions of this Article'.[280]

---

[277] Periods from eight to twenty days.

[278] Judgment of 26 June 1991, *Letellier*, paras 56-57. See also the judgment of 23 November 1993, *Navarra*, paras. 29-30.

[279] Judgment of 30 August 1990, paras 45-46.

[280] Judgment of 29 November 1988, para. 67. See also the judgment of 10 June 1996, *Benham*, para. 50.

As was pointed out by the Court in the *Ciulla* Case, the effective enjoyment of the right guaranteed in paragraph 5 must be ensured in the Contracting States with "a sufficient degree of certainty".[281] In the *Sakik* Case the Court assessed the effectiveness of the application of Article 5(5) by the national authorities. In all the cases in which compensation was payable under the domestic legal provision concerned, it was required that the deprivation of liberty was unlawful. However, the domestic courts considered the detention in accordance with domestic law and the right to compensation depended on the unlawfulness under domestic law. Under these circumstances the effective enjoyment of the right guaranteed by Article 5(5) of the Convention is not ensured with a sufficient degree of certainty.[282]

The damage to be compensated may be material as well as non-material.[283] However, in the *Wassink* Case the Court took the view that the Contracting States are entitled to make the award of compensation dependent of the real existence of any damage resulting from the violation of Article 5.[284] In this case the detention under Article 5(1) was unlawful because there was no registrar present at the hearing, as was required by national law. For this reason it was hard for the applicant to prove any damage; it was uncertain if proceedings conducted in conformity with Article 5 would have led to the release of the applicant. The question of whether damage is involved, concerns the merits and will ultimately have to be decided by the Strasbourg Court.

9.9   DEROGATION

Article 5 is not included in the enumeration of Article 15(2). Under the conditions mentioned in the first paragraph of that article, the Contracting States may, therefore, derogate from the provision of Article 5 if, insofar as, and as long as this is necessary. In the *Brannigan and McBride* Case the derogation made by the United Kingdom Government was upheld by the Court. Surprisingly, the Court held, before examining the derogation, that Article 5(3) and (5) had not been complied with.[285] It is submitted that this consideration should not have been made if indeed the derogation met the requirements of the Convention.[286]

---

[281]   Judgment of 22 February 1989, para 44. See further the judgment of 30 August 1990, *Fox, Campbell and Hartley*, para. 76, and the judgment of 25 October 1990, *Thynne, Wilson and Gunnel*, para. 82.

[282]   Judgment of 26 November 1997, para. 60 and judgment of 11 December 2003, *Yankov*, para. 194.

[283]   Judgment of 22 June 1972, *Ringeisen*, paras 23-26. See also the judgment of 2 December 1987, *Bozano*, paras 6-9.

[284]   Judgment of 27 September 1990, para 38. See also the judgment of 10 March 1972, '*Vagrancy*' Cases, para. 24.

[285]   Judgment of 26 May 1993, para. 37.

[286]   See the declaration of judge Thor Vilhjálmsson, attached to the judgment.

CHAPTER 10
RIGHT TO A FAIR AND PUBLIC HEARING (Article 6)

REVISED BY PIETER VAN DIJK (SECTIONS 1-4)
AND BY MARC VIERING (SECTIONS 5-10)

CONTENTS

10.1 TEXT OF ARTICLE 6

1. *In the determination of his civil rights and obligations or of any criminal charge
    against him, everyone is entitled to a fair and public hearing within a reasonable
    time by an independent and impartial tribunal established by law. Judgment shall
    be pronounced publicly but the press and public may be excluded from all or part
    of the trial in the interest of morals, public order or national security in a democratic
    society, where the interests of juveniles or the protection of the private life of the
    parties so require, or to the extent strictly necessary in the opinion of the court in
    special circumstances where publicity would prejudice the interests of justice.*
2. *Everyone charged with a criminal offence shall be presumed innocent until proved
    guilty according to law.*
3. *Everyone charged with a criminal offence has the following minimum rights:*
    a) *to be informed promptly, in a language which he understands and in detail,
        of the nature and cause of the accusation against him;*
    b) *to have adequate time and facilities for the preparation of his defence;*
    c) *to defend himself in person or through legal assistance of his own choosing
        or, if he has not sufficient means to pay for legal assistance, to be given it free
        when the interests of justice so require;*

d)   *to examine or have examined witnesses against him and to obtain the attendance and examination of witnesses on his behalf under the same conditions as witnesses against him;*

e)   *to have the free assistance of an interpreter if he cannot understand or speak the language used in court.*

10.2   SCOPE OF ARTICLE 6

For the interpretation of Article 6 the Court, in its *Delcourt* judgment, has set forth the following guideline: "In a democratic society within the meaning of the Convention, the right to a fair administration of justice holds such a prominent place that a restrictive interpretation of Article 6(1) would not correspond to the aim and the purpose of that provision."[1]

In thus rejecting a restrictive interpretation, the Court has given guidance not only for its own case law, but also to the national authorities, especially the domestic courts. The Court's case law shows that it considers itself competent to examine in-depth the way in which Article 6 has been interpreted and applied at the national level.

The first issue to be discussed is the scope of Article 6. Thereafter, the various express and implied requirements embodied in the three paragraphs of this provision will be outlined.

10.2.1   DETERMINATION OF CIVIL RIGHTS AND OBLIGATIONS

Unlike the second and the third paragraph of Article 6, which apply exclusively to proceedings concerning criminal charges, the first paragraph also applies to proceedings in which the determination of civil rights and obligations is (also) at issue.

10.2.2   DRAFTING HISTORY

The meaning of the words 'determination of his civil rights and obligations' (*contestations sur ses droits et obligations de caractère civil*) is rather vague and leaves ample scope for 'creative' interpretation and even 'judicial policy'.[2] If, as is the case here, the ordinary meaning to be given to treaty provisions does not provide a suffic-

---

[1]   Judgment of 17 January 1970, para. 25.

[2]   Thus the representative of the Commission, Fawcett, before the Court in the *König* Case, B.25 (1982), p. 179.

iently clear interpretation, recourse may be had to supplementary means of interpretation, including the preparatory work of the treaty and the circumstances of its conclusion.[3] To date the Court has not expressly referred to the preparatory work of the Convention for the interpretation of 'civil rights and obligations'.[4]

The drafting history of the words 'civil rights and obligations' was studied in depth at an early stage by several authors.[5] These studies indicate that the drafting history of Article 14 of the International Covenant on Civil and Political Rights, which was used as a model by the drafters of Article 6 of the Convention, offers a rather strong indication that it was not the drafters' intention to restrict the scope of the right of access to court, apart from determinations of criminal charges, to determinations of rights and obligations of a private-law character. On the contrary, one is struck by the fact that proposals which might imply the risk of such a restriction, were criticised for that reason and rejected or amended.[6]

The *travaux préparatoires* of the European Convention do not contain an indication of a discussion of the formula here at issue in any of the bodies involved in the drafting. In the French text of Article 6 the formula of Article 14 of the Covenant was adopted without any change. In the English text 'rights and obligations in a suit at law' was altered, at the very last stage of the drafting process, to 'civil rights and obligations'. The reason for this is not traceable, but apparently it was not considered to have any implications for the scope of Article 6. One may assume that the only reason for it was that, in the eyes of continental lawyers (and of the linguists involved), 'suit at law' was

---

[3]   Articles 31, para. 1, and 32 of the Vienna Convention on the Law of Treaties; 8 *International Legal Materials* (1969), p. 679.

[4]   With respect to these *travaux préparatoires*, the position was taken in Strasbourg, on the one hand, that they provide no clarity as to the meaning of 'civil rights and obligations' (separate opinion of judge Matscher attached to the judgment of 28 June 1978, *König*), and on the other hand, that they point in the direction of a restrictive interpretation (report of the Commission of 19 March 1970, *Ringeisen*, B.11 (1972), pp. 70-71; joint dissenting opinion attached to the judgments of 29 May 1986, *Feldbrugge* and *Deumeland*), while an extensive interpretation was also considered by some as being in conformity therewith (minority view of the Commission in the *Benthem* Case).

[5]   See, especially, in chronological order: Jacques Velu, 'Le problème de l'application aux juridictions administratives, des règles de la Convention européenne des droits de l'homme relatives à la publicité des audiences et des jugements', *Revue de Droit International et de Droit Comparé* (1961), pp. 129-171; Karl Josef Partsch, *Die Rechte und Freiheiten der europäischen Menschenrechtskonvention*, Berlin (1966), pp. 143-150; Thomas Buergenthal and Wilhelm Kewenig, 'Zum Begriff der Civil Rights in Artikel 6 Absatz 1 der europäischen Menschenrechtskonvention', *Archiv des Völkerrechts* (1966/67), pp. 393-411; Frank C. Newman, 'Natural Justice, Due Process and the New International Covenants on Human Rights: Prospectus', *Public Law* (Winter 1967), pp. 274-313.

[6]   See Velu, *ibidem*, pp. 145-154. See especially his reference, at p. 150, to a statement by the delegate of the USSR, Mr Pavlov. At p. 154 Velu says: "Au fond, toutes les délégations étaient d'accord pour que les garanties de procédures prévues s'appliquent à toutes les juridictions". See also P. Lemmens, *Geschillen over burgerlijke rechten en verplichtingen* [Disputes concerning Civil Rights and Obligations], Antwerp, 1989, pp. 218-220, and M.L.W.M. Viering, *Het toepassingsgebied van artikel 6 EVRM* [The Scope of Article 6 ECHR], Zwolle, 1994, pp. 33-49. Both authors also discuss the intervention by the Danish delegate, Mr Sørensen, who proposed to exclude disputes between a private party and a public authority but did not have a decisive impact on the outcome of the debates on that point.

not the obvious equivalent for '*de caractère civil*'.[7] In conclusion, there is no indication that a restrictive interpretation of 'civil rights and obligations' can be based upon the drafting history of either Article 14 of the Covenant or Article 6 of the Convention. The Committee of Experts on Human Rights of the Council of Europe, when making a comparison between the two provisions, also reached the conclusion with respect to the words here under discussion that 'in view of the fact that the French texts use identical terms (...) the intention was the same'.[8]

It may be true that the original intention of the drafters of a treaty may become less relevant as time lapses, especially after States have become parties whose representatives did not participate in the drafting, but this argument is less convincing as long as there is no common and unambiguous legal opinion and/or uniform practice which deviates from that original intention.

10.2.3 AUTONOMOUS MEANING OF RIGHTS AND OBLIGATIONS

In the *Benthem* Case the Court expressly declined to give an abstract definition of 'civil rights and obligations',[9] notwithstanding the Commission's invitation to do so.[10] That is not to say, however, that the Court has given no guidance as to the interpretation of these words. In its case law the Court has drawn the following main lines.

Although for the determination of whether a right or obligation is at stake the domestic legal system concerned has to be taken as a starting point, the Court has made it clear that, as part of a provision of the Convention, the words 'rights and obligations' have an autonomous meaning. Thus it held in the *König* Case: "The same principle of autonomy applies to the concept in question; any other solution might lead to results incompatible with the object and purpose of the Convention (...). Whilst the Court thus concludes that the concept of 'civil rights and obligations' is autonomous, it nevertheless does not consider that, in this context, the legislation of the State concerned is without importance. Whether or not a right is to be regarded as civil within the meaning of this expression in the Convention must be determined by reference to the substantive content and effects of the right – and not its legal classification – under the domestic law of the State concerned. In the exercise of its

---

[7]   See Velu, *ibidem*, p. 159.

[8]   Council of Europe, *Problems arising from the co-existence of the United Nations Covenants on Human Rights and the European Convention on Human Rights; Differences as regards the Rights Guaranteed*, Report of the Committee of Experts on Human Rights to the Committee of Ministers, Doc. H(70)7, Strasbourg, September 1970, p. 37.

[9]   Judgment of 23 October 1985, para. 35.

[10]   Report of 8 October 1983, *Benthem*, para. 91. More expressly Mr Danelius and Mr Melchior, as delegates of the Commission, in the hearing before the Court; Cour/Misc (85)30, 26 February 1985, pp. 3 and 8 respectively.

supervisory functions, the Court must also take account of the object and purpose of the Convention and of the national legal systems of the other Contracting States (...)."[11]

The first question to be answered is whether a certain claim constitutes a 'right' – or 'legitimate interest?'[12] – under the domestic law of the State concerned for the applicability of Article 6. The Court requires that the determination concerns a right that 'can be said, at least on arguable grounds, to be recognised under domestic law'.[13] The words 'on arguable grounds' leave the Court sufficient room to make an assessment independently of the arguments advanced by the defendant State on the issue.[14] In particular, the Court does not have to be convinced that the legal claim is well-founded under domestic law; it is enough for it to determine that the claim is sufficiently tenable.[15] The fact that the claim concerned was addressed as an issue in national proceedings constitutes sufficient ground for the 'arguability' of the existence of a right.[16]

The viewpoint that Article 6 implies a right of access to court[17] has as a consequence that the fact that a certain claim is not actionable under domestic law, is not decisive for the applicability of Article 6. As the Court stated in the *Al-Adsani*, *McElhinney* and *Fogarty* Cases: "Whether a person has an actionable domestic claim may depend not only on the substantive content, properly speaking, of the relevant civil right as defined under national law but also on the existence of procedural bars preventing or limiting the possibilities of bringing potential claims to court. In the latter kind of case Article 6 para. 1 may be applicable."[18]

Consequently, the doctrine of State immunity does not lead to the conclusion that the person concerned has no right vis-à-vis that State; indeed, the State may waive immunity. The grant of immunity does not qualify a substantive right, but constitutes a procedural bar to have the right determined.[19]

In the *Baraona* Case the Court rejected the Government's submission that the impugned measure had no basis in national law at that time and accordingly could not give rise to liability on the part of the State and could not be the subject of a 'dispute'. The Court adopted the position that it was not for the Court to assess either

---

[11]   Judgment of 28 June 1978, *König*, paras 88-89.
[12]   Judgment of 5 October 2000, *Mennitto*, para. 27.
[13]   Judgment of 21 February 1986, *James and Others*, para. 81; judgment of 12 October 1992, *Salerno*, para. 14; judgment of 10 May 2001, *Z and Others v. the United Kingdom*, para. 87; decision of 14 November 2002, *Berkmann*, para. 2.
[14]   Judgment of 8 July 1987, *O. v. the United Kingdom*, para. 54.
[15]   Judgment of 26 March 1992, *Editions Périscope*, para. 38; judgment of 29 July 1998, *Le Calvez*, para. 56; judgment of 7 November 2000, *Jori*, para. 47.
[16]   Judgment of 26 March 1992, *Editions Périscope*, para. 38; judgment of 5 October 2000, *Mennitto*, para. 27: it was deemed sufficient that the issue 'had given rise to jurisdictional dispute'.
[17]   *Infra*, 4.1.
[18]   Judgments of 21 November 2001, paras 47, 24 and 25, respectively.
[19]   *Ibidem*, paras 48, 25 and 26, respectively.

the merits of the applicant's claim under domestic law or the influence of the revolutionary situation in Portugal on the application of domestic law; this belonged to the exclusive jurisdiction of the national courts. The applicant, however, could claim on arguable grounds to have a right that was recognised under national law as he understood it.[20] And in the *Voggenreiter* Case the Court held that, although according to constant case law of the German Constitutional Court the State cannot be held responsible for legislative acts, the applicant, who complained about the fact that as a result of the adoption of a certain law he had to give up his professional activity, was nevertheless claiming a civil right, since the German Constitution guaranteed the right to the free exercise of one's profession and the right to respect of one's property.[21]

On the other hand, if domestic law expressly excludes the claim, the Court takes the position that 'to this extent' there can be no arguable right which would make Article 6 applicable.[22] The Court may not, by interpreting Article 6 para. 1, create a right that has no basis in the domestic legal system concerned.[23] However, the mere fact that a right has been restricted by the legislator has no effect on the applicability of Article 6.[24] And a court decision to the effect that a certain claim does not exist, cannot remove, retrospectively, the arguability of the claim.[25] However, if the domestic court reaches the conclusion that the claimed right does not exist (any more) under domestic law, Article 6 is no longer applicable and does not guarantee any further access.[26] This may amount to a lack of an effective remedy, but that issue falls under Article 13 and not under Article 6.[27]

The fact that the applicant had also instituted the national proceedings to vindicate the public interest does not stand in the way of the applicability of Article 6, provided that at the same time an individual right was at stake.[28]

The mere fact that the authorities enjoy discretion in their decision-making and that, therefore, the person concerned cannot claim a specific outcome, does not mean that no right of the applicant is involved. He is entitled to the authorities respecting the limits of their discretion. That discretion is not unfettered and has to be exercised within the framework of the applicable law and in conformity with general principles

---

[20]   Judgment of 8 July 1987, paras 40-41.
[21]   Judgment of 8 January 2004, para. 35
[22]   Judgment of 21 February 1990, *Powell and Rayner*, para. 36; judgment of 27 August 1997, *Anne-Marie Andersson*, paras 35-36; decision of 14 November 2002, *Berkmann*, para. 2; judgment of 19 October 2005 (Grand Chamber), *Roche*, paras 119-124.
[23]   Judgment of 10 May 2001, *Z and Others v. the United Kingdom*, para. 98; judgment of 21 November 2001, *Al-Adsani*, para. 47.
[24]   Judgment of 28 June 1990, *Mats Jacobsson*, para. 31; judgment of 28 May 1997, *Pauger*, para. 44.
[25]   Judgments of 10 May 2001, *Z and Others v. the United Kingdom* and *T.P. and K.M. v. the United Kingdom*, paras 89 and 94, respectively.
[26]   Judgment of 10 May 2001, *Z and Others v. the United Kingdom*, para. 97; judgment of 28 June 2001, *Truhli*, para. 27.
[27]   Judgment of 10 May 2001, *Z and Others v. the United kingdom*, paras 102-103.
[28]   Judgment of 27 April 2004, *Lizarraya and Others*, paras 45-48.

of law and good administration.[29] However, if the award of a claimed entitlement is totally left to the court and the case law has not established an obligation on the part of the authorities in situations like the one at issue, no 'actual' right exists.[30]

The determination of the existence of an 'obligation' will be less problematic; that issue has not played an important role in the case law so far.

10.2.4   LEGAL DISPUTE ('CONTESTATION')

From the use of the word '*contestations*' in the French text of Article 6 para. 1, which has no equivalent in the English text, it has been inferred that for Article 6 to be applicable the settlement of a dispute concerning a right or obligation must be at issue.[31] The concept of 'dispute' should not be construed too technically and should be given a substantive rather than a formal meaning: a difference of opinion between two or more (legal) persons who have a certain relation to the right or obligation at issue is sufficient, provided that it is 'genuine and of a serious nature'.[32] One of the (legal) persons may be a public authority whose act or decision affects the other (legal) person.[33] If the act or decision is a favourable one and is not contested by the addressee, but is challenged by another public authority or another (legal) person, the latter has raised a '*contestation*', also in the relation between the former and the competent authority.[34] For the '*contestation*' is not required that damages are claimed.[35]

The '*contestation*' must be of a legal character: it must concern the alleged violation of a right.[36] This does not exclude cases in which the administrative authority has discretionary powers,[37] provided that the way in which these powers have been exercised is challenged on legal and not only on policy grounds.[38] These legal grounds

---

[29]   Judgment of 27 October 1987, *Pudas*, paras 36-37; judgment of 7 July 1989, *Tre Taktörer AB*, paras 39-40; judgment of 25 October 1989, *Allan Jacobsson*, para. 69.

[30]   Judgment of 28 September 1995, *Masson and Van Zon*, para. 51; judgment of 26 March 1996, *Leutscher*, para. 24.

[31]   Judgment of 23 June 1981, *Le Compte, Van Leuven and De Meyere*, para. 45. The Court said, however, "Even if ...". See also the judgment of 23 October 1990, *Moreira De Azevedo*, para. 66: "In so far as the French word '*contestation*' would appear to require the existence of a dispute, if indeed it does so at all ...".

[32]   Judgment of 23 June 1981, *Le Compte, Van Leuven and De Meyere*, para. 45; judgment of 10 May 2001, *Z and Others v. the United Kingdom*, para. 92; judgment of 23 January 2003, *Kienast*, para. 39.

[33]   Judgment of 16 July 1971, *Ringeisen*, para. 94.

[34]   Judgment of 23 October 1985, *Benthem*, para. 33.

[35]   Judgment of 28 September 2004, *Pieniążek*, para. 20.

[36]   Judgment of 23 June 1981, *Le Compte, Van Leuven and De Meyere*, para. 46; judgment of 23 January 2003, *Kienast*, para. 43.

[37]   Judgment of 2 August 2000, *Lambourdiere*, para. 24.

[38]   Judgment of 26 June 1986, *Van Marle and Others*, para. 35; judgment of 27 October 1987, *Pudas*, para. 34.

may relate to the way in which the limits of the discretion set by law have been respected,[39] or to the issue of whether the challenged act is in conformity with generally recognised principles of law and good administration.[40]

The legal-character requirement does not mean that the difference of opinion may not relate to facts, provided that they have some implications for the determination of (the scope of) rights or obligations.[41] In this respect, in our opinion, the *Van Marle* judgment of the Court was not well reasoned.[42] In the national proceedings, which had taken place before a judicial body, the dispute concerned mainly factual aspects, but some of them, such as the calculation of the period of self-employment, had a direct bearing on the entitlement to be registered as an accountant. That complaints about the latter aspects were not pursued in the Strasbourg procedure would seem to be not relevant for the applicability of Article 6, since the issue was rather whether there had been a *contestation* in the domestic proceedings. Indeed, the mere fact that a judicial authority had considered itself competent to deal with the dispute gave the latter a legal character.

The fact that the dispute has been 'settled' by a non-judicial procedure, does not mean that the party who is not satisfied with the settlement no has longer a dispute of a serious and genuine nature.[43]

In the *Moreira de Azevedo* Case the Court held that, although the applicant was only *assistente* in criminal proceedings and had not filed a formal claim for damages, there was a *contestation* concerning his civil rights.[44] It seems to have been deemed crucial that the implications of intervening as an *assistente* were not clear under Portuguese law, because in the subsequent *Hamer* Case the Court reached the conclusion that there had been no 'dispute' over a civil right because of the failure of the applicant to lodge a formal claim for damages.[45]

In most cases, however, where the applicability of Article 6 is at issue the existence of a '*contestation*' is not in dispute.

---

[39]   Judgment of 25 October 1989, *Allan Jacobsson*, para. 69.
[40]   Judgment of 28 June 1990, *Skärby*, para. 28.
[41]   Judgment of 26 June 1986, *Van Marle and Others*, para. 31; judgment of 27 October 1987, *Pudas*, para. 31.
[42]   Judgment of 26 June 1986, paras 31-37. See the concurring opinion of Judges Ryssdal, Matscher and Bernhardt, and the dissenting opinion of Judge Cremona.
[43]   Judgment of 21 September 2004, *Zwiazek Nauczycielstwa Polskiego*, paras 30-34.
[44]   Judgment of 23 October 1990, para. 67.
[45]   Judgment of 7 August 1996, paras 74-79. See also the decision of 10 June 2004, *Garimpo*, which also concerned the position of *assistente* under Portuguese law.

10.2.5 DETERMINATION

The (claimed)[46] judicial proceedings must lead to a 'determination' of civil rights or obligations. The mere communication or warning by a public authority that a certain licence has lapsed *de lege*, is not a 'determination'.[47] However, the mere fact that, at a later stage, the applicant withdrew his action which resulted in the discontinuance of the proceedings, does not affect the applicability of Article 6.[48]

A request for a provisional measure does not result in a (final) determination and, consequently, Article 6 is not applicable.[49] On the other hand, if the determination by a court has taken place but the court decision is not (fully) executed, the claim for (the remainder of the) execution and damages still forms part of the determination and is covered by Article 6.[50]

There must be a connection between the dispute to be solved and a civil right or obligation. A tenuous connection or remote consequence does not suffice.[51] Thus, the Court held that proceedings concerning the licencing of a nuclear power plant did not have a sufficiently direct link with the applicants' rights to adequate protection of their life, physical integrity and property to bring Article 6 para. 1 into play.[52] And proceedings concerning the annulment of a Presidential decree by virtue of an agreement between France and Switzerland, which made enlargement of an airport near the border possible, were deemed not to be sufficiently directly linked to the applicants' right and economic interest to construct an industrial area near the airport.[53] This also means that Article 6 para. 1 does not apply to proceedings instituted by way of *actio populari*.[54] However, the mere fact that the applicant shares the legal connection with several others does not make that connection remote or tenuous.[55]

On the other hand, the 'determination' need not form the main point or even the purpose of the proceedings. It is sufficient that the outcome of the (claimed) judicial

---

[46]   As will be discussed under 'access to court', hereafter under 4.1., according to the Court, Art. 6 para. 1 not only contains procedural guarantees in relation to judicial proceedings, but also grants a right of access to judicial proceedings for the cases mentioned in this article.

[47]   Judgment of 27 March 2001, *Kervoëlen*, paras 28-30.

[48]   Judgment of 14 October 2003, *Ciz*, para. 61.

[49]   Decision of 14 January 2003, *Seija and Vidar Hagman*, para. 1.

[50]   Judgment of 14 October 2003, *Dybo*, paras 20-22.

[51]   Judgment of 23 June 1981, *Le Compte, Van Leuven and De Meyere*, para. 47; judgment of 26 August 1997, *Balmer-Schafroth and Others*, para. 32; judgment of 13 February 2003, *Chevrol*, para. 44.

[52]   Judgment of 26 August 1997, *Balmer-Schafroth and Others*, para. 40; judgment of 6 April 2000, *Athanassoglou and Others*, para. 51.

[53]   Decision of 18 March 2003, *S.A.R.L. du Parc d'Activités de Blotzheim et la S.C.I. Haselaecker*, para. 9.

[54]   Judgment of 6 April 2000, *Athanassoglou and Others*, paras 53-54. See, however, the joint dissenting opinion of Judges Costa, Tulkens, Fischbach, Casadevall and Maruste, who stressed that the decision whether the action had the character of an *actio popularis* required access to a domestic court.

[55]   Judgment of 25 October 1989, *Allan Jacobsson*, para. 70.

proceedings may be 'decisive for',[56] or may 'affect',[57] or may 'relate to'[58] the determination and/or the exercise of the right, or the determination and/or the fulfilment of the obligation, as the case may be. The effects need not be legal; they may also be purely factual.[59] And if the proceedings concern the determination of a civil right or obligation, the same applies to subsequent proceedings concerning legal costs incurred.[60]

The civil right or obligation does not have to constitute the object of the proceedings.[61] If, for instance, the object of the proceedings is the annulment of an administrative decision or sanction, the right or obligation may be the object or one of the objects of that decision or may be implied in the sanction. The civil right may also be a right claimed by a third party who intervenes in criminal proceedings to obtain damages.[62] In the same way, if an administrative decision does (also) affect civil rights of third parties, e.g. the neighbours of a piece of land for which a building permit has been granted or the neighbours of a licensed plant, they also have the right of access to court to challenge the decision.[63] Moreover, the determination need not necessarily concern the actual existence of a right or obligation, but may also relate to its scope or modalities,[64] or to the unlawfulness of interferences with the exercise of a right.[65] The bottom line is reached, however, if the right claimed is not at issue at all in the proceedings concerned. Thus, the Court held Article 6 to be not applicable with regard to one of the applicants in the *McMichael* Case. Mr McMichael had failed to take the requisite prior steps to obtain legal recognition of his parental rights. Therefore, the care-proceedings, instituted by Mr and Mrs McMichael, could not have a connection with the determination of Mr McMichael's rights as a father.[66]

---

[56]   Judgment of 16 July 1971, *Ringeisen*, para. 94. See also, *i.a.*, the judgment of 17 March 1997, *Neigel*, para. 38.

[57]   Judgment of 24 October 1979, *Winterwerp*, para. 73. See also, *i.a.*, the judgments of 23 April 1987, *Ettl and Others; Erkner and Hofauer*; and *Poiss*, paras 32, 62 and 48, respectively.

[58]   Judgment of 28 June 1990, *Skärby*, para. 27; judgment of 4 March 2003, *A.B. v. Slovakia*, paras 46-48.

[59]   Judgment of 23 September 1982, *Sporrong and Lönnroth*, para. 80 in conjuction with para. 63.

[60]   Judgment of 23 September 1997, *Robins*, para. 29. See also, *i.a.*, the judgment of 21 February 2002, *Ziegler*, paras 24-25.

[61]   See the *Winterwerp* Case, where the object was the deprivation of liberty, which had, however, direct consequences for Mr Winterwerp's legal capacity to perform private-law acts; judgment of 24 October 1979, *Winterwerp*, paras 73-74.

[62]   Judgment of 23 October 1990, *Moreira De Azevedo*, paras 66-67.

[63]   Judgment of 6 April 2000, *Athanassoglou and Others*, para. 45.

[64]   Judgment of 23 June 1981, *Le Compte, Van Leuven and De Meyere*, para. 49; judgment of 23 October 1985, *Benthem*, para. 32; judgment of 26 June 1986, *Van Marle and Others*, para. 32.

[65]   Judgment of 23 September 1982, *Sporrong and Lönnroth*, para. 80.

[66]   Judgment of 24 February 1995, para. 77. Decision of 24 June 2004, *Mandela*: the proceedings only concerned a procedural issue and not a determination of the right at issue.

If under domestic law a person may bring a claim for damages incurred by a criminal act in the criminal proceedings, these proceedings are decisive for his 'civil' rights.[67] This also means that the impossibility of taking certain actions to safeguard these rights may amount to lack of access to court.[68] However, if the applicant has failed to lodge a claim in the appropriate proceedings, the proceedings in which he brings the claim cannot be considered to be decisive for the right concerned for the purpose of Article 6 para. 1; consequently, if the latter proceedings are discontinued, the applicant cannot be said to have been denied access to court.[69] Both in the *Hamer* Case and in the *Assenov* Case the applicants had claimed damages as a civil party in criminal proceedings. In the *Hamer* Case the applicant had failed to claim damages at the right stage of the proceedings, which would than have been dealt with by the court in its civil composition. In the *Assenov* Case the applicant could have brought civil proceedings for damages, the outcome of which was, in the opinion of the Court, not determined by that of the criminal proceedings. However, in the *Calvelli and Ciglio* Case the Court decided in respect of Italy that the criminal proceedings were apt to have repercussions on the claims made by the applicants as civil parties.[70] It appears from the facts of the case that there the applicants had also brought a claim in civil proceedings, but the case was struck out of the civil court's list. In any case, if the civil court stays the proceedings to wait for the outcome of the criminal proceedings concerning the criminal issues involved, the Court takes this into account in assessing the reasonableness of the duration of the trial.[71]

In its judgment of 12 Februari 2004 in the *Perez* Case the Grand Chamber considered that the Court's case law concerning civil claims in criminal proceedings might present a number of drawbacks, particularly in terms of legal certainty for the parties, and tended to over-complicate any analysis of the applicability of Article 6 to civil-party proceedings in French law and similar systems. It indicated that it wished to end this uncertainty and held that there can be no doubt that civil-party proceedings constitute (in French law) a civil action for reparation of damages caused by an offence. If the civil component remains closely connected with the criminal component to the extent that the criminal proceedings affect the civil component, Article 6 applies to both components of the proceedings. The damages sought may relate to pecuniary damages, even of a symbolic nature, but also, *e.g.*, to the protection of one's reputation. If, however, the civil action is brought for punitive purposes, Article 6 is not applicable

---

[67]   Judgment of 28 October 1998, *Aït-Mouhoub*, para. 44; judgment of 26 October 1999, *Maini*, paras 28-29; judgment of 3 April 2003, *Anagnostopoulos*, para. 32.

[68]   Decision of 24 February 2005, *Sottani*, para. 2.

[69]   Judgment of 7 August 1996, *Hamer*, paras 74-78; judgment of 28 October 1998, *Assenov and Others*, para. 112.

[70]   Judgment of 17 January 2002, para. 62.

[71]   Judgment of 8 July 2004, *Djangozov*, para. 38.

to the private component of the proceedings, since the Convention does not confer any right to 'private revenge' or to an *actio popularis*.[72]

If a remedy is not provided for under national law, it is not possible to determine what effect the outcome of the proceedings have had or might have had. In those cases the Court investigates whether the challenged decision or refusal to decide was decisive for a civil right or obligation and whether the administrative procedure revealed a *contestation* concerning such a right or obligation.[73]

If the outcome of proceedings concerning procedural requirements determines the merits of the case, these proceedings are decisive for a civil right or obligation, if the merits concern such a right or obligation.[74] The same holds good for non-judicial proceedings which take place in the framework of judicial proceedings determining civil rights and are closely linked to the latter.[75]

10.2.6 AUTONOMOUS MEANING OF 'CIVIL'

The words 'civil rights and obligations' have an autonomous meaning in Article 6.[76] To determine whether a certain right or obligation is a 'civil' right or obligation, one must first examine what the nature of the right or obligation at issue is according to the law of the respondent State.[77] If the right or obligation forms part of private law, it is evident that the first paragraph of Article 6 applies.[78] To this extent the autonomy of the interpretation is a one-way autonomy. The same holds good if the features of private law are 'predominant'.[79] In contrast, the mere fact that the right or obligation at issue is governed by public law does not exclude the applicability of the first paragraph of Article 6; what matters are the contents and effect of that right or obligation rather than its legal classification.[80] In that context the Court also pays attention to the capacity in which a person claims a right and the conditions under which he wishes to exercise it or exercises it.[81] In doing so, it also takes into account the legal systems

---

[72]   Judgment of 12 February 2004, paras 54-71. See also the judgment of 3 April 2003, *Anagnostopoulos*, para. 32.
[73]   Judgment of 27 October 1987, *Bodén*, para. 32; judgment of 28 June 1990, *Skärby*, para. 28.
[74]   Judgment of 19 March 1997, *Paskhalidis*, para. 30.
[75]   Judgment of 28 November 2000, *Siegel*, paras 37-38.
[76]   Judgment of 28 June 1978, *König*, paras 88-89. See also the judgment of 29 September 1998, *Malige*, para. 34; judgment of 5 October 2000, *Maaouia*, para. 34.
[77]   Judgment of 28 June 1978, *König*, para. 89; judgment of 29 May 1986, *Feldbrugge*, para. 28.
[78]   Judgment of 28 November 1984, *Rasmussen*, para. 32.
[79]   Judgment of 29 May 1986, *Feldbrugge*, paras 30-40.
[80]   Judgment of 28 June 1978, *König*, para. 89.
[81]   Judgment of 30 November 1987, *H v. Belgium*, paras 46- 47.

of the other Contracting States.[82] This approach makes the scope of Article 6 para. 1 less dependent on the national legal system concerned.

It is also not decisive for the 'civil' nature of a right or obligation whether the underlying dispute is one between individuals or one between an individual and a public authority. Even if in the latter case that public authority is involved in the proceedings in a sovereign capacity, those proceedings can relate to the determination of 'civil rights and obligations'.[83] It is equally not decisive whether the proceedings take place before a civil court or before another body vested with jurisdiction.[84] And, finally, the fact that in legal relations between individuals great public interests may also be involved, does not bar the applicability of Article 6 para. 1.[85]

Up to the present the Court has held the first paragraph of Article 6 applicable, in addition to proceedings with a private-law character, *inter alia*[86] to the following proceedings as determining civil rights or obligations:
- proceedings concerning a permit, licence or other act of a public authority which constitutes a condition for the legality of a contract between private parties;[87]
- proceedings which may lead to the cancellation or suspension by the public authorities of the qualification required for practising a particular profession;[88]
- proceedings concerning the refusal by the authorities to appoint the applicant to a post that belongs to the liberal professions, or concerning dismissal from such a post,[89] and concerning a decision which prevents the applicant from taking up a certain position;[90]
- proceedings concerning certain financial aspects of public service,[91] and concerning labour contracts for positions in state-owned enterprises;[92]

---

[82] Judgment of 28 June 1978, *König*, para. 89; judgment of 29 May 1986, *Feldbrugge*, para. 29.
[83] Judgment of 28 June 1978, *König*, para. 90; judgment of 23 October 1985, *Benthem*, para. 34.
[84] Judgment of 16 July 1971, *Ringeisen*, para. 94. See also, *i.a.*, the judgment of 8 July 1987, *Baraona*, paras 42-43.
[85] Judgment of 28 November 1984, *Rasmussen*, para. 32.
[86] See also under 2.8.
[87] Judgment of 16 July 1971, *Ringeisen*, para. 94; judgment of 22 October 1984, *Sramek*, para. 34.
[88] Judgment of 28 June 1978, *König*, paras 91-95; judgment of 23 June 1981, *Le Compte, Van Leuven and De Meyere*, paras 46-48; judgment of 10 February 1983, *Albert and Le Compte*, para. 28; judgment of 30 November 1987, *H v. Belgium*, paras 45-47; judgment of 19 April 1993, *Kraska*, para. 25; judgment of 26 September 1995, *Diennet*, para. 27; judgment of 29 September 1999, *Serre*, para. 20; judgment of 10 April 2003, *Bakker*, para. 26; decision of 28 September 2004, *Krokstäde*, para. 1.
[89] Judgment of 6 April 2000, *Thlimmenos*, para. 58; judgment of 15 November 2001, *Werner*, para. 32.
[90] Judgment of 7 November 2000, *Kingsley*, paras 43-45
[91] Judgment of 28 March 2000, *Dimitrios Georgiadis*, para. 21; judgment of 18 July 2000, *S.M. v. France*, para. 19.
[92] Judgment of 30 September 2003, *Sienkiewicz*, impliedly.

- proceedings concerning the grant or revocation of a licence by the public authorities which is required for setting up a certain business or carry out certain economic activities;[93]
- expropriation, consolidation, designation and planning proceedings,[94] proceedings concerning building permits and other real-estate permits,[95] proceedings concerning orders specifying the use of land,[96], proceedings concerning restoration of ownership as a rehabilitation measure[97] and concerning compensation for forefeited property,[98] and more in general proceedings the outcome of which has direct consequences for the right of ownership or has an impact on the use or the enjoyment of property;[99]
- proceedings concerning discrimination when bidding for a public works contract[100] and in access to the civil service;[101]
- proceedings in which a decision is taken on entitlement, under a social security scheme, to health insurance benefits,[102] to industrial-accident insurance benefits,[103] to welfare (disability) allowances,[104] to State pensions,[105] to invalidity pensions,[106] to surviver pensions,[107] and to old-age pensions;[108]

---

[93]   Judgment of 23 October 1985, *Benthem*, para. 36; judgment of 27 October 1987, *Pudas*, para. 37; judgment of 17 July 1989, *Tre Traktörer Aktiebolag*, para. 43; judgment of 18 February 1991, *Fredin*, para. 63; judgment of 21 December 1999, *G.S. v. Austria*, para. 27; judgment of 7 November 2000, *Kingsley*, paras 43-45; judgment of 13 February 2003, *Chevrol*, para. 49.

[94]   Judgment of 23 September 1982, *Sporrong and Lönnroth*, para. 80; judgments of 23 April 1987, *Ettl and Others, Erkner and Hofauer*, and *Poiss*, paras 32, 62 and 48, respectively; judgment of 27 October 1987, *Bodén*, para. 32; judgment of 27 November 1991, *Oerlemans*, para. 48; judgment of 16 December 1992, *De Geouffre de la Pradelle*, para. 28 (impliedly); judgment of 26 October 1999, *Varipati*, para. 21; judgment of 28 March 2000, *Aldo and Jean-Baptiste Zanatta*, para. 24; decesion of 11 May 2004, *Hutten*.

[95]   Judgment of 25 October 1989, *Allan Jacobsson*, para. 73; judgment of 21 February 1990, *Håkansson and Sturesson*, para. 60; judgment of 28 June 1990, *Mats Jacobsson*, para. 34; judgment of 28 June 1990, *Skärby*, para. 29; judgment of 19 February 1998, *Allan Jacobsson* (No. 2), para. 42.

[96]   Judgment of 18 February 1991, *Fredin*, para. 63; judgment of 22 January 2004, *Alge*, para. 20.

[97]   Judgment of 9 November 2000, *Jori*, paras 48-49.

[98]   Judgment of 21 October 2003, *Cegielski*, para. 24.

[99]   Judgment of 23 June 1993, *Ruiz-Mateos*, paras 51-52; judgment of 25 November 1993, *Zander*, para. 27; judgment of 19 June 2001, *Mathieu*, para. 18.; judgment of 20 December 2001, *Ludescher*, para. 16; judgment of 23 October 2003, *Achleitner*, impliedly.

[100] Judgment of 10 July 1998, *Tinnelly & Sons Ltd and Others and McElduff and Others*, paras 61-62.

[101] Judgment of 30 October 2001, *Devlin*, para. 23.

[102] Judgment of 29 May 1986, *Feldbrugge*, paras 26-40; judgment of 26 August 1997, *De Haan*, para. 44.

[103] Judgment of 29 May 1986, *Deumeland*, paras 62-74.

[104] Judgment of 26 February 1993, *Salesi*, para. 19; judgment of 26 November 1997, *Stamoulakatos*, para. 31; decision of 5 February 2004, *Bogonos*, para 1.

[105] Judgments of 26 November 1992, *Francesco Lombardo and Giancarlo Lombardo*, paras 17 and 16, respectively; judgment of 24 August 1993, *Massa*, para. 26.

[106] Judgment of 24 June 1993, *Schuler-Zgraggen*, para. 46; judgment of 19 March 1997, *Paskhalidis*, para. 30.

[107] Judgment of 28 May 1997, *Pauger*, para. 45.

[108] Judgment of 19 March 1997, *Paskhalidis and Others*, para. 30.

- proceedings to obtain allowances under a national health service programme;[109]
- proceedings against public authorities in which rights and obligations concerning family law are at issue;[110]
- proceedings concerning the change of a surname;[111]
- proceedings against the public administration concerning contracts,[112] concerning damages in administrative proceedings[113] or in criminal proceedings,[114] concerning negligence on the part of the authorities[115] and concerncing any (other) tort committed by a person or institution for which the State is responsible;[116]
- proceedings concerning damages as a result of the effects of a land consolidation project;[117]
- proceedings concerning damage caused to one's reputation;[118]
- proceedings relating to compensation for unjustified conviction or detention;[119]
- proceedings concerning public assistance in evicting tenants from a house;[120]
- proceedings concerning the obligation to pay contributions under a social security scheme;[121]
- proceedings concerning the payment of levies for public services;[122]
- patent application proceedings;[123]

---

[109]   Judgment of 5 October 2000, *Mennitto*, para. 27.

[110]   Judgment of 28 November 1984, *Rasmussen*, para. 32; judgments of 8 July 1987, *O. and H. v. the United Kingdom*, paras 54-60 and 69, respectively; judgments of 8 July 1987, *W., B. and R. v. the United Kingdom*, paras 73-79, 73-79 and 78-84, respectively; judgment of 22 June 1989, *Eriksson*, para. 73; judgment of 27 November 1992, *Olsson* (No. 2), para. 97; judgment of 26 May 1994, *Keegan*, para. 57; judgment of 19 February 1998, *Paulsen-Medalen and Svensson*, paras 38-42; judgment of 19 September 2000, *Glaser*, para. 91.

[111]   Decision of 6 December 2001, *Petersen*, para. 4: 'the Court starts with the assumption that Article 6 para. 1 in principle appplies'.

[112]   Judgment of 27 August 1991, *Philis*, para. 65 (impliedly).

[113]   Judgment of 8 July 1987, *Baraona*, para. 44; judgment of 27 April 1989, *Neves e Silva*, para. 37; judgment of 24 October 1989, *H v. France*, para. 47; judgment of 26 March 1992, *Editions Periscope*, para. 40; judgment of 31 March 1992, *X v. France*, para. 30; judgment of 23 September 2003, *Racinet*, impliedly.

[114]   Judgment of 23 October 1990, *Moreira De Azevedo*, para. 66; judgment of 27 February 1992, *Casciaroli*, para. 19 (impliedly); judgment of 24 November 1997, *Werner*, para. 39; judgment of 10 July 2001, *Lamanna*, para. 29.

[115]   Judgment of 19 February 1998, *Kaya*, para. 104; judgment of 28 October 1998, *Osman*, paras 136-139; judgment of 10 May 2001, *Z and Others* v. the United Kingdom, para. 89.

[116]   Judgment of 14 October 2003, *Chaineux*, para. 12; judgment of 21 October 2003, *Broca and Texier-Micault*, para. 26; judgment of 16 December 2003, *Mianowski* (impliedly).

[117]   Judgment of 26 September 2000, *Van Vlimmeren and Van Ilverenbeek*, para. 37 (impliedly).

[118]   Judgment of 15 November 2001, *Werner*, para 33.

[119]   Judgment of 29 May 1997, *Georgiadis*, para. 34; judgment of 24 November 1997, *Szücs*, paras 36-37; judgment of 15 October 1999, *Humen*, para. 57; judgment of 17 November 2000, *Karakasis*, para. 25.

[120]   Judgment of 28 July 1999, *Immobiliare Saffi*, paras 62-63; judgment of 3 August 2000, *G.L. v. Italy*, para. 30.

[121]   Judgment of 9 December 1994, *Schouten and Meldrum*, paras 49-60.

[122]   Judgment of 27 July 2000, *Klein*, para. 29.

[123]   Judgment of 20 November 1995, *British-American Tobacco Company Ltd*, para. 67.

- proceedings concerning the right to register as an association;[124]
- proceedings to have one's legal capacity restored.[125]

10.2.7 PUBLIC LAW PROCEEDINGS WHICH DO NOT FALL WITHIN THE SCOPE OF CIVIL RIGHTS AND OBLIGATIONS

There are still certain administrative proceedings where individual rights or obligations are at stake, with respect to which the Court so far has held that Article 6 para. 1 is not applicable.

10.2.7.1 Proceedings concerning tax duties

In the *Schouten and Meldrum* Case the Court held in an *obiter dictum* that obligations which derive from tax legislation or are otherwise part of normal civic duties in a democratic society, do not fall under the notion of 'civil obligations'.[126] Almost three years before, in the *Editions Périscope* Case, the Court had attributed a decisive meaning to the pecuniary character of the rights and obligations involved rather than to the fact that the dispute concerned damage resulting from the allegedly discriminatory application of tax regulations.[127] And in its judgment in the *National & Provincial Building Society* Case the Court held, referring to its judgment in the *Editions Périscope* Case, that the restitution proceedings were decisive for the determination of private-law rights and that the applicability of Article 6 para. 1 was not affected by the fact that these rights had their background in tax legislation and the obligation of the applicant to account for tax under that legislation.[128] The latter judgment, in particular, cast doubt on the precise direction of the case law.

The *Schouten and Meldrum* line of reasoning was confirmed in the *Ferrazzini* Case by the Grand Chamber, albeit by eleven votes to six. There the Court started its considerations by observing that pecuniary interests are clearly at stake in tax proceedings. However, merely showing that a dispute is pecuniary in nature is not in itself sufficient to attract the applicability of the first paragraph of Article 6 under its 'civil head'. In examining whether interpreting the Convention as a living instrument should lead to the conclusion that developments have occurred in democratic societies that have affected the fundamental nature of the obligation to pay tax, the Court reached the conclusion that "tax matters still form part of the hard core of public-authority

---

[124]   Judgment of 5 October 2000, *APEH Üldözötteinek Szövetsége and Others*, para. 36.
[125]   Judgment of 5 July 1999, *Matter*, para. 51.
[126]   Judgment of 9 December 1994, para. 50.
[127]   Judgment of 26 March 1992, para. 40.
[128]   Judgment of 23 October 1997, para. 97.

prerogatives, with the public nature of the relationship between the taxpayer and the tax authority remaining predominant. (...). It considers that tax disputes fall outside the scope of civil rights and obligations, despite the necessary pecuniary effects which they necessarily produce for the taxpayer."[129]

It is hard to understand why tax procedures, which in all member States of the Council of Europe are governed by rather strict legal rules, do not have to meet the minimum standards of fair trial of Article 6. As judge Lorenzen observed in his dissenting opinion, 'it is now recognised at least in the vast majority of the Contracting Parties that disputes in fiscal matters can be decided in ordinary proceedings by a court or tribunal. It is therefore difficult to see why it is still necessary to grant to the States a special prerogative under the Convention in this field and thus deny litigents in tax proceedings the elementary procedural guarantee of Article 6 para. 1'.[130] In the same dissenting opinion it is stated that the criterion 'normal civic duties in a democratic society', used by the Court, is not suitable to form the basis for a general distinction between 'civil' and 'non-civil' rights and obligations. 'Thus it is difficult to see why, for example, the obligation to hand over property for public use in return for compensation is not a 'normal civic duty' whereas the obligation to tolerate tax-based reductions of the compensation is? (...) Or how can it be explained that an obligation to pay contributions under a social-security scheme is 'civil', but an obligation to pay wage-taxes is not?'[131]

The fact that disputes concerning the obligation to pay taxes are not considered to be 'civil' for the purpose of Article 6 leaves, of course, open the question of the applicability of Article 6 to administrative fines, including fines imposed on taxpayers, under the 'criminal' head.[132] That issue will be discussed at a later stage. It is pointed out in the present context, however, that this applicability under the criminal head has as a result that the protection under Article 6 depends on how the legal framework for tax proceedings is organised in the different legal systems, while even within one and the same legal system it may be coincidental whether penalty proceedings and tax assessment proceedings are joined or not.[133] And why should a person who is charged

---

[129]   Judgment of 12 July 2001, para. 29. See the dissenting opinion of Judge Lorenzen, joined by Judges Rozakis, Bonello, Stráznická, Bîrsan and Fischbach, where it is stated: "It is not open to doubt that the obligation to pay taxes directly and substantially affects the pecuniary interest of citizens and that in a democratic society taxation (...) is based on the application of legal rules and not on the authorities' discretion. Accordingly (...) Article 6 should apply to such disputes (...)".

[130]   Dissenting opinion of Judge Lorenzen, joined by Judges Rozakis, Bonello, Stráznická, Bîrsen and Fischbach, para. 8.

[131]   *Ibidem*, para 6.

[132]   Judgment of 24 February 1994, *Bendenoun*, para. 52; judgment of 16 December 2003, *Faivre*, para. 21. See, however, the decision of 3 June 2003, *Morel*.

[133]   Thus also the dissenting opinion, para. 8.

with a fine for not complying with his tax duties, enjoy more legal protection than those who appeal against a tax duty imposed upon them?

10.2.7.2 Proceedings concerning admission and expulsion of aliens

The Commission had adopted the view that the first paragraph of Article 6 does not apply to proceedings concerning admission and expulsion of aliens.[134] The Commission seemed to indicate that this would be different if the right to respect for family life as a 'civil right' was at issue[135] or if expulsion constituted a violation of the right to education,[136] but in a later decision it held that the expulsion decision as such did not determine the right to respect of family life.[137] Since the applications were declared inadmissible by the Commission, the Court could not pronounce on the issue. The first opportunity presented itself when a case was directly referred to the Court in virtue of Protocol No. 11.

While the Court left the issue open initially,[138] in the *Maaouia* Case the Grand Chamber took a principled position in the matter. There the Court concluded from Article 1 of Protocol No. 7, which contains procedural guarantees for the expulsion of aliens, that "the States were aware that Article 6 para. 1 did not apply to procedures for the expulsion of aliens and wished to take special measures in that sphere."[139] This led the Court to hold that "the proceedings for the rescission of the exclusion order, which form the subject-matter of the present case, do not concern the determination of a 'civil right' for the purposes of Article 6 para. 1. The fact that the exclusion order incidentally had major repercussions on the applicant's private and family life or on his prospects of employment cannot suffice to bring those proceedings within the scope of civil rights protected by Article 6 para. 1 of the Convention."[140]

To indicate that the case was meant to be a 'pilot case' the Court reached the following general conclusion, which extended beyond the facts of the case before it: "Decisions regarding the entry, stay and deportation of aliens do not concern the determination of an applicant's civil rights or obligations or of a criminal charge against him, within the meaning of Article 6 para. 1 of the Convention."[141]

---

[134] Appl. 3225/67, *X, Y, Z, V and W v. the United Kingdom*, Coll. 25 (1968), p. 117 (122-123) (admission) and Appl. 9285/81, *X, Y and Z v. the United Kingdom*, D&R 29 (1982), p. 205 (212) (expulsion).

[135] Appl. 3225/67, *X, Y, Z, V and W v. the United Kingdom*, Coll. 25 (1968), p. 122. See also Appls 2991 and 2992/66, *Alam, Kahn and Singh v. the United Kingdom*, Yearbook X (1967), p. 478 (500-504).

[136] Appl. 7841/77, *X v. the United Kingdom* (not published).

[137] Appl. 8244/78, *Singh Uppal and Others*, D&R 17 (1980), p. 149 (157).

[138] Decision of 4 May 1999, *S.N. v. The Netherlands*, para. 3: "even supposing that the proceedings concerning the grant of residence permits and the expulsion of aliens were to come within the ambit of Article 6".

[139] Judgment of 5 October 2000, para. 36.

[140] *Ibidem*, para. 38.

[141] *Ibidem, para. 40*. The position adopted is still standing case law: decision of 29 June 2004, *Taheri Kandomabadi*.

It is not self-evident, to put it mildly, that for the interpretation of a provision of the Convention conclusions may be drawn from an instrument which was adopted more than thirty years later and has not yet been ratified by all the States parties to the Convention. It is even less evident, from the text of Article 1 of Protocol No. 7 and its Explanatory Note, that Protocol No. 7 may be considered a *lex specialis* with respect to (all) the procedural guarantees of the first paragraph of Article 6.[142] Indeed, "Protocols add to the rights of the individual; they do not restrict or abolish them".[143] The Explanatory Note states that Article 1 of the Protocol 'does not affect' the position adopted by the Commission that Article 6 does not apply to deportation procedures,[144] which does not imply that, according to the drafters of the Protocol, the said position was the only correct interpretation of Article 6. Moreover, the statement in the Explanatory Note only refers to deportations and, thus, does not give ground for any conclusion as to alien procedures in general.[145]

Moreover, in the light of the observation by the Court that the exclusion order incidentally had major repercussions on the applicant's private and family life or on his prospects of employment, it is difficult to understand how the Court's conclusion is to be reconciled with its case law that for the applicability of the first paragraph of Article 6 it is sufficient that the dispute concerned 'relates' to the scope of a civil right and the manner of its exercise.[146]

In *F. v. the United Kingdom* the Court observed that an issue may exceptionally be raised under Article 6 by an expulsion order in circumstances where the person being expelled has suffered or risks suffering a flagrant denial of fair trial in the receiving country.[147] This, of course, is a different issue than that here under discussion.

10.2.7.3 Proceedings concerning civil servants' employment rights

In the *Pellegrin* Case the Court very extensively dealt with the much debated issue of whether and to what extent disputes relating to the recruitment, career and termination of service of civil servants fall within the scope of Article 6 para. 1. Standing case law held that this was not the case.[148] However, the three categories of disputes were restrictively defined. Disputes that exclusively related to pecuniary rights – or rights of a purely or essentially economic character – did not fall under these categories and

---

[142] See the concurring opinion of Judge Costa and the dissenting opinion of Judge Loucaides joined by Judge Traja.
[143] Dissenting opinion of Judge Loucaides joined by Judge Traja.
[144] Explanatory Note, para. 16.
[145] Thus also Judge Costa in his concurring opinion.
[146] Judgment of 28 June 1990, *Skärby*, para. 27.
[147] Judgment of 22 June 2004, para. 2.
[148] Judgment of 24 August 1993, *Massa*, para. 26. See also, *i.a.*, the judgment of 24 August 1998, *Benkessiouer*, para. 30.

were considered to concern civil rights in the sense of Article 6.[149] The guiding criterion was supposed to be whether the claim by the civil servant mainly called into question the authorities' discretionary power in the recruitment, career or termination of service of civil servants.[150] If, however, the pecuniary right claimed directly depended on a decision concerning recruitment, career or termination of service – or indeed re-instatement – the main rule of inapplicability was held to apply.

In the *Pellegrin* Case the Court admitted that this case law contained "a margin of uncertainty for Contracting States as to the scope of their obligations under Article 6 para. 1 in disputes raised by employees in the public sector over their conditions of service." It continued its considerations as follows: "The criterion relating to the eco-nomic nature of a dispute, for its part, leaves scope for a degree of arbitrariness, since a decision concerning the 'recruitment', 'career' or 'termination of service' of a civil servant nearly always has pecuniary consequences. (...) The Court therefore wishes to put an end to the uncertainty which surrounds application of the guarantees of Article 6 para. 1 to disputes between States and their civil servants. (...) The Court accordingly considers that it is important, with a view to applying Article 6 para. 1, to establish an autonomous interpretation of the term 'civil service' which would make it possible to afford equal treatment to public servants performing equivalent or similar duties in the States party to the Convention, irrespective of the domestic system of employment and, in particular, whatever the nature of the legal relation between the official and the administrative authority (whether stipulated in a contract or governed by statutory and regulatory conditions of service). To that end, in order to determine the applicability of Article 6 para. 1 to public servants, whether established or employed under contract, the Court considers that it should adopt a functional criterion based on the nature of the employee's duties and responsibilities. In so doing, it must adopt a restrictive interpretation, in accordance with the object and purpose of the Con-vention, of the exceptions to the safeguards afforded by Article 6 para. 1. (...) The Court therefore rules that the only disputes excluded from the scope of Article 6 para. 1 of the Convention are those which are raised by public servants whose duties typify the specific activities of the public service in so far as the latter is acting as the depository of public authority responsible for protecting the general interests of the State or other public authorities. A manifest example of such activities is provided by the armed forces and the police. (...) Accordingly, no disputes between administrative authorities and employees who occupy posts involving participation in the exercise of powers conferred by public law attract the application of Article 6 para. 1 since the Court intends to establish a functional criterion (...). Disputes concerning pension

---

[149] Judgment of 26 November 1992, *Giancarlo Lombardo*. para. 16. See also, *i.a.*, the judgment of 24 August 1998, *Benkessiouer*, para. 30.

[150] Judgment of 17 March 1997, *Neigel*, para. 44. See, however, the dissenting opinion of Judge Palm. See also, *i.a.*, the judgment of 24 August 1998, *Benkessiouer*, paras 29-30.

all come within the ambit of Article 6 para. 1 because on retirement employees break the special bond between themselves and the authorities; they, and *a fortiori* those entitled through them, then find themselves in a situation exactly comparable to that of employees under private law in that the special relationship of trust and loyalty binding them to the State has ceased to exist and the employee can no longer wield a portion of the State's sovereign power (...)."[151]

The judgment is quoted extensively because it reflects the clear – and not very common – intention of the Court to not only judge on the case before it but draw the lines for future cases. The great advantage of the Court's reasoning is undoubtedly that it puts an end to the many uncertainties which its previous case law and that of the Commission on the matter had created, especially concerning the criterion of the measure of discretion on the part of the authority which took the challenged decision.[152] It is also to be welcomed that the Court dissociates itself from the view that a distinction should be made between civil servants and those in public service who are employed under a contract.[153]

However, by introducing the 'functional criterion' the Court gave rise to a new set of uncertainties and of possible unequal treatment. Indeed, it will be difficult to determine – and even more difficult to predict – in each individual case whether the civil servants concerned "occupy posts involving participation in the exercise of powers conferred by public law".[154] And, indeed, shortly afterwards, in the *Frydlender* Case, where the position of the applicant civil servant would seem very similar to that of Mr Pellegrin, the Court did hold Article 6 to be applicable.[155] The Court itself seems to struggle with the distinction at times, apparently prefering to leave the issue open.[156]

The criterion of 'exercise' is not clear and the separation between administrative acts of a public law and those of a private law character is not drawn in the same way in the different legal systems. The criterion is also problematic, as becomes strikingly clear when it is applied in such a way that the legal position of judges falls outside the guarantees of Article 6, which weakens their independence vis-à-vis the executive.[157]

The – rather remarkable – reference by the Court to a list of posts and activities within the European Commission, that was drafted for quite a different purpose and could only take into account the situation in the member States of the European Union, will provide some but not sufficient guidance as to the 'functional criterion'. Moreover, it has to be pointed out that Article 6 classifies rights and obligations and

---

[151]   Judgment of 8 December 1999, paras 60-66.
[152]   On that criterion, see the previous edition of the present book, pp. 405-406. In his separate opinion in the *Pellegrin* Case Judge Traja calls the previous use of that criterion 'a cautious approach'.
[153]   See also the judgment of 27 June 2000, *Frydlender*, paras 29-32.
[154]   See, *e.g.* the judgment of 30 October 2001, *Devlin*, para. 26.
[155]   Judgment of 27 June 2000, Frydlender, paras 34-41
[156]   Judgment of 21 November 2001, *Fogarty*, para. 28.
[157]   Decision of 8 February 2001, *Pitkevich*, para. 1.

not the subjects or objects thereof; civil rights claims do not depend on any classification of public employees.[158] And "the criterion used will create a new type of discrimination between public sector workers, depending on whether or not they exercise powers conferred by public law."[159] Moreover, the Court maintains a difference of legal protection between employees in the public sector and those in the private sector without an express justification as to the difference on the basis of a legitimate aim and proportionality between the impact of the difference and that aim, while the 'old' Court had found reason in the requirement of equal treatment between civil servants and employees in the private sector to extend the applicability of Article 6.[160] As the dissenting judges put it: "First of all, we do not see how the existence of such a bond [of trust and loyalty] can be a sufficiently weighty argument for the purposes of determining the scope of Article 6 since there may be a similar bond in other employment relationships. Why, for example, would it be right for a policeman not to be protected by Article 6 when an employee of a private security service, with the same duties of maintaining order, would be protected? Secondly, we do not understand why someone who participates in the exercise of powers conferred by public law, and who, under domestic law, has access to an independent tribunal in connection with disputes concerning employment, is not entitled to a judicial decision within a reasonable time. Lastly, although loyalty is relevant above all where it is a matter of appointment to or dismissal from the most sensitive public duties, we fail to see why loyalty should make a difference where it is a matter of disputes over salary or other payments."

In the *Frydlender* Case the Court indicated that it will apply the criterion of 'acting as a depository of public authority', as an exception to the entitlement of civil servants to the protection of Article 6, in a restrictive way in accordance with the object and purpose of the Convention.[161] Indeed, later on several functions were considered not to be covered by the *Pellegrin* criterion.[162] And, as was indicated in the *Pellegrin* judgment, claims of civil servants relating to their retirement, such as pensions, do not come under the exception, as retirement breaks the special bond.[163] On the other

---

158   Judge Traja in his separate opinion, and Judges Tulkens, Fischbach, Casadevall and Thomassen in their joint dissenting opinion.

159   Joint dissenting opinion of Judges Tulkens, Fischbach, Casadevall and Thomassen.

160   Judgment of 26 November 1992, *Francesco Lombardo*, para. 17; judgment of 24 August 1993, *Massa*, para. 26.

161   Judgment of 27 June 2000, para. 40.

162   See, *e.g.*, the judgment of 30 March 2000, *Procaccini*, para. 13; judgment of 18 July 2000, *S.M. v. France*, para. 19; judgment of 2 August 2000, *Lambourdiere*, para. 23; judgment of 26 October 2000, *Castanheira Barros*, para. 32; judgment of 30 October 2001, *Devlin*, para. 26; judgment of 15 November 2001, *Werner*, para. 34.

163   See also the judgment of 14 December 1999, *Antonakopoulos, Vortsela and Antonakopoulou*, para. 21; judgment of 28 March 2000, *Dimitrios Georgiadis*, para. 21; judgment of 18 July 2000, *S.M. v. France*, para. 19. However, Article 6 was held not to apply to the pension rights of a former MP: decision of 11 October 2005, *Papon*.

hand, the Court seems inclined to apply the criterion in a strictly formal way: a civil servant who belonged to the National Fire Service but occupied the position of teacher at the National Fire Academy, was deemed to carry 'considerable responsibilities in the sphere of national defence' with a reference to his research work.[164]

As far as military personnel and the police are concerned, in the *Kerojärvi* Case the Court held that a dispute concerning the entitlement to compensation under the 1948 Military Injuries Act came within the 'civil right' scope of Article 6. The Court saw no reason "to distinguish this case from previous cases in which it has found that disputes over benefits under a social-security scheme concern 'civil rights'."[165] In the *Truhli* Case the Court treated the right to a military pension as a 'civil' right.[166] It was to be expected, however, that the *Pellegrin* line would bring personnel cases concerning the military and the police under the exception of 'depositary of public authority responsible for protecting the general interests of the State'.[167] The cases mentioned above fit into that line "because on retirement employees break the special bond between themselves and the authorities".[168] A reserve officer, who will be called on duty only at intervals, is treated in this respect as still being on duty.[169]

In the present situation, where civil servants as a rule have access to a court for the settlement of disputes with their public employer, it is difficult to understand why the Court excludes them from the right to such access. Most applications filed with the Court in this area concern the reasonable time requirement. As the dissenting judges indicated, this raises the question why domestic courts with jurisdiction in civil servant disputes, which in all other respects fulfil the requirements of Article 6, should not be placed under the obligation to give judgment within a reasonable time.

10.2.8 ARE ALL CONVENTION RIGHTS AND FREEDOMS 'CIVIL'?

Unlike Article 13, Article 6 does not refer to the 'rights and freedoms as set forth in this Convention' but to 'civil rights and obligations'. The two concepts are not co-extensive, although there may be some overlapping.[170]

It is self-evident that the rights laid down in the Convention are 'rights' in the sense of Article 6. But are they also 'civil' rights in that sense? They certainly do have that character to the extent that they have a 'horizontal effect' within the domestic legal

---

[164] Decision of 11 July 2000, *Kepka*, para. 2.
[165] Judgment of 19 July 1995, para. 36; judgment of 12 June 2001, *Trickovic*, para. 40.
[166] Judgment of 28 June 2001, para. 26.
[167] The Court made the express observation (para. 65) that "A manifest example of such activities is provided by the armed forces and the police".
[168] *Ibidem*, para. 66. See also the judgment of 13 November 2003, *Papazoglou and Others*, impliedly.
[169] Judgment of 27 February 2001, *R. v. Belgium*, para. 44.
[170] Judgment of 21 February 1975, *Golder*, para. 33; judgment of 8 January 2004, *Voggenreiter*, para 35.

order, since rights and obligations between private parties are 'civil' in character. Thus an individual's right to respect for his reputation by a private person was considered to be a 'civil right'.[171]

However, the civil rights protected in the Convention may also come under Article 6 if they are vindicated *vis-à-vis* a public authority. Thus, in the *Werner* Case the right of protection of one's good reputation against the public authorities, including the courts, was recognized as a 'civil right' in the sense of Article 6.[172] The same was held in the *Ciz* Case with respect to an alleged defamation by a member of Parliament.[173]

In the *Balmer-Schafroth* Case and the *Athanassoglou* Case the right to have one's physical integrity adequately protected from the risks entailed by the use of nuclear energy was recognized as a right in the sense of Article 6, since it was regulated in the Swiss Nuclear Energy Act and emerged from the constitutional right to life; however, the link between the proceedings concerned and that right was considered to be insufficiently direct to make Article 6 applicable.[174] The right to life also constitutes a civil right for the relatives of the deceased in combination with a claim for damages.[175]

In the *Aerts* Case the Court adopted the position that the right to liberty is a 'civil' right.[176] In the *Paulsen-Medalen and Svensson* Case the right to respect of family life was dealt with as a 'civil' right,[177] as was in the *Petersen* Case (on assumption) the claim relating to a change of a child's surname, as being an element of family life.[178] And in the *Ganci* Case the Court held that complaint procedures against a special detention regime with severe restrictions as to visits by relatives, use of telephone and conduct of financial transactions, concerned the detainee's civil rights.[179] In the *APEH Üldözötteinek Szövetsége* Case the right to register as an association, as part of the right to freedom of association, was held to be a 'civil' right, since "it was (…) the applicant association's very capacity to become a subject of civil rights and obligations (…) that was at stake in the registration proceedings".[180] In the *Tinnelly & Sons Ltd and McElduff*

---

[171] Judgment of 29 October 1991, *Helmers*, para. 29; judgment of 13 July 1995, *Tolstoy Miloslavsky*, para. 58; judgment of 15 November 2001, *Werner*, para. 33; judgment of 3 June 2004, *De Jorio*, para. 18; judgment of 8 July 2004, *Djangozov*, para. 41.; judgment of 28 September 2004, *Pieniazek*, para. 18. If statements made in Parliament are involved, Article 6 is also applicable but access to court may be blocked by the principle of 'parliamentary immunity', see *infra*, 10.4.6.2.

[172] Judgment of 15 November 2001, para. 33. See also the judgment of 12 November 2003, *Bartre*, impliedly.

[173] Judgment of 14 October 2003, *Ciz*, para. 61.

[174] Judgment of 26 August 1997, paras 33-34; judgment of 6 April 2000, para. 44.

[175] Judgment of 22 January 2004, *Sekin and Others*, (impliedly).

[176] Judgment of 30 July 1998, para. 59. See also the decision of 18 March 2003, *Fabre* (impliedly).

[177] Judgment of 19 February 1998, paras 38-42.

[178] Judgment of 6 December 2001, para. 4: "the Court starts with the assumption that Article 6 para. 1 in principle appplies".

[179] Judgment of 30 October 2003, paras 23-26; judgment of 11 January 2005, *Musumeci*, para. 36.

[180] Judgment of 5 October 2000, para. 36.

Case the right not to be discriminated against on grounds of religious belief or political opinion when bidding for a public works contract was held to be a 'civil' right.[181] The same position was taken with respect to discrimination in the area of recruitment for the civil service.[182]

As far as the right to the peaceful enjoyment of possessions is concerned, in the case of expropriation and consolidation decisions and in the case of forfeiture of property, the proceedings in which the legitimacy and/or the damages are determined, are considered to be a 'determination of a civil right'.[183] Equally, the decision to place a bank in compulsory administration, which has a decisive impact on the right of the bank to administer its own property and assets, concerns a civil right of the bank.[184] And if a certain claim is combined with a claim for damages, the Court is inclined to consider the proceedings as being closely connected to a claim of a pecuniary nature and as decisive for the determination of civil rights.[185]

For the rights and freedoms laid down in the Convention that are of a political character the situation is less clear. In the *Pierre-Bloch* Case the Court held that the right to stand for elections is a 'political' and not a 'civil' one and that, therefore, disputes concerning the exercise of that right lie outside the scope of Article 6, even if economic interests are involved.[186] The mere fact that in the dispute concerned the applicant's pecuniary interests were also at stake, did not make Article 6 applicable, because these interests were closely connected with the exercise of the political right.[187]

A claim which has a certain connection with the Convention but is not guaranteed as a right there, does not, on that sole basis, come under the protection of Article 6. If the claim concerned is also not recognized as a right under the applicable domestic law, Article 6 is not applicable. Thus, in the *Gutfreund* Case the Court held Article 6 to be not applicable to proceedings concerning legal aid in a civil case, because the right to legal aid in civil cases is not recognized in Franch law nor, in the circumstances of the case, in Article 6 of the Convention.[188] It reached the same conclusion with respect to proceedings relating to the decision to subject a detainee to a high-security regime.[189]

Thus, it may be concluded that most of the rights and freedoms laid down in the Convention, also in relation to the public authorities, have been recognized by the

---

[181]   Judgment of 10 July 1998, paras 61-62.
[182]   Judgment of 30 October 2001, *Devlin*, paras 25-26.
[183]   Judgments of 2 April 1987, *Ettl and Others, Erkner and Hofauer*, and *Poiss*, paras 32, 62 and 48, respectively; judgment of 27 October 1987, *Bodén*, para. 32; judgment of 23 June 1993, *Ruiz-Mateos*, paras 58-59; judgment of 21 October 2003, *Cegielski*, para. 24; judgment of 13 July 2004, *Beneficio Cappella Paolini*, para. 28.
[184]   Jugdment of 21 Ocotber 2003, *Credit and Industrial Bank*, para. 64-67.
[185]   Judgment of 13 November 2003, *Napijalo*, paras 47-50.
[186]   Judgment of 21 October 1997, paras 50-51; decision of 27 May 2004, *Guliyev*, para. 3; decision of 14 December 2004, *Krasnov and Skuratov*, para. 1.
[187]   *Ibidem*, para. 51.
[188]   Judgment of 12 June 2003, paras 31-43.
[189]   Decision of 28 August 2001, *Lorsé and Others*, para. 3. See, however, note 179.

Court as 'civil' rights unless their political character prevails. To the extent that the applicability of Article 6 is (still) not recognized, Article 13 of the Convention does, of course, apply.[190]

10.2.9 CONCLUDING OBSERVATIONS

The Strasbourg case law concerning 'civil rights and obligations' still lacks clarity and certainty in certain respects in spite of several praiseworthy efforts of the 'new' Court to draw some general lines. It lacks clarity because no general definition of 'civil rights and obligations' can still be inferred from it, while the criteria developed by the Court, such as that of the effect which the outcome of the proceedings may have for a right or obligation of a civil character, are not very specific and sometimes difficult to apply. It lacks certainty because the lines drawn in the case law curve rather frequently and appear still to lead within the Court to different views in concrete cases. In our opinion this lack of clarity and certainty, which constitutes an undesirable situation not only for the individual seeking justice, but also for the public authorities and the courts in the Contracting States, which are called upon to apply Article 6, can only be eliminated if the Court departs from its present casuistic approach and develops a general and readily applicable definition of 'civil rights and obligations', thus fulfilling its function to give direction to the interpretation and application of the Convention.[191] Its judgments in the *Ferrazzini, Maaouia* and *Pellegrin* Cases, although one may not agree with the line of reasoning adopted, are a step in the right direction from that perspective, but even these judgments do not yet offer the clarity and certainty required. Precisely at a moment when several States which have recently acceded to the Convention are in the process of adapting their legislation and reforming their judicial system, more clarity about the scope of Article 6 is urgently needed.

It is submitted that the most satisfactory way to end legal uncertainty and maximize effective legal protection is to recognize – as an example of 'evolutive interpretation' – that the first paragraph of Article 6 is applicable to all cases in which a determination by a public authority of the legal position of a private party is at stake, regardless of whether the rights and obligations involved are of a private character and regardless of whether the claim concerns a public law relationship. The basic principle of the Rule of Law would seem to require that in all cases of government interference with the legal position of a private party the latter has a right of access to court and to a fair

---

[190]   See for a case of privacy affected by aircraft noise, which was not protected under domestic law, the judgment of 7 August 2003, *Hatton and Others*, paras 137-142.

[191]   For this 'constitutional' function, see the judgment of 18 January 1978, *Ireland v. the United Kingdom*, para. 154.

trial.[192] As the Court held in the *Klass* Case, "The rule of law implies, *inter alia*, that an interference by the executive authorities with an individual's rights should be subject to an effective control which should normally be assured by the judiciary, at least in the last resort, judicial control offering the best guarantees of independence, impartiality and a proper procedure."[193]

10.3   CRIMINAL CHARGE

10.3.1   DETERMINATION OF A CRIMINAL CHARGE

The words 'determination of (...) any criminal charge' (*'décidera (...) du bien-fondé de toute accusation en matière pénale'*) also raise problems of interpretation.

From the term 'determination' it follows that the 'criminal' limb of Article 6 is not applicable to every procedure in which an accused or detained person is involved, but only to those proceedings in which the well-foundedness of a charge is at stake. Thus, in the *Ganci* Case the Court held that complaint procedures against restrictions imposed upon a detainee did not concern the determination of a criminal charge, but did indeed concern the determination of the detainee's civil rights.[194]

More problematic is the term 'criminal charge'. On this point the legal systems of the Contracting States show many variations. To avoid differences in the scope of application of Article 6 in the different national legal orders, and also the risk of this application being eroded by the introduction of legal norms and procedures outside the sphere of criminal law, the adoption of an autonomous meaning, independent of the national legal systems, was necessary here as well. In the *Adolf* Case the Court held with respect to 'criminal charge' in so many words: "These expressions are to be interpreted as having an 'autonomous' meaning in the context of the Convention and not on the basis of their meaning in domestic law."[195]

In many cases the criminal character of the proceedings involved is clear, either because of their characterisation under the applicable domestic law or in view of their character and purpose, and the terminology used for their regulation.[196] However,

---

[192]   Thus also the joint dissenting opinion of Judges Tulkens, Fischbach, Casadevall and Thomassen in the *Pellegrin* Case and the dissenting opinion of Judge Loucaides joined by Judge Traja in the *Maaouia* Case. For a proposal to use as a general criterion that the pecuniary interests of an individual are directly affected and the interference is not based on the exercise of discretionary powers, see the dissenting opinion of Judge Lorenzen, joined by Judges Rozakis, Bonello, Stráznická, Bîrsan and Fischbach in the *Ferrazzini* Case.
[193]   Judgment of 6 September 1978, para. 55.
[194]   Judgment of 30 October 2003, para. 22.
[195]   Judgment of 26 March 1982, para. 30.
[196]   Judgment of 23 October 1995, *Gradinger*, para. 36; judgment of 10 June 1996, *Pullar*, para. 29.

there are several cases in which the Court had to draw lines on the basis of an autonomous interpretation.

10.3.2 AUTONOMOUS CONCEPT OF 'CHARGE'

The general point of departure defined in the *Delcourt* Case "that a restrictive interpretation of Article 6 para. 1 would not correspond to the aim and purpose of that provision",[197] also applies here. In addition, in the *Deweer* Case the Court adopted a guideline for the autonomous interpretation of 'charge'. It held that "the prominent place held in a democratic society by the right to a fair trial (...) prompts the Court to prefer a 'substantive', rather than a 'formal', conception of the 'charge' contemplated by Article 6 para. 1."[198] Consequently, the concept is to be understood "within the meaning of the Convention and not solely within the meaning under national law".[199]

In the *Deweer* Case the Court gave the following description of the concept of 'charge' in the sense of Article 6: 'the official notification given to an individual by the competent authority of an allegation that he has committed a criminal offence.'[200] This 'notification' marks the beginning of the 'charge' and, consequently, is also relevant with respect to the period of the procedure to which Article 6 applies, for instance for determining whether the reasonable-time requirement has been met. The relevant period starts with the notification, even if it is formulated in a language which the person concerned does not understand[201] or if it did not reach him.[202]

However, a formal notification is not always required. Examples of possible measures other than an official notification are the search of the person's home and/or the seizure of certain goods,[203] the request that a person's immunity be lifted,[204] and the confirmation by the court of the sealing of a building.[205] In the *Corigliano* Case the Court summarised its case law as follows: "In criminal matters, in order to assess whether the 'reasonable time' requirement contained in Article 6 para. 1 has been complied with, one must begin by ascertaining from which moment the person was 'charged'; this may have occurred on a date prior to the case coming before the trial

---

[197]   Judgment of 17 January 1970, para. 25.
[198]   Judgment of 27 February 1980, para. 44.
[199]   Judgment of 16 December 1997, *Tejedor García*, para. 27.
[200]   Judgment of 27 February 1980, para. 46.
[201]   Judgment of 19 December 1989, *Brozicek*, paras 41-42.
[202]   Judgment of 19 February 1991, *Pugliese*, para. 14 in conjunction with para. 10. For possible consequences of notification not in person, see the judgment of 12 February 1985, *Colozza*, paras 26-28.
[203]   Judgment of 15 July 1982, *Eckle*, para. 74 in conjunction with para. 12.
[204]   Judgment of 19 February 1991, *Frau*, para. 14.
[205]   Judgment of 18 July 1994, *Venditelli*, para. 21.

court (...), such as the date of the arrest, the date when the person concerned was officially notified that he would be prosecuted or the date when the preliminary investigations were opened (...). Whilst 'charge', for the purpose of Article 6 para. 1, may in
general be defined as 'the official notification given to an individual by the competent
authority of an allegation that he has committed a criminal offence', it may in some
instances take the form of other measures which carry the implication of such an
allegation and which likewise substantially affect the situation of the suspect (...)."[206]

From this 'definition' it follows that Article 6 also applies to the pre-trial phase,[207] but
only from the moment a charge has been brought. The mere fact that the police are
carrying out an investigation or witnesses are being heard, or that a judicial organ is
making a preliminary inquiry, does not necessarily mean that a 'criminal charge' exists.

In the *Deweer* Case the Court held that a 'charge' may exist at the stage in which
the prosecuting authorities make a proposal for settlement, even if that proposal is
made in the framework of an inspection that is not performed within the context of
the repression of crime and even if there is no notification of impending prosecution,
while the settlement will prevent such prosecution.[208] And even a summon to appear
as a witness may mark a criminal charge, if the person concerned may deduce from
the circumstances that there is incriminating evidence also against him.[209]

In the *Escoubet* Case the Court adopted the opinion that Article 6 does not apply
to the various preliminary measures which may be taken as part of a criminal investigation before bringing a 'criminal charge', such as the arrest or interviewing of a
suspect (...), measures which may, however, be governed by other provisions of the
Convention, in particular Articles 3 and 5.[210] This reasoning makes the criteria of
'charge' rather difficult to apply. Indeed, in case of the arrest or interviewing of a
suspect, the latter may very well experience this as implying an allegation which substantially affects his situation and may be in need of the guarantees of Article 6 from
that moment on in order to make these guarantees effective.[211]

Article 6 is also applicable to proceedings by which a detention on remand is
reviewed or prolonged on the ground of an existing suspicion, although these proceedings themselves are not directed at the determination of the charge,[212] as well as to
proceedings which ended with the conclusion that the offence was not punishable.[213]

---

[206]   Judgment of 10 December 1982, para. 34.
[207]   Judgment of 16 December 1997, *Tejedor García*, para. 27.
[208]   Judgment of 27 February 1980, paras 42-45.
[209]   Judgment of 20 October 1997, *Serves*, para. 42.
[210]   Judgment of 28 October 1999, para. 34.
[211]   See the joint dissenting opinion of Judges Tulkens, Fischbach and Casadevall, attached to the *Escoubet*
        judgment.
[212]   Judgment of 28 November 1978, *Luedicke, Balkacem and Koç*, para. 49. See also the judgment of 31
        March 1998, *Reinhardt & Slimane-Kaid*, para. 93; judgment of 13 February 2001, *Lietzow*, para. 44.
[213]   Judgment of 26 March 1982, *Adolf*, paras 31-33.

On the other hand, the refusal to pay compensation for damages caused by a public authority in the course of criminal proceedings which are subsequently discontinued, does not amount to a penalty,[214] but may involve a 'civil' right. The mere fact that a criminal prosecution is terminated or results in dismissal of the case does not mean that, in retrospect, Article 6 was not applicable, particularly when the person who was originally accused the prosecution may have left with certain prejudicial consequences.[215]

Whether the criminal proceedings were instituted by a private party or by a public authority is irrelevant to the question of whether a 'charge' was brought, and thus for the applicability of Article 6.[216] However, the private party who takes the initiative to start criminal proceedings is not himself entitled to a determination of the charge by a court; he may be entitled to the determination of his civil rights if a civil claim can be, and actually has been submitted in the criminal proceedings.[217] On the other hand, if a third person's rights are affected adversely by measures consequential upon the prosecution of others, no criminal charge can be said to have been brought against the former, who therefore cannot invoke the guarantees of Article 6 concerning the determination of a criminal charge. This approach, adopted in the *Agosi* Case,[218] led to the conclusion in the *Air Canada* Case that the seizure of an aircraft in which drugs had been brought into the United Kingdom, could not be considered as a 'criminal charge' brought against the airline company. The fact that the company regained the aeroplane only after it had paid an amount of $50,000, did not alter this conclusion.[219] Article 6 may, of course, be applicable under its civil limb.

A tariff-fixing decision by a public authority that determines the period of detention, is itself a sentencing exercise and must comply with the guarantees of Article 6.[220]

---

[214] Decision of 25 January 2000, *Van Leeuwen BV*, para. 1.

[215] Appl. 8269/78, *X v. Austria*, Yearbook XXII (1979), p. 324 (340-342). See also the judgment of 26 March 1982, *Adolf*, para. 33, concerning a decision that an offence was not punishable.

[216] Judgment of 25 March 1983, *Minelli*, para. 28.

[217] Judgment of 23 October 1990, *Moreira De Azevedo*, para. 67; judgment of 17 January 2002, *Calvelli and Coglio*, para. 62. See also *supra*, under 10.2.5.

[218] Judgment of 24 October 1986, para. 65.

[219] Judgment of 5 May 1995, paras 52-53.

[220] Judgment of 16 December 1999, *T. v. the United Kingdom*, paras 106-110; judgment of 12 June 2003, *Easterbrook*, para. 26.

10.3.3   AUTONOMOUS CONCEPT OF 'CRIMINAL'

10.3.3.1 Applicability to Disciplinary Procedures and Administrative Sanctions

The question of whether Article 6 is applicable to disciplinary procedures was answered in the negative by the Commission for a long time.[221] In the *Engel* Case, however, both the Commission and the Court took the position that the character of a procedure under domestic law cannot be decisive for the question of whether Article 6 is applicable, since otherwise the national authorities would be able to evade the guarantees of that provision by introducing disciplinary procedures with respect to offences which, in view of their nature or the character of the sanction imposed, are very similar to criminal offences.[222] As the Court stated in its judgment: "The Convention without any doubt allows the States (...) to maintain or establish a distinction between criminal law and disciplinary law, and to draw the dividing line, but only subject to certain conditions. (...) If the Contracting States were able at their discretion to classify an offence as disciplinary instead of criminal or to prosecute an author of a mixed offence on the disciplinary rather than on the criminal plane, the operation of the fundamental clauses of Articles 6 and 7 would be subordinated to their sovereign will. (...) The Court therefore has jurisdiction, under Article 6 (...), to satisfy itself that the disciplinary does not improperly encroach upon the criminal."[223] The same reasoning was followed in respect of administrative procedures which lead to the imposition of a sanction.[224]

For an answer to the question of whether disciplinary and administrative procedures imply a 'criminal charge' in the sense of Article 6, the Court developed the following criteria in its *Engel* judgment.[225]

10.3.3.2 Classification under Domestic Law

The first criterion to be applied is the classification of the allegedly violated norm under the applicable domestic legal system. Does it belong to criminal law or to disciplinary or administrative law? If the former is the case, the matter is settled, since the autonomy of the interpretation of 'criminal charge' is a one-way autonomy. Domestic

---

[221]   See the case law mentioned in the report of 19 July 1974, *Engel and Others*, B.20 (1978), pp. 68-69.

[222]   *Ibidem*, p. 70 and the judgment of 8 June 1976, para. 81.

[223]   *Ibidem.*

[224]   Judgment of 21 February 1984, *Öztürk*, paras 47-49.

[225]   *Ibidem*, para. 82. In its report of 14 December 1981, *Albert and Le Compte*, B.50 (1986), p. 36, the Commission proposed yet a fourth criterion: the applicable rules concerning evidence. In general, in disciplinary procedures the person concerned has no right to remain silent and no right to invoke professional secrecy. This does not, however, appear to be a correct independent criterion, since it forms a consequence of the choice made by the national legislature between criminal and disciplinary procedures, and moreover a consequence that, if applied as a criterion, would be detrimental to the legal protection of the person concerned.

law is decisive to the extent that, if an act or omission *is* designated as a criminal offence by domestic law, Article 6 is applicable to the proceedings in which the charge related to such act or omission is determined.[226] Criminalisation of certain behaviour may be reviewed for its conformity with other provisions of the Convention,[227] but its justification is not an issue under Article 6.

Only if an offence is not classified as criminal by the relevant legal system or is decriminalised, is there the danger of evasion of the guarantees of Article 6 which makes a further examination of the applicability of that provision necessary. This may require some investigation and interpretation by the Court of the relevant domestic law,[228] its legal history or the case law in relation thereto.[229] Even if Article 6 is found to be applicable, that does not mean that the disciplinary or administrative procedures have to be changed into criminal procedures; the only requirement is that they offer the guarantees of Article 6.

In view of the danger of evasion by defining an offence as 'disciplinary' or 'administrative' under national law, the criterion of the classification serves only as a preliminary point of departure for the ultimate assessment of the applicability of Article 6. This assessment has to be made on the basis of objective principles. For that purpose the Court has developed the following two additional criteria.

10.3.3.3 Scope of the Norm and Purpose of the Penalty

The scope of the norm concerns the circle of its addressees: is the norm only addressed to a specific group or is it a norm of a generally binding character? A provision of disciplinary law only addresses persons belonging to the disciplinary system. Therefore, as a starting point the circle of addressees offers a useful indication, but the same conduct that constitutes an offence under disciplinary law may also amount to an offence under criminal law.[230] On the other hand, there are several criminal law prohibitions which can only apply to certain persons: minors or adults, parents and guardians, spouses, captains, civil servants, *et cetera*. Therefore, the distinguishing feature implied in this criterion is not the number of addressees, but their quality as members of a particular group, combined with the interests protected by the rule.

The indeterminate character of the criterion came clearly to the fore in the *Weber* Case. The applicant had filed a criminal complaint of defamation against the author

---

[226] Judgment of 8 June 1976, *Engel and Others*, para. 81; judgment of 21 October 1997, *Pierre-Bloch*, para. 60.

[227] See the judgment of 22 October 1981, *Dudgeon*, paras 60-61, where the legislation in Northern Ireland, prohibiting homosexual intercourse between consenting male persons over 21 years of age, was held to violate Article 8.

[228] Judgment of 25 March 1983, *Minelli*, para. 28; judgment of 28 June 1984, *Campbell and Fell*, para. 70.

[229] Judgment of 21 February 1984, *Öztürk*, para. 51; judgment of 27 August 1991, *Demicoli*, para. 32.

[230] Judgment of 28 June 1984, *Campbell and Fell*, para. 71.

of a 'reader's letter' in a newspaper. Pending the proceedings he held a press conference to inform the public about his complaint. In summary proceedings he was fined for breaching the secrecy of the investigation. Since his appeal against the conviction was dismissed without public hearing, he claimed that Article 6 had been violated. The Commission had adopted the view that the violated rules were disciplinary rules and that neither the penalty imposed nor the maximum penalty could by their nature make the offence a criminal one.[231] The Court, however, made the following distinction: "Disciplinary sanctions are generally designed to ensure that the members of particular groups comply with the specific rules governing their conduct. Furthermore, in a great majority of the Contracting States disclosure of information about an investigation still pending constitutes an act incompatible with such rules and punishable under a variety of provisions. As persons who above all others are bound by the confidentiality of an investigation, judges, lawyers and all those closely associated with the functioning of the courts are liable in such an event, independently of any criminal sanction, to disciplinary measures on account of their profession. The parties, on the other hand, only take part in the proceedings as people subject to the jurisdiction of the courts, and they therefore do not come within the disciplinary sphere of the judicial system. As Article 185 [of the relevant Swiss Code], however, potentially affects the whole population, the offence it defines, and to which it attaches a punitive sanction, is a 'criminal' one for the purposes of the second criterion."[232]

That this aspect of the second criterion is not an easy one to apply became even clearer when the Court, in the not so dissimilar *Ravnsborg* Case[233] and *Putz* Case,[234] reached the opposite conclusion.

In the *Campbell and Fell* Case the Court, morover, indicated that the distinction between disciplinary and criminal offences is also a relative one. Thus, misconduct by a prisoner is usually no more than a question of internal discipline, but violations of the prison rules may also amount to criminal offences. Relevant indicators are the seriousness of the matter and whether the illegality of the act concerned turns on the fact that it is committed in prison.[235]

The fact that the nature of the offence is only of a minor character is of no relevance under the second criterion. According to the Court, the criminal nature of an offence does not require a certain degree of seriousness.[236]

---

[231]   Report of 16 March 1989, paras 100-111.
[232]   Judgment of 22 May 1990, para. 33. See also the judgment of 27 August 1991, *Demicoli*, para. 33.
[233]   Judgment of 23 March 1994, para. 34.
[234]   Judgment of 22 February 1996, paras 34-38.
[235]   Judgment of 28 June 1984, para. 71; judgment of 9 October 2003 (Grand Chamber), *Ezeh and Connors*, para. 101.
[236]   Judgment of 21 February 1984, *Öztürk*, para. 53; judgment of 9 October 2003 (Grand Chamber) *Ezeh and Connors*, para. 104.

The purpose of the penalty, as the other aspect of the second criterion, mainly serves to distinguish criminal sanctions from purely reparatory or compensatory sanctions. This sub-criterion was introduced in the *Öztürk* Case to determine whether the decriminalisation of certain offences under domestic law had as a consequence that Article 6 would no longer be applicable. The Court held this not to be the case as long as the sanction that could be applied had kept its 'deterrent' and 'punitive' character.[237] In the case of fines a clear criterion is whether the fine is merely intended as pecuniary compensation for damage caused or is punitive or deterrent in nature.[238] The fact that an administrative sanction is imposed on a person who has no personal guilt in the matter does not exclude the sanction from having a punitive character.[239] The criterium of guilt plays a role only in determining the classification of the proceedings under domestic law.[240]

Whereas the three criteria developed by the Court are not cumulative, the two aspects of the second criterion are. This means that an offence which is not criminal under national law, may only be considered criminal in the sense of Article 6 by its nature, if both the scope of the violated norm is of a general character and the purpose of the sanction is deterrent and punitive.[241]

The violation of one and the same legal provision may lead to the imposition of measures which are partly compensatory and partly punitive. Only the latter aspect of the measure brings the proceedings under the category of 'criminal charge'. Thus, under taxation law, if a person has failed to pay the taxes imposed upon him, proceedings instituted against him may result in the decision that he still has to pay a certain amount as compensation for his failure, and a surcharge as a sanction on tax evasion. The latter part is of a punitive character.[242]

The mere fact that a sanction or other measure imposed by the administration or the court is of a severe character with far-reaching consequences for the person concerned, does not mean that the sanction or measure is of a punitive character. If the sanction or measure is only meant to restore, or compensate for, the failure on the part of the person concerned, its character is reparatory rather than punitive,[243] even if full

---

[237] Judgment of 21 February 1984, para. 53. See also the judgment of 2 September 1998, *Lauko*, para. 58.

[238] Judgments of 29 August 1997, *E.L., R.L. and J.O.-L. v. Switzerland* and *A.P., M.P. and T.P. v. Switzerland*, paras 46 and 42, respectively.

[239] Judgment of 29 August 1997, *E.L., R.L. and J.O.-L. v. Switzerland*, paras 42 and 46.

[240] Judgment of 29 August 1997, *A.P., M.P. and T.P. v. Switzerland*, para. 42.

[241] Judgment of 21 February 1984, *Öztürk*, para. 53; judgment of 24 February 1994, *Bendenoun*, para. 47.

[242] Judgment of 24 February 1994, *Bendenoun*, para. 47; judgment of 14 March 1996, *J.J. v. the Netherlands*, para. 37; judgment of 29 August 1997, *E.L., R.L. and J.O.-L. v. Switserland*, para. 46; judgment of 3 May 2001, *J.B. v. Switserland*, paras 47-49.

[243] Judgment of 7 July 1989, *Tre Traktörer AB*, para. 46.

'reparation' is not brought about and is not possible.[244] However, if the sanction or measure is of such a character and severity that it is covered by the third criterion, to be discussed hereafter, Article 6 may still be applicable. This will very rarely be the case, because the person concerned can hardly complain about a measure the only purpose of which is to bring about or promote as closely as possible the situation which he was obliged to create or maintain himself. Possible examples of such severity would be detention to induce the person concerned to fulfil his obligations ('civil detention') and measures of a repetitive character or of such a long duration that the reparatory character will be overshadowed by the punitive side-effects.[245]

The lack of clarity of the (application of the) second criterion and its relation to the third criterion may be illustrated by the *Pierre-Bloch* Case. There the Court examined three kinds of possible sanctions as to their purpose, which surprisingly the Court did under the heading 'nature and degree of severity of the penalty' and not under that of 'nature of the offence'. First, the candidate who violated the Elections Code might be disqualified from standing for election for one year. That sanction was considered not to be 'criminal' since its purpose was to compel candidates to respect the maximum limit of election expenditure and was thus "designed to ensure the proper conduct of parliamentary elections". The severity of the sanction did not make it criminal either, because it was limited to a period of one year.[246] Secondly, the penalty to pay an amount equal to the amount by which the candidate had exceeded the ceiling of election expenditure was considered not to be 'criminal', because it was also "designed to ensure the proper conduct of parliamentary elections".[247] As to its severity the Court observed, *inter alia*, that the penalty was not entered into the criminal record and that in case of failure to pay no imprisonment could be imposed. A fine of FRF 25,000 could be imposed with as an alternative a year's imprisonment, but that eventuality was not considered relevant as no proceedings were brought against the applicant in connection with that possibility.[248] In particular the criterion used by the Court that the penalty concerned had as its purpose to compel the person concerned to respect the law and was therefore not 'criminal', is convincing only if meant in a reparatory or corrective sense. The punitive elements of a penalty also have the aim of compelling respect for the law, but in a preventive way in respect of the future. Indeed, in the *Lauko* Case the Court held the sanction imposed to be punitive, because 'it was intended as a punishment to deter reoffending'.[249]

---

[244]   Judgment of 21 October 1997, *Pierre-Bloch*, para. 58.
[245]   Judgment of 21 October 1997, *Pierre-Bloch*, para. 57.
[246]   *Ibidem*, para. 56.
[247]   *Ibidem*, para. 58.
[248]   *Ibidem*, para. 60.
[249]   Judgment of 2 September 1998, para. 58. See also the judgment of 24 February 1994, *Bendenoun*, para. 47: 'the tax surcharges are intended not as pecuniary compensation for damage but essentially as a punishment to deter reoffending'.

10.3.3.4 Nature and Severity of the Penalty

The third, and in certain cases ultimately decisive criterion is that of the nature and the severity of the penalty with which the violator of the norm is threatened.

The element of the 'nature' of the penalty should not be confused with that of the 'purpose' of the penalty, discussed under the second criterion.[250] If the purpose of the sanction (i.e. deterrence and punishment) does not make the second criterion applicable, the nature and severity of the penalty may still bring the procedure under Article 6.[251] On the other hand, if on the basis of the second criterion the proceedings must be deemed to clearly be of a criminal character, the nature and severity of the penalty are not relevant anymore. The second and third criterions are alternative and not cumulative.[252] On strict logical grounds one might deduct from the *Bendenoun* judgment that the Court changed its position on this point.[253] However, this cannot have been the intention. The case was not referred to the Grand Chamber, which indicates that the Chamber did not think its judgment to be inconsistent with previous case law (see Rule 51 of the then applicable Rules of the Court). And, indeed in the *Ravnsborg* Case the Court took into account 'the three alternative criteria'.[254]

The Court explained its *Bendenoun* judgment in the *Garyfallou AEBE* Case: the second and the third criterion were not cumulative, although they could be taken into consideration together in case a separate analysis of each criterion did not make it possible to reach a clear conclusion as to the existence of a criminal charge.[255] However, the judgment in the *Morel* Case has again contributed to confusion on the matter. In that case a tax penalty of 10% with interest had been imposed. In accordance with its *Bendenoun* judgment the Court concluded that the applicable legislation was of a general character and that the penalty was intended to prevent future violations. Next, again in accordance with its *Bendenoun* judgment, although the first two *Engel*-criteria were met, the Court examined the severity of the penalty. Here it reached the conclusion that the penalty was not sufficiently severe to make Article 6 applicable.[256] In our opinion, and in view of, among others, the *Öztürk* judgment, the Court could have

---

[250] That the Court brings the element of the purpose of the sanction under the second rather than the third criterion is clear from the judgment of 22 May 1990, *Weber*, para. 33: 'As article 185, however, potentially affects the whole population, the offence it defines, and to which it attaches a punitive sanction, is a 'criminal' one for the purposes of the second criterion.'

[251] Judgment of 8 June 1976, *Engel and Others*, para. 85.

[252] Judgment of 21 February 1984, *Öztürk*, para. 54; judgment of 25 August 1987, *Lutz*, para. 55.

[253] Judgment of 24 February 1994, *Bendenoun*, para. 47.

[254] Judgment of 23 March 1994, para. 30.

[255] Judgment of 24 September 1997, para. 33. See also the judgment of 23 July 2002, *Västberga Taxi Aktiebolag and Vulic*, para. 78; judgment of 9 October 2003 (Grand Chamber), *Ezeh and Connors*, para. 86.

[256] Decision of 3 June 2003.

followed that reasoning only, if the first two criteria did not allow for a clear conclusion as to the existence of a criminal charge, which was not the case here.

Imprisonment is considered to be the criminal penalty *par excellence*. Unless it is, by its nature, duration or manner of execution 'not appreciably detrimental', it gives an otherwise disciplinary or administrative procedure a criminal character to such an extent that Article 6 must be held applicable.[257] Thus, in the *Engel* Case, although the Court reached the conclusion that the offences at issue were against norms regulating the functioning of the Dutch armed forces, and therefore they could justly form the object of disciplinary procedures, it held that, since for some of these offences an imprisonment of considerable duration could be imposed, the conditions of Article 6 para. 1 ought to have been observed in the disciplinary procedures in question.[258]

This judgment makes it clear, first of all, that in the opinion of the Court not every limitation of liberty is a deprivation of liberty. This depends on the factual conditions.[259] Moreover, the deprivation of liberty must be 'liable to be imposed as a punishment',[260] which excludes deprivations of liberty such as the detention of mentally ill people or the detention of aliens with a view to deportation or expulsion. Detention to induce the person concerned to fulfil his obligations ('civil detention') would seem to meet the elements of the third criterion, if of a sufficiently long duration.

In the *Kiss* Case, which concerned disciplinary measures against a prisoner, the Commission concluded that Article 6 was not applicable, because it did not consider the possible penalty, loss of the prospect of reduction of the penalty, a deprivation of liberty.[261] However, in the *Campbell and Fell* Case, where the procedure could have resulted in refusal of remission of part of the imprisonment, the Court held that the practice of remission of the penalty creates for the detainee the justifiable expectation that he will be released before the end of the detention period. The procedure might therefore, in the Court's opinion, have such serious consequences for the person concerned as to the duration of his detention that it was to be considered of a criminal

---

[257]   Judgment of 8 June 1976, *Engel and Others*, para 82; judgment of 9 October 2003 (Grand Chamber), *Ezeh and Connors*, para. 126. The same would hold good, *a fortiori*, for capital and corporal punishment, if such punishment would still be allowed under Articles 2 and 3, respectively, in conjunction with Protocols Nos 6 and 13. However, such punishment could hardly be considered of a disciplinary character.

[258]   Judgment of 8 June 1976, para. 85.

[259]   In the *Engel* Case the Commission and the Court differed of opinion as far as the penalty of 'aggravated arrest' was concerned. In the cause of its opinion that no deprivation of liberty was at issue, the Court held it to be decisive that, although under that regime the soldiers, in off-duty hours, had to serve their arrest in a specially designated place which they were not allowed to leave for recreation purposes, they were not 'kept under lock and key'; judgment of 8 June 1976, para. 62.

[260]   *Ibidem*, para. 82. This would seem to indicate that a certain link may exist between the nature and the purpose of the sanction.

[261]   Appl. 6224/73, Yearbook XX (1977), p. 156.

character.[262] It reached the same conclusion in the *Ezeh and Connors* Case, where it also held that the question whether the resulting longer duration of loss of liberty is 'appreciably detrimental' should not be determined by reference to the length of the sentence already being served.[263] In its decision in *X v. Switzerland* the Commission came to the conclusion that isolated confinement of a person who is already detained, as a penalty for late return from leave of absence, is a purely disciplinary matter for which the procedural guarantees of Article 6 para. 1 need not be complied with.[264] The Commission here took into consideration that for a person already deprived of his liberty such a confinement is not of a 'severity' as envisaged in the Court's case law.

The *Engel* judgment also makes it clear that not every deprivation of liberty renders Article 6 applicable. Its effects on the person concerned must be of a certain severity, *inter alia*, due to its duration. Thus, although the 'strict arrest' was held a deprivation,[265] in this case the maximum duration of two days was considered insufficient by the Court for it to be regarded as a criminal penalty,[266] whereas the Court took a different position with regard to the detention of some months to which the applicants De Wit, Dona and Schul could have been sentenced.[267]

The relevant duration is the maximum penalty that *may* be imposed by the authority which is called upon to determine the charge; that is to say that not the penalty actually imposed but the maximum that the person concerned risked when committing the offence is decisive in this respect, even if practice shows that this maximum is seldom, if ever, imposed.[268] This principle of perspective also implies that proceedings where only a financial penalty has been imposed, but failure to pay may lead to alternative imprisonment, may come under Article 6. In the case of a company the latter factor may consist of the possibility of detention of its directors in case of non-payment.[269] However, the judgments in, on the one hand, the *Ravnsborg* Case and the *Putz* Case and, on the other hand, the *Demicoli* Case, the *Schmautzer* Case and *T. v. Austria*, make it difficult to draw a clear line and seem to suggest that factors other than (the duration of) possible (alternative) detention also play a role, especially the

---

[262]   Judgment of 28 June 1984, para. 72.
[263]   Judgment of 9 October 2003 (Grand Chamber), paras 121-124.
[264]   Appl. 7754/77, D&R 11 (1978), p. 216 (218).
[265]   Judgment of 8 June 1976, para. 63.
[266]   *Ibidem*, para. 85.
[267]   *Ibidem*. See also the judgments of 29 September 1999, *Smith and Ford* and *Moore and Gordon*, paras 19 and 18, respectively; judgment of 6 February 2001, *Wilkinson and Allen*, para. 19; judgment of 5 June 2001, *Mills*, para. 20.
[268]   Judgment of 22 May 1990, *Weber*, para. 34: "that the fine could amount to ..."; judgment of 27 August 1991, *Demicoli*, para 34; judgment of 9 October 2003 (Grand Chamber), *Ezeh and Connors*, para. 120.
[269]   Judgment of 24 September 1997, *Caryfallou*, para. 34.

punitive character of the penalty and whether an appeal lies against the decision to convert a fine into a prison sentence.[270]

On the ground of the duration criterion the Commission held in the *Eggs* Case, which also concerned a case of military discipline and in which the penalty imposed was five days of strict arrest in a civil prison: "Although relatively harsh, this freedom-restricting penalty could not, either by its duration or by the conditions of its enforcement in Basle prison, have caused serious detriment to the applicant. It could not, therefore, in this case be classified as criminal."[271]

In the *McFeeley* Case, which concerned IRA prisoners, the Commission took the position that for the determination of the severity of the penalty the cumulative effect of repeatedly imposed penalties should not be taken into account, because for the applicability of Article 6 each sentence must be considered by itself.[272] This position seems to have been confirmed by the Court in the *Ravnsborg* Case[273] and the *Putz* Case.[274] Although the view of the Strasbourg organs is formally correct, it may have the consequence that without any intervention of a court a person may be subjected to restrictions which in combination amount to a much heavier burden for him than the sanction which in a separate case would be of sufficient duration to confer a criminal-law character on the procedure. The question arises whether, if the duration criterion is appropriate at all in cases of deprivation of liberty, one ought not to seek a certain analogy here with the Court's case law concerning Article 5 para. 3 where, for the determination of the reasonableness of the period, successive periods of detention for various charges are also taken into account together,[275] so that the total situation in which the person finds himself is taken as the frame of reference and not the separate measures imposed upon him.

In the *Olivieira* Case and the *Landvreugd* Case the order imposed by the *Burgomaster* to the effect that the applicant was not allowed to enter parts of the city center for fourteen days, was considered to be of a preventive character and not of such a severity to give it a 'criminal' character.[276]

All these elements and conditions as indications of the seriousness of the consequences of the penalty, make the third criterion a rather unpredictable one as long as fixed standards are lacking. It is submitted that it would be desirable and create the required clarity if the third criterion were applied in such a way that in any case where the

---

[270]   Judgment of 23 march 1994, *Ravnsborg*, para. 35; judgment of 22 February 1996, *Putz*, para. 37; judgment of 27 August 1991, *Demicoli*, para. 34; judgment of 23 October 1995, *Schmautzer*, para. 28; judgment of 14 November 2000, *T. v. Austria*, para. 67.

[271]   Report of 4 March 1978, para. 79.

[272]   Appl. 8317/78, D&R 20 (1980), p. 44 (94).

[273]   Judgment of 23 March 1994, para. 35.

[274]   Judgment of 22 February 1996, para. 37.

[275]   Judgment of 27 June 1968, *Neumeister*, para. 6; judgment of 16 July 1971, *Ringeisen*, para. 101.

[276]   Judgments of 6 June 2000, paras 3 and 2, respectively.

penalty may consist of a deprivation of liberty in the sense assigned thereto in the case law concerning Article 5, the guarantees of Article 6 should be observed in the procedure that may result in such a deprivation.[277]

The fact that Article 6 also applies to legal persons raises the issue whether 'deprivation of liberty' of a legal person may also make Article 6 applicable. In its report in the *Kaplan* Case the Commission held that the restrictions imposed by administrative measures on the activities of the company did not concern a 'criminal charge', because these restrictions could not be regarded as equivalent to a penalty.[278]

It is not yet very clear to what extent disciplinary penalties other than deprivations of liberty may be considered severe enough to make Article 6 applicable. In the *Weber* Case, which concerned proceedings where the fine could amount to 500 Swiss francs and could be converted into a term of imprisonment in certain circumstances, the Court held, with a general reference to its third criterion and without further reasoning, that what was at stake was "sufficiently important to warrant classifying the offence as a criminal one under the Convention",[279] leaving it unclear to what extent the fact that the fine could be converted into imprisonment was decisive. The same lack of clarity was left in the *Demicoli* judgment.[280] The more recent *Ravnsborg* Case, *Schmautzer* Case and *Putz* Case seem to make it even more difficult to fathom the Court's case law on this point. In the *Ravnsborg* Case, the imposed maximum fine of 1000 Swedish crowns did not make the sanction a 'criminal' one. In addition to the amount, the Court took into account that the fine was not registered in the police records and that conversion into a term of imprisonment could take place only if a special procedure, including an oral hearing, was followed.[281] This term of imprisonment amounted to at least two weeks. In the subsequent *Schmautzer* Case the Court held that driving without wearing a seat-belt, an administrative offence under Austrian law, was criminal in nature. It used as an additional argument that the imposed fine (of 200 Austrian schillings) had been accompanied by an order for committal to prison in case of non-payment. The maximum term of imprisonment was only 24

---

[277]   Thus judge Cremona in his separate opinion in the *Engel* Case, A.22, pp. 52-53. In its report in the *Albert and Le Compte* Case the Commission indeed observed quite generally with regard to a certain disciplinary measure: "it cannot be treated as being equivalent to a penal sanction, such as the deprivation of liberty"; report of 14 December 1981, *Albert and Le Compte*, B.50 (1986), p. 35. In its decision on Appl. 8209/78, *Sutter v. Switzerland*, para. 2, the Commission also argued quite generally: "The applicant was charged with an offence under the Military Penal Code, punishable by imprisonment, and therefore he was undoubtedly accused of a criminal offence". Also in a general sense: report of 6 May 1981, *Minelli*, B.52 (1986), p. 21.

[278]   Report of 17 July 1980, para. 170. See, however, the judgment of 24 September 1997, *Garyfallou*, para. 34.

[279]   Judgment of 22 May 1990, para. 34.

[280]   Judgment of 27 August 1991, para. 34.

[281]   Judgment of 23 March 1994, para. 35.

hours.[282] In the *Putz* Case, however, the Court held with reference to its reasoning in the *Ravensborg* Case that a possible maximum penalty of 20,000 Austrian schillings, that could have been converted into a term of imprisonment of ten days, did not come within the ambit of Article 6.[283]

The Court went rather far in attributing a decisive character to the severity of a penalty that did not consist in deprivation of liberty in the *Garyfallou AEBE* Case. However, even there the Court took into consideration, in addition to the maximum of the fine and the risk of the company's assets being seized, as "more importantly, for the purposes of the Court's examination" that, in the event of non-payment of the fine, the directors risked detention of up to one year.[284]

The *Malige* Case concerned the measure of docking of points from driving licenses after a conviction for a traffic offence. No possible detention as an alternative was involved. The Court found the measure to be of a severity to make it a criminal sanction. However, in its reasoning the Court seems to have mixed the purpose of the sanction with its severity: "the deduction of points may in time entail invalidation of the licence. It is indisputable that the right to drive a motor vehicle is very useful in everyday life and for carrying on an occupation. The Court, like the Commission, accordingly infers that, although the deduction of points has a preventive character, it also has a punitive and deterrent character and is accordingly similar to a secondary penalty."[285]

The judgment in the *Escoubet* Case suggests that, in the case of two different measures of comparable impact, the connection which a certain measure has with the outcome of criminal proceedings may be decisive for the applicability of Article 6. The Court held with respect to the measure of withdrawal of a driving licence after a road accident: "The immediate withdrawal of a driving licence is a precautionary measure; the fact that it is an emergency measure justifies its being applied immediately and there is nothing to indicate that its purpose is punitive. Withdrawal of a driving licence is distinguishable from disqualification from driving, a measure ordered by the criminal court at the end of criminal proceedings. In such a case, the criminal court assesses and classifies the facts constituting the offence which may give rise to disqualification."[286]

---

[282]   Judgment of 23 October 1995, para. 28. See also, of the same date, five other cases against Austria: *Umlauft*, para. 31; *Gradinger*, para. 36; *Pramstaller*, para. 33; *Palaoro*, para. 35, *Pfarrmeier*, para. 32. In these cases the imposed fines varied from 5,000 Austrian schillings (in the event of default of payment 200 hours of imprisonment) in the *Pfarrmeier* Case to 50,000 schillings (fifty days of imprisonment) in the *Pramstaller* Case. The maximum penalties that could have been imposed varied from 300 schillings (24 hours of imprisonment) in the *Pfarrmeier* Case to 100,000 schillings (three months of imprisonment) in the *Pramstaller* Case.

[283]   Judgment of 22 February 1996, para. 37.

[284]   Judgment of 24 September 1997, para. 34.

[285]   Judgment of 23 September 1998, para. 39.

[286]   Judgment of 28 October 1999, para. 37.

The same kind of reasoning was followed in the *Blokker* Case. The applicant, who had been stopped by the police driving a car with too high an alcohol level in his blood, had been ordered, *inter alia*, to subject to an Educational Measure Alcohol and Traffic, the costs of which he had to pay himself. The Court found the measure not to be of a severity and character to make it a criminal sanction. In the Court's opinion it should be compared with the procedure of issuing a driving licence, aimed at ensuring that the driver possesses the required skills and knowledge of the relevant traffic rules. The costs and time which the applicant had to spend for the Measure were to be compared with the time and costs spent for obtaining a driving licence. The fact that in case of failure to comply with the Measure the driving licence could be declared invalid, did not change the character, since that was to be compared with the consequences of failing to pay for or take an examination for a driving licence, and not with disqualification for driving as a measure in the context of criminal proceedings.[287]

10.3.4 FISCAL PENALTIES

With respect to 'fiscal penalties' the Court has adopted the position that those fiscal penalties which are not compensatory in nature, but are of a punitive character, such as fines, disqualifications and settlements of penalties, give the proceedings a criminal character for the purposes of Article 6.[288]

This was further elaborated upon in the *Bendenoun* Case. Although the tax surcharges imposed upon the applicant were, in the Government's submission, to be considered 'administrative' and not 'criminal' penalties under the applicable French law, the Court did not consider this to be decisive. On the basis of the other criteria of its *Engel* judgment it reached the conclusion that the criminal connotation was predominant, since the surcharges were "intended not as pecuniary compensation for damages but essentially as a punishment to deter reoffending, they were imposed under a general rule, the purpose of which was both deterrent and punitive, and they were very substantial".[289]

10.3.5 DECRIMINALISATION AND 'PETTY OFFENCES'

For a long time there has been a lack of clarity as to whether Article 6 applies to all criminal proceedings, even when offences of a less serious nature are concerned.[290]

---

[287] Judgment of 7 November 2000, para. 1.
[288] Judgment of 7 October 1988, *Salabiaku*, para. 24; judgment of 3 May 2001, *J.B. v. Switzerland*, paras 47-49.
[289] Judgment of 24 February 1994, para. 47; judgment of 3 May 2001, *J.B. v. Switzerland*, para. 48; judgments of 23 July 2002 *Västberga Taxi Aktiebolag and Others*, paras 78-82.
[290] See Appl. 8537/79, *X v. Federal Republic of Germany* (not published).

Since Article 6 does not distinguish between criminal charges of a serious and those of a less serious nature and the determination of a criminal charge concerning a petty offence may be of great importance for the person in question, all proceedings in which there is question of a determination of a criminal charge should fall under the guarantees of Article 6.

This is the view adopted by the Court. In the *Adolf* Case, in which a petty offence was involved, which on that ground was declared non-punishable, the Court held: "non-punishable or unpunished criminal offences do exist and Article 6 of the Convention does not distinguish between them and other criminal offences; it applies whenever a person is 'charged' with any criminal offence."[291] And in the *Öztürk* Case the Court held: "There is in fact nothing to suggest that the criminal offence referred to in the Convention necessarily implies a certain degree of seriousness (...). Furthermore, it would be contrary to the object and purpose of Article 6, which guarantees to 'everyone charged with a criminal offence' the right to a court and to a fair trial, if the State were allowed to remove from the scope of this Article a whole category of offences merely on the ground of regarding them as petty."[292]

The Court indicated in the *Öztürk* Case that it does not conflict with the Convention to distinguish between different categories of offences, but that such a classification is not decisive for the question whether Article 6 is applicable.[293] In this case an offence was involved which was not qualified under German law as a criminal but as a 'regulatory' offence: an *Ordnungswidrigkeit*. Quite in line with its previous case law concerning Article 6 the Court, here again, was on its guard against erosion of the guarantees aimed at in that article: "if the Contracting States were able at their discretion, by classifying an offence as 'regulatory' instead of criminal, to exclude the operation of the fundamental clauses of Articles 6 and 7, the application of these provisions would be subordinated to their sovereign will. A latitude extending thus far might lead to results incompatible with the object and purpose of the Convention."[294]

Consequently, it remains decisive whether the nature of the offence, and that of the sanction that may be imposed, confer a criminal character on the proceedings, irrespective of whether formally they still have that character under domestic law.

10.3.6   ADMISSION, EXPULSION AND EXTRADITION PROCEDURES

The prohibition to enter a country does not amount to a criminal penalty. The same holds good for the removal or expulsion of aliens from the territory, although such

---

[291]   Judgment of 26 March 1982, para. 33.
[292]   Judgment of 21 February 1984, para. 53.
[293]   *Ibidem*, para. 49.
[294]   *Ibidem*, para. 49.

measure may be experienced by the person concerned as a penalty. In the *Maaouia* Case the Court recognised that such measures may be characterized differently in different domestic legal orders and that their characterization as a penalty is not decisive for determining whether or not the penalty is criminal in nature. In that respect the Court noted that, in general, the measure is not characterized as criminal within the member States of the Council of Europe. "Such orders, which in most States may also be made by the administrative authorities, constitute a special preventive measure for the purpose of immigration control and do not concern the determination of a criminal charge against the applicant for the purposes of Article 6 para. 1. The fact that they are imposed in the context of criminal proceedings cannot alter their essentially preventive nature."[295]

The *Maaouia* Case concerned an exclusion order imposed on the applicant by a criminal court in addition to the imprisonment conviction. The Court does not seem to distinguish this order from expulsion orders. However, Judge Costa, in his concurring opinion, defined the order as an 'ancillary penalty' which comes within criminal law. He nevertheless agreed with the majority that Article 6 was not applicable, but for the reason that the charge forming the basis of the order was not challenged by the applicant in the proceedings for the rescission of the order.

Extradition proceedings are also held not to be covered by Article 6, on the ground that a 'determination' involves the full process of the examination of an individual's guilt or innocence, and not the process of determining whether a person can be extradited to another country.[296]

10.3.7 CONCLUDING OBSERVATIONS

As in the case of 'civil rights and obligations', the Court should make further efforts to lift the uncertainty and ambiguity with respect to 'criminal charge' which its case law still leaves, especially concerning the criterion of the nature and severity of the penalty.

As to the nature of the penalty, Article 6 should be held applicable to all those proceedings which may result in the imposition of a punitive sanction that as to its nature and/or its consequences is so similar to criminal sanctions that there is no justification for excluding judicial review, except by free and unambiguous waiver. This includes in particular deprivation of liberty and the imposition of fines, but could also concern restrictions of economic or professional freedom of a punitive character (which, moreover, could affect civil rights and obligations). Since the Court has adopted the position that Article 6 makes no distinction between serious and less serious

---

[295] Judgment of 5 October 2000, para. 39.
[296] Appl. 10227/82, *H v. Spain*, D&R 37 (1984), p. 93 (94).

offences and that it may even apply to proceedings which lead to no penalty at all, the severity of the penalty cannot be a decisive element for its 'punitive' character.

As far as the severity of a non-criminal sanction is concerned, there would seem to be no convincing reason to distinguish between detentions of short and of longer duration, since deprivation of liberty has by definition severe consequences. As to fines, it makes sense to distinguish between small and large amounts. However, the financial situation of the person concerned should then be relevant and, in connection therewith, the possibility that, if the fine is not paid, an alternative detention may be imposed.

10.4 ACCESS TO COURT

10.4.1 INTRODUCTION

Article 6 para. 1 not only contains procedural guarantees in relation to judicial proceedings, but also grants *a right to* judicial proceedings for the cases mentioned there: the right of access to court. This right has not been laid down in express terms in Article 6. Its first paragraph only refers to entitlement to a fair and public hearing by a court, leaving it unclear whether this entitlement only exists in cases where judicial proceedings have been provided for under domestic law, or that provision implies – or rather presupposes – a right to such judicial proceedings.

This unclarity was lifted by the Court in its *Golder* judgment. The Court referred to the reference in the Preamble of the Convention to the rule of law "as one of the features of the common spiritual heritage of the member States of the Council of Europe". According to the Court that reference had to be taken into account when interpreting the terms of Article 6 para. 1 according to their context and in the light of the object and purpose of the Convention. In doing so the Court made the observation that "in civil matters one can scarcely conceive of the rule of law without there being a possibility of having access to the courts". The Court further reasoned that Article 6 must be read in the light of the following two legal principles: (1) the principle whereby a civil claim must be capable of being submitted to a judge, as one of the universally recognised fundamental principles of law; and (2) the principle of international law which forbids the denial of justice.[297] "Taking all the preceding considerations together, it follows that the right of access constitutes an element which is inherent in the right stated by Article 6 para. 1. This is not an extensive interpretation forcing new obligations on the Contracting States: it is based on the very terms of the first sentence of Article 6 para. 1 read in its context and having regard to the object and purpose of the Convention, a lawmaking treaty (...), and to general principles of

---

[297] Judgment of 21 February 1975, paras 34-35.

law. The Court thus reaches the conclusion (...) that Article 6 para. 1 secures to everyone the right to have any claim relating to his civil rights and obligations brought before a court or tribunal."[298]

In conclusion, Article 6 para. 1 also applies to determinations of civil rights and obligations, and of criminal charges, for which domestic law does not provide for judicial proceedings.[299] It does not, however, imply a guarantee against the striking out of a case by the court if there is no sustainable cause of action.[300]

With this extensive, teleological interpretation the Court intended to prevent the States from eroding the guarantees of Article 6 by restricting, or even abolishing, judicial proceedings in some areas and omitting its introduction in others.[301] For the same reason the Court adopted the view that Article 6 also applies to the (non-) implementation of a judicial decision: "to construe Article 6 as being concerned exclusively with access to a court and the conduct of proceedings would be likely to lead to situations incompatible with the principle of the rule of law".[302] Where the competent authorities refuse or fail to comply, or even delay doing so,[303] the guarantees under Article 6 enjoyed by a litigant during the judicial phase of the proceedings, are rendered devoid of purpose. Consequently, the power of the Procurator-General to apply for a final judgment to be quashed infringes the principle of legal certainty and the right of access to court.[304] And the same holds good if private parties refuse to execute a judgment and the judgment is not enforced against them.[305] Execution of a judgment given by a court must, therefore, be regarded as an integral part of the 'trial' for the purposes of Article 6.[306] A stay of execution must itself be subject to effective judicial review.[307]

---

[298] *Ibidem*, para. 36. See, however, the dissenting opinion of judge Fitzmaurice, para. 40.

[299] This was the case, *e.g.*, with the Crown appeal procedure in the Netherlands: judgment of 23 October 1985, *Benthem*, paras 41-44. For a specific administrative review procedure in Sweden that did not meet the requirements, see the judgment of 23 September 1982, *Sporrong and Lönnroth*, para. 86; judgment of 28 June 1990, *Mats Jacobsson*, para. 36.

[300] Judgment of 10 May 2001, *Z and Others v. the United Kingdom*, para. 97.

[301] Judgment of 21 February 1975, *Golder*, para. 35.

[302] Judgment of 19 March 1997, *Hornsby*, para. 40; judgment of 28 July 1999, *Immobiliare Saffi*, para. 63; judgment of 14 December 1999, *Antonakopoulos, Vortsela and Antonakopoulou*, para. 21; judgment of 28 March 2000, *Dimitrios Georgiadis*, para. 25; judgment of 20 July 2000, *Antonetto*, para. 27; judgment of 3 August 2000, *G.L. v. Italy*, para. 33; judgment of 30 November 2000, *Edoardo Palumbo*, para. 42; judgment of 11 January 2001, *P.M. v. Italy*, paras 48-49; judgment of 15 February 2001, *Pialopoulos*, para. 68; judgment of 12 April 2001, *Logothetis*, paras 14-16; judgment of 14 March 2002, *Adamogiannis*, para. 20; judgment of 6 March 2003, *Jasiûnienë*, paras 27-31; judgment of 22 May 2003, *Kyrtatos*, para. 32; judgment of 12 July 2005, *Okyay and Others*, para. 72.

[303] Here, the Court judges on the reasonableness of the delay: decision of 11 January 2005, *Ganenko*.

[304] Judgment of 30 September 1999, *Brumărescu*, para. 62.

[305] Judgment of 22 June 2004, *Pini and Others*, paras 174-189.

[306] Judgment of 22 May 2003, *Kyrtatos*, para. 30; judgment of 23 October 2003, *Timofeyev*, para. 40.

[307] Judgment of 3 August 2000, *G.L. v. Italy*, para. 40; judgment of 30 November 2000, *Edoardo Palumbo*, para. 45.

Lack of financial means is no justification for non-execution,[308] and even if there are compelling reasons for a stay of execution, the authorities must take speedy and adequate measures to create a situation that allows for execution.[309] Consequently, allowing for a final judgment to be quashed at the Procurator-General's application without any time-limit, was considered by the Court to violate the principle of legal certainty and, consequently, the right to a fair hearing.[310] Access to court is also made illusory if the applicant has the possibility of bringing legal proceedings, but is prevented by operation of the law from pursuing his claim.[311]

Interpreted in this way paragraph 1 of Article 6 takes over to a considerable extent the function of Article 13, which guarantees a right to an effective remedy. Article 6 goes even further. Firstly, because it implies a right of recourse to a *court or tribunal* "characterised in the substantive sense of the term by its judicial function, that is to say determining matters within its competence on the basis of rules of law and after proceedings conducted in a prescribed manner".[312] And secondly, because it applies to all determinations of civil rights and obligations and not only to those which are related to one of the rights and freedoms laid down in the Convention. However, Article 13 remains important for cases of violation of rights which according to the Strasbourg case law are not 'civil rights' in the sense of Article 6 para. 1[313] and, indeed, for cases of violation of (the reasonable-time requirement of) Article 6 itself.[314]

The access guarantee of Article 6 covers all the issues related to the dispute concerning civil rights or obligations, including issues concerning the costs involved in having those rights and obligations determined.[315] Domestic law or case law may not exclude these issues from appeal to a court, not even if, in an indirect way, they depend on issues which themselves may be subjected to judicial examination.[316] For the same reason, the possibility of instituting judicial proceedings for damages does not substitute for the right to refer the underlying dispute to a court.[317]

---

[308]   Judgment of 29 June 2004, *Piven*, para. 40; judgment of 27 September 2005, *Amat-G*, para. 48.

[309]   Judgment of 11 January 2001, *Lunari*, para. 45.

[310]   Judgment of 28 October 1999, *Brumarescu*, para. 62. See the concurring opinion of Judge Bratza joined by Judge Zupancic, where it is said that it was rather the right of access to court that was at stake and had been violated. See also the judgment of 24 July 2003, *Ryabykh*, para. 55.

[311]   Judgment of 1 March 2002, *Kutic*, paras 25-33.

[312]   Judgment of 16 December 1992, *Geouffre de la Pradelle*, paras 36-37; judgment of 10 May 2001, *Cyprus v. Turkey*, para. 233; judgment of 22 May 2001, *Baumann*, para. 39.

[313]   Thus the Court in its judgment of 21 February 1975, *Golder*, para. 33.

[314]   Judgment of 26 October 2000, *Kudla*, paras 147-149.

[315]   Judgment of 23 September 1997, *Robins*, para. 28; judgment of 6 February 2001, *Beer*, paras 12-13.

[316]   Judgment of 22 June 1989, *Eriksson*, paras 80-81; judgment of 26 May 1994, *Keegan*, para. 59.

[317]   Judgment of 7 July 1989, *Tre Traktörer AB*, para. 49.

10.4.2 REQUIREMENT OF EFFECTIVENESS

10.4.2.1 General observations

As holds good for all rights laid down in the Convention, the right of access to court must not be theoretical or illusory, but practical and effective.[318] This means that the person concerned not only has a right to apply to a court for the determination of his rights or obligations, but must also be enabled to present his case properly and satisfactorily,[319] which also requires that the proceedings are organized and conducted in a way that takes into account the intellectual abilities of the parties.[320] It further means that the right of access includes the right to obtain a 'determination' of the dispute by the competent court.[321] It also means that there has to be an independent and impartial court with the required jurisdiction to make this determination; otherwise his right of access is not secured.[322] Thus, in its judgments in *W., B.* and *R. v. the United Kingdom* the Court held that, although the parents could apply for judicial review or institute wardship proceedings, and thereby have certain aspects of the authority's access decisions examined by an English court, during the currency of the parental resolutions the court's powers were not of sufficient scope to fully satisfy the requirements of Article 6, as they did not extend to the merits of the matter.[323]

In the *Obermeier* Case the Court held that there had been a violation of the right of access to court, since the court in question could only determine whether the administrative authorities had exercised their discretionary power in a way compatible with the object and purpose of the applicable law.[324] And in the *Tinnelly* Case and the *Devlin* Case the Court adopted the position that the fact that, for national security reasons, the court could not determine the merits of the applicant's complaint concerning discrimination, made the remedy ineffective to an extent that was not justified by the security considerations; it took into consideration that in other contexts it had been found possible to modify judicial proceedings in such a way as to safeguard national security concerns and yet accord the individual a substantial degree of procedural justice.[325]

Consequently, there is a close link between the requirement of effective access to court and the requirement of exhaustion of local remedies, laid down in Article 35

---

[318] Judgment of 9 October 1979, *Airey*, para. 24; judgment of 1 March 2002, *Kutic*, para. 25; judgment of 10 July 2003, *Multiplex*, para. 44.
[319] *Ibidem.*
[320] Judgment of 15 June 2004, *S.C. v. the United Kingdom*, para. 36.
[321] Judgment of 10 July 2003, *Multiplex*, para. 45.
[322] Judgment of 23 June 1981, *Le Compte, Van Leuven and De Meyere*, para. 44; judgment of 23 September 1982, *Sporrong and Lönroth*, para. 80; judgment of 28 May 1985, *Ashingdane*, para. 55.
[323] Judgments of 8 July 1987, paras 81-82, 81-82 and 86-87, respectively.
[324] Judgment of 28 June 1990, paras 69-70.
[325] Judgment of 10 July 1998, paras 77-78; judgment of 30 October 2001, para. 31.

para. 1; if the Court concludes that the local remedies available were not effective it means at the same time, in cases to which Article 6 para. 1 applies, that the applicant did not have effective access to a court.[326]

10.4.2.2 Full Jurisdiction

For the right of access to be effective it is not sufficient that the court has jurisdiction to judge on the merits of the case. The court must have full jurisdiction. This means that the court must have competence to judge both on the facts and on the law as a basis for its 'determination'.[327]

However, the Court recognises that especially in procedures of judicial review of administrative decisions it is a common feature that the courts take a somewhat reserved position in reviewing the establishment of the facts by the administration. In judging on whether that approach is sufficient from the perspective of effective access to court, the Court has regard to such aspects as the subject-matter of the decision appealed against, the manner in which and the procedure according to which that decision was arrived at, and the contents of the dispute. Especially if the subject-matter concerns a specialised area of the law and the facts have been established in the course of a quasi-judicial procedure governed by several of the safeguards required by Article 6, a restricted jurisdiction to re-examine the facts will be acceptable.[328] Thus, on the one hand, in the *Schmautzer* Case the Court held that the appeal from the administrative authorities to the administrative court did not satisfy the requirements of Article 6, since the latter did not have full jurisdiction to review and quash the decision of the administrative body both on questions of fact and of law.[329] There the Court took into consideration that the administrative court was sitting in proceedings that were of a criminal nature for the purposes of the Convention. On the other hand, the judgments in the *Bryan* Case, the *Chapman* Case and the *Jane Smith* Case suggest that in more typically administrative proceedings, if a full review of the facts has been performed by the administrative body, a more restricted jurisdiction may suffice.[330]

---

[326]   Judgment of 22 May 2001, *Baumann*, para. 48.

[327]   Judgment of 23 June 1981, *Le Compte, Van Leuven and De Meyere*, para. 51; judgment of 21 September 1993, *Zumtobel*, para. 29; judgment of 26 April 1995, *Fisher*, para. 28; judgment of 23 October 1995, *Umlauft*, para. 37; judgment of 12 June 2003, *Kück*, para. 48 and judgment of 13 July 2004, *Beneficio Cappella Paolini*, paras 28-29. See, however, the judgment of 22 November 1995, *Bryan*, paras 44-47, and the judgment of 4 October 2001, *Potocka and Others*, paras 52-59, where the Court held that a somewhat restricted jurisdiction could also meet the requirements of Article 6 para. 1 in specific circumstances.

[328]   Judgment of 22 November 1995, *Bryan*, paras 45-47; judgment of 4 October 2001, *Potocka and Others*, para. 53.

[329]   Judgment of 23 October 1995, para. 36; judgment of 20 June 2000, *Mauer*, para. 16.

[330]   Judgment of 22 November 1995, *Bryan*, paras 34-47; judgments of 18 January 2001, *Chapman* and *Jane Smith*, paras 124 and 133, respectively.

Effective access to a court for a determination also means that the final judgment concerning legal issues relevant for the determination rests with the court. Consequently, the practice of the French *Conseil d'Etat* to ask the minister of foreign affairs for a preliminary opinion about the reciprocal character of a treaty, which opinion is then followed by the *Conseil d'Etat* without any possibility for the parties to challenge that opinion, is in violation of the right of access to court.[331]

10.4.2.3 Legal Aid

In the *Airey* Case it was held that, although the right of access to court does not imply an automatic right to free legal aid in civil proceedings, it may imply the obligation on the part of the State to provide for the assistance of a lawyer to persons in financial need. This is the case when legal aid proves indispensable for an effective access to court, either because legal representation is rendered compulsory or by reason of the procedural complexity of the case. The State may also, if appropriate and possible, opt for abolition of compulsory representation and simplification of procedure to the effect that effective access to the court no longer requires a lawyer's assistance.[332] Moreover, a certain financial threshold for the legal costs to be incurred may be acceptable.[333]

In the *Aerts* Case the Court adopted the opinion that legal aid may not be refused by the competent authority on the sole basis of the latter's assessment of the prospects of success of the review, unless the assessment is made by a court.[334] In the *Gnahore* Case the Court specified this by stating that the fact that representation by a lawyer was obligatory, had been decisive. It accepted the refusal of legal aid for reason of lack of any serious cassation ground in a case where legal representation was not required and the procedure of selection offered several guarantees.[335] The same position was adopted in the *Essaadi* and *Del Sol* Cases.[336] If an *ex gratia* offer has been made, but is refused by the applicant, the latter cannot complain about lack of effective access.[337]

10.4.2.4 Other Aspects of Effectiveness

In the *De Geouffre de la Pradelle* Case the Court held that if the law regulating the access to court is so complex and unclear that it creates legal uncertainty, access of court cannot be said to be effective.[338]

---

[331] Judgment of 13 February 2003, *Chevrol*, paras 83-84.
[332] Judgment of 9 October 1979, paras 24-26.
[333] Judgment of 19 September 2000, *Glaser*, para. 99.
[334] Judgment of 30 July 1998, para. 60.
[335] Judgment of 19 September 2000, paras 40-41.
[336] Judgments of 26 February 2002, paras 33-36 and 23-26, respectively.
[337] Judgment of 9 October 1997, *Andronicou and Constantinou*, para. 200.
[338] Judgment of 16 December 1992, paras 33-34.

In the *Golder* Case the Court attached to its view that Article 6 implies a right of access to court and that "hindering the effective exercise of a right may amount to a breach of that right, even if the hindrance is of a temporary character", the consequence that a refusal to permit detainees to correspond with persons providing legal aid or their counsel is contrary to this provision.[339] Moreover, the detainee has a right to have contact with counsel or a person providing legal aid without the presence of a prison authority.[340]

Effective access to a court also requires that the applicant has access to the judgment. However, if a copy of the judgment is sent to the applicant in a normal way, the fact that he lives far away and has not indicated his intention to receive the copy at a certain address is at his own risk.[341]

10.4.3   ACCESS TO COURT IN CRIMINAL CASES

For criminal cases and for cases with criminal features which make Article 6 applicable, the right of access to court implies that the person who is 'charged', has the right that any ultimate determination of that charge is made by a court which fulfils the requirements of Article 6 para. 1. It does not imply that the person 'charged' may demand the continuation of the prosecution and an ultimate trial by a court, but only that, when a determination is made, this is done by a court.[342] However, if the charge is dropped on the basis of a financial transaction between the accused and the prosecuting authority, without a free choice on the part of the accused, he is actually denied access to court contrary to Article 6.[343] In other situations, too, a waiver of the right of access by an accused should not be assumed lightly and may be overruled by an important public interest.[344] And if the case is dropped under circumstances in which the odium of guilt would continue to cling to the person in question, Article 6 has nevertheless been violated; this also in the light of the presumption of innocence of the second paragraph.[345]

---

[339]   Judgment of 21 February 1975, para. 40. See also the judgment of 25 March 1983, *Silver and Others*, para. 82; judgment of 28 June 1984, *Campbell and Fell*, paras 106-107.

[340]   Judgment of 28 June 1984, *Campbell and Fell*, paras 111-113.

[341]   Decision of 5 February 2004, *Bogonos*, para. 1.

[342]   Report of 18 October 1985, *Lutz*, para. 48.

[343]   Judgment of 27 February 1980, *Deweer*, paras 49-54. In this case the person in question was subject to the threat that his shop would be closed if he did not agree to the transaction.

[344]   Judgment of 15 June 2004, *Thompsom*, para. 43.

[345]   Judgment of 25 March 1983, *Minelli*, paras 34-41. See, however, the judgment of 26 March 1996, *Leutscher*, paras 30-32: The applicant had been tried at first instance *in absentia*. He instituted an appeal, but the appeal proceedings ended in the court of appeal declaring the prosecution time-barred. The applicant's request for reimbursement of legal costs was refused on the ground that suspicion still weighed against the applicant. In the opinion of the Court the result was not a violation

The right of access to court does not imply the right for the victim of a criminal offence to institute criminal proceedings himself or to claim prosecution by the public prosecutor.[346] However, if the criminal proceedings are the only possibility for him to vindicate his civil right to damages as a civil party, this may be different.[347]

Against the background of the Court's judgment in the *Airey* Case concerning 'effective' access[348] the Commission's view that the fact that excessive costs are involved for the accused in taking evidence does not imply a violation of Article 6, had to be modified.[349] It did so in an unpublished decision of 1984, where the Commission concluded that in certain circumstances the high costs could raise a problem under Article 6 para. 1.[350]

The decision in the *Golder* judgment, referred to under 10.4.2.4, that the right of access to court implies the right of free correspondence and consultations in private with a lawyer,[351] also holds good for criminal cases, to the extent that this guarantee does not already follow from the third paragraph under (b). Moreover, the right of (effective) access to court may also play a role in assessing whether free legal aid should have been granted under paragraph 3(c)[352] and whether the State should be held responsible for a manifest failure by a legal aid counsel to provide effective representation.[353]

10.4.4 ACCESS TO JUDICIAL APPEAL PROCEEDINGS

The possibility of appeal to a higher court constitutes a domestic remedy that has to be previously exhausted according to Article 35. In fact, an appeal court may remedy the fact that the proceedings in the first instance were not in conformity with Article 6 in all respects.[354]

The right of appeal to a higher court is not laid down, and is also not implied, in Article 6 para. 1.[355] However, if appeal *is* provided for and has been lodged, and the court in that instance is called upon to make a 'determination', Article 6 para. 1 ap-

---

of Article 6 para. 2, since the applicant had been able to exercise the rights of the defence and the decision on reimbursement did not involve a reassessment of the applicant's guilt.

[346] Judgment of 29 October 1991, *Helmers*, para. 29.
[347] *A contrario*, see the judgment of 28 October 1998, *Assenov and Others*, paras 111-112.
[348] Judgment of 9 October 1979, *Airey*, para. 24.
[349] Appl. 1982/63, *X v. Austria* (not published).
[350] Appl. 9379/81, *X v. Switzerland* (not published).
[351] Judgment of 21 February 1975, para. 40.
[352] Judgment of 28 March 1990, *Granger*, paras 44-48.
[353] Judgment of 19 December 1989, *Kamasinski*, para. 65.
[354] Judgment of 16 December 1992, *Edwards*, paras 38-39; judgment of 26 August 1997, *De Haan*, para. 54.
[355] Judgment of 23 July 1968, *Belgian Linguistic Case*, para. 9; judgment of 17 January 1970, *Delcourt*, para. 25; judgments of 11 October 2001, *Hoffmann* and *Sommerfeld*, paras 65 and 64, respectively.

plies.[356] This also means that, if domestic law provides for the remedy of appeal, access to that remedy may not be limited in its essence or in a disproportionate way.[357] If its limitation has a discriminatory effect, this also amounts to a violation of Article 6 in addition to Article 14.[358]

The same holds good for appeal to a constitutional court,[359] unless its review concerns exclusively the constitutionality of the previous judicial decision and not a full 'determination'.[360] It is not easy to understand how and in what situations such a distinction may be made. In fact, the decisive criterion is whether there is a close link between the subject-matter of the proceedings before the constitutional court and that of the proceedings which led to the referral of the matter to the constitutional court.[361]

Article 6 may also be applicable to proceedings concerning a so-called 'special remedy'. Thus the Court held Article 6 applicable to the proceedings concerning a request for revision and retrial.[362] However, the Court took into consideration that the request for revision could also relate to the way the domestic court had applied the law, and in fact replaced the appeal for cassation. As a rule Article 6 does not apply to requests for revision or reopening.[363]

Article 6 does not debar States from laying down regulations governing the access to an appellate or cassation court, provided that their purpose is to ensure the proper administration of justice. Consequently, there is no violation of Article 6 where an applicant is refused access to such a court due to his own procedural mistake. If the rejection of a petition for review or cassation is, however, the result of an omission on the part of the court, the right of access is violated by that rejection.[364]

The decision of the appellate court declaring the appeal inadmissible on the ground that the appellant no longer had a legal interest, does not limit the right of access in

---

[356]   Judgment of 17 January 1970, *Delcourt*, para. 25; judgment of 22 February 1984, *Sutter*, paras 26-28; judgment of 29 May 1986, *Deumeland*, para. 77; judgment of 2 March 1987, *Monnell and Morris*, para. 54; judgment of 26 May 1988, *Ekbatani*, para. 26; judgment of 19 December 1989, *Kamasinki*, para. 106; judgment of 28 August 1991, *F.C.B. v. Italy*, paras 29-33; judgment of 22 April 1992, *Vidal*, paras 30-35; judgment of 12 October 1992, *T. v. Italy*, paras 24-25; judgment of 16 December 1992, *Hadjianastassiou*, paras 29-31; judgment of 23 November 1993, *Poitrimol*, paras 28-29; judgment of 25 March 1998, *Belziuk*, para. 37.

[357]   Judgment of 23 November 1993, *Poitrimol*, paras 35-38; judgments of 29 July 1998, *Omar* and *Guérin*, paras 41-42 and para. 43, respectively; judgment of 14 December 1999, *Khalfaoui*, paras 42-54; judgment of 15 February 2000, *Garcia Manibardo*, paras 44-45.

[358]   Judgment of 11 October 2001, *Hoffmann*, para. 66.

[359]   Judgment of 16 September 1996, *Süszmann*, para. 41; judgment of 1 July 1997, *Pammel*, para. 53; judgment of 21 October 1997, *Pierre-Bloch*, para. 48; judgment of 12 June 2001, *Trickovic*, para. 39; judgment of 18 October 2001, *Mianowicz*, para. 45; judgment of 20 February 2003, *Kind*, para. 43.

[360]   Judgment of 22 October 1984, *Sramek*, para. 35.

[361]   Judgment of 23 June 1993, *Ruiz-Mateos*, para. 59.

[362]   Judgment of 29 July 2004, *S.L. Band Club*, paras 40-48. See, however, the judgment of 8 April 2003, *Jussy*, para. 18.

[363]   Decision of 9 December 2004, *"Energia" Producers' Cooperation*.

[364]   Report of the Commission of 21 October 1998, *Bogdanska Dimova*, paras 52-59.

its essence, especially not if he has had the full benefit of a first (and possibly second) instance that was in conformity with Article 6 para. 1.[365]

If Article 6 is applicable, the specific characteristics of the appeal proceedings in question must be taken into account with regard to the question of whether Article 6 has been complied with.[366] Thus, for instance, it must be examined whether the requirement of publicity of the trial in appeal proceedings[367] and in cassation proceedings[368] has the same fundamental importance as is the case for first instance proceedings. The same even applies to the strict requirement of publicity of the judgment,[369] and the requirement of the presence in person of the person charged.[370] However, the principle of equality of arms has to be respected at every instance.[371]

The Commission has held a few times that Article 6 was not applicable to proceedings in which a decision is taken about leave of appeal, for instance the procedure by which three judges of the *Bundesverfassungsgericht* take a decision about the admission of a *Verfassungsbeschwerde*.[372] It is disputable, however, whether this view is correct in its generality, since in these proceedings a negative decision may also be based on the manifestly ill-founded nature of the appeal, which in fact implies a 'determination'.[373] A more correct view was adopted by the Commission in the *Monnell and Morris* Case, in which Article 6 was deemed to be applicable on account of the close connection of the decision about admission of the appeal with the merits of the appeal proceedings themselves, and because these preliminary proceedings may already lead to an extension of the detention.[374]

In some legal systems the person who has been convicted at first instance, but for whom some remedies against this sentence are still available, is no longer regarded as one against whom a charge is pending, but as a convicted person, so that in such a case, strictly speaking, Article 6 would not be applicable. However, in the *Delcourt* Case, in which the Court stressed the desirability of an extensive interpretation of

---

[365] Decision of 29 January 2002, *Venema and Others*, para. 3.

[366] Judgment of 17 January 1970, *Delcourt*, para. 26; judgment of 25 April 1983, *Pakelli*, para. 29; judgment of 8 December 1983, *Pretto and Others*, para. 23; judgment of 28 March 1990, *Granger*, para. 44; judgment of 19 December 1997, *Brualla Gómes de la Torre*, para. 37.

[367] Judgment of 26 May 1988, *Ekbatani*, paras 27-28; judgments of 29 October 1991, *Helmers, Andersson*, and *Fejde*, paras 36, 27 and 31, respectively.

[368] Judgment of 22 February 1984, *Sutter*, para. 30.

[369] Judgment of 10 July 2001, *Lamanna*, para. 32.

[370] Judgment of 21 September 1993, *Kremzow*, para. 58; judgment of 25 March 1998, *Belziuk*, para. 37; judgment of 6 July 2004, *Dondarini*, para. 27.

[371] Judgment of 20 February 1996, *Lobo Machado*, para. 31; judgment of 25 March 1998, *Belziuk*, para. 37; judgment of 6 February 2001, *Beer*, paras 17-18.

[372] Appl. 9508/81, *X v. Federal Republic of Germany* (not published); Appl. 6916/75, *X, Y and Z v. Sweden*, D&R 6 (1977), p. 101 (107); Appl. 10663/83, *X v. Denmark* (not published).

[373] Cf. the report of 15 March 1985, *Adler*, paras 48-50.

[374] Report of 11 March 1986, paras 125-127, followed by the Court in its judgment of 2 March 1987, para. 54.

Article 6, it held that the charge has not yet been determined in the sense of Article 6 as long as the verdict of acquittal or conviction has not become final.[375] On the one hand this means that, although Article 6 does not grant a right of appeal for criminal cases[376] (Protocol No. 7 contains such a right in Article 2 with regard to those States which have ratified that Protocol), the proceedings in appeal and in cassation do form part of the 'determination', and, therefore, must equally satisfy the minimum standard laid down in Article 6.[377] The fact that in its examination the court of cassation is confined to the legal grounds on which the lower court has based its sentence, does not stand in the way of applicability of Article 6,[378] nor does the circumstance that in some cases appeal and cassation no longer relate to the validity of the criminal prosecution as such, but exclusively to the penalty imposed.[379] On the other hand, procedures in which a decision is taken on requests for conditional release, revision, pardon or mitigation of penalty are not covered by Article 6, since in those cases there has already been a determination which has acquired the force of *res judicata*.[380] However, in the case of a revocation of a conditional release there is the question of 'determination of a criminal charge' in the sense of Article 6, because such a procedure may result in a renewed imposition of a penalty.[381] And in the above-mentioned cases Article 6 *is* of course applicable if the proceedings also involve civil rights or obligations.[382]

10.4.5   NO RIGHT OF ACCESS TO COURT IN EACH STAGE OF THE PROCEDURE

In its judgment in the *Le Compte, Van Leuven and De Meyere* Case the Court held that Article 6 para. 1 does not prescribe the Contracting States "to submit '*contestations*' (disputes) over 'civil rights and obligations' to a procedure conducted at each of its stages before 'tribunals' meeting the Article's various requirements. Demands of flexibility and efficiency, which are fully compatible with the protection of human rights, may justify the prior intervention of administrative or professional bodies and,

---

[375]   Judgment of 17 January 1970, paras 25-26.
[376]   *Ibidem.*
[377]   *Ibidem.*
[378]   *Ibidem*, paras 24-25; judgment of 22 February 1984, *Sutter*, para. 30.
[379]   Appl. 4623/70, *X v. the United Kingdom*, Yearbook XV (1972), p. 376 (394-396).
[380]   Appl. 1760/63, *X v. Austria*, Yearbook IX (1966), p. 166 (174) and the case law mentioned there. See also Appl. 9813/82, *X v. the United Kingdom* (not published), concerning a change of prison location, and Appl. 10733/84, *Asociación De Aviadores de La República, Mata and Others*, D&R 41 (1985), p. 211 (224): a decision concerning an amnesty after conviction does not determine a 'criminal charge'.
[381]   Appl. 4036/69, *X v. the United Kingdom*, Coll. 32 (1970), p. 73 (75).
[382]   Thus implicitly also the Commission: Appl. 1760/63, *X v. Austria*, Yearbook IX (1966), p. 166 (174).

a fortiori, of judicial bodies which do not satisfy the said requirements in every respect."[383]

In the *Albert and Le Compte* Case the Court elucidated this as follows: "in such circumstances the Convention calls at least for one of the two following systems: either the jurisdictional organs themselves comply with the requirements of Article 6, paragraph 1, or they do not so comply but are subject to subsequent control by a judicial body that has full jurisdiction and does provide the guarantees of Article 6, paragraph 1."[384]

This means that, for instance, the situation where objection or appeal against administrative action lies with an administrative body does not conflict with Article 6, also not if this objection or appeal procedure amounts to a determination of civil rights and obligations or a criminal charge, provided that there is in the last resort access to review by a court with full jurisdiction. It was precisely that last requirement which, in the opinion of the Court,[385] had not been fulfilled in the Dutch procedure of Crown appeal.[386] It also means that in the case of a criminal charge the penalty may be determined by an administrative body, *e.g.*, the Revenue,[387] the public prosecutor,[388] local or regional authorities,[389] or the Minister of the Interior,[390] provided that from this decision appeal lies to a court with full jurisdiction. In those cases it has to be examined whether appeal is effectively open in all cases to the appellate body that is indicated by the respondent Government as satisfying Article 6 and whether this is a full appeal.[391]

In the *De Cubber* Case the Court qualified its viewpoint that only the last stage of the proceedings has to fulfil all the requirements of Article 6. It adopted the position that this holds good only for those cases in which under domestic law the proceedings are not of a civil or criminal but, *e.g.*, of a disciplinary or administrative character, and moreover the decision is not in the hands of what within the domestic system are con-

---

[383] Judgment of 23 June 1981, para. 51.

[384] Judgment of 10 February 1983, para. 29. See also the reports of 8 July 1986, *Van Lierde* (not officially published), para. 44 and *Houart*, paras 36-38; judgment of 22 June 1989, *Langborger*, para. 30 and judgment of 27 May 2003, *Crisan*, para. 25.

[385] The Dutch government had argued that, if one looked 'beyond the appearances', the Administrative Litigation Division of the Council of State in fact acted as a court.

[386] Judgment of 23 October 1985, *Benthem*, paras 38-43. See, however, the judgment of 27 November 1991, *Oerlemans*, paras 53-57, where the Court accepted the argument of the Dutch Government that, since the *Benthem* judgment, the procedure of Crown appeal left open access to review by a civil court on the basis of the latter's supplementary jurisdiction.

[387] Judgment of 24 February 1994, *Bendenoun*, para. 46.

[388] Judgment of 16 December 1992, *Hennings*, para. 26 in conjunction with para. 10.

[389] Judgment of 2 September 1998, *Lauko*, para. 64.

[390] Judgment of 23 September 1998, *Malige*, para. 45.

[391] See in particular the report of 3 July 1985, *Ettl and Others*, paras 76-90. In its judgment of 23 April 1987 in that case, paras 42-43, the Court held that there was no question of violation of Article 6, since Austria had made a reservation in this respect upon ratification of the Convention.

sidered 'courts of the classic kind'. If, on the contrary, proceedings are concerned which are to be classified as 'civil' or 'criminal', both in virtue of the Convention and under domestic law, and if the 'detetermination' is made by a body that is a 'proper court in both the formal and the substantive meaning of the term', Article 6 applies to this body irrespective of whether its decision is open to appeal. The flexible standpoint with regard to disciplinary and administrative proceedings, according to the Court, "cannot justify reducing the requirements of Article 6, paragraph 1 in its traditional and natural sphere of application. A restrictive interpretation of this kind would not be consonant with the object and purpose of Article 6, paragraph 1."[392]

This position, which did not receive sufficient attention in legal practice and literature, was reconfirmed in the *Findlay* Case with respect to the requirement of independence and impartiality,[393] and in the *Riepan* Case with respect to the requirement of publicity.[394] In proceedings before courts 'of the classic kind' the parties are entitled to a first instance tribunal that fully meets the requirements of Article 6 para. 1.

10.4.6 LIMITATIONS OF THE RIGHT OF ACCESS TO COURT

10.4.6.1 General observations

The right of access to court laid down in Article 6 is not an absolute right. First of all, it may be waived, provided that this has been done unambiguously.[395] That waiver may concern the right of access as such or certain of its elements, *e.g.*, the publicity of the proceedings[396] – provided that the public interest of publicity does not overrule the interests of the parties in this respect – or the applicant may have limited the judicial review as *dominus litis*.[397] There are also certain implicit restrictions, for instance in the sense that a criminal prosecution may also be terminated without intervention of the court, provided that this does not lead to a formal or factual 'determination'. Moreover, there may be procedural limitations such as time limits,[398] provided that they are not unreasonably short,[399] the requirement of an interest to

---

392   Judgment of 26 October 1984, para. 32.
393   Judgment of 25 February 1997, *Findlay*, para. 79.
394   Judgment of 14 November 2000, *Riepan*, para. 18.
395   Judgment of 7 May 1974, *Neumeister*, paras 33-36.
396   Judgment of 23 June 1981, *Le Compte, Van Leuven and De Meyere*, para. 59; judgment of 10 February 1983, *Albert and Le Compte*, para. 35; judgment of 12 February 1985, *Colozza*, para. 28.
397   Judgment of 5 May 1995, *Air Canada*, paras 61-62.
398   Including civil limitation periods: judgment of 22 October 1996, *Stubbings and Others*, paras 51-57.
399   A time-limit of one week was not considered by the Court to amount to a denial of access; judgment of 16 December 1992, *Hennings*, paras 26-27. See also the judgment of 11 October 2001, *Rodriguez Valin*, para. 28. See, however, the judgment of 28 October 1998, *Pérez de Rada Cavanilles*, paras 46-49

sue,[400] court fees that are not excessive,[401] security for costs to be incurred by the other party,[402] the obligatory assistance of a lawyer[403] and other admissibility requirements, and even prior authorization to proceed with the claim.[404] As the Court held in the *Ashingdane* Case: "Certainly, the right of access to the courts is not absolute but may be subject to limitations; these are permitted by implication since the right of access 'by its very nature calls for regulation by the State, regulation which may vary in time and in place according to the needs and resources of the community and of individuals'. (...) In laying down such regulation, the Contracting States enjoy a certain margin of appreciation. Whilst the final decision as to the observance of the Convention's requirements rests with the Court, it is no part of the Court's function to substitute for the assessment of the national authorities any other assessment of what might be the best policy in this field. (...)."[405]

10.4.6.2 Limitation must not impair the essence of access

The limitations prescribed by law or applied by the courts must not restrict or reduce the access in such a way or to such an extent that the very essence of the right is impaired.[406] They must also be sufficiently clear or the provisions concerned must contain safeguards against misunderstanding.[407] In that context, too, the Court's scrutiny is based on the principle that the Convention is intended to guarantee not rights that are theoretical or illusory but rights that are practical and effective.[408]

---

and the judgment of 10 July 2001, *Tricard*, paras 30-33, where a time limit of three and five days, respectively, was found to be too short.

[400] Judgment of 28 June 1990, *Obermeier*, para. 68; decision of 29 January 2002, *Venema and Others*, para. 3.

[401] Judgment of 19 June 2001, *Kreuz*, paras 58-66.

[402] *Ibidem*, para. 54.

[403] Judgment of 24 November 1986, *Gillow*, para. 69.

[404] Judgment of 28 May 1985, *Ashingdane*, para. 59; judgment of 19 June 2001, *Kreuz*, para. 54.

[405] Judgment of 28 May 1985, para. 57. See also *i.a.* the judgment of 14 December 1999, *Khalfaoui*, paras 35-36; judgment of 10 May 2001, *Z and Others v. the United Kingdom*, para. 93; judgment of 25 September 2003, *Pages*, para. 30; judgment of 28 October 2003, *Stone Court Shipping Company S.A.*, para 34; judgment of 21 September 2004, *Zwiazek Nauczycielstwa Polskiego*, para. 28.

[406] Judgment of 28 May 1985, *Ashingdane*, para. 57; judgment of 9 December 1994, *Holy Monasteries*, para. 83; judgment of 22 October 1996, *Stubbings and Others*, para. 52; judgment of 16 December 1997, *Canea Catholic Church*, para. 41; judgments of 6 December 2001, *Yagtzilar and Others* and *Tsironis*, paras 23 and 26, respectively; judgment of 28 October 2003, *Stone Court Shipping Company S.A.*, para. 35.

[407] Judgment of 4 December 1995, *Bellet*, paras 36-37; judgment of 16 December 1992, *Geouffre de la Pradelle*, paras 31-35; judgment of 30 October 1998, *F.E. v. France*, para. 47; judgment of 10 October 2000, *Lagrange*, paras 40-42.

[408] Judgment of 9 October 1979, *Airey*, para. 24. See also *i.a.* the judgment of 19 June 2001, *Kreuz*, para. 57; judgment of 12 July 2001, *Prince Hans-Adam II of Liechtenstein*, para. 45.

Thus, in the *Canea Catholic Church* Case the Court held that an unforeseeable calling into question of the legal personality of the applicant church imposed a limitation upon the latter that impaired the very substance of its right to a court.[409]

A special category of restrictions is that of immunities. Although immunity does not affect the applicability of Article 6, it may block access to court to a very large extent. For that reason the Court emphasizes that the States must observe restraint in granting and honouring immunity. In the first place, the persons and organs who enjoy immunity must be narrowly defined. In the *Al-Adsani* Case the Court made it clear that conferring, without restraint or control, immunity on large groups or categories of persons would be inconsistent with the basic principle underlying Article 6.[410]

In the second place, the acts in respect of which immunity is claimed must directly relate to the function for which immunity is granted. Thus, a member of Parliament may enjoy immunity in direct relation to his parliamentary work,[411] but not for acts committed outside that specific context.[412] In the third place, the Court examines whether a fair balance has been struck between the public interests which the grant of immunity serves and the interest of unrestricted access to court. Thus, in the *Osman* Case the Court reached the conclusion that the automatic application of a rule which amounts to the grant of immunity to the police, without having regard to competing public-interest considerations, amounted to an unjustifiable restriction.[413]

Parliamentary immunity as such is considered not to constitute a disproportional restriction of access to court, since it reflects a principle that has been generally recognized in the member States of the Council of Europe.[414] The same holds good for restrictions to bring a civil action against judges, since these serve the proper functioning of the judiciary and are common in domestic and international legal systems.[415] Recognition of immunity to States and State organs in accordance with international treaty law and customary law, even when the civil action concerns *ius cogens*, was deemed proportional by the Court on the ground that the State concerned is in compliance with the international requirement of good inter-state relations.[416] However, the Court indicates in its case law that in assessing the proportionality of

---

[409]   Judgment of 16 December 1997, para. 41.
[410]   Judgment of 21 November 2001, para. 47.
[411]   Judgment of 17 December 2002, *A. v. the United Kingdom*, paras 66-89.
[412]   Judgment of 19 June 2001, *Kreuz*, para. 56; judgment of 30 January 2003, *Cordova (No. 1)*, paras 62-63; judgment of 3 June 2004, *De Jorio*, paras 29-30. In the *Ciz* Case the issue of immunity of a member of Parliament against an accusation of defamation was not even raised; judgment of 14 October 2003, *Ciz*, para. 61.
[413]   Judgment of 28 October 1998, paras 151-153.
[414]   Judgment of 17 December 2002, *A. v. the United Kingdom*, paras 78-83.
[415]   Judgment of 15 July 2003, *Ernst and Others*, para. 50.
[416]   Judments of 21 November 2001, *Al-Adsani, Fogarty and McElhinney*, paras 54-56, 35-39 and 36-40, respectively.

restrictions resulting from immunity, it takes into consideration whether and to what extent reasonable alternatives were available to the applicant to have his claim examined.[417]

The availability (at a later moment) of alternatives also played an important role in assessing the proportionality of the restriction in the *Klass* Case. There the Court made the following observation in respect of the complete exclusion of judicial review: "As long as it [i.e. the security control] remains validly secret, the decision placing someone under surveillance is thereby incapable of judicial control on the initiative of the person concerned, within the meaning of Article 6; as a consequence, it of necessity escapes the requirements of that Article."[418] However, the Court added the following observation: "According to the information supplied by the Government, the individual concerned, once he has been notified of such discontinuance [of the security control], has at his disposal serveral legal remedies against the possible infringements of his rights; these remedies would satisfy the requirements of Article 6."[419]

Access to court may also be unduly restricted or taken away by the court itself or by a higher court. In the *Todorescu* Case the courts of first and second instance had examined the applicants' claim for restitution of confiscated property. The court of second instance had decided in favour of the applicants, which decision was upheld by the court of appeal. However, the Supreme Court, at the request of the Procurate General, annulled the second instance judgment and decided that the courts did not have jurisdiction to review the constitutionality of the decree by which the confiscation was ordered. This judgment amounted to barring access to court for the applicants to have their civil right determined. The Court held that the annulment by the Supreme Court of a final judgment was in contravention of the principle of legal certainty and violated the right of access to court.[420]

These cases indicate that the Court is not inclined to leave a very broad margin of appreciation to the national authorities and courts in restricting access to court. In addition, although the Court has repeatedly stated that "its task is not to substitute itself for the competent domestic authorities in determining the most appropriate means of regulating access to justice, nor to assess the facts which led those courts to adopt one decision rather than another,"[421] it does consider it to be its task to examine errors of fact or law allegedly committed by a national court, if these may have resulted

---

[417] Judgment of 18 February 1999, *Waite and Kennedy*, para. 68; judgment of 15 July 2003, *Ernst and Others*, para. 54; judgment of 3 June 2004, *De Jorio*, para. 32.
[418] Judgment of 6 September 1978, para. 75.
[419] *Ibidem.*
[420] Judgment of 30 September 2003, paras 37-40. The line for this case law was set by the Grand Chamber in its judgment of 30 September 1999, *Brumarescu*, paras 61-62.
[421] Judgment of 19 June 2001, *Kreuz*, para. 56.

in denial of access to court.[422] This may be the case, for instance, if the applicable time limit for instituting proceedings has not been correctly applied by the court.[423] The Court goes very far in examining whether the procedural rule concerned is reasonable in itself and has been applied in a reasonable way, taking into account such factors as the strictness of the rule, whether or not the applicant had the assistance of a lawyer, and whether the applicant has taken the necessary precautions.[424] The Court, although recognising the appropriateness of the rule concerned, is even prepared to substitute its own assessment for that of the domestic court and conclude that the rule has been applied in such a strict way that the applicant was in fact deprived of his access to court.[425] In this way the Court approaches the role of a fourth instance.

10.4.6.3 Legitimate aim and proportionality

A limitation is not compatible with Article 6 para. 1 if it does not pursue a legitimate aim and if there is no reasonable relationship of proportionality between the means employed and the aim sought to be achieved.[426]

Examples of a legitimate aim are the good or fair administration of justice,[427] limitations aimed at preventing the courts from becoming overloaded,[428] proper functioning of the judiciary,[429] legal certainty,[430] good international relations which may require the grant of State immunity,[431] and the public interest in regaining sovereignty.[432] Even if the limitation serves a legitimate aim, its application must not be arbitrary[433] nor be disproportional.[434]

---

[422]   Judgment of 12 July 2001, *Prince Hans-Adam II of Liechtenstein*, para. 49; decision of 2 December 2004, *Falcon Rivera*, para. 1.
[423]   Judgment of 26 October 2000, *Leoni*, paras 25-27.
[424]   Judgment of 11 October 2001, *Rodriguez Valin*, paras 23-28.
[425]   Judgment of 25 January 2000, *Miragall Escolano and Others*, para. 38 (see also the critical dissenting opinion of judge Pellonpää); judgment of 16 November 2000, *Société Anonyme 'Sotiris and Nikos Koutras Attee'*, paras 21-23; judgment of 11 January 2001, *Platakou*, paras 32-49; judgment of 6 December 2001, *Tsironis*, paras 27-30.
[426]   Judgment of 28 May 1985, *Ashingdane*, para. 57. For a comprehensive review of these criteria, see the judgment of 21 September 1994, *Fayed*, paras 68-83.
[427]   Judgment of 13 July 1995, *Tolstoy Miloslavsky*, para. 61; judgment of 14 November 2000, *Annoni di Gussola and Others*, para. 51; judgment of 11 October 2001, *Rodriguez Valin*, para. 22; judgment of 28 October 2003, *Stone Court Shipping Company S.A.*, para. 34.
[428]   Judgment of 19 December 1997, *Brualla Gómez de la Torre*, para. 36.
[429]   Judgment of 15 July 2003, *Ernst and Others*, para. 50.
[430]   Judgment of 10 July 2001, *Tricard*, para. 29; judgment of 11 October 2001, *Rodriguez Valin*, para. 22.
[431]   Judgments of 21 November 2001, *Al-Adsani*, *Fogarty* and *McElhinney*, paras 54, 34 and 35, respectively.
[432]   Judgment of 12 July 2001, *Prince Hans-Adam II of Lichtenstein*, para. 69.
[433]   Judgment of 13 July 1995, *Tolstoy Miloslavsky*, para. 65.
[434]   Judgment of 21 September 2004, *Zwiazek Nauczycielstwa Polskiego*, para. 38. For an example of clear disproportionality, see the judgment of 31 July 2001, *Mortier*, paras 36-39.

The proportionality of a limitation depends on many aspects. The Court has recognised that limitations on access to court may be more extensive when regulation of activities in the public sphere is at stake than in relation to litigation over the conduct of persons acting in their private capacity.[435] It has also held that measures which reflect generally recognised rules of public international law on State immunity cannot in principle be regarded as imposing a disproportionate restriction on the right of access to court.[436] International standards may also be a yardstick for the proportionality of statutes of limitation.[437]

In the *Al-Adsani* Case the argument put forward by a minority of the Court, that rules concerning State immunity must yield for provisions of the Convention that reflect *jus cogens* on the basis of the 'normative hierarchy theory', and, consequently, in such cases do not serve a legitimate aim, was not followed by the majority.[438] However, the Court *did* stress that because immunity rules result in removal from the jurisdiction of the courts of a group of civil claims, the States must exercise restraint in claiming immunity, and such claims must be subject to control by the Court.[439]

Although Article 6 does not guarantee a right of appeal, if a limitation rule amounts to taking away the right of appeal, that effect may well be disproportionate. This is the case, for instance, if appeal is not open to an accused who has failed to surrender to custody, notwithstanding the existence of a warrant for his arrest,[440] or who has failed to pay a bail instead.[441] It may also be the case if the appeal is only admissible if the appellant has deposited the amount for which he was convicted at first instance and the court has not taken into consideration the actual financial situation of the appellant.[442] However, in the *Eliazer* Case the limitation that no appeal in cassation lies against judgments pronounced following proceedings *in absentia* was not considered to be disproportionate.[443] The reasoning followed by the Court to distinguish

---

[435]   Judgment of 21 September 1994, *Fayed*, para. 75.

[436]   Judgments of 21 November 2001, *Al-Adsani, Fogarty* and *McElhinney*, paras 54, 35-39 and 36-40, respectively; judgment of 12 December 2002, *Kalogeropoulou*, para. 1.

[437]   Judgment of 22 October 1996, *Stubbings and Others*, para. 53.

[438]   Dissenting opinion of Judges Rozakis, Caflisch, Wildhaber, Costa, Cabral Barreto and Vajić.

[439]   Judment of 21 November 2001, *Al-Adsani*, para. 47.

[440]   Judgment of 23 November 1993, *Poitrimol*, paras 35-38; judgments of 29 July 1998, *Omar* and *Guérin*, paras 41-42 and para. 43, respectively; judgment of 14 December 1999, *Khalfaoui*, paras 42-54; judgments of 20 March 2001, *Goedhart* and *Stroek*, paras 31-32 and 29-30, respectively; judgment of 18 December 2003, *Skondrianos*, para. 27.

[441]   Judgment of 1 July 2004, *Walser*, para. 29.

[442]   Judgment of 15 February 2000, *Garcia Manibardo*, paras 44-45; judgment of 14 November 2000, *Annoni di Gussola and Others*, paras 49-59; judgment of 31 July 2001, *Mortier*, paras 34-39. In its judgment of 25 September 2003, *Pages*, paras 32-36, the Court seems to have reversed the burden of proof: the applicant had not shown that his financial situation was such that removal of his appeal form the role because of lack of execution was disproportional. See, however, the judgment of the same date, *Bayle*, para. 43, where the Court held the financial position of the applicant to be clear.

[443]   Judgment of 16 October 2001, para. 33-36.

its judgment in that case from its *Poitrimol* judgment is not very convincing.[444] It may well be that Eliazer was not obliged to surrender to custody as a precondition, but that does not alter the fact that the reason for his absence was specifically fear of arrest. The Court also held that the applicant could still open the path to the court of cassation by appearing at the objection proceedings, but that would seem to lead to a circular reasoning, since the very issue was the legitimacy of the requirement of his appearing. The Court also took into consideration the fact that it is of capital importance that a defendant should appear at his trial and the legitimate aim to discourage unjustified absences which outweighs the accused's concern to avoid the risk of being arrested by attending his trial,[445] but these considerations would seem to have also been valid in the *Poitrimol* Case.

In the *Sejdovic* Case, where the complaint concerned the refusal of a new trial after conviction *in absentia*, the Court held that a person convicted *in absentia* who could not be considered to have unequivocally waived the right to appear, should in all cases be able to obtain a new ruling by a court.[446]

A short time limit for bringing an action may be proportionate under normal circumstances, but disproportionate in cases where there are special complications[447] or if the applicant lives far away.[448] If in setting the amount of security for the payment of a possible fine the court has not taken into account that the person concerned had no financial resources, this may in practice amount to depriving him of his recourse before that court.[449] And if, in connection with the amount of court fees to be paid, the domestic court relied on the fact that the applicant was a businessman and should have taken into account the need to secure in advance sufficient funds for court fees, without taking into account the link of the proceedings to the business activity and the actual financial situation of the applicant, the fees may be disproportionate.[450]

If the domestic court applies a certain admissibility requirement in too formalistic a way, this may amount to a disproportional restriction, especially if the applicant is not given the opportunity to correct his mistake.[451]

---

[444]   See the dissenting opinion of Judges Türmen and Maruste.
[445]   Judgment of 16 October 2001, *Eliazer*, paras 32.
[446]   Judgment of 10 November 2004, para. 30.
[447]   Judgment of 28 October 1998, *Pérez de Rada Cavanilles*, paras 45-49.
[448]   Judgment of 10 July 2001, *Tricard*, paras 30-34.
[449]   Judgment of 28 October 1998, *Aït-Mouhoub*, paras 57-61. See also the judgment of 13 July 1995, *Tolstoy Miloslavsky*, paras 59-67: in the circumstances of the case, even the obligation to pay an amount of 124,900 English pounds as security for costs to pursue an appeal did meet the requirement of proportionality.
[450]   Judgment of 19 June 2001, *Kreuz*, paras 62-63. See also the decision of 9 December 2004, *V.M. v. Bulgaria*.
[451]   Judgment of 28 October 2003, *Stone Court Shipping Company S.A.*, paras 36-43; judgment of 20 April 2004, *Bulena*, para. 35; judgment of 25 May 2004, *Kadlec and Others*, paras 26-30; judgment of 27 May 2004, *Boulougouras*, paras 26-27.

10.4.6.4 Retrospective legislation with effect on access

In the case of retrospective legislation which has the effect of influencing the judicial determination of a dispute to which a State is a party, respect for the rule of law requires that any reason adduced to justify such measure be treated with the greatest possible degree of circumspection.[452] Even the fact that access to court is restored by subsequent legislation does not put an end to the violation of the right of access to court if that access was stayed for a considerable period of time.[453] Exceptionally, however, a retrospective limitation may be justified if the legislative action is intended to put an end to the efforts of the applicants to frustrate the clear intention of the legislature,[454] or serves other 'compelling grounds of the general interest'.[455] However, a mere financial risk on the part of the government cannot warrant such legislative interference.[456] Even though a situation where a significant number of legal suits claiming large sums of money are lodged against the State may call for some further legislation, the measures taken must be compatible with Article 6 para. 1.[457]

Procedural law amendments which limit the right of appeal may have some retroactive effect for pending cases. According to the Court this is in conformity with a generally recognised principle that, save where expressly provided to the contrary, procedural rules apply immediately to proceedings that are under way. Here the same test applies that such a limitation must serve a legitimate aim, may not impair the very essence of the right of access and must be proportionate; and here again less strict criteria apply if the limitation concerns access to a court of appeal or a court of cassation.[458]

10.4.6.5 Limitations with respect to specific groups

The authorities may lay down specific restrictive rules for access to court with regard to, for instance, minors, prisoners or persons of unsound mind,[459] but in those cases

---

[452] Judgment of 9 December 1994, *Stran Greek Refineries and Stratis Andreadis*, para. 49; judgment of 28 October 1999, *Zielinski and Pradal & Gonzalez and Others*, paras 57-61; judgment of 7 November 2000, *Anagnostopoulos and Others*, paras 20-21; judgment of 28 June 2001, *Agoudimos and Cefallonian Sky Shipping Co.*, para. 30.

[453] Judgment of 1 March 2002, *Kutić*, paras 30-33; judgment of 10 July 2003, *Multiplex*, paras 49-55.; judgment of 9 October 2003, *Acimovic*, para. 42.

[454] Judgment of 23 October 1997, *The National & Provincial Building Society and Others*, para. 112.

[455] Judgments of 28 October 1999, *Zielinsky and Pradel & Gonzalez*, para. 57; judgment of 28 June 2001, *Agoudimos and Cefallonian Sky Shipping Co.*, para. 30; judgment of 10 July 2003, *Multiplex*, para. 52.

[456] Judgments of 28 October 1999, *Zielinsky and Pradel & Gonzalez*, paras 58-59.

[457] Judgment of 10 July 2003, *Multiplex*, para. 52.

[458] Judgment of 19 December 1997, *Brualla Gómes de la Torre*, paras 35-39.

[459] Judgment of 21 February 1975, *Golder*, paras 37-40; judgment of 10 May 2001, *Z and Others v. the United Kingdom*, para. 93.

as well the 'special status' of the individual concerned cannot warrant the total absence of access.[460]

10.4.6.6 Limitations warranted by security reasons

In the *Klass* Case a drastic restriction was imposed on the right of access to court. Article 6 was invoked by the applicants because the challenged legislation, which permitted interference with correspondence and wire-tapping for security reasons without the knowledge of the person concerned, excluded the normal recourse to a court and replaced it by supervision by a parliamentary committee. Leaving open the question of whether this case concerned civil rights or a criminal charge, the Court held that a distinction should be made between two stages. In the first stage the measures are still applied without the person's knowledge and as a consequence are incapable of judicial control on the initiative of the person concerned and, thus, of necessity escape the requirements of Article 6. In the stage in which the measures have been terminated and in which, consequently, there is no longer any ground for secrecy, they come within the ambit of Article 6.[461]

The Court was faced here with the dilemma between, on the one hand, the guarantee of effective access to court and, on the other hand, the necessity for the national authorities to be able to carry out an effective security control for the protection of the democratic values underlying the Convention. The Court observed with respect to the alleged violation of Article 8: "The rule of law implies, *inter alia*, that an interference by the executive authorities with an individual's rights should be subject to an effective control which should normally be assured by the judiciary, at least in the last resort, judicial control offering the best guarantees of independence, impartiality and a proper procedure."[462] Nevertheless, the Court opted for the security interest, imposing restrictions on the effective access to court via what might be called a systematic interpretation of the first paragraph of Article 6 in connection with the second paragraph of Article 8. But the Court also emphasized – as had been done by the German *Bundesverfassungsgericht* – that the secrecy vis-à-vis the person concerned must not last any longer than is required for the protection of the interest envisaged by the measures, after which period access to court must be fully open again for the person in question.[463] The said parliamentary committee will then have to take particular care that the person in question is indeed informed as soon as the situation permits, since otherwise national judicial review as well as the Strasbourg review might be rendered completely illusory.

---

[460]   Judgment of 24 October 1979, *Winterwerp*, para. 75.
[461]   Judgment of 6 September 1978, para. 75.
[462]   *Ibidem*, para. 55.
[463]   *Ibidem*, para. 75 in conjunction with para. 71.

In the *Leander* Case, which also concerned secret surveillance, the Commission had declared the complaint concerning Article 6 incompatible with the Convention *ratione materiae* on the basis of its case law that litigation concerning access to or dismissal from the civil service falls outside the scope of Article 6.[464] Consequently, the Court could not pronounce on the issue. However, it nevertheless gave a clear indication of its point of view by following, with respect to Article 13, its *Klass* judgment in holding that "an effective remedy under Article 13 must mean a remedy that is as effective as can be, having regard to the restricted scope for recourse inherent in any system of secret surveillance for the protection of national security."[465]

In its report in *R.V. v. the Netherlands*, which concerned a request of access to information held by the Dutch Military Intelligence Services (MIS), although no complaint under Article 6 had been lodged but only under Article 8, the Commission based its conclusion that the interference was not 'in accordance with the law', *inter alia*, on the fact that the Royal Decree governing the activities of the MIS did not contain any safeguard mechanism, thus leaving it open whether the safeguards referred to in the Government's observations, which were provided for in a broader framework (investigation by a parliamentary committee and by the National Ombudsman), were sufficiently effective.[466]

10.5 THE RIGHT TO A FAIR TRIAL

10.5.1 INTRODUCTION

Article 6 requires a 'fair hearing'. The notion of 'hearing' may be equated with that of 'trial' or 'trial proceedings'. This follows firstly from the French wording of the provision: '*toute personne a droit à ce que sa cause*(!) *soit entendue*'. Secondly, the right to be heard within a reasonable time, embodied in the first paragraph, refers to the proceedings as a whole[467] and, thirdly, the second sentence of the first paragraph allows the exclusion of the public and the press from all or part of the *trial*. Thus, the notion of 'hearing' should not be seen as equivalent to 'hearing in person' or 'oral hearing', although these two aspects may be elements of the notion of 'fair and public hearing' as contained in Article 6.[468]

When is a hearing 'fair'? In the *Kraska* Case the Court took as a starting-point that the purpose of Article 6 is, *inter alia*, "to place the 'tribunal' under a duty to conduct

---

[464]   Appl. 9248/81, D&R 34 (1983), p. 78 (83).
[465]   Judgment of 26 March 1987, para. 84.
[466]   Report of 3 December 1991, paras 45-46.
[467]   See *infra* 10.7.2.
[468]   See *infra* 10.5.4.

a proper examination of the submissions, arguments and evidence adduced by the parties, without prejudice to its assessments of whether they are relevant to its decision."[469]

However, the Court has avoided giving an enumeration of criteria in the abstract. In each individual case the course of the proceedings has to be assessed to decide whether the hearing concerned has been a fair one. What counts is the picture which the proceedings as a whole present,[470] although certain aspects *per se* may already conflict with the principle of a fair hearing in such a way that an opinion can be given about the fairness of the trial irrespective of the further course of the proceedings, *e.g.*, the way in which the evidence is collected during a preliminary hearing. Depending on the stage of the proceedings and its special features, the manner of application of Article 6 may differ.[471] The publicity requirement, for example, may be less strict as far as cassation proceedings are concerned.[472]

Certain aspects of a 'fair hearing' are expressly outlined for criminal cases in paragraphs 2 and 3 of Article 6. These aspects in principle also apply to civil cases (and to administrative cases if covered by Article 6). However, from the lack of such an enumeration with regard to civil cases, the Court has concluded that the requirements inherent in the notion of a 'fair hearing' in civil cases are not necessarily identical to the requirements in criminal cases and that there exists a 'greater latitude' for the national authorities when dealing with civil cases than when dealing with criminal procedures.[473]

Although the enumeration in the third paragraph might create a different impression, the content of the term 'fair hearing' in 'criminal' cases is not confined to the provisions of paragraph 3 of Article 6.[474] The guarantees implied in the requirement of a 'fair hearing' in paragraph 1 fully apply to criminal proceedings as well. Consequently, the finding that the proceedings are in conformity with the requirements of the third paragraph does not make a review for their conformity with the 'fair-hearing' principle superfluous in all cases. The proceedings as a whole may, for instance, create the picture that the accused has had insufficient opportunity to conduct an optimal defence, although none of the explicitly granted minimum guarantees has been

---

[469]   Judgment of 19 April 1993, para. 30. See also, *e.g.*, the judgment of 6 December 1988, *Barberà, Messegué and Jabardo*, para. 68.

[470]   See, *e.g.*, the judgment of 6 December 1988, *Barberà, Messegué and Jabardo*, para. 68; judgment of 20 November 1989, *Kostovski*, para. 39.

[471]   See, *e.g.*, the judgment of 26 May 1988, *Ekbatani*, para. 27; judgment of 29 October 1991, *Helmers*, para. 36.

[472]   See *infra* 10.6.

[473]   Judgment of 27 October 1993, *Dombo Beheer B.V.*, paras 32-33; judgment of 9 March 2004, *Pitkänen*, para. 59.

[474]   See, *e.g.*, the judgment of 25 February 1993, *Funke*, para. 44; judgment of 7 December 2000, *Zoon*, paras 32-50.

violated. As the Commission observed in the *Adolf* Case: "Article 6(3) merely exemplifies the minimum guarantees which must be accorded to the accused in the context of the 'fair trial' referred to in Article 6(1)."[475] This implies, on the one hand, that a negative answer to the question of whether the first paragraph has been violated renders an investigation of an alleged infringement of the third paragraph superfluous,[476] while, on the other hand, the investigation of a possible violation of the fair-trial principle laid down in the first paragraph must not be confined to an examination of the third paragraph. As a result of an extensive and functional interpretation of the third paragraph in the Strasbourg case law, however, examination for compatibility with the third and with the first paragraph is in fact likely to more or less coincide.

Various aspects of the right of a 'fair trial' are discussed in the following sections. Sometimes it is very difficult to distinguish those aspects, since they are often closely connected. In criminal cases the Court regularly uses the rather vague notion of 'rights of the defence'. This wording seems equal to the concept of a 'fair trial'.[477]

10.5.2 EQUALITY OF ARMS

An important element of the fair hearing requirement is the principle of equality of arms. This principle implies, as the Court held in the *Dombo Beheer B.V.* Case, with regard to civil proceedings "that each party must be afforded a reasonable opportunity to present his case – including his evidence – under conditions that do not place him at a substantial disadvantage *vis-à-vis* his opponent."[478]

For criminal cases, where the very character of the proceedings involves a fundamental inequality of the parties, this principle of 'equality of arms' is even more important, and the same applies, though to a lesser degree, to administrative procedures.[479] The principle can play a role in every stage of the proceedings and with regard to many issues.

The principle of 'equality of arms', that is closely connected to the right to adversarial proceedings, entails that the parties must have the same access to the records and other documents pertaining to the case, at least insofar as these may play a part in the formation of the court's opinion.[480] However, the access to the file may be

---

[475]   Report of 8 October 1980, B.43 (1985), p. 29.
[476]   *Ibidem*. See also the judgment of 27 February 1980, *Deweer*, para. 56.
[477]   See, *e.g.*, the judgment of 24 February 1994, *Bendenoun*, para. 52.
[478]   Judgment of 27 October 1993, para. 33. See also the judgment of 22 September 1994, *Hentrich*, para. 56, and the judgment of 9 December 1994, *Stran Greek Refineries and Stratis Andreadis*, para. 46.
[479]   Judgment of 29 May 1986, *Feldbrugge*, para. 44.
[480]   Judgment of 15 July 2003, *Ernst and Others*, paras 60-61.

restricted to an accused's lawyer.[481] A particular way in which the information from the file must be given or be available does not follow from this principle, provided that no insuperable obstacles are created which in fact amount to withholding information.[482] The parties should in principle have the opportunity to make copies of the relevant documents belonging to the case-file. The case law on this point is not clear, although the Court in the *Schuler-Zgraggen* Case, when deciding the question of whether the access of the applicant to the case-file did meet the requirements of Article 6, expressly mentioned the ability of the applicant to make copies.[483] A lack of access to the case-file may be remedied by an appeal court.[484]

Each party must be given the opportunity to oppose the arguments advanced by the other party.[485] In the *Feldbrugge* Case, for example, the Court came to the conclusion that Article 6(1) had been violated, since the applicant had not been given the opportunity to comment upon the report of a medical expert, which was of decisive importance for the outcome of the proceedings.[486] In the *Hentrich* Case the Revenue exercised the right of pre-emption because it held the sale price of a piece of land contained in the contract of sale to be too low. The applicant did not get a real opportunity to challenge the decision of the Revenue, because the tribunals, on the one hand, refused her the possibility to prove that the sale price corresponded to the real market value of the land and, on the other hand, allowed the Revenue to give a meaningless motivation for its decision to exercise the right of pre-emption.[487] These facts amounted to a breach of Article 6(1).[488] In the *Yvon* Case the applicant claimed that the principle of equality of arms had been breached in the proceedings to determine compensation before the expropriation judge. In the proceedings, the expropriated party was not only faced by the expropriating authority but also by the Government Commissioner, who was competent to present oral observations and file submissions, that must include a reasoned valuation of the compensation. The Court took into account that the Government Commissioner and the expropriating authority had full access to the land charges register, which listed all property transfers, where the expropriated parties had only limited access. Moreover, the Government Commissioner's submissions seemed to be of particular significance where they tended towards a lower valua-

---

[481]   Judgment of 19 December 1989, *Kamasinski*, para. 88; judgment of 21 September 1993, *Kremzow*, para. 52.

[482]   Appl. 8289/78, *X v. Austria*, D&R 18 (1980), p. 160 (167-168).

[483]   Judgment of 24 June 1993, paras 50-52.

[484]   *Ibidem.* Cf. also the judgment of 21 September 1993, *Zumtobel*, para. 35.

[485]   See, *e.g.*, the judgment of 23 June 1993, *Ruiz-Mateos*, para. 63; judgment of 24 November 1997, *Werner*, para. 65; judgment of 6 February 2001, *Beer*, para.17; judgment of 20 December 2001, *Buchberger*, para. 50.

[486]   Judgment of 29 May 1986, para. 44. See also, *e.g.*, the judgment of 23 June 1993, *Ruiz Mateos*, paras 61-68; judgment of 19 April 1994, *Van de Hurk*, paras 56-57.

[487]   The Revenue confined its motivation to stating that the price was too low.

[488]   Judgment of 22 September 1994, para. 56.

tion than proposed by the expropriating authority. If that was the case, the judge who rejected the Government Commissioner's submissions must specifically state the reasons for such a rejection. Therefore, the principle of equality of arms had been breached.[489]

In many cases the Court had to deal with the question whether the participation of the advocate-general or a similar officer in the deliberations of the Court of Cassation or Supreme Court had constituted a violation of the principle of equality of arms. Initially, in the *Delcourt* Case, the Court answered the question in the negative, because of the independent position of the *Procureur général* in relation to the Minister of Justice and the fact that the latter cannot give orders or instructions to the *Procureur général* in concrete cases.[490] The Court changed its view in the *Borgers* Case. It emphasised the correctness of the *Delcourt* judgment in as far as the independence and impartiality of the Court of Cassation and its *Procureur général* are concerned, but nevertheless concluded that the *Procureur général*, in recommending that an appeal on points of law should be allowed or dismissed, appeared to be an ally or opponent to one of the parties. Therefore, his participation in the deliberations had constituted a violation of the principle of equality of arms.[491] This point of view may be regarded as settled case law in criminal[492] as well as in civil cases.[493]

A different, although connected issue, namely the impossibility for the parties to reply to the advocate-general's submissions, is discussed regularly under the head of the adversarial principle. However, in the *Apeh Üldözötteinek Szövetsége* (Alliance of APEH's persecutees) Case that impossibility amounted to a breach of the equality of arms requirement. The case concerned non-contentious proceedings with a view to registering the applicants' association. The Hungarian Tax Authority (APEH), who learnt about the founding of the association from the press, complained that the name of the association was defamatory for APEH. The public prosecutor's office intervened in the registration proceedings and proposed that the request for registration be rejected because there was no approval of APEH for the use of its name. The Court held that the failure of the national courts to notify the applicants of this intervention and likewise of the submissions of the Attorney General's Office to the Supreme Court had violated the principle of equality of arms.[494]

---

[489] Judgment of 24 April 2003, paras 29-37.
[490] Judgment of 17 January 1970, para. 32.
[491] Judgment of 30 October 1991, para. 26.
[492] See, *e.g.*, the judgment of 22 February 1996, *Bulut*, para. 48.
[493] See, *e.g.*, the judgments of 20 February 1996, *Vermeulen*, para. 34 and *Lobo Machado*, para. 32; judgment of 7 June 2001, *Kress*, paras 82-87; judgment of 21 March 2002, *Immeubles Groupe Kosser*, para. 27.
[494] Judgment of 5 October 2000, paras 39-44. See also, with regard to criminal proceedings, the judgment of 22 February 1996, *Bulut*, para. 49; judgment of 31 January 2002, *Lanz*, paras 55-60; judgment of 17 January 2002, *Josef Fischer*, paras 16-22.

Another inequality occurred in the *Platakou* Case. The Greek code of civil procedure provided that all statutory time-limits were suspended in favour of the State during the holiday season from the first of July until September the fifteenth. The Court held that this provision placed the applicant, whose claim for indemnification after expropriation proceedings had been belated and, therefore, declared inadmissible, at a substantial disadvantage to the opposing party.[495]

The principle further entails that the parties are afforded the same opportunity to summon witnesses. In the *Dombo Beheer B.V.* Case the central question in the national proceedings was whether a certain agreement had been concluded between the applicant company and its bank. The person who represented the bank at the meeting where the alleged agreement was concluded, was allowed to testify before the court. The person who represented the applicant company, however, could not give evidence, because the national court identified him with the company itself. Thus, there was 'a substantial disadvantage' for the company vis-à-vis the bank in breach of Article 6.[496] In many legal systems, persons closely related to parties in civil proceedings cannot be heard as witnesses under oath. In the *Ankerl* Case the inability of Mrs Ankerl to give evidence under oath on the allegedly agreed lease between her husband and another party did not amount to a breach of Article 6. The Court held that under national law the court could freely assess the results of the "measures taken to obtain evidence". Furthermore, the national court did not attach any particular weight to the testimony of the other party on account of his having given evidence on oath and the court had relied on evidence other than just the statements in issue.[497] Therefore, the giving of evidence on oath by Mrs Ankerl could not have influenced the outcome of the proceedings.

In the *Pisano* Case the applicant claimed that the refusal of the national courts to summon a witness had violated the applicants' right to a fair trial. Italian law legally restricted the possibility to summon witnesses *à decharge* who had not been listed seven days before the first court hearing, to cases in which the judge considered their citation as absolutely necessary. The same limitation did not apply to witnesses *à charge*. Due to the fact that the applicant did not contest the legitimacy of the refusal, but its correctness, it appeared to the Court not to be necessary to give its express view about this difference. It limited itself to the assessment that the applicant had the opportunity to present his arguments before the courts and that the reasoning in the judgments made clear why the witness had not been summoned. Therefore, Article 6 had not been violated.[498] In the *Vidal* Case the request of the applicant to hear four persons as

---

[495]   Judgment of 11 January 2001, paras 45-48.
[496]   Judgment of 27 October 1993, paras 33-35.
[497]   Judgment of 23 October 1996, para. 38.
[498]   Judgment of 27 July 2000, paras 22-29.

defense witnesses had been rejected implicitly. The complete silence of the judgment on the request did violate Article 6.[499]

In addition, the parties must have the same possibility to call experts and these should in turn receive the same treatment. In the *Bönisch* Case the Court found that the expert involved in the proceedings and the powers given to him insufficiently guaranteed the latter's neutrality, so that he had to be considered as a witness for the prosecution rather than as an expert. Since the accused had not been given the same opportunity to call such an 'expert', the principle of 'equality of arms' had been violated.[500]

Phases in the examination during which neither of the parties was present fulfil the principle of 'equality of arms'. In the *Niteröst-Huber* Case the Court established that the observations of the cantonal court had not been communicated to either of the parties to the dispute before the Federal Court. As the cantonal court could not be regarded as the opponent of either of the parties, the requirement of equality of arms had not been infringed.[501] However, a problem did arise with regard to the right to adversarial proceedings, which is discussed further in the following section.

10.5.3 THE RIGHT TO ADVERSARIAL PROCEEDINGS; EVIDENCE

The right to adversarial proceedings entails in principle the opportunity for the parties to have knowledge of and comment on all evidence adduced or observations filed, even those coming from an independent member of the national legal service.[502] It may be deduced from the extensive case law that it is immaterial whether a person has chosen not to be legally represented,[503] whether the documents or observations in issue are important for the outcome of the proceedings,[504] whether the omission to communicate the document in issue has caused any prejudice,[505] or whether the observations

---

[499]   Judgment of 22 April 1992, para. 34.

[500]   Judgment of 6 May 1985, paras 33-35. The mere fact that an expert is a member of the staff of an institute which reported the initial suspicions, does not suffice to regard the expert as a 'witness for the prosecution': judgment of 28 August 1991, *Brandstetter*, para. 45.

[501]   Judgment of 18 February 1997, *Niteröst-Huber*, para. 23. See also the judgment of 7 June 2001, *Kress*, para. 73; judgment of 21 March 2002, *Immeubles Groupe Kosser*, para. 23.

[502]   See, *e.g.*, the judgment of 20 February 1996, *Vermeulen*, para. 33; judgment of 25 June 1997, Van Orshoven, para. 41; judgments of 27 March 1998, *K.D.B. v. the Netherlands*, and *J.J. v. the Netherlands*, para. 44 and para. 43, respectively; judgment of 18 February 1997, *Niteröst-Huber*, para. 24; judgment of 9 November 2000, *Göç*, paras 31-37; judgment of 7 June 2001, *Kress*, para. 65. See for a rare exception the judgment of 15 June 2004, *Stepinska*, paras 17-19.

[503]   See, *e.g.*, the judgment of 8 February 2000, *Voisine*, para. 33; judgment of 27 February 2001, *Adoud et Bosoni*, para. 20; judgment of 26 April 2001, *Meftah and Others*, para. 42.

[504]   See, *e.g.*, the judgment of 19 July 1995, *Kerojärvi*, paras 39-42; judgment of 28 June 2001, *F.R.. v. Switzerland*, para. 37; judgment of 21 February 2002, *Ziegler*, para. 38.

[505]   Judgment of 3 June 2003, *Walston (No. 1)*, para. 58.

present any fact or argument which already appeared in the impugned decision. It is a matter for the parties to assess whether a submission deserves a reaction.[506] In the *Reinhardt and Slimane-Kaïd* Case concerning French cassation proceedings, the Court found a twofold breach of the adversarial requirement: neither the reporting judge's report, which had been disclosed to the advocate-general, nor the submissions of the latter had been communicated to the parties.[507] However, the Court also held that the subsequent changed French practice did meet the requirements of Article 6.[508] This practice implies that the parties and the advocate-general receive only the first section of the reporting judge's report, which includes an analysis of the case, while on the day preceding the hearing the advocate-general informs the parties' lawyers of the tenor of his submissions.[509] They are entitled to reply by means of a memorandum for the deliberations and in cases where there is an oral hearing they may reply to his submissions orally. In the *Kress* Case, with regard to a similar practice before the French *Conseil d'Etat*, the Court reached the same conclusion.[510] In the *Immeubles Groupe Kosser* Case the Court held that the fact that the memorandum was received the day after the public hearing, whilst the deliberations of the *Conseil d'État* took place directly after the hearing, did not constitute a breach of the adversarial principle.[511]

Evidence obtained contrary to the norms laid down in the Convention itself, such as statements extracted via torture or other inhuman treatment contrary to Article 3, or evidence collected by means of encroachment on privacy contrary to Article 8, conflicts on that ground alone with the Convention. However, the Convention does not lay down rules on evidence as such. The Court, therefore, does not exclude as a matter of principle and in the abstract that evidence obtained in breach of provisions of domestic law may be admitted. It is a matter for the national courts to assess the obtained evidence and its relevance.[512] Nevertheless, the Court has adopted the view

---

[506]   See, *e.g.*, the judgment of 18 February 1997, *Nideröst-Huber*, para. 29, and *mutatis mutandis* the judgment of 22 February 1996, *Bulut*, para. 49; judgment of 31 January 2001, *Lanz*, para. 58; judgment of 15 July 2003, *Fortum Corporation*, para. 42.

[507]   Judgment of 31 March 1998, paras 105-106; see also, *e.g.*, the judgments of 27 March 1998, *K.D.B. v. the Netherlands*, and *J.J. v. the Netherlands*, para. 44 and para. 43, respectively; the judgment of 3 December 2002, *Berger*, paras 42-43. In the judgment of 27 November 2003, *Slimane-Kaïd (No. 2)*, para. 17, the omission to communicate the draft judgment, which had been communicated to the advocate-general, to the party also amounted to a breach of Article 6.

[508]   Judgment of 31 March 1998, para. 106; judgment of 2 November 2004, *Fabre*, paras 31-32.

[509]   In the judgment of 26 July 2002, *Meftah and Others*, paras 49-52, the Court reached the conclusion that a person who has chosen to defend himself without representation should benefit from the same practice.

[510]   Judgment of 7 June 2001, para. 76; see also the judgment of 21 March 2002, *APBP*, paras 23-27; judgment of 10 October 2002, *Theraube*, paras 31-32.

[511]   Judgment of 21 March 2002, para. 26.

[512]   See, *e.g.*, the judgment of 12 July 1988, *Schenk*, para. 46; judgment of 26 September 1996, *Miailhe (No. 2)*, para. 43; judgment of 18 March 1997, *Mantovanelli*, para. 34.

that the principle of 'fair hearing' may entail specific requirements with respect to evidence.

The notion of a fair criminal trial implies that the public interest in the fight against crime cannot justify the use of evidence obtained as a result of police incitement.[513] From the fact that an accused person is entitled in principle to "take part in the hearing and to have his case heard", the Court has deduced that "all the evidence must in principle be produced in the presence of the accused (...) with a view to adversarial argument."[514] The principle of immediacy is a guarantee of fairness as the observations made by the court about the credibility of a witness may have important consequences for an accused. A change in the composition of the trial court after the hearing of an important witness should, therefore, normally lead to a rehearing of that witness.[515] The evidence produced must be sufficiently 'direct' to actually make refutation possible during the public hearing.[516] In the *Bricmont* Case the lack of confrontation between the accused persons and a member of the Belgian royal family, as the party seeking damages, amounted to a breach of paragraphs 1 and 3 of Article 6 taken together.[517]

The case law with regard to the opportunity of the accused to challenge and question a witness is further discussed in subsection 10.10.5. As will be seen, it may be concluded from this case law that a court decision which is exclusively or almost exclusively based upon indirect evidence of witnesses, has not been taken in accordance with the fair-trial requirement, unless in some way or another an adequate possibility for contradiction and counter-evidence has been afforded. The same holds good with respect to other evidence, such as tape recordings; defence against its contents must be allowed and still be practicable. According to the Court Article 6(1) does not require access to the tape itself. Its relevance for the fairness of the trial depends, *inter alia*, on the vital character of the contents of the tape for the evidence, while it is also relevant whether the transcript of the tape has been verified by an independent person.[518] Although the national authorities have greater latitude when dealing with

---

[513]   Judgment of 9 June 1998, *Teixeira de Castro*, paras 34-36; judgment of 22 July 2003, *Edwards and Lewis*, para. 49 and judgment of 27 October 2004, *Edwards and Lewis* (Grand Chamber).

[514]   Judgment of 6 December 1988, *Barberà, Messegué and Jabardo*, para. 78. See also the judgment of 20 November 1989, *Kostovski*, para. 41; judgment of 27 September 1990, *Windisch*, para. 26.

[515]   Judgment of 9 March 2004, *Pitkänen*, para. 58. The same rule seems to hold good in civil cases: *ibidem*, para. 62.

[516]   In the *Kamasinski* Case, the Commission held it to be in violation of Article 6(1) that no note had been given to the applicant or his representative of the contents of the information which the judge, acting as rapporteur, had obtained by telephone from the judge of the regional court who had presided over the trial; report of 5 May 1988, paras 188-195.

[517]   Judgment of 7 July 1989, paras 78-85.

[518]   Judgment of 24 November 1986, *Gillow*, para. 71. See also the judgment of 12 July 1988, *Schenk*, paras 39-49, and the judgment of 2 July 2002, *S.N. v. Sweden*, paras 46-52, with regard to a recorded interview of a minor who was the perceived victim of a sexual offence.

civil cases than they have when dealing with criminal cases, as a rule the principle of immediacy also seems to apply to civil cases.[519]

In the *Mantovanelli* Case the applicants applied to the administrative courts for a ruling that the hospital where their daughter had received medical treatment, was liable for her death. In Strasbourg they complained that the procedure followed in preparing the expert medical opinion ordered by the national administrative court had not been in conformity with the adversarial principle. The Court firstly concluded that it was not disputed that the 'purely judicial' proceedings had complied with the adversarial principle. The applicants could have made submissions to the national court on the content and findings of the report of the expert. Nevertheless, the Court doubted whether they had had a real opportunity to comment effectively on it. The question that had to be answered by the expert concerned a technical field that was not within the judge's knowledge and, therefore, the report was likely to have a preponderant influence on the assessments of the facts by that court. The Court further took into account that no practical difficulties stood in the way of the applicants being associated in the process of producing the rapport, and the fact that the people to be interviewed by the expert were employed by the hospital, the opposing party in the proceedings. Finally the Court concluded that the applicants had not been able to comment effectively on the main piece of evidence and therefore Article 6 had been breached.[520]

The prosecuting authorities are obliged 'to disclose to the defence all material evidence for or against the accused',[521] but the right to disclosure is not an absolute one. In criminal proceedings there may be competing interests, such as national security, the need to protect witnesses or keep secret police methods of investigation of crime.[522] However, only such restrictions as are strictly necessary, are permissible and any difficulties caused to the defence by a limitation of its right must be sufficiently counterbalanced.[523] In principle it is a matter for the national courts to decide whether the non-disclosure of evidence was strictly necessary.[524] The Court scrutinizes whether the decision-making procedure applied in each case complied, as far as possible, with the adversarial principle and the principle of equality of arms, and incorporated adequate safeguards to protect the rights of the accused. In this regard it seems crucial whether the defence is informed, can make submissions and can participate in the

---

[519]   Judgment of 9 March 2004, *Pitkänen*, paras 59-65.
[520]   Judgment of 18 March 1997, paras 35-36.
[521]   Judgment of 16 December 1992, *Edwards*, para. 36.
[522]   See, *e.g.*, the judgment of 26 March 1996, *Doorson*, para. 70; judgment of 16 February 2000, *Rowe and Davis*, para. 61.
[523]   Judgment of 23 April 1997, *Van Mechelen and Others*, para. 58; judgment of 16 February 2000, *Rowe and Davis*, para. 61.
[524]   Judgment of 16 February 2000, *Rowe and Davis*, para. 61.

decision-making process. The Court futher attaches great importance to the fact that the need for disclosure is under constant assessment of the judge, who may monitor throughout the trial the fairness or otherwise of the disclosed evidence.[525]

In the *Fitt* Case the Court concluded, by nine votes to eight, that their had not been a violation of Article 6. In the national proceedings the prosecution had made an *ex parte* application to the trial judge for an order authorising non-disclosure. The defence were told that the material in question related to sources of information and they were able to make submissions to the judge outlining the defence case. The Court based its conclusion *inter alia* on the facts that the material formed no part of the prosecution case and was never put to the jury and that the need for disclosure was at all times under the assessment of a judge. The minority, however, took the view that the surveillance of the judge could not remedy the unfairness created by the defence's absence from the *ex parte* proceedings.[526] In the *Jasper* Case the defence were not (even) told of the category of material that the prosecution sought to withhold, but here again, by nine votes to eight, the Court held that Article 6 had not been violated.[527] A different conclusion was reached in the *Rowe* and *Davis* Case. During the applicant's trial at first instance the prosecution withheld, without notifying the judge, certain relevant evidence on grounds of public interest. The absence of any scrutiny of the undisclosed evidence by the trial judge could not be remedied in the appeal proceedings. The Court held that the trial judge was fully versed in all the evidence, saw witnesses give their testimony and would have been in a position to monitor the need of disclosure throughout the trial. The judges in the Court of Appeal however, were dependent for their understanding of the relevance of the undisclosed evidence on the transcripts of the hearing of the court in first instance and on the information of the prosecuting counsel. Therefore, the lack of scrutiny of the withheld material deprived the applicants of a fair trial.[528] In the *Edwards* and *Lewis* Case the applicants complained that the undisclosed evidence substantiated their claim that they had been the victims of entrapment. Since they were denied access to the evidence, they were not able to argue the case in full before the judge. According to the Court the matters raised by the applicants were of determinative importance to the applicants' trials. The Court reached the conclusion that the trial had not been fair, taking into account that the judge, who subsequently rejected the defence submissions on entrapment, had already seen prose-

---

[525] See, *e.g.*, the judgment of 16 February 2000, *Rowe and Davis*, para. 62-67; judgment of 25 September 2001, *P.G. and J.H. v. the United Kingdom*, paras 69-71.

[526] Judgment of 16 February 2000, paras 47-50; see also the judgment of 25 September 2001, *P.G. and J.H. v. the United Kingdom*, paras 70-73.

[527] Judgment of 16 February 2000, paras 54-58.

[528] Judgment of 16 February 2000, paras 65-69. See also the judgment of 16 December 1992, *Edwards*, paras 35-39; judgment of 19 September 2000, *I.J.L., G.M.R. and A.K.P. v. the United Kingdom*, para. 118; judgment of 19 June 2001, *Atlan*, paras 41-46.

cution evidence which may have been relevant to the issue, and also the lack of adequate safeguards to protect the interests of the accused.[529]

10.5.4 THE RIGHT TO BE PRESENT AT THE TRIAL AND THE RIGHT TO AN ORAL HEARING

The precept of a 'fair hearing' in principle entails the right of the parties to be present in person at the trial. This right is closely connected to the right to defend oneself in person as stipulated in Article 6(3) subparagraph (c),[530] the right to an oral hearing[531] and the right to be able to follow the proceedings.[532] In the *Colozza* Case the Court held that, "although this is not expressly mentioned in para. 1 of Article 6, the object and the purpose of the Article as a whole show that a person 'charged with a criminal offence' is entitled to take part in the hearing."[533]

There may be exceptions to this principle as far as trials at second or third instance are concerned. However, an exception is not allowed where an appellate court has to examine a case both as to the facts and the law and make a full assessment of the issue of guilt or innocence. In that case the direct assessment of the evidence given in person by the accused for the purpose of proving that he did not commit the alleged offence, is required.[534] Moreover, in principle an exception is permissible only if the accused was entitled to be present at the hearing at first instance.[535] In addition, the Court takes

---

[529] Judgment of 22 July 2003, paras 50-59, confirmed by the Court in its judgment of 27 October 2004 (Grand Chamber), para. 47. See also the judgment of 9 May 2003, *Papageorgiou*, paras 30-40, where essential items of evidence had not been produced or adequately examined at the trial.

[530] See, *e.g.*, the judgment of 25 November 1997, *Zana*, para. 68. See on the right to defend oneself in person *infra* 10.10.4.

[531] See the judgment of 23 February 1994, *Fredin (No.2)*, para. 21, and the judgment of 26 April 1995, *Fischer*, para. 44.

[532] Judgment of 23 February 1994, *Stanford*, para. 26. In this case the applicant complained about the poor acoustics of the courtroom.

[533] Judgment of 12 February 1985, para. 27. See also, *e.g.*, the judgment of 2 March 1987, *Monnell and Morris*, para. 58; judgment of 19 December 1989, *Brozicek*, para. 45.

[534] Judgment of 25 July 2000, *Tierce and Others*, para. 95; judgment of 6 July 2004, *Dondarini*, para. 27. However, in the judgment of 19 February 1996, *Botten*, para. 39 and paras 48-53, and the judgment of 15 July 2003, *Sigurthor Arnarsson*, para. 30-38, the Court chose a different approach, where it stated that 'even if the court of appeal has full jurisdiction to examine both points of law and of fact, Article 6 para. 1 does not always require a right to a public hearing or, if a hearing takes place, a right to be present in person'.

[535] In many judgments the Court stated that the notion of a 'fair trial' implies that persons charged with a criminal offence, *as a principle*, are entitled to be present at the first instance trial. See, *e.g.*, the judgment of 26 May 1988, *Ekbatani*, para. 25; judgment of 25 March 1998, *Belziuk*, para. 37; judgment of 3 October 2000, *Pobornikoff*, para. 24. However, there does not seem to be much room for an exception to this principle. In cases where the Court accepted the non-entitlement for the accused to be present at the second or third instance trial, the accused had in fact been present at first instance.

into account the nature of the national (appeal) system,[536] the scope of the powers of the national (appeal) court[537] and the "manner in which the applicant's interests were actually presented and protected" before the national (appeal) court.[538] In the appeal proceedings in the *Kremzow* Case the accused risked a serious increase in sentence. Therefore, the Court held that the gravity of what was at stake implied that the applicant ought to have been able to defend himself in person.[539] A different conclusion was reached in the *Jan Åke Andersson* and *Fejde* Cases. The Court attached importance to the fact that the appeal raised questions which could be decided on the basis of the case-file, to the minor character of the offence and to the prohibition against the increase of the sentence on appeal.[540]

The rule that the person concerned is entitled to be present at the hearing at first instance seems less strict in civil proceedings.[541] However, in the *Helmers* Case, concerning the 'civil' right to enjoy a good reputation, the Court developed with regard to the entitlement of the applicant to be present at the appeal hearing the same line of reasoning as in criminal cases.[542] The seriousness of what was at stake – the professional career of the applicant – did not justify an encroachment on the right to be present.[543]

In civil proceedings the right to be present at the trial may be waived, although the waiver must be made in an unequivocal manner.[544] The same holds good for

---

[536] See, *e.g.*, the judgment of 2 March 1987, *Monnell and Morris*, paras 56-70; judgment of 21 September 1993, *Kremzow*, para. 63; judgment of 8 February 2000, *Josef Prinz*, paras 36-37.

[537] See, *e.g.*, the judgment of 8 February 2000, *Josef Prinz*, para. 43; judgment of 3 October 2000, *Pobornikoff*, paras 29-33; judgment of 23 January 2003, *Richen and Gaucher*, paras 35-36.

[538] See, *e.g.*, the judgment of 29 October 1991, *Helmers*, paras 36-39; judgments of 8 February 2000, *Michael Edward Cooke* and *Josef Prinz*, para. 38 and paras 37 and 44, respectively.

[539] Judgment of 21 September 1993, *Kremzow*, para. 67. See also the judgment of 19 February 1996, *Botten*, paras 48-53, concerning a judgment of the Norwegian Supreme Court in which it had made its own assessment of the facts without hearing the applicant and the judgment of 8 February 2000, *Michael Edward Cooke*, para. 42.

[540] Judgments of 29 October 1991, *Jan-Åke Andersson*, paras 29-30; *Fejde*, para. 33. The latter aspect, the impossibility of increasing the sentence, is not – at least not in itself – decisive. See the judgment of 3 October 2000, *Pobornikoff*, para. 31, where the imposed sentence could not be increased in the appeal proceedings, but nevertheless the applicant had the right to be present at the trial. See also the judgment of 8 February 2000, *Josef Prinz*, paras 40-44, in which the absence of the applicant in the proceedings before the Austrian Supreme Court with regard to the question whether the conditions for the applicant's placement in an institution for mentally ill offenders were met, had not violated Article 6 and the judgment of 3 October 2002, *Kucera*, para. 29.

[541] See the judgment of 23 February 1994, *Fredin (No. 2)*, para. 22; judgment of 19 February 1998, *Allan Jacobsson (No. 2)*, para. 49. Compare also the judgment of 1 June 2004, *Valová, Slezák and Slezák*, paras 63-69.

[542] In particular, its *Jan Åke Andersson* and *Fejde* judgments of 29 October 1991.

[543] Judgment of 29 October 1991, paras 36-39. See also, *e.g.*, the judgment of 23 February 1994, *Fredin (No. 2)*, para. 22; judgment of 12 July 2001, *Malhous*, para. 60.

[544] See, *e.g.*, the judgment of 24 June 1993, *Schuler-Zgraggen*, para. 58; judgment of 21 September 1993, *Zumtobel*, para. 34.

criminal cases.[545] In case the accused has not been notified in person of a hearing, particular diligence is required in assessing whether the accused has waived his right to be present.[546] In the *Sejdovic* Case the Italian authorities took the view that the applicant had waived his right to appear at his trial because he had become untraceable after the allegedly committed crime. However, according to the Court there was nothing to prove that the applicant knew of the proceedings against him and even supposing that he knew, it could not be concluded that he had unequivocally waived his right to appear at his trial. In these circumstances the applicant should have been able to obtain a new ruling by a court on the charges brought against him. Since Italian law did not guarantee with sufficient certainty that the applicant would have the opportunity to appear at a new trial to present his defence, Article 6 had been violated.[547] Moreover, the Court held that the violation of the Convention was the result of the shortcoming in the Italian legal system, which meant that every person convicted *in absentia* could be deprived of a retrial.[548] National legislation may discourage the unjustified absence of an accused at the trial, although there are important restrictions. The right of counsel who attends the trial to conduct the defence in absence of the accused[549] may not be impaired[550] and the measures taken may not be disproportionate otherwise.[551] In the *Medenica* Case, where the absence of the accused, who had received the summons to appear, without a valid excuse barred the rehearing of the case, this requirement of proportionality had been met.[552]

The foregoing, of course, does not bar judgment by default, provided that the person in question has been summoned by the prescribed procedure and sufficient guarantees are attached to this procedure. If it is not certain whether the accused was really aware that proceedings against him were taking place and that he had been summoned for a hearing, the Court examines the carefulness of the procedure by means of which contact was sought with him.[553] In any case, the fact that the accused is detained, is no reason for his not being heard, at least not at a first instance trial.[554]

---

[545]   Judgment of 12 February 1985, *Colozza*, para. 29; judgment of 21 September 1993, *Kremzow*, paras 66 and 68; judgment of 8 February 2000, *Josef Prinz*, para. 33 in conjunction with para. 44; judgment of 13 February 2001, *Krombach*, para. 85; judgment of 14 June 2001, *Medenica*, para. 54.

[546]   Judgment of 27 May 2004, *Yavuz*, paras 49-51, where the accused had been summoned via counsel.

[547]   Judgment of 10 November 2004, paras 34-42.

[548]   *Ibidem*, para. 44.

[549]   See *infra* 10.10.4.3.

[550]   Judgment of 21 January 1999, *Van Geyseghem*, para. 34; judgment of 23 May 2000, *Van Pelt*, para, 67; judgment of 13 February 2001, *Krombach*, para. 89.

[551]   Judgment of 23 November 1993, *Poitrimol*, para. 35.

[552]   Judgment of 14 June 2001, para. 57. See also the judgment of 16 October 2001, *Eliazer*, paras 30-36.

[553]   Judgment of 12 February 1985, *Colozza*, paras 27-28; judgment of 28 August 1991, *F.C.B. v. Italy*, paras 33-36; judgment of 12 October 1992, *T v. Italy*, paras 27-30; judgment of 18 May 2004, *Somogyi*, paras 66-76.

[554]   The judgment of 19 December 1989, *Kamasinski*, paras 104-108, seems to indicate a different point of view with regard to appeal proceedings.

10.5.5 VARIOUS OTHER REQUIREMENTS

While in criminal matters the *nulla poena sine lege*-rule applies, in civil matters, in principle, the legislature is not precluded from adopting new retrospective provisions to regulate rights arising under existing laws. However, the principle of the rule of law and the notion of fair trial embodied in Article 6 preclude any interference by the legislature with the administration of justice designed to influence the judicial determination of the dispute. For this reason the Court held in the *Stran Greek Refineries and Stratis Andreadis* Case that Greece had violated the applicants' rights under Article 6 by enacting a law that influenced the proceedings already pending before the courts, between the applicants and the Greek State, in a way favourable to the State.[555] Such interference by the legislature can only be justified on compelling grounds of interest.[556] In many cases this requirement had not been met,[557] but things turned out differently in the case of *The National & Provincial Building Society*. The effect of the British Finance Act 1992 was to deprive building societies of their chances of winning already pending proceedings against the Inland Revenue. Amongst other arguments, the Court took into account the fact that the interference caused by the Act was of a much less drastic nature than the interference in the *Stran Greek Reference* Case, in which the applicants and the State had been engaged in litigation for many years and the applicants had an enforceable judgment against the State. The judicial proceedings by the building societies had just been started. Furthermore, the intervention of the legislature had been foreseeable and the Finance Act 1992 concerned the tax sector, an area where recourse to retrospective legislation was not confined to the United Kingdom. The Court concluded that there had been no violation of Article 6.[558]

The 'fair hearing' requirement implies the right of the accused 'not to contribute to incriminating himself'.[559] This right is focused on respecting the will of an accused

---

[555]   Judgment of 9 December 1994, paras 42-50. See also *supra* 10.4.6.4.

[556]   See, *e.g.*, the judgment of 28 October 1999, *Zielinski and Pradal and Gonzalez*, para. 57; judgment of 28 June 2001, *Agoudimos and Cefallonian Sky Shipping Co*, para. 30; judgment of 22 April 2002, *Smokovitis*, para. 23.

[557]   See, *e.g.*, the judgment of 22 October 1997, *Papageorgiou*, paras 37-40, where the Greek Government took the position that the dispute in issue, whose outcome had been influenced by the contested Act, was not a dispute between the applicants and the State, because the party in the proceedings was a private-law, not a public-law, entity. However, the Court rejected this argument (para. 27). In this respect, see also the judgment of 28 October 1999, *Zielinski and Pradal and Gonzalez*, para. 60; judgment of 28 June 2001, *Agoudimos and Cefallonian Sky Shipping Co*, para. 34.

[558]   Judgment of 23 October 1997, paras 105-113. See also the judgment of 27 May 2004, *OGIS-Institut Stanislas, OGEC St. Pie X and Blanche de Castille and Others*, paras 61-72, and the judgment of 27 April 2004, *Gorraiz Lizzaragga and Others*, paras 64-73, where the Court held that, although the enactment of the law in issue had indisputably been unsupportive of the applicants' submissions, it could not be said to have been intended to circumvent the principle of the rule of law.

[559]   Judgment of 25 February 1993, *Funke*, para. 44.

person to remain silent. It does not extend to the use in criminal proceedings of material which may be obtained from the accused through the use of compulsory powers, but which has existence independent of the will of the suspect.[560] It applies to criminal proceedings in respect of all types of criminal offences without distinction, from the most simple to the most complex.[561] Although the right not to incriminate oneself and to remain silent lie at the heart of the notion of a fair hearing,[562] these rights are not absolute rights.[563] However, the very essence of these rights may not be destroyed. Therefore, the threat and imposition of a criminal sanction on the accused, such as accumulating fines[564] or a prison sentence,[565] because he fails to supply information to the authorities investigating the alleged commission of crimes, violates the fair hearing requirement.[566]

In the *Saunders* Case the applicant, who had not been charged (yet), had been legally obliged under the Companies Act to give evidence to the inspectors appointed by the Secretary of State for Trade and Industry. The function of the inspectors was an inquisitorial and not a judicial function. It was their task "to conduct an investigation designed to discover whether there are facts which may result in others taking action". The applicant, who risked the imposition of a fine or a prison sentence in case of non-compliance with the obligation, did give evidence. In the subsequent criminal proceedings the transcripts of the interviews which he gave to the inspectors were read out to the jury by the prosecution over a three day period. In these circumstances the Court held that the subsequent use of the statements was intended to incriminate the applicant and constituted an infringement of the right not to incriminate oneself.[567]

---

[560]   Judgment of 17 December 1996, *Saunders*, para. 69. See also the judgment of 22 June 2000, *Coëme and Others*, para. 128.

[561]   Judgment of 17 December 1996, *Saunders*, para. 74. See also the judgments of 21 December 2000, *Heaney and McGuines* and *Quinn*, para. 57 and para. 58 respectively.

[562]   Judgment of 25 February 1993, *Funke*, para. 44.

[563]   Judgments of 21 December 2000, *Heaney and McGuines* and *Quinn*, para. 47 and para. 47, respectively. In these judgments the Court has referred to the judgment of 8 February 1996, *John Murray*, para. 47, in which case the Court held explicitly that the right to remain silent is not absolute, which would seem to imply that the right not to incriminate oneself is also not absolute. In its judgment of 17 December 1996, *Saunders*, para. 74, the Court explicitly refused to answer the question of whether the right not to incriminate oneself is absolute or not.

[564]   Judgment of 25 February 1993, *Funke*, para. 44.

[565]   Judgments of 21 December 2000, *Heaney and McGuines* and *Quinn*, paras 47-56 and paras 47-56, respectively.

[566]   Although not clear, this might be different if statements made by the accused will not be admissible in evidence against him. See the judgments of 21 December 2000, *Heaney and McGuines* and *Quinn*, paras 52-55 and paras 52-54, respectively.

[567]   Judgment of 16 December 1996, paras 67-75. See also the judgment 19 September 2000, *I.J.L., G.M.R. and A.K.P. v. the United Kingdom*, paras 79-83, concerning three persons who were tried together with the applicant in the *Saunders* Case and the judgment of 27 April 2004, *Kansal*, para. 29.

However, the use of compulsory powers to obtain information against the person concerned outside the context of criminal proceedings is in itself not prohibited.[568]

In the *John Murray* Case the Court sought to strike the balance between the right to remain silent and the circumstances in which an adverse inference, regulated by law, may be drawn from silence. In its lengthy reasoning the Court took account of several safeguards designed to respect the rights of the defence. For instance, the fact that the applicant had been warned that adverse inferences might be drawn from this silence, and the fact that the adverse inferences could only be drawn if a failure to express oneself might "as a matter of common sense" lead to the conclusion that the accused had been guilty and if there existed very strong other evidence against the accused.[569] The Court concluded that there had been no violation of Article 6.[570] Things were different in the *Condron* Case, in which the Court held that the trial judge's omission to direct the jury that it could only draw an adverse inference if satisfied that the applicants' silence at the police interview could only sensibly be attributed to their having no answer or none that would stand up to cross-examination, was incompatible with the exercise of their right to remain silent.[571]

A fair trial may imply the right to have the assistance of a lawyer, including during the phase preceding the trial. This aspect will be discussed under paragraph 3(c) of Article 6. Is it also possible to infer a right to free legal aid from the principle of fair hearing? From paragraph 3(c) it might be concluded *a contrario* that this is not the case.[572] In fact, paragraph 3(c) only guarantees this right for criminal proceedings, and even then only 'when the interests of justice so require'. However, if one party does have the means to secure legal aid and the other does not, there is no 'equality of arms' if the latter does not obtain the assistance of a lawyer as well.[573] Above, in section 10.4.2.3, the view of the Court was mentioned that the mere right of 'access to court' which is implied in Article 6(1), entails the obligation for the Contracting States to make legal aid available, or at least financially possible, if the person in question would otherwise be faced with an insuperable barrier to defend himself adequately. In that context the Court will make an independent examination of the complexity of the case and other

---

[568]   Decision of 10 September 2002, *Allen*, 76574/01, with regard to the requirement to make a declaration of assets to the tax authorities; judgment of 8 July 2004, *Weh*, paras 47-57, where the Court by four votes to three held that the obligation of the registered car owner to provide information about who had driven a motor vehicle identified by the number plate at a certain time, did not violate Article 6. It appeared crucial that the link between the applicant's obligation to disclose the driver of the car and possible criminal proceedings for speeding against him was remote and hypothetical.

[569]   Judgment of 8 February 1996, paras 44-58. In the judgment of 20 March 2001, *Telfner*, paras 15-20, the drawing of adverse inferences was not allowed under Article 6(2) because there was no other strong evidence.

[570]   The same conclusion was reached in the judgment of 6 June 2000, *Averill*, paras 38-52.

[571]   Judgment of 2 May 2000, paras 55-62.

[572]   See, *e.g.*, Appl. 6202/73, *X and Y v. the Netherlands*, D&R 1 (1975), p. 66 (71).

[573]   See, *mutatis mutandis*, the judgment of 4 March 2003, *A.B. v. Slovakia*, para. 61.

relevant factors such as the applicable rules of evidence and the emotional involvement of the applicant in the outcome of the proceedings.[574] Other expenses, too, for instance those for a translator or an interpreter, may be so onerous that the principle of 'fair trial' is at stake.[575]

The same applies to the question of whether under Article 6(1) the parties are entitled to have witnesses and experts summoned and examined. From the fact that Article 6(3)(d) contains explicit provisions about this for criminal cases, it might be inferred *a contrario* that such a right does not hold good for the parties in civil proceedings. However, here again, the case law recognises the possibility that the court's refusal to have a particular witness summoned by a party to a dispute, or to hear him, constitutes an encroachment on the right to a fair hearing.[576] That right does not require, however, that a national court appoints, at the request of the defence, another expert when the opinion of the court-appointed expert supports the prosecution case.[577]

Finally, an additional element of 'fair hearing' is the requirement that the judicial decision must state the reasons on which it is based. The extent to which the requirement applies depends on 'the nature of the decision' and can only be assessed in the circumstances of each individual case.[578] According to the Court it is, moreover, necessary to take into account the differences existing in the Contracting States with regard to *inter alia* the presentation and drafting of judgments.[579] It is clear that the court is not obliged to give a detailed answer to every argument.[580] When a motivation is lacking altogether, the remedies provided for are likely to become illusory.[581] The detail into which the statement of the reasons must go is, therefore, determined by what an effective remedy against the decision requires in each particular case.[582]

From this point of departure the practice existing in some countries to provide certain judgments in criminal cases with a motivation only after an appeal has been instituted, seems questionable. However, in the *Zoon* Case the Court held that it cannot

---

[574]   Appl. 9353/81, *Webb v. the United Kingdom*, D&R 33 (1983), p. 133 (138-141).
[575]   Report of 18 May 1977, *Luedicke, Belkacem and Koç*, B.27 (1982), p. 26.
[576]   Judgment of 15 July 2003, *Sigurthor Arnarsson*, paras 31-38.
[577]   Judgment of 28 August 1991, *Brandstetter*, para. 46. The judgment of 2 October 2001, *G.B. v. France*, paras 64-70, constitutes an exception, where the court-appointed expert at the trial, to the detriment of the accused, changed his point of view radically after a brief examination of a prior psychiatric report written by another expert.
[578]   See, *e.g.*, the judgments of 9 December 1994, *Ruiz Torija*, and *Hiro Balani*, para. 29 and para. 27, respectively; judgment of 19 February 1998, *Higgins and Others*, para. 42.
[579]   Judgment of 21 May 2002, *Jokela*, para. 72.
[580]   See, *e.g.*, the judgment of 19 April 1994, *Van de Hurk*, para. 61; judgments of 9 December 1994, *Ruiz Torija*, and *Hiro Balani*, para. 29 and para. 27, respectively; judgment of 21 January 1999, *Garcia Ruíz*, para. 26.
[581]   See the judgment of 16 December 1992, *Hadjianastassiou*, paras 34-36 and *infra* 10.10.3.
[582]   See the judgment of 1 July 2003, *Suominen*, paras 37-38.

be said that the applicant's rights were unduly affected by the absence of a complete judgment or by the absence from the judgment in abridged form of a detailed enumeration of the items of evidence relied on to ground his conviction.[583] In case a judgment only refers to the wording of the law without any detailed reasons Article 6 may be violated.[584] In dismissing an appeal an appellate court may, in principle, simply endorse the reasons of the lower court's decision. However, in such a case Article 6 requires that the court "did in fact address the essential issues which were submitted to its jurisdiction and did not merely endorse without further ado the findings reached by the lower court".[585] In the *Hirvisaari* Case the endorsement by the national court of the reasoning of the Pension Board, which had found the applicant partly capable of working, violated Article 6. Since the applicant's main complaint in his appeal had been the inadequacy of the Pension Board's reasoning, the court should have given proper reasons of its own.[586]

A remarkable situation occurred in the *Schuler-Zgraggen* Case. The national court based its decision with regard to the alleged entitlement of the female applicant to an invalidity pension on the mere assumption that "women give up work when they give birth to a child". This reasoning amounted to a breach of Article 6 in conjunction with Article 14.[587] In the *Van Kück* Case the applicant claimed that the German court proceedings concerning her claims for reimbursement of medical expenses in respect of gender re-assignment measures had been unfair. In the special circumstances of the case the Court held that the interpretation by the national court of the term "medical necessity" and evaluation of evidence in this respect had not been reasonable and that the approach in examining the question of whether the applicant had deliberately caused her transsexuality, had not been appropriate. Therefore, the proceedings in question did not satisfy the requirements of a fair hearing.[588]

10.6 PUBLIC TRIAL AND THE PUBLIC PRONOUNCEMENT OF THE JUDGMENT

Article 6(1) requires that the hearing shall be public. In the *Pretto* Case the Court set forth the rationale of this requirement as follows: "The public character of proceedings

---

[583]   Judgment of 7 December 2000, paras 32-50 and *infra* 10.10.3.

[584]   Judgment of 29 May 1997, *Georgiadis*, paras 41-43; judgment of 15 January 2004, *Sakkopoulos*, paras 50-52; judgment of 19 February 2004, *Yiarenios*, paras 21-23.

[585]   Judgment of 19 December 1997, *Helle*, para. 60; judgment of 27 September 2001, *Hirvisaari*, para. 30.

[586]   Judgment of 27 September 2001, paras 31-32. See also the judgment of 7 July 2004, *H.A.L. v. Finland*, paras 49-52.

[587]   Judgment of 24 June 1993, paras 66-67.

[588]   Judgment of 12 June 2003, paras 46-64.

before the judicial bodies referred to in Article 6 para. 1 (...) protects litigants against the administration of justice in secret with no public scrutiny; it is also one of the means whereby confidence in the courts, superior and inferior, can be maintained. By rendering the administration of justice visible, publicity contributes to the achievement of the aim of Article 6 para. 1 (...) namely a fair trial, the guarantee of which is one of the fundamental principles of any democratic society, within the meaning of the Convention."[589]

In addition to the interest which the parties to the dispute may have in a public hearing, it serves a public interest as well: verifiability of and information about, and thus confidence in the administration of justice. Consequently, the question arises whether the parties can waive their right to a public hearing to an unlimited degree or, on the contrary, the court may only comply with a request to that effect if one of the grounds explicitly mentioned for this in Article 6 presents itself. In *Le Compte, Van Leuven and De Meyere*[590] and in *H v. Belgium*[591] the Court seemed to have taken the first position. This was confirmed by the *Håkansson and Sturesson* judgment, where the Court held that "neither the letter, nor the spirit" of the provision oppose an express or tacit waiver of the right to a public hearing, although the waiver must be made in an unequivocal manner and "must not run counter to any important public interest".[592] In this case the Court concluded that a tacit waiver had occurred. The proceedings concerning the lawfulness of an auction sale usually took place *in camera*. For this reason, in the Court's view, the omission of the applicants to ask the competent authorities for a public hearing could be regarded as a waiver of their entitlement to have their case heard in public.[593] The Court has elucidated its point of view in its subsequent case law. A failure to request a hearing is not to be considered a waiver, where the law explicitly excludes a hearing,[594] or where, though the law does not contain a special rule, the court's practice is never to hold one.[595] In case the court's practice is not to hold one of their own motion, but where the law explicitly provides for the possibility to request one,[596] or where it is at least the practice to hold one upon a party's request,[597] a failure to request a hearing is considered an unequivocal waiver.

---

[589]   Judgment of 8 December 1983, para. 21. See also, *e.g.*, the judgment of 22 February 1984, *Axen*, para. 25; judgment of 26 September 1995, *Diennet*, para. 33; judgment of 24 November 1997, *Werner*, para. 45; judgment of 12 July 2001, *Malhous*, para. 55.

[590]   Judgment of 23 June 1981, para. 59.

[591]   Judgment of 30 November 1987, para. 54.

[592]   Judgment of 21 February 1990, para. 66.

[593]   *Ibidem.*

[594]   Judgment of 26 September 1995, *Diennet*, para. 34; judgment of 21 march 2002, *A.T. v. Austria*, para. 37.

[595]   Judgment of 24 November 1997, *Werner*, para. 48; judgment of 20 May 1998, *Gautrin*, paras 38 and 42; judgment of 21 March 2000, *Rushiti*, para. 22.

[596]   Judgment of 21 September 1993, *Zumtobel*, para. 34; judgment of 24 June 1993, *Schuler-Zgraggen*, para. 58; judgment of 1 July 1997, *Rolf Gustafson*, para. 47.

[597]   Judgment of 28 May 1997, *Pauger*, paras 60-61.

With a view to the public interest which is served by publicity, in particular in criminal cases, it will, however, have to be assumed that there is merely a possibility of waiving the right to a public hearing, not a right to a hearing *in camera*, and that, if a request for a hearing *in camera* is made, the court may refuse this on the ground of the weighing of the interest of the party concerned against the public interest.[598] The court then will, of course, also have to take into account the protection of the private life of the party concerned, as one of the explicitly mentioned grounds of restriction, and also the danger which publicity may constitute for the presumption of innocence protected in the second paragraph.

The text of Article 6 does not contain any qualification of the right to a public hearing as far as the phase of the proceedings is concerned. However, the Court makes a distinction between a trial before a court at first instance and a trial before an appeal court, also with respect to the public interests involved: "The Court fully recognises the value attaching to the publicity of the proceedings such as those indicated by the Commission (...). However, even where a court of appeal has jurisdiction to review the case both as to facts and as to law, the Court cannot find that Article 6 always requires a right to a public hearing irrespective of the nature of the issues to be decided. The publicity requirement is certainly one of the means whereby confidence in the courts is maintained. However, there are other considerations, including the right to trial within a reasonable time and the related need for expeditious handling of the court's case-load, which must be taken into account in determining the necessity of a public hearing at stages in the proceedings subsequent to the trial at first instance. Provided a public hearing has been held at first instance, the absence of such a hearing before a second or third instance may accordingly be justified by the special features of the proceedings at issue. Thus, leave to appeal proceedings and proceedings involving only questions of law, as opposed to questions of fact, may comply with the requirements of Article 6, although the appellant was not given an opportunity of being heard in person by the appeal or cassation court."[599]

In the *Tierce and Others* Case the Court added: "However, where an appellate court has to examine a case to the facts and the law and make a full assessment of the issue of guilt or innocence, it cannot determine the issue without the direct assessment of the evidence given in person by the accused for the purpose of proving that he did not commit the act allegedly constituting a criminal offence. The principle that hearings should be held in public entails the right for the accused to give evidence in person to an appellate court."[600]

---

[598]   Judgment of 21 February 1990, *Håkansson and Sturesson*, para. 67.

[599]   Judgments of 29 October 1991, *Helmers*, para. 36; *Jan-Åke Andersson*, para. 27 and *Fejde*, para. 31. See further, *e.g.*, the judgment of 22 February 1996, *Bulut*, para. 41-42.

[600]   Judgment of 25 July 2000, para. 95.

As far as the publicity requirement is concerned, these quotations do *per se* not raise any difficulty. However, the last clause in the Swedish cases, "although the appellant was not given an opportunity of being heard in person by the appeal or cassation court", and the statement in the *Tierce and Others* Case that the right to a public hearing entails the right to give evidence in person to an appellate court, may cause confusion. The question whether a person should be heard in person has strictly speaking nothing to do with the publicity requirement. In fact, the Court confuses the right to a public hearing – that means a public *trial* – with the right to be heard in person. In fact, in these cases the crucial question did not concern the publicity requirement but appeared to be whether the court of appeal could properly decide to examine the case without the applicants having a right to present their arguments at a hearing.[601]

The form of publicity to be given to the judgment under domestic law must be assessed in the light of the special features of the proceedings.[602] For pragmatic reasons the opinion would seem to be justified that the requirement of a public judgment has been complied with if during a public session the reading is confined to that of the operational part of the judgment,[603] and that even this may be omitted if the operational part contains no more than the determination that the appeal has been rejected or the case is referred back.[604] In that case the parties must receive a copy of the text of the judgment as soon as possible, while the publication of those judgments in which legal questions of a more public interest are at issue, is also of special importance for the verifiability.[605] In case proceedings have been conducted in chambers in order to protect the privacy of children and parties, the pronouncement of the judgment in public may to a large extent frustrate these aims. Despite the fact that Article 6 permits restrictions exclusively with respect to the public nature of the proceedings, not with respect to the public nature of the judgment, the Court has held that in such a case it suffices that anyone who can establish an interest may consult or obtain a copy of the judgment, as long as cases of special interest are routinely published, to enable the

---

[601]   Judgments of 29 October 1991, *Helmers*, para. 38; *Jan-Åke Andersson*, para. 29; and *Fejde*, para. 33; judgment of 25 July 2000, *Tierce and Others*, paras 99-102; the question whether a person has the right to be present at the trial is discussed *supra* 10.5.4.

[602]   See, *e.g.*, with regard to cassation proceedings and proceedings before the supreme court the judgments of 8 December 1983, *Pretto and Others* and *Axen*, para. 27 and para. 31, respectively; judgment of 22 February 1984, *Sutter*, para. 34 (proceedings before the Swiss Military Court of Cassation).

[603]   Judgment of 8 December 1983, *Pretto*, paras 25-28.

[604]   Report of 14 December 1979, *Le Compte, Van Leuven and De Meyere*, B.38, p. 24; report of 15 March 1985, *Adler*, D&R 46 (1986), p. 36 (45).

[605]   See *ibidem*, p. 24 and p. 45, respectively.

public to study the judgments.[606] A failure to deliver the judgment publicly may be remedied on appeal.[607]

With respect to the possibilities of restricting publicity the following observations may be made. Although in some cases the Court examined *ex officio* whether one of the exceptions had been applicable,[608] it may be presumed that it is for the national authorities to invoke explicitly the exceptions of Article 6.[609] On the one hand, the Court has shown to be willing to leave the national authorities, and specifically the national courts, a certain 'margin of appreciation' in the assessment of the question whether there is any reason for application of one of the restrictions, as is the case with respect to the grounds of restriction included in other provisions of the Convention.[610] On the other hand, the Court has also itself shown to be prepared to make an independent examination of the reasons for the restriction,[611] in which context the Court is not prepared to accept simply a developed practice, but requires that it be set forth specifically for each case which ground of restriction is invoked.[612] However, in principle, it is not inconsistent with Article 6 for a State to designate an entire class of cases, *e.g.*, proceedings concerning minors, as an exception to the general rule.[613] In fact the opposite problem occurred in *T. and V. v. the United Kingdom*, concerning two eleven-year-old boys who had been accused of abduction and murder. The applicants complained that they had been deprived of the opportunity to participate effectively in the criminal proceedings because of the massive press attention in and outside court and the fact that the trial had been conducted with the formality of an adult criminal trial, albeit modified to a certain extent in view of the defendants' age. The Government disputed that the public nature of the trial breached the applicants' rights and stressed that the publicity of the trial ensured the fairness of the proceedings. The Court took into account that, according to psychiatric evidence, the ability of the applicants to understand the proceedings in court and to instruct their lawyers was limited and held it "highly unlikely that the applicants would have felt sufficiently uninhibited in the tense courtroom and under public scrutiny" to consult with their lawyers during the trial or that they would have been capable outside the courtroom

---

[606] Judgment of 24 April 2001, *B. and P. v. the United Kingdom*, paras 45-49.

[607] Judgment of 10 July 2001, *Lamanna*, para. 30-34, and implicitly the judgments of 24 November 1997, *Werner* and *Szücs*, paras 54-60 and 43-48, respectively.

[608] See the judgment of 29 September 1999, *Serre*, para. 22; judgment of 8 February 2000, *Stefanelli*, para. 21.

[609] This point of view seems to be confirmed by the judgment of 23 April 1997, *Stallinger and Kuso*, para. 51; judgment of 20 May 1998, *Gautrin*, para. 42.

[610] See also *supra* 10.4.6.3.

[611] See, *e.g.*, the judgment of 23 June 1981, *Le Compte, Van Leuven and De Meyere*, paras 59-61; judgment of 10 February 1983, *Albert and Le Compte*, paras 34-37.

[612] Judgment of 8 June 1976, *Engel*, para. 89. See also the judgment of 3 October 2000, *Eisenstecken*, para. 34-35.

[613] Judgment of 24 April 2001, *B. and P. v. the United Kingdom*, para. 39.

to co-operate with them and give them relevant information for the defence. Thus, the defendants' rights to participate effectively in the proceedings had been violated.[614]

In relation to the restriction ground of the protection of public order one is inclined to think of the prevention of disorder. When Article 14 of the International Covenant on Civil and Political Rights was drafted, this interpretation was indeed advocated, on the part of Great Britain, and on that ground objections were raised – in vain – to the addition of the French term *ordre public* in the English text.[615] Now that the text of Article 6 in its present form has been adopted in terms equal to those of Article 14 of the Covenant, a comparison with Articles 10(2) and 11(2), where for the protection of public order the English text has 'the prevention of disorder' and the French text '*la défense de l'orde*', renders it difficult to maintain the British interpretation, although, on the other hand, the English and the French text of Article 9(2) show that the drafters have not been very consistent in this matter. However this may be, the prevention of disorder in the courtroom may in any case be brought under the ground 'the interests of justice'.[616] What then does 'public order' mean in this context? In the *Le Compte, Van Leuven and De Meyere* Case, the Belgian Government invoked this ground, alleging that publicity of the medical disciplinary cases might lead to violation of medical professional secrecy. The Commission indeed examined this aspect under that denominator.[617] This seems to point in the direction of public order in the sense of *ordre public*. Medical professional secrecy was also invoked in the *Diennet* Case, where the French Government tried to justify the fact that disciplinary proceedings against a medical practitioner had been held *in camera*. However, according to the Court the proceedings in question concerned only 'the method of consultation by correspondence' adopted by the applicant and thus, in principle, not the private life of patients of the applicant.[618]

So far the interest of national security has hardly played a part, if at all, in the Strasbourg case law with respect to the public nature of the trial, but it is easy to conceive of situations in which proceedings deal with State secrets or other information that is security-sensitive. The court will then have to form an independent opinion about

---

[614] Judgments of 16 December 1999, paras. 80-89 and paras 81-91, respectively. See also the judgment of 15 June 2004, *S.C. v. the United Kingdom*, paras 27-37, concerning an eleven- year-old boy with limited intellectual capacity, where the Court held that he should have been tried in a specialist tribunal which was able to give full consideration to and make proper allowance for the handicaps under which he laboured and to adopt its procedure accordingly.

[615] See E/CN.4/SR.318, p. 10: "the proper conception was that closed hearings could be held with a view to preventing disorder".

[616] See the judgment of 14 November 2000, *Riepan*, para. 34, where the Court held that in exceptional cases the public may be excluded from the trial for security concerns.

[617] See the report of 14 December 1979, B.38 (1984), pp. 43-44. See also the report of 14 December 1981, *Albert and Le Compte*, B.50 (1986), pp. 40-41.

[618] Judgment of 26 September 1995, para. 34.

this. Everything that the authorities prefer to be kept secret does not for that reason alone concern national security.

Cases involving the protection of the private life of the parties, except for cases in which the interests of minors are involved,[619] require proceedings *in camera* only if the parties appear to appreciate such protection.[620]

The last ground of restriction – the interests of justice – is explicitly left to the opinion of the domestic court concerned. On occasion it may be necessary to limit the public nature of the proceedings to protect, for instance, the safety and privacy of witnesses; they, too, can claim a 'fair trial'.[621] Here again, however, an ultimate supervision by the Strasbourg Court is fitting. The interests of justice may also require that the space available for the public does not become overcrowded and that agitators are excluded. But, on the other hand, the interest of publicity requires that the administration of justice takes place at locations where reasonable accommodation for the public is available. If the trial takes place outside a regular courtroom, to which the general public in principle has no access (*e.g.* a prison), the national authorities have to take compensatory measures in order to ensure that the public and the media are duly informed about the place of the hearing and are granted effective access.[622]

10.7 THE REASONABLE-TIME REQUIREMENT

10.7.1 INTRODUCTION

Article 6 stipulates in its first paragraph that the hearing of the case by the court must take place 'within a reasonable time' (*dans un délai raisonnable*). Just as with regard to these same words in Article 5(3) this raises the difficult question as to what criteria have to be applied for the assessment of what is reasonable and also what period has to be taken into account in this respect.

In the case of Article 5(3) it is in any event clear what is to be considered as the beginning of the relevant period: this is the moment of the arrest. The rationale of that provision is that the detention on remand does not last longer than is strictly necessary. The purpose of the reasonable-time requirement of Article 6(1), however, is to guarantee that within a reasonable time, and by means of a judicial decision, an end is put to the insecurity into which a person finds himself as to his civil-law position or on account of a criminal charge against him; in the interest of the person in question

---

[619] Judgment of 24 April 2001, *B. and P. v. the United Kingdom*, paras 35-41.
[620] Thus apparently also the Commission in its report in the *Albert and Le Compte* Case, B.50, pp. 40-41.
[621] See on this *infra* 10.10.5.
[622] Judgment of 14 November 2000, *Riepan*, paras 28-31.

as well as of legal certainty. This rationale entails that the provision also applies in cases where there is no question of detention on remand.[623]

The judgments with regard to the reasonable-time requirement are quite numerous. However, around the middle of the eighties of the twentieth century the main lines seem to have been charted.

10.7.2   THE RELEVANT PERIOD

10.7.2.1 Dies a Quo

In the determination of the relevant period the jurisdiction *ratione temporis* must be taken into account. Thus, in the case of an individual complaint concerning proceedings which were already in progress at the moment the State concerned became a party to the Convention – or recognised the individual's right of complaint under former Article 25 – only the length of the period from that moment can be taken into account. However, for the assessment of the reasonableness of that period the stage at which the proceedings were at that moment is also taken into consideration.[624]

With respect to the determination of civil rights and obligations, the beginning of the period is in general taken to be the moment at which the proceedings concerned are instituted[625] or at which, within the framework of other proceedings, such a right or obligation is put forward in a defence. If prior to the judicial proceedings another action, such as an administrative objection[626] or a request for formal confirmation,[627] must have been brought, the beginning is shifted to the moment of that action.[628] A negotiation phase preceding the proceedings, however, is not counted as part of the relevant period.[629]

---

[623]   For the relationship between the two provisions, see the judgment of 10 November 1969, *Stögmüller*, paras 4-5.

[624]   See, *e.g.*, the judgment of 10 December 1982, *Foti*, para. 53; judgment of 26 October 1988, *Martins Moreira*, para. 43; judgment of 25 March 1996, *Mitap and Müftüoglo*, para. 31; judgment of 15 July 2002, *Kalashnikov*, para. 124.

[625]   See, *e.g.*, the judgment of 23 November 1993, *Scopelliti*, para. 18; judgment of 23 March 1994, *Muti*, para. 12; judgment of 27 October 1994, *Katte Klitsche de la Grange*, para. 50.

[626]   Judgment of 28 June 1978, *König*, paras 28 and 101.

[627]   Judgment of 9 December 1994, *Schouten and Meldrum*, paras 61-62.

[628]   Compare the *Vallee* Case, judgment of 26 April 1994, para. 133, where the submission of the preliminary claim for compensation to the administrative authority, required under national law, constituted the starting-point of the relevant period. See also the judgment of 9 June 1998, *Cazenave de la Roche*, para. 46; judgment of 7 June 2001, *Kress*, para. 90.

[629]   Judgment of 8 July 1986, *Lithgow*, para. 199. See, however, also the judgment of 23 April 1996, *Phocas*, para. 69, concerning, *inter alia*, negotiations, expressly recognised by law, prior to formal expropriation proceedings before a court. The Court did assess whether the duration of the preliminary proceedings was reasonable.

With respect to criminal cases the Court has held that the beginning of the relevant period must be taken as the moment at which a 'criminal charge' is brought, since it is only from that moment that the 'determination of (...) any criminal charge' can be involved.[630] However, the rationale mentioned above implies that the period does not in all cases begin at the moment at which the person in question is officially indicted. Even before that he may have been aware of the fact that he is suspected of a criminal offence, so that from that moment he has an interest in a speedy decision about this suspicion being made by the court. This is quite evident in those cases where an arrest precedes the moment of the formal charge.[631] It is, therefore, important here as well that in the Strasbourg case law an autonomous meaning is assigned to the concept of 'charge', the starting-point being that a substantive and not a formal concept of 'charge' must be used because of the great importance of the principle of a fair trial for a democratic society.[632] As the Court held in the *Foti* Case and in the *Corigliano* Case: "Whilst 'charge' (...) may in general be defined as the official notification given to an individual by the competent authority of an allegation that he has committed a criminal offence, it may in some instances take the form of other measures which carry the implication of such an allegation and which likewise substantially affect the situation of the suspect."[633]

Thus, the existence of a 'charge' is not always dependent on an official act.[634] Examples of such 'other measures' are the search of the person's home,[635] the request that a person's immunity be lifted,[636] and the moment the person concerned is informed by the Tax Authority of its intention to impose additional taxes and tax surcharges on him.[637] However, the imposition of fiscal penalties on companies does not imply that the managing director of the companies is charged personally.[638] In some cases the 'charge' does not constitute the *dies a quo* of the relevant period: if the accused did not receive the official notification and was tried in absence, one has to presume that

---

[630] Judgment of 27 June 1968, *Neumeister*, para. 18; judgment of 27 February 1980, *Deweer*, para. 46.

[631] In its judgment of 27 June 1968, *Wemhoff*, para. 19, the Court assumed that the two moments coincided. See further, *e.g.*, the judgment of 28 March 1990, *B v. Austria*, paras 9 and 48; judgment of 19 February 1991, *Alimena*, para. 15; judgment of 25 February 1993, *Dobbertin*, paras 9 and 138. In the latter case there seems to be a clear difference between the moment of arrest and the formal 'charge'. The Court took the moment of arrest as a starting-point.

[632] See *supra* 10.2.1.

[633] Judgments of 10 December 1982, para. 52 and para. 34, respectively.

[634] Initially the Court took a formal criterion to determine the starting-point of the relevant period: judgment of 27 June 1968, *Neumeister*, para. 18. Subsequently, it developed a substantive approach in the judgment of 15 July 1982, *Eckle*, para. 73, which culminated in the judgments of 10 December 1982, *Foti*, and *Corigliano*, para. 52 and para. 34, respectively.

[635] See, *e.g.*, the judgment of 23 October 2003, *Diamantides*, para. 21; judgment of 28 October 2003, *Lopez Sole y Martin de Vargas*, para. 26.

[636] Judgment of 19 February 1991, *Frau*, para. 14.

[637] Judgments of 23 July 2002, *Västberga Taxi Aktiebolag and Vulic*, and *Janosevic*, para. 104 and para. 92, respectively.

[638] Judgment of 22 May 1998, *Hozee*, paras 44-45.

there exists a 'charge',[639] but the reasonable-time requirement is not at stake (yet), because the accused did not live under the pressure of being prosecuted.[640] The period that an accused, who is aware of the 'charge', is on the run, is excluded from the calculation of the relevant period.[641]

10.7.2.2 Dies ad Quem

The above-mentioned rationale of the reasonable-time requirement of Article 6 entails that the end of the period to be taken into consideration is the moment at which the uncertainty concerning the legal position of the person in question has ended. In civil proceedings that is the moment the asserted legal position is determined in a final way.[642] That is not, therefore, the moment at which the hearing in court starts, but the moment at which the decision is taken at highest instance[643] or has become final through the expiration of the time-limit for appeal.[644] Thus, as far as appeal or cassation proceedings 'are capable of affecting the outcome of the dispute', these proceedings must be taken into account in determining the relevant period.[645] Moreover, even stages subsequent to a judgment on the merits, such as enforcement proceedings[646] and proceedings concerning costs,[647] fall under the scope of the reasonable time requirement. However, the lapse of time caused by preliminary proceedings under Article 234 of the EC Treaty [former Article 177] before the Court of Justice of the European Communities is not taken into consideration in the assessment of the length of the proceedings.[648] The same holds good for the institution of extraordinary remedies.

---

[639]   Judgment of 12 February 1985, *Colozza*, para. 29. The applicant was sentenced by default and did have, according to the Court, a right to a 'fresh determination of the merits of the charge'. Compare also the judgment of 23 October 2003, *S.H.K. v. Bulgaria*, para. 26.

[640]   This consequence does not fully correspond with the definition of 'charge' as cited from the *Foti* judgment. The contradiction can be lifted by deleting the word 'likewise'.

[641]   Judgment of 19 February 1991, *Girolami*, para. 15; judgment of 12 October 1992, *Boddaert*, para. 35; judgment of 26 May 1993, *Bunkate*, para. 21.

[642]   See, *e.g.*, the judgments of 26 September 1996, *Di Pede*, and *Zappia*, para. 22 and para 18, respectively; judgment of 28 October 1998, *Pérez de Rada Cavanilles*, para. 39.

[643]   See, *e.g.*, the judgment of 24 May 1991, *Vocaturo*, para. 14; judgment of 12 October 1992, *Salerno*, para. 18.

[644]   See, *e.g.*, the judgment of 24 May 1991, *Pugliese (No. 2)*, para. 16; judgment of 27 February 1992, *Diana*, para. 14.

[645]   See, *e.g.*, the judgment of 23 April 1987, *Poiss*, para. 52; judgment of 21 November 1995, *Acquaviva*, para. 52. The same holds good with regard to proceedings before a Constitutional Court: see *e.g.* the judgment of 23 June 1993, *Ruiz-Mateos*, para. 35; judgments of 1 July 1997, *Probstmeier*, and *Pammel*, paras 46 and 48 and paras 51 and 53, respectively.

[646]   See, *e.g.*, the judgment of 23 March 1994, *Silva Pontes*, paras 35-36; judgment of 19 March 1997, *Hornsby*, para. 40; judgment of 7 June 2000, *Nuutinen*, para. 109.

[647]   Judgment of 23 September 1997, *Robins*, para. 28.

[648]   Judgment of 26 February 1998, *Pafitis*, para. 95.

The Court has chosen the same approach in 'criminal' cases. As the Court held in its *Wemhoff* judgment: "there is (...) no reason why the protection given to the persons concerned against the delays of the courts should end at the first hearing in a trial: unwarranted adjournments or excessive delays on the part of trial courts are also to be feared."[649]

The determination of the charge, also that by, for example, acquittal or dismissal, must be final.[650] As far as convictions are concerned the determination of the penalty affords the certainty to the accused,[651] and then only at the moment at which he can reasonably be assumed to have been informed of the final verdict and its motivation.[652] The decision to refrain from further prosecution may also imply the final determination of the 'charge'.[653]

10.7.3 REASONABLE TIME

After the length of the relevant period has been established, it must be determined whether this period is to be regarded as reasonable. In many cases the Court only makes an overall assessment,[654] while in other cases it assesses the lapse of time in each stage of the proceedings.[655] The reasonableness cannot be judged in the abstract but has to be assessed in view of the circumstances of each individual case.[656] The interests of the person concerned in as prompt a decision as possible will have to be weighed against the demands of a careful examination of the case and a proper conduct of the proceedings.[657]

According to established case law, when assessing the reasonableness of the relevant period the Court applies, in particular, three criteria: a) the complexity of the case, b) the conduct of the applicant, and c) the conduct of the authorities concerned. However, in an increasing number of cases the Court applies, in connection with the con-

---

[649] Judgment of 27 June 1968, para. 18.
[650] See, *e.g.*, the judgments of 19 February 1991, *Pugliese (No. 1)*, para. 18; *Viezzer*, para. 17; *Angelucci*, para. 15.
[651] Judgment of 15 July 1982, *Eckle*, para. 77.
[652] Report of 8 May 1984, *Vallon*, pp. 22-23.
[653] Judgment of 23 October 2003, *S.H.K. v. Bulgaria*, para 27.
[654] See, *e.g.*, the judgment of 19 February 1991, *Colacioppo*, para. 15; judgment of 18 July 1994, *Venditelli*, para. 22; judgment of 26 October 2000, *G.J. v. Luxembourg*, paras 28-36; judgment of 20 December 2001, *Janssen*, paras 40-53.
[655] See, *e.g.*, the judgment of 23 November 1993, *Scopelliti*, paras 22-26; judgment of 23 March 1994, *Silva Pontes*, paras 40-41; judgment of 6 April 2000, *Comingersoll S.A.*, para. 22.
[656] See, *e.g.*, the judgments of 19 February 1991, *Santilli*, and *Maj*, para. 20 and para. 15, respectively; judgment of 23 July 2002, *Rajcevic*, para. 36.
[657] See, *e.g.*, the judgment of 8 July 1987, *H v. the United Kingdom*, paras 71-86; judgment of 31 March 1992, *X v. France*, para. 32; judgment of 23 March 1994, *Silva Pontes*, para. 39.

---

duct of the authorities, a fourth criterion: d) the importance of what is at stake for the applicant.[658]

The question of whether a case is complex is, in general, hard to answer. The Court has attached importance to several factors such as the nature of the facts to be established,[659] the number of accused persons[660] and witnesses,[661] the need to obtain the file of a trial conducted abroad,[662] the joinder of the case to other cases,[663] the intervention of other persons in the procedure[664] and the need to create a special computer program.[665] The complexity may concern questions of fact as well as legal issues.[666]

An attitude or behaviour of the party in question which led to a delay, weakens his complaint about that delay.[667] However, an accused person is not required to co-operate actively in expediting the proceedings which may lead to his own conviction.[668] This may be different for parties to civil proceedings.[669] A party to proceedings cannot be blamed for making use of his right to lodge an appeal.[670] It is evident that this prolongs the proceedings, but this prolongation, too, must stand the test of reasonableness.[671]

With regard to the third criterion, the conduct of the authorities, only delays attributable to the State may cause a violation of the reasonable-time requirement.[672] In particular, the efforts the judicial authorities have made to expedite the proceedings

---

[658]   See, e.g., the judgment of 25 November 1992, *Abdoella*, para. 24; judgment of 30 October 1998, *Styranowski*, para. 47; judgment of 15 October 1999, *Humen*, para. 60; judgment of 27 February 2003, *Niederböster*, para. 39; judgment of 9 March 2004, *Jablonska*, para. 39.

[659]   See, e.g., the judgment of 19 February 1991, *Triggiani*, para. 17; judgment of 30 October 1991, *Wiesinger*, para. 55; judgment of 27 February 1992, *Vorrasi*, para. 17; judgment of 25 February 1993, *Dobbertin*, para. 42; judgment of 1 August 2000, *C.P. v. France*, para. 30.

[660]   Judgment of 19 February 1991, *Angelucci*, para. 15.

[661]   Judgment of 27 February 1992, *Andreucci*, para. 17.

[662]   Judgment of 19 February 1991, *Manzoni*, para. 18.

[663]   Judgment of 27 February 1992, *Diana*, para. 17.

[664]   Judgment of 27 February 1992, *Manieri*, para. 18.

[665]   Judgment of 28 November 2000, *Rösslhuber*, para. 27.

[666]   Judgment of 27 February 1992, *Lorenzi, Bernardini, and Gritti*, para. 16; judgment of 27 October 1994, *Katte Klitsche de la Grange*, para. 55.

[667]   See, e.g., the judgment of 16 July 1971, *Ringeisen*, para. 110; judgment of 15 July 1982, *Eckle*, para. 82; judgment of 23 September 1998, *I.A. v. France*, para. 121; judgment of 31 July 2000, *Barfuss*, para. 81.

[668]   See, e.g., the judgment of 15 July 1982, *Eckle*, para. 82; judgment of 25 February 1993, *Dobbertin*, para. 43; judgment of 25 November 1997, *Zana*, para. 79.

[669]   Judgment of 23 March 1994, *Muti*, para. 16.

[670]   See, e.g., the judgment of 15 July 1982, *Eckle*, para. 82. Compare also the judgment of 24 October 1994, *Katte Klitsche de la Grange*, para. 56. The applicant had applied to the Court of Cassation for a preliminary ruling on jurisdiction of the lower court. Although he could have made a subsequent appeal, his conduct was not open to criticism.

[671]   Judgment of 23 April 1987, *Lechner and Hess*, para. 59.

[672]   See, e.g., the judgment of 20 February 1991, *Vernillo*, para. 14; judgment of 16 December 1997, *Proszak*, para. 40; judgment of 15 October 1999, *Humen*, para. 66.

as much as possible are an important factor.[673] A special duty rests upon the court concerned to see to it that all those who play a role in the proceedings do their utmost to avoid any unnecessary delay. This holds good as well in criminal as in civil cases, where the initiative in the proceedings in principle may be left to the parties.[674] In the *Capuano* Case the Italian Government drew attention to the fact that the delays in the proceedings in first instance, which lasted for more than six years, were attributable to the experts, who filed their opinions too late. The Court held the court concerned responsible for the delays in preparing expert opinions in proceedings under the court's supervision.[675] In the *Idrocalce* and *Tumminelli* Cases the Court reached the same conclusion with reference to the delays in hearing witnesses.[676] If in a criminal case with two accused persons one of them retards the case, the prosecutor must separate the cases, if possible, in order that the other accused does not become the victim of the delay.[677] Legislation or a judicial practice placing obstacles in the way of a plaintiff for a prompt institution of proceedings, as well as legislation enabling him to leave the other party for a long time in uncertainty as to whether or not an action will be brought, without a reasonably short term of limitation preventing this, does not satisfy Article 6(1). On the other hand, the mere fact that the national authorities fail to comply with legal time-limits is in itself not contrary to Article 6(1).[678]

Under the fourth criterion, the importance of what is at stake for the applicant, the Court pays attention to special interests which may be involved. Thus in *H v. the United Kingdom*, which concerned the length of the proceedings instituted by the applicant regarding her claimed access to her child, who had been entrusted to the care of a local authority, the Court put special emphasis on the importance of what was at stake for the applicant in the proceedings in question. Not only were these proceedings decisive for her future relations with her child, but they also had a particular quality of irreversibility, involving as they did what the High Court graphically described as the 'statutory guillotine' of adoption. In these circumstances the Court expected exceptional diligence on the part of the authorities.[679] Subsequently the Court has held that a particular diligence is required in cases concerning civil status and

---

[673] See, *e.g.*, the judgment of 28 June 1978, *König*, paras 104-105; judgment of 28 March 1990, *B v. Austria*, para. 54; judgment of 23 March 1994, *Silva Pontes*, para. 39.

[674] Judgment of 20 February 1991, *Vernillo*, para. 30.

[675] Judgment of 25 June 1987, para. 30. See also the judgment of 26 February 1992, *Nibbio*, para. 18; judgment of 23 November 1993, *Scopelliti*, para. 23.

[676] Judgments of 27 February 1992, para. 18 and para. 17, respectively. See also from the same date *Cooperativa Parco Cuma*, para. 18.

[677] Appl. 6541/74, *Bonnechaux*, D&R 3 (1976), p. 86 (87).

[678] Judgment of 27 February 1992, *G. v. Italy*, para. 17.

[679] Judgment of 8 July 1987, para. 85.

capacity,[680] employment disputes,[681] including pension disputes,[682] and determinations of compensation for the victims of road accidents[683] and for persons infected with HIV as the result of blood transfusion at hospitals.[684] Moreover, the (old) age of the person concerned may urge for swift proceedings.[685] Special diligence is also required in cases where a person is detained pending the determination of the criminal charge against him.[686]

Overburdening of the judiciary in general is not recognised as an excuse, since the Contracting States have the duty to organise the administration of justice in such a way that the various courts can meet the requirements of Article 6.[687] According to constant case law Contracting States are not liable in the event of a temporary backlog of business in their courts, provided that they take, with the requisite promptness, remedial action to deal with an exceptional situation of this kind. The measures taken are assessed as to their effectiveness and it is also ascertained whether they have been taken in good time;[688] measures taken afterwards cannot make up for the fact that the reasonable period has been exceeded.[689] When making this assessment the Court is prepared to take into consideration the political and social background in the country concerned.[690] In the *Bottazzi* Case the Court drew attention to the fact that it had found

---

[680]   Judgment of 29 March 1989, *Bock*, para. 49. See also, *e.g.*, the judgments of 27 February 1992, *Taituti*, para. 18; *Masciariello*, para. 18; and *Gana*, para. 17.

[681]   See, *e.g.*, the judgment of 28 June 1990, *Obermeier*, para. 72; judgment of 24 May 1991, *Vocaturo*, para. 17; judgment of 16 July 2002, *Davies*, para. 26.

[682]   Judgments of 26 February 1992, *Nibbio*, and *Borgese*, para. 18 and para. 18, respectively; judgment of 27 February 1992, *Ruotolo*, para. 17; judgment of 11 October 2001, *H.T. v. Germany*, para. 37.

[683]   See, *e.g.*, the judgment of 26 October 1988, *Martins Moreira*, para. 46; judgment of 23 March 1994, *Silva Pontes*, para. 39; judgment of 14 October 2003, *Signe*, paras 28 and 38.

[684]   See, *e.g.*, the judgment of 31 March 1992, *X. v. France*, para. 32; judgment of 8 February 1996, *A. and Others v. Denmark*, para. 78. Compare also the judgment of 4 April 2000, *Dewicka*, paras 55-56, with regard to the installation of a telephone line in the apartment of an old, disabled woman.

[685]   Judgment of 9 March 2004, *Jablonska*, para. 43; judgment of 6 April 2004, *Krzak*, para. 42.

[686]   Initially, the Court took this position with regard to the reasonable time requirement of Article 5 (3). See, *e.g.*, the judgment of 27 August 1992, *Tomasi*, para. 84; judgment of 24 September 1992, *Herczegfalvy*, para. 71. However, the same holds good for Article 6(1). See, *e.g.*, the judgment of 25 November 1992, *Abdoella*, para. 24; judgment of 21 December 2000, *Jablonski*, para. 102; judgment of 26 July 2001, *Kreps*, paras 52-54.

[687]   See, *e.g.*, the judgment of 26 October 1984, *De Cubber*, para. 35; judgment of 26 November 1992, *Francesco Lombardo*, para. 23; judgment of 21 December 1999, *G.S. v. Austria*, para. 35; judgment of 20 December 2001, *Ludescher*, para. 23.

[688]   Judgment of 13 July 1983, *Zimmermann and Steiner*, paras 29-32; judgment of 25 June 1987, *Baggetta*, paras 22-25; judgment of 26 October 1988, *Martins Moreira*, paras 53-61.

[689]   Report of 12 March 1984, *Marijnissen*, D&R 40 (1985), p. 83 (90).

[690]   See, *e.g.*, the judgment of 25 June 1987, *Milasi*, paras 17-20, where the Court took into account the disturbances in the Region concerned, and the judgment of 7 July 1989, *Unión Alimentaria S.A.*, para. 40. In its decision of 2 March 2005, *Maltzan and Others*, paras 133-134, the Court (Grand Chamber) took into account the wish of the Federal Constitutional Court to group together all cases on similar issues so as to obtain a comprehensive view of the matter, as well as the large flux of constitutional applications following German reunification.

numerous violations of the reasonable time requirement concerning civil proceedings before the civil courts of the various regions of Italy. Therefore, it concluded "that there is an accumulation of identical breaches which are sufficiently numerous to amount not merely to isolated incidents. Such breaches reflect a continuing situation that has not yet been remedied and in respect of which litigants have no domestic remedy (…). This accumulation of breaches accordingly constitutes a practice that is incompatible with the Convention."[691] Subsequently, with reference to its *Bottazzi* judgment, the Court held many complaints against Italy to be well-founded without making a case-to-case assessment on the merits.[692]

The application of the criteria – the complexity of the case, the conduct of the applicant, the conduct of the authorities and what was at stake for the applicant - separately or in combination, may lead to different conclusions. In the *Bunkate* Case, for instance, a criminal case, the relevant period lasted two years and ten months. This lapse of time was amongst other factors caused by a period of total inactivity of fifteen and a half months between the filing of the appeal on points of law and the reception of the case-file by the registry of the Supreme Court. This period in itself infringed the reasonable-time requirement.[693] On the other hand, in the *Boddaert* Case it took slightly more than six years to determine the 'criminal charge'. This lapse of time did not violate Article 6.[694] Comparable differences may be noted as far as civil proceedings are concerned. In the *Ciricosta and Viola* Case an overall period of more than 15 years did meet the requirements of Article 6(1),[695] but a lapse of time that lasted four years and five months in the *Pugliese II* Case did not pass muster.[696]

The requirement of a trial within a reasonable time equally entails that this time may not be unreasonably short, in consequence of which it is not possible for the parties to prepare the case properly. What is expressly provided in paragraph 3(b) for criminal proceedings by virtue of the general requirement of a fair hearing in the first paragraph, applies to civil proceedings as well.

---

[691] Judgment of 28 July 1999, paras 22-23. Moreover, in its subsequent case law the Court has added, that such a practice constitutes an aggravating circumstance of the violation of Article 6 (1). See, *e.g.*, the judgments of 5 October 2000, *Giomi* and *Mennitto*, para. 12 and para. 30, respectively; judgment of 28 February 2002, *Christina Cardo*, para. 10; judgment of 9 July 2002, *Fragnito*, para. 14. Under certain circumstances such a practice may also violate Article 13. See the judgment of 26 October 2000, *Kudla*, paras 146-160.

[692] See, *e.g.*, the judgment of 16 November 2000, *Dorigo*, paras 9-10; judgment of 11 December 2001, *Vanzetti*, paras 10-11; judgment of 9 July 2002, *Nazarro and Others*, paras 14-15.

[693] Judgment of 26 May 1993, paras 20-23.

[694] Judgment of 12 October 1992, paras 35-40.

[695] Judgment of 4 December 1995, paras 23-32.

[696] Judgment of 24 May 1991, paras 50-63.

Article 6(1) does not stipulate what the consequences for the proceedings are, if the reasonable-time requirement has not been met. It would seem to ensue from this provision that, if the reasonable time has been exceeded and, consequently, the determination can no longer be made within a reasonable time, the proceedings would have to be stopped and the civil action or criminal charge to be declared inadmissible. However, in the Strasbourg case law a more flexible view has been adopted: "an excessive length of criminal proceedings can in principle be compensated for by measures of the domestic authorities, including in particular a reduction of the sentence on account of the length of procedure."[697]

Although this point of view does not easily fit into the text of Article 6(1), it offers the most appropriate solution in certain cases. In civil proceedings the applicant, who has an interest in a final determination, should not become the victim of an unreasonable delay for which the public authorities are to be blamed; both parties can be victims of the delay and be entitled to some form of just satisfaction. And in criminal procedures the public interest in the prosecution and conviction of the criminal may be so great that the prosecution should not be stopped for the sole reason that the reasonable time has been transgressed; another, more proportionate compensation should be awarded to the victim of that transgression. In administrative procedures the interests of third parties may also have to be taken into account.

The Italian legislator has tried to stop the numerous violations of the reasonable time requirement by enacting the so-called Pinto Act, which enables parties concerned to seek reparation for losses they have sustained as a result of inordinate delays in proceedings before the domestic courts to which they have been parties. However, in a series of cases the Court held that the sums awarded by the Italian courts for non-pecuniary damage did not constitute a proper and adequate reparation for the violations of the reasonable time requirement.[698] In these judgments the Court has set out with regard to the just satisfaction under Article 41 of the Convention the criteria to be used to calculate compensation for non-pecuniary damage in length of proceedings cases.

---

[697]   Report of 12 December 1983, *Neubeck*, D&R 41 (1985), p. 13 (34). See also the judgment of 15 July 1982, *Eckle*, paras 87 and 94. In the judgment of 8 February 2000, *Majaric*, paras 47-48, the Court rejected the request of the applicant to order a retrial, because it has no jurisdiction under the Convention to order such a measure.

[698]   See, *e.g.*, the decision of 27 March 2003, *Scordino*; judgment of 29 July 2004, *Scordino*, paras 65-70 and 113-115; judgments of 10 November 2004, *Apicella*, and *Cocchiarella*, paras 17-23, 26-30 and paras 17-23, 27-31, respectively.

10.8 INDEPENDENT AND IMPARTIAL TRIBUNAL

10.8.1 INTRODUCTION

The first paragraph of Article 6 provides that the determination there referred to, be made by an independent and impartial tribunal, established by law. The tribunal need not be "a court of law of the classic kind, integrated within the standard judicial machinery of the country".[699] For the notion of 'tribunal' it is essential that there exists a power to decide matters "on the basis of rules of law, following proceedings conducted in a prescribed manner",[700] and that the judicial body has 'full jurisdiction, including the power to quash in all respects, on questions of fact and law, the challenged decision'.[701] The latter requirement had not been met in the *Chevrol* Case, concerning the practice of the French *Conseil d'État* to ask preliminary questions to the Minister of foreign affairs with regard to international treaties. In the instant case, the position taken by the minister that the treaty in issue was not of a reciprocal character, was decisive for the outcome of the proceedings. The applicant did not have any opportunity to give her opinion on the use of the referral procedure or the wording of the question, or to submit a reply to the minister's point of view. The *Conseil d'État* based its decision solely on the opinion of the minister and, in so doing, considered itself to be bound by that opinion. Thus, according to the Court, the *Conseil d'État* voluntarily deprived itself of the power to examine and take into account factual evidence that could have been crucial for the practical resolution of the dispute before it. In these circumstances the Court considered that the applicant did not have access to a tribunal with full jurisdiction.[702] Inherent in the very notion of a 'tribunal' is also that the decision taken by the tribunal may not be deprived of its effect by a non-judicial authority to the disadvantage of the individual party.[703] Moreover, Contracting

---

[699] Judgment of 28 June 1984, *Campbell and Fell*, para. 76; judgment of 22 October 1984, *Sramek*, para. 36. See also the judgment of 24 February 1995, *McMichael*, para. 80, with regard to an adjudicatory body composed of three 'specially trained persons with substantial experience of children' and the judgment of 20 November 1995, *British-American Tobacco Company Ltd.*, para. 77, concerning patent application proceedings.

[700] Judgment of 22 October 1984, *Sramek*, para. 36 and the report of 8 December 1982 in this case, p. 31. See also the judgment of 23 October 1985, *Benthem*, para. 40; judgment of 30 November 1987, *H v. Belgium*, para. 50; judgment of 27 August 1991, *Demicoli*, para. 39.

[701] Judgments of 23 July 2002, *Västberga Taxi Aktiebolag and Vulic*, and *Janosevic*, para. 93 and para. 81, respectively. See also, *e.g.*, the judgment of 24 February 1994, *Bendenoun*, para. 46; judgments of 23 October 1995, *Schmautzer*, and *Pfarrmeier*, para. 36 and para. 40, respectively.

[702] Judgment of 13 February 2003, paras 76-84. See also the judgment of 17 December 1996, *Terra Woningen B.V.*, para. 54.

[703] See, *e.g.*, the judgment of 19 April 1994, *Van de Hurk*, paras 45-52; judgment of 28 October 1999, *Brumarescu*, para. 61; judgment of 26 February 2002, *Morris*, para. 73.

State's domestic legal systems must guarantee the implementation of judicial decisions, otherwise the right of access to a court would be illusory.[704]

The adjectives 'independent' and 'impartial' are the expression of two different concepts. The notion of 'independence' refers to the lack of any connection between the tribunal and other parts of government, whereas the 'impartiality' must exist in relation to the parties to the suit and the case at issue. However, the Court has not always drawn a clear borderline between the two concepts, and often considers both concepts together, as will be seen in the next sections.[705]

The principles established in the Court's case law with regard to the notions of independence and impartiality apply to professional judges as well as to lay judges and jurors.[706] Where a complaint concerns lack of impartiality on the part of the decision-making body, the concept of full jurisdiction demands that the reviewing court not only considers the complaint but also has the power to quash the impugned decision and either take a new decision or remit the case for a new decision by an impartial body.[707]

10.8.2 INDEPENDENCE

In the *Ringeisen* Case the Court held that the Regional Commission could be regarded as a 'tribunal' as it was "independent of the executive and also of the parties". The latter element, however, refers in fact not to the independence but to the impartiality of the court. The Court added that the members of the Regional Commission had been appointed for five years and the proceedings before it did offer the necessary guarantees.[708] A comparable line of reasoning was developed in the *Langborger* Case: "In order to establish whether a body can be considered 'independent' regard must be had, *inter alia*, to the manner of appointment of its members and their term of office, to the existence of guarantees against outside pressures and to the question whether the body presents an appearance of independence."[709]

---

[704]   See, *supra*, 10.4.

[705]   See, *e.g.*, the judgment of 25 February 1997, *Findlay*, para. 73; judgment of 9 June 1998, *Incal*, para. 65.

[706]   Judgment of 22 June 1989, *Langborger*, para. 30; judgment of 23 April 1996, *Remli*, paras 46-48; judgment of 10 June 1996, *Pullar*, paras 31-32; judgment of 25 February 1997, *Gregory*, paras 43-50; judgment of 9 May 2000, *Sander*, paras 22-35.

[707]   Judgment of 28 May 2002, *Kingsley* (Grand Chamber), para. 58, in which the Court held that the High Court and the Court of Appeal did not have full jurisdiction with regard to the decision taken by the Panel of the Gaming Board.

[708]   Judgment of 16 July 1971, para. 95.

[709]   Judgment of 22 June 1989, para. 32. See also, *e.g.*, the judgment of 28 September 1995, *Procola*, para. 43; judgment of 22 November 1995, *Bryan*, para. 37; judgment of 26 February 2002, *Morris*, para. 73.

These various characteristics of the notion of independence seem to fall into three categories. Firstly, the tribunal must function independently of the executive (and the legislature) and base its decisions on its own free opinion about facts and legal grounds. Secondly, there must be guarantees to enable the court to function independently.[710] As far as the latter requirement is concerned, it is not necessary that the judges have been appointed for life, provided that they cannot be discharged at will or on improper grounds by the authorities.[711] The absence of a formal recognition of the irremovability of judges during their terms of office does not imply a lack of independence as long as it is recognised in fact and the other necessary guarantees are present.[712] Thirdly, even a semblance of dependence must be avoided. In the *Bryan* Case the Court held that the very existence of the power of the Secretary of State to revoke the power of an inspector to decide an appeal under the Town and Country Planning Act, was enough to deprive the inspector of the appearance of independence.[713] And in the *Sramek* Case, where a member of the court was hierarchically subordinate to one of the parties to the suit, the Court held: "Litigants may entertain a legitimate doubt about his independence. Such a situation seriously affects the confidence which the courts must inspire in a democratic society."[714] However, strictly speaking, the latter aspect no longer refers to the independence, but to the impartiality of the court.

As to the independence of the tribunal vis-à-vis the legislature, the fact that the Council of State of the Netherlands – like similar institutions in other member States – has an advisory function in the legislative process, does not affect its independence as a judicial body.[715]

10.8.3 IMPARTIALITY

For impartiality it is required that the court is not biassed with regard to the decision to be taken, does not allow itself to be influenced by information from outside the court room, by popular feeling, or by any pressure whatsoever, but bases its opinion on objective arguments on the ground of what has been put forward at the trial. Although a judge, as a matter of course, has personal emotions, including during the

---

[710] In the judgments of 2 September 1998, *Lauko* and *Kadubec*, paras 63-65 and 56-58, respectively, the administrative authorities who had been entrusted with the prosecution and punishment of minor offences, appeared not to be independent of the executive because of the manner of appointment of the officers of the local and district offices and the lack of guarantees against outside pressures.

[711] Implicitly the judgment of 16 July 1971, *Ringeisen*. With regard to military tribunals, see the judgment of 8 June 1976, *Engel*, para. 89.

[712] Judgment of 28 June 1984, *Campbell and Fell*, para. 80; judgment of 26 February 2002, *Morris*, para. 68.

[713] Judgment of 22 November 1995, para. 38.

[714] Judgment of 22 October 1984, para. 42.

[715] Judgment of 6 May 2003 (Grand Chamber), *Kleyn and Others*, paras 193-195.

proceedings, he must not allow himself to be led by them during the hearing of the case and in the formation of his opinion.[716] And although judges may have a political preference and/or adhere to a specific religion or philosophy of life, and although it is right that the various political streams, religions and philosophies of life are also 'represented' within the judiciary, it must not make any difference for the person involved whether he is tried by a judge with one or other preference.

Publicity surrounding a criminal case, where the difference between 'suspected of' and 'guilty of' is not always taken into account, in addition to putting at issue the presumption of innocence-principle of the second paragraph of Article 6, may constitute a threat to the right to a fair and impartial trial, in particular also when this publicity proceeds from the authorities, e.g., from the public prosecutor charged with the examination.[717] The judge must duly take this risk into account when forming his opinion. In cases with a markedly political background the said risk and the necessity for the court to be on the alert against improper influences applies to an even higher degree.[718] In the Strasbourg case law it is assumed, however, that a professional judge will in general be aware of these external factors and will not readily allow himself to be influenced thereby,[719] while moreover on appeal the higher court, in this respect, too, may control and compensate for the attitude of the lower court. Thus, in the *Menten* Case the Commission held that the great publicity and the utterance of hostile feelings in this case could not be avoided, but that the Supreme Court had accurately ascertained on what testimony the lower courts had based their considerations.[720] In cases of trial by jury the risk of the jury being influenced by public opinion or by biassed statements of witnesses or experts is more likely.[721]

The requirement of Article 10(2) that the freedom of expression may be restricted 'for maintaining the authority and impartiality of the judiciary' is closely connected with the point of publicity surrounding a trial. This restriction, which relates to the prohibition of 'contempt of court' embedded in Anglo-American law, was discussed at length in Strasbourg in the *Sunday Times* Case. The complaint concerned the prohibition, imposed by the English courts up to the highest instance, on publishing during a given time an article about the so-called 'thalidomide children', who had been born with serious physical deformities in consequence of the use of the sedative

---

[716]   See Appl. 1727/62, *Boeckmans*, Yearbook VI (1963), p. 370 (416-420), where the complaint concerned a judge who, in his indignation about a specific defence, uttered a warning that its upholding might lead to an increase of the penalty. Later on this case was settled: report of the subcommittee of 17 February 1965.

[717]   Appl. 8403/78, *Jespers*, D&R 22 (1981), p. 100 (127).

[718]   Appls 8603, 8722, 8723 and 8729/79, *Crociani and Others*, D&R 22 (1981), p. 147 (222-223 and 227).

[719]   Judgment of 5 December 2002, *Craxi*, para. 104.

[720]   Appl. 9433/81, *Menten*, D&R 27 (1982), p. 233 (238).

[721]   This risk was emphasised several times by the Commission. See, e.g., Appl. 7542/76, *X v. the United Kingdom* (not published), where in a case which attracted much publicity the Commission attached great importance to the fact that the judge had drawn the jury's attention to the risk of prejudice.

thalidomide by their mothers during pregnancy. The prohibition had been imposed because, at that moment, various proceedings against the manufacturer of thalidomide were pending and the publication might have led to 'contempt of court'. The Court, although with a narrow majority, came to the conclusion that in this case the prohibition was not justified. They took into account, *inter alia*, that a court is not readily influenced by publications of this kind.[722]

In testing whether a 'tribunal' or judge has been prejudiced, the Court makes a distinction between a subjective and an objective approach to impartiality. The subjective approach refers to the personal impartiality of the members of the tribunal involved; this impartiality is presumed as long as the contrary has not been proved.[723] The establishment of a personal bias is difficult. Even when a judicial decision has been amply reasoned, it is difficult to ascertain by what motives a court was led. It will, therefore, only be possible to conclude that a judge is biassed when this is evident from his attitude during the proceedings or from the content of the judgment.[724] It will be even more difficult to prove the prejudice of (members of) a jury, because a decision of the jury does not include a written statement of reasons.[725]

The objective approach refers to the question of whether the way in which the tribunal is composed and organised, or a certain coincidence or succession of functions of one or more of its members, may give rise to doubt as to the impartiality of the tribunal or that member. If there is justified reason for such doubt, even if subjectively there is no concrete indication of bias of the person in question, this already amounts to an inadmissible jeopardy of the confidence which the court must inspire in a democratic society.[726] The fear that the tribunal or a particular judge lacks impartiality must be such that it can "be held to be objectively justified"; consequently, the standpoint of the accused on this matter, although important, is not decisive.[727]

This objective-approach-test has been applied in several cases. Despite the casuistic case law some main lines can be discerned. As the Court held in the *Buscemi* Case, the

---

[722] Judgment of 26 April 1979, paras 65-68.

[723] See, *e.g.*, the judgment of 1 October 1982, *Piersack*, para. 30; judgment of 24 May 1989 *Hauschildt*, para. 45; judgment of 25 June 1992, *Thorgeir Thorgeirson*, para. 49; judgment of 24 February 1993, *Fey*, para. 28; judgment of 22 April 1994, *Saraiva de Carvalho*, para. 33.

[724] See, *e.g.*, the judgment of 27 January 2004, *Kyprianou*, paras 38-42. See also the judgment of 6 May 2003 (Grand chamber), *Kleyn and Others*, para. 195.

[725] Compare the judgment of 10 June 1996, *Pullar*, paras 31-32; judgment of 25 February 1997, *Gregory*, para. 44; judgment of 9 May 2000, *Sander*, paras 25-26.

[726] See, *e.g.*, the judgment of 1 October 1982, *Piersack*, para. 31; judgment of 26 October 1984, *De Cubber*, para. 30; judgment of 22 April 1994, *Saraiva de Carvalho*, para. 35; judgment of 26 February 2002, *Morris*, para. 58; judgment of 6 May 2003 (Grand chamber), *Kleyn and Others*, para. 191.

[727] See, *e.g.*, the judgment of 24 May 1989, *Hauschildt*, para. 48; judgment of 26 February 1993, *Padovani*, para. 27; judgment of 22 April 1994, *Saraiva de Carvalho*, para. 35; judgment of 20 May 1998, *Gautrin and Others*, para. 58; judgment of 9 June 1998, *Incal*, para. 71; judgment of 6 May 2003 (Grand Chamber), *Kleyn and Others*, para. 194.

judicial authorities are required to exercise maximum discretion with regard to the cases with which they deal in order to preserve their image as impartial judges and, therefore, they should not make use of the press, even when provoked. Accordingly, the fact that the president of the court publicly used expressions which implied that he had already formed an unfavourable opinion of the applicant's case before presiding over the court that had to decide it, clearly violated the requirement of impartiality.[728] And in the special circumstances of the *Sigurdsson* Case Article 6 had been violated because of, in short, the existence of strong financial links between the judge's husband and one of the parties to the suit, the National Bank of Iceland.[729]

The fact that a judge has taken decisions in the case prior to the trial and subsequently officiates as a trial judge is in itself not incompatible with the requirement of impartiality. What matters is the 'scope and nature' of the measures or decisions taken prior to the trial.[730] The fear of prejudice cannot, for instance, be justified solely by the fact that the judge has taken decisions on the prolongation of the detention on remand. Only special circumstances can give rise to a different conclusion.[731] Such special circumstances did occur in the *Hauschieldt* Case. In ordering the continued pre-trial detention the judge had to be convinced that there was 'a very high degree of clarity as to the question of guilt'. The difference between this assessment and the assessment that had to be made when giving judgment thus became (too) tenuous.[732] On the contrary, in case the prolongation of the detention on remand may be ordered if the judge is convinced that there exists '*prima facie* evidence', no problem with regard to the impartiality arises.[733] In the *Piersack* Case the fact that the president of the tribunal had been involved in an earlier phase of the case as a public prosecutor amounted to a violation of Article 6.[734] In the *De Cubber* Case a judge was involved who had previously in the same case acted as an investigating judge and as a president

---

[728]   Judgment of 16 September 1999, paras 67-69; judgment of 28 November 2002, *Lavents*, paras 119-120.

[729]   Judgment of 10 April 2003, paras 37-41. See also the judgment of 17 June 2003, *Pescador Valero*, paras 23-29.

[730]   Judgment of 24 August 1993, *Nortier*, para. 33; judgment of 22 April 1994, *Saraiva de Carvalho*, para. 35. In the judgment of 24 February 1993, *Fey*, para. 30, the Court held 'the extent and nature' to be decisive.

[731]   Judgment of 24 May 1989, *Hauschieldt*, para. 50; judgment of 16 December 1992, *Sainte-Marie*, para. 32.

[732]   Judgment of 24 May 1989, paras. 51-53. See also the judgment of 25 July 2002, *Perote Pellon*, paras 46-52 and the judgment of 22 April 2004, *Cianetti*, paras 41-45.

[733]   Judgment of 24 August 1993, *Nortier*, para. 35; judgment of 22 April 1994, *Saraiva de Carvalho*, paras. 38-40; judgment of 26 February 1993, *Padovani*, paras 28-29; judgment of 22 February 1996, *Bulut*, para. 34; judgment of 10 February 2004, *Depiets*, paras 37-43.

[734]   Judgment of 1 October 1982, paras 30-32. See also the judgment of 25 July 2000, *Tierce and Others*, paras 78-81.

of a chamber respectively. The Court held that these facts created too much doubt about the impartiality of the judge concerned in an objective sense.[735]

Doubt about impartiality is also justified in case a judge who participated in a judgment at first instance also participates in the hearing of an appeal against the same judgment.[736] The requirement of impartiality does not imply, however, that a superior court which quashes the decision of a lower court, is obliged to refer the case to another court or to a differently composed chamber of the lower court.[737] In the *Rojas Morales* Case the written statements of a judgment concerning a co-accused created the impression that the applicant was guilty. Therefore, the participation of the same judges in the applicant's trial created objectively justified doubts with regard to their impartiality.[738] In the *Werner* Case the requirement of impartiality had been violated because the judge who submitted to the court a motion for the applicant to be dismissed as a liquidator subsequently participated in the court's decision on this motion.[739]

The consecutive carrying out of an advisory and a judicial function in the same case was at stake in the *Procola* Case. Procola, an association under Luxembourg law, challenged the lawfulness of four ministerial orders for the Judicial Committee of the *Conseil d'Etat*. In deciding the case the Judicial Committee also had to give its opinion on the lawfulness of a regulation that had been the subject of an advisory opinion of the *Conseil d'Etat*. In fact, the *Conseil d'Etat* had recommended the inclusion of the very provision that was challenged by Procola. The Judicial Committee was composed of five members. The fact that four of them had pronounced on the lawfulness of the regulation in their advisory capacity, was, according to the Court, sufficient reason for casting doubt on the structural impartiality of the Luxembourg *Conseil d'Etat*.[740] The Court reached the same conclusion in the *McGonnell* Case. It held that the mere fact that the deputy Bailiff presided over the States of Liberation when the draft developing plan in issue was adopted, was capable of casting doubt on his impartiality

---

[735]   Judgment of 26 October 1984, *De Cubber*, paras 29-30; The Court reached the same conclusion in the judgment of 27 January 2004, *Kyprianou*, paras 34-37, where a charge of contempt of court had been tried by the same judges before whom the contempt allegedly had been committed. See also, e.g., the judgment of 29 April 1988, *Belilos*, para. 67, and the judgment of 7 August 1996, *Ferrantelli and Santangelo*, paras 53-59.

[736]   Judgment of 25 May 1991, *Oberschlick*, paras 50-52; judgment of 26 August 1997, *De Haan*, paras 47-51; judgment of 28 October 1998, *Castillo Algar*, paras 46-51; judgment of 29 July 2004, *San Leonard Band Club*, paras 61-66.

[737]   Judgment of 16 July 1971, para. 97; judgment of 26 September 1995, *Diennet*, paras 36-39. See also the judgment of 10 June 1996, *Thomann*, paras 27-37, concerning a criminal trial *in absentia* and retrial in the presence of the accused by the same judges.

[738]   Judgment of 16 November 2000, paras 33-35.

[739]   Judgment of 15 November 2001, paras 41-47. In the judgment of 6 June 2000, *Morel*, paras 42-50, the insolvency judge did meet the requirements of impartiality.

[740]   Judgment of 28 September 1995, paras 44-45.

when he subsequently determined, as the sole judge of the law in the case, the applicant's planning appeal.[741]

In the *Kleyn* Case the applicants claimed that the institutionalised simultaneous exercise of both advisory and judicial functions by the Dutch Council of State was incompatible with the required objective impartiality, since no separation was made between the members involved in the exercise of the advisory functions and those involved in the exercise of the judicial functions. However, the Court distinguished that case from the *Procola* Case, because the advisory opinions on the Transport Infrastructure Planning Act and the subsequent judicial proceedings concerning the appeals against the railway routing decision, which was based on the Planning Act, did not concern 'the same case' or 'the same decision'.[742] The Court made, however, the observation, as a warning for possible complaints in the future, that it was not as confident as the Dutch Government that the arrangements made by the Council of State with a view to giving effect to the *Procola* judgment, were such as to ensure that the Administrative Jurisdiction Division of the Council of State constitutes in all cases an 'impartial tribunal' for the purposes of Article 6(1) of the Convention.[743]

The independence and impartiality of the members of the *Procureur général*'s department of the Belgian Court of Cassation was tested in the *Borgers* Case. The Court concluded, affirming its previous case law, that on this point no violation of Article 6 arose. A similar conclusion was reached with regard to the *Commissaire du Gouvernement* in French administrative proceedings.[744]

In the *Daktaras* Case the Court reached the opposite conclusion with regard to the role of the president of the criminal division of the supreme court of Lithuania, who was in effect taking up the case of the prosecution and also constituted the court which had to decide the case.[745]

The practice of having courts composed in whole or in part by the military to try members of the armed forces is not contrary to the notion of an independent and impartial tribunal, as long as sufficient safeguards are in place to guarantee the compliance with these concepts.[746] In a series of cases the Court had to deal with the independence and impartiality of British courts-martial convened pursuant to the Army and Air Force Acts 1955. In these cases the role of the convening officer appeared to

---

[741]   Judgment of 8 February 2000, paras 49-58.
[742]   Judgment of 6 May 2003 (Grand Chamber), paras 195-202. See also the judgment of 22 June 2004, *Pabla Ky*, paras 31-35, concerning a member of Parliament who participates as an expert lay member in the decision making in a court.
[743]   Judgment of 6 May 2003 (Grand Chamber), *Kleyn and Others*, para. 198.
[744]   Judgment of 30 October 1991, para. 26, and judgment of 7 June 2001, *Kress*, para. 71. See, on the position of the *Avocat général* and similar officers and the (im)possibility to react to their submissions, *supra*, 10.5.2.
[745]   Judgment of 10 October 2000, paras 33-38.
[746]   Judgment of 26 February 2002, *Morris*, para. 59.

be crucial. This officer had the final decision on the nature and detail of the charges to be brought and was responsible for convening the court-martial, whose members were subordinate in rank to him. Moreover, the convening officer acted as a confirming officer: the decision of the court-martial was not effective until confirmed by him. According to the Court, these fundamental flaws in the court-martial system were not remedied by the presence of safeguards and, therefore, it held the misgivings of the accused persons about the independence and impartiality of the tribunals which dealt with their cases to be objectively justified.[747] Subsequently, the British legislator changed the impugned provisions. In the *Cooper* Case, concerning an air-force court-martial, the Court held that the Armed Forces Act of 1996 did meet the requirements of Article 6. In particular, the presence in a court-martial of the Judge Advocate, a legally qualified civilian, constituted a significant guarantee of the independence of the court-martial proceedings. The Judge Advocate sums up the evidence and delivers further directions to the other members of the court-martial beforehand and he can refuse to accept a verdict if he considers it 'contrary to law' in which case he gives the members of the court-martial further directions in open court, following which those members retire again to consider verdict.[748] Moreover, with regard to the ordinary members of the court-martial,[749] the Court considered that the so-called Briefing Notes not only instructed members of the need to function independently, but also provided a significant impediment to any inappropriate pressure being brought to bear.[750] In the *Grieves* Case the Court concluded that the Judge Advocate in a naval court-martial, who is not a civilian but a serving naval officer who, when not sitting in a court-martial, carries out regular naval duties, cannot be considered a strong guarantee of the independence of a naval court-martial.[751]

In several cases the composition of the Turkish National Security Courts has been at issue. These courts are composed of three judges, one of whom is a regular officer and member of the Military Legal Service. In the *Incal* Case the applicant had been convicted by the Izmir Security Court for disseminating leaflets capable of inciting people to resist the Government and to commit criminal offences. The applicant

---

[747] See, e.g, the judgment of 25 February 1997, *Findlay*, paras 73-80; judgment of 24 September 1997, *Coyne*, paras 56-58; judgment of 18 February 1999, *Cable and Others*, paras 20-22; judgment of 5 June 2001, *Mills*, paras 22-27.

[748] Judgment of 16 December 2003 (Grand Chamber), para. 117.

[749] Those members, who were appointed on an ad hoc basis and had no legal qualifications and relatively little court-martial experience, remained subject to RAF discipline in a general sense since they remained RAF officers. However, they could not be reported upon in relation to their judicial decision-making.

[750] Judgment of 16 December 2003, *Cooper* (Grand Chamber), para. 117. In the judgment of 26 February 2002, *Morris*, paras 66-79, the Court has reached a different conclusion. In that case the United Kingdom Government had omitted to submit to the Court important information with regard to the practice of court-martial. This new information appeared to be crucial in the *Cooper* Case.

[751] Judgment of 16 December 2003 (Grand Chamber), paras 82-91. See also the judgments of 15 June 2004, *G.W. v. the United Kingdom* and *Le Petit*, paras 43-49 and paras 21-24, respectively.

submitted that his conviction had infringed Article 10 and Article 6 of the Convention. As far as Article 6 was concerned, the Court, taking the concepts of independence and impartiality together, firstly took stock of the legal system. It noted that the status of military judges as members of the Security Courts did provide certain guarantees of independence and impartiality. They underwent the same professional training, when sitting enjoyed the same constitutional safeguards as their civilian counterparts and, according to the Turkish Constitution, had to be free from the instructions of public authorities. However, other aspects made the independence and impartiality of military judges questionable: the judges concerned belonged to the army, which takes its orders from the executive; they remained subject to military discipline and assessment reports; decisions pertaining to their appointment were to a great extent taken by the administrative authorities and the army, and, finally, their term of office as National Security Court judges was only four years and could be renewed.[752] The Court further attached special importance to the fact that a civilian had to appear before a court partly composed of members of the armed forces. The Court concluded that because one of the judges of the National Security Court was a military judge, the applicant could legitimately fear that it might allow itself to be unduly influenced by considerations which had nothing to do with the nature of the case. Therefore, he had legitimate doubts about the independence and impartiality of the court.[753] As far as the composition of the Turkish National Security Courts is concerned the *Incal* Case may be regarded as standing case law.[754]

The requirement of impartiality may under circumstances restrict the participation of substitute judges, especially in view of any other profession exercised by them, *e.g.*, that of a practising lawyer. In the *Wettstein* Case the applicant was confronted with a substitute judge who had acted in a similar procedure as the legal representative of the opposing party. Although no material link existed between these two cases, in view of the fact that the proceedings partly overlapped in time, the Court concluded that the applicant could have had reason for concern that the judge would continue to see in him the opposing party.[755]

The mere fact that lay assessors also sit on a tribunal, as is frequently the case in disciplinary tribunals, does not mean on this ground alone that they are not impartial,

---

[752] Judgment of 9 June 1998, para. 68.

[753] *Ibidem*, paras 65-73.

[754] See, *e.g.*, the judgment of 28 October 1998, *Çiraklar*, paras 38-41; judgment of 8 July 1999, *Sürek (No. 1)*, paras 66-76; judgment of 14 October 2004, Yanikoglui, paras 23-25. See, with regard to a Turkish Martial Law Court, *e.g.*, the judgment of 25 September 2001, *Sahiner*, paras 33-47; judgment of 22 June 2004, *Ahmet Koc*, paras 30-32.

[755] Judgment of 21 December 2000, paras 44-50. In the judgment of 23 November 2004, *Puolitaival and Pirttiaho*, paras 45-54, the Court reached a different conclusion, taking into account, *inter alia*, the fact that the functions of the person concerned as counsel and judge had not overlapped in time, and the remoteness in time and subject-matter of both sets of proceedings.

even in cases where they constitute a majority.[756] But if persons are involved who are closely allied to one of the parties, which is often the case in arbitration tribunals, their impartiality may be open to doubt. An issue under Article 6(1) will then arise only when not all the parties or their interests are equally represented in the tribunal in question. Thus, in the *Le Compte, Van Leuven and De Meyere* Case, where three medical practitioners had been summoned before a disciplinary tribunal on account of their opposition to the obligatory membership of a professional association of medical practitioners, the Commission reached the conclusion that there was no impartial course of proceedings, since the tribunal judging at first instance, the Provincial Council, was composed largely of persons who had been elected by members of the professional association, while the Appeal Council consisted of medical practitioners and judges on a fifty-fifty basis. The fact that appeal to the Court of Cassation was also possible did not, in the Commission's opinion, eliminate this defect, because review was possible only on the ground of procedural errors or misapplication of the law.[757] The Court, however, did not follow the Commission. Since an appeal had been lodged with the Appeal Council, in the Court's view the impartiality of the Provincial Council did not require examination. With regard to the Appeal Council, the Court held that the impartiality of such a tribunal must be presumed, unless the contrary can be proved, which had not been done in the present case in the Court's opinion.[758]

In the *AB Kurt Kellerman* Case the applicant company claimed that the Swedish labour court could not be composed of members representing the industrial union, since the court had to examine the applicant company's argument that the industrial union action, including a possible blockade of the company, had to be proportionate and socially relevant. The Court applied the objective-impartiality-test and held that the deciding issue was whether the balance of interests in the composition of the labour court was upset, and, if so, whether any such lack of balance would result in unfair proceedings. In the circumstances of the case, with five votes to two, the Court answered the first question in the negative and, therefore, a violation of Article 6 did not occur.[759] A comparable line of reasoning lead in the *Holm* Case to the conclusion that the impartiality (and independence) of the jury was open to doubt,[760] but in the *Pullar* Case the fact that a member of the jury was a junior employee in the firm of one of the witnesses for the prosecution, could pass the objective-impartiality-test: Article 6 had not been violated.[761] When serious allegations are made that racist com-

---

[756]   See, *e.g.*, the judgment of 23 April 1987, *Ettl*, paras 38; judgment of 23 April 1997, *Stallinger and Kuso*, para. 37.

[757]   Report of 14 December 1979, B.38 (1984), pp. 40-42.

[758]   Judgment of 23 June 1981, para. 58; judgment of 10 February 1983, *Albert and Le Compte*, para. 32; judgment of 28 June 1984, *Campbell and Fell*, para. 84.

[759]   Judgment of 26 October 2004, paras 60-69. The Court reached a different conclusion in the judgment of 22 June 1989, *Langborger*, paras 31-36.

[760]   Judgment of 25 November 1993, paras 30-33.

[761]   Judgment of 10 June 1996, paras 33-41.

ments have been made by jurors, called upon to try a person of different ethnic origin, the court should take sufficient steps to check whether, as constituted, it is 'an impartial tribunal' in the meaning of Article 6. In the *Remli* Case[762] and the *Sander* Case[763] the reaction of the judge concerned appeared not to be sufficient. However, in the circumstances of the *Gregory* Case, where the allegation of racial bias was vague and imprecise, the Court held that the redirection of the jury did constitute a sufficient reaction.[764]

In the *Bulut* Case the question arose whether the applicant had waived his right under domestic law to object to the participation of a judge in a criminal trial, who had taken part previously in the questioning of two witnesses. The approach of the Court in this case seems to be ambiguous. On the one hand, it held that it was irrelevant whether a waiver had been made or not, because it was anyhow incumbent on the Court to assess whether the composition of the trial court could cast doubt on its impartiality.[765] On the other hand, however, it concluded that the objective approach could offer the applicant no success, since he had refrained from his right to challenge the composition of the Court.[766] In the *McGonnell* Case the Court held that the question whether the applicant ought to have taken up his complaint with regard to the lack of independence and impartiality with the national judicial authorities, depended on what was reasonable in the circumstances of the case. With reference to the national case law and taking into account the fact that the argument of waiver was not raised before the Commission but for the first time before the Court, the latter concluded that the failure to challenge the domestic tribunal could not be said to have been unreasonable and could not amount to a tacit waiver of the right to an independent and impartial tribunal.[767]

10.8. 4 ESTABLISHED BY LAW

The prescription that the tribunal must be 'established by law' implies the guarantee that the organisation of the judiciary in a democratic society is not left to the discretion of the executive, but is regulated by law. The phrase covers not only the legal basis for the very existence of a 'tribunal'. In the opinion of the Commission the organization and functioning of the tribunal must also have a legal basis.[768] The Court left the issue

---

[762]   Judgment of 23 April 1996, paras 46-48.
[763]   Judgment of 9 May 2000, paras 22-35.
[764]   Judgment of 25 February 1997, paras 43-50.
[765]   Judgment of 22 February 1996, para. 30.
[766]   *Ibidem*, para. 34.
[767]   Judgment of 8 February 2000, paras 44-45; judgment of 15 June 2004, *Thompson*, paras 44-45.
        See, *mutatis mutandis*, also the judgment of 17 June 2003, *Pescadore Valero*, paras 23-26.
[768]   Report of 13 May 1981, *Piersack*, B.47 (1986), p. 23.

undecided in the *Piersack* Case,[769] but in the *Posokhov* Case it held that the requirement also covers the composition of the bench in each case.[770] As a rule the Court takes the interpretation of national law by the domestic judicial authorities more or less for granted,[771] unless there appears to be a flagrant breach of the law.[772]

In the *Coëme and Others* Case four people had been accused of, in short, forgery and fraud. The criminal proceedings took place before the Belgian court of cassation as court of first instance, because the charges against them were closely linked to the prosecution of a former minister before the same court. Since Article 103 of the Belgian Constitution provided only for jurisdiction of the court of cassation as court of first instance in case of the prosecution of (former) ministers, the Court held, with regard to the proceedings against the four, that the court of cassation had not been established by law.[773] In the *Posokhov* Case, the failure to compile a list of lay judges implied the lack of any legal grounds for the participation of the lay judges in the administration of justice on the day of the applicant's trial and, therefore, amounted to a violation of Article 6.[774]

10.9 THE PRESUMPTION OF INNOCENCE

10.9.1 INTRODUCTION

Article 6(2) sets forth that the person who is charged with a criminal offence, has to be presumed innocent until proved guilty according to law. As in the case of the third paragraph, this paragraph deals with a special aspect of the general concept of 'fair trial' in criminal cases. For that reason no further inquiry is made as to a possible violation of this provision when a violation of the first paragraph has already been found.[775] However, in the *Delta* Case the Court suggested that in special circumstances there is room for a separate investigation under paragraph 2, despite the fact that a violation of the first paragraph has been established already.[776]

From the case law concerning the autonomous meaning of the concept of 'criminal charge' in the first paragraph it follows that the second and third paragraphs are also applicable to proceedings other than criminal proceedings – *e.g.*, disciplinary procee-

---

769   Judgment of 1 October 1982, para. 33.
770   Judgment of 4 March 2003, para. 39.
771   See, *e.g.*, the judgment of 22 February 1996, *Bulut*, para. 29.
772   Judgment of 28 November 2002, *Lavents*, para. 114.
773   Judgment of 22 June 2000, para. 105-108.
774   Judgment of 4 March 2003, paras. 41-42.
775   Judgment of 27 February 1980, *Deweer*, para. 56.
776   Judgment of 19 December 1990, para. 38.

dings[777] and administrative proceedings[778] – which are to be equated with criminal proceedings by means of the criteria developed in the *Oztürk* Case. In the *Phillips* Case the Court held that Article 6(2) was not applicable to confiscation proceedings pursuant to the British Drug Trafficking Act 1994. The Court considered the procee- dings, which enabled the national court to assess the amount at which the confiscation order should properly be fixed, as analogous to the determination by a court of the amount of a fine or the length of a prison sentence and, therefore, the proceedings did not constitute any new "charge".[779] However, the Court held Article 6(1) to be applicable because Article 6(1) applies throughout the entirety of proceedings for "the determination (…) of any criminal charge", including proceedings whereby a sentence is fixed.[780]

In the *Minelli* Case the second paragraph was defined by the Court in the sense that this provision has been violated if "without the accused's having previously been proved guilty according to law and, notably, without his having had the opportunity of exercising his rights of defence, a judicial decision concerning him reflects an opinion that he is guilty."[781] A reasoning by which it is only suggested that the person in question is guilty is already sufficient for such a violation.

However, the presumption may be violated not only by a court but also by other public authorities,[782] including the legislator.[783]

10.9.2   WITH RESPECT TO EVIDENCE

The most important aspect of the presumption of innocence concerns the foundation of the conviction. This aspect is very closely connected with the requirement of the court's impartiality discussed above.[784] The court has to presume the innocence of the accused without any prejudice and may sentence him only on the basis of evidence

---

[777]   Judgment of 10 February 1983, *Albert and Le Compte*, paras 38-42.

[778]   See with regard to tax penalties the judgments of 29 August 1997, *A.T., M.P. and T.P. v. Switzerland* and *E.L., R.L. and J.O.-L. v. Switzerland*, paras 37-43 and 42-48, respectively. In the judgment of 22 September 1994, *Hentrich*, paras 62-64, the exercise of the right of pre-emption by the French tax authorities because the sale price of land declared in the contract of sale was too low, was deemed not to imply an accusation of tax evasion and, accordingly, could not lead to a violation of Article 6(2).

[779]   Judgment of 5 July 2001, paras 28-36.

[780]   *Ibidem*, paras 37-39.

[781]   Judgment of 25 March 1983, para. 37. See also, *e.g.*, the judgments of 25 August 1987, *Lutz, Englert*, and *Nölkenbockhoff*, paras 59-60, 36-37 and 36-37, respectively; judgment of 10 October 2000, *Daktaras*, para. 41.

[782]   Judgment of 10 February 1995, *Allenet de Ribbemont*, para. 36.

[783]   Judgment of 7 October 1988, *Salabiaku*, paras 15-16.

[784]   Compare, *e.g.*, the judgment of 28 November 2002, *Lavents*, paras 119-121 and 125-128, and the judgment of 27 January 2004, *Kyprianou*, paras 51-58.

put forward during the trial, which moreover has to constitute 'lawful' evidence recognised as such by law. The Court has formulated the essence of the principle as follows: "Paragraph 2 embodies the principle of the presumption of innocence. It requires, *inter alia*, that when carrying out their duties, the members of a court should not start with the preconceived idea that the accused has committed the offence charged; the burden of proof is on the prosecution, and any doubt should benefit the accused. It also follows that it is for the prosecution to inform the accused of the case that will be made against him, so that he may prepare and present his defence accordingly, and to adduce evidence sufficient to convict him."[785]

The evidence put forward at the trial may refer back to statements previously made by the accused or testimony by witnesses, provided that the latter can be revoked or refuted during the trial.[786] If a witness does not wish to act as a witness during the trial and can advance a legitimate reason for it, there is no objection to a reading of previous testimony, provided that the right of the defence to question witnesses is sufficiently upheld, *e.g.*, by having provided the opportunity to interrogate and contradict that witness in an earlier phase of the proceedings. If this condition has not been met, the verdict must not be based exclusively or largely on such testimony.[787]

Every instance giving rise to the least doubt with regard to the evidence has to be construed in favour of the accused.[788] This does not necessarily mean that the evidence put forward must be absolutely conclusive – in several legal systems ultimately the conviction on the part of the court is the point that matters – but it does mean that the court must base its conviction exclusively on the evidence put forward during the trial. A sentence may of course also be based on a confession of guilt on the part of the accused. In that case, however, the court will have to ascertain thoroughly that this confession has been made in complete freedom.[789] From a statement of the accused which is not intended to be a confession of guilt, no such confession may be inferred. Article 6(1) embodies the right of the accused not to incriminate himself and the right to remain silent, which is closely linked to the presumption of innocence. In the *John Murray* Case, in which the prosecution had build up a 'formidable' case against the applicant, the Court held that the drawing of adverse inferences from the applicant's silence had not violated Article 6(1).[790] In the *Telfner* Case, however, it reached a different conclusion. The drawing of inferences from the applicant's silence had constituted

---

[785]   Judgment of 6 December 1988, *Barberà, Messegué and Jabardo*, paras 67-68; See also, *e.g.*, the judgment of 20 March 2001, *Telfner*, para. 15.

[786]   See *infra* 10.10.5.

[787]   Judgment of 24 November 1986, *Unterpertinger*, A.110, paras 31-33. On the issue of anonymous witnesses, see *infra* 10.10.5.

[788]   Judgment of 6 December 1988, *Barberà, Messegué and Jabardo*, para. 77.

[789]   Insofar as the confession has been extorted by illegal means, such as physical or mental torture, this follows already from the words 'according to law'; report of 31 March 1963, *Pfunders (Austria v. Italy)*, *Yearbook* VI (1963), p. 784.

[790]   Judgment of 8 February 1996, paras 44-58.

a violation of Article 6(2) because the prosecution had not been able to establish a convincing *prima facie* case against the applicant.[791]

If during the trial statements are made or produced by the prosecutor, witnesses or experts from which bias on their part is evident, the court has to make a stand against those statements if it is to avoid the semblance of being biassed as well. If the court does so, the accused can no longer complain of such bias on the part of the first-mentioned persons.[792] The same holds good if a sentence which the accused alleges to have been dictated by bias, has been upheld on appeal, while the court of appeal has made an inquiry into this very matter. In that case the accused will be able to complain only of bias on the part of this court of appeal or of the fact that the injury caused by the bias of the lower court has not been redressed by the higher court.[793]

If there has been publicity surrounding the proceedings in which publicity the guilt of the accused is assumed, the latter will have to prove to some extent that his ultimate conviction was also influenced by that publicity. This will not be easy.[794] With respect to the possible violation of the presumption of innocence by public authorities the Court has emphasised "the importance of the choice of words by public officials" in their statements before an accused has been tried.[795] In particular, when those statements are made in a context independent of the criminal proceedings, prudence is called for.[796] However, the mere assertion by a prosecutor to the press that there is sufficient evidence to support a finding of guilt by a court does not violate the presumption of innocence.[797]

---

[791]   Judgment of 20 March 2001, paras 17-20. See on the right to remain silent *supra* 10.5.5.

[792]   Report of 31 March 1963, *Pfunders (Austria v. Italy)*, Yearbook VI (1963), p. 740 (784); report of 15 March 1961, *Nielsen*, Yearbook IV (1961), p. 490 (568). See also the judgment of 23 April 1998, *Bernard*, paras 37-41, where the Court held that the psychiatric experts appointed by the investigating judge logically had to start from the working hypothesis that the applicant had committed the crimes, which had given rise to the prosecution.

[793]   Report in the *Pfunders* Case, *ibidem*.

[794]   See, *e.g.*, Appls 7572/76, 7586/76 and 7587/76, *Ensslin, Baader and Raspe*, Yearbook XXI (1978), p. 418 (462). The applicants alleged violation of Art. 6(2) on account of the press campaign against them, in which they were called criminals and murderers, and on account of the exceptional security measures around the suit, which could not but create an impression of guilt. The Commission took the position that the challenged publications and measures were a reaction to their own declarations and behaviour and were not aimed at creating an atmosphere unfavourable for the accused, and that a professional judge is sufficiently immune to any influence that might result from this.

[795]   Judgment of 10 October 2000, *Daktaras*, para. 41.

[796]   *Ibidem*, para. 44 and the judgment of 26 March 2002, *Butkevicius*, para. 52.

[797]   Judgment of 26 March 2002, *Butkevicius*, para. 52. However, the declarations by the Chairman of the national Lithuanian Parliament of the applicant's guilt did violate Article 6(2) (paras 53-54). See also the judgment of 28 October 2004, *Y.B. and Others*, paras 43-51, where the combination of, on the one hand, the press release issued by the police, which could have been construed as confirmation that, according to the police, the applicants had committed the offences of which they were accused, and, on the other hand, the press conference at which journalists were able to take photographs of the applicants, amounted to a violation of the presumption of innocence.

The practice where during the trial the criminal record, if any, of the accused is brought to the notice of the court, does not constitute a conflict with Article 6(2).[798] It is obvious, however, that such information may promote a presumption of guilt on the part of the court or the jury, so that the person in question has at least to be given an opportunity to advance evidence that the criminal record has unduly influenced the court.

The presumption of innocence requires that criminal liability does not survive the person who has allegedly committed the criminal act.[799]

10.9.3 WITH RESPECT TO TREATMENT OF THE ACCUSED

In addition to the establishment of guilt, Article 6(2) also has consequences for the treatment of the accused; in this respect, too, his innocence must be presumed. This applies to the treatment of the accused during the preliminary examination and the trial, as well as to the treatment of a person detained on remand: that treatment may not have a punitive character.[800] However, as the Court held in the *Peers* Case, Article 6 does not require separate treatment for convicted and accused persons in prisons.[801]

10.9.4 WITH RESPECT TO THE PRESUMPTION OF ACCOUNTABILITY

The principle embodied in paragraph 2 also applies in those criminal cases where the issue of guilt is not a central issue. In the *Salabiaku* Case the Court held that the Contracting States are in principle free, subject to certain conditions, to establish an offence on the basis of an objective fact as such, irrespective of whether it results from criminal intent or from negligence. The applicant was convicted not for the mere possession of unlawfully imported prohibited goods, but for smuggling such goods, while the legal presumption of accountability was inferred from their possession which led to his conviction. The Court stressed the relative nature of the distinction between presumption of accountability and presumption of guilt. Presumptions of fact or of law operate in every legal system; this is not contrary to the Convention. The Contracting States

---

[798] Judgment of 10 February 1983, *Albert and Le Compte*, para. 40.
[799] Judgments of 29 August 1997, *A.T., M.P. and T.P. v. Switzerland* and *E.L., R.L. and J.O.-L. v. Switzerland*, paras 44-48 and paras 49-53, respectively.
[800] See the judgment of 5 July 2001, *Erdem*, para. 49, where the Court held, however, that is was not necessary to investigate the complaint under Article 6(2), because it had already found a violation of the reasonable time requirement of Article 5(3).
[801] Judgment of 19 April 2001, para. 78. See, however, the Standard Minimum Rules for the Treatment of Prisoners.

are, however, under the obligation to remain within reasonable limits in this respect as regards their criminal law provisions, taking into account the importance of what is at stake, and to maintain the rights of the defence. Indeed, the guarantee of Article 6(2) must also be respected by the legislature while, according to the Court, the words 'according to law' are not to be construed exclusively with reference to domestic law but contain a reference to the fundamental principle of the rule of law.[802]

In the *Phillips* Case national law required, in short, the court sentencing a person of a drug trafficking offence to assume that any property appearing to have been held by him during the period of six years before the date on which the criminal proceedings were commenced, was received as a payment or reward in connection with drug trafficking. The Court held that the confiscation proceedings conducted against the applicant pursuant to this law had been fair. Although the assumption was mandatory, the legal system was not without safeguards, especially because the assumption could have been rebutted if the defendant had shown, on the balance of probabilities, that he had acquired the property other than through drug trafficking.[803]

In the *Radio France and Others* Case the director of the radio station and two journalists had been convicted for the broadcasting of news bulletins mentioning an article which alleged that a Deputy Prefect had overseen the deportation of thousand Jews in 1942 and 1943. The applicants complained that the Audiovisual Communication Act created an irrefutable presumption that the editorial director of the radio station was liable for the broadcasting of the defamatory accusations. The Court, however, taking into account what was at stake, i.e. the need to prevent the broadcasting of damaging statements in the media by obliging the editorial director to exercise prior control, concluded that the presumption of the Audiovisual Communication Act remained within the requisite 'reasonable limits'.[804]

10.9.5 WITH RESPECT TO POST-TRIAL DECISIONS

Article 6(2) may even be relevant after the formal determination of the 'charge', for instance when a decision has to be taken with regard to the costs of the suit or the compensation for pre-trial detention claimed by the former suspect.

Article 6 applies to these decisions as long as the question to be answered can be regarded as "a consequence and, to some extent, the concomitant of the criminal

---

[802]   Judgment of 7 October 1988, para. 28. See also the judgment of 25 September 1992, *Pham Hoang*, para. 33.

[803]   Judgment of 5 July 2001, paras 40-47. The Court discussed the matter under Article 6(1), because it held Article 6(2) not to be applicable.

[804]   Judgment of 30 March 2004, para. 24.

proceedings".[805] In the *Minelli* Case, where the court had concluded that the plaintiffs in an action for insult could not sue since the period of limitation had expired, but still had condemned the defendant to pay two thirds of the trial costs and to pay compensation in respect of the prosecutor's expenses, because in the court's opinion he would in all probability have been found guilty if the limitation had not barred the continuance of the proceedings, the Court held that the fact that the accused is made to pay some of the costs of the suit if he is discharged need not yet in itself conflict with Article 6(2), but that this *is* the case if the presumable guilt of the accused is used as the criterion for it, without the guarantees of Article 6 being observed.[806] In the *Sekanina* Case the Court held that "the voicing of suspicions regarding an accused's innoncence" following a final aquittal on the merits, is no longer admissible;[807] not even in case the accused had been given the benefit of the doubt[808] and in case the accused is acquitted for technical reasons only.[809] The same holds good for compensation proceedings instituted by the victim of the alleged crime.[810] In the *Lutz, Englert* and *Nölkenbockhoff* Cases the Court held that the decision to refuse reimbursement to a person 'charged with a criminal offence' in the event of discontinuance of the proceedings against him, may raise an issue under Article 6(2) if the supporting reasons amount in substance to a determination of the guilt of the accused without his having previously been proved guilty according to the law, in particular without having had an opportunity to exercise the right of defence.[811] Within this scope the Court distinguished in the *Baars* Case between decisions which describe a 'state of

---

[805] Judgment of 25 August 1993, *Sekanina*, para. 22; judgments of 25 August 1987, *Lutz*, para. 56 and *Nölkenbockhoff*, para. 35. This was not the case in the judgment of 11 February 2003, *Ringvold*, concerning the compensation claim of the victim of alleged sexual abuse. Despite the applicant's acquittal in the criminal proceedings it was legally feasible to award compensation. Therefore the Court held that the compensation case was not a direct sequel to the criminal trial.

[806] Judgment of 25 March 1983, paras 37-38.

[807] Judgment of 25 August 1993, *Sekanina*, para. 30; judgments of 11 February 2003, *O. v. Norway*, and *Hammern*, para. 39 and para. 47, respectively. See, however, also the judgment of 28 November 2002, *Marziano*, where the Italian court decided to discontinue the criminal proceedings against the applicant, who was accused of sexual abuse of his daughter. According to the Court (paras 29-36) the grounds stated in the decision that the child's statements were true in substance but that, as they contained contradictions, the accused could not be convicted, did not violate the presumption of innocence.

[808] Judgment of 21 March 2000, *Rushiti*, paras 31-32; judgment of 10 July 2001, *Lamanna*, paras 38-40; judgment of 20 December 2001, *Weixelbraun*, paras 25-31.

[809] Judgment of 9 November 2004, *Del Latte*, paras 32-34, where the national court based its decisions on the consideration that the applicants would inevitably have been convicted on the facts at issue if the prosecution had charged them with "threatening to commit a crime directed against life" instead of attempted murder/manslaughter.

[810] Judgment of 11 February 2003, *Y. v. Norway*, paras 43-47.

[811] Judgments of 25 August 1987, paras 58-64, 37-41 and 35-41, respectively. See also, *e.g.*, the judgment of 26 March 1996, *Leutscher*, paras 30-32.

suspicion' and decisions which contain a 'finding of guilt' and held that only the latter category is incompatible with Article 6(2) of the Convention.[812]

10.10   MINIMUM RIGHTS FOR THE CRIMINAL SUSPECT

10.10.1   INTRODUCTION

Article 6(3) contains an enumeration of the minimum rights to which everyone charged with a criminal offence is entitled. This provision, unlike the first paragraph, does not relate to proceedings concerning the determination of civil rights and obligations. On the one hand, however, if a party to civil proceedings is denied the rights mentioned in paragraph 3, under certain circumstances this may entail that there is no 'fair hearing' in the sense of the first paragraph.[813] On the other hand, the fact that 'civil rights and obligations' are at issue does not exclude that the proceedings have a criminal character.[814]

The specific enumeration in the third paragraph for criminal proceedings does not imply that an examination for compatibility with the third paragraph makes an examination for compatibility with the first paragraph superfluous, since the guarantees contained in the third paragraph of Article 6 are constituent elements, *inter alia*, of the general notion of a fair trial.[815] The enumeration of the third paragraph is not limitative in that respect, and it is therefore possible that, although the guarantees mentioned there have been satisfied, the trial as a whole still does not satisfy the requirements of a fair trial. As a result of an extensive and functional interpretation of the third paragraph in the Strasbourg case law, however, examination for compatibility with the third and with the first paragraph is in fact likely to more or less coincide. At all events, in the case of a negative outcome of the examination for compatibility with the first paragraph an examination with regard to the third paragraph is deemed superfluous.[816]

Article 6 – and especially its paragraph 3 – applies not only to criminal court proceedings, but is also relevant to pre-trial proceedings, because an initial failure to

---

[812]   Judgment of 28 October 2003, paras 26-32.
[813]   The lack of free legal aid may, for instance, bar the exercise of the right of 'access to court'; see *supra* 10.4.2.3.
[814]   Judgment of 25 March 1983, *Minelli*, para. 28.
[815]   Judgment of 9 April 1984, *Goddi*, para. 28; judgment of 12 February 1985, *Colozza*, para 26.
[816]   Judgment of 27 February 1980, *Deweer*, para. 56.

comply with the provisions of paragraph 3 before a case is sent for trial, may jeopardize the fairness of the trial.[817]

10.10.2 INFORMATION OF THE ACCUSED

Under paragraph 3(a) the accused is granted the right to be informed promptly, in a language which he understands and in detail, of the nature and cause of the accusation against him. This right, which constitutes an 'essential prerequisite' for a fair trial,[818] is very closely related to the right granted under paragraph 3(b) that he must have adequate time and facilities for the preparation of the defence.[819] As the Court held in the *Pélissier and Sassi* Case, the provision implies the right of the accused "to be informed not only of the cause of the accusation, that is is to say the acts he is alleged to have committed and on which the accusation is based, but also the legal characterisation given to those facts".[820] However, in this phase it is not yet necessary to furnish any evidence in support of the charge.[821] The obligation to inform the defendant, which rests entirely on the prosecuting authorities, cannot be complied with passively by making information available without notifying the defence.[822]

The question of whether the required information has been furnished promptly (*dans le plus court délai*), has to be assessed in each individual case on the basis of its specific circumstances. In order to enable the accused to prepare his defence the prosecutor will have to inform him as soon as it has been decided to institute criminal proceedings and, if necessary, make provisions for a translation or for the presence of an interpreter. On that occasion he will have to provide the relevant data available at that moment, which afterwards are to be supplemented, if need be, particularly when the summons is issued. However, adequate defence may already be of great importance in the phase preceding the ultimate decision as to whether or not to institute proceedings and it may even affect this decision, so that it results from the

---

[817] See, *e.g.*, the judgment of 24 November 1993, *Imbrioscia*, para. 36; judgment of 8 February 1996, *John Murray*, para. 62; judgment of 20 June 2002, *Berlinski*, para. 75.

[818] See, *e.g.*, the judgment of 25 March 1999, *Pélissier and Sassi*, para. 52; judgment of 1 March 2001, *Dallos*, para. 47; judgment of 17 July 2001, *Sadak and Others*, para. 49.

[819] See, *e.g.*, the judgment of 25 July 2000, *Mattoccia*, para. 60.

[820] Judgment of 25 March 1999, para. 52. See also, *e.g.*, the judgment of 21 February 2002, *Sipavicius*, para. 27; judgment of 1 March 2001, *Dallos*, para. 47.

[821] Appl. 7628/76, *X v. Belgium*, D&R 9 (1978), p. 169 (173); report of 5 May 1983, *Collozza and Rubinat*, A.89, p. 28.

[822] Judgment of 25 July 2000, *Mattoccia*, para. 65.

rationale of paragraphs 3(a) and 3(b) that even before this formal decision the accused must be kept informed as fully as possible of the suspicion against him.[823]

Paragraph 3(a) requires that the information must be furnished 'in detail', but does not impose any special formal requirement as to the manner in which the defendant is to be informed.[824] The extent of details depends on the particular circumstances of the case, although it is clear that the information provided must suffice to understand fully the charges with a view to preparing an adequate defence.[825] An alternative charge satisfies the requirement of specificity.[826]

The reclassification of an offence in the course of the proceedings may impair the accused in his defence. Therefore, he must be made aware that the offence may be reclassified.[827] In case the reclassification concerns only an element intrinsic to the original accusation, the Court holds the view that the accused must be considered to have been aware of the possible reclassification.[828]

From the words 'in a language which he understands' it follows that if the accused has an insufficient mastery of the vernacular, the information must be translated for him. For this no particular form is prescribed, but the Court seems to require a written translation. An oral elucidation by the person who serves the writ of summons upon the accused, or by an interpreter would seem to be an insufficient basis for the preparation of his defence.[829] It also seems dubious whether paragraph 3(a) has been

---

[823]   In the judgment of 14 November 2000, *T. v. Austria*, the Court held Article 6 (1), taken in conjunction with Article 6(3) subparagraph (a) and (b), to have been violated. The district court had ordered the applicant to supplement his legal aid request, but it had not informed him of the suspicion that he had made false statements in his previous request. Subsequently the district court imposed a fine for abuse of process. The applicant learned about the accusation only when the district's court decision was served on him.

[824]   Judgment of 19 December 1989, *Kamasinski*, para. 79; judgment of 25 March 1999, *Pélissier and Sassi*, para. 53.

[825]   Judgment of 25 July 2000, *Mattoccia*, para. 60. In this case Article 6 had been violated *inter alia* because the information in the accusation had been vague on essential points concerning time and place and had been repeatedly contradicted and amended in the course of the trial (paras 63-72). See also the judgment of 27 January 2004, *Kyprianou*, paras 65-68, where the material facts which appeared to be crucial for the court's decision to impose on the applicant the sentence of imprisonment, were not disclosed before that decision, which amounted to a violation of the presumption of innocence.

[826]   Appl. 3894/68, *X v. the Netherlands*, Coll. 32 (1970), p. 47 (50).

[827]   Judgment of 25 March 1999, *Pélissier and Sassi*, para. 56; judgment of 1 March 2001, *Dallos*, para. 48; judgment of 17 July 2001, *Sadak and Others*, para. 52. A proposal made by the public authorities, acting as a civil party, to the registry of the Court of Appeal to reclassify the criminal acts, without informing the defendant of this proposal, was considered by the Commission to violate the third paragraph under (a): Report of 16 March 1989, *Chichlian and Ekindjian*, p. 52. Before the Court gave judgment, a friendly settlement was reached.

[828]   Judgment of 24 October 1996, *De Salvador Torres*, paras 30-33, with respect to an aggravated circumstance. In the judgment of 25 March 1999, *Pélissier and Sassi*, paras 57-61, the Court held that 'aiding and abetting criminal bankruptcy' did not constitute an intrinsic element of 'criminal bankruptcy'.

[829]   Judgment of 19 December 1989, *Kamasinski*, para. 79.

satisfied if the information is sent to counsel who has mastery of the vernacular and may find ways to inform his client, since in this way the authorities shift an obligation resting upon them on to counsel, while it is important for the accused that he himself is also able to follow the defence put forward on his behalf as adequately as possible. In the *Brozicek* Case the Court concluded that, since the applicant was not of Italian origin, did not reside in Italy and informed the judicial authorities that he did not understand the Italian language, it was for the judicial authority to procure a translation unless it could be established that the person concerned was objectively capable of understanding the content of the notification.[830]

10.10.3 TIME AND FACILITIES FOR THE DEFENCE

Under paragraph 3(b) the accused is guaranteed the right to have adequate time and facilities for the preparation of his defence. Apart from the above-mentioned relation with paragraph 3(a) there is also a close connection with paragraph 3(c), regulating legal aid. In that context the Commission has emphasised that here not only the rights of the accused are concerned, but equally the rights of counsel, so that for the assessment of the overall situation the position of both of them has to be taken into account.[831] In the *Makhfi* Case, after a session that lasted almost sixteen hours, counsel for the accused addressed the jury at 4.25 in the morning. The judge and jury, who held their deliberations between 6.15 and 8.15 in the morning, found the applicant guilty and sentenced him to eight years imprisonment. These facts amounted to a violation of the first paragraph taken together with the third paragraph of Article 6, since the Court considered it essential that not only the accused but also his counsel should be able to make their submissions without suffering from excessive tiredness.[832]

The question of whether the accused has been allowed adequate time for the preparation of his defence will have to be decided afterwards, according to the circumstances in which both the accused and his counsel found themselves, and on the basis of the nature of the case.[833] If the accused has great confidence in a particular lawyer, who is very occupied at the relevant time, the judicial authorities will have to take this

---

[830] Judgment of 19 December 1989, para. 41.
[831] Appl. 524/59, *Ofner*, Yearbook III (1960), p. 322 (352). The question whether the surveillance of the contacts of a detainee with his lawyer is permissible, will be discussed under paragraph 3(c).
[832] Judgment of 19 October 2004, paras 34-42.
[833] See, *e.g.*, the judgment of 12 March 2003, *Öcalan*, paras. 167-169, where Article 6 was found to have been violated, inter alia, because of the fact that the defence received a 17,000 page file approximately two weeks before the beginning of the trial and also the fact that the lawyers had only limited access to their client; Appl. 7909/77, *X and Y v. Austria*, D&R 15 (1979), p. 160 (162-163), where the Commission, notwithstanding the fact that counsel could communicate with his client only with difficulty because of her poor psychological and physical condition, held that the time of ten working days available to him was adequate, considering the complexity of the case.

into account as much as possible. On the other hand, in that case the accused cannot advance the resulting delay as a ground for violation of the first paragraph of Article 6. If for one reason or another the accused has to change counsel, the new lawyer will have to be given adequate time to become acquainted with the case.[834] If there is a right to free legal aid, a lawyer has to be assigned in good time.[835] The accused, however, cannot complain if through his own fault he has created a situation in which a lawyer has to be appointed shortly before the hearing is to be held.[836]

The 'facilities' do not include the possibility to choose counsel or have one assigned, since the right to legal aid is separately provided for under paragraph 3(c).

If appeal is open, the time-limit has to be such that a thorough study of the judgment can be made to enable a decision as to whether an appeal should be brought, while the moment of the hearing of the appeal in turn will have to leave adequate time for the preparation of the hearing.[837] The words 'preparation of his defence', therefore, may not be interpreted to mean that the provision of paragraph 3(b) is not applicable to the appeal proceedings in case the accused has been convicted at first instance and, consequently, acts not as defendant but as plaintiff in these proceedings. In the *Hadjianastassiou* Case the applicant had to give notice of appeal on points of law within a time-limit of five days without having the opportunity to take cognisance of the written version of the judgment. The Court took the view that it is essential for the exercise of the defendant's right of appeal that the national courts indicate unambiguously the reasons on which they base their verdicts. As the applicant was barred in the circumstances of the case from submitting an additional memorial, the Court concluded that paragraph 3(b) in conjunction with paragraph 1 had been violated.[838] In the *Zoon* Case the Court held that it had been possible for the applicant, well before the expiry of the fourteen-day time-limit for lodging an appeal, to take cognisance of the judgment in abridged form of the Dutch regional court. Moreover, in the circumstances of the case the judgment did contain sufficient information. Therefore, the rights of the defence had not been unduly affected by the absence of a complete

---

[834]   See, *mutatis mutandis*, the judgment of 9 June 1998, *Twalib*, para. 40, and, with regard to subparagraph 3 (c), the judgment of 21 April 1998, *Daud*, para. 38.

[835]   Appl. 7909/77, *X and Y v. Austria*, D&R 15 (1979), p. 160 (162), where the Commission stated that the question what period is adequate cannot be answered *in abstracto*.

[836]   Appl. 8251/78, *X v. Austria*, D&R 17 (1980), p. 166 (169-170).

[837]   In the judgment of 21 September 1993, *Kremzow*, para. 48, a period of three weeks between the receipt of the Attorney General's position paper (the so-called *croquis*) and the hearing of the Supreme Court did suffice to formulate a reply to the croquis. See for a case where the date for filing the grounds of appeal had not been fixed, but the appellant was informed about the date of the hearing: the judgment of 17 December 1996, *Vacher*, paras 22-30.

[838]   Judgment of 16 December 1992, paras 34-37.

judgment or a detailed enumeration of the items of evidence relied on to ground the conviction of the applicant.[839]

The reclassification of an offence in the course of proceedings does not violate subparagraph (b) as long as the defendant has adequate opportunity to reorganise his defence accordingly.[840]

In the *Bricmont* Case the Commission stated that subparagraph (b) recognises the right of the accused to have at his disposal, for the purposes of exonerating himself or obtaining a reduction of his sentence, all relevant elements that can be collected by the competent authorities.[841] The accused cannot complain about lack of facilities if he does not co-operate in producing elements to his defence.[842]

Finally, the possibility of inspection of the files must also be mentioned as an important element of the 'facilities'.[843] The case law of the Court indicates that the right of access is incorporated in the provision under (b), although restriction of this right to the defendant's counsel is not incompatible with Article 6,[844] provided that the evidence is made available to the accused before the hearing and the lawyer of the accused has had the opportunity to comment on it.[845] A lack of adequate time for the preparation of the defence may be cured by way of review proceedings.[846]

10.10.4 THE RIGHT TO DEFEND ONESELF IN PERSON OR THROUGH LEGAL ASSISTANCE

10.10.4.1 General observations

Paragraph 3(c) guarantees the right of the accused to defend himself in person or through legal assistance of his own choosing or (and), if he has not sufficient means to pay for legal assistance, to be given it free when the interests of justice so require. In the *Pakelli* Case the Court, referring to "the object and purpose of this paragraph, which is designed to ensure effective protection of the rights of the defence", opted

---

[839] Judgment of 7 December 2000, paras 32-50.

[840] Judgment of 25 March 1999, *Pélissier and Sassi*, para. 62; judgment of 17 July 2001, *Sadak and Others*, para. 57.

[841] Report of 15 October 1987, A.158, p. 47. See also the judgment of 16 December 1992, *Edwards*, para. 36.

[842] Report of 15 October 1987, *Bricmont*, A.158, p. 49.

[843] At least from the moment of the charge: Appl. 4622/70, *X v. Austria*, Coll. 40 (1972), p. 15 (18).

[844] Judgment of 19 December 1989, *Kamasinski*, para. 88; judgment of 21 September 1993, *Kremzow*, para. 52.

[845] Judgment of 12 March 2003, *Öcalan*, para. 50.

[846] Judgment of 20 October 1997, *Serves*, para. 51. The judgment of 9 June 1998, *Twalib*, seems to provide another example. See, however, the criticism expressed in the partly dissenting opinion. See with respect to complaints against reclassification: the judgment of 1 March 2001, *Dallos*, paras 49-52; judgment of 21 February 2002, *Sipavicius*, paras 32-33.

for the '*et*' in the French text, and not for the 'or' in the English text. This resulted in the following interpretation by the Court: "a 'person charged with a criminal offence' who does not wish to defend himself in person must be able to have recourse to legal assistance of his own choosing; if he does not have sufficient means to pay for such assistance, he is entitled under the Convention to be given it free when the interests of justice so require."[847] There are, therefore, three juxtaposed rights included in this provision, which will be dealt with consecutively hereafter.

The manner in which the provision applies (in conjunction with the first paragraph of Article 6) in appeal and cassation proceedings or during a preliminary investigation depends on the characteristics of the proceedings in question.[848]

In as far as the rights of the defence have not been irretrievably prejudiced, a failure to comply with the requirement of paragraph 3(c) may in principle be cured in appeal on the condition that the appeal court may carry out a full review.[849]

The provision under paragraph 3(c) does not contain an "unlimited right to use any defence arguments". It does not in principle offer protection against a subsequent prosecution of the accused because he made "false suspicions of punishable behaviour" concerning another person.[850]

The fact that the applicant has not suffered any damage from the non-fulfilment of the requirement under paragraph 3(c) does not exclude that this provision has been violated.[851]

10.10.4.2 In Person

The right for the accused to defend himself in person is closely related to the right to be present at the hearing,[852] which in principle demands that a person charged with a criminal offence is entitled to be present at least at the first-instance trial hearing. With regard to appeal and cassation proceedings Article 6 does not always entail the right to be present in person.[853]

In the *Gillow* Case the Court accepted the requirement of representation by a lawyer to lodge an appeal as "a common feature of the legal systems in several member

---

847   Judgment of 25 April 1983, para. 31.
848   See *e.g.* the judgment of 2 March 1987, *Monnell and Morris*, para. 56; judgment of 22 February 1994, *Tripodi*, para. 27; and with regard to the preliminary investigation: judgment of 24 November 1993, *Imbrioscia*, para. 38; judgment of 20 June 2002, *Berlinski*, para. 75.
849   Judgment of 24 May 1991, *Quaranta*, para. 37.
850   Judgment of 28 August 1991, *Brandstetter*, paras 50-54.
851   Judgment of 19 February 1991, *Alimena*, para. 20.
852   See, *e.g.*, the judgment of 25 November 1997, *Zana*, para. 68; judgment of 27 May 2004, *Yavuz*, paras 45-52. See on the right to be present *supra* 10.5.4.
853   See, *e.g.*, the judgment of 21 September 1993, *Kremzow*, para. 58; judgment of 25 March 1998, *Belziuk*, para. 37, and see *supra* 10.5.4.

States of the Council of Europe".[854] From paragraph 3(c) it then results that, if the national law stipulates or the judicial authorities decide that the accused must be assisted by a lawyer, he must be able himself to choose this lawyer and, in case of inability to pay for such legal aid, must have a lawyer assigned to him; indeed, in that case such legal aid is evidently considered necessary by national law or the judicial authorities in the interests of justice.

In the *Meftah* Case the applicants complained that they, unlike specialist lawyers, could not make oral representations in the proceedings before the Court of Cassation. The Court held that the special characteristics of cassation proceedings may justify specialist lawyers being reserved a monopoly on making oral representations. Since the applicants had had the choice of whether or not to be represented by a specialist lawyer, the Court rejected their claim.[855]

Although some restrictions of the right of the accused to defend himself in person are permitted, these restrictions cannot go so far that the protection offered by the Convention becomes illusory. In the *Kremzow* Case the situation at issue was that national legislation granted the right of a detained person to be present at the hearing of an appeal against his sentence only if the person concerned made a request to this effect in his appeal. The applicant had failed to make such a request. Nevertheless, because the applicant risked a substantial increase of his sentence of imprisonment, the Court held that the national authorities had been obliged to enable the applicant to be present at the hearing and to 'defend himself in person'. The failure to fulfil this duty amounted to a breach of paragraph 6(1) in conjunction with the provision under paragraph 3(c).[856]

10.10.4.3 Legal Assistance and Implied Rights

In the *John Murray* Case the Court held that, if domestic law attaches consequences to the attitude of the accused at the initial stage of police interrogation, Article 6 in principle requires that the accused be allowed the benefit from the assistance of a lawyer in the pre-trial phase.[857] Subsequently, in the *Magee* Case the Court reformulated this rule in a more general way: "Article 6 will normally require that the accused be allowed to benefit from the assistance of a lawyer already at the initial stages of

---

[854] Judgment of 24 November 1986, para. 69.

[855] Judgment of 26 July 2002, paras 40-48.

[856] Judgment of 21 September 1993, paras 65-69; See also the judgments of 8 February 2000, *Michael Edward Cooke*, and *Josef Prinz*, paras 40-44 and paras 39-46 respectively. The former judgment is on crucial points almost identical to the *Kremzow* Case, but in the latter, concerning proceedings before the Austrian Supreme Court with regard to the question whether the conditions for the applicant's placement in an institution for mentally ill offenders were met, the absence of the applicant had not violated Article 6. Compare also the judgment of 3 October 2002, *Kucera*, para. 29.

[857] Judgment of 8 February 1996, *John Murray*, para. 63.

police interrogation [although] this right, which is not explicitly set out in the Convention, may be subject to restriction for good cause."[858]

In the *John Murray* Case the applicant had been denied access to a lawyer for the first 48 hours of police interrogation. He had been told by the police that he had the right to remain silent but that adverse inferences could be drawn from his silence. Thus, he had been confronted at the beginning of the interrogation with a "fundamental dilemma" concerning his defence. The Court held that in this situation the denial of access to a lawyer had constituted a breach of Article 6(1) in conjunction with paragraph 3(c).[859] In the *Öcalan* Case the Court reached the same conclusion; where the applicant did not receive legal assistance for a period of seven days and made several self-incriminating statements that subsequently appeared to be crucial elements of the indictment, the decision to deny access to a lawyer might irreparably prejudice the defendant's rights.[860] However, in the *Brennan* Case the Court held that the 24 hour deferral period did not constitute a violation of Article 6, because the applicant had made no incriminating statements during that period and no inferences had been drawn from the statements or omissions made by him.[861]

The provision under sub-paragraph (c) embodies the right of an accused to communicate with his counsel out of hearing of a third person. Without this requirement the guarantee offered by the Convention would not be practical and effective.[862] However, the right of access to a solicitor may – here again – be subject to restrictions "for good cause" as long as the proceedings as a whole are fair.[863] The defendant must be able to claim to have been directly affected by the restriction in the exercise of his right of defence, but it is not necessary for him to prove that the restriction had a prejudicial effect on the course of the trial.[864] In the *Öcalan* Case the restriction of number and length of the visits by the applicant's lawyers to a rhythm of two one-hourly meetings per week, violated the principle of fair trial in view of the highly complex charges and voluminous case file.[865] In the *Lanz* Case the Court held that only "very weighty reasons" could have justified the surveillance by the investigating judge of the contacts of a detainee with his defence counsel. The mere risk of collusion did

---

[858] Judgment of 6 June 2000, *Magee*, para. 41; judgment 20 June 2002, *Berlinski*, para. 75. See also, thoughless clear, the judgment of 11 July 2000, *Dikme*, para. 108.

[859] Judgment of 8 February 1996, paras 66-70. See also the judgment of 6 June 2000, *Averill*, paras 55-62, concerning a denial of access to a solicitor during the first 24 hours.

[860] Judgment of 12 March 2003, paras 140-143. See also the judgment of 6 June 2000, *Magee*, para. 42-46; judgment of 22 April 2004, *Sarikaya*, paras 67-68.

[861] Judgment of 16 October 2001, paras 44-48.

[862] Judgment of 28 November 1991, *S v. Switzerland*, para. 48. The Court reached this conclusion by referring to the Standard Minimum Rules for the Treatment of Prisoners and the European Agreement Relating to Persons Participating in Proceedings of the European Commission and Court of Human Rights.

[863] Judgment of 16 October 2001, *Brennan*, para. 58.

[864] *Ibidem.*

[865] Judgment of 12 March 2003, para. 154.

not meet the criterion because this was the very reason for which detention had already been ordered.[866] However, the "extraordinary features" of the *Kempers* Case, where the defendant had been suspected of being the member of a gang and utmost confidentiality had been necessary in order to catch the other members, justified the restriction in issue.[867]

The Court has attached to the right of access to court, implied in Article 6(1), the consequence that this right has been violated if a detainee is not permitted to correspond with a lawyer or another person giving legal assistance. The Court held that "hindering the effective exercise of a right may amount to a breach of that right, even if the hindrance is of a temporary character."[868] Consequently, as soon as a detainee wants to institute an action or wishes to prepare his defence against a criminal charge, such contact must be possible. This may hold good in the pre-trial phase[869] and even with regard to an internal preliminary inquiry.[870]

Searching of counsel and inspection of the correspondence of counsel with his detained client by the prison authorities are in principle also incompatible with the position of counsel. Measures of this kind are justified only in very exceptional circumstances, where the authorities have sound reasons to assume that counsel himself is abusing his position or is allowing it to be abused.[871]

The provision under paragraph 3(c), in conjunction with the first paragraph of Article 6, also implies that counsel who attends the trial must be enabled to conduct the defence also in the absence of the accused, regardless of whether or not there exists an excuse for the latter's absence[872] and whether or not it is possible to apply to have a conviction entered in default set aside.[873] Although in principle national legislation may discourage the unjustified absence of an accused at the trial,[874] this implied aspect

---

[866] Judgment of 31 January 2002, para. 52. In the judgment of 28 November 1991, *S v. Switzerland*, para. 49, the fear that the lawyer of the applicant would collude with the lawyer of a co-accused was based on the fact that the lawyers proposed to coordinate their defence-strategy. This fact, too, could not justify the restriction on the free communication of the accused and his lawyer.

[867] In the judgment of 31 January 2002, *Lanz*, para. 52, the Court refers to and endorses the decision on admissibility by the Commission in the *Kempers* Case, Appl. 21842/93, 27 February 1997.

[868] Judgment of 21 February 1975, *Golder*, para. 26.

[869] Judgment of 8 February 1996, *John Murray*, paras 66-70.

[870] Appl. 7878/77, *Fell*, D&R 23 (1981), p. 102 (113). See also the report of 12 May 1982, *Campbell and Fell*, A.80, pp. 76-77.

[871] See the judgment of 28 June 1984, *Campbell and Fell*, para. 108-11; the judgment of 15 November 1996, *Domenichini*, paras 35-39, where Article 6 subparagraph (b) had been found to have been breached because the monitoring of the letter of a detainee to his lawyer had caused a delay in sending the letter and consequently his lawyer had not been able to file in due time the grounds that supported an appeal on points of law.

[872] Judgments of 22 September 1994, *Lala*, and *Pelladoah*, para. 33 and para. 40, respectively.

[873] See, *e.g.*, the judgment of 13 February 2001, *Krombach*, para. 85; judgment of 16 May 2002, *Karatas and Sari*, para. 54.

[874] See *supra* 10.5.4. However, see also *supra* 10.4.6.3.

of subparagraph 3(c) may not be impaired because the legislator "cannot penalise the accused by creating exceptions to the right of legal assistance".[875]

10.10.4.4 Legal Assistance and the Right to Choose a Lawyer

In the *Ezeh and Connors* Case the right to choose a lawyer had been violated because national law did not provide for a 'right' to legal representation in the adjudication proceedings which could lead to the award of 'additional days' of imprisonment to detained persons who had committed disciplinary offences.[876] On the other hand, a legal requirement that an accused be assisted by counsel in criminal proceedings is in itself not incompatible with the right to choose a lawyer.[877]

According to Strasbourg case law the right of the accused to choose his own lawyer is not an absolute right; he is bound by the provisions applying in the relevant legal system with regard to the question as to who may act as counsel in court.[878] In the *Croissant* Case the Court expressed as its opinion that national courts when appointing defence counsel must take into account the accused's wishes, although those wishes may be overridden if required "in the interests of justice".[879] In any case, if such an unsatisfactory relationship between the accused and the lawyer assigned to him is found to exist that an adequate defence is impossible, or if the qualifications of the assigned lawyer are found to be inadequate considering the nature and/or complexity of the case, paragraph 1 and paragraph 3(b) may imply that another lawyer must be assigned to the accused at the latter's request.[880] In the *Kamasinski* Case, however, the Court held that the responsibility rests in the first place on the applicant: "the competent national authorities are required under Article 6(3)(c) to intervene only if a failure by legal aid counsel to provide effective representation is manifest or sufficiently brought to their attention in some other way."[881]

---

[875] See, *e.g.*, the judgment of 21 January 1999, *Van Geyseghem*, para. 34; judgment of 23 may 2000, *Van Pelt*, para. 67; judgment of 13 February 2001, *Krombach*, para. 89.

[876] Judgment of 15 July 2002, paras 103-106 and the judgment of 9 October 2003 (Grand Chamber), paras 132-134. See also the judgment of 20 June 2002, *Berlinski*, paras 77-78: Article 6 had been violated because the applicant had no defence council for more than a year, without any justification, and the judgment of 15 June 2004, *Thompson*, para. 47.

[877] Judgment of 25 September 1992, *Croissant*, para. 50.

[878] Appl. 722/60, *X v. Federal Republic of Germany*, Yearbook V (1962), p. 104 (106); Appls 7572/76, 7586/76 and 7587/76, *Ensslin, Baader and Raspe*, Yearbook XXI (1978), p. 418 (464).

[879] Judgment of 25 September 1992, para. 29. In this case the applicant contested the necessity of the appointment of a third defence counsel.

[880] See the judgment of 21 April 1998, *Daud*, paras 38-43.

[881] Judgment of 19 December 1989, *Kamasinski*, para. 65. See also the judgment of 24 November 1993, *Imbrioscia*, para. 41. In the *Kamasinski* Case, the Court expressly mentioned that the responsibility rests in the first place on the defendant "whether counsel be appointed under a legal aid scheme or be privately financed". This passage was lacking in the *Imbrioscia* Case. Compare further the judgment of 22 February 1994, *Tripodi*, para. 30.

In this context the Court emphasised in the *Artico* Case that the authorities have not complied with their obligation by the mere assignment of a lawyer, since Article 6(3)(c) speaks of 'assistance' and not of 'nomination', so that it must be sufficiently ensured that real assistance is provided.[882] Here again, however, the accused can forfeit his right by personally creating the situation in which at the very last moment before the hearing another lawyer must be nominated.[883] In the *Lagerblom* Case the Court considered it not unreasonable, in view of the general desirability of limiting the total costs of legal aid, that national authorities take a restrictive approach to requests to replace public defence counsel once they have been assigned to a case and have undertaken certain activities.[884] In the *Mayzit* Case the national court refused to authorize the applicant's sister and mother to act as defenders instead of professional advocates, which in itself was permissible under national law, because as lay persons they would not be able to ensure the applicant's efficient defence. According to the Court, this approach was not inconsistent with Article 6.[885]

10.10.4.5 Free Legal Assistance

Article 6(3)(c) stipulates that legal assistance should be given free to the accused if he has not sufficient means to pay for it and when the interests of justice so require. This provision does not exclude that an accused is required to pay a contribution to the cost of legal assistance, as long as he has sufficient means to pay.[886] A system that does not contain any obligation for the accused who is acquitted to pay for his defence, but requires the reimbursement of the costs of appointed lawyers in case the person concerned is convicted, is in itself not incompatible with the Convention. Surprisingly, the Court left open the question whether it would be consistent with the provision under (c) for the national authorities to seek partial or even full reimbursement after it had been established in enforcement proceedings subsequent to the trial that the convicted person lacks sufficient means to pay the costs of his defence.[887] It is submitted that on this point the text of Article 6(3)(c) leaves no room for doubt: if the accused has insufficient means to bear the costs of legal assistance which is required in the 'interests of justice', it should be given to him free, without restrictions and regardless of the outcome of the case.

The concept of "interests of justice" as yet lacks clarity. In many cases the Court has applied two criteria to establish whether free legal aid is required: the seriousness

---

[882]   Judgment of 13 May 1980, para. 33. See also the judgment of 21 April 1998, *Daud*, para. 38; judgment of 10 October 2002, *Czekalla*, paras 60-71.
[883]   Appl. 8251/78, *X v. Austria*, D&R 17 (1980), p. 166 (169-170).
[884]   Judgment of 14 January 2003, para 59.
[885]   Judgment of 20 January 2005, para. 66.
[886]   Judgment of 26 February 2002, *Morris*, paras 88-89.
[887]   Judgment of 25 September 1992, *Croissant*, paras 33-38.

of the alleged offence in conjunction with the severity of the penalty that the accused risks and, secondly, the complexity of the case.[888] The personal circumstances and development of the accused seem to fall within the framework of the latter criterium.[889] In *R.D. v. Poland* the Court referred to these criteria but also formulated a more general test: "There is, however, a primary, indispensable requirement of the 'interests of justice' that must be satisfied in each case. That is the requirement of a fair procedure before courts, which, among other things, imposes on the State authorities an obligation to offer an accused a realistic chance to defend himself throughout the entire trial."[890]

In this case the national court had refused to grant the applicant further free assistance and had communicated its decision to him eight days before the expiry of the time-limit for the submissions of his cassation appeal. Because of the shortness of time left to the applicant for appointing a lawyer of his own choice and for preparing the intended cassation appeal, the Court held that the applicant did not have "a realistic opportunity" to defend his case in the cassation court in a "concrete and effective way". Therefore, Article 6 had been violated.[891] Since the Court in its reasoning did not pay any attention to the two criteria mentioned above, it remains unclear how the test applied in *R.D. v. Poland* relates to these criteria. In the subsequent *Lagerblom* Case the more general test disappeared. The Court only referred to the seriousness of the offence, the severity of the penalty and the complexity of the case.[892] Be that as it may, where deprivation of liberty is at stake the interests of justice in principle call for legal representation,[893] and for the legal representative to be duly heard.[894]

If on the ground of the requirements of a fair hearing of the first paragraph an accused is entitled to free legal aid, that aid will also have to be considered to be required in the interests of justice, while the general interest of the case exceeding the interests of the accused may also call for legal assistance. If it has been recognised with regard to the written phase of the proceedings that the interests of justice require the assignment of legal aid, as a rule, and even *a fortiori*, this will also apply for the subsequent oral phase.[895]

---

[888]   See, *e.g.*, the judgment of 28 March 1990, *Granger*, paras 46-48; judgment of 24 May 1991, *Quaranta*, paras 32-38; judgment of 10 June 1996, *Benham*, paras 60-64; judgment of 9 June 1998, *Twalib*, para. 52; judgment of 26 September 2000, *Biba*, para. 29.

[889]   Judgment of 24 May 1991, *Quaranta*, para. 35. See also the judgment of 25 September 1992, *Pham Hoang*, paras 39-41.

[890]   Judgment of 18 December 2001, para. 49. This test is not completely new (compare for instance the judgment of 24 May 1991, *Quaranta*, para. 36) but the way the Court presents it, is.

[891]   *Ibidem*, paras 50-52.

[892]   Judgment of 14 January 2003, para 51.

[893]   Judgment of 24 May 1991, *Quaranta*, para. 33; judgment of 10 June 1996, *Benham*, para. 61;

[894]   Judgment of 16 November 2004, *Hooper*, para. 20.

[895]   Judgment of 25 April 1983, *Pakelli*, paras. 36-40.

If a lawyer has been assigned to an accused, but the behaviour of the latter has induced counsel to withdraw, the refusal of the court to assign a new lawyer may be in conformity with the 'interests of justice', provided that from that moment the accused himself is given sufficient opportunity to defend himself in person.[896]

10.10.5 THE RIGHT TO SUMMON AND EXAMINE WITNESSES

Paragraph 3(d) grants to the accused the right to examine or have examined witnesses against him, and to obtain the attendance and examination of witnesses on his behalf under the same conditions as witnesses against him. This provision is closely related to the principle of 'equality of arms' as an element of a 'fair hearing' in the sense of the first paragraph. Consequently, the Court often examines an alleged violation of the provision under sub-paragraph (d) under the two provisions taken together. Although paragraph 3(d) is included among the guarantees applying specifically to criminal proceedings, in the case law the possibility has been recognised that the refusal by the court to permit a party to civil proceedings to have a particular witness summoned or examined constitutes a violation of the right to a fair hearing.[897]

The notion of 'witness' is interpreted autonomously. Statements not made in court in person, but for example to the police, are to be regarded as statements of 'witnesses' as far as the national courts take account of these statements,[898] irrespective of whether the statement is made by a co-accused or a third person.[899] Complaints concerning the hearing or summons of an expert do not fall under the provision of paragraph 3(d) but under the general rule of the first paragraph of Article 6.[900]

Paragraph 3(d) does not grant the accused an unlimited right to secure the appearance of witnesses in court. In principle it is for the national courts to consider whether a particular witness should be heard.[901] Therefore, it is not sufficient for an applicant to complain in Strasbourg that he has not been allowed to question a certain witness; in addition he must explain why it is important for the witness concerned to be heard and the evidence must be necessary for the establishment of the truth.[902]

---

[896]   Appl. 8386/78, *X v. the United Kingdom*, D&R 21 (1981), p. 126 (130-132).

[897]   Judgment of 27 October 1993, *Dombo Beheer B.V.*, para. 33-35. See also *supra* 10.5.2.

[898]   See, *e.g.*, the judgment of 19 December 1990, *Delta*, para. 34; judgment of 19 February 1991, *Isgrò*, para. 33; judgment of 28 August 1992, *Artner*, para. 19; judgment of 10 June 1996, *Pullar*, para. 45.

[899]   Judgment of 27 February 2001, *Lucà*, para.41.

[900]   Judgment of 6 May 1985, *Bönisch*, para. 29; judgment of 28 August 1991, *Brandstetter*, para. 42. See *supra* 10.5.2.

[901]   See, *e.g.*, the judgment of 22 April 1992, *Vidal*, para. 33; judgment of 26 March 1996, *Doorson*, para. 82; judgment of 27 July 2000, *Pisano*, para. 23; judgment of 6 May 2003, *Perna*, (Grand Chamber), para. 29; judgment of 3 February 2004, *Laukanen and Manninen*, para. 35.

[902]   Judgment of 6 May 2003, *Perna*, (Grand Chamber), para. 29.

In principle the Court does not assess whether statements of witnesses have been properly admitted as evidence.[903] Thus, it is a matter for the domestic courts to assess whether a statement given by a witness in open court and under oath should be relied on in preference to another statement of the same witness, even when the former is contradictory to the latter.[904]

The Court has deduced from the fact that an accused person is "entitled to take part in the hearing and to have his case heard in his presence by a tribunal", that all the evidence should "in principle be produced in the presence of the accused at a public hearing with a view to adversarial argument".[905] In the *Hulki Günes* Case the lack of any confrontation with the witnesses who had identified the applicant as the person who had taken part in an armed attack during which one soldier died, deprived him of a fair trial, since the judges had not been able to study their demeanour while giving evidence and form a personal opinion as to their credibility.[906] However, it is not inconsistent with paragraph 3(d) and paragraph 1 to use as evidence statements made at the pre-trial stage as long as the accused has been given "an adequate and proper opportunity to challenge and question a witness against him, either at the time the witness was making his statement or at some later stage of the proceedings."[907] If the accused did not have "an adequate and proper opportunity" to question the witness, his conviction cannot solely or mainly be based on the testimony of the latter.[908] The case law does not seem to leave much room for exceptions to this rule. The use as evidence of a statement made in the pre-trial phase by a person who subsequently, in accordance with national law, refuses to give evidence in court, is in itself not incompatible with the Convention. However, it may lead to a conviction only if there exists evidence that corroborates the statement.[909] The same holds good for a statement of a witness who has disappeared and, therefore, cannot be summoned to appear in court.[910]

---

[903]   See, *e.g.*, the judgment of 6 December 1988, *Barberà, Messegué and Jabardo*, para. 68; judgment of 20 November 1989, *Kostovski*, para. 39; judgment of 31 October 2001, *Solakov*, para. 57.

[904]   Judgment of 26 March 1996, *Doorson*, para. 78.

[905]   See, *e.g.*, the judgment of 6 December 1988, *Barberà, Messegué and Jabardo*, para. 78; judgment of 15 June 1992, *Lüdi*, para. 47; judgment of 23 April 1997, *Van Mechelen*, para. 51.

[906]   Judgment of 19 June 2003, paras 86-96.

[907]   Judgment of 20 November 1989, *Kostovski*, para. 41. See also, *e.g.*, the judgment of 24 November 1986, *Unterpertinger*, para. 31; judgment of 26 April 1991, *Asch*, para 27; judgment of 20 September 1993, *Saïdi*, para. 43; judgment of 2 July 2002, *S.N. v. Sweden*, para. 44; judgment of 5 December 2002, *Craxi*, para. 86.

[908]   Judgment of 20 November 1989, *Kostovski*, para. 44; judgment of 27 September 1990, *Windisch*, para. 31; judgment of 19 February 1991, *Isgrò*, para 35; judgment of 28 August 1992, *Artner*, para. 22; judgment of 20 September 1993, *Saïdi*, para. 44.

[909]   Judgment of 24 November 1986, *Unterpertinger*, paras 31-33; judgment of 26 April 1991, *Asch*, paras 28-31.

[910]   Judgment of 28 August 1992, *Artner*, paras 22-24. In the judgment of 13 November 2003, *Rachdad*, paras 22-25, Article 6 was deemed to have been violated despite the existing difficulty in ascertaining the whereabouts of the witness and the fact that the applicant had contributed to that difficulty by

This approach is also reflected in the case law with regard to the admissibility of the testimony by anonymous witnesses. In the *Doorson* Case the Court held that "a conviction should not be based either solely or to a decisive extent on anonymous statements".[911] It seemed to allow no exceptions to this rule. In this respect the judgment in the *Kostovski* Case had been less clear, where the Court, without formulating a similar starting-point, had concluded that the handicaps of the defence that had been caused by the anonymous statements, were not "counterbalanced by the procedures followed by the judicial authorities". Thus, the Court suggested that a conviction could have been based mainly on anonymous, but sufficiently counterbalanced statements.[912] This uncertainty had not been, at least not clearly, lifted in the *Windisch* Case.[913]

Moreover, the use of anonymous statements seems to be permissible only if they meet strict requirements. In the *Doorson* Case the Court took as a starting-point that the interests of the defence should be balanced "against those of witnesses or victims called upon to testify".[914] Subsequently it took account of the circumstances of the case, which concerned the prosecution of a drug dealer, and concluded that the reasons to maintain the anonymity of some witnesses were relevant and sufficient. Furthermore, the Court held that the handicaps of the defence were "sufficiently counterbalanced by the procedures followed by the judicial authorities"[915] and based its conclusion on several facts: the witnesses had been questioned by an investigating judge who was aware of their identity, the national court had been able due to the report of the investigating judge to draw conclusions about the reliability of the witnesses, counsel of the defence had been offered the opportunity to question them except in so far as their identity was concerned, and the witnesses had identified the applicant from a photograph.[916]

In case the anonymous witnesses are members of the police force the lack of direct confrontation seems (even) more difficult to repair. In the *Van Mechelen* Case the

---

failing to comply with court summonses and thus causing the courts to convict him in his absence. See also the judgment of 18 May 2004, *Destrehem*, paras 45-47, where the court of first instance acquitted the applicant after the hearing of several witnesses. The court of appeal convicted him grounding its decision on a new interpretation of the evidence given by witnesses it had not itself examined, notwithstanding the applicant's requests to that effect. In these circumstances the defence rights had been considerably restricted and the refusal to hear the witnesses constituted a violation of Article 6.

[911] Judgment of 26 March 1996, para. 76.
[912] Judgment of 20 November 1989, para. 43.
[913] Judgment of 27 September 1990, *Windisch*, paras 26-32.
[914] Judgment of 26 March 1996, para. 70.
[915] In the judgment of 20 November 1989, *Kostovski*, para. 43, and the judgment of 27 September 1990, *Windisch*, para 28, the Court held that the lack of a direct confrontation with the witnesses could not be repaired by the opportunity to put written questions. The awareness of the identity of the witnesses was of crucial importance to enable the defence to challenge their statements. A sufficient counterbalance also did not exist in the judgment of 17 July 2001, *Sadak and Others*, paras 60-68; judgment of 28 March 2002, *Birutis*, para. 34; judgment of 14 February 2002, *Visser*, paras 47-52.
[916] Judgment of 26 March 1996, paras 71-75.

officers in question had been in a separate room in the presence of the investigating judge, from which the accused and counsel had been excluded. All communication took place by way of a direct communication channel. Since the defence had not only been unaware of the identity of the police officers but also had been prevented from observing their demeanour under direct questioning, the Court held that the handicaps of the defence had not been sufficiently counterbalanced and the Court rejected the argument of the Dutch Government that the anonymity had been justified by operational needs of the police.[917] In the *Lüdi* Case, however, with respect to an undercover agent, a sworn police-officer whose function was known to the investigating judge, Article 6 did not object to the examination by the defence of an undercover agent without revealing the *real* identity of the agent, because the accused knew the agent by physical appearance.[918]

For criminal proceedings concerning sexual offences the Court accepted, with reference to the position of the perceived victim and taking into account that a minor was involved, that the provision under subparagraph (d) cannot be interpreted as requiring in all cases that questions be put directly by the accused or his or her defence counsel, through cross-examination or by other means.[919] In this case the Court noted that the videotape of the first police interview of the victim had been shown during the trial and appeal hearings, the record of the second interview had been read out before the District Court and the audiotape of that interview had been played back before the Court of Appeal. According to the Court these measures were sufficient to enable the defence to challenge the statements made by the perceived victim.[920] In this case the defence was aware of the victim's identity. Therefore, the question remains what approach the Court will choose in case the perceived victim wants to remain anonymous.[921]

Thus far the question of whether a testimony of a so-called crown witness, who receives benefits in exchange for his testimony, is permissible, has not been brought frequently before the Strasbourg authorities. The Court has recognised that an issue

---

[917]   Judgment of 23 April 1997, paras 56-65. Moreover, the Court held that the conviction was based to a decisive extent on the anonymous statements (para. 63).

[918]   Judgment of 15 June 1992, *Lüdi*, para. 49. (Article 6 had nevertheless been violated because the defence did not have any opportunity to question the undercover agent.) Compare also the reference of the Court in the judgment of 23 April 1997, *Van Mechelen*, para. 60, to the Dutch Act of 11 November 1993 with regard to the use of make-up or disguise and the prevention of eye contact.

[919]   Judgment of 2 July 2002, *S.N. v. Sweden*, para. 52.

[920]   *Ibidem.* The requirements of Article 6 were found not to have been met in the judgment of 14 December 1999, *A.M. v. Italy*, paras 26-28, and the judgment of 10 November 2005, *Bocos-Cuesta*, paras 64-74.

[921]   In the *Baegen* Case, report of 20 October 1994, A.327-B, pp. 44-45, prior to the *Doorson* Case, the conviction of the applicant for rape had been based partly on the anonymous statements of the victim. The Commission held that, despite the lack of any opportunity for the applicant or his lawyer to examine the victim directly, the proceedings had not been unfair. The case has not been pursued before the Court.

under Article 6 may arise, but seems to have no objections of principle to this practice. In the *Erdem* Case the Court declared a complaint with regard to the use of a crown-witness inadmissible. Amongst other things it took into account that the crown witness had not been granted complete immunity but only a reduction of his prison sentence, that no financial benefits had been promised but benefits with regard to police protection and a new identity and that the German practice of granting benefits to crown-witnesses had been regulated by law.[922]

Sub-paragraph (d) does not contain any restriction with respect to the questions which the accused wants to ask the witnesses against him. However, in the case law of the Commission this provision has been deprived of a great deal of its effect because the Commission left very wide discretion to the national court as to which interrogation it allows.[923] If in this respect the court gives evidence of bias, the right to a fair hearing has been violated,[924] but this can hardly be proved. It is submitted that the rationale of paragraph 3(d) is satisfied only if the court affords the accused or counsel ample opportunity for the examination and only makes restrictions in case of manifest abuse or improper use of the right to examination, or if the proceedings are delayed to an unacceptable degree.

In the *Unterpertinger* Case the Commission took the position that the provision of paragraph 3(d) had not been violated, because the prosecution, too, had not had the opportunity to examine the persons concerned.[925] Fortunately this position was not adopted by the Court. Here the Commission transposed the equality principle, which is of decisive importance for the second limb of paragraph 3(d), *viz.* the right to summon witnesses for the defence, to the right to examine witnesses for the prosecution. That position is untenable already from a systematic and grammatical point of view.[926] Moreover, an inequality occurs if the prosecution puts forward a testimony made in a previous phase, since in that previous phase the prosecution has had the opportunity to examine the person in question, albeit perhaps only *via* the police, while the accused has not.

The second limb of paragraph 3(d) clearly allows for discretion on the part of the national court because its only requirement is that the prosecution and the accused receive equal treatment in this respect. With regard to the summoning of witnesses

---

[922] Decision of 9 December 1999. See also the decisions of 27 January 2004, Lorsé, and *Verhoek*; decision of 25 April 2004, *Cornelis*.
[923] See Appl. 4428/70, *X v. Austria*, Yearbook XV (1972), p. 264 (282); Appl. 8417/78, *X v. Belgium*, D&R 16 (1979), p. 200 (207); report of 15 October 1987, *Bricmont*, A.158, p. 45.
[924] This possibility was recognised by the Commission in its decision on Appl. 4428/70, *X v. Austria*, Yearbook XV (1972), p. 264 (284-286).
[925] Report of 11 October 1984, A.110, pp. 19-20.
[926] See the dissenting opinion of Commission member Trechsel, *ibidem*, p. 25.

for the defence and their examination, domestic law and the courts may set conditions and impose restrictions, provided that these equally apply in respect of the witnesses for the prosecution.[927] Moreover, some initiative on the part of the accused may be required as to the calling of witnesses, as well as, of course, during the examination; the court need not call witnesses of its own accord.[928] However, here again the fact that paragraph 3(d) has not been violated does not yet mean that the requirements of the first paragraph have been satisfied. Moreover, the Strasbourg Court has restricted the discretion of the courts somewhat by requiring that the national courts should state the reasons for rejecting a request of the accused to summon a witness.[929]

10.10.6 THE RIGHT TO THE FREE ASSISTANCE OF AN INTERPRETER

Paragraph 3(e), finally, grants to the accused the right to have the free assistance of an interpreter if he cannot understand or speak the language used in court. Thus, the fact that counsel of the accused understands the language used in court does not do away with the latter's right to an interpreter. From paragraph 3(e) it follows that the accused cannot claim that the trial or the examination be conducted in a language other than the official vernacular.

Sub-paragraph (e), too, is linked so closely with the principle of a 'fair hearing' of the first paragraph that also in cases of a determination of civil rights and obligations the necessary costs for a translator or an interpreter may be so burdensome for a party to the proceedings, that non-reimbursement may conflict with the first paragraph.[930]

The right to interpretation is not limited to the trial, but also applies to the pre-trial investigations.[931] In the *Luedicke, Belkacem and Koç* Case the Court held that paragraph 3(e) relates to "all those documents or statements in the proceedings instituted against him which it is necessary for him to understand in order to have the benefit of a fair trial."[932] However, according to the Court, this does not imply that all items of written evidence or official documents have to be translated. The requirement of sub-

---

[927]   Judgment of 22 April 1992, *Vidal*, p. 32.
[928]   Appl. 5881/72, *X v. the United Kingdom* (not published). In its decision the Commission stated that the calling of witnesses "was a matter which was within the discretion of the applicant's solicitor and counsel and the fact that they apparently chose to call only one medical witness does not suggest in any way that the applicant's rights under this provision [i.e. Art. 6(3)(d)] were not respected".
[929]   Judgment of 22 April 1992, *Vidal*, para. 34; judgment of 27 July 2000, *Pisano*, para. 24.
[930]   Report of 18 May 1977, *Luedicke, Belkacem and Koç*, B.27 (1982), p. 26, and report of 9 March 1977, *Airey*, B.30 (1983), p. 32.
[931]   Judgment of 19 December 1989, *Kamasinski*, para. 74.
[932]   Judgment of 28 November 1978, p. 20.

paragraph (e) is met if the accused is enabled to follow, and form an opinion of, the proceedings, so that he can put before the court his comment on the events.[933]

In the *Kamasinski* Case the questions put to the witnesses were not interpreted separately. The interpretation at the trial was "consecutive and summarising". This does in itself not amount to a violation of subparagraph (e). Neither does the absence of a written translation of the verdict, as long as the accused has sufficient knowledge of the judgment and its reasoning to judge whether he should give notice of appeal.[934]

The obligation to appoint an interpreter rests on the competent authorities, although some personal initiative of the accused may be required.[935] In the *Cuscani* Case the requirements of Article 6 had not been satisfied by leaving it to the applicant to invoke the untested language skills of his brother. Since the judge had been alerted to counsel's own difficulties in communicating with the applicant, the verification of the applicant's need for interpretation facilities was a matter for the judge to determine.[936] The obligation to appoint an interpreter is not fulfilled by merely appointing one. If the authorities "are put on notice in the particular circumstances, [it] may also extend to a degree of a subsequent control over the adequacy of the interpretation provided".[937]

In German legal practice paragraph 3(e) was applied in such a way that an interpreter was indeed freely made available to begin with, but the expense involved was ultimately made to fall under the general regulation concerning the costs of the suit. This was considered by the Court to be contrary to the word 'free'.[938] Moreover, the Court indicated that paragraph 3(e) refers not only to the expenses of an interpreter, but also to translation expenses, and then not only to the expenses relating to the hearing itself, but also to those concerning the translation of the charge brought against the accused, as referred to in Article 6(3)(a), and of the reasons for the arrest and the charges.

---

[933] Judgment of 19 December 1989, *Kamasinski*, para. 74; judgment of 14 January 2003, *Lagerblom*, para. 61.

[934] Judgment of 19 December 1989, para. 83.

[935] Appl. 2689/65, *X v. Belgium*, Yearbook X (1967), p. 282 (318).

[936] Judgment of 24 September 2002, para. 38.

[937] Judgment of 19 December 1989, *Kamasinski*, para. 74.

[938] Judgment of 28 November 1978, *Luedicke, Belkacem and Koç*, paras 39-46.

CHAPTER 11
FREEDOM FROM RETROSPECTIVE EFFECT OF PENAL LEGISLATION
(Article 7)

REVISED BY EDWIN BLEICHRODT

CONTENTS

11.1 TEXT OF ARTICLE 7

1. *No one shall be held guilty of any criminal offence on account of any act or omission which did not constitute a criminal offence under national or international law at the time when it was committed. Nor shall a heavier penalty be imposed than the one that was applicable at the time the criminal offence was committed.*
2. *This Article shall not prejudice the trial and punishment of any person for any act or omission which, at the time when it was committed, was criminal according to the general principles of law recognised by civilised nations.*

11.2 THE SCOPE OF ARTICLE 7

The first paragraph of Article 7 contains the following two separate principles, which are essential elements of the Rule of Law: (1) a criminal conviction can only be based on a norm which existed at the time of the incriminating act or omission *(nullum crimen sine lege);* and (2) on account of the infringement of that norm no heavier penalty may be imposed than the one that was applicable at the time the offence was committed *(nulla poena sine lege).* Thus, Article 7 intends to offer "essential safeguards against arbitrary prosecution, conviction and punishment".[1] In this way it occupies a primordial place in the Convention system of protection, as is underlined by the fact that no derogation from it is permissible under Article 15 in time of war or other public emergency.

In addition to the principles of *nullum crimen* and *nulla poena* the Court has distinguished a third principle: the authority applying criminal law shall interpret it not extensively, for instance by analogy, to the accused's detriment. From this third principle follows, according to the Court, that an offence must be clearly defined in law.[2] New, more severe legislation cannot be applied to an ongoing situation that arose before it came into force.[3] It is submitted, however, that this third principle is not a separate one, but is embodied in the rationale of the *nullum crimen* and *nulla poena sine lege* principles.

The principles *nulla crimen sine lege* and *nulla poena sine lege* are two separate principles. That means, *inter alia,* that even a purely declaratory judgment in which a norm of criminal law is applied with retrospective effect and is declared to have been infringed, but in which no punishment or other measure is imposed on the offender, constitutes a violation of Article 7. This is not without importance, because such a declaratory judgment, when registered, may still have prejudicial consequences for the person in question, even apart from the social repercussions that it may entail.

11.3 NULLUM CRIMEN NULLA POENA SINE LEGE

By virtue of the wording of Article 7 the 'penalty' must be imposed following a conviction for a 'criminal offence'. The Court takes this as a starting-point. It seems to be obvious that the meaning of the words 'criminal offence' is closely related to the notion of 'criminal charge' in Article 6. Thus, it is appropriate to argue that Article 7 is also applicable to those disciplinary and administrative convictions which come within the scope of Article 6. In the *Dogan* Case the Court noted that the alleged eviction of the applicants from their homes and the restrictions on their return to their village did not concern 'a criminal charge' against them within the meaning of Article 6 (1). The Court held that it followed that the events and the measures complained of in the instant case did not concern 'a criminal offence' for the purpose

---

[1] Judgment of 25 May 1993, *Kokkinakis,* para. 52; Judgment of 22 November 1995, *S.W. and C.R. v. the United Kingdom,* paras 35 and 33; judgment of 22 July 2003, *Gabarri Moreno,* para. 22.

[2] Judgment of 25 May 1993, *Kokkinakis,* para. 52; judgment of 22 June 2000, *Coëme,* para. 145.

[3] Judgment of 10 November 2004, *Achour,* para. 37. This judgment has been referred to the Grand Chamber.

of Article 7 either.[4] It may, therefore, be concluded that the terms 'criminal offence' and 'criminal charge' have the same scope.

The term 'penalty' is also autonomous in scope. To render the protection afforded by Article 7 effective the Court can go behind appearances and assess for itself whether a particular measure amounts in substance to a 'penalty' within the meaning of this provision.[5] The text of the Convention is the starting-point for such an assessment whether or not Article 7 is applicable. The Court may also use other sources, such as the *travaux préparatoires*. It may also take into consideration the notions currently prevailing in democratic States.[6] Factors that may be relevant are: the characterisation of the measure under national law, its nature and purpose, the procedures involved in the making and implementation of the measure and its severity.[7] The fact that the applicant feels that the effects of the sanction are punitive, is not sufficient to establish that the sanction has a punitive purpose under Article 7;[8] the purpose of the sanction must be established in an objective way. In the *Welch* Case the Court concluded that a confiscation order imposed in addition to a sentence of imprisonment did constitute a 'penalty'. The fact that the confiscation order had also reparative and preventive aims was not decisive.[9] In view of the combination of punitive elements, the confiscation order turned into a penalty.[10] In the *Jamil* Case it was held that the prolongation of a term of imprisonment in default resulted in the applicability of Article 7.[11] The Court took into account that the sanction was ordered by a criminal court, was intended to be deterrent and could have led to a punitive deprivation of liberty. A demolition order, which did not depend on any finding of guilt and which had a restorative aim, did not constitute a 'penalty' within the meaning of Article 7.[12]

It follows from Article 7 that an offence must be clearly defined in law. The term 'law' in Article 7 alludes to the same concept as the one to which the Convention refers elsewhere when using that term.[13] The provisions have to be sufficiently foreseeable

---

[4] Judgment of 29 June 2004, para. 126. See also the judgment of 7 July 1989, *Tre Traktörer Aktiebolag*, para. 46.

[5] Judgment of 9 February 1995, *Welch*, para. 27; judgment of 10 November 2004, *Achour*, para. 34.

[6] See, *e.g.*, the judgment of 6 November 1980, *Guzzardi*, para. 95 and the judgment of 22 June 2000, *Coëme*, para. 145.

[7] Judgment of 9 February 1995, *Welch*, para. 28; judgment of 8 June 1995, *Jamil*, para. 31.

[8] Decision of 26 January 1999, *Adamson*.

[9] Judgment of 9 February 1995, paras 27-35; judgment of 8 June 1995, *Jamil*, para. 32.

[10] Judgment of 9 February 1995, *Welch*, para. 35. The Court distinguished several punitive elements. The combination of these gave the confiscation order the character of a 'penalty'. The Court stressed, however, that the severity of the order was not in itself decisive because "many non-penal measures of a preventive nature may have a substantial impact on the person concerned".

[11] Judgment of 8 June 1995, paras 34-36.

[12] Decision of 23 November 2004, *Saliba*.

[13] See, *e.g.*, the judgment of 22 June 2000, *Coëme*, para. 145.

and accessible.[14] This requirement serves to avoid a criminal conviction being based on a legal norm of which the person concerned could not, or at least need not, have been aware of beforehand. This condition is satisfied if the individual may know from the wording of the relevant provision and, if need be, from the relevant case law, what acts and omissions will make him liable.[15] In the *Grigoriades* Case the Court held that the offence of insulting the army was couched in very broad terms, but nonetheless met the standard of foreseeability.[16] The Court took into consideration that, however clearly drafted a legal provision may be, there is always an inevitable element of judicial interpretation. It is inevitable for the making of legal provisions that more or less vague wordings are used. The Court also accepts that legal provisions must have a certain flexibility to handle changing circumstances and to avoid excessive rigidity. In that context the area of the legal provision seems to be relevant for the degree of discretion of the national authorities. The *Başkaya and Okçuolu* Case was related to the Turkish Prevention of Terrorism Act 1991, in which the "dissemination of propaganda against the indivisibility of the State" was construed as an offence. The Court recognised that in the area under consideration it may be difficult to frame laws with absolute precision and that a certain degree of flexibility may be called for to enable the national courts to assess whether a publication should be considered separatist propaganda against the indivisibility of the State.[17]

Not only statutory law, but also rules of common law or customary law may provide a sufficient legal basis for a criminal conviction, provided that the law is adequately accessible and is formulated with sufficient precision to enable the person concerned to regulate his conduct.[18] In the *Kokkinakis* Case the Court based its decision on the existence of a constant case law. The Court held that the applicant, who was born in an orthodox family, could have known that the conversion to the religion of the Jehovah's witnesses made him liable under the Greek law that declared proselytism a criminal offence. It did so by referring to its conclusion in the same judgment, under Article 9 of the Convention: the legal limitation of the freedom of religion met the requirement 'prescribed by law' because there existed an established case law concerning the relevant legal provision, that was "published and accessible".[19]

Since common law is by definition law developed by courts, Article 7(1) may raise special problems there. In *S.W. v. the United Kingdom* and *C.R. v. the United Kingdom*

---

14 Judgment of 27 September 1995, *G. v. France*, paras 24-25.
15 See, *e.g.*, the judgment of 22 November 1995, *S.W. and C.R. v. the United Kingdom*, paras 35 and 33; judgment of 21 January 2003, *Veeber*, para. 31; decision of 30 March 2003, *Radio France*, para. 20.
16 Judgment of 25 November 1997, para. 38.
17 Judgment of 8 July 1999, para. 39. See also the judgment of 7 February 2002, *E.K. v. Turkey*, para. 52.
18 Appl. 8710/79, *X Ltd. and Y v. the United Kingdom*, D&R 28 (1982), p. 77 (80-81). For these conditions, cf. the judgment of 26 April 1979, *Sunday Times*, para. 49.
19 Judgment of 25 May 1993, para. 52 in conjunction with paras 37-41. See also: judgment of 24 February 1998, *Larissis*, para. 34.

the Court held that Article 7 "cannot be read as outlawing the gradual clarification of the rules of criminal liability through judicial interpretation from case to case, provided that the resultant development is consistent with the essence of the offence and could reasonably be foreseen."[20] In these cases the Court reached the conclusion that the decision of the national courts to lift the immunity of a man from prosecution for rape of his wife constituted a "reasonably foreseeable development of law". Moreover, since the "essentially debasing character of rape" was manifest, the applicants could not claim that they had been subjected to an arbitrary prosecution, conviction and punishment.[21] Is seems to have been relevant that values that the Convention tries to protect were at issue. The same approach provides for a clearer understanding of the two judgments with regard to the murder of a number of people who had attempted to escape from the former German Democratic Republic (GDR) between 1971 and 1989 by crossing the border between the two German States. The Court considered, in order to assess whether the conviction of murder was lawful, the relevant rules of the GDR's written law and the nature of the GDR's State practice. A complicating factor was that there was a contradiction between the legal provisions on the one hand and the very repressive practice of the border-policy regime on the other. The Court took into account that the State practice not only contradicted the GDR's Constitution and legal provisions, but was also in breach of the obligation to respect human rights, i.e. the right of life. In those circumstances State practice cannot be condidered as 'law' within the meaning of Article 7. A State practice such as the GDR's border-policing policy, which flagrantly infringed human rights and above all the right to life, the supreme value in the international hierarchy of human rights, could not be covered by the protection of Article 7(1) of the Convention. The Court held that, at the time when they were committed, the applicants' acts constituted offences defined with sufficient accessibility and foreseeability by GDR law and by the rules of international law concerning the protection of human rights.[22]

In the *Cantoni* Case criminal law contained the term 'medicinal products' instead of describing each product that fell within the scope of the law separately. The existence of a 'grey area' does not in itself make a provision incompatible with Article 7, provided that it proves to be sufficiently clear in the large majority of cases. The role of the courts is to dissipate such interpretational doubts as remain, taking into account the changes in everyday practice. The Court considered that the scope of the notion of foreseeability depends to a considerable degree on the content of the text in issue, the field it is designed to cover and the number and status of those to whom it is addressed. Persons carrying on a professional activity can be expected to take special

---

[20]   Judgments of 22 November 1995, para. 36 and para. 34, respectively.
[21]   *Ibidem*, paras 44-45 and para. 42, respectively.
[22]   Judgment of 22 March 2001, *Streletz, Kessler and Krenz*, paras 53-91; judgment of 22 March 2001, *K.-H. W. v. Germany*, paras 48-91.

care in assessing the risks that such activity entails. The Court held that Mr Cantoni, who was the manager of a supermarket, should have appreciated at the material time that, in view of the line of case law, he ran a real risk of prosecution for unlawful sale of medicinal products.[23] In the *Coëme* Case the question arose whether the immediate application of the extension of a limitation period after the prosecution had started, entailed an infringement of Article 7. In the Court's view Article 7 cannot be interpreted as prohibiting an extension of limitation periods through the immediate application of a procedural law where the relevant offences have never become subject to limitation.[24] The Court did not answer the question whether Article 7 would be infringed if a legal provision would restore the possibility of punishing offenders for acts which were no longer punishable because they had already become subject to limitation.

When the national court has relied on previous case law, the Court has to be on the alert that this case law does not imply in fact an aggravation of the norm since the time the act was committed.

In principle the national legislature is free to decide what act or omission is to be qualified as an offence and has to be penalised. Article 7 is not in issue there. The European review in that case is confined to the question of whether or not any of the other provisions of the Convention has been violated by that legislation.

The word 'heavier' in the second sentence of Article 7(1) seems to refer merely to the severity of the punishment, but the rationale for this provision entails that also a punishment of a different kind than the one formerly provided for, which reasonably may be felt as more burdensome by the person in question, shall not be applied with retrospective effect.

The *nulla poena* principle with its requirement of legal certainty does not go to such lengths that the exact measure of the penalty, or an exhaustive enumeration of alternatives, must be laid down in the criminal law provision. If, as is customary in several legal systems, only the maxima are indicated, the legal subjects know what is the maximum penalty they may incur upon violation of the norm. The Court examines whether the maximum penalty is not exceeded.[25] If a violation of the norm is penalised without a maximum being laid down, in the literal sense there can be no question of 'a heavier penalty (...) than the one that was applicable at the time the criminal offence was committed', unless at the latter time a different penalty was provided for. In that case, however, the second sentence of Article 7(1) will have to be interpreted to mean

---

[23]   Judgment of 22 October 1996, para. 35. See also the judgment of 17 February 2005, *K.A. and A.D. v. Belgium*, paras 56-58.
[24]   Judgment of 22 June 2000, para. 149.
[25]   See, *e.g.*, the judgment of 22 July 2003, *Gabarri Moreno*, para. 33.

that the 'applicable penalty' is the penalty which is usually inflicted for that particular offence within the legal system concerned, or which in any event was reasonably to be expected for the offender.

What is the situation if after the time the offence was committed, but before the trial, the norm of criminal law or the penalty has been modified in a sense which is more favourable for the accused? Do the courts then have to apply that modified provision? Article 15 of the UN Covenant on Civil and Political Rights expressly provides as follows: "If, subsequent to the commission of the offence, provision is made by law for the imposition of a lighter penalty, the offender shall benefit thereby." Such a provision is lacking in Article 7 of the Convention. The words 'at the time the criminal offence was committed' suggest that this provision does not confer a right to application of the norm as subsequently alleviated, or of the lowered penalty.[26] However, as observed above, Article 7 clearly does not prohibit such an application either. It may even be prescribed by domestic law, as was the case in *G. v. France*.[27] The lack of a provision of this import in Article 7 is to be regretted, but it may be hoped that every court, except in special circumstances, will exercise this clemency if its domestic law leaves any scope for doing so.

It is possible that the way of execution of the sentence is heavier than was reasonably foreseeable at the time the sentence was imposed. In general the way of execution of a sentence falls beyond the scope of Article 7. In the *Grava* Case the Court held that a system of remission does not influence the heaviness of a penalty because it concerns the execution of the sentence and not the sentence as such.[28] The Court referred to a similar opinion of the Commission about parole. However, the distinction between the penalty and the execution of the penalty is not always so strict as the Court suggests, especially when changes of the applicable law have consequences for the length of the penalty. It is desirable that, just like the interpretation of the term 'criminal charge', not only the classification is considered relevant, but also the assessment of whether or not the nature of the penalty in essence has become heavier.

---

[26]   Appl. 3777/68, *I. v. the United Kingdom*, Coll. 31 (1970), p. 120 (122); Appl. 7900/77, *X v. Federal Republic of Germany*, D&R 13 (1979), p. 70 (71-72).

[27]   Judgment of 27 September 1995.

[28]   Judgment of 10 July 2003, para. 51.

11.4 APPLICATION WITH RETROSPECTIVE EFFECT

Article 7 prohibits the retrospective application of criminal law to the detriment of the accused. Article 7 clearly does not oppose retrospective application of criminal law in favour of the accused.[29] The use of the term 'retrospective effect' in the title of this subsection is misleading insofar that under Article 7(1) it is of course equally prohibited to continue to apply in the old form any norms of criminal law or sanctions which had already been repealed or modified before the time of the offence.[30] Accordingly, it also forms part of the review by the Court to examine whether and to what extent the norm of criminal law applied still had effect at the relevant time. Since this is essentially a question of national (constitutional) law, the answer will be guided to a high degree by the opinion of the national courts on the matter.[31] Nevertheless, it is ultimately incumbent upon the Court to decide whether Article 7 has been correctly applied.

If it is evident from the legal practice in the country concerned that a particular norm of criminal law has fallen completely into desuetude, so that the offender could not reasonably presume that acting contrary to this norm would result in prosecution, it conflicts with Article 7 if that norm is applied in his case. It is, however, obvious that in such a case a heavy burden of proof rests on the applicant.

The words 'be held guilty' and 'be imposed' at first sight point in the direction that Article 7 can only be held to have been violated if a norm of criminal law has actually been applied with retrospective effect, and not merely on the basis of the fact that such a retrospective effect has been made possible by the legislature.[32] However, one should not overlook the fact that the Convention is addressed to the Contracting States and accordingly to all the organs of these States, including the legislature. If the legislature gives retrospective effect to a provision of criminal law, Article 7 of the Convention has been violated. It is true that such a violation in general cannot be the object of an individual complaint, because it is not yet possible to speak of a victim.[33] It is, however, one of the characteristic features of the equally provided possibility of State complaints that legislation may be submitted *in abstracto* to review for its compatibility with the Convention without it being necessary to allege that there are (already) individual victims of the application of that law.

---

[29] Judgment of 25 May 1993, *Kokkinakis*, para. 52.

[30] Appl. 1169/61, *X v. Federal Republic of Germany,* Yearbook VI (1963), p. 520 (588); Appl. 7721/76, *X v. the Netherlands,* D&R 11 (1978), p. 209 (211).

[31] *Ibidem.*

[32] This view seems to be implied in the report in the *Greek* Case, Yearbook XII (1969), p. 185: "It is not disputed that the penalties provided (...) have not been imposed in any actual case".

[33] In specific cases, however, the mere existence of a criminal law provision, even when it has not yet been applied in a concrete case, may hinder a person so much in his freedom of action that he can already be regarded as a victim. See *supra,* 1.13.3.3. concerning 'potential victim'.

Problems may arise in the case of continuous offences, i.e. a type of crimes committed over a period of time, while the conviction is based on a law that has entered into force in the course of this period. If an accused is charged with a continuing offence, the principle of legal certainty requires that the acts which make up that offence and which entail his criminal liability, be clearly set out in the bill of indictment.[34] The decision by the domestic court must make it clear that the conviction and sentence are based on evidence concerning the ingredients of a continuing offence. In the *Veeber* Case, a considerable number of the acts on the basis of which the applicant was convicted, took place before the extension of the law. The Court observed that it could not be concluded with any certainty that the domestic courts' approach had no effect on the severity of the punishment or did not entail tangible negative consequences for the applicant. Article 7 was violated.[35]

11.5 NATIONAL OR INTERNATIONAL LAW

Article 7 refers to 'a criminal offence under national or international law'. With respect to the word 'national' the question arises whether exclusively the national law of the State concerned is meant or whether this State may also attach certain criminal law consequences to the violation, within another State, of a provision of the criminal law of the latter State which does not form part of the criminal law of the first-mentioned State. On this point the Strasbourg case law does not provide clarity. It is submitted that the words 'national (...) law' must be understood to mean that a criminal judgment can be based only on the national law of the State in question and not on the law of another State; but the wording of Article 7 would not appear to exclude the possibility that certain consequences are attached in State A to a judgment pronounced in State B on the basis of the criminal law applying in State B at that time, even if the fact concerned is not punishable according to the law of State A. The Court has held it to be legitimate for a State governed by the rule of law to bring criminal proceedings against persons who have committed crimes under a former regime. The courts of such a State, having taken the place of those which existed previously, cannot be criticised for applying and interpreting the legal provisions in force at the material time in the light of the principles governing a State subject to the rule of law.[36]

The reference to international law in the first paragraph of Article 7 raises the question of the internal effect of international law within the national legal order. In Chapter I it has already been pointed out that, according to prevalent opinion,

---

[34]   Judgment of 27 February 2001, *Ecer and Zeyrek*, para. 33.
[35]   Judgment of 21 January 2003, para. 36.
[36]   Judgment of 22 March 2001, *Streletz, Kessler and Kreuz*, para. 81; judgment of 22 March 2001, *K.-H.W. v. Germany*, para. 84.

international law as it stands does not oblige States to give internal effect to provisions of international law without their prior 'transformation' into domestic law. Neither does such an obligation ensue from the Convention. The effect of international law within the national legal order is regulated by national constitutional law. In those Contracting States where international law has no internal effect, this effect cannot be given in incidental cases to an international criminal law provision. Here again compliance with Article 7 depends on whether the person concerned could reasonably know that the offence committed by him was prohibited and punishable within the relevant legal system at that time, either by virtue of a national legal provision or by virtue of a directly applicable international legal provision with internal effect.[37]

11.6 THE EXCEPTION IN THE SECOND PARAGRAPH

The second paragraph of Article 7 contains an exception to the first paragraph for the case of the trial and punishment of an act or omission which, at the time when it was committed or omitted, was a criminal offence according to general principles of law. Although this provision is formulated in a general way, it has evidently been incorporated in particular to enable the application of the national and international legislation, enacted during and after World War II, in respect of war crimes, collaboration with the enemy and treason, to facts committed during the war.[38] In that sense it constitutes a codification of the principles laid down by the tribunals of Nuremberg and Tokyo.[39]

However, the second paragraph may also apply to cases other than those mentioned above. In fact, it does not relate exclusively to war crimes, but to all acts and omissions which are criminal 'according to the general principles of law recognised by civilised nations'. Since Article 7(2) does not refer to 'the principles of law common to the Contracting States', but to 'the general principles of law recognised by civilised nations', the Contracting States may not be treated as an isolated group in this respect. The legal rule concerned will also have to be recognised outside this circle by a 'representative' group of States, if the principle of law is to be regarded as a general one. In addition, or frequently also in correlation therewith, general principles of law may emerge from international law as it develops, usually on the basis of a pattern of

---

[37] *Ibidem*, paras 91 and 93, respectively.

[38] Thus also the Commission in its decision on, *e.g.*, Appl. 1038/61, *X v. Belgium*, Yearbook IV (1961), p. 324 (336).

[39] See Principle II of the Nuremberg Principles as formulated in 1950 by the International Law Commission, Yearbook I.L.C., 1950, Vol. II, p. 379: "The fact that international law does not impose a penalty for an act which constitutes a crime under international law does not relieve the person who committed the act from responsibility under international law."

treaties which have been concluded and/or of an international practice which has been or is in the process of being formed. They can then hardly be distinguished from customary international law. Be this as it may, the concept of general principles of law as here referred to requires that the facts concerned are not only made punishable in the legal systems of nearly all countries and/or under international law, but that their punishable character ensues from a fundamental and generally recognized principle of law. Indeed, otherwise the guarantee of the first paragraph would be seriously jeopardised in all those cases where the legislature deliberately derogates from the criminal law as it applies in most countries in a way which is detrimental for the accused.

All this makes it difficult to establish with any accuracy what offences are meant by Article 7(2). This is particularly the case because here not the responsibility of the State but the responsibility of individuals is at issue, a matter which usually is not regulated by international law. In addition to the above-mentioned war crimes one will have to think in particular of the so-called crimes against peace and crimes against humanity. A definition is contained in the Charter of the International Military Tribunal,[40] but in later documents the category of crimes against humanity has also been placed outside the war context.[41] It seems logical to also link the general principles of law of Article 7(2) with fundamental principles in the field of human rights such as the prohibition of torture and racial discrimination. For the applicability of Article 7(2) it is required that the violation of these principles by individuals is punishable according to the national law of (practically) all countries, or that under international law not only the State but also the offender individually is responsible for it. Only then is it possible to speak of a 'criminal act or omission'.[42] Violation of the above-mentioned fundamental rights will be punishable in one form or another in most national systems. However, to the extent that general principles of international law have not been incorporated in one way or another in domestic law, they can serve as a basis for the conviction of individuals only in those cases where the violation of these principles can be qualified as a 'crime against humanity'.[43] In other cases, in our

---

[40]   See Art. 6 of the Charter of the International Military Tribunal, AJIL 39, 1945, Supplement, p. 257.

[41]   Art. I(b) of the Convention on the Non-Applicability of Statutory Limitations to War Crimes and Crimes against Humanity (ILM 8, 1969, p. 68), speaks of "crimes against humanity, whether committed in time of war or in time of peace", and mentions as examples "inhuman acts resulting from the policy of apartheid and the crime of genocide". Compare also the enumeration in the Statute of the International Tribunal for the Prosecution of Persons Responsible for Serious Violations of International Humanitarian Law Committed in the Territory of the Former Yugoslavia since 1991, UN Doc. S25704.

[42]   For war crimes and crimes against humanity this individual responsibility has been laid down in the above-mentioned documents. See also Art. I of the Convention on the Prevention and Punishment of the Crime of Genocide; Art. 1(2) of the International Convention on the Suppression and Punishment of the Crime of Apartheid; and Art. 7 of the Statute of the Yugoslavia Tribunal.

[43]   'Crimes against humanity' used in the sense of also including war crimes, genocide, apartheid and the most fundamental human rights. See the two preceding notes.

opinion, individual responsibility is not yet established clearly enough under international law as it stands at present.

11.7 DEROGATION

According to Article 15(2) the guarantee implied in Article 7(1) is non-derogable. As has been observed, however, the consequence of the second paragraph of Article 7 is that with respect to certain offences this guarantee is not an absolute one, neither in the situations referred to in Article 15(1) nor in other cases.

CHAPTER 12
RIGHT TO RESPECT FOR PRIVACY
(Article 8)

REVISED BY AALT WILLEM HERINGA AND LEO ZWAAK

CONTENTS

12.1   TEXT OF ARTICLE 8

1. *Everyone has the right to respect for his private and family life, his home and his correspondence.*
2. *There shall be no interference by a public authority with the exercise of this right except such as is in accordance with the law and is necessary in a democratic society in the interests of national security, public safety or the economic well-being of the country, for the prevention of disorder or crime, for the protection of health or morals, or for the protection of the rights and freedoms of others.*

12.2   INTRODUCTION

Article 8 protects the rights mentioned in the first paragraph. In particular the notion of private life can be considered to be a rather general one, which is open for interpretation. The Court has so far declined to give an exhaustive definition.[1] The notions

---

[1]   See, *e.g.*, judgment of 16 December 1992, *Niemietz*, para. 29; judgment of 28 January 2003, *Peck*, para. 57.

of family life, home and correspondence have to a great extent been defined in the Court's case law, to which appropriate attention will be paid in the following sections. The notion of private life has been filled by the Court more gradually and at a later moment. An overview was given by the Court in the *Pretty* Case, where it held as follows: "As the Court has had previous occasion to remark, the concept of 'private life' is a broad term not susceptible to exhaustive definition. It covers the physical and psychological integrity of a person (…). It can sometimes embrace aspects of an individual's physical and social identity (…). Elements such as, for example, gender identification, name and sexual orientation and sexual life fall within the sphere protected by Article 8 (…). Article 8 also protects a right to personal development, and the right to establish and develop relationships with other human beings and the outside world (…). Though no previous case law has established any right to self-determination as being contained in Article 8 of the Convention as such, the Court considers that the notion of personal autonomy is an important principle underlying the interpretation of its guarantees."[2]

This interpretation, as will be shown *infra*, has led the Court to give a broad interpretation to the notion of private life and the underlying principles. However, the use of the notion of private life or privacy to indicate the whole of the rights in Article 8 might be misleading. The Court seems willing to accept that Article 8 is to be understood as containing various guarantees to personal autonomy, personal privacy, personal identity, personal integrity, personal development, personal identification and similar concepts linked to the individual notion of personhood. Article 8, therefore, protects much more than a straightforward 'right to privacy'.

In the *Sidabras and Dziautas* Case the Court accepted the exclusion of former KGB employees from State functions as falling within the scope of Article 8 (for the purposes of the applicability of Article 14). According to the Court this general ban affected private life: the impugned ban affected, to a significant degree, the possibility for the applicants to pursue various professional activities and there were consequential effects for their private life such as "the applicants' ability to develop relationships with the outside world to a significant degree and as regard the possibility to earn their living, with obvious repercussions on their enjoyment of their private life".[3]

Two elements of the right to privacy which are not explicitly mentioned in Article 8 are referred to in Article 10(2) as grounds for restriction of the freedom of expression: the protection of a person's reputation and the prevention of disclosure of information received in confidence. In order to rely on such grounds, however, an express legal basis is required; the restrictions must be such 'as are prescribed by law'. Moreover, it has been recognised by the Court that the right to protection of one's

---

[2]   Judgment of 29 April 2002, para. 60.
[3]   Judgment of 27 July 2004, para. 50.

reputation constitutes a 'civil right' in the sense of Article 6(1).[4] Whether these and other comparable interests also find protection in Article 8 depends on the content given in the national and European case law to the rights expressly mentioned therein. In this context it is noteworthy that, although the *travaux préparatoires* appear to point in a different direction, the Court seems to have implicitly recognised the possibility that attacks on a person's reputation may constitute a breach of Article 8.[5] In the *Niemietz* Case the Court referred to the applicant's 'professional reputation' as a relevant and important element in the context of Article 8.[6] In the *Von Hannover* Case the Court struck a balance between freedom of speech and the freedom of the press to report on public figures, and the latter's right to privacy. In that respect the Court ruled that the privacy of public figures is limited to those areas of their private life where it is obvious that they have retreated in order to be alone.[7]

12.3 PRIVATE LIFE

In accordance with the approach followed by the Court to adopt a broad concept of private life, in this sub-section on private life the following aspects will be discussed: registration (of persons, files and data); medical examination; homosexuality, abortion and transsexualism, grouped together under the heading 'sexual privacy'; name; physical integrity; and personal autonomy. These aspects do not cover all issues that may be related to the private life element of Article 8. One needs only to think of new genetic and medical techniques. However, they do reflect the existing case law of the Court and provide a sufficient framework for discussing that case law.

12.3.1 REGISTRATION

12.3.1.1 Registration of personal data

The registration of personal data has been a vital issue of the notion of privacy. In the Commission's opinion, registration by the police does not conflict with Article 8, not even when the registration concerns persons who do not have any criminal record.[8]

---

4   See *supra* 10.2.8.
5   Judgment of 21 September 1994, *Fayed,* para. 67.
6   Judgment of 16 December 1992, para. 37.
7   Judgment of 24 June 2004, para. 76.
8   See Appl. 5877/72, *X v. the United Kingdom,* Yearbook XVI (1973), p. 328 (388), where the complaint concerned taking photographs of the applicant by the police for possible future identification purposes, and storing these in a file. The Commission evidently considered it decisive here that the photographs had not been released for publication or used for purposes other than police ends.

Without any further qualifications, such a viewpoint would appear to be hardly tenable. It must be examined explicitly whether one of the grounds of restriction mentioned in the second paragraph is applicable. Moreover, a review of the collection and use of the data for its compatibility with the *détournement de pouvoir* prohibition of Article 18 might be required. Such a review actually took place in a case, which concerned the transmission of personal data by the police to a criminal court. The Commission considered this justified in the interest of the prevention of crime, although this case concerned the prosecution of a crime and not its prevention. The Commission left the question of whether the act complained of conflicted at all with the first paragraph open.[9] From the judgment in *P.G. and J.H. v. the United Kingdom* it is evident that the Court will always check the conformity with paragraph 2, even in the case of the registration of data in a police investigation.[10]

In the *Leander* Case the complaint concerned the fact that information derived from the secret police register had prevented the applicant from obtaining permanent employment and had led to his dismissal from provisional employment, while the authorities had refused to disclose that information to him. In that case, review of justification on the basis of the second paragraph was performed after the Court had reached the conclusion that the facts (storing in and release from a secret police-register of information relating to Leander's private life, coupled with a refusal to allow Leander an opportunity to refute it) disclosed an interference with the applicant's right to respect for his private life. The Commission had agreed with the Government that the issue depended on the contents of the register concerned. A register which only contained, for instance, the name and address of an individual did, in their opinion, not normally involve any interference with Article 8. The Court did not make this distinction. It simply stated that it was "uncontested that the secret police-register contained information relating to Mr. Leander's private life."[11] The Court granted a wide margin of appreciation to the respondent State in assessing the pressing social need of the interference, and in particular in choosing the means for achieving the legitimate aim of protecting national security. It held as follows: "There can be no doubt as to the necessity, for the purpose of protecting national security, for the Contracting States to have laws granting the competent domestic authorities power, firstly, to collect and store in registers not accessible to the public information on persons and, secondly, to use this information when assessing the suitability of candidates for employment in posts of importance for national security. Admittedly, the contested interference adversely affected Mr Leander's legitimate interests through the consequences it had on his possibilities of access to certain sensitive posts within the public service. On the other hand, the right of access to public services is not as such

---

9   Appl. 8170/78, *X v. Austria*, Yearbook XXII (1979), p. 308 (320-322).
10   Judgment of 25 September 2001, paras 56-63.
11   Judgment of 26 March 1987, para. 48.

enshrined in the Convention (…), and, apart from those consequences, the interference did not constitute an obstacle to his leading a private life of his own choosing."[12] After a detailed discussion of the intelligence system concerned, *inter alia*, the efficacy of control procedures, the Court concluded as follows: "Having regard to the wide margin of appreciation available to it, the respondent State was entitled to consider that in the present case the interests of national security prevailed over the individual interests of the applicant. The interference to which Mr Leander was subjected cannot therefore be said to have been disproportionate to the legitimate aim pursued."[13]

In the *Murray* Case the Court confirmed that article 8 covers "recording personal details concerning (the applicant) and her family, as well as the photograph which was taken of her without her knowledge or consent."[14] In the *Rotaru* Case, the Court referred to its findings in the *Leander Case* to establish the applicability of Article 8 with respect to secret police files which were kept for fifty years and which were partly of a defamatory content. The Court held: "Public information can fall within the scope of private life where it is systematically collected and stored in files held by the authorities. That is all the truer where such information concerns a person's distant past."[15] The Court concluded that Article 8 had been violated because the interference did not have a sufficient legal basis.

In *X. v. the United Kingdom* the obligation to complete a census form was challenged. The Commission took the view that a compulsory public census, including questions relating to the sex, marital status, place of birth and other personal details, may constitute a *prima facie* interference with the right to respect for private and family life, which fails to be justified under the terms of the second paragraph of Article 8. Here again, however, as in the *Leander* Case, the Commission found that the interference was justified as being necessary in a democratic society – in this case 'in the interest of the economic well-being of the country'.[16]

In the *Filip Reyntjens* Case the Commission dismissed complaints about the Belgian system implying an obligation to carry an identity-card and to show it to the police on request. Since this card only contains information concerning name, sex, date of birth and place of residence, the Commission was of the opinion that there was no interference in the private life of the applicant.[17]

In addition to the registration by the police and the judiciary, and to public census, all of which have a long tradition, registration of all sorts of personal data by public

---

[12]   *Ibidem*, para. 59.
[13]   *Ibidem*, para. 67.
[14]   Judgment of 28 October 1994, para. 84.
[15]   Judgment of 4 May 2000, para. 43.
[16]   Appl. 9702/82, D&R 30 (1983), p. 239 (240-241).
[17]   Appl. 16810/90, D&R 73 (1992), p. 136 (152). See also recommendation No. R(87)15 of the Committee of Ministers to Member States regulating the use of personal data in the police sector, Yearbook XXX (1987), pp. 12-218.

authorities and private institutions is taking place to an increasing degree, in particular as a result of the development of technology, which makes the automatic storage and processing of data possible. In most cases the use that is made of such data cannot be checked by the person concerned, so that, even if he has furnished the data of his own free will, that use may still imply an interference with his private life. In this respect the public authorities are bound by Article 8, and, according to the *Gaskin* judgment, the individual concerned in principle can claim a right to access.[18]

12.3.1.2 Access to data

The *Gaskin* Case concerned a complaint about refusal of access to a file. Mr Gaskin wished to have access to the whole file relating to his period in care. The applicant had been taken into care at a very young age, after the death of his mother and had remained in care until he attained his majority. The complaint was presented against the background of his severe psychological problems, which he ascribed to the way in which he was treated while in care. This case differed from the *Leander* Case as far as the character of the data was concerned, but also in that in the latter case the personal information on file constituted the basis of decisions which Mr Leander complained were detrimental to him, while in the *Gaskin* Case no use at all was currently made of the file in relation to the applicant or any other person. In fact, Gaskin did not complain about the fact that information was compiled and stored about him, nor did he allege that any use was made to his detriment. He challenged rather the failure to grant him unimpeded access to that information.[19] The Court expressly held Article 8 to be relevant. It agreed with the Commission that "[the file] no doubt contained information concerning highly personal aspects of the applicant's childhood, development and history and thus could constitute his principal source of information about his past and formative years. Consequently lack of access thereto did raise issues under Article 8."[20]

This aspect, according to the Court, directly related to a positive obligation on the part of the Contracting State flowing from Article 8. In its judgment the Court concentrated on the question of whether a fair balance had been struck between the general interests of the community and the interests of the individual. It held as follows: "In the Court's opinion, persons in the applicant's situation have a vital interest, protected by the Convention, in receiving the information necessary to know and to understand their childhood and early development. On the other hand, it must be borne in mind that confidentiality of public records is of importance for receiving

---

[18]   Judgment of 7 July 1989, para. 37.
[19]   In the judgment of 9 June 1998, *McGinley and Egan*, para. 99, the Court concluded that the State had made available sufficient procedures for the applicants to have access to their own medical files, containing data provided in connection with a nuclear test and possible exposure to radiation.
[20]   Judgment of 7 July 1989, para. 36.

objective and reliable information and that such confidentiality can also be necessary for the protection of third persons. Under the latter aspect, a system like the British one, which makes access to records dependent on the consent of the contributor, can in principle be considered to be compatible with the obligations under Article 8, taking into account the State's margin of appreciation. The Court considers, however, that under such a system the interests of the individual seeking access to records relating to his private and family life must be secured when a contributor to the records either is not available or improperly refuses consent. Such a system is only in conformity with the principle of proportionality if it provides that an independent authority finally decides whether access has to be granted in cases where a contributor fails to answer or withholds consent. No such procedure was available to the applicant in the present case. Accordingly, the procedure followed failed to secure respect for Mr. Gaskin's private and family life, as required by Article 8 of the Convention. There has therefore been a breach of that provision."[21]

In the *Mikulić* Case the applicant, a 5-year-old girl, complained of the length of a paternity suit which she had brought with her mother and the lack of procedural means available under Croatian law to enable the courts to compel the alleged father to comply with a court order for DNA tests to be carried out. The Court weighed the vital interest of a person in receiving the information necessary to uncover the truth about an important aspect of his or her personal identity against the interest of third parties in refusing to be compelled to make themselves available for medical testing. It found that the State had a duty to establish alternative means to enable an independent authority to determine the paternity claim speedily. It held that there had been a breach of the proportionality principle as regards the interests of the applicant, who had been left in a state of prolonged uncertainty as to her personal identity.[22]

The *Odièvre* Case concerned an adopted child trying to trace her natural mother, by whom she was abandoned at birth and who had expressly requested that information about the birth remained confidential. The issue of access to information about one's origins and the identity of one's natural parents was held to be not of the same nature as that of access to a case record concerning a child in care or to evidence of alleged paternity.[23] The Court observed that there were two competing interests in the case before it: on the one hand, the right to know one's origins and the child's vital interest in its personal development and, on the other, a woman's interest in remaining anonymous in order to protect her health by giving birth in appropriate medical conditions. Those interests were not easily reconciled, as they concerned two adults, each endowed with free will. The Court observed that the applicant had been given access to non-identifying information about her mother and natural family that had

---

[21]   *Ibidem*, para. 49. See also judgment of 24 September 2002, *M.G. v. the United Kingdom*, para. 27.
[22]   Judgment of 7 February 2002, paras 64-66.
[23]   Judgment of 13 February 2003, para. 43.

enabled her to trace some of her roots, while ensuring the protection of third-party interests. In addition, while preserving the principle that mothers were entitled to give birth anonymously, the law of 22 of January 2002 facilitated searches for information about a person's biological origins by setting up a National Council on Access to Information about Personal Origins. The legislation was already in force and the applicant could use it to request disclosure of her mother's identity, subject to the latter's consent being obtained. The French legislation thus sought to strike a balance and to ensure sufficient proportion between the competing interests. Consequently, France had not overstepped the margin of appreciation which it had to be afforded in view of the complex and sensitive nature of the issue of access to information about one's origins, an issue that concerned the right to know one's personal history, the choice of the natural parents, the existing family ties and the adoptive parents. Consequently, there had been no violation of Article 8 of the Convention.[24]

In *M.G. v. the United Kingdom* the applicant complained about a lack of unimpeded access to his social service records held by the local authority. The Court noted that one of the main reasons why the applicant sought access to his records was his sincere belief that he had been physically abused when he was a child by his father and his need to obtain as much information as possible about that period in order to come to terms with the emotional and psychological impact of any such abuse and to understand his own subsequent and related behaviour. The Court observed that the applicant was only given limited access to his records in 1995, compared to the records submitted to the Court by the United Kingdom Government. In addition, he had no statutory right of access to those records or clear indication by way of a binding circular or legislation of the grounds upon which he could request access or challenge a denial of access. Most importantly, he had no appeal against a refusal of access to any independent body. The records disclosed by the Government demonstrated the need for such an independent appeal, given that significant portions of the records were blanked out and certain documents had been retained on the basis that non-disclosure was justified by the duty of confidence to third parties. In such circumstances, the Court concluded that there had been a failure to fulfil the positive obligation to protect the applicant's private and family life in respect of his access to his social service records from April 1995. However, from 1 March 2000 (the date of entry into force of the Data Protection Act 1998) the applicant could have, but had not, appealed to an independent authority against the non-disclosure of certain records on grounds of a duty of confidentiality to third parties. Accordingly, the Court held that there had been a violation of Article 8 in respect of the applicant's access, between April 1995 and 1 March 2000, to his social service records.[25]

---

[24]   *Ibidem*, paras. 48-49.
[25]   Judgment of 24 September 2002, paras 29-31.

12.3.1.3 Disclosure of confidential information

Sensitive information needs to be treated with special care; the disclosure of such information to others must be surrounded by procedural guarantees. In *M.S. v. Sweden* the applicant complained about personal medical information having been made available to the social security authority. In that specific case the Court found no violation since the authority concerned was also under a duty to keep the data confidential and it needed the information in order to come to a good judgment as to the eligibility of the applicant for a benefit.[26]

In *Z. v. Finland* the Court applied a very strict test in view of the fact that the information that was made available concerned a person's HIV infection. The Court held as follows: "The disclosure of such data may dramatically affect his or her private and family life, as well as social and employment situation, by exposing him or her to opprobrium and the risk of ostracism. For this reason it may also discourage persons from seeking diagnosis or treatment and thus undermine any preventive efforts by the community to contain the pandemic (…). The interests in protecting the confidentiality of such information will therefore weigh heavily in the balance in determining whether the interference was proportionate to the legitimate aim pursued. Such interference cannot be compatible with Article 8 of the Convention unless it is justified by an overriding requirement in the public interest. In view of the highly intimate and sensitive nature of information concerning a person's HIV status, any State measures compelling communication or disclosure of such information without the consent of the patient call for the most careful scrutiny on the part of the Court, as do the safeguards designed to secure effective protection (…). At the same time, the Court accepts that the interests of a patient and the community as a whole in protecting the confidentiality of medical data may be outweighed by the interest in investigation and prosecution of crime and the publicity of court proceedings (…), where such interests are shown to be of even greater importance."[27] In this specific case the Court accepted that the medical data could be made available in court proceedings; however, it also found that the possibility under Finnish law to make these medical records available for the public after ten years constituted an impermissible interference.

In general the Court requires that domestic law affords appropriate safeguards to prevent any communication or disclosure of such sensitive data, such as data concerning personal health, that are inconsistent with the guarantees in Article 8 of the Convention.[28]

The question could be asked whether the publication in the media of data which an individual considers to be private also enjoys protection under Article 8 and

---

[26]   Judgment of 27 August 1997, para. 44.
[27]   Judgment of 25 February 1997, paras 96-97.
[28]   *Ibidem*, para. 95.

whether this may also come under the strict scrutiny test applied by the Court in the aforementioned *Z. v. Finland Case*. An indication in this respect can be found in *N.F. v. Italy*. The applicant complained about the publication in the press concerning his membership of the Free Masons. In this specific case the Court did not find that the applicant had suffered any harm. On the contrary, anybody could have found out about his membership. For this reason, the Court concluded that no interference in his private life had taken place.[29] It may be assumed that this could have been different when secret and private data had been divulged.

12.3.1.4 Monitoring

In *P.G. and J.H. v. the United Kingdom* the Court held that there is a zone of interaction of a person with others, even in a public context, which may fall within the scope of private life.[30] In this respect the Court held: "There are a number of elements relevant to a consideration of whether a person's private life is concerned in measures effected outside a person's home or private premises. Since there are occasions when people knowingly or intentionally involve themselves in activities, which are or may be recorded or reported in a public manner, a person's reasonable expectations as to privacy may be a significant, although not necessarily conclusive, factor. A person who walks down the street will, inevitably, be visible to any member of the public who is also present. Monitoring by technological means of the same public scene (for example, a security guard viewing through closed-circuit television) is of a similar character. Private life considerations may arise, however, once any systematic or permanent record comes into existence of such material from the public domain."[31]

Monitoring the actions of an individual in a public place by the use of photographic equipment which does not record the visual data does not, as such, give rise to an interference with the individual's private life.[32] On the other hand, recording of the data and the systematic or permanent nature of the record may give rise to such interference. Accordingly, in the *Amann* Case, the *Rotaru* Case and the *Peck* Case the compilation of data by security services on particular individuals, even without the use of covert surveillance methods, constituted an interference with the applicants' private lives.[33] Publication of the material in a manner or degree beyond what is normally foreseeable may also bring security recordings within the scope of Article 8(1). In the *Peck* Case the disclosure to the media for broadcast use of a video

---

[29]   Judgment of 2 August 2001, para. 39.
[30]   Judgment of 6 February 2001, para. 56.
[31]   *Ibidem*, para. 57.
[32]   Appls 32200/96 and 32201/96, *Herbecq and the association "Ligue des droits de l'homme"*, D&R 92-B (1998), p. 92.
[33]   Judgment of 16 February 2000, *Amann*, paras 65-66; judgment of 4 May 2000, *Rotaru*, paras 43-44; judgment of 28 January 2003, *Peck*, para. 59.

footage of the applicant whose suicide attempt was caught on close circuit television cameras was found to be a serious interference with the applicant's private life, notwithstanding that he was in a public place at the time.[34]

In the *Perry* Case the applicant was filmed on video in the custody suite of a police station. The police regulated the security camera so that it could take clear footage of the applicant in the custody suite and inserted it in a montage of film of other persons to show to witnesses for the purposes of seeing whether they identified the applicant as the perpetrator of the robberies under investigation. The question was whether this use of the camera and footage constituted a processing or use of personal data of a nature to constitute an interference with respect for private life. The Court held that the footage in question had not been obtained voluntarily or in circumstances where it could be reasonably anticipated that it would be recorded and used for identification purposes. The Court considered therefore that the recording and use of the video footage of the applicant in this case disclosed an interference with his right to respect for private life.[35] The interference had not been in accordance with the law because the police had failed to comply with the procedures set out in the applicable code: they had not obtained the applicant's consent or informed him that the tape was being made; neither had they informed him of his rights in that respect.[36]

12.3.2 MEDICAL EXAMINATION/TREATMENT

Another modality of interference with private life is the compulsory subjection to a medical or psychological examination or treatment. As the Commission pointed out: "A compulsory medical intervention, even if it is of minor importance, must be considered as an interference with this right."[37] This aspect of article 8 also includes the right not to be treated medically without consent, while with respect to children it implies that treatment cannot be started without the parents' consent. For this reason the Court found a violation of article 8 in the *Glass* Case.[38] In the *Herczegfalvy* Case the Court also accepted the applicability of Article 8 in the context of the compulsory administering of food. Considering the facts of the case, it dismissed the applicant's allegations because, according to the psychiatric principles generally accepted at the time, medical necessity justified the treatment in issue, and because of the lack of specific information capable of disproving the Government's opinion that the hospital authorities were entitled to regard the applicant's psychiatric illness as rendering him

---

[34]   Judgment of 28 January 2003, para. 59.
[35]   Judgment of 17 July 2003, paras 42-43.
[36]   *Ibidem*, paras 47-49.
[37]   Appl. 8278/78, *X v. Austria*, D&R 18 (1980), p. 155 (156).
[38]   Judgment of 9 March 2004, para. 83.

entirely incapable of taking decisions for himself. Consequently, no violation of Article 8 was found to have been shown in this respect.[39]

Most complaints of persons who had to undergo a compulsory medical or psychological examination as suspects, so far were not based upon Article 8, but upon Articles 3, 5 and 6. The Commission held in those cases that such examinations constituted a normal and frequently also desirable element of the investigations concerned.[40] Had the Commission reviewed, *ex officio*, such examinations for their compatibility with Article 8, it should have ascertained whether they were authorised by law and whether subjection thereto could be justified on the basis of one of the grounds of limitation of the second paragraph. This is the approach adopted by the Court. In the *Matter* Case the issue was that an elderly person could only have his legal capacity restored after having undergone a psychological examination, which he refused. The Court concluded that such examination constituted an interference, but that it could not be considered to be disproportionate, in pursuance of the legitimate aim of protecting the patient's own rights and health.[41] What is remarkable in this case, however, is that the Court accepted the protection of the patient's own rights and health as a legitimate aim while Article 8 only mentions the rights and freedoms of others.

In the *Worwa* Case the Court emphasised that ordering a psychiatric report in order to determine the mental state of a person charged with an offence is a necessary measure and one which protects individuals capable of committing offences without being in full possession of their mental faculties. However, the State authorities are required to make sure that such a measure does not upset the fair balance that should be maintained between the rights of the individual, in particular the right to respect for private life, and the concern to ensure the proper administration of justice.[42]

In the *Pretty* Case, with respect to enforced medical treatment the Court held as follows: "In the sphere of medical treatment, the refusal to accept a particular treatment might, inevitably, lead to a fatal outcome, yet the imposition of medical treatment, without the consent of a mentally competent adult patient, would interfere with a person's physical integrity in a manner capable of engaging the rights protected under Article 8 para. 1 of the Convention."[43] The applicant in that case was prevented by law from exercising her choice to avoid what she considered would be an undignified and distressing end to her life. The Court was not prepared to exclude that this constituted an interference with her right to respect for private life as

---

[39]   Judgment of 24 September 1992, para. 86. For similar reasons the Court also concluded that Art. 3 had not been shown to have been violated.
[40]   Appl. 986/61, *X v. Federal Republic Germany*, Yearbook V (1962), p. 192 (198).
[41]   Judgment of 5 July 1999, para. 72.
[42]   Judgment of 27 November 2003, para. 82.
[43]   Judgment of 29 April 2002, para. 63.

guaranteed under Article 8 (1). The Court did not consider that the blanket nature of the ban on assisted suicide was disproportionate. The Government had stated that flexibility was provided for in individual cases by the fact that consent was needed from the Director of Public Prosecution (DPP) to bring a prosecution and by the fact that a maximum sentence was provided, allowing lesser penalties to be imposed as appropriate. It did not appear to be arbitrary for the law to reflect the importance of the right to life, by prohibiting assisted suicide while providing for a system of enforcement and adjudication which allowed due regard to be given in each particular case to the public interest in bringing a prosecution, as well as to the fair and proper requirements of retribution and deterrence. Nor in the circumstances was there anything disproportionate in the refusal of the DPP to give an advance undertaking that no prosecution would be brought against the applicant's husband. Strong arguments based on the rule of law could be raised against any claim by the executive to exempt individuals or classes of individuals from the operation of the law. In any event, the seriousness of the act for which immunity was claimed was such that the decision of the DPP to refuse the undertaking sought could not be said to be arbitrary or unreasonable. The Court concluded that the interference could be justified as 'necessary in a democratic society' for the protection of the rights of others. There had therefore been no violation of Article 8.[44]

In *Y.F. v. Turkey* the applicant alleged that the forced gynaecological examination of his wife constituted a breach of Article 8. The Court considered that, given her vulnerability in the hands of the authorities who had exercised full control over her during her detention, she could not be expected to have put up resistance to the gynaecological examination. There had accordingly been an interference with her right to respect for her private life. The Government had failed to demonstrate the existence of a medical necessity or other circumstances defined by law. While the Court accepted the argument that the medical examination of detainees by a forensic medical doctor could be an important safeguard against false accusations of sexual harassment or ill treatment, it considered that any interference with a person's physical integrity had to be prescribed by law and required that person's consent. As this had not been the case here, the interference had not been in accordance with the law.[45]

The *Glass* Case concerned the son of the applicants, who was severely mentally and physically disabled and required 24-hour attention. Following an operation, he suffered complications, became critically ill and had to be put on a ventilator. During his treatment, hospital staff informed Ms Glass that her son was dying and that further intensive care would be inappropriate. However, his condition improved and he was able to return home on 2 September 1998. On 8 September 1998, when he was re-admitted to the hospital with a respiratory tract infection, doctors discussed with Ms

---

44   *Ibidem*, paras 76-78.
45   Judgment of 22 July 2003, paras 41-44.

676   Intersentia

Glass the possible use of morphine to alleviate distress. On 20 October 1998, the doctors treating him considered that he was dying and recommended that diamorphine be given to him to relieve his distress. Ms Glass did not agree that her son was dying and was very concerned that the administration of diamorphine (previously morphine had been mentioned) would compromise his chances of recovery. She subsequently asked to take him home if he was dying, but a police officer advised her that if she attempted to remove him, she would be arrested. The following day Ms Glass found that her son's condition had deteriorated alarmingly and was worried that this was due to the effect of diamorphine. The family demanded that diamorphine be stopped. His condition improved and he went home on 21 October 1998. The Court considered that the situation which arose at the hospital between 19 and 21 October 1998 could not be isolated from the earlier discussions between members of the hospital staff and Ms Glass about her son's condition. The doctors at the hospital were obviously concerned about Ms Glass' reluctance to follow their advice, in particular their view that morphine might have to be administered to her son. It had not been explained to the Court's satisfaction why the trust did not at that stage seek the intervention of the High Court. Admittedly, Ms Glass could have brought the matter before the High Court. However, the Court considered that the onus was on the trust to take the initiative and to diffuse the situation in anticipation of a further emergency. The Court accepted that the doctors could not have predicted the level of confrontation and hostility, which in fact arose on 18 October 1998. It was nevertheless the case that the trust's failure to make a High Court application at an earlier stage contributed to the situation. That being said, the Court was not persuaded that an emergency High Court application could not have been made by the trust when it became clear that Ms Glass was firmly opposed to the administration of diamorphine to her son. The trust was able to secure the presence of a police officer to oversee the negotiations with Ms Glass but, surprisingly, did not consider making a High Court application even though it would have been possible at short notice. The Court considered that the decision of the authorities to override Ms Glass's objection to the proposed treatment in the absence of authorisation by a court resulted in a breach of Article 8.[46]

12.3.3 SEXUAL PRIVACY

12.3.3.1 Introduction

Another aspect of private life with regard to which far-reaching restrictions are laid down in the legislation of most of the Contracting States, is that of sexuality: prohibition of sexual intercourse with minors; prohibition of homosexual practices;

---

[46] Judgment of 9 March 2004, paras 78-83.

prohibition of the use (or the sale) of contraceptives; prohibition of abortion and non-recognition or limited recognition of (the consequences of) transsexualism. The Strasbourg case law has expressly recognised that sexual life constitutes an important part of a person's private life.[47]

12.3.3.2 Homosexuality

A general prohibition of homosexual practices was accepted as justified by the Commission in an early decision on the basis of the protection of health and morals relied upon by the respondent State.[48] The Commission did not provide any arguments for this. On a later occasion, with a similar complaint of a person prosecuted for homosexual acts, the Commission showed to be prepared to undertake an inquiry into the justification of the restriction concerned and to take into account new developments within the country in question and elsewhere.[49] In a later stage, a couple of complaints of homosexuals against the United Kingdom, in which a breach of Article 8 was alleged, was declared admissible[50] and examined as to their merits.[51] The first of these cases resulted in a resolution of the Committee of Ministers,[52] the second in a judgment of the Court.[53]

The first case concerned a complaint against application of the English Sexual Offences Act, by which homosexual intercourse with male persons under 21 years of age was declared punishable. Here the Commission – followed in this by the Committee of Ministers – found that the prosecution and the punishment were justified on the ground of 'the protection of the rights and freedoms of others'.[54] The second case concerned a complaint against the legislation in Northern Ireland, prohibiting homosexual intercourse even between consenting male persons over 21 years of age. In this case both the Commission and the Court concluded that this penalisation could not be deemed necessary for the protection of morals in a democratic society, whereas the justification of the prohibition with regard to male persons under 21 years of age,

---

[47]   Judgment of 22 October 1981, *Dudgeon*, para. 41; judgment of 26 October 1988, *Norris*, para. 38, as well as the other judgments mentioned in this sub-section.

[48]   Appl. 104/55, *X v. Federal Republic of Germany*, Yearbook I (1955-1957), p. 228 (229).

[49]   Appl. 5935/72, *X v. Federal Republic of Germany*, Yearbook XIX (1976), p. 277 (284-286), where the Commission took into consideration in particular the then current opinions on the possible effect which a homosexual relationship has on juveniles, and on the question of what age limit should have to be laid down in that respect.

[50]   Appl. 7215/75, *X v. the United Kingdom*, Yearbook XXI (1978), p. 354 (372); and Appl. 7525/76, *X v. the United Kingdom*, Yearbook XXII (1979), p. 156 (184).

[51]   Report of 12 October 1978, *X v. the United Kingdom*, D&R 19 (1980), p. 66; and report of 13 March 1980, *Dudgeon*, B.40 (1984), pp. 32-43.

[52]   Res. DH(79)5 of 12 June 1979, D&R 19 (1980), pp. 82-83.

[53]   Judgment of 22 October 1981, *Dudgeon*.

[54]   Report of 12 October 1978, *X v. the United Kingdom*, D&R 19 (1980), p. 66 (75).

here again, was deemed justifiable by both the Commission and the Court.[55] Another complaint about the Irish legislation penalising certain homosexual acts in private between consenting adult males was dealt with in the *Norris* Case. The Court referred to the *Dudgeon* Case and held that there was no 'pressing social need' to make such acts criminal offences.[56] In the *Modinos* Case, concerning Cyprus, the Court stuck to its previous case law by ruling that a prohibition of homosexual relations in private between consenting adults constitutes an interference. Since the respondent Government did not argue that there existed a justification under paragraph 2 of Article 8, the Court decided that, having regard to its case law in *Dudgeon* and *Norris,* a re-examination of this question was not called for. Accordingly, it concluded that there was a breach of Article 8.[57] This case law was, once again, confirmed in *A.D. v. the United Kingdom.* A homosexual was sentenced for 'gross indecency' for homosexual acts recorded on tape. However, since the acts took place in private and were non-violent (and he was charged for the acts and not for the taping), the State had exceeded the margin of appreciation invoking the protection of health and morals.[58]

The outcome was different in a case concerning homosexuals practicing SM, who were sentenced for assault inflicting bodily harm. Their criminal conviction was upheld by the Court as being justified for the protection of health and morals, even though the activities had taken place in private and with mutual consent. The Court distinguished in the *Laskey, Jaggard and Brown* Case these facts from those in the *Modinos, Norris* and *Dudgeon* Cases by considering as follows: "It is evident from the facts established by the national courts that the applicants' sadomasochistic activities involved a significant degree of injury or wounding which could not be characterised as trifling or transient. This, in itself, suffices to distinguish the present case from those applications which have previously been examined by the Court concerning consensual homosexual behaviour in private between adults where no such feature was present."[59]

In a decision of 1983 (that is before the *Norris* and *Modinos* judgments of the Court) the Commission repeated in a general sense its position that "the prohibition by criminal law of homosexual acts committed in private between consenting males amounts to an interference with the 'private life' of those concerned under Article 8(1)". In this case, however, it opined that such prohibition might properly be considered "necessary in a democratic society for the prevention of disorder".[60] Here the age of the partners, or one of them, was not at issue, but the fact that the

---

[55]   Report of 13 March 1980, *Dudgeon,* B.40 (1984), p. 41; judgment of 22 October 1981, para. 62. See also the Voogd Report on discrimination of homosexuals, submitted to the Parliamentary Assembly of the Council of Europe; Doc. 4755, 8 July 1981.
[56]   Judgment of 26 October 1988, para. 46.
[57]   Judgment of 22 April 1993, para. 26.
[58]   Judgment of 31 July 2000, para. 38.
[59]   Judgment of 19 February 1997, para. 45.
[60]   Appl. 9237/81, *B v. the United Kingdom,* D&R 34 (1983), p. 68 (71-72).

prohibiting regulation concerned soldiers. The Commission here accepted that homosexual conduct by members of the armed forces may pose a particular risk to order within the forces, which would not arise in civilian life. In the *Lustig-Prean and Beckett* and *Smith and Grady* Cases, the Court took a different position. Two gays from the Royal navy, and one gay and one lesbian from the Air Force were dismissed from armed service following an investigation into their private life. The plea of the legitimate aim of an anti-gay policy in the army and the promotion of operational effectiveness were not accepted by the Court as convincing. The probing into the applicants' private lives was too intrusive and the career effects for otherwise good officers were profound. In general the Court considered the anti-gay policy too absolute.[61]

12.3.3.3 Abortion

A complaint against a judgment of the German *Bundesverfassungsgericht* in which provisions in the new German legislation on abortion were declared unconstitutional, and against the amendments subsequently introduced, both challenged, *inter alia,* under Article 8, was declared admissible by the Commission insofar as the two female applicants were concerned. The Commission based its decision on the following, very widely formulated ground: "the Commission considers that pregnancy and the interruption of pregnancy are part of private life, and also in certain circumstances of family life. It further considers that respect for private life 'comprises also, to a certain degree, the right to establish and to develop relationships with other human beings, especially in the emotional field, for the development and fulfilment of one's own personality' (...) and that therefore sexual life is also part of private life; and in particular that legal regulation of abortion is an intervention in private life which may or may not be justified under Article 8(2)."[62]

   This formulation would appear to leave sufficient scope for the admissibility also of complaints of men against a prohibition or restriction of voluntary abortion, but the male applicant in this case had insufficiently proved the injury sustained by him. In its report on the merits of the case the Commission held that the new regulation, adopted in consequence of the decision of the *Bundesverfassungsgericht,* having regard to the weighing of interests on which it was based and taking into account that pregnancy and its termination are not solely a matter of the private life of the mother

---

[61]   Judgments of 27 September 1999, para. 104 and para. 110, respectively. See also judgment of 9 January 2003, *S.L. v. Austria,* para. 44; judgment of 9 January 2003, *L. and V. v. Austria,* para. 54; judgment of 3 February 2005, *Ladner,* para. 25.

[62]   Appl. 6959/75, *Bruggemann and Scheuten v. Federal Republic of Germany,* Yearbook XIX (1976), p. 382 (414).

but is regulated in most Contracting States, did not conflict with Article 8(1).[63] The Committee of Ministers agreed with this point of view.[64]

In *X. v. the United Kingdom* it was submitted that the legislation permitting abortion without the father's consent constituted an interference with the latter's right to respect for his family life. The Commission found that, insofar as abortion constitutes an interference with the right of the father, the interference was justified here for the protection of the rights of another person, since the decision to apply abortion had been taken at the request of the mother in order to protect her physical and mental health. The Commission also adopted the view that the father's right to respect for his family life could not be interpreted so broadly that a right to be consulted beforehand in case of an abortion could be derived from it.[65] The Commission arrived at this latter conclusion "having regard to the right of the pregnant woman". It is not evident, however, that the woman's right to respect for her private life should rule out that the man might in principle derive from his right to respect for his family life a right to be consulted. After all, the second paragraph of Article 8 would seem to leave sufficient room to give priority to the woman's right, should the man refuse his consent.

In an application against Norway the applicant complained about the abortion that his female friend had allowed to be performed on her. The Commission declared his complaints, based upon Articles 2, 3, 6, 8, 9, 13 and 14 of the Convention, inadmissible. In general, the Commission noted that it was clear that national laws on abortion differ considerably: "In these circumstances, and assuming that the Convention may be considered to have some bearing in this field, the Commission finds that in such a delicate area the Contracting States must have a certain discretion."[66] With regard to Article 8 the Commission adopted the following reasoning: "It is true that Articles 8 and 9 of the Convention guarantee the right to respect for private and family life and freedom to manifest one's religion. However, the Commission finds that any interpretation of the potential father's right under these provisions in connection with an abortion which the mother intends to have performed on her, must first of all take into account her rights, she being the person primarily concerned by the pregnancy and its continuation or termination. The Commission therefore finds that any possible interference which might be assumed in the circumstances of the present case was justified as being necessary for the protection of the rights of another person. It follows that this part of the application

---

[63]   Report of 12 July 1977, *Brüggemann and Scheuten* D&R 10 (1978), p. 100 (114-118). See, however, the dissenting opinion of Commission Member Fawcett, *ibidem*, p. 144.

[64]   Res. DH(78)1 of 17 March 1978, D&R 10 (1978), pp. 121-122.

[65]   Appl. 8416/78, D&R 19 (1980), p. 244 (253-254).

[66]   Appl. 17004/90, *Hercz v. Norway*, D&R 73 (1992) p. 155 (168).

is also manifestly ill-founded within the meaning of Article 27 para. 2 of the Convention."[67]

In the *Open Door and Dublin Well Women* Case two of the applicants alleged a violation of Article 8 because they were denied access to information concerning abortion abroad, and two other applicants, counselling organisations, alleged a violation of that article because they were hindered in counselling their clients concerning their privacy rights. The Court, however, did not consider it necessary to examine this part of the claims after it had found a violation of Article 10.[68]

In the *Vo* Case a woman brought an application who had been involuntarily aborted. She complained in this respect about the lack of proper and adequate mechanisms protecting her and punishing the physician. The Court investigated this complaint under the heading of Article 2 (right to life). The Court considered it unnecessary to examine whether the abrupt end to the applicant's pregnancy fell within the scope of Article 2, seeing that, even assuming that that provision was applicable, there had been no failure on the part of France to comply with the requirements relating to the preservation of life in the public-health sphere. The unborn child was not deprived of all protection under French law. Contrary to what had been submitted by Mrs Vo, the States' positive obligation – which in the public-health sphere consisted of adopting appropriate measures for the protection of patients' lives and of holding inquiries into the cause of death – did not necessarily require the provision of a criminal-law remedy.[69]

12.3.3.4 Transsexualism

For a long time the Court refused to honour claims by transsexuals under Article 8. In the *Rees, Cossey, X., Y. and Z. v. the United Kingdom* and *Sheffield and Horsham* Cases the Court emphasised the margin of appreciation of the State in the light of the absence of a common ground between the Contracting States with respect to the legal position of transsexuals. Although Article 8 was held to be applicable, the Court concluded that the State did not disturb the required equilibrium by not giving transsexuals a full legal recognition of their new gender status.[70]

---

[67]   *Ibidem.* See on abortion also Appl. 8416/79, *X v. the United Kingdom*, D&R 19, p. 244. It is open for speculation how the Court would have decided the same issue. In the *Keegan* Case, concerning giving up a child for adoption by the mother, without consulting the father and without the father having a legal remedy, the Court found a violation of Article 8; judgment of 26 May 1994, para.55.

[68]   Judgment of 29 October 1992, para. 83.

[69]   Judgment of 8 July 2004, para. 94.

[70]   In the judgment of 25 March 1992, *B. v. France* , para. 63, the Court concluded that Article 8 had been violated, but this conclusion was due to specific factual circumstances of the case and did not mean a principled deviation from the *Rees* and *Cossey* Cases, as turned out in the 1998 judgment in *Sheffield and Horsham*.

In the *Rees* Case the Court indicated that its reference to the lack of consensus at that time also meant that in due course it might change its interpretation of Article 8. It held as follows: "That being so, it must for the time being be left to the respondent State to determine to what extent it can meet the remaining demands of transsexuals. However, the Court is conscious of the seriousness of the problems affecting these persons and the distress they suffer. The Convention has always to be interpreted and applied in the light of current circumstances (...). The need for appropriate legal measures should therefore be kept under review having regard particularly to scientific and societal developments."[71]

In the *Cossey* Case the Court elaborated on this aspect: "There have been certain developments since 1986 in the law of some of the member States of the Council of Europe. However, the Reports accompanying the resolution adopted by the European Parliament on 12 September 1989 (...) and Recommendation 1117 (1989) adopted by the Parliamentary Assembly of the Council of Europe on 29 September 1989 – both of which seek to encourage the harmonisation of laws and practices in this field – reveal, as the Government pointed out, the same diversity of practice as obtained at the time of the Rees judgment. Accordingly this is still, having regard to the existence of little common ground between the Contracting States, an area in which they enjoy a wide margin of appreciation (...). In particular, it cannot at present be said that a departure from the Court's earlier decision is warranted in order to ensure that the interpretation of Article 8 on the point at issue remains in line with present-day conditions. (...) The Court accordingly concludes that there is no violation of Article 8. The Court would, however, reiterate the observations it made in the Rees judgment (...). It is conscious of the seriousness of the problems facing transsexuals and the distress they suffer. Since the Convention always has to be interpreted and applied in the light of current circumstances, it is important that the need for appropriate legal measures in this area should be kept under review."[72]

In 2002 the Court did indeed change its approach in the light of a grown consensus. In the *Goodwin* Case, which concerned a male to female transsexual, the Court fully accepted a positive obligation for the State to recognise a transsexual's new legal status. With respect to a European and international consensus, the Court stated as follows: "Already at the time of the Sheffield and Horsham case, there was an emerging consensus within Contracting States in the Council of Europe on providing legal recognition following gender re-assignment (...). The latest survey submitted by Liberty in the present case shows a continuing international trend towards legal recognition (...). In Australia and New Zealand, it appears that the courts are moving away from the biological birth view of sex (as set out in the United Kingdom case of *Corbett v. Corbett*) and taking the view that sex, in the context of a transsexual wishing

---

[71]   Judgment of 17 October 1986, para. 47.
[72]   Judgment of 27 September 1990, paras 40-41.

to marry, should depend on a multitude of factors to be assessed at the time of the marriage. The Court observes that in the case of Rees in 1986 it had noted that little common ground existed between States, some of which did permit change of gender and some of which did not and that generally speaking the law seemed to be in a state of transition. In the later case of Sheffield and Horsham, the Court's judgment laid emphasis on the lack of a common European approach as to how to address the repercussions which the legal recognition of a change of sex may entail for other areas of law such as marriage, filiation, privacy or data protection. While this would appear to remain the case, the lack of such a common approach among forty-three Contracting States with widely diverse legal systems and traditions is hardly surprising. In accordance with the principle of subsidiarity, it is indeed primarily for the Contracting States to decide on the measures necessary to secure Convention rights within their jurisdiction and, in resolving within their domestic legal systems the practical problems created by the legal recognition of post-operative gender status, the Contracting States must enjoy a wide margin of appreciation. The Court accordingly attaches less importance to the lack of evidence of a common European approach to the resolution of the legal and practical problems posed, than to the clear and uncontested evidence of a continuing international trend in favour not only of increased social acceptance of transsexuals but of legal recognition of the new sexual identity of post-operative transsexuals."[73]

Interesting to note is the Court's emphasis on the continuing international trend and not so much upon an already existing fully-fledged consensus. It also argued that it had stressed in its previous decisions about transsexuals that it was necessary to keep the need for appropriate legal measures under review. With respect to the margin of appreciation the Court underlined the importance of the principles laid down or inherent in Article 8 that play a role in claims of transsexuals: "Under Article 8 of the Convention in particular, where the notion of personal autonomy is an important principle underlying the interpretation of its guarantees, protection is given to the personal sphere of each individual, including the right to establish details of their identity as individual human beings (...). In the twenty-first century the right of transsexuals to personal development and to physical and moral security in the full sense enjoyed by others in society cannot be regarded as a matter of controversy requiring the lapse of time to cast clearer light on the issues involved. In short, the unsatisfactory situation in which post-operative transsexuals live in an intermediate zone as not quite one gender or the other is no longer sustainable."[74] From this the Court reached its conclusion that Article 8 had been violated: "the Court finds that the respondent Government can no longer claim that the matter falls within their margin of appreciation, save as regards the appropriate means of achieving recognition

---

[73]   Judgment of 11 July 2002, paras 84-85.
[74]   *Ibidem*, para. 90.

of the right protected under the Convention. Since there are no significant factors of public interest to weigh against the interest of this individual applicant in obtaining legal recognition of her gender re-assignment, it reaches the conclusion that the fair balance that is inherent in the Convention now tilts decisively in favour of the applicant. There has, accordingly, been a failure to respect her right to private life in breach of Article 8 of the Convention."[75]

12.3.4   NAME

In *B v. France* the Court had ruled that the refusal to allow the applicant to change her first name was also a relevant factor from the point of view of Article 8.[76] The question whether *in itself* a (first) name does enjoy the protection of Article 8 was not yet settled. In 1994 the Court was confronted with this question. It ruled as follows: "As a means of personal identification and of linking to a family, a person's name (...) concerns his or her private and family life. The fact that society and the State have an interest in regulating the use of names does not exclude this, since these public-law aspects are compatible with private life conceived of as including, to a certain degree, the right to establish and develop relationships with other human beings, in professional or business contexts as in others (...). In the instant case, the applicant's retention of the surname by which, according to him, he has become known in academic circles may significantly affect his career. Article 8 therefore applies."[77]

In the *Stjerna* Case the Court confirmed this approach by again holding that the issue of one's (family) name falls within the scope of private and family life, protected under Article 8. The Contracting States do, however, possess a broad margin of appreciation concerning the rules with regard to the change of names, since these rules still differ significantly among them. The Court adopted the following view: "As to the instances of inconvenience complained of by the applicant, the Court is not satisfied on the evidence adduced before it that the alleged difficulties in the spelling and pronunciation of the name can have been very frequent or any more significant than those experienced by a large number of people in Europe today, where movement of people between countries and language-areas is becoming more and more commonplace. (...) no sufficient grounds have been adduced to justify the Court coming to a conclusion different from that of the Finnish authorities."[78]

---

[75]   *Ibidem,* para. 93.
[76]   Judgment of 25 March 1992, para. 58.
[77]   Judgment of 22 February 1994, *Burghartz,* para. 24.
[78]   Judgment of 25 November 1994, para. 42.

In the *Guillot* Case the parents complained about the prohibition to call their daughter Fleur de Marie. The Court made the following observation: "The Court can understand that Mr and Mrs Guillot were upset by the refusal to register the forename they had chosen for their daughter. It notes that this forename consequently cannot appear on official documents and deeds. In addition, it finds it probable that the difference between the child's forename in law and the forename which she actually uses – she is called "Fleur de Marie" by her family and is known by that name socially – entails certain complications for the applicants when acting as her statutory representatives. However, the Court notes that it is not disputed that the child regularly uses the forename in issue without hindrance and that the French courts – which considered the child's interest – allowed the application made in the alternative by the applicants for registration of the forename "Fleur-Marie". In the light of the foregoing, the Court does not find that the inconvenience complained of by the applicants is sufficient to raise an issue of failure to respect their private and family life under Article 8 para. 1. Consequently, there has not been a violation of Article 8."[79]

12.3.5 PHYSICAL INTEGRITY

The concept of private life also covers a person's physical and moral integrity, as was established in *X and Y v. the Netherlands,* where the issue was sexual assault of a mentally handicapped minor.[80] A State is therefore under an obligation to prosecute and punish infringements of a person's physical integrity such as rape effectively.[81]

In the *Costello Roberts* Case the Court held as follows, with respect to corporal punishment in a school: "The Court does not exclude the possibility that there might be circumstances in which Article 8 could be regarded as affording in relation to disciplinary measures a protection which goes beyond that given by Article 3. Having regard, however, to the purpose and aim of the Convention taken as a whole and bearing in mind that sending a child to school necessarily involves some degree of interference with his or her private life, the Court considers that the treatment complained of by the applicant did not entail adverse effects for his physical or moral integrity sufficient to bring it within the scope of the prohibition contained in Article 8. While not wishing to be taken to approve in any way the retention of corporal

---

[79] Judgment of 24 October 1996, para. 27.
[80] Judgment of 26 March 1985, para. 22.
[81] Recently judgment of 4 December 2004, *M.C. v. Bulgaria.*

punishment as part of the disciplinary regime of a school, the Court therefore concludes that in the circumstances of this case there has also been no violation of that Article."[82]

This approach was confirmed in the *Bensaid* Case. The applicant resided illegally in the United Kingdom and was to be deported to Algeria. He was under treatment for a mental illness, for which he had been receiving medical care in the UK. Apart from Article 3, he also invoked Article 8. The Court held as follows: "Private life is a broad term not susceptible to exhaustive definition (…). Mental health must also be regarded as a crucial part of private life associated with the aspect of moral integrity. Article 8 protects a right to identity and personal development and the right to establish and develop relationships with other human beings and the outside world (…). The preservation of mental stability is in that context an indispensable precondition to effective enjoyment of the right to respect for private life. Turning to the present case, the Court recalls that it has found above that the risk of damage to the applicant's health from return to his country of origin was based on largely hypothetical factors and that it was not substantiated that he would suffer inhuman and degrading treatment. Nor in the circumstances has it been established that his moral integrity would be substantially affected to a degree falling within the scope of Article 8 of the Convention. Even assuming that the dislocation caused to the applicant by removal from the United Kingdom where he has lived for the last eleven years was to be considered by itself as affecting his private life, in the context of the relationships and support framework which he enjoyed there, the Court considers that such interference may be regarded as complying with the requirements of the second paragraph of Article 8, namely as a measure 'in accordance with the law', pursuing the aims of the protection of the economic well-being of the country and the prevention of disorder and crime, as well as being 'necessary in a democratic society' for those aims. Accordingly, it finds that the implementation of the decision to remove the applicant to Algeria would not violate Article 8 of the Convention."[83]

Handcuffing a conscript who evaded military service was not proven to affect him sufficiently physically or mentally, nor meant to humiliate him, so as to constitute an interference of Article 8.[84] A normal limitation of liberties during detention, such as handcuffing, does not constitute an interference of Article 8, since the limitation is

---

[82] Judgment of 25 March 1993, para. 36. See also the report of the Commission in *Y v. the United Kingdom*, A.247-A, p. 15, in which the Commission concluded that the corporal punishment complained of constituted a violation of Article 3. It therefore considered that the Article 8 issue was absorbed by that finding and that there was no need to pursue a separate examination of the applicant's claims of an unjustified interference with his right to respect for private and family life. The Court decided to strike the case off the list, because of a friendly settlement reached by the Government and the applicant; judgment of 29 October 1992.

[83] Judgment of 6 February 2001, paras 47-49.

[84] Judgment of 16 December 1997, *Raninen*, para. 64.

not beyond the normal.[85] In various cases damage (or potential damage) to one's health was considered by the Court under the scope of article 8. The *Lopez Ostra* and *Hatton* Cases (*infra* 12.5.2.) are prime examples. In the *McGinley and Egan* Case the Court accepted the applicability of article 8 with respect to a case in which a person was exposed to possible radiation and contamination, which might have adverse health consequences. The Court held that a positive obligation rested upon the respondent State to provide full information about the health hazards.[86]

12.3.6 PERSONAL AUTONOMY; CHOICE TO DIE

In the *Pretty* Case the Court made the following observations: "The Government have argued that the right to private life cannot encapsulate a right to die with assistance, such being a negation of the protection that the Convention was intended to provide. The Court would observe that the ability to conduct one's life in a manner of one's own choosing may also include the opportunity to pursue activities perceived to be of a physically or morally harmful or dangerous nature for the individual concerned. The extent to which a State can use compulsory powers or the criminal law to protect people from the consequences of their chosen lifestyle has long been a topic of moral and jurisprudential discussion, the fact that the interference is often viewed as trespassing on the private and personal sphere adding to the vigour of the debate. However, even where the conduct poses a danger to health, or arguably, where it is of a life-threatening nature, the case law of the Convention institutions has regarded the State's imposition of compulsory or criminal measures as impinging on the private life of the applicant within the scope of Article 8 para. 1 and requiring justification in terms of the second paragraph (...). While it might be pointed out that death was not the intended consequence of the applicants' conduct in the above situations, the Court does not consider that this can be a decisive factor. In the sphere of medical treatment, the refusal to accept a particular treatment might, inevitably, lead to a fatal outcome, yet the imposition of medical treatment, without the consent of a mentally competent adult patient, would interfere with a person's physical integrity in a manner capable of engaging the rights protected under Article 8 para. 1 of the Convention. As recognised in domestic case law, a person may claim to exercise a choice to die by declining to consent to treatment, which might have the effect of prolonging his life. In the present case, though medical treatment is not an issue, the applicant is suffering from the devastating effects of a degenerative disease which will cause her condition to deteriorate further and increase her physical and mental suffering. She wishes to mitigate that suffering by exercising a choice to end her life with the assistance of her

---

[85]   Judgment of 16 May 2002, *D.G. v. Ireland,* para. 110.
[86]   Judgment of 9 June 1998, para. 102.

husband. As stated by Lord Hope, the way she chooses to pass the closing moments of her life is part of the act of living, and she has a right to ask that this too must be respected. The very essence of the Convention is respect for human dignity and human freedom. Without in any way negating the principle of sanctity of life protected under the Convention, the Court considers that it is under Article 8 that notions of the quality of life take on significance. In an era of growing medical sophistication combined with longer life expectancies, many people are concerned that they should not be forced to linger on in old age or in states of advanced physical or mental decrepitude which conflict with strongly held ideas of self and personal identity. (...) The applicant in this case is prevented by law from exercising her choice to avoid what she considers will be an undignified and distressing end to her life. The Court is not prepared to exclude that this constitutes an interference with her right to respect for private life as guaranteed under Article 8 para. 1 of the Convention. It considers below whether this interference conforms with the requirements of the second paragraph of Article 8."[87] The final outcome of the case was that the Court, referring to the margin of appreciation, found the ban to meet the proportionality requirement and might be deemed justified as necessary in a democratic society for the protection of the rights of others.

In the above-mentioned case law many aspects can be distinguished that support the conclusion that the Court interprets Article 8 to cover a right to personal autonomy. The aforementioned *P.G. and J.H. v. the United Kingdom* Case may be considered as illustrative for the Court's approach.[88] In the *Guerra* Case, the Court recognized under Article 8 the right to determine one's life and the accompanying individual right to and the corresponding obligation for the authorities to provide information about potential threats and environmental hazards.[89]

Illustrative for the Court's approach are also the gypsy cases, mentioned *infra* in 12.5.1.2. (*Buckly, Chapman, Beard, Coster, Lee* and *Jane Smith*). Another example is the *Bensaid* Case about the expulsion of a mentally ill Algerian from the United Kingdom. In this case the Court held with respect to the applicability of Article 8: "The preservation of mental stability is (...) an indispensable precondition to effective enjoyment of the right to respect for private life."[90]

In fact, the broad conception of Article 8 as also encompassing the right to lead one's life, the right to establish personal relations, would seem to lead to the recognition of a right to personal autonomy. However, as was also shown in particular in the gypsy cases, but also in the *Pretty* Case, the broad interpretation of the scope of Article 8 does not always lead to a positive outcome for the applicant, because of a large

---

[87]   Judgment of 29 April 2002, paras 61-67.
[88]   *Supra*, 12.3.1.1. and 12.3.1.4.
[89]   Judgment of 19 February 1998.
[90]   Judgment of 6 February 2001, para. 47.

margin of appreciation. A major impact of the generous interpretation is to be noted, however, in the *Hatton*, *Lopez Ostra* and *Guerra* Cases and more recently in the *Goodwin* Case. It seems fair to conclude that the approach by the Court of Article 8 as a general right of personal autonomy may have great impact on the case law, by closing many gaps in the protection of human rights and giving account of new developments.

12.4 FAMILY LIFE

12.4.1 AUTONOMOUS CONCEPT

The notion of family life in Article 8 is an autonomous concept, which must be interpreted independently of the national law of the Contracting States.[91] Moreover, the family life to be considered is not *de jure* family life, but *de facto* family life. As the Court held: "In the present case, it is clear that the applicants the first and second of whom have lived together for some fifteen years (...), constitute a 'family' for the purposes of Article 8. They are thus entitled to its protection, notwithstanding the fact that their relationship exists outside marriage."[92]

The Court takes the view that the fact of birth, *i.e.* the biological tie between mother and child, as a rule creates family life in the sense of Article 8, also in the case of a mother and an illegitimate child.[93] The Contracting States may, however, set up a procedure to establish the truth of the alleged family links.[94] Decisive is the situation at the moment at which the final national decision in the case was taken.[95]

The traditional European concepts common to the member States of the Council of Europe is not considered decisive; a family composed according to a different cultural pattern – *e.g.* a polygamous family – is equally entitled to protection.[96] The same respect for different cultural patterns applies in principle to the way in which parents raise their children. Respect for family life comprises respect for a style of education, which differs from that which is common in a given society, provided that

---

[91] Thus, for the first time, the Commission in its report of 10 December 1977, *Marckx*, B.29 (1982), p. 44. Ever since this has been standing case law.

[92] Judgment of 18 December 1986, *Johnston*, para. 56.

[93] See *e.g.* the judgment of 13 June 1979, *Marckx*, para. 31, where the Court used the argument that a different standpoint would amount to discrimination on the ground of birth, contrary to Article 14.

[94] Appl. 8378/78, *Kamal*, D&R 20 (1980), p. 168.

[95] Judgment of 31 January 2002, *Yildiz*, para. 34.

[96] Implicitly recognised by the Commission in its decision in Appls 2991/66 and 2992/66, *Alam, Kahn and Singh*, Yearbook X (1967), p. 478. This leaves apart the question of whether a State must permit the practice of polygamy or may set limitations on the ground of the protection of good morals.

the treatment involved is not to be considered criminal and punishable under the general standards prevailing in the Contracting States.[97]

In the *Berrehab* Case the Court held that cohabitation is not an indispensable element for the existence of family life between parents and their minor children: "It follows from the concept of family on which Article 8 is based that a child born of such a union [viz. a lawful and genuine marriage] is *ipso jure* part of the relationship; hence, from the moment of the child's birth and by the very fact of it, a bond exists between him and his parents amounting to 'family life' even if the parents are not then living together."[98]

Subsequent events, of course, may break that tie, but this was not the situation in the *Berrehab* Case, according to the Court, and consequently Article 8 was found to be applicable. It is a little peculiar that the Court here seems to give a special, stronger position to children born out of a lawful marriage precisely in a case where the subsequent divorce indicated that the marriage had ended in a failure. It may, however, safely be assumed from the relevant case law that the Court will not easily accept that the tie between the natural parent and the child has been severed. Attempts to keep in touch and to arrange visits suffice to accept the continuation of family life.[99]

In the *Keegan* Case the Court combined the criteria used in the *Johnston* Case and in the *Berrehab* Case as follows: "The Court recalls that the notion of the 'family' in this provision is not confined solely to marriage-based relationships and may encompass other de facto 'family' ties where the parties are living together outside of marriage (...). A child born out of such a relationship is ipso jure part of that 'family' unit from the moment of his birth and by the very fact of it. There thus exists a bond between the child and his parents amounting to family life even if at the time of his or her birth the parents are no longer co-habiting or if their relationship has then ended (...). In the present case, the relationship between the applicant and the child's mother lasted for two years during one of which they co-habited. Moreover, the conception of their child was the result of a deliberate decision and they had also planned to get married (...). Their relationship at this time had thus the hallmark of family life for the purposes of Article 8. The fact that it subsequently broke down does not alter this conclusion any more than it would for a couple who were lawfully married and in a similar situation. It follows that from the moment of the child's birth a bond existed between the applicant and his daughter amounting to family life."[100]

The importance attached by the Court to the *de facto* situation was made very clear in the *Kroon* Case. The case concerned the impossibility under Dutch law then in force for a biological father to have legally recognised family ties established with his child,

---

[97]   Appl. 9253/81, *X v. Federal Republic of Germany* (not published).
[98]   Judgment of 21 June 1988, para. 21.
[99]   Judgment of 19 February 1996, *Gül*, para. 32.
[100] Judgment of 26 May 1994, para. 44.

if the latter is born out of a relationship with a woman who at that moment was still married to another man. The respondent Government had argued that the relationship between the father and his biological child did not amount to family life, since the child was born out of an extramarital relationship, the father did not live with the woman and the child, and did not contribute to the child's upbringing. The Court adopted the following view: "In any case, the Court recalls that the notion of 'family life' in Article 8 is not confined solely to marriage-based relationships and may encompass other de facto 'family ties' where parties are living together outside marriage (...). Although, as a rule, living together may be a requirement for such a relationship, exceptionally other factors may also serve to demonstrate that a relationship has sufficient constancy to create de facto 'family ties'; such is the case here, as since 1987 four children have been born to Mrs Kroon and Mr Zerrouk. A child born of such a relationship is ipso jure part of that 'family unit' from the moment of its birth and by the very fact of it (...). There thus exists between Samir and Mr Zerrouk a bond amounting to family life, whatever the contribution of the latter to his son's care and upbringing. Article 8 is therefore applicable."[101]

In the *Lebbink* Case the applicant complained about the rejection of his request for access to his daughter, born out of wedlock. The Court noted that the applicant had not sought to recognise his daughter, and he had never formed a "family unit" with her and her mother as they had never cohabited. Consequently, the question arose whether there were other factors demonstrating that the applicant's relationship with his daughter had sufficient constancy and substance to create *de facto* "family ties". The Court did not agree with the applicant that a mere biological kinship, without any further legal or factual elements indicating the existence of a close personal relationship, could be regarded as sufficient to attract the protection of Article 8. However, the Court noted that the child was born out of a genuine relationship between the applicant and Ms B. that lasted for about three years and that, until this institution was abolished when his daughter was about seven months old, the applicant was his daughter's auxiliary guardian. It observed that the applicant's relation with Ms B. ended in August 1996 when the child was about sixteen months old. The Court further noted that, although the applicant never cohabited with Ms B. and his daughter, he had been present when the child was born, that – as from her birth until August 1996 when his relation with the mother ended – he visited Ms B. and his daughter at unspecified regular intervals. In these circumstances the Court concluded that, when the applicant's relationship with Ms B. ended, there existed – in addition to biological kinship – certain ties between the applicant and his daughter, which were sufficient to attract the protection of Article 8 of the Convention.[102]

---

[101]   Judgment of 27 October 1994, para. 30.
[102]   Judgment of 1 June 2004, paras 37-40.

Despite the importance of factual links it goes without saying that a family relationship is not terminated by reason of the fact that the child is taken into public care.[103]

Article 8 also covers relations between an adoptive parent and an adoptive child.[104] The Court has not yet decided whether foster parents and foster children also fall under family life. Since for all practical purposes protection of identical interests is at stake here and the factual situation is also quite similar, it is submitted that this question ought to be answered in the affirmative, no matter whether the foster parent has or has not been (temporarily) entrusted with the guardianship, be it that – especially in the latter case – these interests may have to yield to those of the natural parents.[105] And in any case the private life of the foster parents and foster children may be involved.[106]

With respect to the relationship of a homosexual couple the Commission has taken the view that "despite the modern evolution of attitudes towards homosexuality", that relationship does not fall within the scope of the right to respect for family life, but that, here again, the right to respect for private life may be involved.[107] The Commission did not indicate on which criterion it based its decision. The difference with other extra-martial relationships is not self-evident, while there would seem to be a clear similarity of interests. Developments in the law of the member States of the Council of Europe in this area as well as developments in the Strasbourg case law in the area of transsexualism, discussed *supra,* may be expected to have their impact on former case law on the issue.

The mere existence of a family relationship is not sufficient for the applicability of Article 8; only in the case of a sufficiently close factual tie is there a question of family life.[108] In fact, if the relationship does not imply genuine ties, an *interference*

---

[103]   Judgment of 22 June 1989, *Eriksson,* para.58; and judgment of 25 February 1992, *Margareta and Roger Andersson,* para. 72.

[104]   Judgment of 28 October 1998, *Söderbäck,* para. 24: a husband adopted a child without the natural father's consent: the Court accepted family life with the former. But the granting of an adoption order may constitute an interference with the natural parent's right to respect for his family life of a particularly serious nature; see judgment of 26 May 1994, *Keegan,* para. 55.

[105]   See in this connection the dissenting opinion of Commission member Schermers, attached to the report of the Commission of 14 July 1988, *Cecilia and Lisa Eriksson,* A.156, p. 56: "Normally, there will be family life (as a fact) between foster parents and their children".

[106]   See the judgment of 8 July 1987, *W v. the United Kingdom,* para. 59 and the judgment of 26 May 1994, *Keegan,* para. 55: "As has been observed in a similar context, where a child is placed with alternative carers he or she may in the course of time establish new bonds with them which it might not be in his or her interests to disturb or interrupt by reversing a previous decision as to care (...). Such a state of affairs not only jeopardised the proper development of the applicant's ties with the child but also set a process in motion which was likely to prove to be irreversible, thereby putting the applicant at a significant disadvantage in his contest with the prospective adopters for the custody of the child."

[107]   Appl. 9369/81, *X and Y v. the United Kingdom,* D&R 32 (1983), p. 220 (221).

[108]   See, *e.g.,* the judgment of 13 June 1979, *Marckx,* para. 31: "with the result that a real family life existed and *still* exists between them". See also Appl. 7626/76, *X v. the United Kingdom,* D&R 11 (1978), p. 160 (166).

is not possible. Whether such genuine ties exist, is determined, *inter alia*, by the nature of the family relationship invoked by the applicant. For married couples and children born out of that marriage, and for other close family relationships they are assumed unless their absence is evident or proven.[109] For other relationships the genuineness of the family ties is determined by factual circumstances, *e.g.* by the question whether the persons concerned belong to the same household.[110] In the case of a relationship other than of a couple, consideration is also given to the age and dependence of the alleged victim.[111] Thus, a parent who has been, or threatens to be, separated from her or his under age child will in general have a stronger claim to respect for family life than a person who desires to be reunited with his adult child, brother or sister.[112] And for an adult the fact that he has to live at some distance from his parents abroad, in general will be less likely to constitute an interference with family life than for a minor.[113]

A prolonged voluntary separation creates a presumption that the persons concerned do not feel the need of a close family tie. In the *Moustaquim* Case the Court was not willing to exclude the applicability of Article 8 in a case where the applicant's relations with his family were strained. He had run away and had been imprisoned. However, he had never broken off relations with them.[114] In the *Sen* Case, to be discussed *infra* 12.4.3.1., the Court accepted family life between parents and a nine-year-old daughter, although the former had moved to the Netherlands and the child had been raised in Turkey by relatives.

It is submitted that in cases concerning family ties one must take account, *inter alia*, of the question who took the initiative for the separation in the past, of the nature

---

[109] Thus the Court held in the *Marckx* judgment, para. 45, that 'family life' in the sense of Article 8 "includes at least the ties between near relatives, for instance those between grandparents and grandchildren, since such relatives may play a considerable part in family life". See also the judgment of 21 June 1988, *Berrehab*, para. 21.

[110] Thus, *e.g.*, in the case of an uncle and a nephew: Appl. 3110/67, *X v. Federal Republic of Germany*, Yearbook XI (1968), p. 449 (518). See also Appls 7289/75 and 7349/76, *X and Y v. Switzerland*, Yearbook XX (1977), p. 372 (408-410), which concerned an extra-marital relationship.

[111] Thus, *e.g.*, in the case of a mother-daughter relationship the age of the latter was considered relevant in addition to the fact that she was married, lived together with her husband, and had a full-time job: Appl. 5269/71, *X and Y v. the United Kingdom*, Yearbook XV (1972), p. 564 (574). On the criterion of the 'financial (in)dependency', see Appl. 8157/78, *X v. the United Kingdom* (not published).

[112] See *e.g.* the *Boujlifa* judgment of 21 October 1997, para. 34: His ties with his parents and his brothers and sisters came under private life rather than family life, as he has attained the age of majority. In any event, the strength of the ties concerned had not been clearly established by the documents in the file.

[113] See Appl. 1855/63, *X v. Denmark*, Yearbook VII (1965), p. 200 (204), where a refusal to grant a visitor's permit was deemed not to conflict with Article 8, since the case concerned a 41-year-old son, who had lived abroad already for twenty years and had had an opportunity to visit his parents and other relatives regularly for a reasonable time.

[114] Judgment of 18 February 1991, para. 36.

---

of the continued ties, and of the family traditions within the religious, ethnic, and/or cultural community to which the persons in question belong. For instance, in several cultures it is a self-evident obligation for a grandchild to adopt his grandparent into his household after his parents have died, even if he and his grandparent may have been separated for many years. Furthermore, the degree of dependence of the applicant on his parents or other relatives, in material or in immaterial respects, must be considered.[115] And in any case the mere fact that a person has grown up does not mean that he is no longer entitled to any form of protection of the family unit of which he formed part as a child, not even when he himself has married meanwhile.[116]

In the *Pannullo and Forte* Case the Court decided that a delay (of seven months!) caused by an autopsy and other reasons in returning the dead body of a child to parents raised an issue under the concept of family life. In this particular case the Court concluded that no fair balance had been struck between the right to family life of the parents and the State's interest in crime prevention.[117]

12.4.2   GUARANTEES IMPLIED IN THE OBLIGATION TO 'RESPECT' FAMILY LIFE

The right to respect for family life implies the right to recognition of a legal relationship between members of a family.[118] On that ground Belgian law was found to be contrary to Article 8 insofar as, in addition to the production of the birth certificate of an illegitimate child, it set other conditions for a legal relationship between mother and child to come into existence, such as recognition by the mother or a procedure of legitimisation of the child.[119] And the same view was taken with respect to the denial to an illegitimate child, 'adopted by the mother', of legal relations with the parents of the mother, and the denial to an illegitimate child of rights equal to those of a legitimate child. With respect to legal relationships it has also been recognised that Article 8 does not merely require the State to abstain from interferences, but may also

---

[115] See on the one hand, Appl. 5532/72, *X v. the United Kingdom, Coll.* 43 (1973), p.19 (121) and, on the other hand, Appl. 5269/71, *X and Y v. the United Kingdom,* Yearbook XV (1972), p. 564 (574).

[116] The possibility of violation of Article 8 in such a case was examined by the Commission in the case of Appl. 5269/71, mentioned in the preceding note.

[117] Judgment of 30 October 2001, para. 39.

[118] Judgment of 27 October 1994, *Kroon,* para. 36: "The Court recalls that in the instant case it has been established that the relationship between the applicants qualifies as 'family life' (...). There is thus a positive obligation on the part of the competent authorities to allow complete family ties to be formed between Mr Zerrouk and his son Samir as expeditiously as possible."

[119] Judgment of 13 June 1979, *Marckx,* para. 31. The Commission referred to Article 2 of the Draft General Principles on Equality and Non-Discrimination in respect of Persons born out of Wedlock of the Sub-Commission for the Prevention of Discrimination and for the Protection of Minorities of the UN Commission for Human Rights, *Study of Discrimination against Persons born out of Wedlock,* United Nations, New York, 1967, pp. 225-227.

require certain positive measures. Thus, in the *Rasmussen* Case the Court gave as its opinion that effective respect for family life obliges the Contracting States to make available to the alleged father of a child an effective and accessible remedy by which he can establish whether he is the biological father of the child.[120] The Court did not reach the conclusion that in this case there was a violation of Article 8. It focused its examination on the fact that Mr Rasmussen alleged that his right to contest his paternity of a child born during marriage was subject to time-limits, whereas his former wife was entitled to institute paternity proceedings at any time. The Court did not go into the issue of Article 8 separately, although it declared that the facts of the case fell within the ambit of that article,[121] but directly dealt with the issue of Article 14. It concluded that the difference in treatment was not discriminatory.[122]

The *Johnston* Case concerned the absence of the possibility under Irish law of divorce, and of recognition of the family life of persons living in a family relationship outside marriage after the breakdown of the marriage of one of those persons and a third person. The Court took the position that, while respect for private and family life may require a legal provision relieving parties from the obligation to live together, it must, in principle, be left to the State to decide what form the remedy should take.[123] More or less as a logical consequence of this position the Court took the view that, although a genuine family relationship may exist between two persons living together outside marriage and their child, one could not derive from Article 8 an obligation on the part of Ireland to establish for unmarried couples a status analogous to that of married couples.[124] There is, however, at the very least the obligation of non-interference in the family life between them and the children born out of that new relationship.[125] With respect to the legal status of the child born out of a relationship outside marriage the Court concluded that here Irish law was in violation of Article 8, because it did not recognise family-law relationships between the child and her parents. As a consequence the father was not regarded, as of right, as the legal guardian of his daughter, which involved far-reaching consequences for both of them. In addition the child could never be legitimated, not even after the death of her father's wife. Moreover the succession rights of the child could under certain circumstances be inferior to those of legitimate children. In the Court's view, all this constituted a failure by the State to provide a framework for the proper ordering of relations between the child and her parents, and the appropriate legal regime for the proper development

---

[120]   Judgment of 28 November 1984, para. 33.
[121]   *Ibidem.*
[122]   *Ibidem*, para. 42.
[123]   Judgment of 18 December 1986, para. 55.
[124]   *Ibidem*, para. 57.
[125]   *Ibidem*, para. 72.

of their family lives. The Court found no ground for this failure, which met the requirements of the second paragraph of Article 8.[126]

Article 8 does not contain a specific regulation concerning the question which parent has to be awarded the custody of the children if the family unit is disrupted by divorce or judicial separation; in principle this is left to the national authorities, on the basis of the relevant national law.[127] In the *Hoffmann* Case, however, the Court underlined that in deciding on the question which parent to award parental rights Article 14 has to be taken into account. In that case the national courts heavily relied upon the religion of the mother (a Jehovah-witness) in order to grant parental rights to the father. The Court ruled that essentially a distinction had been made based on a difference in religion alone. This was considered to be a violation of Article 8 taken in conjunction with Article 14.[128] No violation, however, was found with respect to a denial of custody to a homosexual father, because of the margin of appreciation in that respect.[129] Every decision about awarding custody of the children implies by definition an encroachment on the right to respect of family life of one or both of the parents, but in addition of course has consequences for the exercise of the right to respect of family life of the child in question and of any other children forming part of the family unit.

As has been shown in the previous sub-section, the fact that after the divorce not all the members of the family live together any more, does not put an end to their family life nor necessarily to the genuineness of their family ties.[130] If the parents cannot reach agreement on custody or if their proposal is ignored, the national authorities may rely on the restriction ground 'protection of health and morals' or 'protection of the rights and freedoms of others' in the second paragraph. However, for the parent who still has genuine ties with his child but to whom the custody of the child has not been awarded, a right of access follows from Article 8,[131] unless the authorities can invoke one of the grounds of the second paragraph for its denial.[132] The justification for the award of the custody to one parent rather than to the other cannot be automatically relied upon as a ground for the denial of the right of access to the latter; very serious arguments have to be put forward for justifying the complete severance of the ties

---

[126]   *Ibidem*, para. 75.
[127]   Appl. 1449/62, *X v. the Netherlands*, Yearbook VI (1963), p. 262 (266); Appl. 5486/72, *X v. Sweden*, Coll. 44 (1973), p. 128 (129).
[128]   Judgment of 23 June 1993, para. 36.
[129]   Judgment of 26 February 2002, *Fretté*, para. 41.
[130]   Judgment of 21 June 1988, *Berrehab*, para. 21. See also the judgment of 26 May 1994, *Keegan*, para. 44; and the judgment of 27 October 1994, *Kroon*, para. 30.
[131]   Appl. 172/56, *X v. Sweden*, Yearbook I (1955-1957), p. 211 (217); Appl. 7911/77, *X v. Sweden*, D&R 12 (1978), p. 192 (193); report of 8 March 1982, *Hendriks*, D&R 29 (1982), p. 5 (14-16).
[132]   Appl. 5608/72, *X v. the United Kingdom*, Coll. 44 (1973), p. 66 (68-69); Appl. 7911/77, *X v. Sweden*, D&R 12 (1978), p. 192 (193); report of 8 March 1982, *Hendriks*, D&R 29 (1982), p. 37-40.

between parent and child. All this applies in principle equally in the case of the termination of the relationship between a parent and his or her illegitimate child.[133] And the same holds good for the deprivation of parental rights, since that also constitutes a problem directly affecting the right to protection of family life of the persons concerned, because the family ties do not end by the fact that the child is taken into public care.[134] Such a measure will in general meet with few objections in Strasbourg if 'the protection of the rights and freedoms of others', mentioned in the second paragraph, is invoked, because of the very marginal inquiry into the reasonableness of such a justification.[135] The case law of the Court therefore includes many cases in which the Court finds the interference with parents' rights justified under Article 8. In the following cases the Court did not find a violation: *Bronda*: a child who stayed with foster parents was not returned to the parents for the sake of the child;[136] *Buscemi*: both parents were declared unfit for parenthood and the child was taken into public care;[137] *L. v. Finland*: children of a mentally ill father were taken into care;[138] *Scozzari and Giunta*: children were taken out of a deteriorated family with violence and sexual abuse; however, a violation was found with respect to access restrictions and placement in a controversial home;[139] *Glaser*: a divorced father was refused access to his children; since the children were under stress, a fair balance was found to have been struck.[140]

In general a violation does occur when measures taken by the State do not aim at re-uniting a family or may be considered to be disproportional. Thus, a violation was found in *K.and T. v. Finland*. There the children of a mentally ill mother were taken into public care, while lighter measures involving relatives were not even considered.[141] And when deciding on child custody, the reports upon which the decision is based should not be contradictory and must be based upon serious allegation. In the *Kutzner* Case the custody decision was based upon such contradictory reports and was not founded upon serious grounds as, for instance, ill treatment.[142]

In *O. v. the United Kingdom* the applicant alleged a violation of Article 8 by the procedures followed to terminate the applicant's access to his children and because of the absence of a remedy against that decision. The Commission found no violation of Article 8 since it interpreted the complaint as being apparently confined to the absence of an effective remedy against the decision to deprive the applicant of access

---

[133] See Appl. 7658/76, *X v. Denmark*, D&R 15 (1979), p. 128.
[134] Judgments of 8 July 1987, *W., B. and R. v. the United Kingdom*, para. 62, 61 and 67 respectively; judgment of 24 March 1988, *Olsson (No. 1)*, para. 59.
[135] See, *e.g.*, Appl. 5132/71, *X v. Denmark*, Coll. 43 (1973), p. 57 (60-61).
[136] Judgment of 9 June 1998, para. 63.
[137] Judgment of 16 September 1999, para. 63.
[138] Judgment of 27 April 2000, para. 122.
[139] Judgment of 13 July 2000, para. 183.
[140] Judgment of 19 September 2000, para. 87.
[141] Judgment of 27 April 2000, para. 146.
[142] Judgment of 26 February 2002, para. 81.

and not as also alleging that the law was applied in a manner which lacked justification under Article 8(2). Consequently, the Commission concluded that there had been no violation of Article 8 of the Convention as a result of the alleged lack of a right to a hearing before a court and of an effective legal remedy in respect of his claim for access to his children.[143] The Court held with respect to the first part of the complaint that the information provided about the procedures followed was insufficient to establish a violation of Article 8. With respect to the second part the Court had already found a violation of Article 6(1) and did not find it necessary to examine the complaint under Article 8.[144]

H. v. the United Kingdom concerned proceedings instituted by the applicant regarding access to her child. Here the Court held that, in view of the delays, the proceedings had failed to show respect for the applicant's family life since the proceedings related to a fundamental element of family life and the procedural delay led to a *de facto* determination of the matter at issue. The Court, therefore, considered that the duration of the proceedings was a factor that could properly be taken into account in the present context.[145] Gross delays in a national court procedure and in inefficiency with respect to DNA or alternative tests to establish parenthood led the Court to conclude that Article 8 had been violated in the *Mikulic* Case.[146]

In *W., B.* and *R. v. the United Kingdom* the complaints concerned the applicants' access to their children in the care of a local authority. According to the Commission the procedures which led to the determination of issues relating to family life, had to be such as to show respect for family life. In particular, parents normally should have a right to be heard and to be fully informed in this connection.[147] The Court took the view that Article 8 contains no explicit procedural requirements, but that this was not conclusive for the matter. The relevant considerations to be weighed by a local authority in reaching decisions on children in its care must include the views and interests of the natural parents. The decision-making process must therefore be such as to secure that their views and interests are made known to and duly taken into account by the local authority and that they are able to exercise in due time any remedies available to them. In the Court's view, "what therefore has to be determined is whether, having regard to the particular circumstances of the case and notably the serious nature of the decisions to be taken, the parents have been involved in the decision-making process, seen as a whole, to a degree sufficient to provide them with the requisite protection of their interests. If they have not, there will have been a failure to respect their family life and the interference resulting from the decision will not be

---

143   Report of 3 December 1985, A.120, pp. 35-36.
144   Judgment of 8 July 1987, para. 67.
145   Judgment of 8 July 1987, para. 89.
146   Judgment of 7 February 2002, para. 65.
147   Report of 15 October 1985, A.121, p. 45; and reports of 4 December 1985, A.121, pp. 86 and 131.

capable of being regarded as 'necessary' within the meaning of Article 8."[148] The Court found a violation of Article 8 after examining the procedure relating to the authority's decisions to place the children with long-term foster parents with a view to adoption, and to terminate access by the applicants. In the Court's view, it revealed insufficient involvement of the applicants.[149]

The fact that the Court has adopted the view that Article 8 implies certain procedural requirements is especially important in view of the fact, discussed *supra* under Article 6, that Article 6 does not apply to procedures concerning the admission or expulsion of aliens, not even if elements of the right to respect for private or family life are at issue. However, the procedural requirements inherent in Article 8 are not identical to the guarantees laid down in Article 6. According to the Court, Article 6(1) "affords a procedural safeguard, namely the 'right to a court' in the determination of one's civil rights and obligations' (...); whereas not only does the procedural requirement inherent in Article 8 cover administrative procedures as well as judicial proceedings, but is ancillary to the wider purpose of ensuring proper respect for, *inter alia*, family life."[150]

In the *McMichael* Case the violation of Article 8 consisted of the fact that the applicants had been unfairly treated in care-proceedings concerning their child. The content of some relevant documents had not been disclosed to them. This procedural aspect is highly important in family life decisions. In well-established case law the Court requires that national procedures do respect the interests of the parents and their role in the decision-making process. An example is the *Elsholz* Case. The Court concluded that Article 8 had been violated since the father of an illegitimate child had not been granted access rights, while in the procedure leading to this decision a psychological report was lacking, no hearing was held and the father had in general insufficiently been involved in the decision-making process.[151]

In the *Sommerfeld* Case and the *Sahin* Case the applicants complained about German court decisions dismissing his second request for access to his child, born out of wedlock. The Court noted that the District Court had heard the child and the parents and had had regard to material obtained in a first set of access proceedings, *inter alia*, comments filed by a psychologist of the local health services. The Court considered that, given the psychologist's rather superficial submissions in the first set of proceedings and the lapse of time, and bearing in mind what was at stake in the pro-

---

[148]   Judgments of 8 July 1987, paras 64 and 66, respectively.
[149]   *Ibidem*, para. 70.
[150]   Judgment of 24 February 1995, *McMichael*, para. 91.
[151]   Judgment of 13 July 2000, para. 53. See also the judgment of 10 May 2001, *T.P. and K.M. v. the United Kingdom*, para. 83: a parent not sufficiently involved in the decision-making process leading at the removal of a child after sexual abuse allegations; judgment of 20 December 2001, *Buchberger*, para. 45: child taken into care after new evidence was not disclosed to the parent. In the judgment of 11 October 2001, *Hoffmann*, para. 47, it was found that a father was not granted access to his illegitimate child, but was sufficiently involved in the decision-making (no violation).

ceedings, namely the relations between a father and his child, the District Court should not have been satisfied with hearing only the child as to her wishes on the matter without having psychological expert evidence at its disposal in order to evaluate the child's seemingly firm wishes. Correct and complete information on the child's relationship with the applicant as the parent seeking access to the child is an indispensable prerequisite for establishing a child's true wishes and thereby striking a fair balance between the interests at stake. The Court further recalled that the Regional Court, which had full power to review all issues relating to the request for access, endorsed the District Court findings on the basis of the file. In the Court's opinion, the German courts' failure to order a psychological report on the possibilities of establishing contacts between the child and the applicant revealed an insufficient involvement of the applicant in the decision-making process.[152] Both cases were referred to the Grand Chamber. The Grand Chamber stated in the *Sommerfeld* Case that it would be going too far to say that domestic courts were always required to involve a psychological expert on the issue of granting access to a parent not having custody. Having had the benefit of direct contact with the child, the District Court had been well placed to evaluate her statements and establish whether or not she had been able to make up her own mind. In the *Sahin* Case, the Grand Chamber stated that it would be going too far to say that domestic courts should always hear evidence from a child in court on the issue of access. As the child had been only five years old at the relevant time, the court had been entitled to rely on the findings of the expert. There had been no cause to doubt her professional competence. The Grand Chamber was satisfied that the German courts had proceeded reasonably in the circumstances of both cases and had provided sufficient material to reach a reasoned decision on the question of access. The procedural requirements implicit in Article 8 had therefore been met.[153]

In the *Olsson* Case the applicants asserted that the decision to take their children into care, the manner in which the decision had been implemented and the refusals to terminate care, had given rise to violations of Article 8. As regards the procedure of the taking into care and the refusals to terminate care, the Court held the view that the applicants had been involved in the decision-making process, seen as a whole, to a degree sufficient to provide requisite protection of their interests. As to the taking into care, the Court held that it is not a sufficient justification that the child will be better off if placed in care. In order to determine whether the reasons for deciding to take the children into care could be considered 'sufficient' for the purposes of Article 8, the Court held that it must have regard to the case as a whole and notably to the circumstances in which the decision was taken. The decisions were based on social reports supported by statements from persons well acquainted with the case and the

---

152   Judgments of 11 October 2001, paras 43-44, and paras 46-47, respectively.
153   Judgments of 8 July 2003, paras 70-74 and paras 72-78, respectively.

decisions were confirmed by courts which were able to form their own impression of the case and whose judgments were not reversed on appeal. Therefore, the Swedish authorities, having regard to their margin of appreciation, were in the Court's view entitled to think that the taking into care was necessary. However, the implementation of the care decision was held by the Court to be in violation of Article 8. It was not the quality of the care given that was at issue, but the separation of the children and the placement of two of them at a long distance from the applicants' home and the restrictions on their visits, which impeded easy and regular access by the members of the family to each other and thus ran counter to the ultimate aim of their reunification. In these respects, and despite the applicants' uncooperative attitude, the measures of implementation of the care decision were not supported by sufficient reasons justifying them as proportionate to the legitimate aim.[154]

In the *Eriksson* Case the Court was confronted with the question whether the prohibition for the mother to remove her daughter from the foster home and the restrictions on her right of access constituted a violation of Article 8. The child was taken into care one month after she was born. When the child was five years old, the care order was lifted, but in the same decision it was decided to prohibit the mother from removing the daughter from the foster home until further notice. Its effect was that the mother, although there were no longer any reproaches against her for inability to care for her daughter, was still deprived of the factual care. Another effect of the prohibition on removal was that the mother could not secure a formal decision on her right of access to her daughter. The Court found a violation of Article 8, considering the factual and legal situation concerning the possibilities for the applicants to meet and develop their relationship with a view to being reunited.[155]

In the *Margareta and Roger Andersson* Case the Court was confronted with a situation in which the child was placed in a foster home and, together with his mother, complained about restrictions on access, including restrictions on communication by correspondence and telephone. The Court reaffirmed that Article 8 includes a parent's and child's right to the taking of measures with a view to their being reunited. The Court reached the conclusion, after having reviewed all the facts, that during a specific period the restrictions were particularly far-reaching. Therefore, they had to be supported by convincing reasons and to be consistent with the ultimate aim of reuniting the Andersson family in order to be justified under Article 8(2). The Court held as follows: "The reasons adduced by the Government are of a general nature and do not specifically address the necessity of prohibiting contact by correspondence and telephone. The Court does not doubt that these reasons were relevant. However, they do not sufficiently show that it was necessary to deprive the applicants of almost every means of maintaining contact with each other for a period of approximately one and

---

154   Judgment of 24 March 1988, para. 81.
155   Judgment of 22 June 1989, para. 71.

a half years. Indeed, it is questionable whether the measures were compatible with the aim of reuniting the applicants."[156] For this reason the Court concluded that the restrictions imposed on meetings, correspondence and telephone were disproportionate, and therefore not necessary in a democratic society.

In the *Olsson (No. 2)* Case the Court also had to rule upon the legality of restrictions on access and the refusal to terminate the measure. The Court reiterated the principle that Article 8 includes a right for the natural parents to have measures taken with a view to their being reunited with their children and an obligation on the part of the national authorities to take such measures. In this case, however, it concluded that in the light of all the facts and the margin of appreciation "it has not been established that the social welfare authorities failed to fulfil their obligation to take measures with a view of the applicants being reunited with Helena and Thomas."[157]

In the *Elsholz* Case the Court summarised its view concerning the margin of appreciation for the States, and the scope of its review as follows: "The margin of appreciation to be accorded to the competent national authorities will vary in accordance with the nature of the issues and the importance of the interests at stake. Thus, the Court recognises that the authorities enjoy a wide margin of appreciation, in particular when assessing the necessity of taking a child into care. However, a stricter scrutiny is called for in respect of any further limitations, such as restrictions placed by those authorities on parental rights of access, and of any legal safeguards designed to secure an effective protection of the right of parents and children to respect for their family life. Such further limitations entail the danger that the family relations between the parents and a young child would be effectively curtailed (...). The Court further recalls that a fair balance must be struck between the interests of the child and those of the parent (...) and that in doing so particular importance must be attached to the best interests of the child which, depending on their nature and seriousness, may override those of the parent. In particular, the parent cannot be entitled under Article 8 of the Convention to have such measures taken as would harm the child's health and development (...)."[158]

In *K. and T. v. Finland* the Court accepted that when action has to be taken to protect a child in an emergency, it may not always be possible, because of the urgency of the situation, to associate in the decision-making process those having custody of the child. Nor might it even be desirable, even if possible, to do so if those having custody of the child are seen as the source of an immediate threat to the child, since giving them prior warning would be liable to deprive the measure of its effectiveness.

---

[156]   Judgment of 25 February 1992, para. 97. In the judgment of 12 July 2001, *K. and T. v. Finland*, para. 176, the Court also found a violation for a failure to try to reunite the family. In this case, however, the taking into care of the child and the access restrictions were justified.

[157]   Judgment of 27 November 1992, para. 79. See also the judgment of 22 April 1992, *Rieme*, para. 76.

[158]   Judgment of 13 July 2000, paras 49-50; judgment of 8 April 2004, *Haase*, para. 93.

The Court held however that it should be satisfied that the national authorities were entitled to consider that there existed circumstances justifying the abrupt removal of the child from the care of its parents without any prior contact or consultation. In particular, it was for the respondent State to establish that a careful assessment of the impact of the proposed care measure on the parents and the child, as well as of the possible alternatives to the removal of the child from its family, was carried out prior to the implementation of a care measure.[159]

In *K. and A. v. Finland* the Court, furthermore, noted that the fact that a child could be placed in a more beneficial environment for his or her upbringing will not on its own justify a compulsory measure of removal from the care of the biological parents; other circumstances must exist pointing to the 'necessity' for such an interference with the parents' right under Article 8 to enjoy a family life with their child.[160]

In the *Haase* Case the Court held that the sudden taking of six children from their respective schools, kindergarten and home, placing them in unidentified foster homes, and forbidding all contact with their parents, went beyond what was necessary in the situation and could not be accepted as proportionate. In particular, the removal of the newborn baby from the hospital was an extremely harsh measure. It was traumatic for the mother and placed her own physical and mental health under strain. It deprived the newborn baby of close contact with its natural mother and of the advantages of breast-feeding. The removal also deprived the father of close contact with his daughter after her birth. There had to be extraordinarily compelling reasons before a baby could be physically removed from the care of its mother, against her will, immediately after birth, as a consequence of a procedure in which neither she nor her husband had been involved. The Court was not satisfied that such reasons had been shown to exist.[161]

In the *Keegan* Case the applicant maintained that the State failed to respect his family life by facilitating the secret placement of his daughter for adoption without his knowledge or consent and by failing to create a legal nexus between himself and his (illegitimate) daughter from the moment of birth. His relationship with the mother had come to an end before the birth of the child. The Court reiterated the principle established in previous case law, *i.e.* that legal safeguards must be created that render the child's integration in his family possible as from the moment of the birth. The Court then noted, while considering whether the interference was necessary in a democratic society, that where a child is placed with alternative caretakers, he may establish new bonds with them in the course of time which it might not be in his interests to disturb or interrupt by reversing a previous decision as to care. According to the Court: "Such a state of affairs not only jeopardised the proper development of the applicant's

---

ties with the child but also set in motion a process which was likely to prove to be irreversible, thereby putting the applicant at a significant disadvantage in his contest with the prospective adopters for the custody of the child. The Government have advanced no reasons relevant to the welfare of the applicant's daughter to justify such a departure from the principles that govern respect for family ties."[162]

The strictness, by which the Court demands that legally recognised family ties can be established between a father and his child was also reflected in the *Kroon* Case, referred to *supra*. The Court in rather strong terms disapproved of the legislation in force in the Netherlands, that prevented a (biological) father from recognising his child, as long as the mother was still married to another man. In this case the father and the mother already had a few children together. The Court held as follows: "In the Court's opinion, 'respect' for 'family life' requires that biological and social reality prevail over a legal presumption which, as in the present case, flies in the face of both established fact and the wishes of those concerned without actually benefiting anyone. Accordingly, the Court concludes that, even having regard to the margin of apprecia-tion left to the State, the Netherlands has failed to secure the 'respect' to the applicants for their family life to which they are entitled under the Convention."[163]

12.4.3 ADMISSION AND EXPULSION OF ALIENS

12.4.3.1 Admission

The right of a non-citizen to enter or reside in a particular country has not been laid down in the Convention, but the immigration policy of the Contracting States has, of course, to be in conformity with their obligations under the Convention. Thus, the exclusion of a person from a country in which his close relatives reside may raise an issue under Article 8.[164]

In the *Abdulaziz, Cabales and Balkandali* Case applications were lodged by three women who resided lawfully and were permanently settled in the United Kingdom, but whose husbands or prospective husbands were refused permission to stay in the United Kingdom. As to the applicability of Article 8, the Court confirmed the Com-mission's established case law by holding as follows: "although some aspects of the right to enter a country are governed by Protocol No. 4 as regards States bound by that instrument, it is not to be excluded that measures taken in the field of immigration may affect the right to respect for family life under Article 8."[165] The Court also

---

[162] Judgment of 26 May 1994, para. 55.
[163] Judgment of 27 October 1994, para. 40.
[164] See, *e.g.*, Appl. 9492/81, *Family X v. the United Kingdom*, D&R 30 (1983), p. 232 (234).
[165] Judgment of 28 May 1985, para. 60.

observed that, although by guaranteeing the right to respect for family life Article 8 presupposes the existence of a family, this does not mean that all *intended* family life falls entirely outside its ambit. Therefore, even if the family life was not yet fully established for all the applicants at the moment when permission was asked for the men to enter or remain in the United Kingdom, this did not exclude the applicability of Article 8. In this case the Court found sufficient ground for this applicability in the fact that the couples, at least in their own opinion, were married and had lived together or wished to live together.[166]

Next, confirming its case law that there may be positive oligations inherent in an effective 'respect' for the rights protected in Article 8, but that a wide margin of appreciation has to be left to the Contracting States in determining the steps to be taken with due regard to the needs and resources of the community and of individuals, the Court held as follows: "In particular, in the area now under consideration, the extent of a State's obligation to admit to its territory relatives of settled immigrants will vary according to the particular circumstances of the persons involved. Moreover, the Court cannot ignore that the present case is concerned not only with family life but also with immigration and that, as a matter of well-established international law and subject to its treaty obligations, a State has the right to control the entry of non-national into its territory."[167] The Court also made the following observation: "The duty imposed by Article 8 cannot be considered as extending to a general obligation on the part of a Contracting State to respect the choice by married couples of the country of their matrimonial residence and to accept the non-national spouses for settlement in that country."[168] The Court found that the applicants had not shown that there were obstacles to establishing family life in their own or their husbands' home countries, or that there were special reasons why that could not be expected of them, and that all three applicants, at the time of their (planned) marriage, were aware of the risk that their husbands would not get a permanent residence permit for the United Kingdom. It, therefore, concluded that there was no lack of respect for family life and, hence, no breach of Article 8 taken alone.[169] However, the Court *did* find that the applicants were victims of discrimination on the ground of sex, in violation of Article 14 in conjunction with Article 8, because of the difference made in the 1980 Statement of Changes in Immigration Rules as to the possibility for male and female immigrants settled in the United Kingdom to obtain permission for their non-national spouses or fiancé(e)s to enter or remain in the country. The assumed difference between the respective impact of men and women on the domestic labour market was

---

[166] *Ibidem,* paras 64-65.
[167] *Ibidem,* para. 67. See also the judgment of 19 February 1996, *Gül.*
[168] Judgment of 28 May 1985, para. 68.
[169] *Ibidem.*

considered by the Court to be not sufficiently important to justify this difference in treatment.[170]

At an earlier stage, the Commission had adopted the position that the right to respect for family life is not interfered with, if the partner and/or other family members of the applicant have the possibility to unite or re-unite with him in his country of origin, and this may reasonably be required of them.[171] In order to determine whether the person concerned may reasonably be required to continue or reside the family unit abroad, the disadvantages involved for the persons concerned have to be weighed against the interests of the respondent State served by its immigration policy. First of all, reunion abroad must be possible. In the *Gül* Case the question was whether Mr Gül's son's move to Switzerland would be the only way for the applicant to develop family life with his son. Since there were no obstacles for Mr Gül preventing him from developing family life in Turkey, while moreover he had only a residence permit on humanitarian grounds and his son had always lived in Turkey,[172] the Court concluded that Switzerland had not failed to fulfil its obligations arising under Article 8(1), and there had therefore been no interference in the applicant's family life.[173] An obstacle was considered to be present in the *Boultif* Case: the applicant, an Algerian national residing in Switzerland, was convicted. However, he and his Swiss wife could not be expected to build up a family life outside Switzerland; not in Algeria because the Swiss wife had no ties with that country and did not speak Arabic, and not in Italy, since it was not established that they would obtain authorisation to reside there lawfully. It also played a role that the applicant posed only a limited threat to society.[174]

There are also other factors, which are deemed to be relevant for determining whether reunion abroad is possible and can reasonably be expected. If, for instance, the State where the member of the family applying for admission resides, or to which he or she has been or is threatened to be expelled, is not prepared to admit the other member or members of the family, the expulsion or the refusal of admission – if a family relationship is indeed involved – constitutes a breach of Article 8.[175] The same holds true if an inhuman treatment in the sense of Article 3 were to await a member of the family when required to settle abroad.[176] If reunion of the family abroad is possible, but the applicant for admission is a minor, the Commission generally

---

[170]   *Ibidem*, para. 82.

[171]   See Council of Europe, *Case Law Topics No. 2, 'Family Life'* (1972), pp. 6-13.

[172]   Precisely on this aspect the Court distinguished the *Gül* Case from the *Berrehab* Case *(infra)*, in which the daughter was born and raised in the Netherlands and therefore could not be expected to have family life in her father's country (Morocco).

[173]   Judgment of 19 February 1996, para. 43.

[174]   Judgment of 2 August 2001, paras 53-55.

[175]   See Appl. 8061/77, *X v. Switzerland* (not published), where the wife alleged that for that reason she could not follow her husband to Yugoslavia.

[176]   See *supra* 7.6.1.

assumed that the child had the right to be reunited with his parents or guardians in the country of their residence, and that the latter could not reasonably be expected to move abroad in order to join the child.[177] However, in 1996 the Court adopted a more stringent view in this respect.[178] The criterion which the Court applies in determining whether admission is necessary or whether family life can also be exercised in another country, was further clarified in the *Sen* Case. Turkish parents residing in the Netherlands with two children born and raised in the Netherlands asked that a third daughter who was nine years old and born and raised in Turkey, be admitted to the Netherlands. The request was refused. The Court found a violation and explicitly considered in that respect that the aspect distinguishing this case from previous cases in which no violation was found, was the major obstacles for the four persons in the Sen family to return to Turkey. The parents had two children born in the Netherlands. They were raised there and did not have any links with Turkey. Consequently they could not reasonably be required to move with their parents to Turkey. Therefore the only possibility to develop family life with the whole family, including the oldest daughter, was to have her admitted in the Netherlands. To impose upon the parents the choice between severing the family life contacts with their oldest child or abandoning their position in Dutch society was a failure to establish a just equilibrium between the interests of the parents and the family and the interests of the state.[179]

Other aspects which the Commission and the Court have so far involved in their weighing of interests are, *inter alia:* the links with the other country;[180] the prospect of joint residence in the respondent State at the time when the family was founded;[181] the existence of ties in the country of origin with other relatives outside the family;[182] and the economic consequences of a removal to another country.[183] If this weighing

---

[177] See Council of Europe, *Case Law Topics*, No. 2, 'Family Life', 1972, pp. 40-41. See also Appls 2991/66 and 2992/66, *Alam, Kahn and Singh v. the United Kingdom*, Yearbook X (1967), p. 478 (502); Appl. 7816/77, *X and Y v. Federal Republic of Germany*, D&R 9 (1978), p. 219 (221); and report of 17 May 1995, *Salah and Souffane Ahmut v. the Netherlands*, Reports 1996 VI, Vol. 24, paras 50-54.

[178] Judgments of 19 February 1996, *Gül* and of 28 November 1996, *Ahmut.*

[179] Judgment of 21 December 2001, paras 36-41.

[180] Appl. 5301/71, *X v. the United Kingdom, Coll.* 43 (1973), p. 82 (84); judgment of 18 February 1991, *Moustaquim*, A.193, para. 36; judgment of 26 March 1992, *Beldjoudi*, para. 71. Especially foreign children of the 'second generation' appear to have a rather strong position in that respect.

[181] Appls 5445-5446/72, *X and Y v. the United Kingdom, Coll.* 42 (1973), p. 146. See also Appl. 7048/75, *X v. the United Kingdom*, D&R 9 (1978), p. 42 (43), where the Commission decided that Article 8 does not *per se* guarantee the right for a married couple to move their residence to a specific country, where one of the two has a visitor's permit. See also the judgment of 28 November 1996, *Ahmut*, Reports 1996-VI, Vol. 24, para. 71.

[182] Appl. 5269/71, *X and Y v. the United Kingdom*, Yearbook XV (1972), p. 564 (574); judgment of 18 February 1991, *Moustaguim*, para. 36.

[183] Appl. 5269/71, *X and Y v. the United Kingdom*, Yearbook XV (1972), p. 564 (574). See also Appl. 9492/81, *Family X v. the United Kingdom*, D&R 30 (1983), p. 232 (234-235), where the Commission found that the fact that the expulsion would prevent the son from continuing his study in the UK did not constitute an interference with the right of respect for family life.

of interests results in the conclusion that the other members of the family cannot reasonably be required to follow the person in question abroad, and that therefore non-admittance or expulsion would violate the latter's family life, the respondent State may still rely on one of the restriction grounds of the second paragraph.[184]

As was mentioned above, in the *Abdulaziz, Cabales and Balkandali* Case the Court held that although Article 8 presupposes the existence of a family, this does not mean that all *intended* family life falls entirely outside its ambit. There, the Court declared Article 8 also applicable to a situation where admission was applied for in order to get married.[185] The applicants could also have relied on Article 12 in that case.

In the case of a divorce, the parent who is entrusted with the custody over the children can of course not reasonably be required to follow the other parent abroad, with the children, in order to maintain the family ties between the latter and the children. In the *Berrehab* Case, the applicant, a Moroccan national, was divorced from his Dutch wife and was appointed as co-guardian of the child born after the divorce. Because of his divorce he was refused prolongation of his residence permit. This resulted in an expulsion order. The Court took into consideration that until his expulsion from the Netherlands, Mr Berrehab saw his daughter four-times a week for several hours at a time. The fact that there were frequent and regular contacts with his daughter led to the conclusion that it could not be maintained that the ties of 'family life' between them had been broken. Although the Court made allowance for the margin of appreciation that is left to the Contracting States and accepted that the Convention does not in principle prohibit Contracting States from regulating the entry and length of stay of aliens, it found a violation of Article 8, having regard to the particular circumstances, since there was in its opinion a disproportion between the means employed and the legitimate aim pursued.[186]

12.4.3.2 Deportation or exclusion on the ground of criminal behaviour

In the case of *deportation* of foreigners who have committed serious crimes, the ground of prevention of disorder or crime mentioned in the second paragraph of Article 8 in general will provide sufficient justification. However, the Court has indicated that this will not easily be the case if the foreigner concerned is a person of the so-called 'second generation'.

---

[184]   See Appl. 312/57, *X v. Belgium*, Yearbook II (1958-1959), p. 352 (353-354); and Appl. 8061/77, *X v. Switzerland* (not published), where the Commission was of the opinion that there was a justification under the second paragraph and for that reason did not inquire the question of whether the wife could really obtain the required permission of the Yugoslav authorities to join her husband.

[185]   Judgment of 28 May 1985, para. 62. See, however, Appl. 7229/75, *X and Y v. the United Kingdom*, D&R 12 (1978), p. 32 (34).

[186]   Judgment of 21 June 1988, para. 29.

In the *Moustaquim* Case the Belgian authorities intended to deport the applicant, a Moroccan national, living in Belgium, because of his having committed a large number of offences and because of the serious risk of his reoffending. The Court had to assess the necessity of this deportation order, since it interfered with his family life because his parents and other family lived in Belgium. The Court took into consideration that the applicant's offences all went back to the period when he was still an adolescent; that all his close relatives had been living in Belgium for a long while; that he was less than two years old when he arrived in Belgium where he had lived for about twenty years; and that he had returned to Morocco only twice, for holidays, and had received all his schooling in French. For these reasons the Court found that his family life would be seriously disrupted by his expulsion. It concluded that the deportation order was disproportionate.[187]

In the *Beldjoudi* Case the Court also concluded that a deportation order concerning Mr Beldjoudi, who was born in France of parents who originated from a territory which was French at the time, namely Algeria, was not proportionate and did therefore violate Article 8. In this case Mr Beldjoudi's criminal record appeared much worse than that of Mr Moustaquim. However, Mr Beldjoudi spent his whole life in France and was deemed to have lost his French nationality in 1963 as his parents had not made a declaration of recognition. In 1970 he manifested his wish to recover the French nationality and was consequently declared to be fit for national service. His wife was born in France of French parents, had always lived there and had French nationality. The deportation might imperil the unity or even the very existence of the marriage. Because of these reasons the Court concluded, from the point of view of respect for the applicants' family life, that the deportation order was disproportionate.[188]

By contrast, in the *Boujaïdi* Case the Court held that the deportation of the applicant was justified under the second paragraph of Article 8. He had not tried to integrate in France or tried to acquire French nationality, whereas the seriousness of the crimes for which he had been convicted, weighed heavily against him.[189]

In the *Radovanovic* Case the Court considered the need to distinguish from a number of cases concerning the expulsion of second-generation immigrants, in which the Court had found no violation of Article 8 of the Convention. In the present case, despite the shorter duration of the applicant's stay in Austria, the Court attached considerable weight to the fact that although the applicant was convicted of aggravated

---

[187]   Judgment of 18 February 1991, paras 44-45. In the same vein also the following five French cases: judgment of 29 January 1997, *Bouchelkia*; judgment of 21 October 1997, *Boujlifa*; judgment of 19 February 1998, *Dalia*; judgment of 30 November 1999, *Baghli*; judgment of 13 February 2001, *Exxouhdi*. These cases all concerned convicted persons who had however strong ties with France, were not always fluent in Arabic and could therefore not be deported.

[188]   Judgment of 26 March 1992, para. 79.

[189]   Judgment of 26 September 1997, para. 41.

robbery, he was only sentenced to a six-month unconditional term of imprisonment, whereas twenty-four months were suspended on probation. The Austrian authorities balanced his right to respect for private and family life against the public interest and gave priority to the latter interest in order to prevent disorder and crime. Without disregarding the serious nature of the offences, the Court noted that the applicant had committed them as a juvenile, that he had no previous criminal record and that the major part of the relatively high sentence was suspended on probation by the Juvenile Court. Therefore the Court was not convinced by the Government's argument and the administrative authorities' assessment that the applicant constituted a serious danger to public order, which necessitated the imposition of the measure concerned. Given the applicant's birth in Austria, where he later also completed his secondary education and vocational training while living with his family, and also taking into account that his family had already lawfully stayed in Austria for a long time and that the applicant himself had an unlimited residence permit when he committed the offence, and considering that, after the death of his grandparents in Serbia and Montenegro, he no longer had any relatives there, the Court found that his family and social ties with Austria were much stronger than with Serbia and Montenegro. The Court therefore considered that, in the circumstances of the case, the imposition of a residence prohibition of unlimited duration was an overly rigorous measure. A less intrusive measure, such as a residence prohibition of a limited duration would have sufficed. The Court thus concluded that the Austrian authorities had not struck a fair balance between the interests involved and that the means employed were disproportionate to the aim pursued in the circumstances of the case. Accordingly, there had been a violation of Article 8 of the Convention.[190]

In the *Mehemi* Case the Court held that in view of the destructive effect of drugs on people's lives, it understood why the authorities show great firmness with regard to those who actively contribute to the spread of this scourge. The fact that the applicant had participated in a conspiracy to import a large quantity of hashish counted heavily against him. Nevertheless, in view of the applicant's lack of links with Algeria, the strength of his links with France and above all the fact that the order for his permanent exclusion from French territory separated him from his minor children and his wife, the Court considered that the measure in question was disproportionate to the aims pursued. There had accordingly been a breach of Article 8.[191] In the *Mehemi (No. 2)* Case the applicant complained, subsequently, that the French authorities had failed to bring the interference with his right to respect for his private and family life which the Court had found to be disproportionate to an end. He complained that the exclusion order remained in effect and also complained of the conditions imposed on his residence in France after his return. The Court considered that in the interval

---

[190]   Judgment of 22 April 2004, paras 34-38.
[191]   Judgment of 26 September 1997, para. 37.

between its judgment and the applicant's return to France, the authorities had had an obligation to facilitate the applicant's return to his family. In that connection, it noted that the French Government had agreed in principle to the applicant's return. While the Court understood that processing residence permits took time, the relevant authorities had been responsible for delays when they should have acted expeditiously in view of the interests at stake, in particular the fact that the applicant had been separated from his family for three years. However, it considered that the delay of three and a half months could not be regarded as excessive. The authorities had taken reasonable steps to facilitate the applicant's early return and his right to respect for his private and family life had, therefore, not been infringed. As regards the applicant's situation since his return to France, the Court noted that he had managed to re-establish ties with his family. The authorities had granted him a residence permit incorporating a right to work, but subject to his residing in a specified area for so long as the exclusion order remained in effect. The Court considered that those circumstances, and in particular the residence requirements, meant that the exclusion order had no legal effect, so that the applicant was under no imminent or short-term risk of deportation. The Court reiterated that the Contracting States had exclusive power to regulate the entry and residence of aliens, provided that they complied with the provisions of the Convention. Consequently, the applicant had no entitlement to any special immigration status in France. Accordingly, the Court held that there had been no violation of Article 8 after the applicant's return to France.[192]

In the *Nasri* Case the Court again showed its preparedness independently to review a deportation order for its proportionality and its impact on the applicant's family life. The special circumstances in this case make it difficult to draw specific conclusions as to the permissibility of a deportation, other than the willingness of the Court actively and intensely to assess the balance between the reasons leading to the deportation order and the (harsh) consequences for the individual concerned.[193] In the *Boultif* Case, on the contrary, the Court summarised the relevant criteria as follows: "The Court has only to a limited extent decided cases where the main obstacle to expulsion is the difficulties for the spouses to stay together and in particular for a spouse and/or children to live in the other's country of origin. It is therefore called upon to establish guiding principles in order to examine whether the measure was necessary in a demo-cratic society. In assessing the relevant criteria in such a case, the Court will consider the nature and seriousness of the offence committed by the applicant; the length of the applicant's stay in the country from which he is going to be expelled; the time elapsed since the offence was committed as well as the applicant's conduct in that period; the nationalities of the various persons concerned; the applicant's family situa-tion, such as the length of the marriage; and other factors expressing the effectiveness

---

192   Judgment of 10 April 2003, paras 44-52.
193   Judgment of 13 July 1995, para. 46.

of a couple's family life; whether the spouse knew about the offence at the time when he or she entered into a family relationship; and whether there are children in the marriage, and if so, their age. Not least, the Court will also consider the seriousness of the difficulties which the spouse is likely to encounter in the country of origin, though the mere fact that a person might face certain difficulties in accompanying her or his spouse cannot in itself exclude an expulsion".[194]

In the *Amrollahi* Case the applicant complained that, if deported, he would lose contact with his wife, children and stepdaughter, as they could not be expected to follow him to Iran. The Court observed that drugs had a devastating effect on people's lives and that it was understandable for the authorities to show great firmness to those who actively contributed to the spread of that scourge. Even if the applicant had not previously been convicted, that did not detract from the seriousness and gravity of such a crime. However, the Court found nothing to suggest that the applicant had maintained strong links, if any, with Iran, while he had to be considered as having strong ties with Denmark. The applicant's wife had never been to Iran, did not understand Farsi and was not a Muslim. Besides being married to an Iranian man, she had no ties with the country. Even if it were not impossible for the applicant's wife and children to live in Iran, it would, nevertheless, cause them obvious and serious difficulties. In addition, the Court recalled that the wife's daughter from a previous relationship, who had lived with her since her birth in 1989, refused to move to Iran. Taking this fact into account as well, the wife could not, in the Court's opinion, be expected to follow the applicant to Iran. There was no indication either that the applicant and his wife could obtain authorisation to live in any other country but Iran. Accordingly, as a consequence of the applicant's permanent exclusion from Denmark, the family would be separated, since it was effectively impossible for them to continue their family life outside Denmark. The Court therefore held that the expulsion of the applicant to Iran would be in breach of Article 8.[195]

In the *Benhebba* Case the Court noted that the applicant had arrived in France at a very young age, had lived there for most of his life, had received all his education there and had worked there. In the absence of any information to substantiate the applicant's claim that he had lived with a French woman as a couple, the Court decided to examine his application in the light of the ties he had developed with France and the principles it had established in previous similar cases. As regards the seriousness of the offences committed by the applicant, the Court noted that the exclusion order had been made by the Lyon Court of Appeal both on the basis of the offences for which he had been prosecuted and in view of his previous convictions for robbery and the failure of measures to assist his reintegration into society. The Court of Appeal had inferred from the amount of cannabis found at the time of his arrest that his

---

[194]   Judgment of 2 August 2001, para. 48.
[195]   Judgment of 11 July 2002, paras 35-42.

involvement in drugs offences could not have been merely occasional. In that connection, the Court reiterated that it understood why States showed great firmness with regard to those who actively contributed to the spread of the scourge of drugs. That approach, and the fact that within the space of eight years the applicant had been given prison sentences totalling six years, seven months and fifteen days, attested to the seriousness of the offences in question. As regards the applicant's links with France, the Court noted that he had formed most of his social ties there and no longer had any links with his country of origin other than his nationality. Although his family lived in France, the Court nonetheless reiterated that Article 8 of the Convention did not necessarily cover relations between adults unless there was evidence of additional forms of dependency going beyond normal emotional ties. In spite of the strength of the applicant's ties with France, the Court considered that the temporary exclusion order imposed on him could legitimately be regarded as necessary for the prevention of disorder and crime. Having regard to the temporary nature of the measure and the seriousness of the offences committed, the Court considered that the measure complained of had been proportionate to the aims pursued.[196]

In the *Slivenko* Case the applicant and her daughter complained that their removal from Latvia had violated their rights guaranteed by Article 8 in that the measures taken against them in that connection had not respected their private life, their family life and their home in Latvia. The Court noted that both applicants had developed a network of personal, social and economic ties constituting a private life in Latvia, since birth. They also lost the flat where they had lived. Their removal from Latvia therefore constituted an interference with their private life and home. However, the measures taken by the Latvian authorities did not break up their family, since the deportation concerned all three members of the family unit and there was no right under the Convention to choose in which country to continue or re-establish family life. The treaty on the withdrawal of Russian troops – which was the principal legal basis for the applicants' deportation – was not in force when the applicants were registered as 'ex-USSR citizens'. However, domestic law could later be legitimately interpreted and applied in the light of the treaty. In addition, the applicants must have been able to foresee to a reasonable degree, at least with legal advice, that they would be regarded as covered by the treaty. In any event, the decisions of the courts did not appear arbitrary. The applicants' removal could accordingly be considered to have been 'in accordance with the law'. Taking into account the wider context of the constitutional and international law arrangements made after Latvia regained independence, the Court accepted that the treaty and implementing measures had sought to protect the interests of national security. It could also be said that the arrangement respected family life in that it did not interfere with the family unit. The withdrawal of active servicemen and their families could be considered similar to a transfer in the course

---

[196]   Judgment of 10 July 2003, paras 32-37.

of normal service. Moreover, the continued presence of active servicemen of a foreign army might be seen as incompatible with the sovereignty of an independent State and a threat to national security. The public interest in the removal of them and their families would therefore normally outweigh the individual's interest in staying. However, removal measures might not always be justified. For example, they did not apply to the same extent to retired officers and their families. The fact that the husband had retired by the time proceedings were brought concerning the legality of the applicants' stay in Latvia, had made no difference to the determination of their status. Yet, it appeared – from information provided by the Latvian Government about treatment of certain hardship cases – that the authorities considered they had some latitude allowing them to ensure respect for private and family life and home. Although decisions were taken on a case-by-case basis, however, the authorities did not appear to have examined whether each person presented a specific danger to national security or public order, the public interest having been perceived rather in abstract terms. A scheme for withdrawal of foreign troops and their families based on a general finding that their removal was necessary for national security was not as such incompatible with Article 8, but implementation of such a scheme without any possibility of taking individual circumstances into account was. The applicants were integrated into Latvian society at the time and could not be regarded as endangering national security because they were part of the father's family of the first applicant, who had retired in 1986, had remained in the country and was not himself considered to present any such danger. In all the circumstances, the applicants' removal could not be regarded as having been necessary in a democratic society.[197]

In general it may be concluded that, next to the seriousness of the crime committed or any other danger to society, the relevant factors include the question of how long a foreigner has lived in the country that wishes to deport him; the intensity of the links he (still) has with his country of origin, and the harshness of the consequences of a deportation/expulsion. These aspects determine the Court's attitude towards the proportionality of the proposed measure of deportation and its compatibility with Article 8. It even appears that these latter factors are conclusive, whatever the (seriousness of the) offences committed. The nature of the offences could, however, be important in those instances in which there still is a link with the country of origin.

12.4.4 DETENTION

With regard to detainees the Court starts from the point of view that the consequences for private and family life resulting from a detention do not give rise to an interference of Article 8. In this sense it held in *D.G. v. Ireland* as follows: "The

---

[197]   Judgment of 9 October 2003, paras 118-128.

Court recalls that any interference with an individual's right to respect for his private and family life will constitute a breach of Article 8, unless it was 'in accordance with the law', pursued a legitimate aim or aims under paragraph 2, and was 'necessary in a democratic society' in the sense that it was proportionate to the aims sought to be achieved. It is true that the notion of private life may, depending on the circumstances, cover the moral and physical integrity of the person, which in turn may extend to situations covering deprivations of liberty. There may therefore be circumstances in which Article 8 could be regarded as affording protection in respect of conditions of detention, which do not attain the level of severity required by Article 3 (…). However, normal restrictions and limitations consequent on prison life and discipline during lawful detention are not matters which would constitute a violation of Article 8 either because they are considered not to constitute an interference with the detainee's private and family life (…) or because any such interference would be justified (…). In the present case, the applicant maintained that three matters brought his detention beyond the restrictions and limitations normally consequent on prison life. He referred, in the first place, to his detention being unlawful within the meaning of Article 5 para. 1. However, given its reasoning noted above leading to a violation of Article 5 para. 1, the Court does not consider that this issue alone gives rise to any separate issue under Article 8. Secondly, the applicant argued that his detention, as a minor not charged or convicted of a criminal offence and in a penal institution, constituted an unjustifiable interference with his private and family life. The conditions of the applicant' detention in St. Patrick's are noted at paragraph 97 above and the Court has already found his allegations about ill-treatment by fellow inmates to be unsubstantiated (…). The Court has also found the relevant detention orders to have been in accordance with domestic law (…). In such circumstances, the Court concludes that, even assuming the above-described restrictions and limitations consequent on life and discipline in St. Patrick's constituted an interference with the applicant's private and family life, they would be proportionate to the legitimate aims sought to be achieved. Thirdly, he complained about his being handcuffed for his appearances in court. However, the Court does not consider that the present case discloses any interference with the rights guaranteed under Article 8 as regards his being handcuffed (…). Accordingly, the Court concludes that the applicant's complaint concerning the lawfulness of his detention does not give rise to any separate issue under Article 8 and that otherwise there has not been a violation of Article 8 of the Convention."[198]

In a similar vein the Commission had adopted the view that the separation between a detainee and his family, and the distress resulting from it, are inherent in detention.[199] Thus, it held that a general limitation of visiting facilities to relatives and close friends

---

[198]   Judgment of 16 May 2002, paras 104-110.
[199]   See, e.g., Appl. 2676/65, X v. Austria, Coll. 23 (1967), p. 31 (37). See also the report of 18 March 1981, McVeigh, O'Neill and Evans, D&R 25 (1982), p. 5 (51-52).

of the prisoners was reasonable and constituted no interference with the prisoners' right to respect for private life.[200] The touchstone in the final analysis is whether the interference with the right of family life, to which the detainee is also entitled, "goes beyond what would normally be accepted in the case of an ordinary detainee."[201] If the restrictions could not stand this test, the Commission nevertheless appeared to be inclined to allow the national authorities a very wide margin of appreciation in the limitation of family contacts on the basis of one of the grounds of the second paragraph.[202]

The Commission accepted, for instance, the Austrian practice according to which those who are serving a sentence of imprisonment of more than one year are on that ground alone denied visits from their children under age, for the protection of the morals of these minors.[203] In the case of a refusal of the English authorities to permit a detainee to attend his daughter's wedding, and in another case his mother's funeral, the Commission concluded that there was no evidence that the authorities in question did not have sufficient reason to believe that this refusal was necessary on one of the grounds mentioned in the second paragraph.[204] Performed in this way, the international review would seem to have too automatic a character. In addition to an examination as to whether the justification of the restrictions by the national authorities on one of the grounds of paragraph 2 was indeed reasonable in the particular case, the Strasbourg organs should see to it that the restriction is not imposed on the prisoner as a disguised sanction on his behaviour, which would indeed constitute a breach of Article 18. But even in those cases where the restriction is not intended as an additional punishment, it will nevertheless, as a result of the detention, in many cases actually have the same effect. As examples one may think of the detention at a place that is so far removed from where the family members live that regular visits are practically impossible,[205] and of the refusal of (regular) conjugal intercourse for detainees, which still is the rule in most countries.[206]

---

[200]   Appl. 9054/80, *X v. the United Kingdom*, D&R 30 (1983), p. 113 (115).

[201]   Appl. 5712/72, *X v. the United Kingdom*, Coll. 46 (1974), p. 112 (116).

[202]   See, e. g., Appls 1420/62, 1477/62 and 1478/62, *X and Y v. Belgium*, Yearbook VI (1963), p. 90 (628), and Appl. 5712/72, *X v. the United Kingdom*, Coll. 46 (1974).

[203]   Appl. 2306/64, *X v. Austria*, Coll. 21 (1967), p. 23 (33). See also Appl. 6564/74, *X v. the United Kingdom*, D&R 2 (1975), p. 105 (106).

[204]   Appl. 4623/70, *X v. the United Kingdom*, Yearbook XV (1972), p. 370 (374); and Appl. 5229/71, *X v. the United Kingdom*, Coll. 42 (1973), p. 140 (141).

[205]   See, e.g., Appl. 9466/81, *S v. the United Kingdom*, D&R 36 (1984), p. 41 (44).

[206]   See Appl. 3603/68, *X v. Federal Republic of Germany*, Yearbook XIII (1970), p. 332 (338) and the comparative study evidently made there by the Commission. Thus also in Appl. 8166/78, *X and Y v. Switzerland*, D&R 13 (1979), p. 241 (243), where the Commission also refers to the Standard Minimum Rules for the Treatment of Prisoners, recommended by the Committee of Ministers in Resolution (73)5. If in a specific case it is possible for a detainee to reside together with his family in the place of detention, the Commission deems it possible that Art. 8 has been violated if the authorities make the living conditions for the family unbearable; report of 7 December 1978, *Guzzardi*, B.35 (1983), pp. 35-36.

The Court would seem to adopt a point of view that is rather similar to that of the Commission. In the *Messina (No. 2)* Case the Court observed that any detention which is lawful for the purposes of Article 5 of the Convention, entails by its nature a limitation on private and family life. However, it is an essential part of a prisoner's right to respect for family life that the prison authorities assist him in maintaining contact with his close family.[207] In that case the applicant alleged a violation of his right to respect for his family life. He had been subject to a special prison regime which involved restrictions on the number of family visits (not more than two per month) and imposed measures for the supervision of such visits (prisoners were separated from visitors by a glass partition). The Court noted that the regime was designed to cut the links between the prisoners concerned and their original criminal environment, in order to minimise the risk that they would maintain contact with criminal organisations. In particular, it noted that, as the Government pointed out, before the introduction of the special regime imprisoned Mafia members were able to maintain their positions within the criminal organisation, to exchange information with other prisoners and the outside world and to organise and procure the commission of serious crimes both inside and outside their prisons. In that context, the Court took into account the specific nature of the phenomenon of organised crime, particularly of the Mafia type, in which family relations often play a crucial role. Moreover, numerous States party to the Convention had high-security regimes for dangerous prisoners. These regimes were also based on separation from the prison community, accompanied by tighter supervision.[208] The Court noted that the applicant was not subject to the restrictions on family visits for the whole of the period during which the special regime was applied to him. It considered that the restrictions of the applicant's right to respect for his family life did not go beyond what was necessary in a democratic society for the protection of public safety and the prevention of disorder or crime, within the meaning of Article 8(2).[209]

In the *Lorsé* Case and the *Van der Ven* Case the applicants were subjected to a special security regime (the so-called EBI) which involved further restrictions on their private and family life than a regular Netherlands prison regime. Thus, their cells were inspected on a daily basis, their correspondence was read, their telephone conversations and conversations with visitors were monitored, they were allowed to associate with a limited number of fellow prisoners only and they were separated from their visitors by a glass partition except for the possibility of one 'open' visit per month by members of their immediate family whose hand they were allowed to shake at the beginning and end of the visit. The Court observed that the applicants were placed in the EBI because the authorities thought it likely that they might attempt to escape.

---

[207]   Judgment of 28 September 2000, para. 61.
[208]   *Ibidem*, para. 66.
[209]   *Ibidem*, paras 72-74.

The Court considered that the particular features of the above-mentioned Italian special regime and those of the EBI regime effectively illustrated that there was a difference. Thus, in the Italian special regime more emphasis was placed on restricting contacts with other prisoners and with family members than in the EBI regime, whereas in the EBI, security was concentrated on those occasions when, and places where, the prisoner concerned might obtain or keep objects which could be used in an attempt at escape or where he might obtain or exchange information relating to such an attempt. Within these constraints, the applicants were able to receive visitors for one hour every week and to have contact, and take part in group activities, with other EBI inmates, albeit a limited number. Although strict security measures were in place, the applicants and their family members were thus nevertheless able to maintain regular contact. In these circumstances the Court found that the restrictions of the applicants' right to respect for their private and family life did not go beyond what was necessary in a democratic society to attain the legitimate aims intended. Accordingly, there had been no violation of Article 8.[210]

12.5 RESPECT FOR THE HOME AND PROTECTION AGAINST NUISANCE

12.5.1 RESPECT FOR THE HOME

12.5.1.1 Introduction

In the *Hatton* Case the Court gave the following definition of home: "A home will usually be the place, the physically defined area, where private and family life develops. The individual has a right to respect for his home, meaning not just the right to the actual physical area, but also to the quiet enjoyment of that area. Breaches of the right to respect of the home are not confined to concrete or physical breaches, such as unauthorised entry into a person's home, but also include those that are not concrete or physical, such as noise, emissions, smells or other forms of interference. A serious breach may result in the breach of a person's right to respect for his home if it prevents him from enjoying the amenities of his home."[211]

In the *Langborger* Case the Court ruled that the power conferred on the Tenants' Union to negotiate on the tenant's behalf the amount of the rent for the flat in which he lived did not come within the scope of Article 8. The notion of 'home' in this article,

---

[210]   Judgments of 4 February 2003, paras 85-86; respectively paras 69-72.
[211]   Judgment of 7 August 2003, para. 96; judgment of 16 November 2004, *Moreno Gómez*, para. 28.

therefore, does not apply to issues concerning rents, nor to rights and obligations deriving from the lease.[212]

12.5.1.2 Live in one's home

In view of the Court's predominantly restrictive review of the justification of restrictions, the right to respect for the home affords only limited guarantees in most situations, since in many cases of interference with that right the national authorities will be able successfully to invoke one of the grounds of the second paragraph. In fact, as long as the national legislation in question makes this possible, the national authorities may search the home of a suspected person in case of any concrete, but also any vague suspicion of a criminal offence, and also all those other homes where clues might possibly be found.[213] However, in so serious a case of interference with the right to respect for the home as the case of Cypriot citizens being expelled from their homes by the Turkish occupying forces and the latter making return to these homes impossible, the Court concluded that none of the grounds mentioned in the second paragraph could be advanced for its justification.[214] And the Court held in the *Akdivar* Case that the deliberate burning of the applicants' homes constituted a serious interference with their right to respect for their homes for which no justification had been offered by the Turkish Government.[215]

The concept of 'home' was at issue in the *Gillow* Case. Mr and Mrs Gillow owned the house 'Whiteknights' in Guernsey, which they had occupied with their family until they left the country to take employment with the FAO in 1960. During their absence they rented the house to various tenants, but they continued the ownership and retained their furniture in the house. When they returned to Guernsey to live there in 1979, they were not granted the required licence, since they did not fulfil all the requirements, some of which were introduced by legislation during the period of their absence. The Commission considered that ownership of a house is not in itself sufficient to establish it as one's home, when one has never in fact lived in the house. However, where continued ownership follows occupation of a house as one's home, such ownership is evidence of a strong continuing link with the house. In the case of the Gillows this link was further illustrated by the fact that they had left their furniture

---

[212]   Judgment of 22 June 1989, para. 38.

[213]   See, *e.g.*, Appl. 530/59, *X. v. Federal Republic of Germany*, Yearbook III (1960), p. 184 (190).

[214]   Judgment of 10 May 2001, *Cyprus v. Turkey*.

[215]   Judgment of 16 September 1996, para. 88. The Court has followed this line of reasoning in many cases: judgment of 28 November 1997, *Mentes and Others*; judgment of 24 April 1998, *Selcuk and Asker*; judgment of 30 January 2001, *Bilgin*; judgment of 18 June 2002, *Orhan*. In these cases the Court established the facts and found a violation in spite of Turkey's denial. In the following cases the Court concluded that the facts were *not* established beyond reasonable doubt: judgment of 25 May 1998, *Gündem*; judgment of 21 February 2002, *Matyar*; judgment of 14 May 2002, *Semse Onen*, judgment of 1 June 2004, *Altun*.

in the house. The Commission was of the opinion that the question whether the house was still the applicants' 'home' at the time of their return to it in 1979, was in part dependent on their intentions and attitude towards the house prior to and on their return, of which the key element was their actual return in 1979 to live in the house. The Commission concluded that this return was a return to their 'home' within the meaning of Article 8. The fact that they were not granted the licence to live in that home and that proceedings were taken against them for unlawful occupation of the house constituted an interference with their right to respect for their home. The Court, too, found a violation of Article 8 in this case. According to the Court it was not the contested legislation that gave rise to the violation, but the manner in which the Housing Authority had exercised its discretion. The Housing Authority had given insufficient weight to the applicants' particular circumstances. They had built 'Whiteknights' as a residence for themselves and their family. At that time they possessed 'residence qualifications' and continued to do so until the entry into force of the Housing Law of 1969. By letting it over a period of 18 years to persons approved by the Housing Authority, they had contributed to the Guernsey housing stock. On their return in 1979, they had no other 'home' in the United Kingdom or elsewhere; 'Whiteknights' was vacant and there were no prospective tenants. Therefore, the refusals as well as the conviction and fining of the applicants constituted interferences which were disproportionate to the legitimate aim pursued.[216]

In the *Buckley* Case the Court affirmed the approach adopted in the *Gillow* Case and went a step further concerning the applicability of Article 8. In *Buckley* the applicant had bought a piece of land to establish her residence in caravans as a gypsy. For this reason the Court accepted that the refusal to give her the planning permission for the caravans was an interference with her right to respect for her home. The Court declined to define her claims also as private life and family life. Because of the margin of appreciation for the State concerning planning permissions the Court considered the refusal not to be disproportionate.[217] This decision was in fact partially overruled in five parallel Cases: *Chapman, Beard, Coster, Lee* and *Jane Smith*.[218] The major distinction with *Buckley* was that the Court in the latter five cases accepted the applicability of Article 8 both under the aspect of private life and family life, and under that of home. For gypsies, the occupation of a caravan was considered to be an integral part of their ethnic identity. This acceptance did, however, not alter the outcome of the case. The Court held that Article 8 does not necessarily go so far as to allow individuals' preferences as to their place of residence to override the general interest. Like in the *Buckley* Case, the Court found that the national authorities had appropriately weighed the various competing interests. However, in a more recent case the Court reached

---

[216]   Judgment of 24 November 1986, para. 58.
[217]   Judgment of 25 September 1996, para. 84.
[218]   Judgments of 18 January 2001.

a different conclusion with respect to a gypsy family who were ordered to leave the site. Because of the harshness of the measures the Court applied a strict scrutiny test and, balancing the various interests, found a violation of article 8.[219]

In the *Prokopovich* Case the applicant and her partner moved into a flat. They never married, but from 1988 onwards they lived together as husband and wife. The applicant however kept her residence registration at her old address. In August 1998, while the applicant was staying in their country cottage, her partner died in the flat. The applicant only learnt of his death two days later, when he had already been buried in the presence of his son and his two sisters. On 2 September 1998, the applicant filed a request with the housing maintenance authority to be given an occupation certificate for the flat. Her request was refused because on 1 September 1998 an occupation certificate had already been issued to the head of the local police department who was also the hierarchical superior of her deceased partner's son. On 4 September 1998, on returning to the flat, the applicant found that the door had been broken open and that books and other household items were being loaded onto a lorry. Once the removal was completed, the applicant was told to vacate the premises immediately. When she refused to comply with the request, she was thrown out of the flat by force. The Court held that the applicant's eviction from the contested flat by State officials had consti-tuted an interference with her right to respect for her home by a public authority. Article 90 of the relevant Housing Code permitted eviction only on the grounds established by law and only on the basis of a court order. That provision introduced an important procedural safeguard against arbitrary evictions and its wording per-mitted no exceptions. The Government had moreover conceded that the procedure established by Article 90 of the Housing Code should have been followed in the applicant's case, even though her residence had not been legally established. The Court could not discern any circumstances that could have justified in this case a departure from the normal procedure of eviction and the remarkably hasty re-allocation of the flat to a police officer just seven days after the death of the former tenant. It followed that the applicant's eviction could not be considered to have been in accordance with the law.[220]

12.5.1.3 Searches

The *Chappell* Case concerned the search of a house in connection with the suspicion that videocassettes were made in breach of copyright by a company controlled by the applicant. The premises were used for both business and residential purposes. In the Commission's view, although the search was directed against the applicant's and his company's business activities, it indirectly impinged on the applicant's private life and

---

[219]   Judgment of 27 May 2004, *Connors*, paras 92-95.
[220]   Judgment of 18 November 2004, paras 43-45.

the private sphere of items and associations which were attributes of a home. The Commission had left open the question of whether some private papers of the applicant constituted correspondence within the meaning of Article 8, as the interference therewith anyway fell within the private-life sphere. The applicability of Article 8 was no longer contested before the Court. The Court reached the conclusion that the interference was necessary in a democratic society for the protection of the rights of others.[221]

In the *Niemietz* Case and the *Crémieux* Case the Court was also confronted with searches. It dealt with them in the context of Article 8, without explicitly distinguishing between 'private life' and 'home'. It may be concluded from this that an infringement of the right to respect of one's 'home' always also includes an interference with one's 'private life'. With respect to the notion of private life the Court did not consider "it possible or necessary to attempt an exhaustive definition of the notion of 'private life'. However, it would be too restrictive to limit the notion to an 'inner circle' in which the individual may live his own personal life as he chooses and to exclude therefrom entirely the outside world not encompassed within that circle. Respect for private life must also comprise to a certain degree the right to establish and develop relationships with other human beings."[222] According to the Court this implies that there is no reason to exclude activities of a professional or business nature from the concept of private life. And the same is true for the concept of 'home'. The interpretation of the words 'private life' and 'home' as including certain professional and business activities or premises is consonant, according to the Court, with the essential object and purpose of Article 8, namely to protect the individual against arbitrary interference by the public authorities.[223]

Quite explicit was the Court in the *Stés Colas Est* Case about a search of enterprises and the seizure of documents. The Court accepted that legal persons may invoke Article 8 as to the protection of their 'homes', even though the protection enjoyed by a company might not have the same intensity as the right of an individual for his personal home. The Court ruled that Article 8 had been violated: the powers of the authorities had been vast and no order by a court or presence of a judge was necessary. Taking into account the aim of the search, preventing distortion of competition, the Court held that the danger of arbitrariness did exist while the law did not offer sufficient guarantees.[224]

---

[221]   Judgment of 30 March 1989, para. 66. An example of a judgment finding a violation is the judgment of 23 September 1998, *McLeod*, in which the Court found that the police had insufficiently investigated whether an entry with the help of the police of a man in the premises of his ex-wife to collect some belongings was legitimate.

[222]   Judgment of 16 December 1992, *Niemietz*, para. 29.

[223]   *Ibidem*, para. 31.

[224]   Judgment of 16 April 2002, para. 49.

In the *Camenzind* Case the Court summarised its approach with respect to the admissibility of searches and the relevant criteria as follows: "The Contracting States may consider it necessary to resort to measures such as searches of residential premises and seizures in order to obtain physical evidence of certain offences. The Court will assess whether the reasons adduced to justify such measures were relevant and sufficient and whether the aforementioned proportionality principle has been adhered to (…). As regards the latter point, the Court must firstly ensure that the relevant legislation and practice afford individuals 'adequate and effective safeguards against abuse'; notwithstanding the margin of appreciation which the Court recognises the Contracting States have in this sphere, it must be particularly vigilant where, as in the present case, the authorities are empowered under national law to order and effect searches without a judicial warrant. If individuals are to be protected from arbitrary interference by the authorities with the rights guaranteed under Article 8, a legal framework and very strict limits on such powers are called for. Secondly, the Court must consider the particular circumstances of each case in order to determine whether, in the concrete case, the interference in question was proportionate to the aim pursued. (…) Having regard to the safeguards provided by Swiss legislation and especially to the limited scope of the search, the Court accepts that the interference with the applicant's right to respect for his home can be considered to have been proportionate to the aim pursued and thus 'necessary in a democratic society' within the meaning of Article 8. Consequently, there has not been a violation of that provision."[225]

12.5.1.4 Right to housing

In the *Velosa Barreto* Case, the Court explicitly held that "effective protection of respect for private and family life cannot require the existence in national law of legal protection enabling each family to have a home for themselves alone". In this particular case the applicant, who lived with his family and his parents-in-law, inherited from his parents a house. This house had been let, and the applicant started proceedings to have the lease terminated on the ground that he needed the house as his own home. The Portuguese courts, however, held that there was no sufficient 'need' as required by Portuguese legislation to have the lease terminated. Since Article 8 does not contain the right to have a home, it followed, in the Court's opinion, that it "does not go so far as to place the State under an obligation to gave the landlord the right to recover possession of a rented house on request and in any circumstances". Under national law the termination of the lease was possible whenever the landlord needed the property to live there. The Court held that this clause "pursues a legitimate aim, namely the social protection of tenants, and that it thus tends to promote the economic well-being of the country and the protection of the rights of others." In applying this

---

[225]   Judgment of 16 December 1997, paras 45-47.

national provision the Portuguese courts had not acted arbitrarily or unreasonably, neither had they failed to discharge their obligation to strike a fair balance between the respective interests.[226]

It may be inferred from this judgment that Article 8 also applies to relations between individuals and that the Contracting States are under the obligation to effectuate this *Drittwirkung*. However, this horizontal effect implies a balancing between conflicting interests; in the *Velosa Barreto* Case it concerned the right of the landlord to have a home and to be protected in one's home against the same rights of the tenant. The Court seems to allow the national authorities a large discretion in solving this horizontal conflict of interest by introducing the test of 'arbitrariness or unreasonableness'. It is likely that this rather marginal test is influenced, on the one hand, by the broad concept of 'economic well-being of the country' as a ground of restriction invoked in this particular case, and on the other hand by the 'social right' nature of the right at issue: the right to a home. Interference in this matter could easily lead the Court into the thicket of judging upon social and economic issues of housing policies. The absence of a clear emergency situation on the part of the applicant may also explain and justify this approach in this particular case.

It may also be inferred from the *Velosa Barreto* Case that the Court at present does not seem prepared fully to accept that the right to respect for the home also implies a right to a (decent) home.[227] Recognition of such a right would amount to a considerable socialisation of Article 8. The Court may be expected to only recognize a positive obligation as to housing in circumstances in which there is a finding of a serious infringement of one's personal life as well as a disproportional balancing (arbitrariness, unreasonableness) of the conflicting interests. In this respect reference can be made to the aforementioned gypsy cases (*Buckley, Chapman, Beard, Coster, Lee* and *Jane Smith, supra* 12.5.1.2.) in which the Court indeed declined to accept a general overriding of general interests by preferences of individuals as to their place of residence. However, the approach adopted by the Court in balancing the competing interests might leave some room for a gradual expansion of Article 8 by allowing for social rights elements to be included, while taking one step at a time.

12.5.2   PROTECTION AGAINST NUISANCE

A form of indirect interference with the right to respect for the home which does substantially enlarge the scope of Article 8 and which does not stand in the way of direct applicability, are deteriorations of living conditions by certain measures or

---

[226]   Judgment of 21 November 1995, para. 25.
[227]   Thus already the Commission in its decision on Appl. 159/56, *X v. Federal Republic of Germany*, Yearbook I (1955-1957), p. 202 (203).

circumstances. Thus, in the *Arrondelle* Case, which case was declared admissible by the Commission because of its complexity, the applicant complained about violation of Article 8 by the British authorities on account of the great nuisance which she experienced in her home near Gatwick Airport from the descending and ascending aircraft, and from the traffic on the motor road.[228]

In the *Powell and Rayner* Case the Court went along with this approach. Again the case dealt with complaints about excessive noise generated by air traffic, this time in and out of Heathrow Airport. The question before the Court was not whether Article 8 had been violated, but whether both applicants had an arguable claim (within the meaning of Article 13) of a violation of Article 8. The Court held as follows: "In each case, albeit to greatly differing degrees, the quality of the applicant's private life and the scope for enjoying the amenities of his home have been adversely affected by the noise generated by aircraft using Heathrow Airport (...). Article 8 is therefore a material provision in relation to both Mr Powell and Mr Rayner."[229] In view of the "fair balance that had to be struck between the competing interests of the individual and of the community as a whole" and taking into account the measures adopted by the authorities to control, abate and compensate for aircraft noise, the Court reached the following conclusion: "In view of the foregoing, there is no serious ground for maintaining that either the policy approach to the problem or the content of the particular regulatory measures adopted by the United Kingdom authorities give rise to violation of Article 8, whether under its positive or negative head. In forming a judgment as to the proper scope of the noise abatement measures for aircraft arriving at and departing from Heathrow Airport, the United Kingdom Government cannot arguably be said to have exceeded the margin of appreciation afforded to them or upset the fair balance required to be struck under Article 8."[230] Despite the outcome of this case, the principle was firmly established: Article 8 does also cover infringements upon private life and home by noise and disturbances.

This principle was confirmed in the *López Ostra* Case, where a violation was found. The applicant complained about smells, noise and polluting fumes caused by a plant for the treatment of liquid and solid waste sited a few metres away from her home. She held the Spanish authorities responsible, alleging that they had adopted a passive attitude. The Court, after reviewing all events, stated that it only needed to establish whether the national authorities had taken the measures necessary for protecting the applicant's right to respect for her home and for her private and family life under Article 8. It concluded as follows: " The Court notes, however, that the family had to bear the nuisance caused by the plant for over three years before moving house with

---

[228] Appl. 7889/77, D&R 19 (1980), p. 186 (198). In this case a friendly settlement was reached: D&R 26 (1982), p. 5.
[229] Judgment of 21 February 1990, para. 40.
[230] *Ibidem*, para. 45.

all the attendant inconveniences. They moved only when it became apparent that the situation could continue indefinitely and when Mrs Lopez Ostra's daughter's paediatrician recommended that they do so (...). Under these circumstances, the municipality's offer could not afford complete redress for the nuisance and inconveniences to which they had been subjected. Having regard to the foregoing, and despite the margin of appreciation left to the respondent State, the Court considers that the State did not succeed in striking a fair balance between the interests of the town's economic well being – that of having a waste treatment plant – and the applicant's effective enjoyment of her right to respect for her home and her private and family life."[231]

In the *Guerra* Case the Court observed: "The direct effect of the toxic emissions on the applicants' right to respect for their private and family life means that Article 8 is applicable".[232] In the *Surugiu* Case, which concerned various acts of harassment by third parties who entered the applicant's yard and dumped several cartloads of manure in front of the door and under the windows of the house, the Court found that the acts constituted repeated interference by third parties with the applicant's right to respect for his home and that Article 8 of the Convention was applicable."[233]

The applicability of Article 8 in the context of environmental nuisance was further clarified in the *Hatton* Case. As in the *Powell and Rayner* Case, the applicants complained about the noise caused at their homes by aircraft using Heathrow airport. Specifically they complained about the noise generated after the introduction of the 1993 scheme. The question before the Court was whether the Government, in permitting increased levels of noise over the years since 1993, respected their positive obligations under Article 8 to the applicants. After the Chamber had found a violation, the Grand Chamber held as follows: "Article 8 protects the individual's right to respect for his or her private and family life, home and correspondence. There is no explicit right in the Convention to a clean and quiet environment, but where an individual is directly and seriously affected by noise or other pollution, an issue may arise under Article 8. (…). At the same time, the Court re-iterates the fundamentally subsidiary role of the Convention. The national authorities have direct democratic legitimation and are, as the Court has held on many occasions, in principle better placed than an international court to evaluate local needs and conditions (…). In matters of general policy, on which opinions within a democratic society may reasonably differ widely, the role of the domestic policy maker should be given special weight (…). Article 8 may apply in environmental cases whether the pollution is directly caused by the State or whether State responsibility arises from the failure properly to regulate private industry. Whether the case is analysed in terms of a positive duty on the State to take

---

[231]   Judgment of 9 December 1994, para. 57.
[232]   Judgment of 19 February 1998, para. 57.
[233]   Judgment of 20 April 2004, para. 59.

reasonable and appropriate measures to secure the applicants' rights under paragraph 1 of Article 8 or in terms of an interference by a public authority to be justified in accordance with paragraph 2, the applicable principles are broadly similar. In both contexts regard must be had to the fair balance that has to be struck between the competing interests of the individual and of the community as a whole; and in both contexts the State enjoys a certain margin of appreciation in determining the steps to be taken to ensure compliance with the Convention. Furthermore, even in relation to the positive obligations flowing from the first paragraph of Article 8, in striking the required balance the aims mentioned in the second paragraph may be of a certain relevance (…)."[234] The Grand Chamber found in appeal that no violation had occurred.[235]

In the *Kyrtatos* Case the Court held that the Convention does not include a right to environmental protection. In cases related to environmental issues a sufficient objective individual interest must be present. The Court will have to investigate whether the environmental issues falling under the responsibility of public authorities affect the personal situation of the complainant relating to his/her home or health.[236] The *Hatton* and *Kyrtatos* Cases show the borders of the Court's environmental case law under Article 8: in the *Hatton* Case the Grand Chamber, reversing a finding of a violation by the Chamber, allowed a State great deference in setting environmental standards and in changing them. In the *Kyrtatos* Case, the Court clearly indicated that environmental issues can only be investigated within the context of the individual rights contained in Article 8.

In the *Taskin* Case the applicants alleged that both the national authorities' decision to issue a permit to use a cyanidation operating process in a gold mine and the related decision-making process had given rise to a violation of their rights guaranteed by Article 8 of the Convention. The Court pointed out that Article 8 applies to severe environmental pollution which may affect individuals' well-being and prevent them from enjoying their homes in such a way as to affect their private and family life adversely, without, however, seriously endangering their health. The same is true where the dangerous effects of an activity to which the individuals concerned are likely to be exposed have been determined as part of an environmental impact assessment procedure in such a way as to establish a sufficiently close link with private and family life for the purposes of Article 8 of the Convention. If this were not the case, the positive obligation on the State to take reasonable and appropriate measures to secure the applicant's rights under paragraph 1 of Article 8 would be set at nought. With regard to the decision-making process, the Court noted that the decision to grant an operating permit had been preceded by a series of investigations and studies conducted

---

[234] Judgment of 8 July 2003, paras 96-98. See also the decision of 20 January 2004, *Ashworth*.
[235] *Ibidem*, para. 130.
[236] Judgment of 22 May 2003, para. 130.

over a long period. A meeting to inform the population of the region had been organised. The applicants and the inhabitants of the region had had access to all the relevant documents, including the study in the issue. The Supreme Administrative Court had based its decision to set aside the operating permit on those studies and reports. However, although that judgment had become enforceable at the latest when it was served on the administrative authorities on 20 October 1997, the mine's closure had not been ordered until 27 February 1998, more than 10 months after delivery of the judgment and four months after it was served. With regard to the period after 1 April 1998, the Court noted the administrative authorities' refusal to comply with the court decisions and domestic legislation, and the lack of a decision, based on a new environmental-impact report, to take the place of the one that had been set aside by the courts. Moreover, despite the procedural safeguards laid down by Turkish legislation and the practical effect given to those safeguards by judicial decisions, on 29 March 2002, in a decision which was not made public, the Cabinet had authorised the continuation of the activities of the goldmine, which had already begun working in April 2001. In those circumstances, the Court considered that the authorities had deprived the procedural safeguards protecting the applicants of all useful effect. Turkey had thus failed to discharge its obligation to guarantee the applicants' right to respect for their private and family life. The Court accordingly concluded unanimously that there had been a violation of Article 8 of the Convention.[237]

In the *Stubbings* Case the Court held as follows: "Although the object of Article 8 is essentially that of protecting the individual against arbitrary interference by the public authorities, it may involve the authorities' adopting measures designed to secure respect for private life even in the sphere of the relations of individuals between themselves."[238] In the *Moreno Gòmez* Case the applicant complained of noise and of being disturbed at night by nightclubs near her home. She alleged that the Spanish authorities were responsible and that the resulting onslaught of sound constituted a violation of her right to respect for her home, as guaranteed by Article 8. The Court noted that this case did not concern interference by public authorities with the right to respect for the home, but their failure to take action to put a stop to third-party breaches of the right relied on by the applicant. It observed that the applicant lived in an area that was indisputably subject to night-time disturbances that clearly unsettled her as she went about her daily life, particularly at weekends. The existence of the disturbances had been noted on a number of occasions. In the circumstances, there appeared to be no need to require, as the Spanish authorities had done, a person from an acoustically saturated zone to adduce evidence of a fact of which the municipal authority was already officially aware. In view of the volume of the noise, at night and beyond permitted levels, and the fact that it had continued over a number of years,

---

[237]   Judgment of 10 November 2004, paras 120-126.
[238]   Judgment of 22 October 1996, para. 62; judgment of 20 April 2004, *Surugiu*, para. 59.

the Court found that there had been a breach of the rights protected by Article 8. Although the City Council had adopted measures intended to secure respect for the rights guaranteed by the Convention, it had tolerated, and thus contributed to, the repeated flouting of the rules which it itself had established. The Court found that the applicant had suffered a serious infringement of her right to respect for her home as a result of the authorities' failure to take action to deal with the night-time disturbances and held that the respondent State had failed to discharge its obligation to guarantee her right to respect for her home and her private life, in breach of Article 8 of the Convention.[239]

12.6 CORRESPONDENCE

12.6.1 LETTERS

With regard to the right to respect for correspondence, the case law mainly concerns public authorities' opening and censoring letters or interfering with other means of communication.

At first the Commission took the view that reliance on the second paragraph as a justification of interference was not necessary if the censorship or the restriction of correspondence concerned detainees, since such restrictions were to be considered inherent in detention. The Commission did not even deem a reference to paragraph 2 necessary for such serious cases as restriction or delay of the correspondence with defence counsel.[240] The Court, however, in the 'Vagrancy' Cases, and later more clearly in the *Golder* Case, rejected this so-called 'inherent features' theory for provisions like Article 8, where restrictions are expressly provided for, and held that every restriction has to be reviewed for its justification on one of the grounds mentioned explicitly in the second paragraph.[241] At the same time, however, the Court recognised in the *Golder* Case that, in doing so, the special position of the prisoner may be taken into account.[242]

This change in the case law is, of course, hardly of avail to the prisoner, if a very wide discretion is still allowed to the prison authorities and the prosecuting authorities in censoring incoming and outgoing letters and in other interferences with the correspondence of prisoners.[243] However, the Court shows to be prepared to conduct

---

[239] Judgment of 16 November 2004, paras 32-35.
[240] See, *e.g.*, Appl. 2375/64, *X v. Federal Republic of Germany*, Coll. 22 (1967), p. 45 (47).
[241] Judgment of 18 June 1971, para. 93; judgment of 21 February 1975, para. 45. See also the report of 12 December 1980, *Schönenberger and Durmaz*, para. 43.
[242] Judgment of 21 February 1975, para. 45. See also the judgment of 25 March 1983, *Silver*, para. 105.
[243] See Council of Europe, Case Law Topics, No. 1, 'Human Rights in Prison', 1971, pp. 24-30. See also Appl. 6166/73, *Baader, Meins, Meinhof and Grundmann v. Federal Republic of Germany*, Yearbook XVIII (1975), p. 132 (146).

a more independent inquiry into the reasonableness of interference with the correspondence of prisoners by the authorities concerned.

In the *Silver* Case the Court noted that since the Commission's report the practice in England and Wales on the control of prisoners' correspondence had undergone substantial modification, but it held that it was not empowered to review the control regime introduced after the events giving rise to the case.[244] It reached the conclusion that, with the exception of the censorship of those letters in which violence was threatened or crimes were discussed, the grounds on which letters of the detained applicants had been held back could find no justification in the second paragraph, at least not if one considered the way in which the relevant rules had been applied in these cases.[245]

In the *Boyle and Rice* Case the Court found that the Prison Governor stopping a letter to a 'media personality' was in breach of Article 8. The Government had acknowledged before the Court that the rules had been wrongly applied since the letter was a purely personal one and should have been allowed to pass.[246] In the *Schönenberger and Durmaz* Case the Court had to deal with the stopping of a letter addressed by a lawyer to a person held on remand. The Government relied in the first place on the contents of the letter in issue. According to the Government, it gave Mr Durmaz advice relating to pending criminal proceedings, which was of such a nature as to jeopardise their proper conduct. The Court took the view that Mr Schönenberger sought to inform the second applicant of his right 'to refuse to make any statement', advising him that to exercise it would be to his 'advantage': "In that way, he was recommending that Mr Dunnaz adopt a certain tactic, lawful in itself since, under Swiss Federal Court's case law – whose equivalent may be found in other Contracting States – it is open to an accused person to remain silent."[247] The fact that the lawyer was not instructed by Mr Durmaz was of little importance, since Mr Schönenberger was acting on the instructions of Mr Durmaz' wife. The contested interference was deemed not justifiable as necessary in a democratic society.[248]

In the *Pfeifer and Plankl* Case the Court reiterated the applicable principles set forth in the *Silver* Case. In this case the relevant issue concerned the deletion by the investigating judge of certain passages in Mrs Plankl's letter to Mr Pfeiffer. The Court held as follows: "The Court recognises that some measure of control over prisoners' correspondents is not of itself incompatible with the Convention, but the resulting interference must not exceed what is required by the legitimate aim pursued.

---

[244] Judgment of 25 March 1983, para. 68.
[245] *Ibidem*, para. 105. See also Appl. 7630/76, *Reed v. the United Kingdom,* D&R 19 (1980), p. 113 (141).
[246] Judgment of 27 April 1988, para. 50.
[247] Judgment of 20 June 1988, para. 28.
[248] *Ibidem*, para. 30. On controls of correspondence of a prisoner see also the judgment of 30 August 1990, *McCallum*, para. 31, in which the Government, the applicant and the Court agreed with the Commission that Article 8 had been violated.

According to the investigating judge, the deleted passages contained 'jokes of an insulting nature against prison officers' (...). The text was not, however, reconstructed before the Austrian courts. (...) In the case of Silver and Others v. the United Kingdom, the Court held that it was not 'necessary in a democratic society' to stop private letters 'calculated to hold the authorities up to contempt' or containing 'material deliberately calculated to hold the prison authorities up to contempt' (...) The deletion of passages is admittedly a less serious interference, but in the circumstances of the case this too appears disproportionate."[249]

In a number of cases against the Ukraine, the applicants complained that they had been prevented from sending letters to and receiving letters from family, and from receiving postal parcels with warm clothes and food. The Court held that the restrictions had constituted interference by a public authority with the applicants' exercise of their right to respect for their private life and their correspondence. The Court reiterated that such interference had to be in accordance with the law, pursue a legitimate aim and be necessary in a democratic society in order to achieve that aim. In order to satisfy the first of those conditions, the law had to be accessible to the person concerned, who had to be able to foresee its consequences. Although the Correctional Labour Code had provided a legal basis for conditions of detention, the authorities had not referred to its provisions when informing the applicants or their relatives about the rules applicable to death-row inmates. After their sentences had become final, their detention had been governed by an Instruction, which was an internal and unpublished document not accessible to the public. That Instruction had been replaced by the Temporary Provisions, which had entered into force on 11 July 1999 and were accessible to the public. However, these were of no application to the applicants' complaints in respect of the period before 11 July 1999. The interference had not therefore been in accordance with the law and there had been a violation of Article 8.[250]

In the *Campbell* Case the applicant complained that correspondence to and from his solicitor and the Commission was opened and read by the prison authorities. In this case the Court gave additional indications as to when and how the authorities are allowed to open correspondence with lawyers. Its point of departure is that correspondence with lawyers is privileged under Article 8 and, consequently, interference requires solid justification. Said the Court: "This means that the prison authorities may open a letter from a lawyer to a prisoner when they have reasonable cause to believe that it contains an illicit enclosure which the normal means of detection have failed to disclose. The letter should, however, only be opened and should not be read. Suitable guarantees preventing the reading of the letter should be provided, *e.g.*

---

[249]   Judgment of 25 February 1992, paras 46-47.
[250]   Judgments of 29 April 2003, *Poltoratskiy*; *Kuznetsov*; *Nazarenko*; *Dankevich*; *Aliev* and *Khokhlich*.

opening the letter in the presence of the prisoner. The reading of a prisoner's mail to and from a lawyer, on the other hand, should only be permitted in exceptional circumstances when the authorities have reasonable cause to believe that the privilege is being abused in that the contents of the letter endanger prison security or the safety of others or are otherwise of a criminal nature. (...) The possibility of examining correspondence for reasonable cause (...) provides a sufficient safeguard against the possibility of abuse."[251] The Court did not accept the respondent Government's argument that the opening of the applicant's correspondence did not prevent him from having an effective opportunity to communicate in confidence with his solicitor during prison visits. In that respect the Court observed that "[the] right to respect for correspondence is of special importance in a prison context where it may be difficult for a legal adviser to visit his client in person because, as in the present case, of the distant location of the prison (...). Finally, the objective of confidential communication with a lawyer could not be achieved if this means of communication were the subject of automatic control."[252] In the *Foxley* Case the Court followed the approach adopted in the *Campbell* Case. In a bankruptcy case, letters were intercepted from the bankrupt with his legal advisers. In this context the Court argued as follows: "The Court can see no justification for this procedure and considers that the action taken was not in keeping with the principles of confidentiality and professional privilege attaching to relations between a lawyer and his client. It notes in this connection that the Government have not sought to argue that the privileged channel of communication was being abused; nor have they invoked any other exceptional circumstances which would serve to justify the interference with reference to their margin of appreciation."[253]

In the *Erdem* Case the Court accepted monitoring a prisoner's correspondence with his lawyer. The reason was that the case concerned a PKK terrorist and that the State had provided for sufficient supervision. The monitoring needed the authorisation of an independent judge and oral communication between the applicant and his lawyer remained possible. The legislative provisions were precise, contained safeguards against abuse and the war against terrorism constituted sufficient justification to allow for the correspondence with the lawyer to be monitored.[254]

The freedom of correspondence with the Registry of the Court constitutes a separate issue, because the prohibition of interference ensues from the Convention

---

[251]   Judgment of 25 March 1992, paras 48-52.
[252]   *Ibidem,* para. 50.
[253]   Judgment of 20 June 2000, para. 44. Another aspect of the case was that his correspondence was monitored. Since this continued even after the Order had lapsed, the Court concluded also in that respect that Article 8 was violated in the absence of a domestic legal basis. For another example of a case in which a proper legal basis was lacking, see the judgment of 21 December 2000, *Rinzivillo*. A peculiar case was the *William Faulkner* Case, judgment of 4 June 2002: a prisoner's letter to a Scottish Minister was not posted by the prison. This omission led to a violation of Article 8.
[254]   Judgment of 5 July 2001, para. 69.

itself for the authorities of all Contracting States and the restrictions of Article 8(2) should therefore, strictly speaking, not apply. Moreover, this matter has been regulated in more detail in a special convention.[255] In the *Campbell* Case the complaint about interference with the applicant's correspondence with 'Strasbourg' was dealt with together with complaints about other interferences with correspondence. There the Court found a violation of Article 8 because it considered the opening of letters from the Commission to the detained applicant to be not necessary in a democratic society. The Court was of the opinion that there was no compelling reason why letters from the Commission should be opened.[256] This has become standing case law in cases in which correspondence with 'Strasbourg' has been hindered.[257]

12.6.2 PHONE-TAPPING

A case which led to an extensive investigation by the Court into the scope of the possibilities of restriction under the second paragraph with respect to the freedom of correspondence and other forms of communication, is the *Klass* Case. This case concerned German legislation authorising letter-opening and wire-tapping for the protection of the free democratic constitutional order and national security, without notification of the person in question and with exclusion of the normal legal remedies. After an extensive inquiry into the substance and application of the challenged legislation, which application by its very nature called for secrecy, the Court concluded that the German legislature could in reasonableness take the view that the measures in question were necessary for the protection of the above-mentioned interests.[258] This judgment is discussed in detail elsewhere in connection with Articles 6 and 13.[259]

Another case directed against the Federal Republic of Germany concerned wire-tapping of a solicitors' office, a measure which the authorities had carried out on the ground of suspicion that the office played a part in the exchange of information between prisoners who were suspected or convicted of terrorist activities. A number of persons whose conversations with the office had been tape-recorded, complained that, contrary to the decision of the investigating judge, those conversations, which apparently were not incriminating, were not erased immediately after recording. Although the Commission considered it regrettable that the instructions of the investigating judge had not been complied with, it held that this did not constitute

---

[255] See *supra* 1.13.5.
[256] Judgment of 25 March 1992, para. 53.
[257] No compelling reasons and therefore not necessary in a democratic society: judgments of 28 November 2000, *Rehbock*; 19 April 2001, *Peers*; 24 July 2001, *Vala'yinas*; 29 January 2002, *A.B. v. the Netherlands*; 14 March 2002, *Puzinas*.
[258] Report of 9 March 1977, B.26 (1982), pp. 37-39; judgment of 6 September 1978, para. 60.
[259] *Supra*, 10.4.6.6. See also *infra* 32.2.2. and 32.4.

a violation of Article 8. It advanced the argument that the measure, as carried out, had been found by the German court to be in conformity with German law and that this same court had decided that it could not be determined until the end of the proceedings which recordings were and which were not relevant.[260] Here the Commission went very far indeed in sheltering behind the point of view of the national court, without making an independent inquiry into the restrictions of the second paragraph relied upon. In the light of the decision in the above-discussed *Campbell* Case and the Court's case law concerning telephone-tapping, to be discussed *infra (Malone, Kruslin, Huvig)*, it is unlikely that this approach taken by the Commission in 1980 conforms to present-day standards under Article 8.

The Strasbourg review of interception of telephone calls by or at the request of the police in the *Malone* Case was more thorough. Mr Malone was charged with dishonest handling of stolen goods. The police officer in charge of the investigation had ordered interception of a telephone conversation on the authority of a warrant issued by the Secretary of State for the Home Department. Moreover, Mr Malone's telephone had been 'metered' on behalf of the police by a device, which automatically recorded all numbers dialled. The Court agreed with the Commission that the laws and practices existing in England and Wales, which permitted secret surveillance of communications, amounted to an interference with the applicant's rights under Article 8. Although this interference was lawful under the relevant law of England and Wales, the Court reached the conclusion that it was not 'in accordance with the law' in the sense of the second paragraph of Article 8, since the relevant law did not lay down with reasonable clarity the essential elements of the authorities' powers in this domain.[261] As to the 'metering', the Court disagreed with the Government that, since the Post Office only recorded signals sent to itself as the provider of the telephone service and did not intercept conversations, it did not entail interference with any right guaranteed by Article 8. Release of that information without the consent of the subscriber did, in the Court's opinion, amount to such an interference. And since there appeared to be no legal rules concerning the scope and manner of exercise of the discretion enjoyed by the public authorities, this practice also was not 'in accordance with the law' within the meaning of Article 8(2).[262]

This approach was elaborated upon in two cases against France: the *Kruslin* Case and the *Huvig* Case. Undisputed in both cases was that telephone-tapping by the police amounted to an interference by a public authority with the exercise of the applicant's right to respect for his correspondence and his private life. The Court therefore had to assess whether France had acted in conformity with the requirements laid down in paragraph 2. It held as follows: "Tapping and other forms of interception of

---

[260]   Appl. 8290/78, *A, B, C and D v. Federal Republic of Germany*, D&R 18 (1980), p. 176 (180).
[261]   Judgment of 2 August 1984, para. 82.
[262]   *Ibidem*, para. 88.

telephone conversations represent a serious interference with private life and correspondence and must accordingly be based on a 'law' that is particularly precise. It is essential to have clear, detailed rules on the subject, especially as the technology available for use is continually becoming more sophisticated."[263] The Court was of the opinion that French law (written and unwritten) did not "indicate with reasonable clarity the scope and manner of exercise of the relevant discretion conferred on the public authorities. This was truer still at the material time, so that Mr. Kruslin did not enjoy the minimum degree of protection to which citizens are entitled under the rule of law in a democratic society"[264]

In *A. v. France* the Court ruled that the recording of a telephone conversation, even if conducted on the initiative and with the consent of one of the interlocutors and even though it exclusively and deliberately dealt with matters of a criminal nature, did concern the right to respect for the applicant's correspondence. The French Government had argued that the recorded conversation fell outside the scope of private life. The Court, however, ruled that it was not necessary to consider whether the recording also affected the applicant's private life. It concluded that the interference with the right to respect for the correspondence had no basis in domestic law. It therefore found a breach of Article 8.[265]

In *M.M. v. the Netherlands* the question before the Court was whether the 'interference' with the applicant's Article 8 rights – to wit, the recording of telephone conversations which he had with Mrs S. with a view to their use as prosecution evidence against the applicant – was imputable to a 'public authority' or not. The Court found that there had been an interference by a public authority with the applicant's right to respect for his correspondence in that, with the prior permission of the public prosecutor, the police had made a crucial contribution to recording the telephone conversations and had thus engaged the respondent State's responsibility. At the relevant time the tapping or interception of telephone conversations for the purpose of obtaining evidence against a person suspected of committing an offence had required a preliminary judicial investigation and an order by an investigating judge. As neither condition had been met here the interference had not been in accordance with the law.[266]

In the *Lüdi* Case the applicant complained about two infringements of Article 8. His first complaint concerned the use of an undercover agent "who had made use of the personal contact established by deceit to obtain information and influence the conduct of the applicant". The second alleged breach of Article 8 followed from the

---

[263] Judgments of 24 April 1990, para. 33 and para. 32, respectively.
[264] *Ibidem*, para. 36 and para. 35, respectively.
[265] Judgment of 23 November 1993, para. 39; judgment of 8 April 2003, *M.M. v. the Netherlands*, para. 21; judgment of 27 April 2004, *Doerga*, para. 21.
[266] Judgment of 8 April 2003, paras 44-46.

fact that this undercover agent had used technical devices in order to gain access to the applicant's home and record conversations, which had been provoked by trickery and wrongly incriminated him. The Court judged that the activities by the undercover agent, either alone or in combination with the telephone interception, did not affect the applicant's private life within the meaning of Article 8. The reason was that the undercover agent's actions took place within the context of a deal relating to 5 kg cocaine. It held as follows: "Mr Lüdi must therefore have been aware from then on that he was engaged in a criminal act punishable under Article 19 of the Drugs Law and that consequently he was running the risk of encountering an undercover police officer whose task would in fact be to expose him."[267] Concerning the telephone interception the Court agreed with the applicant that it was an interference with his private life and correspondence. It ruled, however, that it was in conformity with the requirements laid down in paragraph 2.[268] In the *Halford* Case the phone (private as well as office) of a female police officer had been tapped. With respect to the private phone the Court concluded that it was in conformity with national law; concerning the office phone the lack of statutory basis led to the finding that Article 8 had been violated.[269]

The consequence of the Court's approach in the *Lüdi* Case apparently is that those who engage in criminal activities take the chance of infringements upon their private lives. Therefore, their private life is not affected when the authorities, through the use of undercover agents, decide to act and to gain information. This – implied – notion of 'estoppel' is an approach that raises many questions. The first is why the Court resorted to it only in the context of the activities of the undercover agent. Is it not true in general that criminals do run the risk of having their phones tapped, and being exposed to all kinds of prosecution techniques and tactics? Still the Court accepted that telephone interception, even of supposed criminals, is an interference with Article 8 and has to meet the standards of the second paragraph. It is submitted that the view that a criminal is estopped from invoking Article 8 in the context of the activities of an undercover agent, amounts to too restrictive an interpretation of the scope of the first paragraph of Article 8. Activities by an undercover agent could very well be taken into account under the requirements of the second paragraph.

The requirement that phone tapping must be based on a precise legal provision appears to be the major protection offered in this respect under Article 8. As the Court stated in the *Valenzuela Contreras* Case: "The requirement that the effects of the 'law' be foreseeable means, in the sphere of monitoring telephone communications, that the guarantees stating the extent of the authorities' discretion and the manner in which it is to be exercised must be set out in detail in domestic law so that it has a binding

---

[267]   Judgment of 15 June 1992, para. 40.
[268]   *Ibidem*, para. 39.
[269]   Judgment of 25 June 1997, para. 60; judgment of 27 April 2004, *Doerga*, para. 54.

force which circumscribes the judges' discretion in the application of such measures (...). Consequently the Spanish law which the investigating judge had to apply should have provided those guarantees with sufficient provision."[270] This means that domestic law must indicate with reasonable clarity the scope and manner of exercise of the discretion. The legal provisions concerned must be clear about the cases in which a phone may be tapped; how long tapping may take place; rules concerning destruction and storing of the tapes; who has access to them, etcetera. Domestic law must also provide for adequate protection against abuse: access to an independent authority, preferably a court, must be foreseen.

12.6.3 LISTENING DEVICES

In *P.G. and J.H. v. the United Kingdom* the Court was asked to review the legality of police action having placed listening devices in the applicant's home, metering his phone calls and secretly taping the voice of the applicant in an interview with the police in order to compare his voice with a voice in previously tapped phone conversations. For all these aspects the Court found Article 8 to be applicable. With respect to the latter aspect the Court stated as follows: "the Court is not persuaded that recordings taken for use as voice samples can be regarded as falling outside the scope of the protection afforded by Article 8. A permanent record has nonetheless been made of the person's voice and it is subject to a process of analysis directly relevant to identifying that person in the context of other personal data. Though it is true that when being charged the applicants answered formal questions in a place where police officers were listening to them, the recording and analysis of their voices on this occasion must still be regarded as concerning the processing of personal data about the applicants. The Court concludes therefore that the recording of the applicants' voices when being charged and in their police cell discloses an interference with their right to respect for private life within the meaning of Article 8 par. 1 of the Convention."[271] The Court concluded that Article 8 had been violated since the recording took place without specific legal authority. At the relevant time there existed no statutory system to regulate the use of covert listening devices by the police on their own premises. Similarly, in the *Khan* Case the absence of statutory rules on the use of covert listening devices led the Court to find a violation.[272]

---

[270] Judgment of 30 July 1998, para. 60. In the *Petra* Case the domestic law did not give any criterion: judgment of 23 September 1998. Phone tapping was also based upon too vague a legal basis in the *Kopp* Case, judgment of 25 March 1998.

[271] Judgment of 25 September 2001, paras 59-60.

[272] Judgment of 12 May 2000, para. 28; judgment of 27 May 2003, *Hewitson*, para. 21; judgment of 16 November 2004, *Wood*, para. 33.

12.7 POSITIVE OBLIGATIONS

12.7.1 GENERAL OBSERVATIONS

Within the scope of Article 8 the Court has frequently made use of the concept of 'positive obligations', the assumption being that the national authorities may be under an obligation actively to respect the individual's rights protected under Article 8. This concept was introduced by the Court in the *Marckx* Case where it held that Article 8(2) does not merely compel the State to abstain from interference; in addition to this primarily negative undertaking, there may be positive obligations inherent in an effective respect for family life.[273]

The issue of the positive obligations involved in Article 8 and their scope were also discussed in *X. and Y. v. the Netherlands*. There a father complained that a person who had sexually abused his mentally handicapped daughter, was not prosecuted by the Dutch authorities, on the mere ground that the victim was incapable of lodging the required complaint and the father was not legally empowered to do so as her substitute. The Court held that the positive obligations inherent in Article 8 may involve the adoption of measures designed to secure respect for private life even in the sphere of the relations of individuals between themselves. It found that neither the protection afforded by Dutch civil law nor that offered by the Criminal Code then in force was sufficient, and that, therefore, taking account of the nature of the wrongdoing in question, the daughter was the victim of a violation of Article 8.[274]

The concept of positive obligations was further developed in the *Rees* Case, the *Powell and Rayner* Case, the *Cossey* Case, *B. v. France,* and the *Lopez Ostra* Case (all discussed above). In these cases the Court considered the term 'respect' in paragraph 1 as being not clear-cut, especially as far as the positive obligations inherent in that concept are concerned. In determining whether a positive obligation exists "regard must be had to the fair balance that has to be struck between the general interests of the community and the interests of the individual".[275]

Within the context of the concept of family life the Court also resorted to the concept of positive obligations. It has become standing case law to deduce from the wording of Article 8 active obligations for the States to promote and guarantee the effective enjoyment of family life. Measures by the State must be aimed at reuniting a family and enable them to establish and develop family ties and legal relationships In the *Kroon* Case the Court summarised its approach in this respect as follows: "The Court reiterates that the essential object of Article 8 is to protect the individual against arbitrary action by the public authorities. There may in addition be positive obligations

---

[273]   Judgment of 13 June 1979, para. 31.
[274]   Judgment of 26 March 1985, paras 29-30.
[275]   Judgment of 27 September 1990, *Cossey,* para. 37.

inherent in effective 'respect' for family life. However, the boundaries between the State's positive and negative obligations under this provision do not lend themselves to precise definition. The applicable principles are nonetheless similar. In both contexts regard must be had to the fair balance that has to be struck between the competing interests of the individual and of the community as a whole; and in both contexts the State enjoys a certain margin of appreciation (...). According to the principles set out by the Court in its case law, where the existence of a family tie with a child has been established, the State must act in a manner calculated to enable that tie to be developed and legal safeguards must be established that render possible as from the moment of birth or as soon as practicable thereafter, the child's integration in his family."[276]

In the *Ignaccolo-Zenide* Case the Court held that the national authorities' obligation to take measures to facilitate reunion was not absolute. The nature and extent of such measures will depend on the circumstances of each case, but the understanding and cooperation of all concerned is always an important ingredient. Whilst national authorities must do their utmost to facilitate such cooperation, any obligation to apply coercion in this area must be limited, since the interests as well as the rights and freedoms of all concerned must be taken into account, and more particularly the best interests of the child and his or her rights under Article 8 of the Convention. Where contacts with the parent might appear to threaten those interests or interfere with those rights, it is for the national authorities to strike a fair balance between them.[277] In the *Iglesias Gil and A.U.I.* Case the Court held in this respect that it was decisive whether the national authorities had taken all the steps that could reasonably be demanded of them to facilitate the execution of the court decisions by which the first applicant had been awarded custody and sole parental responsibility for her child. In that connection, the Court noted that the courts dealing with the case had taken a number of steps in accordance with the legislation in force. However, as the case primarily concerned the removal and wrongful retention of the child, the Court set out to examine, in the light of the international obligations deriving from the Hague Convention, whether the national authorities had made adequate and effective efforts to enforce the first applicant's right to the return of her child and the child's right to join his mother. The Court considered that once the Spanish judicial authorities had found the child's abduction to have been wrongful, the competent national authorities should have taken appropriate measures, as laid down in the relevant provisions of the Hague Convention, to secure the return of the child to his mother. However, none of the measures listed in those provisions had been taken by the authorities to facilitate the execution of the decisions in favour of the first applicant and her child. Accordingly, notwithstanding the respondent State's margin of appreciation in the matter,

---

[276]   Judgment of 27 October 1994, paras 31-32; judgment of 29 April 2003, *Iglesias Gil and A.U.I*, para. 49.
[277]   Judgment of 25 January 2000, para. 94; judgment of 24 April 2003, *Sylvester*, para. 72; judgment of 5 February 2004, *Kosmopoulou*, para. 45.

the Court concluded that the Spanish authorities had failed to make adequate and effective efforts to enforce the first applicant's right to the return of her child and the child's right to join his mother, thereby breaching their right to respect for family life, as guaranteed by Article 8 of the Convention.[278]

In the *Maire* Case the Court had to determine whether the Portuguese authorities had taken all the steps that could reasonably be expected of them to enforce the decisions of the French courts. In that connection, the Court reiterated that in cases of this kind the adequacy of a measure was to be judged by the swiftness of its implementation. Custody proceedings required urgent handling as the passage of time could have irremediable consequences for relations between the child and the parent from whom he or she was separated. Here, although no substantial periods of inactivity were attributable to the authorities dealing with the case during the initial stage of the proceedings, the Court found it hard to understand how those authorities had not managed to summon S.C. to appear. The Court accepted that the difficulties in ascertaining the child's whereabouts had been chiefly due to the conduct of the child's mother, but considered that the authorities should have taken appropriate measures to punish her lack of cooperation. The lengthy period that had elapsed before the child had been found had created a factual situation that was unfavourable to the applicant, particularly in view of the child's tender age. In such circumstances, the Court considered that the Portuguese authorities had not made adequate and effective efforts to enforce the applicant's right to the return of his child.[279]

In the *Hansen* Case the applicant complained that the Turkish authorities had failed effectively to enforce her access rights to her children despite numerous attempts she had made to see them between 1992 and 1998. She had travelled to Turkey from Iceland more than a hundred times in six years with the aim of seeing her daughters. However, her efforts had remained unsuccessful because her former husband had consistently refused to comply with the access arrangements. She pointed out that the Turkish authorities had failed to take effective steps to locate her daughters, who had been hidden by their father prior to each visit by the enforcement officers. The Court recalled that proceedings relating to granting parental responsibility, including execution of the decision delivered at the end of them, required urgent handling, as the passage of time could have irremediable consequences for relations between the children and the parent who did not live with them. During the proceedings in this case, which had lasted six years and five months, the children had been under immense pressure and had been exposed to media and public attention. Even in such difficult circumstances, however, the authorities had not taken any measures to enable Ms Hansen to gain access to them while the lengthy proceedings were pending. In particular, they failed to seek the advice of social services or the assistance of

---

[278]   Judgment of 29 April 2003, paras 57-62; judgment of 26 June 2003, *Maire*, para. 74.
[279]   Judgment of 26 June 2003, paras 74-78.

psychologists or child psychiatrists to facilitate her reunion with her daughters or to create a more cooperative atmosphere between her and her former husband. Although the children had expressed a reluctance to see their mother on several occasions, the Court was of the opinion that they were never given any real opportunity to develop a relationship with her in a calm environment so that they could freely express their feelings for her without any outside pressure. The Court did not agree with the Government's submission that the Turkish authorities did everything that could reasonably be expected of them to enforce the applicant's right of access to her children. It found that the fines imposed on her former husband were neither effective nor adequate. The Turkish authorities therefore failed to make adequate and effective efforts to enforce the applicant's access rights to her children and thereby violated her right to respect for her family life, as guaranteed by Article 8.[280]

In the *Hatton* Case, concerning private life and home, the Court clearly set out how it proceeds in balancing the general interests of the applicant in determining whether a positive obligation exists and has been violated. The Court held as follows: "The Court notes that Heathrow airport and the aircraft which use it are not owned, controlled or operated by the Government or by any agency of the Government. The Court considers that, accordingly, the United Kingdom cannot be said to have 'interfered' with the applicants' private or family life. Instead, the applicants' complaints fall to be analysed in terms of a positive duty on the State to take reasonable and appropriate measures to secure the applicants' rights under Article 8 para. 1 of the Convention (….). Whatever analytical approach is adopted – the positive duty or an interference – the applicable principles regarding justification under Article 8 para. 2 are broadly similar (…). In both contexts, regard must be had to the fair balance that has to be struck between the competing interests of the individual and of the community as a whole. In both contexts the State enjoys a certain margin of appreciation in determining the steps to be taken to ensure compliance with the Convention (…). Furthermore, even in relation to the positive obligations flowing from Article 8 para. 1, in striking the required balance the aims mentioned in Article 8 para. 2 may be of a certain relevance (…). The Court would, however, underline that in striking the required balance, States must have regard to the whole range of material considerations. Further, in the particularly sensitive field of environmental protection, mere reference to the economic well being of the country is not sufficient to outweigh the rights of others. The Court recalls that in the above-mentioned Lopez Ostra v. Spain case and notwithstanding the undoubted economic interest for the national economy of the tanneries concerned, the Court looked in considerable detail at 'whether the national authorities took the measures necessary for protecting the applicant's right to respect for her home and for her private and family life…' (…).

---

[280]   Judgment of 23 September 2003, paras 98-109.

It considers that States are required to minimise, as far as possible, the interference with these rights, by trying to find alternative solutions and by generally seeking to achieve their aims in the least onerous way as regards human rights. In order to do that, a proper and complete investigation and study with the aim of finding the best possible solution which will, in reality, strike the right balance should precede the relevant project."[281] In that case, the Grand Chamber reached a different conclusion on the basis of the (evaluation of the application of the) wide margin of appreciation in environmental issues.[282]

In the *Mikulic* Case the Court concluded that a positive obligation existed for the State to assist the applicant in having established whether the defendant was her father; however a court ordered DNA test had not taken place. The Court held that procedural measures must be set in place when paternity cannot be established by means of DNA testing. According to the Court the inefficiency of the courts had left the applicant in a state of prolonged uncertainty as to her personal identity. The Croatian authorities had therefore failed to secure to the applicant the 'respect' for her private life to which she is entitled under the Convention.[283]

As regards private institutions, the issue of the *Drittwirkung* of Article 8 also arises in the context of positive obligations. The second paragraph of Article 8 expressly mentions 'interference by a public authority'. The development by the Court of the concept of positive obligations, however, leads to an interpretation according to which the Contracting States are under an obligation actively to protect the right of privacy, also against infringements by private parties.[284] In that respect reference may be made to the reasoning of the Court in the *Hatton* Case, cited above. Of course this does not mean that in Strasbourg a complaint against a private individual could be submitted, but it implies that Article 8 could be invoked before the national courts against a private individual in those systems in which the Convention has internal effect. Moreover, Article 8 then would imply the obligation for the Contracting States to assure respect for privacy by individuals to the best of their ability *via* the legislature, the administration and the courts.[285]

In *M.C. v. Bulgaria* the applicant complained that Bulgarian law and practice did not provide effective protection against rape and sexual abuse, as only cases where the victim has resisted actively are prosecuted. The Court considered that the Bulgarian

---

[281]   Judgment of 2 October 2001, paras 95-97.

[282]   Judgment of 8 July 2003 (Grand Chamber), paras 116-130.

[283]   Judgment of 7 February 2002, para. 66.

[284]   Article 3 of the 1981 Council of Europe Convention for the Protection of Individuals with Regard to Automatic Processing of Personal Data (European Treaty Series No. 108) stipulates: 'The Parties undertake to apply the Convention to automated personal data files and automatic processing of personal data in the public and private sectors.'

[285]   In its report of 1 March 1979, *Van Oosterwijck*, B.36 (1983), p. 24, the Commission held that Article 8 does not expressly guarantee the right to be protected by the law against interferences with private life', but in the construction here defended not a legal right but a reflex effect would be in issue.

authorities should have explored all the facts and should have decided on the basis of an assessment of all the surrounding circumstances. The investigation and its conclusions should also have been centred on the issue of non-consent. Without expressing an opinion on the guilt of P. and A., the Court found that the effectiveness of the investigation of the applicant's case and, in particular, the approach taken by the investigator and the prosecutors, fell short of Bulgaria's positive obligations under Articles 3 and 8 of the Convention – viewed in the light of the relevant modern standards in comparative and international law – to establish and apply a criminal-law system effectively punishing all forms of rape and sexual abuse.[286]

Reliance upon the notion of positive obligations under Article 8 evidently also has its limits. In the *Botta* Case the handicapped applicant claimed that access to a beach had to be made possible for him. In this case the Court held Article 8 to be inapplicable. It stated: "In the instant case, however, the right asserted by Mr Botta, namely the right to gain access to the beach and the sea at a place distant from his normal place of residence during his holidays, concerns interpersonal relations of such broad and indeterminate scope that there can be no conceivable direct link between the measures the State was urged to take in order to make good the omissions of the private bathing establishments and the applicant's private life."[287]

The *Pretty* Case and the *Osman* Case (discussed *supra*) are more serious examples of Article 8 cases involving positive obligations in which the Court held that no violation had occurred. In the *Pretty* Case the Court held that the State could reasonably have banned assisted suicide. In the *Osman* Case the Court also applied a reasonableness test. It held as follows: "The Court recalls that it has not found it established that the police knew or ought to have known at the time that Paget-Lewis represented a real and immediate risk to the life of Ahmet Osman and that their response to the events as they unfolded was reasonable in the circumstances and not incompatible with the authorities' duty under Article 2 of the Convention to safeguard the right to life. In the Court's view, that conclusion equally supports a finding that there has been no breach of any positive obligation implied by Article 8 of the Convention to safeguard the second applicant's physical integrity."[288]

---

[286] Judgment 4 December 2003, paras 185-187.
[287] Judgment of 24 February 1998, para. 35.
[288] Judgment of 28 October 1998, para. 128.

12.7.2 POSITIVE OBLIGATIONS AND THE SECOND PARAGRAPH

Does the second paragraph of Article 8 have the same relevance if a positive obligation has been found to exist and to have been violated as in the context of 'negative' interferences? The Court seems to have 'merged' the two tests more or less. It seems less and less inclined to distinguish explicitly between negative and positive obligations in this respect as appears from the *Kroon* judgment, quoted *supra*. However, in a more recent decision the formula used by the Court is slightly different. First of all, the Court held that the applicable principles to be '*broadly*' similar. And secondly the Court added: "Furthermore, even in relation to the positive obligations flowing from the first paragraph of Article 8, in striking the required balance the aims mentioned in the second paragraph may be of a certain relevance."[289] The Court repeated this in the *Hatton* judgment quoted *supra*.

The upshot of the Court's case law seems to be, nevertheless, that for the weighing of the interests involved it is of little relevance whether the alleged violation of Article 8 consists in a violation of a positive obligation on the part of the State or rather in an interference.

12.8 PROCEDURAL SAFEGUARDS

In various cases referred to above the Court has developed specific guarantees inherent in the protection afforded by Article 8. In the *Kruslin* Case and the *Huvig* Case (both dealing with telephone tapping) the Court indicated that certain procedures and guarantees had to be laid down in national law in order to have national law meet the standards implied in the notion 'in accordance with the law' of paragraph 2. The essential requirements in that respect appear from the Court's finding that the French system did not "afford adequate safeguards against various possible abuses. For example, the categories of people liable to have their telephones tapped by judicial order and the nature of the offences which may give rise to such an order are nowhere defined. Nothing obliges a judge to set a limit on the duration of telephone tapping. The procedure for drawing up the summary reports containing intercepted conversations; the precautions to be taken in order to communicate the recordings intact and in their entirety for possible inspection by the judge (who can hardly verify the number and length of the original tapes on the spot) and by the defence; and the circumstances in which recordings may or must be erased or the tapes be destroyed, in particular

---

[289]   Judgment of 9 December 1994, *López Ostra*, para. 51. The Court repeated this in the *Hatton* Case, quoted *supra*.

where an accused has been discharged by an investigating judge or acquitted by a court are similarly unspecified."[290]

In the *Herczegfalvy* Case the Court also dealt with the necessity of protection under national law against arbitrary interferences with the rights safeguarded by paragraph 1. According to the Court it is necessary that national law offers a minimum degree of protection against arbitrariness. And again the basis for this fundamental guarantee, flowing from the rule of law, is to be found in the concept of 'law' in the second paragraph.[291]

Another example of the necessity for adequate legal safeguards and effective domestic judicial proceedings is the *Mikulic* Case, mentioned *supra* 12.7.1. In this case, the lack of effective procedural measures led the Court to find a violation. Another example is the *Kosmopoulou* Case: the applicant had not been sufficiently involved in procedures relating to the right to access to her children.[292]

In the *Niemietz* Case the Court introduced the requirement of specific guarantees by relying upon the 'necessary in a democratic society' clause. It considered that "the search of a lawyer's office [was] not accompanied by any special procedural safeguards, such as the presence of an independent observer."[293] According to the Court, special circumstances deserve special procedural guarantees.[294] In the *Lambert* Case a conversation was intercepted on a third party's phone line. Under French law there was no remedy, in the absence of *locus standi*, to challenge the legality of this interception. According to its established case law on the need for an effective remedy, required under Article 8, the Court held as follows: "However, it has to be recognised that the Court of Cassation's reasoning could lead to decisions whereby a very large number of people are deprived of the protection of the law, namely all those who have conversations on a telephone line other than their own. That would in practice render the protective machinery largely devoid of substance. That was the case with the applicant, who did not enjoy the effective protection of national law, which does not make any distinction according to whose line is being tapped (Articles 100 et seq. of the Code of Criminal Procedure). The Court therefore considers, like the Commission, that the applicant did not have available to him the 'effective control' to which citizens

---

[290] Judgments of 24 April 1990, para. 35 and para. 34 respectively. In its judgment of 6 September 1978, *Klass,* para. 50, the Court already stressed the necessity for the relevant legislation and practice to afford adequate and effective safeguards against abuse. In its judgment of 25 February 1993, *Crémieux,* para. 40, the Court also referred to this principle and reached the conclusion that the legislation in force was insufficient in this respect.

[291] Judgment of 24 September 1992, para. 91.

[292] Judgment of 5 February 2004, para. 49.

[293] Judgment of 16 December 1992, para. 37. In its judgment of 25 February 1993, *Crémieux,* para. 40, the Court, on the ground of the absence of sufficient safeguards against abuse, concluded that the interference was not proportionate to the legitimate aim pursued and therefore not necessary in a democratic society.

[294] Reference may also be had to the *Kopp* Case, judgment of 25 March 1998, about phone tapping in a law-firm, leading the Court also to ask for specific procedures and safeguards.

are entitled under the rule of law and which would have been capable of restricting the interference in question to what was 'necessary in a democratic society'. There has consequently been a violation of Article 8 of the Convention."[295]

From this case law it becomes evident that Article 8 may be said also to include aspects of Articles 6 and 13 of the Convention.

12.9   RESTRICTIONS

12.9.1   PROPORTIONALITY

Restrictions to the rights laid down in the first paragraph of Article 8 may be justified, when they meet the requirements of the second paragraph.

Within the concept of the 'necessary in a democratic society' test, the Court relies heavily upon the principle of 'proportionality'. This enables the Court to balance all the relevant interests and factual circumstances, and also to take into account the intensity of the infringement as well as the question whether the essence of the right invoked has been infringed. The scale the Court utilises seems to imply that the more far-reaching the infringement or the more essential the aspect of the right that has been interfered with, the more substantial or compelling the legitimate aims pursued must be.

In the context of family life this has induced the Court in certain cases to impose upon the Contracting States a heavy burden to prove that an infringement was legitimate. An example of this approach is the *Margareta and Roger Andersson* Case, concerning restrictions of contact between a mother and her child. Here the Court held as follows: "The reasons adduced by the Government are of a general nature and do not specifically address the necessity of prohibiting contact by correspondence and telephone. The Court does not doubt that these reasons were relevant. However, they do not sufficiently show that it was necessary to deprive the applicants of almost every means of maintaining contact with each other for a period of approximately one and a half years. Indeed, it is questionable whether the measures were compatible with the aim of reuniting the applicants. Having regard to all the circumstances of the case, the Court considers that the aggregate of the restrictions imposed by the social welfare authorities on meetings and communications by correspondence and telephone between the applicants was disproportionate to the legitimate aims pursued and, therefore, not 'necessary in a democratic society'. There has accordingly been a breach of Article 8."[296]

---

[295]   Judgment of 24 August 1998, paras 38–41.
[296]   Judgment of 25 February 1992, para. 96.

The heavy burden of proof that is sometimes placed upon the States when family ties and reunification of the family are at issue, also came to the fore in the *Keegan* Case. The Court concluded that the state of affairs complained about "not only jeopardised the proper development of the applicant's ties with the child but also set a process in motion which was likely to prove to be irreversible, thereby putting the applicant at a significant disadvantage in his contest with the prospective adopters for the custody of the child. The Government have advanced no reasons relevant to the welfare of the applicant's daughter to justify such a departure from the principles that govern respect for family ties".[297] The Court's reference to 'such a departure from the principles' should particularly be noted in this quotation. The intensity and effect of the infringement seem to have been conclusive. In the case of deportation the Court also seems to be applying a rather strict approach whenever an applicant's family life is threatened to be interfered with severely.[298]

Some encroachments deserve more justification than others. In the *Niemietz* Case, with respect to the search of a law office, the Court paid special attention to the fact that a lawyer's professional secrecy was involved. It stated the following: "More importantly, having regard to the materials that were in fact inspected, the search impinged on professional secrecy to an extent that appears disproportionate in the circumstances; it has, in this connection, to be recalled that, where a lawyer is involved, an encroachment on professional secrecy may have repercussions on the proper administration of justice and hence on the rights guaranteed by Article 6 of the Convention. In addition, the attendant publicity must have been capable of affecting adversely the applicant's professional reputation, in the eyes both of his existing clients and of the public at large."[299]

In the *Kruslin* Case and the *Huvig* Case the Court apparently differentiated the necessary degree of precision of the 'law' depending of the seriousness of the interference. In these cases the Court argued as follows: "Tapping and other forms of interception of telephone conversations represent a serious interference with private life and correspondence and must accordingly be based on a 'law' that is particularly precise. It is essential to have clear, detailed rules on the subject, especially as the technology available for use is continually becoming more sophisticated."[300]

The relevance of the seriousness of the interference was also reflected in the *Pfeifer and Plankl* Case, concerning the control of letters of a prisoner. In this case letters had not been stopped but some (apparently abusive) passages had been deleted. Still the Court concluded that this violated Article 8. It remarked at the same time that "[t]he

---

297 Judgment of 26 May 1994, para.55.
298 See, *e.g.*, the judgment of 26 March 1992, *Beldjoudi*, paras 75-79.
299 Judgment of 16 December 1992, para. 37. Another example is *Kopp*, judgment of 25 March 1998.
300 Judgments of 24 April 1990, para. 33 and para. 34, respectively.

deletion of passages is admittedly a less serious interference, but in the circumstances of the case this too appears disproportionate".[301]

12.9.2   IMPLIED RESTRICTIONS

As was indicated above, the Court rejects the concept of 'inherent limitations' in the context of Article 8.[302] However, some situations do imply restrictions which the Court is likely to allow, since they are inherent in a specific situation or status like that of soldier or prisoner. This should not imply, however, that in those cases the test under the second paragraph is no longer relevant; it may only imply that the Contracting State may be confronted here with a less severe and less probing attitude on the part of the Court. In actual fact, however, at times the testing under the second paragraph is hardly noticeable or not performed at all.

In the *Campbell* Case the Court concluded "that some measure of control over prisoners' correspondence is called for and is not of itself incompatible with the Convention, regard being paid to the ordinary and reasonable requirements of imprisonment".[303] A similar reasoning was adopted by the Court in the *Costello Roberts* Case, concerning corporal punishment at school. In that respect the Court observed that measures taken in the field of education may, in certain circumstances, affect the right to respect for private life, but not every act or measure which may be said to affect the physical or moral integrity of a person adversely necessarily gives rise to such an interference. Regarding the applicability of Article 8 the Court added that sending a child to school necessarily involves some degree of interference with his or her private life. Therefore the Court considered "that the treatment complained of by the applicant did not entail adverse effects for his physical or moral integrity sufficient to bring it within the scope of the prohibition contained in Article 8."[304] In the *Lüdi* Case the Court accepted an interference with Article 8 by the use and activities of an undercover agent because the applicant must have been aware, by engaging in criminal activities, "that consequently he was running the risk of encountering an undercover police officer whose task would in fact be to expose him."[305]

It may be concluded from this case law that, although in general the Court does not accept the concept of inherent or implied restrictions, in specific cases some restrictions are nevertheless accepted by the Court, if these have their basis in a specific legal situation or status.

---

[301]   Judgment of 25 February 1992, para. 47.
[302]   See *supra* 12.4.4.; see also *supra* 5.4.3.
[303]   Judgment of 25 March 1992, para. 47. See also the judgment of 25 March 1983, *Silver,* para. 98 and the judgment of 25 February 1992, *Pfeifer and Plankl,* para. 46.
[304]   Judgment of 25 March 1993, para. 36.
[305]   Judgment of 15 June 1992, para. 40.

12.9.3 NECESSARY IN A DEMOCRATIC SOCIETY

Application of the 'necessary in a democratic society' concept sometimes implies a very extensive and probing scrutiny by the Court, replacing the opinions of the national authorities by its own judgment and its own criteria. Although the general concept of necessity, as used by the Court, is undoubtedly the same in all cases in which the Court refers to it, nevertheless the intensity of the Court's control does differ and is dependent upon many circumstances. They differ depending on factors like the seriousness of the infringement or the position of the applicant. An example of a very probing scrutiny by the Court is certainly its judgment in the *Campbell* Case. In that judgment the Court adopted a very strict approach as against the national authorities with respect to their opening letters of prisoners. But the Court even went further by giving indications to the Contracting State on how to proceed when wishing to control a prisoner's correspondence with a lawyer.[306]

On the contrary, in the area of orders to place children into care, the Court in general adopts a more restrained attitude. Thus, it held in the *Olsson (No. 2)* Case: "In exercising its supervisory jurisdiction the Court must determine whether the reasons given for the prohibition on removal, its maintenance in force until the transfer of custody and the restrictions on access which were in operation throughout this period were 'relevant and sufficient' in the light of the case as a whole."[307] In order to give some more strictness to this test, however, the Court added an extra requirement for the respondent State: to make efforts for reunification of the family. This still would seem to leave more scope for the States than the Court is prepared to allow, for instance, when control of letters to and from prisoners is concerned.

12.10 DEROGATION

Article 8 does not pertain to the rights that are non-derogable in virtue of Article 15(2). This means that the Contracting States can take measures in derogation of Article 8 in the circumstances referred to in Article 15 and under the conditions laid down therein. In the several cases against Turkey in which a destruction of houses by the security forces was held to constitute a violation of Article 8, Article 15 did not play a role, although the Court mentioned the fact that some regions had been the subject of domestic emergency rule.

---

[306] See *supra* 12.6.1.
[307] Judgment of 27 November 1992, para. 87. See also the judgment of 24 March 1988, *Olsson*, para. 81.

CHAPTER 13
FREEDOM OF THOUGHT, CONSCIENCE AND RELIGION
(Article 9)

REVISED BY BEN VERMEULEN

CONTENTS

13.1 TEXT OF ARTICLE 9

1. *Everyone has the right to freedom of thought, conscience and religion; this right includes freedom to change his religion or belief and freedom, either alone or in community with others and in public or private, to manifest his religion or belief, in worship, teaching, practice and observance.*

2. *Freedom to manifest one's religion or beliefs shall be subject only to such limitations as are prescribed by law and are necessary in a democratic society in the interests of public safety, for the protection of public order, health or morals, or for the protection of the rights and freedoms of others.*

13.2 PROTECTION OF THE FORUM INTERNUM

The right to (inner) freedom of thought, conscience and religion, the inviolability of the *forum internum*, is guaranteed in Article 9 of the Convention without qualification. Restrictions are possible only with respect to the external expressions of thought, conscience and religion, *viz.* in pursuance of the second paragraph of Article 9 with respect to the manifestation of religious and other beliefs,[1] and on the basis of the second paragraph of Article 10 with respect to the expression of one's opinion in general.

This absolute freedom to entertain any thought, moral conviction or religious view is not entirely without practical importance. It is true that thoughts and views, as long as they have not been expressed, are intangible and that convictions are especially valuable for the person concerned if he can express them. But that does not render the (inner) freedom of thought, conscience and religion useless. This guarantee also implies that one cannot be subjected to treatment intended to change the process of thinking ('brain-washing'), that any form of compulsion to express thoughts, to change an opinion, or to divulge a religious conviction is prohibited,[2] and that no sanction may be imposed either on the holding of a view or on the change of a religion or conviction: it protects against indoctrination by the State.[3] On the other hand, the obligation for children to attend moral and social education lessons that do not expose them to religious indoctrination or any other form of indoctrination, does not constitute an interference with the freedom of thought and conscience.[4] Likewise the Court has ruled that the obligation to take part in a school parade without military

---

[1] Judgment of 25 May 1993, *Kokkinakis*, para. 33: "The fundamental nature of the rights guaranteed in Article 9 para. 1 is also reflected in the wording of the paragraphs providing for limitations on them. Unlike the second paragraphs of Articles 8, 10 and 11, which cover all the rights mentioned in the first paragraphs of those Articles, that of Article 9 refers only to "freedom to manifest one's religion or belief".

[2] One can gather from the Teitgen-report that the fathers of the Convention intended the freedom of thought etc. to protect the individual against "ces abominables moyens d'enquête policière ou d'instruction judiciaire qui privent le suspect ou l'inculpé du contrôle de ses facultées intellectuelles et de sa conscience" (*Recueil des "Travaux Préparatoires"*, Vol. I, The Hague 1975, p. 223).

[3] Appl. 23380/94, *C.J., J.J. and E.J. v. Poland*, D&R 84-A (1996), p. 46 (56).

[4] Appl. 17187/90, *Bernard*, D&R 75 (1993), p. 57 (73).

overtones is not such as to offend the parent's religious convictions, and, therefore, does not amount to an interference with the right to freedom of religion.[5]

Even the obligation to reveal one's religion or conviction in a census or other registration would seem to conflict with Article 9 because the freedom to have a religion or conviction includes the right not to disclose it. Furthermore it would seem that the Commission has deduced from Article 9 the right to have one's religion or belief correctly registered by the authorities: it considered that the complaint that the municipal authorities refused to provide a certificate indicating the person's religion falls under the scope of Article 9.[6] Compulsory voting, on the other hand, has not been considered contrary to Article 9, because this is only a duty to attend, and not a duty actually to register one's vote.[7]

13.3 FREEDOM OF CONSCIENCE

The freedom to act in accordance with one's thought, conscience and religion is only guaranteed by Article 9 in as far as it may be regarded – from an objective point of view – as a manifestation of religion or belief (paragraph 4). This implies, for instance, that the freedom to act according to one's (subjective) conscience – external freedom of conscience – is as such not protected by Article 9.

Moreover, on grounds of legal logic it should be ruled out that such freedom might be protected by a general provision in a human rights treaty. While every type of action may have conscience as its motivational base, every legal obligation may function as a restriction of the (external) freedom of conscience. It is clear that such freedom cannot be unlimited. However, the 'boundlessness' of conscience prevents the limitations of this freedom from being laid down in a general, strictly formulated restriction clause. Other human rights such as the freedom of speech or religion are concerned with certain specific areas of action, are connected with social institutions, and have to do with foreseeable patterns of behaviour; this makes it possible to define their restriction clauses in general terms. As the external freedom of conscience lacks such an identifiable object and scope, it is not possible to frame a satisfactory and workable provision containing restrictions. Therefore, it must be assumed on logical grounds that Article 9 does not guarantee the external freedom of conscience.

A systematic argument derived from Article 9 itself supports this narrow interpretation. It must be stressed that the freedom of conscience in Article 9(1) cannot be subjected to limitations: Article 9(2) only allows restrictions of the freedom to

---

[5] Judgment of 18 December 1996, *Valsamis*, paras 34-38; judgment of 18 December 1996, *Efstratiou*, paras 35-39.

[6] Appl. 16319/90, *H. v. Greece* (not published).

[7] Appl. 1718/62, *X v. Austria*, Yearbook VIII (1965), p. 168 (172); Appl. 4982/71, *X v. Austria*, Yearbook XV (1972), p. 468 (472-474).

manifest one's religion or belief(s).[8] If the freedom of conscience would comprise the right to act in accordance with the dictates of conscience, this freedom would be unlimited in the sense that every legal obligation would have to yield to (an appeal to) conscientious objections and convictions. But such unrestricted freedom of conscience in *foro externo* would amount to the abolition of the legal order as a binding system of general rules. Therefore, it must be concluded that the freedom of conscience in Article 9 does not cover the "external manifestations" but only the "inner world" (the *forum internum*).

This interpretation is in conformity with the case law. According to the Commission, "Article 9 primarily protects the sphere of personal beliefs and religious creeds, i.e. the area which is sometimes called the *forum internum*. In addition, it protects acts which are intimately linked to these attitudes, such as acts of worship or devotion which are aspects of the practice of a religion or belief in a generally recognised form".[9] The term "acts which are intimately linked to these attitudes", probably refers to the last part of Article 9(1), the "freedom to manifest his religion or belief". Therefore, the phrase "the sphere of beliefs and religious creeds, i.e. the area which is sometimes called the forum internum" sums up the first part of this provision: the right to "freedom of thought, conscience and religion" and the "freedom to change his religion or belief". This implies that according to the Commission the freedom of conscience in this provision only covers the *forum internum*, i.e. only guarantees the internal freedom of conscience.

In the same vein, the Court ruled in the *Pichon and Sajous* Case concerning pharmacists who refused to sell contraceptive pills because of their religious convictions, "that the main sphere protected by Article 9 is that of personal convictions and religious beliefs, in other words what are sometimes referred to as matters of individual conscience. It also protects acts that are closely linked to these matters such as acts of worship or devotion forming part of the practice of a religion or a belief in a generally accepted form. [...] However, in safeguarding this personal domain, Article 9 of the Convention does not always guarantee the right to behave in public in a manner governed by that belief. The word "practice" used in Article 9 para. 1 does not denote each and every act or form of behaviour motivated or inspired by a religion or a belief". The Court, therefore, concluded that "the applicants cannot give precedence to their religious beliefs and impose them on others as justification for their refusal to sell such products."[10]

---

[8]   Judgment of 25 May 1993, *Kokkinakis*, para. 33.
[9]   Appl. 10358/83, *C. v. the United Kingdom*, D&R 37 (1984), p. 142 (147). See also the report of 12 October 1978, *Arrowsmith*, D&R 19 (1980), p. 5 (19).
[10]   Decision of 2 October 2001.

13.4   CONSCIENTIOUS OBJECTIONS TO MILITARY AND SUBSTITUTE SERVICE

With respect to the exercise of the freedom of conscience both in national and in Strasbourg case law the issue of conscientious objections of a religious or other nature against military and substitute service takes an important place. Several international institutions seem to subscribe to the view that at least conscientious objections against military service are covered by Article 9. In Resolution 337(1967) the Parliamentary Assembly of the Council of Europe inferred from Article 9, *inter alia*, that:

"1. Persons liable to conscription for military service who, for reasons of conscience or profound conviction arising from religious, ethical, moral, humanitarian, philosophical or similar motives, refuse to perform armed service shall enjoy a personal right to be released from the obligation to perform such service.

2. This right shall be regarded as deriving logically from the fundamental rights of the individual in democratic Rule of Law States which are guaranteed in Article 9 of the European Convention on Human Rights."[11]

And in 1987 the Committee of Ministers adopted Recommendation No. R(87)8 on the same subject. There, the "basic principle" is laid down that "Anyone liable to conscription for military service who, for compelling reasons of conscience, refuses to be involved in the use of arms, shall have the right to be released from the obligation to perform such service, on the conditions set out hereafter. Such persons may be liable to perform alternative service."[12]

Neither the Resolution nor the Recommendation is legally binding. Nevertheless, they may be considered as an authoritative interpretation of Article 9, which cannot simply be ignored by the national authorities and the Strasbourg institutions. And indeed the Commission has decided that conscientious objections to military service fall "into the realm of Article 9",[13] probably because such objections should in general be regarded as manifestations of a religion or belief.

It may be assumed that the Court, like the Commission, takes the position that conscientious objections fall within the scope of Article 9. In the *Thlimmenos* Case the

---

[11]   Res. 337(1967), Council of Europe, Cons. Ass., Eighteenth Ordinary Session (Third Part), *Texts Adopted* (1967), reiterated by the Parliamentary Assembly in its Res. 816(1977), adopted on 7 October 1977; *Collected Texts*, pp. 222-223. The European Parliament adopted the same point of view in a Resolution of 7 February 1983.

[12]   Council of Europe, *Information Sheet* No. 21, H/INF(87)1, p. 160. See also Resolution 1987/46 of 10 March 1987 of the United Nations Commission on Human Rights on conscientious objection to military service, where the Commission, *inter alia*, "appeals to States to recognize that conscientious objection to military service be considered a legitimate exercise of the right to freedom of thought, conscience and religion recognized by the Universal Declaration of Human Rights and the International Covenant on Civil and Political Rights."

[13]   Appl. 10410/83, *N. v. Sweden*, D&R 40 (1985), p. 203 (207); Appl. 17086/90, *Autio*, D&R 72 (1992), p. 245 (249); Appl. 20972/92, *Raninen*, D&R 84-A (1996), p. 17 (30).

Court had to deal with the complaint of a Jehovah's Witness who was not appointed as a chartered accountant as a result of his past conviction for insubordination, due to his refusal – prompted by religious conscientious objections – to wear the military uniform. The Court concluded that this set of facts fell within the ambit of Article 9.[14]

The assumption that conscientious objections fall within the ambit of Article 9 does not necessarily imply that punishment of conscientious objectors or imposition of alternative civilian service is not allowed. The Commission has found that the right to conscientious objection is not as such guaranteed by Article 9. On the contrary, it has taken the position that the Convention contains no obligation for the Contracting States to exempt conscientious objectors from compulsory military service. For its position the Commission referred to the words in Article 4(3)b): "conscientious objectors *in countries where they are recognized*" (emphasis added).[15] The argument is evidently that, since the drafters of the Convention intended to leave the States free to recognize or not to recognize conscientious objections to military service, they cannot have intended to deprive them of this same freedom in another provision of the same Convention.

Furthermore, the Commission has argued that, while in Article 4(3)(b) "it is expressly recognized that civilian service may be imposed on conscientious objectors as a substitute for military service, it must be concluded that objections of conscience do not, under the Convention, entitle a person to exemption from such service".[16] Therefore, the Convention probably does not prevent a State from taking measures to enforce performance of substitute civilian service or from imposing sanctions on those who refuse to perform such service.[17]

The Court until now has not clarified its position on these issues. In the *Thlimmenos* Case the Court held that "it does not have to address, in the present case, the question whether, notwithstanding the wording of Article 4 para. 3 (b), the imposition of such sanctions on conscientious objectors to compulsory military service may in itself infringe the right to freedom of thought, conscience and religion guaranteed by Article 9 para. 1."[18]

The fact that conscientious objections fall within the ambit of Article 9 – whether this provision contains a right to object or not – implies that differential treatment between those who do their military service and those who have opted for substitute

---

[14] Judgment of 6 April 2000, *Thlimmenos*, para. 42.
[15] See the report of 29 June 1967, *Grandrath*, Yearbook X (1967), p. 626 (672-674). See also Appl. 5591/72, *X v. Austria*, Coll. 43 (1973), p. 161; Appl. 7565/76, *Conscientious objectors*, D&R 9 (1978), p. 117 (118); Appl. 7705/76, *X v. Federal Republic of Germany*, D&R 9 (1978), p. 196 (203); Appl. 10640/83, *A. v. Switzerland*, D&R 38 (1984), p. 219 (223); Appl. 10410/83, *N. v. Sweden*, D&R 40 (1985), p. 203 (206); Appl. 11850/85, *G. v. the Netherlands*, D&R 51 (1987), p. 180 (182).
[16] Report of 29 June 1967, *Grandrath*, Yearbook X (1967), p. 626 (672-674).
[17] Appl. 10600/83, *Johansen*, D&R 44 (1985), p. 155 (165); Appl. 20972/92, *Raninen*, D&R 84-A (1996), p. 17 (32).
[18] Judgment of 6 April 2000, para. 43.

service has to be justified to the extent that they are in a comparable position. For instance, the difference in duration of military and substitute service is often challenged in courts as being unjustified, though until now without success: according to constant national and international case law, substitute service is to be regarded as less arduous than military service, so that the additional time the conscientious objector has to serve is deemed necessary to avoid refusal of military service for that reason only.[19] Even a system in which the length of the substitute service is twice as long as the length of the military service does not amount to a violation of Article 14 in conjunction with Article 9.[20]

Another consequence of the applicability of Article 14 in conjunction with Article 9 is that differential treatment between various categories of conscientious objectors must have an objective and reasonable justification. On this ground the fact that in some countries (only) Jehovah's Witnesses are exempted from military and substitute service has been and still is severely criticized. However, so far it has been denied that this differential treatment is contrary to Article 14. According to the Commission the certainty provided by the membership of the Jehovah's Witnesses with regard to the genuineness of their objections also guarantees that their privileged position does not undermine the military system itself. It is unlikely that one should join this small, rigid sect in order to avoid doing substitute service. This twofold guarantee is lacking with regard to other groups and persons, which justifies why only the Jehovah's Witnesses and not other 'total objectors' are exempted from substitute service.[21] This issue reveals a complex conflict between freedom and equality. On the one hand: is it justifiable that Jehovah's Witnesses are exempted from military and substitute service while other 'total objectors' are imprisoned?[22] On the other hand: would it be justifiable that Jehovah's Witnesses also have to serve such a sentence in order to be treated in the same way as (comparatively few) other 'total objectors'?

Finally, the applicability of Article 14 in conjunction with Article 9 entails that conscientious objectors should in certain circumstances be treated differently from 'common criminals'. The right not to be discriminated against is also violated when States without an objective and reasonable justification do not distinguish between persons whose situations are significantly different. In the *Thlimmenos* Case the Court considered that "unlike other convictions for serious criminal offences, a conviction

---

[19]   Appl. 11850/85, *G. v. the Netherlands*, D&R 51 (1987), p. 180 (182).

[20]   Appl. 17086/90, *Autio*, D&R 72 (1992), p. 245 (250), concerning the system in Finland (military service lasted 8 months, substitute service lasted 16 months).

[21]   Appl. 10410/83, *N. v. Sweden*, D&R 40 (1985), p. 203 (207); Appl. 20972/92, *Raninen*, D&R 84-A (1996), p. 17 (33.

[22]   According to the Human Rights Committee such differential treatment is incompatible with Article 26 of the Covenant. In its view of 27 July 1993, Communication No. 402/1990, it concluded "that the State party [the Netherlands] should give equal treatment to all persons holding equally strong objections to military and substitute service, and it recommends that the State party review its relevant regulations and practice with a view to removing any discrimination in this respect."

for refusing on religious or philosophical grounds to wear the military uniform cannot imply any dishonesty or moral turpitude likely to undermine the offender's ability to exercise this profession. (...) It follows that the applicant's exclusion from the profession of chartered accountants did not pursue a legitimate aim". Therefore, it concluded that there had been a violation of Article 14 in conjunction with Article 9.[23]

13.5 THE FREEDOM TO HAVE (OR NOT TO HAVE) A RELIGION OR BELIEF, AND TO CHANGE ONE'S RELIGION OR BELIEF

The freedom to have or accept a religion or belief as well as the freedom to change one's religion or belief may not be restricted. This freedom also includes the freedom *not* to have a religion or belief: "it is also a precious asset for atheists, agnostics, skeptics and the unconcerned."[24] And it also comprises the right *not* to be obliged to act in a way that entails the expression of the acceptation of a church, a religion or a belief that one does not share. For instance, requiring Members of Parliament to take the oath on the Gospels is "tantamount to requiring (...) elected representatives of the people to swear allegiance to a particular religion, a requirement which is not compatible with Article 9."[25]

It can be deduced from the Commission's and the Court's case law about church taxes that the obligation to pay such taxes does not violate the freedom of religion or belief, provided that the freedom to resign from the church community is safeguarded.[26] A formal and unambiguous confirmation of such a decision may be required.[27] Furthermore, in the *Darby* Case the Court held that exemptions from these taxes are not be granted in a discriminatory way.[28] Unfortunately the Court examined the problem of church taxes in the *Darby* Case exclusively from the perspective of Article 1 of the First Protocol.[29]

That a church imposes specific restrictions on its ministers and others employed by it, in order to preserve the purity of its doctrine and to guarantee unity in religious profession, has been considered in conformity with Article 9 by the Commission. It

---

[23]   Judgment of 6 April 2000, paras 44-49.
[24]   Judgment of 25 May 1993, *Kokkinakis*, para. 31; judgment of 18 February 1999, *Buscarini and Others*, para. 34; judgment of 13 December 2001, *Metropolitan Church of Bessarabia and Others*, para. 114.
[25]   Judgment of 18 February 1999, *Buscarini and Others*, para. 39.
[26]   Appl. 9781/82, *E. and G.R. v. Austria*, D&R 37 (1984), p. 42 (45).
[27]   Appl. 10616/83, *J. and B. Gottesmann*, D&R 40 (1985), p. 284 (289).
[28]   Judgment of 23 October 1990, paras 31-34.
[29]   The Commission found that the church tax without an exemption possibility violated Article 9 as well as Article 14 in conjunction with Article 9 (Report of 9 May 1989, paras 56-60 and 62-70).

opined as follows: "Through the rights granted to its members under Art. 9, the church itself is protected in its right to manifest its religion, to organise and carry out worship, teaching practice and observance, and it is free to act out and enforce uniformity in these matters. Further, in a State church system its servants are employed for the purpose of applying and teaching a specific religion. Their individual freedom of thought, conscience or religion is exercised at the moment they accept or refuse employment as clergymen, and their right to leave the church guarantees their freedom of religion in case they oppose its teachings. In other words, the church is not obliged to provide religious freedom to its servants and members, as is the State as such for everyone within its jurisdiction."[30]

The obligation to join an association of, *e.g.*, architects, which applies to all persons of this category, has no link with the members' personal beliefs, as it leaves them free to set up separate associations and express their personal ideas in other ways, and is, therefore, not regarded as an interference with Article 9.[31]

It is not clear to what extent the right to have and to change one's religion or belief also implies the right to be protected against the imposition of a particular conception of morals. In this respect the judgment of the Court in the *Johnston* Case is worth mentioning. Here, the applicants complained about the prohibition of divorce in Ireland. One of the applicants invoked Article 9 of the Convention, submitting that the impossibility to live together with one of the other applicants in a marital relationship – because he had already been married with a woman with whom he did not live together anymore – conflicted with his conscience. The Court concluded that in this case there was no violation of Article 9. According to the Court, Article 9, "in its ordinary meaning", was not involved.[32]

13.6   THE FREEDOM TO MANIFEST ONE'S RELIGION OR BELIEF

13.6.1   RELIGION OR BELIEF

Article 9 protects the freedom "to manifest his religion or belief". It does not refer to the freedom of expression in general, a right which finds regulation in Article 10. However, a broad interpretation of the words "religion or belief" seems to be called for. They do not only cover the traditional religions and (non-religious) beliefs, but

---

[30]   Appl. 7374/76, *X v. Denmark*, D&R 5 (1976), p. 157 (158); Appl. 11045/84, *Knudsen*, D&R 42 (1985), p. 247 (257-258); Appl. 12356/86, *Karlsson*, D&R 57 (1988), p. 172 (175).
[31]   Appl. 14331/88 and 14332/88, *Revert and Legallais*, D&R 62 (1989), p. 309 (318).
[32]   Judgment of 18 December 1986, para. 63.

also all kinds of minority views. For instance, pacifism[33] and probably also communism are regarded as a "belief" falling within the ambit of Article 9.[34] Even veganism (strict vegetarianism) may fall within the scope of this article.[35]

This does not mean that every individual opinion, conviction or preference is a "religion or belief".[36] The latter concept would be more akin to the concept of "religious and philosophical convictions" that appears in Article 2 of Protocol No. 1, denoting "views that attain a certain level of cogency, seriousness, cohesion and importance".[37] For instance, the preference for a certain language is not a belief in the sense of Article 9.[38] The magic wishes of a 'Wicca' adept were held not to be protected by Article 9, because the applicant failed to specify the content of the Wicca religion, and the same reasoning was followed with regard to the complaint of a 'Lichtanbeter'.[39] And in a case concerning a soldier who had stated at a private party that the Holocaust was a Zionist lie, the Commission concluded that these remarks "did not reflect a 'belief' within the meaning of Article 9 of the Convention which is essentially destined to protect religions, or theories on philosophical or ideological universal values".[40]

When the criteria of 'cogency, seriousness, cohesion and importance' are fulfilled, the existence of a religion or belief must be assumed. It is not up to the State to withhold protection because this religion or belief is regarded as theologically incorrect, untrue or unacceptable. For instance, in the *Manoussakis* Case the Court held that the freedom of religion "excludes any discretion on the part of the State to determine whether religious beliefs or the means used to express such beliefs are legitimate".[41]

---

[33]   Report of 12 October 1978, *Arrowsmith*, D&R 19 (1980), p. 5 (19); Appls 11567/85 and 11568/85, *Le Court Grandmaison and Fritz*, D&R 53 (1987), p. 150 (160).

[34]   Appls. 16311/90, 16312/90 and 16313/90, *N.H, G.H. and R.A. v. Turkey*, D&R 72 (1992), p. 200 (212).

[35]   Appl. 18187/91, *W. v. the United Kingdom* (not published).

[36]   Judgment of 29 April 2002, *Pretty*, para. 82.

[37]   Judgment of 25 February 1982, *Campbell and Cosans*, para. 36.

[38]   Judgment of 23 July 1968, *Belgian Linguistic Cases*, (A.6 (1968), p. 32).

[39]   Appl. 7291/75, *X. v. the United Kingdom*, D&R 11 (1978), p. 55 (56); Appl. 4445/70, *X v. Federal Republic of Germany*, Coll. 37 (1971), p. 119 (121-122).

[40]   Appl. 19459/92, *F.P. v. Federal Republic of Germany*. The Commission has left undecided whether fascist propaganda may fall within the scope of Article 9: Appl. 6741/74, *X v. Italy*, D&R 5 (1976), p. 83 (85).

[41]   Judgment of 26 September 1996, para. 47.

13.6.2   THE FREEDOM TO MANIFEST ONE'S RELIGION OR BELIEF IN PRACTICE

Article 9 protects the freedom to manifest one's religion or belief, in worship, teaching, practice and observance. The enumeration suggests that Article 9 primarily concerns the 'traditional' manifestations in religious cults and rites,[42] *e.g.* in the observance of regulations concerning clothing and food. But even with regard to 'traditional' religious manifestations the Court sometimes concludes that they fall outside the ambit of Article 9. For instance, in the *Cha'are* Case[43] it was concluded – after the Court had recognized that ritual slaughter was a religious act for the purposes of Article 9 – that there would be interference with the freedom to manifest one's religion only if the illegality of performing ritual slaughter made it impossible for ultra-orthodox (French) Jews to eat 'glatt' meat from animals slaughtered in accordance with the religious prescriptions they considered applicable. Because they could obtain such meat in Belgium the Court found that there was no interference. It is respectfully submitted that the Court's conclusion, that the prohibition to perform ritual slaughter (a religious act) does not constitute an interference with the freedom of religion, is incorrect.

It may be assumed that the enumeration of protected manifestations in Article 9 is not intended to be exhaustive. Furthermore, the term 'practice' leaves room for a broader scope, outside the sphere of traditional religious manifestations. The Strasbourg case law, however, has followed a rather restrictive interpretation, for the first time formulated explicitly in the *Arrowsmith* Case. Arrowsmith had claimed that she was entitled to distribute leaflets (to troops in a British army camp) in which she advocated the view that these troops should not serve in Northern Ireland, as Article 9 gave her the right to express her pacifist belief in this practice. The Commission, however, argued that a subjective criterion would not do: "the term 'practice' as employed in Article 9.1 does not cover each act which is motivated or influenced by a religion or belief". The Commission applied an objective standard: "when the actions of individuals do not actually express the belief concerned they cannot be considered to be as such protected by Article 9.1, even when they are motivated by it", and concluded that, since the pamphlets "did not express pacifist views", the applicant did not manifest her belief in the sense of Article 9 and, therefore, could not invoke this provision.[44]

This line of argument has been consistently followed in later decisions of the Commission and in judgments of the Court. The terms 'manifestation' and 'practice'

---

[42]   For instance propagation of religious beliefs (judgment of 25 May 1993, *Kokkinakis*, para. 31); keeping the fast of Ramadan and attending Friday prayers at the mosque (judgment of 1 July 1997, *Kalaç*, para. 29); ritual slaughter (judgment of 27 June 2000, *Cha'are Shalom ve Tsedek*, para. 74); wearing of the Islamic headscarf (judgment of 29 June 2004, *Leyla Sahin*, para. 71).

[43]   Judgment of 27 June 2000, *Cha'are Shalom Ve Tsedek*, paras 80-83.

[44]   Report of 12 October 1978, D&R 19 (1980) p. 5 (19-20).

do not cover each act which is motivated by a religion or belief;[45] actions which do not actually express a belief are not protected by Article 9.[46] So the Court, although not doubting the firmness of the applicant's views concerning assisted suicide, reflecting her commitment to the principle of personal autonomy, nevertheless found that her seeking the assistance of her husband to commit suicide did not involve a form of manifestation of a religion or belief.[47] Likewise the Court ruled that the refusal of pharmacists to sell contraceptive pills because of their religious convictions could not be regarded as a practice of a religion or belief.[48]

In sum, Article 9 does not protect all actions that are motivated by personal convictions and religious beliefs, but only acts "forming part of the practice of a religion or a belief in a generally accepted form".[49] General and neutral legislation, therefore, in principle cannot be regarded as restricting the freedom of religion and belief.[50] For instance, with regard to the obligation to pay taxes the Commission argued that "Article 9 does not confer on the applicant the right to refuse, on the basis of his convictions, to abide by legislation, the operation of which is provided for by the Convention, and which applies neutrally and generally in the public sphere, without impinging on the freedoms guaranteed by that Article".[51] In the same way it was argued that the duty to participate in a pension scheme does not restrict the freedom to manifest one's (anthroposophic) belief: "the obligation to participate in a pension fund applies to all general practitioners on a purely neutral basis, and cannot be said to have any close link with their religion or beliefs."[52]

This restrictive interpretation would seem unavoidable. A legal system consisting of generally binding rules should not leave the questions of whether a person manifests his religion or belief and whether the subjective convictions of this person fall within the scope of Article 9 unanswered. The legal system itself should provide the answers

---

[45] Appl. 10358/83, *C. v. the United Kingdom*, D&R 37 (1984), p. 142 (147); Appl. 16278/90, *Karaduman*, D&R 74 (1993), p. 93 (108); Appl. 22838/93, *Van den Dungen*, D&R 80-A (1995), p. 147 (150); judgment of 1 July 1997, *Kalaç*, para. 27; judgment of 26 October 2000, *Hasan and Chaush*, para. 60; Decision of 2 October 2001, *Pichon and Sajous*; judgment of 29 April 2002, *Pretty*, para. 82.

[46] Appl. 19898/92, *B.C. v. Switzerland*, D&R 75 (1993), p. 223 (230).

[47] Judgment of 29 April 2002, *Pretty*, para. 82.

[48] Decision of 2 October 2001, *Pichon and Sajous*.

[49] *Ibid.* The Commission used similar terms: only acts "which are aspects of the practice of a religion or belief in a generally recognised form" are protected by Article 9: Appl. no. 10358/83, *C. v. the United Kingdom*, D&R 37 (1984), p. 142 (147); Appl. 10678/83, *V. v. the Netherlands*, D&R 39 (1984), p. 267 (268); Appl. 11308/84, *Vereniging Rechtswinkels Utrecht*, D&R 46 (1986), p. 200 (202).

[50] Judgment of 18 december 1996, *Valsamis*, paras 36-37; judgment of 18 december 1996, *Efstratiou*, paras 37-38.

[51] *E.g.* Appl. 10358/83, *C. v. the United Kingdom*, D&R 37 (1984), p. 142 (147); Appl. 17522/90, *Ortega Moratilla*, D&R 72 (1992), p. 256 (262). The Court held that the fact that a citizen had to pay a special tax to the Church of Sweden although he was not a member of that Church, did not violate his right to freedom of religion, because this tax was proportionate to the costs of the Church's purely civil responsibilities: decision of 21 August 2001, *Lundberg*, and decision of 28 August 2001, *Bruno*.

[52] Appl. 10678/83, *V. v. the Netherlands*, D&R 39 (1984), p. 267 (268).

to these questions based on objective criteria, primarily related to the outward appearance of the expression.

However, for less known minorities that are not to a certain extent affiliated with one of the world religions or ideologies this position entails the danger that their actions will only then be considered the expression of a belief, when a sufficient resemblance can be found with the known patterns of familiar spiritual movements. This problem may be mitigated by giving an applicant who claims that a certain type of behaviour is an expression of his religion or belief, the benefit of the doubt if the claim is not manifestly unfounded.[53]

Furthermore, it must be stressed that the application of general regulations on a neutral basis nevertheless may restrict the freedom of religion and belief in specific circumstances. For example planning legislation, limiting the use of buildings to particular purposes, normally does not interfere with the exercise of the right to freedom of religion, even though it may restrict the possibility to employ it for religious activities.[54] However, when a building is already in use for such activities an issue under Article 9 may arise.[55] And the Court decided in the *Manoussakis* Case that the applicants' conviction for using premises as a place of worship without prior authorisation constituted an interference with the exercise of their freedom of religion, because the authorisation requirement had been used to impose prohibitive conditions on the practice of religious beliefs by certain minority movements.[56]

The freedom to manifest one's religion or belief does not imply a right to be protected against criticism or ridicule by others,[57] because these actions cannot generally be regarded as an interference with this freedom. It is only in extreme cases, when the effect of particular methods of opposing or denying religious or other beliefs can be such as to inhibit those who hold those beliefs from exercising their freedom to hold and express them, that the State may be obliged to repress certain forms of conduct in order to guarantee the right under Article 9 to the holders of these beliefs. However, in the *Otto-Preminger-Institut* Case the Court went much further. The Court ruled that the right to respect for the religious feelings of believers as guaranteed by Article 9 could legitimately be thought to have been violated by *Das Liebeskonzil*, a film supposedly blasphemous in the eyes of the Roman Catholic majority. For this reason it decided that the seizure and forfeiture of the film was justified under Article 10(2),

---

[53]   Cf. the judgment of 29 June 2004, *Leyla Sahin*, para. 71.

[54]   However, in the judgment of 24 June 2004, *Vergos*, paras 36-42 the Court assumed that such legislation restricted the freedom of religion (although justified under Article 9(2)). It is submitted here that, in fact, there was no restriction at all.

[55]   Appl. 20490/92, *ISKCON,* D&R 76-A (1994), p. 90 (106); judgment of 9 December 1994, *Holy Monasteries,* paras 86-87.

[56]   Judgment of 26 September 1996, para. 36.

[57]   Appl. 17439/90, *Choudhury* (not published) concerning the refusal of the authorities to bring criminal proceedings against the author (Rushdie) and the publisher of the book 'Satanic Verses'.

being necessary for the protection of the right of this majority to respect for their freedom as protected by Article 9.[58]

It is respectfully submitted that this decision is incorrect. The screening of the film in no way would have limited or inhibited Roman Catholics in manifesting their religion and, therefore, did not restrict their rights under Article 9. The Court extended one's right to be protected against vicious attacks by fellow-citizens on a religion or belief that could endanger the actual enjoyment of the freedom to manifest this religion or belief – particularly relevant for minorities – to a general right – even of dominant majorities – not to be insulted in one's religious or non-religious views. But such a right, relied upon "to sanction improper attacks on objects of religious veneration" and "to prevent that some people should feel the object of attacks on their religious beliefs in an unwarranted and offensive manner",[59] is not included in Article 9, but is on the contrary inconsistent with the "pluralism indissociable from a democratic society" that depends on Article 9.[60]

13.6.3 THE COLLECTIVE DIMENSION OF THE FREEDOM OF RELIGION AND BELIEF; THE RIGHTS OF CHURCHES AND OTHER ORGANIZATIONS; THE NEUTRALITY OF THE STATE

The freedom to manifest a religion or belief is not an exclusively individual right, but also has a collective dimension, recognized in Article 9 by the words "in community with others". It seems plausible, therefore, that collectivities such as churches should also be regarded as subjects of this right. The Commission initially held that a church, "being a legal and not a natural person, is incapable of having or exercising the rights mentioned in Article 9, paragraph (1) of the Convention", and on that ground cannot claim to be itself the victim of the alleged violation of Article 9.[61] This position of the Commission has rightly been criticized. Whereas the freedom of thought and conscience, as well as the freedom to choose a religion or belief are strictly personal freedoms, the right to freedom of religion does not only have an individual but also a collective dimension, and the entire functioning of churches depends on respect for this right. They appear, therefore, to be eminently deserving in this respect, particularly as Article 34 expressly provides for the possibility of complaints by non-governmental organizations and groups.

---

[58]   Judgment of 20 September 1994, para. 47. In the same vein: judgment of 25 November 1996, *Wingrove*, para. 48.
[59]   Judgment of 20 September 1994, *Otto-Preminger-Institut*, paras 49 and 56.
[60]   Judgment of 25 May 1993, *Kokkinakis*, para. 31.
[61]   Appl. 3798/68, *Church of X v. the United Kingdom*, Yearbook XII (1969), p. 306 (314); Appl. 4733/71, *X v. Sweden*, Yearbook XIV (1971), p. 664 (674).

In a decision of 1979 the Commission revised its position and characterized the distinction between a church body and its members as artificial. It held as follows: "When a Church body lodges an application under the Convention, it does so in reality on behalf of its members. It should therefore be accepted that a church body is capable of possessing and exercising the rights contained in Article 9(1) in its own capacity as a representative of its members."[62] The Court has adopted the same view, *viz.* "that an ecclesiastical body may, as such, exercise on behalf of its adherents the right guaranteed by Article 9 of the Convention."[63]

The collective right to manifest a religion is not restricted to churches. Other organizations such as denominational charities may also be capable of possessing and exercising the right to freedom of religion.[64] And in certain circumstances even a limited liability company may enjoy this freedom.[65]

It is not sufficient for a Contracting State to only guarantee the right of either the individual or the group to manifest a religion. The Commission rightly endorsed the view that "the right to manifest one's religion 'in community with others' has always been regarded as an essential part of the freedom of religion and finds that the two alternatives 'either alone or in community with others' in Article 9(1) cannot be considered as mutually exclusive, or as leaving a choice to the authorities, but only as recognising that religion may be practised in either form".[66]

In recent cases the Court has emphasised the importance of the collective dimension of the freedom of religion or belief, and the necessity that the State does not arbitrarily interfere in the organisation of religious communities but remains neutral and impartial. As the Court ruled in the *Hasan and Chaush* Case, "Where the organisation of the religious community is at issue, Article 9 of the Convention must be interpreted in the light of Article 11, which safeguards the associated life against unjustified State interference. Seen in this perspective, the believers' right to freedom of religion encompasses the expectation that the community will be allowed to function peacefully, free from arbitrary State intervention. Indeed, the autonomous existence of religious

---

[62] Appl. 7805/77, *Pastor X and the Church of Scientology*, Yearbook XXII (1979), p. 244 (246). Cf. also Appl. 12587/86, *Chappell*, D&R 53 (1987), p. 241 (246); Appl. 24019/94, *Finska Församlingen i Stockholm and T. Hautaniemi*, D&R 85-A (1996), p. 94 (96).

[63] Judgment of 27 June 2000, *Cha'are Shalom Ve Tsedek*, para. 72; judgment of 13 December 2001, Metropolitan Church of Bessarabia and Others, para. 101.

[64] Appl. 20490/92, *ISKCON*, D&R 76-A (1994), p. 90 (106).

[65] In Appl. 7865/77, *Company X v. Switzerland*, D&R 16 (1979), p. 85 (87) and Appl. 11921/86, *Verein KONTAKT-INFORMATION-THERAPIE and Hagen*, D&R 57 (1988), p. 81 (88) the Commission held that such a company, given the fact that it concerns a profit-making corporate body, can neither enjoy nor rely on the rights referred to in Article 9. However, in Appl. 20471/92, *Kustannus Oy Vapaa Ajattelija and Others*, D&R 85-A (1996), p. 29 (43) the Commission ruled otherwise: "The Commission would therefore not exclude that the applicant association is in principle capable of possessing and exercising rights under Article 9 para. 1."

[66] Appl. 8160/78, *X v. the United Kingdom*, D&R 22 (1981), p. 27 (34).

communities is indispensable for pluralism in a democratic society and is thus an issue at the very heart of the protection Article 9 affords."[67]

Furthermore, the freedom of religion implies the duty of State authorities to remain neutral and impartial towards religious communities,[68] because it is not their role to determine whether religious beliefs are legitimate[69] or to interfere with the leadership of a religious community.[70] From this principle of neutrality and impartiality flows, that the State should not take sides in religious conflicts within and between religious communities. For instance, refusal of legal recognition of a schismatic church for reasons of religious unity must be regarded as a restriction of religious freedom.[71] Likewise, State action favouring one leader or group of a divided religious community, or undertaken with the purpose of forcing the community to come together under a single leadership against its own wishes would likewise constitute an interference with freedom of religion.[72]

13.6.4 FREELY ACCEPTED OBLIGATIONS LIMITING THE EXPRESSION OF RELIGION OR BELIEF

Article 9 does not necessarily imply that one can back out of one's obligations, consented to or contracted freely and without explicit reservation by claiming the right to manifest one's religion. Often these obligations are not regarded as interfering with the freedom of religion. For instance, in case of a conflict between, on the one hand, an ecclesiastical hierarchy and, on the other hand, a servant or member of the church who no longer agrees with the hierarchy, the individual has to choose between submitting to ecclesiastical discipline or leaving the church.[73] Likewise, a muslim teacher who regularly neglects his duties in order to participate in the common prayer on Friday afternoon in the mosque near the School should have made a choice between

---

[67] Judgment of 26 October 2000, para. 62.

[68] The State must be the "neutral and impartial organizer of the exercise of various religions, faiths and beliefs", judgment of 13 February 2003, *Refah Partisi (the Welfare Party) and Others*, para. 91.

[69] Constant case law since the judgment of 26 September 1996, *Mannoussakis*, para. 47.

[70] Judgment of 26 October 2000, *Hasan and Chaush*, para. 78.

[71] Judgment of 13 December 2001, *Metropolitan Church of Bessarabia and Others*, para. 105.

[72] Judgment of 14 December 1999, *Serif*, paras 52-53; judgment of 26 October 2000, *Hasan and Chaush*, para. 78; judgment of 16 December 2004, *Supreme Holy Council of the Muslim Community*, para. 76-85.

[73] Appl. 7374/76, *X v. Denmark*, D&R 5 (1976), p. 157 (158); Appl. 11045/84, *Knudsen*, D&R 42 (1985), p. 247 (257-258); Appl. 12356/86, *Karlsson*, D&R 57 (1988), p. 172 (175). Cf. also Appl. 12242/86, *Rommelfanger*, D&R 62 (1989), p. 151 (161).

fulfilling this religious prescription and his position as a teacher.[74] Similarly, the compulsory retirement of a judge whose conduct and attitude reveals fundamentalist opinions incompatible with the principles of the secular state does not amount to an interference with Article 9.[75] But this reasoning has its limits. Thus, the Court held that dress regulations that prohibit wearing Muslim headscarves in educational institutions interfered with the applicant's right to manifest her religion, although the applicant had freely entered the institution.[76]

13.6.5 SPECIAL RIGHTS

Special rights can be derived from the profession of a particular religion or belief only if these rights are indispensable for the carrying out of the profession.[77] The Commission, therefore, declared ill-founded a complaint that the non-recognition by the public authorities of a marriage concluded exclusively in accordance with a religious ritual was contrary to Article 9.[78] The Commission relied on Article 12, which leaves the regulation of marriage to national law. It is submitted, however, that the Commission might have confined itself to holding that, as long as the religious celebration of the marriage is not prohibited, the legal requirement of a supplementary non-religious procedure for the marriage to be legally valid does not imply an encroachment on the freedom of religion.

A matter related to that of conscientious objections discussed above is that of the exemption from military service for certain ministers of religious communities. Unlike in the case of recognized conscientious objectors, as a rule no alternative civilian service is imposed on these ministers. A right to such an exemption exists in some States only if such an exemption is necessary for the practice of the religion by the person himself and by the community for which he has been appointed. This surely is in conformity with Article 9. If an arrangement for the exemption of ministers has been made, however, the arrangement itself and its application must not lead to discrimination.[79] The case law relating to this issue will be discussed below with reference to Article 14.

---

[74] Appl. 8160/78, *X v. the United Kingdom*, D&R 22 (1981), p. 27 (33-37). Whether the Court will take a similar position is uncertain. See the judgment of 1 July 1997, *Kalaç*, para. 29, in which the Court concluded *inter alia* that there was no interference with the freedom of religion because the applicant was permitted to attend Friday prayers at the mosque.

[75] Judgment of 1 July 1997, *Kalaç*, para. 30.

[76] Decision of 15 February 2001, *Dahlab* (concerning a teacher at a state school); judgment of 29 June 2004, *Leyla Sahin*, para. 71 (concerning a student at a state university). In both cases, the interference was held to be justified under the second paragraph.

[77] The existence of the religion and its profession by the applicant will then have to be proved: Appl. 7291/75, *X v. the United Kingdom*, D&R 11 (1978), p. 55 (56).

[78] Appl. 6167/73, *X v. Federal Republic of Germany*, D&R 1 (1975), p. 64 (65).

[79] Report of 7 March 1996, *Tsirlis and Koulompas*, paras 112-120. The Court did not decide on this issue: judgment of 29 May 1997, *Tsirlis and Koulompas*, para. 70.

13.7 THE RESTRICTION CLAUSE

The freedom to manifest one's religion or belief can only be restricted by such limitations as are prescribed by law and are necessary in a democratic society in the interests of public safety, for the protection of public order, health or morals, or for the protection of the rights and freedoms of others: Article 9(2). Comparing this clause with Article 8(2), 10(2) and 11(2) it is evident that Article 9(2) comprises a relatively small list of interests as grounds for restriction. Furthermore, Article 9(2) refers to "the protection of public order", whereas the other provisions use the term "the prevention of disorder". In its judgment in the *Engel* Case the Court held that "disorder" refers not only to "public order" but "also covers the order that must prevail within the confines of a special social group."[80] From this it seems to follow that "public order" in Article 9(2) only refers to the notion of "order in places accesible to everyone". However, in more recent cases the Court has used a much broader concept of "public order", that also comprises the order within a specific group or organisation,[81] and the maintenance of a peaceful order between rival religious factions.[82] It may be assumed, therefore, that there is no fundamental difference between "prevention of disorder" in the restriction clauses of Articles 8, 10 and 11 and "public order" in the restriction clause of Article 9.

There seems to be no difference between the way the Strasbourg organs apply the restriction clause of Article 9 and the restriction clauses of Article 8, 10 and 11. The emphasis is laid on whether a restriction is necessary; what interest is involved is of less importance.

Article 9(2) stipulates that the State may restrict the freedom of religion or belief only when the interference is prescribed by law. Such a law must be accessible and foreseeable; it must be formulated with sufficient precision to enable the individual to regulate his conduct.[83] The law must afford a measure of legal protection against arbitrary interferences by public authorities with the freedom of religion or belief: therefore, it must indicate with sufficient clarity the scope of their discretion and the manner of its exercise. For instance, if the law does not provide for any substantive criteria, nor procedural safeguards, State interference with the internal organisation of a religious community cannot be regarded as being "prescribed by law".[84]

---

[80]   Judgment of 8 June 1976, para. 98.
[81]   Judgment of 29 June 2004, *Leyla Sahin*, para. 99.
[82]   Judgment of 14 December 1999, *Serif*, para. 45; judgment of 16 December 2004, *Supreme Holy Council of the Muslim Community*, para. 92.
[83]   Judgment of 24 February 1998, *Larissis and Others*, para. 40.
[84]   Judgment of 26 October 2000, *Hasan and Chaush*, paras 84-86; cf. also the judgment of 13 December 2001, *Metropolitan Church of Bessarabia and Others*, para. 109.

The Contracting States have a certain margin of appreciation in assessing the existence and extent of the necessity of an interference. However, this margin is limited when the freedom of religion or belief is concerned. Restrictions on this freedom call for very strict scrutiny by the Court.[85] In several cases the Court has concluded that Article 9 was violated.

In the *Kokkinakis* Case the Court decided that the conviction of a Jehovah's Witness for proselytism formed a breach of this provision because it was not shown that the applicant's conviction was justified in the circumstances of the case by a pressing social need: the Greek courts had established his liability by merely reproducing the relevant section of the law without specifying in what way he had attempted to convince his neighbour by improper means. Therefore, the measure taken did not appear to be proportionate to the aim pursued (the protection of the rights and freedoms of others).[86] Although the outcome of the *Kokkinakis* Case is satisfactory, the Court's reasoning may be criticized. In concentrating on the application of the legislation the Court sidestepped the issue of whether the legislation as such constitutes a breach of Article 9.[87]

In the *Manoussakis* Case the Court had to rule on the compatibility with Article 9 of a conviction of Jehovah's Witnesses for having set up and operated a place of worship without the authorisation of the Minister of Education and Religious Affairs. According to the Court the right to freedom of religion excludes any discretion on the part of the State to determine whether religious belief or means used to express such beliefs are legitimate. The authorisation requirement was consistent with Article 9 only in so far as it was intended to allow the Minister to verify whether formal conditions laid down in the relevant enactments were satisfied. The Court observed that the State tended to use this requirement to impose rigid, or indeed prohibitive, conditions on the practice of religious beliefs by certain non-orthodox movements. Moreover, to that date (1996) the applicants had not received an express decision on their requests made in 1983/1984. The Court concluded that the impugned conviction could not be regarded as proportionate to the aim pursued, nor could it be regarded as necessary in a democratic society.[88] On the other hand, the objective application of planning regulations resulting in the refusal to give permission to build a prayer-house will often be regarded as justified for reasons of the public interest in rational planning.[89]

---

[85] Judgment of 26 September 1996, *Manoussakis and Others*, para. 44.

[86] Judgment of 25 May 1993, para. 49. The Court ruled likewise in its judgment of 24 February 1998, *Larissis and Others*, para. 59. However, it also found that the conviction of military persons for the proselytism of subordinates was, in view of the special character of the relationship between a superior and a subordinate in the army, not disproportionate to the aim pursued, "the protection of the rights and freedoms of others" (*ibidem*, para. 54).

[87] Cf. the opinions of Judges Pettiti, De Meyer and Martens.

[88] Judgment of 26 September 1996, paras 45-53.

[89] Judgment of 24 June 2004, *Vergos*, paras 38-42.

When the State is not neutral and impartial, but takes sides in order to exclude minority denominations or to enforce religious unity, its interference by definition is not necessary under Article 9(2). In the *Buscarini* Case the Court found that requiring Members of Parliament to take an oath on the Gospels was tantamount to swearing allegiance to a particular religion and found that that limitation could not be regarded as necessary in a democratic society.[90]

Generally, however, it is concluded that the interference is not necessary or proportionate to the legitimate aim pursued. For instance, a system of prior authorisation (*e.g.* to build a church) depending on the authorisation by a recognized ecclesiastical authority of the dominant religion is irreconcilable with Article 9(2).[91] Witholding legal recognition of a schismatic church for reasons of religious unity must be regarded as a disproportionate restriction of religious freedom.[92] Likewise, State action favouring one leader or group of a divided religious community, or undertaken with the purpose of forcing the community to come together under a single leadership against its own wishes, is not necessary. In democratic societies the State does not need to take measures to ensure that religious communities are brought under a unified leadership. The role of the State is not to remove the cause of tension by eliminating pluralism, but to ensure that the competing groups tolerate each other.[93]

On the other hand, interferences resulting from *prima facie* neutral regulations are in principle compatible with Article 9(2), as necessary in order to pursue a legitimate aim. For instance, the objective application of general planning regulations will often be regarded as justified for reasons of the public interest in rational planning.[94] Dress regulations, that prohibit wearing Muslim headscarves in public educational institutions, can often be justified by the principle of state neutrality.[95] And the requirement to take off head-covering for a security check at an airport may be regarded as necessary in the interest of public safety, even though it is applied to a Sikh wearing a turban for religious reasons.[96]

---

[90]   Judgment of 18 February 1999, paras 39-40.
[91]   Judgment of 24 June 2004, *Vergos*, para. 34.
[92]   Judgment of 13 December 2001, *Metropolitan Church of Bessarabia and Others*, para. 129.
[93]   Judgment of 14 December 1999, *Serif*, paras 52-53; judgment of 26 October 2000, *Hasan and Chaush*, para. 78; Judgment of 17 February 2002, *Agga*, paras 59-60; judgment of 16 December 2004, *Supreme Holy Council of the Muslim Community*, paras 96-99.
[94]   Judgment of 24 June 2004, *Vergos*, paras 38-42.
[95]   Decision of 15 February 2001, *Dahlab* (concerning a teacher at a state school); judgment of 29 June 2004, *Leyla Sahin*, paras 104-114 (concerning a student at a state university).
[96]   Decision of 11 January 2005, *Phull*.

13.8 DEROGATION

Article 9 does not belong to the provisions included in the second paragraph of Article 15 as non-derogable. On this point the Convention differs from the Covenant, where in Article 4(2) the freedom of thought, conscience, and religion laid down in Article 18 is declared non-derogable. For those Contracting States that are also parties to the Covenant, the prohibition on derogating from the obligation that is incumbent on them under Article 18 of the Covenant also applies under the Convention. In fact, Article 15(1) of the Convention provides that the measures taken by a State must not be "inconsistent with its other obligations under international law", while Article 53 excludes any reference to the Convention which would have the effect of limiting or derogating from any obligation incumbent on the contracting States under other conventions in the field of human rights.

At the beginning of the present section a distinction was made between the right to freedom of thought, conscience and religion, on the one hand, and the freedom to express one's thoughts, conscience and religion on the other hand. With regard to the former right – the inviolability of the *forum internum* – it is doubtful whether the derogations permitted under Article 15 could have any application. Of course, a provision of the Convention cannot be brought under the special protection of the second paragraph of Article 15 if it is not expressly mentioned there, however desirable the incorporation of Article 9 into that provision *de lege ferenda* may be. On the other hand, even for those States which are not parties to the Covenant it will be extremely difficult, if not impossible, to make it plausible that any interference with the freedom of thought, conscience, and religion *per se* is "strictly required by the exigencies of the situation" in the sense of Article 15(1). It is precisely on a point where the European norm is lower than the universally accepted one, that a very critical examination of that necessity by the national organs and the Strasbourg Court would seem appropriate.

CHAPTER 14

FREEDOM OF EXPRESSION (Article 10)

REVISED BY ARJEN VAN RIJN

CONTENTS

14.1 TEXT OF ARTICLE 10

1. *Everyone has the right to freedom of expression. This right shall include freedom to hold opinions and to receive and impart information and ideas without interference by public authority and regardless of frontiers. This Article shall not prevent States from requiring the licensing of broadcasting, television or cinema enterprises.*

2. *The exercise of these freedoms, since it carries with it duties and responsibilities, may be subject to such formalities, conditions, restrictions or penalties as are prescribed by law and are necessary in a democratic society, in the interests of national security, territorial integrity or public safety, for the prevention of disorder or crime, for the protection of health or morals, for the protection of the reputation or rights of others, for preventing the disclosure of information received in confidence, or for maintaining the authority and impartiality of the judiciary.*

14.2 INTRODUCTION

Article 10 takes up a special position between the rights and freedoms which are protected by the Convention. The reason is that the freedom of expression has a fundamental significance for the well-functioning of the democratic process. According to the Court's well-established case law "freedom of expression constitutes one of the essential foundations of a democratic society and one of the basic conditions for its progress and each individual's self-fulfilment".[1] On this basis the Court has developed a set of principles in order to assess whether article 10 can be invoked and whether a given expression is permissible or not.

As to the scope of article 10, the Court holds that the freedom of expression is applicable not only to information or ideas that are favourably received or regarded as inoffensive or as a matter of indifference, but also to those that offend, shock or disturb: "Such are the demands of pluralism, tolerance and broadmindedness, without which there is no 'democratic society'". This freedom is subject to the exceptions set out in the second paragraph of Article 10.

As to these exceptions, the Court holds that they must be construed strictly: "The need for any restrictions must be established convincingly". This implies the existence of a 'pressing social need'. The authorities have a certain margin of appreciation in

---

[1] Since judgment of 7 December 1976, *Handyside*, para. 49. See also: Judgment of 8 July 1986, *Lingens*, para. 41; judgment of 23 May 1991, *Oberschlick*, para. 57; judgment of 23 April 1992, *Castells*, para. 42; judgment of 23 September 1994, *Jersild*, para. 31; judgment of 27 March 1996, *Goodwin*, para. 39; judgment of 16 November 2004, *Karhuvaara and Iltalehti*, para. 37; judgment of 21 December 2004, *Busuioc*, para. 58; judgment of 15 February 2005, *Steel and Morris*, para. 87.

assessing whether such a need exists, but it goes hand in hand with a European supervision, embracing both the legislation and the decisions applying it, even those given by an independent court. The Court is, therefore, empowered to give the final ruling on whether a restriction is permissible. In order to be able to do so the Court must look at the impugned interference in the light of the case as a whole, including the content of the alleged expressions and the context in which they were made. In particular, it must be determined whether the interference in issue was 'proportionate to the legitimate aims pursued' and whether the reasons adduced by the national authorities to justify it were 'relevant and sufficient'. In doing so the Court has to satisfy itself that the national authorities applied standards which were in conformity with the principles embodied in Article 10 and, moreover, that they based themselves on an acceptable assessment of the relevant facts.

In this connection reference is made to "the essential function the press fulfils in a democratic society. Although the press must not overstep certain bounds, particularly as regards the reputation and rights of others and the need to prevent the disclosure of confidential information, its duty is nevertheless to impart – in a manner consistent with its obligations and responsibilities – information and ideas on all matters of public interest". Not only does the press have the task of imparting such information and ideas, with regard to the print media as well as to the audio-visual media,[2] the public also has a right to receive them: "Were it otherwise, the press would be unable to play its vital role of 'public watchdog'".[3] Simultaneously the Court is mindful of the fact that journalistic freedom also covers possible recourse to a degree of exaggeration, or even provocation;[4] however with the proviso that the limits of permissible criticism are narrower in relation to a private citizen than with respect to politicians and governments. Thus, the essential function of the press is always taken into account when an assessment is made whether in the given situation a restriction of the freedom of expression is permissible or not.

---

[2]   Judgment of 23 September 1994, *Jersild*, para. 31.

[3]   See, *inter alia*, the judgment of 26 February 2002, *Unabhängige Initiative Informationsvielfalt*, para. 37; judgment of 6 May 2003, *Perna*, para. 39; judgment of 27 May 2004, *Vides Aizsardzibas Klubs*, para. 42; judgment of 15 June 2004, *Sirbu and Others*, para. 17; judgment of 21 December 2004, *Busuioc*, para. 56.

[4]   Judgment of 26 April 1995, *Prager and Oberschlick*, para. 38. See, *inter alia*, judgment of 28 September 2000, *Gomes da Silva*, para. 34; judgment of 19 June 2003, *Pedersen and Baadsgaard*, para. 65; judgment of 6 May 2003, *Perna*, para. 39; judgment of 29 March 2005, *Ukrainian Media Group*, para. 40.

14.3 THE SCOPE OF THE FREEDOM OF EXPRESSION

14.3.1 EVERYONE

Article 10 may be invoked by natural and legal persons.[5] With regard to the former it is irrelevant for the applicability of Article 10 whether they have a special status like servicemen[6] or civil servants[7], or a special function like police officials[8] or judges.[9] Similarly, it is irrelevant whether the natural or legal person who invokes Article 10 acts as an individual citizen or forms part of the press respectively the journalistic profession. However, the special status, function or position may be relevant under the second paragraph of Article 10.[10]

In the 1980's the Court accepted a major exception to the principle that every natural person can invoke Article 10, irrespective of status, function or position. The exception is based on the assumption that in general Article 10 does not prohibit making access to certain professions subject to regulations, not even when the exercise of those professions consists mainly in the expression of opinions. For the person in question access to such a profession as a rule does not in itself constitute a means which has an independent significance for expressing a specific opinion; the normal channels for doing this are not cut off or restricted if he is not admitted to that profession. Only if a person wishes to exercise a profession or start an enterprise precisely in order to be able to express his opinion in a certain way or by certain means – one might think of a publisher publishing manuscripts which may be assumed not to be accepted elsewhere or of a publisher who wishes to start a periodical of a specific character – is Article 10 at issue and can the person concerned be considered a direct or indirect victim of the violation of that article in case the possibility to exercise the profession or start the enterprise is restricted by certain regulations or other measures. In the *De Becker* Case, in which the Commission concluded that Article 10 had been violated, the penal sanctions imposed on De Becker also comprised the prohibition to exercise the profession of publisher. However, it cannot be clearly inferred from the words which the Commission used in referring to these sanctions – "insofar as

---

[5]   Judgment of 22 May 1990, *Autronic AG*, para. 47.

[6]   Judgment of 8 June 1976, *Engel and Others*, para. 100; judgment of 16 December 1992, *Hadjianastassiou*, para. 39; judgment of 19 December 1994, *Vereinigung Demokratischer Soldaten Österreichs and Gubi*, para. 27.

[7]   Judgment of 26 September 1995, *Vogt*, para. 43.

[8]   Judgment of 20 May 1999, *Rekvényi*.

[9]   Judgment of 28 October 1999, *Wille*, para. 42.

[10] See *infra* 14.4.4.

they affect freedom of expression"[11] – whether the Commission considered this part of the prohibition also to constitute a violation.

If the legal requirements for appointment to a certain office directly concern the freedom of opinion or expression, Article 10 is applicable. The Commission took that position in the *Kosiek* Case and the *Glasenapp* Case, both concerning teaching jobs. Mr Kosiek was an active member of the National Democratic Party of Germany and Mrs Glasenapp was alleged to support the policies of the Communist Party of Germany. The Commission took the view that the provision of the German Civil Servants Act, prescribing that every civil servant owed an obligation of loyalty and allegiance to the Constitution as a condition for appointment and for continued employment in the civil service, directly circumscribed and impinged upon the right guaranteed by paragraph 1 of Article 10.[12]

Both cases were referred to the Court, which first dealt with the Government's argument that the cases concerned the right – not guaranteed under the Convention – of access to a post in the civil service, and not Article 10 of the Convention. With respect to Mrs Glasenapp the Court noted that under the Land Civil Servants Act the applicant could only become a secondary school teacher with the status of probationary civil servant, if she afforded a guarantee that she would consistently uphold the free democratic constitutional system within the meaning of the Basic Law. This requirement, according to the Court, "applies to recruitment to the civil service, a matter that was deliberately omitted from the Convention, and it cannot in itself be considered incompatible with the Convention."[13] In relation to Mr Kosiek the Court adopted a comparable reasoning.[14] In both cases the Court came to the conclusion that in the light of the facts of each case access to the civil service lay at the heart of the issue submitted to it. In refusing such access the authority took account of the applicants' opinions and attitude merely in order to satisfy itself as to whether they possessed one of the necessary personal qualifications for the post in question. There was, therefore, in the Court's view no interference with the exercise of the right protected in paragraph 1 of Article 10.[15]

A more recent case on this matter is the *Vogt* Case, which concerned the dismissal of a teacher from the civil service because of her political activities on behalf of the German Communist Party. The Court held Article 10 to be applicable because "civil servants do not fall outside the scope of the Convention" but, nevertheless, stuck to

---

[11] Report of 8 January 1960, para. 263. The Court struck the case off the list on account of an interim adaptation of the Belgian legislation: judgment of 27 March 1962, pp. 23-27.

[12] Reports of 11 May 1984, paras 63 and 70, respectively.

[13] Judgment of 28 August 1986, para. 52.

[14] Judgment of 28 August 1986, para. 37.

[15] *Ibidem,* paras 53 and 39, respectively. See also the judgment of 26 March 1987, *Leander,* para. 72.

its point of view in the *Kosiek* Case and *Glasenapp* Case by stressing that the *Vogt* Case did not concern the right to recruitment to the civil service.[16]

It is submitted, with due respect, that the Court should have followed the opinion of the Commission in the *Kosiek* Case and *Glasenapp* Case. It is not the intended purpose of a certain regulation and its application, but its effects on the freedom of expression of the person concerned that are decisive for the question of whether Article 10 is applicable. In the *Kosiek* Case and *Glasenapp* Case it was evident that the applicants could have access to the desired posts only by accepting certain restrictions on their freedom of expression. Consequently, the Court should have examined whether these resulting restrictions were justified under paragraph 2 of Article 10.[17]

Nevertheless, the Court affirmed its point of view once more in the *Sidabras and Džiautas* Case. Two Lithuanian officials had been dismissed from their position as a tax inspector and a prosecutor, once it was discovered that they were former KGB employees. The Court ruled that Article 10 was not applicable, because the recruitment to the civil service was at stake. The officials had not met the conditions for appointment.[18]

14.3.2 OPINIONS, INFORMATION AND IDEAS

As is expressly provided for in the first paragraph of Article 10, the freedom of expression includes 'the freedom to hold opinions and to receive and impart information and ideas'. The 'freedom to hold opinions' can hardly be distinguished from the 'freedom of thought' discussed under Article 9.[19] The freedom to impart information and ideas can still be regarded as an expression of an opinion of the informant himself or of a third person. The seeking of information, however, precedes the formation of an opinion by the person who seeks the information, and consequently also its expression.

In its report in *Geïllustreerde Pers N.V. v. the Netherlands* the Commission distinguished between 'information' and 'ideas'. A publisher claimed that Article 22 of the Dutch Broadcasting Act, which prohibited publication of radio and television programmes in any other way than on behalf or by authorisation of the Netherlands Broadcasting Foundation NOS was contrary to Article 10 of the Convention. In the case of information, according to the Commission, the only one who has the right of free distribution of that information is the party who is 'the author, the originator or otherwise the intellectual owner' of the information in question.[20] The publisher,

---

[16] Judgment of 26 September 1995, para. 44.
[17] This criticism holds good also for the judgment of 26 March 1987, *Leander*.
[18] Judgment of 27 July 2004, para. 68-71.
[19] See *supra*, 13.2. The correspondence between Art. 9 and Art. 10 will be discussed *infra*, 14.3.7.
[20] Report of 6 July 1976, D&R 8 (1977), p. 5 (13).

therefore, did have a protected right to publish the programmes if he himself had drawn up a survey of them on the basis of information which he had sought from the individual broadcasting licensees, but no right to copy the survey coordinated by the NOS. The Commission did not elaborate on the question of what rule applies with respect to the distribution of ideas. Its reasoning seems to imply, however, freedom of such distribution irrespective of the source from which those ideas are derived, subject to such limitations as are prescribed by law in conformity with the second paragraph. This distinction between information and ideas would seem rather far-fetched and not corroborated by the text of Article 10. In fact, the Commission seemed to disregard altogether the words 'to receive (...) information'. These words indicate that the collection of information from any source whatever should in principle be free, although restrictions can be made under paragraph 2. It is submitted, therefore, that the Commission should have found that the restriction imposed upon the publisher was contrary to the first paragraph of Article 10, and subsequently should have ascertained whether this restriction was justified on the basis of one or more of the restrictions of the second paragraph, in particular the one of 'protection of the (...) rights of others'.

The freedom 'to receive and impart information and ideas' has been frequently at issue before the Court. The Court has so far expressly refused to give a definition of these terms,[21] but it is clear that the first paragraph of Article 10 offers a broad protection. Thus, *inter alia*, photos[22], medical secrets,[23] the search for the historical truth,[24] factual statements in interviews,[25] television commercials,[26] and advertisements in news-papers[27] fall under information and ideas. The fact that the information concerned is of a commercial nature[28] or that the freedom of expression is not exercised in a discussion of matters of public interest[29] is also irrelevant for the applicability of Article 10. The content of the expressions seems to be irrelevant, too, as the Court has held, with reference to the demands of a democratic society, that Article 10 is also applicable to information or ideas that offend, shock or disturb.

The fact that Article 10 protects the free expression of opinions implies that a rather strong emphasis is laid on the protection of the specific means by which the opinion is expressed. The Court has expressly upheld that Article 10 protects not only the

---

[21]   Judgment of 28 March 1990, *Groppera Radio AG and Others*, para. 55.
[22]   Judgment of 24 June 2004, *Von Hannover*.
[23]   Judgment of 18 May 2004, *Plon (société)*.
[24]   Judgment of 29 June 2004, *Chauvy and Others*.
[25]   Judgment of 16 November 2004, *Selistö*.
[26]   Judgment of 28 June 2001, *VGT Verein gegen Tierfabriken*.
[27]   Judgment of 11 December 2003, *Krone Verlag GmbH & Co KG*.
[28]   Judgment of 20 November 1989, *Markt intern Verlag GmbH and Klaus Beermann*, para. 26; judgment of 24 February 1994, *Casado Coca*.
[29]   Judgment of 23 June 1994, *Jacubowski*; judgment of 14 March 2002, *Diego Nafría*.

substance of ideas and information but also the form in which they are conveyed.[30] Even protesting against fox hunting and disrupting the hunt by diverting the dogs' attention with the aid of a hunting horn constitutes an expression of opinion.[31] The same applies to the publication of photos[32] and news reporting based on interviews.[33] According to the Court it is not for judges "to substitute their own views for those of the press as to what technique of reporting should be adopted by journalists".[34] Any restriction of the means will, therefore, imply a restriction of the freedom 'to receive and impart information and ideas'.[35] However, the means by which a particular opinion is expressed are protected only insofar as they are means which have an independent significance for the expression of the opinion.

If the person who provides the means is not the holder of the opinion, he is also protected by Article 10. Thus, in the *Müller* Case the organisers of the exhibition of Mr Müller's paintings were considered to have exercised their freedom of expression.[36] On the other hand, Article 10 does not bestow any freedom of forum for the exercise of the freedom of expression. Although demographic, social, economic and technological developments are changing the way in which people move around and come into contact with each other, the Court does not consider that this requires unrestricted entry to private property, or even, necessarily, to all publicly owned property. Only if the bar on access to property has the effect of preventing any effective exercise of freedom of expression or if the essence of that right would be destroyed, could a positive obligation arise for the State to regulate property rights.[37]

On the basis of its liberal approach the Court has been able to assess a wide range of situations. It is once more worth mentioning the *Müller* Case, which concerned a conviction for having published obscene material and confiscation of the paintings concerned. In this case the Court concluded that the freedom of artistic expression of a painter, although not mentioned expressly, is also covered by Article 10.[38] Other remarkable cases concern, *inter alia,* the complaint about the conviction of a publisher for having in his possession copies of the 'Little Red School Book' and their destruction as pornography;[39] the injunction of the Irish Supreme Court restraining companies

---

30   See, *inter alia*, the judgment of 11 January 2000, *News Verlags GmbH & Co KG*, para. 39; judgment of 26 February 2002, *Unabhängige Initiative Informationsvielfalt*, para. 38; judgment of 6 May 2003, *Perna*, para. 39.

31   Judgment of 25 November 1999, *Hashman and Harrup*, para. 28.

32   See, *e.g.*, the judgment of 24 June 2004, *Von Hannover*, para. 59.

33   Judgment of 17 December 2004, *Pedersen and Baadsgaard*.

34   Judgment of 11 January 2000, *News Verlags GmbH & Co KG*, para. 39.

35   Judgment of 22 May 1990, *Autronic AG*, para. 47. See also the judgment of 23 September 1994, *Jersild*, para. 31; judgment of 23 May 1991, *Oberschlick*, para. 57.

36   Judgment of 24 May 1988, para. 27.

37   Judgment of 6 May 2003, *Appleby*, para. 47.

38   Judgment of 24 May 1988, para. 27.

39   Judgment of 7 December 1976, *Handyside*.

from giving information to pregnant women about the possibility of obtaining abortions abroad;[40] the seizure and subsequent forfeiture of a film;[41] the refusal of the competent authorities to add a magazine to the list of periodicals distributed by the Austrian army,[42] and the amount of damages awarded by a court for libel.[43]

As a consequence of the great weight the Court attaches to the freedom of the press for the concept of a democratic society and to its vital role of public watchdog, it has also brought the protection of journalistic sources under the scope of Article 10. In the *Goodwin* Case a journalist had received information about the financial problems of a company. When he contacted the company to verify the facts, it appeared that the information had been derived from a confidential company report. These events eventually resulted in an injunction restraining the journalist (and the publishers he worked for) from publishing the information and a court order to disclose the identity of Goodwin's source. The Court held that the disclosure order had to be examined under the second paragraph of Article 10 and thus took for granted that the protection of a journalistic source – in itself not an expression of an opinion – comes within the ambit of Article 10.[44] This was undisputed by the British Government.

When a parliamentarian complained about the fact that a motion proposed by him had not been placed on the agenda and invoked Article 10 for this, his complaint was declared inadmissible by the Commission.[45] The Commission gave no further reasoning for its decision. That reasoning might have been that the procedural decision about which the parliamentarian complained formed part of the very means which he wished to use for the expression of his opinion: Parliament.

In the *Agee* Case a former CIA agent claimed that his expulsion from England was contrary, *inter alia*, to Article 10, because his opportunity to exercise the right conferred therein was restricted by the expulsion. The Commission took the position that the right to stay in a country and the right to freedom of expression have to be distinguished.[46] Abode in a country does not constitute an independent means or independent condition for the expression of one's opinion, unless it were to be firmly established that no other country is to be found in which that particular opinion may be put forward. In the latter case the expelling country is responsible for that situation abroad; it may then only proceed to expel the person concerned on grounds mentioned in the second paragraph.

---

[40]   Judgment of 29 October 1992, *Open Door and Dublin Well Woman*.
[41]   Judgment of 20 September 1994, *Otto-Preminger-Institut*. See also the report of the Commission of 14 January 1993, *Scherer*, para. 50-67.
[42]   Judgment of 19 December 1994, *Vereinigung Demokratischer Soldaten Österreichs and Gubi*.
[43]   Judgment of 13 July 1995, *Tolstoy Miloslavsky*.
[44]   Judgment of 27 March 1996, para. 28.
[45]   Appl. 7758/77, *X v. Switzerland*, D&R 9 (1978), p. 214 (218).
[46]   Appl. 7729/76, D&R 7 (1976), p. 164 (174).

However, as the *Piermont* Case shows, an expulsion order may also come within the ambit of Article 10 if the expulsion order is specifically aimed at the restriction of the freedom of expression. This case concerned an order directing the expulsion of the applicant from the French Polynesia territory and a ban on re-entering as well as an order prohibiting her to enter the territory of New-Caledonia. Mrs Piermont had taken part in a demonstration on the territory of French Polynesia in favour of the independence of French Polynesia and during that demonstration had made a speech in which she supported the anti-nuclear and independence positions of some of the local political parties. The orders in question had been imposed by the French authorities and had the clear intention of preventing Mrs Piermont from supporting publicly the opposition against the French authorities in French Polynesia and New-Caledonia. According to the Court, the expulsion order coupled with the prohibition to re-enter French Polynesia as well as the ban on entering New-Caledonia constituted an interference with the freedom of expression.[47]

The right to receive and impart information and ideas also includes the right to do this by means of radio and television. The broadcasting of programmes over the air and cable transmissions of such programmes fall within the scope of Article 10,[48] while the same holds good for setting up a radio or television station.[49] However, the extent of this right is subject to a special arrangement, which is laid down in the third sentence of paragraph 1 of Article 10. According to the Court, Article 10(1) makes it clear that States are permitted to regulate by a licensing system the way in which broadcasting is organised in their territories, particularly in its technical aspects but also with regard to other considerations, including such matters as the nature and objectives of a proposed station, its potential audience at national, regional or local level, the rights and needs of a specific audience and the obligations deriving from international instruments. This may lead to interferences whose aim will be legitimate under the third sentence of paragraph 1, even though they do not correspond to any of the aims set out in paragraph 2. Subsequently, the compatibility of such interferences with the Convention must nevertheless be assessed in the light of the other requirements of the second paragraph of Article 10.[50]

According to the Commission the right to impart and distribute information does not include a general and unfettered right to have access to broadcasting time on radio

---

[47] Judgment of 27 April 1995, paras 51 and 80. With regard to the ban on entering New-Caledonia the Commission had reached a different conclusion; report of 20 January 1994, *Vella*, A.314, para. 96.

[48] Judgment of 28 March 1990, *Groppera AG and Others*, para. 55. See also Appl. 8962/80, *X and Y v. Belgium*, D&R 28 (1982), p. 112 (124), where the Commission held that a conviction for having used a transceiver for private purposes without the required authorisation constituted an interference with the right to receive and impart information and ideas.

[49] Judgment of 24 November 1993, *Informationsverein Lentia and Others*, para. 26.

[50] *Ibidem*, para. 32. See *infra* 14.3.6.

or TV.[51] This still stands to reason, just as it does not imply a right to have one's information inserted in a daily or weekly paper. However, the Commission added that certain circumstances may occur in which the barring of a specific person or group may result in a violation of Article 10, either in combination with Article 14 or by itself.[52]

Comparetively new means to provide and receive information, for instance over the internet, are increasingly important. Since the case law attributes to the first paragraph of Article 10 a broad protection, one may assume that these new means, as far as they have an independent significance for the expression of opinions, also come within the ambit of Article 10. However, until now there is no case law regarding these new means of communication.

14.3.3   THE RIGHT TO REMAIN SILENT

The freedom of expression entails the right not to express oneself. In the *Young, James and Webster* Case a connection was made by the Commission and the Court between compulsory membership of a trade union and Article 10: as a result of that compulsory membership the employee in question was no longer free to dissent from a view propagated by the trade union.[53] The Commission took the same approach in *K v. Austria,* where it held Article 10 to be applicable to a suspect who refused to give evidence.[54] It held that forcing the applicant to testify against his will constituted an interference with the negative aspect of his right to freedom of expression; his right to remain silent.

14.3.4   WITHOUT INTERFERENCE BY PUBLIC AUTHORITY

Article 10 guarantees the freedom of expression 'without interference by public authority'. In the *Casado Coca* Case the Spanish Government tried to escape from its responsibility by submitting that the disciplinary penalty imposed on a member of the Bar for contravening the ban on advertising, had been imposed by the Barcelona Bar Council and, therefore, not by a 'public authority'. This argument was rejected by the Court. It held that, according to Spanish law, the Bar Council was a public law

---

51   Appl. 4515/70, *X and Association of Z v. the United Kingdom,* Coll. 38 (1972), p. 86 (88).
52   *Ibidem.*
53   Report of 14 December 1979, para. 175; judgment of 13 August 1981, para. 57.
54   Report of 13 October 1992, para. 46.

corporation, that the Bar served the public interest and, moreover, that the penalty had been upheld by the Spanish courts, all of which are State institutions.[55]

14.3.5 REGARDLESS OF FRONTIERS

The words 'regardless of frontiers' in the first paragraph of Article 10 indicate that the authorities must also admit information from beyond the frontiers of the country and allow the imparting of information from across those frontiers, subject, of course, to the possibilities of restriction laid down in the second paragraph.[56] In this connection the Court held in the *Association Ekin* Case that the legal obligation to submit publications of foreign origin or written in a foreign language to a public authority before distribution, is not *a priori* incompatible with the Convention, but must be formulated very strictly and scrutinized very thoroughly under the second paragraph of Article 10 in order to prevent arbitrary application.[57]

The applicability of Article 10 to information from beyond the frontiers of a country does, of course, not offer a guarantee that such information is not held back outside the frontiers, since the State concerned bears no responsibility for measures taken to that effect abroad.[58]

14.3.6 DRITTWIRKUNG AND POSITIVE OBLIGATIONS ON THE PART OF THE AUTHORITIES

Article 10 can be invoked before the Court not only in vertical relations but also in horizontal relations, where a State has taken, or has failed to take certain measures, for instance to protect the reputation or the rights of others as referred to in the second paragraph. This opens up a wide range of possibilities to intervene in conflicts between private parties, as a court decision in a conflict between private individuals is also considered as a measure of the State.[59]

Although the Court has been hesitant to embrace the *Drittwirkung* of Article 10 in so many words,[60] in the *Fuentes Bobo* Case it recognized that a positive obligation can rest with the authorities to protect the freedom of expression against infringe-

---

[55]   Judgment of 24 February 1994, para. 39.
[56]   Judgment of 28 March 1990, *Groppera Radio AG and Others*, and judgment of 22 May 1990, *Autronic AG*, concerning the imparting and receiving of information from abroad.
[57]   Judgment of 17 July 2001, *Association Ekin*, para. 58.
[58]   Appl. 7597/76, *Bertrand Russell Peace Foundation Ltd.*, D&R 14 (1979), p. 117(124).
[59]   See, *e.g.*, judgment of 2 May 2000, *Bergens Tidende and Others*.
[60]   On *Drittwirkung*, see *supra* 1.7.

ments, even by private persons.[61] The applicant, who had been working as a producer with the Spanish public broadcasting company TVE, was fired after having criticised the staff policy of his employer in interviews with another private radio station. The Court held that Article 10 not only applies to relations between employer and employee which are governed by public law, but also to relations which are governed by private law. The Court did not explain which specific obligations the authorities could have had in the concrete situation, but it is evident that in principle the authorities may be held responsible if they do not take appropriate measures to protect freedom of expression in relations governed by private law.

In the *VGT Verein gegen Tierfabriken* Case the Court referred to Article 1 of the Convention and held again that in addition to the primarily negative obligation of a State to abstain from interference in Convention guarantees "there may be positive obligations inherent" in such guarantees. "The responsibility of a State may then be engaged as a result of not observing its obligation to enact domestic legislation."[62] However, the Court "does not consider it desirable, let alone necessary, to elaborate a general theory concerning the extent to which the Convention guarantees should be extended to relations between private individuals *inter se*."[63] It was sufficient in the instant case that the refusal of a commercial television company to broadcast a commercial against the ill-treatment of animals was based on a section of the Swiss Federal Radio and Television Act which prohibits 'political advertising' and, therefore, amounted to an interference by 'public authority'.[64]

In determining whether a positive obligation for the State exists to protect the freedom of expression, regard must be had to the fair balance that has to be struck between the general interest of the community and the interests of the individual. The scope of this obligation will inevitably vary, having regard to the diversity of the situations obtaining in Contracting States and the choices which must be made in terms of priorities and resources. Nor may such an obligation be interpreted in such a way as to impose an impossible or disproportionate burden on the authorities. Against this background the Court decided in the *Appleby* Case that Article 10 does not bestow any freedom of forum for the exercise of that right and that, therefore, it does not automatically create rights of entry to private property or even to all publicly owned property, but that a positive obligation for the State could arise to regulate property rights, where the bar on access to property has the effect of preventing any effective exercise of freedom of expression or where the essence of the right would be destroyed.[65]

---

[61]   Judgment of 29 February 2000, para. 3.
[62]   *Ibidem*, para. 45.
[63]   Judgment of 28 June 2001, para. 46.
[64]   *Ibidem*, paras 47-48.
[65]   Judgment of 6 May 2003, paras 40 and 47.

In the *Steel and Morris* Case members of a small campaign group had accused McDonald's of abusive and immoral farming and employment practices, deforestation, exploitation of children and their parents through aggressive advertising and the sale of unhealthy food. McDonald's had lodged a claim for defamation. According to the Court it was not in principle incompatible with Article 10 to place on the campaigners in libel proceedings the onus of proving to the civil standard the truth of defamatory statements. The State enjoys a margin of appreciation as to the means it provides under domestic law to enable a company to challenge the truth, and limit the damage, of allegations which risk harming its reputation. In that case, however, it is essential, in order to safeguard the countervailing interests of free expression and open debate, that a measure of procedural fairness and equality of arms is provided for. Because the campaigners had no access to free legal aid, the Court held that there was no correct balance between the need to protect the campaigners' rights to freedom of expression and the need to protect McDonald's rights and reputation.[66]

In this regard, the question of whether freedom of expression implies the right of reply or rectification also deserves attention. This question has not been clarified until now.[67] An affirmative answer seems to have been implied by the Commission, but in the case concerned it did not reach an explicit decision on this point, because in the Commission's opinion the arguments advanced constituted an insufficient ground for the decision that the defendant State was responsible for the impugned publication by the daily papers concerned.[68] Here, too, a complicating issue is that of the *Drittwirkung* of Article 10 and also that of the liability of the State – which is the only party against which a complaint may be brought in Strasbourg – for violation of Article 10 by private parties.[69] Indeed, the publications involved will usually originate from a private party and the publication of the reply or rectification will have to be effected in most cases by a private party as well. From Article 10 might then be derived an obligation on the part of the State to create a legal obligation to publish the reply or rectification and to provide for a remedy, either on the ground of a civil claim to that effect or in combination with a criminal conviction for insult. Such an obligation of publication would not constitute an unlawful interference with the freedom of expression laid down in Article 10 for the person on whom it would be imposed, since the justification

---

[66]   Judgment of 15 February 2005, para. 95.

[67]   Within the framework of the UN a special convention was concluded on this in 1953: the Convention on the International Right of Correction, 435 UNTS, p. 191.

[68]   Appl. 1906/63, *X v. Belgium* (not published).

[69]   In Appl. 4515/70, *X and the Association of Z v. the United Kingdom*, Coll. 38 (1972), p. 86 (88), which concerned complaints about the BBC, the Commission expressly left the question of State liability open. See, however, Appl. 6586/74, *X v. Ireland* (not published), where the Commission took the view that the restraint upon staff expressing their views is a common feature of many working situations arising from the relationships of the people concerned and not from written regulations for which the State could be held responsible.

might be found in the restriction ground 'protection of the reputation or rights of others'.

As far as positive obligations are concerned it is still not clear whether – and if so, to what extent – the freedom to receive information entails an obligation on the part of the authorities to impart information. At first sight the judgment in the *Leander* Case provides an answer in the negative. The competent authorities refused to appoint Mr Leander as a museum technician at the Naval Museum, adjacent to a Naval base, on the basis of secret information. With regard to the refusal to reveal the information to the applicant the Court held as follows: "the right to freedom to receive information basically prohibits a Government from restricting a person from receiving information that others wish or may be willing to impart to him. Article 10 does not, in circumstances such as those of the present case, confer on the individual a right of access to a register containing information on his personal position, nor does it embody an obligation on the Government to impart such information to the individual."[70]

In the *Gaskin* Case, which concerned the failure to grant a person unimpeded access to his case record which had been drawn up while he was in child-care, the Court reached the same conclusion.[71] However, the considerations of the Court were expressly based on the specific circumstances of the case and moreover the Court used the word 'basically' ('*essentiellement*' in the French text). In the *Sirbu* Case the Court took the position that the freedom to receive information "cannot be construed as imposing on a State, in circumstances such as those of the present case, positive obligations to disclose to the public any secret documents and information concerning its military, intelligence service or police."[72] Here again, the Court is relying on the specific circumstances of the case and its conclusion is confined to highly sensitive information.

Consequently, there still seems to be some room to argue that the freedom of expression may entail a duty on the part of the authorities to impart information of public interest. An interpretation to that effect is contained in a resolution of the Consultative (Parliamentary) Assembly of the Council of Europe, a document which is not legally binding, but which may be taken to indicate a trend in the legal opinion within the Contracting States or at least some of them. This resolution sets forth with respect to the right to freedom of expression: "This right shall include freedom to seek, receive, impart, publish and distribute information and ideas. There shall be a corresponding duty for the public authorities to make available information on matters of

---

[70]   Judgment of 26 March 1987, para. 74.
[71]   Judgment of 7 July 1989, para. 56.
[72]   Judgment of 15 June 2004, para. 18.

public interest within reasonable limits and a duty for mass communication media to give complete and general information on public affairs."[73]

A comparable matter concerns the question of whether the right to receive information calls for pluriformity in imparting information, which then has to be guaranteed by the authorities, for instance by making grants to persons and institutions imparting information, where this is necessary for such pluriformity.[74] In the *Vereinigung Demokratischer Soldaten Österreichs and Gubi* Case the Austrian army had been distributing free of charge its own publications and publications of private associations of soldiers in all the country's barracks, but had refused to distribute *Der Igel*, a magazine published by the first applicant. The Court held that this difference in treatment considerably reduced the chances of *Der Igel* to increase its readership among service personnel and as a result constituted a violation of Article 10.[75] Having regard to this judgment and the fact that the Court regards pluralism as being of particular importance as far as the press is concerned,[76] it is evident that the authorities, once they proceed to subsidise or in any other way support persons and institutions imparting information, have the duty to do so without discrimination.

14.3.7 RELATION TO OTHER CONVENTION RIGHTS

Article 10 has often been invoked in close connection with other articles of the Convention.

In *K v. Austria* the applicability of Article 10 and Article 6 coincided. The applicant claimed that his obligation to testify in a criminal procedure implied an obligation to testify against himself, contrary to Article 6,[77] and that the imposition of a fine and detention for his refusal to give evidence constituted a breach of Article 10. In deciding whether the interference of Article 10 could be regarded as 'necessary' the Commission took into account the principle of a fair trial embodied in Article 6. It concluded that there had been a violation of Article 10 and that, therefore, it was unnecessary to consider the complaint under Article 6 separately.[78]

---

[73] Res. 428(1970), Council of Europe, Cons. Ass., Twenty-First Ordinary Session (Third Part), 22-30 January 1970, *Texts Adopted*.

[74] In its decision on Appl. 6452/74, *Sacchi*, D&R 5 (1976), p. 43 (50), the Commission held as regards its previously given opinion that Art. 10(1) does not rule out a government monopoly for TV broadcasts: "the Commission would not now be prepared purely and simply to maintain this point of view without further consideration". However, it did not answer the question.

[75] Judgment of 19 December 1994, paras 39-40.

[76] See, *inter alia*, judgment of 7 December 1976, *Handyside*, para. 49; judgment of 24 November 1993, *Informationsverein Lentia and Others*, para. 38.

[77] See also *supra* 14.3.3.

[78] Report of 13 October 1992, paras 41-57. Strictly speaking the Commission concluded (para. 57) that Art. 6 had not been violated, but this conclusion would seem to be inaccurate since it cannot be deduced from the preceding arguments. Due to a friendly settlement the case was struck off the list by the Court, judgment of 2 June 1993.

The *Nikula* Case concerned a lawyer who had been convicted for insulting a public prosecutor while defending her client during a court session. The Court made a connection with Article 6 and held that the right to a fair trial implies a free and even heated exchange of views between the parties. It is the task of councel to defend the interests of his client fervently. Only in exceptional situations will there be a pressing social need for a restriction of the freedom of expression of councel during a court session.[79] In the *McVicar* Case the Court concluded in relation to Article 6(1) that the applicant had not been prevented from presenting his defence to a defamation action effectively in the High Court, nor were the proceedings made unfair, by reason of his ineligibility for legal aid. Therefore, there was no interference with the applicant's right to freedom of expression.[80] The same applied for the exclusion of evidence. The Court found the rules in this respect clear and unambiguous. The applicant and his legal representative could have taken steps earlier in the proceedings which might have had a bearing on the decision to exclude that evidence, but failed to do so. The exclusion had been ordered following detailed analysis by the trial jude and Court of Appeal of the competing interests at stake and the balance which had to be struck between those interests on the facts of the applicant's case.[81]

Since correspondence, telephone and similar means of communication, protected in Article 8, also constitute means for the expression of an opinion, there is a close connection between that article and Article 10. This connection was put forward in the *Silver* Case, which concerned the right of detainees to respect for their correspondence. Both the Commission and the Court took the view that in the examination of the complaints with respect to Article 8, the freedom of expression via correspondence had already been dealt with at such length that a separate examination with regard to Article 10 was not necessary.[82] However, in the subsequent *McCallum* Case, also concerning the correspondence of a detainee, the Commission took a somewhat different approach by stating that "where interference is alleged in the communication of information by correspondence, Article 8 is the *lex specialis* and no separate issues arise under Article 10."[83] This appears to be too general a statement, since the aim of the two articles is not identical: in Article 8 the main point is the protection of the private character of the means of communication referred to, while in Article 10 its

---

[79]   Judgment of 21 March 2002, *Nikula*, para. 55.
[80]   In the *Steel and Morris* Case, however, the lack of free legal aid led to a breach of the obligation of the authorities to protect the freedom of expression; judgment of 15 February 2005, para. 95.
[81]   Judgment of 7 May 2002, paras 74-77.
[82]   Report of 11 October 1980, para. 428; judgment of 25 March 1983, para. 107. See also the judgment of 20 June 1988, *Schönenberger and Durmaz*, para. 71.
[83]   Report of 4 May 1989, para. 63. The claim under Article 10 was not pursued before the Court. The Commission had taken the same position in Appl. 8383/78, *X v. Federal Republic of Germany*, D&R 17 (1980), p. 227 (228-229).

character as a means of expressing an opinion and of providing and receiving information is at issue.

A somewhat remarkable decision of the Commission is the one in which a complaint concerning Article 10 by a prisoner convicted for homosexual practices was declared admissible. The applicant had claimed, *inter alia*, that his right to express feelings of love for other men was interfered with by his detention. The Commission held with respect to this "that there may be an issue under Article 10 regarding his (...) claim that the fact of imprisonment denied him his right to express feelings of love for other men".[84] While in the *Bruggemann and Scheuten* Case sexual intercourse had been brought under Article 8,[85] in *X v. the United Kingdom* thus the possibility of a connection with Article 10 was left open. In its report on the merits of the latter case, however, the Commission took the position, on the ground of the text of paragraph 2, that: "the concept of 'expression' in Art. 10 concerns mainly the expression of opinion and receiving and imparting information and ideas (...). It does not encompass any notion of the physical expression of feelings in the sense submitted by the applicant'."[86]

In the *Crémieux* Case the Commission rejected the claim of the applicant that the seizure of private correspondence at his home was contrary to Article 8 and Article 10 of the Convention. With regard to Article 8 the Commission found the infringement to be justified under the second paragraph. With regard to Article 10, however, the reasoning was rather concise and poor. The Commission simply held that it failed to see how there could have been an infringement.[87] A remarkable example of imparting information was involved in a case where two persons complained that during a 45 hour detention they had been prevented from contacting their wives. The Commission declared the complaints admissible on account of their complexity.[88] In its report the Commission dealt with this complaint in conjunction with Article 8. After having found a breach of Article 8 it considered it unnecessary to decide the issue under Article 10.[89]

In the *Guerra* Case the applicants complained, *inter alia*, that the authorities had violated Article 10 by failing to inform the public of the risks involved in the operation of the chemical factory in their vicinity, and of what was to be done in the event of an accident connected with the factory's operation. The Court held that the freedom to receive information cannot be construed as imposing on a State, "in circumstances

---

[84] Appl. 7215/75, *X v. the United Kingdom*, Yearbook XXI (1978), p. 354 (374).

[85] See *supra* 12.3.3.3.

[86] Report of 12 October 1978, D&R 19 (1980), p. 66 (80). The conclusions of the report were adopted by the Committee of Ministers in Res. DH(79)5 of 12 June 1979.

[87] Report of 8 October 1991, para. 60. In its judgment of 25 February 1993, paras 28-41, the Court concluded that there had been a breach of Art. 8 and deemed it unnecessary to consider Art. 10 separately.

[88] Appls 8022/77, 8025/77 and 8027/77, *X, Y and Z v. the United Kingdom*, D&R 18 (1980), p. 66 (76).

[89] Report of 18 March 1981, *McVeigh, O'Neill and Evans*, D&R 25 (1982), p. 15 (53).

such as those in the present case", positive obligations to collect and disseminate information of its own motion. It concluded that this part of the complaint had to be considered under Article 8.[90]

The freedom of expression is closely related to the freedom of thought, conscience and religion in Article 9 of the Convention. This is the more so to the extent that in the case of freedom of expression emphasis is laid upon the content of the opinion expressed. This does not alter the fact that Article 10 has a wider scope than Article 9. While for the applicability of Article 9 it is required that the opinion which is expressed reflects the conviction of the person who puts this opinion forward,[91] Article 10 envisages the protection of every expression of an opinion, be it that the measure of protection may vary according to the nature of the opinion expressed.[92]

There is also a close connection between Article 10 and the freedom of assembly protected in Article 11. In the *Ezelin* Case concerning a disciplinary penalty imposed on a lawyer because he had participated in a demonstration in which protests were made against judicial decisions and had refused to give evidence to the investigating judge, the Court held that "the protection of opinions, secured by Article 10, is one of the objectives of freedom of peaceful assembly and freedom of expression as enshrined in Article 11."[93] Articles 10 and 11 are both applicable in those situations where several persons jointly express a given opinion. Thus, a demonstration always constitutes an expression of opinion, even if it has the character of a silent procession; at the same time there is an assembly. This overlap need not, however, give rise to problems in practice, since the restrictions on the two rights partly coincide, while the specific restrictions of Article 10 clearly refer to the opinion expressed, and not to the question of whether it has been expressed by one person or by several persons jointly. The approach of the Court on this point seems to differ from case to case. In the *Ezelin* Case the Court held that in the circumstances of the case Article 11 should be regarded as a *lex specialis* in relation to Article 10.[94] In the *Sigurdur A. Sigurjónsson* Case, however, in which the compulsory membership of a organisation for taxicab operators was at stake, the Court concluded that there had been a violation of Article 11 and that there was no need to consider whether there had also been breaches of Articles 9 and 10.[95] Finally, in the *Vogt* Case the Court took the position that the dismissal of a teacher from civil service because of her political activities on behalf of the German Communist Party amounted to a breach of Articles 10 and 11. With regard to the latter

---

[90]   Judgment of 19 February 1998, paras 53-55.
[91]   Report of 12 October 1978, *Arrowsmith,* D&R 19 (1980), p. 5 (19-20).
[92]   See *supra,* 14.3.2.
[93]   Judgment of 26 April 1991, para. 38. See also the judgment of 26 September 1995, *Vogt,* para. 64.
[94]   Judgment of 26 April 1991, para. 35.
[95]   Judgment of 30 June 1993, para. 42. See also the judgment of 13 August 1981, *Young, James and Webster,* para. 65; judgment of 2 July 2002, *Wilson, National Union of Journalists and Others,* paras 48-50.

article the Court based its decision in particular on the arguments adduced with regard to Article 10.[96]

The emphasis on the question of whether the means of expression have an independent significance may delimit the applicability of Article 10 vis-à-vis other freedoms, which are related to the possibility of expressing specific opinions, but cannot be considered as means which have an independent significance apart from other means available to the person concerned. Thus, in the *Belgian Linguistic* Case the Commission took the position that freedom of expression does not comprise the right to be offered the opportunity to express one's opinion in a language of one's choice, the consequence of which would be the right to being taught that language.[97] Here, Article 2 of Protocol No. 1 is at issue, not Article 10. This would only be otherwise if, for instance, an immigrant were denied access to being taught the vernacular or if the required facilities for this were not provided, since he would then be deprived of an independent means of expression: expression in a locally understood language. However, in such a case, too, it would seem to make more sense to invoke Article 2 of Protocol No. 1.

That the right to vote is not protected by Article 10 constitutes established case law of the Commission.[98] No arguments have been adduced for this. It can hardly be denied that taking part in elections is a form of expressing an opinion. Article 3 of Protocol No. 1 refers to 'the free expression of the opinion of the people'. Nor can it be subject to doubt that it constitutes a means for the expression of that opinion which has an independent character. On the other hand, however, it seems logical to assume that the drafters of Article 10 did not intend to include the right to vote. This may be inferred from the incorporation of a specific provision concerning elections into Protocol No. 1. The duty to vote is not in violation of Article 10 – nor of Article 9 – as long as the secret character is guaranteed; in that case the person concerned is free to express any opinion or no opinion at all.

---

[96] Judgment of 26 September 1995, para. 65.
[97] Appl. 1474/62, Yearbook VI (1963), p. 332(342); Appl. 1769/62, *X v. Belgium*, Yearbook VI (1963), p. 444 (454-456).
[98] See, *e.g.*, Appl. 6573/74, *X v. the Netherlands*, D&R 1 (1975), p. 87 (89) and Appl. 6850/74, *Association X, Y and Z v. Federal Republic of Germany*, D&R 5 (1976), p. 90 (93).

14.4   RESTRICTION OF THE FREEDOM OF EXPRESSION

14.4.1   GENERAL OBSERVATIONS

In addition to restrictions the second paragraph of Article 10 also mentions formalities, conditions and penalties as measures to which the freedoms of the first paragraph may be subjected.[99] At first sight it is remarkable that precifically with respect to the right to freedom of expression, to which Western democracies attach such great value, the restrictions are formulated more broadly than with respect to other rights and freedoms. However, in practice this broad formulation is of little impact. The imposition of conditions or formalities in fact also amounts to restrictions, while on the other hand the failure to observe a restriction prescribed by law will also be subject to a sanction in most cases. It does not matter much, therefore, whether the complaint is directed against the application of the legal norm restricting the exercise of the freedom or against the penalty imposed for having violated that norm. Indeed, the restriction implied in the imposition of a penalty may also not serve the mere purpose of a retaliation, but should be designed to protect the interests enumerated in paragraph 2.

As was pointed out, the Court has taken the position that the exceptions to the freedom of expression 'must be narrowly interpreted and the necessity for any restrictions must be convincingly established'.[100] This applies even more to preventive restraints on publications. Such restraints are as such not incompatible with Article 10, but call for the most strict supervision of the Strasbourg organs since, even if they are temporary, they may deprive the information to be published from all its interests.[101] For this reason the relevant law must clearly indicate the circumstances when prior restraints on publications are permissible and, *a fortiori*, when the consequences of the restraint are to block publication of a periodical completely.[102] The strict supervision of preventive restraints is also reflected in those cases where the Court held that the intended purpose of the ban on publication, the prevention of the disclosure of information, could no longer justify the prohibition because the information had already become public on the basis of another source.[103]

---

[99]   See, *inter alia*, judgment of 6 November 2003, *Krone Verlag GmbH & Co KG*; judgment of 22 February 2005, *Pardemirli*.

[100]   Judgment of 26 November 1991, *The Observer and Guardian*, para. 59. See also *supra* 14.1.

[101]   Judgments of 26 November 1991, *The Observer and Guardian*, and *The Sunday Times (No. 2)*, para. 53 and para. 51, respectively; judgment of 17 July 2001, *Association Ekin*, para. 56.

[102]   Judgment of 14 March 2002, *Gaweda*, para. 40.

[103]   Judgments of 26 November 1991, *The Observer and Guardian* and *The Sunday Times (No. 2)*, paras 66-70 and paras 52-56, respectively. See also the judgment of 22 May 1990, *Weber*, para. 51, *juncto* para. 13; judgment of 9 February 1990, *Bluf*, para. 45.

A clear example of the narrow interpretation of the exceptions of the freedom of expression in the second paragraph can be found in the many Turkish cases the Court had to deal with in connection with critical articles in the press and other statements in the public debate. The Court has applied a consistent line. Even when statements paint an extremely negative picture of the Turkish State and thus give the narrative a hostile tone, they can be permissible as long they do not encourage violence, armed resistance or insurrection and do not constitute hate speech.[104]

In assessing whether an infringement of the first paragraph has been 'necessary', the Court has often referred to the 'duties and responsibilities' mentioned in the second paragraph of Article 10 of those who exercise the freedom of expression. This concept will be discussed in sections 14.4.3, 14.4.4 and 14.4.5.

The grounds enumerated in the second paragraph are not identical to the interests mentioned in Articles 8, 9 and 11 of the Convention. Therefore, three of the grounds laid down in the second paragraph of Article 10 deserve special attention: 'territorial integrity', 'preventing the disclosure of information received in confidence', and 'maintaining the authority and impartiality of the judiciary'.

The 'freedom to hold opinions', mentioned separately in Article 10, can hardly be distinguished from the 'freedom of thought' provided for in Article 9. As has been observed with regard to Article 9, here again it is submitted that the restrictions mentioned in the second paragraph should not be applied to this 'freedom to hold opinions'.[105] The following analysis focuses on a number of aspects to the restrictions contained in Article 10(2) as well as on the case law related to it.

14.4.2 FACTS AND VALUE JUDGMENTS

According to the Court, in assessing whether there is a pressing social need capable of justifying interference with the exercise of the freedom of expression, a careful distinction needs to be made between facts and value judgments, because "The existence of facts can be demonstrated, whereas the truth of value judgments is not susceptible of proof. The requirement to prove the truth of a value judgment is impossible to fulfil and infringes freedom of opinion itself, which is a fundamental

---

[104] See, *inter alia*, judgment of 10 November 2004, *Dicle*, paras 12-18.

[105] Thus also the Report of the Committee of Experts on Human Rights to the Committee of Ministers, *Problems arising from the Co-Existence of the United Nations Covenants on Human Rights and the European Convention on Human Rights*, Doc. H(70), p. 45, with the argument that "any restrictions on this right would be inconsistent with the nature of a democratic society".

part of the right secured by Article 10."[106] This means that, in general, people may be expected to act more prudently when stating facts than when making value judgments. An interference with the freedom of expression is more likely to be justifiable when it concerns a factual statement which can be proved than when it concerns a value judgment. However, it may sometimes be difficult to distinguish between assertions of facts and value judgments. For this and for other reasons it is also difficult to make an absolute distinction in treatment between the two categories.[107]

A value judgment may nevertheless be impermissible, since even a value judgment without any factual basis to support it may be excessive.[108] In those circumstances an interference by the authorities can be proportional. In other words, an excessive value judgment needs some kind of factual basis in order to be permissible.

On the other hand, requirements as to the proof of factual statements may not be such that these hamper the freedom of the press. In the Court's case law the starting point is that protection of the right of journalists to impart information on issues of general interest requires that they should act in good faith and on an accurate factual basis and provide reliable and precise information in accordance with the ethics of journalism. This also includes the duty to verify any information before publishing it.[109] Under the terms of paragraph 2 of Article 10 the freedom carries with it duties and responsibilities, which also apply to the press. "Moreover, these 'duties and responsibilities' are liable to assume significance when there is a question of attacking the reputation of a named individual and infringing the 'rights of others'. Thus, special grounds are required before the media can be dispensed from their ordinary obligation to verify factual statements that are defamatory of private individuals. Whether such grounds exist depends in particular on the nature and degree of defamation in question and the extent to which the media can reasonably regard their sources as reliable with respect to the allegations."[110] Thus, the need to verify a factual statement increases with the increase of the defamatory character of the statement.

---

[106]   Judgment of 15 February 2005, *Steel and Morris*, para. 87; judgment of 21 December 2004, *Busuioc*, para. 61; judgment of 17 December 2004, *Cumpana and Mazare*, para. 98. See also the judgment of 13 November 2003, *Scharsach*: the use of the word 'Kellernazi' in relation to a Austrian FPÖ-politician was a permissible value judgment. In the judgment of 26 February 2002, *Dichand*, para. 50, a journalist had criticised the chairperson of a parliamentary committee who was also a lawyer. The committee dealt with a legislative amendment which was favourable for one of the lawyer's clients. The parliamentarian had omitted to lay down his function as a lawyer. Criticising this was a fair comment, according to the Court.

[107]   Judgment of 27 May 2004, *Vides Aizsardzibas Klubs*, para. 43.

[108]   Judgment of 27 February 2001, *Jerusalem*, para. 43; judgment of 27 May 2004, *Rizos and Daskas*, para. 45; judgment of 27 May 2004, *Vides Aizsardzibas Klubs*, para. 99; judgment of 20 July 2004, *Hrico*, para. 40; judgment of 15 February 2005, *Steel and Morris*, para. 87; judgment of 29 March 2005, *Sokolowski*, para. 48; judgment of 29 March 2005, *Ukrainian Media Group*, para. 42.

[109]   Judgment of 21 December 2004, *Busuioc*, para. 69. See also the judgment of 26 April 1995, *Prager and Oberschlick*, para. 37.

[110]   Judgment of 17 December 2004, *Pedersen and Baadsgaard*, para. 78; judgment of 7 May 2002, *McVicar*, Reports 2002-III, para. 84.

In the *Colombani* Case the Court found the conviction of the publisher and a journalist of *Le Monde* because of defamation of the Moroccan king impermissible. The newspaper had given an account of a report of the European Commission dealing with drugs trade from Morocco. The Court held that the press must be able to rely on an official report without having the duty to investigate the facts on which the report is based.[111] The Court had come to the same conclusion in the *Tromsø and Stensaas* Case. The newspaper and its publisher had based their articles dealing with seal hunting on an official report which had been presented to the Ministry of Fishing. The accusations in the report could not be proved. Nevertheless, the Court considered Tromso and Stensaas' conviction for defamation disproportional and, therefore, impermissible, because they had acted in good faith.[112]

In the *Pedersen and Baadsgaard* Case the Court also attached importance to the fact that under Article 6 paragraph 2 individuals have the right to be presumed innocent of any criminal offence until proven guilty. The journalists had made two television documentaries in which they suggested that the police had not correctly judged available evidence in a murder case. As a result the journalists were convicted for defamation of the Chief Superintendent. After a thorough investigation of all elements of the case the Court found with the Danish Supreme Court that there was no sufficient factual basis for the allegation made by the journalists and that the national authorities thus were entitled to consider that there was a pressing social need to take action against them. Neither were the penalties excessive in the circumstances or of such a kind as to have a chilling effect on media freedom.[113]

An example of close scrutiny is the *Nilsen and Johnsen* Case.[114] Trade union officials had accused the independent researcher Mr. Bratholm of 'pure misinformation intended to harm the police', 'deliberate lies', 'frivolous allegations' and attempts to undermine the dignity and authority of the police. After having observed that the case had its background in a long and heated public debate in Norway on investigations into allegations of police violence, notably in the city of Bergen, and after having noted that there is little scope under Article 10(2) for restrictions on political speech or on debate on questions of public interest, the Court found that only the accusation of deliberate lies exceeded the limits of permissible criticism. This could be regarded as an allegation of fact susceptible to proof, for which there was no factual basis and which could not be warranted by Mr. Bratholm's way of expressing himself. The other statements were opinions and thus rather akin to value judgments.[115]

---

[111] Judgment of 25 June 2002, *Colombani*, para. 65.
[112] Judgment of 20 May 1999, para. 65.
[113] *Ibidem*, paras 92-93. See also judgment of 7 May 2002, *McVicar*, paras 86-87; judgment of 17 December 2004, *Cumpana and Mazare*, paras 101-110.
[114] Judgment of 25 November 1999.
[115] *Ibidem*, paras 49-50. See for a differentiated approach also judgment of 21 December 2004, *Busuioc*, as from para. 76.

In the *Sokolowski* Case the Court had to decide whether an accusation of theft was a statement of fact or value judgment. The case concerned the behaviour of the councillors of election committees. The Court noted that the applicant's criticism, couched in ironical language, was meant to stress that the functions in the election committees should have been assigned to those inhabitants of the municipality who where financially worse off than the councillors themselves. The income to be earned for their work in the committees was then compared to the market prices of various goods at that time. It was further suggested that the councillors, by receiving that money paid from the local taxes, would 'take away' these goods from the reader of the leaflet, in which the applicant had written down his criticism. In the Court's view a serious accusation of theft could not be justifiably read into such a statement, particularly when the satirical character of the text and the irony underlying it were taken into account. Therefore, the Court considered that it should be qualified as a value judgment.[116]

14.4.3   PUBLIC DEBATE AND ITS ACTORS

The Court attaches great importance to the freedom of the press.[117] It is the right and task of the press "to impart information and ideas on political issues just as on those in other areas of public interest,"[118] which also includes those relating to justice and the functioning of the judiciary.[119] This emphasis on the public interest is reflected in the case law concerning the restrictions on the freedom of expression.

In the *Lingens* Case the Court stressed the importance of the "freedom of political debate", which is "at the very core of the concept of a democratic society", and then held as follows: "The limits of acceptable criticism are accordingly wider as regards a politician as such than as regards a private individual. Unlike the latter, the former inevitably and knowingly lays himself open to close scrutiny of his every word and deed by both journalists and the public at large, and he must consequently display a greater degree of tolerance."[120]

In the *Ukrainian Media Group* Case the Court observed that the applicants' publications contained criticism of two politicians in strong, polemical, sarcastic language.

---

[116]   Judgment of 29 March 2005, paras 46-47.
[117]   See *supra* 14.1.
[118]   Judgment of 8 July 1986, *Lingens*, para. 41. See also the judgment of 23 May 1991, *Oberschlick*, para. 58; judgment of 23 April 1992, *Castells*, para. 43; judgment of 25 June 1992, *Thorgeir Thorgeirson*, para. 63; judgment of 23 September 1994, *Jersild*, para. 31; judgment of 21 January 1999, *Fressoz and Roire*, para. 45; judgment of 2 May 2000, *Bergens Tidende and Others*, para. 18; judgment of 28 September 2004, *Sabou and Pircalab*, para. 33. The wording in these cases is not fully identical.
[119]   Judgment of 20 July 2004, *Hrico*, para. 40; judgment of 27 May 2004, *Rizos and Daskas*, para. 42.
[120]   Judgment of 8 July 1986, para. 42. See also, *inter alia*, judgment of 29 March 2005, *Ukrainian Media Group*, para. 39.

Subsequently, the Court stated as follows: "No doubt the plaintiffs were offended thereby, and may have even been shocked. However, in choosing their profession, they laid themselves open to robust criticism and scrutiny; such is the burden which must be accepted by politicians in a democratic society."[121] All this applies, in particular, when the politicians themselves make public statements that are susceptible to criticism.[122]

In the *Castells* Case the Court introduced a further refinement where it held that the bounds of permissible criticism are even wider with regard to the Government than in relation to a politician.[123] Similarly, limits of acceptable criticism in respect of civil servants exercising their powers may in some circumstances be wider than those with respect to private individuals. However, civil servants do not knowingly expose themselves to close scrutiny of every word and deed to the same extent as politicians do; consequently, they should not be treated on an equal footing with politicians when it comes to the criticism of their actions. Moreover, civil servants must enjoy public confidence in conditions free of undue perturbation if they are to be successful in performing their tasks. It may, therefore, prove necessary to protect them from offensive, abusive or defamatory attacks when acting in their official capacity.[124]

For the same reason as politicians who must display a greater degree of tolerance because they enter the public arena voluntarily, private individuals or associations also expose themselves to scrutiny when they enter the arena of public debate.[125]

The Court has taken the position that reporting details of the private life of public figures may contribute to a debate of general interest and may, therefore, be permissible. This is particularly the case where politicians are concerned. Nevertheless, in balancing the protection of private life against the freedom of expression the Court reached the conclusion that the publishing of photos of Princess Caroline of Monaco was not allowed, because the published photos and accompanying commentaries did not come within the sphere of any political or public debate but related exclusively to details of the princess's private life. The Court noted explicitly that Princess Caroline did not exercise any function on behalf of the State of Monaco or one of its institutions.[126]

---

[121]   Judgment of 29 March 2005, para. 67. See also the judgment of 22 February 2005, *Pakdemirli*, para. 52: it is also against the spirit of the convention to offer special protection to Heads of State as privileged persons.

[122]   Judgment of 27 February 2001, *Jerusalem*, para. 38.

[123]   Judgment of 23 April 1992, para. 46. In its judgment of 16 November 2004, *Karkuvaara and Iltalekti*, para. 40, the Court considered politicians and governements as being in the same category.

[124]   Judgment of 11 December 2003, *Yankov*, para. 129; judgment of 27 May 2004, *Rizos and Daskas*, para. 48; judgment of 19 June 2003, *Pedersen and Baadsgaard*, para. 66; judgment of 29 March 2001, *Thoma*, para. 42.

[125]   Judgment of 27 February 2001, *Jerusalem*, para. 38.

[126]   Judgment of 24 June 2004, *Von Hannover*, paras 62-64.

As to the necessity to protect the private life of a public figure, the Court ruled in the *Plon (société)* Case that the proportionality of measures to forbid the publication of details from the medical file of the former President of the French Republic, Mr. Mitterand, was influenced by the length of time between the death of Mr. Mitterand and the publication of the medical data.[127] In the *Tammer* Case a woman who had had a relationship with, and had a child with the former Minister of the Interior of Estonia, who was married to another woman at that time, had been described as a person breaking up another's marriage and as an unfit and careless mother deserting a child, after she had published her memoirs. The Court held these remarks to be impermissible because they related to aspects of the woman's private life which she described in her memoirs that were written in her private capacity. Although she herself made these details public, the justification of the use of the actual words by Mr. Tammer in the circumstances of the case had to be examined against the background which prompted their utterance as well their value to the general public. The Court found that the criticism could have been formulated in a less offensive and insulting manner. It noted that the use of the impugned expressions were not justified by considerations of public concern and that they did not bear on a matter of general importance. Neither had the woman's private life been among the issues that affected the public at the time Mr. Tammer's remarks had been made. Those remarks could therefore scarcely be regarded as serving the public interest.[128] The case shows how meticulously the Court examines the question of whether the public debate on a matter of public interest is at stake. It also shows how difficult it is to predict the outcome of these types of cases.[129]

It should be pointed out that not only journalists may claim the high level of protection afforded to the press under Article 10. What counts is the contribution to the public debate on matters of general public interest. Consequently, in a democratic society even small and informal campaign groups may claim this protection, because they must be able to carry out there activities effectively and because there is a strong public interest in enabling such groups and individuals outside the mainstream to contribute to the publice debate.[130] Similarly, the Court also set forth that the freedom of expression is especially important for an elected representative of the people and that, therefore, "interferences with the freedom of expression of an opposition Member of Parliament call for the closest scrutiny on the part of the Court".[131]

---

[127]   Judgment of 18 May 2004, para. 53.

[128]   Judgment of 6 February 2001, *Tammer*, paras 66-68.

[129]   The public debate on a matter of general interest was also at stake in the case of a company chairman who had received large pay increases while at the same time opposing his employees' claims for a rise; judgment of 21 January 199, *Fressoz and Roire*, para. 50.

[130]   Judgment of 15 February 2005, *Steel and Morris*, para. 89.

[131]   *Idem*. See also judgment of 27 April 1995, *Piermont*, para. 76; judgment of 27 February 2001, *Jerusalem*, para. 36; judgment of 22 February 2005, *Pakdemirli*, para. 33.

The safeguard afforded to journalists by Article 10 in relation to reporting on issues of general interest is subject to the proviso that they act in good faith in order to provide accurate and reliable information in accordance with the ethics of journalism. The same principle must apply to others who engage in the public debate.[132]

The case law mentioned so far in this subsection concerned "information and ideas" on issues of public interest. The *Markt Intern Verlag and Klaus Beerman* Case concerned the question of freedom of the press in business matters. The applicants, a publishing company and its editor, had reported on a dissatisfied client of a mail-order firm. The mail-order firm obtained an injunction, prohibiting publication of the article. According to the Court the contested article did not directly concern the public as a whole and contained information of a commercial nature.[133] This conclusion appeared to be relevant with regard to the margin of appreciation of the national authorities. The Court held as follows: "Such a margin (...) is essential in commercial matters and, in particular, in an area as complex and fluctuating as that of unfair competition. Otherwise, the European Court of Human Rights would have to undertake a re-examination of the facts and all the circumstances of each case. The Court must confine its review to the question whether the measures taken on the national level are justifiable in principle and proportionate."[134] On the basis of this point of view the Court reached the conclusion – by nine votes to nine, with the casting vote of the President – that the requirements of the protection of 'rights of others' carried more weight than the publication of the information concerned.[135]

In the *Casado Coca* Case a member of the Spanish bar complained about the disciplinary penalty that had been imposed on him for breaching the prohibition of commercial advertising. The approach of the Court in assessing whether the penalty was 'necessary' in the interests of 'the protection of the (...) rights of others' would seem to be somewhat ambiguous. On the one hand the Court reiterated its position in the *Markt Intern Verlag and Klaus Beerman* Case, just quoted, thus leaving a broad margin of appreciation to the national authorities. On the other hand it held that "in some contexts, the publication of even objective, truthful advertisements might be restricted (...) Any such restrictions must, however, be closely scrutinised by the Court."[136] Finally, the Court referred to the differences that exist between the regulations in the Contracting States and concluded that the national authorities were in

---

[132] Judgment of 15 February 2005, *Steel and Morris*, para. 90; judgment of 16 November 2004, *Selistö*, para. 54.

[133] Judgment of 20 November 1989, para. 26.

[134] *Ibidem*, para. 33.

[135] *Ibidem*, para. 35. The Commission had reached a different conclusion where it had held that the approach of the domestic courts failed to distinguish between the freedom of the business-oriented press to impart specialist information on the one hand and a competitor's advertising interests on the other. This failure rendered the injunction disproportionate. *Ibidem*, paras 224-252.

[136] Judgment of 24 February 1994, para. 51.

a better position to determine the right balance between the various interests concerned.[137]

The *Jacubowski* Case concerned the prohibition on distributing a circular under the Unfair Competition Act. The supervision of the Court with regard to the question of whether the interference was necessary appeared to be rather loose. The Court left a considerable margin of appreciation to the German courts and based its conclusion that Article 10 had not been violated, amongst other arguments, on the fact that Mr Jacubowski could use other means to express his opinions.[138] Having regard to the *Markt Intern Verlag and Klaus Beerman* Case, the *Casado Coca* Case and the *Jacubowski* Case, it may be concluded that the margin of appreciation of the national authorities increases when commercial speech is involved, while the Strasbourg supervision becomes less strict.[139]

The *Barthold* Case shows that the Strasbourg supervision may be critical towards the question of whether the information or ideas expressed are of a commercial character. The case concerned an interview given by the applicant, in which he made it known that his veterinary clinic provided a night service on a voluntary basis. He had further expressed the view that a regular night service should be established with the participation of private veterinary surgeons. The interview was accompanied by the applicant's photograph and mentioned his name as well as the name of his clinic. A court action alleging unfair competition led to an injunction against the applicant prohibiting him, under penalty of a fine or imprisonment, from repeating the statements concerned in the press. Both the Commission and the Court held that the publication was a normal press interview and not an advertisement in the sense in which this term is generally understood. It was held to be not necessary in a democratic society to restrict the freedom of expression of members of a liberal profession by forbidding them to disclose their identity and function when expressing an opinion on matters of public concern, even if this information relates to their sphere of professional activity.[140]

14.4.4   DUTIES AND RESPONSIBILITIES AND SPECIAL STATUS

It is clear from the text of the second paragraph of Article 10 that everyone – including artists and those who promote their work[141] – who exercises the right contained in the

---

[137]   *Ibidem,* paras 52-55. See also report of the Commission of 19 October 1992, *Colman,* paras 38-39.
[138]   Judgment of 23 June 1994, para. 29.
[139]   At an early stage the Commission had taken the same view: Appl. 7805/77, *Pastor X and Church of Scientology,* Yearbook XXII (1979), p. 244 (252-254).
[140]   Report of 13 July 1983, paras 75-82; judgment of 25 March 1985, paras 57-59.
[141]   Judgment of 24 May 1988, *Mutter and Others,* para. 34.

first paragraph bears 'duties and responsibilities'. Those words imply the possibility to differentiate, in assessing the necessity of restricting the freedom of expression, according to 'the particular situation of the person exercising freedom of expression and the duties and responsibilities attaching to that situation'.[142] For the person concerned that special responsibility may lead to a broader or a narrower interpretation of the possibilities to restrict his freedom of expression. Although the Court has often referred to the 'duties and responsibilities', it appears that this concept plays an important part particularly in three circumstances. Firstly, as discussed in the preceding subsection, if the freedom of the press is involved. Secondly, in case the person who exercises the freedom of expression possesses a special status, such as a serviceman or a civil servant, and thirdly, if the restriction of the protection of morals is involved.

The concept of 'duties and responsibilities' of a person with a special status will be discussed below. In subsection 14.4.6 attention will be paid to the protection of morals.

In the *Engel* Case the position of the Dutch Government that the prohibition imposed on soldiers from publishing and distributing a stencilled sheet was necessary in a democratic society, found favour with the Court mainly on the basis of the special duties and responsibilities of members of the armed forces.[143] One may wonder about the Court's approach in this case. The mere fact that a person has a special status does not yet provide a sufficient reason for a special treatment. There has to be a relationship between the special status of the person in question, the content of the opinion expressed or to be expressed, and/or the medium chosen for it. This relationship is quite evident in the case of the dissemination of information which is available to a person by virtue of his function. The Court seems to have adopted this approach in the *Hadjianastassiou* Case, where it held that the applicant, a captain in the air force who had been in charge of an experimental missile programme, "was bound by an obligation of discretion in relation to anything concerning the performance of his duties".[144]

In the *Vereinigung Demokratischer Soldaten Österreichs and Gubi* Case the Austrian army had been distributing free of charge its own publications and publications of private associations of soldiers in all the country's barracks. However, the Minister for Defence had refused to distribute *Der Igel,* a magazine published by the first applicant. According to the Government, the content of *Der Igel* was a threat to military discipline. The Court referred to the *Engel* Case but this time contrasted its own view with regard to the content of the magazine with that of the Government.

---

[142] Report of 30 September 1975, *Handyside,* para. 141. See also the judgment of 7 December 1976 in this case, para. 49; report of 11 May 1984, *Kosiek,* para. 110; judgment of 26 September 1995, *Vogt,* para. 53.

[143] Judgment of 8 June 1976, para. 98.

[144] Judgment of 16 December 1992, para. 46.

It held that the criticism in *Der Igel* did not overstep "the bounds of what is permissible (...) in the army of a democratic State".[145] The difference between the *Vereinigung Demokratischer Soldaten Österreichs and Gubi* Case and the *Engel* Case can be explained, according to the Court, by the fact that in the former case the Austrian authorities refused to distribute the magazine in all the barracks, while in the latter the banned magazine had been distributed in only one barrack where unrest had occurred.[146]

The special status of civil servants was at issue in the reports of the Commission in the *Glasenapp* Case and the *Kosiek* Case.[147] The Commission pointed to the fact that the rule contained in Article 11(2) permitting certain restrictions on the exercise of freedom of assembly and association on members of the armed forces, of the police and of the administration of the State, is not expressly included in Article 10(2). However, in the opinion of the Commission, this was not sufficient ground for arguing that the drafters of the Convention had not intended to impose specific restrictions of the kind included in Article 11(2) also on the freedom of opinion. The effect of the provision in Article 11(2) may be to limit some forms of expression of opinion, such as membership of political organisations by certain categories of government employees. According to the Commission, the connection between the two provisions is reflected in the requirement laid down in Article 10(2) that the restriction imposed must be necessary in a democratic society in the light of the actual duties and responsibilities which the exercise of freedom of expression and opinion by the person concerned carries with it; its necessity must flow from the applicant's circumstances. On this basis the Commission adopted the view that the requirement that a schoolteacher dissociated herself completely from the German Communist Party could not be considered a necessary condition and restriction on her freedom of opinion and expression,[148] whereas the dismissal of a lecturer on the basis of his personal and public identification with the extreme policies of the National Democratic Party of Germany, in which he was a leading figure, was considered justified, because the dismissal could be deemed necessary and proportionate.[149]

The *Vogt* Case concerned the dismissal of a teacher from the civil service because of her political activities on behalf of the German Communist Party. The Court took the position that the Contracting Parties are entitled to require civil servants to be loyal

---

[145] Judgment of 19 December 1994, para. 38.

[146] *Ibidem,* para. 39.

[147] The Court held Art. 10 not to be applicable because the 'access to the civil service', a right not secured in the Convention, lay at the heart of the case. Judgments of 28 August 1986, para. 53 and para. 39 respectively. See also *supra* 14.2.1.

[148] Report of 11 May 1984, *Glasenapp*, para. 95 and para. 128.

[149] Report of 11 May 1984, *Kosiek*, paras 87-88 and 112-115.

to their constitutional values[150] and held that the 'duties and responsibilities' are 'to a certain extent' also incumbent on teachers outside school.[151] However, in this case the Court found the circumstances adduced by the Government not sufficient to justify the dismissal. The Court referred, *inter alia*, to the fact that Mrs Vogt, in the performance of her duty, had been beyond reproach, that the German Communist Party had not been banned and that there was no evidence, even outside the school, of any anti-constitutional statements on her part. As a result, the dismissal was considered disproportionate to the aim pursued.[152]

In the *Rekvényi* Case the ban contained in the Hungarian Constitution on political activities by police officials was at issue. The Court held this ban to be permissible. Under the given circumstances it found the term 'political activities' clear enough to regulate the behaviour of the police officials. In view of the fact that the police had been an instrument in the hands of the communist party until 1989, the purpose of having a politically neutral police force could be considered a pressing social need, which made the interference proportional.[153]

In 1995 the President of the Administrative Court of Liechtenstein gave a lecture on questions of constitutional jurisdiction. His discourse included a statement on the competences of the Constitutional Court under Article 112 of the Liechtenstein Constitution. It was the President's view that the term 'Government' used in this provision included the Prince, an opinion allegedly in conflict with the principle of the Prince's immunity from the jurisdiction of the Liechtenstein judiciary. Subsequently, the Prince sent a letter to the President announcing his decision not to appoint him to a public office in the future anymore. According to the Court this action was disproportionate to the aim pursued and, therefore, impermissible. First, the Court stated: "Although it is legitimate for a State to impose on civil servants, on account of their status, a duty of discretion, civil servants are individuals and, as such, qualify for the protection of Article 10 of the Convention."[154] Subsequently, although the Court accepted that the President's lecture inevitably had political implications, it held that this element alone should not have prevented the applicant from making any statement on the matter. The Court stressed that the opinion expressed by the President could not be regarded as an untenable proposition since it was shared by a considerable number of persons in Liechtenstein. Moreover, there was no evidence

---

[150]   Judgment of 26 September 1995, para. 59.
[151]   *Ibidem*, para. 60.
[152]   *Ibidem*, para. 61. The Court did not express clearly which aim was involved. The Government relied on the interest of national security, the prevention of disorder and the protection of rights of others; *ibidem*, para. 49.
[153]   Judgment of 20 May 1999, paras 47-49.
[154]   Judgment of 28 October 1999, *Wille*, para. 62.

to conclude that the President's lecture contained any remarks on pending cases, severe criticism of persons or public institutions or insults of high officials or the Prince.[155]

This case law shows that the Court, as far as servicemen, civil servants and other public officials are concerned, is not inclined to accept easily that the special 'duties and responsibilities' may lead to a restriction of the freedom of expression. Therefore, the *Engel and Others* Case may in retrospect be regarded as a false start.[156]

14.4.5   SPECIAL STATUS OF PRISONERS

With regard to Article 10 prisoners stand out as a special group in the case law too, not in connection with the above-mentioned special duties and responsibilities which may be incumbent on a person in a particular capacity, but on the basis of the special requirements assumed to be involved in detention. While here again in some cases the Commission has taken the view that certain restrictions on the freedom to receive and impart information and ideas are inherent in detention and consequently are not contrary to the right laid down in the first paragraph,[157] in other cases such restrictions have been considered justified on the basis of the second paragraph, in particular on the basis of a very broad interpretation of the restriction 'prevention of disorder'. On that ground, for instance, the Commission considered justifiable the refusal by the prison authorities to make available, at the prisoner's request, a copy of the provisional regulations on the execution of penalties; this was because he wanted to use the information in a discussion with the press.[158] The prohibition on a Buddhist prisoner from sending an article to a Buddhist journal was also permissible in the eyes of the Commission,[159] as was the prison rule that in principle no journals from outside the United Kingdom were admitted.[160]

The *Yankov* Case concerned a prisoner who had criticised the way prisoners were treated by the warders. He had claimed that the prisoners were given very bad and insufficient food, that the warders shouted, cursed and hit prisoners who stayed more than two minutes in the lavatory with truncheons, and that the criminal proceedings against him were unjust and unlawful. The Court considered that, having regard to the particular vulnerability of persons in custody, the punishment of prisoners for

---

[155]   *Ibidem*, para. 67.

[156]   See also judgment of 14 March 2002, *Diego Nafría*, in which the dismissal of a high public bank official was held disproportionate.

[157]   Thus, *e.g.* in Appl. 2795/66, *X v. Federal Republic of Germany*, Yearbook XII (1969), p. 192 (204), where the applicant alleged that he had been given insufficient opportunity to consult an annotated text of the German Criminal Code for the preparation of his request for a new hearing of his case. See also Appl. 4517/70, *Huber*, Yearbook XIV (1971), p. 548 (568).

[158]   Appl. 1860/63, *X v. Federal Republic of Germany*, Yearbook VIII (1965), p. 204 (216).

[159]   Appl. 5442/72, *X v. the United Kingdom*, D&R 1 (1975), p. 41 (42).

[160]   Appl. 5270/72, *X v. the United Kingdom*, Coll. 46 (1974), p. 54 (59-60).

having made allegedly false accusations concerning the conditions of detention and acts of the penitentiary authorities require particularly solid justification in order to be considered necessary in a democratic society.[161] The Court added that it was struck by the fact that the prisoner was punished for having written down his own thoughts in a private manuscript which, apparently, he had not shown to anyone at the time it was seized. The prisoner had neither uttered nor disseminated any offensive or defamatory statements. The manuscript was seized when the applicant was about to hand it over to his lawyer to 'impart' its contents. This was the reason the Court did not take the freedom of thought under Article 9 or the prisoner's right for respect of his private life under Article 8 into consideration. Nonetheless, the fact that the prisoner's remarks were never made public was relevant to the assessment of the proportionality of the interference under Article 10: "The Court notes in this respect, in addition, that the manuscript was not in a form ready for publication and that there was no immediate danger of its dissemination, even if it had been taken out of prison."[162] The Court found subsequently that the need to ensure that civil servants enjoy public confidence in conditions free of undue perturbation can justify an interference with the freedom of expression only where there is a real threat in this respect. "The applicant's manuscript obviously did not pose such a threat".[163] Therefore, the seven days confinement in a disciplinary cell was disproportionate.

Although the Court's judgment was favourable to the prisoner, it makes clear that the Court still adopts quite a reticent attitude towards the review of interferences of the freedom of expression of prisoners, while there would seem to be room for a stricter necessity test.[164]

14.4.6 DUTIES AND RESPONSIBILITIES AND PROTECTION OF MORALS

The concept of 'duties and responsibilities' also seems to play an important part if 'the protection of morals' has been invoked to justify a restriction of the freedom of expression. In the *Handyside* Case the Government of the United Kingdom relied on this aim to justify the conviction of a publisher for having in his possession copies of the 'Little Red School Book' and their destruction as pornography. The reference to

---

[161] Judgment of 11 December 2003, para. 134.
[162] *Ibidem*, para. 141.
[163] *Ibidem*.
[164] See also the judgment of 27 May 2003, *Skalka*, in which a prisoner had criticised a judge. The Court found the sentence of eight months imprisonment disproportionately severe.

the special responsibility of the publisher constituted an argument for a reserved Strasbourg review.[165]

This case may be compared with the *Otto-Preminger-Institut* Case, concerning the seizure and subsequent forfeiture of a film. According to the Austrian authorities this film had disparaged the Roman Catholic religious doctrine. The Government relied on 'the protection of (...) rights of others'. This was accepted by the Court, but it indicated that in this case that aim came very close to the concept of 'morals'. The Court referred to the 'duties and responsibilities'. It held as follows: "Amongst them – in the context of religious opinions and beliefs – may legitimately be included an obligation to avoid as far as possible expressions that are gratuitously offensive to others and thus an infringement of their rights, and which therefore do not contribute to any form of public debate of furthering progress in human affairs."[166] The Court concluded that Article 10 had not been violated.

In the *Murphy* Case the Court again pointed out that one of the duties and responsibilities the freedom of expression carries with it is the general requirement to ensure the peaceful enjoyment of the rights guaranteed under Article 9 to the holders of such beliefs, including a duty to avoid as far as possible an expression that is, in regard of objects of veneration, gratuitously offensive to others and profane. The Court held that, therefore, "a wider margin of appreciation is generally available to the Contracting States when regulating freedom of expression in relation to matters liable to offend intimate personal convictions within the sphere of morals or, especially, religion. Moreover, as in the field of morals, and perhaps to an even greater degree, there is no uniform European conception of the requirements of 'the protection of the rights of others' in relation to attacks on their religious convictions. What is likely to cause substantial offence to persons of a particular religious persuasion will vary significantly from time to time and from place to place, especially in an era characterised by an ever growing array of faiths and denominations. By reason of their direct and continuous contact with the vital forces of their countries, State authorities are in principle in a better position than the international judge to give an opinion on the exact content of these requirements with regard to the rights of others as well as on the 'necessity' of a 'restriction' intended to protect from such material those whose deepest feelings and convictions would be seriously offended."[167]

The case law mentioned makes it clear that the reference to 'duties and responsibilities' leads to a broad margin of appreciation if at the same time on good grounds the concept of 'morals' is invoked.

---

[165]   Judgment of 7 December 1976, para. 49. See also, less clear, the judgment of 24 May 1988, *Mutter and Others*, para. 33.
[166]   Judgment of 20 September 1994, para. 49. See also the judgment of 13 September 2005, *I.A. v. Turkey*, paras 28-32.
[167]   Judgment of 10 July 2003, *Murphy*, paras 65 and 67.

14.4.7 LICENSING OF BROADCASTING, TELEVISION OR CINEMA ENTERPRISES

For the most important media in addition to written publications, *viz.* broadcasting, television and cinema, Article 10 provides that they may be subjected to a licensing system. This provision is contained in the first, not the second paragraph. Therefore, at first sight one would expect that when refusing a licence, the authorities are not confined to the restriction grounds mentioned in the second paragraph. However, in the *Groppera Radio AG* Case the Court developed a different approach. The case concerned the ban on cable retransmissions in Switzerland of programmes that had been broadcasted by a radio station from Italy. The Court held that the third sentence of the first paragraph permits the Contracting States 'to control the way in which the broadcasting is organised', especially with regard to 'technical aspects', but that otherwise the licensing measures had to comply with the requirements of the second paragraph.[168]

This point of view was further elucidated in the *Informationsverein Lentia* Case. The applicants complained that the impossibility of setting up a radio and television station because of the monopoly of the Austrian broadcasting company, constituted a breach of the third sentence of the first paragraph. The Court referred to its judgment in the *Groppera Radio AG* Case and held as follows: "the purpose of that provision is to make clear that States are permitted to regulate by a licensing system the way in which broadcasting is organised in their territories, particularly in its technical aspects. (…) Technical aspects are undeniably important, but the grant or refusal of a licence may also be made conditional on other considerations, including such matters as the nature and objectives of a proposed station, its potential audience and the obligations deriving from international legal instruments. This may lead to interferences whose aims will be legitimate under the third sentence of paragraph 1, even though they do not correspond to any of the aims set out in paragraph 2. The compatibility of such interferences with the Convention must nevertheless be assessed in the light of other requirements of paragraph 2."[169]

As far as the aims are concerned, the Contracting States do have considerable freedom in setting up a licensing system. Thus, if the licensing system is 'prescribed by law', the guarantees offered by Article 10 in this respect seem to lie mainly in the necessity-test of the second paragraph. The supervision of the Court may be rather strict on this point. In the *Groppera Radio AG* Case the ban on cable transmissions from a foreign radio station was considered permissible because the station was a pirate and wanted

---

[168] Judgment of 28 March 1990, paras 59-61. See also the judgment of 22 May 1990, *Autronic AG*, para. 53.
[169] Judgment of 24 November 1993, para. 32.

to circumvent the rules of the Swiss broadcasting system. In such circumstances a State has a right to take measures in order to protect its own system. This view fits in with the decision of the Commission in *X v. the United Kingdom*. There the Commission took the view that, since the first paragraph envisages legislation requiring the licensing of broadcasting organisations, a State is also allowed to take measures against those who seek to promote or encourage unlicensed 'pirate' stations by advertising them or making them known in some other way.[170] In the *Autronic AG* Case, however, the refusal of the Swiss authorities to authorise a company to receive, by means of a private dish aerial uncoded, legally broadcast television programmes, in absence of the consent of the broadcasting State, did not meet the requirements of the necessity-test.[171]

In the *Informationsverein Lentia* Case the Court held that the impossibility of setting up a radio and television station did not meet these requirements either. The Court referred to the fundamental role of freedom of expression in a democratic society, in particular where, through the press, it serves to impart information and ideas of general interest, which the public moreover is entitled to receive. According to the Court, such an undertaking cannot be successfully accomplished unless it is grounded in the principle of pluralism, of which the State is the ultimate guarantor. This observation holds true particularly in relation to audio-visual media, whose programmes are often broadcasted very widely. Of all the means to ensure that these values are respected, a public monopoly is the one which imposes the greatest restrictions on the freedom of expression. Therefore, these restrictions may only be justified if they correspond to a pressing need. As a result of the technical progress made over the last few decades, justification of these restrictions can no longer today be found in considerations relating to the number of frequencies and channels available.[172]

In the *Tele 1 Privatfernsehgesellschaft mbH* Case the Court held that the refusal to grant a licence for terrestrial television broadcasting is only permissible if cable television broadcasting offers private broadcasters a viable alternative, which is the case when almost all households receiving television in a certain area have the possibility of being connected to the cable network.[173] In the *Demuth* Case the Court accepted the refusal to grant a licence for cable television to a private broadcaster whose programme was mainly aimed at the promotion of automobiles, given the specific Swiss political and cultural context and the requirements which the federal structure sets on a pluralistic programme supply.[174]

Under Article 14 no discrimination is permitted in the granting of licences and, in case of a State monopoly, the broadcasting time granted to a political party, trade union or other institution of a specific political, religious, philosophical or ethical

---

[170]   Appl. 8266/78, D&R 16 (1979), p. 190 (192).
[171]   Judgment of 22 May 1990, paras 60-63.
[172]   Judgment of 24 November 1993, paras 38-39.
[173]   Judgment of 21 September 2000, para. 18.
[174]   Judgment of 5 November 2002, para. 44.

character may not be disproportionate. For the assessment of whether discrimination or disproportionality has occurred, all facets of the political, religious and social climate of the community concerned have to be taken into account. Thus, departure from the arithmetical proportionality on the ground that otherwise a small political party would not be entitled to any broadcasting time at all, or to a uselessly short time only, does not constitute discrimination.

The *Jersild* Case concerned the criminal liability of a television journalist who had taken the initiative of making a television programme about a group of young people who were known for their racist ideas. Subsequent to the broadcasting of a summary of the interview in which the members of the group ventilated their racist statements and insulted various people, criminal proceedings were instituted and Mr Jersild was convicted and sentenced for aiding and abetting the dissemination of racist statements. According to the national courts Mr Jersild had not sufficiently counterbalanced the expressed racist views. In assessing the claim of the applicant about violation of Article 10 the Court accepted that the interference pursued 'the protection of the reputation or rights of others'. Next, the Court made a distinction between print media and audio-visual media by explaining that the audio-visual media "have often a much more immediate and powerful effect". However, according to the Court, this fact did not justify the Court or the national courts substituting "their own views for those of the press as to what technique of reporting should be adopted by journalists".[175] Moreover, the Court seemed to leave no margin of appreciation to the national authorities with regard to evaluating the attitude of the applicant. The Court expressly disagreed with the national courts and held that Mr Jersild clearly dissociated himself from the person interviewed. Accordingly, Article 10 had been breached.[176]

In the *Murphy* Case a general ban on the broadcasting of any religious advertising was considered permissible. The Court took into account that a provision allowing one religion, and not another, to advertise would be difficult to justify and saw some force in the Irish Government's argument that the exclusion of all religious grouping from broadcasting advertisements generates less discomfort than any filtering of the amount and content of such expression by such groupings. The Court also observed that there appears to be no clear consensus between the Contracting States as to the manner in which to legislate for the broadcasting of religious advertisements and that, for example, Greece, Switzerland and Portugal had similar prohibitions.[177]

---

[175]   Judgment of 23 September 1994, para. 31.
[176]   *Ibidem*, paras 33-37.
[177]   Judgment of 10 July 2003, paras 77-81.

14.4.8   PROTECTION OF JOURNALISTIC SOURCES

In the *Goodwin* Case the applicant, a British journalist, had received information about the financial problems of a company. When he contacted the company to verify the facts, it appeared that the information had been derived from a confidential company report. These events eventually resulted in an injunction restraining the journalist (and the publishers he worked for) from publishing the information and a court order to disclose the identity of Goodwin's source. With regard to the question of whether the alleged interference was 'necessary in a democratic society' to protect the company's rights the Court labelled the protection of journalistic sources as "one of the basic conditions for press freedom" and held that "limitations on the confidentiality of journalistic sources call for the most careful scrutiny".[178] The Court took the position that the purpose of the injunction – the prevention of the dissemination of the confidential information – and of the disclosure order had been basically the same and, therefore, the disclosure order was not supported by sufficient reasons for the purpose of the second paragraph. The interest of the company to unmask a disloyal employee, who had disclosed the secret plan, did not constitute a sufficient reason for the disclosure order either. Consequently, the Court reached the conclusion that the disclosure order and the fine imposed upon the journalist for having refused to comply with the order had been contrary to Article 10.[179]

In the *Ernst* Case the massive search of the premises of journalists and the confiscation of their documents and computer data in the context of a criminal case, in which the journalists were not suspects or otherwise involved, was considered disproportional. In addition, more proportionate measures should have been taken to reach the legitimate aim.[180] It is clear that the Convention offers very strong, albeit not absolute, protection for journalistic sources.

14.4.9   TERRITORIAL INTEGRITY

In the *Piermont* Case the French Government relied on 'territorial integrity' to justify an infringement of the first paragraph of Article 10. Mrs Piermont had taken part in a demonstration on the territory of French Polynesia in favour of the independence of French Polynesia. During that demonstration she had made a speech in which she supported the anti-nuclear and independence demands of some of the local political parties. The applicant claimed that Article 10 had been violated by the subsequent

---

[178]   Judgment of 27 March 1996, para. 40.
[179]   *Ibidem,* paras 37-46.
[180]   Judgment of 15 July 2003, paras 99-105 See also the judgment of 25 February 2003, *Roemen and Schmitt,* paras 49-60.

order by the French authorities, directing her expulsion from the French Polynesian territory coupled with a ban on re-entering, and the order prohibiting her from entering the territory of her next destination, New-Caledonia. The Court accepted that the interference pursued two aims, the prevention of disorder and the interest of territorial integrity.[181] With regard to the necessity-requirement the Court referred, *inter alia*, to the importance of a free political debate, the fact that the speech had been held during an authorised and non-violent demonstration and that the demonstration had not been followed by any disorder.[182] The Court reached the conclusion that the orders had not been 'necessary in a democratic society'.[183]

14.4.10 PREVENTING THE DISCLOSURE OF INFORMATION RECEIVED IN CONFIDENCE

The wide formulation of the restriction 'for preventing the disclosure of information received in confidence' overlaps with other grounds. Insofar as it refers to the right of the authorities to take measures against the leakage of State secrets, the ground 'in the interests of national security, territorial integrity or public safety' would appear to sufficiently serve that purpose. And insofar as it refers to the possibility of being exempted from a legal duty to impart information when information received in confidence is involved, for instance as a witness in judicial proceedings, what is involved is not a restriction, but on the contrary a confirmation of the freedom of expression, since the first paragraph entails the right to be silent.[184] And if the protection of a person's privacy is concerned, the restriction 'protection of the reputation or rights of others' will suffice. Neverless, cases may occur in which information received in confidence is revealed without one of the above-mentioned interests being applicable, such as when a civil servant reveals or intends to reveal on his own initiative an official secret which does not affect either national security or the rights of others.[185]

---

[181] Judgment of 27 April 1995, para. 70 and (less clear) paras 82-85.
[182] In its judgment of 25 August 1993, *Chorherr*, paras 32-33, the Court accepted a reference by the Austrian Government to the fear of disorder during a military parade and held that Art. 10 had not been violated.
[183] Judgment of 27 April 1995, paras 73-78 and 86. The Government relied also on Articles 63 and 16 to justify the interference. The Court rejected these arguments, paras 23 and 64, respectively.
[184] This does not hold true if the first paragraph is also taken to contain a right to seek information and accordingly a duty of the authorities to enforce the ('horizontal') obligation to impart information. On this, see *supra* 14.3.6.
[185] See, *e.g.*, Appl. 4274/69, *X v. Federal Republic of* Germany, Yearbook XIII (1970), p. 888 (892).

14.4.11 MAINTAINING THE AUTHORITY AND IMPARTIALITY OF THE JUDICIARY

Another specific feature of the second paragraph of Article 10, in comparison with the restrictions in other articles of the Convention, is the restriction ground 'for maintaining the authority and impartiality of the judiciary'. This ground would seem to have been included mainly with a view to the prohibition, familiar from Anglo-Saxon law, of 'contempt of court', which is intended to prevent the authority and the independence of the court, as well as the rights of the parties to the proceedings,[186] from being impaired by publications and other acts. In the *Weber* Case, the Court held that the application of a provision of the criminal code was intended 'to ensure the proper conduct of the investigation' and, therefore, also came within the ambit of this restriction ground.[187]

The restriction was discussed at length in the *Sunday Times* Case. In this case the publisher, the editorial staff and the general editor of the Sunday Times complained about the ban for a given period, imposed by an English court, on the publication of an article concerning the so-called 'thalidomide children', *i.e.* children born with serious malformations of limbs, because their mothers had used the sedative thalidomide during pregnancy. The reason given for the prohibition was the prevention of 'contempt of court', because at that time claims for damages were pending before the English courts. In order to be able to answer the question of whether the ban on publication could be justified on this ground the Commission undertook an independent inquiry into the circumstances under which the prohibition had been imposed. In the final analysis it concluded that the nature of the prohibited publication did not tend to affect the impartiality of the court, since the article contained only information with which the court had already become familiar from another source. Nor could the authority of the court be impaired by the publication. In fact, at the moment of the prohibition, in the majority of the cases the parties were negotiating in order to reach a friendly settlement, while the role of the court consisted only in approving such a settlement if reached and in protecting the interests of the minors concerned. Moreover, the proposed publication was also specifically meant to protect the interests of those minors. In this particular situation, therefore, the domestic courts were not called upon to pronounce on the liability of the producer of the medicine, the issue which the publication dealt with. And as to the few cases in which the parents were quite averse to reaching a settlement, the proceedings, in the opinion of the majority of the Commission, were still in so early a stage that the influence of the publication on the outcome was negligible. Moreover, the Commission took into

---

[186] Judgment of 26 April 1979, *The Sunday Times*, para. 56; judgment of 26 November 1991, *The Observer and Guardian*, para. 56.

[187] Judgment of 22 May 1990, para. 45.

consideration the circumstance that, although this was a civil action, a public interest was involved in the case as well. Since that public interest had not been brought out, either in a criminal prosecution or in an inquiry instituted by the authorities, only very compelling reasons could justify a prohibition of information being imparted by private persons. The Commission considered that no such compelling reasons existed.[188] The Court basically concurred – though with the bare majority of 11 votes to 9 – with the opinion of the majority of the Commission.[189]

The *Observer and Guardian* Case concerned interlocutory injunctions restraining two newspapers from publishing, pending proceedings which had been instituted by the Attorney General to obtain permanent injunctions, details of the manuscript of a book (Spycatcher) containing the memoirs of a former agent of the British Security Service. The Court held that the injunction had been permissible initially, but could no longer be justified once the book had been published in the United States, because from that very moment the confidentiality of the material had been destroyed.[190]

Ensuring the proper conduct of investigation may not be the only reason for the last restriction of paragraph 2. The aim is wider. According to the Court in the *Skalka* Case, the work of the courts, which are the guarantors of justice and which have a fundamental role in a State governed by the rule of law, needs to enjoy public confidence. It should, therefore, be protected against unfounded attacks. However, as with all public institutions, the courts are not immune from criticism and scrutiny. In this respect a clear distinction must be made between criticism and insult. If the sole intent of any form of expression is to insult a court or members of a court, an appropriate punishment would not, in principle, constitute a violation of Article 10(2).[191] The Court declared the statement in a letter to the President of the Katowice Regional Court that all judges of that court were 'irresponsible clowns' and calling an unnamed judge 'a small-time cretin', 'an illiterate', 'a fool' and 'such a limited individual' impermissible, but nevertheless it considered a prison sentence of eight months disproportionately severe.[192]

In the *Barfod* Case a journalist had been convicted for writing an article of an allegedly defaming character. In his article he criticised a judgment in a case in which two lay judges had participated, who were both employed as civil servants in the local government, which was the defendant party in that case. The applicant's conviction

---

[188] Report of 18 May 1977, paras 231-248.

[189] Judgment of 26 April 1970, paras 42-68. The issue of 'contempt of court' also arose in Appl. 10038/82, *Harmon*, D&R 38 (1984), p. 53 (61-63), where a lawyer had given access to a journalist to documents which were exclusively meant for purposes of the trial.

[190] Judgment of 26 November 1991, para. 68. See also the judgment of 26 November 1991, *The Sunday Times (No. 2)*, para. 54.

[191] Judgment of 27 May 2003, para. 34. See also the judgment of 27 May 2004, *Rizos and Daskas*, para. 43.

[192] Judgment of 27 May 2003, *Skalka*, para. 41.

was based on the fact that he suggested that the two lay judges had cast their votes rather as employees of the local government than as independent and impartial judges. In the opinion of the Commission this statement concerned matters of public interest involving the functioning of the public administration, including the judiciary. According to the Commission, in such a case the test of necessity of the interference must be a particularly strict one: "It follows that even if the article in question could be interpreted as an attack on the integrity or reputation of the two lay judges, the general interest in allowing a public debate about the functioning of the judiciary weighs more heavily than the interest of the two judges in being protected against criticism of the kind expressed in the applicant's article."[193] The Commission further-more indicated that the aim mentioned in Article 10(2) to maintain the authority of the judiciary cannot be used as a basis for restraining criticism of the composition of a court which is improperly constituted under the applicable rules. Unlike the Com-mission, the Court held that the interference with the applicant's freedom of expression did not aim at restricting his right under the Convention to criticise publicly the composition of the court in question. It was quite possible to question the composition of that court without at the same time attacking the two lay judges personally. The State's legitimate interest in protecting the reputation of the two lay judges was accordingly not in conflict with the applicant's interest in being able to participate in free public debate on the question of the structural impartiality of the High Court.[194] The Court reached the conclusion that the conviction could not be regarded as disproportionate and that, therefore, Article 10 had not been violated. It is submitted with due respect that it is difficult to make a distinction between the 'personal attack' on the two judges and the complaint about the improper constitution of the Court, and that the review by the Court in this case should have been more strict, precisely for the reasons given by the Commission. The same doubts arise concerning the judgment in the *Prager and Oberschlick* Case concerning a journalist and a publisher convicted for defamation of a judge. The rejection of their complaint was partly based on the Court's opinion that the classification of the insults in the published article as allegations of fact and value-judgments comes within the ambit of the margin of appreciation of the national authorities.[195]

In the *Amihalachioaie* Case the Court referred to the right of the public to also be informed about questions which concern the functioning of the judiciary. In an interview a lawyer had criticised the Constitutional Court of Moldavia as being not constitutional and had argued that it was likely that the judges of that court did not recognise the Strasbourg Court's authority. The Constitutional Court had ruled that a legal provision which obliged lawyers to be a member of the national bar association

---

[193]   Report of 16 July 1987, para. 71.
[194]   Judgment of 22 February 1989, para. 34.
[195]   Judgment of 26 April 1995, para. 36.

was contrary to the Constitution. The Court held that the statement contributed to a question of general interest, which was the object of a controversial debate and polemic between the members of the legal profession and had been caused by the decision of the Constitutional Court itself. Also taking into consideration that the lawyer had denied saying everything which had been stated in the interview and that he could not be held responsible for the whole content of that interview, the Court held that the punishment imposed on the lawyer constituted a violation of Article 10.[196]

14.5 DEROGATION

Article 10 is not mentioned in the enumeration of Article 15(2), and the right to freedom of expression, therefore, is not a non-derogable right. In the *Greek* Case, accordingly, a violation of the Convention on account of a breach of Article 10 could only be established after the Commission had examined whether the Greek Government had rightly invoked Article 15, and after it had reached a negative conclusion in that respect.[197]

As has been submitted with regard to Article 9, here again it may be submitted that in fact the exceptions provided for in Article 15 can never be applicable to the 'freedom to hold opinions' contained in Article 10, since an exception to that right can in no circumstance be 'strictly required' in the sense of Article 15(1).

---

[196]   Judgment of 20 April 2004, paras 31-40.
[197]   Report of 5 November 1969, Yearbook XII (1969), p. 1 (75-76 and 100).

CHAPTER 15

FREEDOM OF ASSOCIATION
AND ASSEMBLY (Article 11)

REVISED BY AALT WILLEM HERINGA AND FRIED VAN HOOF

CONTENTS

15.1   TEXT OF ARTICLE 11

1. *Everyone has the right to freedom of peaceful assembly and to freedom of association with others, including the right to form and to join trade unions for the protection of his interests.*
2. *No restrictions shall be placed on the exercise of these rights other than such as are prescribed by law and are necessary in a democratic society in the interests of national security or public safety, for the prevention of disorder or crime, for the protection of health or morals or for the protection of the rights and freedoms of others. This Article shall not prevent the imposition of lawful restrictions on the exercise of these rights by members of the armed forces, of the police or of the administration of the State.*

15.2 INTRODUCTION

In the Convention the freedom of association and that of peaceful assembly are contained in one and the same provision. Freedom of association in fact presupposes freedom of assembly, since without regular meetings of its members an association cannot lead an effective existence. Freedom of assembly is also important, however, outside the framework of associations, for instance in connection with the right to freedom of expression laid down in the preceding article and in connection with the periodical free elections by secret ballot guaranteed in Article 3 of Protocol No. 1.[1]

Both the freedom of association and the freedom of assembly are closely connected with the freedom of thought, conscience and religion provided for in Article 9, and with the freedom of expression of Article 10. In fact, the exercise of the right to freedom of association and of the right to freedom of assembly will generally involve the holding and propagation of specific opinions. This was expressly indicated by the Court in the *Young, James and Webster* Case. The Court treated the freedoms set forth in Articles 9 and 10 as elements of Article 11 and considered their violation as constituting an additional argument for the finding of a violation of Article 11.[2] This interpretation is now established case-law since the Court invariably repeats its opinion that Article 11 must also be considered in the light of Articles 9 and/or 10.[3] In the *Ezelin* Case the Court added that "(t)he protection of personal opinions, secured by Article 10, is one of the objectives of freedom of peaceful assembly as enshrined in Article 11".[4]

The link between Articles 11 and 10 has also led to an importation of the standard of review developed by the Court in the context of public speech under Article 10 into Article 11. This is most notable in cases concerning political parties. In the *United Communist Party of Turkey* Case the Court first set forth that Article 11 must be considered in the light of Article 10, all the more in relation to political parties in view of their essential role in ensuring pluralism and the proper functioning of democracy. It subsequently held as follows: "the exceptions set out in Article 11 are, where political parties are concerned, to be construed strictly; only convincing and compelling reasons can justify restrictions on such parties' freedom of association. In determining whether a necessity within the meaning of Article 11 para. 2 exists, the Contracting States possess only a limited margin of appreciation, which goes hand in hand with rigorous

---

[1]   See the report of 5 November 1969, *Greek* Case, Yearbook XII (1969), pp. 170-171.

[2]   Judgment of 13 August 1981, para. 57. Recent examples of the link between Article 11 and Article 10: *Refah Partisi (Prosperity Party) and Others*, judgment of 31 July 2001; *Freedom and Democratic Party (ÖZDEP)*, judgment of 8 December 1999.

[3]   An example is the *Chassagnou* Case, judgment of 29 April 1999, para. 100: an obligation to join an association is an interference with the 'negative' freedom of association and is, therefore, considered by the Court under Article 11 in the light of Article 9, since protection of personal opinions is one of the purposes of the freedom of association.

[4]   Judgment of 26 April 1991, para. 37.

European supervision embracing both the law and the decisions applying it, including those given by independent courts. The Court had already held that such scrutiny was necessary in a case concerning a Member of Parliament who had been convicted of proffering insults (...); such scrutiny is all the more necessary where an entire political party is dissolved and its leaders banned from carrying on any similar activity in the future."[5]

In some cases the facts do give rise to a violation of Article 10 as well as of Article 11. In the *Vogt* Case the relevant issue was the compatibility with Articles 10 and 11 of the dismissal of the applicant from her post as a civil servant on the ground of her having persistently refused to dissociate herself from the DKP (the German Communist Party), claiming that membership of that party was not incompatible with her duty of loyalty. The Court first concluded that Article 10 had been violated. It then held that the facts which gave rise to that conclusion also constituted a breach of Article 11. Its main argument was that the requirements of paragraph 2 of Article 11 are identical to those laid down in paragraph 2 of Article 10 (with the exception of the last sentence of paragraph 2 of Article 11). The finding that there had been a disproportionality with respect to the legitimate aim pursued in the context of Article 10, therefore, automatically resulted in the conclusion that there also had been a violation of Article 11.[6]

This approach implies that the Court's method of interpretation and the margin of appreciation it accords to a State is influenced, also in the context of Article 11, by the basic principle that freedom of expression (and consequently also the freedom of association) is one of the essential foundations of a democratic society. Interferences with the freedom of association will, therefore, be reviewed more strictly whenever political associations or opinions are concerned, in line with the Court's approach towards 'political speech'. These different approaches, varying according to the nature of the opinion or association involved, can be clearly discerned when comparing the *Vogt* Case with the *Gustafsson* Case. In the latter case the Court granted the respondent Government a wider margin of appreciation because in this case the freedom of association did not involve political associations or opinions but trade union freedom and the freedom not to participate in collective bargaining.[7]

However, the parallel approach does not imply an identical approach. In the *Gorzelik* Case the Polish authorities had refused to register the 'Union of People of Silesion Nationality'. Under Article 10 the Court has been very strict in its assessment of preventive permission (censorship) pertinent to publications. In the *Gorzelik* Case

---

[5]   Judgment of 30 January 1998, para. 46. Also the judgment of 25 May 1998, *Socialist Party and Others*, para. 50.
[6]   Judgment of 26 September 1995, paras 64-65.
[7]   Judgment of 25 April 1996, para. 45.

the Court seems to have applied less strict standards with respect to prior control under Article 11. It stated as follows: "the applicants could easily have dispelled the doubts voiced by the authorities, in particular by slightly changing the name of their association and by sacrificing, or amending, a single provision of the memorandum of association (…). Those alterations would not, in the Court's view, have had harmful consequences for the Union's existence as an association and would not have prevented its members from achieving the objectives they set for themselves. The Court would also point out that pluralism and democracy are, by the nature of things, based on a compromise that requires various concessions by individuals and groups of individuals. The latter must sometimes be prepared to limit some of their freedom so as to ensure the greater stability of the country as a whole."[8]

Therefore, although Article 10 has an important impact upon the interpretation of Article 11, this does not go so far as to amount to identical interpretation. The test applied by the Court is that of proportionality. In the *Sidiropoulos* Case the Court found a violation because the refusal to register the applicants' association was disproportionate to the objectives pursued. One of the aspects taken into account by the Court was the possibility under Greek law to dissolve the association whenever the association might pursue an aim contrary to law, morality or public order. This seems to point at a strict approach. The Court also held that the exceptions listed in Article 11, paragraph 2, are to be construed strictly: "only convincing and compelling reasons can justify restrictions on freedom of association".[9]

The Court's decisions in the *Gorzelik* Case and the *Sidiropoulos* Case, and the differences in outcome, can be explained from the fact that the Polish authorities were willing to register the association, however with some (small) changes, whereas in Greece the refusal was an absolute one. When no special circumstances are present justifying an absolute ban the Court will find it to be a disproportionate interference.

The Court has refrained from interpreting the right to freedom of expression and accordingly, to peaceful assembly, as creating automatic rights of access to private property or to all publicly owned property.[10] Nevertheless, the Court has not excluded that a positive obligation could arise for the State to protect the enjoyment of the rights guaranteed by Articles 10 and 11 by regulating property rights. Thus a ban on access to private or certain types of public property, which has the effect of preventing any effective exercise of the freedoms of expression and/or assembly, could possibly give rise to a violation of the Convention on the part of the State.

---

[8] Judgment of 20 December 2001, paras 65-66.
[9] Judgment of 10 July 1998, para. 40.
[10] Judgment of 6 May 2003, *Appleby and Others*, para. 47.

15.3 PEACEFUL ASSEMBLY

Although, as the Commission held, the right to freedom of peaceful assembly, like the right to freedom of expression, "is a fundamental right in a democratic society and (...) is one of the foundations of such a society",[11] freedom of assembly still has not played an important part in the Strasbourg case law.

In the *Ezelin* Case, which concerned a lawyer who had been disciplined for having participated in a peaceful assembly, the Court referred to "the special importance of freedom of peaceful assembly and freedom of expression, which are closely linked in this instance". The Court proceeded to apply *de facto* a test which has the same strictness as that applied in 'pure' freedom of expression cases. It held as follows: "The Court considers, however, that the freedom to take part in a peaceful assembly – in this instance a demonstration that had not been prohibited – is of such importance that it cannot be restricted in any way, even for an advocate, so long as the person concerned does not himself commit any reprehensible act on such an occasion."[12]

In the *Vogt* Case, the Court applied the criteria which it had elaborated in the context of freedom of expression, equally in order to review the compatibility with Article 11.[13] It may, therefore, safely be assumed that peaceful assemblies (including demonstrations) are to be judged on the basis of the same strict standards as other means of expression. It would seem to be preferable, however, that the Court formulates these strict standards *expressis verbis* for all freedoms and activities covered by Article 11.

The adjective 'peaceful' has restricted the scope of the protection offered by the first paragraph to a very large extent. If the authorities concerned could reasonably have believed that a planned assembly would not have a peaceful character or if this has become apparent during the assembly, its prohibition or restriction does not conflict with the first paragraph of Article 11. Consequently, the second paragraph need not be relied upon in that case and it is not, therefore, required that the prohibition or restriction be 'prescribed by law'. However, a peacefully organised demonstration that runs the risk of resulting in disorder by developments beyond the control of the organisers, for example through a violent counter-demonstration, does not for that reason fall outside the scope of Article 11 of the Convention.[14]

It is the Court itself that examines whether a State can claim that an assembly is or is not peaceful. In the *Stankov and the United Macedonian Organisation Ilinden* Case the government had disputed the applicability of Article 11 on the basis of its doubts

---

[11] Appl. 8191/78, *Rassemblement jurassien et Unité jurassienne*, D&R 17 (1980), p. 93 (119).
[12] Judgment of 26 April 1991, para. 53.
[13] Judgment of 26 September 1995, paras 64-65.
[14] Appl. 8440/78, *Christians against Racism and Fascism*, D&R 21 (1981), p. 138 (148); Appl. 10126/82, *Plattform Ärzte für das Leben*, D&R 44 (1985), p. 65 (72).

as to the peaceful character of the applicant association's meetings. The Court dismissed this argument and accepted applicability. It held that, "having carefully studied all the material before it, the Court does not find that those involved in the organisation of the prohibited meetings had violent intentions".[15] It may, therefore, be safely concluded that the Court indeed relates the applicability of Article 11 to the non-violent intentions of those involved in the assembly, and not of those not involved. The Court considers it also its duty to examine independently whether the assembly may be considered to be peaceful, i.e. to be based upon the non-violent intentions of the organisers.

Particularly with regard tot assemblies of a public character the above observations mean that they may be subjected to a system of periods. In the *Stankov* Case the Court laid down some criteria as to the standard of scrutiny in this respect and the balancing of interests. The standard of scrutiny relates to the link between Article 10 and Article 11 ("Article 11 must also be considered in the light of Article 10"). The Court held as follows: "Such a link is particularly relevant where – as here – the authorities' intervention against an assembly or an association was, at least in part, in reaction to views held or statements made by participants or members. Freedom of expression constitutes one of the essential foundations of a democratic society and one of the basic conditions for its progress and for each individual's self-fulfilment. Subject to paragraph 2 of Article 10, it is applicable not only to 'information' or 'ideas' that are favourably received or regarded as inoffensive or as a matter of indifference, but also to those that offend, shock or disturb. Such are the demands of pluralism, tolerance and broadmindedness without which there is no 'democratic society' (…). Likewise, the freedom of assembly as enshrined in Article 11 of the Convention protects a demonstration that may annoy or give offence to persons opposed to the ideas or claims that it is seeking to promote. The Court has to satisfy itself that the national authorities applied standards which were in conformity with the principles embodied in Article 11 and, moreover, that they based their decisions on an acceptable assessment of the relevant facts (…). There is little scope under Article 10 paragraph 2 of the Convention for restrictions on political speech or on debate on questions of public interest (…). One of the principal characteristics of democracy is the possibility it offers of resolving a country's problems through dialogue, without recourse to violence, even when those problems are irksome. Democracy thrives on freedom of expression. From that point of view, there can be no justification for hindering a group solely because it seeks to debate in public the situation of part of the State's population and to find, according to democratic rules, solutions capable of satisfying everyone concerned (…). An essential factor to be taken into consideration is the question whether there has been a call for the use of violence, an uprising or any other form

---

[15]   Judgment of 20 December 2001, para. 78.

of rejection of democratic principles."[16] This description of the level of scrutiny and the criteria that might be relevant (non-violence, open public debate, reluctance to accept content related control) are similar to the ones under Article 10, although the Court has shown itself to be aware of the special circumstances related to assemblies.

In the *Stankov* Case the Court left open the general question of which requirements have to be met by the national authorities when imposing a system of permits.[17] In any case, if the adjective 'peaceful' allows for the use of a standard that does not need to be covered by the restrictions of the second paragraph, such a system of permits and its application may then only relate to that peaceful character and must not affect the right of assembly as such. The latter, for instance, is the case if the prohibition has a general character or concerns a very wide category of assemblies.[18] One of the factors taken into account by the Court in the *Stankov* Case was "the practice of imposing sweeping bans on Ilinden's meetings".[19] In general, it may be assumed that the more general the ban, the less likely that it will respond to a pressing social need.

In the *Djavit* Case the Court found a violation of Article 11 because of the repeated refusal on the part of the Turkish authorities to allow the applicant to cross the 'green line' in order to participate in bi-communal meetings with Greek Cypriots. As at the time of the events complained of there was no law applicable regulating the issuance of permits to Turkish Cypriots living in northern Cyprus to cross the 'buffer zone' into southern Cyprus in order to engage in peaceful bi-communal assemblies, the Court concluded that the interference with the applicant's exercise of his freedom of assembly was not 'prescribed by law' and therefore, could not be justified by concerns pertaining to security reasons and public interest.[20]

The prohibition may also not be of such a nature that an independent means of expression is thus in fact excluded altogether for one or more groups. This requirement also seems to flow from the link between Article 10 and Article 11 and the implied necessity to see to it that minority views are also protected. In that respect the Court held in the *Stankov* Case as follows: "The national authorities must display particular vigilance to ensure that national public opinion is not protected at the expense of the assertion of minority views no matter how unpopular they may be".[21] This flows from the need to protect also those opinions that offend, shock or disturb.

In the aforementioned *Ezelin* Case the Court was confronted with a demonstration that had not been prohibited, but during which some disturbances had occurred. The

---

[16]   *Ibidem*, paras 85-90.
[17]   In the context of Article 10 prior control may also be exercised by the authorities. However, "the dangers inherent in prior restraints are such that they call for the most careful scrutiny on the part of the Court"; judgment of 26 November 1991, *The Sunday Times (No. 2)*, para. 51.
[18]   Appl. 8440/78, *Christians against Racism and Fascism*, D&R 21 (1981), p. 138 and Appl. 8191/78, *Rassemblement jurassien et Unité jurassienne*, D&R 17 (1980), p. 93.
[19]   Judgment of 2 October 2001, para. 109.
[20]   Judgment of 20 February 2003, para. 18.
[21]   *Ibidem*, para. 107.

applicant had been disciplined for not having dissociated himself from offensive and insulting acts committed by other demonstrators.[22] From the position adopted by the Court in that case it may be concluded, in the first place, that an individual participating in an assembly that has not been prohibited cannot afterwards be confronted with allegations that he took part in a non-peaceful assembly that lacks the protection of Article 11. Secondly, an individual participant enjoys the full protection of Article 11 ("his right cannot be restricted in any way") as long as he abstains from non-peaceful behaviour.

Article 11 also imposes on national authorities an obligation to safeguard the right of assembly of aliens without legal residence status in the country in which the assembly takes place, provided their protest is of a peaceful nature. In the *Cisse* Case the applicant was an illegal immigrant who together with a group of aliens took collective action to draw attention to the difficulties they were experiencing in obtaining a review of their immigration status in France. With the acquiescence of parish authorities the group occupied a church for nearly two months. Eventually the church premises were forcefully evacuated by the police as there had been a marked deterioration of sanitary conditions. The Court held that the fact that the applicant was an illegal immigrant did not suffice to justify a breach of her freedom of assembly. And although the Court regretted the intervention methods used by the police, which were deemed to have gone beyond what was reasonable for the authorities to do when curtailing the freedom of assembly, in the particular circumstances of the case it was concluded that the interference complained of was necessary and proportionate to the purposes of paragraph 2 of Article 11.[23]

15.4 ASSOCIATION

15.4.1 AUTONOMOUS MEANING

An autonomous meaning is to be assigned to the word 'association'. The legal form chosen and the legal consequences attached thereto by national law cannot be decisive here, since otherwise the guarantee of Article 11 might be rendered illusory by the national legislature, and great differences in scope of that guarantee might exist among the legal systems of the various Contracting States. In the *Chassagnou* Case the Court stated as follows: "The term 'association' therefore possesses an autonomous meaning: the classification in national law has only relative value and constitutes no more than a starting point."[24] A brief definition was given by the Court in the *Gorzelik* Case,

---

[22]   Judgment of 26 April 1991, para. 53.
[23]   Judgment of 9 April 2002, para. 53.
[24]   Judgment of 29 April 1999, para. 100.

discussed *supra*. The Court held as follows: "The Court recalls at the outset that the right to form an association is inherent in the right laid down in Article 11, even if that provision only makes express reference to the right to form trade unions. The most important aspect of the right to freedom of association is that citizens should be able to create a legal entity in order to act collectively in a field of mutual interests. Without this, that right would have no meaning."[25]

An association is a legal entity, intended to operate as such in a specific area. The right to freedom of association implies the right to form one and it includes the right not to be forced to be a member of an association.[26] An inherent part of the freedom of association is the recognition of the association as a legal entity. Therefore refusals of registration are fully covered by the scope of Article 11.

By expressly mentioning the trade unions in Article 11, the drafters obviously wanted to put it beyond doubt that the right to trade union freedom falls under the protection of this provision, irrespective of whether according to national law a trade union can be considered an association. As the Court puts it: "the right to form and join trade unions in Article 11 is an aspect of the wider right to freedom of association".[27] That political parties also fall under the term 'association' was implicitly assumed by the Commission in its *KPD* decision,[28] and subsequently also by the Court in the *Vogt* Case, in which it found that the dismissal of the applicant from a post as a civil servant on the ground that she had persistently refused to dissociate herself from the KDP, constituted an interference with the right protected by paragraph 1 of Article 11.[29] More recently the Court was confronted with various political party cases, which will be dealt with in greater detail hereafter in sub-paragraph 11.3.2.

The *Vogt* Case also indicates that the freedom of association is involved when an individual has been punished, harassed or otherwise sanctioned or treated unfavourably because of his or her membership of an association. Similarly, the Court decided in the *Grande Oriente d'Italia di Palazzo Giustiani* Case that Article 11 was violated by requiring that candidates for public functions declare themselves not to be members of the Free Masons. The Court does not accept such an infringement, where membership of legal organisations is at stake; it considers this to be a disproportional restriction to discourage those running for public office from being a member of legal organisations.[30] In a parallel case the Court concluded that Article 11 had been violated because the requirement for judges to dissociate themselves from the Free Masons had

---

[25]   Judgment of 20 December 2001, para. 55.
[26]   An example of the latter aspect, outside the area of trade-unions, to be discussed *infra*, is the judgment of 29 April 1999, *Chassagnou*, para. 103.
[27]   See, *e.g.*, the judgment of 30 June 1993, *Sigurdur A. Sigurjónsson*, para. 32.
[28]   Appl. 250/57, *Kommunistische Partei Deutschland*, Yearbook I (1955-1957), p. 222.
[29]   Judgment of 26 September 1995, para. 65. The respondent Government had not contested the applicability of Article 11.
[30]   Judgment of 2 August 2001, paras 25-26.

not been laid down in a law, as required under paragraph 2 of Article 11.[31] Recently, the Court confirmed its previous decisions finding a violation of Article 11 on the basis of the lack of foreseeability of existing Italian law aimed at regulating the exercise of judicial functions on the part of members of the Free Masons.[32]

15.4.2 VOLUNTARY ORGANISATION: PRIVATE VERSUS PUBLIC ASSOCIATIONS

In the *Young, James and Webster* Case, in respect of one of the allegations of the British Government, the Commission took the position that the term 'association' presupposes a voluntary organisation for a common purpose, and that there was no such organisation in the case of the mere relationship among employees of the same employer, since that relationship is based on the contractual connection between the employee and the employer.[33] In its decision in *Association X v. Sweden* the Commission gave the following definition of 'freedom of association': "a general capacity for the citizens to join without interference by the State in associations in order to attain various ends".[34] It may, therefore, be assumed that this freedom includes any voluntary association by several natural and/or legal persons for a certain period of time with an institutional structure and for common purposes.[35]

A professional organisation established by the Government and governed by public law, which as a rule is intended not only to protect the interests of the members, but also certain public interests, is not an 'association' in the sense of Article 11. The Commission and the Court adopted this opinion in the *Le Compte, Van Leuven and De Meyere* Case with regard to the Belgian *Ordre des médecins*. On the other hand, Article 11 was considered to be involved if the existence of such a public law institution ruled out the voluntary association of the colleagues in question in private professional organisations.[36] In the aforementioned *Sigurdur A. Sigurjónsson* Case the Court explicitly answered the question whether the 'trade union' involved ('Frami') was a public-law association outside the ambit of Article 11 or a private-law association

---

[31] Judgment of 2 August 2001, *N.F. v. Italy*, paras 31-32.
[32] Judgment of 17 February 2004, *Maestri*.
[33] Report of 14 December 1979, B.39 (1984), p. 47.
[34] Appl. 6094/73, D&R 9 (1978), p. 5 (7).
[35] In Appl. 7729/76, *Agee*, D&R 7 (1977), p. 164 (174), a former CIA agent invoked for his complaint against his expulsion, *inter alia*, Article 11, referring to his regular contacts in England with foreign intelligence agents. The Commission here left open the question of whether such a loose relation could still be considered as an association. In its decision on Appl. 8317/78, *McFeeley*, D&R 20 (1980), p. 44 (97-98), however, the Commission submitted that freedom of association 'does not concern the right of prisoners to share the company of other prisoners or to "associate" with other prisoners in this sense'.
[36] Report of 14 December 1979, B.39 (1984), p. 23 and judgment of 23 June 1981, paras 64-66, respectively. *See* also the judgment of 10 February 1983, *Albert and Le Compte*, para. 44.

within the meaning of this article. It held as follows: "Frami performed certain functions which were to some extent provided for in the applicable legislation and which served not only its members but also the public at large (...). However, the role of supervision of the implementation of the relevant rules was entrusted primarily to another institution, namely the Committee, which in addition had the power to issue licences and to decide on their suspension and revocation (...). Frami was established under private law and enjoyed full autonomy in determining its own aims, organisation and procedure. According to its Articles, admittedly old and under revision, the purpose of Frami was to protect the professional interests of its members and promote solidarity among professional taxicab drivers; to determine, negotiate and present demands relating to the working hours, wages and rates of its members; to seek to maintain limitations on the number of taxicabs and to represent its members before the public authorities (...). Frami was therefore predominantly a private-law organisation and must thus be considered an 'association' for the purposes of Article 11."[37]

Here the Court explicitly referred to the distinction between private and public associations. Recently, in the *Chassagnou* Case, the Court also referred to this distinction. The Government had claimed that the associations in question were "public law para-administrative institutions whose internal governing bodies admittedly resembled those of associations, but whose constitution clearly distinguished them from ordinary associations, since they were subject to a mixed legal regime containing elements of both private and public law." The Court, after having noted that the term association has an autonomous meaning, specifically looked into the private law and public law aspects. It remarked in that respect that the hunters' associations (ACCAs) "owe their existence to the will of parliament, but (...) that they are nevertheless associations set up in accordance with the Law of 1 July 1901, and are composed of hunters or the owners of land or hunting rights, and therefore of private individuals, all of whom, a priori, wish to pool their land for the purpose of hunting. Similarly, the fact that the prefect supervises the way these associations operate is not sufficient to support the contention that they remain integrated within the structures of the State (...). Furthermore, it cannot be maintained that under the Loi Verdell ACCAs enjoy prerogatives outside the orbit of the ordinary law, whether administrative, rule making or disciplinary, or that they employ processes of a public authority, like professional organisations."[38]

The present model, adopted and applied by the Court in the *Sigurdur A. Sigurjónsson* Case, serves to carefully examine the dominant features of an association

---

[37]   Judgment of 30 June 1993, para. 31.
[38]   Judgment of 29 April 1999, paras 98-101.

in order to determine its public or private law aspects.[39] In this respect it is an autonomous concept; the Court, as confirmed in the *Chassagnou* Case, carefully looks for predominant private law or public law characteristics.

15.4.3 POLITICAL PARTIES

In a number of cases the Court was confronted with complaints pertaining to bans and dissolutions of political parties. In dealing with these complaints the Court invariably referred to the essential role of political parties in ensuring pluralism and the proper functioning of democracy, and, consequently, adopted a very strict approach vis-à-vis the necessity of any restrictions on the freedom of association of political parties protected by Article 11 of the Convention. The basic principles concerning the interpretation of Article 11 with regard to political parties were laid down in several judgments against Turkey: the *United Communist Party of Turkey* Case,[40] the *Socialist Party* Case,[41] the *Freedom and Democracy Party (ÖZDEP)* Case,[42] and the *Refah Partisi (Prosperity Party)* Case.[43] These cases involved sensitive issues pertaining to considerations of national security, territorial integrity, the protection of minorities and the maintenance of political and social order.

In the *Freedom and Democracy Party (ÖZDEP)* Case the Court held that, although the political design proposed by the party concerned could be considered incompatible with the current principles and structures of the Turkish State, this in itself did not mean that it infringed democratic rules. The Court reasoned that it was of the essence of democracy to allow diverse political projects to be proposed and debated, even those

---

[39] The distinction between public and private law did not receive any attention from the Commission in a number of previous cases in which compulsory membership was at issue. Thus, in a case involving the compulsory membership of the *Landbouwschap,* a Dutch public agricultural organisation, the Commission confined itself to the general observation that this organisation formed part of "an elaborate system for organising effectively the economic life of the country", and that the challenged system of organisation was not contrary to the Convention; Appl. 2290/64, *X v. the Netherlands,* Coll. 22 (1967), p. 28 (32). And for dairy farmers the compulsory membership of a health service was accepted without any further argument; Appl. 1068/61, *X v. the Netherlands,* Yearbook V (1962), p. 278 (284). In *Association X v. Sweden,* the Commission considered it to be characteristic of a professional organisation that it "upholds ethics and discipline within the profession or defends its members' interests in outside disputes", and of a trade union that it "shall represent [its members] in a labour conflict situation against an employer", (Appl. 6094/73, D&R 9 (1978), p. 5 (8)). This served to show that a students' association belongs to neither of the two categories. With respect to a complaint that membership of a particular students' association was required for admission to a certain university, the Commission adopted the view that this association was to be regarded as part of the university, a State institution, so that Article 11 was not applicable. (Ibidem).

[40] Judgment of 30 January 1998, paras 42-47.

[41] Judgment of 15 May 1998, paras 41-50.

[42] Judgment of 8 December 1998, paras 37-48.

[43] Judgment of 31 July 2001, paras 64-84.

which called into question the way a State was organised – its constitutional and legal order – provided they did not harm democracy itself. It was further considered that there could be no justification for hindering a political group solely because it sought to initiate dialogue about irksome national issues (i.e. the Kurdish question) as long as the group did not propagate or take recourse to violence.

On similar grounds the Court found a violation of Article 11 in the *United Community Party of Turkey* and the *Socialist Party* Cases. It was held that only convincing and compelling reasons could justify restrictions on political parties' freedom of association. Any restrictions would not be justified if (i) a party is promoting change, which, although bearing on the existing structures of the State and its established order, is in itself compatible with fundamental democratic principles, and (ii) the means proposed to effectuate such change are legal and democratic.

The general principles developed by the Court in the aforementioned judgments were further elaborated in the more recent case of *Refah Partisi (Prosperity Party)*. Great emphasis was placed on the examination of the existence of a 'pressing social need', which according to the Court was of fundamental importance to the determination of the necessity of State interference with the freedom of association. The Court considered that in order to establish whether the refusal to register the political party concerned met a pressing social need, it had to examine: (i) whether the risk to democracy was sufficiently imminent, (ii) whether the acts and speeches of the leaders of the party under consideration, on the basis of which the party's freedom of association had been restricted, could be imputed to the party itself, and (iii) whether the acts and speeches imputable to the party constituted a whole, which gave a clear picture of the model of society advocated by the party, and whether this model was compatible with the concept of 'democratic society'. The overall analysis in this regard, according to the Court, had to also take into account the historical context in which a refusal to register a given party had taken place. In light of Refah Partisi's plans to establish a plurality of legal systems in which a sharia-based regime would be re-introduced in the Turkish State and the failure of Refah's leaders to dissociate themselves from members of the party who publicly called for the use of force, the Court found that the refusal of the authorities to register the party was necessary as it served a pressing social need. Refraining from expressing an opinion in the abstract on the advantages and disadvantages of a plurality of legal systems, the Court considered that the re-introduction of a sharia-based regime would be incompatible with the democratic principles on which the Convention is based. Furthermore, taking into account the political momentum, which Refah Partisi was gaining, the Court deemed justified the national authorities' restrictions imposed on the party as there was a highly likely prospect that Refah would win the forthcoming general elections.

The reasoning developed in Refah Partisi was confirmed by the Court in the *Partidul Comunistilor (Nepeceristi) and Ungureanu* Case.[44] However, in this case Romania was found in violation of Article 11 for its refusal to register the party concerned without there being any pressing social need justifying the restriction imposed.

The Court has also pronounced on national regulations imposing restrictions on the political activities of civil servants, members of the armed forces and the police, members of the judiciary and other members of the public service. Unlike the judgments discussed *supra*, these cases concerned general bans on the participation of specific persons or groups in political parties rather than restrictions on the activities of parties themselves.

The *Ahmed* Case concerned a regulation imposing restrictions on civil servants' activities in the political parties of which they were members. The Court found this particular interference with the right protected under Article 11 (as it also did with respect to Article 10) to be justified and proportionate. It based its conlusion on the fact that the regulation concerned was limited to restricting the extent of the applicants' participation in an administrative and representative capacity in the political parties of which they were members but it did not restrict their right to join any political party of their choosing.[45] In the *Rekvényi* Case[46] the Court dealt with a fully fledged prohibition on members of the army, the police and the security forces from participating in politics and being members of political parties. In this case the Court – rather remarkably – reasoned that the restriction concerned was intended to depoliticise the police and security services and thereby, to contribute to the conso-lidation and maintanance of pluralistic democracy. As such the prohibition com-plained of was considered by the Court to be compatible with democratic principles. Special emphasis was placed on Hungary's totalitarian past where the ruling regime to a great extent relied on the direct commitment of the army, police, and security forces.

The second sentence of paragraph 2 of Article 11, authorising lawful restrictions with regard to members of the armed forces, of the police, or of the administration of the State, however, does not apply to members of parliament or to members of the elected bodies of local authorities. In the *Ždanoka* Case the Court found that the applicant's disqualification from standing for election to parliament and local councils on account of her active participation in the Communist Party of Latvia, maintained more than a decade after the events held against that party, was disproportionate to the aim pursued (i.e. the protection of national security) and, consequently, not neces-

---

[44]   Judgment of 3 February 2005, paras 50-60.
[45]   Judgment of 2 September 1998, para. 70.
[46]   Judgment of 20 May 1999, paras 46-50.

sary in a democratic society.[47] The Court concluded that there had been a violation of Article 11 on the part of the Latvian State in this regard.

15.4.4   TRADE UNIONS

It is remarkable that Article 11 mentions only with respect to trade unions the right to *form* an association. However, it was held in the *Gorzelik* Case, discussed *supra*, that this aspect is implied in the freedom of association as such. Indeed, if people want to associate in a new association, the right to set up an association forms a necessary condition for the exercise of the freedom of association.

Since Article 11 refers to 'the right (...) to join trade unions', the question arises whether this implies at the same time protection against compulsory membership. This is important in particular with regard to the practice of compulsory trade union membership, the so-called 'closed shop' system. From the *travaux préparatoires* of Article 11 one might conclude that the drafters did not intend to prohibit such a practice.[48] The Commission, however, opined as early as in its decision on *X v. Belgium* that "the very concept of freedom of association with others also implies freedom not to associate with others or not to join unions".[49] In that case the Commission held the complaint on this point to be manifestly ill-founded. In later cases the Commission characterised this problem as very complex and declared admissible complaints concerning compulsory membership of a professional organisation or a trade union.[50]

In the first two of these cases the question was not examined any further, because the Commission and the Court held that the professional association in question was not an association in the sense of Article 11.[51] In the *Young, James and Webster* Case, however, the question of compulsory membership was discussed at length. There the complaint concerned the discharge of the applicants on account of their refusal to join a trade union. Both the Commission and the Court considered the *travaux préparatoires* not decisive for answering the question of whether the closed-shop system was contrary to Article 11.[52] Both organs, however, avoided making a general pronouncement on the compatibility of the closed-shop system with Article 11, but confined themselves to holding that Article 11 had been violated in this particular case. The Court left open the question of whether compulsory membership of a trade union

---

[47]   Judgment of 17 June 2004, para. 110.
[48]   *See* the quotation in the judgment of 13 August 1981, *Young, James and Webster*, para. 52.
[49]   Appl. 4072/69, Yearbook XIII (1970), p. 708 (718). *See* also Appl. 9926/82, *X v. the Netherlands*, D&R 32 (1983), p. 274 (280).
[50]   Appl. 6878/75, *Le Compte v. Belgium*, Yearbook XX (1977), p. 254 (276); Appl. 7238/75, *Van Leuven and De Meyere v. Belgium*, Yearbook XX (1977), p. 348 (368); and Appl. 7601/76, *Young and James v. the United Kingdom*, Yearbook XX (1977), p. 520 (564).
[51]   See *supra* 15.4.2.
[52]   Report of 14 December 1979, B.39 (1984), p. 46; judgment of 13 August 1981, para. 52.

is always contrary to Article 11, but regarded the threat of discharge for those who did not wish to join a given union as a form of coercion which affects the essence of the freedom guaranteed in Article 11. The Court also took into account that the compulsory membership had been introduced after the applicants had entered into employment, while it also referred to the fact that the number of unions from which they could choose was extremely limited.[53] Finally, the Court expressed as its opinion that the compulsion imposed on the applicants could not be deemed to be 'necessary in a democratic society' in the sense of the second paragraph.[54] In the same case the Court also assigned to Article 11 a certain *Drittwirkung* by recognising the liability of the British authorities for a violation by an enterprise of Article 11 such as was at issue here. Practices like those complained of in this case are therefore prohibited under Article 11, regardless of whether they are imposed by the authorities or not, and can be put forward in Strasbourg whenever the national legislation of the respondent State allows such practices.[55]

In 1993, in the *Sigurdur A. Sigurjónsson* Case, the Court went beyond its *Young, James and Webster* judgment by concluding that "Article 11 must be viewed as encompassing a negative right of association".[56] It, however, did not go so far as to accept a full-blown substantive negative right of association, because the Court added that it "is not necessary for the Court to determine in this instance whether this right is to be considered on an equal footing with the positive right".[57] The most important reason for the Court to accept in principle the negative right of association was the emergence of common ground at the international level and in the legal orders of the Contracting States as to the recognition and protection of the negative right of association. The Court devoted much attention to many international treaties and recommendations as well as to national legislation: "Compulsory membership of this nature, which, it may be recalled, concerned a private-law association, does not exist under the laws of the great majority of the Contracting States. On the contrary, a large number of domestic systems contain safeguards which, in one way or another, guarantee the negative aspect of the freedom of association, that is the freedom not to join or to

---

[53]   Judgment of 13 August 1981, paras 53-56.
[54]   *Ibidem,* para. 29.
[55]   See *infra* 15.5. In the *Sibson* Case the Court stuck to its opinion that Article 11 does not *per se* prohibit a compulsion to join a particular trade union; only a form of such compulsion which strikes at the very substance of the freedom of association guaranteed by Article 11 constitutes an interference. In the particular case the Court concluded that the applicant "was not subjected to a form of treatment striking at the very substance of the freedom of association guaranteed by Article 11"; judgment of 20 April 1993, para. 29. An important distinction with the *Young, James and Webster* Case was that the three applicants in the latter case were faced with a threat of dismissal involving loss of livelihood, whereas for Mr Sibson alternative employment was available with no significantly less favourable working conditions.
[56]   Judgment of 30 June 1993, para. 35.
[57]   *Ibidem.*

withdraw from an association. A growing measure of common ground has also emerged in this area at the international level. As observed by the Commission, in addition to the above mentioned Article 20 para. 2 of the Universal Declaration (...), Article 11 para. 2 of the Community Charter of the Fundamental Social Rights of Workers adopted by the Heads of State or Government of eleven member States of the European Communities on 9 December 1989, provides that every employer and every worker shall have the freedom to join or not to join professional organisations or trade unions without any personal or occupational damage being thereby suffered by them. Moreover, on 24 September 1991 the Parliamentary Assembly of the Council of Europe unanimously adopted a recommendation, amongst other things, to insert a sentence to this effect into Article 5 of the 1961 European Social Charter (...). Even in the absence of an express provision, the Committee of Independent Experts set up to supervise the implementation of the Charter considers that a negative right is covered by this instrument and it has in several instances disapproved of closed-shop practices found in certain States Parties, including Iceland. With regard to the latter, the Committee took account of, *inter alia*, the facts of the present case (...). Following this, the Governmental Committee of the European Social Charter issued a warning to Iceland (...). Furthermore, according to the practice of the Freedom of Association Committee of the Governing Body of the International Labour Office (ILO), union security measures imposed by law, notably by making union membership compulsory, would be incompatible with the Conventions Nos. 87 and 98".[58]

On that basis the Court concluded that Article 11 had been violated, because the applicant ran a risk of losing his taxi-licence as a result of his unwillingness to become a member of a specific private-law association. The Court also attached importance to the fact that the applicant objected to being a member of the association in question "partly because he disagreed with its policy in favour of limiting the number of taxicabs and, thus, access to the occupation". This aspect led the Court to consider Article 11 also "in the light of Articles 9 and 10", and to the conclusion that the very essence of Article 11 had been infringed.[59]

Summing up it may be concluded that the Strasbourg case-law has now recognised that Article 11 also protects the freedom not to join an association or trade union. Recent developments in the Court's case law have brought Article 11 in this respect in line with other international instruments. The negative right of association is not only interfered with after a dismissal, but also when other serious 'sanctions' have been imposed, or in case the individual's refusal to become a member is inspired by personal convictions or opinions. In the latter case the protection offered by Article 11 gathers strength because of the direct link it presents with Articles 9 and 10.

---

[58]   *Ibidem.*
[59]   *Ibidem*, para. 37.

15.4.5 OTHER TRADE UNION RIGHTS

The case law has gradually refined the right to freedom of association – and in particular that of trade union freedom – in the sense that this right now also includes those rights and freedoms which are important for its enjoyment.

Above the example has been given of the right to *form* an association.[60] In its decision in *X v. Ireland* the Commission, referring to Convention No. 87 of the International Labour Organisation, held that the freedom of association concerned not only an unobstructed membership, but that intimidation of an employee to make him relinquish his function within the trade union might likewise constitute an encroachment on this freedom.[61] In the aforementioned *Vogt* Case the Court held that the dismissal of the applicant from a post as a civil servant because she had refused to dissociate herself from a particular political party constituted a violation of Article 11.[62] Reference should also be made here to the cases discussed *supra*: the *Grande Oriente d'Italia* Case and *N.F. v. Italy*, as well as the *Ahmed* Case and the *Rekvényi* Case: all cases in which there was a relationship between membership of and involvement in a political party, and status as a public official. In its decision in the *Van der Heijden* Case the Commission likewise gave as its opinion that a court decision terminating an employee's contract because of his activity in a political party constituted an interference with the exercise of the right guaranteed by this provision. In this case the Commission concluded that the interference could be held to be necessary in a democratic society for the protection of the rights of others, as the political party in question was known to have objectives opposed to those of the employer, a foundation concerned with the welfare of immigrants.[63]

On the other hand, the State must protect the individual against abuse by associations of their dominant position. Expulsion from a trade union in breach of the union's rules or on the basis of arbitrary rules, or entailing exceptional hardship for the individual concerned, may constitute such an abuse.[64]

In principle the right to form trade unions involves the right of trade unions to draw up their own rules, to administer their own affairs and to establish and join trade union federations. Such trade union rights are explicitly recognised in Articles 3 and 5 of ILO Convention No. 87, which must be taken into account in the context of Article 11. Accordingly, in principle trade union decisions in these domains must not be subject to restrictions and control by the State except on the basis of the second paragraph of Article 11.[65]

---

[60] See *supra* 15.4.1.
[61] Appl. 4125/69, Yearbook XIV (1971), p. 198 (222).
[62] Judgment of 26 September 1995, para. 65.
[63] Appl. 11002/84, D&R 41 (1985), p. 264 (271).
[64] Appl. 10550/83, *Cheall*, D&R 42 (1985), p. 178 (186).
[65] *Ibidem*, p. 185.

In three judgments concerning trade union freedom, on the basis of the words 'for the protection of his interests' in paragraph 1, the Court took the position that this freedom entitles the union members to a union that is able to serve their interests as workers. It is, therefore, incumbent on the authorities to allow the unions sufficient scope in this respect. This implies, for instance, that the trade union must be heard by the authorities in order that it may be able to stand up for those interests, although the Court held that this obligation does not necessarily take the specific form that the authorities have to consult the unions before taking certain decisions,[66] or that the authorities as employers are obliged to conclude a collective agreement with a particular union.[67] With regard to other employers, too, Article 11 does not entail a *right* for trade unions to conclude collective agreements, which the authorities would then be obliged to uphold, but only the *freedom* to conclude them, which the authorities must help to make possible.[68] If one were to assume such a *right,* to be upheld by the authorities, a more far-reaching obligation would be construed than the Contracting States have undertaken under Article 6(2) of the European Social Charter, *viz.*: "to promote, where necessary and appropriate, machinery for voluntary negotiations between employers and employers' organizations and workers' organizations, with a view to the regulation of terms and conditions of employment by means of collective agreements."[69]

In the *Gustafsson* Case the Court referred to Article 6 of the European Social Charter in order to deem protected trade union activities that were aimed at forcing an employer to submit himself to a system of collective agreements.[70] The employer concerned alleged that he had suffered considerable losses because of trade union action, consisting of a boycott. The Court argued that the union action pursued legitimate interests consistent with Article 11. With respect to the right not to enter into a collective agreement, alleged by the applicant, the Court held that Article 11 does not as such guarantee the negative right not to participate in collective bargaining. Thus, the Court seemed to draw such conclusions from the fact that, in its opinion, Article 11 does not guarantee a positive right to participate in collective bargaining either. The Court also concluded that the freedom of association had not been significantly affected to such an extent as to conclude that it had been violated.[71] Judge Martens dissented from the Court's reasoning and against the outcome. He observed that the freedom to negotiate labour agreements is necessarily inherent in the freedom

---

66   Judgment of 27 October 1975, *National Union of Belgian Police,* para. 39.
67   Judgment of 6 February 1976, *Swedish Engine Drivers' Union,* paras 39-40. The same applies to the collective bargaining as such: Appl. 7361/76, *Trade Union X v. Belgium,* D&R 14 (1979), p. 40 (47).
68   *See,* for example, Appl. 9792/82, *Association A v. Federal Republic of Germany,* D&R 34 (1983), p. 173 (174).
69   Thus the Court in its judgment of 6 February 1976, *Swedish Engine Drivers' Union,* para. 39.
70   Judgment of 25 April 1996, para. 53.
71   *Ibidem,* para. 52.

of association. In this respect he referred to Articles 5 and 6 of the European Social Charter and the findings of the Committee of Independent Experts, as well as to the conclusions of the ILO Committee on Freedom of Association.[72]

More recently the Court upheld its previous decisions maintaining that collective bargaining is not indispensable for the effective enjoyment of trade union freedom.[73] Employers are under no obligation to either recognise a trade union or accept compulsory collective bargaining. Irrespective of the wide margin of appreciation which States enjoy in deciding how union freedom may be secured, this freedom must however be effective. In the *Wilson, National Union of Journalists and Others* Case the Court held that by permitting employers to use financial incentives to induce employees to surrender union rights, in particular to acquiesce to the termination of their exisiting collective bargaining agreement, the State has failed in its positive obligation to secure the enjoyment of the rights protected by Article 11.[74]

Strikes are considered by the Strasbourg organs as a very important, but not an exclusive means for union members to protect their interests. Referring to the European Social Charter, the Court held that a right to strike, assuming that it is protected by Article 11, may be subjected to restrictions by the national legislature.[75] The authorities have to leave the trade unions sufficient scope to stand up for the interests of the affiliated employees, since trade union freedom would otherwise be illusory, but it is largely for the authorities to decide the means which they allow unions tot have tot achieve this end.

15.5 POSITIVE OBLIGATIONS/HORIZONTAL EFFECT

It is established case-law that the Convention does not merely oblige the authorities of the Contracting States to respect the rights and freedoms embodied in it, but in addition requires them to secure the enjoyment of these rights and freedoms by preventing and remedying any breach thereof, and that, therefore, the obligation to secure the effective exercise of Convention rights may involve positive obligations on the part of the State, even involving the adoption of measures in the sphere of the relations between individuals. On that basis the Court took the view that the right to freedom of assembly includes the right to protection against counter-demonstrators, because it is only in this way that its effective exercise can be secured to groups wishing to demonstrate with regard to highly controversial issues. If the protection provided by

---

[72]   Dissenting opinion of judge Martens.
[73]   Judgment of 2 July 2002, para. 44.
[74]   *Ibidem*, para. 48.
[75]   Judgment of 6 February 1976, *Schmidt and Dahlström*, para. 36.

the authorities proves to be insufficient to enable a free exercise of the right to freedom of assembly, this amounts to a restriction which has to be reviewed for its justification on the basis of the second paragraph.

Thus, in the *Plattform Ärzte für das Leben* Case the Court reviewed the measures taken to protect the two demonstrations involved against interference by counter-demonstrators for their reasonableness and appropriateness to enable the demonstrations to proceed peacefully. The Court held that the participants of a demonstration must "be able to hold the demonstration without having to fear that they will be subjected to physical violence by their opponents; such a fear would be liable to deter associations or other groups supporting common ideas or interests from openly expressing their opinions on highly controversial issues affecting the community. In a democracy the right to counter-demonstrate cannot extend to inhibiting the exercise of the right to demonstrate". The Court concluded from this that "Genuine, effective freedom of peaceful assembly cannot, therefore, be reduced to a mere duty on the part of the State not to interfere: a purely negative conception would not be compatible with the object and purposes of Article 11. Like Article 8, Article 11 sometimes requires positive measures to be taken, even in the sphere of relations between individuals, if need be".[76] With respect to the content of these measures, the Court held that the Contracting States have a wide discretion in the choice of the means to be used.[77]

The same approach had been taken by the Court in the *Young, James and Webster* Case,[78] and has been continued in more recent cases. In the *Sibson* Case the Court reiterated that even if a case involves no direct interference on the part of the State, the responsibility of the State would nevertheless be engaged if the infringement of the rights under Article 11 resulted from a failure on its part to secure those rights in its domestic law.[79]

In the *Gustafsson* Case the Court further elaborated upon its approach to accept State responsibility in the case of infringements committed by private individuals. The issue in dispute was the permissibility of union action against the applicant's business in order to force him to meet the union's demand to become a party to a collective agreement. The Court laid down the following general principles in this respect: "The matters complained of by the applicant, although they were made possible by national law, did not involve a direct intervention by the State. The responsibility of Sweden would nevertheless be engaged if those matters resulted from a failure on its part to secure from harm under domestic law the rights set forth in Article 11 of the Convention (...). Although the essential object of Article 11 is to protect the individual

---

[76]   Judgment of 21 June 1988, para. 32.
[77]   *Ibidem*, para. 34.
[78]   Judgment of 13 August 1981, para. 52.
[79]   Judgment of 20 April 1993, para. 27.

against arbitrary interferences by the public authorities with his or her exercise of the rights protected there may in addition be positive obligations to secure the effective employment of these rights. (...) national authorities may, in certain circumstances be obliged to intervene in the relationships between private individuals by taking reasonable and appropriate measures to secure the effective enjoyment of the negative right to freedom of association (...). In view of the sensitive character of the social and political issues involved in achieving a proper balance between the competing interests and, in particular, in assessing the appropriateness of State intervention to restrict union action aimed at extending a system of collective bargaining, and the wide degree of divergence between the domestic systems in the particular area under consideration, the Contracting States should enjoy a wide margin of appreciation in their choice of the means to be employed".[80]

In Article 11, paragraph 1, the words 'for the protection of his interests' are grammatically exclusively related to the trade union freedom, not to the freedom of association in general. However, associations other than trade unions are also set up precisely for the promotion and protection of common interests, and it may, therefore, be concluded with regard also to those associations that, lest the freedom of association should be illusory, once they have been set up, the authorities have the obligation to leave them sufficient scope to function as associations. It is self-evident that Article 11 does not guarantee that the objectives of an association are actually realised,[81] but efforts to that end must not be interfered with, except on the basis of the restrictions set forth in the second paragraph.[82]

From this obligation of the authorities ensues a *Drittwirkung* also in relation to associations in general. The Court had at first expressly left undecided the question as to "the applicability, whether direct or indirect, of Article 11 to relations between individuals *strictu sensu*".[83] However, the Court's position that "the Convention requires (...) that under national law trade unions should be enabled, in conditions

---

[80] Judgment of 25 April 1996, para. 45.

[81] Appl. 6094/73, *Association X v. Sweden*, D&R 9 (1978), p. 5 (7). See also Appl. 7990/77, *X v. the United Kingdom*, D&R 24 (1981), p. 57 (63), where the Commission stated. that the authorities are not required to actively support a union or an individual union member in a particular case.

[82] In its decision on Appl. 9234/81, *X Association v. Federal Republic of Germany*, D&R 26 (1982), p. 270 (271), the Commission states that "private associations should be able to pursue their statutory aims by all lawful means, but this does not imply the right to have *locus standi* on all matters falling within the ambit of the statutory activities".

[83] Judgment of 6 February 1976, *Swedish Engine Drivers' Union*, para. 37; judgment of 6 February 1976, *Schmidt and Dahlström*, para. 33.

not at variance with Article 11, to strive for the protection of their members' interests"[84] in fact implies that Article 11 has an indirect *Drittwirkung* in the form of an obligation for the authorities to enable the (trade) unions, also vis-à-vis third parties, to enjoy the rights and freedoms set forth in that article.

This likewise implies that national law must enable legal personality for associations, or at least sufficient legal status for them to be able to stand up effectively for the interests of their members. A consequence on the international plane ought to be that associations must also be able to file on their own account an application under Article 34, not only in the case of a violation of Article 11, but in all those cases where they allegedly have been prejudiced by a violation of one of their own rights or of rights of their members which they have to protect.

15.6 RESTRICTIONS

In addition to the 'usual' restrictions, the second paragraph of Article 11 provides for the possibility that, with regard to members of the armed forces, the police and the administration of the State, lawful restrictions may be imposed on the exercise of the rights laid down in Article 11. Although most complaints of violation of Article 11 hitherto examined by the Court actually concerned police officers, civil servants or members of the armed forces, in most cases this provision was not applied.[85] In the *Vogt* Case the Court observed that the notion of 'administration of the State' should be interpreted narrowly, and in the light of the post held by the civil servant concerned.[86] Consequently, the Court is prepared to independently review the necessity of the restrictions imposed. In the *Vogt* Case this review took the form of a proportionality test. In the case at hand the Court concluded that the dismissal of the applicant was disproportionate to the legitimate aim pursued (national security, prevention of disorder, rights and freedoms of others).[87] The applicability of the last sentence of the second paragraph does not, therefore, stop the Court from examining whether the other conditions set forth in the second paragraph have been met. The 'lawful restrictions' that can be imposed on members of the police, the army and the administration of the State are judged on the basis of the standards of legitimate aim, pressing social need and proportionality.

---

[84] Judgment of 27 October 1975, *National Union of Belgian Police*, para. 39. In its report in the *Swedish Engine Divers' Union* Case, the Commission speaks of 'to promote their members' economic and social interests against interference by the State and by employers, B.18 (1977), p. 49. In the *Gustafsson* Case, the Court also stated that the words 'for the protection of their interests' show that Article 11 safeguards freedom to protect the occupational interests of trade union members by trade union action.

[85] The Court referred to the provision in its judgment of 8 June 1976, *Engel*, para. 54.

[86] Judgment of 26 September 1995, paras 60-65.

[87] *Ibidem.*

In the *Rekvényi* Case the Court followed a similar approach to the one in the *Vogt* Case. It reviewed the compatibility of the interference (prohibition on members of the army, police and security forces) with the requirements of the second paragraph. It concluded in that respect that the interference satisfied those conditions. Subsequently it held that "it is not necessary in the present case to settle the disputed issue of the extent to which the interference in question is, by virtue of the second sentence of Article 11 para. 2, excluded from being subject to the conditions other than lawfulness enumerated in the first sentence of that paragraph."[88]

The Commission did apply the second sentence of the second paragraph once, *viz.* in an unpublished decision, in which it considered the prohibition on setting up a trade union, imposed on a Belgian police officer, to be justified on that ground.[89] This decision would appear to be questionable on the ground that the Commission did not apply the necessity test. As a result of such an approach the person concerned can be completely deprived of trade union freedom, while it is undoubtedly intended that restrictions can be imposed only with regard to particular ways of exercising this freedom, since a restriction may never affect a right in its essence. Although it is not prescribed with regard to the restriction in question that it must be 'necessary in a democratic society', it is submitted that the test should be applied in that case as well, since the purposes of the Convention and the legal order established by it imply that for any restriction of the rights and freedoms laid down in the Convention such a necessity and the proportionality is a *condition sine qua non.*[90]

15.7 DEROGATION

Article 11 is not listed in the enumeration in Article 15(2) of provisions which are non-derogable. It has to be taken into account, however, that the right to trade union freedom has developed, in particular in the International Labour Organisation, into a right which has to be respected by the States regardless of whether they have undertaken to do so in a treaty.

---

[88]   Judgment of 20 May 1999, para. 61.

[89]   Mentioned by F. Castberg, *The European Convention on Human Rights*, Leyden, 1974, p. 152. *See* also Appl. 10365/83, *S v. Federal Republic of Germany*, D&R 39 (1984), p. 237 (240), where the Commission held that a disciplinary penalty imposed on a civil servant who was a committee member of a union, and who called on civil servants to strike, did not constitute a violation of the right to exercise freedom of association, since in this case the right to strike was prohibited by law for civil servants and that prohibition as such was not inconsistent with the right of freedom of association.

[90]   In its judgment of 2 August 2001, *Grande Oriente d'Italia di Palazzo Giustiniani*, para. 31, the Court did not have to pronounce on the issue, since it held the second sentence not to be applicable.

CHAPTER 16

THE RIGHT TO MARRY AND TO
FOUND A FAMILY (Article 12)

REVISED BY PIETER VAN DIJK

CONTENTS

16.1 TEXT OF ARTICLE 12

*Men and women of marriageable age have the right to marry and to found a family,
according to the national laws governing the exercise of this right.*

16.2 THE SCOPE OF ARTICLE 12

The right to marry and to found a family, laid down in Article 12, has a clear
connection with the right to respect for private and family life of Article 8. Reliance
by an applicant on the former right is, therefore, usually combined with reliance on

the latter.[1] However, after two persons have got married, interference with their marital life constitutes an issue under Article 8 and not under Article 12.[2] Nevertheless, the Court sometimes separately examines the complaint under Article 12, for instance because not the right to marry but the right to found a family is at issue.[3]

Article 12 does not include a second paragraph laying down possibilities for restrictions. However, from the inclusion of the formula 'according to the national laws governing the exercise of this right', it is evident that Article 12 does not guarantee an unlimited right. The national legislature has been left a certain margin for subjecting the exercise of the right laid down in Article 12 to certain conditions, regulating the legal consequences of marriage and laying down provisions concerning the resulting family ties. However, the scope afforded to national law is not unlimited, since that would make Article 12 redundant. The limitations ensuing from national law must not restrict or reduce the right to marry in such a way or to such an extent that the very essence of the right is impaired.[4]

While Article 12 thus does not imply an absolute obligation on the part of the authorities to refrain from interference with regard to the exercise of the right to marry and to found a family, it does also not entail a positive obligation for the authorities in concrete cases to provide the material means which must enable the persons concerned to marry and to found a family.[5] However, if they proceed to do so, they may not discriminate.[6] And more generally their regulations and policies have to be of such a nature that the exercise of the right to marry and to found a family is not substantially interfered with.[7]

The right to marry and to found a family entails for the authorities a prohibition on putting a sanction on the marital and/or parental status. Thus, in general, the Government as an employer (and private employers, via the horizontal effect of Article 12) is not allowed to discharge an employee on the mere ground that the person has married or has become a parent.[8] However, loss of, *e.g.*, disability benefits because of marriage is not a sanction and does not constitute an interference with the exercise of the right to marry.[9] The same may be presumed to hold for the implication that a marriage may lead to a change of name.[10] Discharge does not constitute a violation

---

[1] See, *e.g.*, the decision of 7 September 2000, *E.P. v. Italy*, para. 2.

[2] Decision of 9 November 1999, *Schober*, para. 1.

[3] Decision of 7 March 2000, *K.S. v. the United Kingdom*, para. 4.

[4] Judgment of 17 October 1986, *Rees*, para. 50.

[5] Appl. 25928/94, *Cannatella* (not published); decision of 7 June 2000, *Ivanov*, para. 5.

[6] With respect to a complaint by a Turkish Cypriot against Cyprus concerning allegedly discriminatory legislation, a friendly settlement was reached after new legislation had been enacted: judgment of 16 July 2002, *Selim*.

[7] Report of 13 December 1979, *Hamer*, para. 62.

[8] See Appl. 35426/97, *Staiku*; the complaint concerned was, however, declared inadmissible *ratione temporis*.

[9] Appl. 10503/83, *Kleine Staarman*, D&R 42 (1985), p. 162 (165).

[10] Appl. 20798/92, *Maleville*, para. 1. See also Appl. 25080/94, *Wolf*.

either when the person concerned has promised *in full freedom* not to marry, or at least has accepted the consequence that marriage will constitute a ground for discharge. That situation occurs, for instance, when a Roman Catholic priest is relieved from his priestly and directly related functions after having given up his celibate status. Toleration of this by the authorities does not then conflict with Article 12. On the other hand, Article 12 also implies the right not to marry, with the same prohibition on putting a sanction on not being married.

In the *Marckx* Case Article 12 had been put forward because under Belgian law the granting to an illegitimate child of the same status as a legitimate child was linked with his or her legitimisation, which could only take place through the marriage of the natural parents. The Court was of the opinion that there was no need for it to pronounce on the question of whether the Convention also protects the right not to marry, since in the Court's view the freedom to marry or not was not at issue, and the discrimination against a child born out of wedlock fell outside the scope of Article 12.[11]

In the *Johnston* Case the Commission held it to be clear that the concept of 'family life' under Article 8 is not limited to the marriage-based family, but refers to people actually living together as a genuine family. However, according to the Commission, Article 8 does not oblige the State to grant a right to custody and care to a natural father of a child born out of wedlock where the parents were free to marry but had chosen not to do so.[12] That 'family' in the meaning of Article 8 is a broader concept than the marriage-based family has also been recognised by the Court, although in the *Berrehab* Case the members of a family based on a 'lawful and genuine marriage' were still given a certain preferential – "*ipso jure*" – treatment.[13] An equally broad interpretation of 'family' has not yet been adopted for Article 12.

In the *Abdulaziz, Cabales and Balkandali* Case the Court held that the expression 'family life' in the case of a married couple normally comprises cohabitation. In the Court's view this proposition is reinforced by Article 12, 'for it is scarcely conceivable that the right to found a family should not encompass the right to live together'.[14]

In *P., C. and S. v. the United Kingdom* the Court made it clear that Article 12 does not concern the circumstances in which interferences with family life between parents and a child may be justified. It held that Article 8 was to be regarded as the *lex specialis*, and that no separate issue arose under Article 12.[15]

That Article 12, according to the Commission, does not include the right to marry a deceased person posthumously, can hardly have come as a surprise.[16]

---

[11]   Judgment of 13 June 1979, para. 67.
[12]   Report of 5 March 1985, para. 106.
[13]   Judgment of 21 June 1988, para. 21.
[14]   Judgment of 28 May 1985, para. 62.
[15]   Judgment of 16 July 2002, para. 142.
[16]   Appl. 10995/84, *M v. Federal Republic of Germany*, D&R 41 (1985), p. 259 (261).

16.3 THE RIGHT TO MARRY

16.3.1 NATIONAL LAW

Article 12 refers to national law and, consequently, accepts the possibility that, on the issues concerned, the legal systems may vary among the Contracting States. In some Contracting States, for instance, the law attaches to the religious marriage ceremony the legal consequences of matrimony, whereas in other Contracting States this is not the case. The refusal to register a marriage which has not been concluded according to the procedure legally prescribed, does not constitute a violation of Article 12.[17] And the question of when a person has reached marriageable age also needs not to be answered the same way in all Contracting States. However, this does not mean that there are no common minimum norms which national law and those applying it have to respect and against which that law and that application can be reviewed in Strasbourg. The very fact that Article 12 puts the *right* first and foremost, implies that domestic regulations concerning the exercise of that right must not be of such a nature that the right itself would be affected in its essence. As the Commission opined in its report in the *Hamer* Case: "Whilst this is expressed as a 'right to marry (...) according to the national laws governing the exercise of this right', this does not mean that the scope afforded to national law is unlimited. If it were, Art. 12 would be redundant. The role of national law, as the wording of the Article indicates, is *to govern the exercise* of the right."[18]

Formalities required by national law for getting married are as a rule accepted as justified, but they may not cause an excessively long delay,[19] nor be applied in a discriminatory way.[20] A provision of domestic law prohibiting marriage between a former parent-in-law and the former child-in-law as long as their former spouses are still alive, was found to violate Article 12.[21]

If the right to marry is denied to a person who is already married, this may be justified on the ground that the legislation prohibiting bigamy is so firmly anchored in the national legal order of most of the Contracting States that the Convention was not intended to change this, and that for a person who is already married the essence

---

[17]   Appl. 6167/73, *X v. Federal Republic of Germany*, D&R 1 (1975), p. 64 (65).
[18]   Report of 13 December 1979, para. 60 (emphasis added). See also the report of 10 July 1980, *Draper*, para. 47. The Commission refers to the case law of the Court to the effect that measures concerning the exercise of a right "must never injure the substance of the right".
[19]   Appl. 31401/96, *Sanders*, para.1; Appl. 33257/96, *Klip and Krüger para. 2.*
[20]   Appl. 30309/96, *K.M. v. the United Kingdom*, para.2. See also the decisions as to the admissibility of 18 September 2001, *Selim*, where the complaint has been declared admissible concerning a legal regulation in Cyprus that makes contracting a civil marriage impossible for persons professing the Moslem faith.
[21]   Judgment of 13 September 2005, *B. and L. v. the United Kingdom*, paras 37-40.

of the right to marry is not affected by this prohibition.[22] The same holds good for the denial of admission of an alien for family reunion in a situation where his first wife is living in his home State.[23] Similar reasoning applies with regard to the legislation according to which the right to marry is denied to persons below a given age. As long as there is a reasonable relation between that age limit and the concept of 'marriageable age', the essence of the right is not affected with respect to them. If the right to marry is denied to a person because of his limited mental faculties, his state of health, or his financial situation, the relevant national law cannot be said not to affect the essence of that right, assuming of course that such persons can be deemed capable of determining their free will to consent to the marriage.

The conditions and restrictions set by domestic law may not amount to a violation of any of the other provisions of the Convention and its Protocols. Reference has already been made to Article 14, which prohibits the national authorities from discriminating in regulating the enjoyment of the rights and freedoms.[24] Another relevant provision is the prohibition of inhuman treatment in Article 3; preventing a person from marrying or founding a family – one may think, for instance, of laws permitting compulsory sterilisation in certain cases – may assume the character of an inhuman treatment.[25] That Article 8 would entail restrictions for regulating the right to marry is less imaginable, since both provisions are interpreted in close correlation.[26]

Article 12 does not provide a solution for cases in which the conclusion of a marriage involves links with various legal systems. The general reference to national law implies that this is left to the rules of private international law (conflicts of law) applying in the country where the marriage is to take place.[27] This means, for instance, that a person whose national law permits polygamy cannot rely on this law under Article 12 in a country where polygamy is prohibited by law and this norm is applied as being one of public policy. Here again, of course, application of a certain rule of private international law may not lead to discrimination. Because of the implications

---

[22]   In the Judgment of 18 December 1986, *Johnston*, para. 52, the Court, in general refers to "a society adhering to the principle of monogamy".

[23]   See Appl. 23860/94, *Khan*, which was, however, declared inadmissible for non-compliance with the 'six months' rule.

[24]   The equality of the spouses as to marriage, during marriage and in the event of its dissolution is provided for in Art. 5 of Protocol No. 7 and will be discussed *infra*.

[25]   The prohibition imposed on a detainee from marrying during his detention was not considered by the Commission as an inhuman or degrading treatment: Appl. 6564/74, *X v. the United Kingdom*, D&R 2 (1975), p. 105.

[26]   *Ibidem*. See, also, Appl. 8041/77, *X v. Federal Republic of Germany* (not published), where the applicant submitted that his deportation to the United States would destroy his marriage, because his wife would not be admitted to the United States. The Commission took the position that, since it had concluded that a violation of the first paragraph of Art. 8 found its justification in the second paragraph, it did not have to review the matter independently for its conformity with Art. 12. See the decision of 7 March 2000, *K.S. v. the United Kingdom*, para. 4, where the Court did not even examine the complaints separately under Article 12.

[27]   Appl. 9057/80, *X v. Switzerland*, D&R 26 (1982), p. 207 (208).

of nationality in this respect, changing a person's nationality may, under certain circumstances, entail restrictions on his possibility of marrying. In the *Beldjoudi* Case the Commission addressed this issue but did not find, in the facts submitted to it by the applicants, any appearance of a violation of Article 12.[28]

16.3.2 THE RIGHT TO MARRY OF PERSONS OF THE SAME SEX AND OF TRANSSEXUALS

An issue that still seems not to have been firmly settled is that of how to regard national legislation which only permits marriage between persons of the opposite sex. Can homosexuals and lesbians of marriageable age claim a right to marry a person of the same sex, submitting that marriage with a person of the opposite sex does not present a genuine marriage for them? It may safely be assumed that, when the text of Article 12 was drafted, the term 'marriage' alluded exclusively to an institutionalised relationship between two persons of the opposite sex.

In its report in the *Van Oosterwijck* Case the Commission emphasises that "a marriage requires the existence of a relationship between two persons of the opposite sex".[29] The complaint concerned the fact that under Belgian law Van Oosterwijck, who had been entered in the birth registry as a woman, was prohibited from marrying a woman. Van Oosterwijck submitted that he was mentally as well as physically a man, so that according to that submission this would not be a marriage between partners of the same sex. The Commission held that "by raising in advance to any application to marry an indirect objection based merely on the statements in the birth certificate and the general theory of the rectification of civil status certificates without examining the matter more thoroughly, the government has in fact failed in the instant case to recognise the applicant's right to marry and found a family within the meaning of Article 12 of the Convention."[30] The words 'without examining the matter more thoroughly' would seem to leave the door open for recognition of the applicant's right to marry.[31] The applicant's complaint was based on Articles 8 and 12. According to the Commission the Belgian State had violated both articles.

However, some years later, in the *Rees* Case, the Commission changed or clarified its position.[32] In the Commission's unanimous opinion Article 12 had not been

---

[28]   Report of 6 September 1990, para. 83.

[29]   Report of 1 March 1979, B.36 (1983), pp. 27-28. See also the opinion of the Commission members Fawcett, Tenekides, Gözübüyük, Soyer and Batliner annexed to the report of 12 December 1984, *Rees*, and the Court's judgment of 17 October 1986, *Rees*, para. 49.

[30]   *Ibidem*.

[31]   See, however, the dissenting opinion of the Commission members Sperduti and Kiernan, annexed to the report.

[32]   Report of 12 December 1984, para. 53.

violated, but the Commission was divided as to the reasons for this conclusion. Five members of the Commission were of the opinion that the complaint under Article 12 was closely connected to that of violation of Article 8: "There is no reason to believe that once this obstacle [the applicant is not recognised as a 'man'] has been removed the applicant is still not able to marry."[33] The other five members of the Commission wanted to separate the application of Article 8 from the application of Article 12: "The protection of private life includes (…) the recognition (…) of a person's civil status as a man or a woman (…), but the national law can clearly require men and women protected by Article 8 (…) to satisfy specific requirements in order to marry and found a family with respect to the formalities required for contracting a marriage (…), and may also exclude certain specified categories of men and women."[34] These members based their view that Article 12 was not violated on the interpretation that the 'social purpose' of Article 12 includes the physical capacity to procreate since the "references to marriageable age and to the different sex of the spouses are obviously intended to refer to the physical capacity to procreate". This led them to the following conclusion: "It follows that a Contracting State must be permitted to exclude from marriage persons whose sexual category itself implies a physical incapacity to procreate either absolutely (in the case of a transsexual) or in relation to the sexual category of the other spouse (in the case of individuals of the same sex)."[35]

The question whether, assuming that the latter interpretation was correct for the moment the Convention was drafted, this social purpose may have lost that exclusive orientation in the years in which the Convention has been in existence as a 'living instrument', was not expressly addressed. The view expressed by the latter five Commission members was in clear contradiction with the earlier statement of the Commission in the *Van Oosterwijck* Case that "there is nothing to support the conclusion that the capacity to procreate is an essential condition of marriage or even that procreation is an essential purpose of marriage."[36]

However, their opinion received support from the Court. In the *Marckx* Case the Court had already indicated that all the legal effects attaching to marriage do not have to apply equally "to situations that are in certain respects comparable to marriage".[37] In its *Rees* judgment the Court held without much argument that "the right to marry guaranteed by Article 12 refers to the traditional marriage between persons of the opposite biological sex. This appears also from the wording of the Article which makes it clear that Article 12 is mainly concerned to protect marriage as the basis of the family."[38] The Court was of the opinion that a legal impediment to the marriage of

---

[33]   Opinion of Frowein, Busuttil, Trechsel, Carrilo and Schermers, *ibidem*.
[34]   Opinion of Fawcett, Tenekides, Gözübüyük, Soyer and Batliner, *ibidem*.
[35]   *Ibidem*.
[36]   Report of 1 March, 1979, *Van Oosterwijck*, B.36 (1983), p. 28.
[37]   Judgment of 13 June 1979, *Marckx*, para. 67.
[38]   Judgment of 17 October 1986, *Rees*, para. 49.

persons who are not of the opposite biological sex cannot be said to restrict or reduce the right in such a way or to such an extent that the very essence of the right is impaired.

In the *Cossey* Case the Commission, by a majority of ten to six and basing itself on the fact that the applicant was anatomically no longer of male sex and had a partner wishing to marry her, held that the situation of this transsexual fell under the protection of Article 12: "The Commission agrees, in principle, with the Court, that Article 12 refers to the traditional marriage between persons of opposite biological sex. It cannot, however, be inferred from Article 12 that the capacity to procreate is a necessary requirement for the right in question. Men or women, who are unable to have children, enjoy the right to marry just as other persons. Therefore, biological sex cannot for the purpose of Article 12 be related to the capacity to procreate."[39]

The Court did not follow the majority of the Commission. By fourteen votes to four it held as follows: "Although some Contracting States would now regard as valid a marriage between a person in Miss Cossey's situation and a man, the developments which have occurred to date (...) cannot be said to evidence any general abandonment of the traditional concept of marriage. In these circumstances, the Court does not consider that it is open to it to take a new approach to the interpretation of Article 12 on the point at issue."[40] The Court also repeated its view that the legal impediment on the marriage of persons who are not of the opposite biological sex cannot be said to impair the very essence of the right to marry.[41]

Of the members belonging to the minority, judge Martens presented an extensive and comprehensive dissenting opinion. In his view, a true reconsideration of the issues arising under Article 12 should have led the Court to conclude that the *Rees* judgment was wrong "or at least that present-day conditions warranted a different decision in the *Cossey* case". As to the Court's view that the right to marry was not impaired in its essence by the impediments in question, judge Martens observed that the Court could take that position only because it based itself on the restrictive position that Article 12 confines the right to marry to persons who are of the opposite *biological* sex. Although he agreed with the Court that Article 12 applied to marriage as the union of two persons of the opposite sex, in his opinion that did not necessarily mean that 'sex' in this context must be interpreted as 'biological sex'. Finally, with respect to the relevance of the ability to procreate, judge Martens stated in what may well be called his 'panegyric on marriage': "Marriage is far more than a sexual union, and the capacity for sexual intercourse is therefore not 'essential' for marriage. Persons who are not or are no longer capable of procreating or having sexual intercourse may also

---

[39]   Report of 9 May 1989, paras 45-46.
[40]   Judgment of 27 September 1990, *Cossey*, para. 46.
[41]   *Ibidem*, para. 43.

want to and do marry. That is because marriage is far more than a union which legitimates sexual intercourse and aims at procreating: it is a legal institution which creates a fixed legal relationship between both the partners and third parties (including the authorities); (…) it is, moreover, a species of togetherness in which intellectual, spiritual and emotional bonds are at least as essential as the physical one."[42]

In *B v. France*, where the Court reached a conclusion with respect to Article 8 which differed from that in the *Rees* Case and the *Cossey* Case by distinguishing the facts in the former case from those in the two latter cases,[43] Article 12 had not been relied upon by the applicant and, therefore, was not addressed by the Court. There was, therefore, some expectation that the changing attitude towards the situation which confronts transsexuals, which the Court showed in *B v. France*, would also lead to a change in the Court's case law with respect to Article 12.

However, in the *Sheffield and Horsham* Case the Court repeated the position adopted in the *Rees* Case that Article 12 refers to the traditional marriage between persons of opposite biological sex and that the legal impediment on the marriage of persons who are not of the opposite biological sex, does not impair the very essence of the right to marry. The Court was of the opinion that this attachment to the traditional concept of marriage in Article 12 provided sufficient reason for the continued adoption by a State of biological criteria for determining a person's sex for the purposes of marriage within the State's power to regulate by national law the exercise of the right to marry.[44] Here again, the majority did not accept the argument that, even if Article 12 refers to marriages between persons of the opposite sex, the gender reassignment following a surgical operation should be recognised as implying that the person concerned should be considered as a person of the new sex for legal purposes.[45]

In *X, Y and Z v. the United Kingdom*, which concerned a transsexual who claimed the right to be recognised as the father of the child born to his partner as a result of artificial insemination by a donor, the Commission found a violation of Article 8. Article 12 was not relied upon by the applicants. The Commission held that this case had to be distinguished from the *Kerkhoven* Case concerning two lesbian partners, in that in the former case there has been a re-assignment of gender which meant that

---

[42]   Dissenting opinion of Judge Martens attached to the judgment of 27 September 1990, *Cossey*. See also the joint dissenting opinion of judges Palm, Foighel and Pekkanen: "The fact that a transsexual is unable to procreate cannot, however, be decisive. There are many men and women who cannot have children but, in spite of this, they unquestionably have the right to marry".

[43]   Judgment of 25 March 1992, para. 63. The Court took great effort to leave the impression that the fact that it reached a different conclusion here, found its reason merely in differences between the French and English systems; see *ibidem*, para. 51. In para. 48 the Court states in so many words that "there is as yet no sufficiently broad consensus between the Member States of the Council of Europe to persuade the Court to reach opposite conclusions to those in its Rees and Cossey judgments".

[44]   Judgment of 30 July 1998, paras 66-67.

[45]   See the dissenting opinion of Judge Van Dijk, para. 8.

the two partners no longer were of the same sex.[46] The Court reached the conclusion that Article 8 had not been violated. It held that the lack of common ground amongst the European States regarding the parental rights of transsexuals afforded the Contracting States a wide margin of appreciation.[47]

Ultimately, in the *Goodwin* Case,[48] the Court changed its position. In relation to Article 8 it held, on the basis of striking a fair balance between the public interests involved and the interests of the applicant, that this provision contained a positive obligation for the States to recognize for legal purposes the results of gender re-assignment surgery. It held that, if domestic law would not take the resulting change of gender into account, a "conflict between social reality and law arises which places the trans-sexual in an anomalous position, in which he or she may experience feelings of vulnerabiltiy, humiliation and anxiety".[49] In relation to Article 12, too, the Court distanced itself from its previous case law: "Reviewing the situation in 2002, the Court observes that Article 12 secures the fundamental right of a man and woman to marry and to found a family. The second aspect is not however a condition of the first and the inability of any couple to conceive or parent a child cannot be regarded as per se removing their right to enjoy the first limb of this provision. The exercise of the right to marry gives rise to social, personal and legal consequences. It is subject to the national laws of the Contracting States but the limitations thereby introduced must not restrict or reduce the right in such a way or to such an extent that the very essence of the right is impaired (...). It is true that the first sentence refers in express terms to the right of a man and woman to marry. The Court is not persuaded that at the date of this case it can still be assumed that these terms must refer to a determination of gender by purely biological criteria (...). There have been major social changes in the institution of marriage since the adoption of the Convention as well as dramatic changes brought about by developments in medicine and science in the field of transsexuality. The Court has found above, under Article 8 of the Convention, that a test of congruent biological factors can no longer be decisive in denying legal recognition to the change of gender of a post-operative transsexual. There are other important factors – the acceptance of the condition of gender identity disorder by the medical professions and health authorities within Conctracting States, the provision of treatment including surgery to assimilate the individual as closely as possible to the gender in which they perceive that they properly belong and the assumption by the transsexual of the social role of the assigned gender."[50]

---

[46] Report of 27 June 1995, para. 55. See, however, the concurring opinion of Mr. Schermers, who rejects the distinction made.
[47] Judgment of 22 April 1997, para. 44.
[48] And in the judgment in *I. v. the United Kingdom* of the same date.
[49] Judgments of 11 July 2002, para. 76.
[50] *Ibidem*, paras 98-100.

The point of view that the prohibition on a transsexual from marrying a person of (previously) the same sex does not limit his or her right to marry in its essence, was also now abandoned by the court: "In that regard, it finds that it is artificial to assert that post-operative transsexuals have not been deprived of the right to marry as, according to law, they remain able to marry a person of their former opposite sex. The applicant in this case lives as a woman, is in a relationship with a man and would only wish to marry a man. She has no possibility of doing so. In the Court's view, she may therefore claim that the very essence of her right to marry has been infringed."[51]

Finally, the Court held that the fact that fewer countries permitted the marriage of transsexuals in their assigned gender than recognized the change of gender itself, did not lead it to a different conclusion as to the violation of Article 12 than it had reached as to the violation of Article 8: "The Court is not persuaded that this supports an argument for leaving the matter entirely to the Contracting States as being within their margin of appreciation. This would be tantamount to finding that the range of options open to a Contracting State included an effective bar on any exercise of the right to marry. The margin of appreciation cannot extend so far. While it is for the Contracting State to determine inter alia the conditions under which a person claiming legal recognition as a transsexual establishes that gender re-assignment has been properly effected or under which past marriages cease to be valid and the formalities applicable to future marriages (including, for example, the information to be furnished to intended spouses), the Court finds no justification for barring the transsexual from enjoying the right to marry under any circumstances."[52]

Thus, the *Goodwin* judgment finally confirmed the right of transsexuals to marry a person of the (previous) same sex. The more general, and indeed different, question of whether homosexuals and lesbians have the right under Article 12 to marry a person of the same sex, has not been answered by this judgment. Given the fact that, so far, only a few member States of the Council of Europe have recognized such a right in their domestic law, does not make it likely that the Court would draw the line of *Goodwin* all the way in that direction in the near future.

16.3.3 DIVORCE AND REMARRIAGE

As the exercise of the right to marry always depends on the free consent of the partners, the right to marry cannot be invoked against a law which makes divorce at the request

---

51   *Ibidem*, para. 101.
52   *Ibidem*, para. 103.

of the other partner possible.[53] But does the right to marry include the right to divorce and to make a new marriage possible?

In the *Johnston* Case a complaint had been lodged against Ireland where divorce is not permitted. The Court held that Article 12 did not oblige the Contracting States to provide the legal possibilities to dissolve a marriage. For an *a contrario* argument the Court referred to Article 16 of the Universal Declaration of Human Rights which, in addition to the right to marry and to found a family, provides for the entitlement to 'equal rights as to marriage, during marriage and at its dissolution', words which were deliberately left out of the Convention. The Court concluded that "the *travaux préparatoires* disclose no intention to include in Article 12 any guarantee of a right to have the ties of marriage dissolved by divorce".[54] The applicants had referred to the judgment of the Court in the *Marckx* Case, where it was upheld that the Convention is a living instrument which ought to be interpreted in the light of the present-day conditions. To this the Court responded as follows: "However, the Court cannot, by means of an evolutive interpretation, derive from these instruments a right that was not included therein at the outset. This is particularly so here, where the omission was deliberate."[55]

The Court furthermore pointed out that the right to divorce was also not included in Protocol No. 7 to the Convention. The opportunity was not used to deal with this question in Article 5 of the Protocol, which guarantees certain additional rights to spouses, notably in the event of dissolution of marriage. Indeed, paragraph 39 of the Explanatory Report to the Protocol states that the words 'in the event of its dissolution' in Article 5 "do no imply any obligation on a State to provide for dissolution of marriage or to provide any special forms of dissolution".[56]

With respect to the applicant's view that the prohibition of divorce was to be seen as a restriction on the capacity to marry the Court held that, even if this was the case, such a restriction could not be regarded as injuring the substance of the right to marry "in a society adhering to the principle of monogamy".[57] Against the phrase between quotation marks it might be argued, however, that in many cases the possibility of divorce would precisely serve to avoid situations of factual bigamy.

In *F. v. Switzerland* the complaint concerned Article 150 of the Swiss Civil Code, which provided for a prohibition of remarriage for a period ranging from one to three years, to be imposed by the court on the party at fault in the event of divorce granted on the ground of adultery. This provision had been applied to the applicant for the maximum period. The Court rejected the Government's argument that the system of temporarily

---

53   Appl. 33597/96, *Slimani*, para. 2.
54   Judgment of 18 December 1986, para. 52.
55   *Ibidem*, para. 54.
56   *Ibidem*.
57   *Ibidem* para. 52.

prohibiting remarriage served to protect the institution of marriage and the rights of others. The Court expressed doubts as to whether the system was an appropriate means for protecting the stability of marriage. It was of the opinion that the interests of the future spouse were not protected by it and that the interests of the child born out of the relationship could be harmed. Subsequently, the Court distinguished the case from the *Johnston* Case by holding that "If national legislation allows divorce, which is not a requirement of the Convention, Article 12 secures for divorced persons the right to remarry without unreasonable restrictions."[58]

The Court reached the conclusion that the disputed measure, which affected the very essence of the right to marry, was disproportionate to the legitimate aim pursued. Thus the Court not only addressed the question of whether the right to marry was affected in its essence, but in reaching a positive conclusion also applied the criterion of proportionality.[59]

The procedure of separation from bed and board, which exists in several legal systems instead of, or as an alternative to divorce, does not lead to a dissolution of the marriage and, consequently, does not concern the right to remarry. A complaint about the long protraction of the procedure alleging a violation of Article 12 was, therefore, declared manifestly ill-founded.[60]

Article 12 does not deal with the legal consequences attached to the dissolution of marriage such as the right to wardship and to keep contact with the children. However, Article 8 does apply here.

16.4 THE RIGHT TO FOUND A FAMILY

With respect to the right to found a family as well, Article 12 does not imply a positive obligation guaranteeing a socio-economic right to, for instance, sufficient living accommodation and sufficient means of subsistence to keep a family.[61] It primarily contains a prohibition on the authorities from interfering with the founding of a family. Here again, it will have to be assumed that 'the national laws governing the exercise of this right' may regulate the enjoyment of this right, but may not exclude it altogether or affect it in its essence, for instance by prescribing the compulsory use of contraceptives, ordering a non-voluntary sterilisation or abortion, or tolerating the

---

[58] Judgment of 18 December 1987, para. 38.

[59] See also the decision of 11 December 2001, *Truszkowska*, para. 3: the complaint was held to be unsubstantiated because the applicant had not shown that she actually wanted to re-marry. More or less the same line of reasoning had been adopted in the decision of 7 September 2000, *E.P. v. Italy*, para. 2: the applicant complained that he was prevented from re-marrying on account of his forced cohabitation with his relatives. The Court held that he had failed to prove that he intended to live in the apartment in question.

[60] Appl. 27962/95, *D.P. v. Italy*; Appl. 37175/97, *Bolignari*.

[61] Appl. 11776/85, *Andersson and Kullman*, D&R 46 (1986), p. 251 (253).

performance thereof. As has been observed before, the victim of such a measure may also invoke Article 3, and in case of abortion perhaps also Article 2. Whether such an interference against the will of the person concerned is permitted in case of medical necessity depends on the question of whether the right to life has to be considered an inalienable right, for the protection of which ultimately the authorities bear responsibility.

If the person who is most directly concerned consents to the medical treatment leading to sterilisation or abortion, but the partner does not, the question arises whether the interests of the latter are also protected by Article 12, provided that the treatment in question is permitted by law. Since Article 12 refers to both partners, in principle the answer has to be in the affirmative. However, a conflict may arise between the rights and interests of the two partners, while in the case of abortion the issue of possible rights and interests of the foetus may also play a part. The national authorities have to resolve this conflict in their law and legal practice by weighing all the interests involved. The result of this may then ultimately be submitted to the Court for review of its conformity with, *inter alia*, Article 12.

Although no concrete solution can be worked out here, it is submitted that Article 12 entails the positive obligation that the law prescribes that before the treatment in question takes place, a reasonable effort should be made to obtain the consent of both partners. If no agreement is reached, in case of sterilisation the right of the most directly affected person to have control of her or his own body will have to be decisive. In the case of abortion the situation is different insofar as there the two partners have already taken a first step – whether intentional or not – to found or increase a family. If they do not agree on the question of whether the pregnancy is to continue, here again consultation of both partners should be prescribed, but ultimately the rights and interests of the woman should have priority over those of the man. Indeed, her body is most directly concerned and possibly her health and even her life may be at stake. In general, therefore, the consequences for the woman of the performance or non-performance of abortion will be greater than for the man. This leaves open the question of whether and, if so, how the rights and interests of the woman have to be weighed against any possible rights and interests of the foetus.[62]

The important question of whether the exposure of a person to nuclear detonations which allegedly made him sterile, may constitute an interference with the right to found a family, has not yet been answered. A complaint to that effect was declared inadmissible because it was introduced out of time.[63]

---

[62] For the above issues, reference is made to the discussion of Articles 2 and 3, *supra*.
[63] Appl. 21825/93, *McGinley*, *sub* F.

As regards adoption, the Commission took the position that a family may also be founded by means of adopting a child,[64] but that Article 12 does not guarantee a *right* to adopt or otherwise integrate into the family a child who is not the natural child of the couple concerned.[65] The two views would seem to contradict one another. In fact, if it is recognised that there are different ways of founding a family, why should only one of those ways form part of the right conferred in Article 12, even in those cases where for the person(s) in question the other way is in fact the only possible way to found a family? Of course, the national authorities will have to be allowed ample scope for regulating the conditions for adoption,[66] in which context the rights of the persons concerned will have to be weighed carefully against those of others, especially the natural parents, while the rights and interests of the child should be predominant. However, this need not bar the recognition of the right as such. In the *Singh* Case the Court declared admissible the complaint that the refusal of familiy reunion with an adopted child for the reason that the adoption had not been in conformity with domestic rules and procedures, violated Article 12 alone or in conjunction with Article 14.[67]

If every accessible method of artificial reproduction is prohibited by domestic law that would seem to affect the right to found a family in its essence for the person concerned, unless adoption is facilitated and considered by the persons concerned as an equivalent alternative. There is, however, no case law on the matter.

In *X, Y and Z v. the United Kingdom* a female to male transsexual and his female partner had claimed in vain legal recognition of the former as the father of a child born to the latter as a result of artificial insemination by a donor. In that case the Commission found a violation of Article 8,[68] whereas the Court reached the opposite conclusion.[69] Article 12, which could be relevant to the situation concerned, was not relied upon by the applicants. Article 12 *was* invoked by a woman who as a single person wished to adopt a child, which was refused because the request did not come within the categories of cases in which Italian law allowed for adoption by a single person. The Commission decided that Article 12 presupposed a couple and did not imply a right to found a family for singles.[70] The Court adopted the same position with respect to an applicant whose request for adoption of a child was refused on the ground that he was single and a homosexual.[71]

---

[64]   Appl. 7229/75, *X and Y v. the United Kingdom*, D&R 12 (1978), p. 32 (34). See also the report of 1 March 1979, *Van Oosterwijck*, B.36 (1983), p. 28.

[65]   Appl. 7229/75, *X and Y v. the United Kingdom*, D&R 12 (1978), p. 32 (34).

[66]   Appl. 8896/80, *X v. the Netherlands*, D&R 24 (1981), p. 176 (177).

[67]   Decision of 3 September 2002.

[68]   Report of 27 June 1995, paras 62-69.

[69]   Judgment of 22 April 1997, paras 41-52.

[70]   Appl. 31924/96, *Di Lazzaro*.

[71]   Decision of 12 June 2001, *Fretté*, para. 1. See also the judgment of 26 February 2002, *Fretté*, paras 37-43.

The question of whether the right to found a family also implies the right to increase the family, or on the contrary that right materializes with the birth or adoption of the first child, was expressly left open by the Commission.[72] It is submitted here that the question has to be answered in the former sense. After the birth of their first child some parents may take the view that they have thus founded the family they wanted, but for others this is the case only after two or more children. Since the Convention does not provide any indication in this respect and could not very well do so, it must be assumed that in national law, too, no limit may be set, since such a limitation would affect the right in its essence for some people, even apart from the possible conflict with Article 9. Family planning may be stimulated on a voluntary basis only.[73]

Unlike Article 8 the concept of 'family' in Article 12 is confined to the circle of parents and children. A complaint that the applicants were prevented from founding a larger family by having grandchildren, because their children had taken a vow of celibacy, was declared incompatible *ratione materiae*: "the right to have grandchildren and the right to procreation is not covered by Article 12".[74]

16.5 THE RELATIONSHIP BETWEEN THE RIGHT TO MARRY AND THE RIGHT TO FOUND A FAMILY

Is the right to found a family connected with the right to marry, in the sense that exclusively married couples have the former right? This was almost certainly the original intention, considering the fact that the two rights are merged into one right in Article 12 in the words 'the exercise of this right', while the words 'of marriageable age' also point in that direction.[75] And, indeed, the Court held in the *Rees* Case that "Article 12 is mainly concerned to protect marriage as the basis of the family".[76]

However, just as was observed with regard to the concept of 'family life' in Article 8, here again it may be submitted that since the drafting of the Convention the views with respect to the monopoly of marriage have been subject to great changes, while

---

[72] Appl. 6564/74, *X v. the United Kingdom*, D&R 2 (1975), p. 105 (106).

[73] Cf. Art. 16 of the Proclamation of Teheran of 1968; United Nations, *Human Rights; a Compilation of International Instruments*, Vol. 1 (First Part), New York, 1994, p. 54: "Parents have a basic human right to determine freely and responsibly the number and the spacing of their children".

[74] Decision of 6 March 2003, *Šijakova and Others*, para. 3.

[75] Thus also the Commission in its decision on Appl. 6482/74, *X v. Belgium and the Netherlands*, D&R 7 (1977), p. 75 (77). See also the opinion of Commission members Fawcett, Tenekides, Gözübüyük, Soyer and Batliner, laid down in the report of the Commission of 12 December 1984 in the *Rees* Case, para. 55.

[76] Judgment of 17 October 1986, para. 49.

other forms of cohabitation, with family relations adapted thereto, are finding increasing recognition, also juridically. The text of Article 12 would seem to leave sufficient scope for an interpretation of the concept of 'founding a family' in which these developments are taken into account. In *X v. Belgium and the Netherlands* a bachelor invoked Article 12 in a complaint against the application of Articles 227 and 228 of the Dutch Civil Code, which made adoption possible only for married couples. In its decision the Commission left open the question of whether "the right to found a family may be considered irrespective of marriage", although according to the formulation chosen it appears to be inclined to answer this question in the negative. It did, however, infer from the text of Article 12 that for the exercise of that right "[t]he existence of a couple is fundamental".[77] The issue raised here is also of direct relevance for the question of whether a provision of national law which makes a differentiation between married and unmarried couples in respect of the right to found a family, will have to be reviewed for its compatibility with Article 14.

16.6   DEPORTATION AND EXTRADITION

It is recognised in the case law that from Article 12, too, restrictions may ensue for the authorities of the Contracting States of their power of deportation or extradition, and their power to refuse aliens access to their territory. As regards the right to marry, however, Article 12 can be invoked successfully only against an (imminent) measure of deportation or extradition, or against a refusal of access, if the person in question can make it sufficiently plausible that he or she has concrete plans to marry and cannot reasonably be expected to realise those plans outside the country concerned.[78] And with regard to the right to found a family, just as in the case of Article 8, the Commission adopted the view that deportation, extradition and refusal of access to the territory of the State do no constitute a violation of Article 12, if the partner is in a position to follow the person concerned to the country of deportation or extradition, or to the country of the latter's residence or any other country, and if this may reasonably be required of the former.[79]

In the *Abdulaziz, Cabales and Balkandali* Case the Court held that, although by guaranteeing the right to respect for family life Article 8 presupposes the existence of a family, "this does not mean that all intended family life falls entirely outside its

---

[77]   Appl. 6482/74, D&R 7 (1977), p. 75 (77).

[78]   Appl. 7175/75, *X v. Federal Republic of Germany*, D&R 6 (1977), p. 138 (140).

[79]   See, *e.g.*, Appl. 2535/65, *X v. Federal Republic of Germany*, Coll. 17 (1966), p. 28 (30), where the Commission furthermore took into account that the applicant, when she married, knew that her husband did not have a residence permit. For a case of refusal of admission, see Appl. 5301/71, *X v. the United Kingdom*, Coll. 43 (1973), p. 82 (84).

ambit".[80] This implies that couples who apply for admission of one of them in view of their intention to marry, may rely on Article 8 and that, here again, the Court will not be inclined to investigate an alleged violation of Article 12 separately after it has found a violation or non-violation of Article 8. In fact, in the *Abdulaziz, Cabales and Balkandali* Case Article 12 was not invoked by the applicants.

If the persons concerned *are* married, the refusal of entry or the expulsion of one of them does not interfere with their right to marry and found a family. Article 12 does not impose a general obligation upon Contracting States to respect a married couple's choice of the place where they wish to found a family or to accept non-national spouses for settlement to facilitate that choice.[81] There may, however, be an issue under Article 8.[82]

On the same ground the refusal of entry for the reason that the alien concerned had the intention of getting married to a partner from her home State and, consequently, was not seeking family reunion in the host State, was not considered to be in violation of Article 12: she could live her marriage with her husband in their home country.[83]

16.7 DETAINED PERSONS

With regard to Article 12, too, the question has arisen whether inherent limitations ensue from detention for the exercise of the rights provided in that article.

The complaint of a person detained on remand about the refusal of the German authorities to give their consent to his getting married during his detention was dismissed by the Commission as manifestly ill-founded. The Commission did not advance its own reasons for this, but confined itself to mentioning the grounds on which the *Landgericht* had based its decision, *viz.* that it was expected that the person in question would be detained for a long time, so that he would not be able to cohabit with his future wife for a long time to come, which would be required to give a sound basis to marriage; that in view of his personality and the unusually long engagement period it could not be assumed that he seriously intended to marry; and that marriages of prisoners inevitably tended to affect the maintenance of order in a prison.[84]

The first ground would seem to be irrelevant since, even apart from the violation of the presumption of innocence, it is not for the authorities to prescribe to a married couple a given type of conjugal life, and this certainly cannot be made a condition.

---

[80]   Judgment of 28 May 1985, para. 62.
[81]   Appl. 25050/94, *Yavuz*. See also the judgment of 28 May 1985, *Abdulaziz, Cabales and Balkandali*, para. 68 (in relation to Article 8).
[82]   Appl. 34025/96, *Gelaw*.
[83]   Appl. 31042/96, *K.-V v. Switzerland*, para. 1.
[84]   Appl. 892/60, *X v. Federal Republic of Germany*, Yearbook IV (1961), p. 240 (256).

Many years later, in its reports in the *Hamer* Case and the *Draper* Case, this was recognised by the Commission. In its report in the *Hamer* Case the Commission opined as follows: "In considering whether the imposition of such a delay [in consequence of the detention] breached the applicant's right to marry, the Commission does not regard it as relevant that he could not have cohabited with his wife or consummated his marriage, whilst serving his sentence. The essence of the right to marry, in the Commission's opinion, is the formation of a legally binding association between a man and a woman. It is for them to decide whether or not they wish to enter such an association in circumstances where they cannot cohabit."[85]

For the second ground, insufficient arguments were advanced, at least judging from the decision as it was published. In cases where persons who are not detained, wish to get married, their possible intention to conclude a fictitious marriage is not examined and rightly so; at best, certain legal consequences are denied to what is obviously a fictitious marriage, for instance admission to the country or acquisition of a nationality. The argument of the fictitious marriage, therefore, can be used against a prisoner only if it is likely that the marriage ceremony is intended in reality, for example, to enable his escape, in which case there is indeed an abuse of right. It is only in the case of the third ground that an inherent limitation may be at issue, albeit a very broad and vague one, which is related to the purpose and the execution of the detention.

The doctrine of inherent limitations has been rejected by the Court, at least for those provisions of the Convention in which the restrictions are enumerated expressly, and then also exhaustively.[86] Such an enumeration does not occur in Article 12; the only restriction mentioned there is the general phrase 'according to the national laws governing the exercise of this right'. May national law contain special restrictions for prisoners? The Commission was faced with this question in the *Hamer* Case, where the complaint concerned the refusal of a request by a prisoner for temporary leave with a view to the conclusion of a marriage. Here the Commission departed from its earlier – almost automatic – decisions concerning inherent limitations for prisoners and decided that prisoners who are of the requisite age and further satisfy the legal conditions have the right to marry. If on the basis of national law restrictions may be imposed with respect to this right at all, according to the Commission – which referred to the judgments of the Court in the *Belgian Linguistic* Case[87] and the *Golder* Case[88] – these restrictions must not be of such a nature as to affect the essence of the right to marry. This means that "national law may not otherwise deprive a person or

---

[85]   Report of 13 December 1979, para. 71. Similar wording is to be found in the report of 10 July 1980, *Draper*, para. 60.

[86]   Judgment of 21 February 1975, *Golder*, para. 38.

[87]   Judgment of 23 July 1968, para. 5.

[88]   Judgment of 21 February 1975, para. 38.

category of persons of full legal capacity of the right to marry. Nor may it substantially interfere with the exercise of the right."[89] Although admitting that some administrative arrangements have to be made by the prison authorities before a prisoner can marry, the Commission was of the opinion that some positive action is required on their part to make the right effective.[90] The Commission subsequently concluded that when a person is obliged by the authorities to defer the marriage for a considerable time (in this case, for two years), in general this affects the right to marry in its essence, regardless of whether the delay is due to legislation which is only intended to regulate the exercise of that right, to an administrative act, or to a combination of the two. In the Commission's opinion the mere fact of the detention does not provide a justification for thus affecting the said right, since "no particular difficulties are involved in allowing the marriage of prisoners".[91]

When a prisoner complained that he was not allowed conjugal life and thus also could not increase his family, the Commission – leaving open the question of whether a person who already has a child, can still invoke Article 12 – held that Article 12 indeed contains an absolute right, but does not imply for that reason that a person must at all times be given the actual possibility to beget offspring, and that the applicant had to blame himself for this temporary impossibility.[92] Leaving aside the additional remark about the blameworthiness, which, even if tenable according to modern doctrines of criminology and forensic psychiatry, may nevertheless not be used as a justification of restrictions which are not justified otherwise, the Commission would appear to differentiate here between the possibility of founding a family in general and that possibility at a given moment. In the Commission's opinion measures in consequence of which a person is temporarily unable to found a family or increase his family do not constitute a violation of Article 12, since considering the preceding and the subsequent possibilities, on the whole the person in question has not been deprived of that right. It does not appear from its decision that the Commission took into account the length of the detention, but it is obvious that this point is of relevance for the legitimacy of the reasoning followed by the Commission since, here as well, the exercise of the right may not be substantially interfered with.

In a later decision the Commission apparently followed a different line of reasoning. The case concerned a complaint of a husband and wife who were both detained in the same prison for pre-trial investigations and who had been refused a common cell. Here, the Commission interrelated the right to protection of privacy and family life in Article 8 and the right to found a family in Article 12. After first having concluded that the restrictions imposed upon the married couple with respect

---

[89] Report of 13 December 1979, *Hamer*, para. 62.
[90] *Ibidem*, para. 68.
[91] *Ibidem*, paras 70-73.
[92] Appl. 6564/74, *X v. the United Kingdom*, D&R 2 (1975), p. 105 (106). The Commission quotes that passage in its report of 13 December 1979, *Hamer*, para. 58.

to their right to privacy and to respect for their family life could find their justification in the second paragraph of Article 8, the Commission subsequently held that restrictions which are not contrary to Article 8 on that ground cannot constitute a conflict with the right granted in Article 12 either.[93] Phrased in this general way the argument would seem to be incorrect. The fact that Article 12 is incorporated in the Convention independently of Article 8 also applies with regard tot the second element: the right to found a family. Given the notable fact that the drafters of the Convention have not included an enumeration of restrictions in Article 12, this provision cannot be subjected to the regime of the second paragraph of Article 8. However, the argumentation of the Commission is correct insofar as it amounts to declaring Article 8, and not Article 12, applicable to a measure by which the couple is temporarily deprived of the opportunity to have sexual intercourse. Even if the desired sexual intercourse would actually be aimed at the foundation or increase of a family, it cannot be said that their right to do so is substantially restricted by such a temporary measure. The same applies, for instance, with regard to conscript soldiers, who during a given period are unable to lead a normal conjugal life. The situation will, however, have to be judged separately for each individual case, because in the case of a measure applied for a longer period Article 12 may indeed come into issue. In this context it is noteworthy that the Commission has opened the door for a dynamic development by referring expressly and with approval to "the reformative movement in several European countries as regards an improvement of the conditions of imprisonment and the possibilities for detained persons of continuing their conjugal life to a limited extent."[94]

In a rather specific case, where the wife of a prisoner required medical surgery to be able to conceive a child, but the surgery could only be successful if within a short period thereafter conception took place, the Commission followed its traditional line. It considered the interference justified under the second paragraph of Article 8 for the prevention of disorder or crime, and held that an interference justified under Article 8 could not at the same time constitute a violation of Article 12. The exceptional circumstances of the case did not lead the Commission to the conclusion that the right of the couple to found a family was restricted in its essence. It took into consideration that during the short period concerned artificial insemination was not impossible. The objection by the applicants that artificial insemination was not an option for them as practising Catholics was answered as follows: "Article 9 of the Convention, which protects the freedom to manifest one's religious beliefs, does not guarantee the right

---

93   Appl. 8166/78, *X and Y v. Switzerland*, D&R 13 (1979), p. 241 (242-244).
94   *Ibidem*. Thus also earlier in Appl. 3603/68, *X v. Federal Republic of Germany*, Coll. 31 (1970), p. 48 (50).

to be exempted from rules which apply generally and neutrally, such as rules prohibiting 'conjugal visits' in prison."[95]

With due respect it is submitted that the Commission here places too much emphasis on the justification of the interference under Article 8, seen in separation. It should at least have left open the possibility that the evaluation of that justification may have a different outcome, when considered in conjunction with Articles 12 and 9.

16.8 DEROGATION

Article 12 does not belong to the category of the rights which are non-derogable by virtue of Article 15(2).

---

[95] Appls 32094/96 and 32568/96, *H and H v. the United Kingdom*, para. 2.

CHAPTER 17

RIGHT TO THE PEACEFUL ENJOYMENT OF ONE'S POSSESSIONS
(Article 1 of Protocol No. 1)

REVISED BY ARJEN VAN RIJN

CONTENTS

17.1 TEXT OF ARTICLE 1 OF PROTOCOL NO. 1

Every natural or legal person is entitled to the peaceful enjoyment of his possessions. No one shall be deprived of his possessions except in the public interest and subject to the conditions provided for by law and by the general principles of international law. The preceding provisions shall not, however, in any way impair the right of a State to enforce such laws as it deems necessary to control the use of property in accordance with the general interest or to secure the payment of taxes or other contributions or penalties.

17.2 INTRODUCTION

The classification of the right to the enjoyment of one's possessions – at least in an unqualified form – among the human rights is not unchallenged. Indeed, the UN Covenant on Civil and Political Rights contains no provision equivalent to Article 17 of the Universal Declaration of Human Rights. That the drafters of the Convention also hesitated about the status and exact formulation of this right may appear from the fact that it was not included among the original rights and freedoms of the Convention, but was added later by Protocol No. 1.[1] Indeed, the right of property has lost a good deal of its inviolability, also in the Member States of the Council of Europe, under the influence of modern social policy *(Sozialstaat)*. This fact is reflected in the very far-reaching limitations which Article 1 allows.

As the Court has often held, Article 1 comprises three distinct rules. The first rule, which is expressed in the first sentence and is of a general nature, lays down the principle of peaceful enjoyment of property. The second rule, in the second sentence, covers deprivation of possessions and makes it subject to certain conditions. The third rule, laid down in the second paragraph, recognises that the Contracting States are entitled, amongst other things, to control the use of property in accordance with the general interest, by enforcing such laws as they deem necessary for the purpose. However, these rules are not 'distinct' in the sense of being unconnected. The second and the third rule are concerned with particular instances of interference with the right to peaceful enjoyment of property. They must, therefore, be construed in the light of the general principle laid down in the first rule.[2] Each of the two forms of interference must comply with the principle of lawfulness and pursue a legitimate aim by means that are reasonably proportionate to the aim sought to be realised.[3]

The essential object of Article 1 of Protocol No. 1 is to protect a person against unjustified interference by the State with the peaceful enjoyment of his or her possessions. However, the positive obligations which rest on the Contracting Parties by virtue of Article 1 of the Convention, may require the State also to take measures necessary to protect the right of property. The boundaries between the State's positive and negative obligations under Article 1 of Protocol No. 1 do not lend themselves to precise definition. The applicable principles are nonetheless similar. Whether the case

---

[1]   This Protocol entered into force on 18 May 1954. For the state of ratifications, see Appendix I.

[2]   See, among others, judgment of 23 September 1982, *Sporrong and Lönnroth*, para. 61; judgment of 21 February 1986, *James and Others*, para. 37; judgment of 8 July 1986, *Lithgow and Others*, para. 106; judgment of 24 October 1986, *AGOSI*, para. 48; judgment of 23 April 1987, *Erkner and Hofauer*, para. 73; judgment of 23 April 1987, *Poiss*, para. 63; judgment of 18 February 1991, *Fredin*, para. 41; judgment of 16 September 1996, *Matos e Silva, Lda. and Others*, para. 81; judgment of 22 June 2004, *Broniowski*, para. 134; judgment of 16 November 2004, *Bruncrona*, para. 65.

[3]   See, *inter alia*, judgment of 5 January 2000, *Beyeler*, paras 108-114; judgment of 16 November 2004, *Bruncrona*, para. 66.

is analysed in terms of a positive duty on the State or in terms of an interference by a public authority which requires justification, the criteria to be applied do not differ in substance. In both contexts regard must be had to the fair balance to be struck between the competing interests of the individual and of the community as a whole. In both contexts the State also enjoys a certain margin of appreciation in determining the steps to be taken.[4]

As with other rights and freedoms of the Convention, the Court has recognised that in principle, the State may be responsible under Article 1 for interferences with the peaceful enjoyment of possessions resulting from transactions between private individuals. However, for the State's responsibility to be engaged it is necessary that the facts complained of are the result of an exercise of State authority and that they do not concern exclusively contractual relations between private individuals.[5]

Before turning to the case law with respect to the above-mentioned three rules, attention will be paid to a particular question related to the applicability of Article 1, that is: the meaning of the term 'possessions'.

17.3   PEACEFUL ENJOYMENT OF POSSESSIONS

17.3.1   POSSESSIONS

In the *Marckx* Case the Court held that "Article 1 is in substance guaranteeing the right of property".[6] However, the concept of 'possessions' in the first sentence of Article 1 should not be understood in the technical-juridical meaning of the word; it is wider, as also appears from the French word *'biens'*.

In its judgment in the *Gasus Dosier- und Fördertechnik GmbH* Case the Court confirmed that the notion of 'possessions' has an autonomous meaning which is not limited to ownership of physical goods: certain other rights and interests constituting assets can also be regarded as property rights and thus as 'possessions'. In that case the Court considered it immaterial whether the applicant's right to a concrete-mixer (which had been seised and sold by the Dutch tax authorities) was a right of ownership

---

4   Judgment of 22 June 2004, *Broniowski*, paras 143-144.
5   See judgment of 25 April 1996, *Gustafsson*, para. 60 (applicability of Art. 1 denied). See also judgment of 21 February 1986, *James and Others*, para. 35, in which the Court endorsed the view of the Commission that its examination of the applicants' complaints had to focus on the practical effects of the legislation on ownership rights in relation to the individual transactions between private persons, and on the issue whether that legislation was compatible with the Convention rather than these individual transactions.
6   Judgment of 13 June 1979, para. 63.

or a security right *in rem*.[7] This autonomy does not mean that domestic law is completely irrelevant for determining whether there is a 'possession'. When, in the *Pressos Compania Naviera S.A* Case, the Belgian Government invoked the autonomy of the term 'possession' in order to argue that Article 1 was inapplicable to the applicants' claim under domestic tort law, the Court responded by stating that it may have regard to the domestic law where there is nothing to suggest that that law runs counter to the object and purpose of Article 1. On this basis the Court accepted that the rules in question were rules of tort. Subsequently, however, it held that where the domestic law of tort creates a right of compensation as soon as the damage occurs, the resulting claim constitutes an asset and, therefore, amounts to a 'possession' within the meaning of Article 1.[8]

As a consequence, Article 1 may come into play in relation to a variety of claims constituting assets. As the case law on this point is still developing, it is difficult to deduce precise criteria. However, the case law offers some general pointers.

The basic point of departure appears to be the economic value of the right or interest: where State measures do not affect this economic value, no responsibility under Article 1 is engaged. For example, the right to live in a home which one does not own is not a 'possession' within the meaning of Article 1.[9] Neither does Article 1 protect a particular quality of living environment, although a high level of noise nuisance may infringe the right to peaceful enjoyment of one's possessions on account of a drop in the value of real property.[10] However, a person who had illegally built a house on State property and had been living in the house for five years, which had been tolerated by the authorities, appeared to have a justified claim under Article 1 that the State would reduce the risks related to a adjoining landfill.[11]

As will be become clear in the remainder of this section, many rights or interests other than ownership may represent an economic value and thus constitute assets for the purpose of Article 1. The more recent case law of the Commission suggested a certain link with the notion of 'civil rights and obligations' of Article 6(1) of the Convention. Where the latter provision is not applicable because no 'determination of civil rights and obligations' is at issue, the Commission has been reluctant to accept

---

[7]   Judgment of 23 February 1995, para. 52. See also the judgment of 16 September 1996, *Matos e Silva, Lda. and Others*, para. 75: although the applicants' ownership of land under domestic law was contested, the Court held that their unchallenged rights over the land for almost a century and the revenues they derived from working the land did qualify as 'possessions'.

[8]   Judgment of 20 November 1995, para. 25.

[9]   Appl. 19217/91, *Durini*, D&R 76-A (1994), p. 76 (79).

[10]   Appl. 13728/88, *S v. France*, D&R 65 (1990), p. 250 (261).

[11]   Judgment of 18 June 2002, *Öneryildiz*.

the applicability of Article 1 of Protocol No. 1.[12] The Court, too, assumes a connection between both Articles. The *Yagtzilar* Case concerned the expropriation of an olive yard, which had taken place without any compensation. The entitled party had submitted a claim in 1933. In 1995 the claim was declared inadmissible because it had expired at least since 1971. According to the Court Article 6 had been violated. The fact that in the national procedure the State had invoked the expiration only in a very late stage had deprived the entitled party from his possibilities to receive compensation. This constituted a violation of Article 1 of Protocol No. 1 as well.[13]

The object of the possessions must be adequately definable in relation to the claims based thereupon. Thus, with regard to pension schemes and social security systems the Commission has differentiated between, on the one hand, systems according to which, by the payment of contributions, an individual share in a fund is created, the amount of which can be determined at each particular moment, and, on the other hand, systems according to which the relation between the contributions being paid and the later benefit is much looser, which makes the object of the possessions less adequately definable. The first is a property-creating system and claims to benefits constitute 'possessions' in the sense of Article 1, while the second system "is based on the principle of solidarity which reflects the responsibility of the community as a whole" and does not create for the participant any claim to an identifiable share, but only an expectation the amount of which depends on the conditions prevailing at the time the pension is being paid.[14] The latter pensions are based on the principle of collective security and are not funded by contributions which can be individualised in any way.[15] In the latter case, too, there may be a right to certain benefits as long as the system is in force and the participant fulfils the prevalent conditions.[16] However, in that case the right guaranteed by Article 1 is not a right to a particular amount, since

---

[12]   Appl. 21775/93, *Aires*, D&R 81-B (1995), p. 48 (52); Appl. 20714/92, *Henry*, D&R 81-B (1995), p. 24 (34). Similarly, the Court appears to have transposed the requirement under Art. 6(1) that the 'right' be of a pecuniary nature to the context of Art. 1: see judgment of 16 September 1996, *Gaygusuz*, paras 41 and 55.

[13]   Judgment of 6 December 2001, *Yagtzilar*, paras 36-42. See also the judgment of 11 January 2001, *Platakou*, discussed *infra* in 17.3.2; judgment of 21 July 2005, *Natalya Gerasimova*, para. 25.

[14]   See in particular Appl. 4130/69, *X v. the Netherlands*, Yearbook XIV (1971), p. 224 (244). See also Appl. 5763/72, *X v. the Netherlands*, Yearbook XVI (1973), p. 274 (290-292) concerning amounts deducted from a Dutch social security pension in respect of pension payments received under a Norwegian pension scheme.

[15]   Appl. 10094/82, *G. v. Austria*, D&R 38 (1984), p. 84 (85-86) concerning a claim of entitlement to a survivor's pension for civil servants.

[16]   See Appl. 7624/76, *X v. Austria*, D&R 19 (1980), p. 100 (104-105), where the reduction of an old age pension was due to the fact that the person in question did not satisfy the conditions for a full pension due to the amount of his monthly contributions. See also Appl. 7995/77, *National Federation of Self-Employed*, D&R 15 (1979), p. 198 (201), where the Commission brought an increase of contributions, without a proportional increase of pension claims in return, under the justification of the second paragraph of Art. 1 'in the general interest'.

it may be subject to fluctuations, *inter alia* due to legal regulation. Fluctuations in the amount of the benefit may only amount to a violation of Article 1 if a very substantial reduction of the benefit is concerned.[17] And even if the right guaranteed extends, in principle, to periodic increases, it may be subjected to restrictions if the pension is to be paid abroad, since many countries apply specific restrictions to the payment of benefits to foreign countries.[18] However, pension rights which fall within the scope of Article 1 may not be honoured in a discriminatory way.[19]

In the *Feldbrugge* Case and the *Deumeland* Case the minority of the Commission put forward that even under a social security scheme the insurance of risks is financed by methods based on classical insurance techniques. In their view it is incorrect to argue that a property right is involved in old age insurance only if it is financed by a funding system, and that this is not the case if the insurance is based on the pay-as-you-go system. In the minority's view the important point is that, particularly in sickness and accident insurance, the benefits are financed by contributions directly or indirectly deducted from the worker's remuneration. They argue as follows: "The part borne directly by the worker is of course a deduction from the income earned by his work. But the contribution borne by the employer is in fact, indirectly, a similar deduction. If there was no compulsory insurance (...) this contribution would be added to the worker's net remuneration (...) The fact that in certain cases the scheme is also funded by State contributions in addition to those of the employers does not alter the nature of the scheme involved which remains an insurance scheme."[20]

Until now the Court has seen no reason to follow the Commission's approach concerning the importance to be attached to the distinction between contributory and not-contributory systems. In a judgment concerning an Austrian scheme, under which emergency assistance was granted to persons who had exhausted their entitlement to unemployment benefit, the Court, while noting that the entitlement emergency assistance was linked to the payment of contributions to the unemployment insurance fund, simply held "that the right to emergency assistance – insofar as provided for in the applicable legislation – is a pecuniary right for the purposes of Article 1 of Protocol No. 1. That provision is therefore applicable without it being necessary to rely solely

---

[17]   Report of 1 October 1975, *Mutter*, Yearbook XIX (1976), p. 996 (1018-1020). Such a substantial and therefore inacceptable reduction was held to have taken place, judgment of 12 October 2004, *Kjartan Ásmundsson*, paras 39-45. See also the judgment of 2 September 2005, *Goudswaard – van der Lans*.
[18]   Appl. 9776/82, *X v. the United Kingdom*, D&R 34 (1983), p. 153 (154).
[19]   Judgment of 4 juni 2002, *Wessels-Bergervoet*, para. 43; judgment of 11 June 2002, *Willis*, paras 48-50.
[20]   Reports of 9 May 1984, paras 14-17, and paras 14-17, respectively.

on the link between entitlement to emergency assistance and the obligation to pay 'taxes or other contributions'."[21]

Furthermore, the right or interest can only constitute a 'possession' if it is sufficiently established to be enforceable.[22] There is no question of possessions until the moment at which one can lay claim to the property concerned. A person complaining of an interference with his property right must show that such right existed. According to constant case law, 'possessions' may be either existing possessions or valuable assets, including claims, in respect of which the applicant can argue that he has at least a 'legitimate expectation' of obtaining effective enjoyment of a property right.[23] Examples of such assets are debts, either recognised[24] or following from the law[25], claims against fiscal authorities on restitution of tax money,[26] and final and binding judgment debts.[27] The mere hope of recognition of the survival of an old property right which it has long been impossible to exercise effectively, cannot be considered as a "possession" within the meaning of Article 1, nor can a conditional claim which lapses as the result of the non-fulfilment of the condition.[28]

---

[21]   Judgment of 16 September 1996, *Gaygusuz,* para. 41. The Court found a violation of Art. 14 in conjunction with Art. 1 of Protocol No. 1, as the scheme distinguished between nationals and non-nationals, a distinction which lacked an objective and reasonable justification (see para. 50 of the judgment). In its report in this case, the Commission had adopted the view that, since the obligation to pay 'taxes or other contributions' *(cf.* the second paragraph of Art. 1) falls within the field of application of Art. 1, the ensuing benefits also fall within its scope; report of 11 January 1995, *C.G. v. Austria,* para. 47). See also the judgment of 21 February 1997, *Van Raalte,* paras 34-35; judgment of 6 July 2005, *Stec and Others,* paras 47-56.

[22]   See the judgment of 9 December 1994, *Stran Greek Refineries and Stratis Andreadis,* para. 59; judgment of 18 November 2004, *Pravednaya,* para. 38.

[23]   See judgment of 23 November 1983, *Van der Mussele,* para. 48; judgment of 29 November 1991, *Pine Valley Developments Ltd and Others,* para. 50; judgment of 20 November 1995, *Pressos Compania Naviera S.A. and Others,* para. 25; judgment of 24 June 2003, *Stretch,* para. 35; judgments of 24 February 2005, *Veselinski* and *Djidrovski,* para. 75 and para. 80, respectively.

[24]   Judgment of 11 January 2000, *Almeida Garrett, Mascarenhas Falcao and Others,* para. 46; judgment of 20 December 2001, *F.L. v. Italy,* para. 23.

[25]   Judgment of 29 July 2004, *Mora do Vale and Others,* para. 38.

[26]   Judgment of 16 April 2002, *S.A. Dangeville,* paras 44-48; judgment of 3 July 2003, *Buffalo Srl,* paras 27-29; judgment of 22 July 2003, *SA Cabinet Diot and SA Gras Savoye;* para. 26; judgment of 27 May 2004, *OGIS-Institut Stanislas, OGEC St. Pie X en Blanche de Castille and Others,* paras 77-78.

[27]   Judgment of 9 November 2004, *Svetlana Naumenko,* para. 104; judgment of 18 November 2004, *Pravednaya,* para. 39. The quashing of a final and binding judgment therefore constitutes an interference with the right to property; see the judgment of 9 April 2002, *Anghelescu,* paras 63-65; judgment of 16 July 2002, *Ciobanu,* paras 49-52; judgments of 2 November 2004, *Ionescu* and *Chivorchian,* paras 44-46 and paras 48-51, respectively; judgment of 2 November 2004, *Tregubenko,* paras 50-51; judgment of 18 January 2005, *Popov,* para. 57.

[28]   Judgment of 12 July 2001, *Prince Hans-Adam II of Liechtenstein,* para. 83. See also judgment of 26 October 2004, *Pistorová,* para. 38: Article 1 applies only to existing possessions and does not guarantee a right to acquire property.

As pointed out above, a claim as such may constitute a 'possession' in the sense of Article 1,[29] but it should then be a concrete and adequately specified claim. Thus, the Commission decided that the claim of a notary to payment for his services does not find protection in Article 1 until it is an actual claim based on services rendered. His expectation that the applicable provisions about notarial fees were not going to be modified, does not find protection in Article 1.[30] Nor do claims which a person has as an heir during the testator's lifetime fall under the protection of Article 1, because this provision protects existing property and not the right to acquire property. It does of course protect the right of the testator to dispose of his patrimonial rights and the rights which have already been acquired by inheritance even before distribution of assets.[31]

In the *Stran Greek Refineries and Stratis Andreadis* Case the Greek Government argued that the applicants had no claim against the State, as neither a judgment of a domestic court of first instance nor an arbitration award was sufficient to establish the existence of such a claim. In order to determine whether the applicants had a 'possession', the Court examined whether the domestic judgment and arbitration award concerned "had given rise to a debt in their favour that was sufficiently established to be enforceable".[32] The Court then distinguished between the judgment and the award. The former was a preliminary decision which, while apparently accepting the principle that the State owed a debt to the applicants, ordered that witnesses be heard before a ruling could be made on the existence and extent of the alleged damage. According to the Court: "The effect of such a decision was merely to furnish the applicants with the hope that they would secure recognition of the claim put forward. Whether the resulting debt was enforceable would depend on any review by two superior courts. This is not the case with regard to the arbitration award, which clearly recognised the State's liability (...). According to its wording, the award was final and binding; it did not require any further enforcement measure and no ordinary or special appeal lay against it (...). Under Greek legislation arbitration awards have the force of final decisions and are deemed to be enforceable (...); no provision is made for an appeal on the merits."[33] The Court concluded that the arbitration award conferred

---

[29]   See also Appl. 7742/76, *A, B and Company A.S. v. Federal Republic of Germany*, D&R (1979), p. 146 (168).

[30]   Appl. 8410/78, *X v. Federal Republic of Germany*, D&R 18(1980), p. 216(219-220). See also Appl. 10426/83, *Pudas*, D&R 40 (1985), p. 234 (241); Appl. 10438/83, *Batelaan and Huiges*, D&R 41 (1985), p. 170 (173); and Appl. 19819/92, *Størksen*, D&R 78-A (1994), p. 88 (94-95): expectations for future earnings can only be considered to constitute a 'possession', if the income had already been earned or where an enforceable claim exists.

[31]   Judgment of 13 June 1979, *Marckx*, para. 51 and paras 63-64, respectively; judgment of 28 October 1987, *Inze*, para. 43.

[32]   Judgment of 9 December 1994, para. 59. See also Appl. 9676/82, *Sequaris*, D&R 29 (1982), p. 245 (249).

[33]   *Ibidem*, paras 61-62.

on the applicants a right in the sums awarded. Although this right was revocable since the award could still be annulled, the ordinary courts had already twice held that there was no ground for such annulment. Therefore, the applicants' right constituted a 'possession' within the meaning of Article 1.

Two complaints of an Austrian lawyer that his obligation to render *pro deo* services as counsel was contrary to Article 1, were declared admissible by the Commission.[34] In these cases, however, a friendly settlement was reached.[35] In the *Van der Mussele* Case the Court held that the absence of remuneration of expenses made by the applicant for public services was unrelated to the 'peaceful enjoyment' of applicant's existing possessions. The Court held that, since the expenses were relatively small and resulted from obligations to accomplish work compatible with Article 4 of the Convention, there was no breach of Article 1.[36]

In a number of cases the issue was examined whether a licence for carrying out certain activities constitutes a 'possession'. In its decision on admissibility in the *Pudas* Case the Commission had to answer the question whether a licence to conduct certain economic activities gives the licence-holder a right protected by Article 1. The Commission opined as follows: "the answer will depend *inter alia* on the question whether the licence can be considered to create for the licence-holder a reasonable and legitimate expectation as to the lasting nature of the licence and as to the possibility to continue to draw benefits from the exercise of licensed activity."[37]

And indeed, in the *Tre Traktörer Aktiebolag* Case, where the complaint concerned the decision to revoke the applicant's licence to serve beer, wine and other alcoholic beverages, the Commission held that the economic interests connected with the applicant company's restaurant business were 'possessions' within the meaning of Article 1. Since that licence was an important element in the running of the restaurant and the applicant company could legitimately expect to keep the licence as long as it did not infringe the conditions thereof, the revocation of the licence was an interference with the company's rights under Article 1.[38] The Court essentially endorsed the Commission's view, adding that the withdrawal of the licence had adverse effects on the goodwill and value of the restaurant.[39] A licence is often granted under certain conditions. If a licence-holder no longer meets the conditions, he cannot be considered to have a legitimate expectation to continue his activities.[40] Similarly, a licence-holder

---

[34]   Appls 4897/71 and 5219/71, *Gussenbauer*, Coll. 42 (1973), pp. 41 and 94, respectively.

[35]   Report of 8 October 1974, Yearbook XV (1972).

[36]   Judgment of 23 November 1983, paras 25-26. See also Appl. 8682/79, *X v. Federal Republic of Germany*, D&R 26 (1982), p. 97 (99-100), where the Commission held that Article 1 is not violated when an officially appointed defence counsel is obliged to repay an advance on his fees for not having assured the accused's defence up to the end of the proceedings.

[37]   Appl. 10426/83, D&R 40 (1985), p. 234 (241).

[38]   Report of 10 November 1987, para. 111.

[39]   Judgment of 7 July 1989, para. 53.

[40]   Appl. 10438/83, *Batelaan and Huiges*, D&R 41 (1985), p. 170 (173).

cannot be considered to have a reasonable and legitimate expectation to continue his activity if the licence is withdrawn in accordance with the provisions of the law which was in force when the licence was issued.[41]

In the *Van Marie* Case the Court stated that it agreed with the Commission that the 'goodwill' relied upon by the applicants may be "likened to the right of property embodied in Article 1: by dint of their own work, the applicants had built up a clientele; this had in many respects the nature of a private right and constituted an asset and, hence, a possession within the meaning of Article 1."[42]

On the other hand, the Commission rejected complaints by Greek customs officers about loss of income due to the abolition of customs barriers within the European Union. The Commission noted that in Greece the occupation of customs officer is a liberal profession, with no fixed income and no guaranteed turnover, but which is subjected to the hazards of economic life. The customs officers could not claim to be entitled to a guaranteed volume of business which could have qualified as a 'possession'.[43]

Measures which are taken in order to establish who is entitled to a certain property – for instance seizure[44] – and conditions with regard to the evidence of that entitlement, in themselves do not constitute violations of Article 1, unless such conditions impose an unreasonably heavy burden of proof on the person laying claim to the property.[45]

17.3.2 PEACEFUL ENJOYMENT

Article 1 protects 'peaceful enjoyment'. That implies that this provision may also have been violated when a person has not been affected as to his property or possessions *per se,* but is not accorded an opportunity to use that property, for instance because a necessary permit is refused to him,[46] or because in some other way such restrictions

---

[41] Appl. 19819/92, *Størksen,* D&R 78-A (1994), p. 88 (94).

[42] Judgment of 26 June 1986, para. 41. See however the decision of the Commission on Appl. 10438/83, *Batelaan and Huiges,* D&R 41 (1985), p. 170 (173): the goodwill of a professional practice is an element in its valuation but does not constitute a 'possession' to the extent that it is not necessarily linked with the profession in question. See for law practices and their goodwill: judgment of 24 May 2005, *Buzescu,* para. 81 and paras 88-98, respectively.

[43] Appl. 24581/94, *Greek Federation of Customs Officers, Galouris, Christopoulos and 3,333 other customs officers,* D&R 81-B (1995), p. 123 (128).

[44] Appl. 7256/75, *X v. Belgium,* D&R 8 (1977), p. 161 (165-166).

[45] See Appl. 7775/77, *Pacheco,* D&R 15 (1979), p. 143, which was declared inadmissible by the Commission.

[46] See, *e.g.,* Appl. 7456/76, *Wiggins,* D&R 13 (1979), p. 40 (46-47), concerning the refusal of a housing licence to the applicant to live in his own house.

ensue from the legislation or from government measures to the extent that there is
no longer any question of a 'peaceful enjoyment'.[47]

In the *Loizidou* Case, which concerned denial of access to property situated in the
area occupied by Turkish Cypriot forces following the civil war in Cyprus, the
Commission was of the opinion that the right to the peaceful enjoyment of possessions
did not include as a corollary a right of freedom of movement. However, the Court
took the position that the applicant's complaint was wider: she had complained that
the denial of access over a period of 16 years had gradually affected her right as a
property owner and in particular her right to a peaceful enjoyment of her possessions.
Against this background the Court did not accept the characterisation of her complaint
as being limited to the right of freedom of movement. Article 1 was thus held to be
applicable.[48]

That Article 1 applies to restrictions on the possibilities of using property is also
clear from the second paragraph, which employs the words 'to control the use of
property'. However, the distinction between 'deprivation of possessions' and 'control
of the use of property' is a fluid one in certain situations. In some cases the Court
appears to have difficulties in bringing the case under either the second sentence of
Article 1 (deprivation of possessions) or the second paragraph of that article (control
of use of property), although the right to peaceful enjoyment of possessions is clearly
affected. In such circumstances the case is decided on the basis of the "general rule"
laid down in the first sentence.

In the *Sporrong and Lönnroth* Case, although the expropriations left intact in law
the owners' right to use and dispose of their possessions, they nevertheless in practice
significantly reduced the possibility of its exercise. The expropriation measures also
affected the very substance of ownership in that they recognised before the event that
any expropriation would be lawful and authorised the City of Stockholm to expropriate
whenever it found it expedient to do so. In the Court's view the applicants' right of
property thus became precarious and defeasible.[49]

In the *Erkner and Hofauer* Case and in the *Poiss* Case the applicants submitted that
the provisional transfer of their land to other landowners, who were partners to a
consolidation scheme, interfered with their right of property. The Court noted that

---

[47]   Report of 8 October 1980, *Sporrong and Lönnroth*, para. 103, concerning, *inter alia*, restrictions on
the possibility to build on land held in freehold. See also Appl. 7889/77, *Arrondelle*, D&R 19 (1980),
p. 186, where the complaint concerned the nuisance caused to the owner of a house by the
neighbouring airfield. In this case a friendly settlement has been reached; report of 13 May 1982,
D&R 26 (1982), p. 5. See, *e.g.*, judgment of 27 March 2003, *Satka and Others*, paras 44-50.
[48]   Judgment of 18 December 1996, paras 60-61.
[49]   Judgment of 23 September 1982, para. 60. See also the report of 8 October 1987, *Jacobsson*, paras
129-130, where the Commission considered that the continued building prohibition on the
applicant's property constituted an interference with his right to the peaceful enjoyment of
possessions.

the Austrian authorities did not effect either a formal expropriation or a *de facto* expropriation (Article 1, second sentence). The transfer carried out was a provisional one; only the entry into force of the consolidation plan would make it irrevocable. The applicants would, therefore, recover their land if the final plan could not confirm the distribution made at an earlier stage of the proceedings. Nor was the provisional transfer essentially designed to restrict or control the 'use' of the land (second paragraph), but to achieve an early restructuring of the consolidation area with a view to improved, rational farming by the 'provisional owners'.[50] Impliedly the Court recognised here that apart from formal expropriations the second sentence of Article 1 may also extend to *de facto* expropriations which "can be assimilated to a deprivation of possessions".[51]

However, in a case where the Court concluded that there had been a *de facto* expropriation, it did not specify which sentence of Article 1 applied. In the *Papamichalopoulos* Case the applicants' land had been occupied by the Greek military authorities without any compensation. Although the Greek courts had subsequently recognised the applicants' rights to the land, it had not been returned to them. Neither had any compensatory measures been effected. Thus, the applicants, although technically still the owners of the land, were unable to dispose of it in any way. The Court had little difficulty in finding a violation: "The loss of all ability to dispose of the land in issue, taken together with the failure of the attempts made so far to remedy the situation complained of, entailed sufficiently serious consequences for the applicants *de facto* to have been expropriated in a manner incompatible with their right to the peaceful enjoyment of their possessions."[52]

From this formulation it is unclear whether the Court applied the first sentence or the second sentence of Article 1, or a combination of the two rules. Conversely, in the *Hentrich* Case the Court did specify that there had been a deprivation of possessions to which the second sentence applied, but it did not respond to the applicant's contention that there had been a *de facto* expropriation.[53]

In other cases in which the first sentence was identified as the applicable rule the Court gave some criteria for its choice. In its judgment in the *Matos e Silva, Lda. and Others* Case the Court examined a number of measures interfering with the applicants' right to the peaceful enjoyment of their possessions (parcels of land). These included so-called public interest declarations, issued as a preliminary to expropriation for the purpose of creating a nature reserve, and prohibitions on all building and on any change in the use of the land. The Court held that there was no formal or *de facto*

---

[50] Judgments of 23 April 1987, para. 74 and para. 64, respectively. See also the judgment of 30 October 1991, *Wiesinger*, para. 72.
[51] Judgments of 23 April 1987, *Erkner and Hofauer* and *Poiss*, para. 74 and para. 64, respectively.
[52] Judgment of 24 June 1993, para. 45.
[53] Judgment of 22 September 1994, para. 34.

deprivation of possessions in this case, as the effects of the measures were not irreversible as had been the case in *Papamichalopoulos*: "The restrictions on the right to property stemmed from the reduced ability to dispose of the property and from the damage sustained by reason of the fact that expropriation was contemplated. Although the right in question had lost some of its substance, it had not disappeared. The Court notes, for example, that all reasonable manner of exploiting the property had not disappeared seeing that the applicants continued to work the land. The second sentence of the first paragraph is therefore not applicable in this case."[54]

In the *Phocas* Case the Court held the first sentence to be applicable because the applicant did not complain about a deprivation of property or of specific measures restricting the use of it, but of an infringement resulting from the authorities' general conduct.[55] In the *Elia S.r.l.* Case the Court held explicitly that the second sentence of the first paragraph was not applicable, after having observed that the applicant company was not denied access to its land and did not lose control of it and that, although it became more difficult to sell the land, that possibility in principle subsisted. Because the measures did not amount to a control of the use of property within the meaning of the second paragraph either, the situation fell to be dealt with under the first sentence of Article 1.[56]

However, the importance of the classification of cases under the three rules of Article 1 should not be exaggerated. As was recalled in section 17.1 above, the Court has always held that these three rules are not unconnected: the rule concerning deprivation of possessions and that concerning control of the use of property should be construed in the light of the general principle laid down in the first sentence: the right to the peaceful enjoyment of possessions. This is made clear also by the main test applied for establishing whether or not Article 1 has been violated.

The Court confirmed this point of view in the *Beyeler* Case concerning the question who was the owner of a painting of Vincent van Gogh. In 1977 a Roman art collector sold the painting to a person who six years later appeared to have acted as the agent of the applicant. When, in 1988, the applicant sold the painting to the Peggy Guggenheim Collection in Venice, the Italian State exercised its right of pre-emption in respect of the 1977 sale, notwithstanding the two-months time-limit which applies for exercising this right, and prevented the transfer of the painting to Venice. The Court did not consider it necessary to rule on whether the second sentence of the first paragraph of Article 1 applied to this case: "The complexity of the factual and legal position prevents its being classified in a precise category". The situation envisaged in the second sentence of Article 1 is only a particular instance of interference with

---

[54]   Judgment of 16 September 1996, para. 85.
[55]   Judgment of 23 April 1996, para. 54 (urban development scheme which impeded the development of the applicant's property without any compensation for more than 16 years).
[56]   Judgment of 2 August 2001, *Elia S.r.l.*, paras 56-57.

the right to peaceful enjoyment of property as guaranteed by the general rule set forth in the first sentence. The Court, therefore, considered that it should examine the situation in the light of that general rule.[57]

Under each of the three rules the Court applies a 'fair balance' test: "The Court must determine whether a fair balance was struck between the demands of the general interest of the community and the requirements of the protection of the individual's fundamental rights. The search for this balance is inherent in the whole of the Convention and is also reflected in the structure of Article 1."[58] Here, as with other proportionality tests under the Convention, the Court accepts that a margin of appreciation must be left to the national authorities. In the context of Article 1 this margin of appreciation is usually wide.

The case law with respect to the first sentence shows that there are two – often combined – aspects to the protection offered by the fair balance requirement: (formal) protection against lack of procedural guarantees or against protracted proceedings, and (substantive) protection against arbitrary action by the State,[59] or action which puts an individual and excessive burden on the applicant. The absence of any compensation may also be a relevant factor under the fair balance test.

In order to determine whether a 'fair balance' had been achieved in the *Sporrong and Lönnroth* Case the Court examined the possibilities for the applicants to seek a reduction of the time limits within which the expropriation of their properties might be effected or to claim compensation for the damages suffered during the extremely long period during which the enjoyment of their property right had been impeded. Because remedies to that effect were not available, the Court decided that Article 1 had been violated.[60]

Conversely, the fair balance will not be upset where the applicant has failed to make proper use of available procedures for remedying the interferences complained of, even where these interferences were *prima facie* incompatible with the fair balance requirement and even where the conduct of the authorities was not beyond reproach. Thus, in the *Phocas* Case the Court first noted with regard to the restrictions imposed on the applicant's property on account of a development scheme for improving the

---

[57] Judgment of 5 January 2000, para. 106. See also the judgment of 12 July 2005, *Solodyuk*, para. 29.

[58] Judgment of 23 September 1982, *Sporrong and Lönnroth*, para. 69 (with respect to the first sentence of paragraph 1). See, for the second sentence of paragraph 1, judgment of December 1994, *Holy Monasteries*, para. 70. For the second paragraph, see judgment of 21 November 1995, *Velosa Barreto*, para. 23.

[59] Like a Supreme Court decision which is contrary to legitimate expectations; judgments of 24 February 2005, *Veselinski* and *Djidrovski*, paras 81-82 and paras 86-87, respectively.

[60] Judgment of 23 September 1982, paras 69-74. See also the Court's focus on procedural issues, including the length of the land consolidation proceedings, in the *Erkner and Hofauer* and *Poiss* Cases, judgments of 23 April 1987, para. 77 and para. 68, respectively; likewise judgment of 30 October 1991, *Wiesinger*, para. 77.

crossroads where his property was situated: "The threat of expropriation and the restrictions on building were undoubtedly an obstacle to continuing to run his business on the premises and made it doubtful that he could sell them or let them as a trader. Nor was the applicant able to convert his building as he wished, since three of his applications for planning permission were adjourned and one refused. (...) Such a situation is in principle incompatible with the fair balance required by Article 1 of Protocol No. 1."[61] However, the Court then observed that a remedy had been available to the applicant: he could have taken steps to have his land purchased by the local authority for whose benefit the land had been reserved under the development plan within three years of the application. Failing agreement, an application could be made to the expropriations judge to fix the price. Having regard to the applicant's conduct – he twice renewed his application to the local authority instead of turning to the expropriations judge, with the result that, when he finally did apply to the judge, his application was out of time so that the judge had to decline jurisdiction – the Court found that the failure of these proceedings was attributable to him, "even if the authorities delayed in replying to Mr Phocas's applications". The Court concluded that Article 1 had not been violated.[62]

The Court reached the opposite conclusion with respect to the interferences with the applicants' property rights in the above-mentioned *Matos e Silva, Lda. and Others* Case. Although it recognised that the various measures complained of did not lack a reasonable basis, the Court observed as follows: "in the circumstances of the case the measures had serious and harmful effects that have hindered the applicants' ordinary enjoyment of their rights for more than thirteen years during which virtually no progress has been made in the proceedings. The long period of uncertainty both as to what would become of the possessions and as to the question of compensation further aggravated the detrimental effects of the disputed measures. As a result, the applicants have had to bear an individual and excessive burden which has upset the fair balance which should be struck between the requirements of the general interest and the protection of the right to the peaceful enjoyment of one's possessions."[63]

---

61   Judgment of 23 April 1996, Vol. 7, p. 544.
62   *Ibidem*, p. 545. Failure to make use of available remedies was also held against the applicant in the judgment of 27 October 1994, *Katte Klitsche de la Grange*, para. 46. In the *Phocas* Case, judges Foighel and Palm dissented, agreeing with the Commission that the acts of the French authorities and courts had made the applicant's right of property unstable and uncertain over a very long period. Pointing to a lack of diligence on the part of the authorities and of indications given by them which could reasonably lead to applicant to believe that negotiations were continuing and that a solution was imminent, these judges disagreed with the majority that the failure of the domestic proceedings was attributable to the applicant alone.
63   Judgment of 16 September 1996, p. 1115. The 'individual an excessive burden' criterion was applied by the Court for the first time under the first sentence of paragraph 1 in the judgment of 23 September 1982, *Sporrong and Lönnroth*, para. 73. As regards the second sentence of paragraph 1, see the judgment of 22 September 1994, *Hentrich*, para. 49. See also the judgment of 2 August 2001, *Elis S.r.l.*, para. 83.

In the *Stran Greek Refineries and Stratis Andreadis* Case the applicants complained of the Greek legislature's intervention which annulled an arbitration award that was in their favour and had become final and binding. In this case domestic courts of first instance and of appeal had already held that there were no grounds for annulment of the arbitration award when, at the State's request, the date for the hearing by the Court of Cassation was postponed on the ground that a draft law on the case was before Parliament. Just before the hearing took place a law was enacted which, *inter alia,* annulled the award. Subsequently, this part of the law was not held unconstitutional by the Court of Cassation. The Court, referring to the case law of international courts and arbitration tribunals, did no question the right of the State to terminate contracts with private individuals provided it pays compensation and with the exception of arbitration clauses. The domestic courts of first instance and of appeal had recognised in this case that arbitration clauses are autonomous. Moreover, they had found that the unilateral termination of the contract by the Greek State had not invalidated the applicants' existing claims. The Court concluded that Greece was "under a duty to pay the applicants the sums awarded against it at the conclusion of the arbitration procedure, a procedure for which it had itself opted and the validity of which had been accepted until the day of the hearing in the Court of Cassation. (...) By choosing to intervene at that stage of the proceedings in the Court of Cassation (...) the legislature upset, to the detriment of the applicants, the balance that must be struck between the protection of the right of property and the requirements of public interest."[64] The straightforward reasoning of the unanimous Court in this case may be explained by the dubious, *ad hoc* character of the legislation in question. As the Court observed, "the real objective of the legislature" was to close the domestic proceedings in the present case once and for all.[65]

17.4 DEPRIVATION OF POSSESSIONS

17.4.1 IN THE PUBLIC INTEREST

The most important restriction to be imposed by the authorities on the peaceful enjoyment of one's possessions is regulated explicitly in the second sentence: deprivation of property in the public interest.[66] Under this head the Court examines 1) whether the deprivation had a 'public interest' aim; 2) whether the measure was

---

[64] Judgment of 9 December 1994, para. 74.

[65] *Ibidem,* para. 69.

[66] On the question of whether this sentence applies also to *de facto* expropriation, see section 17.2 *supra.*

proportionate in relation to the aim pursued; and 3) whether the measure was lawful, *i.e.* 'provided for by law' and by 'the general principles of international law'.[67]

Such a test is of course not necessary when the circumstances are clear. Thus the Court held in the *Sîrbu* Case that by failing to comply with the judgments of the Centru District Court the national authorities prevented the applicants from having their compensation paid and from enjoying the possession of their money: "The Government have not advanced any justification for this interference and the Court considers that lack of funds cannot justify such an omission."[68]

Whether a particular expropriation has been performed in the public interest will be subjected by the Court to a very limited review only, the main objective being to detect cases of *détournement de pouvoir*[69] or of manifest arbitrariness.[70] As the Commission stated in its report in the *Handyside* Case in connection with the fact that the first paragraph speaks of 'in the public interest' and not of 'necessary in a democratic society': "Clearly the public or general interest encompasses measures which would be preferable or advisable, and not only essential, in a democratic society."[71]

In the *James* Case the Court held with respect to the State's margin of appreciation as follows: "Furthermore, the notion of 'public interest' is necessarily extensive. In particular, as the Commission noted, the decision to enact laws expropriating property will commonly involve considerations of political, economic and social issues on which opinion within a democratic society may reasonably differ widely. The Court, finding it natural that the margin of appreciation available to the legislature in implementing social and economic policies should be a wide one, will respect the legislature's judgment as to what is 'in the public interest' unless that judgment be manifestly without

---

[67] See the judgment of 22 September 1994, *Hentrich,* where the Court examined all three requirements. In most judgments, however, the 'lawfulness' of the deprivation measure is not at issue; in fact, such measures normally take the form of legislation. In its judgment of 18 November 2004, *Fotopoulou,* para. 38, the Court stated that the legal basis for the demolition of a wall failed. Thus, Article 1 had been violated.

[68] Judgment of 15 June 2004, para. 32. See also the judgment of 14 September 2004, *Timbal,* para. 25; judgment of 2 November 2004, *Tregubenko,* para. 54. In its judgment of 9 November 2004, *Svetlana Naumenko,* para. 104, the Court noted that the impossibility for the applicant to obtain enforcement of the judgment recognising her status of a "Chernobyl relief worker" for an unreasonably long period of time constituted an interference with her right to the peaceful enjoyment of her possessions.

[69] See Appl. 3039/67, *A, B, C and D v. the United Kingdom,* Yearbook X (1967), p. 506 (516-518), where the Commission uses the doctrine of the margin of appreciation also on this point. See also the Court's judgment of 9 December 1994, *Holy Monasteries,* para. 67 (doubts as to real reasons of a legislative measure; see *infra*).

[70] Report of 30 September 1975, *Handyside,* para. 163; judgment of 21 February 1986, *James,* para. 46.

[71] *Ibidem.*

reasonable foundation."[72] Regarding the meaning of 'the public interest' the Court held as follows: "a deprivation of property effected for no reason other than to confer a private benefit on a private party cannot be 'in the public interest'. Nonetheless, the compulsory transfer of property from one individual to another may, depending upon the circumstances, constitute a legitimate aim for promoting the public interest."[73] The Court added that a taking of property effected in pursuance of legitimate, social, economic or other policies may be 'in the public interest', even if the community at large has no direct use or enjoyment of the property taken.[74]

It is, therefore, not surprising that the Court has, so far, never ruled that a deprivation of possessions was not 'in the public interest'. For example, it accepted that the prevention of tax evasion is a legitimate objective which is in the public interest.[75] Likewise, the purpose of constructing housing for a category of disadvantaged persons constitutes a public interest aim.[76] In the *Pressos Compania Naviera S.A.* Case the Court accepted that a law depriving the applicants of their property pursued such an aim, without commenting in any specific way on the reasons put forward by the Belgian Government.[77]

The Court's deference to the national legislature's assessment of what is in the public interest appears very clearly from the judgment in the *Holy Monasteries* Case. This case concerned a Greek law effectively transferring full ownership of land held by the monasteries to the State. The reasons given for this measure were to end illegal sales of the land, encroachments on it and its abandonment or uncontrolled development. The Court expressed some doubts on this point on account of the fact that the law gave the State optional power whether or not to transfer the land for use by farmers and that it mentioned also public bodies in the list of possible beneficiaries. Nonetheless, it accepted that the overall objective of the law was legitimate.[78]

When the Court had to judge the expropriation of property of the former King of Greece, it followed the same approach. It first stated "that because of their direct knowledge of their society and its needs, the national authorities are in principle better placed than the international judge to appreciate what is 'in the public interest'." Subsequently the Court noted "that there is no evidence to support the Government's

---

[72]   Judgment of 21 February 1986, para. 46. See also the judgment of 8 July 1986, *Lithgow and Others*, para. 122; judgment of 20 November 1995, *Pressos Compania Naviera S.A. and Others*, para. 37; judgment of 23 November 2000, *The former King of Greece and Others*, para. 87; judgment of 22 June 2004, *Broniowski*, para. 149.

[73]   Judgment of 21 February 1986, para. 40.

[74]   *Ibidem*, paras 47-49.

[75]   Judgment of 22 September 1994, *Hentrich*, para. 39.

[76]   Judgment of 7 August 1996, *Zubani*, p. 1077.

[77]   Judgment of 20 November 1995, para. 34. The Belgian Government had sought to justify the interference (a law which retroactively deprived the applicants of civil law claims against the State) by referring to the need to protect the State's financial interests, the need to re-establish legal certainty and the need to bring Belgian legislation in line with that of neighbouring countries.

[78]   Judgment of 9 December 1994, para. 69.

argument on the need to protect the forests and archaeological sites. On the other hand, it does not doubt that is was necessary for the Greek State to resolve an issue which it considered to be prejudicial for its status as Republic. The fact that the constitutional transition from a monarchy to a republic took place in 1975, namely almost twenty years before the enactment on the contested Law, might inspire some doubt as to the reasons for the measures, but it cannot suffice to deprive the overall objective of Law no. 2215/1194 of its legitimacy as being 'in the public interest'."[79] These considerations show the very reticent attitude of the Court towards this question.

17.4.2   PROPORTIONALITY OF THE MEASURE

The review by the Court is more extensive as concerns the proportionality requirement, although a wide margin of appreciation for national legislatures is normally also accepted on this score. As was already pointed out in section 17.2.2 above, the Court assesses the proportionality of the contested measure by determining whether a 'fair balance' has been struck between the interest of the community and the requirements of the protection of the individual's fundamental rights. This means, in particular, that there must be a reasonable relationship of proportionality between the means employed and the aim sought to be realised by any measure depriving a person of his possessions.[80]

According to the Court compensation terms are material to the assessment of whether the contested measure respects the requisite fair balance and whether or not it imposes a disproportionate burden. In this connection the Court holds that the taking of property without payment of an amount reasonably related to its value will normally constitute a disproportionate interference.[81] However, legitimate objectives of "public interest may call for less than reimbursement of the full market value".[82] A total lack of compensation can be considered justifiable only in exceptional circumstances.[83] Such a lack of compensation does not make a deprivation *eo ipso*

---

[79]   Judgment of 23 November 2000, *The former King of Greece and Others*, para. 88.

[80]   See the judgment of 21 February 1986, *James and Others*, para. 50; judgment of 8 July 1986, *Lithgow and Others*, para. 120; judgment of 9 December 1994, *Holy Monasteries*, para. 70; judgment of 20 November 1995, *Pressos Compania Naviera S.A. and Others*, para. 33; judgment of 23 November 2000, *The former King of Greece and Others*, para. 89.

[81]   See, *inter alia*, the judgment of 11 January 2001, *Platakou*, para. 55.

[82]   See the judgment of 9 December 1994, *Holy Monasteries*, paras 70-71; judgment of 25 March 1999, *Papachelas*, para. 48; judgment of 16 November 2004, *Bruncrona*, para. 68.

[83]   Judgment of 9 December 1994, *Holy Monasteries*, para. 73; judgment of 20 November 1995, *Pressos Compania Naviera S.A. and Others*, para. 31; judgment of 23 November 2000, *The former King of Greece and Others*, para. 89. In its judgment of 21 February 1986, *James*, para. 54, and in its judgment of 8 July 1986, *Lithgow and Others*, para. 120, the Court had already referred to this in terms of a principle applying under the legal systems of the Contracting States, adding that the protection afforded by Article 1 would be largely illusory in the absence of any equivalent principle.

wrongful, provided that the interference in question satisfies the requirement of lawfulness and is not arbitrary. Decisive is, whether in the context of a lawful expropriation a disproportionate and excessive burden has been imposed on the individual.[84] This requires an overall examination of the various interests in issue, baring in mind that the Convention is intended to safeguard rights that are 'practical and effective'. Therefore, it is necessary to look behind appearances and investigate the realities of the situation complained of. That assessment may involve not only the relevant compensation terms, but also the conduct of the parties. In that context uncertainty is a factor to be taken into account in assessing the State's conduct. Public authorities have to act in good time as well as in an appropriate and consistent manner.[85]

These principles were applied in the *Broniowski* Case. The Court had to judge the way the Polish authorities had handled their obligation to compensate nearly 80,000 people who had lost property as a result of their repatriation following the territorial changes between Poland en the Soviet-Union after the Second World War. The Polish State had recognised the claims, but practical and legislative obstacles had made it almost impossible to realise them. The Court recognised that during the political, economic and social transition undergone by Poland in recent years, it was necessary for the authorities to resolve exceptionally difficult situations, involving complex, large-scale decisions. The vast number of persons involved and the very substantial value of their claims certainly had to be taken into account in ascertaining whether the requisite 'fair balance' was struck. The Court also accepted that in the case before it, involving a wide-ranging but controversial legislative scheme with significant economic impact for the country as a whole, the choice of measures may necessarily involve decisions restricting compensation for the taking or restitution of property to a level below its market value. Still there should be a reasonable relation to the real value of the property. An earlier compensation to the applicant of 2% did in any case not suffice to cut him off from broader compensation measures, which were to be rewarded to persons who had not yet received any compensation at all.[86]

After Greece had become a republic in 1974, possessions of the Greek Church and of the former royal family were expropriated. In both cases not any compensation was provided for by the legislator who had decided the expropriations. In the *Holy Monasteries* Case the Court disagreed with the Commission that exceptional circumstances existed which would justify the total lack of compensation. The special relationship between the Greek Church and the State was not sufficient to justify the measures taken, which imposed a considerable burden on the applicant monasteries. When

---

[84]   Judgment of 23 November 2000, *The former King of Greece and Others, supra*, para. 90. See also the judgment of 21 February 1986, *James and Others*, para. 50; judgment of 22 September 1994, *Hentrich*, para. 49; judgment of 22 June 2004, *Broniowski*, para. 150.

[85]   Judgment of 22 June 2004, *Broniowski*, para. 151.

[86]   *Ibidem*, paras 162-186. See as to the former GDR: judgment of 30 June 2005, *Jahn and Others*.

resorting to similar expropriation measures in 1952, the State had provided for compensation to the monasteries of one-third of the real value of the land. No compensation measures had been taken in the case at hand. The Court concluded that Article 1 had been violated.[87] In the *The former King of Greece* Case the Court held that the Greek State could have considered in good faith that exceptional circumstances justified the absence of compensation, but that this assessment was not objectively substantiated. The Court pointed out that at least part of the expropriated property was purchased by the applicants' predecessors in title and paid out of their private funds. Moreover, compensation was provided for the last time the property was expropriated in 1973. Therefore, the applicants had a legitimate expectation to be compensated by the Greek legislature for the taking of their estates.[88]

The judgment in the *Pressos Compania Naviera S.A.* Case confirms the Court's critical attitude towards legislative interference with the judicial process and the importance it attaches to rule of law considerations.[89] The Court considered that the Belgian law at issue quite simply extinguished, with retrospective effect going back thirty years and without compensation, claims for very high damages that the victims of the pilot accidents could have pursued against the Belgian State or against the private companies concerned, and in some cases even in proceedings that were already pending. The serious financial considerations cited by the Government could warrant prospective legislation to derogate from the general law of tort but not legislating with retrospective effect with the aim and consequence of depriving the applicants of their claims for compensation. Such a fundamental interference with the applicants' rights is inconsistent with preserving a fair balance between the interests at stake.[90]

Although legitimate objectives of public interest may call for compensations which do not reflect the full market value, it is self-evident that in less exceptional circumstances reimbursement of the full market value should stay the rule. And even this can turn out to be insufficient in specific situations. In the *Hentrich* Case the applicant complained of measures taken by the French tax authorities under which she was deprived of the real property which she had purchased. French law recognised a right of pre-emption by the Revenue, where the latter considered the sale price to be too low. This right, a deterrent against tax evasion, was to be exercised by offering to pay the purchaser the sale price plus a ten percent premium. The Court first stated that, in order to assess the proportionality of this interference, it had to look at the degree of protection from arbitrariness that was afforded by the proceedings in this case. In this instance domestic law did not require that reasons be given for the decision to

---

87   Judgment of 9 December 1994, *Holy Monasteries*, paras 74-75.
88   Judgment of 23 November 2000, *supra*, para. 98.
89   See also the judgment in *Stran Greek Refineries and Stratis Andreadis*, discussed in section 17.3.2 *supra*.
90   Judgment of 20 November 1995, paras 39-44 See also the judgment of 29 July 2004, *Scordino*, para. 79.

exercise the right of pre-emption. The right of pre-emption allowed the tax authorities to substitute themselves for any purchaser, even one acting in perfectly good faith, for the sole purpose of general deterrence against tax evasion. In addition this right of pre-emption, which does not exist in other States, was not exercised systematically every time the sale price was too low, but only rarely and scarcely foreseeable. The Court, after having pointed to other suitable methods for discouraging tax evasion, and having regard to the risk run by any purchaser that he will lose his property and the "definite level of severity" of the consequences of a pre-emption measure, considered that "merely reimbursing the price paid – increased by 10 percent – and the costs and expenses of the contract cannot suffice to compensate for the loss of a property acquired without any fraudulent intent". Having regard to all these factors the Court considered that, as a selected victim of the exercise of the right of pre-emption, Mrs Hentrich bore an individual and excessive burden which could have been rendered legitimate only if she had had the possibility – which was refused to her – of effectively challenging the measure taken against her.[91] A particular feature of this case was the fact that, although compensation had been given to the applicant, the Court found that the French system offered insufficient protection from arbitrary deprivation of property.[92]

In the *Lallement* Case a farmer had lost 60% of his lands, which he used for milk production. The land was needed for the building of a road. The farmer was compensated fully for the expropriation of the land. However, he argued that he had also to be compensated for the loss of his production resources, because of the inextricable connection between the possession of the whole parcel of land and the possibility to continue his milk producing activities. The Court held that a compensation which did not cover the loss of his possibilities to continue his milk producing activities as well created an excessive burden to the farmer and, therefore, constituted a violation of Article 1.[93]

In the same vein the Court saw an excessive burden for a person who had been expropriated, as the authorities postponed the land use measures for which the expropriation had taken place for a very long time. According to the Court the applicant had to be compensated additionally for the increase in value of the land since the moment of the expropriation 19 years earlier.[94]

---

[91] Judgment of 22 September 1994, paras 43–49.
[92] In this connection, it should be noted that the Court also reached a negative conclusion as concerns the lawfulness of the interference See also the judgment of 7 August 1996, *Zubani*, para. 49, where the Court found a violation on account of the way the national authorities had handled the applicants' situation, in spite of the fact that a considerable compensation had been awarded to them.
[93] Judgment of 11 April 2002, para. 24.
[94] Judgment of 2 July 2002, *Motais de Narbonne,* paras 16–23.

17.4.3 PROVIDED FOR BY LAW AND BY THE GENERAL PRINCIPLES OF INTERNATIONAL LAW

Expropriations are permissible only if the conditions provided for by law and by the general principles of international law have been observed. As regards compliance with national legal conditions, here again the Court does not examine whether national law has been applied correctly. It takes the position that in this matter it has to refer to the judgment of the national court in the case concerned and that it must not function as a 'fourth instance'. Nonetheless, the Court has recalled, also in the context of Article 1, that the notion of 'law' within the meaning of the Convention requires the existence of and compliance with adequately accessible and sufficiently precise domestic legal provisions.[95] Furthermore, there must be protection, in the form of procedural safeguards, from arbitrariness.[96]

With respect to the reference to international legal principles one is inclined to think first of all of the obligation to pay damages, as this obligation exists under international law or at all events existed according to the prevalent view at the moment when Protocol No. 1 was drafted. In fact the Commission has taken that general principle of international law into consideration. It came, however, with reference to the genesis of Article 1, to the conclusion that this principle relates exclusively to the nationalisation of foreign property and cannot be invoked against the national State of the owner. This has led the Commission to conclude that in the case of public interest expropriation of property owned by the State's own subjects, the State is under no obligation to pay damages if this is not provided for in national law.[97]

According to this interpretation Article 1 of Protocol No. 1 permits a difference in treatment between the State's own nationals and aliens, this contrary to the purpose of the Convention to secure to everyone the same enjoyment of the rights and freedoms, as laid down in Articles 1 and 14, and Protocol No. 12. This result is all the more curious as the derogation from that purpose is an implied one and this even to the detriment of the State's own nationals, while other derogations are laid down expressly, *viz.* in Article 16 of the Convention and Article 3 of Protocol No. 4, and are to the detriment of aliens. However, in the case of Article 1 of Protocol No. 1 this does not create a fundamental difference between nationals and aliens, but one which exists only insofar and as long as general principles of international law actually prescribe a specific treatment of foreign property and these principles are different from those applying under the law of the State in question with regard to the treatment of the

---

[95] See the judgment of 8 July 1986, *Lithgow and Others,* para. 110; judgment of 22 September 1994, *Hentrich,* para. 42.

[96] Judgment of 22 September 1994, *Hentrich,* para. 42 Here, the Court criticised the discretionary nature of the exercise of the State's right of pre-emption and the unfairness of the procedure (no adversarial proceedings respecting the principle of equality of arms).

[97] See, *e.g.,* Appl. 511/59, *Gudmundsson,* Yearbook III (1960), p. 394 (422-424).

property of its own nationals. If any differences on this point still exist at present, developments within international law go into the direction of their minimisation.[98] It should be added that also developments in the case law of the Court as regards compensation for deprivation of property of nationals tend to result in a relativisation of these differences.[99]

In the *James* Case and in the *Lithgow* Case the Court, too, held that the reference to the general principles of international law in Article 1 means that those principles are incorporated into that article, but only as regards those acts to which they are normally applicable, that is to say acts of a State in relation to non-nationals. For this interpretation the Court referred to Article 31 of the Vienna Convention on the Law of Treaties: the words of a treaty should be understood to have their ordinary meaning.[100] On that ground it rejected the grammatical argument of the applicants, based upon Article 1, that all elements of that article applied to everyone. The Court also rejected the argument of the applicants that the interpretation according to which the principle in question only applied to non-nationals, would make the reference in Article 1 to the general principles redundant since non-nationals already enjoyed the protection thereof. In the Court's view the inclusion of the reference could be seen to serve at least two purposes: "Firstly, it enables non-nationals to resort directly to the machinery of the Convention to enforce their rights on the basis of the relevant principles of international law, whereas otherwise they would have to seek recourse to diplomatic channels or to other available means of dispute settlement to do so. Secondly, the reference ensures that the position of non-nationals is safeguarded, in that it excludes any possible argument that the entry into force of Protocol No. 1 has led to a diminution of their rights."[101] The Court also indicated that the difference in treatment did not constitute discrimination, since the differences in treatment had an 'objective and reasonable justification': "Especially as regards a taking of property effected in the context of a social reform, there may well be good grounds for drawing

---

[98]   See the Charter of Economic Rights and Duties of States, adopted by Res. 3281 (XXIX) of the General Assembly of the UN on 12 December 1974, *International Legal Materials* (1975), p. 251

[99]   See the observations made above as concerns the Court's critical attitude in cases where there has been a total lack of compensation. A further way of minimising the differences in protection between nationals and aliens appears from the Commission's report in the *Gasus Dosier und Fördertechnik* Case, report of 21 October 1993, paras 57-64. This was a (rare) case of interference with property rights of an alien (a foreign company). The Commission considered that the seizure of the applicant company's machine – in actual possession of a Dutch company which went bankrupt – by the Dutch tax authorities for the purpose of securing payment of the taxes owed by the bankrupt company, constituted a deprivation of possessions. Nevertheless, the Commission said that this particular form of deprivation of possessions could not be compared to measures of confiscation, nationalisation or expropriation in regard to which international law provides special protection to foreign citizens and companies. The Court did not pronounce o this aspect of the case, as it examined it under the second paragraph of Art. 1.

[100]   Judgment of 21 February 1986, para. 61; judgment of 8 July 1986, para. 114.

[101]   *Ibidem*, para. 62 and para. 118, respectively.

a distinction between nationals and non-nationals as far as compensation is concerned."[102] In the Court's view non-nationals are more vulnerable to domestic legislation since, unlike nationals, they will generally have played no part in the elections. Secondly, although the taking of property must always be effected in the public interest, different considerations may apply to nationals and non-nationals and there may well be a legitimate reason for requiring nationals to bear a greater burden in the public interest than non-nationals. Finally, the Court pointed to the fact that also the *travaux préparatoires* and Resolution (52)1 of 19 March 1952 approving the text of the Protocol revealed that the reference to the general principles of international law was not intended to extend to nationals.[103] In both cases the Court found that no violation of Article 1 had been established, since in the exercise of its margin of appreciation the United Kingdom was entitled to adopt the compensation provisions as applied to the applicants and these provisions and their application were deemed by the Court not to be unreasonable.

17.5   THE RESTRICTIONS UNDER THE SECOND PARAGRAPH

17.5.1   CONTROL OF THE USE OF PROPERTY

The second paragraph of Article 1 allows the national authorities an almost unlimited power to impose restrictions on the use of property in accordance with the general interest. It does not concern the deprivation of property itself but rather restriction of its use. In this context it is remarkable that with regard to this restriction it is provided that it must be necessary, while with respect to the expropriation itself it is not.[104]

However, the judgment as to what is necessary in the general interest is expressly left to the State: 'as it deems necessary'. Taken literally, this phrase appears to suggest that the relevant national legislation and its application can be reviewed by the Court only for their conformity with the prohibition of discrimination of Article 14, with the prohibition of *détournement de pouvoir* laid down in Article 18, and possibly with Article 17.[105] This was indeed the view taken by the Court in the *Handyside* Case: "this

---

102   *Ibidem.*

103   *Ibidem,* para. 64 and para. 117, respectively.

104   The submission by an applicant that in his case the deprivation of property could not be deemed to have been necessary was not, therefore, examined by the Commission: Appl. 3039/67, *A, B, C and D v. the United Kingdom,* Yearbook X (1967), p. 506 (516).

105   In Appl. 4984/71, *X v. Federal Republic of Germany,* Coll. 43 (1973), p. 28 (35-36), the Commission nevertheless seems to have reviewed the measure by which a prisoner was prohibited from spending his money, be it in a very marginal way, for its necessity in the public interest.

paragraph sets the Contracting States up as sole judges of the 'necessity' for an interference. Consequently, the Court must restrict itself to supervising the lawfulness and the purposes of the restriction in question."[106]

However, a more extensive supervision has gradually been developed in the case law. In its report in the *Sporrong and Lönnroth* Case the Commission concluded from the slightly modified wording used by the Court in the *March* judgment[107] that the Court recognises the States as the 'sole judges' only with respect to the law on which the restrictions are based, but not in relation to the necessity of the measures themselves. As regards the latter, in the Commission's opinion, the possibility of review by the Strasbourg organs goes further and includes, for instance, the proportionality between those measures and the purpose of the law on which they are based.[108]

In its judgment in the *AGOSI* Case the Court adopted a similar approach, but later judgments show that the Court applies a fair balance test to assess the proportionality of the interference, both as concerns enforcement measures and the underlying legislation.[109] As the Court held in the *Allan Jacobsson* Case: "Under the second paragraph of Article 1 of Protocol No. 1, the Contracting States are entitled, amongst other things, to control the use of property in accordance with the general interest, by enforcing such laws as they deem necessary for the purpose. However, as this provision is to be construed in the light of the general principle enunciated in the first sentence of the first paragraph, there must exist a reasonable relationship of proportionality between the means employed and the aim sought to be realised. In striking the fair balance thereby required between the general interest of the community and the requirements of the protection of the individual's fundamental rights, the authorities enjoy a wide margin of appreciation."[110]

Given the flexibility of the 'reasonable relationship of proportionality' criterion and the wide margin of appreciation, the Court will not easily conclude that a fair

---

[106] Judgment of 7 December 1976, para. 62.
[107] Judgment of 13 June 1979, para. 65.
[108] Report of 8 October 1980, para. 103.
[109] Judgment of 24 October 1986, para. 52 (distinction between the importation prohibition as such and the enforcement of this prohibition).
[110] Judgment of 25 October 1989, para. 55. See also the judgment of 18 February 1991, *Fredin*, para. 51; judgment of 18 January 2001, *Jane Smith*, paras 121-125; judgment of 26 October 2004, *Rajnai*, paras 21-24, in which the Court approved restrictions on bee-keeping for reasons of public health on the applicant's property. This fair balance test applies also to legislative measures: see the judgment of 19 December 1989, *Mellacher and Others*, para. 48; judgment of 28 September 1994, *Spadea and Scalabrino*, para. 40; judgment of 2 December 2004, *Yarolslavtsev*, paras 32-35, in which the Court approved of the rule preventing registration of vehicles in respect of which the lawfulness of there acquisition could not be shown.

balance has not been achieved, not even when it entertains doubts on this score.[111] Generally speaking the fair balance will be lacking where the applicant has to bear an individual and excessive burden.[112] Invoking such burden has good chances of success, notably where the applicant can show that the control of the use of his property suffered from procedural irregularities such as non-implementation of recognised claims resulting from expropriation,[113] a legislatory amendment which prevented from awarding legal costs in pending procedures despite legitimate expectations on the basis of the previous legislation,[114] unreasonable delay in the restitution of tax payments,[115] the excessive term of a court procedure for the benefit of establishing property rights,[116] the six year long impossibility to get police assistance for the eviction of tenants,[117] contradictory urban planning legislation,[118] non-implementation of domestic court judgments, or (otherwise) a lack of application of domestic law.[119]

As concerns the 'general interest' aim of the interference, the Court, accepting a wide margin of appreciation, has stated that "it will respect the legislature's judgment as to what is in the general interest unless that judgment be manifestly without reasonable foundation."[120] Thus, a wide variety of aims have been considered to be in the general interest, such as social and economic policy aims in the fields of housing, town planning and alcohol consumption, but also the protection of the environment, the need to combat international drugs trafficking, the need to preserve evidence of offences and to prevent aggravation of offences, the need to avoid unregulated hunting

---

[111] Judgment of 25 October 1989, *Allan Jacobsson,* para. 63. In the judgment of 16 April 2002, *S.A. Dangeville,* paras 59-61, the fair balance was held to be lacking because of the absence of a sufficient remedy to claim payment of a government debt. The Court did not answer the question whether this absence constituted a deprivation or a control of the use of property. In the judgment of 29 April 1999, *Chassagnou and Others,* paras 80-85, the statutory obligation to transfer hunting rights for landowners opposed to hunting, who, by definition, do not wish to derive any advantage or profit from a right to hunt which they refuse to exercise because this is totally incompatible with their beliefs, had disturbed the fair balance.

[112] Judgment of 23 February 1995, *Gasus Dosier- und Fördertechnik,* para. 67. In later judgments the Court spoke of "a disproportionate and excessive burden"; see the judgment of 5 January 2000, *Beyeler,* para. 121. In that case such a burden existed, because the authorities had derived an unjust enrichment as far a the price of a Van Gogh painting concerned, as they had waited to exercise their right of pre-emption for several years, while claiming to pay only the old value of the painting.

[113] Judgment of 11 January 2000, *Almeida Garrett, Mascaranhas Falcao and Others,* paras 49-55; judgment of 30 January 2003, *Ahmet Acar,* paras 25-29; judgment of 29 July 2004, *Mora do Vale and Others,* paras 38-45.

[114] Judgment of 19 October 2000, *Ambruosi,* paras 29-34.

[115] Judgment of 3 July 2003, *Buffalo Srl,* para. 39.

[116] Judgment of 17 January 2002, *Tsirikakis,* paras 60-61.

[117] Judgment of 28 July 1999, *Immobiliare Saffi,* para. 59; judgment of 11 January 2001, *Lunari,* paras 31-34.

[118] Judgment of 27 March 2003, *Satka and Others,* paras 48-49.

[119] Judgment of 22 February 1994, *Raimondo,* para. 36; judgment of 18 July 1994, *Venditelli,* para. 40; judgment of 29 September 1994, *Scollo,* para. 40.

[120] Judgment of 19 December 1989, *Mellacher and Others,* para. 44; judgments of 28 September 1995, *Spadea and Scalabrino* and *Scollo,* para. 29 and para. 28 respectively.

and encourage the rational management of game stocks and the control by the State of the market in works of art for the purpose of protecting a country's cultural and artistic heritage.[121] In the pursuance of modern social policies the States are entitled even to take measures which affect existing contracts: "The Court observes that, in remedial social legislation and in particular in the field of rent control, it must be open to the legislature to take measures affecting the further execution of previously concluded contracts in order to attain the aim of the policy adopted."[122]

Various factors may play a role in the proportionality test. The Court has, for example, on occasion referred to the fact that avenues of judicial review of the contested measures had been available to the applicant.[123] Similarly, the fact that the applicant was engaged in a commercial venture which by its very nature involved an element of risk, the circumstance that the applicant could have sought to reduce this risk, the fact that the applicant must have been aware of the possibility of restrictions on the use of his property, as well as the fact that the duration of a bankruptcy procedure was due to the lack of funds and that the State had no influence as to this aspect.[124] In the *OGIS-Institut Stanlislas, OGEC St. Pie X en Blanche de Castille* Case the public interest of equal treatment of all schools prevailed over the confidence of some individual schools that overpayments would be restituted.[125]

Although the second paragraph of Article 1 does not explicitly require that the control of use of property be in accordance with the law (as does the second sentence of the first paragraph), the Court has taken the position that it may review the 'lawfulness' of the measures interfering with the use of property. Consequently, even if the Court's review of compatibility with domestic law as such is limited, the usual requirements of foreseeability and accessibility of the law, as well as that of legal

---

[121]   See, respectively, the judgment of 19 December 1989, *Mellacher and Other*, para. 47 (housing); judgment of 25 October 1989, *Allan Jacobsson*, para. 57 (town planning); judgment of 7 July 1989, *Tre Traktörer*, para. 56 (alcohol consumption); judgment of 1 February 1991, *Fredin*, para. 50 (protection of nature); judgment of 29 November 1991, *Pin Valley and Others*, para. 57 (protection of the environment); judgment of 5 May 1995, *Air Canada*, para. 39 (combatting international drugs trafficking); judgment of 18 July 1994, *Venditelli*, para. 38 (preservation of evidence of offences and prevention of aggravation of offences); judgment of 29 April 1999, *Chassagnou and Others*, para. 79 (avoiding unregulated hunting); judgment of 5 January 2000, *Beyeler*, paras 112-113 (control of the market in works of art).

[122]   Judgment of 19 December 1989, *Mellacher and Others*, para. 51.

[123]   Judgment of 23 February 1995, *Gasus Dosier- und Fördertechnik GmbH*, para. 73; judgment of 5 May 1995, *Air Canada*, para. 46.

[124]   See, respectively, the judgment of 29 November 1991, *Pine Valley and Others*, para. 59; judgment of 23 February 1995, *Gams*, para. 73; judgment of 18 February 1991, *Fredin*, para. 51; judgment of 20 December 2001, *F.L. v. Italy*, paras 29-34; in the latter case the Court concluded that there was a violation of Article 13.

[125]   Judgment of 27 May 2004, para. 87.

protection against interference by public authorities, apply also in the context of the second paragraph.[126]

17.5.2   SECURE THE PAYMENT OF TAXES OR OTHER CONTRIBUTIONS OR PENALTIES

A broad margin of discretion also applies in the case of the second element of the second paragraph: securing the payment of taxes or other contributions and penalties. In its older case law the Commission seemed to read this element as not placing any particular limit on national measures in this area.[127] Under this approach the power of the national authorities to levy taxes, to impose penalties (duly respecting Article 7), to make social security contributions compulsory and to impose other levies[128] was deemed to be in accordance with Article 1 as long as it had a legal basis, no discrimination was involved, and the power was not used for a purpose other than that for which it had been conferred.[129]

However, the Commission gradually moved to an interpretation which affords a wider protection. It accepted that a taxation scheme did not escape its powers of review under the second paragraph of Article 1, notably as concerns the requirements of a 'fair balance' and a 'reasonable relationship of proportionality'. In the area of taxes and other contributions the Commission has taken the position that "the financial liability arising out of the raising of tax or contributions may adversely affect the guarantee secured under this provision if it places an excessive burden on the person or the entity concerned or fundamentally interferes with his or its financial position."[130]

Nevertheless, the States Parties have a wide margin of appreciation in deciding on the type of tax or contribution they wish to levy given the assessment of political economic and social considerations that is involved. Thus, in a case where the Com-

---

[126]   Judgment of 7 July 1989, *Tre Traktorer,* para. 58; judgment of 18 February 1991, *Fredin,* para. 50; judgment of 5 May 1995, *Air Canada,* para. 46. In its judgment of 22 February 1994, *Raimondo,* para. 36, the Court found a violation under this head (unexplained delay in execution of domestic court judgment). See also the judgment of 24 March 2005, *Frizen,* para. 36, in which the legal basis for the decision lacked completely. The Court has treated lack of compliance with domestic law also as being relevant under the proportionality test (see *supra*).

[127]   In its report in the *Greek* Case, therefore, the Commission held with regard to this latter provision that it does not prescribe any limitation, either of form or of size; Yearbook XII (1969), p. 185.

[128]   *E.g.* a levy for the construction of a road: Appl. 7489/76, *X v. Federal Republic of Germany,* D&R 9 (1978), p. 114. See also Appl. 7669/76, *Company X v. the Netherlands,* D&R 15 (1979), p. 133 (134): contribution to a professional organisation, required in virtue of a collective agreement declared generally binding by the Government.

[129]   A complaint of discrimination in relation to tax legislation was upheld by the Court in its judgment of 23 October 1990, *Darby,* para. 34.

[130]   Appl. 13013/87, *Wasa Liv Omsesidigt,* D&R 58 (1988), p. 163 (188); Appl. 15117/98, *Travers and 27 Others,* D&R 80 (1995), p. 5 (11).

mission recognised that a particular system of deducting tax advances created a substantial burden for taxpayers, it nevertheless considered that "the applicants have not proved that such a burden seriously undermined their financial situation".[131]

A considerable margin of appreciation is also accepted in relation to measures taken by tax authorities to enforce tax obligations. In the *Gasus Dosier- und Fördertechnik GmbH* Case the Court held, with respect to Dutch legislation which enabled the authorities to recover tax debts against a third party's assets, as follows: "in passing such laws, the legislature must be allowed a wide margin of appreciation, especially with regard to the question whether – and if so, to what extent – the tax authorities should be put in a better position to enforce tax debts than ordinary creditors are in to enforce commercial debts. The Court will respect the legislature's assessment unless it is devoid of reasonable foundation."[132] Nevertheless, the Court went on to examine the case on the basis of the requirements of a 'fair balance' and of a 'reasonable relationship of proportionality'. The applicant company in this case had complained that, by seizing and selling its possessions which were held by a third party which went bankrupt, the Dutch authorities had deprived it of its property in order to secure payment of a tax debt owed by that third party, for which debt it was in no way responsible. The Court held that such a system of recovery of debts was not uncommon and not incompatible *per se* with the requirements of Article 1. The Court pointed, amongst other things, to the fact that the applicant company was engaged in a commercial venture which naturally entailed risks (in this case: bankruptcy of a debtor), which it could have sought to reduce or eliminate in various ways. The Court, considering also that the tax authorities have fewer possibilities than commercial creditors to protect themselves against insolvency of debtors and that a legal remedy against the seizure had been available to the applicant, concluded that the proportionality requirement had been satisfied in this case.[133]

Outside the area of taxation, as well, enforcement measures such as forfeiture, or even preventive measures such as seizure, have been examined for their compatibility

---

[131] Appl. 15117/89, *Travers and 27 Others*, D&R 80 (1995), p. 5 (12). One may assume that this wide margin of appreciation will apply *a fortiori* in relation to the *level* of taxation. See, however, the Court's judgment of 23 February 1995, *Gasus Dosier- und Fördertechnik*, para. 60, which left open the question of whether the State's right to 'enact (...) laws (...) to secure the payment of taxes' is limited to procedural tax laws or whether it also covers substantive tax laws (laws that define the circumstances under which tax is due and the amounts payable). This rather mysterious statement could be taken to mean that the Court reserved the question of whether it is competent to review taxation levels under Art. 1.

[132] Judgment of 23 February 1995, para. 60.

[133] *Ibidem*, paras 67-74.

with the second paragraph of Article 1.[134] The *AGOSI* Case concerned a forfeiture, by court order, of smuggled gold coins belonging to a third party and the subsequent refusal by the customs authorities to restore the goods. The Commission observed that AGOSI complained not of the seizure of the coins, but of their forfeiture and the denial of their return. It was not for the Commission to decide upon AGOSI's innocence or complicity in smuggling, but to examine whether the decision not to restore the coins to the applicant and the procedure which had led to that decision satisfied the procedural requirement inherent in Article 1. The Commission first recalled its case law that forfeiture constitutes a control of the use of property, not a deprivation. In this case, since the smuggling of the coins was intended to circumvent customs legislation, the forfeiture found its justification in the security which the authorities sought to obtain for the payment of customs duties and penalties. The forfeiture presupposes that the smuggler owns the property. If he does not and if the lawful owner is unaware of the smuggling and suffers loss, the specific justification for forfeiture may be absent and it may amount to confiscation without any specific justification *vis-à-vis* the owner. In the opinion of the Commission the rule of proportionality requires that the innocent owner be given an opportunity to assert his property right and show that he is an innocent owner, this being a necessary balancing factor to the State's forfeiture powers. The Commission concluded that this proportionality requirement was not fulfilled by the legislation and the procedures concerned.[135] Unlike the Commission, the Court concluded that it was not established that the British system failed either to ensure that reasonable account be taken of the behaviour of the applicant company or to afford it a reasonable opportunity to put its case.[136]

17.6   DEROGATION

Since Article 5 of Protocol No. 1 provides on the one hand that 'all the provisions of the Convention shall apply accordingly', while on the other hand no separate mention is made of Article 15(2), it follows from this that none of the rights mentioned in Protocol No. 1 is non-derogable.

---

[134] As concerns preventive measures, see the judgment of 22 February 1994, *Raimondo*, paras 26-33 (seizure and confiscation not held disproportionate, having regard to the importance of the fight against the mafia); a violation was found because the confiscation continued even after a domestic court had ordered that the possessions be returned. See also judgment of 18 July 1994, *Venditelli*, paras 35-40 (sequestration of a flat – to preserve evidence of an offence and prevent any aggravation of the offence – which lasted well beyond the judgment ending the criminal proceedings, placed a disproportionate burden on the applicant).

[135] Report of 11 October 1984, A.108, paras 80-92.

[136] Judgment of 24 October 1986, para. 60.

CHAPTER 18
THE RIGHT TO EDUCATION
(Article 2 of Protocol No. 1)

REVISED BY BEN VERMEULEN

CONTENTS

18.1 TEXT OF ARTICLE 2 OF PROTOCOL NO. 1

No person shall be denied the right to education. In the exercise of any functions which it assumes in relation to education and to teaching, the state shall respect the right of parents to ensure such education and teaching in conformity with their own religious and philosophical convictions.

18.2 THE RIGHT TO EDUCATION

18.2.1 GENERAL

Article 2 of Protocol No. 1 (hereafter also: Article 2) comprises two different, though interconnected rights. While its first sentence guarantees a right to education, its second sentence obliges the state to respect the right of parents to ensure education for their children in conformity with their fundamental convictions. The right to education is the primary right[1]: the article "constitutes a whole that is dominated by its first sentence (...). The right set out in the second sentence is an adjunct of this fundamental right to education".[2]

The right to education in the first sentence can be invoked by children[3] or by their parents representing them.[4] The right in the second sentence can only be invoked by parents.[5] According to the Commission an association or a foundation cannot claim to be a victim of Article 2. Solely the members of the association or foundation, as individuals, can claim to be victims of a violation of this right, which by its nature is not susceptible of being exercised by an association or foundation.[6]

The negative formulation of the first sentence seems to emphasize that the right to *freedom of* education is involved here rather than the social and cultural *right to* education entailing a positive obligation on the part of the state. And indeed, in the *Belgian Linguistic* Cases the Court held that Article 2 does not require that the Contracting States ensure at their own expense, or subsidize, education of a particular type, but merely implies for those who are under the jurisdiction of one of the Contracting States the right 'to avail themselves of the means of instruction existing at a given time'.[7] Therefore, its primary objective is to guarantee a right of equal access to the existing educational institutions.

In addition, according to the Court, Article 2 obliges the State to give official recognition in one form or another to those who have completed a given type of studies with good results, since otherwise the exercise of this right would not be very effective.[8] Whether this also applies to education pursued abroad has been left open so far. In

---

[1] Report of 21 March 1975, *Kjeldsen, Busk Madsen and Pedersen*, B.21 (1979), para. 149.

[2] Judgment of 7 December 1976, *Kjeldsen, Busk Madsen and Pedersen*, para. 52; Judgment of 25 February 1982, *Campbell and Cosans*, para. 40.

[3] For example Report of 23 January 1987, *Townend*; report of 16 July 1987, *Durairaj and Baker*; report of 16 July 1987, *Brant and Others*.

[4] For example the judgment of 25 February 1982, *Campbell and Cosans*, para. 39.

[5] Judgment of 22 June 1989, *Eriksson*, para. 93.

[6] Decision of 7 April 1997, *Scientology Kirche Deutschland*, para. 1.

[7] Judgment of 23 July 1968, *Belgian Linguistic Cases*, para. 3 (A.6 (1968), p. 31).

[8] *Ibidem.*

any case the person in question may be required to undergo an examination in the country where recognition of those studies abroad is requested.[9]

As the Court observed in its judgment in the *Belgian Linguistic* Cases, the right to education in Article 2 comprises the right to avail oneself of the 'means of instruction existing at a given time'. This implies that the scope of the right to education may vary from one country to another and may be subject to developments within a particular country. If in a given country a new branch or a new type of education is introduced, persons in that country have a right of access to it, provided that they satisfy the conditions of entry. This right of access refers to all levels of education. As the Commission held in the *Belgian Linguistic* Cases, it 'includes entry to nursery, primary, secondary and higher education'.[10] The position the Commission has taken in more recent cases, *viz.* that the 'right to education envisaged in Article 2 is concerned primarily with elementary education',[11] is corroborated neither by the text of Article 2 nor by the court's case-law. According to the Court's interpretation Article 2 does not require from the states a particular level of education – in the member states of the Council of Europe elementary education must be assumed to be the absolute minimum – but it does oblige them to give access to everyone to all existing educational institutions in accordance with the relevant rules.

The right to education by its very nature calls for a certain regulation on the part of the Government. This regulation may vary in time and place taking into account the needs and resources of the community and individuals concerned. However, this regulation may never be of such a nature and scope that the essence of the right[12] is affected, or that one of the other rights and freedoms guaranteed by the Convention is violated as a result. The Government has to find a balance between the protection of the general interest of the community and respect of fundamental human rights . of individuals while giving particular importance to the latter.[13]

This was confirmed by the court in its judgment in the *Campbell and Cosans* Case. In this case the parents complained, *inter alia*, that their children were actually denied the right to education because they did not receive the guarantee that at the school in question no corporal punishment would be applied, while there was no alternative for them. Since the refusal of Jeffrey Cosans to accept that he should receive corporal

---

[9]   Appl. 7864/77, *X v. Belgium*, D&R 16 (1979), p. 82 (83-84); Appl. 11655/85, *Glazewska*, D&R 45 (1986), p. 300 (302).

[10] See the judgment of 23 July 1968, *Belgian Linguistic Cases*, para. 1 (A.6 (1968), p. 22). *Cf.* also Appl. 5492/72, *X v. Austria*, Coll. 44 (1973), p. 63 (64).

[11] Appl. 5962/72, *X v. the United Kingdom*, D&R 2 (1975), p. 50; Appl. 7010/75, *X v. Belgium*, D&R 3 (1976), p. 162 (164); Appl. 14524/89, *Yanasik*, D&R 74 (1993), p. 14 (27); Appl. 24515/94, *Sulak*, D&R 84-A (1996), p. 98 (99).

[12] For the question as to what this 'essence' is, the difference between elementary and other education has to be taken into consideration.

[13] Judgment of 23 July 1968, *Belgian Linguistic Cases*, para. 5 (A.6 (1968), p. 32).

punishment in a concrete case had resulted in suspension, and the requirement itself to submit to that kind of punishment conflicted with the parents' right laid down in the second sentence of Article 2, in the Court's opinion there was no longer any question of a reasonable regulation of access to education and it consequently concluded that the right to education had been violated.[14]

On the other hand reasonable disciplinary measures are undoubtedly compatible with Article 2. For instance, it is not incompatible with this provision for pupils who have committed disciplinary offences or who have been caught cheating, to be suspended or expelled from the institute where they study.[15]

Although Article 2 in principle confers a right of access to any type and any level of education existing in the country concerned, the conditions for access and admittance as well as the duration of the possibility to study may be regulated.[16] It is an inherent feature of education that one can complete a particular kind of studies or training successfully only when one has reached the required level. Conditions of entry referring to an objective assessment of this level, therefore, are not contrary to the freedom of education.[17] The same holds good for restrictions resulting from admission decisions, fixed numbers of entries, limits as regards the length of the period one is allowed to spend on one's studies and the like, caused by the limited availability of facilities at a given moment in relation to the demand. Since Article 2 does not imply the obligation to increase this availability, once again there is no question of violation of the Convention as long as no discrimination takes place in the admission.

The obligation to wear a school uniform does not constitute an interference with the right to education.[18] In the *Leyla Şahin* Case the Court concluded that the ban on wearing the Islamic headscarf in higher-education institutions did not constitute a violation of article 9 of the Convention, because the ban was prescribed by law, pursued the legitimate aims of protecting the rights and freedoms of others and protecting the public order and was necessary in a democratic society taking into account the margin of appreciation left to the Contracting States. Because there was no violation of Article 9, no separate question arose under Article 2 of Protocol No. 1.[19]

---

14   Judgment of 25 February 1982, para. 41.
15   Appl. 14524/89, *Yanasik*, D&R 74 (1993), p. 14 (27); Appl. 24515/94, *Sulak*, D&R 84-A (1996), p. 98 (100).
16   Appl. 5492/72, *X v. Austria*, Coll. 44 (1973), p. 63 (64).
17   Appl. 6598/74, *X v. Federal Republic of Germany* (unpublished). See also Appl. 8844/80, *X v. the United Kingdom*, D&R 23 (1981), p. 228 (229), in which it was found compatible with Art. 2 of Protocol No. 1 that a person was not readmitted to the university because of the fact that he failed the first-year examination and had a poor attendance record.
18   Appl. 11674/85, *S. v. the United Kingdom*, para. 3.
19   Judgment of 29 June 2004, para. 117.

18.2.2   THE POSITIVE OBLIGATION TO SET UP AND SUPPORT A SYSTEM OF EDUCATION

The primary objective of Article 2 of Protocol No. 1 is to guarantee a right of non-discriminatory access to the existing educational facilities. This provision does not in general require that the Contracting States establish or subsidize education of a particular type or at a particular level.[20] They are, for instance, not obliged to provide for particular types of adult education.[21] They are also not required to establish or subsidize schools in which education is provided in a given language,[22] nor is it their duty to guarantee the availability of schools which are in accordance with a certain religious conviction of the parents.[23] Furthermore, they are not obliged to provide free transport to the school of one's choice where an alternative is available which would involve free transport and which has not been shown to conflict with the parent's convictions[24] or to recognize and subsidize private denominational schools.[25] The Contracting States are equally not required to place a dyslexic child in a private specialized school, with fees paid by the State, when a place is available in an ordinary State school which has special teaching facilities for disabled children.[26]

However, the exercise of the right to education, understood as a right of equal access, requires by implication the existence and the maintenance of a minimum of education provided by the State, since otherwise that right would be illusory, in particular for those who have insufficient means to maintain their own institutions. Denying a person the possibility to receive primary education has such far-reaching consequences for his development and for his chances to enjoy the rights and freedoms of the Convention to the full, that such treatment is contrary, if not to the letter of Article 2, at all events to the object and purpose of the whole system of the Convention, in the light of which Article 2 has to be interpreted.

In the *Belgian Linguistic* Cases, the Court stated that the right to education would be meaningless if it did not imply the right to be educated in the national language or in one of the national languages.[27] In *Cyprus v. Turkey* the Court concluded that

---

[20]   Judgment of 23 July 1968, *Belgian Linguistic Cases*, para. 3 (A.6 (1968), p. 31), followed by the Commission: Appl. 6853/74, *40 Mothers v. Sweden*, Yearbook XX (1977), p. 214 (238); Appl. 7527/76, *X and Y v. the United Kingdom*, D&R 11 (1978), p. 147 (150); Appl. 9461/81, *X and Y v. the United Kingdom*, D&R 31 (1983), p. 210 (211); Appl. 23419/94, *Verein Gemeinsam Lernen*, D&R 82-A (1995), p. 41 (45).

[21]   Appl. 7010/75, *X v. Belgium*, D&R 3 (1976), p. 162 (164).

[22]   Judgment of 23 July 1968, *Belgian Linguistic Cases*, para. 7 (A.6 (1968), p. 42).

[23]   Appl. 7527/76, *X and Y v. the United Kingdom*, D&R 11 (1978), p. 147 (150).

[24]   Decision of 28 February 1996, *Cohen*, para. 1.

[25]   Appl. 7782/77, *X. v. the United Kingdom*, D&R 14 (1979), p. 179 (181); Appl. 11533/85, *Ingrid Jordebo Foundation of Christian Schools*, D&R 51 (1987), p. 125 (128).

[26]   Appl. 14688/89, *Simpson*, D&R 64 (1990), p. 188 (195).

[27]   Judgment of 23 July 1968, *Belgian Linguistic Cases*, para. 3 (A.6 (1968), p. 31).

the abolishment of the facility for children of Greek-Cypriot parents in Northern Cyprus wishing to pursue a secondary education in the Greek language constituted an interference with Article 2. The children had already received primary education in a Greek-Cypriot school there and for this reason the possibility to continue education in the North (in the Turkish language) was not a viable one. The possibility to transfer the children to the South to pursue education in the Greek language did not fulfill the obligation of Article 2 because of the impact on family life.[28]

In the *Scozzari and Giunta* Case the applicant complained that her children, who were placed in the Il Forteto community in accordance with a care order, did not have adequate schooling and that the only education they would be receiving was that provided within the community. The Court concluded that there was no violation of Article 2 because the elder son began school shortly after arriving at the community and the younger son had just reached school age and was attending a nursery school.[29]

In three cases concerning gypsies the applicants complained that the refusal to allow them to remain on their own land where they lived in a caravan without a planning permission, resulted in their children being denied access to satisfactory education. The Court, however, concluded that the applicants had failed to substantiate their complaints that their children were effectively denied the right to education. In the *Coster* Case the applicants' oldest children, at the moment of the judgment over 16 years of age, had left school to work and their youngest children were attending school near their new home.[30] In the *Lee* Case the applicants' grandchildren had been attending school near their home on the applicant's land.[31] In the *Jane Smith* Case the applicant had remained on her land since the moment she had bought it.[32]

In the *Durmaz, Isik, Unutmaz and Sezal* Case, where the applicants complained that they had to interrupt their studies in order to serve their prison sentences, the Court concluded that "the fact that the applicants were only prevented during the period corresponding to their lawful detention after conviction by a court to continue their full-time education, cannot be construed as a deprivation of the right to education within the meaning of Article 2".[33] From this decision it may be concluded that the right to education at a certain institution can be restricted as a result of a prison sentence after conviction by a court. But as will be pointed out in 18.4, prisoners have a right to education that is available for them and which they can follow without unacceptable consequences for the execution of the penalty - for instance a correspondence course.

---

[28]   Judgment of 10 May 2001, paras 273-280.
[29]   Judgment of 13 July 2000, paras 238-243.
[30]   Judgment of 18 January 2001, para. 137.
[31]   Judgment of 18 January 2001, para. 125.
[32]   Judgment of 18 January 2001, para. 129.
[33]   Decision of 4 September 2001, para. 4.

The above mentioned case-law recognizes that there exists an obligation for the state to guarantee access to the existing educational facilities. This access may not be made illusory by the non-existence of a minimum of education, the non-continuance of education in a given language, a care order, the refusal of a planning permission or a prison sentence. However, there is no obligation for the State to guarantee access to a specific institution. This becomes clear from the *Coster* Case, where the Court concluded that the fact that the children had to change schools, did not constitute a substantiated complaint that the children were effectively denied the right to education. Prisoners, too, only have a right to the educational facilities available to them as prisoners. The fact that they have to intermit their studies and change for example to a school that teaches by correspondence, does not constitute a violation of Article 2.[34]

18.2.3   COMPULSORY EDUCATION

Does the freedom of education also imply the freedom not to receive education? In other words: is a system of compulsory education contrary to Article 2? Article 2 protects free access to, and a certain degree of free choice of education, but does not seem to prohibit compulsory education in which sufficient scope is left for such a free choice. Accordingly, the Commission adopted the view that "it is clear that Article 2 of Protocol No. 1 implies a right for the State to establish compulsory schooling, be it in State schools or private tuition of a satisfactory standard, and that verification and enforcement of educational standards is an integral part of that right." In that particular case the Commission concluded "that to require the applicant parents to cooperate in the assessment of their children's educational standards by an education authority in order to ensure a certain level of literacy and numeracy, whilst, nevertheless, allowing them to educate their children at home, cannot be said to constitute a lack of respect for the applicant's rights under Article 2 of Protocol No. 1."[35]

It is interesting to note that the Commission did not attach so much weight to the form of the (primary) education, but rather to the responsibility of the State for its quality: to guarantee a certain level of literacy and numeracy, whilst leaving the rights of the parents unimpaired as much as possible. After all, even though compulsory education is not contrary to Article 2, it is limited by certain rights of the children and their parents, in particular the right to respect for their convictions and private lives.

---

[34]   *Ibidem.*
[35]   Appl. 10233/83, *Family H. v. the United Kingdom*, D&R 37 (1984), p. 105 (108).

18.2.4 THE RIGHT TO ESTABLISH PRIVATE SCHOOLS

The question arises whether the right to education only comprises the right to receive education or also implies the right to provide for education. Does it, for instance, include the right to provide for private education outside the system of public schools?

Since the first sentence of Article 2 of Protocol No. 1 only refers to education, while the second sentence distinguishes between education and teaching, the interpretation that it includes the right to provide for (private) education does not seem to have originally been intended. In its report in the *Kjeldsen, Busk Madsen and Pedersen* Case, however, the Commission took the view that the right to "the establishment of and access to private schools or other means of education outside the public school system" falls under the provision of Article 2.[36] And in its judgment in the same case the Court, too, by reference to the *travaux préparatoires*, seems to have recognized that the freedom to provide for private education, though not expressly set forth in the text of Article 2, had been present to the minds of the drafters in the different phases of the drafting process, so that an interpretation which also covers this right is not excluded.[37] However, this right is subject to regulation by the State in order to ensure a proper educational system as a whole. In the *Ingrid Jordebo Foundation of Christian Schools and Ingrid Jordebo* Case the Commission found the refusal to permit the Foundation to run the upper stage of the compulsory school compatible with Article 2, because the education offered at this level did not meet the quality conditions provided in the School Act.[38] Furthermore, the right to establish and run a private school does not contain a positive obligation for the State to fund it.[39]

18.3 PARENTAL RIGHTS

18.3.1 SCOPE

The second sentence of Article 2 does not concern the freedom of education of those receiving education, but the right of parents to ensure education for their children in conformity with their own religious and philosophical convictions.[40] This right has

---

[36] Report of 21 March 1975, B.21 (1975-76), p. 44. This position would seem to imply that the Commission then also ought to revise its standpoint that legal persons cannot complain on their own account about violation of Art. 2 (Appl. 3798/68, *Church of X v. the United Kingdom*, Yearbook XII (1969), p. 306 (314)).

[37] Judgment of 7 December 1976, *Kjeldsen, Busk Madsen and Pedersen*, para. 50.

[38] Appl. 11533/85, D&R 51 (1987), p. 124 (128).

[39] Appl. 23419/94, *Verein Gemeinsam Lernen*, D&R 82-A (1995), p. 41 (45).

[40] The question as to who are to be considered in a concrete case as the parents of a minor is determined by national law; in this context awards of guardianship, adoptions and the like also have to be taken into account. See Appl. 7626/76, *X v. the United Kingdom*, D&R 11 (1978), p. 160 (167-168).

to be *respected*; it is not sufficient that it is taken into account. The Court rejected the defense of the British Government that it fulfilled the obligation of Article 2 with regard to parents that objected to corporal punishment at school, since it pursued a policy of gradual abolition of this punishment. Referring to the *travaux préparatoires*, the Court held: "As is confirmed by the fact that, in the course of the drafting of Article 2, the words 'have regard to' were replaced by the word 'respect' (...), the latter word means more than 'acknowledge' or 'take into account'; in addition to a primarily negative undertaking, it implies some positive obligation on the part of the state."[41]

In the *Valsamis* Case and the *Efstratiou* Case the Court reaffirmed its earlier case law that "democracy does not simply mean that the views of a majority must always prevail: a balance must be achieved which ensures the fair and proper treatment of minorities and avoids any abuse of a dominant position".[42]

In the *Kjeldsen, Busk Madsen and Pedersen* Case, in which the Danish legislation was challenged which made sex education obligatory at public schools, as integrated with the teaching of other subjects, so that the parents could avoid such education for their children only by sending them to a private school, the Court clearly stated that the subjective views of the parents are not decisive for the question of whether the content of the instruction is in conformity with their religious and philosophical convictions: this question should be examined by reference to objective criteria.[43] The Court held that the second sentence of Article 2 "aims in short at safeguarding the possibility of pluralism in education, which possibility is essential for the preservation of the 'democratic society' as conceived by the Convention". And "in view of the power of the modern State, it is above all through State teaching that this aim must be realized".[44] As the Government is responsible for the curriculum, it is entitled to include in the teaching also the transmission of information of a directly or indirectly religious or philosophical kind, integrated with other subjects, since they will inevitably be implied in the subject-matter to be taught. Article 2 has been violated only if the transmission of ideas does not take place in an objective, critical and pluralistic way, but on the contrary assumes the character of indoctrination. The question of whether the latter was the case here, was examined independently by the Court; it took into account particularly the purpose of sex education, the general character of the instruction which did not amount to indoctrination, the fact that the instruction given did

---

[41]   Judgment of 25 February 1982, *Campbell and Cosans*, para. 37.

[42]   Judgment of 18 December 1996, para. 27, and judgment of 18 December 1996, para. 28.

[43]   Judgment of 7 December 1976, para. 53. *Cf.* the judgment of 18 December 1996, *Valsamis*, paras 28-33, and the judgment of 18 December 1996, *Efstratiou*, paras 29-34: the court could not discern any military overtones in the school parade, in which the child of Jehovah's Witnesses had to take part, that could possibly offend their pacifist convictions to an extent prohibited by the second sentence of Article 2.

[44]   Judgment of 7 December 1976, *Kjeldsen, Busk Madsen and Pedersen*, para. 50.

not affect the rights of parents to advise and guide their children in line with their convictions, and the possibility of taking action against abuse at a particular school or by a particular teacher.[45]

If the State prescribes a certain instruction it must not be indoctrinating but objective and pluralistic. In the case of such integrated instruction, this requirement of pluralism always applies. On the other hand religious instruction based on a particular State religion provided at a public school is not necessarily contrary to Article 2, provided that parental beliefs are respected by granting exemptions.[46] From the prohibition of discrimination in Article 14 it follows that the State, when granting exemptions on the ground of religious belief, should also allow exemptions on the ground of non-religious philosophical convictions.[47]

The second sentence of Article 2 refers to *all* activities of the Government and consequently also implies an obligation concerning the organization of public education.[48] At the same time, however, the Court held that the fact that the State makes an essential contribution to the defrayment of the costs of private education must be taken into consideration when deciding whether the obligation ensuing from Article 2 has been fulfilled.[49] How much weight the Court is prepared to attach to this aspect in a concrete case was not revealed, since it reached the conclusion that the obligatory sex education was of such a nature as not to conflict with the interests of the parents protected in Article 2.

In its report in the *Campbell and Cosans* Case, in regard to the argument advanced by the British Government that there existed private schools where the challenged corporal punishment was not applied, the Commission took the position that this did not absolve the Government from the obligation to respect at public schools the religious and philosophical conviction of the parents, while the fact that private schools required a high financial contribution from the parents or that these schools were situated at a great distance could render the alternative unrealistic.[50] In a later decision,

---

[45] *Ibidem*, paras 53-54. See also the Commission, Appl. 6853/74, *40 Mothers v. Sweden*, Yearbook XX (1977), p. 214 (238-240), and Appl. 7527/76, *X and Y v. the United Kingdom*, D&R 11 (1978), p. 147 (151). Furthermore, see Appl. 8811/79, *Seven individuals v. Sweden*, D&R 29 (1982), p. 104 (116): reference to policy statements of a general character in official publications cannot be held to be indoctrination.

[46] Appl. 10491/83, *Angeleni*, D&R 51 (1987), p. 41 (46).

[47] However, the Commission seemed to accept that exemptions of moral and social education lessons are exclusively conditional on adherence to a religious belief: Appl. 17187/90, *Bernard and Others*, D&R 75 (1993), p. 57 (74-75).

[48] Judgment of 7 December 1976, *Kjeldsen, Busk Madsen and Pedersen*, para. 50. This point of view was followed by the Commission in its decision on Appl. 6853/74, *40 Mothers v. Sweden*, Yearbook XX (1977), p. 214 (238).

[49] Judgment of 7 December 1976, *Kjeldsen, Busk Madsen and Pedersen*, para. 50. See also Appl. 7782/77, *X v. the United Kingdom*, D&R 14 (1979), p. 179 (181).

[50] Report of 16 May 1980, B.42 (1985), pp. 38, 39.

however, the Commission did away without any argument with the factor that the parents could not afford private education as an alternative.[51]

In the above-mentioned judgment in the *Kjeldsen, Busk Madsen and Pedersen* Case the Court rejected the submission of the Danish Government that the second sentence of Article 2 refers exclusively to specific religious instruction. According to the Court, in *all* education activities with which the Government is concerned the right of parents ensured in Article 2 has to be respected.[52]

Although parents have the right to keep their children away from religious instruction at a public school, they cannot lay claim to separate instruction as an alternative. The State is not required to provide for special facilities to accommodate their particular convictions;[53] nor is the State obliged to set up and support schools serving such beliefs.[54]

It has not yet been decided whether opinions of parents about the appropriate school for their disabled child can be said to be based on philosophical convictions. Even assuming that this is the case, the wide measure of discretion left to the authorities implies that the second sentence of Article 2 does not require the placing of such a child in a regular school with additional facilities rather than in an available place in a special school,[55] nor *vice versa*.[56]

Since Article 2 in principle also refers to secondary and higher education to the extent available, it must be assumed that the obligation of the State to ensure pluriformity in religious and philosophical respects in providing for education applies also to education for adults. For this they may rely on the first sentence of Article 2, interpreted in the light of the whole of Article 2.

18.3.2   RELIGIOUS AND PHILOSOPHICAL CONVICTIONS

In the *Campbell and Cosans* Case the Court gave a description of the concept of 'convictions'. It did not equate these convictions with 'mere' opinions or ideas: "the

---

[51]   Appls 10228/82 and 10229/82, *W. & D.M.* and *M. & H.I. v. the United Kingdom*, D&R 37 (1984), p. 96 (100). See also its decision on Appl. 7527/76, *X and Y v. the United Kingdom*, D&R 11 (1978), p. 147 (151), where the Commission took into consideration that the parents had been offered a place for their son at a Roman Catholic school in a neighbouring municipality.

[52]   Judgment of 7 December 1976, para. 51.

[53]   Appl. 7782/77, *X. v. the United Kingdom*, D&R 14 (1979), p. 179 (180); Appl. 13887/88, *Graeme*, D&R 64 (1990), p. 158 (165); Appl. 25212/94, *Klerks*, D&R 82-A (1995), p. 129 (132).

[54]   Appl. 7527/76, *X. v. the United Kingdom*, D&R 11 (1978), p. 147 (151); Appl. 9461/81, *X and Y v. the United Kingdom*, D&R 31 (1983), p. 210 (211).

[55]   Appl. 14135/88, *P.D. and L.D. v. the United Kingdom*, D&R 62 (1989), p. 292 (297); Appl. 13887/88, *Graeme*, D&R 64 (1990), p. 158 (166); Appl. 25212/94, *Klerks*, D&R 82-A (1995), p. 129 (133).

[56]   Appl. 14688/89, *Simpson*, D&R 64 (1990), p. 188 (195).

word 'conviction', taken on its own, is not synonymous with the words 'opinions' and 'ideas', such as are utilised in Article 10, which guarantees freedom of expression; it is more akin to the term 'beliefs' (...) appearing in Article 9 – which guarantees freedom of thought, conscience and religion – and denotes views that attain a certain level of cogency, seriousness, cohesion and importance."[57]

The Court clarified the concept of 'religious convictions' in the *Valsamis* Case and the *Efstratiou* Case concerning Jehovah's Witnesses. The Court held that "Jehovah's Witnesses enjoy both the status of a 'known religion' and the advantages flowing from that as regards observance." For this reason the applicants were entitled to rely on the right to respect for their religious convictions within the meaning of Article 2 of Protocol No. 1.[58] The Court clarified the concept of 'philosophical convictions' in the *Campbell and Cosans* Case: "Having regard to the Convention as a whole, including Article 17, the expression 'philosophical convictions' in the present context denotes, in the Court's opinion, such convictions as are worthy of respect in a 'democratic society' (...) and are not incompatible with human dignity; in addition, they must not conflict with the fundamental right of a child to education, the whole of Article 2 being dominated by its first sentence."[59] In that context and with respect to objections submitted to corporal punishment, the Court held as follows: "The applicant's views relate to a weighty and substantial aspect of human life and behaviour, namely the integrity of the person, the propriety or otherwise of the infliction of corporal punishment and the exclusion of the distress which risk of such punishment entails. They are views which satisfy each of the various criteria listed above; it is this that distinguishes them from opinions that might be held on other methods of discipline or on discipline in general."[60]

Respect for 'philosophical convictions' does not extend to the domain of language. In the *Belgian Linguistic* Cases the Court concluded that Article 2 "does not require of States that they should, in the sphere of education or teaching, respect parents' linguistic preferences, but only their religious and philosophical convictions. To interpret the terms 'religious' or 'philosophical' as covering linguistic preferences

---

[57]   Judgment of 25 February 1982, para. 36.
[58]   Judgment of 18 December 1996, para. 26; judgment of 18 December 1996, para. 27.
[59]   Judgment of 25 February 1982, para. 36. See also Appl. 8566/79, *X, Y and Z v. the United Kingdom*, D&R 31 (1983), p. 50 (53). *Cf.* the definition of the Commission in its report of 16 May 1980, B.42 (1985), p. 37: 'those ideas based on human knowledge and reasoning concerning the world, life, society, etc., which a person adopts and professes according to the dictates of his or her conscience. These ideas can more briefly be characterized as a person's outlook on life including, in particular, a concept of human behaviour in society'. See also *ibidem*, p. 36, where the Commission abandoned its much narrower interpretation in the *Belgian Linguistic Cases* that 'philosophical opinions were added in order to cover agnostic opinions'.
[60]   Judgment of 25 February 1982, *Campbell and Cosans*, para. 36. In order to be respected, those philosophical convictions must of course first have been brought to the attention of the authorities: see Appl. 8566/79, *X, Y and Z v. the United Kingdom*, D&R 31 (1983), p. 50 (53).

would amount to a distortion of their ordinary and usual meaning and to read into the Convention something which is not there."[61]

Neither does respect for 'philosophical convictions' extend to parental opinions concerning the appropriate school for their disabled child.[62]

18.3.3   EDUCATION AND TEACHING

In its *Campbell and Cosans* judgment the Court also gave a definition of the words 'education' and 'teaching': "the education of children is the whole process whereby, in any society, adults endeavour to transmit their beliefs, culture and other values to the young, whereas teaching or instruction refers in particular to the transmission of knowledge and to intellectual development."[63] On the basis of these definitions the submission of the British Government that discipline at school does not form part of these concepts was rejected: "it is (...) an integral part of the process whereby a school seeks to achieve the object for which it was established, including the development and moulding of the character and mental powers of its pupils."[64]

Furthermore, it was clearly established that, once the Government has assumed responsibility for education, no distinction can be made between aspects of education falling under that responsibility and aspects not falling under it; certainly not where education at public schools is concerned. That responsibility, therefore, extends beyond the curriculum and also embraces the way in which discipline is maintained at the school, even though the Government does not concern itself with such maintenance day by day.[65]

18.3.4   PARENTAL AUTHORITY

The broad definition of 'education' set forth in the *Campbell and Cosans* Case implies that the second sentence also applies to situations outside the framework of teaching institutions. In the *Olsson* Case parents complained of a violation of that provision because their son had been placed in a foster family that belonged to a religious denomination and attended church with him, whereas they did not wish their children to receive a religious upbringing. The Commission first referred to its earlier case law

---

[61]   Judgment of 23 July 1968, para. 6 (A.6 (1968), p. 32).
[62]   Appl. 14135/88, *P.D. and L.D. v the United Kingdom*, D&R 62 (1989), p. 292 (297); Appl. 13887/88, *Graeme*, D&R 64 (1990), p. 158 (166); Appl. 14688/89, *Simpson*, D&R 64 (1990), p. 188 (195); Appl. 25212/94, *Klerks*, D&R 82-A (1995), p. 129 (133).
[63]   Judgment of 25 February 1982, para. 33.
[64]   *Ibidem.*
[65]   *Ibidem*, para. 34.

that in case of adoption or when the courts have removed a parent's right to custody, that parent no longer has the right to determine the child's education, since this is an integral part of the right to custody (and *a fortiori* of the rights of adoptive parents). Whether Article 2 imposes on the public authorities an obligation not to transfer parental authority over a child to persons who do not share the convictions of the natural parents in matters of education, was expressly left open by the Commission.[66] Subsequently, it held that a decision to take a child into care was of a different character and did not mean that the right to custody was removed from the parents. However, since a care order temporarily transfers certain parental rights to the public authorities, it is inevitable, according to the Commission, that the contents of the parent's rights in Article 2 must be reduced accordingly. On the other hand, the responsible authorities must, in the exercise of their rights under a care order, have due regard to these rights. In the case under consideration the Commission, followed by the Court, concluded that there were no serious indications that the applicants had, prior to the care order, been particularly concerned with giving their children a non-religious upbringing and that, moreover, there was no reason to believe that the religious education of their son in the foster home would be in conflict with the education previously given by the applicants.[67]

18.4 FOREIGNERS AND DETAINEES

A foreigner cannot, by referring to Article 2, claim admittance to a Contracting State in order to receive education there at one of the existing institutions, since only those who are already under the jurisdiction of the Contracting State may derive rights from Article 2. If, however, Article 2 is interpreted to include the right to give instruction, this may imply that, for instance, a religious group established in the country may claim admittance for its members to attend a congress, a course of study, and the like, or may claim the admittance of a person who is specifically qualified to teach.[68]

Can a foreigner challenge the refusal of the legalization of his stay or extension of his stay permit by referring to Article 2? This was done by fifteen foreign students in a complaint against the United Kingdom. The Commission, however, declared this complaint manifestly ill-founded, holding that the power of the States to decide for themselves who may reside in their territory is not limited by Article 2, unless perhaps

---

[66] See Appl. 7626/76, *X v. the United Kingdom*, D&R 11 (1978), p. 160 (167); Appl. 7911/77, *X v. Sweden*, D&R 12 (1978), p. 192 (194).

[67] Report of 2 December 1986, paras 184-185; Judgment of 24 March 1988, *Olsson*, para. 95.

[68] The Commission, however, rejected such a construction in its decision on Appl. 3798/68, *Church of X v. the United Kingdom*, Yearbook XII (1969), p. 306 (320-322), after it had first taken the disputable view that an organization cannot derive an independent right from Article 2 of Protocol No. 1.

in cases where expulsion might result in the person concerned being deprived of any elementary education.[69] It would seem that with respect to the right to primary education the line would have to be followed that the situation outside the country in question must also be included in the assessment of a possible violation of the Convention (as is the case in expulsion cases where Articles 3, 6, 8 and 12 are invoked).

As long as a foreigner resides lawfully in a Contracting State, he of course also has the right to education. However, this does not imply the right to receive education in his own vernacular if that is not already offered by the State concerned; there is only a right of access to the existing educational facilities (cf. section 18.2). In the Court's opinion the right to have one's children educated in one's own language or in the language of one's choice is also not protected by the second sentence of Article 2, because an interpretation of the terms 'religious and philosophical convictions' in that sense "would amount to a distortion of their ordinary and usual meaning", while it is evident from the *travaux préparatoires* that this provision was not intended "to secure respect by the State of a right for parents to have education conducted in a language other than that of the country in question".[70] The question remains, however, whether in virtue of the first sentence of Article 2 it is not at least incumbent on the Government to create additional facilities within the existing educational institutions for the benefit of those aliens, having taken up residence in the territory, who do not yet have sufficient command of the language in which education is conducted; otherwise the right to education will remain illusory for them for a long time. At least as regards elementary education this question may be answered in the affirmative on the same grounds as have been given above for minimum provisions for elementary education in general (section 18.2).

Article 2 does not contain a restriction clause, which raises the difficult question as to what extent foreigners without a residence permit can derive from this provision a right to education. As was observed in section 18.2, this article primarily guarantees a right of *equal access* to the existing educational institutions. Is the fact that these persons do not have a stay permit a sufficient reason for differential treatment by denying them the right of access to educational institutions that nationals and legally residing foreigners have? It seems that at least with regard to primary education this is not the case[71] as far as it concerns foreigners who, although not legally residing here, are likely to stay here for a considerable period of time (for instance because they cannot be expelled for humanitarian reasons). Denying these persons the possibility to receive primary education has such far-reaching consequences, that the fact that

---

[69]   Appl. 7671/76 and fourteen other complaints, *15 foreign students v. the United Kingdom*, D&R 9 (1978), p. 185 (186-187).

[70]   Judgment of 23 July 1968, *Belgian Linguistic Cases*, para. 6 (A.6 (1968), p. 32).

[71]   Appl. 7671/76 and fourteen other complaints, *15 foreign students v. the United Kingdom*, D&R 9 (1978), p. 185 (186-187), points in this direction: expulsion is not limited by Article 2, unless perhaps in cases where it might result in the person concerned being deprived of any elementary education.

they do not legally reside here is not a reasonable justification for this differential treatment, which therefore is contrary to Article 2 (independently or in conjunction with Article 14).

With regard to detainees the question of inherent limitations arises, since Article 2 does not contain an enumeration of restrictions. As was mentioned before, the Court concluded in the *Durmaz, Isik, Unutmaz and Sezal* Case that "the fact that the applicants were only prevented during the period corresponding to their lawful detention after conviction by a court to continue their full-time education, cannot be construed as a deprivation of the right to education within the meaning of Article 2."[72] However, prisoners, too, are in principle entitled to make use of the existing educational facilities if this is compatible with the rationale of the detention on remand or the penalty of imprisonment, taking also into consideration changing views of penitentiary policy. Thus, correspondence courses or courses *via* radio, subject to the necessary security measures, must as a rule be permitted, as must also the acquirement of books for purposes of study. In our view the argument advanced by the Commission that no facilities for the desired education were available within the prison,[73] is in itself insufficient. If a type of education is available which prisoners can follow without unacceptable consequences for the execution of the penalty - for instance a correspondence course – it is difficult to understand why they should not have the right "to avail themselves of the means of instruction existing at a given time". But it follows from the negative formulation of Article 2 that the Government is not obliged to defray the costs.

18.5 DEROGATION

Article 2 of Protocol No. 1 is not exempted from Article 15(1) of the Convention. This means that derogating measures may be taken under the conditions laid down in Article 15.

---

[72]   Decision of 4 September 2001, para. 4.
[73]   Appl. 5962/72, *X v. the United Kingdom*, D&R 2 (1975), p. 50.

CHAPTER 19

FREE ELECTIONS BY SECRET BALLOT
(Article 3 of Protocol No. 1)

REVISED BY JEROEN SCHOKKENBROEK

CONTENTS

19.1   TEXT OF ARTICLE 3 OF PROTOCOL NO. 1

The High Contracting Parties undertake to hold free elections at reasonable intervals by secret ballot, under conditions which will ensure the free expression of the opinion of the people in the choice of the legislature.

19.2   INTRODUCTION

The importance of Article 3 does not in the first instance consist of the obligation of the States to hold free elections at reasonable intervals by secret ballot, but in the connection between those elections and the composition of the legislature. In fact this means that Article 3 presupposes the existence of a representative legislature, elected at reasonable intervals, as the basis of a democratic society.[1]

Since such an important role has been assigned to the national legislature in ensuring the enjoyment of the rights and freedoms set forth in the Convention as well as in subjecting certain of these rights and freedoms to rules which may restrict their enjoyment, it is of eminent importance that this legislature consists of democratically elected representatives of the holders of those rights and freedoms. Therefore, properly speaking, Article 3 should have preceded the provisions of Section I of the Convention as a further elaboration of the concept of 'effective political democracy' referred to in the Preamble and of 'democratic society' mentioned in various provisions of the Convention. In its first judgment with regard to Article 3 the Court emphasised that "since it enshrines a characteristic principle of democracy, Article 3 of Protocol No. 1 is accordingly of prime importance in the Convention system".[2] The centrality of the concept of democracy in the Convention was also underlined in the *United Communist Party* Case, where the Court considered that democracy is without doubt a fundamental feature of the European public order and that democracy "appears to be the only political model contemplated by the Convention and, accordingly, the only one compatible with it".[3]

19.3 THE OBLIGATION TO HOLD FREE ELECTIONS AT REASONABLE INTERVALS

With respect to both its formulation and its content Article 3 constitutes an exception among the rights and freedoms laid down in the Convention and its Protocols. It is formulated neither as a right or freedom nor as an obligation for the national authorities to refrain from interfering with the exercise of a right or freedom, but as an undertaking on the part of the Contracting States to do something; an express and not only an implied positive obligation.

What does that obligation imply for the States? From the text of Article 3 it follows that elections must be held at regular intervals, that those elections must be free, *i.e.* without any pressure as regards to choice, and that the secrecy of the votes cast must be safeguarded. Moreover, it follows from the word 'choice' in Article 3 that there must be a real choice, which implies that the States must make possible the creation and functioning of political parties and must enable the latter – apart from the possible

---

[1]   See the report of 5 November 1969 in the *Greek* Case, Yearbook XII (1969), p. 179.
[2]   Judgment of 2 March 1987, *Mathieu-Mohin and Clerfayt*, para. 47.
[3]   Judgment of 30 January 1998, para. 45.

applicability of Article 17[4] – to present candidates for the elections.[5] A one-party system imposed by the State, therefore, would be contrary to Article 3.[6] Indeed, the Court has stressed that there can be no democracy without pluralism and that political parties play an essential role in ensuring such pluralism and the proper functioning of democracy. The obligation under Article 3 to hold elections is an expression of the State's responsibility as the ultimate guarantor of the principle of pluralism. According to the Court the "free expression of the opinion of the people in the choice of the legislature" is "inconceivable without the participation of a plurality of political parties representing the different shades of opinion to be found in a country's population".[7] And although Article 3 does not prescribe any particular form of government, it follows from the tenor of Article 3 that the legislative power must rest with the body constituted as a result of those free elections, while the possibility for the Head of State or Government to rule by decree without a parliamentary mandate would be contrary to that tenor.

Conditions for the admission of a group of persons as a political party to the elections were considered permissible if these conditions serve the purpose of guaranteeing the public character of the political process and of avoiding confusion of the electorate by groups which cannot assume political responsibility, provided that they do not essentially interfere with free choice.[8] Requirements as to the language in which a list is submitted for registration normally do not constitute such an interference, since Article 3 does not guarantee a right to use a given language for elections.[9] The requirement of the production of a given number of signatures was considered justified, since groups standing any chance at all in the elections will easily be able to satisfy such a requirement, while groups evidently unable to bear political responsibility will thereby be excluded.[10] In a later decision the Commission pursued this line further with respect to the requirement that an appeal against the way in which the elections have been conducted must be supported by a given number of signatures.

---

[4]   On Art. 17, see *infra* Chapter 36.

[5]   Report of 5 November 1969, *Greek* Case, Yearbook XII (1969), p. 180. See also Appl. 7140/75, *X v. the United Kingdom*, D&R 7 (1977), p. 95 (96).

[6]   However, a guarantee of the right to free political opposition, which appeared in the European Movement's draft, was not included in the final text. In practice, most aspects of that right are protected by other provisions of the Convention, such as Article 10 and, for political parties in particular, Article 11. There is no doubt that political parties come within the scope of Article 11, and that Article 11 also offers protection against measures such as dissolution of a party: see, *inter alia*, the judgment of 30 January 1998, *United Communist Party and Others*, paras 25 and 33.

[7]   Judgment of 30 January 1998, *United Communist Party and Others*, paras 43 and 44.

[8]   Appl. 6850/74, *Association X, Y and Z v. Federal Republic of Germany*, D&R 5 (1976), p. 90 (93-94). For conditions in regard to the objectives of political parties, see the discussion of Article 17, *infra* Chapter 36.

[9]   Appl. 34184/96, *Andecha Astur v. Spain*, where the Commission specified that this Asturian party wished to take part in nation-wide elections and that it had been given an opportunity to resubmit its application for registration in Spanish (Castilian).

[10] *Ibidem.*

The Commission adopted the following view: "having regard to the principles of a democratic society that the procedural rights related to the exercise of the right to stand as a candidate or to propose candidates, reflect the character of the elections as a public political process, and that these rights are accordingly circumscribed in such a way that they cannot be exercised by an individual acting alone, but only with the support of a certain minimum number of persons holding the same views."[11]

Likewise the Commission accepted as legitimate a French rule according to which lists standing in general elections must pay a deposit, which will only be reimbursed to lists having obtained at least five percent of the votes cast. This system was "designed to promote the emergence of sufficiently representative currents of thought", a legitimate aim for the purposes of Article 3.[12]

The system according to which political parties are subsidised by the Government on the basis of the results of the elections, too, was deemed permissible as one which protects the parties from undue outside pressure and at the same time reflects the real importance of each of them.[13] The latter justification (representativity) also applied to a system whereby small political parties were awarded less broadcasting time than bigger ones.[14]

Both the constituency voting system of elections within a certain district[15] and the system of proportional representation[16] are compatible with Article 3. The same must be assumed to apply to a system of indirect elections, since the word 'direct' does not appear in Article 3 and the people may be able freely to express their opinion on the ultimate composition of the legislature *via* such a system as well. In the same vein it was held by the Court in the *Mathieu-Mohin and Clerfayt* Case that Article 3 of Protocol No. 1 "does not create any obligation to introduce a specific system, (...) such as proportional representation or majority voting with one or two ballots".[17] The Court further emphasised that any electoral system must be assessed in the light of the political evolution of the country concerned, so long as the free expression of the opinion of the people in the choice of the legislature is ensured. In the Court's opinion it does not follow from Article 3 that "all votes must necessarily have equal weight as

---

[11]   Appl. 8227/78, *X v. Federal Republic of Germany,* D&R 16 (1979), p. 179 (180-181).

[12]   Appl. 12897/87, *Desmeules v. France,* D&R 67 (1991), p. 166 (173). The Commission added that it did not consider arbitrary or disproportionate the way this rule was applied in the instant case.

[13]   Appl. 6850/74, *Association A, Y and Z v. Federal Republic of Germany,* D&R 5 (1976), p. 90 (93-94); Appl. 40436/98, *New Horizons and Others v. Cyprus*; Appl. 58333/00, *Antonopoulos v. Greece.*

[14]   Appl. 58333/00, *Antonopoulos v. Greece.*

[15]   In this sense, concerning a complaint of a member of the British Liberal Party: Appl. 7140/75, *X v. the United Kingdom,* D&R 7 (1977), p. 95 (96-97).

[16]   Appl. 8364/78, *Lindsay v. the United Kingdom,* D&R 15 (1979), p. 247 (251), with regard to a complaint about the electoral system of Northern Ireland in connection with the elections for the European Parliament. See also Appl. 8765/79, *The Liberal Party, Mrs R. and Mr P. v. the United Kingdom,* D&R 21 (1981), p. 211 (223).

[17]   Judgment of 2 March 1987, para. 54.

regards the outcome of the election or that all candidates must have equal chances of victory. Thus no electoral system can eliminate 'wasted votes'."[18]

The aim of electoral systems is to organise and render possible persons' participation in the political life of the country, not to restrict such participation. In the *Aziz* Case the Court expressed this in the following general consideration: "Although the Court notes that States enjoy considerable latitude to establish rules within their constitutional order governing parliamentary elections and the composition of the Parliament, and that the relevant criteria may vary according to the historical and political factors peculiar to each State, these rules should not be such as to exclude some persons or group of persons from participating in the political life of the country and, in particular, in the choice of the legislature, a right guaranteed by both the Convention and the Constitutions of all Contracting States."[19]

The Court also confirmed the Commission's constant case law according to which setting thresholds (a certain minimum percentage of votes) for obtaining a seat in the legislative body is compatible with Article 3. Such a system is designed to promote the emergence of sufficiently representative currents of thought; it exists in several European legal systems, and even a relatively high threshold may be regarded as falling within the wide margin of appreciation permitted to States in the choice of electoral system.[20]

Once the people can participate in the composition of the legislature at regular intervals, the requirements set by Article 3 regarding participation in government have been satisfied. In particular this provision does not require that the people shall be consulted *via* referendum about certain legislative acts.[21]

In a case concerning the electoral system of Niedersachsen (Germany), the Commission examined whether a five-year period still constituted a 'reasonable interval' within the meaning of Article 3. It found that this question should be determined by reference to the purpose of parliamentary elections: ensuring that fundamental changes in the prevailing public opinion are reflected in the opinions of the representatives of the people. Too short an interval might impede longer-term planning for the implementation of the will of the people, while too long a period may lead to a composition of Parliament which no longer bears any resemblance to the prevailing will of the

---

[18] *Ibidem.* See also Appl. 8765/79, *The Liberal Party, Mrs R and Mr P v. the United Kingdom*, D&R 21 (1981), p. 211 (224), and Appl. 8941/80, *X v. Iceland*, D&R 27 (1982), p. 145 (150).

[19] Judgment of 22 June 2004, para. 28.

[20] Decision of 2 July 2002, *Gorizdra* (with references to earlier decisions of the Commission), where the complaint concerned a 4% threshold applied in Moldova.

[21] Appl. 6742/74, *X v. Federal Republic of Germany*, D&R 3 (1976), p. 98 (103), concerning the conclusion of a treaty. Complaints about limitations of the right to vote in referendums have consistently been rejected as falling outside the scope of Article 3: see *infra* 19.5.

electorate. The Commission considered that a five-year interval gave appropriate weight to these various considerations and duly reflected the will of the people.[22]

19.4 THE RIGHT TO VOTE AND TO STAND FOR ELECTION

19.4.1 GENERAL

The formulation of Article 3 as a government undertaking to hold elections and not as an individual right, might give rise to the assumption that this provision can only be the object of a complaint by a State and not of an individual complaint. The Commission never went that far, although its observation quoted above that the right of appeal against the way elections have been conducted is a right which "cannot be exercised by an individual acting alone"[23] seems to go somewhat in the direction of excluding a complaint by an individual.

At first the Commission drew from the text of Article 3 the general conclusion that this provision does not imply a right of the individual citizens to vote and to stand for election. Exclusion from the franchise, not only of particular persons,[24] but also of groups of persons,[25] was, therefore, considered admissible on that ground, be it under the condition that "such exclusion does not prevent the free expression of the opinion of the people in the choice of the legislature".[26] This view of the Commission was corroborated to some extent by the *travaux préparatoires*: in fact, the word 'universal' was deleted from the original draft,[27] from which it might be inferred that the drafters did not wish to include a guarantee for universal suffrage. In later decisions, however, the Commission took the position that the obligation imposed on the Contracting States does imply "the recognition of universal suffrage".[28] It added, however, that this did not mean that the right to take part in the elections was ensured to everyone without any restriction.

---

[22]   Appl. 27311/95, *Timke v. Federal Republic of Germany*, D&R 82 (1995), p. 158 (160).

[23]   In that context it is rather surprising that on the other hand the Commission still left open the question of whether a political party may be the victim of a violation of Art. 3: Appl. 8765/79, *The Liberal Party, Mrs R and Mr P v. the United Kingdom*, D&R 21 (1981), p. 211 (223).

[24]   Thus, *e.g.*, of a detainee: Appl. 530/59, *X v. Federal Republic of Germany*, Yearbook III 1960 p. 184 (190), and of a collaborator: Appl. 787/60, *X v. the Netherlands*, Coll. 7 (1962), p. 75 (79), and Appl. 6573/74, *X v. the Netherlands*, D&R 1 (1975), p. 87 (89-90).

[25]   *E.g.* the exclusion of Belgian residents in Belgian Congo from the elections in Belgium: Appl. 1065/61, *X v. Belgium*, Yearbook IV (1961), p. 260 (268).

[26]   *Ibidem.*

[27]   See the *Collected Edition of the 'travaux préparatoires' of the European Convention on Human Rights*, Vol. VI, Dordrecht 1985, pp. 30 and 44, in comparison to the earlier version on pp. 8 and 12.

[28]   Appl. 2728/66, *X v. Federal Republic of Germany*, Yearbook X (1967), p. 336 (338).

In a decision of May 1975 the Commission clearly expressed its view in the following words: "it follows both from the preamble and from Article 5 of Protocol No. 1 that the rights set out in the Protocol are protected by the same guarantees as are contained in the Convention itself. It must, therefore, be admitted that, whatever the wording of Article 3, the right it confers is in the nature of an individual right, since this quality constitutes the very foundation of the whole Convention."[29] Repeating thereupon its position that Article 3 recognises universal suffrage, the Commission concluded "that Article 3 guarantees, in principle, the right to vote and the right to stand for election to the legislature".[30] Here again, however, the Commission emphasised that this does not mean that it is an absolute or unlimited right. From the words 'under conditions which will ensure the free expression of the opinion of the people in the choice of the legislature' it inferred that the Contracting States are allowed to impose certain restrictions on the right to vote and to stand for election, provided that this is not done arbitrarily and does not constitute interference with the free expression of the people's opinion as such. In the final analysis it is for the Strasbourg organs to judge whether this condition has been fulfilled.[31]

The Commission's view was endorsed by the Court in 1987. The Court held that "the inter-State colouring of the wording of Article 3 does not reflect any difference of substance from the other substantive clauses of the Convention and Protocols. The reason for it would seem to lie rather in the desire to give greater solemnity to the commitment undertaken and in the fact that the primary obligation in the field concerned is not one of abstention or non-interference, as with the majority of the civil and political rights, but one of adoption by the State of positive measures to 'hold' democratic elections."[32]

The Court approved the Commission's interpretation of the right embodied in Article 3 as a subjective right of participation, but also recognised that there are implied limitations which leave the States a wide margin of appreciation in making the rights to vote and to stand for election subject to certain conditions. The Court has to satisfy itself that these conditions do not curtail the rights in question to such an extent as to impair their very essence and deprive them of their effectiveness, that they are imposed in pursuit of a legitimate aim and that the means employed are not disproportionate. In particular such conditions must not thwart 'the free expression of the opinion of the people in the choice of the legislature'.[33] Moreover, the Court emphasised that the phrase 'conditions which will ensure the free expression of the opinion

---

[29]   Appls 6745 and 6746/74, *W, X, Y and Z v. Belgium,* Yearbook XVIII (1975), p. 236 (244).
[30]   *Ibidem.*
[31]   *Ibidem.*
[32]   Judgment of 2 March 1987, *Mathieu-Mohin and Clerfayt,* para. 50.
[33]   Ibidem, para. 52. These criteria were confirmed in subsequent judgments: cf., *e.g.,* judgment of 18 February 1999, *Matthews,* para. 63.

of the people in the choice of the legislature' "implies essentially – apart from freedom of expression (already protected under Article 10 of the Convention) – the principle of equality of treatment of all citizens in the exercise of their right to vote and their right to stand for election."[34]

A touchstone for the admissibility of limitations of the right to vote will, therefore, have to be, in addition to the prohibition of arbitrariness, the question whether the right to vote and to stand for election has been conferred in a sufficiently wide and representative way to make it possible to speak of a free expression of the people's opinion as such. Furthermore, the restrictions have to be reviewed, by virtue of Article 5 of Protocol No. 1, for their conformity with the whole of the Convention, in particular with the prohibition of discrimination of Article 14. The establishment of a minimum age for the exercise of the right to vote and to stand for election in principle meets the criteria contained in the case law.[35] However, when this limit is appreciably higher than is the case in most other member States of the Council of Europe, the question of its reasonableness and the impact on the representative character of the elections will have to receive special attention.

19.4.2 THE RIGHT TO VOTE

In the *Mathieu-Mohin and Clerfayt* Case the Belgian 1980 Special Act was at issue, which required that candidates elected for the Flemish Council should take their parliamentary oath in Dutch. The applicants complained that this requirement prevented French-speaking electors from voting for a candidate who was likewise French-speaking. The Commission agreed that the Act had as an effect that a substantial minority in the district concerned could not have its own representatives on the Flemish Council and, therefore, constituted restrictions which were not compatible with Article 3 of Protocol No. 1, taken on its own. Having reached that conclusion, the Commission found it unnecessary to give its opinion on whether Article 14 of the Convention had also been violated.[36]

The Court, by thirteen votes to five, reached a different conclusion. It attached great importance to the fact that the Act fitted into a general institutional system of the Belgian State, based on the territoriality principle, and was designed to achieve an equilibrium between the Kingdom's various regions and cultural communities by means of a complex pattern of checks and balances, and to defuse the language disputes in the country by establishing more stable and decentralised organisational structures. Against that background and given the State's margin of appreciation, the

---

[34]   Judgments of 2 March 1987, *Mathieu-Mohin and Clerfayt*, para. 54.
[35]   Appls 6745 and 6746/74, *W, X, Y and Z v. Belgium*, Yearbook XVIII (1975), p. 236 (244-246).
[36]   Report of 15 March 1985, paras 100-112.

system – which was still incomplete and provisional – was not considered unreasonable by the Court. The fact that the French-speaking electors must vote either for candidates who will take the parliamentary oath in French and will accordingly join the French-language group in the (central) House of Representatives or the Senate and sit on the (regional) French Community Council, or else for candidates who will take the oath in Dutch and so belong to the Dutch-language group in the House of Representatives or the Senate and sit on the Flemish Council, was considered by the Court not to be a disproportionate limitation such as would thwart 'the free expression of the opinion of the people in the choice of the legislature'. For the same reason the Court held that there was no discrimination prejudicial to the applicants in violation of Article 14.[37]

In the *Matthews* Case, however, the Court was faced with a situation where the whole population of a territory (Gibraltar) could not take part in the election for the European Parliament at all. After having found that Article 3 applied to these elections (see section 15.4 *infra*), the Court held that the very essence of the applicant's right to vote was denied.[38]

In the *Aziz* Case the Court criticised the fact that the Cypriot legislature had failed to lay down rules allowing the applicant and other members of the Turkish Cypriot community living in the Government-controlled part of Cyprus to vote in parliamentary elections. The 1960 Cypriot Constitution had provided for two separate electoral lists, one for each community. However, this system had not been applied since the 1960s, due to the special situation on the island. Members of the Turkish Cypriot community (some 1000 people) were thereby prevented from voting in the elections, since they could not be registered on the Greek-Cypriot electoral roll. The Court observed that the system envisaged by the Constitution had been rendered ineffective and that there was a manifest lack of legislation to solve the ensuing problems. Consequently, the applicant 'was completely deprived of any opportunity to express his opinion in the choice of the members of the House of Representatives of the country of which he is a national and where he has always lived.'[39] This amounted to both an impairment of the very essence of his right to vote and to discrimination within the meaning of Article 14 of the Convention.[40]

Denying the right to vote to women is contrary to the tenor of Article 3 as well as to the prohibition of discrimination. As to the restriction of the right to vote to citizens only, this question is more difficult to answer. Article 16, which allows restriction of the political activities of aliens in certain cases, has not been linked to Article 3 of

---

[37]   Judgment of 2 March 1987, paras 57 and 59.
[38]   Judgment of 18 February 1999, paras 64 and 65.
[39]   Judgment of 22 June 2004, para. 29.
[40]   *Idem*, paras 30 and 36-38.

Protocol No. 1 but may operate *via* Article 14 of the Convention.[41] It is true that the above-mentioned important role which is assigned by the Convention to the legislature in ensuring and further regulating the enjoyment of the rights and freedoms, points to an equal interest of aliens in the composition of the legislature in their host country, since Article 1 of the Convention confers the enjoyment of those rights and freedoms on them as well, while these rights and freedoms may be restricted in particular by the legislator.

Similarly, one of the reasons which led the Court to find a violation in the *Matthews* Case was the fact that the applicant, as resident of Gibraltar, was completely denied the right to vote in the European Parliament elections, in spite of the fact that the legislation which emanates from the EC forms part of the legislation in Gibraltar and that the applicant was directly affected by it.[42] This reasoning would seem to also apply, in respect of national elections, to aliens lawfully residing in the country. On the other hand, the Court held in its *Mathieu-Mohin and Clerfayt* judgment that Article 3 "implies essentially equality of treatment of all *citizens* in the exercise of their right to vote and to stand for election".[43]

Restriction of the franchise to the State's own nationals is still fairly common and was even more so at the time Article 3 was drafted, so that it is not very likely that the drafters have wished to exclude such a system for the future.[44] However, if they have intended to express this by the word 'people', this is inadequate; it can hardly be argued that those aliens who have been residents of a given country for a long time and as such contribute to the economic, social and cultural life of that country, without, for whatever reason, having become citizens thereof, do not belong to the 'people' of that country. It is, therefore, not a matter of course to deny the franchise to them when one takes seriously the principle of representative democracy, as laid down in Article 3. Although the idea of granting the right to vote to aliens, in particular in local elections,

---

[41] Whatever the relevance of Article 16 may be, it is clear that it has further diminished, and even disappeared in discrimination cases under Protocol No. 12 to the Convention, as a result of the fact that Article 16 has not been made applicable to the general prohibition of discrimination guaranteed by this new Protocol.

[42] Judgment of 18 February 1999, para. 64.

[43] Judgment of 2 March 1987, para. 54 (emphasis added).

[44] Thus impliedly also the Commission: Appl. 7566/76, *X v. the United Kingdom*, D&R 9 (1978), p. 121 (122), and Appl. 7730/76, *X v. the United Kingdom*, D&R 15 (1979), p. 137 (138).

is gaining more ground,[45] it may hardly be expected that the Strasbourg case law will force a break-through on this point.[46]

In several member States the law provides that citizens may take part in elections in the country in question only if they also have residence in that country. The Commission considered this restriction as being in conformity with Article 3 and advanced the following justifications for such a restriction: (1) non-residents are less directly or less continuously concerned with and less well informed on the day-to-day problems in the country; (2) candidates for the elections have less easy access to non-residents to present the different electoral issues so as to secure a free expression of opinion; (3) non-residents have less influence on the selection of candidates and the formulation of their electoral programmes; and (4) the correlation between the right to vote and being directly affected by acts of the bodies elected is less.[47] The Court essentially endorsed this set of justifications, whilst stressing, in addition, the legitimate concern that the legislature may have to limit the influence of citizens living abroad in elections on issues which, while admittedly fundamental, primarily affect persons living in the country.[48] Both the Commission and the Court recognised that not all of these various justifications may be fully applicable in each individual case, because some people may have maintained ties with their country of origin. However, "the law cannot take account of every individual case but must lay down a general rule", and "the applicant cannot argue that he is affected by the acts of political institutions to the same extent as resident citizens. Thus the applicant's situation is different from that of a resident citizen, and that justifies the residence requirement."[49]

---

[45]   See, for example, the 1992 Council of Europe Convention on the Participation of Foreigners in Public Life at Local Level, *ETS* 144, Art. 6 of which contains an undertaking, as concerns local elections, to grant the right to vote and to stand for election to every foreign resident provided he has been a lawful and habitual resident for the five years preceding the elections. This Convention has so far been ratified by Italy, Norway, Sweden, the Netherlands, Denmark, Finland and Iceland. For European Union citizens, a right to vote and to stand for election in local and European Parliament elections in the EU member State where they have their residence has also been recognised (Article 19 of the EC Treaty and Article I-10, para. 2(b) of the Treaty establishing a Constitution for Europe (not yet entered into force)).

[46]   While the Commission referred to developments in this field (Appl. 7730/76, *X v. the United Kingdom*, D&R 15 (1979), p. 137 (138)), it also considered that citizenship is frequently applied by States Parties as one of the criteria conditioning the right to vote: Appl. 27614/95, *Luksch v. Italy*.

[47]   Appl. 7730/76, *X v. the United Kingdom*, D&R 15 (1979), p. 137 (139) (this decision also dealt with an complaint about discrimination: the fact that in some countries nationals residing abroad who are working there in the service of their country do have the right to vote, does not in the Commission's opinion constitute discrimination in the sense of Article 14, because in view of their function they still keep a closer link with their country). See also Appl. 7566/76, *X v. the United Kingdom*, D&R 9 (1978), p. 121 (122), and with regard to the elections for the European Parliament, Appl. 8612/79, *Alliance des Belges de la Communauté européenne v. Belgium*, D&R 15 (1979), p. 259 (264).

[48]   Appl. 31981/96, *Hilbe v. Liechtenstein*.

[49]   *Ibidem*; see, as regards the Commission, Appl. 35385/97, *Luksch v. Germany*.

In *X v. the United Kingdom* the applicant, a resident of Jersey, complained about the fact that he could not participate in elections for the United Kingdom Parliament. Although this Parliament does have legislative competence with regard to Jersey (which it exercises occasionally) and residents of Jersey are in that respect British subjects, they are not considered residents of the United Kingdom. Accordingly, they cannot participate in elections for Parliament. The Commission, after considering the specific constitutional relationship between Jersey and the United Kingdom and after considering that Jersey has its own elected legislature, concluded that there was no breach of Article 3.[50] Specific residence requirements with respect to the right to vote in elections for *regional* representative bodies – to the extent that they are covered by the notion of 'legislature' (see *infra* 19.5) – may also be permitted under Article 3, especially where they serve the legitimate and important aim of protecting minorities living in the region from a risk of 'dilution'.[51]

With regard to the right to vote of prisoners, whose invocation of Article 3 found no hearing under the old case law of the Commission,[52] the Strasbourg case law has long remained extremely restrictive. In the case of a Dutch conscientious objector, who complained about a rule in the Netherlands according to which every prison sentence of more than one year automatically resulted in a suspension of the exercise of the right to vote for three years, the Commission concluded that, taking into account the legislator's margin of appreciation, such a measure does not go beyond the restrictions justifiable in the context of Article 3 of Protocol No. 1.[53] In the more recent case of an Irish prisoner, who was disenfranchised because the law simply did not foresee a right for prisoners to vote, the Commission referred to its case law and held that the fact that all of the convicted prisoner population cannot vote does not affect the free expression of the opinion of the people in the choice of the legislature. It added that the position under Irish law could not be considered to be arbitrary in view of the margin of appreciation and the jurisprudence of the Convention organs.[54]

It is submitted, however, that the way in which the Netherlands and the Irish authorities, respectively, have used the margin of appreciation in these cases leads to a disproportionate limitation such as thwarts the free expression of the opinion of the people in the sense of Article 3. If the law foresees that the (temporary) loss of the franchise may be imposed by a judge as a penalty for particular offences, such a

---

[50] Appl. 8873/80, D&R 28 (1982), p. 99 (104).

[51] Appl. 23450/94, *Polacco and Garofalo* (a 4-year residence requirement held to be acceptable even though the applicants had strong links with the region; applicants did not belong to the linguistic (German and Ladin) minorities that the Statute of the Region of Trentino Alto-Adige sought to protect).

[52] Appl. 530/59, *X v. Federal Republic of Germany*, Yearbook III (1960), p. 184 (188); Appl. 2728/66, *X v. Federal Republic of Germany*, Yearbook X (1967), p. 336 (338).

[53] Appl. 9914/82, *H v. the Netherlands*, D&R 33 (1983), p. 242 (245-246).

[54] Appl. 24827/94, *Holland v. Ireland*.

restriction would be in conformity with principles of democracy and the rule of law.[55] However, this is different with a general or automatic prohibition for prisoners to participate in elections, not as a punitive measure, but as a measure for maintaining order, and even less so when this is left to the discretion of the prison authorities. Since special regulations for the voting of prisoners can be made without difficulty, a general exclusion would amount to an exclusion of a group of the population which is insufficiently justified by their special status. The Commission sought to justify the Dutch and the Irish restrictions by reference to the notion of dishonour that certain convictions carry with them for a specific period, which may be taken into consideration by the legislation in the respect of the exercise of political rights. This cannot, however, serve as sufficient justification for a general exclusion of broad categories of convicted prisoners, let alone of all of them. The latter would be tantamount to saying that the opinions of convicted prisoners form no part of the 'opinion of the people', which would be difficult to reconcile with modern penological views regarding the purposes of prison sentences.

The Court has not yet pronounced itself definitively on this precise question, but there are several indications that the Court might depart from the Commission's case law. In the *Labita* Case the applicant's voting rights had been automatically suspended as a result of the special police supervision measure that had been imposed on him, even though he had been finally acquitted in the criminal proceedings brought against him. The Court noted that, under Italian law, persons subject to such supervision forfeit their civil rights because they represent a danger to society or, as in the present case, are suspected of belonging to the mafia. The Government feared that their right to vote might be exercised in favour of other members of the mafia. The Court had "no doubt that temporarily suspending the voting rights of persons against whom there is evidence of Mafia membership pursues a legitimate aim". However, the special supervision measure which had triggered the suspension of voting rights was applied after the applicant had been acquitted on the ground that he had not committed the offence. There was, therefore, no concrete evidence on which a suspicion of Mafia membership could be based and the Court, holding that the removal of the applicant from the electoral register was not proportionate, found a violation of Article 3.[56] Although this judgment is not concerned with convicted prisoners, it does suggest that,

---

[55] See the *Code of Good Practice in Electoral Matters,* drawn up by the Council of Europe's European Commission for Democracy Through Law (Venice Commission) in 2002, which also takes the position that the withdrawal of political rights may only be imposed by express decision of a court of law (principle 1.1 d. under v.).

[56] Judgment of 6 April 2000, paras 202-203. See, as regards disenfranchisement as a consequence of special police supervision in Italy, also the judgment of 1 July 2004, *Santoro*, paras 58-59, where an excessive delay in executing this special measure (with the result that the applicant missed the opportunity to vote in two elections) was held to be neither in accordance with law nor necessary.

for the Court, the nature of the offence committed constitutes a relevant factor in assessing whether restrictions of the right to vote are justified.

With respect to another complaint against Italy the Court regarded the duration of a temporary suspension of the right to vote as an important factor for determining whether such a measure was arbitrary or disproportionate.[57] This would seem to rule out any generic or automatic deprivation of political rights in respect of persons convicted to custodial sentences. Finally, a case is currently pending before the Court's Grand Chamber in which the Chamber had ruled that the United Kingdom's system, involving an automatic and blanket bar on voting by any serving prisoner in any circumstances, transgressed the wide margin of appreciation available to national legislatures in this area.[58]

It goes without saying that the exercise of the right to vote will frequently be conditioned by certain formalities which individuals must fulfil beforehand, such as ensuring that they are properly registered as voters within the applicable time-limit. Such formalities serve a legitimate aim, namely to ensure the proper conduct of the elections and avoid electoral fraud.[59]

19.4.3 THE RIGHT TO STAND FOR ELECTION

The right to stand for election to the legislature is also not unlimited. Here the same general conditions apply as with regard to restrictions of the right to vote. The Court has confirmed this in a series of judgments.

Some cases concerned restrictions of the right to stand for election which applied in respect of civil servants. At issue in the *Gitonas* Case was a Greek rule which precluded certain categories of holders of public office from standing for election and being elected in any constituency where they have performed their duties for more than three months in the three years preceding the elections. The Court held that "[s]uch disqualification, for which equivalent provisions exist in several member States of the Council of Europe, serves a dual purpose that is essential for the proper functioning and upholding of democratic regimes, namely ensuring that candidates of different political persuasions enjoy equal means of influence (since holders of public office may on occasion have an unfair advantage over other candidates) and protecting the electorate from pressure from such officials who, because of their position, are called upon to take many – and sometimes important – decisions and enjoy substantial

---

[57] Appl. 58540/00, *M.D.U. v. Italy*, concerning a two-year suspension of the right to vote as an accessory sanction imposed by a court in criminal proceedings.

[58] Judgment of 30 March 2004, *Hirst (No. 2)*, para. 51.

[59] Appl. 51685/99, *Benkadour*.

prestige in the eyes of the ordinary citizen, whose choice of candidate might be influenced."[60]

While admitting that the Greek system was complex as concerns the precise categories of public officials covered by the restriction, the Court did not consider it to be arbitrary or disproportionate. The fact that it was based on objective criteria for disqualification, which prevented the Greek Special Supreme Court from having regard to any special features of each case, was not unreasonable "having regard to the enormous practical difficulty in proving that a position in the civil service had been used to electoral ends." The Court also accepted as reasonable the Greek court's assimilation of the applicants' situations (for example, Gitonas had been on secondment from an investment bank to the Prime Minister's office) to the posts explicitly described in the relevant legislation, this being an issue of interpretation of domestic law and thus a matter primarily left to the national authorities.[61]

In the *Ahmed* Case the Court concluded that the restrictions applicable to local civil servants in the United Kingdom (who were prevented from standing for election as long as they held politically restricted posts) did not violate Article 3. The relevant regulations had a legitimate aim, namely to secure the political impartiality of senior officers. Nor could it be maintained that the restrictions limited the very essence of the applicants' rights under Article 3 having regard to the fact that they only operate as long as the persons concerned occupy politically restricted posts; furthermore, any of the applicants wishing to run for elected office was at liberty to resign from his post.[62]

In the *Podkolzina* Case, which concerned language requirements attached to the right to stand for election to the Latvian Parliament, the Court confirmed that States have a broad latitude to establish constitutional rules on the status of members of Parliament, including criteria for declaring them ineligible. Such criteria vary in accordance with the historical and political factors specific to each State; the multiplicity of situations provided for in the constitutions and electoral laws of numerous member States of the Council of Europe shows the diversity of possible approaches in this area.[63] However, the Court also referred to the principle that Convention rights must be concrete and effective, not theoretical or illusory: "The right to stand as a candidate in an election, which is guaranteed by Article 3 of Protocol No. 1 and is inherent in the concept of a truly democratic regime, would only be illusory if one could be arbitrarily deprived of it at any moment. Consequently, while it is true that States have a wide margin of appreciation when establishing eligibility conditions in the abstract, the principle that rights must be effective requires the finding that this or that

---

[60]   Judgment of 1 July 1997, para. 40.
[61]   *Ibidem*, para. 44.
[62]   Judgment of 2 September 1998, para. 75.
[63]   Judgment of 9 April 2002, para. 33.

candidate has failed to satisfy them to comply with a number of criteria framed to prevent arbitrary decisions. In particular, such a finding must be reached by a body which can provide a minimum of guarantees of its impartiality. Similarly, the discretion enjoyed by the body concerned must not be exorbitantly wide; it must be circumscribed, with sufficient precision, by the provisions of domestic law. Lastly, the procedure for ruling a candidate ineligible must be such as to guarantee a fair and objective decision and prevent any abuse of power on the part of the relevant authority."[64]

The Court accepted that it is in principle for the State alone to choose the working language of the national parliament and that, having regard to their margin of appreciation, requiring candidates in parliamentary elections to have a sufficient knowledge of the official language pursues the legitimate aim of ensuring the normal functioning of the State's institutional system. However, the Court found that, in the absence of any guarantee of objectivity, the procedure followed was incompatible with the above-cited requirements of procedural fairness and legal certainty that must be satisfied in relation to candidates' eligibility.[65] The decision to strike Ms Podkolzina off the list of election candidates was, therefore, disproportionate and violated Article 3.

Various conditions or restrictions attached to the right to stand for election have been considered compatible with Article 3 of the Protocol. For example, the condition that to be eligible one must not be a member of another legislature was not held to be inconsistent with Article 3 of the Protocol.[66] This holds true also for a prohibition of dual citizenship for candidates to parliamentary elections,[67] and for a condition that candidates present a certain number of signatures.[68] In the *Masson* Case the Court accepted that the French statutory provisions setting a ceiling on election campaign expenditure and providing for a system of expenditure control served a legitimate aim, namely to ensure a certain equality between candidates and thus to help guarantee 'the free expression of the will of the people in the choice of the legislature'. The threat of ineligibility was considered to be an adequate means for ensuring respect of the relevant rules. The Court went on to examine whether the way the provisions had been applied in the decision of the Constitutional Council, was tainted by arbitrariness or disproportionality; this was held not to be the case.[69]

---

[64]   *Ibidem*, para. 35.
[65]   *Ibidem*, paras 34 and 36. Although the applicant was in the possession of a valid language certificate, she was, on a very dubious legal basis, with only a few other candidates selected for a second examination, carried out by a single official who was not bound by any procedural rules or official assessment criteria, thus possessing an exorbitant power of assessment. The examiner apparently also questioned the applicant about the reasons for her political orientation (see para. 36 of the judgment).
[66]   Appl. 10316/83, *M. v. the United Kingdom*, D&R 37 (1984), p. 129 (133-134).
[67]   Appl. 28858/95, *Ganchev*.
[68]   Appl. 23151/94, *Asensio Serqueda v. Spain*, D&R 77 (1994), p. 122.
[69]   Appl. 41944/98, decision of 14 September 1999.

On the other hand, in the *Melnychenko* Case formal application of a residence requirement as ground for refusal to register a candidate having his legal residence in the country but actually living abroad as a refugee, was found to be in breach of Article 3. The Court accepted that stricter requirements may be imposed on the eligibility to stand for election to parliament, as distinguished from voting eligibility (see *supra* 19.4.2); it would not preclude a five-year continuous residence requirement for potential parliamentary candidates as this might be appropriate to enable such persons to familiarise themselves with the issues associated with the parliament's work. Moreover, it would correspond to the interests of a democratic society that the electorate be in a position to assess the candidate's personal qualifications and ability to best represent its interests in parliament. On the specific facts of the case, however, the Court found a violation, since the authorities had applied the residence requirement in a formalistic manner and because it found the applicant's hasty flight from the country and his fear of persecution understandable.[70] Furthermore, it remains to be seen what the Court's final assessment will be in a Latvian case concerning the applicant's continuing ineligibility on account of her active participation in the Latvian Communist Party in 1991, without her ever having been convicted in a criminal procedure. This case raises important questions of principle concerning political pluralism in newly democratic States and the extent to which it entails participation rights for those who in the past have been hostile to the democratic process, at a time when that process was still fragile.[71]

Quite logically, the Court has interpreted the right to stand for election as also including a right of the person elected to (continue to) exercise the mandate received. In the *Selim Sadak* Case the Court affirmed the Commission's case law in this sense and found a violation of Article 3. The applicants, who were elected parliamentarians and members of a pro-Kurdish party, were automatically prohibited from exercising their parliamentary mandates as a result of the dissolution of that party. The Court noted that the dissolution of the political party by the Constitutional Court was based on grounds unrelated to the applicants personal political activities. In view also of the extreme severity of the measure inflicted upon them the Court found that the sanction was disproportionate and incompatible with the very essence of the right to stand for election and to exercise their mandate which Article 3 granted to them. It added that

---

[70]   Judgment of 19 October 2004, paras 57-58, 63 and 65-66.
[71]   Chamber judgment of 17 June 2004 in the Case of *Ždanoka* (violation of Article 3 of Protocol No. 1), currently pending before a Grand Chamber.

the measure had also infringed the sovereign power of the electorate that had elected them to parliament.[72]

However, also the right to exercise an electoral mandate may be subjected to certain formalities such as an oath, provided they do not conflict with other Convention rights. Thus, while an oath of allegiance to the Queen may reasonably be attached to taking up one's parliamentary seat in a monarchy,[73] obliging a newly elected parliamentarian to take an oath on the Gospels was considered to be a disproportionate interference with (negative) freedom of religion.[74]

Article 3 also gives protection to candidates who have suffered from irregularities in the way the elections have been conducted, to the extent that there has been an interference with the free expression of the opinion of the people in the choice of the legislature. However, where a competent national authority has duly examined the complaint and ruled that the irregularities could not have prejudiced the outcome of the election, the European review will be limited to whether or not that finding was arbitrary.[75]

In the *Pierre-Bloch* Case the Court held that disputes by candidates about the arrangements for the exercise of the right to stand for election, such as those concerning the obligation of candidates to limit their campaign expenditure, fall outside the scope of Article 6, paragraph 1, of the Convention, since the right to stand for election is a political one and not a 'civil' one within the meaning of that Article, notwithstanding possible pecuniary or economic aspects of the proceedings.[76]

---

[72]   Judgment of 11 June 2002, paras 33 and 37-40. By contrast, in the Case of *Refah Partisi (the Welfare Party) and Others*, the fact that the leaders of a dissolved political party were unable to stand for election, was not examined under Article 3. In its judgment of 13 February 2003, the Court found that this measure was only a secondary effect of their party's dissolution which the Court had found not to be in breach of Article 11 of the Convention (para. 139 of the judgment).

[73]   Appl. 39511/98, *McGuinness*, decision of 8 June 1999.

[74]   Judgment of 18 February 1999, *Buscarini and Others*, para. 39.

[75]   Appl. 18997/91, *I.Z. v. Greece*, D&R 76 (1994), p. 65 (68); Appl. 43476/98, *Babenko*. Conversely, the Court rejected a complaint from a candidate who claimed to have suffered from such a formality (the requirement that the records of voting results be signed by the President of the polling station, failing which the votes concerned were invalid). Such formalities are not arbitrary; on the contrary, they constitute safeguards against irregularities or fraud (Appl. 74287/01, *Tsimas*).

[76]   Judgment of 21 October 1997, paras 50-51; see also Appl. 41944/98, *Masson*, and Appl. 35584/02, *Guliyev*. In the first two cases, the Court also examined whether Article 6 applied under its 'criminal' head and concluded that neither the legal classification of the offence under domestic law and its very nature, nor the nature and degree of severity of the penalties were such as to make Article 6 applicable in its criminal aspect.

19.5   CHOICE OF THE LEGISLATURE

What is meant in Article 3 by 'legislature' (French: '*corps législatif*')? Does Article 3 relate to the election of the highest legislative bodies in the Contracting States only, or of all bodies having legislative powers? Does it also apply to international legislative bodies?

Several elements of the notion of 'legislature' have emerged in the Strasbourg case law. First, the body must have a real power which must be of a legislative nature. A body which can only propose bills, but cannot itself adopt them, does not belong to the 'legislature'.[77] Purely deliberative powers do not suffice; a body which has no power 'to promulgate any form of binding norm or decision' will in any case not qualify as a 'legislative' body.[78] Similarly, according to constant case law, Article 3 does not apply to the right to vote in referendums.[79] Furthermore, the Commission has indicated that the power must be a 'rule-making power'.[80]

The Commission has also held that Article 3 is not applicable to the election of a Head of State and that there was no indication that the powers of the President of Lithuania could be construed as 'legislature'.[81] So far the Court seems to follow a less categorical approach. It denied applicability of Article 3 to the Presidential elections in Azerbaijan and in "the former Yugoslav Republic of Macedonia", but it reached that conclusion after an examination of the constitutional rules defining the extent and nature of the President's involvement in the legislative process. In the *Guliyev* Case the Court found that the President, although he was head of the executive, had some powers linked to Parliament's legislative power. The President's powers (to issue decrees and orders, to sign or veto legislative acts adopted by Parliament) were accessory to the legislative power of Parliament and part of the system of checks and balances in the Republic.[82] In the *Boskoski* Case the Court indicated that it did not exclude the possibility of applying Article 3 to presidential elections. Referring to the *Matthews* judgment (see *infra* in this Chapter), the Court held that regard should be had not only to the strictly legislative powers which a body has, but also to that body's role in the overall legislative process. Should it be established that the office of the Head of State had been given the power to initiate and adopt legislation or enjoys wide powers to control the passage of legislation or the power to censure the principal

---

[77]   Appls 6745 and 6746/74, *W, X, Y and Z v. Belgium,* Yearbook XVIII (1975), p. 236 (240-244).

[78]   Appl. 31699/96 *Lindsay and Others* (concerning the Northern Ireland Forum).

[79]   See, *e.g.,* Appl. 27881/95, *Nurminen and Others* (with references to older case law); Appl. 26633/95, *Bader;* Appl. 31981/96 *Hilbe;* Appl. 54767/00, *Borghi;* Appl. 399/02, *Bocellari and Rizza.*

[80]   Appl. 23450/94, *Polacco and Garofalo.*

[81]   Appl. 41090/98, *Baskauskaite.* The applicant unsuccessfully argued that the President signs and issues laws, and that he has the right to propose new legislation and to decline to sign a law and remit it back to Parliament for re-consideration.

[82]   Appl. 35584/02, *Guliyev.*

legislation-setting authorities, then it could arguably be considered to be a 'legislature' within the meaning of Article 3 of Protocol No. 1. This was held not to be the case regarding the Macedonian President.[83]

It is submitted that the reasoning in *Boskoski* is not convincing. The *Matthews* judgment seems to offer little precedent value on this specific point, since that judgment's focus on the criterion of the 'body's role in the overall legislative process' was the direct consequence of the Court's view that the European Community had a *sui generis* nature, which does not follow the pattern found in many States of a more or less strict division of powers between the executive and the legislature, but is rather marked by a legislative process involving the participation of the European Parliament, the Council and the European Commission. More importantly, accepting that a single (elected) official may constitute a 'legislature' within the meaning of Article 3 would seem to sit ill with the concepts of pluralism and representative democracy embraced by the Convention (see notably *supra* 19.2), and could even result in monarchies with a non-elected, hereditary monarch, being in violation of Article 3.

Finally, as a further element of the notion of 'legislature', the power and competence vested in a body must be sufficiently wide, but neither the Commission nor the Court have specified what the minimum scope of such competence is for there to be a legislative power.[84] Rather, they stressed that the notion of 'legislature' has to be interpreted in the light of the constitutional structure of the State concerned, particularly the origin of the power in question.

In the *Mathieu-Mohin and Clerfayt* Case the Court took the position that the word 'legislature' does not necessarily mean the national parliament only. According to the Court its meaning has to be interpreted in the light of the constitutional structure of the State in question. On that basis the Court held that, further to the 1980 constitutional reform, the Flemish Council in Belgium was vested with competences and powers wide enough to make it, alongside the French Community Council and the Walloon Regional Council, a constituent part of the Belgian 'legislature' in addition to the House of Representatives and the Senate.[85]

This confirms earlier case law of the Commission according to which the constitutional law of the Contracting State in question is decisive in this respect. The Commission added the criterion that the legislative power has to be an autonomous power. With regard to bodies which have indeed legislative powers, but only by virtue of delegation by a superior legislator, and with regard to bodies whose legislative powers only concern a limited circle of persons, the obligation to hold free elections

---

[83] Appl. 11676/04, *Boskoski*.

[84] Judgment of 2 March 1987 in the *Mathieu-Mohin and Clerfayt* Case, para. 53; Appl. 46813/99, *Malarde*.

[85] Judgment of 2 March 1987, para. 53.

does not apply.[86] The body concerned must, in that opinion, be the legislative body which derives its legislative powers directly from the written or unwritten constitution.

For those States which are a federation, such as the Federal Republic of Germany, Austria, Switzerland and Russia, the highest legislative bodies of the constituent states, too, will have to be considered as belonging to the 'legislature', since they do not exercise their legislative powers by virtue of delegation by the federal legislator, but derive these powers directly from the federal constitution.[87]

The situation in respect of regions is less clear-cut, no doubt because they have varying levels of autonomy in different countries (and sometimes even within one country). The Court accepted that, by analogy to the constituent states of Federal States, the legislative assemblies of the autonomous communities in Spain qualify as 'legislature' within the meaning of Article 3: they participate in the exercise of legislative power in Spain.[88] As regards the regional councils in Italy, the Commission had left open the question of whether they might be part of the legislature in the country.[89] However, the matter was settled by the Court in the *Santoro* Case. It referred to the constitutional provisions according to which "the regional councils are competent to enact, within the territory of the Region to which they belong, laws in a number of pivotal matters in a democratic society, such as administrative planning, local policy, public-health care, education, town planning and agriculture (...). The Court therefore considers that the Constitution vested the regional councils with competence and powers wide enough to make them a constituent part of the legislature in addition to the Parliament."[90]

On the other hand, Santoro's complaint was declared inadmissible in so far as it concerned the provincial councils in Italy: the Constitution did not confer on the provincial authorities any legislative power within the meaning of Article 3.[91] Likewise, the Regional Council of Brittany in France was not considered to be part of the French legislature, but the Court's reasoning here was more focused on the fact that legislative power in France is reserved to Parliament. The competence of regional councils under French law is limited to regulating, *through deliberations*, the economic, social, cultural

---

[86]   Appl. 5155/71, *X v. the United Kingdom*, D&R 6 (1977), p. 13, and Appl. 9926/82, *X v. the Netherlands*, D&R 32 (1983), p. 274 (281).

[87]   See, as regards the Diets of the German *Länder*, Appl. 27311/95, *Timke v. Germany*, D&R 82 (1995), p. 158. As regards Austria, see Appl. 7008/75, *X. v. Austria*, D&R 6 (1977), p. 120. It should be noted that the Court cited these two decisions of the Commission in its judgment of 18 February 1999 (para. 40) in the *Matthews* Case in support of its affirmation that 'legislature' does not necessarily mean the national parliament. As concerns the Parliaments of Russia's 'subjects of the Federation', see Appl. 51501/99, *Cherepkov*.

[88]   Decisions of 7 July 2001, *Hormaechea Cazon*, and *Federacion Nacionalistica Canaria*.

[89]   Appl. 27614/97, *Luksch*, and 23450/94, *Polacco and Garofalo*.

[90]   Judgment of 1 July 2004, para. 52.

[91]   Appl. 36681/97, *Santoro*.

and scientific affairs of the region as well as health matters.[92] From these decisions it would appear that, as far as regional bodies in unitary States are concerned, the degree of regulatory autonomy recognised within the State's constitutional framework will be largely determinative for the applicability of Article 3.

The case law is clearer as regards municipal councils and similar organs of local authority possessing – sometimes fairly broad – regulatory powers. In its judgment in the *Ahmed* Case the Court still left open the question of applicability of Article 3 to local elections in the United Kingdom,[93] but soon thereafter it adopted the position that "the power to make regulations and by-laws which is conferred on the local authorities in many countries is to be distinguished from legislative power, which is referred to in Article 3".[94]

Whilst this position has the advantage of being clear and simple, it is submitted that it may do insufficient justice to the high degree of local autonomy recognised in some countries. Where such autonomy, with attendant regulatory competence, flows directly from the constitution, it would be more in line with the growing importance attached to local democracy in Europe and with the Court's general 'constitutionalist' approach under Article 3 to hold the latter provision applicable. Any presumption against its applicability to local elections should, therefore, at least be rebuttable.[95]

The question of whether Article 3 also applies to international legislative bodies has been addressed in cases concerning the European Parliament. The matter was settled by the Court in its landmark judgment in the *Matthews* Case.[96] According to an annex to the 1976 Act concerning elections to the European Parliament (a treaty concluded within the legal order of the European Community), the residents of Gibraltar could not take part in the elections for that Parliament. After holding that the United Kingdom was responsible under Article 1 of the Convention (*inter alia* because EC legislation affects the population of Gibraltar in the same way as 'purely' domestic legislation; furthermore, the country's responsibility derives from the fact that it has entered into treaty commitments subsequent to the applicability of Article 3 to Gibraltar), the Court examined whether Article 3 was applicable to the European Parliament. It did so in two stages. First, it addressed the government's general thesis that a supranational organ such as the European Parliament fell outside the scope of Article 3. This had also been the view of the majority of the Commission in this case,

---

[92] Decision of 5 September 2000, *Malarde*.

[93] Judgment of 2 September 1998, para. 76.

[94] Decision of 25 January 2000, *Cherepkov*. See also the decision of 12 October 2000, *Salleras Llinares*; decision of 2 July 2002, *Gorizdra*; and decision of 6 March 2003, *Ždanoka*.

[95] See the decision of 6 March 2003, *Ždanoka*, where the Court did verify the position of municipal councils under the Latvian Constitution.

[96] Judgment of 18 February 1999.

who had referred to the fact that the drafters of Article 3 could not have intended to make it applicable to an organ that did not even exist at that time.[97] This latter point was rejected by the Court on the basis of the principle that the Convention is a living instrument which must be interpreted in the light of present-day conditions: "The mere fact that a body was not envisaged by the drafters of the Convention cannot prevent that body from falling within the scope of the Convention. To the extent that Contracting States organise common constitutional or parliamentary structures by international treaties, the Court must take these mutually agreed structural changes into account in interpreting the Convention and its Protocols."[98]

The Court recalled the case law of the Court of Justice of the European Community according to which it is an inherent aspect of EC law that such law sits alongside, and indeed has precedence over, domestic law as well as its own case law, underlining that Article 3 enshrines an characteristic of effective political democracy. It held that that there was no indication of any alternative means of providing for electoral representation of the population of Gibraltar and that "to accept the Governments contention that the sphere of activities of the European Parliament falls outside the scope of Article 3 of Protocol No. 1 would risk undermining one of the fundamental tools by which 'effective political democracy' can be maintained."[99] Having thus found that the supranational nature of the European Parliament was not a reason for excluding it from the scope of Article 3, the Court went on to examine in more detail whether that Parliament possessed the characteristics of a 'legislature' in Gibraltar. In determining that question the Court first observed that it "must bear in mind the sui generis nature of the European Community, which does not follow in every respect the pattern common in many States of a more or less strict division of powers between the executive and the legislature. Rather, the legislative process in the EC involves the participation of the European Parliament, the Council and the European Commission."[100] Therefore, regard should be had not only to the strictly legislative powers of a body, but also to that body's role in the overall legislative process. The Court carried out a three-pronged test. Firstly, it noted that since the Maastricht Treaty the powers of the European Parliament are no longer expressed as 'advisory and supervisory', which must be taken as an indication that it has moved away from being a purely consultative body towards being a body with a decisive role in the legislative process. However, this is not sufficient: "only an examination of the European Parliament's actual powers in the context of the EC legislative process as a whole will determine whether it qualifies as 'legislature' within the meaning of Article 3". The Court then listed those 'actual powers': the different modalities of the Parliament's involvement

---

[97]   *Ibidem*, para. 38.
[98]   *Ibidem*, para. 39.
[99]   *Ibidem*, para. 43.
[100] *Ibidem*, para. 48.

in the passage of legislation, its democratic control functions in relation to the European Commission and the budget, and the right to request that the Commission submit proposals for Community acts. Finally, under the third limb of the test, *i.e.* the context in which the European Parliament operates, the Court took "the view that the European Parliament represents the principal form of democratic, political accountability in the Community system. The Court considers that whatever its limitations, the European Parliament, which derives democratic legitimation from the direct elections by universal suffrage, must be seen as that part of the European Community structure which best reflects concerns as to 'effective political democracy'."[101] And it concluded: "The Court thus finds that the European Parliament is sufficiently involved in the specific legislative processes leading to the passage of legislation under Articles 189b and 189c of the EC treaty, and is sufficiently involved in the general democratic supervision of the activities of the European Community, to constitute part of the 'legislature' of Gibraltar for the purposes of Article 3 of Protocol No. 1."[102]

Having established that Article 3 applied to the present case the Court had no difficulty in finding a violation. The applicant had been completely denied any opportunity to express her opinion in the choice of the members of the European Parliament, even though legislation emanating from the EC was part of the legislation in Gibraltar and the applicant was directly affected by it. Thus, the 'very essence' of her right to vote had been denied.[103]

Certainly, the *Matthews* judgment could be criticised for attaching too little importance to the – still very limited – actual legislative powers of the European Parliament and for the circularity of the argument that that body is elected 'by universal suffrage'. It is submitted, however, that the specificity of the EC's legal order rightly pushed the Court to adopt a *sui generis* approach and attach greater importance to the 'context' in which the Parliament operates.[104] There is no doubt that the judgment provides important support for the position of the European Parliament as the main democratic component of the EC. On the other hand, the specificity of the Court's approach also means that the judgment will probably be of limited guidance to future questions concerning the applicability of Article 3 in other international contexts.

---

[101]   *Ibidem*, para. 52.
[102]   *Ibidem*, para. 54.
[103]   *Ibidem*, paras 64-65.
[104]   The specificity of that legal order may also operate in favour of Contracting States: see as concerns Article 14, *e.g.*, the judgment of 18 February 1991, *Moustaquim*.

19.6 DEROGATION

From the fact that Protocol No. 1 does not contain a reference to Article 15(2) of the Convention, it follows also for Article 3 that it does not belong to the provisions which are non-derogable. On the other hand, it was observed above that the principle of democratic representation in the legislative bodies forms one of the basic conditions for the effectiveness of the Convention. In the supervision of the application of Article 15, and particularly in the assessment of the necessity of the temporary derogation from this principle, this fundamental character should weigh very heavily. If the derogation is broad in scope and of a rather long duration, the question even arises whether the country in question does not lose by this very fact the basis for its membership of the Council of Europe.

CHAPTER 20
PROHIBITION OF DEPRIVATION OF LIBERTY ON THE GROUND OF INABILITY TO FULFIL A CONTRACTUAL OBLIGATION
(Article 1 of Protocol No. 4)

REVISED BY JEROEN SCHOKKENBROEK

CONTENTS

20.1   TEXT OF ARTICLE 1 OF PROTOCOL NO. 4

No one shall be deprived of his liberty merely on the ground of inability to fulfil a contractual obligation.

20.2   SCOPE

This provision contains a further restriction of the powers of the authorities to deprive a person of his liberty. It supplements Article 5 of the Convention and refers to the notion of 'deprivation of liberty' contained in that Article.[1] Specifically, it limits the possibility of deprivation of liberty mentioned in that article sub (1)(b) 'for non-compliance with the lawful order of a court in order to secure the fulfilment of any obligation prescribed by law'. In those States which have ratified Protocol No. 4,[2] the

---

[1]   Appl. 32190/96, *Luordo*.
[2]   Protocol No. 4 entered into force on 2 May 1968. For a state of ratifications see Appendix I.

courts will not be allowed to give such an order merely on the ground that the person in question is unable to pay a debt or to meet some other contractual obligation.

Article 1 speaks of 'inability'. If a debtor is able to pay, but refuses to do so, Article 1 does not exclude deprivation of liberty. Moreover, there is the word 'merely'. If a debtor acts in a fraudulent or malicious way, Article 1 does not bar his detention on that ground, even if it is established or it appears afterwards that he was unable to pay his debt.[3] A person whose detention had been ordered by the court because at the request of the creditor he had refused to make an affidavit in respect of his property contrary to the law, was deemed not to be entitled to the protection of Article 1.[4] In its report to the Committee of Ministers, the Committee of Experts gives the following examples of cases to which Article 1 does not apply: a person orders a meal at a restaurant knowing that he is unable to pay; through negligence a person fails to supply goods when he is under a contract to do so; a debtor is preparing to leave the country to avoid meeting his commitments.[5] This literal interpretation of the word 'merely' seems to be followed in the case law on Article 1, which tends to conclude to non-applicability of this provision.[6] As a result the prohibition which it contains has only a very limited scope.

20.3 DEROGATION

As to the question of whether the rights and freedoms are non-derogable, for Protocol No. 4 the same reasoning applies as that set out above with regard to Protocol No. 1: since Article 6(1) of Protocol No. 4 declares that all the provisions of the Convention are applicable and does not make any addition to the enumeration of Article 15(2), it must be assumed that, under the circumstances and conditions referred to in Article 15(1), derogations from the provisions of Protocol No. 4 are allowed.

---

[3] See the Explanatory Reports on the Second to Fifth Protocols to the European Convention for the Protection of Human Rights and Fundamental Freedoms, submitted by the Committee of Experts to the Committee of Ministers, H(71)11 (1971), pp. 39-40.

[4] Appl. 5025/71, *X v. Federal Republic of Germany*, Yearbook XIV (1971), p. 692 (696-698).

[5] See the Explanatory Reports on Protocol No. 4, para. 6 of the Commmentary.

[6] See, *e.g.*, Appl. 27373/95, *Ninin*; Appl. 28346/95, *Pietrzyk*.

CHAPTER 21
THE RIGHT TO LIBERTY OF MOVEMENT (Article 2 of Protocol No. 4)

REVISED BY BEN VERMEULEN

CONTENTS

21.1 TEXT OF ARTICLE 2 OF PROTOCOL NO. 4

1. *Everyone lawfully within the territory of a State shall, within that territory, have the right to liberty of movement and freedom to choose his residence.*
2. *Everyone shall be free to leave any country, including his own.*
3. *No restrictions shall be placed on the exercise of these rights other than such as are in accordance with law and are necessary in a democratic society in the interests of national security or public safety, for the maintenance of "ordre public", for the prevention of crime, for the protection of health or morals, or for the protection of the rights and freedoms of others.*
4. *The rights set forth in paragraph 1 may also be subject, in particular areas, to restrictions imposed in accordance with law and justified by the public interest in a democratic society.*

21.2 INTRODUCTION

Within the framework of the discussion of some of the other rights and freedoms it has been highlighted that the Convention does not provide for a general right to be admitted to the territory of the Contracting States.[1] Protocol No. 4 ensures such a right only to the nationals of the Contracting State in question, viz. in Article 3, to be discussed below. Admission of aliens has so far been left by the Convention to national legislation and national policy, provided that the rights and freedoms ensured in the Convention are respected.

21.3 LIBERTY OF MOVEMENT AND FREEDOM TO CHOOSE RESIDENCE

The starting point of non-interference with the admission policy of the national authorities with regard to aliens is expressed in Article 2 of this Protocol in the words 'lawfully within the territory of a State' in the first paragraph. Indeed, without these words the national authorities would be prohibited, on grounds other than those mentioned in the third and fourth paragraphs, from expelling an alien who has managed to enter the country illegally. It is precisely with a view to keeping the discretion of the national authorities in this respect as wide as possible that the word 'legally' ('*légalement*') in the original draft was replaced by 'lawfully' ('*régulièrement*').[2]

It follows from the fact that Article 3 of this same Protocol contains the obligation to admit the State's own nationals and prohibits their expulsion that a national is always lawfully within the territory of his own State. It is rather curious that this consequence of Article 3 has not been explicitly included in Article 2. In a recent series of decisions involving Russia's treatment of its nationals of non-Russian descent who were trying to enter the country, the question of the lawfulness in the light of Article 2 of impediments to movement by nationals within their country has been raised.[3]

A person who has been admitted to a given country is lawfully there only as long as in compliance with the conditions under which admittance was granted.[4] His presence becomes unlawful after the expiration of the period for which the stay permit applies, but also, for instance, when the admitted person no longer has sufficient means of livelihood, in violation of the conditions of admission made in that respect. The

---

[1]   See, especially, *supra*, under Article 3 and Article 8.
[2]   See the *Explanatory Reports on the Second to Fifth Protocols on the European Convention for the Protection of Human Rights and Fundamental Freedoms*, submitted by the Committee of Experts to the Committee of Ministers, H(71)11 (1971), para. 7.
[3]   Decision of 30 March 2004, *Gartukayev*, and decision of 30 March 2004, *Timishev*.
[4]   See Appl. 14102/88, *Aygun*, D&R 63 (1989), p. 195.

same applies from the moment an expulsion order on public order grounds is served upon a person.[5] These conditions, however, apart from the cases mentioned in the third and the fourth paragraph, may not restrict his freedom of movement itself in the country and his freedom to choose his residence there, since the first paragraph of Article 2 would then not contain any guarantee; indeed, a right the enjoyment of which completely depends on the discretion of the authorities is not a right, but only a favour.[6]

The restrictions of the third paragraph also apply to those persons who have always resised in the country and not only to those who have been admitted under certain conditions. Thus, with respect to a woman who was convicted of running a 'disorderly house or brothel', the order imposed upon her to close down her business, which according to her complaint resulted in her no longer being able to reside with her husband, was considered justified as a measure necessary for the prevention of crime and for the protection of health and morals.[7]

It may not always be easy to determine whether the first paragraph of Article 2 of Protocol No. 4 or some other provision of the Convention applies. This may be the case, for example, with the right to a home (Article 8),[8] the right to respect for private life (Article 8),[9] the right to the peaceful enjoyment of one's possessions (Article 1 of Protocol No. 1)[10] or the right to personal freedom protected by Article 5.[11] On the last point the Court has held that placing a person under special police supervision may be considered to fall under Article 2 of Protocol No. 4, while this measure does not amount to a deprivation of liberty within the meaning of Article 5. In this case the special supervision of the applicant consisted of a prohibition to leave his home without informing the police, an obligation to report to the police on specified dates and an obligation to stay at home at night unless there were valid reasons not to do so which he had first submitted to the authorities. The Court considered that, in view of the Mafia threat to a democratic society, the measures were in principle necessary

---

5   Judgment of 27 April 1995, *Piermont*, para. 44.

6   In a different sense, the Committee of Experts, Explanatory Reports *supra* note 2, para. 8, where these conditions are mentioned as examples of possible conditions.

7   Appl. 8901/80, *X v. Belgium*, D&R 23 (1981), p. 237 (243).

8   Judgment of 24 November 1986, *Gillow*, para. 58 (a case dealt with under Article 8; the respondent State (the United Kingdom) had not ratified Protocol No. 4).

9   Appl. 16810/90, *Reijntjes*, D&R 73 (1992), p. 136 (152-153): in the absence of special circumstances the obligation to carry an identity card and to show it to the police whenever requested constitutes neither an interference with private life nor a restriction of liberty of movement.

10   Concerning denial of access to property in the area of Cyprus occupied by the Turkish Cypriot forces, see the judgment of 18 December 1996, *Loizidou*, para. 60: denial of access over a period of 16 years gradually affected the applicant's right as a property owner. The complaint therefore did not concern the right to freedom of movement.

11   In a judgment of 8 April 2004, *Assanidze*, para. 194, the Court found that it was unnecessary to examine the alleged restriction of movement as it had already found that the arbitrary detention of the applicants was a breach of Article 5.

in a democratic society for the maintenance of "*ordre public*" and for the prevention of crime. However, insofar as there had been a delay in notifying the applicant of a court order lifting the police supervision, the Court found a violation of Article 2 as this interference was neither provided by law nor necessary.[12] Similar preventive police supervision was at issue in the *Labita* Case. The Court in that case deemed the police supervision 'not necessary in a democratic society', as the applicant, who had been suspected of having ties to the Mafia, had been acquitted in court and the only reason to continue to supervise him was that his wife was the sister of an already deceased Mafia boss.[13]

In a case where the applicant, who was opposed to abortion on religious grounds, had been prohibited by court order from entering the immediate vicinity of an abortion clinic where he had previously distributed anti-abortion material, the Commission noted that the injunction was of limited duration (six months) and applied to a specified, limited area. This restriction of his liberty of movement was considered proportionate to the legitimate aim of the protection of the rights of others and, therefore, 'necessary in a democratic society'.[14] A similar situation may arise with respect to orders given by the local authorities prohibiting a person from being present in a specific area on the ground of the maintenance of public order or prevention of crime, as was the case in two judgments concerning hard-drug users in the Netherlands.[15]

With regard to the freedom to choose residence two decisions involving Russia have raised the question whether a local authorities' rejection of an applicant's address as his actual place of residence (ensuing forcible deportation) and the refusal to register a national at the address of their choice respectively is compatible with Article 2(1).[16]

21.4 RIGHT TO LEAVE THE COUNTRY

The right to leave the country, conferred in the second paragraph, has not a very broad effective scope, because practically all conceivable motives on the part of the authorities to refuse a person this right can be brought under the restrictions of the third paragraph.

Thus, the ground of 'the maintenance of '*ordre public*' or of 'the prevention of crime' may be invoked against a person who is serving a term of imprisonment, who is detained on remand, or whose extradition has been decided on, should he claim

---

[12]   Judgment of 22 February 1994, *Raimondo*, paras 39-40.
[13]   Judgment of 6 April 2000, paras 195-197.
[14]   Appl. 22828/93, *Van den Dungen*, D&R 80 (1995), p. 147 (151-152).
[15]   Judgment of 4 June 2002, *Landvreugd*, paras 68-72 and judgment of 4 June 2002, *Olivieira*, paras 61-65.
[16]   Decision of 8 July 2004, *Bolat* and decision of 20 January 2005, *Tatishvili*, respectively.

the right to leave the country.[17] A series of cases brought against Italy, however, have shown that the prohibition of a bankrupt to leave the place where bankruptcy proceedings have been started cannot be continued indefinitely. The necessity to remain at the same place of residence in order to protect the rights of creditors will diminish over time and in these cases "the length of the proceedings upset the balance that had to be struck between the general interest (...) and the applicant's personal interest."[18]

The grounds of the third paragraph may also justify measures which are aimed at preventing a person from leaving the country, such as the requirement imposed upon an accused or convicted person to surrender his passport as a condition for provisional or conditional release.[19] However, in the *Baumann* Case the French authorities' refusal to return the applicant's passport which had been seized during the investigation of a crime in which the applicant was not involved because he was imprisoned in Germany for another crime at the time of the request, was not a measure 'necessary in a democratic society.' The fact that the applicant was unable to exercise his freedom of movement because he was detained, did not provide the French authorities with a legitimate reason not to return the passport as the applicant had not been implicated in the French crime.[20]

The Committee of Experts, referring to the words 'any country' (*'n'importe quel pays'*), assigned a certain external effect to the second paragraph. Although, of course, only the Contracting States are bound by this provision, it may have as a consequence that a court, when it has to pronounce on the question of whether a person has lawfully left the territory of a non-Contracting State, should decide that reference to the law of that State is accepted only insofar as that law does not prejudice the principle of freedom to leave a country.[21]

The Commission has accepted a fairly wide interpretation of the expression 'any country'. In a case concerning a passport refusal by Finnish authorities to a person who had failed to report for military service and who was resident in Sweden and could travel freely without a passport between the Nordic countries, the Commission nevertheless considered that the refusal interfered with his right: the freedom to leave 'any country' implies the right to leave for a country of the person's choice to which he may be admitted. However, the Commission did not consider that the measure

---

[17]   See Appls. 3962/69, 4256/69, 4436/70 and 7680/76, all of them directed against the Federal Republic of Germany, Yearbook XIII (1970), p. 688 (690); Coll. 37 (1971), p. 67 (68-69); Yearbook XIII (1970), p. 1028 (1032-1034); D&R 9 (1978), p. 190 (193). See also Appl. 8988/80, *X v. Belgium*, D&R 24 (1981), p. 198 (204): forbidding a bankrupt from absenting himself was considered necessary for the maintenance of the '*ordre public*' and for the protection of the rights and freedoms of others.

[18]   See, among others, the judgment of 17 July 2003, *Luordo*, para. 96 and the decision of 14 December 2004, *Fedorov*.

[19]   Appl. 10307/83, *M v. Federal Republic of Germany*, D&R 37 (1984), p. 113 (118-119).

[20]   Judgment of 22 May 2001, paras 66-67.

[21]   Explanatory Reports, *supra* note 2, para. 11.

went beyond the limits of paragraph 3 in view of the wide margin of appreciation to which the Contracting States are entitled in the organisation of their national defence.[22]

21.5 RESTRICTIONS IN PARTICULAR AREAS

Besides the grounds of restrictions in the third paragraph, which do not differ from the 'usual' list,[23] in the fourth paragraph a special ground for restricting the rights conferred in the first paragraph has been included: the public interest in a democratic society. Restrictions which are justified on this ground may be imposed in particular areas.

This restriction has been the subject of a good deal of discussion within the Committee of Experts, as is evident from its report.[24] It was intended to make possible restrictions which serve the public interest of the country in situations where it cannot be clearly established that the '*ordre public*' is also involved. Although the majority of the Committee was opposed to the express inclusion of 'economic welfare' as a ground for restriction, the chosen formulation 'in the public interest' is so wide that the economic welfare of society as a motive for the imposition of restrictions does not appear to be excluded by it. The grant of a housing licence only to those who have an economic link with the municipality in question might be justified on that ground, and so might, for instance, the transfer of government departments, with the obligation for those employed by those departments to move on penalty of loss of their job. The scope of application or the ground of application of the restrictive measures, however, will have to be localised, according to the text of the fourth paragraph, within particular areas – *e.g.* areas with an extraordinarily dense population or with a high unemployment rate – and, consequently, may not apply to the country as a whole. Furthermore, obviously, here again no discrimination is permitted in the application of the restrictions.

The restriction under the fourth paragraph does not apply to the freedom to leave the country, regulated in the second paragraph. A Contracting State may not, therefore, prohibit emigration in the public interest on purely economic grounds, *e.g.* in order to prevent a 'brain drain'.

---

[22] Appl. 19583/92, *Peltonen*, D&R 80 (1995), p. 38 (43). See also Appl. 21228/93, *K.S. v Finland*, D&R 81 (1995), p. 42 (46).

[23] See the cases cited in the previous footnote as well as the judgment of 22 February 1994, *Raimondo*, para. 39 and judgment of 23 May 2001, *Denizci*, paras 405-406, in which a restriction of the applicants movements in the Southern part of Cyprus was neither in accordance with the law nor pursuing a legitimate aim.

[24] Explanatory Reports, *supra* note 2, paras 38-42.

21.6   TERRITORIAL APPLICATION

Article 5(4) of Protocol No. 4 provides that, if a Contracting State has declared the Protocol to be applicable to any territory for whose foreign relations it is responsible, this territory and the territory of the Contracting State to which the Protocol already applies by virtue of the ratification itself shall be treated as separate territories for the application of Article 2. Thus, the Court treated French Polynesia as being a separate territory, where different rules applied concerning the entry and residence of aliens as compared with metropolitan France, which is relevant to the question whether someone is 'lawfully' within the territory concerned.[25]

21.7   DEROGATION

None of the rights mentioned in Protocol No. 4 is non-derogable.

---

[25]   Judgment of 27 April 1995, *Piermont*, paras 43-44.

CHAPTER 22
PROHIBITION OF EXPULSION OF NATIONALS AND THE RIGHT OF NATIONALS TO ENTER THEIR OWN COUNTRY (Article 3 of Protocol No. 4)

REVISED BY JEROEN SCHOKKENBROEK

CONTENTS

22.1 TEXT OF ARTICLE 3 OF PROTOCOL NO. 4

1. *No one shall be expelled, by means either of an individual or of a collective measure, from the territory of the State of which he is a national.*
2. *No one shall be deprived of the right to enter the territory of the State of which he is a national.*

22.1 PROHIBITION OF EXPULSION OF NATIONALS

Although the term expulsion is usually used in connection with aliens and not with the State's own nationals, the drafters of Article 3 preferred the word 'expelled' to 'exiled', because exile is a word pregnant with meaning, which might raise many interpretation problems. Article 3 not only prohibits exile as a penalty or as a political measure, but any expulsion of a national from the territory.

According to a definition used in Strasbourg case law, expulsion is involved when "a person is obliged permanently to leave the territory of the State (...) without being left the possibility of returning later".[1] The words 'permanently' and 'without being left the possibility of returning later' in this definition may create the wrong impression that temporal expulsion of nationals would be permitted. According to the Commission, these words have been included to make it clear that extradition does not fall under the concept of expulsion, and consequently not under the prohibition of Article 3 either.[2] The Commission could rely on the *travaux préparatoires* for its point of view. In fact in its report to the Committee of Ministers the Committee of Experts set forth: "It was understood that extradition was outside the scope of this paragraph".[3] This does raise the question why the drafters did not bring out this intention somewhat more clearly in the formulation of Article 3. As this provision is now worded, on the basis of an extensive interpretation of the word 'expelled' one might conclude that a national enjoys protection against any measure according to which he has to leave his country under compulsion; in fact, in its report the Committee of Experts itself puts the very wide interpretation of 'to drive away from a place' on the word 'expel'.[4] At any rate case law has recognised that extradition – of aliens as well as of nationals – may constitute a violation of one of the other rights and freedoms, specifically of the prohibition of inhuman treatment and of the right to respect of family life.[5]

Case law concerning the prohibition of expulsion of nationals remains scant. The Court described this prohibition as being absolute, which means that no restrictions or exceptions are permitted.[6] In the case of *Denizci v. Cyprus* the Court refused to consider the applicants' complaint concerning their 'expulsion' to Northern Cyprus in the light of Article 3 of Protocol No. 4, since this was not a removal to the territory of another State.[7]

---

[1]   Appl. 6189/73, *X v. Federal Republic of Germany*, Coll. 46 (1974), p. 214; Appl. 33878/96, *A.B. v. Poland*.

[2]   *Ibidem*. Two weeks later, in its decision on Appl. 6242/73, *Brückmann v. Federal Republic of Germany*, Yearbook XVII (1974), p. 458 (478), the Commission took the same position with the following definition of the two concepts: "Expulsion is the execution of an order to leave the country, while extradition means the transfer of a person from one jurisdiction to another for the purpose of his standing trial or for the execution of a sentence imposed upon him".

[3]   Explanatory Report on Protocol No. 4, para. 21 of the Commentary.

[4]   *Ibidem*.

[5]   *Supra*, Articles 3 and 8, respectively.

[6]   Appl. 48321/99, *Slivenko v. Latvia*.

[7]   Judgment of 23 May 2001, paras 410-411.

22.3   THE RIGHT OF NATIONALS TO ENTER THEIR OWN COUNTRY

The second paragraph of Article 3, which contains without any restriction the right to be admitted to the State of which one is a national, would particularly confront the United Kingdom with serious problems, since numerous people outside the United Kingdom, particularly in the Commonwealth countries, acquired British nationality by birth. However, the United Kingdom has not ratified Protocol No. 4. This does not alter the fact that, if that country, in admitting people having its nationality, should discriminate with respect to a particular racial group, it could still come into conflict with its obligations under the Convention; not under Article 14, which in that case indeed could only have been violated in conjunction with Article 3 of Protocol No. 4[8], but because such discrimination may constitute a degrading treatment in the sense of Article 3 of the Convention.[9]

The same could apply in relation to a discriminatory denial of the right of entry to a national in the case that the State Party has limited its obligations through a valid reservation to Article 3 of Protocol No. 4.[10]

In its Explanatory Report the Committee of Experts states that the proposal to include the word 'arbitrarily' in the second paragraph, in accordance with Article 12(4) of the UN Covenant on Civil and Political Rights, was expressly rejected, but that the members of the Committee agreed that the right of the national to be admitted to his State does not confer on him an absolute right to stay within that State. The Report gives the example of a national who, after first having been extradited to another country, takes refuge again in his own State, and of a national who, after having served in the army of another State, wishes to return to his own country.[11]

These examples, however, would seem to create the wrong impression. Indeed, in those cases the absolute character of the prohibition under the second paragraph of Article 3 is not affected, but in the first example the State has the right to decide to extradite the person again, and in the second example it has the right to impose the sanction of forfeiture of nationality and of the rights associated with it on service in the army of another State. The Court has indeed confirmed that the prohibition of

---

[8]   See, in contrast, the general prohibition of discrimination under Protocol No. 12, which entered into force on 1 April 2005.

[9]   *Supra*, 7.6.1.

[10]   See Appl. 15344/89, *Habsburg-Lothringen v. Austria*, D&R 64 (1989), p. 210 (219-220): even though it accepted the validity of the Austrian reservation with respect to Art. 3 of Protocol No. 4, the Commission went on to examine the complaint about discrimination based on the applicant's family origin under Articles 3 and 14 of the Convention; it found that the situation complained of had not been shown to constitute a distinction the effects of which were contrary to Art. 3 of the Convention, either alone or taken together with Art. 14.

[11]   Explanatory Report on Protocol No. 4, para. 28 of the Commentary.

deprivation of the right to enter one's own country is absolute (leaving aside the possibility of derogation under Article 15).[12] On the other hand, case law makes clear that this prohibition does not apply to measures that merely diminish one's desire to return to one's own country.[13]

22.4 TERRITORIAL APPLICATION

With respect to the inhabitants of colonies and other territories for whose international relations a Contracting State is responsible, the Protocol itself provides for a possibility of avoiding certain consequences in case of ratification. And this in connection with the first as well as the second paragraph of Article 3. First of all, at the moment of ratification States may indicate under Article 5 to what extent they wish this Protocol to apply to these territories; this, irrespective of the extent to which they have declared the Convention itself applicable. Thus, they are able to declare that some articles of the Protocol are applicable to these territories and others are not. Moreover, the fourth paragraph of Article 5 provides in relation to Article 3 that, where there is a reference to 'the territory of a State', the territory of the Contracting State itself and these territories are treated as separate territories.

22.5 ACQUISITION AND LOSS OF NATIONALITY

Can a State evade its obligations under Article 3 by depriving a person of his nationality? In principle the Convention leaves it to the States to regulate the acquisition and the loss of nationality; a right to a nationality, such as it is incorporated in Article 15 of the Universal Declaration of Human Rights, does not form part of the rights and freedoms laid down in the Convention. However, if a person can be deprived of his nationality for the sole purpose of his expulsion or refusal to admit him, the protection of Article 3 may be rendered illusory.

It appears from the Explanatory Report that the Committee of Experts was aware of this problem, but that it rejected a proposal to include a provision in Article 3 according to which 'a State would be forbidden to deprive a national of his nationality for the purpose of expelling him'. Although the Committee stated that it approved of the underlying principle, the majority thought that "it was inadvisable in Article

---

[12]   Appl. 48321/99, *Slivenko v. Latvia*.
[13]   Appl. 22012/93, *C.B. v. Germany* (an arrest warrant issued against the applicant does not amount to a deprivation within the meaning of Article 3, paragraph 2).

3 to touch on the delicate question of the legitimacy of measures depriving individuals of nationality".[14]

This does not answer the above question, for even though in its generality Article 3 leaves the right of the State to decide to whom it will grant its nationality and whom it will deprive of it intact, still such a decision by the national authorities in a given case may involve a violation of that article. Thus, with regard to a refusal of nationality combined with an order of expulsion it was expressly recognised by the Commission that the link between the two decisions could create the presumption that the refusal of nationality had the mere purpose of making the expulsion possible.[15] Indeed, a measure of the national authorities which has as its sole object evasion of an obligation under the Convention is equivalent to a violation of that provision. A rule to that effect must be deemed to be implicit in the Convention as an essential requirement for the maintenance of the effective enjoyment of its rights and freedoms and is also in conformity with the rationale underlying Article 17. However, it may be assumed only in very evident cases that the national authorities *exclusively* intended to evade the operation of the Convention by their measure. In the above-mentioned decision the Commission in fact adopted the view that in this case nothing justified such a conclusion.[16]

The Court has held that, for the purposes of Article 3, whether a person has the 'nationality' of a given State must be determined in principle by reference to the national law of that State. It has also admitted that, although a right to nationality or 'citizenship' is not guaranteed by the Convention or its Protocols, an arbitrary denial of nationality may under certain circumstances amount to an interference with the rights under Article 8 of the Convention.[17] It has thus reserved a – modest – possibility to review denials or losses of nationality under the Convention, but rather under Article 8 of the Convention than under Article 3 of Protocol No. 4.

22.6   DEROGATION

To Article 3 again the above statement applies that none of the rights incorporated in Protocol No. 4 are non-derogable.[18]

---

[14]   *Ibidem*, para. 23.
[15]   Appl. 3745/68, *X v. Federal Republic of Germany*, Coll. 31 (1970), p. 107 (110).
[16]   *Ibidem*, p. 111.
[17]   Appl. 48321/99, *Slivenko v. Latvia*; Appl. 31414/96, *Karassev and Family v. Finland*.
[18]   See *supra* 20.3.

CHAPTER 23

PROHIBITION OF COLLECTIVE EXPULSION OF ALIENS (Article 4 of Protocol No. 4)

REVISED BY JEROEN SCHOKKENBROEK

CONTENTS

23.1 TEXT OF ARTICLE 4 OF PROTOCOL NO. 4

Collective expulsion of aliens is prohibited.

23.2 INTRODUCTION

Article 4 only prohibits the collective expulsion of aliens, but this without any possibility of restriction other than under Article 15. In addition to the general prohibition of expulsion of a State's own nationals as laid down in the above-mentioned Article 3, the Consultative Assembly wished to make the expulsion of aliens in this article subject to stringent conditions. According to its draft, expulsion of an alien lawfully residing in a Contracting State would be permitted only on grounds of danger to national security or violation of the *ordre public* or morality. However, the Committee of Experts did not adopt this part of the draft and proposed an entirely new provision, referring exclusively to collective expulsion.[1]

---

[1] Explanatory Reports on Protocol No. 4, paras 34-35 of the Commentary.

The first argument advanced by the Committee was that the subject matter brought up in the draft of the Consultative Assembly had already been regulated in the European Convention on Establishment of 1955.[2] Against this, however, it may at once be argued that this renders regulation in Protocol No. 4 by no means superfluous, since the Establishment Convention only confers protection on the nationals of the other States Parties to that Convention and not, as would be the case in the proposal of the Consultative Assembly, on all aliens residing in one of the Contracting States. Moreover, the Establishment Convention lacks an international supervisory procedure as provided for in the Convention. And since the text of the draft of the Consultative Assembly was almost identical to that of the Establishment Convention, there was no reason to fear that those Contracting States, which have also ratified the Establishment Convention, would have to confer a more far-reaching protection, *via* the operation of Articles 14 and 53 of the Human Rights Convention, on these 'other' aliens (*i.e.* those aliens who are not nationals of one of the other States Parties to the Establishment Convention) than that which Article 4 of Protocol No. 4 itself would oblige them to confer.

The second argument put forward in favour of the cancellation – and the one, which was no doubt decisive – is that the majority of the Committee did not wish to restrict the grounds for expulsion and did not wish the motives, which induce a State in each individual case to expel an alien, to be subjected to international supervision.[3]

Meanwhile Protocol No. 7 has entered into force on 1 November 1988, Article 1 of which provides for certain procedural guarantees in the case of expulsion of individual aliens who are lawfully resident in the territory of a Contracting State. That provision will be discussed separately hereafter.

23.3 SCOPE OF THE PROHIBITION

Even in its present formulation Article 4 is not entirely devoid of importance, considering such practices, also existing within countries of the Council of Europe, as the expulsion of groups of Roma/gypsies seeking a camp or groups of migrant workers seeking employment.

The effect of Article 4 depends largely on the interpretation that is put on the word 'collective'. Is this to refer to the expulsion of *all* aliens residing in a given State or at least of all aliens of *one particular nationality*? This would deprive Article 4 of any practical value, since it is likely that Article 15 would be brought into play in situations where a need is felt for such extreme measures. It must, therefore, be assumed that

---

[2]   *Ibidem.* The Convention has been published in *European Treaty Series*, No. 19.
[3]   *Ibidem.*

the Contracting States did not mean to restrict Article 4 to these very exceptional cases of collective expulsion, but wanted to prohibit any expulsion of aliens *as a group*.

Even then, however, the question of what exactly distinguishes the expulsion of a group of aliens from the expulsion of a number of individual aliens has not yet been answered. How large must such a group be? Is the expulsion of an entire family to be considered a collective expulsion? And is this the case, for instance, for the expulsion of an orchestra or sport team consisting of foreigners? If so, why then do such 'groups' deserve more protection than a foreigner who lives on his own or an individual foreign musician or sportsman? This problem can be solved only if one uses neither the number of which the group consists nor the link knitting together the members of that group as the decisive criterion for the application of Article 4, but the procedure leading to the expulsion. If a person is expelled along with others without his case having received individual treatment, his expulsion is a case of collective expulsion.

This is the view taken by the Court, which confirmed the earlier case law of the Commission on this question. The Court gave the following definition of 'collective expulsion of aliens': "any measure compelling aliens, as a group, to leave a country, except where such a measure is taken on the basis of a reasonable and objective examination of the particular case of each individual alien of the group."[4] At first sight it would appear as if the Court introduced a restriction to the absolutely formulated prohibition of Article 4, since Article 4 does not make any exception for cases where an examination such as that mentioned in the definition by the Court has taken place with regard to each member of the group. However, this is not really the case. In fact, the national authorities can always evade the absolute prohibition of Article 4 by following a procedure in which there is no question of a collective expulsion in the proper sense. In the opinion of the Court a *pro forma* individual approach by national authorities is not enough for compatibility with the prohibition of Article 4. This means, *inter alia*, that each person must be given "the opportunity to put arguments against his expulsion to the competent authorities on an individual basis."[5] This in fact introduces certain minimum procedural guarantees, although, as was pointed out

---

[4]   Appl. 45917/99, *Andric v. Sweden*, referring to the Commission's decision in Appl. 14209/88, *A. and Others v. the Netherlands*, D&R 59 (1989), p. 274 (277). The definition given in the *Andric* decision was also adopted in the Court's judgment of 5 February 2002 in the Case of *Čonka v. Belgium*, para. 59.

[5]   Appl. 45917/99, *Andric v. Sweden*.

above, a proposal to that effect had been expressly rejected by the Committee of Experts.[6]

In the *Čonka* Case the Court formulated an important additional requirement. The case concerned a group of Slovak gypsies who, pending their appeals against the refusals to grant asylum, were asked to report to the police station in order to 'complete their asylum request files'. However, upon their arrival at the police station removal orders were served upon them and a few hours later they were detained in a holding centre and subsequently removed to Slovakia. The Court held that the fact that a "reasonable and objective examination of the particular case of each individual alien of the group" has taken place (as was the case here) does not mean that the circumstances surrounding the implementation of the expulsion decisions play no role in the determination of whether Article 4 has been respected. In this particular case the Court expressed doubts as to the legal basis for the manner in which the Belgian authorities had proceeded, also in view of the large numbers of individuals of the same origin that were concerned. These doubts were reinforced by a set of circumstances: the fact that the political authorities had announced beforehand that operations of this type would be held and had given instructions for them; the simultaneous convocation to report to the police station; the identical wording of the arrest and expulsion orders; the great difficulty for the persons concerned to contact a lawyer; and the fact that the asylum procedure had not been completed. The Court concluded that "at no stage in the period between the service of the notice on the aliens to attend the police station and their expulsion did the procedure afford sufficient guarantees demonstrating that the personal circumstances of each of those concerned had been genuinely and individually taken into account."[7]

As was observed above, the Convention has been supplemented by Protocol No. 7, stipulating in Article 1 minimum procedural rights for aliens lawfully within a Contracting State, who are confronted with expulsion. The above-mentioned case law suggests that, in cases of simultaneous expulsion of a group of aliens, most of those procedural rights are to some extent already protected by Article 4 of Protocol No. 4. This is all the more striking in that not all States that have ratified Protocol No. 4

---

[6]   The definition given by the Court, however much it has to be welcomed *per se*, raises the problem that for the expulsion of an alien who forms part of a particular group certain procedural requirements are developed, which are not necessarily prescribed for the expulsion of other aliens. However, this seems to be the logical and unavoidable consequence of the need to attach some practical meaning to the term "collective", as discussed above. Stronger safeguards seem justified on the ground that simultaneous expulsion of members of the same group may give rise to a suspicion that these persons were expelled merely on the ground of their membership of the group, i.e. without individual examination of each individual case. Thence an obligation for the State to demonstrate convincingly that such a suspicion is unfounded.

[7]   Judgment of 5 February 2002, para. 63.

have also ratified Protocol No. 7, and that the protection of Article 4 is not limited to aliens "lawfully resident" in the State Party.[8]

Finally, it should again be pointed out that the expulsion of aliens may also constitute a violation of the Convention on other grounds. One may think in particular of those cases in which the consequences of the expulsion are such that it entails an inhuman treatment contrary to Article 3 or a severance of family ties contrary to Article 8.[9]

24.4 DEROGATION

As has been stated above, none of the provisions of Protocol No. 4, including Article 4, are non-derogable.

---

[8]   See the decisions of 14 March 2002, *Sulejmanovic and Sultanovic* and *Sejdovic and Sulejmanovic* (aliens not considered lawfully resident in Italy; complaint under Article 1 of Protocol 7 rejected on that ground, but complaint under Article 4 of Protocol No. 4 declared admissible). In its judgment of 8 November 2002 in these cases concerning the expulsion of Roma to Bosnia and Herzegovina, the Court noted the friendly settlement reached between the parties (involving, *inter alia*, withdrawal of the expulsion orders, the applicants' return to Italy, providing them with a residence permit, efforts to find an appropriate camp for them) and struck the cases off its list.

[9]   See *supra* under these articles.

CHAPTER 24
ABOLITION OF THE DEATH PENALTY
(Article 1 of Protocol No. 6)

REVISED BY JEROEN SCHOKKENBROEK

CONTENTS

24.1 TEXT OF ARTICLE 1 OF PROTOCOL NO. 6

The death penalty shall be abolished. No one shall be condemned to such penalty or executed.

24.2 INTRODUCTION

The abolition of the death penalty has since long been a matter of concern in- and outside the Council of Europe. As early as 1957 the European Committee on Crime Problems studied the problem of capital punishment in the States of Europe. The Parliamentary Assembly also regularly dealt with this question. In 1980 it adopted two resolutions, in which, on the one hand, it appealed to national parliaments to abolish capital punishment from their penal systems, if they had not already done so,[1] and, on the other hand, called upon the Committee of Ministers to 'amend Article 2 of the European Convention on Human Rights to bring it into line with Resolution 727'.[2] In December 1982 the Committee of Ministers adopted the text of draft Protocol No. 6, prepared by the Steering Committee for Human Rights, and opened it for

---

[1]   Res. 727 of the Parliamentary Assembly, 32nd Session, 22 April 1980, Yearbook XXIII (1980), p. 66.
[2]   Res. 891 of the Parliamentary Assembly, 32nd Session, 22 April 1980, Yearbook XXIII (1980), p. 66.

signature and ratification by the member States of the Council of Europe on 28 April 1983. The Protocol entered into force on 1 March 1985 after it had received five ratifications.[3]

Until the 1990s no death sentences had been executed in the member States of the Council of Europe for many years. However, the enlargement of this organisation since 1990 made this a matter of topical concern. The Parliamentary Assembly made the willingness to sign Protocol No. 6 within one year and ratify it within three years from the time of accession and to introduce a moratorium upon accession a prerequisite for membership to the Council of Europe on the part of the Assembly. In spite of this some of the new member States have carried out executions after their accession to the Council of Europe.[4] However, this is no longer the case: all member States have now abolished the death penalty and ratified Protocol No. 6, with the exception of Russia where a moratorium applies since 1996.

24.3 SCOPE OF THE PROHIBITION

Article 1 of the Protocol must be read in conjunction with Article 2 of the Convention. It follows from this that a State, which wants to become a party to the Protocol may no longer rely on the exception mentioned in Article 2 and has to delete the death penalty from its criminal law. The second sentence of Article 1 underlines that it contains not only an obligation, but also a right: every individual has the right not to be condemned to the death penalty or to its not being executed.

However, the scope of the obligation to abolish the death penalty is limited to acts committed in peacetime. Protocol No. 6 does not apply to acts committed in times of war or of imminent threat of war, provided that the law lays down the instances in which the death penalty may be applied and that the relevant provisions of the law are communicated to the Secretary General of the Council of Europe. It follows from the wording of Article 2 of Protocol No. 6 that, even after a State has ratified the Protocol, it may introduce the death penalty for those situations.[5] It may, of course, withdraw or modify this legislation later on and notify the Secretary General of this. The requirement in those situations that the death penalty shall be applied only in the instances laid down in the law in fact is superfluous since this also stems from Article

---

[3]   For an overview of the Contracting States which have ratified Protocol No. 6, see Appendix 1.

[4]   See *Report on the Abolition of the Death Penalty in Europe* (Committee on Legal Affairs and Human Rights, rapporteur: Mrs Wohlwend) of 25 June 1996, Parliamentary Assembly, Document 7589.

[5]   Art. 2 of the Protocol reads as follows: "A State may make provisions in its law for the death penalty in respect of acts committed in time of war or of imminent threat of war; such penalty shall be applied only in the instances laid down in the law and in accordance with its provisions. The State shall communicate to the Secretary General of the Council of Europe the relevant provisions of the law". What is meant by the phrase 'imminent threat of war' is not made clear in the Protocol or the Explanatory Report thereto.

7 of the Convention. However, Article 2 of Protocol No. 6 adds that this penalty shall only be applied 'in accordance with' the law, which also concerns the way the death penalty is executed.

Following a proposal of the Parliamentary Assembly that a new additional protocol be drawn up abolishing the death penalty also in wartime,[6] instructions were given by the Committee of Ministers to the Steering Committee for Human Rights which led to the entry into force of Protocol 13 to the Convention, on 1 July 2003, providing for the abolition of the death penalty under all circumstances.

There is so far little case law concerning Protocol No. 6, which may be explained by the fact that the States Parties to the Convention refrained from ratifying this Protocol before first abolishing the death penalty within their own legal system. However, Article 1 of Protocol No. 6 may also be relevant in expulsion and extradition cases, on the basis of the reasoning followed by the Court in the *Soering* Case.[7] There, the Court accepted that Article 3 of the Convention could not be interpreted as generally prohibiting the death penalty, because the existence of Protocol No. 6 shows that the intention of the drafters was to use the normal method of amendment of the text to introduce an obligation to abolish capital punishment. However, the circumstances relating to a death sentence may be such as to give rise to an issue under Article 3. Article 3 in its turn prohibits expulsion or extradition in case a person would face a real risk of exposure to inhuman or degrading treatment or punishment in the receiving State. The *Soering* Case concerned extradition by a State not bound by Protocol No. 6, but where the State is so bound, Article 1 of the Protocol may be violated if the State extradites or expels a person to another State where he is at serious risk that he will be sentenced to death and that sentence will be executed. In the latter cases there is no need for the Court to proceed in an indirect manner by examining, under Article 3, the circumstances relating to the death sentence. The key question is whether extradition or expulsion would expose the applicant to a real risk of being subjected to capital punishment.[8]

---

[6]   See Recommendation 1246 (1994) on the abolition of capital punishment.

[7]   This case is discussed *supra*, under 7.6.1.

[8]   Appl. 22742/93, *Aylor-Davis v. France*, D&R 76-B (1994), p. 164 (170); the Commission does not exclude State responsibility under Protocol No. 6; assurances obtained from US authorities by France such as to exclude the risk of the applicant being sentenced to death; extradition thus not liable to expose applicant to serious risk of treatment or punishment prohibited by Art. 3 of the Convention or Art. 1 of Protocol No. 6. The same approach is followed by the Court: see, *e.g.* decision of 14 December 2000, *Nivette*; decision of 15 March 2001, *Ismaili*. As concerns expulsion, see Appl. 16531/90, *Y v. the Netherlands*, D&R 68 (1991), p. 299 (304): the Commission left open whether Art. 1 of Protocol No. 6 was applicable, but it went on to consider that no real risk had been shown that the death penalty would be imposed. Applicability of Protocol 6 was implicitly accepted in the decision of 25 October 1996, *Kareem*; decision of 26 October 2004, *B. v. Sweden* (expulsion cases; applicant's statements not credible), and decision of 7 September 1998, *Özdemir* (expulsion; no risk shown).

Finally, in view of the rejection of the death penalty by the member States of the Council of Europe,[9] the question arises whether today, as opposed to the year 1989 (when the *Soering* judgment was rendered), and notwithstanding the point made in that judgment about the existence of Protocol No. 6, there is consensus among the Contracting States that the exception to the right to life made in the second sentence of Article 2, paragraph 1, of the Convention should be deemed to have been abrogated. This question received a provisional answer from the Court in the *Öcalan* Case. Put briefly, the extensively reasoned judgment referred to the considerable evolution of the legal position as regards the death penalty (at the time of the judgment: *de jure* abolition in 43 of the 44 member States; all member States having signed Protocol No. 6 and all but one of them having ratified it). Against this consistent background the Court expressed the view that capital punishment in peacetime has come to be regarded as an unacceptable, if not inhuman, form of punishment, which is no longer permissible under Article 2 of the Convention. However, the Court found it not necessary to reach a firm conclusion on this point since it construed Article 2 of the Convention as prohibiting the *implementation* of the death penalty in respect of a person who has not had a fair trial and Article 3 of the Convention as prohibiting the *imposition* of the death penalty after an unfair trial, as such imposition would amount to inhuman treatment.[10]

In the *Ilascu* Case a Grand Chamber had already held that the anxiety and suffering engendered by a death sentence "can only be aggravated by the arbitrary nature of the proceedings which led to it, so that, considering that a human life is at stake, the sentence thus becomes a violation of the Convention." In this case the Court found a violation of Article 3 in respect of the first applicant on account of the death sentence coupled with the conditions and the treatment suffered during his detention.[11]

---

[9] See, *e.g.*, the *Guidelines on Human Rights and the Fight against Terrorism*, adopted by the Committee of Ministers on 15 July 2002, Article X, para. 2, of which provides: 'Under no circumstances may a person convicted of terrorist activities be sentenced to the death penalty; in the event of such a sentence being imposed, it may not be carried out.'

[10] Judgment of 12 March 2003, paras 195-196; 198, and 202-207. The reasoning was followed by the Grand Chamber, judgment of 12 May 2005, paras 162-175.

[11] Judgment of 8 July 2004, paras 431 and 440. The Court considered that the facts complained of did not call for a separate examination under Article 2 of the Convention, since the risk of enforcement of the death penalty was now more hypothetical than real (Mr Ilascu having been released and living in Romania with that country's nationality) (paras 416-417 of the judgment).

24.4 DEROGATION

The prohibition of the death penalty is non-derogable.[12] Moreover, according to Article 4 of the Protocol it is not possible to make any reservation in respect of the provisions of the Protocol.

---

[12]   Art. 3 of the Protocol.

CHAPTER 25

EXPULSION OF ALIENS (Article 1 of Protocol No. 7)

REVISED BY CEES FLINTERMAN

CONTENTS

25.1 TEXT OF ARTICLE 1 OF PROTOCOL NO. 7

1. *An alien lawfully resident in the territory of a State shall not be expelled therefrom except in pursuance of a decision reached in accordance with law and shall be allowed:*
   a) *to submit reasons against his expulsion,*
   b) *to have his case reviewed, and*
   c) *to be represented for these purposes before the competent authority or a person or persons designated by that authority.*
2. *An alien may be expelled before the exercise of his rights under paragraph 1(a), (b) and (c) of this Article, when such expulsion is necessary in the interests of public order or is grounded on reasons of national security.*

25.2 INTRODUCTION

As is clear from the text of the article, and as is emphasised in the Explanatory Report,[1] the guarantees laid down therein only apply to certain categories of aliens, and even then not in all circumstances. Indeed, Article 1 only concerns aliens lawfully resident in the territory of the State in question. The word 'resident' is intended to exclude any alien who has arrived at the border or (air)port, but has not yet passed through immigration control. Aliens who have been admitted for the purpose of transit or for other non-residential purposes, or who are waiting for a decision on a request for a residence permit, are also excluded from the scope of this article.

The term 'lawfully' refers to domestic law. It is up to domestic law to determine the conditions for a person's presence in the territory to be considered 'lawful'. As soon as an alien no longer complies with one or more of these conditions, his presence can no longer be considered 'lawful'.

According to the Explanatory Report the phrase 'expulsion' must be considered as an autonomous concept, independent of any domestic definition. It refers to any measure compelling the departure of an alien from the territory except extradition.[2]

25.3 REQUIREMENTS OF THE FIRST PARAGRAPH

The Convention contains implied guarantees in several articles for aliens against whom a measure of expulsion is taken. First of all, Article 4 of Protocol No. 4 contains the prohibition of collective expulsion of aliens. In addition, in individual cases Articles 3, 5(1)(f), and 8, in conjunction with Article 13, do provide some guarantees against measures of expulsion.[3] Article 1 of Protocol No. 7 has been added "in order to afford minimum guarantees to such persons (aliens) in the event of expulsion from the territory of a Contracting Party".[4] And minimal they are indeed.

Expulsion may take place only "in pursuance of a decision reached in accordance with law". The word 'law' refers to domestic law. It is, therefore, up to domestic law to determine which authority is competent to decide on expulsion and the procedure to be followed, provided that the requirement of an effective remedy of Article 13 of the Convention is met. A judicial authority is not required, as Article 6 of the Convention does not apply to cases of expulsion. However, within the framework of

---

[1]   Explanatory Report on Protocol No. 7 to the Convention for the Protection of Human Rights and Fundamental Freedoms, para. 9.

[2]   *Ibidem,* para. 10.

[3]   See *supra* for Articles 3, 5 and 8, and *infra* for Article 13.

[4]   Explanatory Report, *supra* note 1, para. 9.

the procedure the alien concerned has some minimum rights, as set forth in paragraph 1(a)-(c).[5]

As regards the first right: to submit reasons against his expulsion, here again it is up to domestic law to determine the conditions governing the exercise of this right. This right may, however, also be exercised in the first phase of the procedure and not only at the review stage, as is clear from its formulation separately from (b).[6]

As regards the second right: to have his case reviewed, it is emphasised in the Explanatory Report that this does not necessarily imply "a two-stage procedure before different authorities, but only that the competent authority should review the case in the light of the reasons against expulsion submitted by the person concerned."[7] This 'competent authority' may be the same authority that took the original decision or a higher authority. The form of the review, again, is determined by domestic law.

The minimal approach, which overshadowed the preparation of the Protocol, can be clearly inferred from the Explanatory Report where it expressly states that Article 1 does not relate to the stage of proceedings, existing in some States, in which aliens have the possibility of lodging an appeal against the decision taken following the review of their case: "The present Article (...) does not therefore require that the person concerned should be permitted to remain in the territory of the State pending the outcome of the appeal introduced against the decision taken following the review of his case."[8]

Also for the third right: to be represented before the competent authority or a person or persons designated by that authority, it is up to domestic law to determine the form of representation and the competent authority. There is no requirement for the representative to be a lawyer or for the competent authority to be a judicial organ. The authority is not even required to be the authority which finally decides on the expulsion. In order to comply with this article, it is sufficient that the competent judicial or administrative authority makes a recommendation to an(other) administrative authority, which then decides on the expulsion measure.[9] The provision does not give the alien or his representative the right to be physically present when the case is considered, nor does the procedure have to include an oral hearing; the whole procedure may be a written one.[10]

---

[5]   See also Article 5 of the Convention.
[6]   Explanatory Report, *supra*, note 1, para. 13.1.
[7]   *Ibidem*, para. 13.2.
[8]   *Ibidem*.
[9]   *Ibidem*, para. 13.3.
[10]   *Ibidem*, para. 14.

In the *Maaouia* Case[11], the European Court of Human Rights held that Article 6 paragraph 1 does not apply to procedures for the expulsion of aliens. According to the Court it was obvious that by adopting Article 1 of Protocol no. 7 the Contracting States had clearly indicated their intention not to include proceedings for the expulsion of aliens within the scope of Article 6. Furthermore the Court held that proceedings for the rescission of the exclusion order do not concern the determination of a civil right for the purposes of Article 6 paragraph 1, nor do excluding orders concern the determination of a criminal charge.

25.4 EXCEPTIONS

As a rule the alien concerned has the right to make use of the minimum guarantees laid down in the first paragraph of Article 1 before being expelled. The second paragraph, however, allows for exceptions to this rule "when such expulsion is necessary in the interests of public order or is grounded on reasons of national security". The words 'in a democratic society', which are part of the necessity requirement in the several provisions of the Convention, which allow for restrictions of the rights embodied therein, are lacking here for unclear reasons. However, Strasbourg case law has not (yet) made these words play a distinctive role. With reference to that case law the Explanatory Report states that the exceptions have to be applied "taking into account the principle of proportionality as defined in the case law of the European Court of Human Rights".[12]

When a State relies on the interest of public order, it is up to that State to show why in the particular case or cases that exception was necessary. If, however, a State grounds the exception on reasons of national security, according to the Explanatory Report 'this in itself should be accepted as sufficient justification'.[13] Since this view would imply that review by the Strasbourg organs is not possible at all, it would run counter to the purpose of the Protocol to place the rights embodied therein under the supervisory system of the Convention; especially the necessity requirement must be subject to the review of the Court, be it that the latter may leave a margin of discretion to the national authorities in that respect. In the above-mentioned cases it is only scant comfort for the alien concerned to know that he may still exercise his rights under paragraph 1 of this article after his expulsion.

---

[11]   Judgment of 5 October 2000.
[12]   Explanatory Report, *supra* note 1, para. 15.
[13]   *Ibidem.*

25.5 DEROGATION

Article 1 is not a non-derogable right under Article 15 of the Convention.

CHAPTER 26
THE RIGHT TO A REVIEW BY A HIGHER TRIBUNAL (Article 2 of Protocol No. 7)

Revised by Cees Flinterman

CONTENTS

26.1 TEXT OF ARTICLE 2 OF PROTOCOL NO. 7

1. *Everyone convicted of a criminal offence by a tribunal shall have the right to have his conviction or sentence reviewed by a higher tribunal. The exercise of this right, including the grounds on which it may be exercised, shall be governed by law.*

2. *This right may be subject to exceptions in regard to offences of a minor character, as prescribed by law, or in cases in which the person concerned was tried in the first instance by the highest tribunal or was convicted following an appeal against acquittal.*

26.2 SCOPE

The scope of this article is essentially determined by the concepts of 'criminal offence', 'tribunal' and 'conviction or sentence'. It seems to be obvious that the meaning of the words 'criminal offence' is closely related to the notion of 'criminal charge' of Article 6 of the Convention. Thus, it would seem appropriate to argue that Article 2 of Protocol

No. 7 also applies to those disciplinary and administrative sanctions that fall within the scope of Article 6. It seems to be inapplicable, however, to preventive measures, deportation orders and decisions concerning extradition as far as no criminal law elements are involved.

Article 2 presupposes the existence of a 'conviction or sentence', which notions are to be interpreted autonomously. Article 2 is to be inapplicable if a person is not convicted and also not sentenced in view of lack of evidence or guilt.

In the first sentence of paragraph 1 it is emphasised that the conviction must have been imposed 'by a tribunal'. According to the Explanatory Report this phrase was added to make it clear that the right laid down in this provision is not applicable to "offences which have been tried by bodies which are not tribunals within the meaning of Article 6 of the Convention".[1] At first sight this is a somewhat remarkable restriction, since Article 6 of the Convention requires that the determination of criminal charges be made by an independent tribunal. Therefore, trial of a criminal offence by a non-judicial organ would in itself be a violation of the Convention. However, since Strasbourg case law has accepted the possibility that the determination of a criminal charge is made, in the first instance, by a non-judicial body, provided that from that determination appeal lies to a tribunal, the drafters must be assumed to have intended to make it clear that this first appeal to a tribunal is not a review in the sense of Article 2; its decision on appeal must be open to review by a higher instance, which has to meet the standards of an independent tribunal.

26.3 RIGHT TO A REVIEW

The first sentence of paragraph 1 provides that everyone has the right to have the 'conviction or sentence' reviewed. The reason for using the word 'or' instead of 'and'[2] is, again according to the Explanatory Report[3], that it is not required that in every case both the conviction and the sentence should be reviewed. For example, if a person has pleaded guilty and has been convicted, the right of review may be restricted to the review of the sentence. Here, too, the line of reasoning is not very convincing. Although in most cases in which a suspect has pleaded guilty the review will in fact mainly focus on the sentence, it may be necessary also to review the way the confession was obtained, and, therefore, the basis of the conviction. On the other hand, a review of the conviction alone, without the sentence also being reviewed, is only possible in those cases in which the suspect has been found guilty, but no sentence has been

---

[1]   Explanatory Report on Protocol No. 7 to the Convention for the Protection of Human Rights and Fundamental Freedoms, para. 17.

[2]   Art. 14(5) of the Covenant on Civil and Political Rights uses the word 'and'.

[3]   Explanatory Report, *supra* note 1, p. 17.

imposed. Just as in the corresponding Article 14(5) of the Covenant on Civil and Political Rights, it would, therefore, have been better if the word 'and' instead of 'or' had been used.

As is made clear in the second sentence of the first paragraph, exercising this right of appeal shall be governed by law. In other words, the modalities of the review are left for determination by domestic law. The Explanatory Report adds to this that the review may either concern a review of findings of facts and questions of law, or be limited to questions of law. According to the Court in the *Krombach* Case, States have a wide margin of appreciation to determine how the right secured by Article 2 of Protocol No. 7 to the Convention is to be exercised.[4] The Court set forth that "thus, the review by a higher court of a conviction or sentence may concern both points of fact and points of law or be confined solely to points of law. Any restrictions contained in domestic legislation on the right to a review guaranteed by this provision must, by analogy with the right of access to a court embodied in Article 6 para. 1 of the Convention, pursue a legitimate aim and not infringe the very essence of that right."[5] It may be deduced from this that the Court will not accept a restricted form of review of questions of law which cannot result in an annulment or alteration of the conviction or sentence concerned as sufficient.

Some countries have a system according to which persons who wish to appeal to a higher tribunal must in certain cases first apply for leave of appeal. According to the Explanatory Report such a procedure is in itself to be regarded as a form of review within the meaning of the present article.[6] Whether this interpretation is in conformity with the text of the article may be doubted. The decision to grant or refuse leave of appeal may be based upon reasons of expediency and does not necessarily imply a substantive review of the conviction or sentence as Article 2 would seem to guarantee, but may rather block such a review. Moreover, one may wonder whether such a decision can be said always to amount to a review 'by a higher tribunal'. It is submitted that the Court should be guided by the text and purpose of Article 2 rather than by the restrictive interpretation given in the Explanatory Report on this point.

26.4   EXCEPTIONS

The second paragraph of Article 2 contains three exceptions to the right laid down in the first paragraph.

---

[4]   Judgment of 13 February 2001, para. 96.
[5]   Explanatory Report, *supra* note 1, para. 18.
[6]   Explanatory Report, *supra note* 1, para. 19.

The first exception concerns offences of a minor character. In practice it will not always be clear where the dividing line between serious and minor offences lies. The Explanatory Report proposes as an important criterion the question of whether the offence is punishable by imprisonment or not.[7]

Although this criterion is a clear one, it is unlikely to lead to a common scope or autonomous meaning of the concept of 'offences of a minor character'. Since the question of imprisonment is entirely regulated by domestic law, major differences may occur between the Contracting States. More importantly, in several States a great many minor offences, such as infringements of traffic rules, are made punishable by imprisonment, though such sentences are never imposed in practice. It is unlikely that the drafters of the Protocol wished to make the right of review by a higher tribunal also obligatory in such cases.

The second exception concerns cases in which a person has been tried in the first instance by the highest tribunal. It refers to cases in which domestic law has assigned the highest tribunal as a court of first instance because of the status of the accused as a minister, judge or other high official, or because of the nature of the offence. It is obvious that in those cases review by a higher tribunal is not even possible.

The third exception is more controversial. It concerns cases where the conviction has been pronounced following an appeal against acquittal. For the person concerned this exception can be very unsatisfactory, especially when he thinks that the court of second instance has made an error of fact or law. In most member States of the Council of Europe, however, the convicted person will normally have the right of appeal in cassation to a third instance. In that case, at least any error of law can be restored. The assumption must be that the third exception does not apply in the case that the acquittal has been pronounced by a non-judicial body. Since Article 6 of the Convention requires that the determination of criminal charges be made by an independent tribunal, no consequences should ensue from a decision of a non-judicial body in this respect.

26.5 DEROGATION

Article 2 does not belong to the non-derogable rights in the sense of Article 15(2) of the Convention.

---

[7]   *Ibidem*, para. 21.

CHAPTER 27

COMPENSATION FOR MISCARRIAGE OF JUSTICE (Article 3 of Protocol No. 7)

REVISED BY CEES FLINTERMAN

CONTENTS

27.1 TEXT OF ARTICLE 3 OF PROTOCOL NO. 7

When a person has by a final decision been convicted of a criminal offence and when subsequently his conviction has been reversed, or he has been pardoned, on the ground that a new or newly discovered fact shows conclusively that there has been a miscarriage of justice, the person who has suffered punishment as a result of such conviction shall be compensated according to the law or the practice of that State concerned, unless it is proved that the non-disclosure of the unknown fact in time is wholly or partly attributable to him.

27.2 SCOPE

The right to compensation for miscarriage of justice, which is acknowledged in article 3 of Protocol 7 should not be confounded with the right to compensation for unlawful detention.[1] Both rights are distinct rights. Under a miscarriage of justice is understood: "some serious failure in the judicial process involving grave prejudice to the convicted

---

[1] Which is guaranteed by article 5(5) ECHR.

person."[2] Article 3 of Protocol No. 7 applies only if seven preconditions have been fulfilled.

Firstly, Article 3 presupposes the existence of a 'criminal offence'. It seems to be obvious that the notion of 'criminal offence' is closely related to the notion of 'criminal charge' of Article 6 of the Convention. Thus, it is appropriate to argue that Article 3 also applies to those disciplinary and administrative sanctions that fall within the scope of Article 6.

Secondly, the person concerned must have been 'convicted'. Consequently, the article does not apply in cases where the charge is dismissed or the accused is acquitted.[3]

Thirdly, the person concerned must have been convicted by a 'final decision'. A decision is final "if, according to the traditional expression, it has acquired the force of *res judicata*. This is the case when it is irrevocable, that is to say when no further ordinary remedies are available or when the parties have exhausted such remedies or have permitted the time-limit to expire without availing themselves of them."[4]

Fourthly, the person concerned must, as a result of this final decision, have suffered punishment. Thus, if the suspect has been found guilty, but no sentence has been imposed or the sentence has not (yet) been executed, Article 3 does not apply.

Fifthly, the right laid down in this article can only be exercised, if the conviction has been reversed or pardoned.

Sixthly, the reversal or pardon must have taken place because of new or newly discovered facts. In the latter case an assessment must moreover be made into whether the circumstance that these facts were not disclosed in time is wholly or partly attributable to the person concerned. It is obvious that if a person is willingly withholding relevant information, he loses his right to compensation because the prejudice suffered is (partly) due to his own conduct. If, besides the convicted person, others are also responsible for the fact that certain relevant facts were not disclosed, it may not always be fair to put the blame solely on the former by fully denying him a right to compensation. In that case a partial compensation may be more appropriate.

Seventhly, the new or newly discovered facts on the basis of which the person's conviction has been reversed or the pardon has been awarded must conclusively show that there has been a miscarriage of justice. Reversal or pardon on other grounds – pardon may often especially be granted on other grounds – does not create a right to compensation. According to the Explanatory Report the intention is that compensa-

---

[2]   Explanatory Report on Protocol No. 7 to the Convention for the Protection of Human Rights and Fundamental Freedoms, para. 23.

[3]   Explanatory Report, *supra* note 2, para. 22. Under circumstances the fifth paragraph of Art. 5 of the Convention may offer compensation.

[4]   *Ibidem*, with reference to the *Explanatory Report of the European Convention on the International Validity of Criminal Judgments, Commentary on Article 1(a)*, Council of Europe, Strasbourg, 1970, p. 22.

tion should be paid only in "clear cases of miscarriage of justice, in the sense that there would be acknowledgement that the person concerned was clearly innocent".[5] In what follows the Explanatory Report seems to imply that reversal on the ground that new facts have been discovered which introduce a reasonable doubt as to the guilt of the accused is not enough.[6]1 It is submitted that this interpretation would seem to be too strict, especially in view of the right to be presumed innocent, laid down in Article 6(2) of the Convention, which implies that reasonable doubt and clear innocence should lead to the same result.

27.3 RIGHT TO COMPENSATION

If all conditions have been fulfilled, Article 3 provides that the person who has suffered punishment as a result of such conviction shall be compensated according to the law[7] or the practice of the State concerned.

What the phrase 'the practice of the State concerned' means is rather unclear. The Explanatory Report does not clarify it any further than by providing that "the State should provide for the payment of compensation in all cases to which the Article applies".[8] It is submitted that this phrase, which does not appear anywhere else in the Convention, is rather unfortunate. It does not add anything to the reference that is already made to national law and it may lead to confusion as to its meaning. Article 5(5) of the Convention, which establishes a right to compensation for victims of arrest or detention in contravention of the provisions of Article 5, uses the words 'an enforceable right to compensation'. This phrase should also have been adopted here.

In the event of absence of a law which provides for compensation for miscarriage of justice, the State must be deemed not to be relieved of its obligation to pay compensation for miscarriage of justice. The state remains bound by international standards.[9]

---

5   *Ibidem,* para. 25.

6   *Ibidem.*

7   Article 14(6) ICCPR recognizes the same right. According to this article, compensation should be paid by the State according to law. The Human Rights Committee in its General Comment No.13, para. 18, has made it clear that this means that States must enact laws which provide compensation to victims of miscarriages of justice.

8   Explanatory Report, *supra,* note 1, para. 25.

9   See in this regard Article 27 Vienna Convention on the Law of Treaties, which reads: "A party may not invoke the provisions of its internal law as justification for its failure to perform a treaty."

27.4 DEROGATION

Article 3 does not belong to the non-derogable rights in the sense of Article 15(2) of the Convention.

CHAPTER 28

NE BIS IN IDEM (Article 4 of Protocol No. 7)

REVISED BY EDWIN BLEICHRODT

CONTENTS

28.1 TEXT OF ARTICLE 4 OF PROTOCOL NO. 7

1. *No one shall be liable to be tried or punished again in criminal proceedings under the jurisdiction of the same State for an offence for which he has already been finally acquitted or convicted in accordance with the law and penal procedure of that State.*
2. *The provisions of the preceding paragraph shall not prevent the re-opening of the case in accordance with the law and penal procedure of the State concerned, if there is evidence of new or newly discovered facts, or if there has been a fundamental defect in the previous proceedings, which could affect the outcome of the case.*
3. *No derogation from this Article shall be made under Article 15 of the Convention.*

28.2 SCOPE

The aim of article 4 of Protocol No. 7 is to prohibit the repetition of criminal proceedings that have been concluded by a final decision.[1] The Article is not applicable in cases where different sanctions are issued at the same time by two different

---

[1]   Judgment of 23 October 1995, *Gradinger*, para. 53; judgment of 20 July 2004, *Nikitin*, para. 35.

authorities, i.e. a criminal and an administrative authority.[2] The principle that nobody may be tried or punished again is limited to 'criminal proceedings'. In the *Gradinger* Case the applicant had been convicted and punished by a criminal court. Subsequently the administrative authorities imposed a fine on him. The latter punishment was based on the same facts. The applicant complained that the decision of the administrative authorities amounted to a violation of Article 6 of the Convention[3] and Article 4 of Protocol No. 7. The Court had first to asses whether Article 6 did apply to the administrative proceedings. It answered this question in the affirmative with reference to the criteria developed in its case law. With regard to Article 4 of Protocol No. 7 the Court took the existence of the 'criminal proceedings' for granted.[4] It may be concluded that the notion of 'criminal' in Article 4 of Protocol No. 7 is identical to the term 'criminal' in Article 6 of the Convention. In the *Göktan* Case the Court held that the notion of what constitutes a 'penalty' cannot vary from one Convention provision to another. It concluded that imprisonment in default of payment of customs fine was not a means of enforcing the fine, but a penalty within the meaning of Article 7 of the Convention and of Article 4 of Protocol No. 7.[5]

Article 4 only applies to criminal proceedings under the jurisdiction of one and the same State, thus limiting its scope to the national level. It, therefore, still allows that a person is punished more than once for the same facts in two or more countries, depending on the rules on jurisdiction of the States involved.[6]

Paragraph 1 of Article 4 further provides that the *ne bis in idem* principle is only applicable if the conviction or acquittal has become final. Here again, just as in the preceding Article 3, according to the Explanatory Report to Protocol No. 7, a decision is to be considered final if, according to the traditional expression, it has acquired the force of *res judicata*. This is the case when it is irrevocable, that is to say when 'no further ordinary remedies are available or when the parties have exhausted such remedies or have permitted the time-limit to expire without availing themselves of them.'[7] In the *Nikitin* Case the Russian applicant was acquitted. The Russian procedural law at the time allowed certain officials to challenge a judgment within one year after it had taken effect. The grounds for this 'supervisory review' were the same as for bringing an ordinary appeal. The Court considered that a supervisory request for annulment of a final judgment is a form of extraordinary appeal as it is not accessible to the defendant in a criminal case directly. The Court considered the appeal judgment by which the acquittal acquired final force as the 'final decision' referred to in Article

---

[2]   Decision of 30 May 2000, *R.T. v. Switzerland.*
[3]   The applicant contended that he did not have access to a 'tribunal'.
[4]   Judgment of 23 October 1995, paras 61 and 65-66. See also, *e.g.*, the decision of 21 November 2000, *Luksch.*
[5]   Judgment 2 July 2002, para. 48.
[6]   Decision of 28 June 2001, *Amrollahi.*
[7]   Explanatory Report, para. 29 *juncto* para. 22.

4 of Protocol No. 7. In the case the request for supervisory review was not, however, accepted, which meant that the applicant was not 'tried again' within the meaning of Article 4 para. 1.[8]

28.3   SAME OFFENCE

In the *Gradinger* Case the question arose whether the 'offence' the applicant had been tried and punished for by the criminal court – causing death by negligence, while driving his car – concerned the same 'offence' as his subsequent conviction of driving under the influence of alcohol by the administrative authorities. The former offence constituted a violation of the Criminal Code and the latter came under the Road Traffic Act. The relevant provisions differed with regard to their nature and purpose. Nevertheless, the Court reached the conclusion that Article 4 of Protocol No. 7 did apply and had been violated. It appeared to be crucial in the Court's view that the decision of the criminal court under the Criminal Code and the decision of the administrative authorities under the Road Traffic Act "were based on the same conduct".[9] The criterion of 'the same conduct' suggests that the (former) accused derives a large amount of protection from Article 4 of Protocol No. 7, because in national legal systems one and the same set of facts may constitute various different offences.

However, later case law makes clear that the protection has a more limited scope. In the *Oliveira* Case the applicant was first convicted by the police magistrate for failing to control her vehicle as she had not adapted her speed to the road conditions. Subsequently, she was convicted by the criminal court of causing physical injury by negligence. The Court concluded that there had been no violation of Article 4 of Protocol No. 7, considering that it presented a typical example of a single act constituting various offences. According to the Court, there is nothing in that situation which infringes Article 4 of Protocol No. 7, since that provision only prohibits people being tried twice for the same offence.[10]

The Court's approach would seem to be contradictory. In his dissenting opinion judge Repik observes that there is no difference between the *Gradinger* Case and the *Oliveira* Case that can justify these two wholy conflicting decisions. Did the Court take into account that the offences in the *Oliveira* case could have been tried at the same time and that the highest penalty absorbed the lowest? Or may the different result be explained by the order of the proceedings or by the fact that the two judgments in the

---

[8]   Judgment of 20 July 2004, paras 42-49.

[9]   Judgment of 23 October 1995, para. 66.

[10]   Judgment of 30 July 1998, para. 26. See for a similar result the decision of 14 September 1999, *Ponsetti and Chesnel*.

Gradinger Case were contradictory? None of these factual differences are decisive as appears from the *Fischer* Case, where the Court noted that the question whether the *non bis in idem* principle is violated concerns the relationship between the two offences at issue and can, therefore, not depend on the order in which the respective proceedings are conducted. Moreover, it considered that Article 4 of Protocol No. 7 is not confined to the right not to be *punished* twice but extends to the right not to be *tried* twice. Decisive is whether the offences in question differ in their essential elements. The mere fact that one act constitutes nominally different offences is not contrary to Article 4 of Protocol No. 7. Where different offences based on one act are prosecuted consecutively, one after the final decision of the other, the Court examines whether such offences have the same essential elements.[11] Although the Court tries to uphold that the *Gradinger* judgment is in conformity with later case law, it may be concluded that the Court has abandoned the criterion of 'the same conduct' that was used in the *Gradinger* judgment.

In the *Franz Fischer* Case the Court considered that the administrative offence of drunken driving of the Austrian Road Traffic Act, and the special circumstances under Article 81 para. 2 of the Criminal Code, namely driving a vehicle while having a certain blood alcohol level, as interpreted by the national courts, did not differ in their essential elements.[12] In the *Bachmaier* Case the applicant was prosecuted for causing death by negligence in particularly dangerous conditions, *i.e.* under influence of alcohol. He was acquitted of these charges without any further consideration of the application's state of drunkenness. The additional element of drunkenness was only considered in the subsequent administrative criminal proceedings. In the particular circumstances of the case the Court held that the applicant had not been 'tried again' within the meaning of Article 4 of Protocol 7.[13] This conclusion is remarkable, because the element of the influence of alcohol was also crucial in the indictment in the criminal proceedings, irrespective the acquittal.

28.4   RE-OPENING OF THE CASE

The second paragraph of Article 4 provides that the *ne bis in idem* principle does not prevent that a case to be re-opened if there is evidence of new or newly discovered facts, irrespective of the question whether this is in favour or to the detriment of the person concerned. According to the Explanatory Report, the term 'new or newly discovered facts' also 'includes new means of proof relating to previously existing

---

[11]   Judgment of 29 May 2001, *Franz Fischer*, para. 25; judgment of 6 June 2002, *Sailer*, para. 26.
[12]   Judgment of 29 May 2001, para. 27.
[13]   Decision of 2 September 2004.

facts'.[14] What is exactly meant by these words is not clear, but it seems to be apt to lead to misuse. Is the meaning of this phrase that new technologies or previously forbidden forms of collecting evidence may lead to a re-opening of a case, if that technology or form has become available after the closing of a case? Especially when these 'facts' may also lead to a situation detrimental to the person concerned, this might create legal uncertainty for that person. In fact, a person may, even after an acquittal, be found guilty after the re-opening of a case as a result of new technologies or a change in the caselaw concerning proof. This would practically mean that an accused may only feel safe after the prosecution for a criminal offence has become barred by limitation.

Re-opening of the proceedings and any other changing of the judgment, again according to the Explanatory Report, may also take place on other grounds, if this is in favour of the convicted person.[15]

The Court makes a clear distinction between a second prosecution or trial which is prohibited by the first paragraph of this Article, and the resumption of a trial in exceptional circumstances, which is provided for in its second paragraph. Article 4(2) of Protocol No. 7 expressly envisages the possibility that a case is re-opened following the emergence of new evidence or the discovery of a fundamental defect in the previous proceedings. A system which allows for revision of a decision on the grounds of a judicial error on points of law and procedure can also be regarded as a special type of re-opening falling within the scope of the second paragraph of Article 4.[16]

28.5   DEROGATION

According to the third paragraph of Article 4, the principle of *ne bis in idem* is non-derogable in the sense of Article 15(2) of the Convention.

---

[14]   Explanatory Report, para. 31.
[15]   *Ibidem.*
[16]   Judgment of 20 July 2004, *Nikitin*, paras 45-46.

CHAPTER 29
EQUALITY OF RIGHTS AND RESPONSIBILITIES BETWEEN SPOUSES DURING AND AFTER MARRIAGE
(Article 5 of Protocol No. 7)

REVISED BY CEES FLINTERMAN

CONTENTS

29.1   TEXT OF ARTICLE 5 OF PROTOCOL NO. 7

Spouses shall enjoy equality of rights and responsibilities of a private law character between them, and in their relations with their children, as to marriage, during marriage and in the event of its dissolution. This Article shall not prevent States from taking such measures as are necessary in the interests of the children.

29.2   RELATIONS OF A PRIVATE-LAW CHARACTER

The rights and obligations to which the equality principle of Article 5 refers are of a private-law character; the equality concerns only the relations between the spouses themselves, with respect to their personal status or their property, and their relations with their children.[1] As the Explanatory Report puts it, "the Article does not apply to other fields of law, such as administrative, fiscal, criminal, social, ecclesiastical or labour laws".[2] Since under the system of the Convention complaints can be lodged against States only, the scope of the Strasbourg review is rather restricted and mainly concerns the obligation of the State to enact and enforce the appropriate legislation. It is, however, clear that Article 5 implies *Drittwirkung*.[3] In the *Cernecki* Case the Court held that States are under a positive obligation to provide a satisfactory legal framework under which spouses have equal rights.[4] Other international human rights bodies have adopted the same conclusion. The Human Rights Committee, in its General Comment No. 18 (non-discrimination), held that "it is a positive duty of States parties to make certain that spouses have equal rights as required by the Covenant."[5] The Committee on the Elimination of Discrimination Against Women is of the same opinion.[6]

To a large extent the equality of spouses is already secured by Article 8, in conjunction with Article 14, of the Convention. In the *Hokkanen* Case the applicant complained that, in breach of Article 8 of the Convention and Article 5 of Protocol No. 7, the public authorities had not taken the necessary steps to facilitate the speedy reunion of the applicant and his daughter. The Commission declared the complaint under both these articles admissible. However, it finally reached the conclusion, as did the Court, that Article 8 of the Convention had been violated and that no separate issue arose under Article 5 of Protocol No. 7.[7]

29.3 DURING AND AFTER MARRIAGE

The rights and obligations 'as to marriage' relate to the legal effects connected with the conclusion of marriage.[8] Article 5 is not applicable to the period preceding marriage. It also is not concerned with the conditions of capacity to enter into mar-

---

[1] Article 23(4) of the UN Covenant on Civil and Political Rights and Article 16 of the Convention on the Elimination of all Forms of Discrimination Against Women recognize the same right. Both Conventions, however, are more detailed in this matter than Protocol No. 7.

[2] Explanatory Report on Protocol No. 7 to the Convention for the Protection of Human Rights and Fundamental Freedoms, para. 35.

[3] On this, see *supra* 1.7.

[4] Decision of 11 July 2000, para. 15.

[5] Human Rights Committee, General Comment No. 18 (non-discrimination), 37th session 1989, para. 5, UN doc. HRI/GEN/1/Rev. 7, 12 May 2004, p. 146

[6] Committee on the Elimination of Discrimination Against Women, General Recommendation No. 21, 13th session, 1994, Equality in marriage and family relations, para. 49, UN Doc. HRI/GEN/1/Rev. 7, 12 May 2004, p. 253

[7] Report of 22 October 1993, para. 150; judgment of 23 September 1994, para. 66.

[8] Explanatory Report, *supra* note 2, para. 37.

riage.[9] It is, therefore, left to the States to determine these conditions. It would, for instance, be allowed for States to make a difference between men and women with regard to the minimum age required for marriage, since this concerns the premarital period, provided of course that this difference is in conformity with Article 12 in conjunction with Article 14 of the Convention. This approach is different from the approach of the Convention on the Elimination of all Forms of Discrimination Against Women. Article 16 CEDAW contains provisions which are applicable to the period preceding marriage.[10] The same applies to article 23 of the UN Covenant on Civil and Political Rights.[11]

The words 'in the event of its dissolution' in Article 5 do not imply a right to divorce. States are not obliged to provide for dissolution of marriage. In this context it is noteworthy that the phrase referring to the dissolution of marriage in the present article and in the corresponding Article 23(4) of the UN Covenant on Civil and Political Rights is identical in the French version, but not in the English version. In the French version both articles speak of '*lors de sa dissolution*'. In the English version, Article 23(4) of the UN Covenant on Civil and Political Rights uses the words 'at its dissolution',[12] while Article 5 of Protocol No. 7 states 'in the event of its dissolution'. Apparently this change has been introduced to take into consideration the situation in some member States of the Council of Europe where the dissolution of a marriage is still prohibited.

---

[9] *Ibidem.*

[10] The text of article 16(1)(a) and (b) reads as follows: "State Parties shall take all appropriate measures to eliminate discrimination against women in all matters relating to marriage and family relations and in particular shall ensure, on a basis of equality of men and women:
(a) The same right to enter into marriage;
(b) The same right freely to choose a spouse and to enter into marriage only with their free and full consent."

[11] Article 23 ICCPR reads as follows:
1. The family is the natural and fundamental group unit of society and is entitled to protection by society and the State.
2. The right of men and women of marriageable age to marry and to found a family shall be recognized.
3. No marriage shall be entered into without the free and full consent of the intending spouses.
4. State Parties to the present Covenant shall take appropriate steps to ensure equality of rights and responsibilities of spouses as to marriage, during marriage and at its dissolution. In the case of dissolution, provision shall be made for the necessary protection of any children.

[12] Article 16 para. 1(c) of the Convention on the Elimination of all forms of Discrimination Against Women also uses the phrase 'at its dissolution'.

29.4 EXCEPTION TO THE EQUALITY OF RIGHTS AND RESPONSIBILITIES

The second sentence of Article 5 contains an exception to the equal enjoyment of the rights and responsibilities. The Contracting States may take such measures as are necessary in the interests of the children, even if this results in inequality between the spouses. The Explanatory Report states in too broad a phrase that Article 5 "should not be understood as preventing the national authorities from taking due account of all relevant factors when reaching decisions with regard to the division of property in the event of dissolution of marriage".[13] To the extent that these 'relevant factors' are related to the interests of the children, it follows from the express provision in Article 5 itself. However, since Article 5 contains no other exceptions – at least not expressly – it is submitted that any other limitations of the right to equal enjoyment will have to meet the requirement of an objective and reasonable justification and that of reasonable proportionality, which have been developed in the Strasbourg case-law with respect to Article 14. The exception of the second sentence of Article 5 is also reflected in similar provisions in Article 23 of the UN Covenant on Civil and Political Rights and Article 16(1)(d) of the Convention on the Elimination of All Forms of Discrimination Against Women; the exception is based on the consideration that the best interests of the child shall always be paramount.

29.5 DEROGATION

Article 5 does not belong to the non-derogable rights in the sense of Article 15(2) of the Convention.

---

[13]   Explanatory report, *supra* note 2, para. 38.

CHAPTER 30
GENERAL PROHIBITION OF DISCRIMINATION (Article 1 of Protocol No. 12)

REVISED BY FRIED VAN HOOF

CONTENTS

30.1 TEXT OF ARTICLE 1 OF PROTOCOL NO. 12

Article 1:
1. *The enjoyment of any right set forth by law shall be secured without discrimination on any ground such as, sex, race, colour, language, religion, political or other opinion, national or social origin, association with a national minority, property, birth or other status.*
2. *No one shall be discriminated against by any public authority on any ground such as those mentioned in paragraph 1.*

30.2 INTRODUCTION

In 2000 a 12th Protocol was adopted containing a general (and non-accessory) non-discrimination clause. This Protocol entered into force for the ratifying States on April 1ˢᵗ, 2005.

Protocol No. 12 intends to remedy the major weakness of Article 14 of the Convention: its accessory nature. Under Article 14 only those equality issues that are related to a substantive provision in the Convention or one of its Protocols can be addressed. Although the Court has gradually expanded the scope of Article 14 by giving a wide interpretation to these provisions (*e.g.* Article 1 of the First Protocol: the right to property), Article 14 cannot be invoked in various important areas of social life (housing, employment to name but a few).[1]

In this respect the European Convention was by-passed by Article 26 of the International Covenant on Civil and Political Rights. The Charter of Fundamental Rights of the European Union also prohibits any discrimination on enumerated grounds without any limitation as to the rights covered. Consequently, the Explanatory Report to Protocol 12 refers to the need to introduce a general substantive equality and non-discrimination clause.[2]

30.3 SCOPE OF THE PROHIBITION

It is important to note that Article 1 of Protocol No. 12 contains a general prohibition of discrimination. The Preamble, however, does mention the principle of equality before the law and equal protection of the law. According to the Explanatory Report "the non-discrimination and equality principles are closely intertwined. For example, the principle of equality requires that equal situations are treated equally and unequal situations differently. Failure to do so will amount to discrimination unless an objective and reasonable justification exists".[3] Unequal treatment, for which no justification exists, is in this approach an instance of prohibited discrimination.

It seems to have been the intention to follow the case law of the Court under Article 14 with respect to defining what constitutes discrimination, i.e. unjustified unequal treatment: "A difference of treatment is discriminatory if it has no objective and reasonable justification, that is if it does not pursue a 'legitimate aim' or if there is not a 'reasonable relationship of proportionality between the means employed and the aim sought to be realised'."[4]

The list of non-discrimination grounds in Article 1 is identical to that in Article 14. It has been expressly decided not to add new grounds such as disability, sexual orientation and age, "not because of a lack of awareness that such grounds have become particularly important ... but because such an inclusion was considered unnecessary from a legal point of view since the list of non-discrimination grounds is not exhaustive, and because inclusion of any particular additional ground might give rise to unwarranted a contrario interpretations as regards discrimination based on grounds not so included."[5]

---

[1] See *infra*, Chapter 33.
[2] Explanatory Report, para. 1.
[3] Explanatory Report, para. 15.
[4] Explanatory Report, para. 18, citing judgment of 28 May 1985, Abdulaziz, Cabales and Balkandali, para. 72.
[5] Explanatory Report, para. 20.

In addition to Article 14, Article 1(1) of the Protocol offers protection against discrimination in the enjoyment of any right granted to an individual under national law. Even though there does not have to be a relation to a right protected by the Convention, the applicability of Protocol No. 12 is related to different treatment as to the enjoyment of rights granted under domestic law.

Additionally the second paragraph of Article 1 covers discrimination by a public authority. This applies to discretionary acts, as well as clear legal obligations imposed upon it, and also other acts or omissions by a public authority. It can be assumed that Article 1 also offers protection against private law acts by public authorities, so that a public authority is always bound by Article 1, paragraph 2, whatever powers, acts, or omissions are at stake.

The prime objective of Article 1 was to embody a negative obligation for the Parties: the obligation not to discriminate against individuals. It "is not intended to impose a general positive obligation on the Parties to take measures to prevent or remedy all instances of discrimination in relations between private persons."[6] Although positive obligations might not be intended they cannot be excluded either. Occasionally the duty to 'secure' under Article 1 of the Convention might entail positive obligations. "Regarding more specifically relations between private persons, a failure to provide protection from discrimination in such relations might be so clear-cut and grave that it might engage clearly the responsibility of the State and then Article 1 of the Protocol could come into play".[7] However, the extent of positive obligations will be, according to the Explanatory Report, limited: "any positive obligation in the area of relations between private persons would concern, at the most, relations in the public sphere normally regulated by law, for which the state has a certain responsibility (for example, arbitrary denial of access to work, access to restaurants, or to services which private persons may make available to the public such as medical care or utilities such as water and electricity, etc.)."[8]

It seems that the Explanatory Report reflects a compromise. On the one hand it seemed not a good idea to exclude the notion of positive obligations altogether, because this might hinder the Court in fitting in Article 1 of the Protocol in its general framework of interpretation, including the incorporation of appropriate positive obligations in order to secure the effectiveness of a substantive provision. On the other hand, some States had to be reassured that Article 1 of the Protocol could not lead to the development of obligations to set up affirmative action programmes or to interfere extensively in private matters. The compromise relates therefore to arbitrary (discriminatory) access to socially important (but privately run) institutions and

---

[6]   Explanatory Report, para. 25.
[7]   Explanatary Report, para. 26.
[8]   Explanatory Report, para. 28.

facilities. These openings might give the Court sufficient room for interpretation to prudently include positive obligations within the context of Article 1 of the 12th Protocol.

CHAPTER 31
ABOLITION OF THE DEATH PENALTY
IN TIME OF WAR (Article 1
of Protocol No. 13)

REVISED BY JEROEN SCHOKKENBROEK

CONTENTS

31.1 TEXT OF ARTICLE 1 OF PROTOCOL NO. 13

The death penalty shall be abolished. No one shall be condemned to such penalty or executed.

31.2 INTRODUCTION

Protocol No. 13, concerning the abolition of the death penalty in all circumstances, seeks to remove the last remaining possibility for Contracting States to have recourse to this form of punishment. While Protocol No. 6 went a very long way towards the abolition of the death penalty – thus rendering largely obsolete the second sentence of the first paragraph of Article 2 of the Convention (right to life) – it still contained an exception in Article 2 of the Protocol according to which a State may make provision in its law for the death penalty in respect of crimes committed in time of war or of imminent threat of war. In the light of the strong trend in Europe and beyond in favour of abolition of the death penalty in general, it is hardly surprising that the specific issue of the use of the death penalty in time of war came on the political agenda of the organs of the Council of Europe. It was raised for the first time by the

Parliamentary Assembly in Recommendation 1246 (1994), in which it recommended that the Committee of Ministers draw up an additional protocol to the Convention, providing for the abolition of the death penalty both in peace- and in wartime. While a large majority of the Steering Committee for Human Rights at the time advised that a favourable response be given to the recommendation by the Committee of Ministers, the latter considered that the political priority was to obtain and maintain moratoria on executions, to be consolidated by complete abolition of the death penalty.[1] Indeed, as was noted in Chapter 24 above, around the mid-1990s some newer member States still continued to execute death sentences.

Only a few years later almost all Contracting States had ratified Protocol No. 6 and a moratorium on executions was firmly in place in the few States that had not yet done so. The European Ministerial Conference on Human Rights, held in November 2000 on the occasion of the 50th anniversary of the Convention, agreed in its Resolution No. II (para. 14) to invite the Committee of Ministers to consider the feasibility of an additional protocol to the Convention which would exclude the possibility of maintaining the death penalty in respect of acts committed in time of war or of imminent threat of war. In January 2001 the Committee of Ministers gave instructions to the Steering Committee for Human Rights to study the proposal and give its views as to the feasibility of a new protocol on this matter. The Steering Committee presented a draft text in November 2001. The Committee of Ministers adopted the text of Protocol No. 13 on 21 February 2002 and opened it for signature on 3 May 2002.[2] It entered into force on 1 July 2003 after it had received ten ratifications.[3]

31.3 SCOPE OF THE PROHIBITION

Article 1 of Protocol No. 13 is identical to Article 1 of Protocol No. 6. The additional protection offered by Protocol No. 13 as compared to Protocol No. 6 lies in the fact that the exception provided in Article 2 of Protocol No. 6 (death penalty for acts committed in time of war or of imminent threat of war) is not included in the new Protocol. This means, having regard also to the fact that the protocol does not allow any reservations or derogations (Articles 2 and 3 of the Protocol), that the prohibition of the death penalty contained in Protocol No. 13 is complete and absolute. The Explanatory Report indicates that, as an additional protocol, it does not, from a technical point of view, supersede Article 2 of the Convention, since the first sentence of paragraph 1 and the whole of paragraph 2 of that article still remain valid, even for States Parties to this Protocol. However, it is clear that the second sentence of

---

[1]   See the Explanatory Report on Protocol No. 13, para. 9.
[2]   See paras 10-13 of the Explanatory Report.
[3]   For an overview of the Contracting States which have ratified Protocol No. 13, see Appendix 1.

Article 2(1) of the Convention is no longer applicable in respect of those States; this holds true also for the possibility provided for in Article 2 of Protocol No. 6.[4]

Most certainly as a reflection of the evolution of the political and legal position on the death penalty in Europe since the 1980s, the Protocol places the abolition of the death penalty squarely in the context of the right to life, much more clearly than Protocol No. 6 did. The preamble to Protocol No. 13 expresses the conviction that "everyone's right to life is a basic value in a democratic society and that the abolition of the death penalty is essential for the protection of this right and for the full recognition of the inherent dignity of all human beings". Noting the exception still permitted by Protocol No. 6, it describes Protocol No. 13 as a "final step in order to abolish the death penalty in all circumstances". For this reason it would not be justified to regard the existence of Protocol No. 13 as a valid argument against an evolutive interpretation of Article 2 of the Convention as far as the abolition of the death penalty in time of peace is concerned.[5] On the contrary, the preamble's strong emphasis on the right-to-life context of abolition of the death penalty, as an authoritative expression of contemporary opinion as to the scope and implications of that right, rather militates in favour of such an evolutive interpretation.

For the same reasons as were expressed in relation to Protocol No. 6, it is unlikely that Protocol No. 13 will give rise to an important case law about the application of the death penalty within the legal orders of the Contracting Parties. However, as with Protocol No. 6, it is not excluded that it may be invoked in relation to measures of extradition or expulsion to States not bound by the Protocol.[6]

Finally, mention should be made of the fact that the Protocol takes a very restrictive view as to the possibility for States Parties to withdraw or modify any declarations made concerning the territorial application of Protocol No. 13. While Article 4(3) of the Protocol does allow for such withdrawal or modification (following a similar provision of Article 5 of Protocol No. 6), the Explanatory Report specifies that this is allowed only on formal grounds, in cases where the State concerned ceases to be responsible for the international relations of the territory in question and not in order to permit the re-introduction of the death penalty in such a territory.[7]

---

[4]   See para. 18 of the Explanatory Report.
[5]   See the discussion of the *Soering* judgment and the *Öcalan* judgment in Chapter 24, *supra*.
[6]   A first decision of admissibility in a case of this kind was given in the decision of 26 October 2004, *Bader and Others v. Sweden* (expulsion to Syria where the first applicant had been sentenced to death).
[7]   See paragraph 17 of the Explanatory Report.

31.4 DEROGATION

No derogations from the provisions of Protocol No. 13 are permitted. It should be recalled that the very object and purpose of the Protocol are to abolish the death penalty in all circumstances, including in time or war or of imminent threat of war.[8]

---

[8]   See Article 2 of the Protocol and paragraph 15 of the Explanatory Report.

CHAPTER 32

RIGHT TO AN EFFECTIVE REMEDY BEFORE A NATIONAL AUTHORITY
(Article 13)

REVISED BY YUTAKA ARAI

CONTENTS

32.1   TEXT OF ARTICLE 13

Everyone whose rights and freedoms as set forth in this Convention are violated shall have an effective remedy before a national authority notwithstanding that the violation has been committed by persons acting in an official capacity.

32.2   GENERAL OBSERVATIONS

32.2.1   ANCILLARY CHARACTER

Ideally, a general guarantee of an effective remedy should be provided for anyone who alleges that one of his/her rights has been violated by the authorities or by an individual. The concept of the rule of law, which along with the idea of democracy constitutes one of the pillars of the Council of Europe,[1] would justify a broader construction of the requirements of Article 13. However, as can be seen from the words 'whose rights and freedoms as set forth in this Convention are violated', Article 13, instead of embodying such a general guarantee, refers exclusively to cases in which the alleged violation concerns one of the rights and freedoms of the Convention.[2] The applicability of Article 13 depends on the finding that the principal complaints are not declared incompatible *ratione materiae*, and that they are arguable. Article 13 cannot be invoked independently from, but only in conjunction with, one or more of substantive rights and freedoms of the Convention (Articles 2-12, or Article 14),[3] or of its Protocols.

Both the rule on exhaustion of domestic remedies under Article 35(1) and the requirement of effective remedies available at national level under Article 13 embody the principle of subsidiarity, according to which the Convention system is subsidiary to the primary responsibility of national constitutional systems for safeguarding fundamental rights.[4] The fact that the procedural rule under Article 35(1) presupposes the existence of an effective domestic remedy suggests a 'close affinity' between the

---

[1]   See in particular, the Preamble and Article 3 of the Statute of the Council of Europe; and the Preamble of Resolution (78) 8 on Legal Aid and Advice, adopted by the Committed of Ministers on 2 March, 1978 at the 284th meeting of the Ministers' Deputies, where 'the right of access to justice' is described as an 'essential feature of any democratic society'.

[2]   For the case law of the Commission, see, for instance, Appl. 6753/74, *X and Y v. the Netherlands*, D&R 2 (1975), p. 118 (119), and the report of 17 July 1980, *Kaplan*, DR 21 (1981), p. 5 (35). For the case law of the Court, see, for example, decision of 18 May 2004, *Eccleston*, para. 4.

[3]   Though rejected in the specific facts of the case, the Court examined the possibility of a violation of two 'ancillary' provisions of Articles 13 and 14 in, judgment of 27 April 1988, *Boyle and Rice*, paras 85-86.

[4]   Judgment of 23 September 2004, *Rachevi*, para. 61.

two provisions, but Article 13 establishes an 'additional guarantee' for an individual.[5] According to the *travaux préparatoires*, Article 13 aims to accord a means whereby individuals can obtain relief at a national level for violations of their Convention rights before having recourse to the Strasbourg supervision.[6]

The ancillary character of the right to an effective remedy under Article 13 prompted Judges Matscher and Pinheiro Farinha to aver in their dissenting opinions in *Malone* that "Article 13 constitutes one of the most obscure clauses in the Convention (...) [with] the Convention institutions (...) for the most part advancing barely convincing reasons".[7] The subsequent development of case law, especially that of the new Court, however, has provided some guidelines for the application of this important procedural right.

32.2.2   INHERENT LIMITATIONS

The Court has taken the view that the absence of any limitation clauses under Article 13 does not mean that this right is absolute; this provision should be construed as having inherent limitations.[8] The standard of remedy that must be provided is "a remedy that is as effective as can be having regard to the restricted scope for recourse inherent in [the particular context]".[9] The theory of inherent limitations has been invoked to support the argument that Article 13 does not recognise constitutional judicial review, which would allow a Member State's laws to be challenged before a national authority as being incompatible with the Convention.[10] The Court has, however, emphasised the need to minimise such implied restrictions.[11] It is possible to argue that one of the jurisprudential rationales for such inherent limitations lies in the 'positive' nature of the State obligations under Article 13. The scope of positive obligations depends on the nature of the complaint,[12] including the nature of the substantive rights invoked in conjunction, with a more stringent and broader obligation recognized in the case of alleged violations of fundamental rights of non-

---

[5]   Judgment of 28 July 1999, *Selmouni*, para. 74 ; and judgment of 26 October 2000, *Kudla*, para. 152.

[6]   *Collected Edition of the 'Travaux Préparatoires' of the European Convention on Human Rights*, vol. II, pp. 485 and 490, and vol. III, p. 651; cited in judgment of 26 October 2000, *Kudla*, para. 152.

[7]   Partly dissenting opinion of judges Matscher and Pinheiro Farinha in judgment of 2 August 1984, *Malone*, para. 1; the concurring opinion of judges Bindschedler-Robert, Gölcuklu, Matscher and Spielman in judgment of 21 February 1986, *James and Others*, para. 1.

[8]   See, for instance, judgment of 26 March 1987, *Leander*, para. 79.

[9]   Judgment of 6 September 1978, *Klass and Others*, para. 31, para. 69; judgment of 26 October 2000, *Kudla*, para. 151.

[10]   Judgment of 26 October 2000, *Kudla*, para. 151. See also judgment of 21 February 1986, *James and Others*, para. 86; and judgment of 26 March 1987, *Leander*, para. 79.

[11]   Judgment of 26 October 2000, *Kudla*, para. 152.

[12]   See, for example, decision of 31 August 2004, *Toimi*.

derogable nature, such as the right to life and the freedom from torture or other forms of ill-treatment.

32.2.3 MEANING OF THE WORDS 'ARE VIOLATED' AND 'HAS BEEN COMMITTED'

The words 'are violated' and 'has been committed' (in French, 'ont été violés' and 'aurait été commise') literally denote that a violation of a substantive right or freedom of the Convention has occurred or has been established. However, such interpretation would run afoul of the Convention's underlying objective of establishing an international supervisory system, depriving Article 13 of its meaning, as the very establishment of a violation by a national tribunal may suggest that the applicant has had an effective remedy in the national system. The Court has enunciated that this phrase should be interpreted as "guaranteeing an 'effective remedy before a national authority' to everyone who *claims* that his rights and freedoms under the Convention have been violated".[13]

The approach of the Strasbourg organs has been to shift their focus from the literal construction of the phrase 'are violated' and 'has been committed', to the examination of the two following substantive issues: firstly, the question of the scope of application *ratione materiae* of a claimed right, examining whether the principal complaint as to a substantive right falls within the scope of the Convention;[14] and secondly, the analysis of the arguability of the principal complaint, as discussed below. Even if the Court has found no violation of a substantive right, the Contracting State remains obliged to provide an effective remedy for the examination of the alleged violation. In that sense, while being invoked only in conjunction with one of the other Convention rights, Article 13 embodies an independent right.

32.3 THE ARGUABILITY TEST (*LE CARACTÈRE 'DÉFENDABLE'*)

32.3.1 MEANING

According to the case law, where an individual has an 'arguable claim' to be a victim of a breach of the Convention rights, national authorities must provide him with a

---

13   Judgment of 6 September 1978, *Klass and Others*, para. 64 (emphasis added).
14   Judgment of 21 October 1997, *Pierre-Bloch*, paras 62-64; decision of 8 December 1997, *Kaukonen*, D&R 91-A (1997), p. 14; decision of 23 September 2004, *Vjekoslav Baneković*.

remedy that is capable of determining his claim and, if appropriate, of securing redress.[15] The arguability test, which the Court has developed since the *Silver* case,[16] has not been fully elaborated in the case law. The approach of the Strasbourg organs is to avoid an abstract definition of the notion of arguability[17] and to examine this notion on a case-by-case basis, with special regard to the particular facts and the nature of the legal issues raised.[18] A close examination of the case law provides some guidelines for the meaning of this test. The Strasbourg organs have repeatedly emphasised that Article 13 does not require a remedy in domestic law to be established in relation to *any* alleged grievance of a Convention right, irrespective of how unmeritorious such a grievance may be.[19] In *Boyle and Rice* the Commission defined the arguability test as requiring that a claim "only needs to raise a Convention issue which merits further examination".[20]

32.3.2   COMPARISON WITH THE NOTION OF MANIFESTLY ILL-FOUNDED

The arguability test, which requires assessment of the substance of claims, is closely related to the manifest ill-foundedness test, which is used to screen frivolous cases at the admissibility stage. In the *Boyle and Rice* Case the Court held that the notion of non-arguability is not the same as manifest ill-foundedness, suggesting that a complaint declared manifestly ill-founded may retain arguability. Invoking the judgment in the *Airey* Case,[21] in which the notion of manifest ill-foundedness was equated to the absence of even a *prima facie* case,[22] the Court conceded that "it is difficult to

---

15   See, for instance, judgment of 25 March 1983, *Silver and Others*, para. 113; judgment of 26 March 1987, *Leander*, para. 77; judgment of 19 February 1998, *Kaya*, para. 106; and judgment of 26 October 2000, *Kudla*, para. 157.

16   Judgment of 25 March 1983, *Silver and Others*, para. 114. A rudimentary form of this test was recognized in the earlier case of *Klass and Others*, judgment of 6 September 1978, para. 64, in which the Court held that "Article 13 (...) requires that where an individual considers himself to have been prejudiced by a measure allegedly in breach of the Convention, he should have a remedy before a national authority in order both to have his claim decided and, if appropriate, to obtain redress".

17   Judgment of 27 April 1988, *Boyle and Rice*, para. 55; and judgment of 21 June 1988, *Plattform 'Ärzte für das Leben'*, para. 27.

18   *Ibidem.*

19   Judgment of 27 April 1988, *Boyle and Rice*, para. 52.

20   The Commission's position before the Court in judgment of 27 April 1988, *Boyle and Rice*, para. 53.

21   Judgment of 9 October 1979, para. 18.

22   Judgment of 27 April 1988, *Boyle and Rice*, para. 54.

conceive how a claim that is 'manifestly ill-founded' can nevertheless be 'arguable', and vice versa".[23]

The confusion as to the two concepts has been compounded by the fact that though both notions call for examinations of the merit of the claim, their operational spheres differ, with the notion of manifest ill-foundedness appearing at the admissibility stage and the arguability test applied at the merit phase. It is submitted that the notion of arguability must be distinguished from that of manifestly ill-founded in that the admissibility decisions as to the latter concept are not confined to determining whether or not the applicant has made a *prima facie* case, but cover a fully-fledged review of the merits. However, analysis of the case law suggests that while the possibility of discrepancy between the two concepts is not ruled out, this is very unlikely in view of the Court's deference to the reasoning of an admissibility decision.[24]

In order to better grasp this issue, it is essential to carry out closer examinations of the approaches followed by the Commission and the Court in two marked cases: the *Boyle and Rice* Case and the *Powell and Rayner* Case. In the *Boyle and Rice* Case the Commission's delegate submitted that the concept of manifestly ill-founded under former Article 27(2) entailed a "spectrum of standards that encompassed but ranged beyond absence of arguability", suggesting that the threshold of this concept can be set higher than that of arguability under Article 13.[25] The Court stressed that when evaluating the complaints under Article 13, it needs to take the 'arguability' or not of the claims of the violation of the substantive provisions into account, and noted that the Commission's admissibility decision as to the underlying claims and the reasoning therein can form a 'significant'[26] or 'useful',[27] if not decisive, indication as to the arguable character of the claims for the purpose of Article 13.[28] The methodology in the *Boyle and Rice* judgment suggests that while allowing the possibility of setting the threshold of manifestly ill-founded under Article 35 differently from that of arguability under Article 13, the admissibility decision based on the former notion can exert considerable influence on the appraisal of the latter.

---

[23] Judgment of 27 April 1988, *Boyle and Rice*, para. 54. In this regard, the Court recalled the *Airey* case in which it found that the rejection of a complaint as 'manifestly ill founded, amounted to a decision that 'there is not even a *prima facie* case against the respondent State' (judgment of 9 October 1979, para. 18). See also the respondent State's submission in: judgment of 21 June 1988, *Plattform 'Ärzte für das Leben'*, para. 26.

[24] See, for instance, judgment of 21 February 1990, *Powell and Rayner*, para. 33.

[25] The Delegate of the Commission added that "to be arguable a claim '*only* needs to raise a Convention issue which merits further examination', whereas a conclusion that a complaint is manifestly ill founded may be reached after *considerable* written and oral argument" (emphasis added), judgment of 27 April 1988, *Boyle and Others*, para. 53.

[26] *Ibidem*, para. 54.

[27] Judgment of 21 June 1988, *Plattform 'Ärzte für das Leben'*, para. 27.

[28] Judgment of 27 April 1988, *Boyle and Rice*, para. 54; and Judgment of 21 June 1988, *Plattform 'Ärzte für das Leben'*, para. 27.

In the subsequent *Powell and Rayner* Case the majority of the Commission adhered to its position in the *Boyle and Rice* Case, drawing a distinction between the notion of 'manifest ill-foundedness' and the absence of 'arguability', and recognising the possibility that the threshold of the former notion could go higher than that of the latter notion. They opined that it was implicit in the Commission's established case law that the term 'manifestly ill-founded' extends further than the literal meaning of the word 'manifestly' would suggest at first reading, and that some serious claims might give rise to a *prima facie* issue but, after 'full examination' at the admissibility stage, ultimately be rejected as manifestly ill-founded notwithstanding their arguable character.[29] The respondent State and the minority of the Commission found it inconsistent that a substantive claim of violation was at one and the same time 'manifestly ill-founded' under ex Article 27(2) and 'arguable' under Article 13.[30]

The Court, in turn, seems to have felt need to clarify and settle its hitherto ambiguous position on the matter. After adverting to its *Boyle and Rice* judgment, in which the Court conceded the incongruency of recognising different standards for the two notions at issue,[31] the Court held: "Furthermore, Article 13 and Article 27(2) (...) are concerned, within their respective spheres, with the availability of remedies for the enforcement of the same Convention rights and freedoms. The coherence of this dual system of enforcement is at risk of being undermined if Article 13 (...) is interpreted as requiring national law to make available an 'effective remedy' for a grievance classified under Article 27(2) (...) as being so weak as not to warrant examination on its merits at international level. Whatever threshold the Commission has set in its case law for declaring claims 'manifestly ill-founded' under Article 27(2), in principle it should set the same threshold in regard to the parallel notion of 'arguability' under Article 13."[32] This paragraph, which cautions the potential discrepancy of the standard of the two comparable concepts, indicates a departure from the Court's subtle approach in its *Boyle and Rice* judgment which, albeit with circumspection, recognised possibly distinct thresholds for the two concepts. The Court's reasoning in its *Powell and Rayner* judgment demonstrates that it rejected the Commission's pattern of holding claims to be arguable under Article 13, despite their 'manifestly ill-founded' character under the principal complaint. The *Powell and Rayner* judgment suggests that the Court has become more convinced of the need to apply the same threshold to the two concepts 'in principle'.

Such inference can be reinforced by another statement in the same judgment. The Court observed that the determination of arguability for the purposes of Article 13

---

[29]   Report of 19 January 1989, para. 59.
[30]   See the judgment of 21 February 1990, para. 32.
[31]   Judgment of 27 April 1988, para. 54.
[32]   Judgment of 21 February 1990, *Powell and Rayner*, para. 33.

requires the examinations of the particular facts and the nature of the legal issues, "notably in the light of the Commission's admissibility decisions and the reasoning contained therein", but that "a claim is not necessarily rendered arguable because, before rejecting it as inadmissible, the Commission has devoted careful consideration to it and to its underlying facts."[33] This statement would imply that the process of examinations, however lengthy and thorough it may be, matters less than the result that the claim is declared inadmissible as being manifestly ill-founded. Declaring a complaint inadmissible by reference to the notion of manifest ill-foundedness would virtually exclude the claim's being arguable for the purpose of Article 13 and prevent the notion of arguability having a threshold different from that of manifest ill-foundedness. It is odd that after a detailed review of Article 8 claims, the Court was quick to conclude that there was 'no arguable claim' of violation of Article 8,[34] denying the basis for the entitlement to a remedy under Article 13.[35] The Court's approach should again mark a stark contrast to the Commission's stance in the relevant case. In relation to Mr Rayner's claims, the Commission defended its finding of a violation of Article 13 on the ground that "the 'careful consideration' which had had to be given to Mr Rayner's claim under Article 8 (…) at the admissibility stage and the facts underlying it persuaded the Commission that it was an arguable claim for the purposes of Article 13".[36]

In the subsequent *Plattform 'Ärzte für das Leben'* Case the Court followed its methodology of the *Powell and Rayner* Case. It engaged in meticulous examinations of the question of arguability under Article 13 with respect to the implied positive obligations on a respondent State to take 'reasonable and appropriate measures' so as to protect a public demonstration from a counter-demonstration under Article 11. While the Court found the Austrian authorities to have taken such necessary protective measures, it is again striking that its own lengthy discussions on this question did not make the applicant organisation's claim under Article 11 arguable for the purposes of Article 13.[37] By subsuming the arguability test into the assessment of a substantive provision with a limitation clause, the Court set a considerably high threshold for applying this test. The Court's approach leaves doubt as to whether that threshold was made contingent on violation of a substantive right, with the arguability test mixed up with the question of a violation of a substantive provision (Article 11).

---

[33] Judgment of 21 February 1990, para. 33. See also judgment of 27 April 1988, *Boyle and Rice*, paras 68-76, and 79-83; and judgment of 21 June 1988, *Plattform 'Ärzte für das Leben'*, paras 28-39.

[34] The Court found that there was 'no serious ground' for holding that the policy approach or the content of regulatory measures breached either positive or negative obligations of Article 8: judgment of 21 February 1990, *Powell and Rayner*, paras 43-45.

[35] *Ibidem*, para. 46.

[36] *Ibidem*, para. 38.

[37] Judgment of 21 June 1988, in particular paras 34-39.

Since the new supervisory system has come into operation, the Committee of three judges entrusted with screening the cases at the admissibility stage has followed the Court's approach in the *Powell and Rayner* Case,[38] recognising the interlocking relationship between the two concepts in question. When a complaint under a substantive right is declared manifestly ill-founded, the Court tends to deny the arguability of that complaint under Article 13 on the basis of the same reasoning, rendering Article 13 inapplicable.[39]

32.3.3   COMPARISON WITH THE 'GENUINE AND SERIOUS' NATURE OF A CLAIM UNDER ARTICLE 6(1)

The standard of arguability may also be compared with the test of the 'genuine and serious' nature of a claim, which needs to be demonstrated to make Article 6(1) applicable. In the context of Article 6(1) the Court has emphasised that the applicability of this provision requires, *inter alia*, that the dispute in question be 'genuine and serious', which may be related to the existence of a right or to its scope and the manner of its exercise.[40] The Court has held that a claim submitted to a domestic tribunal can be presumed to be both 'genuine and serious', except in case of clear indications to the contrary, as in the case of the claim that is frivolous or vexatious, or lacking in foundation.[41] It is this requirement of a 'genuine and serious' nature of the dispute that raises a question whether its threshold is comparable to that of arguability under Article 13. Two differences between the nature of disputes under Article 6(1) and the nature of complaints under Article 13 must be highlighted. First, Article 6(1) concerns a dispute over any civil right or obligation, the category of which naturally goes beyond the Convention rights. Second, Article 6(1) concerns a dispute that must be raised before a domestic tribunal, whereas a remedy under Article 13 does not have to be judicial in the strict sense. Bearing in mind these differences, one can note that both the literal construction of the 'genuine and serious' nature of the claim and the thorough manner in which the Court examines the genuine and serious nature of a

---

[38]   Judgment of 21 February 1990, para. 33.

[39]   See, for instance, decision of 5 October 2004, *Igor Vrabec*; decision of 28 September 2004, *Milan Šulva*; and decision of 28 September 2004, *Koray Düzgören* (in relation to Article 8 and Article 1 of Protocol No. I).

[40]   See, for instance, judgment of 28 June 1990, *Skärby*, para. 27; judgment of 19 April 1993, *Kraska*, para. 24; judgment of 25 November 1993, *Zander*, para. 22; judgment of 19 July 1995, *Kerojärvi*, para. 32; and judgment of 21 November 1995, *Acquaviva*, para. 46.

[41]   Judgment of 1 July 1997, *Rolf Gustafson*, para. 39; and decision of 16 March 2004, *Törmälä and Others*.

dispute over a civil right,[42] suggest that its threshold may be higher than that of arguability under Article 13.

32.4 THE REQUIREMENT OF EFFECTIVENESS

Prior to undertaking detailed examinations of what specific elements the notion of effectiveness has yielded in the development of the case law under Article 13, this sub-section provides two preliminary observations. First, the 'authority' before which an effective remedy must be available within the meaning of Article 13 need not be a judicial authority but, if it is not, both the powers and the procedural guarantees that it affords are considered as 'relevant' factors for determining the effectiveness or not of the remedy at issue.[43] Second, when ascertaining effectiveness of remedies, the Strasbourg organs have allowed a cumulative evaluation in favour of national authorities in that although no single remedy may itself entirely satisfy the requirements of Article 13, the aggregate of remedies provided for under domestic law may do so.[44]

In order to flesh out the substance of the requirements under Article 13 the Court has consistently invoked the principle of effective protection, which serves as one of the 'constitutional' underlying principles of the Convention. The application of this principle under Article 13 suggests that the exercise of domestic remedies must not be unjustifiably hindered by acts or omissions of the authorities of the respondent State.[45] Further, the notion of effectiveness is construed as ensuring either the prevention of the alleged violation, or the provision of adequate redress, including compensation, for a victim of a violation.[46] In the case of complaints of the length of proceedings, such alternative nature of Article 13 requirements demands that remedies must be capable either of expediting a decision by the courts, or of providing the litigant with adequate redress for delays in proceedings.[47]

---

[42]   See, for instance, judgment of 1 July 1997, *Rolf Gustafson*, para. 39.

[43]   Judgment of 6 September 1978, *Klass and Others*, para. 67; judgment, *Silver and Others*, para. 113; judgment of 26 March 1987, *Leander*, para. 77; judgment of 26 October 2000, *Kudla*, para. 157; and decision of 31 August 2004, *Toimi*.

[44]   See, for instance, judgment of 25 March 1983, *Silver and Others*, para. 113; judgment of 26 March 197, *Leander*, para. 77; judgment of 15 November 1996, *Chahal*, para. 145; judgment of 26 October 2000, *Kudla*, para. 157; and decision of 31 August 2004, *Toimi*.

[45]   Judgment of 18 December 1996, *Aksoy*, para. 95; judgment of 25 September 1997, *Aydin*, para. 103; judgment of 19 February 1998, *Kaya*, para. 89; judgment of 27 June 2000, *Ilhan*, para. 97; judgment of 26 October 2000, *Kudla*, para. 157; judgment of 17 February 2004, *İpek*, para. 197; judgment of 8 April 2004, *Özalp and Others*, para. 59; judgment of 30 January 2001, *Dulaş*, para. 65; judgment of 24 July 2003, *Yöyler*, para. 87; and judgment of 1 June 2004, *Altun*, para. 70.

[46]   See, for instance, judgment of 26 October 2000, *Kudla*, paras 158; and decision of 31 August 2004, *Toimi*.

[47]   Judgment of 26 October 2000, *Kudla*, para. 159.

The evolution of effective investigations obligations under Articles 2 and 3 in the case law since the 1990s has provided an impetus for the Court to clarify the corresponding requirement of effective investigations under Article 13. In particular, the parallel relationship between the procedural limb of obligations under Article 2 and Article 13 is readily discernible in the Court's methodology. In order to obtain a useful insight into the notion of effectiveness under Article 13, it is necessary to make brief discussions on the effective investigations requirement under Article 2. Since the mid-1990s the Court has elaborated upon the requirement of effective investigations under Article 2. For inquiries into an alleged unlawful killing by State agents to be effective for the purposes of Article 2, several subsidiary requirements must be complied with. The first requirement is related to institutional elements, demanding that the persons responsible for and conducting the investigation must be independent from those implicated in the alleged killing or disappearance.[48] The notion of independence goes beyond the mere absence of hierarchical or institutional connection, calling for 'practical independence'.[49] This requirement is purported to bolster the objective nature of inquiries and the public confidence in their legitimacy.[50] Second, the notion of effectiveness is broadened to include procedural elements, requiring not only the possible determination of the lawfulness of the force used in the impugned fatal incident but also the identification and punishment of those responsible.[51] On this matter the Court stressed that while this investigative obligation is not that of result, but of means, the procedural duties must be capable of securing the necessary evidence to determine the cause of death or the responsible person,[52] by means of, *inter alia*, eye witness testimony,[53] forensic tests, ballistic examinations of bullets and autopsy.[54] The third subsidiary requirement implicit in the procedural/investigative limb of positive duties under Article 2 is that of promptness and reasonable expedition.[55] This

---

[48] Judgment of 27 July 1998, *Güleç*, paras 81-82; and judgment of 20 May 1999, *Oğur*, paras 91-92; judgment of 4 May 2001, *Kelly and Others*, para. 114; judgment of 18 June 2002, *Orhan*, para. 348; and judgment of 17 February 2004, *İpek*, para. 170.

[49] Judgment of 28 July 1998, *Ergi*, paras 83-84; and judgment of 4 May 2001, *Kelly and Others*, para. 95.

[50] A. Mowbray, *The Development of Positive Obligations under the European Convention on Human Rights by the European Court of Human Rights*, (Oxford: Hart, 2004), at 32-33.

[51] Judgment of 20 May 1999, *Oğur*, para. 88; judgment of 4 May 2001, *Kelly and Others*, para. 96; judgment of 17 February 2004, *İpek*, para. 170.

[52] Judgment of 17 February 2004, *İpek*, para. 170.

[53] For witnesses, see judgment of 8 July 1999, *Tanrikulu*, para. 109; judgment of 27 July 1998, *Güleç*, para. 82; judgment of 10 October 2000, *Akkoç*, para. 98.

[54] Judgment of 19 February 1998, *Kaya*, para. 89; judgment of 28 March 2000, *Mahmut Kaya*, para. 104; judgment of 14 December 2000, *Gül*, para. 89; and judgment of 10 April 2001, *Tanli*, para. 150.

[55] Judgment of 2 September 1998, *Yaşa*, paras 102-104; judgment of 8 July 1999, *Çakici*, paras 80, 87, 106; judgment of 8 July 1999, *Tanrikulu*, para. 109; judgment of 28 March 2000, *Mahmut Kaya*, paras 106-107; judgment of 4 May 2001, *Kelly and Others*, para. 97; judgment of 17 February 2004, *İpek*, para. 171; and judgment of 20 April 2004, *Buldan*, para. 84.

---

requirement is of decisive importance to allegations of disappearance in detention,[56] but it also entails a public dimension in that by averting any appearance of collusion or tolerance of unlawful acts on the part of authorities, it serves to maintain public confidence in the rule of law.[57] Fourth, the Court demands "a sufficient element of public scrutiny of the investigation or its results", which is designed to "secure accountability in practice as well as in theory".[58] The absence of thorough and prompt investigations of alleged detention of family members in life-threatening or inhuman environments may involve a concurrent breach of the parallel, positive obligation to conduct effective investigations under Article 5.[59]

An influx of cases alleging killings, disappearances and ill-treatment committed by Turkish security forces in South-eastern Turkey, a region beset by terrorist/insurgent activities, prompted the Court to formulate a judicial strategy based on the combined strengths of effective investigation obligations under Articles 2 and/or 3 on the one hand, and Article 13 on the other. The Court has repeatedly emphasised that once an individual makes out an 'arguable claim' relating to the substance of the complaints under Articles 2 or/and 3, the notion of effectiveness under Article 13 entails the institutional and investigative/procedural elements parallel to those established under Article 2 or 3.

First, in relation to the institutional obligations under Article 13, the Court stressed the need not only of the absence of hierarchical or institutional connection but also of 'practical independence' of the persons responsible for carrying out the investigations into alleged killings or ill-treatment.[60] In *Khan v. UK*, which involved the complaint of the use of covert listening devices in breach of Article 8, the Court found that recourse to the Police Complaints Authority did not meet the requirement of effectiveness under Article 13 in that this authority lacked necessary independence, with its members subject to appointment, remuneration and even dismissal by the Secretary of State.[61]

Second, as regards the investigative/procedural limb, the effective inquiries requirement under Article 13 demands "a thorough and effective investigation" that can lead to the "identification and punishment of those responsible" for violations of Article 2 or 3 (killings, torture or other proscribed forms of ill-treatment, or destruction of

---

[56]   Judgment of 18 June 2002, *Orhan*, para. 336.
[57]   Judgment of 4 May 2001, *Kelly and Others*, para. 97; judgment of 4 May 2001, *McKerr*, paras 108-115; judgment of 10 July 2001, *Avşar*, paras 390-395; judgment of 17 February 2004, *İpek*, para. 171; and judgment of 20 April 2004, *Buldan*, para. 84.
[58]   Judgment of 4 May 2001, *Kelly and Others*, para. 98.
[59]   Judgment of 17 February 2004, *İpek*, paras 189-191.
[60]   Judgment of 20 May 1999, *Oğur*, para. 91; and judgment of 20 July 2004, *Mehmet Emin Yüksel*, para. 37.
[61]   Judgment of 12 May 2000, para. 47. See also report of 14 January 1998, *Govell*, paras 68-70.

properties) and that ensures "effective access" by the complainant or the relatives to the investigatory procedure.[62] The effectiveness of a remedy for the purpose of Article 13 does not hinge on the certainty of a favourable outcome for an applicant.[63] Such obligation is deemed as inherent both in the substantive right under Article 2 or 3, and in the general duty under Article 1 of the Convention. The Court held that while lacking a provision calling for the investigative duty akin to Article 12 of the 1984 United Nations Convention against Torture and Other Cruel, Inhuman or Degrading Treatment or Punishment, which imposes a duty to proceed to a 'prompt and impartial' investigation whenever there is a reasonable ground to believe that an act of torture has been committed, such an inquiry requirement is implicit in the notion of an 'effective remedy' under Article 13.[64] Third, the requirement of promptness and reasonable expedition is held as inherent in the notion of effectiveness, so as to call for prompt investigations into alleged killings or ill-treatment contrary to Article 2 or 3.[65] The Court emphasised that the requirement of promptness under Article 13 ensures both the maintenance of public confidence in the rule of law and the prevention of any appearance of collusion in, or tolerance of, unlawful acts.[66]

The requirement of effectiveness under Article 13 can be usefully compared with the meaning of 'remedies' under Article 35, which need to be exhausted before an applicant brings complaints before the Strasbourg Court. Recognising the 'close affinity' between Articles 13 and 35 (1) of the Convention,[67] the Court emphasised that the concept of 'effective' remedy as required under Article 35(1) corresponds to the alternative nature of the obligations under Article 13, namely, either the duty to provide

---

[62]   Judgment of 18 December 1996, *Aksoy*, para. 98; judgment of 25 September 1997, *Aydin*, para. 103; judgment of 19 February 1998, *Kaya*, paras 106-107; judgment of 8 January 2004, *Ayder and Others*, para. 98; judgment of 17 February 2004, *İpek*, para. 198; judgment of 30 March 2004, *Nuray Şen (No. 2)*, para. 191; judgment of 27 June 2000, *Salman*, para. 121; judgment of 8 April 2004, *Özalp and Others*, para. 60; judgment of 20 April 2004, *Buldan*, para. 103; judgment of 29 June 2004, *Doğan and Others*, para. 106; judgment of 20 July 2004, *Mehmet Emin Yüksel*, para. 36; judgment of 27 July 2004, *Ağdaş*, para. 109; judgment of 29 July 2004, *Mehmet Şirin Yilmaz*, para. 93. The Court applied the same dictum to cases involving destruction of home and possessions: judgment of 28 November 1997, *Menteş and Others*, para. 89; judgment of 1 June 2004, *Altun*, para. 71.

[63]   Judgment of 30 October 1991, *Vilvarajah and Others*, para. 122; and judgment of 20 July 2004, *Balogh*, para. 63. See also judgment of 25 March 1993, *Costello-Roberts*, paras 37-40.

[64]   Judgment of 18 December 1996, *Aksoy*, para. 98. Compare this reasoning with that in *Soering*, in which the Court, by way of effective and teleological construction, recognised the obligation of non-refoulement as inherent in Article 3: judgment of 7 July 1989, *Soering*, para. 88.

[65]   Judgment of 2 September 1998, *Yasa*, paras 102-104; judgment of 8 July 1999, *Çakici*, paras 80, 87, 105-106; judgment of 28 March 2000, *Mahmut Kaya*, paras 106-107; and judgment of 26 October 2004, *Çelik and İmret*, para. 59.

[66]   Judgment of 26 October 2004, *Çelik and İmret*, para. 55.

[67]   Judgment of 26 October 2000, *Kudla*, para. 152.

an alleged violation through expediting a decision by the courts, or the duty to provide adequate redress for delays.[68]

The Court has demonstrated that 'remedies' for addressing breaches of the Convention rights under Article 35 must meet the tests of accessibility and effectiveness. The construction of 'remedies' under Article 35 is guided by the principle of effective protection, according to which the existence of such domestic remedies must be "sufficiently certain not only in theory but also in practice".[69] The effective protection principle also entails significant implications for the distribution of the burden of proof, which is inherent in Article 35(1). The respondent State needs to establish that "the remedy was an effective one available in theory and in practice at the relevant time, that is to say, that it was accessible, was one which was capable of providing redress in respect of the applicant's complaints and offered reasonable prospects of success".[70]

The *Doğan* Case illustrates the closely intertwined relationship between issues of exhaustion of domestic remedies under Article 35(1) and the requirement to safeguard an effective remedy under Article 13. There the Court found that the forced eviction of the applicants from their village and the inability to return to their homes and livelihood constituted violations of Article 1 of Protocol No 1, and of Articles 8 and 13 of the Convention. In relation to the preliminary objection, the Court found that the Government failed to establish the availability of a remedy that could provide redress for the applicants' Convention complaints with reasonable prospects of success.[71] This failure was held to constitute a violation of Article 13 as well,[72] with no need for separate reasoning. Similarly, in the *Rachevi* Case the Court's appraisal of the exhaustion of domestic remedies in response to the preliminary objections under Article 35(1) was determinative of the conclusion that the remedies under the Bulgarian Code of Civil Procedure were not effective for the purposes of Article 13.[73]

---

[68]   Decision of 11 September 2002 (Grand Chamber), *Mifsud*, para. 17; and decision of 29 January 2004, *Davenport*. See also judgment of 26 October 2000, *Kudla*, para, 158.

[69]   See, *inter alia,* judgment of 20 February 1991, *Vernillo*, para. 27; judgment of 19 February 1998, *Dalia*, para. 38; decision of 11 September 2002 (Grand Chamber), *Mifsud,* para. 15; judgment of 16 September 1996, *Akdivar and Others*, para. 66; decision of 20 January 2004, *Pihlak,*; and judgment of 23 September 2004, *Rachevi*, para. 62.

[70]   Judgment of 20 February 1991, *Vernillo*, para. 27; judgment of 28 July 1999, *Selmouni*, para. 76; judgment of 13 July 2004, *Zynger,* para. 62; and judgment of 23 September 2004, *Rachevi*, para. 63.

[71]   Judgment of 29 June 2004, para. 110.

[72]   *Ibidem,* para. 164.

[73]   Judgment of 23 September 2004, paras 60-68 and 96-104. Note that in that case, the Court separated the question of the delays in proceedings under Article 6(1) from the question of the lack of effective procedures to complain of such delays. While as regards the former question the Court conducted a thorough examination on the basis of the established criteria, the Court regarded the latter question as more affiliated with the question of the exhaustion of local remedies, applying its conclusion on the latter to the issue under Article 13.

32.5   THE RELATIONSHIP BETWEEN ARTICLE 13 AND SUBSTANTIVE RIGHTS AND FREEDOMS

32.5.1   INTRODUCTION

In order to shed light on the relationship between Article 13 as an ancillary right and substantive provisions (Articles 2-12 and 14 of the Convention, as well as provisions of the Protocols), the following analysis focuses on three areas: the effective investigation obligations guaranteed under Article 13 and the concomitant obligations derived from non-derogable rights under Article 2 or 3; issues of the length of proceedings discussed under Article 5(4) or Article 6(1) in conjunction with Article 13; and whether or not to dispense with the need to find a separate violation of Article 8 or 10 in tandem with Article 13.

32.5.2   ARTICLE 13 AND ARTICLE 2 OR 3

When a grievance relates solely to a breach of a substantive duty, that is the duty not to commit torture or other proscribed form of ill treatment, it is incumbent on the Court to carry out a separate appraisal under Article 13.[74] In the case of an alleged breach of the procedural limb of the positive obligations under Article 2 or Article 3 (namely, the effective investigation obligations), there is an overlapping relationship between such obligation and the effectiveness requirements under Article 13. This would raise the question whether holding a respondent State to have breached the inquiries obligations under Article 2 or 3 would justify abandoning a separate examination and a finding of a breach of the corresponding obligations under Article 13, or conversely whether such obligations can be ascertained solely in the context of Article 13.

In admissibility decisions, the examinations of whether complaints under Article 2 or 3 are manifestly ill-founded under Article 35(3) are closely intertwined with examinations of Article 13. In case complaints under Article 2 or 3 are declared

---

[74]   See, for instance, judgment of 4 February 2003, *Lorsé and Others*, paras 74 and 87-96 (finding of a breach of a 'negative' obligation under Article 3, in respect of 'inhuman and degrading treatment at the 'Extra Security Institution', but no breach of effective investigation obligations under Article 13); and judgment of 26 November 2002, *E. and Others v. the United Kingdom*, paras 101, and 106-116 (breach of a 'positive' obligation, under Article 3, to protect the applicants from child abuse constituting inhuman and degrading treatment, and a breach of Article 13 in respect of the lack of means to obtain a determination of alleged failure of the local authorities to protect them). See also the judgment of 13 September 2005, *Ostrovar*, paras 90 and 112; judgment of 21 September 2005, *Dizman*, paras 85-86 and 99-100; judgment of 2 February 2006, *Iovchev*, paras 135-138 and 146-148; and judgment of 21 February 2006, *Doğanay*, paras 33 and 41-42.

admissible as well as well-founded, the Court does not engage in detailed examinations of the complaint under Article 13, declaring it admissible for the same reason.[75] Similarly, the combined assessment of the effective inquiries obligation under Article 2 or 3 and the corresponding duties under Article 13 can be seen in the course of examinations of the merits of complaints at the admissibility stage.[76] The Court may join the question of exhaustion of domestic remedies to the merits of the case on the basis that the grievances concerning effective investigations are closely connected with the substance of the complaints under the two provisions.[77] Surely, it is also conceivable that issues of non-exhaustion of local remedies in relation to substantive provisions other than Articles 2 and 3 can be joined to the merits of the complaint under Article 13,[78] but such possibility seems more pervasive in the context of Articles 2 and 3. Further, when examining the merits in their admissibility decisions, the Court seems to equate the notion of manifest ill-foundedness to that of 'arguability' under Article 13.[79] Such parallel move may be seen in the approach whereby the Court made the admissibility of the complaint as to the absence of compensation for alleged killing or ill-treatment under Article 13 dependent on the outcome of both substantive and procedural limbs of Article 2 or Article 3.[80]

Once the complaints are declared admissible, another array of salient features may be revealed at the merits phase. First, even if the Court has found the applicant to fail the test of proof beyond reasonable doubt as to a respondent State's implication in the disappearance, killing or ill-treatment under the heading of 'negative' obligations under Articles 2 and/or 3, this does not detract from the arguable nature of the complaint in relation to these substantive provisions for the purposes of Article 13.[81]

---

[75] See, for instance, decision of 30 March 2004, *Koval* (complaints relating to the conditions of detention, and insufficient medical treatment and assistance). For such combined assessment of the notion of manifest ill-foundedness under other substantive provisions and Article 13, see, for instance, decision of 18 March 2004, *Russian Conservative Party of Entrepreneurs, Zhukov and Vasilyev* (Article 3 of Protocol I and Article 13).

[76] See, for instance, decision of 19 October 2004, *Siddik Aslan, Yasin Aslan, Türkan Aslan and Nihari Aslan*.

[77] *Ibidem*. At the admissibility stage, the preliminary objections that criminal investigations into alleged killing or ill treatment were still pending, with the applicant's complaints being premature, are likely to be joined to the merits of the complaints: decision of 8 June 2004, *Afanasyev* (alleged ill-treatment).

[78] Decision of 5 February 2004, *Kirilova and Others, Metodeiva, Ilchev, Shoileva-Stambolova and Shoilev, (joined)* (the question of exhaustion of domestic remedies in relation to the complaints under Article 1 of Protocol I joined to the merits of the complaint under Article 13).

[79] See, for instance, decision of 15 January 2004, *Menesheva* (lack of an effective remedy against ill-treatment); decision of 19 October 2004, *Siddik Aslan, Yasin Aslan, Türkan Aslan and Nihari Aslan*.

[80] Decision of 8 June 2004, *Afanasyev*.

[81] See, for instance, judgment of 18 June 2002, *Orhan*, para. 386; judgment of 19 February 1998, *Kaya*, pp. 330-31, para. 107; and judgment of 2 September 1998, *Yaşa*, para. 113; judgment of 15 January 2004, *Tekdağ*, para. 97; judgment of 30 March 2004, *Nuray Şen (No. 2)*, para. 192; judgment of 20 April 2004, *Buldan*, para. 104; judgment of 27 July 2004, *Ağdaş*, para. 110. This principle can be deduced from the Court's approach in judgment of 27 April 1988, *Boyle and Rice*, para. 52.

This can be readily explained by the fact that the standard of evidence beyond reasonable doubt[82] is much more onerous than the more 'lax' notion of arguability. Conversely, the 'arguable' nature of grievances concerning alleged killing, disappearance or ill-treatment can be *ipso facto* assumed, once such grievances are found to constitute a violation of Article 2 or 3 of the Convention.[83] Second, according to the Court's reasoning, the scope of positive obligations under Article 13 hinges on the nature and gravity of the interference complained of under the Convention rights, especially the nature of the rights guaranteed under Articles 2 and 3.[84] The non-derogable nature of Articles 2 and 3 rights are more susceptible to a separate and stringent appraisal of the requirements of Article 13 than in instances involving other provisions.[85]

Third, the Court has stated that the requirements of Article 13 are 'broader' than the obligation of investigation imposed by Article 2.[86] This dictum brings us back to the question whether finding a breach of a duty to mount an effective investigation under Article 2 would necessarily entail a concurrent violation of Article 13, or whether such a finding would make a separate examination under Article 13 redundant. The Court has more or less consistently[87] shown a willingness to find concurrent violations

---

[82]   Note that this standard, while being suitable for criminal proceedings, is criticized for being too harsh in a discrimination context. See the applicants' submissions under Article 14 in: judgment of 26 February 2004, *Nachova and Others*, para. 153.

[83]   Judgment of 30 January 2001, *Dulaş*, para. 67; judgment of 1 June 2004, *Altun*, para. 72. This dictum is based upon an *a contrario* interpretation that was developed in judgment of 27 April 1988, *Boyle and Rice*, para. 52, and the cases concerning killing: judgment of 19 February 1998, *Kaya*, para. 107, and the judgment of 2 September 1998, *Yaşa*, para. 113.

[84]   Judgment of 15 November 1996, *Chahal*, paras 150-51; judgment of 18 December 1996, *Aksoy*, para. 95; judgment of 25 September 1997, *Aydin*, para. 103; and judgment of 19 February 1998, *Kaya*, para. 89; judgment of 15 January 2004, *Tekdağ*, para. 95; and judgment of 8 April 2004, *Özalp and Others*, para. 60.
     See also judgment of 28 November 1997, *Menteş and Others*, para. 89 (in the context of Article 8).

[85]   Judgment of 19 February 1998, *Kaya*, para. 107; judgment of 15 January 2004, *Tekdağ*, para. 96. In the case of Article 3, while stressing the 'irreversible nature' of the harm that might occur, the Court demanded an 'independent and rigorous scrutiny' of a complaint of a 'real risk' that an applicant would be subjected to ill-treatment within the meaning of Article 3: See, *inter alia*, judgment of 11 July 2000, *Jabari*; and decision of 16 March 2004, *Kasem*.

[86]   Judgment of 19 February 1998, *Kaya*, para. 107; judgment of 27 June 2000, *Salman*, paras 104-109 and 123; judgment of 27 July 2004, *Ağdaş*, para. 111; judgment of 29 July 2004, *Mehmet Şirin Yilmaz*, para. 94. See also judgment of 18 June 2002, *Orhan*, para. 387; judgment of 28 March 2000, *Kiliç*, para. 93; judgment of 17 February 2004, *İpek*, para. 198; and judgment of 30 March 2004, *Nuray Şen (No. 2)*, para. 193.

[87]   So far, there exist only few cases in which the chamber held that the effective investigation obligation under Article 13 was absorbed into the same obligation under Article 2, and that a breach of the latter obligation was sufficient: judgment of 26 February 2004, *Nachova and Others*, paras 115-141 and 146; judgment of 20 December 2004, *Makavatzis*, paras 71-72, 78-79 and 86 (violation of both substantial and procedural limbs of Article 2); and judgment of 10 November 2005, *Ramsuhai and Others*, paras 407-408, 430-431 and 437-438 (violation only of a procedural limb under Article 2).

of Article 2 and Article 13.[88] The Court's methodology is not to engage in a detailed, separate assessment under Article 13, but to reiterate its findings concerning the lack of effective investigations under a substantive provision (Article 2 or 3) to justify its separate finding of a breach of Article 13.[89] In the *İpek* Case, in view of serious deficiencies of the investigations conducted by the relevant Turkish authorities, which consisted, *inter alia*, of the absence of independence of the body responsible for inquiries, the lack of due diligence and vigour in investigations, and the failure to seek evidence from eye-witnesses, the Court found a breach of the duty to engage in effective investigation under Article 2.[90] Such findings were automatically, and without any further separate examinations, translated into the finding of the absence of a thorough and effective investigation in breach of Article 13.[91] A similar approach can be discerned in other cases involving inadequate inquiries into the death of family members, with the Court holding such investigative defects as amounting to combined violations of Articles 2 and 13.[92]

The Court's policy remains obscure, however, in respect of the relationship between the requirement to mount an effective investigation into alleged ill-treatment under Article 3 and the corresponding requirement under Article 13.[93] The Court's methodology in respect of alleged violations of both Articles 3 and 13 is distinct from that established in the case of combined assessment of Articles 2 and 13, in that the Court may incorporate examinations of the procedural limb of Article 3 in the context of Article 13. Such a reasoning process has been established since the *Ilhan* judgment, in which the Grand Chamber found that the applicant's complaints concerning the lack of effective investigations by the authorities into the cause of his injuries fell to

---

[88] See, for instance, judgment of 19 February 1998, *Kaya*, para. 107; judgment of 27 June 2000, *Salman*, para. 123, judgment of 15 January 2004, *Tekdağ*, paras 98-99; judgment of 27 July 2004, *Ağdaş*, para. 111; judgment of 27 July 2004, *İkincisoy*, paras 76-80 and 119-126; judgment of 29 July 2004, *Mehmet Şirin Yilmaz*, para. 94.

[89] See, for instance, judgment of 19 February 1998, *Kaya*, paras 89-92 and 108; judgment of 29 July 2004, *Mehmet Şirin Yilmaz*, paras 80-87 and 94.

[90] Judgment of 17 February 2004, paras 173-177.

[91] *Ibidem*, paras 200-201.

[92] Apart from the *İpek* Case, which is discussed here, for cases involving such concurrent identification of breaches of Articles 2 and 13, see, for instance, judgment of 30 March 2004, *Nuray Şen (No. 2)*, paras 174-179 and 193-194; judgment of 8 April 2004, *Özalp and Others*, paras 43-47, and 62-65; judgment of 20 April 2004, *Buldan*, paras 85-90, 105-106.

[93] Under Article 13, the Court has established virtually the same principles as those that are applicable under Article 3. The Court held that "[w]here an individual has an arguable claim that he has been tortured or subjected to serious ill-treatment by agents of the State, the notion of an 'effective remedy' entails, in addition to the payment of compensation where appropriate, a thorough and effective investigation capable of leading to the identification and punishment of those responsible and including effective access for the complainant to the investigatory procedure": judgment of 18 December 1996, *Aksoy*, para. 98; judgment of 20 July 2004, *Mehmet Emin Yüksel*, para. 36; judgment of 27 June 2000, *Salman*, para. 121-122; and judgment of 27 July 2004, *İkincisoy*, para. 123.

be dealt with under Article 13.[94] The Court has asserted that in case of alleged breaches of the positive obligations to conduct effective inquiries under Article 3, the examinations of such procedural obligations can be dispensed with, stating that they are subsumed into the appraisal under Article 13.[95] The Chamber's approach in the subsequent case of *Mehmet Emin Yüksel* follows the methodology seen in *Ilhan*. The Chamber dispensed with a separate finding of Article 3 in respect of the absence of effective inquiries, holding that it was satisfied with the finding of a breach of the substantive obligation (to refrain from torture), and that the investigation requirement could be 'more appropriately' dealt with under Article 13.[96] However, in the more recent case of *Menesheva*, another chamber has departed from the Grand Chamber's methodology in *Ilhan* and identified a concurrent violation both of Article 13 and of the procedural limb of Article 3.[97]

Beyond the general and rather obscure statement in the *Ilhan* Case that "[w]hether it is appropriate or necessary to find a procedural breach of Article 3 will (…) depend on the circumstances of the particular case",[98] the Grand Chamber provided neither clear guidelines nor rationales for obliterating the need for separate appraisal and findings of a violation of the procedural/investigative limb of Article 3, in conjunction with Article 13. This question, which links the procedural duties of Article 3 and Article 13, is closely intertwined with the inconsistency of the approaches followed by the Court in relation to the question whether the finding of a substantive violation of Article 3 (breach of obligations not to commit torture or other maltreatment) can justify the exclusion of determining a breach of the effective investigation obligation under the same provision.[99] In the *Ilhan* Case the Grand Chamber failed to explain why issues of investigative obligations under Article 3 can be so differentiated from

---

[94]   Judgment of 27 June 2000 (Grand Chamber), *Ilhan*, paras 92-93.

[95]   Judgment of 28 March 2000, *Mahmut Kaya*, para. 120; judgment of 20 July 2004, *Mehmet Emin Yüksel*, para. 32; judgment of 20 July 2004, *Balogh*, para. 60 (in the latter case, while finding a violation of the substantive limb of Article 3, the Court was satisfied that the applicant had an effective remedy within the meaning of Article 13 in relation to his complaint under Article 3); and judgment of 26 October 2004, *Çelik and İmret*, para. 50.

[96]   Judgment of 20 July 2004, para. 32.

[97]   Judgment of 9 March 2006, paras 68 and 74. In that case, the chamber also found a breach of the substantive limb of Article 3 (paras 59-60).

[98]   Judgment of 27 June 2000 (Grand Chamber), para. 92.

[99]   On this matter, compare the Grand Chamber's refusal of a separate finding of the procedural limb under Article 3 in *Ilhan*, with inconsistent approaches disclosed by Chambers in judgment of 28 October 1998, *Assenov and Others*; judgment of 11 April 2000, *Sevtap Veznedaroglu*; judgment of 10 October 2000, *Satik and Others* (findings of violation of Article 3 in both substantive and procedural limbs); and judgment of 23 May 2001, *Denizci and Others*, (finding of inhuman treatment but no separate examination of effective inquiries under Article 3).

the comparable obligations under Article 2 as to exempt an independent finding of a violation under Article 3.[100]

32.5.3 ARTICLE 13 AND THE RIGHT TO PROCEEDINGS BEFORE A COURT UNDER ARTICLE 5(4) AND ARTICLE 5(5)

The Court has consistently asserted that in the case of deprivation of liberty and compensation for unlawful detention, paragraphs 4 and 5 of Article 5 constitute a *lex specialis* in relation to the more general requirements of Article 13.[101] At the admissibility level the policy of the Court is that, as in the case of Articles 2 and 3, once the complaints under Article 5(4) are declared admissible as being not manifestly ill-founded, the Court, for the same reason and without any separate examinations, tends to admit the complaint under Article 13.[102] However, on the merits phase the tendency is that the finding of a violation of the right to a prompt review of the lawfulness of the detention by a court under Article 5(4) is considered as sufficient to dispense with a separate examination under Article 13.[103] In *De Wilde, Ooms and Versyp* (*Vagrancy Cases*), where the vagrants arrested and brought before the police court complained of guarantees inferior to those recognized in criminal proceedings, the Court was satisfied to find a violation only of Article 5(4), to the exclusion of a separate appraisal under Article 13.[104] Similarly, in *De Jong, Baljet and Van den Brink* both the Commission and the Court, after having found a violation of Article 5(4), decided to abandon the examination of the alleged violation of Article 13 on the basis that Article 5(4) guarantees a right to proceedings before a 'court', which is considered as a *lex specialis* with respect to the general obligation under Article 13 to provide an effective remedy before an authority of unspecified status.[105] In *Brannigan and McBride* the Court ruled out the examinations under Article 13, holding that detainees could challenge the lawfulness of their detention by recourse to habeas corpus proceedings, as found in

---

[100] Evidently, when a grievance relates solely to a breach of substantive duty not to commit torture or other proscribed form of ill treatment, it is incumbent on the Court to carry out a separate appraisal under Article 13. See, for instance, judgment of 4 February 2003, *Lorsé and Others*, paras 74 and 87-96 (finding of inhuman and degrading treatment in breach of Article 3, but no violation of Article 13).

[101] Decision of 9 September 2004, *Stoichkov*, para. 5. As to the habeas corpus provision of Article 5(4), see also decision of 23 November 1999, *M.A. and M.M.* For the right to compensation under Article 5(5), see, for example, judgment of 29 May 1997, *Tsirlis and Kouloumpas*, para. 73.

[102] See, for instance, decision of 15 January 2004, *Menesheva*, (absence of effective remedies against the imposition of the 'administrative' detention); decision of 29 June 2004, *Falkovych*.

[103] See, for example, judgment of 22 June 2004, *Pavletić*, para. 100; judgment of 21 June 2005, *Kolanis*, paras 82 and 86; and judgment of 8 November 2005, *Gorshkov*, paras 46-47.

[104] Judgment of 18 June 1971, paras 74-80, and 95.

[105] Report of 11 October 1982, para. 32; and judgment of 22 May 1984, para. 60. See also judgment of 29 February 1988, *Bouamar*, para. 65.

the *Brogan* Case.[106] However, in his dissenting opinion Judge Walsh averred that the habeas corpus remedies, which depended on showing a breach of national laws, did not satisfy the requirements of Article 13, stating that the Court's judgment overlooked the fact that the arrested person was "held incommunicado and without legal assistance" within the crucial first forty-eight hours of detention.[107]

As with the complaints of concurrent violations of Articles 6(1) and 13 with respect to the delay in proceedings, the gist of complaints under Article 13 is specifically directed to the absence of an effective remedy, whether judicial or not, which would have allowed a complaint of the absence of a prompt judicial review to be heard. In that sense, a separate appraisal under Article 13 can hardly be considered as superfluous.[108]

32.5.4   ARTICLE 13 AND THE RIGHT OF ACCESS TO COURT UNDER ARTICLE 6

The Court has consistently held that Article 6 constitutes the *lex specialis* in relation to Article 13 and that the requirements under the latter provision are 'less strict than', and susceptible to absorption by, those of Article 6.[109] In case the Court reaches the conclusion that Article 6 is not violated in view of the absence of the determination of a 'civil right', a separate inquiry into a possible violation of Article 13 may be required. Article 13 grievances would relate specifically to the question of excessive length of proceedings concerning such putative, though rejected, civil rights. On the other hand, if a violation of Article 6 *has* been found, it may be questioned whether a further inquiry under Article 13 is superfluous, to the extent that the guarantees of the two provisions overlap or that the requirements of Article 13 are subordinate to those of Article 6. Even if the Court, after finding a violation of Article 6(1) with respect to effective access to a court and/or length of proceedings, carries out

---

[106]   Judgment of 26 May 1993, para. 76.

[107]   *Ibidem*, dissenting opinion of Judge Walsh, paras 12-15.

[108]   See, for instance, judgment of 27 July 2004, *İkincisoy*, in which the finding of violations both of Article 5(4) as regards the dilatory nature of a judicial remedy for determining lawfulness of detention under Article 5(4) and of Article 5(5) with respect to the absence of compensation for unlawful arrest or detention, did not stop the Court from making a separate appraisal under, and finding a violation of, Article 13.

[109]   Judgment of 9 October 1979, *Airey*, para. 35; judgment of 21 February 1975, *Golder*, para. 33; judgment of 23 September 1982, *Sporrong and Lönnroth*, para. 88; judgment of 8 July 1987, *W*, para. 86; judgment of 27 October 1987, *Pudas*, para. 43; judgment of 7 July 1989, *Tre Traktörer AB*, para. 51; judgment of 25 October 1989, *Allan Jacobsson (No. 1)*, para. 78; and judgment of 19 December 1989, *Kamasinski*, para. 110. For more recent cases, see, for instance, decision of 4 May 2004, *Ahlskog and Oy Maple House AB*; decision of 4 May 2004, *Ziliberberg*; and decision of 28 September 2004, *Krokstäde*.

examinations under Article 13, it may find no violation under Article 13.[110] In a number of cases, the Court abandoned the examination of the complaint under Article 13, on the ground that the requirements of Article 13 are absorbed by more stringent obligations under Article 6.[111] However, as some judges pointed out in their separate opinion,[112] the finding of a violation of Article 6 may precisely raise the question of whether against such a violation, namely, excessively lengthy proceedings, an effective remedy within the meaning of Article 13 was available.[113]

This 'absorption approach' cannot be assumed in relation to all procedural requirements of Article 6. The Court has held that the decision to dispense with a separate examination under Article 13 can be warranted in circumstances where a substantive right in relation to which the right to a fair trial under Article 6(1) is allegedly infringed concerns a 'civil right'.[114] The Court applied the same reasoning to cases where the complaints relate to the adequacy of an existing appellate or cassation 'criminal' procedure.[115]

---

[110]   For admissibility decisions, see, for instance, decision of 8 January 2004, *Užkurėlienė and Others*, (admissible as to the complaint under Article 6 of the non-execution of the Supreme Court judgment, but inadmissible as to the same complaint under Article 13); decision of 31 August 2004, *Toimi*, (admissible as to the complaints concerning effective access to a court and the length of proceedings under Article 6(1) but inadmissible with respect to an effective remedy requirement under Article 13).

[111]   See, *inter alia*, judgment of 23 September 1982, *Sporrong and Lönnroth*, para. 88; judgment of 25 March 1983, *Silver and Others*, para. 110; judgment of 28 June 1984, *Campbell and Fell*, para. 123; judgment of 8 July 1987, *O*, para. 69; judgment of 27 October 1987, *Pudas*, para. 43; and judgment of 23 September 1994, *Hokkanen*, para. 74.

[112]   In the joint separate opinion in *W. v. the United Kingdom*, Judges Pinheiro Farinha and De Meyer opined: "it was only with some hesitation that we concurred in the decision that it was not necessary to examine the case under Article 13 of the Convention. We are not quite sure that such examination was made superfluous by the finding of a violation … of the entitlement to a hearing by a tribunal within the meaning of Article 6, para. 1. Are the 'less strict' requirements of Article 13 truly 'absorbed' by those of Article 6, para. 1? Do these provisions really 'overlap'? It appears to us that the relationship between the right to be heard by a tribunal, within the meaning of Article 6, para. 1, and the right to an effective remedy before a national authority, within the meaning of Article 13, should be considered more thoroughly"; judgment of 8 July 1987, *W. v. the United Kingdom*, para. III. See also the partly dissenting opinion of Mr Schermers, joined by Mr Jörundsson, annexed to the report of the Commission in this case, A. 121, pp. 55-56.

[113]   Appl. 7987/77, *Company X v. Austria*, D&R 18, (1980), p. 31 (46). In such a case it will have to be a judicial remedy, since appeal to a non-judicial authority against an act or omission of a judicial organ would impair the independence of the court, which is guaranteed under Article 6. See the individual opinion of Commissioner Trechsel in report of 17 July 1980, *Kaplan v. the United Kingdom*, DR 21 (1981), p. 5 (37).

[114]   Judgment of 23 September 1982, *Sporrong and Lönnroth*, para. 88 (in contrast, the Commission found a separate violation of Article 13); judgment of 8 July 1987, *W v. the United Kingdom*, para. 86; judgment of 27 October 1987, *Pudas*, para. 43; judgment of 7 July 1989, *Tre Traktörer AB*, para. 51; judgment of 25 October 1989, *Allan Jacobsson*, para. 78 (the Commission dispensed with a separate finding under Article 13); and judgment of 19 December 1997, *Brualla Gómez de la Torre*, para. 41.

[115]   Judgment of 19 December 1989, *Kamasinski*, para. 110.

As regards the requirement of holding a trial within a reasonable time, in the *Kudla* Case the Court made a crucial departure from precedents, considering it necessary to make a further examination under Article 13, as distinct from the finding of a violation of Article 6(1). According to the Court the requirements of Article 13 should be considered as 'reinforcing' those of Article 6(1), rather than being absorbed by the obligation to prohibit inordinate delays in legal proceedings under Article 6(1).[116] In the *Kudla* Case the Court distinguished the complaints under the two headings, holding that while the complaints under Article 6(1) concerned criminal charges, the thrust of the applicant's complaints under Article 13 related to the unreasonable length of proceedings. In the previous cases of a comparable nature the Court, however, evaded a separate evaluation under Article 13 when it already found a breach of the 'reasonable time' requirement under Article 6(1).[117] The Court invoked institutional problems to justify the review of the case law. It pointed out that both the growing accumulation of applications concerning excessive delays in the administration of justice and the absence of domestic remedies for such delays in certain Member States[118] risked seriously undermining the rule of law.[119] The Court's wariness as to such systematic shortcomings is bolstered by the concern of judicial economy. Unless a violation of Article 13 is established to highlight the absence of domestic remedies to cure those institutional shortcomings, the Court will be inundated with complaints relating to the same matter. The thrust of argument for a separate appraisal under Article 13 is that there is no overlap between the complaint of the unreasonably dilatory nature of proceedings for determining civil rights and obligations or a criminal charge under Article 6(1) on one hand, and the grievance concerning the lack of an effective remedy to ventilate a complaint of such undue delays under Article 13 on the other.[120]

Since then, the Court's policy in respect of excessive length in proceedings is generally to follow the *Kudla* approach with the need to carry out a separate examination under Article 13.[121] At the admissibility level the general policy seems to be that when complaints of the absence of access to a court under Article 6(1) are declared

---

[116]   Judgment of 26 October 2000, *Kudla*, para. 152.
[117]   See, for instance, judgment of 26 February 1993, *Pizzetti*, para. 21; judgment of 7 December 1999, *Bouilly*, para. 27; and judgment of 25 January 2000, *Giuseppe Tripodi*, para. 15.
[118]   Judgment of 28 July 1999, *Bottazzi*, para. 22; judgment of 28 July 1999, *Di Mauro*, para. 23; judgment of 28 July 1999, *A.P. v. Italy*, para. 18; judgment of 28 July 1999, *Ferrari*, para. 21. See also the Committee of Ministers of the Council of Europe's Resolution DH (97) 336 of 11 July 1997 (Length of civil proceedings in Italy: supplementary measures of a general character).
[119]   Judgment of 26 October 2000, *Kudla*, para. 148.
[120]   *Ibidem*, para. 147.
[121]   Note, however, *Association Ekin*, in which the Court was satisfied with the finding of violations of Articles 10 and 6(1) with regard to the ban on the book at issue and the length of proceedings to review such a measure, finding it unnecessary to examine under Article 13 the question of absence of access to an urgent procedure before an administrative court: judgment of 17 July 2001, paras 60-62, 73 and 75. See also the judgment of 17 May 2005, *Horváthová*, paras 37 and 41.

admissible and well-founded, this would induce the Court to adopt the same conclusion under Article 13 without any separate examinations.[122] At the merits phase the Court is very likely to find concurrent breaches of both the 'reasonable time' requirement under Article 6(1) and the requirement to establish an 'effective remedy' within the meaning of Article 13 so as to enforce the rights under Article 6(1). This approach is seen not only in relation to the right to a 'hearing within a reasonable time',[123] but also in relation to the right to secure the execution of a judgment given by a court.[124] This methodology is characterised by the Court as one of adducing the findings under Article 6(1) to support the conclusion under Article 13 with little separate assessment.[125] In some instances, however, the Court felt need to engage in a thorough appraisal under Article 13, duly separating the length of proceedings under Article 6(1) from the absence of procedures to complain of such delays under Article 13. In this scenario the appraisal of the issues under Article 6(1) may have little bearing on issues under Article 13 beyond the preliminary question of arguability.[126]

The survey of the case law reveals another dimension of the Court's methodology, with the gravity of appraisal shifted to grievances under Article 13. In a manner diametrically opposed to the approach followed in the pre-*Kudla* decisions, in a number of Turkish cases alleging inadequacy of investigations, the Court suggested that the complaint of a violation of Article 6 can be absorbed into the examinations of the broader and more general obligations under Article 13, obliterating a separate assessment under Article 6. In *Kaya* the Court observed as follows: "the applicant's grievance under Article 6(1) of the Convention is inextricably bound up with his more general complaint concerning the manner in which the investigating authorities treated the death of his brother and the repercussions which this had on access to effective remedies which would help redress the grievances which he and the deceased's family harboured as a result of the killing. It is accordingly appropriate to examine the

---

[122] See, *inter alia*, decision of 15 January 2004, *Sukhorubchenko*; decision of 30 March 2004, *Jonasson*; and judgment of 27 July 2004, *Romashov*, paras 29-35. See also decision of 29 January 2004, *Grubišić*, (admissible as to complaints of restrictions on the right of access to a court under Article 6(1) and the right to an effective remedy under Article 13, which were raised in conjunction).

[123] See, for example, judgment of 13 July 2004, *Zynger*, paras 58 and 65.

[124] Judgment of 27 July 2004, *Romashov*, paras 42-47 and judgment of 27 September 2005, *"Amat-G" Ltd and Mebaghishvili*, paras 49-50. The right to have a final, binding judicial decision executed is recognized on the basis of the effective interpretation of Article 6(1): judgment of 19 March 1997, *Hornsby*, para. 40; and judgment of 27 July 2004, *Romashov*, para. 42.

[125] See, for instance, judgment of 29 January 2004, *Kormacheva*, paras 60-64; judgment of 27 April 2004, *E.O. and V.P.*, paras 83-86, and 97-98; judgment of 29 April 2004, *Plaksin*, paras 37-44, and 49-50. Contrast these with judgment of 13 July 2004, *Zynger*, where the Court undertook a relatively lengthy assessment in response to the Government's submissions under Article 13 (*ibidem*, paras 62-65).

[126] Judgment of 23 September 2004, *Rachevi*, para. 99. In that case, the Court's elaborate examinations of the effectiveness of domestic remedies under Article 35(1) in relation to the preliminary objections were decisive for the conclusion as to the issues of Article 13: *ibidem*, paras 60-68, and 96-104.

applicant's Article 6 complaint in relation to the more general obligation on Contracting States under Article 13 of the Convention to provide an effective remedy in respect of violations of the Convention including Article 2 thereof, which, it is to be noted, cannot be remedied exclusively through an award of compensation to the relatives of the victim."[127]

Such methodology is conspicuously seen in cases involving grievances as to the failure of national authorities to mount an effective criminal investigation into the death of a family member[128] or into the destruction of home and possessions.[129]

32.5.5   ARTICLE 13 AND THE RIGHTS UNDER ARTICLE 8

The relationship between Article 13 and Article 8 may provide a basis for surmising how the Strasbourg Court has dealt with the alleged concurrent violations of Article 13 and substantive rights of the Convention, other than non-derogable rights under Articles 2 and 3, or due process rights under Articles 5 and 6. The assessment of the case law reveals a certain unevenness in the Court's methodology. In most cases the Court followed an 'absorption approach', invoking a finding of a violation of a substantive right to justify the exclusion of a separate examination of a grievance under Article 13. Absence of an examination even in a cursory manner under Article 13 may give reason to think that in such circumstances the Court has reduced the independent character of Article 13 to the vanishing point.[130]

In the *Malone* Case, where the interception of postal and telephone communications as well as the release of information obtained from the 'metering' of telephones were found to contravene Article 8, the Court dispensed with the need to rule on the alleged breach of Article 13 without any further argument.[131] Such absorption approach was followed in a number of subsequent cases. In *X and Y v. the Netherlands* the Court justified the exclusion of a separate examination under Article 13 on the ground that its evaluation under Article 8 took into account the absence of adequate means of

---

[127]   Judgment of 19 February 1998, *Kaya*, para. 105. See also judgment of 29 June 2004, *Doğan and Others*, para. 123.

[128]   Judgment of 18 December 1996, *Aksoy*, paras 93-94; judgment of 25 September 1997, *Aydın*, paras 100-03; judgment of 19 February 1998, *Kaya*, para. 106; judgment of 8 April 2004, *Özalp and Others*, paras 54-55; judgment of 27 July 2004, *Ağdaş*, para. 108; and judgment of 27 July 2004, *İkincisoy*, paras 114 and 119-126.

[129]   Judgment of 1 June 2004, *Altun*, paras 66-67; and judgment of 26 October 2004, *Çaçan*, para. 75.

[130]   With respect to Articles 8 and 10, see also judgment of 24 September 1992, *Herczegfalvy*, paras 95-96.

[131]   Judgment of 2 August 1984, paras 90-91.

obtaining a remedy for Miss Y, a mentally handicapped victim of rape.[132] Similarly, in the *Herczegfalvy* Case the Court did not pursue the issue of the alleged Article 13 violation, stressing that it was sufficient to find violations of Articles 8 and 10 with respect to forced medical treatment and feeding, as well as to the refusal to send on the applicant's correspondence.[133]

Yet, in some cases the Court did not recoil from carrying out a separate appraisal, and even in a thorough manner. It is submitted that the ancillary, but autonomous, character of Article 13 demands a separate appraisal and finding under Article 13. An example of this approach has occasionally surfaced in the case law, albeit without guidelines as to when such concurrent finding was deemed necessary. In the *Campbell and Fell* Case the complaint under Article 8 was mainly directed to the two issues: the refusal to allow confidential correspondence by a prisoner with his lawyer and the restrictions on his personal correspondence. The fact that the Court found a violation of Article 8 in these respects[134] did not prevent the Court from examining the alleged violation of Article 13 on both counts.[135]

In more recent cases the Court showed a greater willingness to apply the methodology of pursuing separate appraisal, and such tendency can be exemplified, most notably, in two areas of complaints directed against English remedies under Article 8: intrusions into privacy of homosexuals in the army, and use of surveillance devices. On issues of homosexuals the Court justified its progressive construction of Article 8 in tandem with Article 13 on the basis of the emerging European consensus on more tolerant attitudes of homosexuality. In the *Smith and Grady* Case concerning the privacy of homosexuals in the army the Court, after finding a violation of Article 8, concluded that the English remedies, including judicial review proceedings, did not satisfy the requirement of effectiveness under Article 13.[136] As regards issues of secret surveillance, a series of complaints were directed to a legal loophole by reference to

---

[132]   Judgment of 26 March 1984, paras 35-36. See also the *Hokkanen* Case, in which the Court, while finding the non-enforcement of the applicant's right to access [to his daughter] for 3 years and five months to contravene Article 8, concurred with the Commission, considering it unnecessary to make a separate examination of the grievance under Article 13: judgment of 23 September 1994, paras 73-74.

[133]   Judgment of 24 September 1992, paras 95 and 96.

[134]   Judgment of 28 June 1984, paras 110 and 120.

[135]   *Ibidem,* paras 124-128 (violation of Article 13 on both accounts).

[136]   Judgment of 27 September 1999, paras 135-139. See also the subsequent case of judgment of 22 October 2002, *Beck, Copp and Bazeley,* para. 58. Compare these with *Christine Goodwin*, which involves encroachments on the right of transsexuals. There, the Court found a violation of Articles 8 and 12 in relation to the lack of legal recognition of the transsexual applicant's changed gender in the UK. As regards claims under Article 13, the Court did not outright reject a separate evaluation under this provision, albeit it did not find a breach of Article 13 on the basis that Article 13 does not call for a remedy against the state of domestic law through a requirement to incorporate the Convention. The Court held that since the Human Rights Act 1998 took effect on 2 October, 2000, the applicant could have availed herself of remedies before domestic courts: judgment of 11 July 2002, *Christine Goodwin*, paras 109-114.

Articles 8 and 13. In *Kahn* the finding of a violation of Article 8 in respect of the use of covert listening devices did not prevent the Court from thoroughly examining whether the remedies suggested by the United Kingdom government for ventilating the complaint of violation of Article 8 were effective.[137]

Even with regard to other types of grievances under Article 8 the case law of the Court does not seem to exclude the possibility of separate appraisal under Article 13.[138] Yet, beyond a series of complaints against English remedies, it is not certain whether the Court has now come to espouse the *general* policy of pursuing separate examinations under Article 13. The Court has failed to provide guidelines as to circumstances that would necessitate the concurrent examinations of Article 13 in tandem with Article 8, beyond its assertion that the scope of obligations under Article 13 depends on the nature of the rights at issue and the particular circumstances of the case. Such an approach can be contrasted to the Court's approach in cases involving alleged violations of Articles 10 and 13. The Court's methodology emerging from a much smaller number of relevant cases seems to be that the finding of a violation of Article 10 does not make it purposeless to engage in a separate appraisal under Article 13.[139] A similar approach was adopted as regards the allegation of concurrent violations of Articles 9 and 13.[140] However, in relation to an equally small number of cases alleging violations of Articles 11 and 13, the Court seems to be satisfied with a finding of a violation of Article 11, to the exclusion of a separate appraisal and finding under Article 13.[141]

---

[137]   Judgment of 12 May 2000, *Khan*, paras 28 and 47 (violation of Article 13 as well). See also the subsequent cases dealing with the use of surveillance measures: judgment of 5 November 2002, *Allan*, paras 36 and 55; judgment of 12 June 2003, *Chalkley*, paras 25 and 27 (in those two cases, the Government accepted the violations of Articles 8 and 13, following the judgment in *Kahn*.

[138]   In *Sabou and Pircalab*, the Court found a violation of Article 8 with respect to the complaint raised by the first applicant, a journalist, that he was condemned to detention by virtue of alleged defamation against a judge, and that he was also deprived of parental rights. This again, however, did not deter the Court from pursuing a separate appraisal of the absence of effective remedies and finding a violation of Article 13 taken in conjunction with Article 8: judgment of 28 September 2004, *Sabou and Pircalab*, paras 44-56.

[139]   See, for instance, judgment of 19 December 1994, *Vereinigung Demokratischer Soldaten Oesterreichs and Gubi*, A 302, paras 40 and 53 (violations of both Articles 10 and 13); judgment of 28 October 1999, *Wille*, paras 70, 76-78 (violations of both Articles 10 and 13); and judgment of 28 June 2001, *Vgt Verein gegen Tierfabriken*, paras 79-83 (violation of Article 10 but not of Article 13).

[140]   See, for instance, judgment of 13 December 2001, *Metropolitan Church of Bessarabia and Others* (concurrent violations of Articles 9 and 13); and judgment of 16 December 2004, *Supreme Holy Council of the Muslim Community* (finding of a violation of Article 9, and a separate appraisal under Article 13, albeit with no finding of a breach of the latter provision).

[141]   See, for instance, judgment of 13 August 1981, *Young, James and Webster*, paras 65 and 67. However, see Commission's Report of 10 January 1995, *Gustafsson*, as referred to, in: judgment of 25 April 1996, paras 43, 46 and 69 (the Court, while finding Article 11 to be applicable, concluded that there was violation neither of Article 11 nor of Article 13).

32.6 NOTWITHSTANDING THAT THE VIOLATION HAS BEEN COMMITTED BY PERSONS IN AN OFFICIAL CAPACITY

32.6.1 EXCLUSION OF IMMUNITIES AND IMPLICATIONS FOR DRITTWIRKUNG

From the words 'notwithstanding that the violation has been committed by persons acting in an official capacity' one can infer that the Convention purports to deny the legal effect of national laws providing to public officials immunity from responsibility of human rights violations under the Convention. Further, this wording may suggest the broader interpretation that an effective legal remedy within the meaning of Article 13 must also, and *a fortiori*, be furnished when the violation has been committed by a private individual, raising the possibility of the indirect *Drittwirkung* (third-party effect) of the Convention rights between citizens. It is possible to find the jurisprudential rationale for *Drittwirkung* to lie in the combined effect of the principle of effective protection and the general obligation to guarantee the rights and freedoms under Article 1 of the Convention. Yet, in view of the principle of subsidiarity underlying the application of Article 13, this possibility should be restricted to cases of positive obligations to protect individuals against risk of serious violations stemming from other individuals, as in the case of the duty to protect individuals against life-threatening risk under Article 2 or risk of ill-treatment under Article 3.

32.6.2 POSITION OF THE LEGISLATOR

As to the words 'persons acting in an official capacity', the Commission opined that this term did not include the legislator, on the ground that this would be tantamount to the requirement to establish a kind of judicial review of national legislation. According to the Commission, the words 'notwithstanding that the violation has been committed by persons acting in an official capacity' indicates "that the Article is concerned with individuals acting for the State".[142] The Court's position on this matter is consistent in asserting that national authorities are given a margin of appreciation in assessing the manner in which the Convention rights are secured, including as to the

---

[142] The Commission continued to observe as follows: "Even if these words are mainly directed to exclude any doctrine of immunity of State organs, they can be used as an element to show the scope of the Article. Article 13 does not relate to legislation and does not guarantee a remedy by which legislation could be controlled as to its conformity with the Convention"; report of 14 December 1979, *Young, James and Webster*, B. 39, (1984), p. 49. See also report of 17 July 1980, *Kaplan*, DR 21 (1981), p. 5 (36).

form of remedies in the case of an alleged breach of those rights, with no duty of incorporating the Convention into domestic law.[143] This means that Article 13 does not guarantee either a remedy that would allow a Contracting State's laws as such to be challenged before a national authority on the ground of being contrary to the Convention or equivalent domestic norms,[144] or a remedy that would make available a constitutional review allowing an individual to challenge the terms of subordinate legislation.[145] What matters most is that such remedies, whatever form may be secured in domestic legal order, must be able to enforce and claim non-compliance with the substance of the Convention rights and freedoms.[146]

In the *Boyle and Rice* Case the Court avoided addressing the general question as to the nature of the remedy required by Article 13 when the applicable national norms are themselves compatible with the substantive provisions of the Convention.[147] With specific regard to the English judicial review proceedings the old Court had found them to be an effective remedy in general.[148] Yet, later on the Court held that they did not

---

[143]   Judgment of 26 November 1991, *The Observer and Guardian*, para. 76. Judge Valticos, however, noted that States are under a duty to give effect to the Convention and that the obligation to give effect is often best fulfilled where the terms of the Convention are transposed into the domestic legal system: separate opinion of Judge Valticos, *ibid.*, p. 45. Note also the separate opinion of Judge De Meyer, joined by Pettiti, in which it is stated as follows: "The question whether a certain treaty is, or is not, 'incorporated into domestic law' (…) has no relevance when fundamental rights are concerned; these are of such a nature that it cannot be necessary to have them formally 'incorporated into domestic law' (…) the object and purpose of the European Convention on Human Rights was not to create, but to recognize rights which must be respected and protected even in the absence of any instrument of positive law. It has to be accepted that, everywhere in Europe, these rights 'bind the legislature, the executive and the judiciary, as directly applicable law' and as 'supreme law of the land (…) anything in the constitution or laws of any State to the contrary notwithstanding"; *ibidem*, p. 44.

[144]   See, for instance, judgment of 26 March 1987, *Leander*, para. 77; judgment of 21 February 1986, *James and Others*, para. 85; judgment of 9 December 1994, *Holy Monasteries*, para. 90; judgment of 23 September 1998, *A. v. the United Kingdom*, paras 112-113; and judgment of 27 May 2004, *Connors*, para. 109.

[145]   Judgment of 8 July 1986, *Lithgow and Others*, para. 206; and judgment of 27 April 1988, *Boyle and Rice*, para. 87.

[146]   See, *inter alia*, judgment of 21 February 1986, *James and Others*, para. 84; judgment of 8 July 1986, *Lithgow and Others*, para. 205; judgment of 27 April 1988, *Boyle and Rice*, para. 52; judgment of 15 November 1996, *Chahal*, para. 145; judgment of 18 December 1996, *Aksoy*, para. 95; judgment of 25 September 1997, *Aydin*, para. 103; judgment of 19 February 1998, *Kaya*, para. 89; and judgment of 15 January 2004, *Tekdağ*, para. 95.

[147]   Judgment of 27 April 1988, para. 87. In this regard, the Court referred to judgment of 25 March 1983, *Silver and Others*, para. 118; and judgment of 21 February 1987, *James and Others*, para. 86.

[148]   Judgment of 7 July 1989, *Soering*, paras 122-124. In *Vilvarajah and Others* the Court concluded that '[w]hile it is true that there are limitations to the powers of courts in judicial review proceedings…these powers, exercisable as they are by the highest tribunals in the land, do provide an effective degree of control over the decisions of the administrative authorities in asylum cases and are sufficient to satisfy the requirements of Article 13': judgment of 30 October 1991, para. 126. Note however, that Judges Walsh and Russo dissented on this point, arguing, *inter alia*, 'the claim of the U.K. Government that judicial review "controls" the decision of immigration authorities must be qualified, by the fact that in English law judicial review controls only the procedure and not the merits of the impugned decision'. They concluded that 'a national system which it is claimed provides an

satisfy the requirements of Article 13, with the test of 'Wednesbury unreasonableness' and irrationality[149] being placed much higher than justified by the principle of proportionality as understood in the Strasbourg case law.[150]

It must be noted that the Strasbourg organs have recognised that in certain circumstances a mere existence of a law as such may constitute a violation of Article 8 of the Convention without any specific application to alleged victims.[151] This means that in contrast to cases where applicants complain of specific measures, applicants claiming to be victims of infringement of their right by virtue of an impugned law in itself are excluded from raising the question of effective remedies under Article 13. Once such a law is applied to the alleged victim, the Court's willingness to review the effectiveness of remedies under Article 13 depends on whether or not it has found the law as such to be in conformity with the substantive provisions of the Convention, such as Articles 6 and 8. If this is the case, the Court tends to conclude that no violation of Article 13 occurred.[152] If not, the Court may heighten the standard of review under Article 13.[153]

---

effective remedy for a breach of the Convention and which excludes the competence to make a decision on the merits cannot meet the requirements of Article 13': *ibidem*, partly dissenting opinion of Judge Walsh, joined by Judge Russo, paras 1 and 3.

[149] *Associated Provincial Picture Houses Ltd*, [1948] 1 KB 223, *Per* Lord Greene M.R. at pp. 230, 233. In the judgment of Sir Thomas Bingham MR, the test of 'irrationality' applied in judicial review proceedings was described as follows: "a court was not entitled to interfere with the exercise of an administrative discretion on substantive grounds save where the court was satisfied that the decision was unreasonable in the sense that it was beyond the range of responses open to a reasonable decision-maker. In judging whether the decision-maker had exceeded this margin of appreciation, the human rights context was important, so that the more substantial the interference with human rights, the more the court would require by way of justification before it was satisfied that the decision was reasonable'; referred to in: judgment of 27 September 1999, *Smith and Grady*, para. 137. See also judgment of 28 January 2003, *Peck*, para. 99.

[150] See, among others, judgment of 27 September 1999, *Smith and Grady*, paras 136-139; and judgment of 28 January 2003, *Peck*, paras 105-107.

[151] See, for instance, judgment of 22 October 1981, *Dudgeon*; judgment of 26 October 1988, *Norris*; and judgment of 22 April 1993, *Modinos* (The mere existence of a law criminalizing private homosexual conduct between consenting adults was found to contravene the right to private life of homosexuals, who were recognised as potential victims, irrespective of whether the law has been applied to them).

[152] See judgment of 21 February 1986, *James and Others*, para. 86; and judgment of 8 July 1986, *Lithgow and Others*, para. 207.

[153] Judgment of 28 May 1985, *Abdulaziz, Cabales and Balkandali*, paras 92-93.

CHAPTER 33
PROHIBITION OF DISCRIMINATION
(Article 14)

REVISED BY AALT WILLEM HERINGA AND FRIED VAN HOOF

CONTENTS

33.1 TEXT OF ARTICLE 14

The enjoyment of the rights and freedoms set forth in this Convention shall be secured without discrimination on any ground such as sex, race, colour, language, religion, political or other opinion, national or social origin, association with a national minority, property, birth or other status.

33.2 INTRODUCTION

Like Article 13, Article 14 according to its formulation does not grant an independent right, in this case the right to freedom from discrimination. However, Protocol No. 12 has entered into force in 2004, containing an independent equality / non-discrimination clause.[1]

With Protocol No. 12 the Convention has caught up with the developments at the global level, where the elimination of discrimination has received and still receives a good deal of attention, as has been expressed in a number of treaties: the 1952 UN Convention on the Political Rights of Women, the 1951 and 1958 Conventions of the International Labour Organisation on Equal Remuneration and on Discrimination in Employment and Occupation respectively, the 1960 UNESCO Convention against Discrimination in Education, the 1965 UN Convention on the Elimination of All Forms of Racial Discrimination, the 1979 UN Convention on the Elimination of All Forms of Discrimination against Women, and last but not least Article 26 of the UN Covenant on Civil and Political Rights.

33.3 ACCESSORY CHARACTER

The case law of the Court concerning Article 14 presents a rather complex picture because of the necessary relationship between Article 14 and the other substantive Convention provisions and because of the inherent complex nature of questions related to non-discrimination and equality.

Two closely connected questions concerning the relationship between Article 14 and the rights and freedoms of Section I of the Convention and the Protocols are more or less interwoven in the case law. On the one hand, there is the question whether Article 14 has its own significance independently of the rights and freedoms protected in the Convention. On the other hand, there is the question whether, in relation to those rights and freedoms, Article 14 grants an autonomous or only an accessory protection, that is whether it can be applied only when any of those rights or freedoms has been violated. These questions have been answered by the Court in a standard formula, according to which "Article 14 complements the other substantive provisions of the Convention and the Protocols. It has no independent existence, since it has effect solely in relation to 'the enjoyment of the rights and freedoms' safeguarded by those provisions. Although the application of Article 14 does not necessarily presuppose a breach of those provisions – and to this extent it is autonomous – , there can be no

---

[1]   About this protocol see *supra*, Chapter 30.

room for its application unless the facts at issue fall within the ambit of one or more of the latter."[2]

This formula makes clear that Article 14 is not independent in the sense that there has to be at least some kind of relation with any of the rights and freedoms of the Convention; differential treatment in a field which falls outside the scope of the Convention cannot amount to a violation of Article 14. At the same time the case law referred to bears out that Article 14 is autonomous in the sense that its application does not require the simultaneous violation of one of the Convention's rights or freedoms.[3]

This autonomous character of Article 14 had been recognised earlier by the Court in the *Belgian Linguistic* Case, where it held as follows: "While it is true that this guarantee [*viz.* the one laid down in Article 14] has no independent existence in the sense that under the terms of Article 14 it relates solely to 'rights and freedoms set forth in the Convention', a measure which in itself is in conformity with the requirements of the Article enshrining the right or freedom in question may however infringe this Article when read in conjunction with Article 14 for the reason that it is of a discriminatory nature."[4]

In the *Thlimmenos* Case the Court showed its willingness to be generous in accepting the applicability of a substantive provisions in order to conclude that Article 14 is relevant. Under the facts of this case the applicant had been refused an appointment as an accountant for his being convicted of a felony. His felony had consisted of refusing to serve in the army on religious grounds. The Court noted "that the applicant was not appointed a chartered accountant as a result of his past conviction for insubor-

---

2   Judgment of 28 May 1985, *Abdulaziz, Cabales and Balkandali*, para. 71. *See* also the judgment of 28 November 1984, *Rasmussen*, para. 29; judgment of 23 November 1983, *Van der Mussele*, para. 43; judgment of 28 October 1987, *Inze*, para. 36; judgment of 23 October 1990, *Darby*, para. 30 (the duty to pay taxes falls within the field of application of Article 1 of Protocol No. 1); judgment of 18 July 1994, *Karlheinz Schmidt*, para. 22; judgment of 16 September 1996, *Gaygusuz*, para. 36; judgment of 21 February 1997, *Van Raalte*, para. 33; judgment of 24 February 1998, *Botta*, para. 39 (since Article 8 was not applicable, Article 14 did not apply).

3   In the judgment of 12 July 2001, *Prince Hans-Adam III of Liechtenstein*, para. 91, the Court seemed to require a violation of one of the substantive provisions. In the judgment of 27 June 2000, *Jewish Liturgical Association Cha'are Shalom Ve Tsedek*, para. 87, the Court also rejected the applicability of Article 14 because of a link between the absence of a violation of Article 9 and the therefore limited nature of the difference of treatment. These judgments seem to be exceptions to the general rule.

4   Judgment of 23 July 1968, para. 9 (of the operative part of the judgment). In later case law the Court took a similar view. In its judgment of 27 October 1975, *National Union of Belgian Police*, para. 44, it held: "Although the Court has found no violation of Article 11(1), it has to be ascertained whether the difference in treatment complained of by the applicant union contravenes Articles 11 and 14 taken together (...) A measure which in itself is in conformity with the requirements of the Article enshrining the right or freedom in question may therefore infringe this Article when read in conjunction with Article 14 for the reason that it is of a discriminatory nature". For the Court's view, see also the judgment of 6 February 1976, *Swedish Engine Drivers' Union*, and the judgment of 13 June 1979, *Marckx*.

dination consisting in his refusal to wear the military uniform. He was thus treated differently from the other persons who had applied for that post on the ground of his status as a convicted person. The Court considers that such difference of treatment does not generally come within the scope of Article 14 in so far as it relates to access to a particular profession, the right to freedom of profession not being guaranteed by the Convention. However, the applicant does not complain of the distinction that the rules governing access to the profession make between convicted persons and others. His complaint rather concerns the fact that in the application of the relevant law no distinction is made between persons convicted of offences committed exclusively because of their religious beliefs and persons convicted of other offences. (…) In essence, the applicant's argument amounts to saying that he is discriminated against in the exercise of his freedom of religion, as guaranteed by Article 9 of the Convention, in that he was treated like any other person convicted of a felony although his own conviction resulted from the very exercise of this freedom. Seen in this perspective, the Court accepts that the 'set of facts' complained of by the applicant (….) 'falls within the ambit of a Convention provision', namely Article 9."[5]

In the *Karlheinz Schmidt* Case the Court investigated the claim based upon Article 14 and Article 4(3)(d) after having established that the obligation to pay a financial contribution in lieu of service in the fire brigade fell within the scope of the latter provision. The Court held as follows: "Like the participants in the proceedings, the Court considers that compulsory fire service such as exists in Baden-Wurttemberg is one of the 'normal civic obligations' envisaged in Article 4 para. 3 (d). It observes further that the financial contribution which is payable – in lieu of service – is, according to the Federal Constitutional Court (...), a 'compensatory charge'. The Court therefore concludes that, on account of its close links with the obligation to serve, the obligation to pay also falls within the scope of Article 4 para. 3 (d). It follows that Article 14 read in conjunction with Article 4 para. 3 (d) applies."[6] According to the Court, Article 14 constitutes as it were "an integral part of each of the Articles laying down rights and freedoms".[7]

Sometimes the Court refrains from looking into Article 14 because it is of the opinion that the same guarantees are to be found in the 'main' provision of the Convention. This has been the case in respect of Article 6: "The Court judges it superfluous to examine the contested facts also under Article 14 since in the present

---

[5]   Judgment of 6 April 2000, para. 42. In the judgment of 27 July 2004, *Sidabras and Dziautas*, para. 50 the Court found that Article 8 in conjunction with Article 14 applied to the access to jobs in private employment.
[6]   Judgment of 18 July 1994, para. 23.
[7]   Judgment of 23 July 1968, *Belgian Linguistic Cases*, para. 9.

context the rule of non-discrimination laid down in that provision is already embodied in Article 6 para. 3(e)."[8]

In summary, the case-law leads to the conclusion that Article 14 contains an autonomous, though complementary guarantee in relation to the rights and freedoms protected in Section I. Even though the 'main' provision on itself has not been violated, the facts may show a violation of that provision in conjunction with Article 14 and a broad interpretation of the scope of the 'main' provision will lead to an expansion of the applicability of Article 14. In the *Gaygusuz* Case, for instance, the Court held that Article 1 of Protocol No. 1 includes pecuniary rights, such as social security benefits.[9] This means that Article 14 also covers distinctions made in a social security system. In the *Petrovic* Case, concerning alleged discrimination with respect to the Austrian system of parental leave allowances, the Court found that Article 8 did apply (and therefore also Article 14) because the allowance enables a State to demonstrate respect for family life.[10] A rare example of non-application of Article 14 because of the denial of applicability of a substantive provision in the Convention was the *Botta* Case.[11]

33.4 THE SUBSIDIARY GUARANTEE OF ARTICLE 14

When a violation of one of the articles from Section I is actually found, the Court generally takes the position that it is not necessary anymore to make an inquiry into the possible violation of that article in conjunction with Article 14. In other words: in such cases Article 14 is not treated as an autonomous and complementary, but only as a subsidiary guarantee.

In its judgment in the *Airey* Case the Court formulated this view, which was repeated in later judgments, as follows: "Article 14 has no independent existence; it constitutes one particular element (non-discrimination) of the rights safeguarded by the Convention (...). The Articles enshrining those rights may be violated alone and/or in conjunction with Article 14. If the Court does not find a separate breach of one of those Articles that has been invoked both on its own and together with Article 14, it must also examine the case under the latter Article. On the other hand, such an examination is not generally required when the Court finds a violation of the former

---

[8]   Judgment of 19 December 1989, *Kamasinski*, para. 75. Recently: judgment of 12 June 2003, *Van Kück*, para. 91-92.

[9]   Judgment of 16 September 1996, para. 41. See also the judgment of 21 February 1997, *Van Raalte*, para. 34.

[10]   Judgment of 27 March 1998, *Petrovic*, para. 29.

[11]   Judgment of 24 February 1998, para. 39. See also the judgment of 13 January 2004, *Haas*.

Article taken alone. The position is otherwise if a clear inequality of treatment in the enjoyments of the right in question is a fundamental aspect of the case."[12]

Even apart from the fact that the meaning of the formulation 'clear inequality of treatment' is left vague and therefore allows for different interpretations in a concrete case,[13] the line followed by the Court would appear not to be very consistent. It cannot be appreciated why Article 14 should have another character in cases where a violation of another article of the Convention has been found than in cases where there is no question of a violation of any of these articles as such. As Judge Evrigenis rightly observed in his dissenting opinion in the *Airey* Case: "Discrimination in the enjoyment of a right protected by the Convention contravenes Article 14 irrespective of whether such discrimination lies within or outside the area of violation of that right. The word 'enjoyment', within the meaning of Article 14, must cover all situations that may arise between, at the one extreme, plain refusal of a right protected by the Convention and, at the other, full embodiment of that right in the domestic system."[14]

In the *Dudgeon* Case the Court gave the following argument for the distinction it made with regard to Article 14: "Once it has been held that the restriction on the applicant's right to respect for his private sexual life gives rise to a breach of Article 8 by reason of its breadth and absolute character (...) there is no useful legal purpose to be served in determining whether he has in addition suffered discrimination as compared with other persons who are subject to lesser limitations on the same right."[15]

From the argumentation of the Court it appears that it has in mind in particular a 'useful legal purpose' from the viewpoint of the individual applicant concerned. Even leaving aside whether in the case at issue the applicant took the same view, and whether the Court's approach not to investigate all the elements of the complaint is correct from a procedural point of view,[16] in our opinion this argument would seem to ignore the fact that decisions of the Court, as the highest organ competent to interpret the Convention, have an effect far exceeding the concrete aspects of the case submitted

---

[12] Judgment of 9 October 1979, para. 30. See also the judgment of 22 October 1981, *Dudgeon*.

[13] See the dissenting opinions of Judge Evrigenis in the *Airey* Case (judgment of 9 October 1979) and of the Judges Evrigenis and Garcia De Entecre in the *Dudgeon* Case (judgment of 24 February 1983), who, unlike the majority of the Court, concluded that in these cases there was decidedly a question of a 'clear inequality of treatment'.

[14] Dissenting opinion of Judge Evrigenis.

[15] Judgment of 22 October 1981, para. 69.

[16] See the position of Judge Matscher in his dissenting opinion in the *Dudgeon* Case: "In my view, when the Court is called on to rule on a breach of the Convention which has been alleged by the applicant and contested by the respondent Government, it is the Court's duty, provided that the application is admissible, to decide the point by giving an answer on the merits of the issue that has been raised. The Court cannot escape this responsibility by employing formulas that are liable to limit excessively the scope of Article 14 to the point of depriving it of all practical value".

to it, and that these decisions may therefore also have implications of a more general character.[17]

Nevertheless, the Court's position has become standing case law. In recent cases the Court did not even adduce arguments anymore for its position. Thus, after having found a violation of Article 8 with respect to one of the applicants – an illegitimate child whose legal situation under Irish law differed considerably from that of a legitimate child – the Court held with respect to the allegation that Article 14 had been violated: "Since succession rights were included among the aspects of Irish law which were taken into consideration in the examination of the general complaint concerning the third applicant's legal situation (...) the Court (...) does not consider it necessary to give a separate ruling on this allegation."[18]

In the *Philis* Case, the Court held that it would serve "no useful purpose (...) in determining whether [the applicant] has suffered discrimination" since the Court had established that the right of access to a court had been violated.[19] And in the *Castells* Case, the Court refused to deal with a claim based upon Article 14, since it considered this question not to be "a fundamental aspect of the case".[20]

However, in recent case law the Court seems to nuance this subsidiary character. In a few cases, after having concluded that a substantive article has been violated, the Court has continued and investigated the alleged violation. It is too early to tell in what cases the Court will resort to this new approach and whether the nuance will signal a change in its case law or simply constitute an exception to the general rule.

---

[17]   *Cf.* in this context also what has been observed *supra* 2.3.3., with regard to the public-interest considerations in deciding to strike a case from the list.

[18]   Judgment of 18 December 1986, *Johnston*, para. 79. See also the judgment of 21 September 1993, *Kremzow*, para. 80; judgment of 26 March 1992, *Beldjoudi*, para. 81; and judgment of 22 September 1994, *Hentrich*, para. 66. In the *Johnston* Case there was one separate opinion in this respect, partly dissenting and partly concurring, of Judge De Meyer, who stated as follows: "I consider that in the present case the Court should, as in the *Marckx* Case, have found not only a violation of the right to respect for private and family life but also a violation, as regards that right, of the principle of non-discrimination. In my view, the latter violation arises from the very fact that, on the one hand, the legal situation of the third applicant, as a child born out of wedlock, is different from that of a child of a married couple and that, on the other hand, the legal situation of the first and second applicants [the unmarried parents of the third applicant] in their relations with or concerning the third applicant is different from that of parents of a child of a married couple in their relations with or concerning that child". In later cases the Court unanimously considered it unnecessary to examine the complaint under Article 14 when a violation of a substantive Convention provision had been established. See, *e.g.* the judgment of 8 December 1999, *Freedom and Democracy Party (ÖZDEP)*, para. 49: the complaints under Article 14 related to the same matters as those considered under Article 11; therefore it is not necessary to consider them separately under Article 14.

[19]   Judgment of 27 August 1991, para. 68.

[20]   Judgment of 23 April 1992, para. 52. In the judgment of 25 February 1997, *Gregory*, para. 54, the Court said there was no separate issue under Article 14, since it had found no violation of Article 6 in a case of alleged racial bias in a jury.

In the *Özgür Gündem* Case[21] the Court had decided that Article 10 had been violated because of a lack of necessity as regards the aims pursued by the government (national security, territorial integrity, the prevention of crime and disorder). Because of the existence of legitimate aims under Article 10, the Court found that there was no reason to believe that the restrictions under Article 10 could be attributed to a difference of treatment based on the applicants' national origin or association with a national minority. It therefore rejected the claim based upon Article 14. Also in the *VGT Verein gegen Tierfabriken* Case[22] the Court found a violation of Article 10 but subsequently still proceeded with the alleged violation of Article 14 and concluded in that respect that no violation of that article had occurred.

However, the Court's case law in this respect is complicated. In the *Prince Hans-Adam II of Liechtenstein* Case[23] the Court concluded first that there had not been an interference with a right under Article 1 of the First Protocol (right to property) and for that reason the applicant could not claim, according to the Court, that in those respects he had been discriminated against in the enjoyment of his property rights. This meant that Article 1 of the First Protocol did apply, but that, in the absence of an interference, the applicant did not suffer any harm and therefore was not discriminated against. This situation is to be distinguished from the cases where the Court found an interference, but also concluded that the interference was justified. In that situation a difference in treatment might be present, in which case the Court has to look for an objective and reasonable justification.

In the *Jewish Liturgical association Cha'are Shalom Ve Tsedek* Case[24] the Court had concluded that Article 9 had not been violated; after this conclusion it referred in the context of Article 14 to its findings under Article 9 and found no violation of Article 14.

33.5 THE SCOPE OF ARTICLE 14

33.5.1 GENERAL

The concept of equality and the ensuing prohibition of discrimination constitute one of the most complex legal principles. This is not the place to extensively deal with the concept of equality.

The general model under which the Court will review differences in treatment is the model, as recently laid down in the *Koua Poirrez* Case: "According to the Court's

---

[21]   Judgment of 16 March 2000, para. 71.
[22]   Judgment of 28 June 2001, paras 83-89.
[23]   Judgment of 12 July 2001, paras 93-94.
[24]   Judgment of 27 June 2000, paras 87-88.

case law, a distinction is discriminatory, for the purposes of Article 14, if it has 'no objective and reasonable justification', that is if it does not pursue a 'legitimate aim' or if there is not a 'reasonable relationship of proportionality between the means employed and the aim sought to be realised'. Moreover the Contracting States enjoy a certain margin of appreciation in assessing whether and to what extent differences in otherwise similar situations justify a different treatment."[25]

Here it suffices to briefly outline the elements which should be taken into account if a given treatment or situation is reviewed for its conformity with the principle of equality and the prohibition of discrimination. These elements are the following. A violation of the principle of equality and non-discrimination arises if there is (a) differential treatment of (b) equal cases, (c) without there being an objective and reasonable justification, or if (d) proportionality between the aim sought and the means employed is lacking.

33.5.2   DIFFERENCE IN TREATMENT

As far as the first element is concerned, it should be observed from the outset that Article 14 – despite the French text 'sans distinction aucune' – does not prohibit every difference in treatment. On the contrary, the obligation contained therein may even entail unequal treatment. Indeed, Article 14 is not only concerned with *formal* equality – equal treatment of equal cases – but also with *substantive* equality: unequal treatment of unequal cases in proportion to their inequality. In other words, a difference in treatment which is aimed at eliminating an existing inequality creates substantive equality and is consequently in conformity with Article 14.

In the *Hoffmann* Case, which dealt with the legality of taking into account the religion of one of the parents when deciding about awarding parental rights over the children after divorce, the Court first examined whether the applicant could claim to have undergone differential treatment. It was only after having accepted that there had been a difference in treatment, based on the ground of religion, that the Court set out to investigate whether this difference amounted to discrimination within the meaning of Article 14.[26] In the *Prince Hans-Adam II of Liechtenstein* Case it also became clear that Article 14 can only be relied upon when a distinction (in that case called a discrimination) can be shown.[27]

In the *Thlimmenos* Case the Court for the first time recognised that Article 14 also covers situations in which persons in different situations have been treated alike: "The

---

[25]   Judgment of 30 September 2003, para. 46.
[26]   Judgment of 23 June 1993, paras 31-36. The Court's reasoning concerning the justification for the difference in treatment will be dealt with *infra*.
[27]   Judgment of 12 July 2001, paras 92-94.

Court has so far considered that the right under Article 14 not to be discriminated against in the enjoyment of the rights guaranteed under the Convention is violated when States treat differently persons in analogous situations without providing an objective and reasonable justification (…). However, the Court considers that this is not the only facet of the prohibition of discrimination in Article 14. The right not to be discriminated against in the enjoyment of the rights guaranteed under the Convention is also violated when States without an objective and reasonable justification fail to treat differently persons whose situations are significantly different."[28]

Basically the Court is inclined to deal under Article 14 only with those differences of treatment which are related to personal characteristics ('status') by which persons or groups of persons are distinguishable from each other.[29]

33.5.3 EQUAL CASES

The second comparative element of the concept of equality consists of the question as to whether the cases at hand are equal or unequal in the relevant respects. In order to be able to answer that question, a yardstick has to be developed, which has to be applied to both cases, and on that basis the ensuing results have to be compared. The crux of the matter are the yardstick or the criteria used for the comparison. Since two cases can always be said to be equal in some respects and unequal in others, for the comparability test to be meaningful, the criteria used have to be adequately related to the object of the provision which prescribes equal treatment. To the extent that such is the case, the comparison which is inherent in the equality test puts in focus the goals underlying the provisions concerned.

Consequently, in many cases the comparability test is skipped or merged into the third element – the justification test. In principle this merger seems to be an appropriate approach. The comparability can be best tested within the context of the justification test because comparability only exists in relation to the aims and the ratio of the differential treatment and the underlying legal rule. A negative answer to the question of comparability, without linking this answer to the question of justification, leads to the justification test being ignored. This would also mean that there would be no link between the comparability and the – objective and reasonable – ratio of the justification. In the *Edoardo Palumbo* Case, about the protection of tenants, the Court held as follows: " The Court notes that the applicant seeks to compare himself to his tenant. In view of the fundamental differences between a landlord and a tenant, the

---

[28]   Judgment of 6 April 2000, para. 44; confirmed in the judgments of 18 January 2001, *Chapman, Beard, Lee* and *Jane Smith*, para. 129, and in the judgment of 6 July 2005, *Nachova and Others*, para. 145

[29]   Judgment of 7 December 1976, *Kjeldsen, Busk Madsen and Pedersen*, para. 56. Other examples: judgment of 8 July 1999, *Gerger*, para. 69 and the judgment of 6 June 2000, *Magee*, para. 50.

Court does not find that these two situations can be compared as being analogous and considers therefore that no question of discrimination arises in the present case."[30]

The Court does not always provide clear guidance about its approach. Sometimes it performs the comparability test, *e.g.* in its *Van der Mussele* judgment and its judgment in the *Johnston* Case. In the first-mentioned case it was alleged, *inter alia*, that Belgian *avocats*, unlike medical practitioners, veterinary surgeons, pharmacists, and dentists, were required to provide their services free of charge to indigent persons and that such a difference in treatment constituted arbitrary inequality. The Court pointed out that between the Bar and the other professions cited fundamental differences existed as to legal status, conditions for entry to the profession, nature of the functions involved, manner of exercise of those functions, *etc.* The Court, consequently, did not find any similarity between the disparate situations in question, because each one was characterised by a corpus of rights and obligations of which it would be artificial to isolate one specific aspect.[31]

In the *Johnston* Case, the two applicants alleged violation of Article 14 on the basis of the fact that the first applicant was unable to obtain a divorce in order subsequently to marry the second applicant, whereas other persons resident in Ireland and having the necessary means could obtain a divorce abroad which could be recognised *de jure* or *de facto* in Ireland. The Court, however, noted that under general Irish rules of private international law foreign divorces are recognised in Ireland only if they have been obtained by persons domiciled abroad and that, therefore, the situations of such persons and of the first and the second applicants could not be regarded as analogous.[32]

In the *Fredin* Case, the Court extensively investigated the question whether the closure of applicants' pit amounted to a violation of Article 14. The applicants had not forwarded any arguments (other than their dissimilar treatment) supporting their claim that they had been discriminated against. From this, under the heading of the comparability test, the Court inferred a rule of evidence: "In their submissions to the Court the applicants did not try to refute the Commission's assessment, nor did they adduce other evidence. Their main argument was, since theirs was the only ongoing business to have been stopped (...), it was for the Government to explain in what respect their case was dissimilar to those of the other enterprises which had been allowed to continue their activities or to give a plausible reason for their exceptional treatment. The Court cannot subscribe to this argument. It is true that, in the absence of further information from the Government with regard to the implementation of the 1964 Act and, in particular, the 1973 amendment thereto (...), the Court has to

---

[30] Judgment of 30 November 2000, para. 52. *See* also the judgment of 11 January 2001, *P.M. v. Italy*, para. 55.
[31] Judgment of 23 November 1983, para. 46.
[32] Judgment of 18 December 1986, para. 60.

presume that the applicants' pit is the only one to have been closed by virtue of that amendment. However, this is not sufficient to support a finding that the applicants' situation can be considered similar to that of other ongoing business which have not been closed."[33]

In the *Sunday Times* and *The Observer and Guardian* Cases the Court held with respect to the comparability test: "Article 14 affords protection against different treatment, without an objective and reasonable justification, of persons in similar situations (...). If and so far as foreign newspapers were subject to the same restrictions as [the Sunday Times, the Observer and the Guardian], there was no difference in treatment. If and so far as they were not, this was because they were not subject to the jurisdiction of the English courts and hence were not in a situation similar to that of [the Sunday Times, the Observer and the Guardian]."[34] And in the *Spadeo and Scalabrino* Case the Court held as follows: "Article 14 will be breached where, without objective and reasonable justification, persons in 'relevantly' similar situations are treated differently. For a claim of violation of this Article to succeed, it has therefore to be established, *inter alia*, that the situation of the alleged victim can be considered similar to that of persons who have been better treated."[35]

The category of cases just referred to in fact presents relatively few difficulties, because the comparability test is clearly performed instead of being merged into the justification test, or even skipped completely.[36] Obviously, this is not to say that the comparability test may not be very complex. It is not always easy to decide whether the situations concerned are different or equal, or rather to select the relevant criteria on which that decision has to be based. It requires an intensive investigation into the relevance of the criteria used. In this respect the Court does not go at length in analysing the (dis)similarity of the cases at hand. In most of the cases mentioned *supra* the Court readily accepts the relevance of dissimilarity which can be traced to national jurisdiction, national (or EU) citizenship and the like.

In the *VGT Verein gegen Tierfabriken* Case the question before the court related to a difference of treatment between commercial advertisements and commercials by

---

[33] Judgment of 18 February 1991, para. 61.
[34] Judgments of 26 November 1991, paras 58, 73 and 73, respectively.
[35] Judgment of 28 September 1995, para. 45.
[36] The comparability test seems to have been skipped in many cases of suspect classifications: *See,* for instance, the judgment of 28 May 1985, *Abdulaziz;* judgment of 22 February 1994, *Burghartz;* judgment of 18 July 1994, *Karlheinz Schmidt;* judgment of 1 February 2000, *Mazurek;,* judgment of 3 October 2000, *Camp and Bourini;* judgment of 11 October 2001, *Sahin;* judgment of 26 February 2002, *Fretté;* judgment of 4 June 2002, *Wessels-Bergervoet;* judgment of 11 June 2002, *Willis;* judgment of 11 October 2001, *Sommerfeld;* judgment of 24 July 2003, *Karner and Others.* Occasionally, when there is doubt as to the comparability the Court, however, does pay attention to it. See *e.g.* the judgment of 16 September 1996, *Gaygusuz;* judgment of 21 February 1997, *Van Raalte;* judgment of 27 March 1998, *Petrovic;* judgment of 13 February 2003, *Odièvre;* judgment of 30 September 2003, *Koua Poirrez.*

the applicant against the meat industry. The Court simply said that promotions of the meat industry were economic in nature in that they aimed at increasing the turnover, whereas the applicant association's commercial, exhorting reduced meat consumption, was directed against industrial animal production and related to animal protection. "As a result, the applicant association and the meat industry cannot be considered to be "placed in comparable situations" as their commercials differed in their aims."[37] Indeed, there is a difference between a meat commercial and an anti-meat commercial; on the other hand, they are similar in that they are both commercials. The question therefore is which aspect has to prevail. It is submitted that this question can best be answered by also taking into account the relevant justification in national law for a distinction between the two sorts of commercials. This means that the comparability question has to be linked with the justification argument. If not, the Court runs the risk of making an arbitrary determination pertinent to the comparability issue.

It seems that the Court relies on the comparability test only in order to dismiss cases; in those cases where the petitioner is able to show some merits in his claim, the Court will investigate the matter and check the validity of the justifications forwarded, including the comparability of the situation.

33.5.4   EVIDENCE OF DISCRIMINATION

In the *Fredin* Case the Court stated as a rule of evidence that it is up to the applicant to come forward with relevant information leading to the conclusion that his case is a similar case.[38] In the *Eisholz* Case the Court seemed to introduce a new criterion in order to assess the applicability of Article.14. It said in a case about an alleged distinction between fathers of children born out of wedlock and divorced fathers that the facts of the case did not substantiate that "a divorced father would have been treated more favourably".[39] This would, indeed, seem to concern the most important and relevant factor pertinent to the applicability of Article 14: has there been a difference in treatment which created a disadvantage for the applicant. This can be

---

[37]   Judgment of 28 June 2001, para. 88. Similarily the judgment of 16 October 2001, *Eliazer*, para. 41: "the situation of a person convicted *in absentia* is not comparable to that of a person convicted following adversarial proceedings in that the latter has attended his trial and the former has not."

[38]   Judgment of 18 February 1991, para. 61. *See* also the judgment of 28 November 1997, *Mentes and Others*, paras 95-96 (unsubstantiated allegations about discrimination); judgment of 19 February 1998, *Kaya*; judgment of 24 February 1998, *Larissis and Others*; judgment of 24 April 1998, *Selcuk and Asker*; judgment of 25 May 1998, *Kurt*; judgment of 9 June 1998, *Tekin*; judgment of 8 July 1999, *Tanrikulu*; judgment of 8 July 1999, *Cakici*; judgment of 27 February 2001, *Cicek*; judgment of 12 July 2001, *Feldek*; judgment of 21 February 2002, *Matyar*; judgment of 21 March 2002, *Vasilopoulou*; judgment of 14 May 2002, *Semse Onen*.

[39]   Judgment of 13 July 2000. In three later cases the Court concluded that in those cases the fathers of children born out of wedlock were put in a different, less favourable position, than divorced fathers: *Sahin*, *Hoffmann* and *Sommerfeld*, 11 October 2001; about these tree cases *infra* 33.5.7.

established on the basis of the facts of a case and is therefore a better criterion than the comparability aspect, which is linked to the justification aspect as well.[40] It is, therefore, submitted that the Court should start from an alleged difference in treatment, which has harmed the applicant. After that it should continue and assess the comparability and justifications. The applicant has to put forward proof as to the likelihood of him having undergone a difference in treatment. The State concerned will then be asked to submit objective and reasonable justifications.

Whenever an individual complains about a certain treatment on the ground of racial bias underlying this treatment, a violation of Article 14 will only be accepted by the Court if this bias has been clearly proven. In the *Velikova* Case a prisoner had died while being in police custody. The State had not provided any plausible indication as to the circumstances of the prisoner, nor had it explained why no inquest had been set up. In that respect the applicant complained about racial prejudice. The Court said, however, that the standard of proof required under the Convention is "proof beyond reasonable doubt".[41] In this case there was insufficient evidence that racial prejudice was a relevant factor. In the *Avsar* Case the Court decided that there was no significant evidence to justify the findings that persons had been the victims of intimidation based on their ethnic status or political opinions.[42]

Recently, in four parallel cases (*Hugh Jordan, McKerr, Kelly and Others,* and *Shanagan*) the Court nuanced this strict approach, by accepting, in theory, that statistics, if undisputed, might indicate a difference in treatment, even though no direct racial or other unlawful prejudice could be proven: an indirect approach. The Court stated as follows: "The Government replied that there was no evidence that any of the deaths which occurred in Northern Ireland were analogous or that they disclosed any difference in treatment. Bald statistics (the accuracy of which was not accepted) were not enough to establish broad allegations of discrimination against Catholics or nationalists. Where a general policy or measure has disproportionately prejudicial effects on a particular group, it is not excluded that this may be considered as discriminatory notwithstanding that it is not specifically aimed or directed at that group. However, even though statistically it appears that the majority of people shot by the security forces were from the Catholic or nationalist Community, the Court does not consider that statistics can in themselves disclose a practice which could be classified as discriminatory within the meaning of Article 14. There is no evidence before the Court which would entitle it to conclude that any of those killings, save the

---

[40] In a similar vein the judgments of 22 March 2001, *Streletz, Kesslet and Krenz* and *K.-H.W.*: the principles applied by the national court had general scope and were equally valid; no difference in treatment.

[41] Judgment of 18 May 2000, para. 94.

[42] Judgment of 10 July 2001, para. 435.

four which resulted in convictions, involved the unlawful or excessive use of force by members of the security forces."[43]

In the admissibility decision in the *Hoogendijk* Case the Court provided further guidance about the level of evidence required in indirect discrimination cases: "the Court considers that where an applicant is able to show, on the basis of undisputed official statistics, the existence of a prima facie indication that a specific rule – although formulated in a neutral manner – in fact affects a clearly higher percentage of women than men it is for the respondent Government to show that this is the result of objective factors unrelated to any discrimination on grounds of sex."[44]

33.5.5   JUSTIFICATIONS

In the above-mentioned cases the discussion goes to the heart of the matter, *i.e.* whether the situations at hand are equal or unequal. In most instances of the Strasbourg case-law, however, the comparability test is glossed over, and the emphasis is (almost) completely on the justification test.[45] This ensues from the approach which the Court takes with respect to Article 14. According to the Court, for the purposes of Article 14 a difference of treatment is discriminatory if it has no objective and reasonable justification, that is if it does not pursue a legitimate aim or if there is no reasonable relationship of proportionality between the means employed and the aim sought to be realised.[46] This approach was developed by the Court in its judgment in the *Belgian Linguistic* Case.[47] According to this scheme, discrimination contrary to Article 14 occurs when in a given case the existence of the following three elements can be established: "(a) the facts found disclose a differential treatment; (b) the distinction does not have a legitimate aim, i.e. it has no objective and reasonable justification having regard to the aim and effects of the measure under consideration; and (c) there is no reasonable proportionality between the means employed and the aim sought to be realized."[48]

Review of an allegedly discriminatory act on the part of a Contracting State by reference to the above criteria has become established case law of the Court. Since the

---

[43]   Four judgments of 4 May 2001, paras 147-148.

[44]   Decision of 6 January 2005.

[45]   *E.g.* the judgment of 28 September 1995, *Spadea and Scalabrino*, paras 45-47. In this case the Court first noted that the similarity of the legal situation of the persons involved had to be established. Subsequently it did not do so, but immediately answered the question whether the distinction drawn was objective and reasonable given the aim of the legislation.

[46]   *See*, for instance, the judgment of 21 February 1986, *James*; judgment of 8 July 1986, *Lithgow*; judgment of 28 October 1987, *Inze*; judgment of 23 October 1990, *Darby*; judgment of 23 June 1993, *Hoffmann*; and judgment of 24 February 1995, *McMichael*.

[47]   Judgment of 23 July 1968, para. 41.

[48]   *See* the report of 6 July 1976, *Geïllustreerde Pers N.V.*, D&R 8 (1977), p. 5 (14-15).

criteria are cumulative and not alternative, the finding that one of them has not been met may make the investigation of the other ones superfluous.[49]

Gradually the approach has been summarised in the following formula: "Article 14 of the Convention prohibits a difference in treatment of persons in analogous situations without providing an objective and reasonable justification".[50]

The judgment in the *Pretty* Case aptly summarises the case law of the court as to its general approach: "The Court has found above that the applicant's rights under Article 8 of the Convention were engaged (…). It must therefore consider the applicant's complaints that she has been discriminated against in the enjoyment of the rights guaranteed under that provision in that domestic law permits able-bodied persons to commit suicide yet prevents an incapacitated person from receiving assistance in committing suicide. For the purposes of Article 14 a difference in treatment between persons in analogous or relevantly similar positions is discriminatory if it has no objective and reasonable justification, that is if it does not pursue a legitimate aim or if there is not a reasonable relationship of proportionality between the means employed and the aim sought to be realised. Moreover, the Contracting States enjoy a margin of appreciation in assessing whether and to what extent differences in otherwise similar situations justify a different treatment (…). Discrimination may also arise where States without an objective and reasonable justification fail to treat differently persons whose situations are significantly different (…). Even if applied to the applicant's situation, however, there is, in the Court's view, objective and reasonable justification for not distinguishing in law between those who are and those who are not physically capable of committing suicide. Under Article 8 of the Convention, the Court has found that there are sound reasons for not introducing into the law exceptions to cater for those who are deemed not to be vulnerable (…). Similar cogent reasons exist under Article 14 for not seeking to distinguish between those who are able and those who are unable to commit suicide unaided. The borderline between the two categories will often be a very fine one and to seek to build into the law an exemption for those judged to be incapable of committing suicide would seriously undermine the protection of life which the 1961 Act was intended to safeguard and greatly increase the risk of abuse. Consequently, there has been no violation of Article 14 in the present case."[51]

As was already observed, this approach implies that the interests or goals embodied in the comparability test are intertwined with those in the context of the objective and reasonable justification test.

In recent case law there seems to be a tendency to more specifically address the fairness or reasonableness of the justifications which have been advanced. The Court has shown an inclination not to accept biased ideas, or generalities or subjective criteria. In the *L. and V. v. Austria* Case (criminalisation of homosexual activities) the Court found that the Criminal Code embodied a predisposed bias: "these negative attitudes cannot

---

[49]   Judgment of 21 February 1997, *Van Raalte*, para. 44.
[50]   E.g. the judgment of 6 April 2000, *Thlimmenos*, para. 44, and the judgment of 16 October 2001, *Eliazer*, para. 40.
[51]   Judgment of 29 April 2002, paras 86-89.

of themselves be considered by the Court to amount to sufficient justification for the differential treatment".[52] In the *Palau-Martinez* Case (about the refusal to award custody to a Jehova's Witness) it was held that "the Court of Appeal (...) asserted generalities concerning Jehova's Witnesses. [The Court] notes the absence of any direct, concrete evidence demonstrating the influence of the applicant's religion on her two children's upbringing and daily life."[53] And in the *Buchen* Case the Court condemned the utilization of subjective criteria in the realm of employment.[54]

Recently, the Court has also referred to the restriction criteria laid down in the second paragraphs of Articles 8-11 of the Convention as reasonable justifications within he context of Article 14. It stated in the *Sidabras and Dziautas* Case as follows: "the Court accepts that the restriction of the applicants' employment prospects under the Act, and hence the difference of treatment applied to them, pursued the legitimate aims of protection of national security, public order, the economic well-being of the country and the rights and freedoms of others."[55]

33.5.6 MARGIN OF APPRECIATION

In general, the Court leaves a wide margin of appreciation to the national authorities in appreciating the weight of the public interest concerned as compared with the individual interests at stake. In fact, as an element of the above-mentioned criteria of equal treatment in the case-law it is sometimes added that "the Contracting States enjoy a certain margin of appreciation in assessing whether and to what extent differences in otherwise similar situations justify a different treatment in law".[56] Clearly, this approach would seem to further detract from the importance of Article 14 in the case law.

An example of this approach is the *Rasmussen* Case.[57] In this case Mr Rasmussen alleged violation of Article 14, because under a Danish Act of 1960 his right to contest his paternity of a child born during marriage was subject to time-limits, whereas his former wife was entitled to institute paternity proceedings at any time. The Court started by skipping the comparability test. It felt that it did not have to deal with the question of whether or not husband and wife were placed in analogous situations,

---

[52] Judgment of 9 January 2003, para. 52.
[53] Judgment of 16 December 2003, para. 42.
[54] Judgment of 26 November 2002, para. 75.
[55] Judgment of 27 July 2004, para. 55.
[56] See, *e.g.*, the judgment of 8 July 1986, *Lithgow*, para. 122, where the Court further observed that "the scope of this margin will vary according to the circumstances, the subject-matter and its background". *See* also the judgment of 28 May 1985, *Abdulaziz, Cabales and Balkandali*, para. 78 and the judgment of 18 July 1994, *Karlheinz Schmidt*, para. 24.
[57] Judgment of 28 November 1984.

because "the positions and interests referred to are also of relevance in determining whether the difference of treatment was justified".[58] With respect to this latter question the Court subsequently relied on the margin of appreciation to be granted to the Contracting States, and pointed out that one of the relevant factors in this respect might be the existence or non-existence of common ground between the laws of the Contracting States on the issue concerned. The Court found no such common ground, as the position of the mother and that of the husband were regulated in different ways in the various legal systems and, therefore, concluded that the Danish authorities were entitled to think that the difference made was justified.[59] In the same vein the Court finally decided that the proportionality requirement was fulfilled: "the competent authorities were entitled to think that as regards the husband the aim sought to be realized would be most satisfactorily achieved by the enactment of a statutory rule, whereas as regards the mother it was sufficient to leave the matter to be decided on a case-by-case basis".[60]

No matter whether one agrees or disagrees with the Court on the outcome of this case, the approach taken by the Court would seem to water down the significance of Article 14 to the bare minimum. In many other cases the Court applied the regular justification test, with no further bite.[61] As noted, this justification test with a large margin of appreciation for the State is applied specifically in those areas where no common ground seems to exist. In the *Sheffield and Horsham* Case the Court relied upon the margin granted to the State in a matter involving the legal position of transsexuals. In this case the Court's conclusion that the State had not violated Article 8 (a fair balance was said to exist) also led it to the finding that Article 14 had not been vioated.[62]

Once a difference in treatment has been established, it is primarily incumbent upon the applicant to substantiate his claim of unjustified disadvantages. The burden of evidence is subsequently on the State to adduce relevant reasonable and objective justifications. This rule has been established by the Court in the *Larkos* Case about the difference in treatment between government tenants who were not protected against eviction and private tenants who were. The Court observed "that the respondent State has sought to justify the difference in treatment between government tenants such as the applicant and other private tenants renting from private landlords by pointing

---

58   *Ibidem*, para. 37.
59   *Ibidem*, paras 41-42.
60   *Ibidem*, para. 41.
61   E.g. the Case of *National & Provincial Building Society, The Leeds Permament Building Society and the Yorkshire Building Society*, judgment of 23 October 1997, paras 89-92: no violation of Article 14 in a case in which one Building Society had obtained a national court judgment in its favour, whereas the others, which did not go to court, were subjected to less favourable new legislation.
62   Judgment 30 July 1998, para. 58.

to the duties which the Constitution imposes on the authorities as regards the administration of the property of the State. While the Court accepts that a measure which has the effect of treating differently persons in a relevantly similar situation may be justified on public interest grounds, it considers that in the instant case the respondent Government have not provided any convincing explanation of how the general interest will be served by evicting the applicant."[63] This burden of proof, the necessity to forward relevant reasons, has also to meet certain standards of specificity. Since the Court assesses the situation at hand, it will not suffice that the States simply invoke the general interest without being specific as to the fair balance between the treatment of the applicant and a legitimate aim.

Thus, a progressive income tax is not discriminatory provided the progressive measure is proportional and consequently results in a fairer distribution of income than would be the case without it. Obviously, what may be called 'fair' and 'proportional' in such cases is to a large extent still dependent upon the national situation, so that the reasonableness of the national authorities' views on this matter can be reviewed only marginally in Strasbourg. This may explain why a complaint concerning a difference in treatment under the fiscal legislation was declared 'manifestly ill-founded' by the Commission on the basis of the very general argument "that it is a common incident of taxation laws that they apply in different ways or in different degrees to different persons or entities in the community".[64]

It is important to note that the scope or the intensity of the review of the Court may and probably will vary according to the grounds of the distinction made. *Infra* it will be concluded from the case law of the Court that some distinctions have to be treated with a more strict scrutiny than others. Crucial seems to be whether a common ground can be said to exist. Another factor, however, that could play a role is the area in which a specific distinction has been made. When it concerns purely economic regulations the Court probably will be more reluctant to interfere than when it has to cope with a distinction that touches upon essential elements of freedom rights.

In some recent cases the Court seems to have strengthened its hold upon Article 14.

Firstly, it should be noted that the Court, in the context of Article 14, apart from the examples referred to *supra*, does not frequently refer to the margin of appreciation doctrine.

Secondly, the Court is not inclined to be of any help to the Contracting States in looking for 'justifications'. Thus, in the *Pine Valley Developments LTD* Case the Court ruled that there had been a violation of Article 14 since, *inter alia*, the Government

---

[63]   Judgment 18 February 1999, para. 31. See also the judgment of 29 April 1999, *Chassagnou and Others*, para. 121: the State had not put forward any objective and reasonable justification for the difference in treatment.

[64]   Appl. 511/59, *Gudmundsson*, Yearbook III (1960), p. 394 (424).

did not "advance any other justification for the difference of treatment between the applicants and the other holders of permissions in the same category as theirs".[65]

Thirdly, the Court is gradually developing a course whereby some distinctions need to be scrutinised more strictly. In the following sub-paragraph this new category will be elaborated upon, which can be described as the 'suspect classifications'.

33.5.7 SUSPECT CLASSIFICATIONS

This category has in common that the relevant distinctions lead to Court to leave a small (if any) margin of appreciation to the States. These distinctions do not need a simple justification, but "very weighty reasons"; in some cases the Court even held that "a distinction based essentially on a difference in religion is not acceptable".

So far, the following 'suspect classifications' can be detected in the Court's case-law: a. distinctions between legitimate and illegitimate children;[66] b. distinctions on the basis of sex;[67] c. distinctions based upon religion;[68] and d. distinctions based upon nationality.[69]

In the area of the first distinction a decisive aspect in the Court's case-law is the common ground to be detected in the member States of the Council of Europe. In the *Marckx* Case the Court held that the distinction, made on different points in the Belgian legislation, between legitimate and illegitimate children, was contrary to the Convention.[70] Recently this approach was confirmed in the *Mazurek* Case about a difference in treatment of illegitimate children in inheritance rights: because of a European consensus as to the equality of treatment of illegitimate children the Court concluded that only very strong reasons ("très fortes raisons") can justify a distinction on the basis of being born out of wedlock. Since these do not exist, the more so since the illegitimate children cannot be blamed for their being born out of wedlock, the Court held the distinction to amount to a violation of Article 14.[71]

---

[65]   Judgment of 29 November 1991, para. 64. See also the judgment of 23 October 1990, *Darby*, para. 33: "In fact, the Government stated at the hearing before the Court that they did not argue that the distinction in treatment had a legitimate aim. In view of the above, the measure complained of cannot be seen as having had any legitimate aim under the Convention."

[66]   *E.g.* Judgment of 13 June 1979, *Marckx*; judgment of 29 November 1991, *Vermeire*.

[67]   *E.g.* Judgment of 28 May 1985, *Abdulaziz, Cabales and Balkandali*; judgment of 24 June 1993, *Schuler-Zgraggen*; judgment of 22 February 1994, *Burghartz*; judgment of 18 July 1994, *Karlheinz Schmidt*; judgment of 21 February 1997, *Van Raalte*.

[68]   *E.g.* Judgment of 23 June 1993, *Hoffmann*.

[69]   *E.g.* Judgment of 16 September 1996, *Gaygusuz*.

[70]   Judgment of 13 June 1979, paras 43, 48, 59 and 65. See also the judgment of 28 October 1987, *Inze*, paras 43-45.

[71]   Judgment of 1 February 2000, para. 49. See also the judgment of 3 October 2000, *Camp and Bourimi*, para. 38.

The qualification of distinctions between legitimate and illegitimate children as 'suspect' does, however, not mean that all distinctions between natural and married fathers have to be judged with the same strict standard. In the *McMichael* Case[72] the Court applied the objective and reasonable justification standard without the same strictness as in the *Marckx* Case. The Court did not offer an explanation for this different approach. The conclusion that seems to may be drawn, however, is that the Court is careful in expanding the scope of the classifications here identified as 'suspect'. But in the three Cases of *Sahin*, *Sommerfeld* and *Hoffmann* the Court repeated with regard to distinctions between fathers of children born out of wedlock and divorced fathers that "very weighty reasons need to be put forward before a difference in treatment on the ground of birth out of wedlock can be regarded as compatible with the Convention."[73]

In the *Abdulaziz, Cabales, and Balkandali* Case the Court concluded that there was a violation of Article 14 because of discrimination on the ground of sex, since the British immigration rules made it more difficult for women than for men to obtain a permit to enter and stay for their foreign spouses. As a justification the British Government had adduced the aim of protecting the domestic labour market. In the view of the Court this was not enough reason to justify the difference in treatment, the main argument being that "the advancement of the equality of the sexes is today a major goal in the member States of the Council of Europe".[74]

With regard to the second category of distinctions the Court added in the *Abdulaziz, Cabales and Balkandali* Case, the *Schuler-Zgraggen* Case, the *Burghartz* Case, the *Karlheinz Schmidt* Case and the *Van Raalte* Case that, since the advancement of the equality of the sexes is a major goal, very weighty reasons would have to be advanced before a difference of treatment on the ground of sex could be regarded as compatible with the Convention.[75] However, in the *Petrovic* Case a distinction on the basis of sex with respect to parental leave allowances (only to mothers) was found not to be in violation of Article 14 (in conjunction with Article 8). In this case the Court granted the respondent State a large margin (even though it concerned a distinction on the basis of sex) because of the great disparity between the legal systems of the Contracting States in this field. It held that there was no common ground as to a system of parental leave allowances.[76]

---

[72]   Judgment of 24 February 1995, *McMichael*, paras 97-99
[73]   Judgments of 11 October 2001, paras 57, 54 and 56, respectively.
[74]   Judgment of 28 May 1985, para. 78.
[75]   Respectively the judgment of 28 May 1985, para. 78; judgment of 24 June 1993, para. 67; judgment of 22 February 1994, para. 27; judgment of 18 July 1994, para. 24; judgment of 21 February 1997, para. 39.
[76]   Judgment of 27 March 1998, paras 42-43.

With respect to distinctions on the basis of religion no such reasoning, based upon common ground between the Member States, has been given by the Court. In the *Hoffmann* Case the Court simply held as follows: "Notwithstanding any possible arguments to the contrary, a distinction based essentially on a difference in religion is not acceptable. The Court therefore cannot find that a reasonable relationship of proportionality existed between the means employed and the aim pursued; there has accordingly been a violation of Article 8 taken in conjunction with Article 14."[77]

In the *Thlimmenos* Case the Court did not refer to religion as a suspect criterion either. This judgment, however, also shows the strictness of the scrutiny of the Court when it rules upon a distinction on the ground of religion. This case concerned the exclusion of certain professions of people with a criminal conviction, even those whose criminal conviction was related to the refusal of military service on religious grounds. The Court held the exclusion to constitute a further sanction and therefore to be disproportionate. It followed therefrom that the exclusion did not pursue a legitimate aim. For that reason there existed no objective and reasonable justification "for not treating the applicant differently from other persons convicted of a felony."[78]

In two cases where the facts were comparable in the sense that in the one case a national court had taken a decision about parental custody basically upon the (homo)sexual orientation of the father, while in the other case the religion of the mother was the crucial issue, the Court came to an identical outcome leaving no margin of appreciation for the State.[79] A restrictive interpretation of these two judgments might lead to the conclusion that the Court simply ruled that religion and sexual orientation were irrelevant arguments in the context of parental custody and that in other areas these two grounds would not necessarily lead to the adoption of their suspectness.[80]

That this interpretation seems plausible can be inferred from the *Fretté* Case, which dealt with a refusal for a single homosexual to adopt a child. The Court referred to the large margin of appreciation for the Contracting States for the reason that there was no common ground about the possibility for homosexuals to adopt a child. The outcome of the case was that the refusal did not amount to a violation of Article 14 because of the presence of objective and reasonable justifications (the interest of the

---

[77]   Judgment of 23 June 1993, para. 36. In the judgment of 27 June 2000, *C'ha'are Shalom Ve Tsedek* and in the judgment of 16 December 2003, *Palau-Martinez*, the Court did not mention the suspect nature of the distinction on the ground of religion but did apply a strict scrutiny test, similar to the very weighty reasons test.

[78]   Judgment of 6 April 2000, para. 47.

[79]   Judgment of 23 June 1993, *Hoffmann*, para. 36, and judgment of 21 December 1999, *Salgueiro da Silva Mouta*, para. 36.

[80]   However, the facts and the friendly settlement in *Sutherland*, judgment of 27 March 2001, might suggest that in the area of homosexuality, whithout any room for justification, the same age limits ought to apply as for heterosexual contacts.

child). Specifically the facts that scientific literature was divided about this issue and that public opinion was very much divided as well lead the Court to conclude that the national authorities reasonably could have decided not to allow adoption and that, considering the prime importance of the interests of the child, the principle of proportionality had not been violated.[81]

Recently, however, in *L. and V. v. Austria* the Court made it abundantly clear that sexual orientation indeed is a suspect ground within Article 14: "Just like differences based on sex, differences based on sexual orientation require particularly serious reasons by way of justification."[82]

With regard to distinctions on the basis of nationality the Court held in the *Gaygusuz* Case that "very weighty reasons would have to be put forward before the Court could regard a difference of treatment based exclusively on the ground of nationality as compatible with the Convention".[83]

This marginal approach of the review does not seem to be followed when the Court has to investigate an unequal treatment on the basis of nationality concerning decisions in the area of entrance and expulsion of aliens. In the *Moustaquim* Case the Court was asked to pronounce upon the unequal treatment of foreigners from third States as compared to foreigners from European Community member States. The Court held as follows: "As for the preferential treatment given to nationals of the other member States of the Communities, there is objective and reasonable justification for it as Belgium belongs, together with those States, to a special legal order. There has accordingly been no breach of Article 14 taken together with Article 8."[84]

With respect to civil status and race the Court has never pronounced on the suspect character of a differentiation. Recent judgments however seem to indicate that the Court will treat differentiations on any of these grounds as leading to the application of a strict scrutiny. This can be inferred for civil status from the *Wessels-Bergervoets* Case, in which the Court simply stated: "The Court considers that very weighty reasons have to be put forward before it could regard a difference in treatment based on the ground of sex and marital status as compatible with the Convention."[85]

The self evident nature of race as a suspect classification comes to the surface in the *Nachova* Case, in which the Court stated that the prohibition of discrimination in general and of racial and ethnic discrimination in particular reflects basic values.[86]

---

[81]   Judgment of 26 February 2002, paras 40-43.
[82]   Judgment of 9 January 2003, para. 45, confirmed in the judgment of 24 July 2003, *Karner*, para. 37.
[83]   Judgment of 16 September 1996, para. 42. In the same vein the judgment of 30 September 2002, *Koua Poirrez*, para. 46: social security and nationality.
[84]   Judgment of 18 February 1991, para. 49.
[85]   Judgment of 4 June 2002, para. 49.
[86]   Judgment of 26 February 2004, para. 155.

33.5.8 NO EXHAUSTIVE ENUMERATION OF DISCRIMINATION GROUNDS

As appears from the words 'on any ground such as' ('*ou toute autre situation*'), the enumeration of grounds for a difference in treatment which constitute discrimination is not exhaustive.[87] No distinctive feature or distinctive situation whatsoever may constitute a ground for an unequal treatment, unless that inequality serves an objective and reasonable purpose or is precisely intended to remove for the person concerned the disadvantages resulting from the distinctive feature or the distinctive situation.

In the *Botta* Case the applicant invoked Article 14 alleging an unequal treatment on the ground of disability. Whether Article 14 also covers this distinction was not decided by the Court since it concluded that Article 14 did not apply because of the inapplicability of Article 8.[88] It can be inferred, however, from the *Pretty* Case that distinctions based upon disability are covered by Article 14.[89]

In the *Salgueiro da Silva Mouta* Case the Court explicitly held that sexual orientation was covered by Article 14. It referred in that respect to the indicative and not limitative nature of this article.[90]

In the *Magee* Case the Court made a subtle distinction between the grounds mentioned in Article 14 and other grounds. The applicant complained about differences in criminal procedure between England and Wales, and Northern Ireland. The applicant had argued that these were distinctions on the basis of national origin. The Court held as follows: "For the Court, in so far as there exists a difference in treatment of detained suspects under the 1988 Order and the legislation of England and Wales on the matters referred to by the applicant, that difference is not to be explained in terms of personal characteristics, such as national origin or association with a national minority, but on the geographical location where the individual is arrested and detained. This permits legislation to take account of regional differences and characteristics of an objective and reasonable nature. In the present case, such a difference does not amount to discriminatory treatment within the meaning of Article 14 of the Convention."[91]

Thus it seems that differences of treatment on other grounds than those mentioned in Article 14 cannot be classified as discriminatory treatment if they are not 'personal characteristics'. It is, however, respectfully submitted that the Court would seem to mix up the consecutive steps under Article 14. It ought not to be relevant whether a distinction is discrimination in order to invoke the applicability of Article 14.

---

[87] See, for instance, the judgment of 21 February 1986, *James*, para. 74.
[88] Judgment of 24 February 1998, para. 39.
[89] Judgment of 29 April 2002, paras 87-90.
[90] Judgment of 21 December 1999, para. 28.
[91] Judgment of 6 June 2000, para. 50.

Whenever a difference of treatment has been established, the next step ought to be whether a justification for such different treatment exists.

33.6   THE SOCIALISING EFFECT OF ARTICLE 14

Article 14 may have a socialising effect on the rights and freedoms laid down in the Convention. The Convention is concerned mainly with what might broadly be called freedom rights, which by their nature do not in general require a specific performance on the part of the authorities,[92] but oblige them to refrain from restrictive interference. If, however, the authorities proceed in one way or another to specific performance in a field connected with one or more of the rights in question, they are obliged to do so without discrimination. If, for instance, they proceed to subsidise a particular religious community or to promote education in a particular language, other religious communities or other linguistic communities are in principle entitled to the same treatment. Such a right in itself is not laid down in the Convention, but derives its protection from the operation of Article 14. Here again, however, such a right does not arise when the preferential treatment by the authorities is intended precisely to remove an existing inequality or – according to the case law developed by the Commission and the Court – may be justified on other objective and reasonable grounds.

---

[92]   Leaving apart the doctrine of 'positive obligations' developed by the Court and discussed *passim* in connection with the relevant rights.

CHAPTER 34

DEROGATION FROM THE RIGHTS AND FREEDOMS IN CASE OF A PUBLIC EMERGENCY (Article 15)

REVISED BY CEES FLINTERMAN

CONTENTS

34.1 TEXT OF ARTICLE 15

1. *In time of war or other public emergency threatening the life of the nation any High Contracting Party may take measures derogating from its obligations under this Convention to the extent strictly required by the exigencies of the situation, provided that such measures are not inconsistent with its other obligations under international law.*
2. *No derogation from Article 2, except in respect of deaths resulting from lawful acts of war, or from Articles 3, 4 (paragraph 1) and 7 shall be made under this provision.*

3. *Any High Contracting Party availing itself of this right of derogation shall keep the Secretary General of the Council of Europe fully informed of the measures which it has taken and the reasons therefore. It shall also inform the Secretary General of the Council of Europe when such measures have ceased to operate and the provisions of the Convention are again being fully executed.*

34.2 INTRODUCTION

Article 15 contains a general authorisation for temporary derogation from the rights and freedoms laid down in the Convention – insofar as they are not exempted in the second paragraph – in case of a public emergency threatening the life of the nation. As the former Secretariat of the Commission observed in a publication, here "the overriding rights of the State to protect its democratic institutions" are concerned.[1] This general authorisation for derogations is additional to the special restriction clauses which are incorporated into some articles of the Convention and in which 'national security' and 'public safety' are also mentioned as grounds for such restrictions.[2]

When a Contracting State avails itself of the possibility of derogation provided for in Article 15, the consequences may be so far-reaching and the number of people affected may be so large that effective supervision on the part of the Court is of the utmost importance. Indeed, particularly in times of emergency threatening the life of the nation protection of human rights at the national level is likely to be defective. At the same time victims of violations in cases of emergency may, in general, be expected to be hesitant to lodge complaints while national courts may be under considerable pressure, assuming that possibilities for lodging complaints and for judicial review are not suspended at all precisely as a result of the derogation on the part of the State concerned.

Up until April 2005 only six States had availed themselves of the possibility of derogation of the Convention.[3] Especially the United Kingdom and Turkey have used the derogation clause in their 'wars against terrorism'. Only in some cases the Strasbourg organs have held the derogation to be unwarranted.[4] However, it should be observed at the outset that effective Strasbourg supervision with respect to Article

---

[1]   *Case law Topics*, No. 4, 'Human Rights and their limitations', Strasbourg, 1973, p. 3.

[2]   See Articles 8(2), 9(2), 10(2) and 11(2) of the Convention; Article 2(3) of Protocol No. 4; and Article 1(2) of Protocol No. 7.

[3]   These States are Belgium, France, Greece, Ireland, the United Kingdom and Turkey.

[4]   Report of 5 November 1969, *Denmark, Norway, Sweden and the Netherlands v. Greece*, Yearbook XII, pp. 42-43; report of 10 July 1976, *Cyprus v. Turkey*; report of 4 October 1983, *Cyprus v. Turkey*; judgment of 18 December 1996, *Aksoy*, para. 84; judgment of 26 November 1997, *Sakik and Others*, para. 39; judgment of 23 September 1998, *Demir and Others*, paras 52-57; judgment of 17 June 2003, *Nuray Sen*, para. 28.

15 has not yet materialized. This is mainly due to the approach taken by the Court (and earlier the Commission) on the basis of the doctrine of the margin of appreciation.

At the moment of writing (April 2005) no case law of the Court exists concerning a situation that a Contracting Party relies on Article 15 on the basis of an imminent danger which does not occur in the Contracting State itself but in a third State. Maybe this will change in the near future as the United Kingdom has proclaimed a derogation from Article 5 of the Convention after the September 11, 2001 attacks on the USA.

Article 15 is more than just a derogation clause. Its purpose is to protect the essence of the Convention during the time of a derogation and to make sure that the Convention will be fully applied again after the emergency has ceased to exist. Its object is to guarantee the continuing existence of the democratic rule of law.[5] It is for this reason that Article 18 of the Convention does not allow Article 15 to be used for other purposes. Article 15 cannot be invoked if the State concerned tries to achieve anti-democratic, authoritarian or dictatorial purposes. Moreover, a derogation can only be made in public emergency situations in which the normal measures are not sufficient. This has repeatedly been confirmed by the Court.[6]

34.3 ARTICLE 15 AND THE DOCTRINE OF THE MARGIN OF APPRECIATION

In connection with the application of Article 15, just as with respect to the special restriction clauses, two questions arise: (1) are the values (*i.e.* the life of the nation) which are to be protected by means of the derogation from or restriction of rights and freedoms threatened, and (2) are the legislation enacted, the measures taken, or the penalties imposed 'necessary' or, as Article 15 formulates it even more restrictively, 'strictly required' to safeguard these values?

The demarcation between, on the one hand, the discretion of the national authorities and, on the other hand, the review of its use within the framework of the Strasbourg mechanism, was defined by the Commission in its report in the first case in which Article 15 was at issue: *Greece v. the United Kingdom.* In this case the Commission took the position that, on the one hand, the (former) Commission and the Court were competent to institute an inquiry into both the above-mentioned

---

[5]   According to the Human Rights Committee in its General Comment No. 29, concerning Article 4 of the Covenant on Civil and Political Rights (the counterpart of Article 15 of the Convention) "the restoration of a state of normalcy where full respect for the Covenant can again be secured must be the predominant objective of a State party derogating from the Covenant". Human Rights Committee, General Comment No. 29, States of Emergency (Article 4), CCPR/C/21/Rev.1/Add. 11, 31 August 2001, p. 2.

[6]   In the *Lawless* Case, the *Brannigan and McBride* Case and the *Aksoy* Case.

questions, but that, on the other hand "the Government should be able to exercise a certain measure of discretion in assessing the extent strictly required by the exigencies of the situation".[7]

Although, in its report in the *Greek* Case, the Commission referred to the 'margin of appreciation' of the Greek Government,[8] it subsequently gave a negative answer to the first question on the basis of a detailed examination of testimony, publications in the press and other information besides the views of the Governments involved.[9] There is hardly any evidence in that report of a restriction to a marginal review of the reasonableness of the position of the Greek Government.

In the *Lawless* Case the Court set forth as a starting point for the Strasbourg supervision that "it is for the Court to determine whether the conditions laid down in Article 15 for the exercise of the exceptional right of derogation have been fulfilled in the present case".[10] Subsequently, with regard to the first of the above-mentioned questions, the Court held that "the existence at the time of a 'public emergency threatening the life of the nation' was *reasonably* deduced by the Irish Government from a combination of several factors".[11] However, with regard to the second question the Court appeared to institute an independent inquiry, which then resulted in the conclusion that the condition that the measures taken must be 'strictly required' had been satisfied.[12]

If on the basis of the above-mentioned case law a lack of clarity concerning the attitude of the Strasbourg organs has arisen, this seems to have been removed by the Court in *Ireland v. the United Kingdom*. There the Court adopted the line of the 'margin of appreciation' with respect to Article 15, which, like the Commission, it had followed with respect to the imposition of special restrictions in the *Belgian Linguistic* Case and in the *Handyside* Case. The judgment of the Court granting the State quite a wide margin of appreciation contains the following observations: "It falls in the first place to each Contracting State, with its responsibility for 'the life of [its] nation', to determine whether that life is threatened by a 'public emergency' and, if so, how far it is necessary to go in attempting to overcome the emergency. By reason of their direct and continuous contact with the pressing needs of the moment, the national authorities are in principle in a better position than the international judge to decide both on the presence of such an emergency and on the nature and scope of derogations necessary to avert it. In this matter Article 15 para. 1 leaves those authorities a wide margin of appreciation. Nevertheless, the States do not enjoy an unlimited power in

---

7   Report of 2 October 1958, Yearbook II (1958-1959), p. 174 (176).
8   Report of 5 November 1969, Yearbook XII (1969), p. 72.
9   *Ibidem*, pp. 73-76.
10   Judgment of 1 May 1961, para. 22.
11   *Ibidem*, para. 28 (emphasis added).
12   *Ibidem*, paras 31-37.

this respect. The Court, which (…) is responsible for ensuring the observance of the States' engagements (Article 19), is empowered to rule on whether the States have gone beyond the 'extent strictly required by the exigencies' of the crisis (...). The domestic margin of appreciation is thus accompanied by a European supervision."[13]

In exercising in this case the European supervision, mentioned at the end of the quotation, the Court indeed gave evidence of instituting an independent inquiry into the necessity of the derogations, but with respect to those points where differences of opinion were possible as to the interpretation of facts and the effectiveness of measures, it confined itself to an assessment of the reasonableness of the position taken in the matter by the respondent Government.[14] The Court has persisted in this approach up to the present. In a later case dealing with Article 15 it was argued by the applicants as well as by a number of authoritative non-governmental organisations that strict scrutiny was required by the Court when examining derogation from fundamental guarantees for the protection of detainees. Nevertheless, the Court explicitly held that also in such matters like these a wide margin of appreciation had to be left to the national authorities.[15]

Several concurring and dissenting opinions quite severely criticised this approach favoured by the Court's majority. Judge Pettiti opined that "Even if it is accepted that States have a margin of appreciation (...), the situation relied on must be examined by the European Court."[16] He concluded that in the *Brannigan and McBride* Case "the Government's action fell outside the margin of appreciation which the Court is able to recognise".[17]

Judge Martens concurred with the majority, but "only after considerable hesitation".[18] He criticised the majority's margin of appreciation approach for being solely based on an old precedent, *i.e.* the above-mentioned 1978 *Ireland v. the United Kingdom* judgment. His line of reasoning is noteworthy: "Since 1978 'present day conditions' have considerably changed. (...) the situation within the Council of Europe has changed dramatically. It is therefore by no means evident that standards which may have been acceptable in 1978 are still so. The 1978 view of the Court as to the margin of appreciation under Article 15 was, presumably, influenced by the view that the majority of the then member States of the Council of Europe might be assumed to be societies which (...) had been democratic for a long time and, as such, were fully aware both of the importance of the individual right to liberty and of the inherent

---

[13] Judgment of 18 January 1978, para. 207.
[14] *Ibidem,* paras 212-214 and 243, respectively.
[15] Judgment of 26 May 1993, *Brannigan and McBride,* para. 43.
[16] Dissenting opinion of Judge Pettiti in the case referred to in the previous note.
[17] *Ibidem.*
[18] Concurring opinion of Judge Martens in the same case, para. 1.

danger of giving too wide a power of detention to the executive. Since the accession of eastern and central European States that assumption has lost its pertinence."[19]

It is interesting to compare this view with judge Makarczyk's observations on the same topic: "The principle that a judgment of the Court deals with a specific case and solves a particular problem does not, in my opinion, apply to cases concerning the validity of a derogation made by a State under Article 15 of the Convention. A derogation made by any State affects not only the position of that State, but also the integrity of the Convention system of protection as a whole. It is relevant for other member States – old and new – and even for States aspiring to become Parties which are in the process of adapting their legal systems to the standards of the Convention. For the new Contracting Parties, the fact of being admitted, often after long periods of preparation and negotiation, means not only the acceptance of the Convention obligations, but also recognition by the community of European States of their equal standing as regards the democratic system and the rule of law. In other words, what is considered by the old democracies as a natural state of affairs, is seen as a privilege by the newcomers which is not to be disposed of lightly. A derogation made by a new Contracting Party from Eastern and Central Europe would call into question this new legitimacy and is, in my opinion, quite improbable. Any decision of the Court concerning Article 15 should encourage and confirm this philosophy. In any event it should not reinforce the views of those in the new member States for whom European standards clash with the interests which they have inherited from the past. I am not convinced that the reasoning adopted by the majority fulfils these requirements."[20]

Judge Martens rejects the majority's formula by which the national authorities are granted a wide margin of appreciation not only because he is of the opinion that it is outdated, but also for reasons of principle. As to the question of whether there is an objective ground for derogating which meets the requirements laid down in the opening words of Article 15, judge Martens holds as follows: "Inevitably, in this context, a certain margin of appreciation should be left to the national authorities. There is, however, no justification for leaving them a *wide* margin of appreciation because the Court, being the 'last-resort' protector of the fundamental rights and freedoms guaranteed under the Convention, is called upon to strictly scrutinise every derogation by a High Contracting Party from its obligations."[21] Furthermore, the question as to whether the derogation is to the extent strictly required by the exigencies of the situation, according to judge Martens, "calls for a closer scrutiny than the words 'necessary in a democratic society' which appear in the second paragraphs of Articles

---

[19]   *Ibidem*, para. 3.
[20]   Dissenting opinion of Judge Makarczyk in the same case, para. 1.
[21]   Concurring opinion, para. 4.

8-11. Consequently, with respect to this (...) question there is, if at all, certainly no room for a *wide* margin of appreciation."[22]

Judge Makarczyk also questioned the position taken by the majority on the margin of appreciation as far as its consequences with respect to the issue of the duration of a derogation were concerned by observing that the approach of the majority "does not contribute to reassure the international community that the Court is doing all that is legally possible for the full applicability of the Convention to be restored as soon as possible. On the contrary, the present wording of the judgment tends rather to per-petuate the *status quo* and opens, for the derogating State, an unlimited possibility of applying extended administrative detention for an uncertain period, to the detriment of the integrity of the Convention system and, I firmly believe, of the derogating State itself."[23]

The latter observation implies, it might be added, that in judge Makarczyk's opinion the Court's *Brannigan and McBride* judgment has also an effect to its own detriment; the judgment has not fostered confidence that the Court is able to provide an effective type of supervision with respect to Article 15. This raises the question of whether the Court is the most appropriate body to conduct the examination on the basis of which it has to be judged whether the situation in a State meets the require-ments laid down in Article 15(1) and, if so, whether the measures taken by the national authorities are strictly required in the light of that situation. At any rate it is clear that the Court is prepared to grant the Contracting States a very wide margin of apprecia-tion and this attitude does not fail to make its impact felt on the interpretation and application of the various elements of Article 15.

34.4   THE SCOPE OF THE FIRST PARAGRAPH

34.4.1   TIME OF WAR

The interpretation of the term 'time of war' in the first paragraph of Article 15 does not raise great problems. This situation is present at any rate in case of an official declaration of war on the part of, or directed against, the State in question, or when that State is actually involved in an international armed conflict. Whether a 'time of war' may also be considered to exist in case of a civil war or a 'war against terrorism', a question that is of great importance for the applicability of humanitarian law of war,

---

[22]   *Ibidem.*
[23]   *Dissenting opinion, para. 2.*

is not relevant here on account of the addition 'or other public emergency threatening the life of the nation'.[24]

34.4.2 PUBLIC EMERGENCY THREATENING THE LIFE OF THE NATION

In its report in the *Lawless* Case the Commission gave the following definition of 'public emergency threatening the life of the nation': "an exceptional situation or crisis of emergency which affects the whole population and constitutes a threat to the organised life of the community of which the State is composed".[25]

This definition was adopted by the Court in its judgment in this case.[26] In that judgment the Court held that the Irish Government could have reasonably deduced that there was a 'public emergency' at a given moment, on the basis of a combination of the following factors: (1) the existence in the territory of the Republic of a secret army which was engaged in unconstitutional activities and was using violence to attain its ends; (2) the fact that this army was also operating outside the territory of the State, thus seriously jeopardising the relation of the Republic with its neighbour; and (3) the steady and alarming increase in terrorist activities in the period preceding the decisive moment.[27]

In the *Greek* Case the above-mentioned definition was elaborated by the Commission. It pointed out beforehand that the French – authentic – text of the *Lawless* judgment, in which the Court adopted its definition, mentioned not only the word '*exceptionnel*', but also the word '*imminent*'.[28] In the opinion of the Commission an emergency must have the following characteristics if it is to be qualified as a 'public emergency' in the sense of Article 15: 1) it must be actual or imminent, 2) its effects must involve the whole nation, 3) the continuance of the organised life of the community must be threatened, and 4) the crisis or danger must be exceptional, in that

---

[24]   The counterpart of Article 15 of the Convention in Article 4 of the Covenant on Civil and Political Rights, makes no distinction between war and public emergency threatening the life of the nation. However, according to the Human Rights Committee in its General Comment No. 29, Article 4 of the Covenant "requires that even during an armed conflict measures derogating from the Covenant are allowed only if and to the extent that the situation constitutes a threat to the life of the nation. If States parties consider invoking Article 4 in other situations than an armed conflict, they should carefully consider the justification and why such a measure is necessary and legitimate in the circumstances". CCPR/C/21/Rev. 1/Add. 11, 31 August 2001, para. 3.

[25]   Report of 19 December 1959, B.1, p. 82.

[26]   Judgment of 1 July 1961, para. 28.

[27]   *Ibidem.*

[28]   The French version stated that "qu'ils désignent, en effet, une situation de crise ou de danger exceptionnel et imminent qui affecte l'ensemble de la population et constitue une menace pour la vie organisée de la communauté composant de l'Etat"; *ibidem.*

the normal measures or restrictions, permitted by the Convention for the maintenance of public safety, health and order, are plainly inadequate.[29]

Before dealing with the specific arguments of the Greek Government in this case, it is appropriate to make a few notes on the above-mentioned characteristics. First, the inclusion of the term 'imminent' is vital. Imminent either means that the danger is about to happen or to occur at any moment. The state must perceive the danger as unavoidable and non-evadable. Second, the whole nation has to be endangered. This notion has been relaxed somewhat in later case law: a derogation may apply to only a part of the territory and the danger may affect only a part of the population.[30] As long as the danger stays confined to one region of the State, the declaration remains confined to the afflicted area and does not apply to the nation as a whole.[31] Third, the threat to the organized life of the community means either a threat to the physical integrity of the population, the territorial integrity of the state, or the functioning of the organs of the state. Fourth, the fact that the danger must be exceptional requires the exhaustion of those measures normally used to deal with infractions of public order.

The arguments of the Greek Government for its submission that there was a 'public emergency' were summarised as follows by the Commission: (1) communist danger, (2) crisis of constitutional government, and (3) crisis of public order.[32] In support of its submission the Greek Government had put forward in particular that the communists were preparing an armed revolt within the State and from outside and were planning to seize power; that the other political parties were collaborating with the communists and were corrupt; that the numerous changes of government had rendered the administration of the country impossible; that constant strikes had brought the State on the verge of bankruptcy; and that the violent demonstrations had led to anarchy.[33] In the Commission's opinion, however, the Government had not thus sufficiently demonstrated that the situation in Greece showed the above-mentioned four characteristics at the decisive moment.[34]

In *Ireland v. the United Kingdom* both the Commission and the Court, on the basis of a very brief finding, concluded that the 'public emergency' invoked by the British Government indeed appeared to exist in Northern Ireland, and observed that this fact had not been contested by Ireland.[35] Since large-scale violent actions by a paramilitary

---

29   Report of 5 November 1969, Yearbook XII (1969), para. 153.
30   Judgment of 18 January 1978, *Ireland v. the United Kingdom*, para. 205; judgment of 26 May 1993, *Brannigan and McBride*, paras 47 and 50; and judgment of 18 December 1996 *Aksoy*, para. 70.
31   In the *Sakik* Case the Court stated that the derogation which was made for the south-east of Turkey, did not extend to the capital. It was therefore that the detention which was based upon this derogation was unjustifiable; judgment of 26 November 1997, para. 39.
32   Report of 5 November 1969, para. 89.
33   *Ibidem*, paras 88-151.
34   *Ibidem*, paras 152-165.
35   Report of 25 January 1976, B.23/I, p. 94; judgment of 18 January 1978, para. 205.

organisation were concerned, which were largely directed against the British security forces, the conclusion of the Commission and the Court can indeed hardly be disputed. The brief finding might, however, create the impression that, if the existence of a 'public emergency' in the sense of Article 15 has not been disputed by the applicant, the Court need not institute an independent inquiry into it anymore. Such an approach would, however, be incorrect. The supervision by the Court has objective elements, especially in the case of inter-state complaints, to maintain the legal order created by the Convention. A passive attitude with respect to the submission of the parties is, therefore, not fitting in the case of derogations which lead to a partial suspension of that legal order.

In the *Brannigan and McBride* Case the Court has avoided creating that impression. The applicants did not dispute the existence of an emergency situation. In this case, too, the Court reached the conclusion that "there can be no doubt that such a public emergency existed at the relevant time" in the light of "the extent and impact of terrorist violence in Northern Ireland and elsewhere in the United Kingdom". The Court was explicitly "[r]ecalling its case law in Lawless v. Ireland (...) and Ireland v. the United Kingdom", but meaningfully added "and making its own assessment".[36] In the *Aksoy* Case the applicants did not dispute the existence of an emergency which threatened the life of the nation either, but the Court reached its conclusion "in the light of all the material before it".[37]

34.4.3 STRICTLY REQUIRED BY THE EXIGENCIES OF THE SITUATION

The condition of 'strictly required by the exigencies of the situation' implies that States have to provide a careful justification for the derogation measures they have taken; the extent of the derogation must be strictly related to the situation. In the determination of the 'strictly required' character of the derogating measures various elements may play a role, notably the necessity of the derogations to cope with the threat and the proportionality of the measures in view of the threat. In its *Brannigan and McBride* judgment the Court found, more specifically, that it had to give appropriate weight to such relevant factors as "the nature of the rights affected by the derogation, the circumstances leading to, and the duration of, the emergency situation."[38]

In the *Lawless* Case the Court held that the requirement of necessity had been satisfied, because the Irish Government had proved that the existing legislation and the normal procedures for the maintenance of the legal order were not sufficient. The

---

[36] Judgment of 26 May 1993, para. 47.
[37] Judgment of 18 December 1996, para. 70.
[38] Judgment of 26 May 1993, para. 43.50.

requirement of proportionality had been satisfied in the Court's opinion, because, on the one hand, the Irish Government had not proceeded to take more far-reaching measures, such as the complete closure of the frontiers, while, on the other hand, in the internment system a number of guarantees against abuse of power by the authorities had been incorporated.[39] In the *Sakik* Case the Court held that if a derogation is made for a certain area in the territory, this derogation cannot be claimed outside this territory. The Court stated as follows: "It should be noted, however, that Article 15 authorizes derogation from the obligations arising from the Convention only 'to the extent strictly required by the exigencies of the situation'. In the present case the Court would be working against the object and purpose of that provision if, when assessing the territorial scope of the derogation concerned, it were to extend its effects to a part of Turkish territory not explicitly named in the notice of derogation. It follows that the derogation in question is inapplicable ratione loci to the facts of the case."[40]

In the *Aksoy* Case the Court held for the first time that a derogation measure which was taken by the Turkish Government was not strictly required by the exigencies of the situation.[41]

There are certain principles the Government (and consequently the Court) has to take into account when determining whether a derogation measure on the basis of Article 15 is strictly required by the exigencies of the situation. Those principles are (1) the necessity of the measure; (2) the proportionality of the measure; and (3) the duration of the measure taken.

Only measures deemed as crucial or strictly necessary against the danger are permitted. The mere fact that a derogation in a certain situation is justified by the exigencies of the situation does not mean that the specific measures taken are also required by the exigencies of the situation. The measures have to be immediately and directly pertinent to the protection against the danger. If a State can deal with the danger with normal measures, those measures have to be taken. In those cases there is no necessity for derogation. In the *Demir* Case the Court held that the incommunicado detention imposed upon the applicants for a period between sixteen to twenty-three days, was not strictly required by the crises relied on by the Government.[42]

As to the proportionality principle, the severity, duration and scope of the measures taken are elements that are particularly relevant. The derogation has to be proportional

---

[39]   Judgment of 1 July 1961, paras 36-37.
[40]   Judgment of 26 november 1997, para. 39.
[41]   Judgment 18 December 1996, para. 83.
[42]   Judgment of 23 September 1998, paras 49-57. The Commission was of the same opinion. In its report it stated that, 'despite the seriousness of the threat posed by terrorism (...) detaining the applicants for twenty-three and sixteen days or more respectively, without bringing them before a judge (...) exceeded the government's margin of appreciation and cannot be held to have been strictly required by the situation'; Report of 29 May 1997, *Demir and others*, para. 57.

to the danger. The measures taken during each phase of the danger must vary accordingly in degree. And the measures must be geographically proportional.

34.4.4 DURATION OF THE EMERGENCY

The issue of the duration of the measures taken by the Irish Government was not examined by the Court in the *Lawless* Case, evidently because the Court held that the situation called for the same stringent measures during the entire relevant period. It is, however, conceivable that, even if it can be established that the 'public emergency' continues, the effect of the measures adopted or of certain developments has been such that from a given moment continuation of the derogations to the same extent can no longer be deemed 'strictly required'.

In *Ireland v. the United Kingdom* it had been argued by the Irish Government that the English internment measures had proved ineffective and after a given point in time had not, therefore, been applied any longer. With respect to this the following position was taken by the Court: "It is certainly not the Court's function to substitute for the British Government's assessment any other assessment of what might be the most prudent or most expedient policy to combat terrorism. The Court must do no more than review the lawfulness, under the Convention, of the measures adopted by that Government from 9 August 1971 onward. For this purpose the Court must arrive at its decision in the light, not of a purely retrospective examination of the efficacy of those measures, but of the conditions and circumstances reigning when they were originally taken and subsequently applied."[43]

A curious reaction to a curious argument! From the side of the applicant State one would have expected the argument that the respondent State has gone to unnecessary lengths with its measures, and in doing so had exceeded the limit of proportionality, while the argument of Ireland seems to have the opposite purport, *viz*, that England had not gone far enough in fighting the IRA. But in itself the argument is valid: if certain measures are not adequate for checking or restricting the dangers against which they are aimed, those measures cannot be considered necessary and must be modified or abolished as soon as that inefficacy is established. It is certainly for the Court to judge whether this has been done and, if so, whether it has been done in good time, although the Court must allow the national authorities sufficient discretion to assess that efficacy themselves. In evident cases of inefficacy, however, the conditions of Article 15 have not been satisfied. By establishing this, the Court indeed does "no more than review the lawfulness, under the Convention, of the measures", since this is a matter of review for conformity with the condition that they must be 'strictly required'.

---

[43]   Judgment of 18 January 1978, para. 214.

In fact, in one of the subsequent paragraphs of the same judgment the Court did go into the obligation of the State to always ascertain, when applying derogations under Article 15, whether and to what extent the scope of these derogations could be restricted. Thus the Court found with respect to the right to judicial review, which Article 5(4) grants to everyone who has been deprived of his liberty, that it would have been preferable if this had been provided for immediately upon the introduction of the internment measures, but that the British Government *might* have been of the opinion that this was not yet possible in the initial period. 'The interpretation of Article 15 must leave a place for progressive adaptations'.[44]

In the *Brannigan and McBride* Case the same issue came up in the form of the question of whether the derogation had been declared prematurely by the British authorities. According to the applicants this was indeed the case because at the time of declaring the emergency the Government had not reached a firm and final view on the need to derogate and had announced that it required a further period of reflection and consultation. The Court rejected this line of reasoning: "The validity of the derogation cannot be called into question for the sole reason that the Government had decided to examine whether in the future a way could be found of ensuring greater conformity with Convention obligations. Indeed, such a process of continued reflection is not only in keeping with Article 15 para. 3 which requires permanent review of the need for emergency measures but is also implicit in the very notion of proportionality."[45]

34.4.5 THE NATURE OF THE RIGHTS AFFECTED

This element in the evaluation of whether a derogation is strictly required also came up in the *Brannigan and McBride* Case. That case concerned Article 5(3) and (5). The Court started out its examination by stressing that "judicial control of interference by the executive with the individual's right to liberty provided for by Article 5 is implied by one of the fundamental principles of a democratic society, namely the rule of law".[46]

Against the background of that point of departure the way in which the Court subsequently dealt with the Government's assertion that control of extended detention by a judge or other officer authorised by law to exercise judicial control was not possible, comes somewhat as a surprise. In the final analysis the Court concluded that the Government had not overstepped its margin of appreciation in deciding against judicial control because "[i]n the context of Northern Ireland, where the judiciary is

---

[44]   *Ibidem*, para. 220.
[45]   Judgment of 26 May 1993, para. 54.
[46]   *Ibidem*, para. 48.

small and vulnerable to terrorist attacks, public confidence in the independence of the judiciary is understandably a matter to which the Government attach great importance."[47]

This is quite a remarkable line of reasoning and it is, therefore, no surprise that various dissenters reacted in quite strong terms against this position of the majority. According to judge Pettiti, "it is difficult to believe that the independence of a judge would be undermined because he took part in proceedings making it possible to grant or approve an extension of detention".[48] In the same vein judge Walsh observed as follows: "The Government's plea that it is motivated by a wish to preserve public confidence in the independence of the judiciary is, in effect, to say that such confidence is to be maintained or achieved by not permitting them to have a role in the protection of the personal liberty of the arrested person. One would think that such a role was one which the public would expect the judges to have. It is also to be noted that neither Parliament nor the Government appears to have made any serious effort to rearrange the judicial procedure or jurisdiction, in spite of being advised to do so by the persons appointed to review the system, to cater for the requirement of Article 5 para. 3 in cases of the type now under review. It is the function of the national authorities so to arrange their affairs as not to clash with the requirements of the Convention. The Convention is not to be remoulded to assume the shape of the national procedures."[49]

On the one hand, in the *Brannigan and McBride* Case, the Court *expressis verbis* did set forth the nature of the right affected as a specific element in the evaluation of whether a derogation is strictly required by the exigencies of the situation. On the other hand, however, the judgment makes it difficult to escape the impression that the Court in fact attached hardly any weight to the nature of the right concerned as a separate element within the framework of the said evaluation. As far as the Convention is concerned it is difficult to come up with a more essential provision than the requirement of judicial control of interference by the executive with the individual's right to liberty which, as the Court itself reiterated, is implied by one of the fundamental principles of a democratic society, namely the Rule of Law.

Despite the fact that this fundamental requirement was at stake in the *Brannigan and McBride* Case and despite convincing arguments to the contrary, as for instance set forth in the dissenting opinions, the Court approved the Government's derogation. As to future cases one wonders what circumstances have to prevail for the Court to consider a derogation not justified on the basis of the nature of the rights affected, particularly when 'less fundamental' rights are concerned.

---

[47]   *Ibidem,* para. 59.
[48]   Dissenting opinion of Judge Pettiti.
[49]   Dissenting opinion of Judge Walsh, para. 10.

34.4.6 PROVIDED THAT SUCH MEASURES ARE NOT INCONSISTENT WITH ITS OTHER OBLIGATIONS UNDER INTERNATIONAL LAW

The provision in Article 15 that the measures adopted must not be inconsistent with the other obligations resting on the State under international law has played little part in the case law thus far.[50] In the *Lawless* Case – *ex officio*[51] –, in *Ireland v. the United Kingdom*[52] and in the *Brannigan and McBride* Case[53] the Court held that no evidence was found of any infringement of this condition. To the extent that obligations under other international conventions concerning human rights are concerned, the same condition also follows from Article 53 of the Convention.[54]

The Court has the duty to test whether the derogating measures of a State are consistent with other obligations of the State concerned under international (human rights and humanitarian) law. In this context it is of interest that Article 4 of the UN Covenant on Civil and Political Rights also provides for the possibility of derogations in case of a 'public emergency', but that more rights are 'non-derogable' there. The enumeration of Article 4(2) of the UN Covenant on Civil and Political Rights also includes Article 11 (the prohibition of imprisonment merely on the ground of inability to fulfill a contractual obligation) and Article 18 (freedom of thought, conscience and religion). A Contracting State which has also ratified the UN Covenant on Civil and Political Rights, therefore, cannot take derogatory measures with respect to those rights either, unless, where the freedom to manifest one's religion or beliefs is concerned, the restriction is one which is supported by the third paragraph of Article 18 of the UN Covenant on Civil and Political Rights. The Court is unlikely to easily reach the conclusion that a Contracting State is in violation of Article 15 because the measures adopted are inconsistent with Article 4 of the UN Covenant on Civil and Political Rights. In the *Brannigan and McBride* Case the applicants alleged a violation of the requirement contained in the Covenant's Article 4 that an emergency has to be officially proclaimed. The Court did go into the plausibility of this argument (and rejected it), but only after having observed that it is not the Court's "role to seek to define authoritatively the meaning of the terms 'officially proclaimed' in Article 4 of the Covenant."[55]

---

[50]   It is interesting to note that this principle of consistency with other obligations under international law is scarcely applied by most of the supervisory bodies. However, in its new General Comment on derogations (General Comment No. 29) the Human Rights Committee mentions this principle, where it did not mention it in General Comment No. 5; see *supra*, note 5.

[51]   Judgment of 1 July 1961, paras 39-41.

[52]   Judgment of 18 January 1978, para. 222.

[53]   Judgment of 26 May 1993, paras 67-73.

[54]   On this, *supra* note 5.

[55]   Judgment of 26 May 1993, para. 72.

In its General Comment No. 29 the Human Rights Committee, however, stresses the obligation of States to comply in a consistent manner with all their obligations under international law.[56] Apart from the UN Covenant on Civil and Political Rights, other provisions that may be thought of are those of the Geneva Conventions (1949) concerning humanitarian law and the Additional Protocols thereto (1977), which are intended to be applied in situations such as those mentioned in Article 15. The wide formulation 'other obligations under international law' also covers obligations under other than human rights and humanitarian conventions, such as customary international law and generally recognised legal principles. It is evident, however, that on this point the Court will not lightly go beyond the scope of conventional law, unless it can rely on clear international case law or an express consensus within the community of States.

Besides the conditions mentioned in Article 15 itself, the exercise of the power of derogation granted in that article is also subject to conditions ensuing from a number of other articles of the Convention, *viz.* Articles 14, 17, 18 and, as pointed out above, Article 53.

34.5 NON-DEROGABLE RIGHTS

The second paragraph of Article 15 contains an enumeration of the provisions of the Convention from which no derogation may be made under any circumstances, not even under those mentioned in the first paragraph: these provisions are non-derogable. Within the survey of the discussion of each individual right and freedom the issue has been addressed whether a particular right or freedom is non-derogable. However, this does not mean that derogable provisions can be derogated from at will; the requirement that the measure be strictly required by the exigencies of the situation obliges the State concerned to make an objective assessment of the actual situation to determine whether derogable rights should be derogated from. Although Article 14 is not mentioned in the second paragraph of Article 15, there are elements or dimensions of the right of non-discrimination that cannot be derogated from under any circumstances.[57] This follows from the condition that a derogation may not be discriminatory in nature.[58]

---

[56]   *Supra*, note 5, paras 9-10.

[57]   The Human Rights Committee concurs with this view in its General Comment No. 29; *supra*, note 5, para. 8.

[58]   Furthermore, the HRC states that some of the principles of fair trial and detention cannot be derogated from: "Safeguards related to derogation, as embodied in article 4 of the Covenant, are based on the principles of legality and the rule of law inherent in the Covenant as a whole. As certain elements of the right to a fair trial are explicitly guaranteed under international humanitarian law during armed conflict, the Committee finds no justification for derogation from these guarantees during other emergency situations. The Committee is of the opinion that the principles of legality

34.6   INFORMATION TO BE PROVIDED TO THE COUNCIL OF EUROPE

The notification principle is regarded as one of the important protective elements of Article 15. It is seen as a safeguard against abuse of the derogation clause. However, as the case law of the Court and the behaviour of States show, both the States and the Court regard this principle as primarily a procedural element and not as a material condition and a safeguard against misuse of the power of derogation. As to the information to be given to the Secretary General of the Council of Europe, as prescribed in the third paragraph, the Court held in the *Lawless* Case that this must take place 'without delay' after the entry into force of the measures concerned. A delay of twelve days was still considered to be in conformity with this obligation.[59] The Commission, in its report, had used the words 'without any avoidable delay',[60] thus evidently indicating that allowance must be made for special difficulties with which a government may be confronted in case of a 'public emergency'. A delay of four months in the *Greek* Case, however, was considered too long by the Commission.[61]

No special form is prescribed for the information nor need it be stated expressly that it is intended as information in the sense of Article 15(3).[62] However, in the words of the Commission, the Government must "furnish sufficient information concerning them [the measures in question] to enable the other High Contracting Parties and the European Commission to appreciate the nature and extent of the derogation from the provisions of the Convention which these measures involve".[63] Moreover, the information must be sufficient to enable the Court to infer therefrom the reasons for the measures.[64] This is important because the information provided constitutes merely a first indication of whether a derogation is justifiable. It is solely for the Court to judge whether the condition of the third paragraph has been fulfilled. However, here again the Court leaves some discretion to the Government concerned.

---

and the rule of law require that fundamental requirements of fair trial must be respected during a state of emergency. Only a court of law may try and convict a person for a criminal offence. The presumption of innocence must be respected. In order to protect non-derogable rights, the right to take proceedings before a court to enable the court to decide without delay on the lawfulness of detention, must not be diminished by a State party's decision to derogate from the Covenant"; *supra*, note 5, para. 16.

59   Judgment of 1 July 1961, para. 47.
60   Report of 19 December 1959, para. 80.
61   Report of 5 November 1969, Yearbook XII (1969), p. 43. See also the dissenting opinion of Commission member Delahaye, *ibidem*, pp. 43-44.
62   Report of 19 December 1959, *Lawless*, B.1, pp. 73-74. See also the judgment of 1 July 1961 in this case, para. 47.
63   *Ibidem.*
64   Judgment of 1 July 1961, *Lawless*, para. 47.

What are the consequences if a Contracting State makes use of the possibilities of derogation provided for in the Convention, but omits to inform the Secretary General thereof in the way prescribed in Article 15(3)? Since the Convention does not explicitly lay down such consequences, two extremes are conceivable. Failure to inform the Secretary General might rule out reliance on Article 15 for the justification of derogation measures taken. On the other hand, there is the possibility that non-observance of Article 15(3) has no (legal) consequences at all.

The question here referred to arose in the joined applications of *Cyprus v. Turkey,* where Cyprus complained about the action of the Turkish invasion forces.[65] In the first Case of *Greece v. the United Kingdom* and in the *Lawless* Case this question had also already arisen, but then in a more indirect way. In these latter cases the Commission had "reserved its view as to whether failure to comply with the requirements of Article 15(3) 'may attract the sanction of nullity or some other sanction'".[66] The question was raised expressly, however, in the joined applications just mentioned. The Turkish Government had not furnished any information as referred to in Article 15(3), because, as it submitted, it had no jurisdiction over the Northern part of Cyprus occupied by the Turkish forces.[67] The Commission, on the contrary, had held in its decision on admissibility that "the Turkish armed forces in Cyprus brought any person or property there 'within the jurisdiction' of Turkey, in the sense of Article 1 of the Convention, 'to the extent that they exercise control over such persons or property'."[68]

During its examination of the merits the Commission was, therefore, confronted with the question of the consequences of the Turkish Government's failure to provide the relevant information. Despite the fact that this question thus became prominent the Commission, curiously enough, began its answer with the following observation: "In the present case the Commission still does not consider itself called upon generally to determine the above question".[69] It continued as follows: "It finds, however, that, in any case, Article 15 requires some formal and public act of derogation, such as a declaration of martial law or state of emergency, and that, where no such act has been proclaimed by the High Contracting Party concerned, although it was not in the circumstances prevented from doing so, Article 15 cannot apply."[70]

Thus, in a case of a failure on the part of the authorities to publicly declare the state of war or other public emergency, it would appear that the State concerned is deprived of the right to invoke Article 15(1). This still leaves open the question of what are the

---

[65]   Appls 6780/74 and 6950/75, Yearbook XVIII (1975), p. 82.
[66]   See the report of 10 July 1976, *Cyprus* v. *Turkey* (not published), para. 526.
[67]   *Ibidem.*
[68]   *Ibidem,* para. 525.
[69]   *Ibidem,* para. 527.
[70]   *Ibidem.* The proclamation of martial law in Turkey itself, which had been notified, according to the Commission could not be deemed 'to cover the treatment of persons brought into Turkey from the northern area of Cyprus'; *ibidem,* para. 530.

consequences if a State has publicly declared such a state, but has failed to inform the Secretary General about it. As relevant case law of the Court on the issue is lacking, the consequences of non-fulfilment of the information obligation laid down in Article 15 have not yet been clarified.

If the derogation measures have ceased to operate and the provisions of the Convention are being fully executed again, a further notification is required under Article 15(3). The rationale behind this is that the Secretary-General and other States will be informed of the termination of the derogation measures and will thus be able to monitor whether the rights under the Convention are being fully respected again.

In the *Brannigan and McBride* Case the Court further held that Article 15(3) implies an obligation to keep the need for emergency measures under permanent review, an obligation implicit in the proportionality of any measures of derogation.[71]

34.7 THE ADEQUACY OF THE SUPERVISION OVER ARTICLE 15

Given the far-reaching consequences of the application of Article 15 it is of the utmost importance that that application in practice is supervised as effectively as possible. Nothing at all is left of the supervision by the Court – which is already very marginal – of the application of Article 15 by the Contracting States if a reservation, as made by France with respect to Article 15, would be accepted.[72] This reservation implies, *inter alia*, that the words 'to the extent strictly required by the exigencies of the situation' must not be interpreted as restrictions on the power of the President of the French Republic to take 'measures required by the circumstances'. The consequence would be that derogation from the rights and freedoms protected in the Convention, with the exception of those mentioned in Article 15(2), remains at the complete discretion of the Contracting State in question, without any real review of the use of that discretion by the Court being possible.

In some situations it may turn out to be difficult to judge the exact scope of the Strasbourg supervision over the observance of Article 15. In a case which has remained unique until now, France, Norway, Denmark, Sweden and the Netherlands alleged a violation of Article 15 on the part of Turkey, but subsequently reached a friendly settlement with the latter.[73] As far as Article 15 was concerned, the applicant States noted that Turkey had in the meantime progressively reduced the geographical scope of martial law and had declared that it would be lifted from the remaining provinces within 18 months, and that a number of decrees and other legal enactments,

---

[71]   Judgment of 26 May 1993, para. 54.
[72]   On the question of whether this French reservation is legitimate or not, see *infra* p. 1113.
[73]   Appls 9940-9944/82, report of 7 December 1985, D&R 44 (1985), p. 31.

mentioned by the applicant Governments in their applications, had been changed or amended.[74] The Commission accepted the settlement by concluding that it had been secured on the basis of respect for human rights in the sense of present Article 38(8).[75] In accordance with Article 30 (old) the Commission's report was confined to a brief statement of the facts and of the solution reached. Consequently, no arguments are to be found in it to support the Commission's conclusion that respect for human rights had indeed been secured.[76]

Turkey had limited its derogation under Article 15 to Article 5 and to a number of specified districts in 1992 and 1993 respectively. In fact, during the whole period Turkey has been switching on and off its obligations under the Convention without any form of supervision being exercised on the part of the Court for some time. More recently, however, some supervision over Turkey has been exercised by the Court.[77]

Even if Strasbourg supervision is exercised, there is no guarantee in the present situation that it is effective. This has become clear from the Court's reaction in its *Brannigan and McBride* judgment to the aftermath of its earlier *Brogan* judgment. The latter judgment had held that the United Kingdom had violated, *inter alia*, Article 5(3) because the applicants, after being detained, were neither brought promptly before a judicial authority nor released promptly following their arrest. As far as Article 15 is concerned the judgment contained the following considerations: "The Government have adverted extensively to the existence of particularly difficult circumstances in Northern Ireland, notably the threat posed by organized terrorism. (...) The Government informed the Secretary General of the Council of Europe on 22 August 1984 that they were withdrawing a notice of derogation under Article 15 which had relied on an emergency situation in Northern Ireland (...). The Government indicated accordingly that in their opinion 'the provisions of the Convention are being fully executed'. In any event, as they pointed out, the derogation did not apply to the area of law in issue in the present case. Consequently, there is no call in the present proceedings to consider whether any derogation from the United Kingdom's obligations under the Convention might be permissible under Article 15 by reason of a terrorist campaign in Northern Ireland."[78]

However, on 23 December 1988 – less than a month after the *Brogan* judgment – the British Government provided the Secretary General with a set of information in order to ensure compliance with its obligations under Article 15(3). The contents

---

[74]   *Ibidem*, p. 39.

[75]   *Ibidem*, p. 41.

[76]   On 25 May 1987, the Turkish Government informed the Secretary General of the Council of Europe that martial law would be lifted in the remaining provinces from 19 July 1987; Council of Europe, *Information Sheet* No. 21, 1987, p. 14.

[77]   See the judgments in the *Aksoy* Case, the *Demir* Case and the *Sakik* Case.

[78]   Judgment of 29 November 1988, para. 48.

of this information was at least confusing and from the perspective of the United Kingdom's obligations under the Convention even dubious. Formally the *Note Verbale* in which the information was contained, could be taken as a notice on the part of the British Government that from 23 December 1988 it was going to make use of the possibility provided for by Article 15 to derogate from certain of the obligations ensuing from the Convention. In a technical sense such a step is fully justified, provided that the Government can convincingly argue that the circumstances prevailing in the country call for the application of Article 15. In the present case, however, that was hard to imagine. Given the above-mentioned position taken by the British Government during the *Brogan* Case, the circumstances requiring application of Article 15 could only have arisen between the date of the Court's judgment and 23 December 1988. The *Note Verbale* did not make this clear at all. On the contrary, reference was made to 'recent years' of campaigns of organised terrorism and to the year 1974, in which the Government found it necessary to introduce special measures to combat this terrorism. Since the Government did not rely on Article 15 in the *Brogan* Case, the position taken in the Note Verbale, in our view, bore witness to bad faith on the part of the British Government as far as the period starting from 23 December 1988 was concerned in order to evade the consequences of the *Brogan* judgment.[79]

In the *Brannigan and McBride* Case the applicants took the similar position alleging that the 1988 derogation on the part of the United Kingdom was the Government's reaction to the *Brogan* judgment and was declared in order to circumvent the consequences of that judgment. The Court first observed that the power of arrest and extended detention had been considered necessary by the British Government in dealing with the threat of terrorism since 1974. Following the *Brogan* judgment, according to the Court, the Government were then faced with the option of either introducing judicial control or lodging a derogation from their Convention obligations in this respect. The Court then simply added: "The adoption of the view by the Government that judicial control compatible with Article 5 para. 3 was not feasible because of the special difficulties associated with the investigation and prosecution of terrorist crime rendered derogation inevitable. Accordingly, the power of extended detention without such judicial control and the derogation of 23 December 1988 being

---

[79] As far as the period between the date of the judgment up to 23 December 1988 was concerned, there was an outright violation of the Convention and the *Note Verbale* did not even bother to conceal it. After recalling that the Court had held that 'even the shortest of the four periods of detention concerned (...) fell outside the constraints as to time permitted by the first part of Article 5(3)", the *Note Verbale* bluntly added that "Following this judgment (...) the Government did not believe that the maximum period of detention should be reduced." Finally it was concluded that "Since the judgment of 29 November 1988 as well as previously, the Government have found it necessary to continue to exercise, in relation to terrorism connected with the affairs of Northern Ireland, the powers described above enabling further detention without charge, for periods of up to five days." (DH(89)1, pp. 10-11).

clearly linked to the persistence of the emergency situation, there is no indication that the derogation was other than a genuine response."[80]

In view of the history of the case the Court's reaction is, first of all, rather concise. Moreover, the attitude of the majority reflects a very loose type of supervision, which squares uneasily with the far-reaching impact of derogation under Article 15. The approach set forth by judge De Meyer in his dissenting opinion would seem to be much more convincing. According to judge De Meyer, given the prevailing situation in Northern Ireland, "[o]ne can (...) understand that (...) the Government of the United Kingdom have, since 1957, repeatedly felt it appropriate to avail themselves of their right of derogation under Article 15 of the Convention. In 1984 they had come to the conclusion that this was no longer necessary. We have been told that one of their reasons for doing so was their belief that detaining for up to seven days a person suspected of terrorism without bringing that person before a judge or other judicial officer was not inconsistent with their obligations under the Convention. In our Brogan and Others v. the United Kingdom judgment of 29 November 1988 we held that this assumption was wrong, and we strongly emphasised the importance of the fundamental human right to liberty and the need for judicial control of interferences therewith. The Government of the United Kingdom have tried to escape the consequences of that judgment by lodging again a notice of derogation under Article 15 in order to continue the practice concerned. In my view, this was not permissible: they failed to convince me that such a far-reaching departure from the rule of respect for individual liberty could, either after or before the end of 1988, be 'strictly required by the exigencies of the situation'. Even in the circumstances as difficult as those which have existed in respect of Northern Ireland for many years it is not acceptable that a person suspected of terrorism can be detained for up to seven days without any form of judicial control. This was, in fact, what we had already decided in the Brogan and Others Case and there was no valid reason for deciding otherwise in the present one."[81]

Similarly, on the basis of a comparable line of reasoning, judge Pettiti concluded in his dissenting opinion that "[t]he State was under a duty to implement mechanisms complying with the Brogan and Other judgment and making it possible to conform thereto without resorting to derogation".[82]

The most recent derogation was declared by the UK after the September 11, 2001 attacks on the Twin Towers in New York. It is most likely that in due time the Court will be seized of this matter.

The possibility of derogation under Article 15 has been made use of several times and by different countries. It goes without saying that an effective protection of the rights

---

[80] Judgment of 26 May 1993, para. 51.
[81] Dissenting opinion of Judge De Meyer.
[82] Dissenting opinion of Judge Pettiti.

and freedoms guaranteed in the Convention requires that derogations from the provisions of the Convention be minimised. This calls for a continuous and strict supervision of the observance of the conditions laid down in Article 15. One may wonder whether the supervision mechanism provided for in the Convention, which comes into operation only after submission of a complaint and consequently has an incidental character, is sufficient in this respect. A better structured approach might be action by the Secretary General under Article 52 at appropriate occasions.

CHAPTER 35
RESTRICTIONS ON THE POLITICAL
ACTIVITY OF ALIENS (Article 16)

Revised by Yutaka Arai

CONTENTS

35.1 TEXT OF ARTICLE 16

Nothing in Articles 10, 11 and 14 shall be regarded as preventing the High Contracting Parties from imposing restrictions on the political activity of aliens.

35.2 INTRODUCTION

With respect to certain rights Article 16 constitutes an exception to the general principle, as embodied in Articles 1 and 14, that the enjoyment of the Convention rights and freedoms is guaranteed to everyone within the jurisdiction of the Contracting States irrespective of nationality. Article 16 is distinct in that the restrictions contemplated under this provision are limited in scope of application *ratione materiae* and *ratione personae*. While the addressees of the restrictions are confined to aliens, Article 16 applies to a specific category of activities, namely, political activities, in the context of particular rights: the freedom of expression under Article 10 and the freedom of association and assembly under Article 11, as well as the freedom from discrimination under Article 14. The provision now laid down in Article 16 was initially not included in the draft of the Consultative Assembly, but was inserted by the Committee of Experts.[1]

35.3 ALIENS

The term 'aliens' ('*étrangers*') refers both to persons having the nationality of one of the other Contracting States (while not also having the nationality of the State in question) and to other foreigners, including stateless persons. Unlike the European Union law with respect to nationals of member States of the Union, the Convention does not grant a privileged position to those aliens who are nationals of one of the member States of the Council of Europe. However, in the *Piermont* Case the Court suggested that a privileged status was accorded to a member of the European Parliament (MEP). In that case a German MEP was invited by local political parties to participate in pro-independence and anti-nuclear weapons demonstrations in French Polynesia. When she was leaving, she was served with an order for her expulsion and denial of re-entry and found herself excluded from entry into New Caledonia, on the ground of the prevention of disorder and of the preservation of territorial integrity. When assessing the term 'aliens' the Commission characterized the Convention as a 'living instrument', which must be interpreted in harmony with present day conditions and the evolution of modern society.[2] It dismissed the applicability of Article 16 and found that justifications for the French authorities' interference could lie only in the second paragraph of Article 10. It attached special importance to the fact that MEPs are supposed to express views and adopt policy stances not only in the European Parliament but also in other fora on political problems of both the Community and its member States, and that the applicant was invited in a capacity as an MEP by local political parties to visit the overseas territories whose citizens took part in the election of MEPs.[3] When ascertaining, *inter alia,* whether Article 16 could be invoked to justify an alleged interference with her freedom of expression under Article 10,[4] the Court agreed with the view of the French Government that the applicant could not rely on European citizenship, because the Community treaties did not then recognize such citizenship. Nevertheless, the Court concluded "that Mrs Piermont's possession of the nationality of a member State of the European Union and her status as a member of the European Parliament do not allow Article 16 of the Convention to be raised against her, especially as the people of the OTs [Overseas

---

[1]   Council of Europe, *Collected Editions of the 'Travaux Préparatoires of the European Convention on Human Rights,* Vol. III, The Hague, 1976, p. 238.
[2]   *Piermont,* report of 20 January 1994, paras 59-61.
[3]   *Ibidem,* paras 65-70.
[4]   *Piermont,* judgment of 27 April 1995, paras 60-64.

Territories] take part in the European Parliament elections".[5] Judges Ryssdal, Matscher, Freeland and Jungwiert, in their partly dissenting opinion, expressed the view that the Court's approach in *Piermont* in effect added a new immunity to members of the European Parliament, aspects of which were already governed by the 1965 Protocol on the privileges and immunities of the European Communities.[6] In their opinion the Court's approach was at odds with the fact that Article 16 unambiguously refers to 'aliens' without express exceptions.[7] This prompted the dissenting judges to argue that 'convincing grounds' need to be adduced to justify an 'inferred' exception to Article 16. They averred that the proportionality appraisal under Article 10(2) should incorporate the object and purpose of Article 16.[8]

It may be argued that underlying the interpretation of the majority of the Court in *Piermont* is the policy approach based on the principle of effective protection, with the need to construe any restrictions on the Convention rights narrowly. The application of this principle can be deemed of special importance with respect to Article 16 in order to minimize any adverse implications of applying this provision, whose *raison d'être* has become increasingly questionable, especially in relation to nationals of other Contracting States.

35.4   POLITICAL ACTIVITY

The scope of application *ratione materiae* of Article 16 depends on the interpretation of the term 'political activity' ('activité politique'). Article 16 does not deprive aliens within the territory of a member State of all the guarantees under Articles 10, 11, and 14, but its restrictive effect extends only to political activities. Insofar as the rights safeguarded under these provisions relate to other than political activities, aliens are entitled to the same guarantees as the nationals of the State in question.

The second paragraph of Articles 10 and 11 enumerate such legitimate aims as 'the interests of national security and public safety',[9] and 'the prevention of disorder',[10] which can justify interfering measures, while the first paragraph of Article 11 speaks of 'peaceful assembly'. These formulae suggest that the drafters of the Convention contemplated the protection of other interests of a State under Article 16. Within the framework of the latter article it needs to be examined whether the interest of good

---

[5]   *Ibidem*, para. 64.
[6]   *Ibidem*, joint partly dissenting opinion of judges Ryssdal, Matscher, Freeland and Jungwiert, para. 4.
[7]   *Ibidem*.
[8]   *Ibidem*, para. 5. In view of the object and purpose of Article 16, as well as of the indiscreet nature of the applicant's public conduct in Polynesia, these judges concluded that there was no breach of proportionality: paras 7-9.
[9]   The second paragraphs of Articles 10 and 11 of the Convention.
[10]   The second paragraph of Article 10 of the Convention.

relations with other (non-contracting) States can justify application of Article 16. It is questionable whether Article 16 can authorize a ban on migrant workers or other lawful residents who have yet to acquire the nationality of the State in question, or indeed political refugees, prohibiting them to participate in demonstrations or to publish political pamphlets in order to criticize a government of a non-contracting State. Both political expression and political demonstration are among the most essential values of democracy underpinning the Convention system. It would even more be unacceptable to invoke Article 16 in order to allow restrictions on the rights under Articles 10, 11 and 14 where the political implications of certain activities exclusively concern the host country itself. Otherwise a Contracting State would be allowed to obstruct migrant workers from advocating their rights, such as improvement in its social security measures and the granting of stay permits, even though such demands do not touch on that State's interests, such as national security or public order. These examples clearly demonstrate that, in its present, unqualified form, Article 16 is hardly compatible with the Convention as a 'living instrument'.

Whether a 'political activity' is involved in a specific case is subject to the supervision by the Court, but this question has not yet been raised so far. It is possible to contemplate that the Court might be tempted to apply the notion of margin of appreciation in assessing this term, as in the case of other possibilities of restrictions. However, it is submitted that the Court should resist such temptation as much as possible and place the onus on the Contracting State to advance reasonable arguments for qualifying certain activities as 'political'.

The application of Article 16 suggests that, insofar as political activities are concerned, a Contracting State may place restrictions on the rights of aliens to freedom of expression under Article 10 and to freedom of association and assembly under Article 11, even without the need for such restrictions to be justified under the second paragraph of those provisions. Another implication of Article 16 is that under Article 14 the national authorities may discriminate against aliens in relation to the rights guaranteed in Articles 10 and 11. In addition, the relationship between Article 16 and the anti-discrimination clause of Article 14 is more complex. The application of Article 16 would 'disable' aliens from invoking Article 14 in relation to rights other than those guaranteed under Articles 10 and 11, which may involve elements of political activities. It is not difficult to conceive the concurrent application of Articles 16 and 14 authorizing restrictions on the right of aliens to vote and to be elected under Article 3 of the First Protocol. Apart from such conspicuous scenarios, it is possible to conceive restrictions on other Convention rights in a more subtle way. The exercise of the right to property under Article 1 of the First Protocol may be related to political activities, as in the case of political parties' use of premises. Similarly, both the right to freedom of religion under Article 9 of the Convention and the right of education under Article 2 of the First Protocol may involve political activities if exercised by a certain political party affiliated with a specific religious group.

35.5 ARTICLE 16 AS AN OBSOLETE PROVISION?

So far the *Piermont* judgment is the only judgment of the Court concerning Article 16.[11] The dearth of case-law and the growing perception that this provision does not conform to the increasingly integrated Europe may explain why the Parliamentary Assembly adopted Recommendation 799 (1977), which urged the Committee of Ministers "[t]o instruct the competent committee of experts to make proposals of the amendment of the European Convention for the protection of Human Rights and Fundamental Freedoms in such a way as to exclude restrictions at present authorised by Article 16 with respect to political activity on the exercise by aliens of the freedoms guaranteed by Article 10 (freedom of expression) and Article 11 (freedom of association)".[12] It is regrettable that this proposal has not been taken up, leaving Article 16 intact even after the major overhaul of the supervisory system effectuated by the entry into force of the 11th Protocol.

Following the Committee on Migration, Refugees and Demography's Report of 22 December 2000,[13] the Parliamentary Assembly of the Council of Europe adopted Recommendation 1500 (2001) on *Participation of immigrants and foreign residents in political life in the Council of Europe member States.*[14] This document recommends the Committee of Ministers, *inter alia*, to reappraise minimum standards of human rights for non-citizens residing in a member State, "with a view to granting the right to vote and stand in elections to all legally established migrants irrespective of their origin, and invite member governments to take all appropriate action to ensure their implementation".[15] It also urges the member States 'to grant the right to vote and stand in local elections to all migrants legally established for at least three years *irrespective of their origin*',[16] and to ratify the European Convention on the Participation of Foreigners in Public Life at a Local Level 1992.[17] Article 6(1) of this Convention specifically recognizes the duty of the State Parties to grant the right to vote and to stand for election in local authority elections to *every* foreign resident, subject to the conditions that they have been a lawful and habitual residents in the State for the 5 years preceding the

---

[11] Note that in *H.N. v. Italy*, the Commission declared the complaint relating to Article 16 incompatible with the Convention's provisions, decision of 27 October 1998, para. 4.

[12] Recommendation 799 (1977) on the political rights and position of aliens, 25 January 1977; Parliamentary Assembly, 28th Ordinary Session, Third part, *Texts Adopted* (1977).

[13] *Participation of immigrants and foreign residents in political life in the Council of Europe member states,* Report by the Committee on Migration, Refugees and Demography (Rapporteur: Mr. Luis), Doc. 8916, 22 December 2000.

[14] Recommendation 1500 (2001), Text adopted by the Assembly on 26 January 2001 (8th Sitting).

[15] *Ibidem*, para. 11 (i).

[16] *Ibidem*, para. 11 (iv) (a), emphasis added.

[17] *Ibidem*, para. 11 (iv) (e).

elections.[18] However, after entering into force in 1997, this Convention has been ratified only by a tiny fraction of member States.[19]

---

[18] However, Article 6(2) of this Convention allows State parties to make a declaration to the effect that they can be exempted from granting to foreign residents the right to stand for election. Further, the rights guaranteed under Article 6(1) are subject to greater restrictions in time of war or other public emergency within the meaning of Article 9.

[19] As of 11 February 2005, only the Scandinavian countries (Denmark, Finland, Iceland, Norway and Sweden), the Netherlands and Italy have ratified this treaty.

CHAPTER 36

PROHIBITION OF ABUSE OF THE RIGHTS AND FREEDOMS SET FORTH IN THE CONVENTION AND OF THEIR LIMITATION TO A GREATER EXTENT THAN IS PROVIDED FOR IN THE CONVENTION (Article 17)

REVISED BY YUTAKA ARAI

CONTENTS

36.1   TEXT OF ARTICLE 17

Nothing in this Convention may be interpreted as implying for any State, group or person any right to engage in any activity or perform any act aimed at the destruction of any of the rights and freedoms set forth herein or at their limitation to a greater extent than is provided for in the Convention.

36.2 INTRODUCTION

The prohibition of abuse of right is considered as one of the 'general principles' of the Convention. This principle corresponds to Article 5 of the International Covenant on Civil and Political Rights.[1] The primary purpose of Article 17, which reiterates this self-evident principle, is two-fold: first, to ensure that individual persons or groups do not abuse their Convention rights in such a manner as to propagate, for example, racial hatred or anti-Semitism as savagely done by the Nazis during the Holocaust; second, to ensure that State authorities do not invoke possibilities of restrictions on the Convention rights based on extraneous motives, or more ominously, with a view to undermining the Convention values and enabling a totalitarian feature to be crept into national societies. In *United Communist Party of Turkey and Others v. Turkey*, the Court observed that the applicability of Article 17 depends on whether the aim of the offending actions is to spread violence or hatred, to resort to illegal or undemocratic methods, to encourage the use of violence, to undermine the nation's democratic and pluralist political system, or to pursue objectives that are racist or likely to destroy the rights and freedoms of others.[2]

From the formulation of Article 17 it is clear that this provision does not have an independent character, and that its violation is necessarily connected with one or more of the rights and freedoms enumerated in Section I of the Convention and its Protocols. The nature and degree of such connection may vary, depending on whether Article 17 is invoked against an individual or against a State.

Article 17 can also be invoked to challenge the applicability of Article 15, though the Strasbourg organs may see fit to incorporate elements of Article 17 into the process of stringently assessing the existence of emergency conditions under Article 15. In the *Greek Case*, the Commission held that since it had already found the existence of a public emergency warranting the application of Article 15 to be absent, there was no further need to examine whether the Greek Government's derogations were excluded by Articles 17 and 18.[3] Yet, the Commission's reasoning does not exclude the possibility that Article 17 (and Article 18) may be invoked to challenge the application of a derogation clause.

---

[1]   See also Articles 29 (2) and 30 of the Universal Declaration of Human Rights.
[2]   Judgment of 30 January 1998, para. 23. See also Appl. 250/57, *The German Communist Party*, Yearbook I (1956-57), p. 222 (the German Constitutional Court's ban on a political party with the objective of gaining power by violent means), at 224, at 224-225; and *Remer*, D&R 82-A (1995), p. 117 (a revisionist editor who was convicted of incitement to hatred and race hatred against Jewish people pursuant to the German Penal Code, in relation to his publication that contained articles denying the existence of gas chambers in Nazi concentration camps).
[3]   Report of 5 November 1969, *Yearbook* XII (1969), at 111-112.

Chapter 36   Prohibition of Abuse of the Rights and Freedoms set Forth in the
Convention and of Their Limitation to a Greater Extent than is Provided for
in the Convention (Article 17)

36.3   THE SCOPE OF ARTICLE 17 VIS-À-VIS
PRIVATE PARTIES

As a general clause Article 17 is unique under the Convention in that the addressees
of this prohibition are not only the Contracting States, but also private individuals
and groups. With regard to individuals and groups the aim of Article 17 is to prevent
them from invoking the Convention rights for the purpose of destroying or limiting
the rights of others.[4] In the *Glimmerveen and Hagenbeek* Case the Commission held
that "Article 17 covers essentially those rights which, if invoked, will facilitate the
attempt to derive therefrom a right to engage in activities aimed at the destruction of
any of the rights and freedoms set forth in the Convention".[5]

Where Article 17 was invoked by a Contracting State, or by the Strasbourg organs
ex officio, to justify restrictions on a right of individual persons, the methodology
followed by the Strasbourg organs may be encapsulated in three approaches.

First, they have invoked Article 17 to negate the protection of certain Convention
rights. In the *Glimmerveen and Hagenbeek* Case the Commission found that both the
conviction of the applicants for possessing leaflets of the anti-immigration political
party '*Nederlandse Volks Unie*', intended for distribution to the public, and the
prevention of their participation in municipal elections were justified under Article
17. The application of Article 17 resulted in the finding that the applicants were
debarred from relying on Article 10 of the Convention or Article 3 of the First
Protocol.[6]

Second, the Strasbourg organs have examined the complaints only under
substantive provisions and discarded the examination under Article 17. The assessment
of the Strasbourg organs has been confined to the statement that the restrictions
concerned were in conformity with the provision in question, ruling out the
examinations of the applicability of Article 17. In *X. v. Austria* the Commission found
no need to examine whether criminal convictions of a National Socialist could be
justified under Article 17 on the ground that it found the penal measures to be justified
under Articles 9(2) and 10(2).[7]

---

[4]   See judgment of 1 July 1961, *Lawless*, para. 6.

[5]   Decision of 11 October 1979, D&R 18 (1980), p. 187, at 195 para. 18. See also a similar case decided
by the Human Rights Committee under Article 5(1) in conjunction with Article 19 of the
International Covenant on Civil and Political Rights: *Faurisson v. France*, Communication No.
550/1993, 8 November 1996, CCPR/C/58/D/550/1993, 16 December 1996.

[6]   Decision of 11 October 1979, D&R 18 (1980), p. 187, at 195, paras 19-22 and 25-27.

[7]   Appl. 1747/62, *X v. Austria, Yearbook* VI (1963), p. 424, at 442-444. See also *Engel and Others,* which,
though Article 17 was directed at a member State rather than at private parties, followed this approach
(an alleged breach of Article 10 coupled with Article 17): Report of 19 July 1974, B. 20 (1978), paras
184-187; judgment of 8 June 1976, para. 104.

Third, the methodology developed by the Commission is to incorporate elements of Article 17 into the appraisal of limitations allowed under the specific provision. This may be described as the 'indirect application' of Article 17. The *Remer* Case concerned a revisionist editor convicted of incitement to hatred and race hatred pursuant to the German Penal Code in relation to his publication that contained articles on the Holocaust denial, including the denial of the existence of gas chambers in Nazi concentration camps, and other articles condemning policies relating to the 'preferential treatment' of asylum-seekers and 'gypsies'. The Commission evaluated the requirements of Article 17 when applying the 'necessary in a democratic society' standard under the second paragraph of Article 10.[8] It concluded that criminal convictions of the applicant were justified by the 'relevant and sufficient reasons' and that there was no appearance of a violation of Article 10.

36.4 THE PRINCIPLE OF PROPORTIONALITY

When ascertaining the applicability of Article 17 (and Article 18) to private individual persons, the Commission emphasized the principle of proportionality in order to constrain potentially far-reaching effects of the application of Article 17 in prohibiting individual persons from exercising Convention rights. In the *De Becker* Case the Commission stressed that "Article 17 is of somewhat limited scope: it applies only to persons who threaten the democratic system of the Contracting Parties and then to an extent strictly proportionate to the seriousness and duration of such threat".[9] As compared with Article 15, which entails the notion of proportionality as a 'built-in' principle, the Commission felt the need to affirm it in the case law of Articles 17 and 18. However, the dearth of the case law involving substantive appraisal of complaints under Article 17 has still left the notion of proportionality at an inchoate stage.

36.5 ASSESSMENT OF ARTICLE 17 TO BE JOINED TO THE MERITS

It is desirable that in case Article 17 is invoked by a respondent State to justify restrictive measures, the Committee of three judges at the admissibility stage, if it does not hold the applicability of Article 17 as manifestly ill-founded, joins its examination to the merits, and that a full-fledged review of the merits is conducted by a Chamber of the Court. Whether or not Article 17 is applicable is largely dependent on the substance of the complaints. The finding that there has been an abuse of rights on the

---

[8]   Appl. 25096/94, D&R 82-A (1995), p. 117, at 122-123.
[9]   Report of 8 January 1960, B.2 (1962), pp. 137-138, para. 279.

Chapter 36 Prohibition of Abuse of the Rights and Freedoms set Forth in the
Convention and of Their Limitation to a Greater Extent than is Provided for
in the Convention (Article 17)

part of individual persons or groups within the meaning of Article 17 inevitably implies that the State concerned has not violated the Convention rights. In the *Lawless* Case the Commission did indeed join the preliminary objection based on Article 17 to the merits.[10]

However, this methodology was not generally followed by the Commission. The *KPD* Case concerned the complaint raised by the *Kommunistische Partei Deutschland* (KPD) that the decision of the German *Bundesverfassungsgericht* had dissolved the applicant party and had declared it a prohibited party. The Commission, apparently *ex officio*, examined the applicability of Article 17 and found, on the basis of depositions made by the KPD during the proceedings before the *Bundesverfassungsgericht*, that the aim of the KPD was to establish a socialist-communist system by means of a proletarian revolution, and that it did not appear to renounce these principles, despite its attempt to seize power via constitutional methods. The Commission concluded that Article 17 was applicable and that there was no violation of any provisions of the Convention. It declared the application inadmissible as being incompatible with the Convention.[11] That the Commission decided the case on the basis exclusively of written proceedings, without regard to activities of the KPD, was all the more problematic because the text of Article 17 refers explicitly to 'activity' and 'act'. To allow the ban on a political party solely on the basis of its aims rather than on its activities, as the Commission did in this case, drastically affects the freedom of expression and the freedom of association, two of the most fundamental values of the Convention indispensable for the healthy functioning of democracy. It is ,therefore, to be welcomed that in *Refah Partisti (the Welfare Party) and Others v. Turkey*, the Grand Chamber, although considering it unnecessary to examine the complaints of abuse of the restrictions by the Turkish authorities under Article 17 (and Article 18), took the position that merely invoking aims and objectives stated in written documents was not sufficient to justify restrictions on political activities.[12]

That the question of applicability of Article 17 should be joined to the merits can also be demonstrated by reference to the *Glimmerveen* and *Hagenbeek* Cases, which concerned complaints directed at the criminal conviction for having possessed leaflets of the anti-immigrant party for the purpose of distribution and at the decision of the Central Voting Boards of Amsterdam to invalidate the list of candidates of this party in a local election. Despite its recognition that the freedom of expression constitutes

---

[10]   Appl. 332/57, Yearbook II (1958-59), p. 308, at 340. In the *De Becker* Case Article 17 was invoked by the Belgian Government only after the declaration of admissibility, during the examination of the merits: Report of 8 January 1960, B.2 (1962), p. 133.

[11]   Appl. 250/57, *Yearbook* I (1955-1957), p. 222, at 224-225.

[12]   Judgment of 13 February 2003 (Grand Chamber), paras 136-137. Judges Fuhrmann, Loucaides and Bratza, in their joint dissenting opinion, on the contrary, placed emphasis on the relevant political party's manifestos and aims, rather than public statements made by members of that party: joint dissenting opinion, paras 5 and 6.

one of the essential foundations of a democratic society, the Commission concluded that pursuant to Article 17, the two applicants could not invoke Article 10 of the Convention alone or in tandem with Article 3 of the First Protocol, and declared the applications 'incompatible with the provisions of the Convention'.[13]

36.6 THE SUBSTANTIVE RIGHTS AFFECTED BY ARTICLE 17 – THE 'LINKAGE REQUIREMENT'

Both the Commission and the Court have introduced a very important constraint on the respondent State's discretion to invoke Article 17 in order to justify restrictive measures. Even if it is firmly established that people aim at destroying or restricting the rights of others, or belong to a group with such an objective, this does not justify depriving them of all their rights recognized under the Convention. Instead, the effect of Article 17 is to disable the operation exclusively of those rights that they abuse for destructive purposes. The applicability of Article 17 depends on the requirement of linkage between Convention rights and the destructive aims pursued. In the *Lawless* Case both the Commission and the Court found little connection between the objectives of the IRA and the rights invoked by the applicant (Articles 5 and 6), thus dismissing the Irish Government's plea based on Article 17. Even though Lawless was involved in IRA activities, he had not relied on the guarantees of Articles 5 and 6 in order to justify or perform these activities.[14]

Similarly, in the *De Becker* Case where the applicant was debarred from exercising the freedom of expression under the Belgian Penal Code owing to his totalitarian views and activities dating from the time of the Nazi occupation, the Commission observed that "Article 17 cannot be used to deprive an individual of his rights and freedoms permanently merely because at some given moment he displayed totalitarian convictions and acted consequently". It was not shown that the applicant would abuse his freedom of expression for totalitarian purposes, and the application of Article 17 in such a circumstance would upset the proportionate balance.[15] The *De Becker* Case is relevant, for instance, to the situation of war criminals and terrorists detained in prison or released on probation. Their past deeds, though relevant to assessment of their contemporary activities, do not provide a sufficient ground for suspending their

---

[13] Appls 8348 and 8406/78, D&R 18 (1980), p. 187, at 194-197.
[14] Judgment of 1 July 1961, paras 4-7, and report of 19 December 1959, B.1 (1961), p. 180, respectively.
[15] Report of 8 January 1960, B. 2 (1962), pp. 137-138, para. 279. The Court did not take a decision on this point, as the case was struck out of the list following the amendment of the relevant Belgian legislation.

Chapter 36   Prohibition of Abuse of the Rights and Freedoms set Forth in the
Convention and of Their Limitation to a Greater Extent than is Provided for
in the Convention (Article 17)

Convention rights.[16] This 'linkage requirement' was reaffirmed in the *Lehideux and Isorni* Case, where the applicants were convicted of public defense of war crimes and crimes of collaboration in relation to the advertisement purported to defend Marshall Pétain. The Commission held that Article 17 could not prevent the applicants from relying on Article 10, as the advertisement in question did not contain terms of racial hatred or other statements calculated to destroy or restrict the Convention rights.[17]

It must be questioned how close a link is required between the right claimed and the activity prohibited under Article 17. When a Swiss company claimed that the confiscation of its property in the Federal Republic of Germany was contrary to Article 1 of the First Protocol, the German Government invoked Article 17, submitting that the aim of the company was to manage and protect real property of the *Kommunistische Partei Deutschland*. However, the applicants submitted that they only claimed compensation, which they guaranteed would not be used for anti-constitutional activities. This submission was, however, declared inadmissible on account of non-exhaustion of the local remedies, so that the Commission did not arrive at a decision on this point.[18]

36.7   LIMITATIONS CLAUSES AND ARTICLE 17 – THE 'ABSORPTION APPROACH'

Where an alleged violation is found to contravene a substantive provision equipped with a limitation clause, the policy of the Strasbourg organs seems to be to dispense with a separate review of the complaint directed against a State under Article 17. Two scenarios may be contemplated. At first glance, it seems reasonable that finding no breach of a principal provision accompanied by a limitation clause is considered to make a separate appraisal under Article 17 (and Article 18) unnecessary.[19] In the *Engel* Case the applicants submitted that the penalty imposed on them for having written an article in a barracks journal could not be justified under Article 10(2) and constituted a violation of Article 17. The Commission declared this part of the complaint

---

[16]   This issue must not be confused with the fact that persons responsible for 'core crimes' such as genocide, crimes against humanity and war crimes are not entitled to statutory limitations. However, even such persons are entitled to a variety of due process guarantees in international criminal proceedings.

[17]   Decision of 24 June 1996, cited with approval in the Court's judgment of 23 September 1998, para. 37.

[18]   *Retimag S.A.*, Yearbook IV (1961), p. 384, at 392-394.

[19]   Apart from the *Refah Partisi* Case discussed here, reference should be made to Decision of 13 December 1969, *X. v. Austria*, Yearbook VI (1963), p. 424, at 442-444. There the Commission found no need to examine whether criminal convictions of a National Socialist could be justified under Article 17, in that it already considered the penal measures to be justified under Articles 9(2) and 10(2).

admissible,[20] but concluded that since the impugned restrictions were found to comport with the purposes of preventing disorder in the army and protecting the reputation or rights of others, the Dutch authorities were not considered to have taken advantage of Convention provisions (Articles 5, 10 and 11) to impose greater restrictions than contemplated by the Convention.[21] Similarly, but in a more curt manner, the Court dismissed the complaints under Article 17 (and Article 18) as unsubstantiated on the basis of the conclusion that the said limitation was justified under the second paragraph of Article 10.[22] Similarly, in the *Refah Partisi (the Welfare Party)* Case the Grand Chamber found that the Party's dissolution and the temporary forfeiture of certain political rights by the other applicants did not disclose any violation of Article 11. It concluded that under the second paragraph of Article 11, these measures were proportionate to the legitimate objectives of forestalling a political party, which did not renounce violent means, from establishing the Islamic theocratic regime based on Sharia law.[23] Even 'the restricted margin of appreciation' that the Grand Chamber conceded to the respondent State was enough to encompass such drastic measures, making the complaints of breaches of Articles 17 and 18 moot, with such complaints subsumed into the appraisal under Article 11 (2).[24] The approaches followed by the Strasbourg organs in those cases, however, leave it unclear in what circumstances they are prepared to proceed to a separate appraisal under Article 17 even after finding a violation of a substantive right provision.

In the *Lehideux and Isorni* Case, the Court was asked to determine whether convictions of public defense of war crimes or crimes of collaboration with respect to advertisement about Marshal Pétain in *Le Monde* were justified under Article 10(2). In that case the Court assessed the question of compliance with Article 10 in the light of Article 17.[25] It distinguished the category of clearly established historical facts such as the Holocaust from the events subject to on-going historical debate, noting that denial or revision of the former category would 'remove ... the protection of Article

---

[20]   Decision of 17 July 1972, Yearbook XV (1972), p. 508, at 556-558.

[21]   Report of 19 July 1974, B. 20, para. 187.

[22]   Judgment of 8 June 1976, para. 104.

[23]   Judgment of 13 February 2003 (Grand Chamber), paras , 116-136 (unanimous). In contrast, the Chamber reached the same conclusion, by a narrow vote of four to three (Judgment of 31 July 2001), with strong dissenting opinion of Judges Fuhrmann, Loucaides and Bratza. On this matter, comparison should be made to *Freedom and Democracy Party (ÖZDEP)*, which, though not involving issues of Article 17, concerned similar issues: radical measures against a political party, the ÖZDEP, including its dissolution with immediate effect, the liquidation of its assets and the ban on its leaders from pursuing similar political activities. The Court found that ÖZDEP's programme did not disclose any call for the use of violence for achieving the self-determination of the Kurds, and that the drastic measures in question were disproportionate: judgment of 8 December 1999, paras 40 and 42-48 (unanimous).

[24]   *Ibidem*, para. 138.

[25]   Judgment of 23 September 1998, para. 38. See also judgment of 30 January 1998, *The United Communist Party of Turkey and Others*, para. 32.

Chapter 36   Prohibition of Abuse of the Rights and Freedoms set Forth in the
Convention and of Their Limitation to a Greater Extent than is Provided for
in the Convention (Article 17)

10 by Article 17".[26] The Court classified the impugned advertisement intended to cast positive light on the role of Marshal Pétain of the Vichy regime as belonging to the latter category, which did not attract automatic application of Article 17. The Court found that the convictions in question were disproportionate in breach of Article 10, and that it was not appropriate to apply Article 17.[27]

While the right to property under Article 1 of the First Protocol is subject to implied limitations under the first sentence of the first paragraph of this provision, there exist two possibilities of express limitations: firstly, 'deprivation' of property under the second sentence of the first paragraph; and 'control' over the use of property under the second paragraph. In the *Lithgow* Case, which concerned the question of deprivation of property in relation to nationalization measures, the Commission did not simply dispense with the assessment under Article 17. It found, first, that the taking of the applicants' property as a result of the nationalization measures was justified under the 'limitation clause' of the second sentence of Article 1 (1) of the First Protocol, and subsequently pursued the appraisal of alleged violation of Article 17. In the final analysis the Commission did not find the measures concerned to have aimed at the destruction of, or excessive limitation on, the applicants' rights.[28] Regrettably, the Court did not deal with this question, as this was not submitted before the Court.

If not invoked by a Contracting State, the issues of Article 17 may be raised by the Court in order to assess whether this provision may be interpreted to strengthen justifications for restrictions under a limitation clause. In the *Glasenapp* Case, which concerned the German loyalty control imposed on a school teacher sympathetic to a banned German communist party, the Commission, *proprio motu*, examined whether or not Article 17 could be applied to reinforce the arguments for 'necessity' under the second paragraph of Article 10. The German Government had submitted that the restrictions on the applicant's freedom of expression were justified by the 'pressing social need' to defend the system of democracy and the rule of law in a country that had experienced National Socialism. The Commission stressed that, since the freedom of expression is "the cornerstone of the principles of democracy and human rights", those restrictions must be scrutinized on the basis of "clearly established" criteria under Article 10 (2).[29] While not assessing the complaints under Article 17, the Commission

---

26   Judgment of 23 September 1998, *Lehideux and Isorni*, para. 47.
27   *Ibidem*, para. 58.
28   Report of 7 March 1984, paras 446-450.
29   The Commission took the following position: "Where a Government seeks to achieve the ultimate protection of the rule of law and the democratic system, the Convention itself recognizes in Article 17 the precedence which such objectives take, even over the protection of the specific rights which the Convention otherwise guarantees. Nevertheless, precisely because of the cardinal importance to be attached to the preservation of the rule of law and the democratic system, the Convention requires a clearly established need for any interference with the rights it guarantees, before such interference can be justified on that basis", *Glasenapp*, report of 11 May 1984, para. 110.

found a violation of Article 10 on the grounds that the applicant had only a limited link to the impugned political party and that the application of the loyalty control was categorical, with no account being taken of the rank or position of the civil servant or nature of civil service concerned.[30]

36.8 IMPLIED LIMITATIONS AND ARTICLE 17

In relation to a provision that excludes a possibility of restrictions, or that recognizes only implied limitations, Article 17 may assume importance as an autonomous or complementary criterion for assessing whether or not an impugned 'restriction' can be justified. Implied limitations have been recognized in relation to certain provisions, such as Article 6(1)[31] of the Convention and to the first sentence of Article 1(1) of the First Protocol. In the *Sporrong and Lönnroth* Case, after having found that the expropriation permits and prohibitions on construction were justified under Article 1 of the First Protocol, the Commission examined whether these restrictions on the right to property exceeded the requirements of Article 17 and unanimously found no violation of this provision.[32] In contrast, the Court applied an 'absorption approach' to the question of Article 17. After finding that there was a violation of Article 1 of the First Protocol, on the ground that a 'fair balance' was upset in applying 'implied limitations' allowed under the first sentence of Article 1(1) of the First Protocol, the Court, without adducing any additional argument, abandoned a separate examination under Article 17.[33]

---

[30] *Ibidem*, para. 128. See also report of 11 May 1984, *Kosiek*, para. 106 (no violation of Article 10 in relation to the dismissal of a lecturer belonging to an extreme right-wing party, NPD, in view of his close involvement in that party). However, in both the *Glasenapp* and the *Kosiek* Cases the Court did not deal with Article 17, reducing the complaints to the question of access to a position of civil service, not covered by the Convention's scope of guarantee *ratione materiae*: judgment of 28 August 1986, *Glasenapp*, para. 53; and judgment of 28 August 1986, *Kosiek*, para. 39.

[31] See judgment of 21 February 1975, *Golder*, paras 37-40 (with respect to an 'inferred' right of access to court). In contrast, the Court, in *Campbell and Fell*, rejected the possibility of implied limitations as to the right to public announcement of decisions under Article 6(1), which is subject to an express list of exceptions under the second sentence. The Court observed that '[b]earing in mind the terms of Article 17 ... and the importance of the principle of publication ... the Court does not consider that that principle may be regarded as subject to an implied limitation as suggested by the Government': judgment of 28 June 1984, para. 90.

[32] Report of 8 October 1980, paras 122-124.

[33] Judgment of 23 September 1982, para. 76.

CHAPTER 37
PROHIBITION OF MISUSE OF POWER IN RESTRICTING THE RIGHTS AND FREEDOMS (Article 18)

REVISED BY YUTAKA ARAI

CONTENTS

37.1 TEXT OF ARTICLE 18

The restrictions permitted under this Convention to the said rights and freedoms shall not be applied for any purpose other than those for which they have been prescribed.

37.2 SUBSIDIARY CHARACTER

Article 18 generally prohibits the Contracting States from using the restrictions permitted under the Convention for any purpose other than those for which they are intended. The subsidiary nature of this provision is demonstrated by the fact that its prohibition cannot constitute the object of an independent complaint but may be advanced only in conjunction with one of the Convention rights,[1] including the free-

---

[1] Report of 14 July 1974, *Kamma*, Yearbook XVIII, (1975), p. 300, at 316; report of 8 October 1980, *Sporrong and Lönnroth*, paras 122-124.

dom from discrimination under Article 14,[2] or with the right of individual communication with the Court under Article 34.[3] However, as is the case with Article 14, Article 18 was given an autonomous character in the case law of the Commission in that this provision could be violated in conjunction with a principal provision, even though the latter was not violated.[4]

In most cases where Article 18 was invoked the Court found it unnecessary to conduct a separate examination under this provision. The Court may, however, also take the approach of not dismissing the complaints under Article 18 (and Article 17) and carry out a combined assessment under a substantive provision and Article 18.[5] The exclusion of a separate examination under Article 18 may be encountered in the following contexts. First, the Court may find that the principal right invoked has not been violated, deeming the alleged violation of Article 18 as unsubstantiated.[6] Second, the Court may be satisfied with finding a violation only of a substantive right, in tandem with which Article 18 has been invoked.[7] In this scenario the Court may consider a separate appraisal under Article 18 as superfluous, holding that the primary

---

[2] See, for instance, judgment of 9 November 2004, *Hasan İlhan*, para. 132; and judgment of 18 January 2005, *Menteşe and Others,* para. 92 (In both cases, the applicants alleged abuse based on discrimination against the Kurds. The Court, however, found neither Article 14, taken together with substantive rights, nor Article 18 to have been violated, on the ground that the allegation was unsubstantiated).

[3] See, for instance, judgment of 18 June 2002, *Orhan*, para. 402. However, the Court did not examine the complaints of a violation of Article 34 in tandem with Article 18, on the ground that aspects of Article 18 were already discussed in the context of Article 38 of the Convention: *ibidem,* para. 274.

[4] In the *Kamma* Case, the Commission observed: "Article 18, like Article 14 of the Convention, does not have an autonomous role. It can only be applied in conjunction with other Articles of the Convention. There may, however, be a violation of Article 18 in connection with another Article, although there is no violation of that Article taken alone"; report of 14 July 1974, *Kamma*, Yearbook XVIII, (1975), p. 300 at 316; and D&R 1 (1975), p. 4. See also decision of 11 May 2000, *Oates*, para. 2; and judgment of 19 May 2004, *Gusinskiy*, para. 73.

[5] See, for instance, judgment of 28 May 1985, *Ashingdane*, paras 43-49.

[6] Judgment of 8 June 1976, *Engel and Others*, para. 108 (no need to examine the complaints under Article 11 taken together with Articles 17 and 18 in view of no 'interference' with the rights under Article 11). See the Court's observation as to an alleged breach of Article 6 taken with Article 18: *ibidem,* para. 93. There, the Court ruled that the examinations of Article 6 in relation to the choice of disciplinary rather than criminal proceedings against the applicants, which resulted in depriving them of guarantees under Article 6, would make it unnecessary to examine the issue under Article 18 (a breach only in respect of the duty to provide public proceedings and no violation in respect of other guarantees under Article 6). Note should also be taken of the *Lynas* Case. There, the Commission found no appearance of violations of Articles 5 and 6, but this did not prevent it from going on to refer to the allege breach of Article 18 coupled with Article 5; decision of 6 October 1976, Yearbook XX (1977), p. 412, at 446.

[7] Judgment of 18 December 1986, *Bozano*, para. 61 (the finding that the deportation procedure at issue contravened Article 5(1) was deemed as sufficient to exclude a separate appraisal under Article 18 taken in tandem with Article 5(1)).

issue of misuse of powers was 'absorbed' into the assessment of that right.[8] Third, the
tendency to exclude a review under Article 18 may de witnessed where the Court has
already examined aims of restricting measures and found them to be 'legitimate' under
a limitation clause[9] without any extraneous motives or aims within the meaning of
Article 18. In a fourth scenario the Court may find it superfluous to make an appraisal
under Article 18, when it has already found impugned aims to be incompatible under
a limitation clause attached to a substantive right.[10]

37.3 GENERAL APPLICABILITY

It appears from its formulation that Article 18 refers to all restrictions allowed under
the Convention.[11] This means that the applicability of Article 18 can be contemplated
in four situations. First and foremost, Article 18 is applied to the limitation clauses
designed to qualify specific rights, such as the second paragraphs of Articles 8-11 of
the Convention, the third paragraph of Article 2 of the Fourth Protocol, and the second
paragraph of Article 1 of the Seventh Protocol. Two possibilities of restrictions
envisaged under Article 1 of the First Protocol, which can be assimilated into the
limitation clauses, must also comply with the requirement of Article 18.[12]

Second, Article 18 should be deemed applicable to cases of so-called 'limitations
by delimitation', where certain Convention provisions expressly exclude specific areas
or persons from their scope of guarantee. This can be seen in relation to Article 4(3)
(exemption of certain work or service from the meaning of 'forced or compulsory
labour'), the third sentence of Article 10 (the licensing of broadcasting, television or
cinema enterprises), the second sentence of Article 11(2) ('lawful restrictions on the

---

[8]   *Ibidem.* See also judgment of 10 May 2001, *Cyprus*, paras 206 and 388 (violations of the rights of
displaced persons to respect for their home and property under Articles 8 and 13 of the Convention,
and Article 1 of the First Protocol).

[9]   See, *inter alia*, judgment of 7 December 1976, *Handyside*, paras 52, 62 and 63-64 (Article 10 of the
Convention and Article 1 of the First Protocol); judgment of 8 June 1976, *Engel and Others*, para.
104 (exclusion of an examination of alleged violation of Article 10 together with Articles 17 and 18
in view of the finding of no violation under Article 10(2)); and judgment of 18 July 2000, *Şener*, paras
61-62 (Article 10). See also *Dickle*. In that case, though finding the criminal convictions based on
publication to be disproportionate, the Court considered the aims pursued to be legitimate, and hence
not to be susceptible to application of Article 18: judgment of 10 November 2004, paras 24-25.

[10]   In this regard, see judgment of 30 January 1998, *The United Communist Party of Turkey and Others*,
para. 62. There, while submitting alleged complaints of violations of Articles 9, 10, 14 and 18 before
the Commission, the applicants did not pursue these complaints before the Court, accepting the
Commission's argument that the finding of a violation of Article 11 would make it unnecessary to
ascertain these complaints. The Court did not make the evaluations *proprio motu*.

[11]   *X. v. Austria*, Coll. 4, (1960).

[12]   In the *Sporrong and Lönnroth* Case, the Commission took account of Article 18 in assessing whether
the restrictions at issue were lawful measures pursuant to the general interest in the sense of Article
1 of the First Protocol: Report of 8 October 1980, paras 122-124.

freedom of assembly and association exercised by members of the armed forces, of the police or of the administration of the State) and Article 12 (national laws 'governing' the exercise of the right to marry).

Third, Article 18 applies to the general restrictions ensuing from Articles 15, 16 and 17. In the *De Becker* Case the Commission relied in part on Article 18 to conclude that measures which were taken in accordance with Article 15 in connection with an emergency situation of the Nazi occupation during the World War II were no longer justified if they contravene the requirements of Article 18. The Commission rejected the Belgian Government's submission that derogating measures under Article 15 would not cease to operate merely because the war was over, noting that such an argument was in breach of the proportionality requirement under Article 15 and of Article 18.[13] In this regard it must be emphasized that since non-derogable rights, as guaranteed under Articles 2-4 and 7 of the Convention and Article 4 of the Seventh Protocol, are formulated in absolute terms, they are not susceptible to any restrictions, express or implicit. Hence, it is logically impossible to conceive violation of Article 18 in relation to any of the four non-derogable rights,[14] the right to security (as opposed to the right to liberty) under Article 5, and the right to conscience under Article 9.

Fourth, it must be questioned whether Article 18 is also applicable to 'inherent limitations'. Insofar as 'inherent limitations' are considered as lawful in the case law, they are to be considered as 'restrictions permitted under this Convention' within the meaning of Article 18, and it must be ascertained whether the application of such limitations has conformed to Article 18. The absence of elaborate criteria for reviewing inherent limitations, such as the principle of proportionality, suggests that apart from Articles 14 and 17, Article 18 would provide an important criterion for assessing the *Conventionnalité* of such limitations.

37.4 BURDEN OF PROOF

Just as in the case of the French public law doctrine of the prohibition of misuse of power (*détournement de pouvoir*), Article 18 proves to be a provision that is hard to apply in practice. First, Article 18 requires an exact determination of the motives on the part of the authorities taking the measure concerned. Second, it must be established that such motives were not in conformity with the aims envisaged under particular provisions of the Convention. Although bad faith does not constitute an element of *détournement de pouvoir*, in most cases determination of the former notion is included

---

[13]   Report of 8 January 1960, B. 2, (1962), para. 271. In its report in the *Greek* Case, the Commission did not examine an alleged abuse of Article 15 under Article 18 (and Article 17) on the ground that the conditions of Article 15 were not fulfilled: Report of 5 November 1969, *Yearbook* XII, (1969), at 111-112.

[14]   Report of 14 July 1974, *Kamma*, Yearbook XVIII, (1975), p. 300, at 316.

in assessing the latter. Unless the intention of the national authorities concerned can be clearly inferred from the nature of the impugned measure, a particularly onerous burden of proof is placed on applicants invoking Article 18.[15] Such onus is aggravated by the fact that even though the Court is not only competent but arguably even obliged to do so under Article 19, it has not shown a readiness to rely on 18 *proprio motu*.

Evidently, circumstances where ulterior motives of restricting Convention rights manifest themselves are seldom. In this regard *Gusinskiy v. Russia* provides an exception that reveals a straightforward breach of Article 18. There the applicant complained that his detention was an abuse of power in that the authorities compelled him to sell his media business to a state petroleum company, Gazprom, on unfavourable terms and conditions. While in prison, the applicant was asked to sign an agreement with Gazprom, which was later endorsed by a State Minister. The signature of this agreement led to the charges against him being dropped. The Court found a violation of Article 18 together with Article 5(1)(c).[16]

37.5 APPLICATION OF ARTICLE 18 IN THE CASE LAW

A preponderant role played by Article 18 was seen in the *Kamma* Case. The applicant complained of a violation of Article 18 in that, while in detention on remand on the suspicion of extortion and attempted robbery, the police took advantage of his detention, which was allowed under Article 5(1)(c), to conduct one-month investigations into a murder case. He submitted that, as a result, his detention on remand was prolonged by one month and that he had been subjected to a more rigorous regime during that period. Under Dutch law the suspicion of murder in itself would have been a sufficient ground for detaining him on remand.[17] However, in this case the Dutch court, when deciding on detention for the period in question, was informed neither of the applicant's detention at the police station nor of the inquiry into the murder, so that the court decision related solely to the suspicion of extortion.[18] In its report, the Commission concluded that there was no violation of Article 18.[19] The Commission found that, though the lawful deprivation of liberty was used for another purpose

---

[15] Note should be taken of the *Engel* Case. In that case, the Court rejected a complaint that the imposition of disciplinary proceedings for writing in a journal in the army had extraneous motives of suppressing trade union activities in violation of Articles 18 in tandem with Articles 10 and 11: judgment of 8 June 1976, paras 104-108.

[16] Judgment of 19 May 2004, *Gusinskiy*, paras 76-77.

[17] If such a decision to detain him had been taken by the court, Article 18 would not have come into play.

[18] The investigating judge, on the contrary, *was* informed of the second suspicion, but apparently did not consider it necessary to take a separate decision.

[19] Report of 14 July 1974, Yearbook XVIII (1975), p. 300, at 316-322.

of investigations in a different case, there was nothing to cast doubt on the validity of his detention at police headquarters. The gist of the complaint under Article 18 was, however, not whether the restrictions on the right to liberty were legitimate as such, but precisely whether those restrictions, assuming that they were justified according to one of the grounds exhaustively enumerated under Article 5 (1), were genuinely imposed pursuant to that ground and not for any ulterior purpose. It is regrettable that the *Kamma* Case was not referred to the Court, but that it was decided by the Committee of Ministers, which, agreeing with the opinion of the Commission, found no violation of the Convention.[20] Nevertheless, the Commission at least noted that "the respondent Government concluded their observations on the merits with an indication that they intend to examine the question as to whether a reform of the relevant legislation is necessary in order to avoid ambiguous situations which may, as in the present case, arise under the existing provisions concerning interrogation by the police of persons already in detention on remand".[21] This observation seem to signal the Commission's misgivings, despite its finding of no breach of the obligation not to misuse powers under Article 18.

Note should also be taken of the *Engel* Case, where two of the conscript applicants, Dona and Schul, complained that disciplinary punishment imposed on them for writing an article in a barracks journal revealed a violation of Article 18 in two ways: first, the authorities classified the offence as a disciplinary rather than a criminal matter in an alleged attempt to deprive the applicants of procedural guarantees under Article 6; and second, the alleged purpose of meting out disciplinary punishment under the Dutch Military Penal Code, for writing articles in a barracks journal, was to restrict their trade union freedom under Article 11.[22] The Commission dismissed the first allegation, opining that Article 18 was applicable only in relation to 'restrictions permitted under this Convention to the said rights and freedoms', as stipulated in that provision, with no relevance to the choice between criminal and disciplinary proceedings under the Military Discipline Act.[23] With respect to the second allegation, the Commission recalled that the restrictions on the freedom of expression were justified by the legitimate aims based on the prevention of disorder and the protection of reputation and rights of others under the second paragraph of Article 10, and that even no interference with Article 11(1) was found.[24] It concluded that there had been no breach of Article 18.[25] The Court did not examine the issues under Article 18 in tandem either with Article 10 or with Article 11.[26]

---

[20]   *Ibidem*, at 302.
[21]   *Ibidem*, p. 322.
[22]   Report of 19 July 1974, B. 20 (1978), pp. 85-86, para. 189.
[23]   *Ibidem*, para. 191.
[24]   *Ibidem*, para. 178.
[25]   *Ibidem*, para. 193.
[26]   Judgment of 8 June 1976, paras 104 and 108.

It is submitted that Article 18 does not refer to 'any purpose in violation of the said rights and freedoms', but to 'any purpose other than those for which they have been prescribed'. Consequently, even if the inquiry under Article 10 may lead to the conclusion that this provision has not been violated, with restrictions being justified under the second paragraph, it is still possible that Article 18 may be breached. If the two applicants concerned, Dona and Schul, would have been able to furnish *prima facie* evidence that the disciplinary measure was imposed to restrain their trade union activities in general in lieu of maintaining order in the barracks, Article 18 would have been violated in conjunction with Article 18.[27] Indeed, review on the basis of the second paragraph of Article 10 provides an answer only to the question of whether or not the authorities could hold that the measure was necessary for the protection of one of the legitimate aims, and investigations into the 'hidden' ulterior motives may be necessary in a separate appraisal under Article 18. The conclusion that, once the review under Article 10(2) has found no violation, this would make it unnecessary to conduct a separate inquiry under Article 18, would remove Article 18 of its autonomous (albeit conjunctive) character. Nevertheless, it would be difficult to imagine how any extraneous motive can operate behind the façade of legitimate aims invoked by a respondent State without being caught by a rigorous examination under this limitation clause.

In its report in the *Handyside* Case the Commission appears to have departed from the outright 'absorption' approach taken in the *Engel* Case. The applicant, a publisher who was prevented from publishing the so-called 'Little Red Schoolbook', submitted that the UK authorities' interference was motivated not by the objective of protecting morals, but by other motives, such as the desire to resist the development of modern teaching techniques at schools. The Commission found that the interference with the applicant's freedom of expression was justified pursuant to a legitimate aim of protecting morals of juvenile readers under the second paragraph of Article 10.[28] However, rather than dismissing the complaints under Article 18 outright, it continued to observe that "an examination of the case (...) does not disclose any evidence which might suggest that the authorities and courts in the United Kingdom in taking the action complained of against the publication and distribution of the Schoolbook, have in any way been guided by motives other than those described in Article 10(2)."[29] On that ground the Commission unanimously concluded that there had been no breach of Article 18. This reasoning suggests that the Commission felt a need to evaluate any motives other than those duly appraised under Article 10(2) under Article 18. The

---

27   This conclusion could be reached regardless of whether the impugned disciplinary measure also conflicted with the requirement of Article 11(2).

28   Report of 30 September 1975, B.22 (1976), para. 157.

29   *Ibidem*, para. 175.

Commission's methodology in the *Handyside* Case was followed only in some of its subsequent cases.[30] but not in the case law of the Court.[31]

In the *Bozano* Case the applicant alleged that his deportation by the French authorities to Switzerland and the ensuing deprivation of his liberty were, *inter alia*, contrary to Article 5. The Commission acceded to these claims and examined whether the unlawfulness of the deportation affected the applicant's detention in respect of Article 18 of the Convention as well. It noted that the French administrative court had found a *détournement de pouvoir*, holding the enforcement of deportation order, and hence the applicant's detention, as unlawful on the ground that the executive had sought to circumvent the competent judicial authority's veto on extraditing the applicant, which was binding on the French Government.[32] The Commission made no express finding in respect of Article 18 but concluded that the applicant's detention had a purpose different from detention with a view to deportation, as provided for in Article 5(1)(f).[33] The Court took an 'absorption' approach and did not deem it necessary to examine this issue under Article 18 taken in tandem with Article 5(1), on the ground that it already found, in connection with Article 5(1) taken alone, that the deportation procedure was 'abused for objects and purposes other than its normal ones'.[34]

The approach taken by the Court in the *Bozano* Case indicates that Article 18 has been made an integral part of those Convention rights that allow some scope of restrictions, express or implied, on the rights guaranteed therein. This marks a contrast to the case law concerning Article 14 and, in some instances, Article 17.

---

[30]   See report of 8 October 1980, *Sporrong and Lönnroth,* paras 122-124; and decision of 10 December 1975, *X v. Federal Republic of Germany,* DR 3 (1976), p. 104 , at 107. In contrast, see *The Sunday Times (No. 1),* B. 28 (1982), report of 18 May 1977 paras 263-265 (the Commission outright dismissing the claim under Article 18 in tandem with Article 10).

[31]   Note that in the *Handyside* Case, the Court found it unnecessary to examine the complaints on Article 18 on the basis that the contested restrictions pursued legitimate aims under Article 10(2) of the Convention and under the second paragraph of Article 1(1) of the First Protocol: judgment of 7 December 1976, paras 52, 62 and 63.

[32]   Report of 7 December 1984, *Bozano,* paras 77-81.

[33]   *Ibidem,* para. 82.

[34]   Judgment of 18 December 1986, *Bozano,* para. 61.

CHAPTER 38

RESERVATIONS (Article 57)

Revised by Cees Flinterman

CONTENTS

38.1 TEXT OF ARTICLE 57

1. *Any State may, when signing this Convention or when depositing its instrument of ratification, make a reservation in respect of any particular provision of the Convention to the extent that any law then in force in its territory is not in conformity with the provision. Reservations of a general character shall not be permitted under this Article.*
2. *Any reservation made under this Article shall contain a brief statement of the law concerned.*

38.2 INTRODUCTION

Under Article 57 of the Convention States Parties may make reservations to their obligations arising under the Convention.[1] Article 57 provides that States may do so for

---

[1]   There is only one exception. According to Article 4 of Protocol No. 6 States are not allowed to make reservations to that Protocol.

only one reason. This reason is that any law in force within the State Party concerned is not in conformity with the particular provision to which the reservation is made. Reservations of an open end character are not allowed.

The inclusion into the Convention of the possibility of making reservations was a controversial matter at the time the Convention was drafted. The Committee on Legal and Administrative Questions of the Consultative Assembly was opposed to giving the States unlimited power to do so: "Such a power would threaten to deprive the latter [the Convention] of its practical effect and in any case of its moral authority". The Committee, therefore, proposed that the validity of a reservation would at the least have to be subjected to the approval of a qualified majority of the other Contracting States, and that the State in question would have to give reasons for each separate reservation. Moreover, it was suggested that a State which made a reservation should submit periodically a report in which the reasons for the maintenance of that reservation would have to be given.[2] These suggestions were not adopted by the Committee of Ministers.

Indeed, the possibility for Contracting States to make reservations would seem to be at odds with the presumption of universality of human rights. By making reservations when ratifying a human rights treaty the State concerned excludes or modifies its obligations under that particular treaty with as a consequence that the acceptance of the human rights standards is not of a common level or intensity. Moreover, the possibility of making reservations is hard to be reconciled with the character and contents of human rights obligations as a minimum standard. As the Human Rights Committee, established under the UN Covenant on Civil and Political Rights, states in its General Comment on Issues Relating to Reservations: "it is desirable in principle that States accept the full range of obligations, because the human rights norms are the legal expression of the essential rights that every person is entitled to as a human being."[3]

What holds good for global human rights systems applies *a fortiori* for the common legal order established by the Convention. Nevertheless, under international law as it stands at present, reservations to human rights treaties are not excluded, as is well illustrated by Article 57 of the Convention. And, in fact, several Contracting States have made reservations in respect of the Convention.[4] Most of these reservations have a limited scope and concern substantive provisions, *i.e.* the rights and freedoms protected by the Convention and the Protocols.

---

[2]   Council of Europe, Cons. Ass., Ordinary Session 1950, Documents, Part II, Doc. 6, p. 534.

[3]   Human Rights Committee, General Comment No. 24 on issues relating to reservations made upon ratification or accession to the Covenant or the Optional Protocols thereto, or in relation to declarations under article 41 of the Covenant, 11 November 1994, para. 4. UN doc HRI/GEN/1/Rev.7 p. 161.

[4]   The reservations made by the different Contracting States can be found at the website of the Council of Europe, http://conventions.coe.int/treaty/en/victor3menutraites.asp.

38.3 SUPERVISION OF THE VALIDITY OF RESERVATIONS

The first general question to be discussed as to the Convention's system of reservations concerns the competence to decide on the legal validity of reservations. As was observed above, the Convention does not stipulate that a reservation requires acceptance by other Contracting States, although State practice shows that States have often raised objections against allegedly invalid reservations. Considering that the Convention embodies a specific mechanism of supervision of its observance, it seems obvious, therefore, that the said competence lies with the Court. It took, however, quite some time before the Strasbourg organs expressed themselves explicitly on the issue of reservations.

In the *Temeltasch* Case the Commission expressly established its competence to review and interpret reservations. Leaving aside the question of whether reservations and declarations may be the subject of express acceptance or objection by other Contracting States, it continued as follows: "However, it emphasises that, even assuming that some legal effect were to be attributed to an acceptance or an objection made in respect of a reservation to the Convention, this could not rule out the Commission's competence to express an opinion on the compliance of a given reservation or an interpretative declaration with the Convention. In this respect, the specific nature of the Convention should be recalled, and particularly the fact that in Section III it establishes organs responsible for supervising the enforcement of its provisions by the Contracting Parties. (...) The latter, in drawing up the Convention, did not intend – as the Commission has already noted – to concede to each other reciprocal rights and obligations in pursuance of their individual national interests, but (...) to establish a common public order of the free democracies of Europe with the object of safeguarding their common heritage of political traditions, ideals, freedoms and the rule of law. (...) The obligations undertaken by States are of an essentially objective character, which is particularly clear from the supervisory machinery established by the Convention. The latter 'is founded upon the concept of a collective guarantee by the High Contracting Parties of the rights and freedoms set forth in the Convention'. In view of the above considerations, the Commission considers that the very system of the Convention confers on it the competence to consider whether, in a specific case, a reservation or an interpretative declaration has or has not been made in accordance with the Convention."[5]

In the *Belilos* Case the Court expressly adopted the same point of view,[6] after having recognised its competence impliedly at two earlier occasions.[7] Indeed, the task

---

[5]   Report of 5 May 1982, D&R 31 (1983), p. 120 (144-145).
[6]   Judgment of 29 April 1988, para. 50.
[7]   Judgment of 16 July 1971, *Ringeisen*, paras 97-98; judgment of 9 October 1979, *Airey*, para. 26.

entrusted to the Court in Article 19 'To ensure the observance of the engagements undertaken by the High Contracting Parties' can only be fulfilled if in the last instance the Court, and not the States, determines the contents of the obligations as well as the validity and scope of reservations pertaining thereto.[8]

The Court's straightforward assertion of jurisdiction should not obscure the fact that in many cases the question as to the validity of reservations remains open as long as it is not raised in proceedings in connection with an alleged violation of one of the rights and freedoms. The Court is only competent to deal with reservations in case of an individual complaint or inter-State complaint. This may lead to protracted uncertainty. It would, therefore, appear to be desirable to set up a special procedure by which the admissibility of reservations can be judged by the Court at the moment at which they are made either *ex officio*, or at the request of a Contracting State or Council of Europe organ.

In its *Belilos* judgment the Court also decided on the important issue of whether, if a reservation is held to be invalid, the State concerned must, as a consequence, be deemed not to be bound by the treaty at all. According to the Court that was not the case in the present instance, since an overall willingness on the part of the State concerned to be bound by the Convention might be presumed.[9] This approach is also followed by the Human Rights Committee.[10] However, it is doubtful whether this approach prevails among (European) States. The International Law Commission, in its Preliminary Conclusions of 15 July 1997 on Reservations to Normative Multilateral Treaties including Human Rights Treaties, adopted the following view: "in the event of inadmissibility of a reservation, it is the reserving State that has the responsibility for taking action. This action may consist, for example, in the State either modifying its reservation so as to eliminate the inadmissibility, or withdrawing its reservation, or forgoing becoming a party to the treaty'."[11]

---

[8]   In its report of 5 May 1982, *Temeltasch*, D&R 31 (1983), p. 120 (145), the Commission has taken the same position.

[9]   Judgment of 29 April 1988, para. 60.

[10]   Human Rights Committee,General Comment no. 24, *supra*, note 3, para. 20. The Human Rights Committee found that "the normal consequence of an unacceptable reservation is not that the Covenant will not be in effect at all for a reserving party. Rather, such a reservation will generally be severable, in the sense that the Covenant will be operative for the reserving party without the benefit of the reservation".

[11]   Preliminary Conclusions of the International Law Commission on Reservations to Normative Multilateral Treaties including Human Rights Treaties, adopted by the Commission, Article 10, *Report of the International Law Commission on the work of its forty-ninth session*, 12 May to 18 July 1997, UN Doc. A/52/10, 1997, at paragraphs 50–157.

38.4 CONDITIONS FOR THE VALIDITY OF RESERVATIONS

The Vienna Convention on the Law of Treaties contains a number of provisions on reservations.[12] The Vienna Convention is, however, only of limited significance. The European Convention on Human Rights contains special rules concerning reservations. Only when the latter is silent on a certain matter may the Vienna Convention contribute to the interpretation of the matter of reservations.

According to Article 19 of the Vienna Convention, which in this respect codifies customary law,[13] the submission of reservations is not allowed if:

a) the reservation is prohibited by the treaty;
b) the treaty provides that only specified reservations, which do not include the reservation in question, may be made; or
c) in cases not falling under subparagraphs (a) and (b), the reservation is incompatible with the object and purpose of the treaty.

As far as the category under (c) is concerned, the International Court of Justice has indicated that the following are relevant factors:

a) whether the principles underlying the treaty concerned are principles which are recognised by civilised nations as binding on States, even without any conventional obligation;
b) whether the obligation concerned is of a universal character; and
c) whether the treaty was adopted for a purely humanitarian purpose in which the States do not have any interest of their own but merely a common interest, *viz.* the accomplishment of that purpose.[14]

In the case of the Convention Article 57 contains an express provision concerning reservations, which makes it clear that it was the intention of the drafters to make reservations possible. It is to be regretted that Article 57 has not been modelled after Article 15 in the sense that it lists the provisions of the Convention with respect to which reservations are not allowed. Now that this has not been done, Article 19 of the Vienna Convention of the Law of Treaties applies, which means that reservations are allowed under Article 57 only if and insofar as they are not incompatible with the object and purpose of the Convention. Therefore, in addition to reviewing reservations

---

[12]   Articles 19-24 Vienna Convention on the Law of Treaties
[13]   Thus also the Commission in its report in the *Temeltasch* Case, D&R 31 (1983), p. 120 (146).
[14]   Advisory opinion of 28 May 1951 on Reservations to the Convention on Genocide, *ICJ Report* 1951, p. 23. Article 19 of the Vienna Convention on the Law of Treaties can be seen as a codification of this point of view.

for their conformity with Article 57 itself,[15] the Court also has to include in its review the principle laid down in Article 19 of the Vienna Convention.[16]

Article 57 provides that:

a) a reservation must be made at the moment the Convention is signed or ratified;
b) a reservation has to concern a particular provision of the ECHR;
c) the domestic law to which a reservation relates must then be in force;
d) a reservation of a general character is not permitted; and
e) a reservation must contain a brief statement of the law concerned.

The requirement that reservations must be made at the moment of signature or ratification of the Convention is in accordance with international law. From this requirement it can be inferred that changes in reservations after ratification are prohibited if they widen the scope thereof. Changes which restrict the scope, however, are allowed. Reservations can be withdrawn at any moment.

The requirement that a reservation must be specific may be inferred from the first sentence of the first paragraph, which provides that a reservation may only concern 'any particular provision'. From this it ensues that, when a reservation is made, the provision of the Convention to which it refers must be expressly mentioned and the effect of the reservation remains confined exclusively to that provision. The requirement of specificity does not mean that a reservation has to relate to an article of the Convention as a whole. Reservations can be made to parts of an article. In view of the exceptional character and far-reaching consequences of reservations the conditions laid down in Article 57 should be interpreted an applied restrictively. That is not, however, the picture the Strasbourg case law has consistently presented. Thus, as far as this specificity requirement is concerned, in its decision on X v. Austria the Commission found as follows: "whereas it is true that this reservation does not make any express reference to Article 6 of the Convention; (...) whereas the Commission, in interpreting the terms of the reservation, has to take into consideration the clear intention of the Government (...); whereas, accordingly, the reservation must be extended to cover not only 'the measures for the deprivation of liberty' but also the

---

[15] See, e.g., the judgment of 29 April 1988, *Belilos*, paras 51-59, and the judgment of 22 May 1990, *Weber*, paras 36-38.

[16] Although the Court did not refer to Art. 19 of the Vienna Convention, that must have been the base of its judgment of 23 March 1995, *Loizidou* (Preliminary Objections), paras 7-89, when it held that the restrictions *ratione loci* attached to the Turkish declaration recognising the competence of the Commission to deal with individual applications under Article 25 (the present Article 34) and the declaration accepting the Court's jurisdiction, were invalid 'Taking into consideration the character of the Convention, the ordinary meaning of Articles 25 and 46 in their context and *in light of their object and purpose* and the practice of the Contracting Parties' (emphasis added).

proceedings leading up to a decision by which an accused person is deprived of his liberty in accordance with the Acts mentioned in the reservation."[17]

The condition of specificity of the reservation also implies that the reservation must be restricted to a specific law or specified legal measures, which must be indicated explicitly in the reservation. This also appears from the second paragraph: 'Any reservation made under this Article shall contain a brief statement of the law concerned'. Austria had made a reservation in respect of Article 1 of Protocol No. 1 in connection with Part IV and Part V of the State Treaty which Austria had concluded with the Western Allies and the Soviet Union in 1955. A complaint directed against Austria was concerned with a law of 1958, which had been enacted in execution of Part IV of the State Treaty, but which had not been mentioned in the reservation. The Commission nevertheless brought the law within the scope of the Austrian reservation, holding that "in making a reservation with respect to Parts IV and V of the State Treaty, Austria must necessarily have had the intention of excluding from the scope of the First Protocol everything forming the subject matter of Parts IV and V of the said Treaty; whereas it follows that the Austrian reservation relating to Parts IV and V of the said Treaty must be interpreted as intended to cover all legislative and administrative measures directly related to the subject matter of Parts IV and V of the State Treaty."[18]

With respect to the condition of the second paragraph of Article 57 that the reservation 'shall contain a brief statement of the law concerned', the Commission concluded in the *Temeltasch* Case that the Swiss interpretative declaration did not comply with that provision. It nevertheless reached the conclusion that "the failure by Switzerland – an omission which it would have been desirable to avoid – (...) did not prove to be decisive in the circumstances of the present case. Indeed, the very terms of the interpretative declaration were sufficient to make the applicant or his lawyer aware that the principle of the free assistance of an interpreter could not as such be invoked against Switzerland."[19]

Later case law, however, shows a somewhat stricter approach. Thus, as to the condition of specificity, the Court held in the *Belilos* Case with respect to an interpreta-

---

[17] Appl. 1452/62, Yearbook VI (1963), p. 268 (276). See also Appl. 473/59, *I. v. Austria*, Yearbook II (1958-1959), p. 400 (406); Appl. 2432/65, *X v. Austria*, Coll. 22 (1967), p. 124 (127); Appl. 4002/69, *X v. Austria*, Yearbook XIV (1971), p. 178 (186). In a later decision the Commission indicated that it wanted to reconsider its position. In Appl. 8180/78, *X v. Austria*, D&R 20 (1980), p. 23 (27-28), it held, after an express reference to the case-law just mentioned as follows: "The Commission has now come to the opinion that in view of the various questions which may be raised by the scope of a reservation and its compatibility with Article 64 (the present Article 57) of the Convention, its previous decisions on this matter could usefully be reconsidered". The reconsideration announced did not take place in this case because the complaint concerned was declared manifestly ill-founded.

[18] Appl. 2765/66, *X v. Austria*, Yearbook X (1967), p. 412 (418). See also Appls 1821-1822/63, *Hudetz, Haiek and Von Beringe v. Austria*, Yearbook IX (1966), p. 214 (236).

[19] Report of 5 May 1982, D&R 31 (1983), p. 120 (151).

tive declaration on the part of the Swiss Government[20] that "By 'reservation of a general character' in Article 64 (the present Article 57) is meant in particular a reservation couched in terms that are too vague or broad for it to be possible to determine their exact meaning and scope. While the preparatory work and the Government's explanations clearly show what the respondent State's concern was at the time of ratification, they cannot obscure the objective reality of the actual wording of the declaration. The words 'ultimate control by the judiciary over the acts or decisions of the public authorities relating to [civil] rights or obligations or the determination of [a criminal] charge' do not make it possible for the scope of the undertaking by Switzerland to be ascertained exactly, in particular as to which categories of dispute are included and as to whether or not the 'ultimate control by the judiciary' takes in the facts of the case. They can, therefore, be interpreted in different ways, whereas Article 64 para. 1 (the present Article 57 para. 1) requires precision and clarity. In short, they fall foul of the rule that reservations must not be of a general character."[21] From this it may be concluded that, according to the Court, the exact scope of the reservation must be deducible from the terms of the reservation.

With respect to the requirement contained in the second paragraph the Swiss Government attempted to justify its failure to comply with that condition by referring to the very flexible State-practice in this respect and by advancing the argument that Article 57 does not take account of the specific and allegedly almost insuperable problems faced by federal States. As to this latter argument, according to the Government, "Switzerland would have had to mention most of the provisions in the twenty-six cantonal codes of criminal procedure and in the twenty-six cantonal codes of criminal procedure, and even hundreds of municipal laws and regulations."[22] Neither of these arguments were honoured. The Commission, referring to its report in the *Temeltasch* Case, had held that the undeniable practical difficulties put forward by the Government could not justify the failure to comply with paragraph 2 of Article 57.[23] The Court agreed with this position, adding that "the 'brief statement of the law concerned' both constitutes an evidential factor and contributes to legal certainty. The purpose of Article 64 para. 2 (the present Article 57 para. 2) is to provide a guarantee (...) that a reservation does not go beyond the provisions expressly excluded by the State concerned."[24]

---

[20] This declaration was worded as follows: "The Swiss Federal Council considers that the guarantee of fair trial in Article 6, paragraph 1 of the Convention, in the determination of civil rights and obligations or any criminal charge against the person in question is intended solely to ensure ultimate control by the judiciary over the acts or decisions of the public authorities relating to such rights or obligations or the determination of such a charge".

[21] Judgment of 29 April 1988, para. 55.

[22] *Ibidem*, para. 57.

[23] Opinion of 7 May 1986, para. 114.

[24] Judgment of 29 April 1988, para. 59.

After this more strict test in the *Belilos* Case the Austrian reservation, which had also been at issue in the above-mentioned Commission decisions, came under review again in the *Chorherr* Case. The Court held that the reservation concerned did not contain the degree of generality prohibited by Article 57, because it 'encompasses a limited number of laws which, taken together, constitute a well-defined and coherent body of substantive and procedural administrative provisions'.[25] Also with respect to the condition that the reservation contains a brief statement of the law concerned the Court took a rather lenient attitude. It accepted the mere reference to the Federal Official Gazette, as that reference made it possible for everyone to identify the precise laws concerned and to obtain any information regarding them, while it also provided safeguards against any interpretation which would unduly extend the field of application of the reservation.[26]

As judge Valticos, not without good reason, observed in his partly dissenting opinion, by merely indicating where the laws in question can be found, the reservation "clearly does not contain a 'brief statement' of the substance of this law which would make it possible to understand the law's contents and its scope, or to determine whether the text amounts to a general reservation which is not permitted under the Convention."[27]

In the *Eisenstecken* Case, however, the Court decided that the absence of a brief statement of the law concerned was a sufficient basis to render the reservation invalid. The Court held that "a reservation which merely refers to a permissive, non-exhaustive, provision of the Constitution and which does not refer to, or mention, those specific provisions of the Austrian legal order which exclude public hearings, does not 'afford to a sufficient degree a guarantee... that [it] does not go beyond the provision expressly excluded by Austria'. Accoringdingly, the reservation does not satisfy the requirements of Article 57 para. 2 of the Convention."[28]

The third condition mentioned in Article 57 implies that the law or legal provisions concerned must have been effective at the time the reservation is made, *i.e.* at the moment of signature or ratification of the Convention by the State in question. This unambiguous provision seems to leave room for no other conclusion than that no later law may be brought within the scope of the reservation once it has been made. However, thus far the Strasbourg organs have not held on to the letter of this provision.

Thus, the Commission declared a complaint inadmissible concerning an Austrian Act of 1960 on road traffic. This Act replaced an Act of 1947 and had been enacted

---

[25]   Judgment of 25 August 1993, para. 18.
[26]   *Ibidem*, para. 20.
[27]   *Partly dissenting opinion of judge Valticos.*
[28]   Judgment 3 October 2000, para. 29.

after the date of the Austrian reservation in question. The Commission considered that the Act of 1960 was covered by the reservation in view of the fact "that the subject matter covered by the Road Traffic Act of 1947 and the Road Traffic Act of 1960 is substantially the same; whereas, therefore, the latter Act does not have the effect of enlarging, a posteriori, the subject matter which is excluded from the competence of the Commission by the above reservation".[29]A similar reasoning was applied by the Court in the *Campbell and Cosans* Case.[30]

38.5 THE PROVISIONS OF THE CONVENTION SUBJECT TO RESERVATIONS

The preceding observations concerned reservations with respect to the substantive provisions of the Convention. In addition thereto, and leaving aside the Convention's final clauses, the Convention comprises two categories of provisions: provisions concerning the enjoyment and the restriction of the rights and freedoms (Articles 1 and 13-18), and provisions concerning the supervisory mechanism (Articles 19-51).

With respect to the former category of provisions reservations would seem to be impermissible. It is true that the text of Article 57 speaks of 'any particular provision', but this cannot be considered conclusive. The obligations ensuing from Articles 1 and 13-18 are of such a fundamental importance for the enjoyment of the rights and freedoms laid down in the Convention that restricting them by means of a reservation would be incompatible with the 'object and purpose' of the Convention and consequently must be considered inadmissible.

It is submitted, therefore, that the reservation which France has made with respect to Article 15 conflicts with the Convention. This reservation is to the effect that the circumstances specified in Article 16 of the French Constitution and other relevant national legislation regarding proclamation of a state of siege or emergency "must be understood as complying with the purpose of Article 15 of the Convention, and (...) secondly, for the interpretation and application of Article 16 of the Constitution of the Republic, the terms 'to the extent strictly required by the exigencies of the situation' shall not restrict the power of the President of the Republic to take 'the measures required by the circumstances'."

Article 15 in itself is already a highly exceptive clause. It confers on the Contracting States the power to derogate from a number of provisions of the Convention in

---

[29]   Appl. 2432/65, *X v. Austria*, Coll. 22 (1967), p. 124 (127). See also Appl. 3923/69, *X v. Austria*, Coll. 37 (1971), p. 10 (15).

[30]   Judgment of 25 February 1982, para. 37, in which it was held that the new legislation was no more than an echo of the identical provision from the old legislation and 'therefore goes no further than a law in force at a time when the reservation was made'.

exceptional cases. As such Article 15 draws the line beyond which the Contracting States may not go under the Convention. It must, therefore, be considered inacceptable that this limit could be shifted even further in favour of the States by means of a reservation. This holds true also for the French reservation, since its formulation is so wide that it in fact eliminates the Strasbourg supervision of the implementation of Article 15 altogether.

From the category of provisions pertaining to the supervisory machinery (Articles 19-51) it may be inferred that the drafters of the Convention intended the supervisory mechanism to operate unabridged with regard to each of the Contracting States. It is submitted that reservations with respect to the mandatory nature of the jurisdiction of the Court (article 32) are incompatible with the 'object and purpose' of the Convention. The same would seem to hold good in respect of the binding effect of decisions of the Court (Article 46) and the reporting procedure at the request of the Secretary General (Article 52). It appears from the Preamble that the purpose of the Convention was "to take the first steps for the collective enforcement of certain of the Rights stated in the Universal Declaration". Any backing out of the mechanism set up for this 'collective enforcement' that goes beyond that expressly permitted by the Convention would, with respect to the State concerned, hamper this 'collective enforcement' and accordingly the purpose of the Convention.

In this respect it is still of interest to note the decision of the Court in the *Loizidou* Cases which concerned the (previously existing) optional competences of the Commission and the Court (former Article 25 and 46).[31] In its declaration pursuant to former Article 25, by which it accepted the competence of the Commission to receive individual applications, Turkey had stated, *inter alia:* "the recognition of the right of petition extends only to allegations concerning acts or omissions of public authorities in Turkey performed within the boundaries of the territory to which the Constitution of the Republic of Turkey is applicable".[32] Turkey's subsequent Article 25 declarations contained a similar reservation,[33] which was also included in its declaration under former Article 46 concerning the jurisdiction of the European Court.[34]

The Court took as a starting point that "the object and purpose of the Convention as an instrument for the protection of individual human beings requires that its provisions be interpreted and applied so as to make its safeguards practical and effective".[35] Building thereupon, the Court held as follows: "If, as contended by the respondent Government, substantive or territorial restrictions were permissible under these provisions, Contracting Parties would be free to subscribe to separate regimes

---

[31]   Judgment of 23 March 1995, Preliminary Objections.
[32]   *Ibidem,* para. 15.
[33]   *Ibidem,* paras 25-26.
[34]   *Ibidem,* para. 27.
[35]   *Ibidem,* para. 72.

of enforcement of Convention obligations depending on the scope of their acceptances. Such a system, which would enable States to qualify their consent under the optional clauses, would not only seriously weaken the role of the Commission and Court in the discharge of their functions but would also diminish the effectiveness of the Convention as a constitutional instrument of European public order *(ordre public)*. (...) In the Court's view, having regard to the object and purpose of the Convention system as set out above, the consequences for the enforcement of the Convention and the achievement of its aims would be so far-reaching that the power to this effect should have been expressly provided for. However, no such provision exists in either Article 25 or Article 46."[36]

This led the Court to the conclusion that the restrictions *ratione loci* attached to Turkey's declarations were invalid.[37] And as it did in its *Belilos* judgment, the Court took the position that the impugned restrictions could be separated from the remainder of the text of the declarations, leaving intact the acceptance of the optional clauses.[38] The above reasoning of the Court in the *Loizidou* Case applies *a fortiori* to the present Article 32 providing for the mandatory nature of the jurisdiction of the Court.

38.6 INTERPRETATIVE DECLARATIONS

The relation between interpretative declarations and reservations was one of the issues in the *Belilos* Case.[39] In addition to two reservations Switzerland had made two interpretative declarations, one of which was relied upon by the Swiss Government. Consequently, the Court was faced with "[t]he question whether a declaration described as 'interpretative' must be regarded as a 'reservation'".[40] The Court took as a starting point that "it is necessary to ascertain the original intention of those who drafted the declaration"[41] and that "in order to establish the legal character of such

---

[36]   *Ibidem*, para. 75. In the same vain the Human Rights Committee in its General Comment concerning its competence to consider individual communications under the Optional Protocol to the International Covenant on Civil and Political Rights: 'And because the object and purpose of the first Optional Protocol is to allow the rights obligatory for a State under the Covenant to be tested before the Committee, a reservation that seeks to preclude this would be contrary to the object and purpose of the first Optional Protocol, even if not of the Covenant'; UN Doc. CCPR/C/2 I/Rev. I/Add. 6, 11 November 1994, para. 13.

[37]   *Ibidem*, para. 89.

[38]   *Ibidem*, para. 97.

[39]   The Commission had pronounced on the issue in its report in the *Temeltasch* Case, D&R 31 (1983), p. 120 (146-148).

[40]   Judgment of 29 April 1988, para. 49.

[41]   *Ibidem*, para. 48.

a declaration, one must look behind the title given to it and seek to determine the substantive content."[42]

This led the Court to examining the validity of the interpretative declaration in question, as in the case of a reservation, in the context of Article 57.[43] This flexible approach carries with it the disadvantage of legal uncertainty as to the exact scope of a State's obligations under the Convention, while a State should be aware of the difference between reservations and interpretative declarations and its possible legal implications. On the other hand, the decision of the Court is fully in line with Article 2 of the Vienna Convention, which, in its paragraph 1(d), defines a reservation as 'a unilateral statement, however phrased or named'.

38.7   CONCLUDING OBSERVATIONS

Are the object and purpose of the Convention static concepts? The Convention as a whole is considered by the Court to be a 'living instrument' that must be interpreted and applied according to the circumstances which prevail at that particular moment.[44] This implies that the will of the States at the moment of drafting the provisions of the Convention is considered by the Court not to be decisive for their scope. If the Court has thus created a certain latitude within the Convention for taking into account the evolution of legal and social concepts, there is no reason why the same doctrine should not equally apply to the interpretation and application of Article 57. This was expressly recognised by the Court in its *Loizidou* judgment.[45]

Following that line of reasoning, if one of the purposes of the Convention, according to its Preamble, is to pursue the achievement of greater unity between the member States of the Council of Europe through the maintenance and further realisation of human rights, the unity aimed at may have reached a certain stage at a certain moment where it becomes increasingly problematic to justify differences on important issues between the Member States in the obligations which they have accepted concerning the protection of human rights. Observations like the foregoing may lead the Court to even greater reticence in accepting and interpreting reservations made under Article 57; a reticence which has also been displayed by the Human Rights Committee in its General Comment, to which reference was made *supra*.[46] This attitude would not exclude, of course, that the Court continues to leave the States a certain 'margin of appreciation' in implementing some of these common obligations, allowing for

---

[42]   *Ibidem*, para. 49.
[43]   *Ibidem*.
[44]   See, *e.g.*, the judgment of 25 April 1978, *Tyrer*, para. 31 and the judgment of 22 October 1981, *Dudgeon*, para. 60.
[45]   Judgment of 23 March 1995, para. 71.
[46]   See note 3.

certain variations in interpretation and application as discussed in the introduction. Such variations leave the core of the commitment in tact and do not necessarily lower their level of protection, whereas reservations detract from the integrity and interdependence of these commitments and negatively affect the level of protection.

Ultimately, developments in Europe may have reached such a level of integration that this allows for the conclusion that the common legal order established by the Convention, in view of the generally recognised character of its provisions, the unity aimed at between the Member States of the Council of Europe, and the principle of equality before the law and equal protection of the law which should not only apply within, but also between the States, no longer leaves any room for unilateral reservations. If such a conclusion would be shared by the competent authorities of the Contracting States, it should then be translated into an amendment of Article 57 of the Convention. To gradually bring the Contracting States to accepting such a change, the Secretary General of the Council of Europe might consider using his power under Article 52 to ask those States which have made reservations, to explain, at regular intervals, the reasons and the necessity of maintaining them. A comparison comes to mind here with Article 22 of the European Social Charter, which provides as follows: "The Contracting Parties shall send to the Secretary-General, at appropriate intervals as requested by the Committee of Ministers, reports relating to the provisions of Part II of the Charter which they did not accept at the time of their ratification or approval or in a subsequent notification. The Committee of Ministers shall determine from time to time in respect of which provisions such reports shall be requested and the form of the reports to be provided."[47] And the Human Rights Committee, in its General Comment, opined as follows: "It is desirable for a State entering a reservation to indicate in precise terms the domestic legislation or practices which it believes to be incompatible with the Covenant obligations reserved; and to explain the time period it requires to render its own laws and practices compatible with the Covenant, or why it is unable to render its own laws and practices compatible with the Covenant. States should also ensure that the necessity for maintaining reservations is periodically reviewed, taking into account any observations and recommendations made by the Committee during examination of their reports. Reservations should be withdrawn at the earliest possible moment. Reports to the Committee should contain information on what action has been taken to review, reconsider or withdraw reservations."[48]

A truly common European legal order in the field of human rights presupposes that all Contracting States are under the same obligations in that field. At the moment that clearly still is not the case, although it must be noted that the number of reser-

---

[47] *European Treaty Series*, No. 35, 18 October 1961; 529 UNTS 89.
[48] *Supra*, note 3.

vations submitted by Central and Eastern European States that ratified the Convention over the past 15 years has been remarkably limited.[49]

---

[49]   See *supra*, note 4.

APPENDIX: DATES OF RATIFICATION OF THE ECHR AND ADDITIONAL PROTOCOLS[1]

Dates of entry into force
X = ratified   S = signed
Source: www.echr.coe.int

States	ECHR	P. No. 1	P. No. 4	P. No. 6	P. No. 7	P. No. 9	P. No. 10	P. No. 11	P. No. 12	P. No. 13	P. No. 14
Albania	2/10/96	2/10/96	2/10/96	1/10/00	1/01/97			1/11/98	1/04/05	S	X
Andorra	22/01/96			1/02/96				1/11/98		1/07/03	X
Armenia	26/04/02	26/04/02	26/04/02	1/10/03	1/07/02			26/04/02	1/04/05	S	X
Austria	3/09/58	3/09/58	18/09/69	1/03/85	1/11/88	1/10/94	X	1/11/98	S	1/05/04	X
Azerbaijan	15/04/02	15/04/02	15/04/02	1/05/02	1/07/02			15/04/02	S		X
Belgium	14/06/55	14/06/55	21/09/70	1/01/99	S	1/12/95	X	1/11/98	S	1/10/03	S
Bosnia and Herzegovina	12/07/02	12/07/02	12/07/02	1/08/02	1/10/02			12/07/02	1/04/05	1/11/03	X
Bulgaria	7/09/92	7/09/92	4/11/00	1/10/99	1/02/01			1/11/98		1/07/03	X
Croatia	5/11/97	5/11/97	5/11/97	1/12/97	1/02/98			1/11/98	1/04/05	1/07/03	X
Cyprus	6/10/62	6/10/62	3/10/89	1/02/00	1/12/00	1/01/95	X	1/11/98	1/04/05	1/07/03	X
Czech Republic	1/01/93	1/01/93	1/01/93	1/01/93	1/01/93	1/10/94	X	1/11/98	S	1/11/04	X
Denmark	3/09/53	18/05/54	2/05/68	1/03/85	1/11/88	1/06/96	X	1/11/98	S	1/07/03	X
Estonia	16/04/96	16/04/96	16/04/96	1/05/98	1/07/96	1/08/96	X	1/11/98	S	1/06/04	X
Finland	10/05/90	10/05/90	10/05/90	1/06/90	1/08/90	1/10/94	X	1/11/98	1/04/05	1/03/05	X
France	3/05/74	3/05/74	3/05/74	1/03/86	1/11/88	S	S	1/11/98		S	X

---

[1]   Status as of: 4 September 2006.

States	ECHR	P. No. 1	P. No. 4	P. No. 6	P. No. 7	P. No. 9	P. No. 10	P. No. 11	P. No. 12	P. No. 13	P. No. 14
Georgia	20/05/99	7/06/02	13/04/00	1/05/00	1/07/00			20/05/99	1/04/05	1/09/03	X
Germany	3/09/53	13/02/57	1/06/68	1/08/89	S	1/11/94	X	1/11/98	S	1/02/05	X
Greece	28/11/74	28/11/74		1/10/98	1/11/88	S	S	1/11/98	S	1/06/05	X
Hungary	5/11/92	5/11/92	5/11/92	1/12/92	1/02/93	1/10/94	S	1/11/98	S	1/11/03	X
Iceland	3/09/53	18/05/54	2/05/68	1/06/87	1/11/88			1/11/98	S	1/03/05	X
Ireland	3/09/53	18/05/54	29/10/68	1/07/94	1/11/01	1/10/94	X	1/11/98	S	1/07/03	X
Italy	26/10/55	26/10/55	27/05/82	1/01/89	1/02/92	1/10/94	X	1/11/98	S	S	X
Latvia	27/06/97	27/06/97	27/06/97	1/06/99	1/09/97			1/11/98	S	S	X
Liechtenstein	8/09/82	14/11/95	8/02/05	1/12/90	1/05/05	1/03/96	X	1/11/98	S	1/07/03	X
Lithuania	20/06/95	24/05/96	20/06/95	1/08/99	1/09/95	S		1/11/98		1/05/04	X
Luxembourg	3/09/53	18/05/54	2/05/68	1/03/85	1/07/89	1/10/94	X	1/11/98	1/07/06	1/07/06	X
Malta	23/01/67	23/01/67	5/06/02	1/04/91	1/04/03	S	X	1/11/98		1/07/03	X
Moldova	12/09/97	12/09/97	12/09/97	1/10/97	1/12/97			1/11/98	S	S	X
Monaco	30/11/05	S	30/11/05	1/12/05	1/02/05			30/11/05		1/03/06	X
Netherlands	31/08/54	31/08/54	23/06/82	1/05/86	S	1/10/94	X	1/11/98	1/04/05	1/06/06	X
Norway	3/09/53	18/05/54	2/05/68	1/11/88	1/01/89	1/10/94	X	1/11/98	S	1/12/05	X
Poland	19/01/93	10/10/94	10/10/94	1/11/00	1/03/03	1/02/95	X	1/11/98			S
Portugal	9/11/78	9/11/78	9/11/78	1/11/86	1/03/05	1/02/96	X	1/11/98	S	1/02/04	X
Romania	20/06/94	20/06/94	20/06/94	1/07/94	1/09/94	1/10/94	X	1/11/98	1/11/06	1/08/03	X
Russia	5/05/98	5/05/98	5/05/98	S	1/08/98	1/09/98	X	1/11/98	S	S	S
San Marino	22/03/89	22/03/89	22/03/89	1/04/89	1/06/89	1/10/95	X	1/11/98	1/04/05	1/08/03	X
Serbia	3/03/04	3/03/04	3/03/04	1/04/04	1/06/04			3/03/04	1/04/05	1/07/04	X
Slovakia	1/01/93	1/01/93	1/01/93	1/01/93	1/01/93	1/10/94	X	1/11/98	S	1/12/05	X

States	ECHR	P. No. 1	P. No. 4	P. No. 6	P. No. 7	P. No. 9	P. No. 10	P. No. 11	P. No. 12	P. No. 13	P. No. 14
Slovenia	28/06/94	28/06/94	28/06/94	1/07/94	1/09/94	1/10/94	X	1/11/98	S	1/04/04	X
Spain	4/10/79	27/11/90	S	1/03/85	S			1/11/98	S	S	X
Sweden	3/09/53	18/05/54	2/05/68	1/03/85	1/11/88	1/08/95	X	1/11/98		1/08/03	X
Switzerland	28/11/74	S		1/11/87	1/11/88	1/08/95	X	1/11/98		1/07/03	X
The former Yugoslav Republic of Macedonia	10/04/97	10/04/97	10/04/97	1/05/97	01/07/97			1/11/98	S	1/11/04	
Turkey	18/05/54	18/05/54	S	1/12/03	S	S		1/11/98	S	1/06/06	S
Ukraine	11/09/97	11/09/97	11/09/97	1/05/00	1/12/97			1/11/98	1/07/06	1/07/03	X
United Kingdom	3/09/53	18/05/54	S	1/06/99			X	1/11/98		1/02/04	X

INDEX OF CASES

I. European Court of Human Rights: Decisions

II. European Court of Human Rights: Judgments

III. European Commission of Human Rights: Decisions

IV. European Commission of Human Rights: Reports

INDEX OF SUBJECTS